W9-AAZ-407

PRENTICE HALL

THE AMERICAN NATION

Dr. James West Davidson
Author

Dr. Michael B. Stoff
Author

Dr. Herman J. Viola
Senior Consultant

IN ASSOCIATION WITH
American Heritage®

Upper Saddle River, New Jersey
Needham, Massachusetts

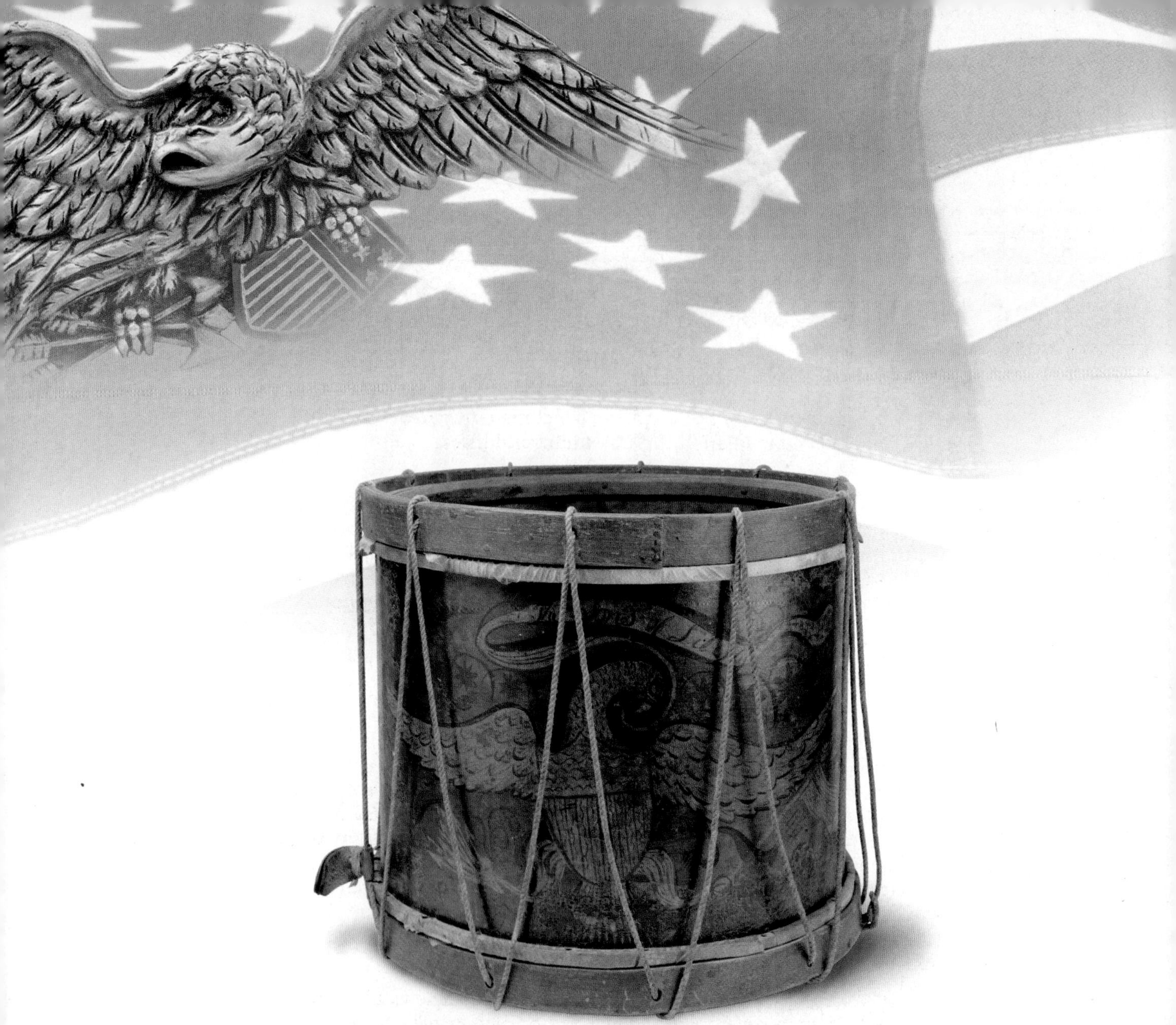

Collections of the Fort Ticonderoga Museum

Acknowledgments appear on page 965, which constitutes an extension of this copyright page.

ISBN 0-13-181715-9
1 2 3 4 5 6 7 8 9 10   07 06 05 04 03

Authors

Dr. James West Davidson is coauthor of *After the Fact: The Art of Historical Detection* and *Nation of Nations: A Narrative History of the American Republic.* Dr. Davidson has taught at both the college and high school levels. He has also consulted on curriculum design for American history courses. Dr. Davidson is an avid canoeist and hiker. His published works on these subjects include *Great Heart,* the true story of a 1903 canoe trip in the Canadian wilderness.

Dr. Michael B. Stoff received his Ph.D. from Yale University and teaches history at the University of Texas at Austin. He is the author of *Oil, War, and American Security: The Search for a National Policy on Foreign Oil, 1941–1947,* coauthor of *Nation of Nations: A Narrative History of the American Republic,* and coeditor of *The Manhattan Project: A Documentary Introduction to the Atomic Age.* Dr. Stoff has won numerous grants, fellowships, and teaching awards.

Senior Consultant

Dr. Herman J. Viola, curator emeritus with the Smithsonian Institution, is a distinguished historian and author. Dr. Viola received his Ph.D. in American history from Indiana University. He founded the scholarly journal *Prologue* at the National Archives. Dr. Viola also served as director of the National Anthropological Archives at the Smithsonian Institution. A nationally recognized authority on American Indians, the history of the American West, and the Civil War, Dr. Viola is the author of many historical works for both adults and young readers.

AmericanHeritage® **American Heritage** magazine was founded in 1954, and it quickly rose to the position it occupies today: the country's preeminent magazine of history and culture. Dedicated to presenting the past in entertaining narratives underpinned by scrupulous scholarship, *American Heritage* today goes to more than 300,000 subscribers and counts the country's very best writers and historians among its contributors.

Program Reviewers

Academic Consultants

David Beaulieu, Ph.D.
Professor, School of Education
University of Wisconsin–Milwaukee
Milwaukee, Wisconsin

William R. Childs, Ph.D.
Associate Professor of History
Ohio State University
Columbus, Ohio

Theodore DeLaney, Ph.D.
Associate Professor of History
Washington & Lee University
Lexington, Virginia

Emma Lapsansky, Ph.D.
Professor of History and
Curator of Special Collections
Haverford College
Haverford, Pennsylvania

William A. McClenaghan
Professor of Political Science
Oregon State University
Corvallis, Oregon

Timothy R. Mahoney, Ph.D.
Professor of History
University of Nebraska–Lincoln
Lincoln, Nebraska

Ralph Mann, Ph.D.
Associate Professor of History
University of Colorado
Boulder, Colorado

Michael Sells, Ph.D.
Professor of Religion
Haverford College
Haverford, Pennsylvania

Teacher Reviewers

Joanne Alexander
Reading Supervisor
Osbourn High School
Manassas, Virginia

Chris Beech
Social Studies Teacher
Lamar Junior High School
Rosenberg, Texas

Bob Borjes
Social Studies Teacher
Hal Peterson Middle School
Kerrville, Texas

Phyllis Bridges
Social Studies Teacher
Chaffin Middle School
Ft. Smith, Arkansas

Clement R. Brown, III
Social Science Teacher
Madison Junior High School
Naperville, Illinois

Susan Buha
Social Studies Teacher
Hobart Middle School
Hobart, Indiana

Steve Bullick
Supervisor of Social Studies
Mt. Lebanon School District
Mt. Lebanon, Pennsylvania

Marilyn Bunner
Social Studies Teacher
Decatur Middle School
Indianapolis, Indiana

Ronald Conklin
Social Studies Teacher
Will Rogers Middle School
Fair Oaks, California

Sandra Lee Eades, Ph.D.
Social Studies Content Leader
Ridgely Middle School
Lutherville, Maryland

Nancy Foss
Social Studies Teacher
Glenn Hills Middle School
Augusta, Georgia

Mike Harter
Social Studies Teacher
Austin Middle School
Amarillo, Texas

Beverly Hooper
Social Studies Teacher
Dartmouth Middle School
San Jose, California

Patricia Mymbs
Social Studies Teacher
Edward H. Cary Middle School
Dallas, Texas

Denis O'Rourke
Social Studies Teacher
Hommocks Middle School
Larchmont, New York

David Peterson
Social Studies Teacher
Fairmont Junior High School
Boise, Idaho

Lauri Rule
Social Studies Teacher
Shackelford Junior High School
Arlington, Texas

Dana Sanders
Social Studies Teacher
Knox County High School
Edina, Missouri

W. David Scott
Social Studies Teacher
Havenview Middle School
Memphis, Tennessee

Bill Speer
Social Studies Teacher
Albright Middle School
Houston, Texas

Donna Wenger
Social Studies Teacher
Wilson Middle School
Plano, Texas

Pamela West
Social Studies Teacher
Greshman Middle School
Birmingham, Alabama

Reading Specialist

Bonnie Armbruster, Ph.D.
Professor of Education
University of Illinois at Urbana-Champaign
Champaign, Illinois

Curriculum and Assessment Specialist

Jan Moberley
Dallas, Texas

Accuracy Panel

Esther Ratner
Greyherne Information Services
Lynn D. Hoover, The Hoover Associates
Jane B. Malcolm, Professional Research Services
Alice Radosh, Ph.D., Academy of Educational Development
Lorrain Rosenberg, Baldwin School District, New York (Ret.)
Cathy S. Zazueta, California State University, Los Angeles

Program Advisors

Michal Howden
Social Studies Consultant
Zionsville, Indiana

Kathy Lewis
Social Studies Consultant
Fort Worth, Texas

Joe Wieczorek
Social Studies Consultant
Baltimore, Maryland

Contents

Hopi kachina doll

UNIT 1 Roots of American History 1

Building the Massachusetts Bay colony

Ratifying the Constitution

UNIT 2 The Revolutionary Era 136

Drum from the American Revolution

The Jefferson Memorial, Washington, D.C.

UNIT 3 THE EARLY REPUBLIC 274

1840 model of frontier log cabin

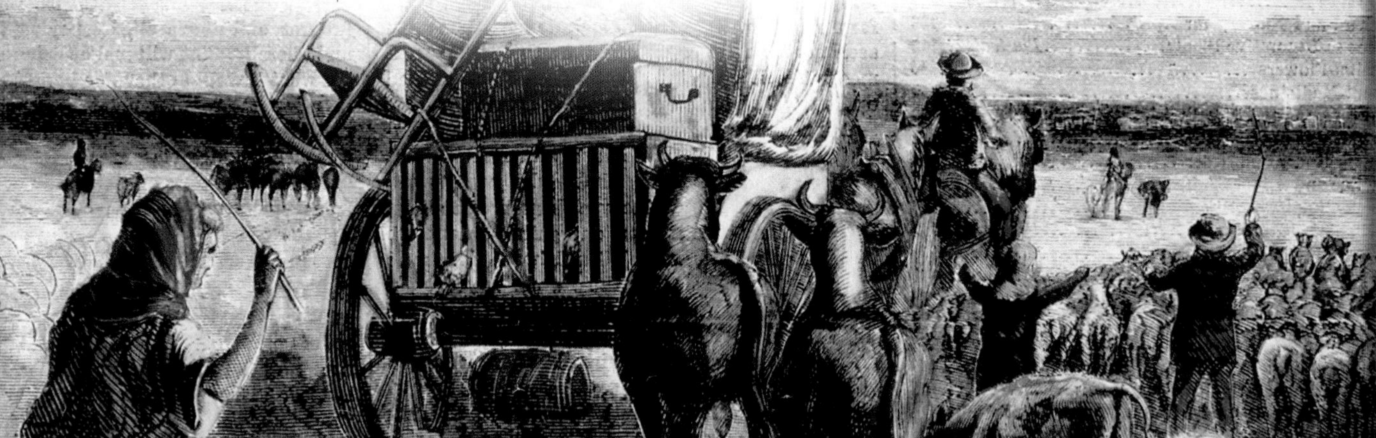
On the Oregon Trail

The 54th Massachusetts Regiment in battle, 1863

UNIT 5 Division and Reunion 456

UNIT 6 TRANSFORMING THE NATION 540

A Plains family and livestock

Theodore Roosevelt leading a charge in Cuba

UNIT 7 A New Role for the Nation 626

A Teddy bear, named for President Theodore Roosevelt

Best-selling novel from the 1920s

Hard times during the Great Depression

Button from the 1970s

Vietnam Veterans Memorial, Washington, D.C.

Special Features

Master skills you will use all your life.

Child labor around 1900

Connecting With...

See how history has fascinating links with other subjects.

Special Features

American Heritage® MAGAZINE

HISTORY HAPPENED HERE

Read about special sites where American history happened.

TEST PREPARATION

History Through Literature

Geography and History

Investigate the connection between history and geography.

Connecting to Today

Explore links between historical events and your world today.

Special Features/Primary Sources

An American Profile

Meet fascinating history makers.

Primary Sources

Relive history through eyewitness accounts, literature, and documents.

Primary Sources

In-text Primary Sources

(continued)

Primary Sources

> **"**This momentous question, like a fire bell in the night, awakened and filled me with terror. I considered it at once as the knell of the Union.... We have the wolf by the ears, and we can neither hold him, nor safely let him go.**"**
>
> —Thomas Jefferson, Letter to John Holmes, April 22, 1820

(continued)

Primary Sources

"This great nation will endure as it has endured, will revive and will prosper. So, first of all, let me assert my firm belief that the only thing we have to fear is fear itself..."

—Franklin D. Roosevelt, Inaugural Address, March 4, 1933

(continued)

Primary Sources/Maps

Chapter Maps

(continued)

Maps

(continued)

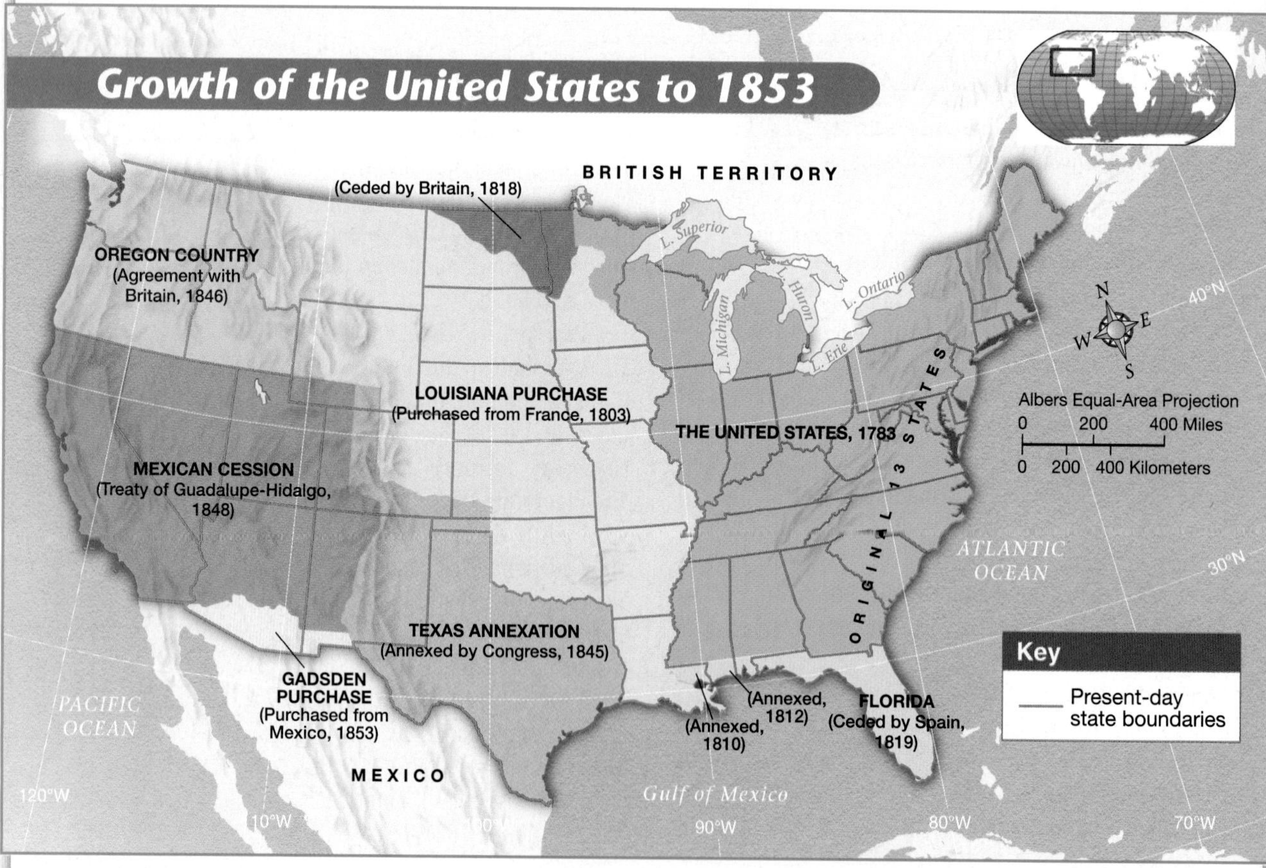

Maps/Political Cartoons

Reference Section Maps

Political Cartoons

The Horse "America" Throwing His Master

Charts and Graphs

Charts and Graphs

Cause and Effect

(continued)

Charts and Graphs

Graphic Organizers

Immigrants: Push and Pull Factors

Push Factors:	Pull Factors:
• Scarce land • Farm jobs lost to new machines • Political and religious persecution • Revolution • Poverty and hard lives	• Promise of freedom • Family or friends already settled in the United States • Factory jobs available

Use This Book for Success

You can use *The American Nation* as a tool to master American history. Spend a few minutes becoming familiar with the way the textbook is set up, and see how you can unlock the secrets of American history.

Read for Content Mastery

Before You Read You will begin each section of the text by reading the Section Objectives. These statements give you a purpose for reading and guide you to the critical content you need to master. Another helpful aid is the **Target Reading Skills** exercise and graphic organizer at the beginning of each section. It encourages you to use reading skills to organize the content of the section. You will learn more about Target Reading Skills on pages xxxii–xxxiii.

As You Read *The American Nation* provides many opportunities for you to strengthen your reading skills. As you read the text, you will see **Target Reading Skills** activities in the side column next to the text. These activities help you practice a reading skill in relation to the content you are actually reading. If you are reading about Native Americans of the Great Plains, it might ask you to construct questions you might have asked the Plains Native Americans about the roles of women. By stopping to think as you read, you will gain a better understanding of the text.

After You Read The questions in the Section Assessment require you to recall what you have read. Use these questions to assess your comprehension. Then, gain additional information by completing the activity. When you do activities, you continue to learn.

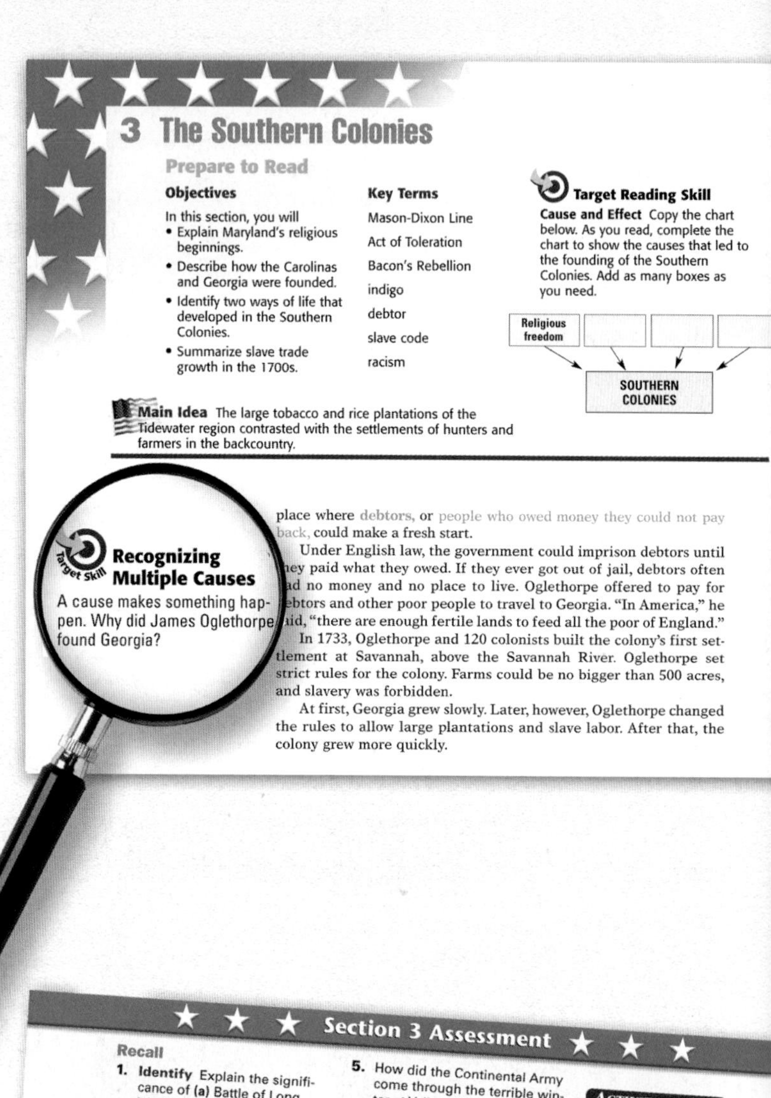

3 The Southern Colonies

Prepare to Read

Objectives

In this section, you will
- Explain Maryland's religious beginnings.
- Describe how the Carolinas and Georgia were founded.
- Identify two ways of life that developed in the Southern Colonies.
- Summarize slave trade growth in the 1700s.

Key Terms

Mason-Dixon Line
Act of Toleration
Bacon's Rebellion
indigo
debtor
slave code
racism

Target Reading Skill

Cause and Effect Copy the chart below. As you read, complete the chart to show the causes that led to the founding of the Southern Colonies. Add as many boxes as you need.

Main Idea The large tobacco and rice plantations of the Tidewater region contrasted with the settlements of hunters and farmers in the backcountry.

Recognizing Multiple Causes A cause makes something happen. Why did James Oglethorpe found Georgia?

place where debtors, or people who owed money they could not pay back, could make a fresh start.

Under English law, the government could imprison debtors until they paid what they owed. If they ever got out of jail, debtors often had no money and no place to live. Oglethorpe offered to pay for debtors and other poor people to travel to Georgia. "In America," he said, "there are enough fertile lands to feed all the poor of England."

In 1733, Oglethorpe and 120 colonists built the colony's first settlement at Savannah, above the Savannah River. Oglethorpe set strict rules for the colony. Farms could be no bigger than 500 acres, and slavery was forbidden.

At first, Georgia grew slowly. Later, however, Oglethorpe changed the rules to allow large plantations and slave labor. After that, the colony grew more quickly.

Section 3 Assessment

Recall

1. **Identify** Explain the significance of **(a)** Battle of Long Island, **(b)** Nathan Hale, **(c)** Battle of Trenton, **(d)** General John Burgoyne, **(e)** Battle of Saratoga, **(f)** Marquis de Lafayette, **(g)** Friedrich von Steuben, **(h)** Thaddeus Kosciusko, **(i)** Valley Forge.
2. **Define (a)** ally, **(b)** cavalry.

Comprehension

3. How did Washington turn retreat into victory in New Jersey?
4. Explain the results of the Battle of Saratoga.
5. How did the Continental Army come through the terrible winter at Valley Forge with new hope?

Critical Thinking and Writing

6. **Exploring the Main Idea** Review the Main Idea statement at the beginning of this section. Then, write a newspaper article celebrating the victory at Saratoga. Why was it a turning point?
7. **Analyzing Information** Why do you think people from other lands, such as Lafayette and Pulaski, were willing to risk their lives to help the American cause?

ACTIVITY

Creating a Dramatic Scene Write a scene in which Benjamin Franklin meets with the French King Louis XVI to convince him to support the Continental Army. Focus on how France and the Continental Army would benefit from such an alliance.

Chapter 6 Section 3 ★ 185

Develop Your Skills

Each chapter has a Skills for Life feature. Use these features to learn and practice social studies skills. These skills will help you be successful in understanding American history. Complete the Skills Assessment at the end of every chapter to apply the skills that you have learned.

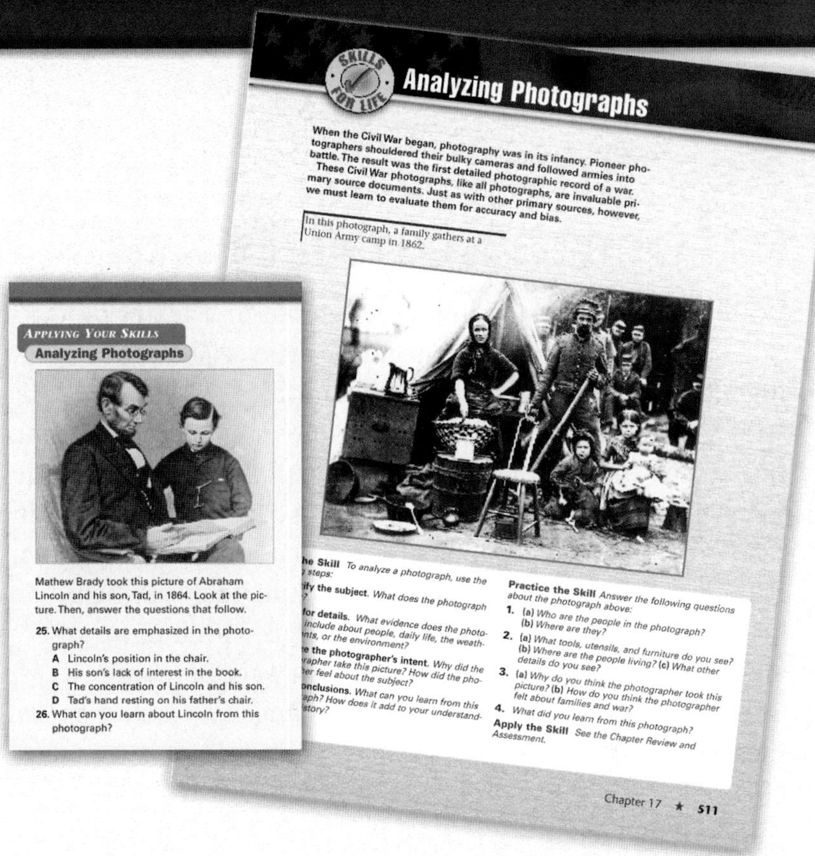

Use the Internet to Explore

With the click of a mouse, the Internet connects you to a wealth of American history resources. Use the Go Online activities to research and learn more about key concepts in American history. The Virtual Field Trips in the American Heritage® History Happened Here feature let you explore historic sites online.

For chapter summaries, Internet activities, and more, use **Web Code mfk-1000.**

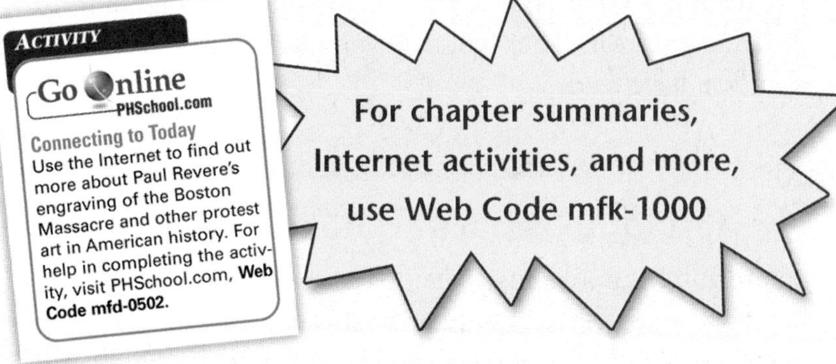

Prepare for Tests

The American Nation helps you prepare for tests. Start by answering the questions at the end of every section and chapter. Go to **PHSchool.com** at the end of each chapter to take the practice Chapter Self-Test. Then, use the Test Preparation pages at the end of the unit to test your knowledge further.

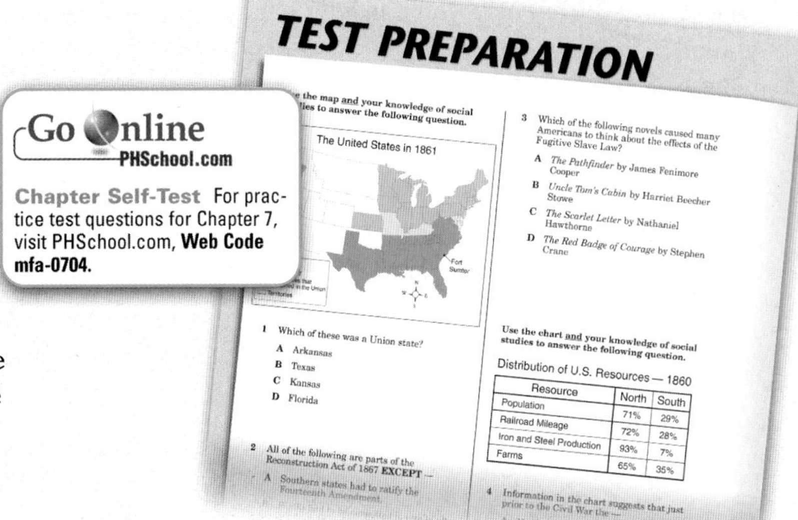

Resource	North	South
Population	71%	29%
Railroad Mileage	72%	28%
Iron and Steel Production	93%	7%
Farms	65%	35%

Reading Informational Texts

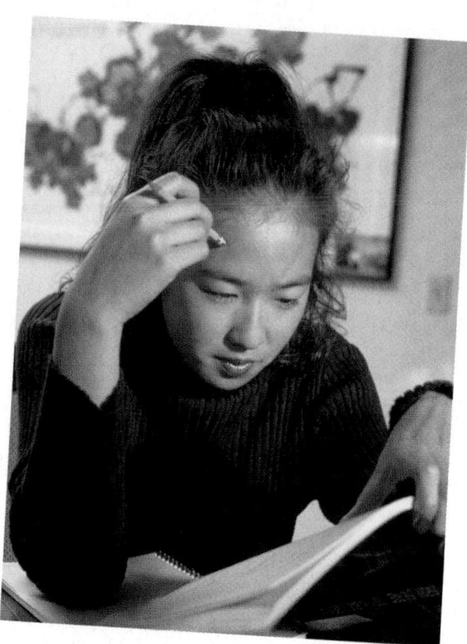

Reading and understanding the material in a textbook is not the same as reading a novel or magazine article. The purpose of reading a textbook is to acquire information. There are many reading strategies that can help you get the most out of reading informational texts. In this section, we will focus on reading strategies that will help increase your comprehension of the information in your textbook. We will also look at ways to develop vocabulary as you read. Finally, we will examine a few skills that will help you read textbooks and other nonfiction materials with a more critical eye. On pages xxxii–xxxiii, you will read about some **Target Reading Skills** that you will have a chance to practice as you read this textbook.

Reading Your Textbook

The reading strategies described below will help you before, during, and after you read. They will help you understand and remember what you have read.

Previewing: Prepare to Read

Before you begin reading a chapter or a section, take a few minutes to preview the text to get an idea of what you will be reading. Previewing will give you an overview of the chapter or section, help you consider what you already know, and give you some idea of what you are expected to learn.

- ❑ Read the chapter or section title.
- ❑ Read the objectives, key terms, and main ideas that begin each section.
- ❑ Check the Target Reading Skill and graphic organizer at the start of each section.
- ❑ Scan the headings and subheadings.
- ❑ Look at photos, maps, and charts.
- ❑ Check highlighted words and definitions.
- ❑ Read the questions at the end of the section or chapter.
- ❑ Read the section summaries that appear in the Chapter Review and Assessments.

Reading: Be an Active Reader

Become an active reader by learning to think about the meanings of new terms, main ideas, and the details that support the main ideas. Use the strategies listed here as you read. They will help you interact with your text.

- ❑ Take notes as you read.
- ❑ Turn headings into questions and look for the answers.
- ❑ Recall related information that you have previously learned.
- ❑ Use context clues and word structure to determine word meanings.
- ❑ Distinguish between facts and opinions.
- ❑ Identify the main ideas of sections, subsections, and paragraphs.
- ❑ Stop every so often and ask yourself, "Do I understand what I have read?"
- ❑ Reread to clarify words or ideas that you might not have understood the first time you read.

After Reading

Take time to be sure you understand and can remember what you have read. Use the strategies listed here to help you review and recall main ideas and details.

- ❑ Review the headings and subheadings.
- ❑ Summarize the main ideas and recall supporting details.
- ❑ Check the notes you took.
- ❑ Understanding informational texts often requires reading more than once. If you need to, read parts or all of the section again.
- ❑ If you still have questions about the content, get help from a classmate or your teacher.

Reading and Writing Handbook

Increase Vocabulary

Good readers try to increase their vocabulary. Using strategies that help you learn new words as you read will help you become a better reader.

Context

When you come across an unfamiliar word, you can sometimes determine its meaning from the context. The context is the surrounding words and sentences. Look for clues in the surrounding words, sentences, and paragraphs to help you understand the meaning of the unfamiliar word.

Word Analysis

Word analysis refers to strategies you can use to determine the meanings of unfamiliar words by breaking them into parts. Many words have a root and a prefix or a suffix. A root is the base of a word. It may be a word that has a meaning by itself. A prefix is placed at the beginning of a root and changes the meaning of the root. Think about the word *justice.* If you add *in-* as a prefix to *justice,* the word becomes *injustice. Justice* means "to be fair, right, or correct," while *injustice* is "the quality of being unfair."

A suffix is placed at the end of a root and changes the word's part of speech. If you add *-ment* to the root *amend,* it becomes *amendment. Amend* is a verb. *Amendment* is a noun.

Analyze Informational Text

Here are several reading strategies to help you think about and analyze informational text. They include analyzing the author's purpose, distinguishing between facts and opinions, identifying evidence, and evaluating credibility.

Analyze the Author's Purpose

Different types of materials are written with different purposes in mind. For example, a textbook is written to teach students information about a subject. The purpose of a technical manual is to teach someone how to use something, such as a computer. A newspaper editorial might be written to persuade the reader to a particular point of view. A writer's purpose influences how the material is presented.

Distinguish Between Facts and Opinions

It is important to distinguish between fact and opinion. A fact can be proved or disproved. An opinion reveals someone's personal viewpoint or evaluation.

For example, the editorial pages in a newspaper offer opinions on current events. You need to read newspaper editorials with an eye for bias and faulty logic. The newspaper editorial shown here shows factual statements in blue and opinion statements in red. The underlined words are examples of highly charged words and exaggerations. They reveal the writer's bias.

More than 5,000 people voted last week in favor of building a new shopping center, but the opposition won out. The margin of victory is irrelevant. Those radical voters who opposed the center are obviously self-serving elitists who do not care about anyone but themselves.

This month's unemployment figures for our area are 10 percent, which represents an increase of about 5 percent over the figures for last year. These figures mean that unemployment is worsening. But the people who voted against the mall probably do not care about creating new jobs.

Identify Evidence

Before you accept a writer's conclusions, you need to make sure that the writer has based the conclusion on enough evidence and on an accurate portrayal of the evidence. A writer may present a whole series of facts to support a claim, but the facts may not tell the whole story.

For example, what evidence does the writer in the newspaper editorial above provide to support his claim that shopping centers create more jobs? Isn't it possible that the shopping center might put local stores out of business, thus increasing unemployment rather than decreasing it?

Evaluate Credibility

Whenever you read informational texts, you need to assess the credibility of the writer. This is especially true of Web sites you may visit on the Internet. Here are some questions to ask yourself when evaluating the credibility of a Web site.

- ❑ Did a respected organization, a discussion group, or an individual create the Web site?
- ❑ Does the Web site creator include his or her name and credentials, as well as the sources he or she used to write the content?
- ❑ Is the information on the site objective or biased?
- ❑ Can you verify the information using two other sources?
- ❑ Is there a date on the Web site?

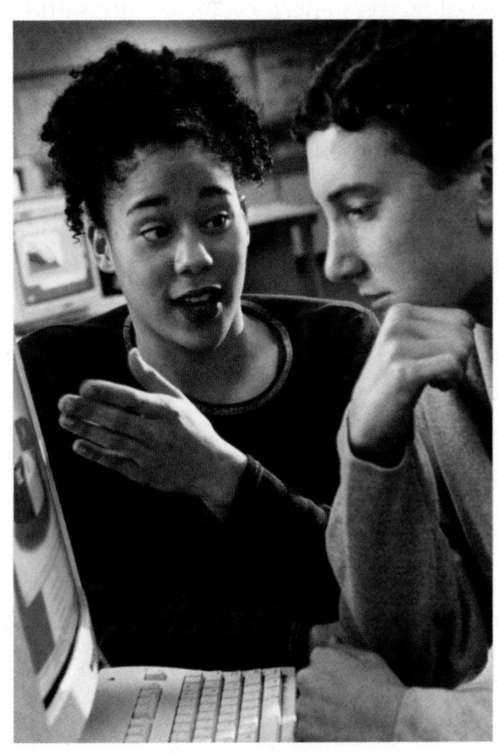

How to Read Social Studies

Target Reading Skills

The Target Reading Skills introduced on this page will help you understand the words and ideas in your textbook. Each chapter contains several of these strategies, and each strategy is paired with a graphic organizer. The graphic organizers help you visualize and organize the content you are reading. In the margins of your textbook, you will find Target Reading Skill sidenotes that will help you use the reading skill and the graphic organizer while you read the text. Good readers develop a bank of reading strategies. Then, they draw on the particular strategies that will help them understand what they are reading.

Reading Process

Reading actively will help you remember what you have read. The paragraphs below describe several ways to read actively. In addition, preparing an outline or using a chart, table, or concept web can help focus your reading.

1 Set a Purpose

When you set a purpose for reading, you give yourself a focus. Before you read a section, study the objectives and look at headings and visuals to see what the section is about.

2 Predict

Making predictions helps you remember what you read. After studying the objectives, headings, and visuals, predict what the text might discuss.

3 Ask Questions

Before you read a section, write down one or two questions that will help you understand or remember something important in the section. Read to answer your questions.

4 Use Prior Knowledge

Your prior knowledge is what you already know about a topic before you read. Building on what you already know helps you learn new information.

Clarifying Meaning

Clarifying meaning helps you understand what you have read. Reread difficult passages. Paraphrase, or restate in your own words, what those passages mean. Summarize, or state in the correct order, the main points you have read. Outlining and filling in charts, tables, or concept webs can help to clarify meaning.

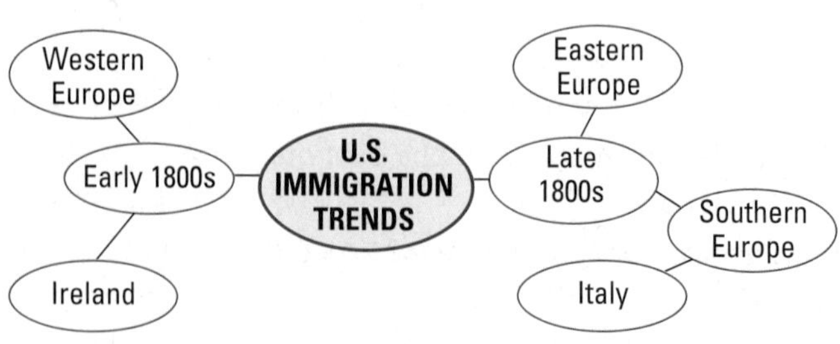

Main Idea

It is impossible to remember every detail that you read. Good readers therefore identify the main idea in every paragraph or section. The main idea is the most important point in a passage. Main ideas are supported by details that add more information. Use outlines and concept webs to help you identify main ideas and supporting details.

I. Differences Between the North and the South
- **A.** Views on slavery
  - **1.** Northern abolitionists
  - **2.** Southern slave owners
- **B.** Economies
  - **1.** Northern manufacturing
  - **2.** Southern agriculture

Comparison and Contrast

Comparing and contrasting can help you sort and analyze information. When you compare, you examine the similarities between things. When you contrast, you look at the differences. A Venn diagram is a good tool for comparing and contrasting people, places, events, or ideas.

FEDERAL POWERS
- coin money
- declare war

SHARED POWERS
- collect taxes
- pass laws

STATE POWERS
- provide schools
- establish local governments

Sequence

A sequence is the order in which a series of events occurs. Noting the sequence of important events can help you understand and remember the events. You can track the order of events by making a flowchart. Write the first event, which sets the other events in motion, in the first box. Then, write each additional event in a box. Use arrows to show how one event leads to the next.

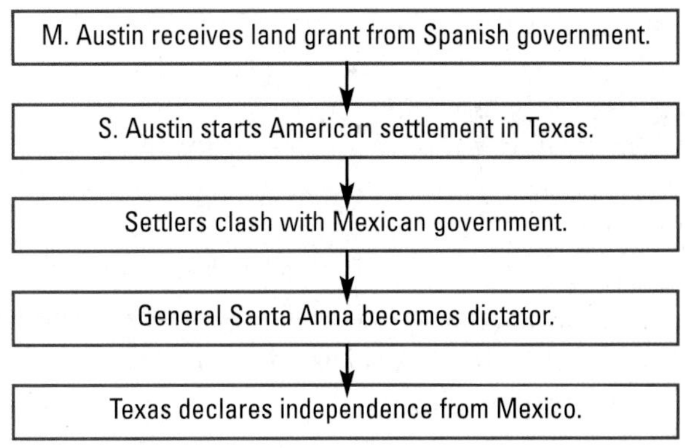

Cause and Effect

Determining causes and effects helps you understand relationships among situations or events. A cause makes something happen. An effect is what happens. Remember that there can be more than one cause for an event and more than one effect. Fill in a cause-and-effect chart to help you understand how causes lead to events and how effects are the results of events.

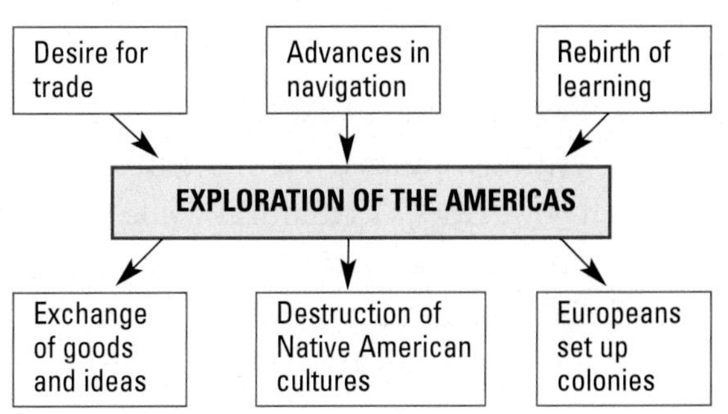

Writing for Social Studies

When you face a writing assignment, do you think, "How will I ever get through this?" Research shows that writing about what you have read actually helps you remember new content. And, of course, good writing skills are important for doing well on tests. Here are some tips to guide you through your social studies writing assignments, whether they are short-answer questions on a test, essays, or research papers.

Types of Writing

There are many different types of writing. Here are six types that are most often assigned:

1. **Narrative Essay**—writing in which you tell a story about a personal experience
2. **Persuasive Essay**—writing in which you support an opinion or a position
3. **Expository Essay**—writing in which you explain a process, compare and contrast, explain causes and effects, or explore solutions
4. **Research Paper**—writing in which you conduct research and write about a specific topic
5. **Writing Extended Responses on a Test**—writing essays for a test
6. **Writing Short Answers on a Test**—writing briefly to respond to short-answer questions

1 Narrative Essay

Writing a narrative essay is a natural form of expression because it involves putting onto paper what we normally do when we tell a good story.

Step 1: Select and Narrow Your Topic

A narrative is a story. In social studies, a narrative essay might focus on how a historical event affected you or your family.

Step 2: Gather Details

Brainstorm for a list of details you want to include in your narrative.

Step 3: Write a First Draft

Start by writing a simple opening sentence that will catch your reader's attention while conveying the main idea of your essay. Continue by writing a colorful story that has interesting details. Write a conclusion that summarizes the significance of the event or situation described in your essay.

Step 4: Revise and Edit

Check to make sure you have not begun too many sentences with the word *I*. Replace general words with more specific, colorful ones.

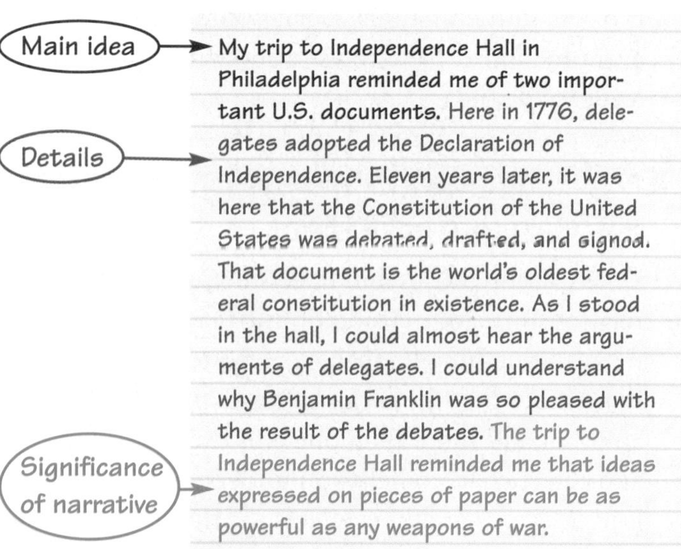

❷ Persuasive Essay

A persuasive essay is writing in which you support an opinion or a position.

Step 1: Select and Narrow Your Topic

Choose a topic that provokes an argument and has at least two sides. Your task will be to persuade most of your readers to understand your point of view.

Step 2: Gather Evidence

Create a table that states your position at the top and lists the pros and cons for your position beneath it.

Step 3: Write a First Draft

Write a strong thesis statement that clearly states your position. Continue by presenting the strongest arguments in favor of your position. Take time to acknowledge and refute opposing arguments, too.

Step 4: Revise and Edit

Check to make sure you have made a logical argument and that you have not oversimplified the argument. Add the following transition words to make your reasoning more obvious:

To show a contrast—*however, although, despite*

To point out a reason—*since, because, if*

To signal a conclusion—*therefore, consequently, so, then*

❸ Expository Essay

An expository essay is writing in which you explain a process, compare and contrast, explain causes and effects, or explore solutions to a problem.

Step 1: Select and Narrow Your Topic

Expository writing is writing that explains something in detail. It might explain the similarities and differences between two or more subjects (compare and contrast). It might explain how one event causes another (cause and effect), or it might explain a problem and describe a solution.

Step 2: Gather Evidence

Create a graphic organizer that identifies details to include in your essay. You might create a Venn diagram for a comparison-and-contrast essay, a diagram showing multiple causes and effects for a cause-and-effect essay, or a web for defining all the aspects of a problem and possible solutions.

Step 3: Write a First Draft

Write a strong topic sentence. Then, organize the body of your essay around the similarities and differences, causes and effects, or problem and solutions. Be sure to include convincing details, facts, and examples.

Step 4: Revise and Edit

Revise to include transition words between sentences and paragraphs.

To show similarities—*all, similarly, both, in the same way, closely related, equally*

To show differences—*on the other hand, in contrast, however, instead, yet*

4 Research Paper

A research paper is writing in which you conduct research and write about a specific topic. Research papers are very different from other types of writing. People who enjoy creative writing may find this form of writing more challenging. Others who do not enjoy creative writing may excel at writing research papers.

Step 1: Select and Narrow Your Topic

Choose something you are interested in, but make sure that the topic is not too broad. For example, instead of writing a paper on Panama, write about the construction of the Panama Canal. Ask yourself, What do I want to know about the topic?

Step 2: Acquire Information

Use several sources of information about the topic from the library, the Internet, or an interview with someone knowledgeable. Before you use a source, make sure that it is reliable and up to date. Take notes using an index card for each detail or subtopic, and note the source of the information. Use quotation marks when you copy the exact words from a source. Create a source index card for each resource, listing the author, title, publisher, and place and date of publication.

Step 3: Make an Outline

Decide on the organization of your report by creating an outline. Sort your index cards into the order of your outline.

Step 4: Write a First Draft

Write an introduction, body, and conclusion. Leave plenty of space between lines so you can go back and add details that you may have left out. Make sure that you have at least one new paragraph on each doubled-spaced page. If you don't, your paragraphs are probably too long and your reader may get lost or lose interest.

Outline
I. Introduction
II. Why the Canal Was Built
III. How the Canal Was Built

Reference
McCullough, David. *The Path Between the Seas: The Creation of the Panama Canal, 1870-1914.* N.Y., Simon and Schuster, 1977.

Good detail for body:
"In 1904, the U.S. government began the largest civil engineering project in its history. An enthusiastic President Theodore Roosevelt set the work in motion by urging the engineers to "Make the dirt fly!"

Building the Panama Canal
Ever since Christopher Columbus first explored the Isthmus of Panama, people had been looking for a water route through it. They wanted to be able to travel from the Atlantic to the Pacific without having to sail around the southern tip of South America. However, it was not until 1914 that the dream became a reality.

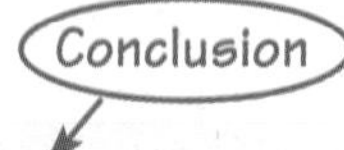

It took eight years and more than 70,000 workers to make the Panama Canal. It remains one of the greatest engineering feats of modern times.

5 Writing Extended Responses on a Test

Step 1: Choose a Writing Prompt and Budget Time

In some testing situations, you may be given a choice of writing prompts, or topics. Before choosing one, consider how much you know about a topic and how much a topic interests you. To budget time, allow about

- 1/4 of your time to prepare to write,
- 1/2 of your time writing a first draft,
- 1/4 of your time revising and editing.

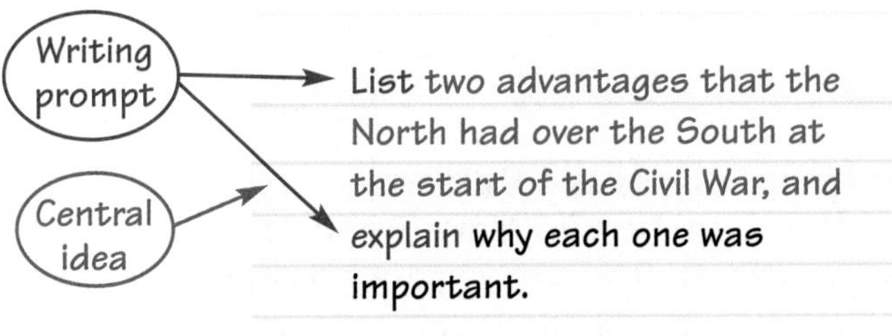

Step 2: Carefully Analyze the Question or Writing Prompt

Pay special attention to key words that indicate exactly what you are supposed to do:

Explain—Give a clear, complete account of how something works or why something happened.

Compare and Contrast—Provide details about how two or more things are alike and how they are different.

Describe—Provide vivid details to paint a word picture of a person, place, or thing.

Argue and Convince—Take a position on an issue and present strong reasons to support your side of the issue.

Summarize—Provide the highlights or most important elements of a subject.

Classify—Group things into categories and define the categories using facts and examples.

Persuade—Provide convincing reasons to accept your position.

Step 3: Gather Details

Take a few minutes to divide your topic into subtopics. Jot down as many facts and details as you can for each subtopic. Create a graphic organizer to organize the details.

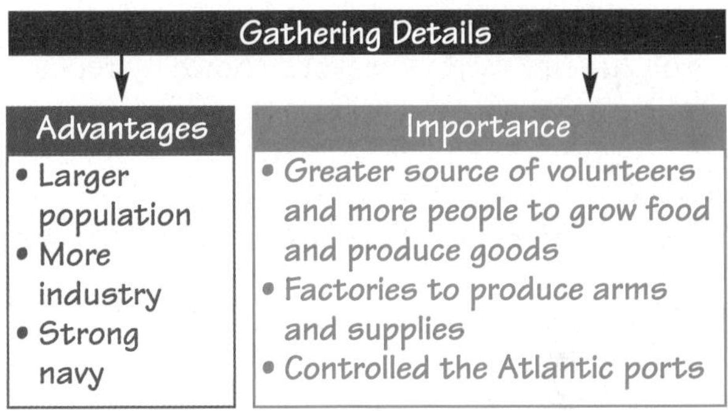

Step 4: Write a First Draft

Write a single sentence that sums up your main point. Use this sentence as the centerpiece of an introductory paragraph. Then, consider the best plan for organizing your essay.

- For a summary or an explanation, organize your details in chronological order, as on a time line.
- For a comparison-and-contrast essay, present similarities first and then differences.
- For a persuasive essay, organize your points by order of importance.

Use the organization you've selected to write your first draft.

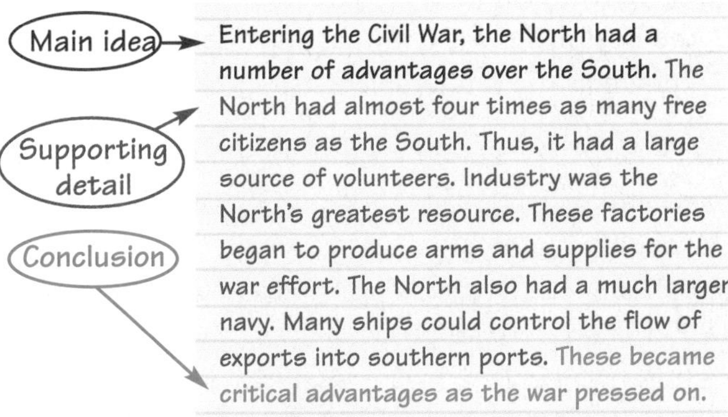

Step 5: Revise

Read your response to make sure that

- the introduction includes a strong main idea sentence and presents subtopics.
- each paragraph focuses on a single topic.
- you have included transition words between sentences and paragraphs, such as *first, for example, because,* and *for this reason.*
- you have revised your word choice by replacing general words with specific ones.

Step 6: Edit and Proof

Read your response to make sure each sentence

- contains a subject and a verb.
- begins with a capital letter.
- ends with a period, question mark, or exclamation point.

Correct any spelling or punctuation errors.

6 Writing Short Answers on a Test

These are questions that require either filling in blanks, paragraph answers, or bullet-point answers.

Step 1: Use Key Words From the Question

Read the question carefully, noting key words.

Step 2: Write in Complete Sentences

When answering a short-answer question, always be clear and concise. Practice writing a structured response. Begin by introducing the key topic words you have jotted down.

Question: What was Great Britain's response to the Boston Tea Party?
Fragment: The Intolerable Acts
Complete sentence: Great Britain responded to the Boston Tea Party by passing a series of laws known as the Intolerable Acts.

Step 3: Follow the Pattern of the Question in Your Answer

Include specific, precise, and detailed information that reflects the wording of the question. Avoid vague answers.

Question: Who was Thomas Jefferson, and why is he remembered today?
Vague response: Jefferson was a Virginian who did many important things in the early days of American history.
Precise response: Jefferson wrote the Declaration of Independence and was the third President of the United States.

Step 4: Write a Draft

Write an introductory sentence. Then, provide an illustration or example that supports the introductory sentence. Be sure to answer only what the question asks.

Evaluating Your Writing: Rubrics

Most essays are scored on the following elements:

Purpose—distinct main idea, theme, or unified point

Organization—clear beginning, middle, and end; obvious relationship between one point and the next and between sentences and paragraphs using transitions

Elaboration—important details and specific, thorough, and correct word choices to explain the topic

Language—strong command of punctuation, capitalization, sentence structure, and spelling

Use the rubric below to help you evaluate your writing.

	Excellent	Good	Acceptable	Unacceptable
Purpose	Achieves purpose—to inform, persuade, or provide historical interpretation—very well	Informs, persuades, or provides historical interpretation reasonably well	Reader cannot easily tell if the purpose is to inform, persuade, or provide historical interpretation	Lacks purpose
Organization	Develops ideas in a very clear and logical way	Presents ideas in a reasonably well-organized way	Reader has difficulty following the organization	Lacks organization
Elaboration	Explains all ideas with facts and details	Explains most ideas with facts and details	Includes some supporting facts and details	Lacks supporting details
Use of Language	Uses excellent vocabulary and sentence structure with no errors in spelling, grammar, or punctuation	Uses good vocabulary and sentence structure with few errors in spelling, grammar, or punctuation	Includes some errors in spelling, grammar, or punctuation	Includes many errors in spelling, grammar, or punctuation

Unit 1 Roots of American History

UNIT OUTLINE

Chapter 1
Geography, History, and the Social Sciences (Prehistory–Present)

Chapter 2
Before the First Global Age
(Prehistory–1600)

Chapter 3
Exploration and Colonization (1492–1675)

Chapter 4
The Thirteen English Colonies
(1630–1750)

An Untouched Landscape
Grand Canyon by William Robinson Leigh captures the natural beauty of the American continent.

“For this is what America is all about. It is the uncrossed desert and the unclimbed ridge. It is the star that is not reached and the harvest sleeping in the unplowed ground.”

—Lyndon B. Johnson, President of the United States (1965)

CHAPTER 1

Geography, History, and the Social Sciences

PREHISTORY–PRESENT

1 Thinking Geographically
2 Lands and Climates of the United States
3 The Tools of History
4 Economics and Other Social Sciences

Early encounter between Europeans and Native Americans

Settlers clearing the land

AMERICAN EVENTS

1500s The first global age begins with the meeting between Europeans and Native Americans.

1600s England sets up colonies in North America.

1700s Thirteen English colonies separate from Great Britain and form the United States of America.

Prehistory | 1500 | 1600 | 1700

WORLD EVENTS

▲ **1500s** Europeans explore the Americas.

▲ **1600s** European nations struggle for control of North America.

Physical Features of the United States

The United States is divided into different physical regions.

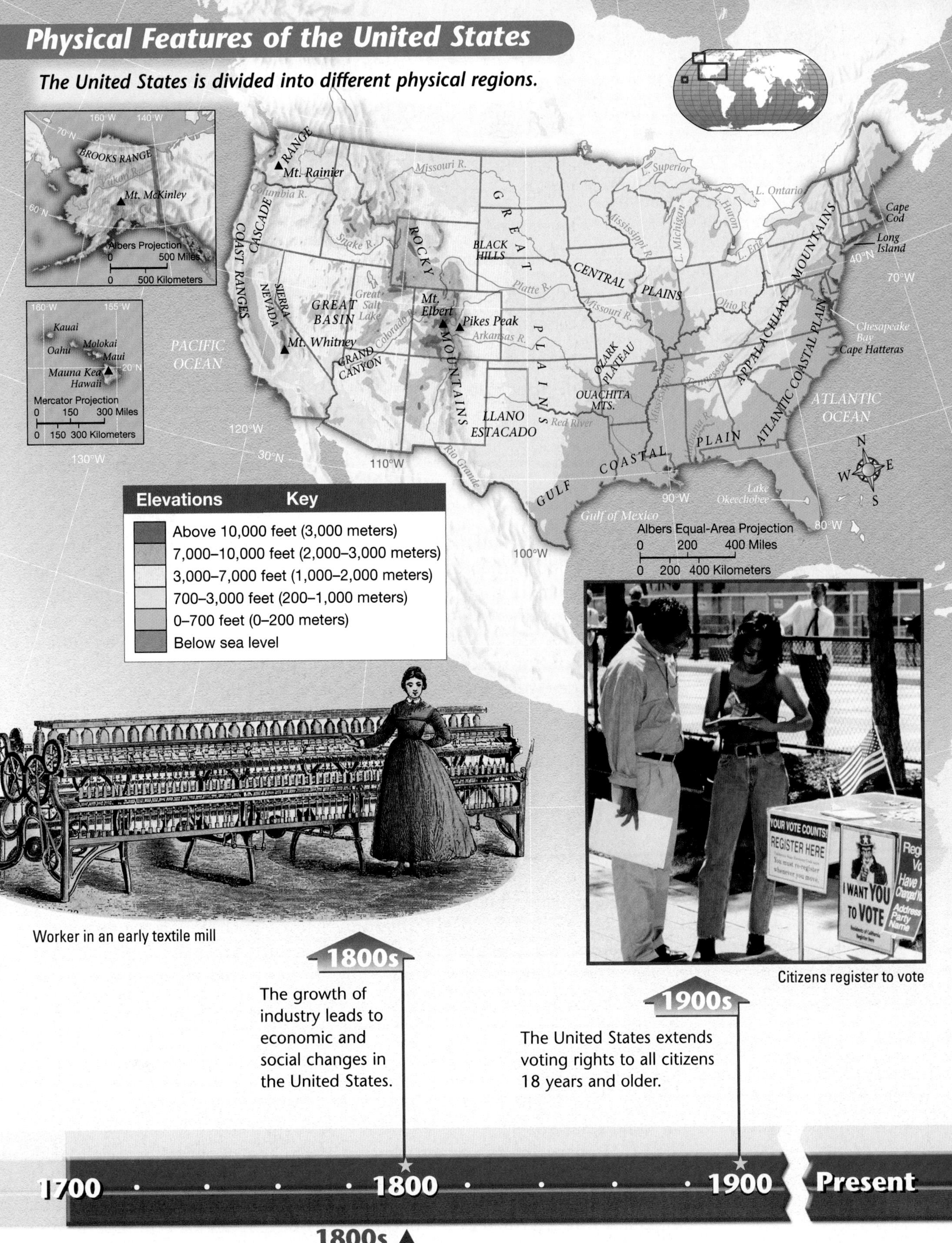

Worker in an early textile mill

Citizens register to vote

1800s

The growth of industry leads to economic and social changes in the United States.

1900s

The United States extends voting rights to all citizens 18 years and older.

1800s ▲

Millions of immigrants move to the United States.

1 Thinking Geographically

Prepare to Read

Objectives

In this section, you will
- Explain how the five themes of geography help define the connections between geography and history.
- Identify how geography influenced population trends in U.S. history.
- Describe how maps are made and used.

Key Terms

geography
latitude
longitude
natural resources
irrigation
cartographer
map projection
thematic map

Target Reading Skill

Reading Process Copy the chart below. As you read, fill in the chart with information about the five themes of geography. Add boxes for the remaining themes.

LOCATION	PLACE
• Exact Location: longitude and latitude	• •

Main Idea Geography helps us to understand the way people have lived in different places throughout history.

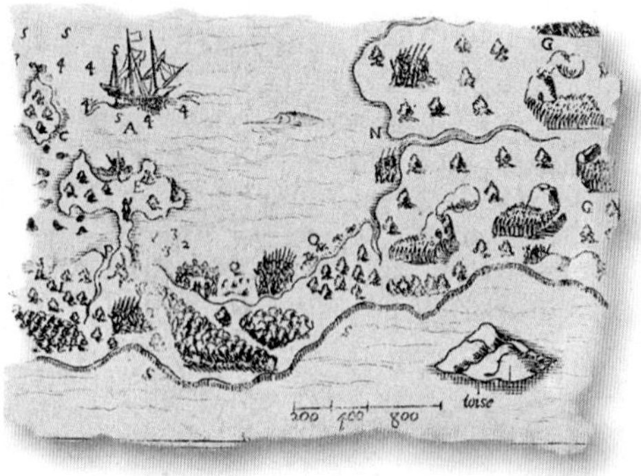

A map by Samuel de Champlain

Setting the Scene In a tiny Native American fishing village, a small group gathered around a man who began to draw in the sand. They watched closely as Samuel de Champlain, a French explorer, drew a sweeping line on the ground. The line represented the coastline where they stood. The local chief drew additional lines. A young man added piles of rocks to represent the village and nearby settlements. When they were done, they had an informal map of the local area.

Champlain and the Native Americans he met on Cape Ann in Massachusetts in the 1600s did not speak the same language. Yet, they both understood the basic language of geography.

Five Themes of Geography

Geography is the study of people, their environments, and their resources. Geographers ask how the natural environment affects the way we live and how we, in turn, affect the environment.

Geography is closely linked to history. Both historians and geographers want to understand how the natural environment affects people and events. To help show these connections, geographers have developed five themes: location, place, interaction between people and their environment, movement, and regions.

Location Often, the most basic question we ask about an event is, "Where did it happen?" The answer to this question involves the geographic theme of location. There are two types of location: exact and relative.

To describe the exact location of a place, geographers use a grid of numbered lines on a map or globe. Lines of **latitude** measure distance north and south from the Equator. The Equator is an imaginary line that lies at 0° (degrees) latitude. It divides the Earth into two halves, called hemispheres. Lines of **longitude** measure distance

The Five Themes of Geography

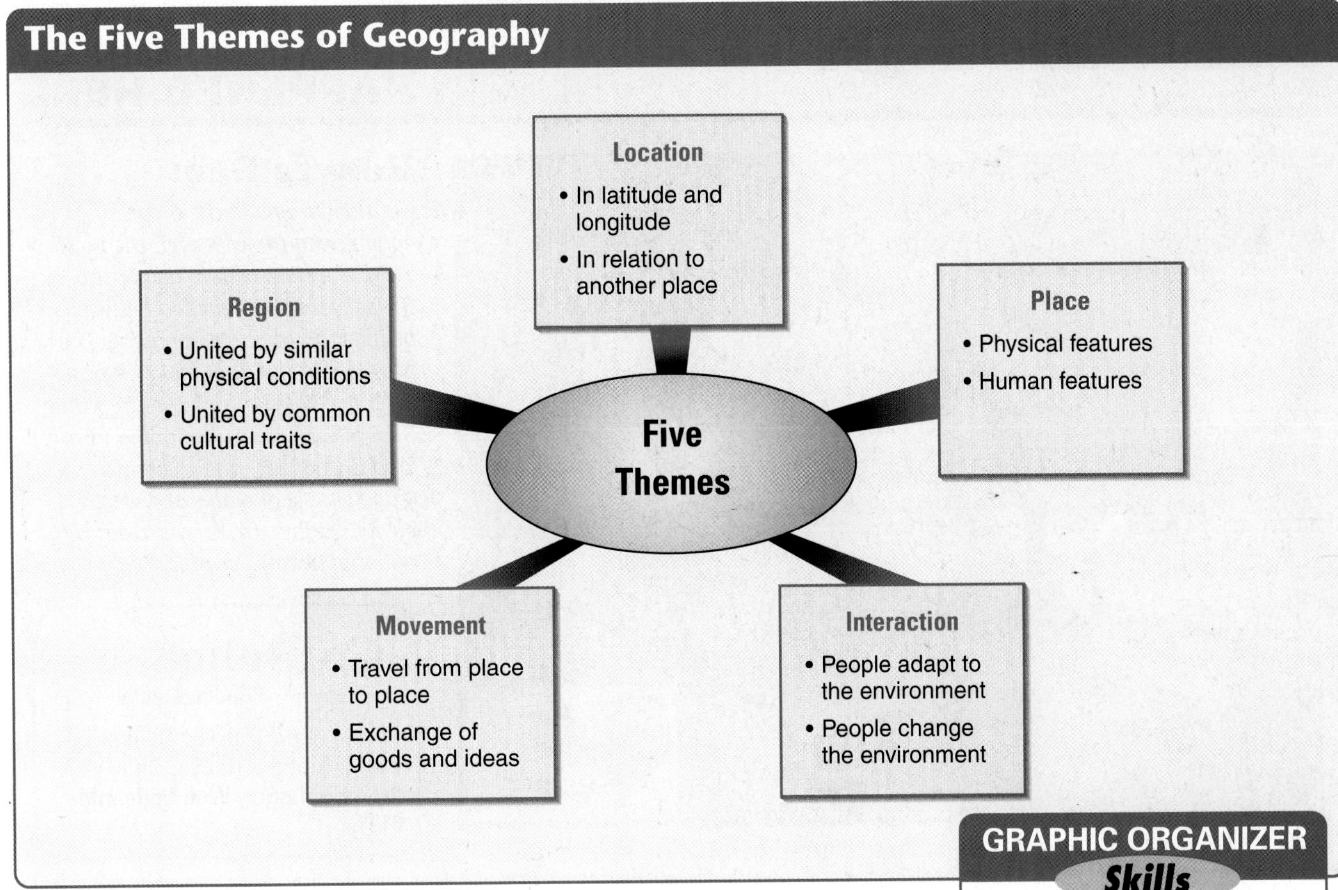

GRAPHIC ORGANIZER *Skills*

Geographers have developed five themes to help us understand the connections between people and the natural environment, and between geography and history.

1. **Comprehension** What are two ways to describe the location of a place?
2. **Critical Thinking Applying Information** Which geographic theme would be most concerned with trade among nations?

east and west from the Prime Meridian, which runs through Greenwich (GREHN ihch), England. For example, the city of San Antonio, Texas, is located at 29 degrees (°) north latitude and 99 degrees (°) west longitude. This location is written as 29°N/99°W. In the same way, New York City is located at 41°N/74°W.

Sometimes, you will find it more useful to know relative location, or the location of a place in relation to some other place. For example, San Antonio is about 125 miles from the Mexican border. New York City is located where the Hudson River empties into the Atlantic Ocean. Relative location can help explain why people settled in certain areas or why battles took place at certain places.

Place Geographers use the theme of place to describe an area's physical and human features. Physical features include climate, soil, vegetation, animal life, and bodies of water. One of the most important aspects of a place is its **natural resources,** materials that humans can take from the environment to survive and satisfy their needs. For example, a mountain range may contain reserves of coal or iron, while a nearby river or ocean may supply fish.

People help shape the character of a place through their ideas and actions. The human features of a place include the kinds of houses people build, their means of transportation, their ways of earning a living, their languages, and their religions.

Interaction Interaction between people and their environment is a third theme of geography. Throughout history, people have adapted

AmericanHeritage
M A G A Z I N E

HISTORY **HAPPENED HERE**

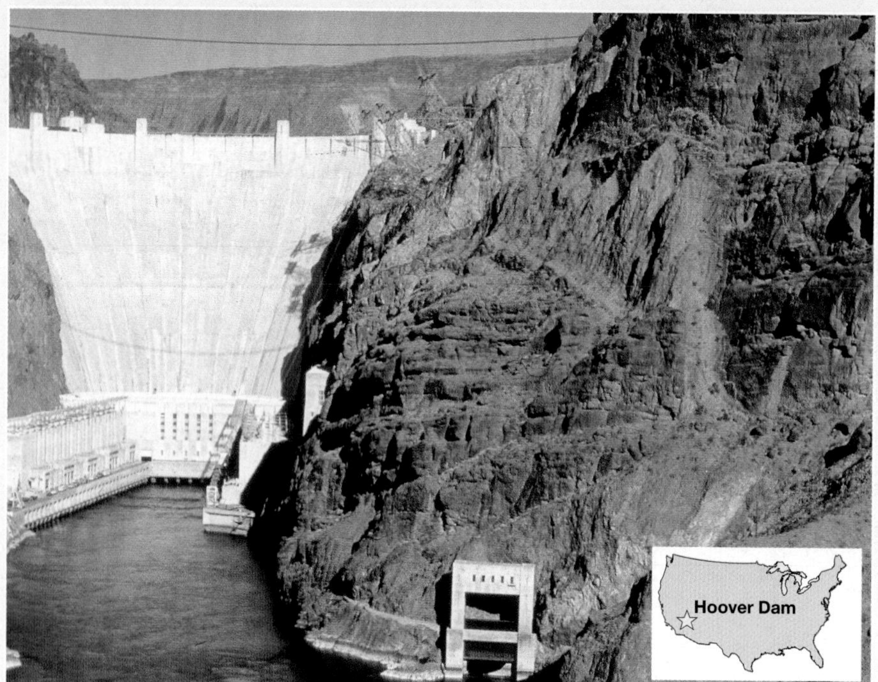

Hoover Dam

Considered one of the greatest engineering projects ever, the building of the Hoover Dam demonstrates the successful interaction between people and their environment. The presence of the dam makes it possible for people to live in an area that is largely desert. Surrounding farmland is irrigated, and there is a ready supply of water and electric power. Today, the Hoover Dam is a national historic landmark.

Virtual Field Trip For an interactive look at the Hoover Dam, visit PHSchool.com, **Web Code mfd-0101.**

to and changed their natural surroundings. Ancient American hunters learned to plant seeds and grow food crops. This adaptation meant they no longer had to move from place to place in search of food. Later, Native Americans in the Southwest developed methods of **irrigation,** or bringing water to dry lands. By digging ditches that channeled water from the Salt and Gila rivers, they turned arid, unproductive desert into farmland.

Today, advanced technology allows people to change their environment in even more dramatic ways. People have wiped out pests that destroyed crops and found ways to take oil from the ocean floor.

Set a Purpose When you set a purpose for reading, you give yourself a focus. Your purpose in this section is to learn about the five themes and complete your chart. How does this paragraph help you meet your goal?

Movement A fourth geographic theme involves the movement of people, goods, and ideas. Movement occurs because people and resources are scattered unevenly around the globe. To get what they need or want, people travel from place to place. As they meet other people, they exchange ideas and technology as well as goods.

History provides many examples of movement. Early hunters populated the Americas as they followed herds of large animals. Much later, people from all over the world moved to the United States in search of opportunity or liberty. They brought customs and beliefs that have helped shape American life.

Regions A region has certain unifying characteristics. It may be defined by its physical characteristics, such as its climates or landforms. For example, the Great Plains is a region with fairly level land, hot summers, cold winters, and little rainfall. In the 1930s, when parts of the plains were hit by drought, the region was called the "Dust Bowl." The Pacific Coast region is known for rugged mountains, dense forests, and scenic ocean shores.

A region's characteristics may also be human and cultural. San Francisco's Chinatown is a region where Chinese Americans have preserved their language and culture. Bourbon Street in the city of New Orleans is associated with jazz.

Case Study: Population Trends and the Five Themes

As you study events and trends in history, you will often need to think geographically. For practice, let us see how population trends throughout the history of the United States relate to the five themes of geography.

When the United States won its independence in 1783, it was made up of 13 states located on the Atlantic coast (*region, exact location*). The majority of the population lived along the coast or near rivers (*relative location*), where water transportation was easy (*movement*). The Appalachian Mountains and other geographic features limited westward movement (*region, movement*). In 1790, the nation's center of population was located in Maryland.

The Nation Expands The United States added vast new territories in the early 1800s, eventually stretching to the Pacific Ocean (*movement, exact location*). As the nation expanded, its rapidly growing population shifted westward (*movement*). Settlers dug canals, built roads and railroads, and cut down forests to clear farmland and build log cabins (*interaction, place*).

A New Trend The westward trend continued in the late 1800s. As white settlers displaced Native Americans, the human and cultural characteristics of the West changed (*place*). By 1900, the center of population had shifted to Indiana.

In the mid-1900s, a new population trend began to emerge. Many people began to move from the Northeast to the Sunbelt, a region stretching from Florida across Texas to California (*region, movement*). Many people were attracted by the area's mild climate (*place*). In 1960, only 2 of the 10 largest American cities were located in the South or West (*region*). By 2000, six of them were: Houston, Dallas, San Antonio, Los Angeles, San Diego, and Phoenix. Furthermore, the center of the nation's population had shifted again, both southward and westward, to Missouri.

Maps and Globes

The most common tools used to understand geography are maps and globes. A map is a drawing of the surface of the Earth or part of the Earth. A globe is a sphere with a map of the Earth printed on it.

Maps and globes have different uses. Because a globe is about the same shape as the Earth, it can accurately show sizes and shapes of landforms. However, compared to a map, a globe is awkward to use. In addition, a map can show more detail than a globe and allows

Map Projections

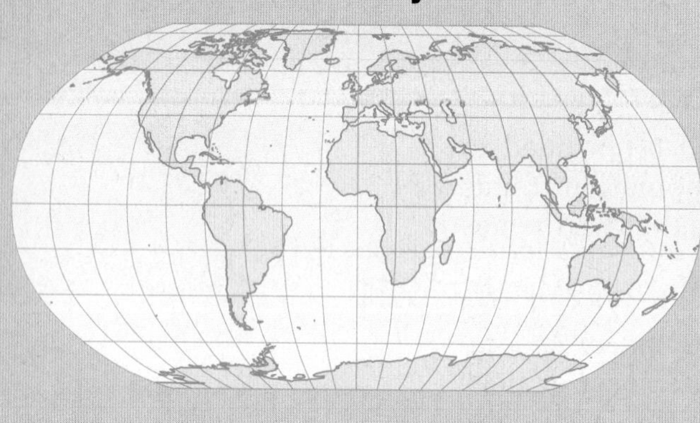

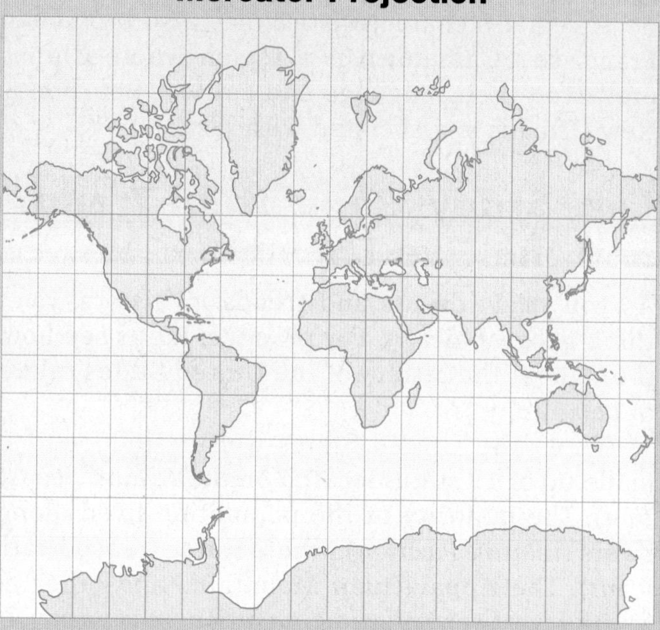

GEOGRAPHY *Skills*

Map projections make it possible for mapmakers to show a round world on a flat map.

1. **Location** On the map, locate **(a)** North America, **(b)** Africa, **(c)** Asia.
2. **Place** What differences appear in the two projections of North America?
3. **Critical Thinking Comparing** On the Mercator map, which areas are most distorted?

you to see all of the Earth's surface at one time. Still, a flat map has the disadvantage that it distorts some parts of the Earth.

Map Projections Mapmakers, or **cartographers,** have developed dozens of ways of drawing the Earth on a flat surface. These methods are known as **map projections.** Each map projection has benefits and drawbacks. Some show the sizes of landmasses correctly but distort their shape. Others give continents their true shape but distort their sizes.

For hundreds of years, the most widely used map projection was the Mercator projection. It was developed in 1569 by the Flemish cartographer Gerardus Mercator. The Mercator projection was valuable because it gave sailors an accurate picture of ocean distances and the shapes of landmasses. Mercator boasted:

> “If you wish to sail from one port to another, here is a chart, and a straight line on it, and if you follow this line carefully you will certainly arrive at your destination.”
>
> —Gerardus Mercator, "To the Readers of This Chart, Greeting!"

However, the Mercator projection distorts size, especially for places that are far from the Equator. For example, on a Mercator map, Greenland appears as big as all of South America, even though South America is more than eight times larger!

Today, many geographers use the Robinson projection. It shows the correct sizes and shapes of landmasses for most parts of the world. The Robinson projection also gives a fairly accurate view of the relationship between landmasses and bodies of water. There are many other types of map projections as well. On each map in this book, you will see a label identifying the type of projection used.

Types of Maps As you study American history, you will use various types of maps. Each one has a special purpose. Physical maps show mountain ranges, bodies of water, and other physical features. Political maps show features that are determined by people. These include the boundaries of countries and states, as well as the location of capitals and other cities. You will see examples of these types of maps in the Geographic Atlas in the Reference Section of this book.

You will also use a wide variety of **thematic maps,** or maps that deal with specific topics, that can help you understand the connections between geography and history. Population maps show the number of people who live in a particular area. Economic maps show how people make a living. Battle maps show the locations of major battles and the routes of advancing and retreating armies. Other thematic maps may provide information on natural resources, rainfall, vegetation, elections, or the religious or ethnic makeup of a place.

Making Accurate Maps The oldest surviving map in the world today was created by an ancient cartographer somewhere around 2300 B.C. Ever since, geographers have worked to make maps more accurate.

Today, cartographers create maps with the help of computers and satellites. This new technology provides incredibly complete information about the most remote corners of the Earth. As a result, today's mapmakers create maps that are more accurate than anyone had previously thought possible.

★ ★ ★ Section 1 Assessment ★ ★ ★

Recall

1. **Define** **(a)** geography, **(b)** latitude, **(c)** longitude, **(d)** natural resources, **(e)** irrigation, **(f)** cartographer, **(g)** map projection, **(h)** thematic map.

Comprehension

2. Briefly describe the five themes of geography.
3. List three population trends in the history of the United States. Give the theme, or themes, of geography illustrated by each.
4. Why does a globe show the Earth more accurately than a flat map?

Critical Thinking and Writing

5. **Exploring the Main Idea** Review the Main Idea statement at the beginning of this section. Name two ways that geography affects life in the community or state where you live. Write your findings in a paragraph.
6. **Synthesizing Information** Study the picture of the Hoover Dam on page 6. How does the dam illustrate the geographic theme of interaction?

ACTIVITY

Connecting to Today
Use the Internet to research the satellite mapping program started in 1972. Choose a site with satellite images of the Earth. Select a picture. Print it out. In a paragraph, describe the picture. Explain how it would be useful to a cartographer. For help in completing the activity, visit PHSchool.com, **Web Code mfd-0102.**

Reviewing Map Skills

SKILLS FOR LIFE

Early maps were crude but useful pictures drawn on animal skins, clay tablets, and cloth. Today, maps are even more important tools in providing information about places on Earth. Learning how to read and interpret a map is also helpful in understanding how geography affects history.

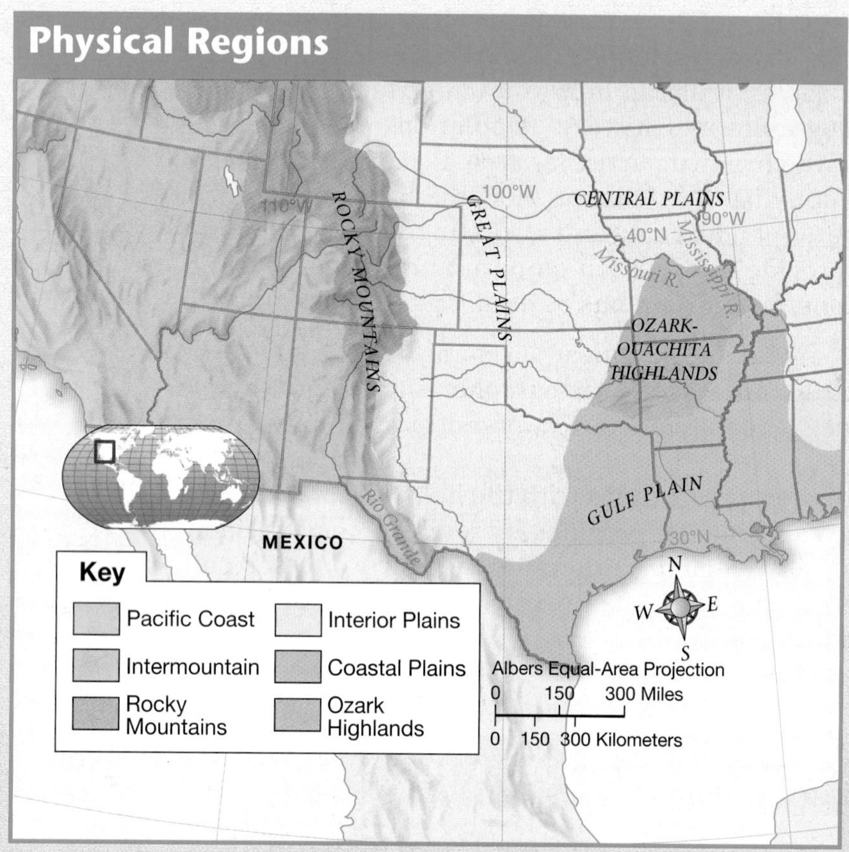

Learn the Skill *To review basic map-reading skills, use the following steps:*

1. **Read the title.** The title summarizes the basic information included on a map.
2. **Refer to the map key.** The key identifies what the different symbols on the map mean.
3. **Find the scales of distance.** Maps are miniature pictures of places on Earth, so they are drawn to scale. To determine actual distance, you need to know how many inches represent miles or kilometers.
4. **Use the compass rose.** The arrows on this symbol indicate directions on a map.
5. **Check for a locator map.** A locator map helps you see where on Earth a place is located.

Practice the Skill *Answer the following questions about the map above:*

1. What is the purpose of this map?
2. **(a)** What does the color tan represent on this map? **(b)** Through which physical regions does the Missouri River flow?
3. How many miles does one-half inch represent?
4. **(a)** What country is south of the United States? **(b)** In what direction are the Great Plains from the Mississippi River?
5. **(a)** What parts of the United States are not shown on the large map? **(b)** How do you know?

Apply the Skill *See the Chapter Review and Assessment.*

2 Lands and Climates of the United States

Prepare to Read

Objectives

In this section you will
- Identify the main physical regions of the United States.
- Explain how rivers and lakes affect American life.
- Describe how climates vary across the United States.

Key Terms

isthmus
elevation
erosion
tributary
weather
climate
precipitation
altitude

Target Reading Skill

Cause and Effect Copy the cause-and-effect chart. As you read, fill in additional factors that explain the causes and effects of climate.

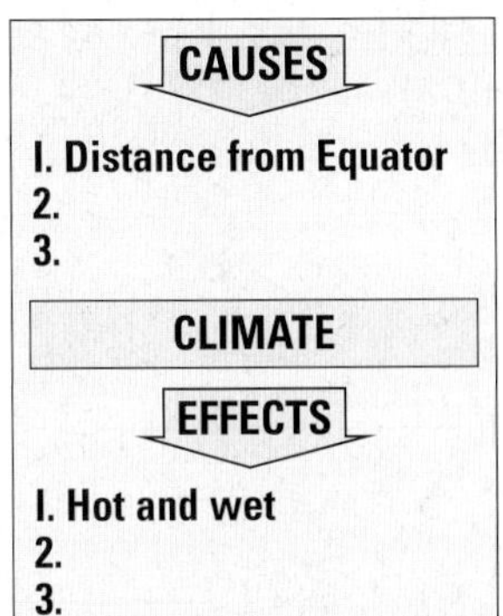

Main Idea The United States is a nation of diverse landforms and climates.

Setting the Scene The view took her breath away. Katharine Lee Bates, a teacher from the East, had journeyed westward to Colorado in 1893. Standing atop the towering Pikes Peak, looking across the "sea-like expanse" below, Bates was moved to write a tribute to her land. Her poem was later set to music:

> "O beautiful for spacious skies,
> For amber waves of grain,
> For purple mountain majesties
> Above the fruited plain!
> America America!
> God shed His grace on thee
> And crown thy good with brotherhood
> From sea to shining sea!"
>
> —Katharine Lee Bates, "America the Beautiful"

Pikes Peak

Besides plains and mountains, the United States is also a land of arid deserts and frozen tundras, quiet forests and crashing seas. This wide variety of climates and landforms has had a powerful impact on American life and history.

Physical Regions of the United States

North America is the world's third largest continent. It is surrounded on three sides by oceans: the Atlantic Ocean to the east, the Pacific Ocean to the west, and the icy Arctic Ocean to the north. To the south, an **isthmus** (IHS muhs), or narrow strip of land, links North America to South America.

The United States is one of the largest countries in the world. Its physical regions offer great contrasts. In some regions, the land is fertile. Other regions have natural resources such as coal and oil.

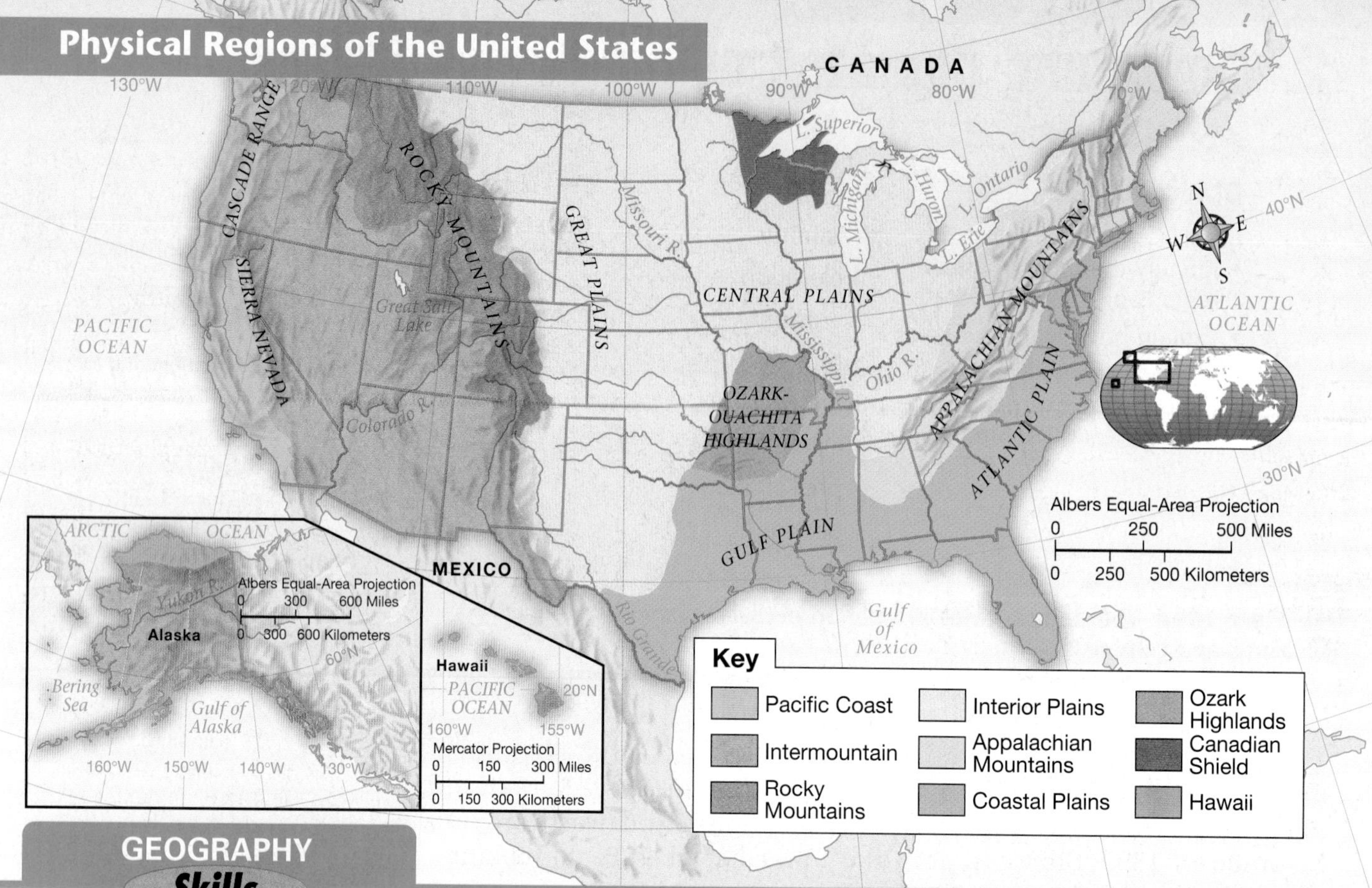

GEOGRAPHY *Skills*

Geographers divide the United States into different physical regions.

1. **Location** On the map, locate **(a)** Sierra Nevada, **(b)** Great Lakes, **(c)** Atlantic Plain, **(d)** Mississippi River, **(e)** Rocky Mountains
2. **Region** Through what three physical regions does the Mississippi River flow?
3. **Critical Thinking Comparing** Compare the Pacific Coast and the Rocky Mountain regions. Why do you think more people live on the Pacific Coast than in the Rocky Mountains?

Geographers divide the United States into different physical regions marked by contrasting landforms and physical features.*

Pacific Coast The westernmost region of North America is the Pacific Coast. It includes high mountain ranges that stretch from Alaska to Mexico. In the United States, some of these western ranges are near the Pacific Ocean. The Cascades and the Sierra Nevada stand a bit farther inland. Important cities of the Pacific Coast region include Seattle, Portland, San Francisco, San Diego, and Los Angeles.

A notable feature of the Pacific Coast region is the San Andreas Fault. This 600-mile fracture in the Earth's crust runs through California from northwest to southeast. Movement of the Earth's crust along this fault can cause earthquakes. For example, powerful quakes shook San Francisco in 1906 and Los Angeles in 1994, causing significant damage and loss of life.

Intermountain Region East of the Pacific Coast mountain ranges lies the Intermountain Region. This region is marked by mountain peaks, high plateaus, deep canyons, and dry, sandy deserts. The Grand Canyon, more than a mile deep, cuts through the Intermountain Region. Another prominent physical feature is the Great Salt Lake of Utah, the nation's largest saltwater lake.

*To review definitions of major landforms and other geographic terms, refer to the Glossary of Geographic Terms at the end of this section.

The rugged terrain limits where people can live in the Intermountain Region. Among the few major cities located there are Phoenix and Salt Lake City.

Rocky Mountains The Rocky Mountains stretch from Alaska through Canada into the western United States. They include the Bitterroot Range in Idaho and Montana, the Big Horn Mountains in Wyoming, and the Sangre de Cristo Mountains in Colorado and New Mexico. In Mexico, the Rockies become the Sierra Madre (MAH dray), or "mother range."

The Rockies include some of the highest peaks in North America—some with an **elevation,** or height above sea level, of more than 14,000 feet. Throughout history, visitors like Katharine Lee Bates have marveled at the beauty and grandeur of the Rocky Mountains. Today, Denver is a major city of the Rocky Mountain Region.

Interior Plains Between the Rockies in the West and the Appalachian Mountains in the East is a large lowland area called the Interior Plains. The dry western part of the region is called the Great Plains. The eastern part is called the Central Plains.

Scientists believe that a great inland sea once covered the Interior Plains. Today, some parts are rich in resources such as coal and petroleum. Other parts offer fertile soil for farming and grasslands for raising cattle. Major cities of the Interior Plains include Dallas, St. Louis, Chicago, Cincinnati, Detroit, and Indianapolis.

Ozark Highlands The Ozark Highlands extend across southern Missouri and northern Arkansas and into eastern Kansas. Thick with forests, the region includes mountains that rise more than 2,000 feet. The highest are the Boston Mountains in Arkansas. Important industries in the region include forestry, agriculture, and mining.

Appalachian Mountains The Appalachian Mountains run along the eastern part of North America. They stretch from Canada in the North to Georgia and Mississippi in the South. The Appalachians have different names in different places. For example, the Green Mountains, Alleghenies, and Great Smoky Mountains are all part of the Appalachians.

The Appalachians are lower and less rugged than the Rockies. The highest peak is Mt. Mitchell in North Carolina, with an elevation of 6,684 feet. Today, hearty hikers enjoy the challenge of walking the Appalachian Trail from Georgia to Maine.

Canadian Shield The Canadian Shield is a lowland area that lies mostly in eastern Canada. The southern part extends into Michigan, Wisconsin, and Minnesota. This region was once an area of high mountains. Centuries of **erosion,** or gradual wearing away, reduced the area to low hills and plains. The Canadian Shield is rich in minerals.

Coastal Plains The easternmost region of North America is called the Coastal Plains, a fairly flat, lowland area. This was the first region settled by Europeans who crossed the Atlantic Ocean. It is made up of two subregions, the Atlantic Plain and the Gulf Plain.

The Atlantic Plain lies between the Atlantic Ocean and the foothills of the Appalachians. The Atlantic Plain is narrow in the North, where major cities such as Boston, New York, and Philadelphia are located. It broadens in the South to include all of Florida.

An American Profile

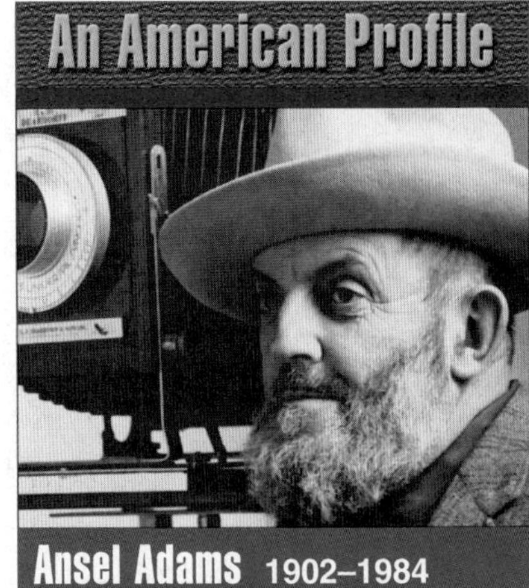

Ansel Adams 1902–1984

Ansel Adams was a landscape photographer known for his dramatic images of the American West.

Adams's photographs (one of which appears on page 14) have inspired millions of people to seek out the wilderness and preserve it.

In 1980, President Jimmy Carter awarded Adams the Medal of Freedom, which is presented to citizens for outstanding achievement in culture, world peace, or public service. "It is through [Adams's] foresight and fortitude," noted Carter, "that so much of America has been saved for future Americans."

How did Adams's art have a political effect?

Viewing History

Regional Contrasts

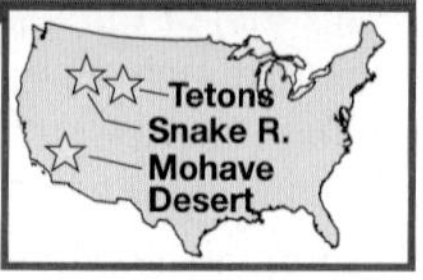

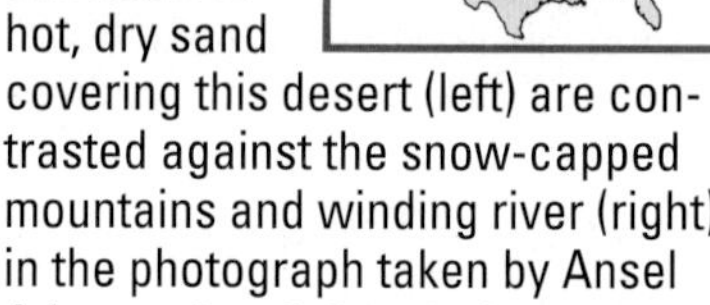

The miles of hot, dry sand covering this desert (left) are contrasted against the snow-capped mountains and winding river (right) in the photograph taken by Ansel Adams. **Applying Information** ***How have people adapted to desert and mountainous conditions?***

The Gulf Plain lies along the Gulf of Mexico. This region is economically important because of its large deposits of petroleum. New Orleans and Houston are major cities of the Gulf Plain.

Hawaiian Islands The Hawaiian Islands lie far out in the Pacific, about 2,400 miles west of California. Much of Hawaii has a wet tropical climate and dense tropical rain forest vegetation. The region includes eight large islands and many smaller ones.

The islands are actually the visible tops of volcanoes that erupted through the floor of the Pacific many centuries ago. Mauna Loa (man uh LOH uh), on the island of Hawaii, is an active volcano that rises 13,680 feet above sea level.

American Rivers and Lakes

Great rivers crisscross North America, linking many of the different physical regions. Many of these rivers begin in the mountains. They collect runoff water from rains and melting snows and carry it to the oceans.

The Mississippi-Missouri River System The Mississippi and Missouri rivers make up the longest and most important river system in the United States. The system carries water thousands of miles through the Interior Plains to the Gulf of Mexico.

In addition to the two main branches, the Mississippi-Missouri river system includes many tributaries. A **tributary** is a stream or smaller river that flows into a larger one. Among the most important tributaries are the Ohio, Tennessee, Arkansas, and Platte rivers. These and other rivers provide water for the rich farmlands of the Interior Plains. The Mississippi River also serves as a means of transportation. Today, as in the past, barges carry freight up and down the river.

Other Rivers The United States includes dozens of other rivers, both large and small. The Colorado River begins in the Rocky Mountains and flows for about 1,450 miles through Colorado, Utah, Arizona, and Nevada. It forms the border between California and Arizona as it winds toward the Gulf of California.

Smaller rivers have also been important in American history. The Hudson River, for example, forms part of the border between New York and New Jersey. Only 306 miles long, it provided a vital link between New York City and the rich farmlands of upstate New York. In the 1960s, efforts to clean up pollution of the Hudson River helped launch the modern environmental movement.

Rivers form political boundaries between the United States and its neighbors. To the south, the Rio Grande forms part of the border between Texas and Mexico. To the north, the St. Lawrence River separates the Northeast from Canada.

The Great Lakes The Great Lakes also form part of the border between the United States and Canada. These five lakes—Superior, Michigan, Huron, Erie, and Ontario—form the largest body of fresh water in the world. Today, artificial waterways connect the Great Lakes to the St. Lawrence and Mississippi rivers. As a result, goods can be shipped from the Central Plains eastward to the Atlantic Ocean and southward to the Gulf of Mexico.

Climate and Weather

The condition of the Earth's atmosphere at a given time and place is its **weather.** The weather in one region can influence the weather in another area. It also affects the jobs we do, the leisure activities we enjoy, and the kinds of homes we build. In history, weather has determined the outcome of battles and even destroyed civilizations.

The average weather of a place over a period of 20 to 30 years is known as **climate.** Two main features that help define an area's climate are temperature and **precipitation** (pree sihp uh TAY shuhn), or water that falls in the form of rain, sleet, hail, or snow. A region may be hot and dry, cold and rainy, or any other combination.

Several factors influence climate. Perhaps the most important is distance from the Equator. Lands near the Equator are usually hot and wet all year. Closer to the North and South poles, temperatures are colder. **Altitude,** or height of the land above sea level, also affects climate. In general, highlands are cooler than lowlands. Other factors that affect climate include ocean currents, wind currents, and location of landforms such as inland mountains, large desert areas, lakes, or forests.

Identify Causes and Effects

Determining causes and effects helps you understand relationships among situations or events. A cause makes something happen. An effect is what happens. What is the effect of altitude on climate? Write the answer in your cause-and-effect chart.

Climates of the United States

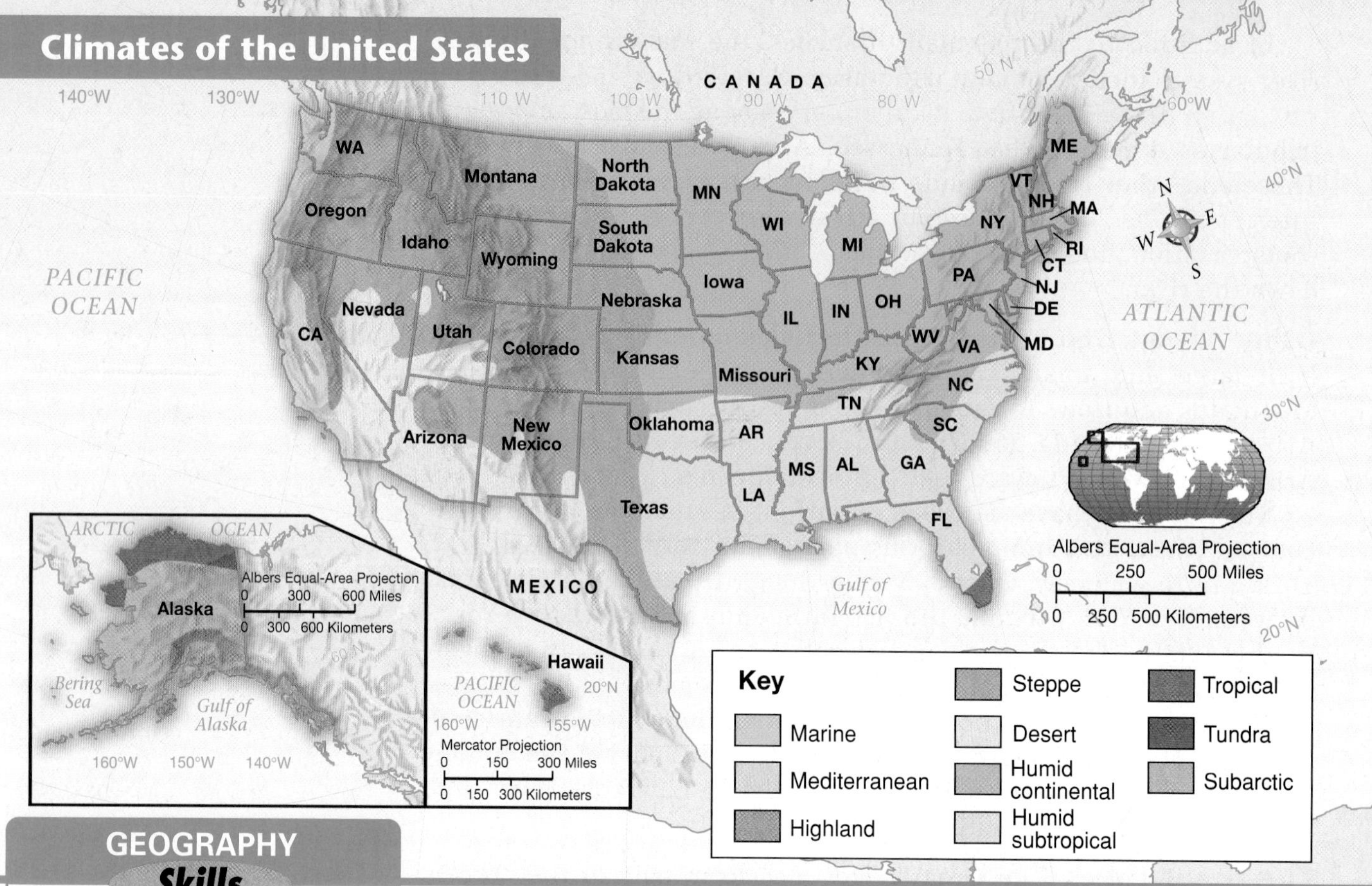

GEOGRAPHY *Skills*

The United States is a land of many climates.

1. **Location** On the map, locate **(a)** an area with a Mediterranean climate **(b)** an area with a desert climate.
2. **Place** What states have three or more different climates?
3. **Critical Thinking Applying Information** **(a)** Identify a state or a part of a state where water is probably scarce. **(b)** Why is water in such short supply there?

Climates of the United States

The United States has 10 major climates. Today, as in the past, these climates strongly influence the nation's population patterns and economic activities.

Marine The strip of land from southern Alaska to northern California is sometimes called the Pacific Northwest. This region has a mild, moist marine climate, with warm summers and cool winters. The Pacific Northwest has many forests, making it a center of the lumber industry.

Mediterranean Much of California has a Mediterranean climate. Winters are mild and wet. Summers are hot and dry. Because of dry conditions, farmers and fruit growers must often irrigate the land. This region produces almost all of the nation's almonds, walnuts, olives, apricots, dates, and figs.

Highland In the Cascades, Sierra Nevada, and Rocky Mountains, a highland climate brings cooler temperatures. Conditions in a highland climate vary according to altitude. For example, Mount Rainier in the state of Washington, at over 14,000 feet above sea level, is snowcapped all year. The highland climate attracts vacationers eager to ski in the winter and escape the heat during the summer.

Desert and Steppe Much of the southwestern United States has a desert climate, with hot days and cold nights. This dry region stretches as far east as the Rockies. The deserts of New Mexico, Nevada,

Arizona, and southeastern California get almost no rainfall. In many places, people irrigate the land so that they can grow crops.

East of the Rockies, the Great Plains have a steppe climate with limited rainfall, hot summers, and cold winters. In the 1800s, settlers brought cattle and built a prosperous beef industry in the region.

Humid Continental The Central Plains and the northeastern United States have a humid continental climate. This climate has more precipitation than the steppe. The seasons are marked by mild summers and cold winters. Tall prairie grasses once covered the Central Plains. Today, American farmers raise much of the world's food in this region.

At one time, the humid continental climate supported forests that covered much of the Northeast. While much of this forestland was cleared to build settlements and grow crops, the region still has a thriving lumber industry.

Tropical and Humid Subtropical Located near the Equator, Southern Florida and Hawaii have tropical climates. The hot, humid conditions make these regions good for growing such crops as pineapples and citrus fruits.

The southeastern United States has a humid subtropical climate. Warm temperatures and regular rainfall make this region ideal for growing crops such as cotton, soybeans, and peanuts.

Tundra and Subarctic Northern and western coastal regions of Alaska have a tundra climate. It is cold all year round. The rest of Alaska, as well as northern Canada, has a subarctic climate with long, cold winters and short summers.

Relatively few people live in these harsh climates. Farming is limited to a small fertile valley in southern Alaska. However, the dense forests that cover almost one third of Alaska are ideal for logging and production of paper pulp.

★ ★ ★ Section 2 Assessment ★ ★ ★

Recall

1. **Define** **(a)** isthmus, **(b)** elevation, **(c)** erosion, **(d)** tributary, **(e)** weather, **(f)** climate, **(g)** precipitation, **(h)** altitude.

Comprehension

2. Name the physical regions of the United States and describe one feature of each region.
3. How do rivers and lakes benefit the economy of the United States?
4. Describe the climate of the region in which you live.

Critical Thinking and Writing

5. **Exploring the Main Idea** List the physical regions and climates of the United States. Then, choose the three regions and climates where you would most like to live. Explain your choices.
6. **Linking Past and Present** **(a)** How do you think the role of rivers and lakes has changed over the course of the nation's history? **(b)** What are the most important roles of rivers and lakes today?

Activity

Mental Mapping Study the physical map of the United States on page 12. On a piece of paper, draw your own sketch map of the United States. Label the major physical features, including mountains, rivers, and other bodies of water. Use colors to outline and shade each physical region.

Glossary of Geographic Terms

The list below includes important geographic terms and their definitions. Sometimes, the definition of a term includes an example in parentheses. An asterisk (*) indicates that the term is illustrated on page 19.

altitude height above sea level

***archipelago** chain of islands (Hawaiian Islands)

basin low-lying land area that is surrounded by land of higher elevation; land that is drained by a river system (Great Basin)

***bay** part of a body of water that is partly enclosed by land (San Francisco Bay)

canal waterway made by people that is used to drain or irrigate land or to connect two bodies of water (Erie Canal)

***canyon** deep, narrow valley with high, steep sides (Grand Canyon)

***cape** narrow point of land that extends into a body of water (Cape Cod)

climate pattern of weather in a particular place over a period of 20 to 30 years

***coast** land that borders the sea (Pacific Coast)

coastal plain lowland area lying along the ocean (Gulf Plain)

continent any of seven large landmasses on the Earth's surface (Africa, Antarctica, Asia, Australia, Europe, North America, South America)

continental divide mountain ridge that separates river systems flowing toward opposite sides of a continent

***delta** land formed by soil that is deposited at the mouth of a river (Mississippi Delta)

desert area that has little or no moisture or vegetation (Painted Desert)

directional arrow arrow on a map that always points north

downstream in the direction of a river's flow; toward a river's mouth

elevation the height above sea level

fall line place where rivers drop from a plateau or foothills to a coastal plain, usually marked by many waterfalls

foothills low hills at the base of a mountain range

***gulf** arm of an ocean or sea that is partly enclosed by land, usually larger than a bay (Gulf of Mexico)

hemisphere half of the Earth (Western Hemisphere)

***hill** area of raised land that is lower and more rounded than a mountain (San Juan Hill)

***island** land area that is surrounded by water (Puerto Rico)

***isthmus** narrow strip of land joining two large areas or joining a peninsula to a mainland (Isthmus of Panama)

***lake** body of water surrounded entirely by land (Lake Superior)

latitude the distance in degrees north and south from the Equator

longitude the distance in degrees east or west from the Prime Meridian

marsh lowland with moist soils and tall grasses

***mountain** high, steep, rugged land that rises sharply above the surrounding land (Mount McKinley)

mountain range chain of connected mountains (Allegheny Mountains)

mouth of a river place where a river or stream empties into a larger body of water

ocean any of the five largest bodies of salt water on the Earth's surface (Arctic Ocean, Atlantic Ocean, Indian Ocean, Pacific Ocean, and Antarctic Ocean)

***peninsula** piece of land that is surrounded by water on three sides (Delmarva Peninsula)

piedmont rolling land along the base of a mountain range

***plain** broad area of fairly level land that is generally close to sea level

***plateau** large area of high, flat, or gently rolling land

prairie large area of natural grassland with few or no trees or hills

***river** large stream of water that empties into an ocean or a lake or another river (Pecos River)

***sea** large body of salt water that is smaller than an ocean (Caribbean Sea)

sea level average level of the ocean's surface from which the height of land or depth of the ocean is measured

***source of a river** place where a river begins

steppe flat, treeless land with limited moisture

strait narrow channel that connects two larger bodies of water (Straits of Florida)

***tributary** stream or small river that flows into a larger river or stream

upstream in the direction that is against a river's flow; toward a river's source

valley land that lies between hills or mountains (Shenandoah Valley)

***volcano** cone-shaped mountain formed by an outpouring of lava—hot, liquid rock—from a crack in the Earth's surface (Mount St. Helens or Mauna Loa)

weather condition of Earth's atmosphere at any given time and place

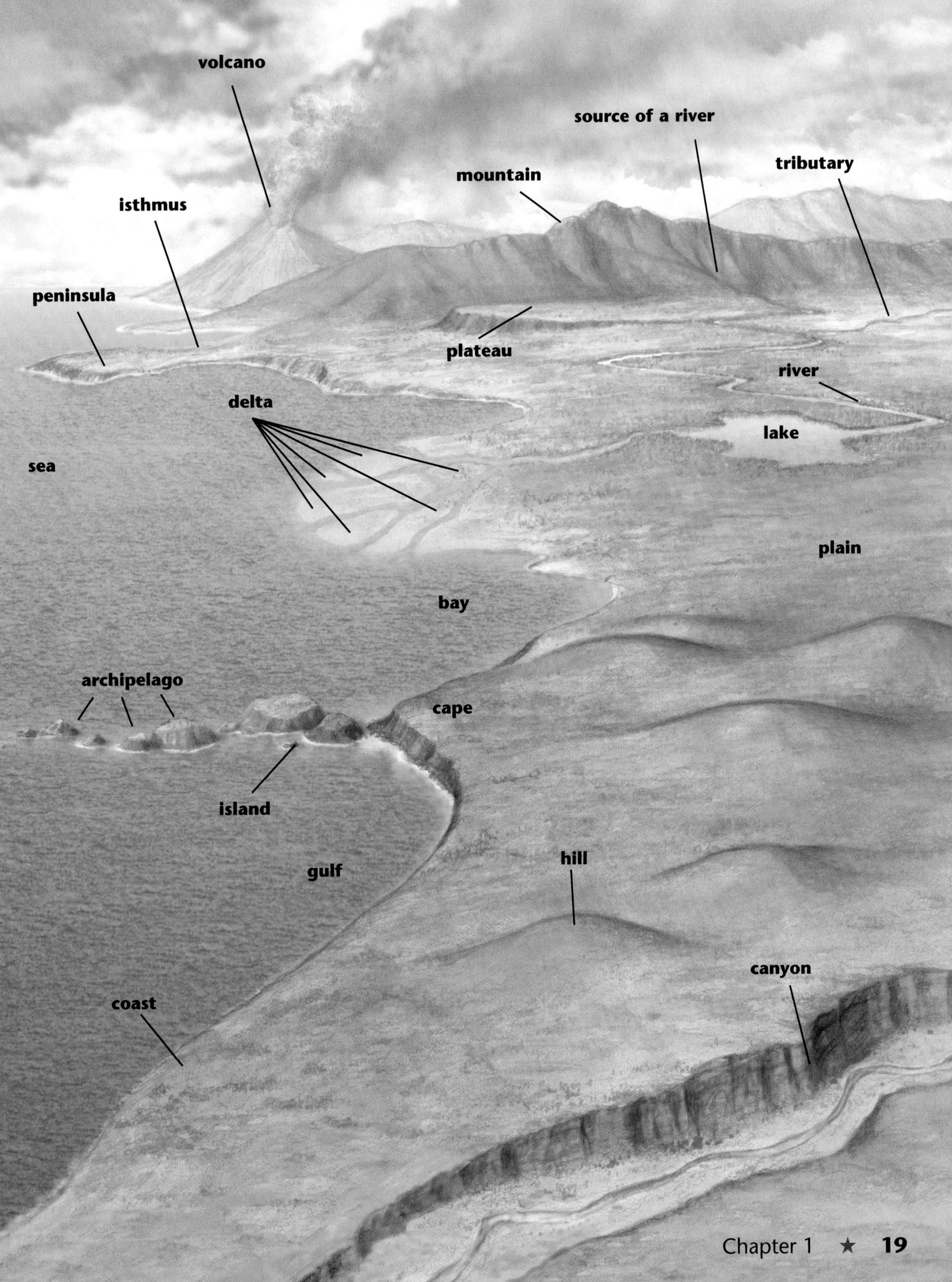
volcano
source of a river
tributary
mountain
isthmus
peninsula
plateau
river
delta
lake
sea
plain
bay
archipelago
cape
island
gulf
hill
canyon
coast

3 The Tools of History

Prepare to Read

Objectives

In this section, you will

- Explain how historians evaluate and interpret historical evidence.
- Summarize how archaeologists add to our knowledge of history.
- Explain what we can learn about history by understanding chronology and eras.

Key Terms

primary source
secondary source
authenticity
bias
artifact
archaeology
culture
chronology

Target Reading Skill

Reading Process As you read, prepare an outline of this section. Use roman numerals to indicate major headings, capital letters for subheadings, and numbers for the supporting details. The sample at right will help you get started.

I. Using Historical Evidence
A. Primary and secondary sources
1. Official documents
2. Eyewitness accounts
B. Evaluating evidence
1.
2.
3.
C. Interpreting evidence
1.
2.
II. Archaeologists Uncover the Past

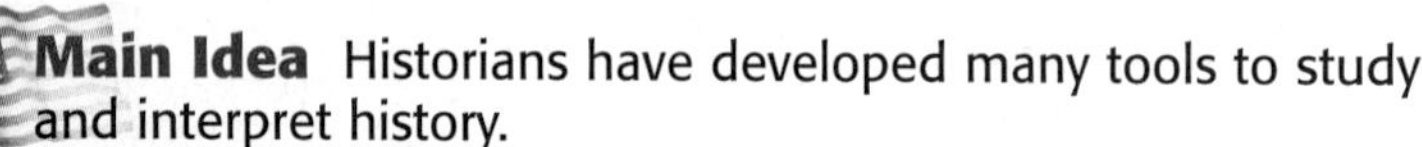

Main Idea Historians have developed many tools to study and interpret history.

David McCullough

Setting the Scene "It has been coming on for a long time," warned David McCullough, "like a creeping disease." McCullough was not talking about a flu epidemic or an outbreak of measles. Instead, he was alarmed that young Americans did not know enough about their nation's past.

> "Everything we have, all our great institutions, hospitals, universities, libraries, this city, our laws, our music, art, poetry, our freedoms, everything is because somebody went before us and did the hard work. . . . Indifference to history isn't just ignorant, it's rude. It's a form of ingratitude."
>
> —David McCullough, *Why History?*

Historians like David McCullough have devoted their lives to making sure we do not forget our shared past and values. They have developed a wide variety of methods to accomplish this goal.

Using Historical Evidence

Studying the lives of people in different times and places is the work of the historian. The most basic tool for this work is historical evidence. Historians collect the evidence, then use it to interpret events.

Primary and Secondary Sources Historians look first for primary sources. A **primary source** is firsthand information about people or events. Primary sources include official documents such as laws or court decisions, public speeches, eyewitness accounts such as diaries and letters, and autobiographies. Primary sources may also include visual evidence such as a news photograph or a videotape. A special type of primary source is oral—or spoken—history, which may be based on interviews with people of today recalling the past.

Historians also make use of secondary sources. A **secondary source** is an account provided after the fact by people who did not directly witness or participate in the event. Secondary sources are usually based on primary sources. This textbook is an example of a secondary source. Encyclopedias, biographies, or books and articles written by historians are also secondary sources.

Evaluating Evidence When dealing with a primary source, the first job of a historian may be to determine whether it is authentic. **Authenticity** refers to whether or not the source is actually what it seems to be. For example, in 1928, a magazine published a series of newly discovered letters that were said to have been written by a young Abraham Lincoln. After careful detective work, historian Paul Angle concluded that the letters were clever forgeries. Angle described some of the questions historians ask when deciding if a source is authentic:

> "Is the paper of the proper age, and is the ink that of the period in which the documents are supposed to have been written? . . . Does [the handwriting] resemble that of letters and papers of undoubted genuineness? . . . Do specific incidents mentioned in the challenged documents check with [provable] historical fact?"
>
> —Paul M. Angle, "The Minor Collection: A Criticism"

After showing that a source is authentic, historians must determine whether it is reliable. Reliability refers to whether or not the source gives an accurate account of the events being described. Was the person describing the event really an eyewitness or just passing on stories told by other people? How accurate was the witness's memory? Do the records of a meeting between two officials report their exact words? What was left out, and why? Such questions help a historian determine reliability.

In evaluating reliability, historians must always be on the lookout for bias. **Bias** is a leaning toward or against a certain person, group, or idea. Cultural background, personal experiences, economic status, and political beliefs may all contribute to bias. An account of a battle given by a soldier on one side may differ widely from an account of the same battle given by a soldier on the other side. A description of a political candidate may be affected by whether the writer is for or against that candidate. In this book, you will find lessons on how to look for signs of bias in order to determine the reliability of sources.

Interpreting Evidence In addition to evaluating sources, historians interpret what the sources mean. Often, the historian's goal is to determine the causes of a certain development or event, such as a war or an economic collapse. By explaining why things happened in the past, the historian can help us understand what is going on today and what may happen tomorrow.

Still, different historians may interpret the same evidence in different ways. Although historians try to be objective, they may be influenced by their own biases. Interpretations of events also change over time, influenced by current events, new ideas, and new sources.

Target Skill

Set a Purpose

When you set a purpose for reading, you give yourself a focus. Your purpose for reading "Evaluating Evidence" might be to find out how historians evaluate evidence. Add this information to your outline.

Primary Source

Preserving Historical Evidence

Historian Robin Winks tells how even the simplest documents can provide important evidence of the past:

"Precisely because the historian must turn to all possible witnesses, he is the most bookish of men. For him, no printed statement is without its interest. For him, the destruction of old cookbooks, gazetteers, road maps, Sears Roebuck catalogues, children's books, railway timetables, or drafts of printed manuscripts, is the loss of potential evidence. Does one wish to know how the mail-order business was operated or how a Nebraska farmer might have dressed in 1930? Look to those catalogues."

—Robin Winks, *The Historian as Detective*

Analyzing Primary Sources

What can the historian learn from the items that Winks mentions?

POLITICAL CARTOON
Skills

Beware the Archaeologist
This cartoon appeared in the British humor magazine *Punch* in 1971. At that time, many amateur archaeologists were traveling to England to search for ancient artifacts.

1. **Comprehension** What kind of work are the three people in the cartoon doing?
2. **Understanding Main Ideas** **(a)** What has Sam pieced together? **(b)** Why is he eager to show it?
3. **Critical Thinking Identifying Points of View** How do you think the cartoonist feels about amateur archaeologists? Explain.

"Good effort, Sam, but it was a water jug!"

Archaeologists Uncover the Past

Most of the evidence that historians use to study American history is in written form. However, when examining the distant past, historians must often rely on **artifacts** (AHRT uh faktz), or objects made by humans. Artifacts include items such as stone tools, weapons, baskets, and carvings.

The Science of Archaeology Artifacts are the building blocks of archaeology (ahr kee AHL uh jee). **Archaeology** is the study of evidence left by early people in order to find out about their way of life.

As ancient cultures disappear, their remains are buried by centuries of sand, dirt, and water. Later people then build new settlements in the same spot, burying the artifacts even deeper. In places like the desert Southwest, archaeologists dig into the earth. They carefully preserve, photograph, and label the artifacts they find. Each new find can provide valuable information about the past.

In laboratories, experts analyze the finds. By testing the level of carbon in a piece of pottery or bone, they can date it to within a few hundred years. They might study kernels of ancient corn through a microscope to find out about the climate in which it grew. They might compare clay pots from different areas to find out about the people who made them.

Studying Ancient Cultures From artifacts and other evidence, archaeologists form theories about the cultures of ancient peoples. A **culture** is the way of life that a people has developed. It includes their homes, clothing, economy, arts, and government. It also includes the customs, ideas, beliefs, and skills that they pass on from generation to generation.

By studying artifacts, archaeologists can determine approximately when the objects were made. They can also form theories about the people who made them. Modern technology, such as computers, helps the archaeologist study artifacts. A finely carved arrowhead suggests that a people knew how to make weapons and hunt. Woven plant fibers suggest that they were skilled basket makers.

In the Americas, archaeologists often focus on the cultures that existed before the arrival of Europeans. Their work has given us valuable insight into the lives of the first Americans, as you will see. Still, some Native Americans have objected to the disturbance of ancient burial grounds or other sites. In recent years, archaeologists have grown more aware of the need to respect Native American landmarks and traditions.

Chronology and Historical Eras

Perhaps you feel that the study of history is a collection of dates, names, and facts. Actually, it is much more than that. It is a story that has many parts.

Learn From the Past When you study history, you learn how the past is linked to the present. As you begin to study the past, you will find that it is like unraveling a fascinating mystery. There is always

Viewing History

Finding Artifacts

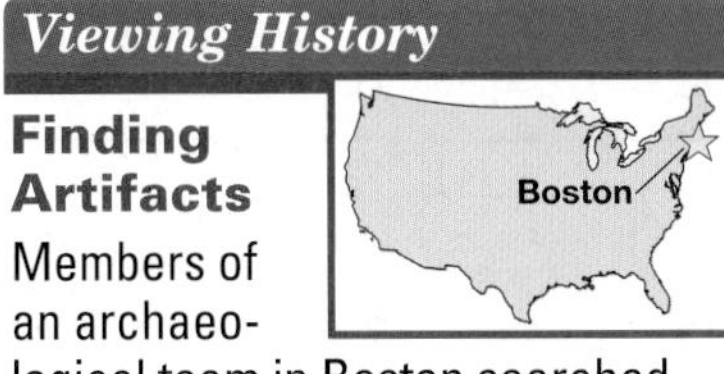

Members of an archaeological team in Boston searched for and found artifacts from colonial Boston. The teapot and glass bottle were found at the site.
Analyzing Information ***What might these items tell archaeologists about the people who used them?***

Eras in American History

Era	Dates	Description
First Americans, or Pre-Columbian	Before 1492	Diverse cultures developed in North America and South America.
Era of Exploration	1492–1600s	Europeans explored and settled in the Americas, resulting in the decline or destruction of a number of Native American cultures.
Colonial Era	1607–1775	The thirteen English colonies were settled in North America. The era ended with the start of the American Revolution.
Revolutionary Era	1763 – 1781	Following a war for independence from Great Britain, the United States became a nation. Some historians mark the end of this era as 1789, when the Constitution went into effect.
Early Republic	1789 – 1828	The new United States government, with George Washington as its first President, took shape. The country began to expand, and its economy began to develop.
Jacksonian Era or the Age of Jackson	1828 – 1840	Andrew Jackson's inauguration symbolized a new era in which the interests of the people were addressed. Democratic rights were extended to more Americans.
Era of Expansion	1840s – 1853	The United States expanded from the Atlantic to the Pacific Ocean, adding many new territories.
Civil War Era	1850s – 1877	Disputes about the growth of slavery, as well as other conflicts, led to the Civil War between the North and South. The era ended with Reconstruction, when the North and South reunited as one nation.
Progressive Era	1898 – 1917	Reformers sought to improve society. They were successful in passing laws for regulating business, limiting child labor, and protecting natural resources.
The Great Depression	1929 – 1941	After the boom of the 1920s, a severe economic crisis affected all Americans. Millions lost jobs as factories closed down.
Post–World War II	1945 – Present	As we get closer to the present day, it becomes more difficult to divide American history neatly. The years after World War II, however, are variously known as the Cold War Era, the Civil Rights Era, the Vietnam Era, the Atomic Age, and the Space Age.

CHART *Skills*

American history can be divided into several eras, or major periods of time.

1. **Comprehension** During which era did the United States begin to establish a new government?
2. **Critical Thinking Applying Information** Why is it useful to organize history into eras?

more to know. Often by studying how people solved problems in the past, we can apply these insights to solving today's problems.

History is the story of the men and women we honor as heroes. These exceptional men and women dared to believe they could change the world—and they did. Some were great leaders such as George Washington. Still others, such as Harriet Tubman; Abraham Lincoln; Dr. Martin Luther King, Jr.; and Charles Lindbergh, changed people's view of the world.

Learn About People History is also the story of ordinary people who do the everyday things that shape the character of our country. It is also the story of how people lived, where they traveled, and how they felt about their lives. Ordinary people work hard, raise families, and fight wars. In addition, ordinary people also settled the frontier, built cities, and participated in protest marches.

Furthermore, there is much that historians can learn from what we consider everyday items. Children's toys and games may give clues about a culture. The clothes people wear, the music they listen to, and even the kind of work people do can give clues to historians.

On the practical side, studying history provides you with useful skills. As you begin to analyze events, you will learn how to research topics, recognize different points of view, make connections, and understand causes and effects.

Absolute Chronology The study of history starts with chronology (kruh NAHL uh gee), the sequence of events over time. Just as geography answers the question *where,* chronology answers the question *when.*

There are two types of chronology: absolute and relative. Absolute chronology refers to the exact time an event took place. Depending on the information available, absolute chronology may be expressed in terms of centuries, years, days, or even hours. For example, according to eyewitnesses, President Abraham Lincoln died of an assassin's bullet on April 15, 1865, at 7:22 A.M.

Relative Chronology The time when an event took place in relation to other events is called relative chronology. For example, in 1773, Britain imposed a tea tax on its American colonies. Later that year, protesters in Boston raided British ships and dumped chests of tea into the harbor. Within three months, the British passed new laws to punish Boston. The phrases "later that year" and "within three months" show the relative chronology of the three events.

Relative chronology helps us understand connections between different events. Still, the fact that one event came before another one does not necessarily mean that the first event caused the second. For example, suppose your neighbor washes his car and an hour later there is a thunderstorm. Did washing the car cause it to rain? In January 1837, Martin Van Buren became President. Two months later the nation faced a terrible economic crisis. Did Van Buren's becoming President cause the crisis? Only careful study can help you decide if and how the two events are linked.

Recall

1. **Define** **(a)** primary source, **(b)** secondary source, **(c)** authenticity, **(d)** bias, **(e)** artifact, **(f)** archaeology, **(g)** culture, **(h)** chronology.

Comprehension

2. What steps must a historian take to evaluate historical evidence?
3. How do archaeologists learn about the past?
4. Why do historians divide history into eras?

Critical Thinking and Writing

5. **Exploring the Main Idea** Review the Main Idea statement at the beginning of this section. List five sources that a historian might use to write a history of your life. Then, evaluate them for authenticity, reliability, and bias.
6. **Solving Problems** How can archaeologists continue to study ancient remains without infringing on the rights of Native Americans?

ACTIVITY

Exploring Primary Sources
Choose an era from the chart on page 24. Then, use the Internet to find a primary source from that era. Write a short summary of the source. Then, analyze it for authenticity, reliability, and bias. For help in completing the activity, visit PHSchool.com, **Web Code mfd-0103.**

4 Economics and Other Social Sciences

Prepare to Read

Objectives

In this section, you will
- Identify the basic questions that economists ask about society.
- List the benefits of free enterprise.
- Explain how the social sciences can support the study of history.

Key Terms

economics
consumer
cash economy
free enterprise system
social sciences
political science
civics
anthropology
sociology
psychology

Target Reading Skill

Main Idea Copy the concept web below. As you read, fill in the blank ovals with information about the study of economics. Add as many ovals as you need.

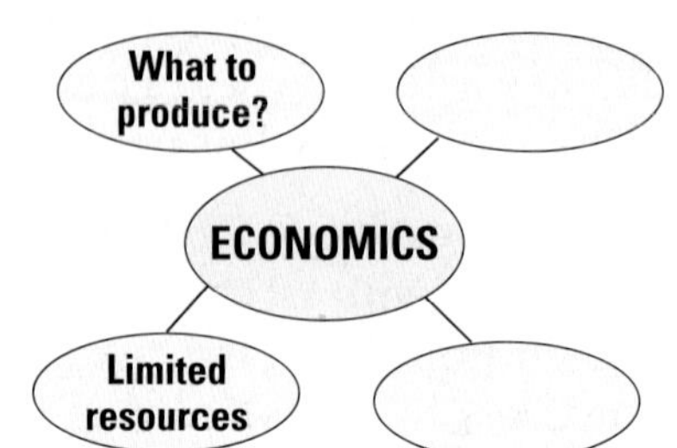

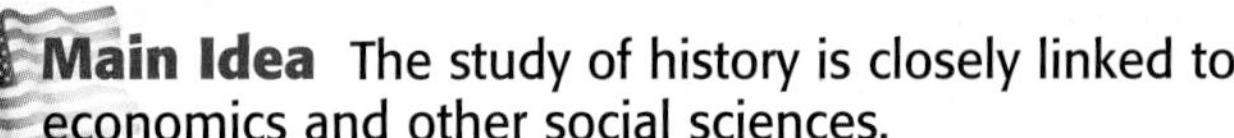

Main Idea The study of history is closely linked to economics and other social sciences.

Stacks of coins

Setting the Scene If you were growing up in an Iroquois village 300 years ago, you would have depended on the local forests and rivers for all your needs. Americans living on the frontier in the 1800s also relied on what they could raise or hunt themselves. A lucky family might expand its supply of goods by growing a few pounds of cotton. They would then trade the cloth they wove from the cotton for a pig or a calf.

Today, Americans take for granted their ability to consume an almost limitless supply of goods from all over the world. With a short trip to the local shopping mall, we buy shoes from Italy or shirts from Hong Kong. Shopping on the Internet can bring leather backpacks and wool sweaters from Australia or stone carvings from Kenya.

People in every society have wants and needs. At the same time, every society—no matter how rich—has limited resources. In this section, we will examine the ways that different societies manage their limited resources to meet their wants and needs.

Three Economic Questions

The study of how people manage their limited resources to satisfy their wants and needs is called **economics.** Every society must answer three basic economic questions: (1) What goods and services should we produce? (2) How should we produce them? (3) For whom should we produce them? The answers to these questions define every society's economic system.

What Goods and Services Should We Produce? A society's first economic task is to fulfill people's basic needs—food, shelter, and clothing. After that, the society must make choices about how to use the rest of its limited resources. Should it focus on producing

consumer goods, such as cars and washing machines? Should it use its resources for education? Should it concentrate on heavy industry such as construction or trucking?

Decisions about what to produce vary according to the time and culture. Developing nations are less concerned about producing private automobiles. They are more concerned with building industries that will provide jobs and improve their quality of life. In the United States, on the other hand, we see cars as a necessity of life. Special situations also affect decision making. During World War II, for example, the United States government limited the manufacture of items such as cars and washing machines in favor of tanks and fighter planes.

How Should We Produce Goods and Services? Even when people agree on what to produce, they must choose how to produce it and how much of it to produce. Technology plays a major role in these decisions. For example, in the past, each family grew enough fruits, grains, and vegetables to meet its needs. Or small, family-run farms grew crops for the local community. With the invention of new farm machinery, agriculture changed. Today in the United States, most of the food we eat is grown on giant mechanized farms run by large corporations.

Advances in technology also changed manufacturing. At one time, most manufactured items were produced by hand in homes or small workshops. Then, the Industrial Revolution introduced new methods and machines that allowed large factories to mass-produce great quantities of manufactured goods. Today, computers and robot technology have once more revolutionized manufacturing.

For Whom Should We Produce Goods and Services? We are all **consumers,** or users of goods and services. However, just as resources are limited, supplies of goods and services are limited. What goods and services should be available to what consumers? How do consumers pay for what they want and need?

In past societies, consumers and producers were often the same people. They consumed the goods they produced themselves. Today, we live in a **cash economy,** that is, an economy where we exchange

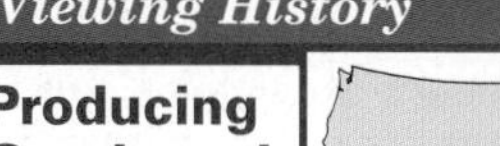

Viewing History

Producing Goods and Services

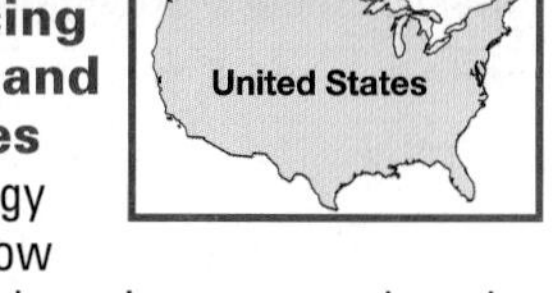

Technology affects how goods and services are produced. On the farm (above) and in the textile factory (inset), machines do much of the work that was once done entirely by hand. **Drawing Conclusions** ***What do you think are some of the economic benefits and drawbacks of technology?***

Identify Supporting Details

What details in this subsection discuss economic systems? Add this information to your concept web.

Glossary of Economic Terms

barter	the direct exchange of one set of goods or services for another
budget	a plan for spending and saving
capital	any human-made resource that is used to create other goods or services
command economy	an economy in which one organization decides what goods are produced and how much stores will charge for these goods
credit	any form of deferred payment
entrepreneur	ambitious leader who combines land, labor, and capital to create and market new goods or services
export	a good that is sent to another country for sale
free enterprise	an economic system characterized by private or corporate ownership of capital goods; investments that are determined by private decision rather than by state control
free market	an economic system in which individuals rather than the government make most of the decisions about economic activities
import	a good that is brought in from another country for sale
labor	the effort that people devote to a task for which they are paid
private property	something owned by an individual; especially land or buildings
profit	the amount of money a company has once it has sold its products
scarcity	limited quantities of resources to meet unlimited wants
supply and demand	a feature of the capitalist economy; when supplies of goods or services are plentiful, prices drop; when supplies are scarce, prices rise
surplus	situation in which quantity supplied is greater than quantity demanded; also known as excess supply

CHART

This glossary gives the meaning of some basic economic terms.

1. **Comprehension** Which term refers to an economic system where ownership of goods can be private or corporate?
2. **Critical Thinking Making Decisions** Why might an entrepreneur be better off in a free-market economy than in a command economy?

money for goods and services. Your income and wealth determine the goods and services you can consume. How to supply basic needs to people who cannot afford to buy them is a difficult issue for governments, charities, religious communities, and individuals.

The American Free Enterprise System

The economy of the United States is based on an economic principle known as free enterprise. In a **free enterprise system,** the government plays a limited role in the economy. Businesses are owned by private citizens. Owners decide what products to make, how much to produce, where to sell products, and what prices to charge. Furthermore, competition is encouraged. Competition gives businesses an incentive, or reason, for working harder. Companies compete for consumers by making the best product at the lowest price.

The free enterprise system began early in the United States. After the War for Independence, Americans were free to engage in any economic activity without government interference. The Framers of the Constitution believed that the prosperity of the nation depended on a free-market economy. Provisions for private property and competition, for example, are included in the Constitution.

Until the late 1800s, the United States government did relatively little to control the economy. Since then, government has gradually taken on a more active role. Many Americans argue that government regulations are needed to end abuses or ensure against economic collapse. Others claim that government interference keeps the free enterprise system from working efficiently.

Despite such disagreements, Americans have long recognized free enterprise as one of the nation's greatest strengths.

The "know-how" of individual American traders, inventors, and investors helped create vast personal fortunes, as well as prosperity for the nation. Today, many nations around the world look to the American free enterprise system as a model.

The free enterprise system also allows consumers freedom to make economic choices. Through their buying decisions, consumers can tell businesses what to make, how much, and at what price. In this respect, the economic system is much like a democracy. People are allowed to express their preferences.

Other Social Sciences

Economics, history, and geography are considered **social sciences** because they relate to human society and social behavior. Other social sciences include political science, civics, anthropology, sociology, and psychology.

Political Science and Civics The study of government is called **political science.** Political scientists look at the ideas behind different forms of government, how these governments are organized, and how they work. Like economics, political science raises many basic questions. Who should have the most power in a government? How are decisions made? How do governments change?

Before 1776, Americans lived as subjects of a foreign king, to whom they owed loyalty and obedience. After throwing off that form of government, they built what Abraham Lincoln called a "government of the people, by the people, for the people." As citizens, Americans owe loyalty to the nation and have a say in their government. The basic principles and organization of American government are contained in the Constitution of the United States. You will learn more about the Constitution in later chapters.

Civics An important branch of political science is **civics,** the study of the rights and responsibilities of citizens. In 1776, the Declaration of Independence stated the idea that every person had basic rights that could not be taken away:

> "We hold these truths to be self-evident, that all men are created equal; that they are endowed by their Creator with certain inalienable rights; that among these are life, liberty, and the pursuit of happiness."
>
> —Declaration of Independence

Throughout the nation's history, Americans have worked to expand and protect the rights of individuals. The addition of the Bill of Rights to the Constitution ensures individual rights to all

Americans. These rights include freedom of speech, which means the newspapers, books, and magazines you read can print the news. Your right to worship as you please and to freely assemble are also guaranteed. Americans have also recognized their responsibility to serve the nation in many ways, including obeying its laws, voting, and serving in the military.

Anthropology, Sociology, and Psychology The study of how people and cultures develop is called **anthropology** (an thruh PAHL uh gee). Anthropologists look at the ways people thought and behaved at different times and places. For example, an anthropologist might examine how the first Americans spread across North and South America and the different ways of life they developed. One branch of anthropology is archaeology, as discussed in Section 3.

Sociology is the study of how people behave in groups. Looking at a particular society, a sociologist might ask: Is this society divided into different social classes? How are families organized? How do the roles of men and women differ? What values and beliefs do people share? Even a single nation, such as the United States, contains many different social groups. For example, a sociologist may be interested in how life in a small farming community in upstate New York differs from life in a big-city neighborhood in New York, Los Angeles, or Houston. A sociologist might even study how different student groups in a middle school relate to one another.

Psychology is the study of how people think and behave. Psychology is linked to history because history is the study of human beings. For example, a person writing a biography of a well-known figure might look to psychology to understand why that person acted in a certain way. Psychology can also help us evaluate primary sources by helping us understand people's views and biases.

Section 4 Assessment

Recall

1. **Define** **(a)** economics, **(b)** consumer, **(c)** cash economy, **(d)** free enterprise, **(e)** social sciences, **(f)** political science, **(g)** civics, **(h)** anthropology, **(i)** sociology, **(j)** psychology.

Comprehension

2. What three basic economic questions must every society answer?
3. Explain why the free enterprise system was developed in the new nation.
4. Choose two of the social sciences discussed in this section. Describe how they support the study of history.

Critical Thinking and Writing

5. **Exploring the Main Idea** Review the Main Idea statement at the beginning of this section. Then, write three questions that you might ask about the development of the economy of the United States from independence to today.
6. **Identifying Alternatives** Why would a developing nation answer the three basic economic questions differently than a country like the United States?

Activity

Creating a Comic Strip **Create a comic strip for Free Enterprise Publishers showing the steps an ambitious young American would take to start and run a new business. Be sure to include a panel showing how our hero would respond to competition from other businesses.**

American Entrepreneurs

American history is filled with stories of successful entrepreneurs. Their success makes it easy to see why the United States is often called the "land of opportunity."

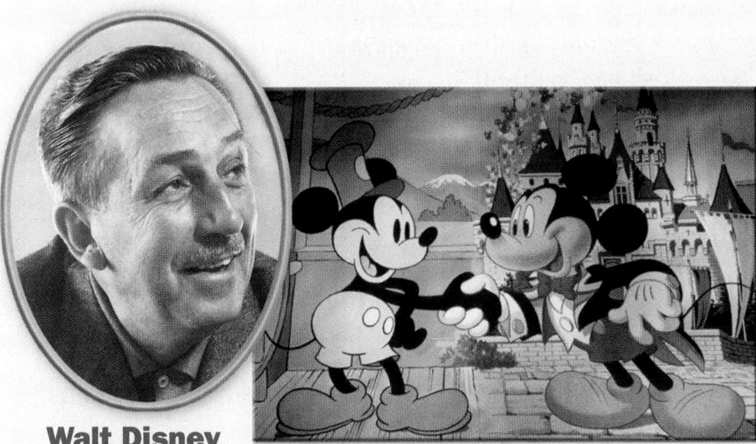

Walt Disney

Walt Disney owed his success to a mouse. In 1928, he introduced Mickey Mouse in the animated cartoon "Steamboat Willie." Mickey's worldwide popularity helped Disney build a business empire that came to include a movie studio and huge theme parks in Florida and California.

Madame C. J. Walker

Madame C. J. Walker's money-making idea was to market hair-care products for African Americans. Starting in 1905, she created her own formulas and sold them door-to-door. Five years later, she was running a factory that provided employment for some 3,000 people. By the time of her death in 1919, Walker was one of the first American women to have become a millionaire through her own efforts.

Junior Achievement

Since 1919, Junior Achievement has worked "to educate and inspire young people to value free enterprise, business, and economics." Junior Achievement volunteers run programs in schools across the country, including a competition in which students have an opportunity to experience running an actual business.

ACTIVITY

With a partner, write a plan for a new business. Describe the goods or services you plan to market, explain who your customers would be, and list what you would need to get started.

CHAPTER 1

Review and Assessment

Chapter Summary

Section 1
Geography is the study of people, their environments, and their resources. Geographers have developed five themes to help explain the connection between geography and history. Maps and globes are pictures of the Earth's surface.

Section 2
The United States is divided into nine physical regions and seven climate regions. Several great river systems and lakes have played important roles in American history.

Section 3
Historical evidence is the basic tool of historians. Archaeologists dig into the earth to find artifacts left behind by ancient cultures. The study of history starts with chronology, the sequence of events over time.

Section 4
Economics is the study of how people manage their resources to satisfy their wants and needs. The U.S. economy is based on the free enterprise system. The social sciences provide important clues about people who lived in the past.

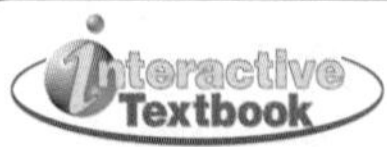

For additional review and enrichment activities, see the interactive version of *The American Nation,* available on the Web and on CD-ROM.

Chapter Self-Test For practice test questions for Chapter 1, visit PHSchool.com, **Web Code mfa-0104.**

Building Vocabulary

Review the chapter vocabulary words listed below. Then, use the words and their definitions to create a matching quiz. Exchange quizzes with another student. Check each other's answers when you are finished.

1. **geography**
2. **cartographer**
3. **climate**
4. **precipitation**
5. **altitude**
6. **primary source**
7. **artifact**
8. **ohronology**
9. **cash economy**
10. **free enterprise**

Reviewing Key Facts

11. What are the different uses for maps and globes? (Section 1)
12. Describe three physical regions of the United States. (Section 2)
13. Name three kinds of evidence that archaeologists study. (Section 3)
14. How does the American free enterprise system work? (Section 4)

Critical Thinking and Writing

15. Connecting to Geography: **Movement** How does the movement of people, goods, and ideas shape a society?
16. **Evaluating Information** Which would be more reliable: a map of North America from the 1500s or a map of North America from the 1900s? Explain your answer.
17. **Synthesizing Information** Look at the picture of Pikes Peak on page 11. **(a)** Describe the physical region in which Pikes Peak is located. **(b)** Describe the climate of that region.
18. **Applying Information** Imagine that you are an archaeologist living 1,000 years from now. What conclusions about our society might you draw from the following artifacts: **(a)** coins and dollar bills, **(b)** automobile, **(c)** fast food containers, **(d)** TV set, **(e)** cell phone?
19. **Making Decisions** Review the discussion on page 28 about the proper role of government in the economy. Do you agree with the Americans who argue for a smaller or a larger government role? Explain your answer.

SKILLS ASSESSMENT

Analyzing Primary Sources

In 1845, Lansford W. Hastings wrote a guide for people traveling to the West. In it, he made the following statements about the West:

> “The time is not distant, when those wild forests, trackless plains, untrodden valleys . . . will present one grand scene of continuous improvements . . . when those vast forests shall have disappeared before the hardy pioneer; those extensive plains shall abound with innumerable herds of domestic animals; those fertile valleys shall groan under the weight of their abundant products.”
>
> —Lansford W. Hastings, from *The Emigrants' Guide to Oregon and California*

20. How do you think Hastings felt about the changes he predicted?
- **A.** He feared them.
- **B.** He was unconcerned.
- **C.** He approved of them.
- **D.** He wanted to prevent them from happening.

21. Hastings probably would have been surprised by the
- **A.** increasing population of the West.
- **B.** emergence of the environmental movement.
- **C.** development of the lumber industry.
- **D.** rise of the beef industry.

APPLYING YOUR SKILLS

Reviewing Map Skills

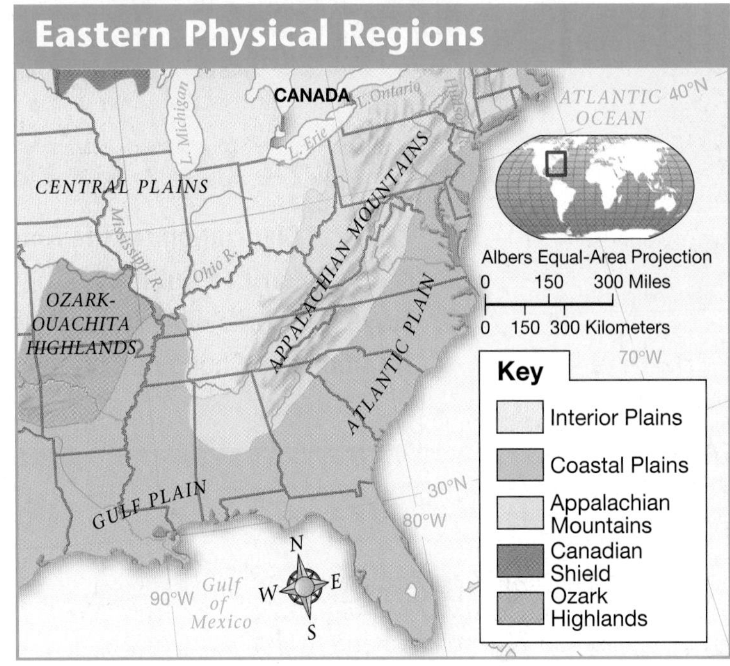

22. What region is northwest of the Appalachian mountains?
- **A.** Ozark Highlands
- **B.** Atlantic Plain
- **C.** Gulf Plain
- **D.** Central Plains

23. Which is the smallest region? Describe its location.

ACTIVITIES

Connecting With . . . Geography

Using the Five Themes Use the five themes of geography to describe the neighborhood, community, or state in which you live. Develop your description by writing one or two sentences for each of the five themes. Consider the following questions:

1. Where is the place located?
2. How do people interact with the environment?
3. How do people and ideas move between places?

Connecting to Today

Creating a Chart Some scientists are worried that human activities such as driving cars and operating factories are causing a dangerous rise in the Earth's temperatures. Other scientists do not agree with this global-warming theory. They point out that the Earth has gone through warm and cold cycles in the past. Use the Internet to find out about the global-warming debate. Create a chart showing the arguments on both sides and the evidence used to support them. For help in starting this activity, visit PHSchool.com, **Web Code mfd-0105.**

CHAPTER 2

Before the First Global Age

PREHISTORY–1600

1. The First Civilizations of the Americas
2. Native American Cultures
3. Trade Networks of Africa and Asia
4. Tradition and Change in Europe

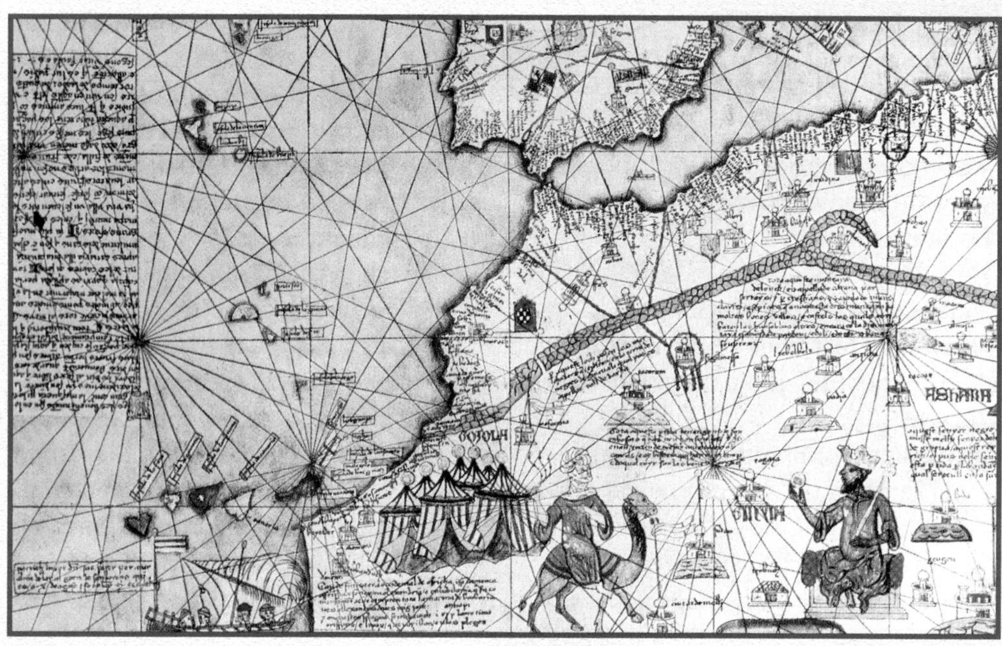

A Spanish map from the 1300s showing Mansa Musa seated on his throne

30,000 to 10,000 years ago
The first people arrive in the Americas.

Early 1300s
The African kingdom of Mali is at its most powerful. Its king, Mansa Musa, makes a famous pilgrimage to Mecca, Islam's holiest city.

Late 1300s
The Renaissance begins in southern Europe.

Prehistory · 1300 · 1400

The World Around 1500

In 1500, the world was on the brink of major changes.

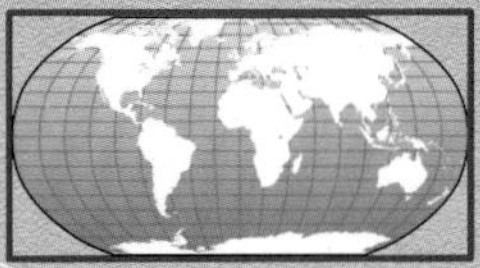

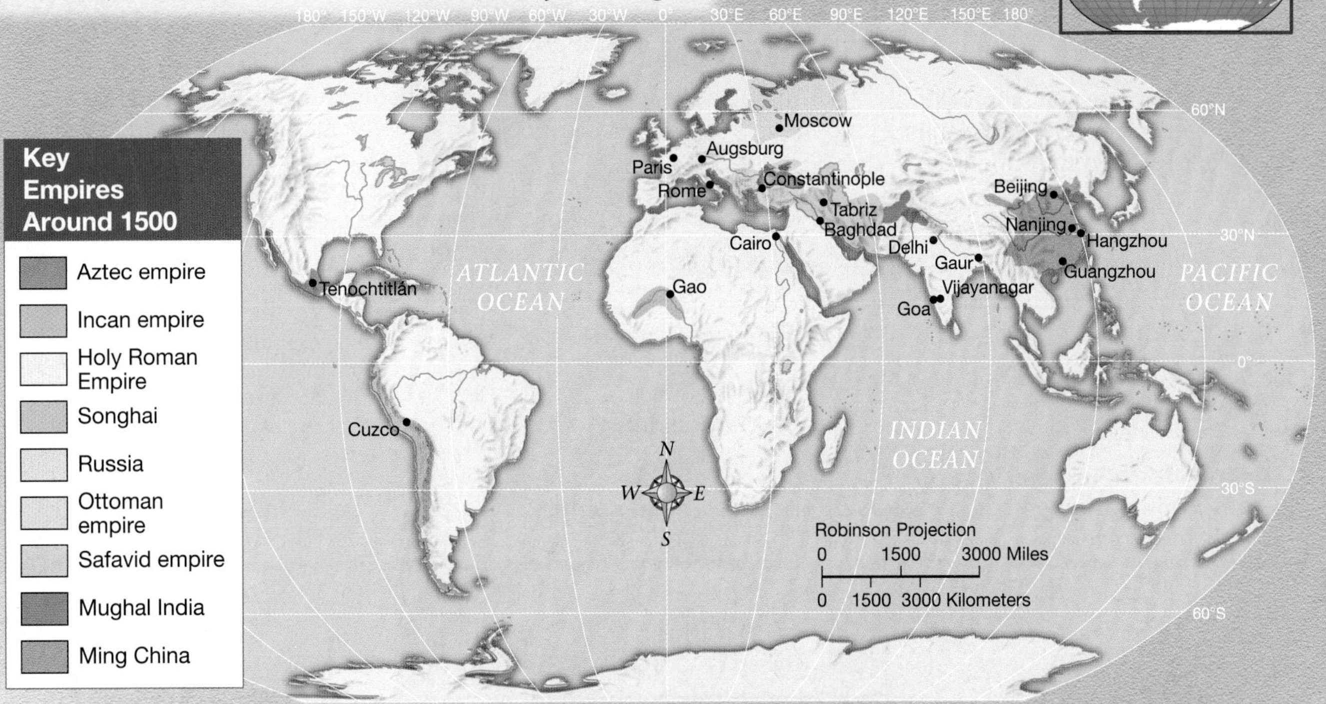

Key
Empires Around 1500

- Aztec empire
- Incan empire
- Holy Roman Empire
- Songhai
- Russia
- Ottoman empire
- Safavid empire
- Mughal India
- Ming China

Robinson Projection

Gutenberg's printing press

A detail from *The Great City of Tenochtitlán,* by Diego Rivera

Mid 1400s

Europe's first books are printed on presses, such as this one built by Johannes Gutenberg.

Late 1400s

Tenochtitlán, capital city of the Aztecs, becomes one of the world's largest cities. The emperor (center) is worshipped and feared.

1591

Songhai empire falls to invaders from Morocco.

1400 · 1500 · 1600

1 The First Civilizations of the Americas

Prepare to Read

Objectives

In this section, you will

- Explain how people first reached the Americas.
- Describe the Olmec, Mayan, Aztec, and Incan civilizations.
- Summarize the development of early cultures in North America.

Key Terms

glacier
surplus
causeway
quipu
terrace
culture
adobe
pueblo
Mound Builders

Target Reading Skill

Comparison and Contrast Copy this incomplete Venn diagram. As you read, write key facts about the Aztecs and the Incas in the appropriate sections. Write common achievements in the overlapping section.

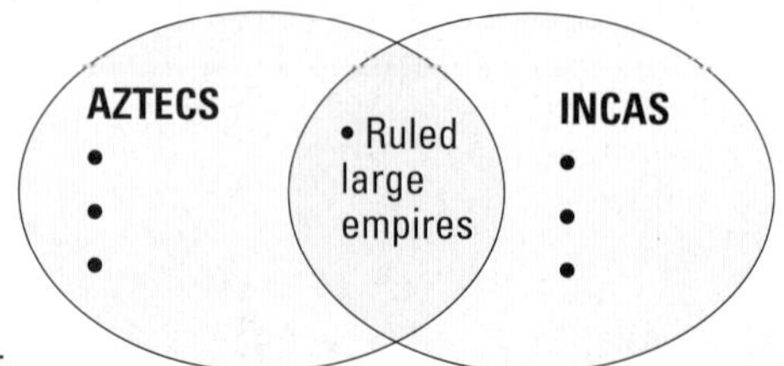

Main Idea In several parts of the Americas, the development of farming enabled some groups of people to build complex civilizations.

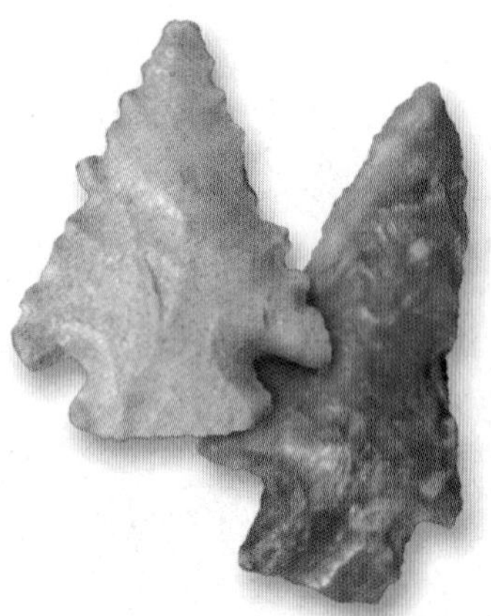
Ancient Indian spear points

Setting the Scene The hunters crept slowly forward. Ahead, a herd of bison grazed near a swamp. At a signal, the hunters leaped up, shouting loudly. The startled herd stampeded into the swamp. As the bison struggled in the deep mud, the hunters hurled their spears.

Scenes much like this took place on North America's Great Plains more than 10,000 years ago. Hunters tracking herds of bison were among the first people to reach the Americas. Over time, their descendants spread out across two continents.

Reaching the Americas

Like other early people around the world, the first Americans left no written records to tell us where they came from or when they arrived. However, scientists have found evidence to suggest that the first people reached the Americas sometime during the last ice age.

According to geologists, the Earth has gone through several ice ages. The last ice age occurred between 100,000 and 10,000 years ago. During that time, thick sheets of ice, called **glaciers,** covered almost one third of the Earth. In North America, glaciers stretched across Canada and reached as far south as present-day Kentucky.

Crossing the Land Bridge Glaciers locked up water from the oceans, causing sea levels to fall and uncovering land that had been under water. In the far north, a land bridge joined Siberia in northeastern Asia to Alaska in North America.

Most scientists think that bands of hunters reached North America across this land bridge. These hunters tracked herds of grazing animals. Other scientists disagree. They think that the first Americans crossed the icy arctic waters by boat, reaching North America by sea. Another theory claims that people could have reached the Americas from

Europe, Africa, or islands in the South Pacific.

Once these early hunters reached the Americas, they had to keep moving in search of food. Slowly, over thousands of years, they spread across North America, Central America, and South America. The lands they settled varied widely. Native Americans settled on mountain plateaus, dry deserts, fertile plains, lush woodlands and thick rain forests. In these very different environments, Native American groups developed many different customs and languages.

Adapting to New Conditions About 12,000 years ago, the last ice age ended. As temperatures rose, the glaciers melted. The land bridge between Siberia and Alaska disappeared under the Bering Strait.

About the same time, some types of large animals died out. This forced hunting bands to adapt to new conditions. Smaller animals, wild berries, nuts, grains, and fish became a larger part of their diets.

About 5,000 years ago, people in Central America learned to grow crops such as corn, beans, and squash. Farming brought great changes to those who practiced it. Farmers no longer had to keep moving to find food. Instead, they stayed in one place and began to build permanent villages. As farming methods improved, people produced more food, which in turn allowed the population to grow.

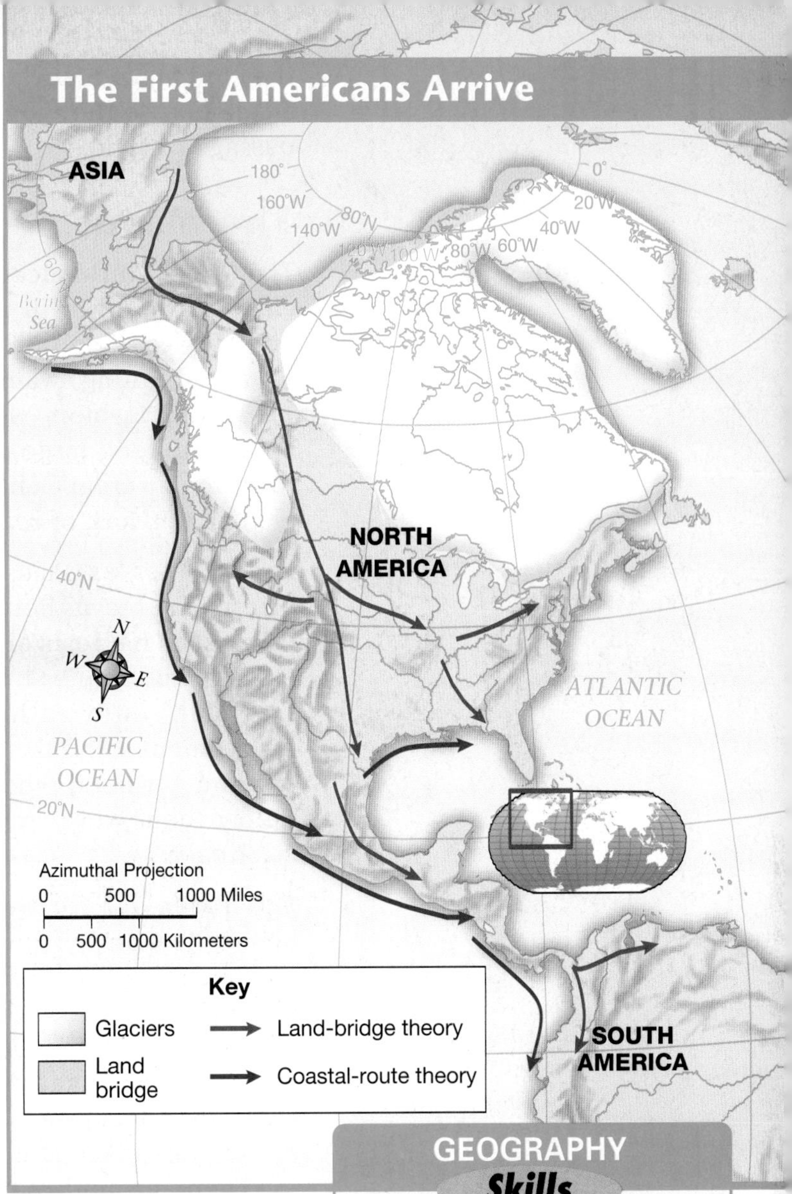

The First Americans Arrive

GEOGRAPHY *Skills*

The first Americans reached North America from Asia. Over thousands of years, these hunters populated two huge continents.

1. **Location** On the map, locate: **(a)** Asia, **(b)** Bering Sea, **(c)** North America, **(d)** South America.
2. **Movement** According to the land-bridge theory, in which direction did early hunters travel once they reached North America?
3. **Critical Thinking Drawing Conclusions** Why do you think many of the first Americans continued to travel south after reaching North America?

Olmec Civilization

Farming was a key advance. In time, some farming communities in Central America grew enough **surplus,** or **extra,** food to support large populations, and the first cities emerged.

Cities marked the rise of the first civilization in the Americas. A civilization is a society that has certain basic features. Among these are cities, a well-organized government, different social classes, a complex religion, and some method of record keeping.

The earliest known civilization in the Americas was that of the Olmecs in Central America. The Olmecs lived in the lowlands along the Gulf of Mexico, about 3,500 years ago. Scientists have found huge stone heads carved by the Olmecs. Some were ten feet tall and weighed several tons. Smaller figures showed creatures that were part human and part animal.

Olmec farmers supplied nearby cities with food. There, powerful leaders built stone temples. The Olmecs left few written records, but they did make many advances. They studied the stars and developed a calendar so they could predict the change of seasons and mark the passage of time.

The Mayas

The Olmecs influenced many later peoples, including the Mayas. The early Mayas lived in the rain forests of what are today Guatemala and Mexico. About 3,000 years ago, they began clearing the rain forest and draining swamps to create farmland.

Mayan farmers were able to produce great harvests of corn, enough to feed large cities. As Mayan population grew, cities began to spring up from Central America to southern Mexico. Trade flowed along a network of roads that linked inland cities and the coast.

Social Classes Priests held great power in Mayan society. Only priests, the Mayas believed, could perform the ceremonies needed to bring good harvests or victory in battle. Priests conducted these ceremonies in temples built on top of huge stone pyramids.

Nobles enjoyed high status, too. They served as warriors and government officials. Near the bottom of Mayan society were laborers and farmers, who grew corn, squash, and many other crops. Below them were slaves, most of whom were prisoners of war or criminals.

Advances in Learning Mayan priests had to know exactly when to honor the many gods who were thought to control the natural world. Every day, priests anxiously studied the sun, moon, and stars. They learned much about the movement of these bodies.

Based on their observations, priests made impressive advances in astronomy and mathematics. They learned to predict eclipses and created an accurate, 365-day calendar. They also developed a system of numbers that included the concept of zero.

Then, around A.D. 900, the Mayas abandoned their cities. Historians are not sure why. Perhaps they did so because of warfare, a drought—or both. The rain forests swallowed up the great Mayan temples and palaces. Although Mayan cities decayed, the Mayan people survived. Today, more than 2 million people in Guatemala and southern Mexico speak Mayan languages.

Compare and Contrast

As you read about the Aztecs and the Incas, check to see if you understand how their accomplishments were similar and how they were different. How were Tenochtitlán and Cuzco similar? How were they different?

The Aztecs

Long after the Mayan cities were abandoned, a new civilization rose far to the north. Its builders were the Aztecs. The early Aztecs were nomads, people who moved from place to place in search of food. In the 1300s, the Aztecs settled around Lake Texcoco (tay SKOH koh) in central Mexico. From there, they built a powerful empire.

Tenochtitlán On an island in the middle of the lake, the Aztecs built their capital, Tenochtitlán (tay noch tee TLAHN). They constructed a system of **causeways**, or raised roads made of packed earth. The causeways linked the capital to the mainland.

The Aztecs learned to farm the shallow swamps of Lake Texcoco. In some places, they dug canals, using the mud they removed to fill in parts of the lake. In other places, they attached reed mats to the lake bottom with long stakes. Then, they piled mud onto the mats to create farmland. Aztec farmers harvested several crops a year on these *chinampas,* or floating gardens.

With riches from trade and conquest, Tenochtitlán prospered. Its markets offered a wide variety of goods. "There are daily more than 60,000 people bartering and selling," wrote a Spanish visitor in the 1500s.

Religion Like the Mayas, Aztec priests studied the heavens and developed complex calendars. Such calendars gave them the ability to tell their people when to plant or harvest. Priests also performed rituals designed to please the many Aztec gods.

The Aztecs paid special attention to the sun god. They believed that each day the sun battled its way across the heavens. They compared the sun's battle to their own, calling themselves "warriors of the sun." They believed that the sun required human sacrifices in order to rise each day. The Aztecs therefore sacrificed thousands of captives each year to please this powerful god.

A Powerful Empire By 1500, the Aztecs ruled a huge empire. It stretched from the Gulf of Mexico to the Pacific Ocean and included millions of people. The Aztecs took great pride in their empire and their capital. "Who could conquer Tenochtitlán?" boasted an Aztec poet. "Who could shake the foundation of heaven?"

The Aztec world was far from peaceful, however. Heavy taxes and the sacrifice of huge numbers of prisoners of war sparked many revolts. Across the empire, people conquered by the Aztecs were eager for revenge. As you will read in Chapter 3, enemies of the Aztecs would help outsiders from distant lands destroy the Aztec empire.

GRAPHIC ORGANIZER *Skills*

Like many other ancient civilizations, Aztec society was strictly divided into social classes.

1. **Comprehension**
   (a) Who occupied the highest position in Aztec society? **(b)** Which classes of people were equal to one another?
2. **Critical Thinking**
   Analyzing Information
   How does this graphic organizer suggest the importance of warfare in Aztec society? Give two examples.

The Incas

Far to the south of the Aztecs, the Incas built one of the largest empires in the Americas. By 1500, their empire stretched for almost 2,500 miles along the west coast of South America.

The center of the Incan empire was the magnificent capital at Cuzco (KOO skoh), located high in the Andes. Cuzco was a holy city to the Incas. All nobles in the empire tried to visit it at least once in their lifetimes. The city had massive palaces and temples made of stone and decorated with gold ornaments. At the center was the

An American Profile

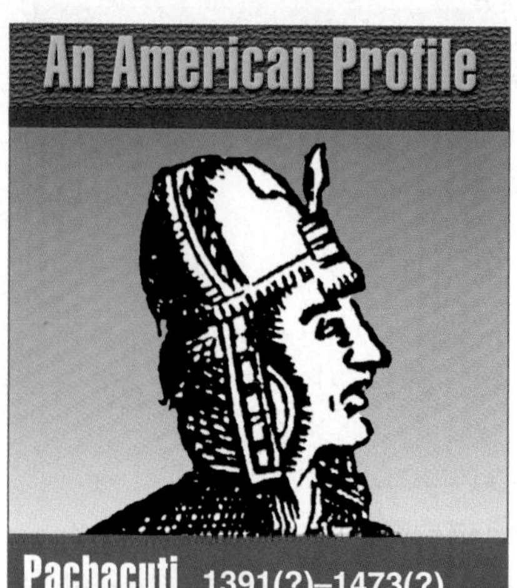

Pachacuti 1391(?)–1473(?)

Cuzco, the Incan capital, was under attack in 1438. The Sapa Inca fled, leaving his son Pachacuti (pah chah KOO tee) to defend the city. Against great odds, Pachacuti drove the enemy back and saved the city.

Pachacuti expanded Incan power. He conquered new lands and built a network of roads to unite his empire. Magnificent new temples and other buildings turned Cuzco into an impressive capital.

Pachacuti imposed a single language and a single government on the empire. Today, many historians rank Pachacuti among the world's greatest empire builders.

How did Pachacuti prove he was a powerful leader?

palace of the emperor, who was known as the Sapa Inca. The emperor was regarded as a god who was descended from the sun god.

From Cuzco, the emperor ruled more than 10 million people. They lived in varied environments, from coastal deserts to lowland jungles to the highlands of the Andes.

The Incan empire was very well organized. The emperor kept well informed about affairs in all parts of his empire. He sent high officials out to act as governors of his domain. The governors made sure that every person worked at least part of the time on projects for the state.

To unite their empire, the Incas maintained a system of roads that covered more than 10,000 miles. Builders carved roads in rock cliffs and stretched rope bridges across deep gorges. Teams of runners quickly spread royal orders across the empire using these roads.

The runners carried with them a device known as a **quipu** (KEE poo). This was a cord or string with knots that stood for quantities. The quantities might be bags of grain, numbers of soldiers, or other amounts. The quipu was also used by government officials to keep records.

The Incas were skilled engineers. They built massive stone temples and forts. With only human labor, ropes, and wooden rollers, they moved stones weighing up to 200 tons. They used all their engineering skills to farm the dry, rugged mountain lands. They became experts at creating **terraces,** or wide steps of land, out of the steep mountainsides. Sturdy stone walls kept rain from washing away the soil.

Early Cultures of North America

Scholars have found evidence of Mayan and Aztec ideas among some groups of people farther north. Traders and migrating people carried foods, goods, arts, and beliefs from Central America and Mexico to the early peoples of North America. This flow of products and ideas helped lead to the development of many distinct cultures in North America. A **culture** is the entire way of life of a people. It includes their homes, clothing, economy, arts, and government.

People of the Southwest At least 3,000 years ago, knowledge of farming spread northward. Gradually, farming societies emerged in what is today the American Southwest. They included the Hohokams (hoh HOH kahmz) and Anasazis (ah nuh SAH zeez).

The Hohokams lived in present-day southern Arizona. About 2,000 years ago, they dug networks of irrigation ditches so they could farm the desert land. The ditches carried water from the Salt and Gila rivers to fields, where farmers produced corn, squash, and beans.

The Anasazis lived in the Four Corners region, where Colorado, Utah, New Mexico, and Arizona meet. Like the Hohokams, the Anasazis irrigated the desert in order to farm. They also created a network of roads to link dozens of towns. Traders traveled these roads, carrying cotton, sandals, and blankets woven from turkey feathers.

Anasazi Houses The Anasazis built large houses with walls of stone and **adobe,** or sun-dried brick. When the Spanish later saw these houses in the early 1500s, they called them **pueblos** (PWEHB lohz), the Spanish word for "village." (They also called the descendants of the Anasazis the Pueblos.)

About 1,000 years ago, some Anasazi villages faced attacks from warlike neighbors. To escape that threat, they built new homes along steep cliffs. Toeholds cut into the rock let people climb the cliff walls. Farmers planted their crops on land above the cliffs.

Mound Builders To the east, other farming cultures flourished in North America. Among them were the **Mound Builders,** various cultures that built large earth mounds beginning about 3,000 years ago. Thousands of these mounds dot the landscape from the Appalachian Mountains to the Mississippi Valley and from Wisconsin to Florida.

The first mounds were used for burials. Later mounds were used for religious ceremonies. They were similar in function to the pyramid temples of the Mayas.

The best-known groups of Mound Builders were the Hopewells and the Mississippians. Between A.D. 700 and 1500, the Mississippians built a large city at Cahokia (kah HOH kee ah) in present-day Illinois. As many as 30,000 people may have lived there at one time.

Viewing History

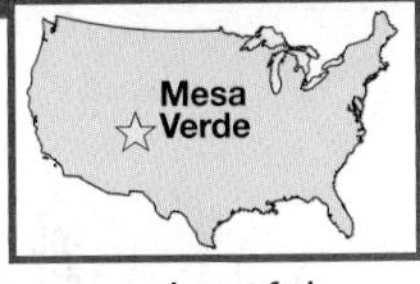

Cliff Dwellings The cliff dwellings of Mesa Verde are examples of the homes of Native Americans in the canyons and cliffs of southwest Colorado. **Drawing Inferences** ***Do you think the inhabitants of these dwellings were a peaceful or a warlike people? Explain.***

★ ★ ★ Section 1 Assessment ★ ★ ★

Recall

1. **Identify** Explain the significance of **(a)** Olmecs, **(b)** Mayas, **(c)** Aztecs, **(d)** Incas, **(e)** quipu, **(f)** Mound Builders.
2. **Define** **(a)** glacier, **(b)** surplus, **(c)** causeway, **(d)** terrace, **(e)** culture, **(f)** adobe, **(g)** pueblo.

Comprehension

3. In the opinion of most scientists, how did the first people reach the Americas?
4. Describe one achievement of each of the following early civilizations in the Americas: **(a)** Mayan, **(b)** Aztec, **(c)** Incan.
5. How did early people adapt to the desert Southwest?

Critical Thinking and Writing

6. **Exploring the Main Idea** Review the Main Idea statement at the beginning of this section. Then, write a paragraph explaining how farming was necessary for the first American civilizations to emerge.
7. **Applying Information** Review the subsection entitled "Early Cultures of North America." Then, make a list showing how the information in this subsection supports the idea that geography affects history.

Activity

Connecting to Today
Mexico City was built on the site of ancient Tenochtitlán. Use the Internet to find out how archaeologists discovered evidence of Aztec life in modern Mexico City. Write a paragraph describing how their findings help Mexicans understand their past. For help in completing the activity, visit PHSchool.com, **Web Code mfd-0201.**

2 Native American Cultures

Prepare to Read

Objectives

In this section, you will
- Describe how people lived in different culture areas of North America.
- Explain how climate and resources affected Native American cultures.
- List the beliefs shared by different Native American groups.
- Summarize life among the Iroquois.

Key Terms

culture area
tribe
diffusion
pit house
potlatch
kachina
clan
League of the Iroquois
sachem

Target Reading Skill

Main Idea Copy the table below. As you read the section, fill in the ways that each Native American culture adapted to the climate and resources in its area.

CULTURE	CLIMATE/ RESOURCES	HOW ADAPTED
• Arctic • Great Basin • Northwest • Southeast • Eastern Woodlands	• Harsh, limited	• Hunted small animals

Main Idea Native American cultures in North America varied greatly due in part to differences in climate and resources.

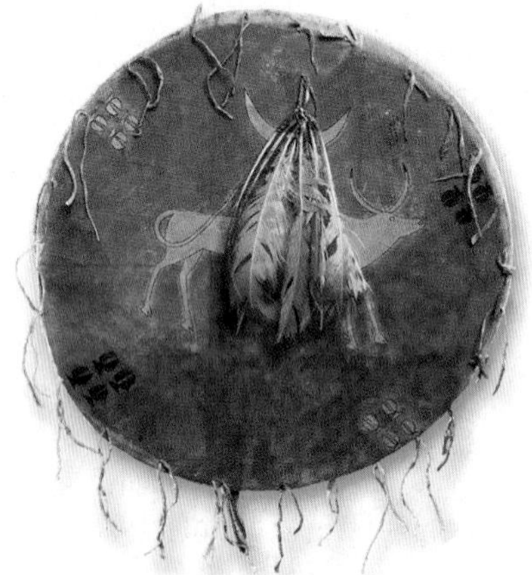

Cheyenne shield made of buffalo hide

Setting the Scene When Christopher Columbus reached the Americas in 1492, he thought he had landed in the East Indies—islands off the coast of Asia. So, he called the people he met "Indios," or "Indians." Other Europeans picked up the term. Even after Europeans realized Columbus's error, they continued to call the people of the Americas Indians.

The term Indian is misleading for another, more important, reason. Native Americans do not belong to a single group. In 1492, as now, Native Americans included many different people with many distinct cultures. In North America alone, there were hundreds of Native American languages spoken. Native American cultures, too, varied greatly, much like the cultures of the people of Europe. In the years that followed Columbus's arrival, Europeans would have difficulty understanding this complexity.

Culture Areas of North America

The map on page 44 shows the major culture areas of North America, north of Mexico, around A.D. 1450. A **culture area** is a region in which people share a similar way of life.

Each culture area was home to many different tribes. A **tribe** is a community of people who share common customs, language, and rituals. Members of a tribe saw themselves as a distinct people who shared a common origin. Tribal leaders often made decisions for the group.

Hunting, Gathering, and Fishing Native Americans developed a variety of ways to meet their basic needs for food, clothing, and shelter. In some culture areas, tribes hunted animals and gathered the nuts and fruits that grew in the wild. Other tribes depended on the sea for food. They made boats out of animal skins or carved canoes out of trees. From their boats and canoes, they speared fish or hunted marine animals such as seals, walrus, and whales.

Farming Other tribes lived mostly by farming, planting corn, beans, and squash. Native American tribes farmed in many parts of North America, from California in the West to the Eastern Woodlands. Over time, farmers improved their crops. For example, more than 5,000 years ago, wild corn was tiny, about the size of a human finger. Indian farmers developed dozens of varieties of corn including ones with larger ears.

Trade Indian tribes traded with one another for goods not found within their own region. Trade networks linked people across large distances. Goods sometimes traveled more than 1,000 miles from where they were made.

In the Northwest, traders met near the Dalles on the Columbia River. Local Indians caught and dried salmon, which they exchanged for goods and produce from other places.

More than goods traveled from Indian group to group. New ideas and skills also spread. This process of spreading ideas from one culture to another is known as **diffusion.** Through diffusion, farming skills spread from one Native American group to another.

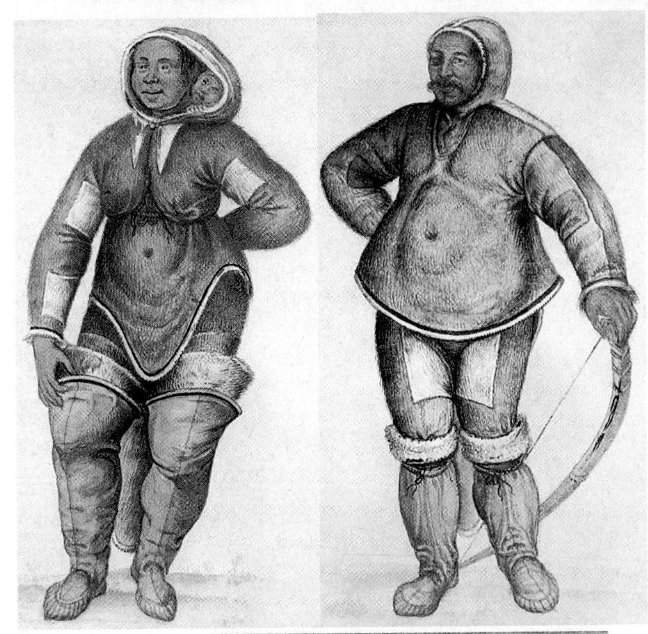

Geography and History

Living With Arctic Cold

The Inuit had to rely on the resources of the icy Arctic environment to survive. They built igloos and insulated them with seal skins and sod. They also used caribou and seal fur to make warm clothing. Because caribou hair is hollow, it traps air and offers good insulation against the cold. So, in the fall and winter, the Inuit wore caribou parkas.

Inuit parkas had two layers. The soft inner layer had the fur facing in. A heavier outer layer had fur on the outside. This design was comfortable and protected the wearer from the cold.

In the spring and summer, the coastal Inuit fished or hunted from boats. Because seal fur repels water, the Inuit wore sealskin during the spring and summer.

How might Inuit culture have been different in a warmer climate?

Climate, Resources, and Culture

Climate and natural resources helped shape Native American cultures in different regions. Climate and natural resources influenced the crops people grew and the animals they hunted. Climate also affected people's needs for clothing and shelter. Resources provided the materials for their clothing and shelter.

Climate and resources affected tribal organization. Where climates were harsh and resources limited, people struggled to find enough food and shelter. In such regions, people were often nomadic. They lived in small hunting bands. Each band included a number of families. In regions with more favorable climates and plentiful resources, people tended to live in larger groups and stay in one place for longer periods.

Cultures of the Far North and Plateau Regions Frozen seas and icy, treeless plains made up the world of the Inuits, who lived in the Arctic region. The Inuits used all the limited resources of their environment. In the short summer season, they collected driftwood along the ocean shore, using it for tools and shelters. For most of the year, the Inuits lived in **pit houses,** houses dug into the ground and covered with wood and skins. Lamps filled with seal oil kept their homes warm even in the bitter cold. Women made warm clothing out of furs and waterproof boots out of sealskins.

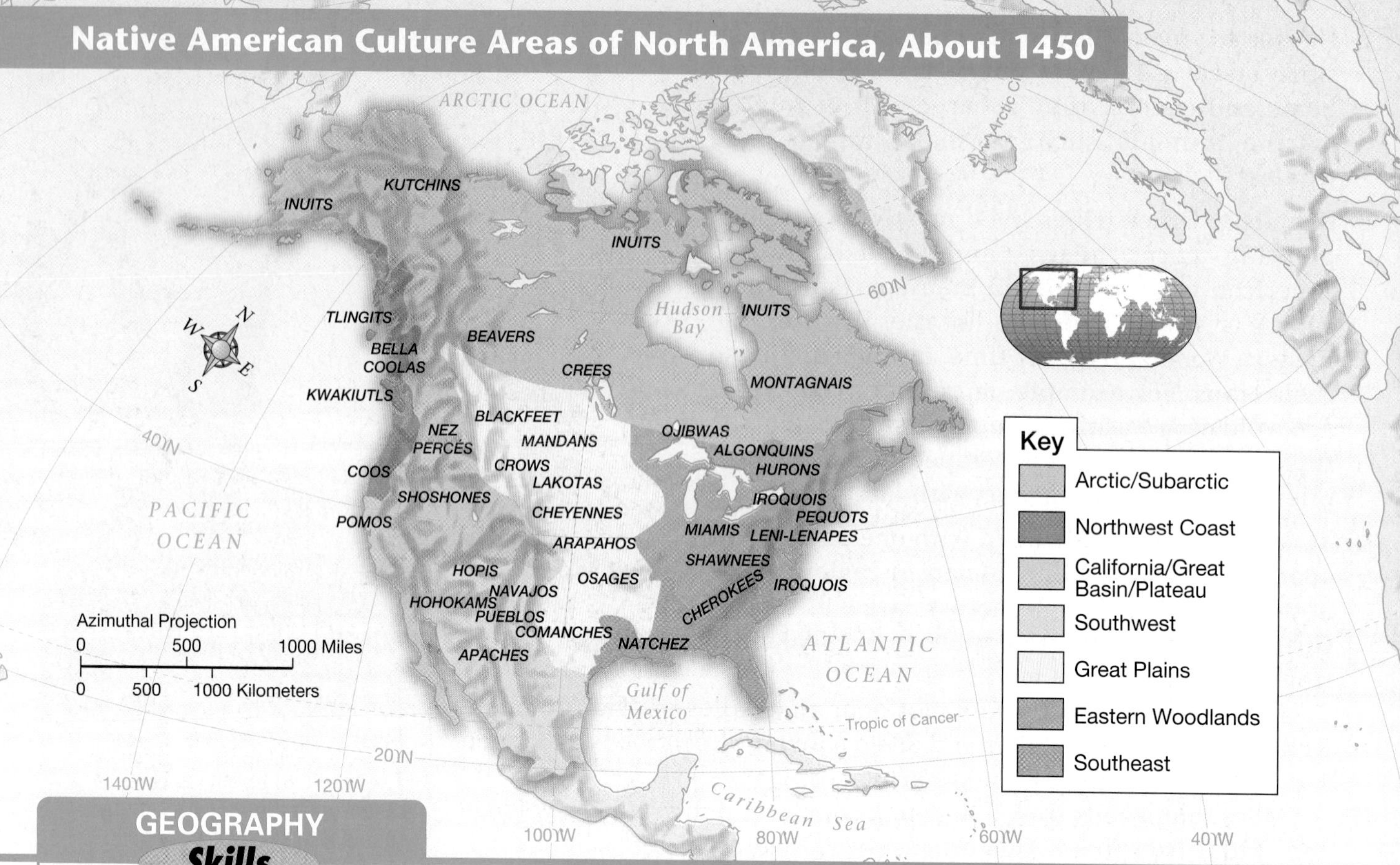

GEOGRAPHY Skills

Native Americans spread out to populate North America. In the process, they developed many different cultures. Within these culture areas, tribes shared similar ways of life.

1. **Location** On the map, locate **(a)** Northwest Coast culture area, **(b)** Eastern Woodlands culture area, **(c)** Great Plains culture area.
2. **Place (a)** Name two tribes in the Southwest culture area. **(b)** With which culture area are the Cherokees associated?
3. **Critical Thinking Analyzing Information** In which culture areas could Native Americans probably not depend on the sea for food? Explain.

The Plateau region has a cold and dry environment. Surprisingly, however, numbers of hardy plants and animals thrive in the region.

Among the people of the Plateau region were the Utes (YOOTZ) and Shoshones (shoh SHOH neez). They collected pine nuts and dug for roots in the dry soil. They also hunted mountain sheep and rabbits. The Native Americans of the region had few possessions beyond digging sticks, baskets, and tools and weapons needed for hunting.

Cultures of the Northwest Elsewhere in North America the climate was kinder, which helped more complex cultures emerge. The people of the Northwest Coast enjoyed milder temperatures and abundant food supplies. They gathered rich harvests of fish from the sea. From nearby forests, they cut down tall cedar trees and split the trunks into planks for houses and canoes.

With plenty of food, the people of the Pacific Northwest stayed in one place. They built permanent villages and prospered from trade with nearby groups.

Within a village, a family gained status according to how much it owned. Families sometimes competed with one another. To improve its standing, a family might hold a **potlatch,** or ceremonial dinner, to show off its wealth. The potlatch could last for many days. The family invited many guests and gave everyone gifts. The more goods a family gave away, the more respect it earned. However, people who received gifts at a potlatch were then expected to hold their own potlatches and give gifts.

Native American Culture Groups of North America

ARCTIC/SUBARCTIC

Beavers, Crees, Inuits, Kutchins, Montagnais
Lived as nomadic hunters and food gatherers in cold climate; honored ocean, weather, and animal spirits

CALIFORNIA/GREAT BASIN/PLATEAU

Nez Percés, Pomos, Shoshones
Lived as hunters and gatherers in small family groups; ate mainly fish, berries, acorns

SOUTHWEST

Apaches, Hohokams, Hopis, Navajos, Pueblos
Lived in villages in homes made of adobe; built irrigation systems to grow corn and other crops; honored earth, sky, and water spirits

SOUTHEAST

Cherokees, Natchez
Grew corn, squash, beans, and other crops; held yearly Green Corn Ceremony to mark end of year and celebrate harvest

GREAT PLAINS

Arapahos, Blackfeet, Cheyennes, Comanches, Crows, Lakotas, Mandans, Osages
Lived in tepees; animals hunted by men; crops grown by women; relied on buffalo to meet basic needs of food, shelter, and clothing

EASTERN WOODLANDS

Algonquins, Ojibwas, Hurons, Iroquois, Leni-Lenapes, Miamis, Pequots, Shawnees
Lived in farming villages, but also hunted for food; long houses shared by several families; women shared social and political power

NORTHWEST COAST

Bella Coolas, Coos, Kwakiutls, Tlingits
Lived in villages; benefited from rich natural resources in forests, rivers, and ocean; held potlatches, or ceremonial dinners, where host families gave gifts to guests to show wealth and gain status

Cultures of the Southeast Many tribes inhabited the southeastern region of North America. Among them were the Natchez (NACH ihz). They benefited from the region's warm, moist climate. They hunted, fished, and farmed along the fertile coast of the Gulf of Mexico.

The Natchez calendar divided the year into 13 months. Each month was named after a food or an animal that the Natchez harvested or hunted. Their months included Strawberry, Little Corn, Mulberry, Deer, Turkey, and Bear.

The ruler of the Natchez was known as the Great Sun and was worshipped as a god. The Great Sun's feet never touched the ground. Either he was carried on a litter or he walked on mats. Below the Great Sun were members of his family, called Little Suns. Next came Nobles, then Honored People, and finally Stinkards, or commoners, who made up the majority of the people.

Marriage laws ensured that membership in each class kept changing. By law, Nobles had to marry Stinkards. Even the Great Sun chose a Stinkard as a wife. In this way, no one family could hold the position of Great Sun forever. In time, even descendants of a Great Sun became Stinkards.

Target Skill — Identify Supporting Details

Which details in this paragraph give examples of how Native American cultures of the Southeast adapted to the climate and environment of their region? Use these details to fill in your table.

Shared Beliefs

The many Native American groups had a wide variety of beliefs. Yet, they shared some basic ideas.

AmericanHeritage MAGAZINE

HISTORY **HAPPENED HERE**

Knife River Indian Villages National Historic Site

For thousands of years, Native American groups were drawn to the Knife River in North Dakota by the herds of buffalo that came to the river to drink. Once the area was dotted with the Indians' earthlodges. Time and weather have destroyed the earthlodges. However, visitors can still see depressions where lodges were located.

Virtual Field Trip For an interactive look at the Knife River Indian Villages, visit PHSchool.com, **Web Code mfd-0202.**

Respect for Nature Central to Native American beliefs was a deep respect for the earth. People felt a close bond to plants, animals, and the forces of nature.

Whether hunting, fishing, farming, or gathering wild plants, Native Americans had a great respect for the natural world. Their prayers and ceremonies were designed to maintain a balance between people and the forces of nature. They believed that they must adapt their ways to the natural world in order to survive and prosper.

Native Americans believed that the world was full of powerful, unseen forces and spirits. They honored those spirits, which were thought to act and feel like humans.

In the Pacific Northwest, many tribes relied on fishing. One such group was the Kwakiutls (kwah kee OOT lz). Each year when they caught their first fish of the season, they chanted this prayer:

> “We have come to meet alive, Swimmer,
> do not feel wrong about what I have done to you,
> friend Swimmer,
> for that is the reason why you came,
> that I may spear you,
> that I may eat you,
> Supernatural One, you, Long-Life-Giver, you Swimmer.
> Now protect us, me and my wife.”
>
> —Kwakiutl Prayer of Thanks

Special Ceremonies In farming areas, tribes held special ceremonies to ensure good rainfall. At midsummer, Pueblo villages in the

Southwest rang with cries of: "The *kachinas* are coming!" **Kachinas** were **spirits, who were represented by masked Native American dancers.** The Pueblos believed that the kachinas had the power to bring good harvests.

At Pueblo festivals, the kachinas danced. Religious leaders prayed to the spirits and gave them gifts. Only if the spirits were treated well would they return each year with rain for the Pueblos' crops.

In the Southeast, many tribes held a Green Corn Ceremony when the corn ripened in the fall. The ceremony lasted for several days. It marked the end of the old year and the beginning of a new one. On the last day, a sacred fire was lighted. Dancers circled the flames, and the people enjoyed a great feast. Women then used coals from the sacred fire to make new fires in their own houses.

Viewing History

Iroquois Women at Work

In several Native American cultures, including the Iroquois, women were responsible for growing and gathering food. Here, Iroquois women collect sap to make maple sugar. **Applying Information** ***How does making maple taffy require both cold and heat?***

The Iroquois Confederacy

Among the many Native American groups in the Eastern Woodlands were the Iroquois (IHR uh kwoi) people. They lived mostly in present-day New York State.

The Iroquois called themselves "The People of the Long House." They took great pride in their sturdy dwellings, called long houses. A typical long house was about 150 feet long and 20 feet wide. Twelve or more families lived in a long house.

Women had a special place in Iroquoian society. They owned all the household property and were in charge of planting and harvesting. When a man married, he moved in with his wife's family.

Women also had political power. They chose clan leaders. A **clan** was a group of two or more related families. If a clan leader did not do his job well, the women could remove him from his position.

The Iroquois included five nations that spoke similar languages: the Mohawk, Seneca, Onondaga (ahn uhn DAW guh), Oneida (oh NI duh), and Cayuga (kay YOO guh). Each nation had its own ruling council. Until the late 1500s, the five nations were frequently at war.

Then, around 1570, the five Iroquois nations formed an alliance to end the fighting. According to legend, a religious leader named Dekanawida (deh kan ah WEE dah) inspired Hiawatha (hi ah WAH thah) to organize the alliance. It became known as the **League of the Iroquois.**

A council of 50 specially chosen tribal leaders, called **sachems,** met once a year. The council made decisions for the League. Here, too, women had a political role because they chose the sachems and watched over their actions.

Looking Ahead

Scholars do not know exactly how many people lived north of Mexico in 1500. Their figures range from about 1 million to 10 million. Many experts put the figure at about 2.5 million.

Across North America, hundreds of tribes followed their own ways of life. Trade and warfare brought some tribes into contact with one another. Yet, those contacts were limited. By the late 1400s, however, events were taking place on far-off continents that would forever change all of the Native American cultures.

★ ★ ★ Section 2 Assessment ★ ★ ★

Recall

1. **Identify** Explain the significance of **(a)** Natchez, **(b)** League of the Iroquois.
2. **Define** **(a)** culture area, **(b)** tribe, **(c)** pit house, **(d)** potlatch, **(e)** kachina, **(f)** clan, **(g)** sachem.

Comprehension

3. List three ways Native Americans in different culture areas met their needs for food, clothing, and shelter.
4. Give three examples of how climate and resources affected Native American cultures.
5. Describe one belief that Native Americans shared.
6. How did women play an important role in Iroquois culture?

Critical Thinking and Writing

7. **Exploring the Main Idea** Review the Main Idea statement at the beginning of this section. Choose the culture area that you think offered the most favorable conditions for people. Then, make a list of at least three reasons for your choice.
8. **Formulating Questions** Study the map and chart on pages 44–45. Then, pose a question that links the two graphics. Exchange questions with a classmate and answer his or her question.

Activity

Design a Magazine Cover **Design a cover for a special issue of a magazine on the variety of Native American cultures. Include a cover illustration as well as the titles of three or four articles that will appear in the magazine.**

Native American Dwellings

Native Americans developed a wide variety of dwellings to suit their different environments. Shown here are a pueblo from the Southwest, a tepee from the Great Plains, and a long house from the Eastern Woodlands.

Pueblo

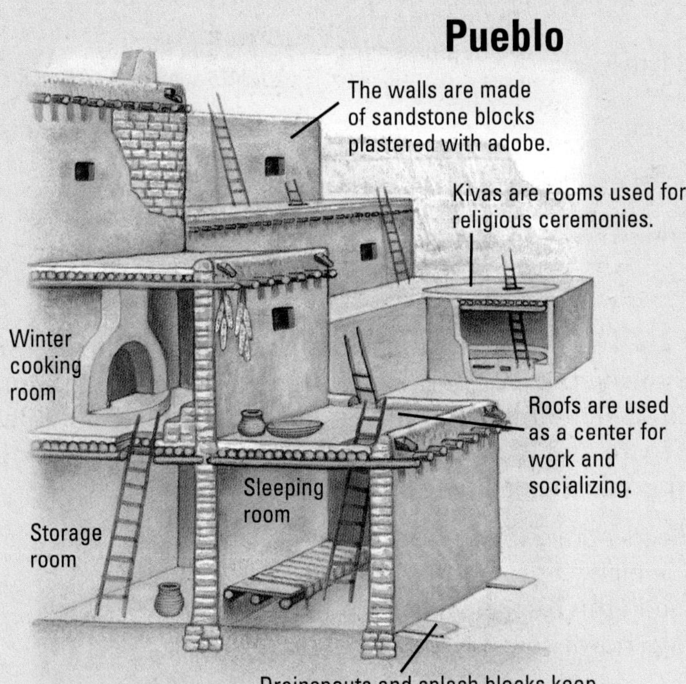

Tepee

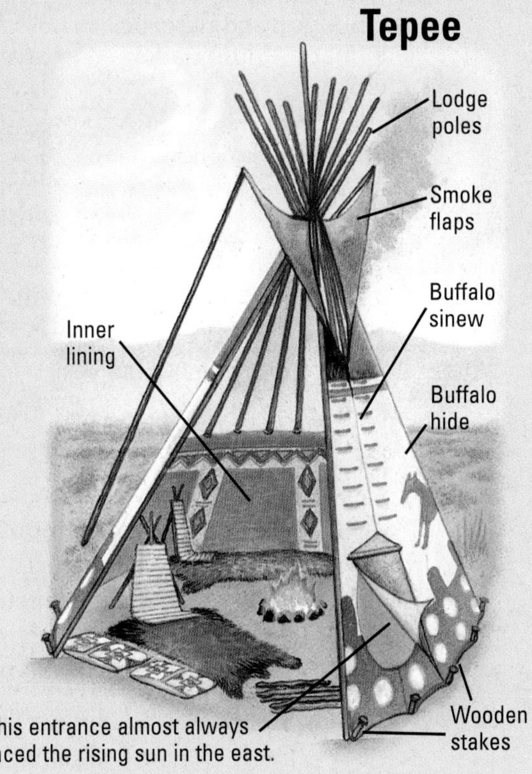

Long House

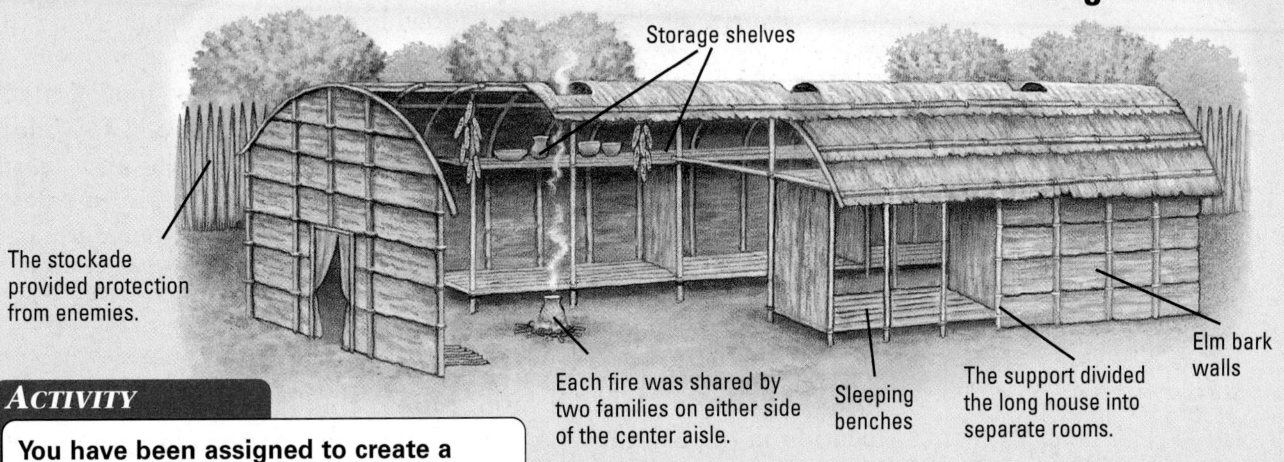

Activity

You have been assigned to create a poster promoting an exhibit on different styles of Native American dwellings. Use the information in this chapter to create an original poster that will make people want to attend the exhibit.

3 Trade Networks of Africa and Asia

Prepare to Read

Objectives

In this section, you will
- Explain why trade flourished in the Muslim world.
- Identify the trading states that rose in Africa, and describe life in many African trading cultures.
- Describe how China's overseas trade expanded in the early 1400s.

Key Terms

first global age
Islam
Quran
Silk Road
caravan
city-state
savanna
extended family
kinship

Target Reading Skill

Main Idea As you read, prepare an outline of this section. Use roman numerals to indicate the major headings of the section, capital letters for the subheadings, and numbers for the supporting details. The outline has been started for you.

I. The Muslim World
  A. Rise and spread of Islam
    1.
    2.
  B. Trade routes
    1.
    2.
  C. Silk Road
II. African Trading States and Cultures
  A. City-states of East Africa
    1.
    2.
  B. Trading kingdoms of West Africa

Main Idea Busy trade networks linked the peoples of Africa and Asia long before Europeans reached the Americas.

Ancient caravans across the desert

Setting the Scene Ibn Battuta was just 21 years old in 1325 when he set off to see the world. During the next 30 years, he would cover more than 73,000 miles. Ibn Battuta visited lands from Spain and North Africa to the Middle East, India, and China. When he finally returned home for good, he wrote proudly of his travels:

> "I have indeed—praise be to God—attained my desire in this world, which was to travel through the earth, and I have attained in this respect what no other person has attained to my knowledge."
>
> —Ibn Battuta, *Rhila (Book of Travels)*, 1355

Ibn Battuta was a scholar from North Africa who wanted to learn all he could about the many lands and the different peoples of the Muslim world. In the 1300s, that world reached from lands along the Atlantic Ocean to the borders of China.

Travelers like Ibn Battuta, as well as trade goods, moved along the land and sea routes that linked the peoples of Africa, the Middle East, and Asia. The amount of long-distance trade and travel increased dramatically in the 1400s. For the first time, far-off parts of the world began to be linked. For this reason, this period marks the beginning of what historians call the **first global age.**

The Muslim World

Arab merchants played a large role in this growing trade. Arabia's location in the Middle East made it a major crossroads of the world. It stood at the center of trade routes that linked the Mediterranean world in the west with Asia in the east and Africa in the south.

Rise and Spread of Islam The growth of trade was also linked to the growth of a new religion. In the early 600s, a new religion, **Islam,**

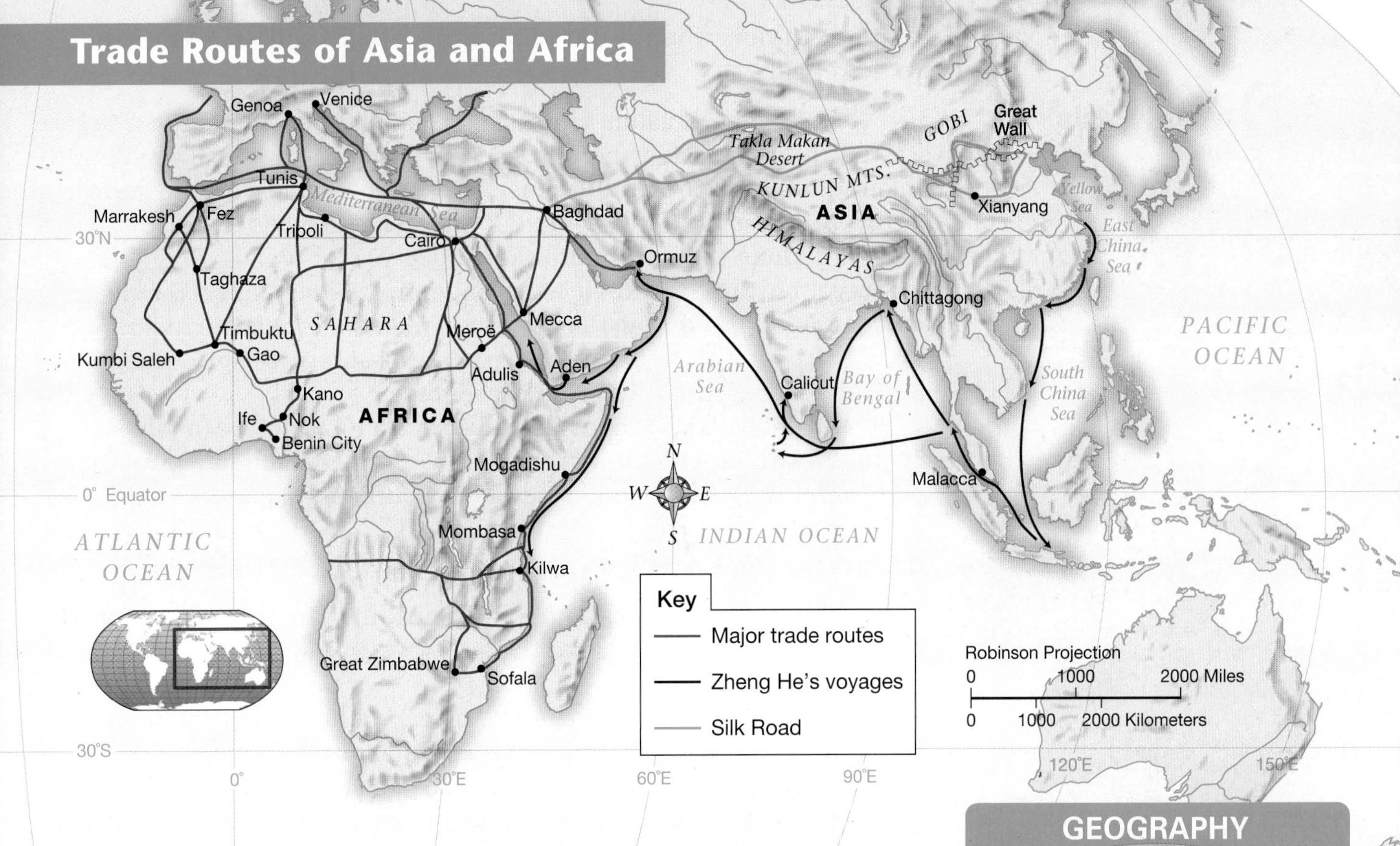

GEOGRAPHY Skills

Before the 1500s, Asian and African cultures had established important trade routes. This enabled the movement of goods and ideas between civilizations that had had few outside contacts.

1. **Location** On the map locate **(a)** the Silk Road, **(b)** Xianyang, **(c)** Baghdad.
2. **Place** Through what Asian desert did the trade route from Xianyang to Baghdad pass?
3. **Critical Thinking Drawing Conclusions** Why might large cities have developed on the eastern and western ends of the Silk Road but not in the middle?

emerged in Arabia. Its founder was the prophet Muhammad. The central teaching of Islam was belief in one God. (The Arabic word for God is *Allah.*) Followers of Islam, called Muslims, believed that the **Quran** (ku RAHN), the sacred book of Islam, contained the exact word of God as revealed to Muhammad.

Muhammad won many followers among the Arabs. After his death in 632, Islam spread rapidly. Devout followers carried Islam across North Africa and into Spain. Islam spread eastward, too, from Persia to India and beyond.

Islam expanded through trade and conquest. Many people in conquered lands chose to convert to the successful new religion. Elsewhere, Muslim merchants carried the new faith to people living along the trade routes of Asia and Africa.

Islam united Muslims from many lands. Muslims had a basic duty to make a pilgrimage, or journey, to the holy city of Mecca at least once in their lives. Every year, people from across the Muslim world traveled to Mecca. Muslims from North Africa, Persia, Afghanistan, India, Spain, and West Africa crowded Mecca's dusty streets. They prayed in Arabic, the language of Islam.

Trade Routes Muslim merchants traded across a vast area. They sailed to ports around the Indian Ocean. Their ships used large, triangular sails that allowed captains to use the wind even if it changed direction.

Muslim sailors had expert knowledge of wind and weather conditions of the Indian Ocean. As a result, merchants in ports around the region knew when the trading ships had to sail and when they would return.

Silk Road Some Muslim traders traveled the overland routes that crossed the grasslands, mountains, and deserts of Central Asia and linked China and the Middle East. These routes had become known as the **Silk Road** because prized Chinese silks had been carried westward along them for more than 2,000 years.

Identify Main Ideas

Which sentence states the main idea under the red head "Silk Road"?

Travel on the Silk Road was dangerous. Desert storms, hunger, and bandits were a constant threat. Traders formed **caravans,** or groups of people who traveled together for safety. Despite the dangers, trade along the Silk Road prospered.

By the 1400s, trade goods flowed across a huge area. Muslim merchants sold fine porcelains from China, cloth from India, ivory and gold from East Africa, and spices from Southeast Asia.

African Trading States and Cultures

Trade routes played a large role in Africa, too. Long-distance trade routes crossed the vast Sahara, the desert linking West Africa and North Africa.

A peaceful afternoon in a West African village might be pierced by sounds of a horn. Children would shout, "Batafo! Batafo!" Traders! Soon, a long line of porters and camels arrived. Villagers watched as the tired travelers unloaded sacks of salt or dried fish. Gold, fabrics, jewelry, and slaves were also part of the caravan.

Primary Source

Timbuktu

Hasan al-Wazan, also known as Leo Africanus, described Timbuktu in 1526:

"The inhabitants are very rich. . . . The royal court is magnificent and very well organized. . . . There are in Timbuktu numerous judges, teachers, and priests, all properly appointed by the king. He greatly honors learning. Many hand-written books . . . are also sold. There is more profit from this commerce than from all other merchandise."

—Hasan al-Wazan, from *The Description of Africa,* 1526

Analyzing Primary Sources

What were some signs of prosperity in Timbuktu?

City-States of East Africa Trade had long flowed up and down the coast of East Africa. Small villages that had good natural harbors grew into busy trading centers.

Gold from Zimbabwe (zihm BAH bweh), a powerful inland state, was carried to coastal cities such as Kilwa and Sofala. From there, ships carried the gold, and prized goods such as hardwoods and ivory, across the Indian Ocean to India and China.

Wealth from trade helped local East African rulers build strong city-states. A **city-state** is a large town that has its own government and controls the surrounding countryside.

Many rulers of these city-states became Muslims. In time, Muslim culture influenced East African traditions. The blend of cultures led to the rise of a new language, Swahili, which blended Arabic words and local African languages.

Trading Kingdoms of West Africa A region of grasslands, called the **savanna,** covers much of West Africa. Several rich trading kingdoms emerged there. Among the best known were Mali and Songhai (SAWNG hi). The city of Timbuktu was the major trading center for both kingdoms.

The kingdom of Mali rose in about A.D. 1200 and flourished for about 200 years. Like the rulers of East Africa's city-states, many rulers in West African kingdoms adopted the religion of Islam.

Mali's most famous ruler, Mansa Musa, was a Muslim. In 1324, the emperor made a pilgrimage to Mecca. On the way, he and his caravan stopped in Cairo, Egypt. His wealth in gold amazed the Egyptians. In time, stories of Mansa Musa's immense wealth reached Europe. A

Spanish map from that time shows Mansa Musa on his throne, holding a golden object. The mapmaker wrote these words nearby:

> “So abundant is the gold in his country that this lord is the richest and most noble king in all the land.”
>
> —Catalan Atlas, 1375

In the 1400s, Songhai emerged as the most powerful kingdom in West Africa. Muslim emperors extended Songhai's power and made Timbuktu into a thriving city.

Village and Family Life Ways of life varied greatly across the huge continent of Africa. While powerful trading states flourished in some regions, most people lived outside these kingdoms. Many lived in small villages. They made a living by herding, fishing, or farming.

Family relationships were important in African cultures. Although family patterns varied across Africa, many people lived within an extended family. In an **extended family,** several generations live in one household. An extended family usually included grandparents, parents, children, and sometimes aunts, uncles, and cousins. The grandparents, or elders, received special respect for their wisdom and knowledge.

Ties of **kinship,** or sharing a common ancestor, linked families. People related by kinship owed loyalty to one another. Kinship ties encouraged a strong sense of community and cooperation.

Religious beliefs varied widely across Africa. Yet, African beliefs reflected some common threads. Links among family members lasted even after a person died. In their rituals and ceremonies, Africans honored the spirits of their ancestors as well as the forces of nature. Powerful spirits, they believed, could harm or could help the living.

Viewing History

Historic Journeys

Between 1405 and 1433, the Chinese admiral Zheng He (bottom left) led a fleet of large ships like this one on journeys of exploration to Southeast Asia, India, and Arabia. By the time of Zheng He's death, Chinese influence had spread across a wide region. **Drawing Inferences** ***What do you think it would take to maintain Chinese influence in these areas of Southeast Asia, India, and Arabia after Zheng He's death?***

Chinese Voyages of Trade and Exploration

Africa had many different cultures and kingdoms. By contrast, in China, power was centered on the emperor. Chinese rulers were often suspicious of outsiders. China was the most isolated civilization of the ancient world. Long distances and physical barriers separated it from Egypt, the Middle East, and India. This isolation contributed to the Chinese belief that China was the center of the Earth and the sole source of civilization. The ancient Chinese looked down on outsiders, who did not speak Chinese or follow Chinese ways.

The Great Treasure Fleet The young emperor who came to power in 1402 was eager for trade. He ordered a huge fleet to be built and named Zheng He (DZUNG HEH) to command it. Zheng He's fleet numbered more than 300 ships. It carried tons of trade goods. The largest ships were more than 400 feet long.

Between 1405 and 1433, Zheng He made seven long voyages. His fleet traded at ports in Southeast Asia, India, Arabia, and East Africa. At every port, Chinese traders carried on a brisk business. They expanded Chinese trade and influence across a wide region.

The Voyages End The great fleet returned home with exotic goods and animals, such as giraffes, that the Chinese had never seen. However, China's overseas voyages soon ended. A new emperor decided that China had nothing to learn from the outside world. He outlawed foreign trade.

What Might Have Been Historians sometimes discuss what might have happened if events had taken a slightly different course. One question historians ponder is what if Zheng He had led his fleet around the southern tip of Africa or across the Pacific?

Chinese ships could certainly have made such long voyages. They were much larger than the ships commanded by Christopher Columbus in 1492. When Columbus sailed westward across the Atlantic Ocean, he had three tiny ships. They carried only 90 sailors, compared to the approximately 28,000 on Zheng He's ships.

If Zheng He had crossed the Pacific Ocean and reached the Americas, American history might have turned out very different. Instead, China stopped its voyages and closed its doors to trade. Within a few years, however, several small European nations began to hunt for new trade routes to Asia. Their eagerness for trade led to daring voyages across the Atlantic Ocean.

Section 3 Assessment

Recall

1. **Identify** Explain the significance of **(a)** Ibn Battuta, **(b)** first global age, **(c)** Islam, **(d)** Quran, **(e)** Silk Road, **(f)** Timbuktu, **(g)** Zheng He.
2. **Define (a)** caravan, **(b)** city-state, **(c)** savanna, **(d)** extended family, **(e)** kinship.

Comprehension

3. How did trade and religion link people in the Muslim world?
4. What were some common values that linked the people of many different African cultures?
5. How did China's emperor encourage overseas trade in the early 1400s?

Critical Thinking and Writing

6. **Exploring the Main Idea** Review the Main Idea statement at the beginning of this section. Then, write a paragraph describing networks linking Africa and Asia in 1400. Explain how these networks helped the movement of goods, people, and ideas.
7. **Solving Problems** Suppose a European ruler wanted to profit from trade with Asia. The routes through the Mediterranean and across Asia were already controlled by others, however. How might the ruler try to get a foothold in the Asian trade?

Activity

Connecting to Today

Use the Internet to find out more about either Ibn Battuta or the Chinese admiral Zheng He. With the information you find, prepare a script for a TV news report. For help in completing the activity, visit PHSchool.com, **Web Code mfd-0203.**

4 Tradition and Change in Europe

Prepare to Read

Objectives

In this section, you will
- Define Jewish and Christian traditions that influenced European civilization.
- Describe how ancient Greek and Roman traditions affected later Europeans.
- List the ways in which the events of the Middle Ages changed Europe.
- Identify the importance of the Renaissance.

Key Terms

salvation
missionary
direct democracy
republic
feudalism
manor
Crusades
astrolabe
Renaissance

Target Reading Skill

Clarifying Meaning Copy the concept web below. Add as many ovals as you need. As you read, fill in each blank oval with important facts about the traditions that shaped European civilization. Two ovals have been completed to help you get started.

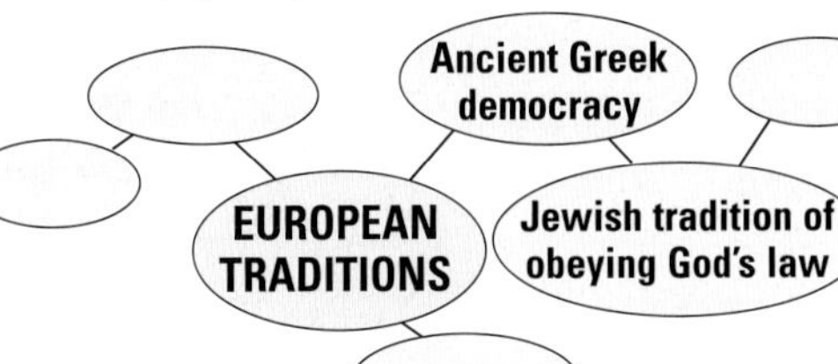

Main Idea European civilization emerged from a long period of isolation during the 1400s.

Setting the Scene The sturdy ship dipped in and out of the rolling waves of the Atlantic Ocean. Above, stars dotted the night sky.

At the first hint of dawn, a cabin boy checked the hourglass, which was used to keep track of time. It took 30 minutes for sand to run from the top half of the glass into the bottom. So every half-hour, the boy had to turn the glass. Afterward, he prayed aloud:

> "Blessed be the light of day and the Holy Cross, we say; and the Lord of Truth and the Holy Trinity. Blessed be the immortal soul and the Lord who keeps it whole."
>
> —Eugenio de Salazar, 1573

Sailing the high seas

The boy's prayer was a tradition on European sailing ships. In the 1400s, bold Europeans set out to explore the world. They brought with them their traditions that, over time, would affect people in many lands.

Jewish and Christian Traditions

European civilization emerged slowly during the long period from about A.D. 500 to 1400. As in other societies, religious beliefs played an important role in European life. They provided moral guidance and helped people understand their place in the world. European beliefs were shaped by two religions of the ancient Middle East, Judaism and Christianity.

Judaism and the Importance of Laws Judaism refers to the religious beliefs of the Israelites, who lived more than 3,000 years ago. (Later, the Israelites became known as Jews.) Jews believe in one God and feel a sacred duty to obey God's rules.

The history and laws of the ancient Jews were recorded in the Torah. The Jews credited Moses with bringing God's laws to them. Those laws included the Ten Commandments, a set of religious and moral rules.

The Jews believed that every Jew must obey the Ten Commandments and other religious laws. No one was above God's laws, even the most powerful ruler. That view differed from most religions of that time, which regarded rulers as gods. More than 2,000 years ago, many Jews left their homeland. This scattering of people sent Jews to different parts of the world. Wherever they settled, Jews maintained their identity as a people by obeying their religion's laws and traditions.

Christianity and the Teachings of Jesus About 2,000 years ago, a Jew named Jesus lived in a province of the Roman empire. Jesus believed in the Ten Commandments and other Jewish traditions. He preached about God's goodness and mercy. Some followers began to call him the Messiah, a savior chosen by God.

The Gospels, which recount the life of Jesus, tell how crowds flocked to hear Jesus teach and perform miracles. Local officials, however, saw Jesus as a political threat. They had him arrested, tried, and crucified—a Roman form of execution.

The life and teachings of Jesus inspired a new religion, Christianity. The new faith included many Jewish traditions, such as belief in one God and the Ten Commandments, along with the teachings of Jesus. Like Jewish teachers, Jesus emphasized love, mercy, and forgiveness.

Jesus taught that anyone, rich or poor, could achieve **salvation**, or everlasting life. That belief, which meant that everyone was equal in the eyes of God, appealed to many people. As Christianity spread across the Roman empire, officials sometimes persecuted Christians. However, the persecutions did not slow the growth of the religion. Eventually, around A.D. 391, Christianity became the official religion of the empire.

By then, Christians had organized a strong church with its own government and officials. The church sent out **missionaries**, people who spread Christian teachings across Europe. Slowly, missionaries brought many non-Christian peoples of Europe into the new faith.

Primary Source

The Greatness of Athenian Democracy

Pericles, a longtime leader of Athens, made a speech that has survived since ancient times. In it, he described Athenian greatness, especially its democracy:

"Our constitution is called a democracy because power is in the hands not of a minority but of the whole people. When it is a question of settling private disputes, everyone is equal before the law. . . .

Here a citizen is interested not just in his own affairs but in the affairs of state as well. Even citizens who are busy with their own affairs are very well-informed on politics. Unlike other states, we do not say that a man who takes no interest in politics is a man who minds his own business. We say that he has no business here at all."

—Pericles, Funeral Oration, 431 B.C.

Analyzing Primary Sources

What is Pericles' view of citizens who do not participate in government?

Greek and Roman Traditions

Two ancient civilizations shaped European traditions over the centuries. They were the civilizations that grew up in ancient Greece and Rome.

Greek Ideas About Government Around 500 B.C., Greece entered a golden age. Greek artists created fine marble statues and designed elegant temples. Poets and playwrights created works that are still read today.

Greek thinkers, such as Socrates and Aristotle, valued human reason. Using reason, they said, individuals could understand the natural world. Other Greek thinkers made important contributions to science and mathematics. They developed the study of geometry and pioneered the idea that all matter is made up of small moving atoms. Greek doctors tried to diagnose and treat diseases using scientific methods. Greek thinkers debated many issues, including the best kind of government. Greek ideas about government would have a great impact on later European thinking.

Unlike in the large empires of the ancient world, the Greeks lived in small city-states. At first, a monarch ruled each city-state. Slowly, some city-states developed other kinds of government. In some, a king ruled. In others, a few wealthy people controlled the government. Ancient Athens, for example, first created direct democracy. **Direct democracy** is a form of government in which ordinary citizens have the power to govern.

Athenians were proud of their government. They believed that people could think and act for themselves. All citizens could attend the assembly and make laws for the city. Athenian democracy was very limited, however. Only free men whose parents had been born in Athens were citizens. Most people in Athens were not citizens. This included all women and slaves and men who came to Athens from other city-states.

Roman Government and Law As the Greeks entered their golden age, a few small villages in Italy were growing into the city of Rome. From a small city-state, Rome would one day become a huge empire. In the process, it absorbed ideas from many other peoples, including the Greeks. It also created its own traditions, especially in the fields of law and government.

In 509 B.C., the Romans overthrew their king and set up a republic. A **republic** is a system of government in which citizens choose representatives to govern them. In the Roman Republic, a senate and assembly made the laws.

As Rome expanded, the republic faced a series of crises that caused military leaders to seize power. Among them was Julius Caesar, who named himself dictator for life. After Caesar's murder, his nephew, Octavian, declared himself emperor in 27 B.C. He received the title Caesar Augustus.

The Roman empire lasted for almost 500 years. Rome spread its language, Latin, and ideas about law across a wide area. In Roman tradition, everyone was equal before the law. Accused people were considered innocent until proven guilty. Rome also set up rules about the use of evidence in court. Roman legal traditions would later influence Europe.

Decline of Rome The Roman empire declined slowly. Invaders attacked and overran many regions. Trade and travel slowed. In place of the Roman empire, Europe was splintered into many small, warring kingdoms.

During this time, the achievements of Greece and Rome were largely forgotten. A few Christian monasteries preserved ancient manuscripts. Others survived in the Islamic world. Much later, as you will read, Europeans would rediscover these ancient texts. Then, Greek and Roman traditions would, in turn, come to play a key role in American history.

Target Skill

Paraphrase

When you paraphrase, you restate in your own words what you have already read. Paraphrase the information about how Roman government and law influenced European traditions. Include this information on your concept web.

Viewing History

Roman Senators

Rome

In the Roman Republic, forms of government were established to take power away from the few and give it to the many. The bas-relief below shows two Roman senators. **Summarizing** ***Based on the information on Roman government, write two sentences explaining how the Romans established traditions of government that would influence later societies.***

The Middle Ages

The period from about A.D. 500 to about 1400 is known as the Middle Ages. During the early Middle Ages, invasion and war were common. Without Roman armies, people had to find other means of defending themselves.

Feudalism A new kind of government evolved during the Middle Ages. Kings and queens divided their lands among warrior nobles. In return, nobles promised to fight for the ruler when asked. This system of rule by lords who ruled their lands but owed loyalty and military service to a monarch is called **feudalism** (FYOOD 'l ihz uhm).

At the top of feudal society stood the king and the most powerful lords. Next came the lesser nobles. Most people in feudal society were peasants who farmed the lord's lands and could not leave the land without the lord's permission.

Viewing History

Peasants and Lords

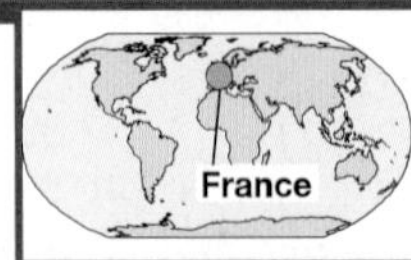

In the Middle Ages, it was the peasants' duty to farm the lord's lands. The lord in his magnificent castle had the duty of protecting the peasants. **Making Predictions** ***Based on this painting from France in the early 1400s, and the information on the Middle Ages, what problems do you think could arise between peasant and lord?***

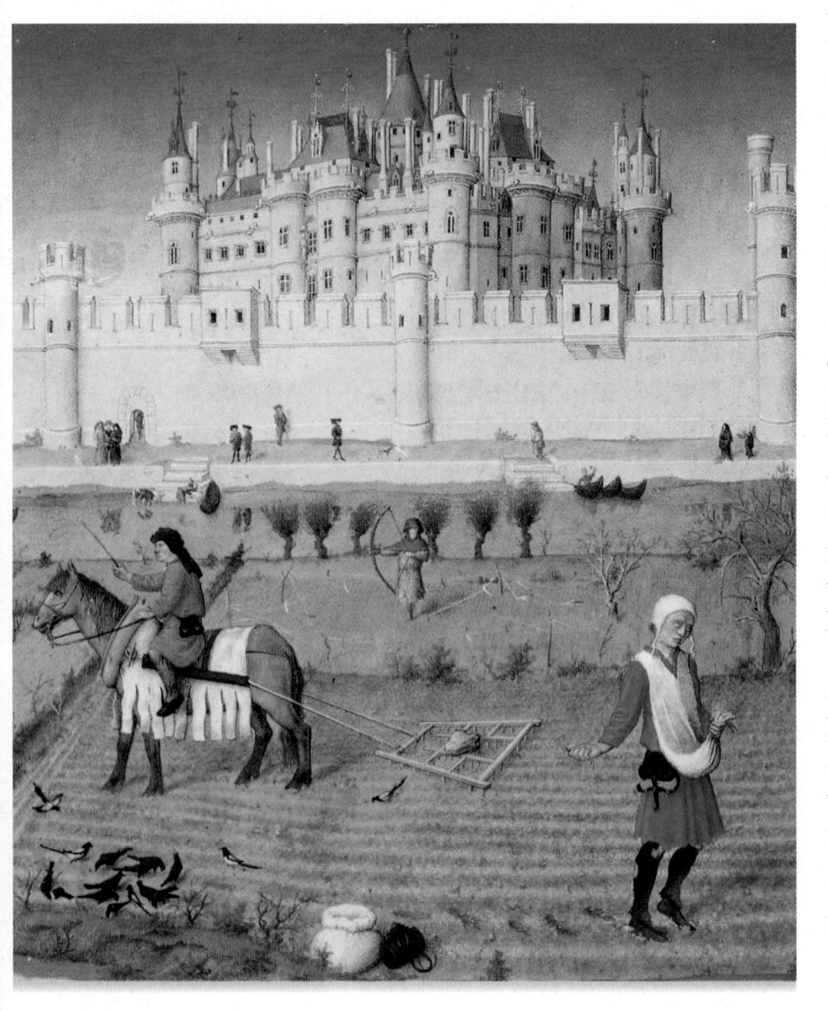

Daily Life Feudal life revolved around the **manor,** which included the lord's castle and the lands around it. Manor lands might include several villages.

Each manor was self-sufficient. That is, people made almost everything they needed. Life for peasants was hard. They struggled to produce enough food just to survive.

The most powerful force was the Roman Catholic Church. It ruled more than religious life. The Church owned large amounts of land and was the source of education. The clergy were often the only people who could read and write. Because of their efforts, much of the learning from the ancient world was preserved.

By about A.D. 900, life began to change. Peasants used new methods of farming to produce more food. Warfare declined and trade began to grow. Slowly, people began to look beyond their isolated villages.

The Crusades The pace of change increased between 1100 and 1300 in part because of the Crusades. The **Crusades** were a series of wars fought by Christians to control the Holy Land. The Holy Land included Jerusalem and the other places where Jesus had lived and taught. Muslims had controlled this region for centuries.

During the Crusades, tens of thousands of Christians journeyed to the Middle East. Fighting between Christians and Muslims continued for almost 200 years. Christians won some victories. But in the end, they failed to win control of the Holy Land.

Growth of Trade The Crusades had important effects on Europe, however. Crusaders traveled beyond their villages and came into contact with other civilizations. In the Middle East, they tasted new foods, such as rice, oranges, dates, and new spices. They saw beautiful silks and woven rugs.

Europe had traded with the Middle East for many years before the Crusades. However, returning Crusaders demanded more of the Asian foods, spices, silks, and rugs. Italian merchants realized that people would pay high prices for such goods. They outfitted ships and increased trade with the Muslim world.

New Tools for Navigation Trade brought new knowledge. From the Muslim world, Europeans acquired sailing skills and the magnetic compass. Muslims had earlier adopted the magnetic compass from the Chinese. The special needle of the compass always pointed north, which helped ships stay on course.

Another useful instrument was the **astrolabe** (AS troh layb), which helped sailors determine their latitude while at sea. These new instruments let Europeans sail far out to sea, beyond sight of land. By 1500, Portugal had taken the lead in this new overseas travel.

Portuguese Routes of Exploration

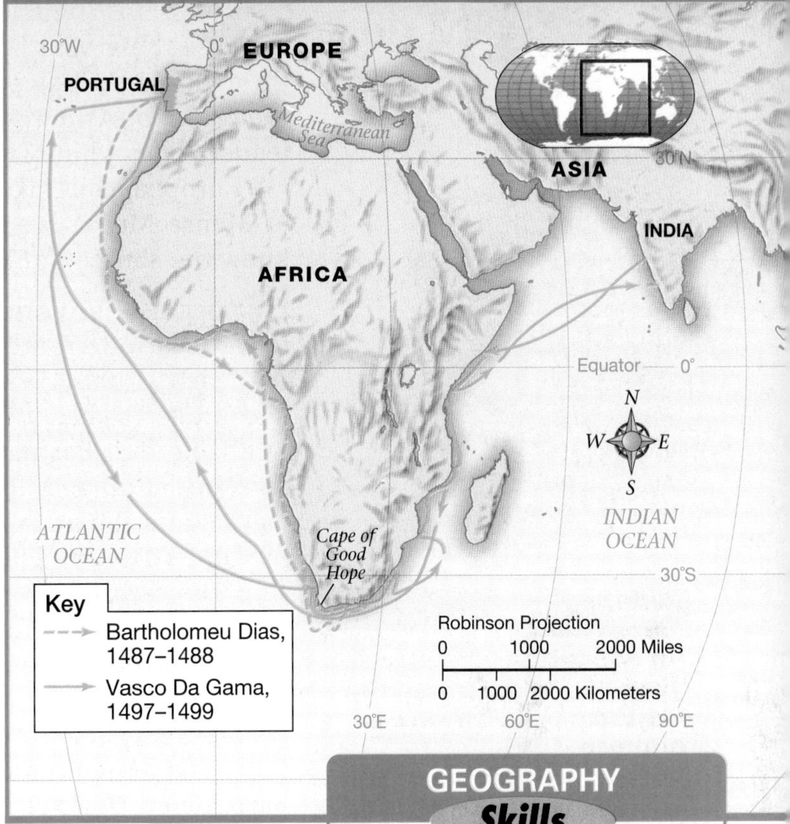

Key
- Bartholomeu Dias, 1487–1488
- Vasco Da Gama, 1497–1499

Robinson Projection

The Renaissance Expands Horizons

Increased trade and travel made Europeans eager to learn more about the wider world. Scholars looked in monastery libraries for manuscripts of ancient Greek and Roman works. Some traveled to the Muslim world, where many ancient works had been preserved.

As scholars studied ancient learning, they began to make their own discoveries. They produced new books on art, medicine, astronomy, and chemistry. This great burst of learning was called the **Renaissance** (REHN uh sahns), a French word meaning rebirth. It lasted from the late 1300s until the 1600s.

A new invention, the printing press, helped to spread Renaissance learning. A German printer named Johannes Gutenberg (GOOT uhn berg) is credited with this invention in the 1430s. Before then, books were scarce and costly because each was copied by hand. With the printing press, large numbers of books could be produced quickly and at a low cost. Soon more people began to read, and learning spread more quickly.

The Search for New Trade Routes During the Renaissance, trade brought new prosperity. European rulers began to increase their power. In England and France, kings and queens tried to bring powerful feudal lords under their control. In Spain and Portugal,

GEOGRAPHY *Skills*

New technologies and new skills allowed Portuguese sailors to make historic voyages along the coast of Africa and across the Indian Ocean to India.

1. **Location** On the map locate **(a)** Portugal, **(b)** Cape of Good Hope, **(c)** Indian Ocean.
2. **Movement** Describe the route taken by Da Gama.
3. **Critical Thinking Drawing Inferences** Why do you think the Cape of Good Hope was an important landmark to sailors?

Christian monarchs drove out Muslim rulers, who had governed there for centuries.

Rulers in England, France, Spain, and Portugal were eager to increase their wealth. They saw the great profits that could be made through trade. However, Muslim and Italian merchants controlled the trade routes across the Mediterranean Sea. So, Western Europe's leaders began hunting for other routes to Asia.

European rulers also looked to Africa as a source of riches. Tales of Mansa Musa's wealth had created a stir in Europe, but no one knew the source of African gold.

Viewing History

An African View of the Portuguese

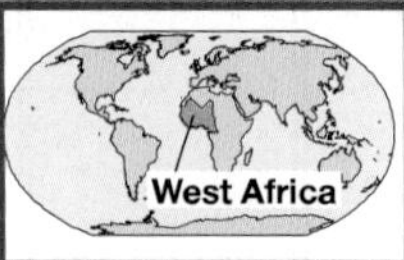

The ivory carving above was done by an African artisan in the 1500s. **Drawing Inferences** ***How do you think Africans perceived the Portuguese?***

Portuguese Voyages Portugal was an early leader in the search for a new trade route to Asia and for the source of African gold. In the early 1400s, Prince Henry, known as Henry the Navigator, encouraged sea captains to sail south along the coast of West Africa. Realizing that Portugal needed better navigators to accomplish the task, he set up an informal school to teach sailors techniques of navigation and the art of shipbuilding.

Under Henry's guidance, the Portuguese designed a new type of ship, the caravel (KAR uh vehl). With triangular sails and a steering rudder, caravels could be sailed into the wind. Portuguese caravels stopped at many places along the coast of West Africa. They traded cloth, silver, textiles, and grain for gold, ivory, and slaves.

Slowly, Portuguese explorers ventured farther south, hoping to find a sea route around Africa to the rich spice trade of Asia. In 1488, Bartolomeu Dias reached the southern tip of Africa.

Nine years later, in 1497, Vasco da Gama rounded the Cape of Good Hope at the southern tip of Africa. He then sailed up the coast of East Africa and across the Indian Ocean to India. The Portuguese pushed on to the East Indies, the islands of Southeast Asia and the source of valuable spices.

★ ★ ★ Section 4 Assessment ★ ★ ★

Recall

1. **Identify** Explain the significance of **(a)** Crusades, **(b)** Renaissance, **(c)** Johannes Gutenberg, **(d)** Prince Henry.
2. **Define** **(a)** salvation, **(b)** missionary, **(c)** direct democracy, **(d)** republic, **(e)** feudalism, **(f)** manor, **(g)** astrolabe.

Comprehension

3. Describe one tradition from Judaism and Christianity that influenced later Europeans.
4. What were three ideas that Europeans learned from ancient Greece and Rome?
5. How did the Crusades help bring changes to Europe?
6. Why did Renaissance rulers in Western Europe want to find new routes to Asia?

Critical Thinking and Writing

7. **Exploring the Main Idea** Review the Main Idea statement at the beginning of this section. Then, identify reasons for the European exploration of North America.
8. **Drawing Conclusions** Write an editorial explaining whether you think the Crusades were a success or a failure.

ACTIVITY

Writing a Diary **You are a sailor on Vasco da Gama's voyage of 1497. With a partner, write two different diary entries that express your hopes and fears about the voyage.**

Finding Main Ideas and Supporting Details

History books are bursting with information. Although you can't remember every fact, you can learn to identify the main ideas and note the details that explain and support them. The passage below describes the growth of trade between Europe and other regions of the world. After you have read the passage, use "Learn the Skill" below to help you identify the main idea.

Toward the end of the Middle Ages, European nations developed an interest in trading with Asia. Several factors contributed to this interest. Perhaps the most important of these was the huge profit that European nations could gain through such trade. Rulers of countries including Spain, France, England, and Portugal quickly saw that increased prosperity from trade could be turned into increased power for them.

Trade with Asia promised several other benefits as well. The shimmering silks and colorful rugs of Asia pleased and intrigued Europeans. So, too, did foreign foods such as oranges, rice, and dates. Exotic spices such as ginger and pepper not only improved food but also helped to preserve it. Still other reasons that Europeans sought trade were a new awareness of the rest of the world and a curiosity to learn more about it.

Learn the Skill *To identify main ideas and supporting details, use the following steps:*

1. **Find the main idea.** The main idea is what the passage is about. Often, the main idea is stated in the first sentence of a paragraph. However, it can occur in other parts of a paragraph as well.
2. **Restate the main idea.** To be sure you understand what a paragraph is about, restate the main idea in your own words.
3. **Look for details.** These include facts, reasons, explanations, examples, and descriptions that tell more about the main idea.
4. **Make connections.** Note how the details support and expand the main idea.

Practice the Skill *Answer the following questions about the paragraphs above:*

1. What is the main idea sentence in each of the two paragraphs?
2. Restate the main idea in each paragraph in your own words.
3. Identify a detail that supports the main idea in the first paragraph.
4. **(a)** How do the details in the first paragraph help explain the main idea of that paragraph? **(b)** How do the details in the second paragraph expand the main idea of that paragraph?

Apply the Skill *See the Chapter Review and Assessment.*

CHAPTER 2

Review and Assessment

Chapter Summary

Section 1
Asian wanderers who came to the Americas on a land bridge had to adjust to new conditions. A number of civilizations thrived in Central and South America. Other cultures blossomed in North America.

Section 2
The climates and resources of North America enabled many different groups to survive there. Native American cultures shared some beliefs. The Iroquois Confederacy linked several Native American nations.

Section 3
As Islam spread, Muslim merchants began to trade across Asia and Africa. The Chinese voyager Zheng He reached as far west as India, Arabia, and East Africa.

Section 4
The modern era has been influenced by many ideas from Jewish and Christian traditions, from Greek and Roman traditions, and from the Renaissance. The Crusades occurred during the Middle Ages.

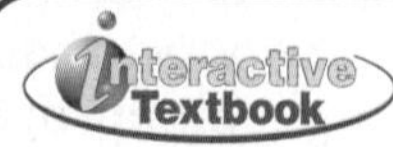

For additional review and enrichment activities, see the interactive version of *The American Nation,* available on the Web and on CD-ROM.

Chapter Self-Test For practice test questions for Chapter 2, visit PHSchool.com, **Web Code mfa-0204.**

Building Vocabulary

Write sentences, using the chapter vocabulary words listed below, leaving blanks where the vocabulary words would go. Exchange your sentences with another student and fill in the blanks in each other's sentences.

1. **glacier**
2. **surplus**
3. **culture area**
4. **pit house**
5. **sachem**
6. **city-state**
7. **extended family**
8. **direct democracy**
9. **republic**
10. **feudalism**

Reviewing Key Facts

11. What civilizations emerged in present-day Mexico? (Section 1)
12. Name two Native American cultures that developed in North America and explain how each adapted to its environment. (Section 2)
13. How did trade affect East Africa and West Africa before the 1500s? (Section 3)
14. How did the Renaissance open new horizons for Europeans? (Section 4)

Critical Thinking and Writing

15. **Comparing** Make a list comparing the methods used by the Aztecs to farm swampy Lake Texcoco to those used by the Anasazi to farm the desert Southwest.
16. **Contrasting** **(a)** Make a list of differences between the cultures of the Great Basin and those of the Southeast. **(b)** Write a paragraph explaining how those differences were related to the climate and resources of each region.
17. **Connecting to Geography: Movement** The movement of people, goods, and ideas is another key link between geography and history. **(a)** Describe the trade networks that had grown up across Africa and Asia by the 1400s. **(b)** Give one example of how trade led to the exchange of ideas.
18. **Synthesizing Information** Write a paragraph describing how the Renaissance led Europeans to explore unfamiliar lands.

SKILLS ASSESSMENT

Analyzing Primary Sources

Not all primary sources consist of words. A painting can also be a primary source. For example, the painting below contains some valuable information about how the Aztecs lived. Study it, and then answer the questions below.

19. The seated person is the emperor. What is the other person doing?
    - A. He is putting on a puppet show.
    - B. He is bringing the emperor gifts.
    - C. He is cleaning up the throne room.
    - D. He is exterminating the throne room.
20. What do you think is the attitude of the person at right?
    - A. He is defiant.
    - B. He is aggressive.
    - C. He is submissive.
    - D. He is confused.

APPLYING YOUR SKILLS

Finding Main Ideas and Supporting Details

Read the passage below, which comes from a high school American history textbook. Then, answer the questions that follow.

> “No matter how Native Americans adapted to their environment, they generally looked to the family to fulfill many of their social needs. Their families provided them with many of the services we expect today, from governments, churches, and private organizations. Such services included medical care, child care, settlement of disputes, and education.”
>
> —Andrew Cayton, *America: Pathways to the Present,* 1998

21. Which statement best reflects the main idea of the selection?
    - A. Families provide medical care.
    - B. Families support people.
    - C. Indian families were not important.
    - D. Families provided for many social needs of Native Americans.
22. What details does the author use to support the main point of the selection?

ACTIVITIES

Connecting With . . . Science and Technology

Identifying Causes and Effects By the 1400s, Europeans were beginning to use new instruments and knowledge about navigation. Several new technologies are discussed in the chapter. Write a news bulletin for two new technologies, describing how each one helped Europeans undertake voyages of exploration.

Evaluating Internet Sites

Reviewing Sites About the First American Civilizations Use the Internet to find at least two sites with visual materials about the Mayas, Aztecs, or Incas. Write a review of these sites. In it, describe the kind of information they gave, the quality and quantity of visuals, and their usefulness in learning about the civilization. Include the addresses of the sites. For help in starting this activity, visit PHSchool.com, **Web Code mfd-0206.**

The Mother of Nations

Joseph Bruchac

Joseph Bruchac

Introduction **Joseph Bruchac is a scholar of Native American culture and an author, poet, novelist, and storyteller. He has written more than 50 books and has won a Lifetime Achievement Award of the Native Writers' Circle of the Americas. Bruchac grew up and still lives in the foothills of the Adirondack Mountains in New York State. His story "The Mother of Nations" deals with the founding of the Iroquois Confederation.**

Vocabulary Before you read the selection, find the meanings of these words in a dictionary: **longhouse, descendent, stockaded, exhort.**

Long ago there was a woman whose longhouse stood to the west at Oniagara. Her people, whom she led, were those known as the Cultivators, the Hadiyent-togeo-no and they were cousins to the Ongwe-oweh.

It was said that this woman was the direct descendent of the first woman born on the Earth. Her name was Jigonsahseh, the Lynx. Her longhouse stood by the warriors' path which ran from east to west. Though she was unable to stop the continual war which tore apart the nations in those days, still her words were respected. She always fed those who passed by her door and she was called by many "The Great Mother."

When The Peacemaker, who brought the great message from the Master of Life, set out into the world he went first to the land of the Cultivators. He crossed Sganya-dai-yo, the Great Beautiful Lake, in his canoe made of white stone. He saw that there were no cornfields planted because of the continual warfare. The towns were stockaded and filled with people who were hungry and quarrelling.

The Peacemaker went to the house of Jigonsahseh. She welcomed him and placed food before him. When he had finished eating she spoke. "You have come to bring a message," she said. "My mind is open to it. I wish to hear."

Then The Peacemaker spoke. He told her he was acting as the messenger of the Maker of Life. He said that his message was to bring justice, peace, and good laws for the people. The wars between the Ongwe-oweh, the True Human Beings, would cease.

"This message is good," said Jigonsahseh. "What form shall it take among the People?"

Then The Peacemaker explained. "It will take the form of the Longhouse. There will be many fires within the Longhouse, many families. But all will live together under the guidance of a wise Clan Mother. The five nations of the Ongwe-oweh will become of one mind and be known as the People of the Longhouse. Together they will seek the way of Peace which would be open to all the nations.

"My hands are open to this message. I reach out and grasp it," said Jigonsahseh.

Then it was decided that, since a woman was the first to accept this new way, from that day on the women would possess the titles and give them to the men who would speak for their nations in the Longhouse. These women would name from their clans the men who would serve the people. The Clan Mothers would give them the horns of office and if they did not do their jobs well the women could take back their titles.

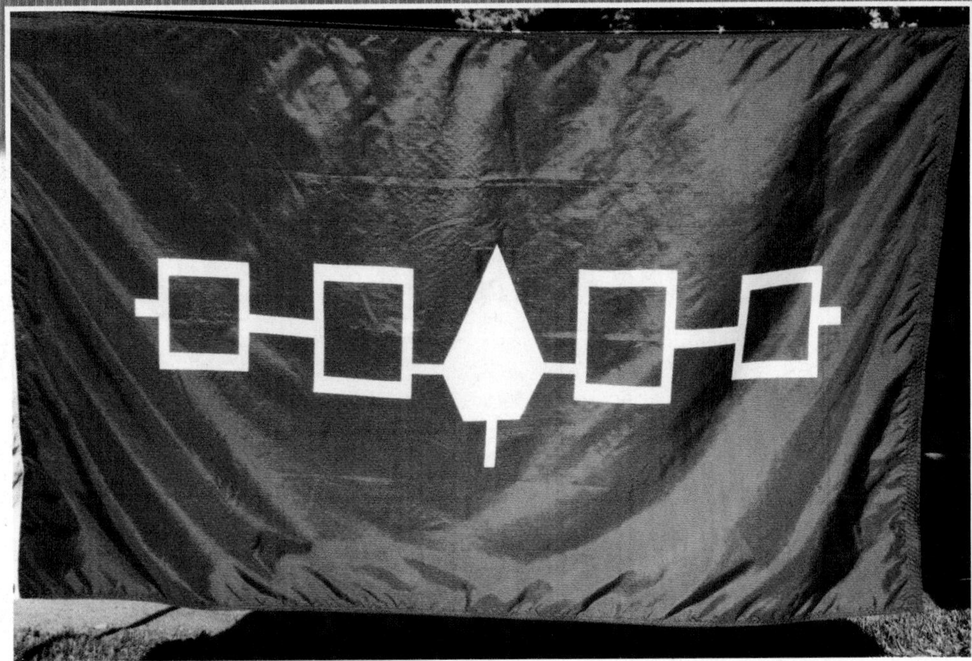

Iroquois flag showing the five-nation symbol

From that day on, the longhouse of Jigonsahseh would be known as the Peace House. All would now call her the Yegowaneh, "The Mother of Nations." In the land of her people there would be no war. The Cultivators would now be known as the Attiwendaronk, "The Neutral Nation."

So it came to be that in the land of the Yegowaneh, the Mother of Nations, there was no war. Her name was passed down from mother to eldest daughter. When it was necessary for the People of the Longhouse to deal with other nations who had not joined the League of Peace or when there were disputes between nations, the War Captains would always pass first through her land and deliver Peace Belts to the Yegowaneh.

She would give them food, as had been the custom of all those who carried the name of Jigonsahseh and were descended from the first woman born on Earth. Then the Mother of Nations would exhort them to seek peace and accept war only as a last resort. So it is said among the People of the Longhouse that the path of war runs through the House of Peace.

Analyzing Literature

1. Why was The Peacemaker troubled when he visited the land of the Cultivators?

- **A** They were not worshipping him in the proper ways.
- **B** They were not planting crops because they were fighting among themselves.
- **C** They had gone off to war in far-off lands, leaving their families behind.
- **D** They spent too much time hunting and trapping and not enough raising crops.

2. How did the longhouse symbolize the Iroquois?

- **A** Many families lived under one roof in the longhouse, just as the tribes lived together in unity in the world.
- **B** The longhouse was made of strong wood, just as the people were strong.
- **C** Women built the longhouse, just as women held titles of power.
- **D** People shared the longhouse, just as they shared land with the woodland animals.

3. **Critical Thinking and Writing** **Comparing** List three ways the information in this story supports the information about the Iroquois in Section 2 of Chapter 2.

CHAPTER 3

Exploration and Colonization

1492–1675

Christopher Columbus

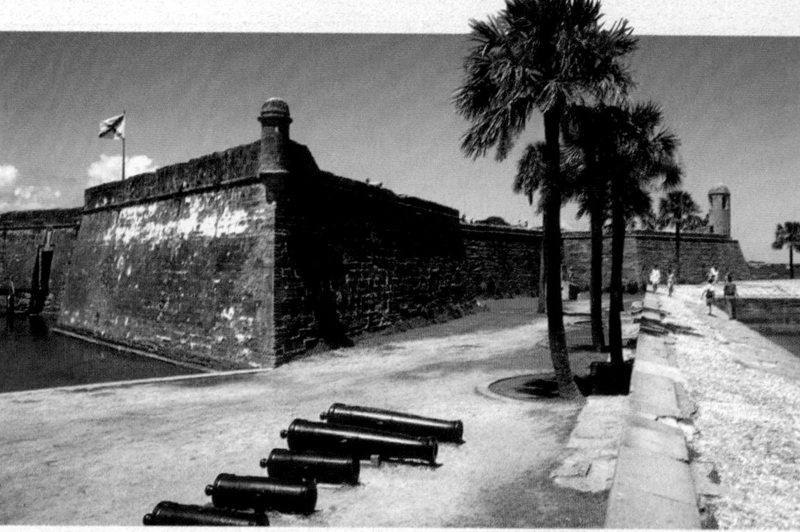

Fort of Castillo de San Marcos at St. Augustine

AMERICAN EVENTS

1492 Seeking a westward route from Europe to Asia, Christopher Columbus reaches the Caribbean. His voyage marks the start of regular contact between Europe and the Americas.

1519 Spanish warrior Hernando Cortés begins conquest of the Aztec empire.

1565 Spain builds a fort at St. Augustine. Today, St. Augustine, Florida, is the oldest city in the United States.

1475 · 1525 · 1575

WORLD EVENTS

1500s ▲ Atlantic slave trade begins.

▲ 1517 Protestant Reformation begins in Europe.

European Voyages of Exploration, 1487–1522

In the late 1400s, European explorers began to sail and chart the oceans of the world.

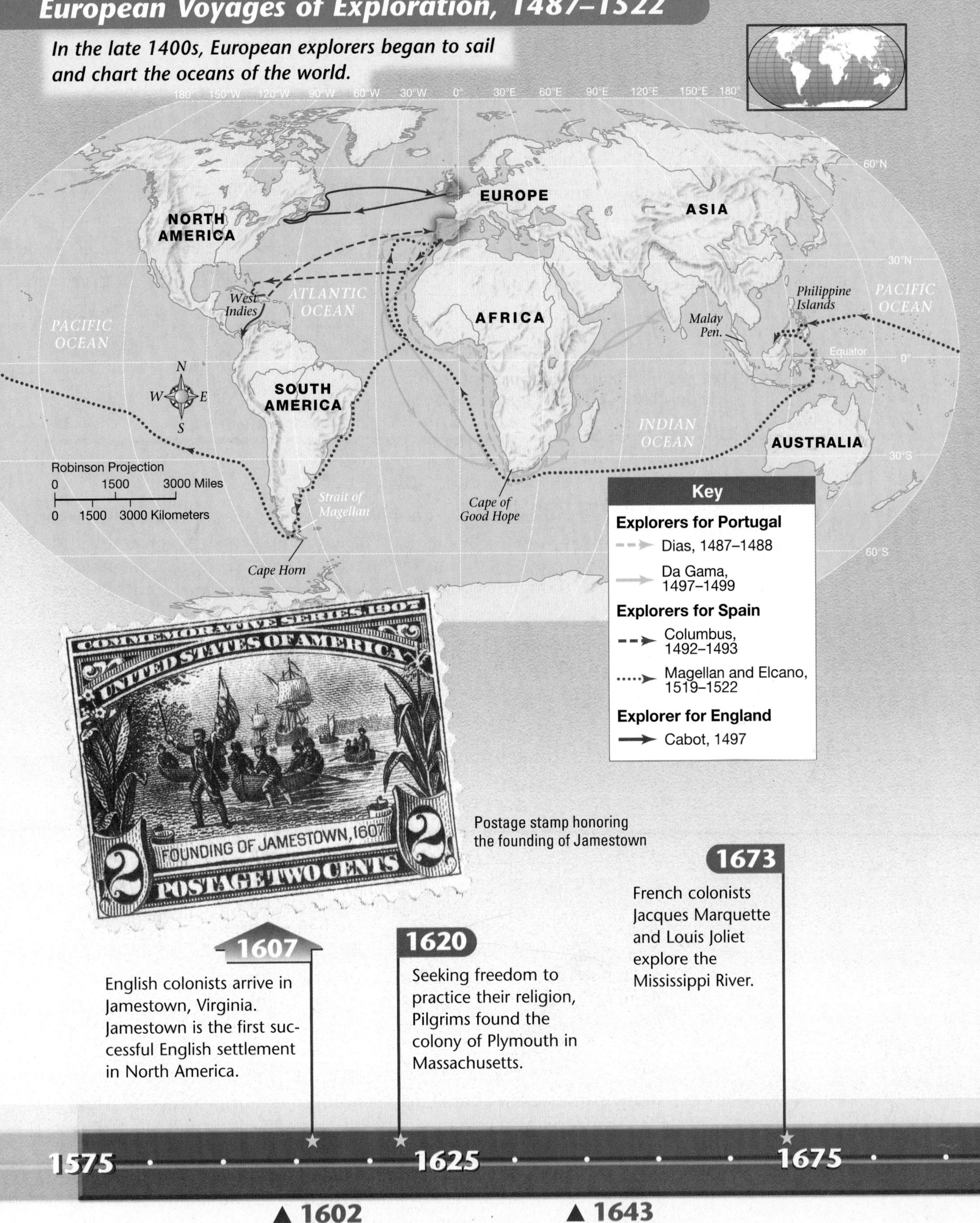

Postage stamp honoring the founding of Jamestown

1607
English colonists arrive in Jamestown, Virginia. Jamestown is the first successful English settlement in North America.

1620
Seeking freedom to practice their religion, Pilgrims found the colony of Plymouth in Massachusetts.

1673
French colonists Jacques Marquette and Louis Joliet explore the Mississippi River.

1575 · · · · 1625 · · · · 1675 · ·

▲ 1602
Dutch East India Company is formed to trade in Asia.

▲ 1643
Louis XIV becomes king of France.

1 An Era of Exploration

Prepare to Read

Objectives

In this section, you will
- Identify the impact of Columbus's voyage.
- Describe how Spanish explorers found a route across the Pacific Ocean.
- Explain how exploration set off a global exchange of goods and services.

Key Terms

colony

turning point

circumnavigate

Columbian Exchange

Cause and Effect Copy the chart below. As you read, complete the chart to show some of the effects of the journey of Christopher Columbus. Add as many boxes as you need.

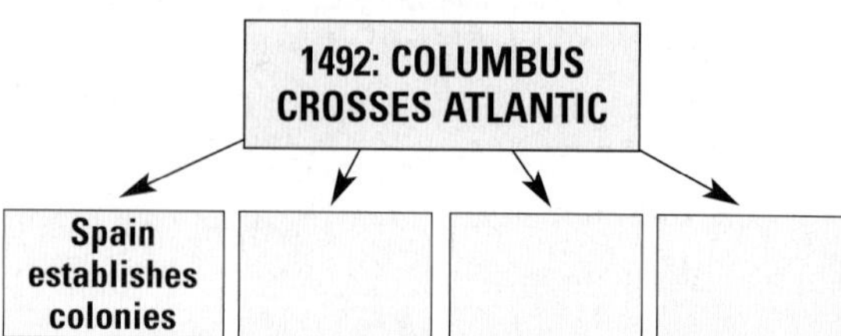

Main Idea Despite some earlier contacts, Europeans began to explore the Americas fully only after Columbus reached the West Indies in 1492.

Viking warriors

Setting the Scene A band of seafarers sailed across the Atlantic to settle at a place they called Vinland. To their surprise, a multitude of kayaks came paddling by one morning—"so many that the bay looked as though it was sown with charcoal." One settler recalled:

> "As soon as [the two peoples] met they began trading together. Most of all, these people wanted to buy red cloth, in return for which they had furs to offer and gray [seal] skins."
>
> —*Saga of Erik the Red*

Trading continued until a large bull that the seafarers had brought with them "ran out of the forest bellowing loudly." The natives, who had never seen such an animal, ran to their kayaks and paddled away.

This meeting took place about 1,000 years ago. It was one of the earliest encounters between Native Americans and Europeans. The people in kayaks were Inuits. The settlers were Vikings, seafaring people from Scandinavia in Northern Europe.

The Vikings abandoned the settlement after only a few years. Nearly 500 years later, an expedition from Spain sailed into the Caribbean Sea. This time, the arrival of Europeans launched an era of exploration that dramatically affected both the Americas and Europe.

Early Voyages to the Americas

Many stories exist about early people from Europe or Asia sailing to the Americas. Yet, real evidence has been hard to find. Most experts agree that such voyages were rare, if they occurred at all.

The Vikings left behind the most detailed record of their voyages. In 1001, Viking sailors led by Leif Ericson reached the northern tip of North America. Today, many archaeologists believe that the Viking settlement of Vinland was located in present-day Newfoundland. The Vikings did not stay in Vinland long and no one is sure why they left. However, Viking stories describe fierce battles with Skraelings, the Viking name for the Inuits.

Some historians suggest that Asians continued to cross the Bering Sea into North America after the last ice age ended. Others believe that ancient seafarers from Polynesia may have traveled to the Americas using their knowledge of the stars and winds. Modern Polynesians have sailed canoes thousands of miles in this way. Still others claim that fishing boats from China and Japan blew off course and landed on the western coast of South America.

Perhaps such voyages occurred. If so, they were long forgotten. The peoples of Asia and Europe had no knowledge of the Americas and their remarkable civilizations.

Columbus Reaches the Americas

As you read, Portuguese sailors pioneered new routes around Africa toward Asia in the late 1400s. Spain, too, wanted a share of the Asian spice trade. King Ferdinand and Queen Isabella agreed to finance a voyage of exploration by Christopher Columbus. Columbus, an Italian sea captain, planned to reach the East Indies by sailing west across the Atlantic.

The Atlantic Crossing In August 1492, Columbus set out with three ships and a crew of about 90 sailors. As captain, he commanded the largest vessel, the *Santa María.* The other ships were the *Niña* and the *Pinta.*

After a brief stop at the Canary Islands, the little fleet continued west into unknown seas. Fair winds sped them along, but a month passed without the sight of land. Some sailors began to grumble. They had never been away from land for so long. Still, Columbus sailed on.

On October 7, sailors saw flocks of birds flying southwest. Columbus changed course to follow the birds. A few days later, crew members spotted tree branches and flowers floating in the water. At 2 A.M. on October 12, the lookout on the *Pinta* spotted white cliffs shining in the moonlight. *"Tierra! Tierra!"* he shouted. "Land! Land!"

At dawn, Columbus rowed ashore and planted the banner of Spain on the beach. He was convinced that he had reached the East Indies in Asia. In fact, he had reached islands off the coasts of North America and South America in the Caribbean Sea. These islands later became known as the West Indies.

For three months, Columbus explored the West Indies. To his delight, he found signs of gold on the islands. Eager to report his success, he returned to Spain.

Spain Authorizes Colonies In Spain, Columbus presented Queen Isabella and King

Viewing History

The *Santa María*

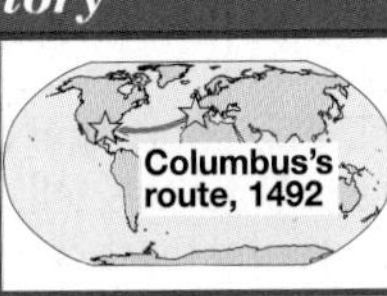

Columbus's report on his first voyage included this picture of the *Santa María.* Improved navigational equipment, such as the astrolabe (inset), enabled Columbus to cross the Atlantic. **Evaluating Information** ***The artist who made this drawing never saw the* Santa María. *Would you consider it a reliable piece of historical evidence? Why or why not?***

Ferdinand with gifts of pink pearls and brilliantly colored parrots. The royal couple listened intently as Columbus described many things that Europeans had never seen before: tobacco, pineapples, and hammocks used for sleeping. Columbus also described the "Indians" he had met, the Tainos (TI nohz). The Tainos, he promised, could easily be converted to Christianity and could also be used as slaves.

The Spanish monarchs were impressed. They gave Columbus the title Admiral of the Ocean Sea. They also agreed to finance future voyages.

Columbus made three more voyages across the Atlantic. In 1493, he founded the first Spanish colony in the Americas, on an island he called Hispaniola (present-day Haiti and the Dominican Republic). A **colony** is a group of people who settle in a distant land but are still ruled by the government of their native land. Columbus also explored present-day Cuba and Jamaica and sailed along the coasts of Central America and northern South America. He claimed all these lands for Spain.

Columbus proved to be a better explorer than a governor. During his third expedition, settlers at Hispaniola complained of his harsh rule. Queen Isabella appointed an investigator, who sent Columbus back to Spain in chains. In the end, the queen pardoned Columbus, but he never regained the honors he had won earlier. He died in 1506, still convinced that he had reached Asia.

Primary Source

Columbus Meets the Tainos

In his journals, Christopher Columbus recorded his first meeting with the Tainos:

"All whom I saw were young, not above thirty years of age, well made, with fine shapes and faces; their hair short, and coarse like that of a horse's tail, combed toward the forehead. . . . It appears to me that the people are ingenious, and would be good servants and I am of opinion that they would very readily become Christians, as they appear to have no religion. They very quickly learn such words as are spoken to them. If it please our Lord, I intend at my return to carry home six of them to your Highnesses, that they may learn our language."

—Christopher Columbus, *Journal*

Analyzing Primary Sources

How would you describe Columbus's attitude toward the Tainos?

A Lasting Impact

Columbus has long been honored as the bold sea captain who "discovered America." Today, we recognize that Native Americans had "discovered" and settled these lands long before 1492. Still, in at least one sense, Columbus deserves the honors history has given him. Europeans knew nothing of the Americas until Columbus told them about this "new world." His daring voyages marked the beginning of lasting contact among the peoples of Europe, Africa, and the Americas.

For a great many Native Americans, contact had tragic results. Columbus and those who followed were convinced that European culture was superior to that of the Indians. The Spanish claimed Taino lands and forced Tainos to work in gold mines, on ranches, or in Spanish households. Many Tainos died from harsh conditions or European diseases. Within 100 years of Columbus's arrival, the Taino population was virtually wiped out.

For better or worse, the voyages of Columbus signaled a turning point for the Americas. A **turning point** is a moment in history that marks a decisive change. Curious Europeans saw the new lands as a place where they could settle, trade, and grow rich.

The Spanish Cross the Pacific

After Columbus, the Spanish explored and settled other Caribbean islands. By 1511, they had conquered Puerto Rico, Jamaica, and Cuba. They also explored the eastern coasts of North America and South America in search of a western route to Asia.

In 1513, Vasco Núñez de Balboa (bal BOH uh) plunged into the jungles of the Isthmus of Panama. Native Americans had told him that a large body of water lay to the west. With a party of Spanish soldiers and Indians, Balboa reached the Pacific Ocean after about 25 days. He stood in the crashing surf and claimed the ocean for Spain.

The Spanish had no idea how wide the Pacific was until a sea captain named Ferdinand Magellan (muh JEHL uhn) sailed across it. The expedition—made up of five ships and about 250 crew members—left Spain in 1519. Fifteen months later, it rounded the stormy southern tip of South America and entered the Pacific Ocean. Crossing the Pacific, the sailors ran out of food. One sailor recalled:

> ❝ We remained 3 months and 20 days without taking in provisions or other refreshments and ate only old biscuit reduced to powder, full of grubs and stinking from the dirt which rats had made on it. We drank water that was yellow and stinking. ❞
>
> —Antoñio Pigafetta, *The Diary of Antoñio Pigafetta*

The Columbian Exchange

From the Americas to Europe, Africa, and Asia

maize
potato
sweet potato
beans
peanut
squash
pumpkin
peppers
pineapple
tomato
cocoa

From Europe, Africa, and Asia to the Americas

wheat
sugar
banana
rice
grape (wine)
olive oil
dandelion
horse
pig
cow
goat
chicken
smallpox
typhus

CHART *Skills*

The four voyages of Christopher Columbus set off a worldwide exchange of goods and ideas.

1. **Comprehension**
   (a) Identify two kinds of livestock that Europeans brought to the Americas.
   (b) Identify two food crops that Europeans carried from the Americas.
2. **Critical Thinking**
   Identifying Causes and Effects What elements shown here led to a decline in Native American population?

Magellan himself was killed in a battle with the local people of the Philippine Islands off the coast of Asia.

In 1522, only one ship and 18 sailors returned to Spain. They were the first people to **circumnavigate,** or sail completely around, the world. In doing so, they had found an all-water western route to Asia. Their voyage made Europeans aware of the true size of the Earth.

A Global Cultural Exchange

The encounter between the peoples of the Eastern and Western hemispheres sparked a global exchange of goods and ideas. Because it started with the voyages of Columbus, this transfer is known as the **Columbian Exchange.** The Columbian Exchange covered a wide range of areas, including food, medicine, government, technology, the arts, and language.

The exchange went in both directions. Europeans learned much from Native Americans. At the same time, Europeans contributed in many ways to the culture of the Americas.

European Influences Europeans introduced domestic animals such as chickens from Europe and Africa. European pigs, cattle, and horses often escaped into the wild and multiplied rapidly. As horses spread through North America, Indians learned to ride them and used them to carry heavy loads.

Plants from Europe and Africa changed the way Native Americans lived. The first bananas came from the Canary Islands. By

1520, one Spaniard reported that banana trees had spread "so greatly that it is marvelous to see the great abundance of them." Oranges, lemons, and figs were also new to the Americas. In North America, explorers also brought such plants as bluegrass, the daisy, and the dandelion. These plants spread quickly in American soil.

Tragically, Europeans also brought new diseases, such as smallpox and influenza. Native Americans had no resistance to these diseases. Historians estimate that within 75 years, diseases from Europe had killed almost 90 percent of the people in the Caribbean islands and in Mexico.

Target Skill: Understand Effects According to this subsection, what effects did Native Americans have on Europeans? Add this information to your chart.

Native American Influences For their part, Native Americans introduced Europeans to new customs and ideas. After 1492, elements of Native American ways of life gradually spread around the world.

Native Americans introduced Europeans to valuable food crops such as corn, potatoes, beans, tomatoes, manioc, squash, peanuts, pineapples, and blueberries. Today, almost half the world's food crops come from plants that were first grown in the Americas.

Europeans carried the new foods with them as they sailed around the world. Everywhere, people's diets changed and populations increased. In South Asia, people used American hot peppers and chilis to spice stews. Chinese peasants began growing sweet potatoes. Italians made sauces from tomatoes. People in West Africa grew manioc and maize.

European settlers often adopted Native American skills. In the North, Indians showed Europeans how to use snowshoes and trap beavers and other fur-bearing animals. European explorers learned how to paddle Indian canoes. Some leaders studied Native American political structures. Benjamin Franklin admired the League of the Iroquois and urged colonists to unite in a similar way.

★ ★ ★ Section 1 Assessment ★ ★ ★

Recall

1. **Identify** Explain the significance of **(a)** Leif Ericson, **(b)** Ferdinand and Isabella, **(c)** Christopher Columbus, **(d)** Vasco Núñez de Balboa, **(e)** Ferdinand Magellan, **(f)** Columbian Exchange.
2. **Define** **(a)** colony, **(b)** turning point, **(c)** circumnavigate.

Comprehension

3. Describe two effects of Columbus's voyage.
4. What route did Magellan's expedition take?
5. **(a)** Identify two European influences on the Americas. **(b)** Identify two Native American influences on the rest of the world.

Critical Thinking and Writing

6. **Exploring the Main Idea** Review the Main Idea statement at the beginning of this section. Then, write a paragraph explaining why historians consider Columbus to be more important than Leif Ericson.
7. **Supporting a Point of View** Today, Columbus Day is a national holiday. Yet, some Americans oppose the celebration. List one reason to support each point of view.

ACTIVITY

Go Online
PHSchool.com

Connecting to Today
Use the Internet to find English words that were borrowed from Indian languages. Create fact cards for three words. State what language each word came from, what it originally meant, and what it means today. For help in completing the activity, visit PHSchool.com, **Web Code mfd-0301**.

Sequencing

When learning about past events, such as Columbus's voyage, you must first understand sequence. In what order did various events take place? How was one event related to another? To start this lesson, read the excerpt and study the timetable below.

The following excerpts are from the log that Columbus kept on his first voyage:

Sunday, 9 September 1492 This day we completely lost sight of land, and many men sighed and wept for fear they would not see it again for a long time. I comforted them with great promises of lands and riches.

Saturday, 15 September 1492 I sailed to the west day and night for 81 miles, or more. Early this morning I saw a marvelous meteorite fall into the sea 12 to 15 miles away to the SW. This was taken by some people as a bad omen . . .

Sunday, 7 October 1492 This morning we saw what appeared to be land to the west . . . the *Niña* . . . ran ahead and fired a cannon and ran up a flag on her mast to indicate that land had been sighted. Joy turned to dismay as the day progressed, for by evening we had found no land . . .

Thursday, 11 October 1492 Then, at two hours after midnight, the *Pinta* fired a cannon, my prearranged signal for the sighting of land.

1492: First Voyage of Columbus

Date	Event
August 3	Sets sail from Palos
August 9	Stops for repairs in Canary Islands
September 6	Sets sail from Canary Islands
September 15	Sees a meteorite
September 24	Writes of trouble with crew
October 7	Alters course to follow birds
October 12	Goes ashore

Learn the Skill *To sequence information, use the following steps:*

1. **Identify the order in which events happen.** Applying absolute and relative chronology gives you a clearer picture of events.
2. **Identify time-order words.** Words such as first, next, and last give helpful time signals. Pay attention to other words such as later, now, then, while, this evening, before, and after.
3. **Figure out time intervals.** Understand how much time takes place between events.
4. **Make connections.** Ask: Are the events related? How does one event lead to the next?

Practice the Skill *Use the log entries and timetable to answer the following questions:*

1. **(a)** On what date did Columbus first set sail? **(b)** On what date did Columbus leave the Canary Islands? **(c)** Did Columbus see a meteorite before or after he changed course?
2. Identify two time words or phrases that Columbus used in his log.
3. **(a)** How much time passed between the false sighting of land and the true one? **(b)** About how much time did Columbus spend in the Canary Islands?
4. **(a)** On September 24, Columbus wrote of trouble with the crew. What earlier event might have contributed to this? **(b)** How might the events of October 7 and October 11 be related?

Apply the Skill *See the Chapter Review and Assessment.*

2 Spain Builds an Empire

Prepare to Read

Objectives

In this section, you will
- Describe how conquistadors defeated two Indian empires.
- Name the areas the Spanish explored.
- Explain how Spain settled its colonies.
- Summarize what life was like for Native Americans under Spanish rule.

Key Terms

conquistador
pueblo
presidio
mission
peninsulare
creole
mestizo
encomienda
plantation

Target Reading Skill

Main Idea Copy the concept web below. As you read, fill in the blank ovals with important facts about Spain's American empire. Add as many ovals as you need.

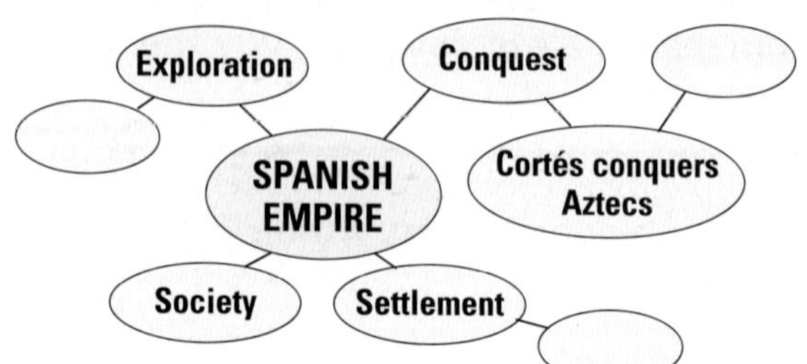

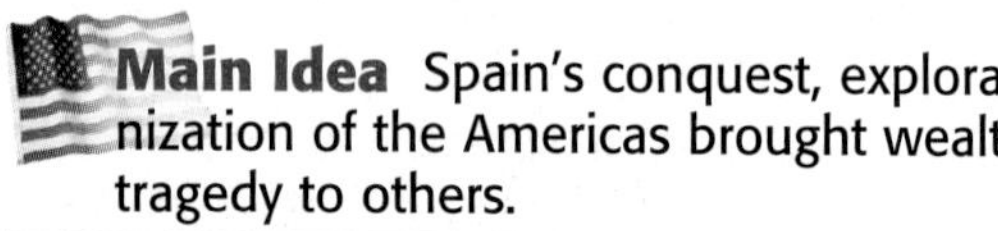

Main Idea Spain's conquest, exploration, and colonization of the Americas brought wealth to some and tragedy to others.

Spanish coin found in Florida

Setting the Scene "What a troublesome thing it is to discover new lands. The risks we took, it is hardly possible to exaggerate." Thus spoke Bernal Díaz del Castillo, one of the many Spanish **conquistadors** (kahn KWIS tuh dorz), or **conquerors**, who marched into the Americas in the 1500s. When asked why they traveled to the Americas, Díaz responded, "We came here to serve God and the king and also to get rich."

In their search for glory and gold, the conquistadors made Spain one of the richest nations in Europe. Spanish colonists followed the conquistadors and created a vast new empire in the Americas.

Spanish Conquistadors

The rulers of Spain gave conquistadors permission to establish settlements in the Americas. In return, conquistadors agreed to give Spain one fifth of any gold or treasure they captured.

Like other conquistadors, Hernando Cortés was eager to win riches and glory. He had heard rumors of a fabulously wealthy Native American empire in Mexico. With only about 600 soldiers and 16 horses, Cortés set sail for Mexico in 1519 in search of gold.

Conquest of the Aztecs Moctezuma (mokt uh ZOO muh), the Aztec emperor who ruled over much of Mexico, heard disturbing reports of a large house floating on the sea. It was filled with white men with long, thick beards. Aztec sacred writings predicted that a powerful white-skinned god would come from the east to rule the Aztecs. As the strangers neared Tenochtitlán, the Aztec capital, Moctezuma decided to welcome them as his guests.

Cortés took advantage of Moctezuma's invitation. Shrewdly, Cortés had already begun to win the support of other Indians who resented Aztec rule. One of his trusted advisors was an Indian

woman the Spanish called Doña Marina. She gave Cortés valuable information about the Aztecs and acted as a translator and negotiator.

On November 8, 1519, Cortés marched into Tenochtitlán. Thousands upon thousands of Aztecs turned out to see the astonishing newcomers riding horses. Díaz recalled:

> “Who could count the multitude of men, women and children which had come out on the roofs, in their boats on the canals, or in the streets, to see us?”
>
> —Bernal Díaz del Castillo, *True History of the Conquest of New Spain*

At first, Cortés was friendly to Moctezuma. Soon, however, he made the emperor a prisoner in his own city. Tensions mounted in Tenochtitlán over the next half year.

Finally, the Aztecs drove out the Spanish. Their victory, however, was brief. Aided by people whom the Aztecs had conquered, Cortés recaptured the city. In the end, the Spanish killed Moctezuma and destroyed Tenochtitlán. The Aztec empire had fallen.

Viewing History

Spanish and Aztecs Meet

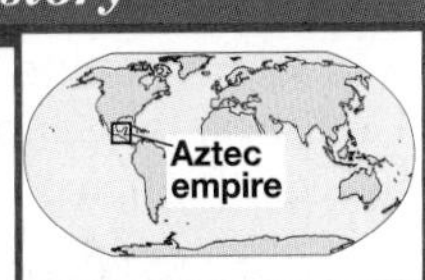

This Aztec drawing depicts a meeting between Spanish conquistadors (left) and Aztecs (right). Not all encounters between the two sides were as peaceful as this one. **Analyzing Information** ***What elements shown here might have seemed unfamiliar to the Aztecs? To the Spanish?***

Conquest of the Incas Another bold conquistador, Francisco Pizarro (pee SAR oh), set his sights on the Incan empire. Pizarro sailed down the Pacific coast of South America with fewer than 200 Spanish soldiers. In 1532, he captured the Incan emperor Atahualpa (ah tuh WAHL puh) and later executed him. Without the leadership of Atahualpa, Incan resistance collapsed. By 1535, Pizarro controlled much of the Incan empire.

Reasons for Spanish Victories How were the Spanish able to conquer two great empires with only a handful of soldiers? First, the Spanish had superior military equipment. They were protected by steel armor and had guns. The Aztecs and Incas relied on clubs, bows and arrows, and spears. Also, the Native Americans had never seen horses. They were frightened by mounted Spanish soldiers.

In addition, the Native Americans did not fight as hard as they might have. The Aztecs hesitated to attack at first because they thought the Spanish might be gods. The Incas were weak from fighting among themselves over control of their government.

Finally, many Indians died from European diseases, such as chickenpox, measles, and influenza. Some historians believe that disease alone would have ensured Spanish victory over the Indians.

Exploring the Spanish Borderlands

The Spanish search for treasure reached beyond the lands of the Aztecs and Incas. Moving north, conquistadors explored the area known as the Spanish borderlands. The borderlands spanned the present-day United States from Florida to California.

Juan Ponce de León (PAWN suh day LAY awn) traveled through parts of Florida in 1513, looking for a legendary fountain of youth. Indians claimed that anyone who bathed in its magical water would remain young forever. Ponce de León found no such fountain.

An Ill-Fated Journey Another explorer, Pánfilo Narváez (nar vah EHS), led an expedition that ended in disaster. In 1528, a storm struck his fleet in the Gulf of Mexico. Narváez and many others were lost at sea. The rest landed on an island near present-day Texas. Indians captured the few survivors and held them prisoner. Álvar Núñez Cabeza de Vaca assumed leadership of the small group.

Cabeza de Vaca, an enslaved African named Estevanico, and two others finally escaped their captors in 1533. The four walked across the plains of Texas, searching for a Spanish settlement. Finally, in 1536, they reached a town in Mexico. They had traveled by foot more than 1,000 miles through the Southwest.

GEOGRAPHY Skills

In the 1500s, the Spanish explored and settled North American lands from Florida to California.

1. **Location** On the maps, locate **(a)** Ponce de León's route, **(b)** De Soto's route, **(c)** St. Augustine, **(d)** San Antonio, **(e)** Santa Fe, **(f)** San Francisco.
2. **Movement** Which Spanish explorers crossed the Rio Grande?
3. **Critical Thinking Linking Past and Present** Compare these maps to a map of the modern United States. Identify three states in which you would expect Spanish influence to be strong.

Spanish Explorers/Spanish Settlements

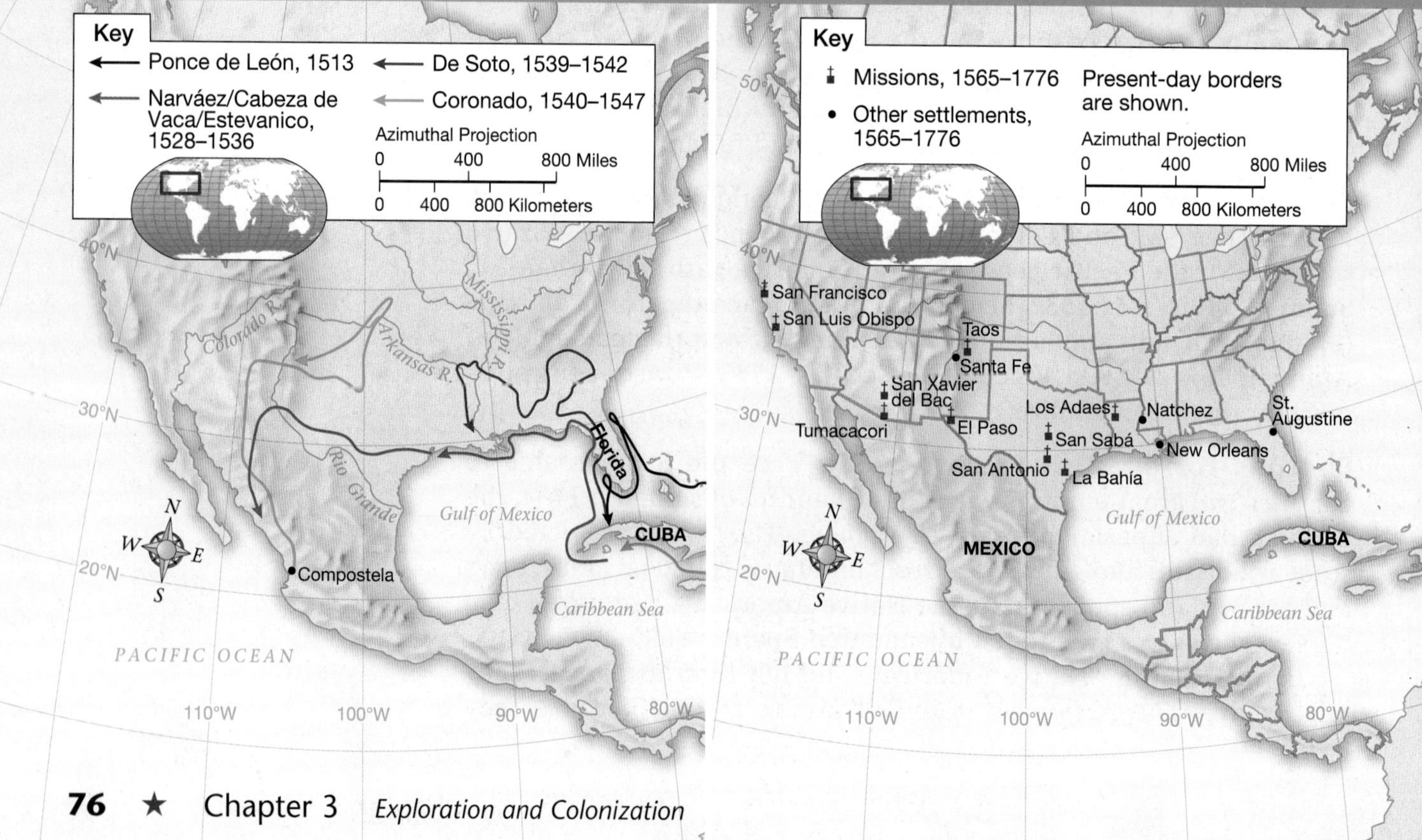

De Soto and Coronado From 1539 to 1542, Hernando De Soto explored Florida and other parts of the Southeast. In his search for gold, he reached the Mississippi River. De Soto died along the riverbank, without finding the riches he sought.

The conquistador Francisco Coronado (koh roh NAH doh) heard legends about "seven cities of gold." In 1540, he led an expedition into the southwestern borderlands. He traveled to present-day Arizona and New Mexico. Some of his party went as far as the Grand Canyon. Still, the Zuñi villages he visited had no golden streets.

The Spanish expeditions into the borderlands met with little success. Faced with strong Indian resistance in the north, Spain focused instead on bringing order to its empire in the south.

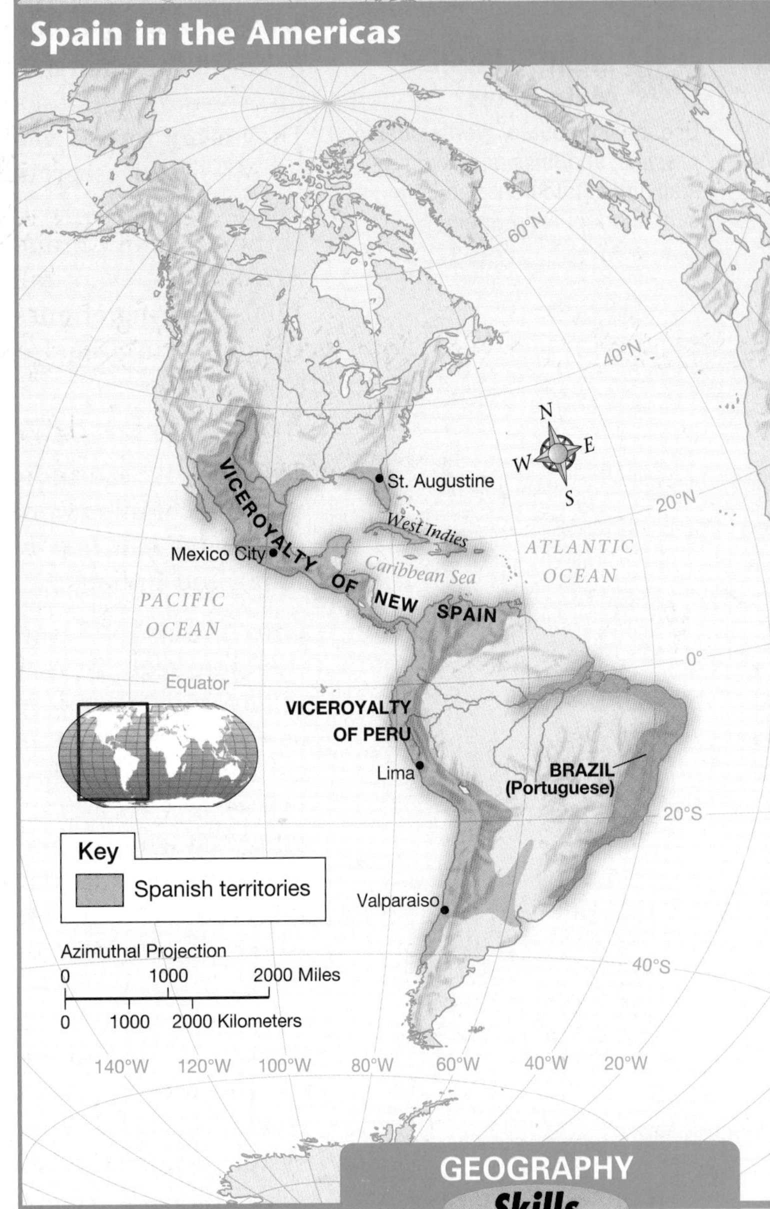

GEOGRAPHY *Skills*

In 1535, the king of Spain divided his American colonies into New Spain and Peru.

1. **Location** On the map, locate **(a)** New Spain, **(b)** Peru, **(c)** West Indies, **(d)** Mexico City.
2. **Region** **(a)** Which viceroyalty included Florida? **(b)** What other European power colonized part of South America?
3. **Critical Thinking Drawing Conclusions** Why was control of the Caribbean Sea important to Spain?

Settling New Spain

At first, Spain let the conquistadors govern the lands they conquered. When the conquistadors proved to be poor rulers, the Spanish king took away their authority. He then set up a strong system of government to rule his growing empire. In 1535, he divided his American lands into New Spain and Peru. The borderlands were part of New Spain. The king put a viceroy in charge of each region to rule in his name.

A code called the Laws of the Indies stated how the colonies should be organized and ruled. The code provided for three kinds of settlements in New Spain: pueblos, presidios (prih SIHD ee ohz), and missions. Some large communities included all three.

Pueblos and Presidios The pueblos, or towns, were centers of farming and trade. In the middle of the town was a plaza, or public square. Here, townspeople and farmers came to do business or worship at the church. Shops and homes lined the four sides of the plaza.

The Spanish took control of Indian pueblos and built new towns as well. In 1598, Juan de Oñate (oh NYAH tay) founded the colony of New Mexico among the adobe villages of the Pueblo Indians. He used brutal force to conquer the Native Americans of the region. Don Pedro de Paralta later founded Santa Fe as the Spanish capital of New Mexico.

Presidios were forts where soldiers lived. Inside the high, thick walls were shops, stables, and storehouses for food. Soldiers protected the farmers who settled nearby. The first presidio in the borderlands was built in 1565 at St. Augustine, Florida.

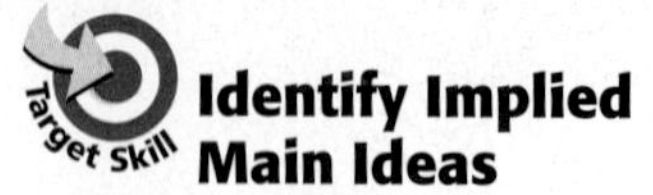

Identify Implied Main Ideas

Use the vocabulary words *pueblo, presidio,* and *mission* to write a main idea statement about the settlement of New Spain.

Missions Like other Europeans in the Americas, the Spanish believed they had a duty to convert Indians to Christianity. They set up **missions,** religious settlements run by Catholic priests and friars. They often forced Indians to live and work on the missions.

Missionaries gradually spread across the Spanish borderlands. The first mission in Texas was founded in 1659 at El Paso. In 1691, Father Eusebio Francisco Kino (KEE noh) crossed into present-day Arizona. He eventually set up 24 missions in the area. By the late 1700s, a string of missions also dotted the California coast from San Diego to San Francisco.

Society in New Spain

The Laws of the Indies also set up a strict social system. People in Spanish colonies were divided into four social classes: peninsulares (puh NIHN suh LAH rayz), creoles (KREE ohlz), mestizos (mehs TEE zohz), and Indians.

Four Social Classes At the top of the social scale were the **peninsulares.** Born in Spain, peninsulares held the highest jobs in government and the Church. They also owned large tracts of land as well as rich gold and silver mines.

Below the peninsulares were the **creoles,** people born in the Americas to Spanish parents. Many creoles were wealthy and well educated. They owned farms and ranches, taught at universities, and practiced law. However, they could not hold the jobs that were reserved for peninsulares.

Below the creoles were people of mixed Spanish and Indian background, known as **mestizos.** Mestizos worked on farms and ranches owned by peninsulares and creoles. In the cities, they worked as carpenters, shoemakers, tailors, and bakers.

The lowest class in the colonies was the Indians. The Spanish treated them as a conquered people. Under New Spain's strict social system, Indians were kept in poverty for hundreds of years.

A Blend of Cultures A new way of life took shape in New Spain that blended Spanish and Indian ways. Spanish settlers brought their own culture to the colonies. They introduced their language, laws, religion, and learning. In 1551, the Spanish founded the University of Mexico.

Native Americans also influenced the culture of New Spain. As you have read, colonists adopted Indian foods and items of Indian clothing, such as the poncho and moccasins. Indian workers used materials they knew well, such as adobe bricks, to build fine libraries, theaters, and churches. Sometimes, Indian artists decorated church walls with paintings of local traditions.

Harsh Life for Native Americans

Spanish colonists needed workers for their ranches, farms, and mines. To help them, the Spanish government gave settlers **encomiendas** (ehn koh mee EHN dahz), land grants that included the right to demand labor or taxes from Native Americans.

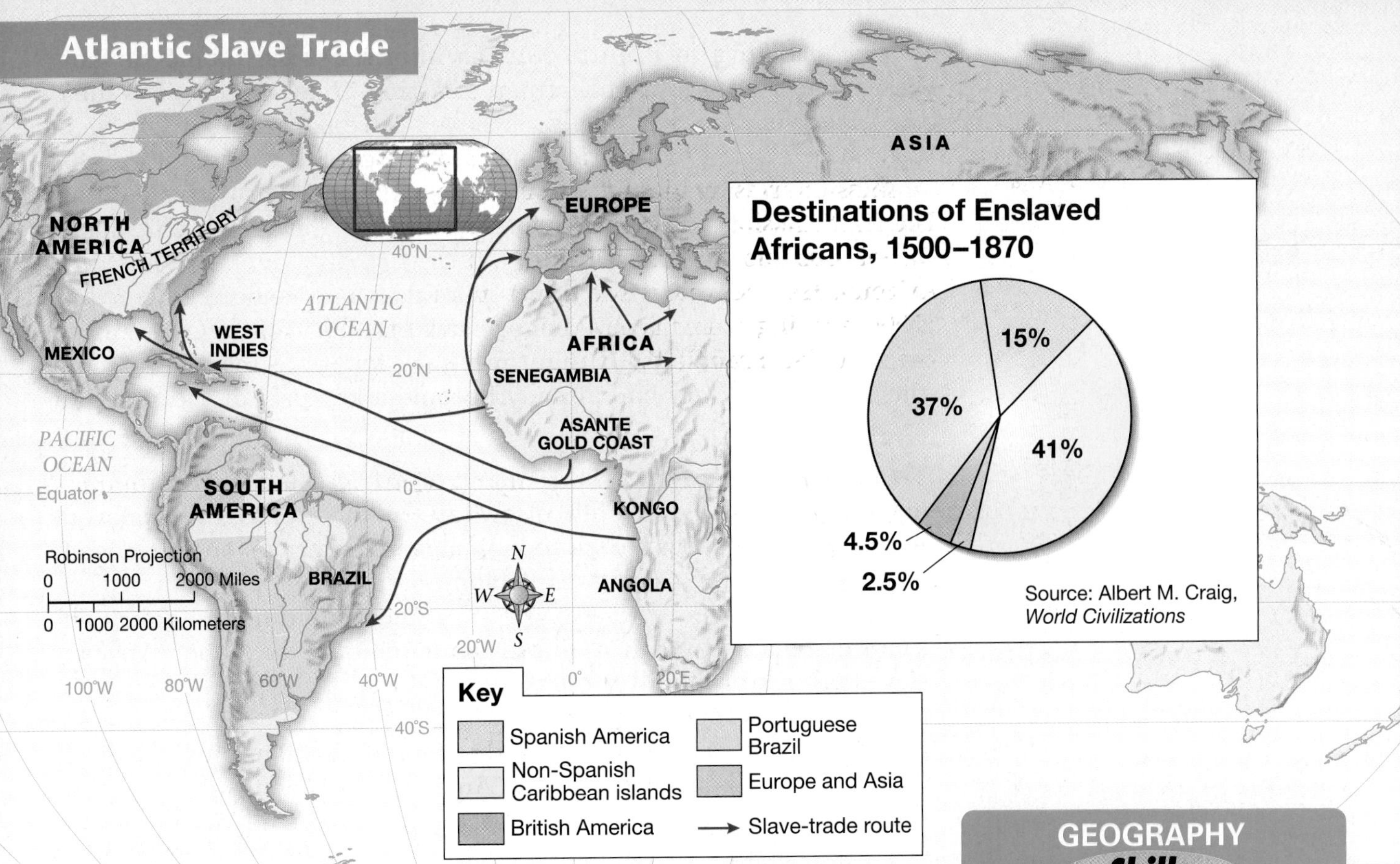

GEOGRAPHY Skills

Destinations of Enslaved Africans

The Atlantic slave trade began with Spain's efforts to supply labor for its American empire.

1. **Comprehension** Which two regions of the Americas received the largest number of enslaved Africans?
2. **Critical Thinking Drawing Conclusions** Why do you think the growth of the slave trade had relatively little effect on eastern Africa?

Hard Labor Mines in Mexico, Peru, and other parts of the Americas made Spain rich. Treasure ships laden with thousands of tons of gold and silver sailed regularly across the Atlantic.

The Spanish forced Native Americans to work in the gold and silver mines. In flickering light, Indians hacked out rich ores in narrow dark tunnels. Many died when tunnels caved in.

These harsh conditions led one priest, Bartolomé de Las Casas (day lahs KAH sahs), to seek reform. Traveling through New Spain, Las Casas witnessed firsthand the deaths of Indians due to hunger, disease, and mistreatment. What he saw horrified him:

> “The Indians were totally deprived of their freedom. . . . Even beasts enjoy more freedom when they are allowed to graze in the field.”
>
> —Bartolomé de Las Casas, *Tears of the Indians*

Las Casas journeyed to Spain and asked the king to protect the Indians. In the 1540s, the royal government did pass laws prohibiting the enslavement of Native Americans. The laws also allowed Indians to own cattle and grow crops. However, few officials in New Spain enforced the new laws.

The Atlantic Slave Trade Begins The death toll among Native Americans continued to rise. Faced with a severe shortage of workers, Spanish colonists looked across the Atlantic Ocean for a new source of labor.

Still seeking to protect Native Americans, Bartolomé de Las Casas made a suggestion that had a lasting, tragic impact. His idea was that Africans be brought as slaves to replace Indian laborers. Las Casas argued that Africans would not catch European diseases and die from them like Native Americans did. He also claimed that Africans would suffer less because they were used to doing hard farm work in their homelands.

By the time he died in 1566, Las Casas had come to regret his suggestion to use African labor. He saw that African slaves suffered as much as the Indians. By that time, however, it was too late to undo the damage. Slavery had already become a key part of the colonial economy.

The Slave Trade Spreads Demand for African labor grew rapidly, not only in New Spain, but elsewhere in the Americas. Enslaved Africans were especially valued on sugar plantations on Caribbean islands and in the Portuguese colony of Brazil. A **plantation** is a large estate farmed by many workers. Sugar could not be grown on small estates because it required too much land and labor. African slaves often worked all through the night cutting sugar, which was then sold in Europe for a large profit.

Some scholars today estimate that more than 10 million enslaved Africans were transported to the Americas between the 1500s and the 1800s. (See the map and chart on page 79.) The vast majority came from West Africa.

Most of the Africans were sent to Brazil or the Caribbean. However, a total of more than 500,000 enslaved Africans would eventually arrive in the British colonies of North America. (You will read more about the effects of the Atlantic slave trade on the Americas and Africa in the next chapter.)

Section 2 Assessment

Recall

1. **Identify** Explain the significance of **(a)** Hernando Cortés, **(b)** Moctezuma, **(c)** Francisco Pizarro, **(d)** Juan Ponce de León, **(e)** Bartolomé de Las Casas.
2. **Define** **(a)** conquistador, **(b)** pueblo, **(c)** presidio, **(d)** mission, **(e)** peninsulare, **(f)** creole, **(g)** mestizo, **(h)** encomienda, **(i)** plantation.

Comprehension

3. Why were the Spanish able to conquer the Americas?
4. What areas of North America did the Spanish explore?
5. How did the Laws of the Indies regulate life in New Spain?
6. **(a)** What was life like for Native Americans under Spanish rule? **(b)** Why did Spain bring Africans to the Americas?

Critical Thinking and Writing

7. **Exploring the Main Idea** Review the Main Idea statement at the beginning of this section. Then, write two generalizations about Spanish rule, from the viewpoints of a peninsulare and of an Indian.
8. **Drawing Inferences** Why do you think Spain reserved the most powerful positions for Spanish-born officials?

Activity

Writing an Obituary
Based on what you have read, write an obituary for one of the figures discussed in this section, such as Hernando Cortés, Estevanico, or Bartolomé de Las Casas. Briefly summarize that person's most notable achievement and express a point of view about him or her.

3 Colonizing North America

Prepare to Read

Objectives

In this section, you will
- Explain why European powers sought a new route to Asia.
- Identify how the Protestant Reformation affected rivalries among European nations.
- Describe how a rivalry developed between New France and New Netherland.

Key Terms

northwest passage

Protestant Reformation

coureur de bois

alliance

Target Reading Skill

Compare and Contrast Copy this incomplete Venn diagram. As you read, fill in key facts about French and Dutch settlements in North America. Write common characteristics in the overlapping section.

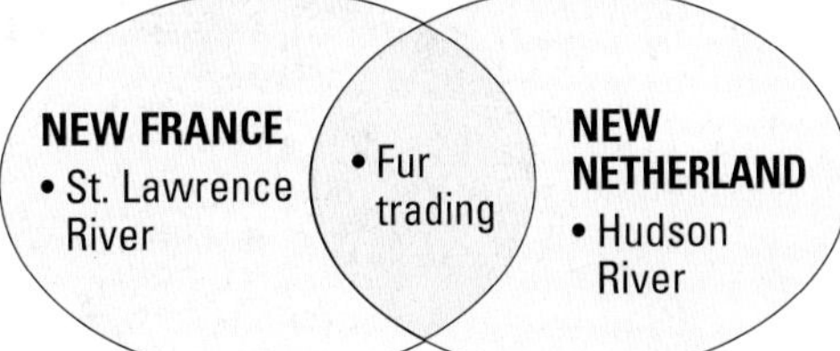

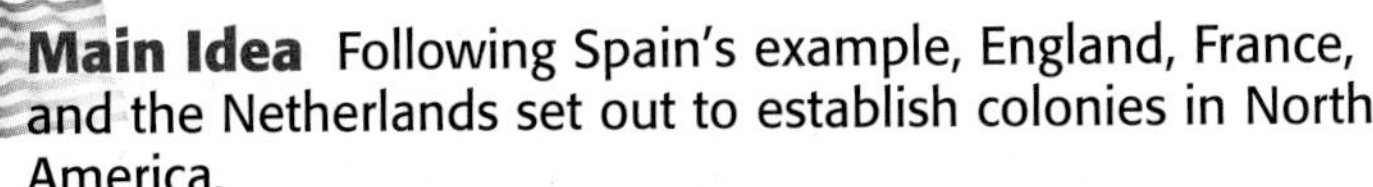

Main Idea Following Spain's example, England, France, and the Netherlands set out to establish colonies in North America.

Setting the Scene The court of King Henry VII of England buzzed with excitement in August 1497. Italian sea captain Giovanni Caboto and a crew of English sailors had just returned from a 79-day Atlantic voyage.

Caboto, called John Cabot by the English, cut a swaggering figure on the streets of London. He dressed himself in fine silks and made such a stir that ordinary Londoners "[ran] after him like madmen," reported one observer. Cabot appeared before King Henry to announce that he had reached a "new-found island" in Asia where fish were plentiful.

Cabot was one of many Europeans who explored North America between the 1400s and 1600s. England, France, and the Netherlands all envied Spain's new empire. They wanted American colonies of their own.

John Cabot

Search for a Northwest Passage

Throughout the 1500s, European nations continued to look for new ways to reach the riches of Asia. Magellan's route around South America seemed long and difficult. They wanted to discover a shorter **northwest passage,** or waterway through or around North America.

Although John Cabot was confident he had found such a passage, he was mistaken. His "new-found island" off the Asian coast in fact lay off the coast of North America. Today, Newfoundland is the easternmost province of Canada.

Exploring for France The French sent another Italian captain, Giovanni da Verrazano (vehr rah TSAH noh), in search of a northwest passage. Verrazano journeyed along the North American coast from the Carolinas to Canada. During the 1530s, Jacques Cartier (kar tee YAY), also sailing for the French, traveled more than halfway up the river now known as the St. Lawrence.

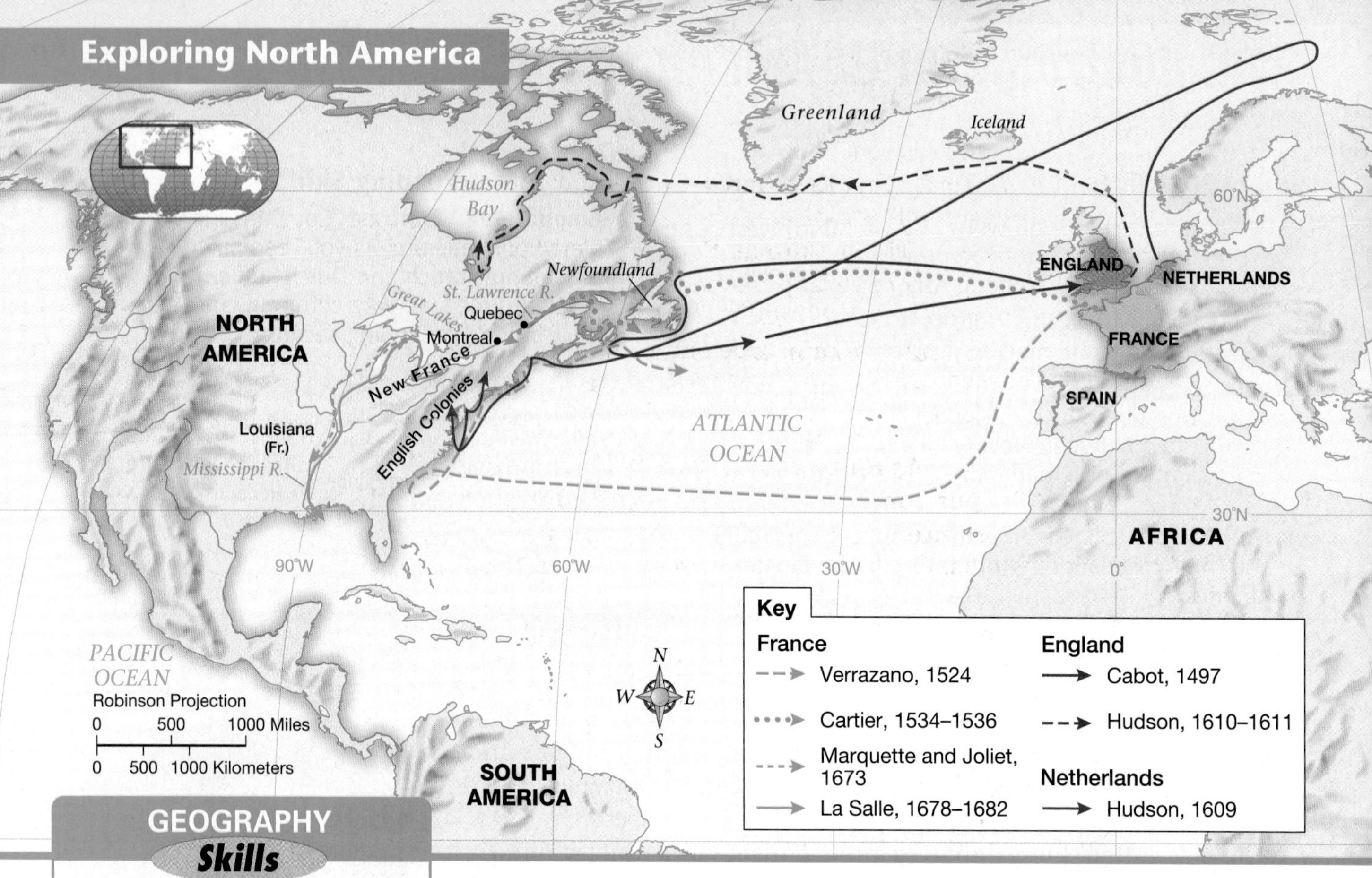

GEOGRAPHY Skills

Explorers from England, France, and the Netherlands competed to find a northwest passage to Asia.

1. **Location** On the map, locate **(a)** New France, **(b)** Newfoundland, **(c)** St. Lawrence River, **(d)** Hudson Bay, **(e)** Mississippi River.
2. **Movement** Describe the route taken by Henry Hudson when he explored for the Netherlands.
3. **Critical Thinking Making Predictions** Based on this map, why might you expect conflict to develop between the English and French in North America?

Henry Hudson In 1609, the English explorer Henry Hudson sailed for the Dutch. His ship, the *Half Moon,* entered present-day New York harbor. Hudson continued to sail some 150 miles up the river that now bears his name.

The following year, Hudson made a voyage into the far north—this time for the English. After spending a harsh winter in present-day Hudson Bay, his crew rebelled. They set Hudson, his son, and seven loyal sailors adrift in a small boat. The boat and its crew were never seen again.

Failure and Success None of these explorers found a northwest passage to Asia. However, they did map and explore many parts of North America. The rulers of Western Europe began thinking about how to profit from the region's rich resources.

Rivalries Among European Nations

European nations began to compete for riches around the world. Religious differences heightened their rivalry. Until the 1500s, the Roman Catholic Church was the only church in Western Europe. That unity ended when a major religious reform movement sharply divided Christians.

Religious Divisions In 1517, a German monk named Martin Luther publicly challenged many practices of the Catholic Church. Soon after, he split with the Church entirely. Luther believed that the Church had become too worldly. He opposed the power of popes. He also objected to the Catholic teaching that believers could gain eternal life by performing good works. Luther argued that people could be saved only by faith in God.

Because of their protests against the church, Luther's supporters became known as Protestants. The **Protestant Reformation,** as the new movement was known, divided Europe. Soon, the Protestants themselves split, forming many different churches.

By the late 1500s, religion divided the states of Western Europe. Roman Catholic monarchs ruled Spain and France. A Protestant queen, Elizabeth I, ruled England. In the Netherlands, the Dutch people were mostly Protestant.

Rivalries in the Americas As Europeans settled in the Americas, they brought their religious conflicts with them. Queen Elizabeth encouraged English adventurers to raid Spanish colonies and capture Spanish treasure fleets. Protestant England also competed with Catholic France for lands in North America.

Not all rivalries were religious. Both the Netherlands and England were Protestant. Still, they competed for control of land in North America and for economic markets all over the world.

Viewing History

Fur Trapper in New France

Coureurs de bois, like the one shown here, depended on beaver furs for a living. By 1675, trappers and traders in New France were exporting nearly 90,000 pounds of beaver pelts a year. **Applying Information** ***Based on what you have read, how does this picture show that* coureurs de bois *made use of Native American technology?***

New France

Samuel de Champlain (sham PLAYN) founded Port Royal, the first permanent French settlement in North America, in 1605. Three years later, he led another group of settlers along the route Cartier had pioneered. On a rocky cliff high above the St. Lawrence River, Champlain built a trading post known as Quebec (kwi BEHK).

Economy of New France Unlike Spain's American empire, New France had little gold or silver. Instead, the French profited from fishing, trapping, and trading.

French colonists who lived and worked in the woods became known as ***coureurs de bois*** (koo RYOOR duh BWAH), or "runners of the woods." The French brought knives, kettles, cloth, and other items for trade with Native Americans. In return, the Indians gave them beaver skins and other furs that sold for high prices in Europe.

Coureurs de bois established friendly relations with the Native Americans. Unlike the Spanish, the French did not attempt to conquer the Indians. Also, because *coureurs de bois* did not build farms, they did not interfere with Indian

lands. Indians taught the French trapping and survival skills, such as how to make snowshoes and canoes. Many coureurs married Indian women.

Missionary Work Catholic missionaries often traveled with fur traders. A missionary is a person who goes to another land to win converts for a religion. French missionaries worked to teach Native Americans about Christianity. They also drew maps and wrote about the lands they explored.

Life was difficult, especially in winter. One French priest recalled traveling on foot through deep snow:

> "If a thaw came, dear Lord, what pain! . . . I was marching on an icy path that broke with every step I took; as the snow softened . . . we often sunk in it up to our . . . waist."
>
> —Paul Le Jeune, quoted in *The Jesuits in North America* (Parkman)

Viewing History

Joliet and Marquette

The journey of Joliet and Marquette to the Mississippi was often difficult. This engraving from the 1900s shows the French explorers portaging, or carrying, their canoe over a waterfall. **Evaluating Information** ***Do you think this is a realistic picture of Joliet and Marquette? Explain.***

Identify Contrasts (Target Skill) As you read about New France, note the missionary work, slavery, and economy. On the following pages, you will contrast these with conditions in New Netherland.

Expansion to the Mississippi French trappers followed the St. Lawrence deep into the heart of North America. Led by Indian guides, they reached the Great Lakes. Here, Indians spoke of a mighty river, which they called Mississippi, or "Father of the Waters."

A French missionary, Father Jacques Marquette (mar KEHT), and a fur trader, Louis Joliet (joh lee EHT), set out to reach the Mississippi in 1673. Led by Indian guides, they followed the river for more than 700 miles before turning back. Nine years later, Robert de La Salle completed the journey to the Gulf of Mexico. La Salle named the region Louisiana in honor of the French king, Louis XIV.

To keep Spain and England out of Louisiana, the French built forts in the north along the Great Lakes. Among them was Fort Detroit, built by Antoine Cadillac near Lake Erie. The French also built New Orleans, a fort at the mouth of the river. New Orleans grew into a busy trading center.

French colonists imported thousands of Africans to work as slaves on nearby plantations. Some slaves, however, joined with the Natchez Indians in a revolt against the French. The French put down the Natchez Revolt in 1729. Some slaves who fought on the side of the French received their freedom. In Louisiana, free and enslaved Africans together made up the majority of settlers.

Government of New France New France was governed much like New Spain. The French king controlled the government directly, and people had little freedom. A council appointed by the king made all decisions.

Louis XIV worried that too few French were moving to New France. In the 1660s, therefore, he sent about a thousand farmers to the colony, including many young women. Despite the king's efforts to increase the population, New France grew slowly. Only about 10,000 settlers lived in the colony by 1680. Of those, one third lived on farms along the St. Lawrence. Many more chose to become *coureurs de bois,* living largely free of government control.

New Netherland

Like the French, the Dutch hoped to profit from their discoveries in the Americas. In 1626, Peter Minuit (MIHN yoo wiht) led a group of Dutch settlers to the mouth of the Hudson River. There, he bought Manhattan Island from local Indians. Minuit called his settlement New Amsterdam. Other Dutch colonists settled farther up the Hudson River. The entire colony was known as New Netherland (now known as New York).

From a tiny group of 30 houses, New Amsterdam grew into a busy port. The Dutch welcomed people of many nations and religions to their colony. A Roman Catholic priest who visited New Netherland in 1643 reported:

> “On the island of Manhattan, and in its environs, there may well be four or five hundred men of different sects and nations: the Director General told me that there were men of eighteen different languages; they are scattered here and there on the river, above and below, as the beauty and convenience of the spot has invited each to settle.”
>
> —Father Isaac Jogues, quoted in *Narratives of New Netherland, 1609–1664* (Jameson)

The Dutch also built trading posts along the Hudson River. The most important one was Fort Orange, today known as Albany. Dutch merchants became known for their good business sense.

The Dutch enlarged New Netherland in 1655 by taking over the colony of New Sweden. The Swedes had established New Sweden along the Delaware River some 15 years earlier.

Rivalry Over Furs Dutch traders sent furs to the Netherlands. The packing list for the first shipment included "the skins of 7,246 beaver, 853 otter, 81 mink, 36 cat lynx, and 34 small rats."

The Dutch and French became rivals in the fur trade. Both sought alliances with Native Americans. An **alliance** is an agreement between nations to aid and protect one another. The Dutch

Cause *and* Effect

Causes

- Europeans want more goods from Asia
- Muslims gain control of trade between Europe and Asia
- Rulers of European nations seek ways to increase their wealth
- European nations look for a sea route to Asia
- Columbus reaches the Americas

EXPLORATION OF THE AMERICAS

Effects

- Spain builds an empire in the Americas
- English, French, and Dutch set up colonies in North America
- Millions of Native Americans die from "European" diseases
- Slave traders bring enslaved Africans to the Americas
- Foods from the Americas are introduced into Europe

Effects Today

- The United States is a multicultural society
- American foods, such as corn and potatoes, are important to people's diets around the world

GRAPHIC ORGANIZER Skills

Exploration had a dramatic impact on the Americas, Europe, Africa, and Asia.

1. **Comprehension** Identify two economic causes of European exploration.
2. **Critical Thinking Linking Past and Present** Based on the chart, what cultures may have helped shape American culture today?

Connecting to Today

From Wall to Wall Street

"How can we protect ourselves from attack?" That was the problem New Amsterdam town leaders met to discuss in March 1653. They decided to build a wall on the northern edge of the city. Less than a mile long, the wooden wall never faced the test of battle. Much of it was dismantled over the years by people needing wood. Dutch colonists later built a road in its place: Wall Street.

Today, Wall Street is the center of banking and business in the United States. It is home to the New York Stock Exchange and many great commercial businesses. The little Dutch road is now a symbol of finance throughout the world.

What streets or other places in your community get their name from their location?

made friends with the Iroquois. The Hurons (HYOO rahnz) helped the French. Fighting raged for years among the Europeans and their Native American allies.

Dutch Ways in North America The Dutch brought many of their customs from Europe to New Netherland. They liked to ice-skate, and in winter, the frozen rivers and ponds filled with skaters. Every year on Saint Nicholas's birthday, Dutch children put out their shoes to be filled with all sorts of presents. Later, "Saint Nick" came to be called Santa Claus.

Some Dutch words entered the English language. A Dutch master was a *boss.* The people of New Amsterdam sailed in *yachts.* Dutch children munched on *cookies* and rode through the snow on *sleighs.*

Impact on Native Americans European settlement of North America brought major changes to Native Americans. As in New Spain, European diseases killed thousands of Indians. Rivalry over the fur trade increased Indian warfare as European settlers encouraged their Native American allies to attack one another. The scramble for furs also led to overtrapping. By 1640, trappers had almost wiped out the beavers on Iroquois lands in upstate New York.

The arrival of Europeans affected Native Americans in other ways. Missionaries tried to convert Indians to Christianity. Indians eagerly adopted European trade goods, such as copper kettles and knives. They also bought muskets and gunpowder for hunting and warfare. Alcohol sold by European traders had a harsh effect on Native American life.

The French, Dutch, and English all waged warfare to seize Indian lands. As Indians were forced off their lands, they moved westward onto lands of other Indians. The conflict between Native Americans and Europeans would continue for many years.

★ ★ ★ Section 3 Assessment ★ ★ ★

Recall

1. **Identify** Explain the significance of **(a)** John Cabot, **(b)** Jacques Cartier, **(c)** Protestant Reformation, **(d)** Samuel de Champlain, **(e)** Marquette and Joliet, **(f)** Peter Minuit.
2. **Define** **(a)** northwest passage, **(b)** *coureur de bois,* **(c)** missionary, **(d)** alliance.

Comprehension

3. Why did Europeans seek a northern route to Asia?
4. **(a)** What religious differences divided Europe? **(b)** How did these differences affect the race for American colonies?
5. How did the rivalry between French and Dutch colonists affect Native Americans?

Critical Thinking and Writing

6. **Exploring the Main Idea** Review the Main Idea statement at the beginning of this section. Then, write a paragraph explaining whether you think the French and Dutch achieved their goals.
7. **Making Decisions** Both *coureurs de bois* and missionaries endured great hardships in New France. For each of them, list two reasons they might have decided to come to North America.

Activity

Making a Map **Suppose you could send a map back through time to Joliet and Marquette or to La Salle. Create a map showing how they could travel by land and water from Newfoundland through New France to the mouth of the Mississippi. Include a list of supplies they might need to complete the journey.**

4 Building the Jamestown Colony

Prepare to Read

Objectives

In this section, you will
- Identify challenges faced by the first English colonies.
- Describe how Virginia began a tradition of representative government.
- Name the groups of people who made up the new arrivals in Virginia after 1619.

Key Terms

charter
burgess
House of Burgesses
representative government
Magna Carta
Parliament

Target Reading Skill

Clarifying Meaning As you read, prepare an outline of this section. Use roman numerals to indicate the major headings, capital letters for the subheadings, and numbers for the supporting details. The sample at right will help you get started.

I. The First English Colony
A. England seeks riches
B.
II. Challenge and Survival
A. Setting up Jamestown
1. King grants charter
2.
B. Early problems
1. Geography
2.

Main Idea Founded in 1607, England's Jamestown colony survived hard times and set up a representative government.

Setting the Scene Thomas Gates was full of plans as he sailed from England to help run the Jamestown Colony in Virginia. The colony had been founded three years earlier, in 1607. Since then, nearly 700 English colonists had crossed the Atlantic Ocean to settle in Jamestown.

Gates was hardly prepared for the sight that greeted him. Of the 700 colonists, only 60 remained. They came staggering out to the shore, he reported, "so lean that they looked like [skeletons], crying out, 'We are starved, we are starved.'" Many had resorted to eating turtles, poisonous snakes, or their own horses.

Discouraged, Gates loaded everyone onto his ships and turned to sail for home. By chance, however, a new fleet from England arrived that day, bringing supplies and more settlers. The colony survived. Yet, it would take more than ten years before the English colony in Virginia put down permanent roots.

Tortoise shell found in Jamestown

The First English Colony

England watched with envy as Spain gained riches from its American colonies. Several ambitious English gentlemen proposed that England settle the Americas as well. With Queen Elizabeth's permission, Sir Walter Raleigh raised money to outfit a colony in North America. In 1585, about 100 men set sail across the Atlantic.

The colonists landed on Roanoke (ROH uh nohk), an island off the coast of present-day North Carolina. Within a year, however, the colonists had run short of food and were quarreling with neighboring Indians. When an English ship stopped in the harbor, the weary settlers sailed home.

In 1587, Raleigh sent John White, one of the original colonists, back to Roanoke with a new group of settlers, including women and children. When supplies ran low, White returned to England, leaving behind 117 colonists. He planned to return in a few months. When he

Viewing History

Jamestown Rebuilt

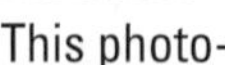

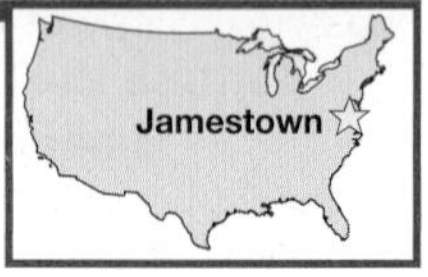

This photograph shows a modern reconstruction of what the early settlement in Jamestown looked like. The strong leadership of Captain John Smith (inset) enabled the struggling colony to survive starvation and disease. **Drawing Conclusions** ***What sources of information might historians use to accurately re-create a historic site like this one?***

got back to England, however, he found the country was then preparing for war with Spain. It was three years before he was able to sail back to Roanoke.

When White arrived, he found the settlement strangely quiet. Houses stood empty. Vines twined through the windows and pumpkins sprouted from the earthen floors. On a tree, someone had carved the word CROATOAN, the name of a nearby island. No other trace of the colonists remained.

White was eager to investigate, but a storm was blowing up and his crew refused to make the trip. To this day, the fate of the "Lost Colony" remains a mystery.

Challenge and Survival in Jamestown

After the failure of Roanoke, nearly 20 years passed before England again tried to establish a colony in North America. In 1606, the Virginia Company of London received a charter from King James I. A **charter** is a legal document giving certain rights to a person or company.

The royal charter gave the Virginia Company the right to settle lands between present-day North Carolina and the Potomac River. The charter also guaranteed that colonists of this land, called Virginia, would have the same rights as English citizens.

A Disastrous Start In the spring of 1607, a group of 105 colonists arrived in Virginia. They sailed into Chesapeake Bay and began building homes along the James River. They named their tiny outpost Jamestown after their king.

The colonists soon discovered that Jamestown was located in a swampy area. The water was unhealthy, and mosquitoes spread malaria. Many settlers suffered or died from disease.

Governing the colony also proved difficult. The Virginia Company had chosen a council of 13 men to rule the settlement. Members of the council quarreled with one another and did little to plan for the colony's future. By the summer of 1608, the colony was near failure.

Starvation and Recovery Another major problem the Jamestown colonists faced was starvation. Captain John Smith, a young soldier and explorer, observed that the colonists were not planting enough crops. He complained that people wanted only to "dig gold, wash gold, refine gold, load gold." As they searched in vain for gold, the colony ran out of food.

Smith helped to save the colony. He set up stern rules that forced colonists to work if they wished to eat. He also visited nearby Indian villages. Powhatan (pow uh TAN), the most powerful chief in the area, agreed to supply corn to the English.

Peaceful relations with Native Americans did not last, however. Whenever the Indians refused to supply food, the colonists used force to seize what they needed. Once, Smith aimed a gun at Powhatan's brother until the Indians provided corn to buy his freedom. Such incidents led to frequent and bloody warfare. Peace was restored briefly when the colonist John Rolfe married Pocahontas, daughter of Powhatan.

Even in times of peace, Jamestown did not prosper. Problems arose soon after John Smith returned to England in 1609. As you read, the colony suffered terribly for the next few years. Desperate settlers cooked "dogs, cats, snakes, [and] toadstools" to survive. To keep warm, they broke up houses to burn as firewood.

A Profitable Crop Jamestown's economy finally improved after 1612, when colonists began growing tobacco. Europeans had learned about tobacco from Native Americans.

King James called pipe smoking "a vile custom." Still, the new fad caught on quickly. By 1620, England was importing more than 30,000 pounds of tobacco a year. At last, Virginians had found a way to make their colony succeed.

Representative Government

For a time, the governors sent by the Virginia Company ran the colony like a military outpost. Each morning, a drumbeat summoned settlers to work at assigned tasks. Harsh laws imposed the death penalty even for small offenses, like stealing an ear of corn. Such conditions were unlikely to attract new colonists. As John Smith commented after his return to England, "No Man will go . . . to have less freedom there than here."

An American Profile

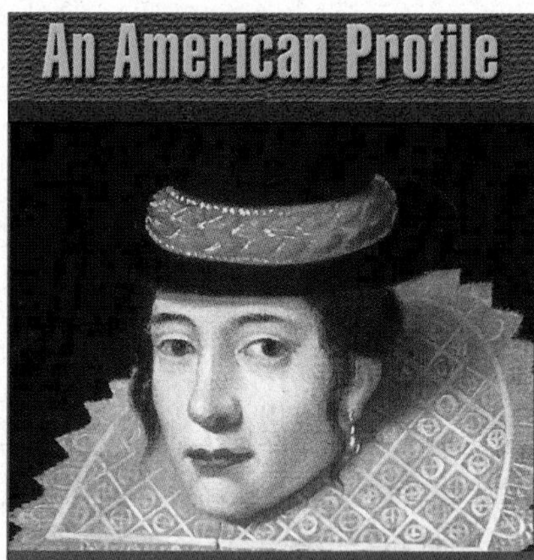

Pocahontas 1596?–1617

As a young woman, Pocahontas, whose name means "playful one," captured the affections of John Rolfe, a Jamestown tobacco planter. They were married in 1614.

In 1616, when she was about twenty years old, Pocahontas accompanied her husband and infant son, Thomas, to England. The English were fascinated by this "Indian princess." She was invited to the court of King James I. A painting shows her dressed as an English noblewoman in velvet and lace. In 1617, as she prepared to return to Virginia, Pocahontas became ill. She died and was buried in England.

Why do you think the English wanted to meet Pocahontas?

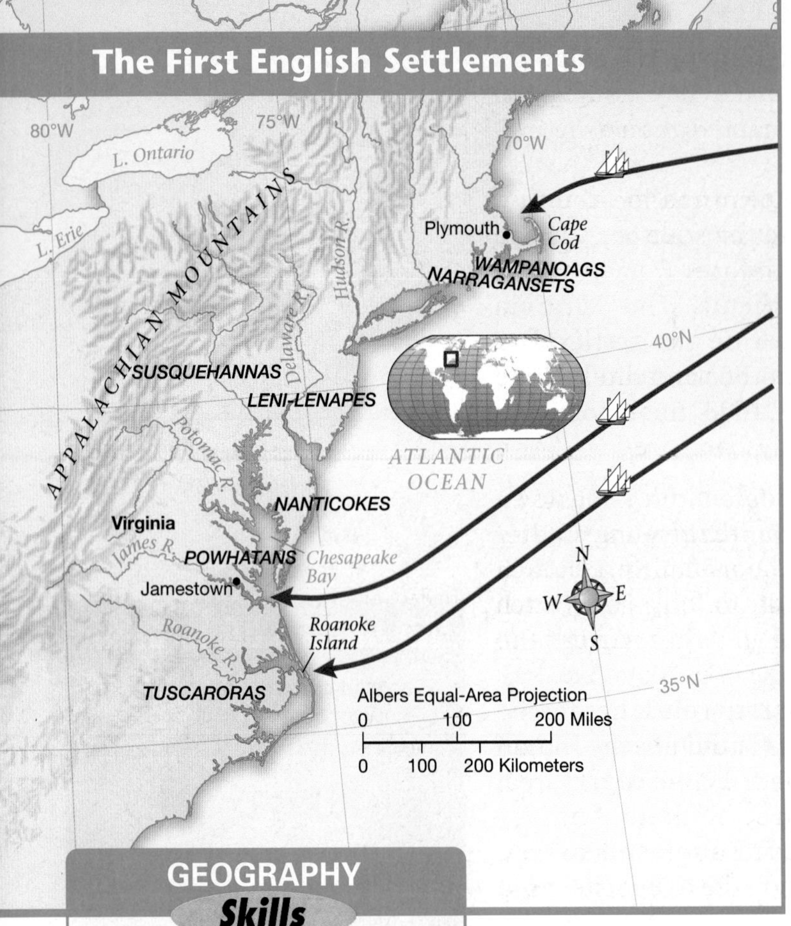

GEOGRAPHY *Skills*

After a difficult start, England finally established successful colonies in North America.

1. **Location** On the map, locate **(a)** Roanoke, **(b)** James River, **(c)** Jamestown, **(d)** Cape Cod, **(e)** Plymouth.
2. **Region** What Native American groups lived near the Jamestown Colony?
3. **Critical Thinking Comparing** What did the first three English colonies in North America have in common? Why?

Reforms of 1619 To attract more settlers, the Virginia Company took steps to establish a more stable government. In 1619, it sent a new governor with orders to consult settlers on all important matters. Male settlers were allowed to elect **burgesses,** or representatives to the government.

The burgesses met in an assembly called the **House of Burgesses.** Together with the governor and his council, they made laws for the colony. The first session met in the Jamestown church in July and August 1619. In steamy weather, the burgesses sat in the church pews, while the governor and council took their places in the choir stalls.

The House of Burgesses marked the beginning of representative government in the English colonies. In a **representative government,** voters elect representatives to make laws for them.

English Traditions The idea that people had political rights was deeply rooted in English history. In 1215, English nobles had forced King John to sign the **Magna Carta,** or Great Charter. This document said that the king could not raise taxes without first consulting a Great Council of nobles and church leaders.

Over time, the rights won by nobles were extended to other people. The Great Council grew into a representative assembly, called **Parliament.** Parliament was divided into the House of Lords, made up of nobles, and an elected House of Commons. Only a few rich men had the right to vote. Still, the English had established the principle that even monarchs had to obey the law.

Virginia's Representative Tradition At first, free Virginians had even greater rights than citizens in England. They did not have to own property in order to vote. In 1670, however, the colony restricted the vote to free, white, male property owners.

Despite these limits, representative government remained important. The idea took root that settlers should have a say in the affairs of the colony. Colonists came to refer to the Virginia Company's 1619 frame of government as their own "Great Charter."

New Arrivals

During the early years of the Jamestown Colony, only a few women chose to make the journey from England. Nor did enough workers come to raise tobacco and other crops.

Women in Virginia The colony's first women arrived in 1608—a "Mistress Forrest" and her maid, Anne Burras. Few others followed until 1619, when the Virginia Company sent about 100 women to help "make the men more settled." This shipload of women quickly found husbands. The Virginia Company profited from the marriages because it charged each man who found a wife 150 pounds of tobacco.

Women survived the hardships of Virginia better than men. One colonist commented that women "escape better than men, either that their work lies chiefly [inside] or because they are of a colder temper." In fact, men were almost twice as likely as women to die from diseases or other causes.

Still, life for women remained a daily struggle. Women had to make everything from scratch—food, clothing, even medicines. Many died young from hard work or childbirth. By 1624, there were still fewer than 300 women in the Jamestown colony, compared to over a thousand men.

The First Africans Africans came to Virginia early on. Recently discovered records show that at least 15 black men and 17 black women were already living there by 1619. That same year, a Dutch ship arrived with about 20 Africans. The Dutch sold the Africans to Virginians who needed laborers to grow tobacco. The colonists valued the agricultural skills that the Africans brought with them.

About 300 Africans lived in Virginia by 1644. Some were slaves for life. Others worked as servants and expected one day to own their own farms. Some Africans did become free planters. Anthony Johnson owned 250 acres of land and employed five servants to help him work it. For a time, free Africans in Virginia also had the right to vote.

In the late 1600s, Virginia set up a system of laws allowing white colonists to enslave Africans for life. As slavery expanded, free Africans lost rights. By the early 1700s, free African property owners could not vote.

Summarize When you summarize, you review and state in the correct order the main points you have read. Write two or three sentences summarizing the impact of the "new arrivals" to the Jamestown Colony in 1619.

★ ★ ★ Section 4 Assessment ★ ★ ★

Recall

1. **Identify** Explain the significance of **(a)** Walter Raleigh, **(b)** John Smith, **(c)** Powhatan, **(d)** House of Burgesses, **(e)** Magna Carta, **(f)** Parliament.
2. **Define** **(a)** charter, **(b)** burgess, **(c)** representative government.

Comprehension

3. **(a)** Describe three problems the Jamestown Colony faced after 1607. **(b)** Why was the colony finally able to survive?
4. What were the origins of representative government in the English colonies?
5. What new arrivals helped the Jamestown Colony thrive?

Critical Thinking and Writing

6. **Exploring the Main Idea** Review the Main Idea statement at the beginning of this section. Then, list what you would consider to be the four most important milestones in the growth of Jamestown.
7. **Linking Past and Present** Name three important features of Jamestown's government. For each item, write a sentence explaining how it is also an element of American representative government today.

ACTIVITY

Creating an Advertisement **You are an investor in the Virginia Company. In order to make a profit, you must encourage people to leave England and move to Jamestown. Create an advertisement describing the advantages of living in Virginia. If possible, include an illustration.**

The House of Burgesses

The House of Burgesses first met in Jamestown, Virginia, on July 30, 1619. That hot day marks the beginning of representative government in what became the United States.

The first session passed a variety of laws. The burgesses decreed:

- that colonists plant mulberry trees and grape vines.
- that penalties be imposed for drunkenness, idleness, and gambling.
- that colonists attend church twice on Sunday—and that they bring their guns and swords with them.
- that "no injury or oppression be [committed] by the English against the Indians."
- that each town and plantation had to educate a number of Indian children.

The first burgesses wore multiple layers of velvets and silks, like upper-class members of the British Parliament (left). But Jamestown's hot, humid July climate proved deadly. Several burgesses got sick, and one died.

The 22 elected burgesses gathered in the Jamestown church. Parson Buck opened the meeting with a prayer. As each burgess heard his name called, he took his seat before the governor.

ACTIVITY

Choose one of the laws listed above. With a partner, enact a discussion in the House of Burgesses about that law. Explain why you think such a law is necessary for the well-being of the colony.

5 Seeking Religious Freedom

Prepare to Read

Objectives

In this section, you will
- Describe how European states controlled or regulated religion.
- Explain why the colonists at Plymouth wanted the Mayflower Compact.
- Identify how the Pilgrims survived early hardships.

Key Terms

Pilgrims
established church
persecution
Mayflower Compact
precedent
Thanksgiving

Target Reading Skill

Sequence Copy this flowchart. As you read, fill in the boxes with the major events and developments relating to the founding of the Plymouth Colony. The first and last boxes have been completed to help you get started. Add as many boxes as you need.

England persecutes Separatists
↓
[ ]
↓
[ ]
↓
[ ]
↓
First successful harvest in Plymouth

Main Idea The Pilgrims founded Plymouth Colony in 1620 in order to practice their religion freely.

Setting the Scene The small sailing ship had been tossed by so many storms that leaks had sprung in the ship's hull. After two hard months at sea, the colonists on board were relieved to see the shores of New England. Still, there were no European colonies for hundreds of miles. Worse, it was already November of 1620, much too late for crops to be planted. One of the voyagers, William Bradford, vividly remembered the situation:

> "Being thus passed the vast ocean . . . they had now no friends to welcome them nor inns to entertain or refresh their weatherbeaten bodies; no houses or much less towns to repair to . . . And for the season it was winter, and they that know the winters of that country know them to be sharp and violent."
>
> —William Bradford, *Of Plymouth Plantation*

Cradle carried on the Mayflower

Despite many hardships, the newcomers made their new colony succeed. Unlike the Jamestown colonists or the Spanish, they sought neither gold nor silver nor great riches. What they wanted most was to practice their religion freely. Years later, the founders of Plymouth became known to history as the **Pilgrims.***

European States and Religion

It was not easy for people to practice religion freely in Europe during the 1500s. As you have read, after the Protestant Reformation, European Christians were divided into Protestants and Roman Catholics. This division led to fierce religious wars. In France, for example, Protestants and Catholics fought each other for nearly 40

*The founders of the Plymouth Colony did not call themselves Pilgrims. However, William Bradford once wrote that they were "pilgrims . . . [who] lifted up their eyes to the heavens, their dearest country." A pilgrim is anyone who makes a long journey for religious reasons.

years. Thousands upon thousands of people were killed because of their religious beliefs.

Most European rulers believed that they could not maintain order unless the state supported a particular religion. The chosen religion was known as the **established church.** In England, for example, the established church was the Anglican church, or Church of England. In the 1530s, Parliament passed laws making the English monarch the head of the Church of England.

In England and other nations, people who did not follow the established religion were often persecuted. **Persecution** is the mistreatment or punishment of certain people because of their beliefs. Sometimes, members of persecuted groups had to worship secretly. If they were discovered, they might be imprisoned or even executed by being burned at the stake.

Separatists Seek Religious Freedom One religious group in England that faced persecution were the people we now call the Pilgrims. At the time, they were known as Separatists. They were called that because, although they were Protestant, they wanted to separate from the Church of England.

The English government bitterly opposed the Separatists. William Bradford remembered what some Separatists suffered:

> “They . . . were hunted and persecuted on every side. . . . For some were taken and clapped up in prison, others had their houses beset and watched night and day . . . and the most were [glad] to flee and leave their houses.”
>
> —William Bradford, *Of Plymouth Plantation*

In the early 1600s, a group of Separatists left England for Leyden, a city in the Netherlands. The Dutch allowed the newcomers to worship freely. Still, the Pilgrims missed their English way of life. They were also worried that their children were growing up more Dutch than English.

Primary Source

The Mayflower Compact

On November 11, 1620, the 41 male passengers on the Mayflower *signed a binding agreement for self-government:*

"We, whose names are underwritten. . . . Having undertaken for the Glory of God, and Advancement of the Christian Faith and honor of our King and country, a voyage to plant the first colony in the northern parts of Virginia, do . . . solemnly and mutually in the presence of God, and one of another, covenant and combine ourselves into a civil body politic . . . to enact, constitute, and frame, such just and equal Laws . . . as shall be thought most [fitting] and convenient for the general Good of the Colony; unto which we promise all due submission and obedience."

—Mayflower Compact

Analyzing Primary Sources

Identify two promises the signers of the Mayflower Compact made with regard to laws for their colony.

The Pilgrim Colony at Plymouth

A group of Separatists decided to return to England. Along with some other English people who were not Separatists, they won a charter to set up a colony in Virginia. In September 1620, more than 100 men, women, and children set sail aboard a small ship called the *Mayflower.* As you have read, the journey was long and difficult.

At last, in November 1620, the *Mayflower* landed on the cold, bleak shore of Cape Cod, in present-day Massachusetts. The passengers had planned to settle farther south along the Hudson River, but the difficult sea voyage exhausted them. The colonists decided to travel no further. They called their new settlement Plimoth, or Plymouth, because the *Mayflower* had sailed from the port of Plymouth, England.

The Mayflower Compact Before going ashore, the Pilgrims realized that they would not be settling within the boundaries of Virginia. As a result, the terms of their charter would not apply to their new colony. In that case, who would govern them? The question was important because not all colonists on the Mayflower were Pilgrims. Some of these "strangers," as the Pilgrims called them, said they were not bound to obey the Pilgrims, "for none had power to command them."

In response, the Pilgrims joined together to write a framework for governing their colony. On November 11, 1620, the 41 male passengers—both Pilgrims and non-Pilgrims—signed the **Mayflower Compact.** They pledged themselves to unite into a "civil body politic," or government. They agreed to make and abide by laws that insured "the general Good of the Colony." (See the Primary Source on the preceding page.)

The Mayflower Compact established an important tradition. When the Pilgrims found themselves without a government, they banded together themselves to make laws. In time, they set up a government in which adult male colonists elected a governor and council. Thus, like Virginia's Great Charter, the Mayflower Compact strengthened the English tradition of governing through elected representatives.

Tradition of Religious Freedom The Pilgrims were the first of many English settlers who came to North America in order to worship as they pleased. Still, as you will read in the next chapter, that did not mean that religious freedom spread quickly through England's colonies. Many settlers who wished to worship as they

Viewing History

Signing the Mayflower Compact

Before the *Mayflower* anchored in what is now Provincetown Harbor off Cape Cod, the male passengers signed the Mayflower Compact. This painting depicts the event. **Drawing Inferences** ***What does this painting suggest about the women aboard the* Mayflower?**

Plimoth Plantation

By 1627, Plymouth was a stable settlement. Using records from that year, historians carefully re-created Plimoth Plantation on the grounds of the old village in Massacusetts. Plimoth is a "living museum," where people in authentic costumes tend crops, make tools, and tell you about their lives. Even the animals at Plimoth are all breeds that were raised by the Pilgrims.

Virtual Field Trip For an interactive look at the Plimouth Plantation, visit PHSchool.com, **Web Code mfd-0302.**

pleased still believed that only their own religious beliefs should be observed. Most of the later English colonies set up their own established churches.

Still, the Pilgrims' desire to worship freely set an important **precedent,** or example for others to follow in the future. Plymouth's leaders announced "that any honest men may live with them, that will carry themselves peaceably and seek the common good." In time, the idea of religious freedom for all would become a cornerstone of American democracy.

Early Hardships

The Pilgrims built their settlement on the site of a Native American village that had been abandoned because of disease. The colonists even found baskets filled with corn that they were able to eat.

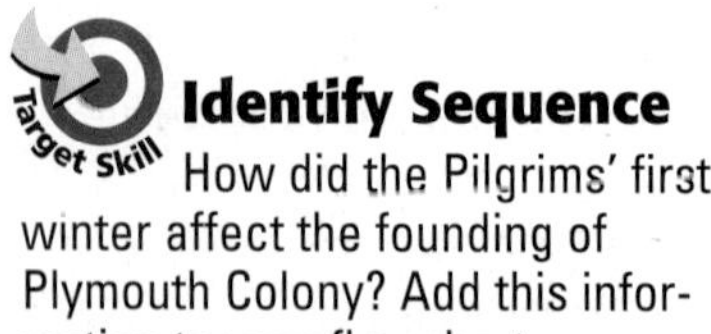

Identify Sequence How did the Pilgrims' first winter affect the founding of Plymouth Colony? Add this information to your flowchart.

First Winter in Plymouth However, the corn was not enough to get the Pilgrims through their first winter. The Pilgrims had failed to bring enough food with them, and it was too late in the season to plant new crops.

The harsh season was also difficult to survive because the Pilgrims had not had enough time to build proper shelters. Most threw together crude houses of sod, or clumps of earth. Some dug themselves into pits in the ground, covered by branches to protect themselves from the weather. Nearly half the settlers perished of disease or starvation.

Among those who died that winter was the colony's first governor. William Bradford was chosen to take his place. Bradford's able leadership helped the colony survive. Reelected many times, he would lead Plymouth for most of the next 36 years.

Despite the great suffering of the "Starving Time," the Pilgrims' religious faith remained strong. They believed that it was God's will for them to remain in Plymouth. "What could now sustain them," wrote Bradford, "but the Spirit of God and His grace?"

Help From Native Americans In the spring, the Pilgrims began to clear land and plant crops. They also received help from neighboring Native Americans. A Pemaquid Indian, Samoset, had learned English from earlier explorers sailing along the coast. He introduced the Pilgrims to Massasoit (MAS uh soit), chief of the local Wampanoag (wahm puh NOH ahg) Indians.

The Wampanoag who helped the Pilgrims most was named Squanto. As a young man, Squanto had been captured by an English expedition led by John Smith. Squanto lived for a time in England, where he learned to speak the language. As a result, he could communicate easily with the Pilgrims.

Squanto brought the Pilgrims seeds of native plants—corn, beans, and pumpkins—and showed them how to plant them. He also taught the settlers how to catch eels from nearby rivers. By treading water, he stirred up eels from the mud at the river bottom and then snatched them up with his hands. The grateful Pilgrims called Squanto "a special instrument sent of God."

In the fall, the Pilgrims had a very good harvest. Because they believed that God had given them this harvest, they set aside a day for giving thanks. In later years, the Pilgrims celebrated after each harvest season with a day of thanksgiving. Americans today celebrate Thanksgiving as a national holiday.

Recall

1. **Identify** Explain the significance of **(a)** William Bradford, **(b)** Pilgrims, **(c)** Mayflower Compact, **(d)** Squanto, **(e)** Thanksgiving.
2. **Define** **(a)** established church, **(b)** persecution, **(c)** precedent.

Comprehension

3. Why did many religious groups in Europe face persecution?
4. **(a)** How did the Mayflower Compact resolve a conflict among the Plymouth settlers? **(b)** Why is this document important?
5. How did Native Americans help the Pilgrims survive?

Critical Thinking and Writing

6. **Exploring the Main Idea** Review the Main Idea statement at the beginning of this section. Then, write a letter from one Separatist in England to another explaining why you have decided to sail on the *Mayflower.*
7. **Comparing** Write a list of three ways the founding of Plymouth was different from or similar to the founding of Jamestown.

ACTIVITY

Exploring Tradition

Freewrite a list of images that might describe the first Thanksgiving. Then, use the Internet to find accounts of the Pilgrims' harvest celebration in 1621. Explain two things you learned that surprised you. For help in completing the activity, visit PHSchool.com, **Web Code mfd-0303.**

CHAPTER 3

Review and Assessment

Chapter Summary

Section 1
Christopher Columbus did not discover a route to Asia, but his voyage had a lasting impact. Explorers who came after Columbus opened a cultural exchange between Europe and the Americas.

Section 2
Conquistadors created a Spanish empire in the Americas when they conquered the Aztecs and Incas. Native American deaths in the Spanish colonies led to the introduction of the slave trade.

Section 3
The French, English, and Dutch competed for the fertile land that they discovered in North America. Native Americans suffered as a result of their encounters with Europeans.

Section 4
Jamestown, in Virginia, became the first permanent English colony in North America. The colonists in Virginia brought their English traditions with them, including the practice of representative government.

Section 5
Religious persecution brought the Pilgrims to North America. They established a colony in Plymouth. After barely surviving their first winter, the Pilgrims planted crops with the help of Native Americans.

Building Vocabulary

Write sentences, using the chapter vocabulary words listed below, leaving blanks where the vocabulary words would go. Exchange your sentences with another student and fill in the blanks.

1. **colony**
2. **circumnavigate**
3. **conquistador**
4. **presidio**
5. **mission**
6. **peninsulare**
7. **northwest passage**
8. **charter**
9. **representative government**
10. **established church**

Reviewing Key Facts

11. Identify one reason Spain financed Columbus's voyage in 1492. (Section 1)

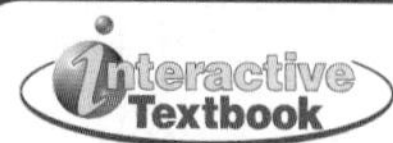

For additional review and enrichment activities, see the interactive version of *The American Nation,* available on the Web and on CD-ROM.

Chapter Self-Test For practice test questions for Chapter 3, visit PHSchool.com, **Web Code mfa-0304.**

12. How were European and Native American cultures blended in New Spain? (Section 2)
13. How did Dutch ways help shape American culture? (Section 3)
14. Describe two English political traditions of the Jamestown Colony. (Section 4)
15. Why did the Pilgrims decide to start a colony? (Section 5)

Critical Thinking and Writing

16. **Recognizing Points of View** For each of the following, write one sentence describing the person's feelings about Bartolomé de Las Casas: **(a)** a Native American working on a Caribbean plantation; **(b)** a Spanish plantation owner; **(c)** a slave trader in East Africa; **(d)** an African sent to the Americas as a slave.
17. Connecting to Geography: **Movement** Look at a world map or a map of North America. **(a)** Write a description of a possible northern sea route around the Americas to Asia. **(b)** Based on what you know of this part of the world, why do you think the British, French, or Dutch never found a northwest passage?
18. **Comparing (a)** List one similarity and one difference between Jamestown's "Great Charter" of 1619 and the Mayflower Compact. **(b)** Write a paragraph evaluating the importance of these documents.

Skills Assessment

Analyzing Primary Sources

Read the following excerpt from Jacques Marquette's journal and answer the questions that follow:

> "We slept in the chief's cabin, and on the following day we took leave of him, promising to pass again by his village, within four moons. He conducted us to our canoes, with nearly 600 persons who witnessed our embarkation, giving us every possible sign of the joy that our visit had caused them. For my own part, I promised . . . that I would come the following year, and reside with them to instruct them."
>
> —Jacques Marquette, quoted in *The Jesuit Relations and Allied Documents* (Thwaites)

19. When Marquette wrote that he would return "within four moons," he probably meant that he would be back in about four

A. days.
B. weeks.
C. months.
D. years.

20. Upon his return to the village, Marquette probably intended to teach the Indians about

A. the art of making canoes.
B. Christianity.
C. how to tell time using a watch or clock.
D. the shortest route to the Mississippi.

Applying Your Skills

Sequencing

Below are some key events relating to the first English colonies. The events are not listed in correct time sequence. Look at the events and answer the questions that follow.

I.	House of Burgesses is formed
II.	Pilgrims leave England
III.	Jamestown Colony is founded
IV.	Mayflower Compact is signed
V.	Roanoke colonists disappear
VI.	Squanto teaches Pilgrims
VII.	Colonists begin to grow tobacco

21. In which set below are the events listed in the correct sequence?

A. VII, IV, II
B. V, I, VI
C. III, VI, IV
D. II, VII, VI

22. Choose two events from the list above. Identify the correct time sequence and explain how the two events are related.

Activities

Connecting With . . . Geography

Creating a Thematic Map With the class, create a map of the Era of Exploration and Colonization. Use the information found on the various maps in this chapter. (Your teacher may suggest that you look at additional maps as well.) Draw a large base map of the world. Label important continents, countries, oceans, and rivers. Create a color key for the major European powers discussed in the chapter. Choose who you consider to be the 10 most important explorers and show their routes on the map. Then, color in the areas of the Americas that were colonized by European nations. Use the same color key to show a nation, its explorers, and its colonies.

Exploring Historical Scholarship

Summarizing Use the Internet to find one theory about the disappearance of the colony at Roanoke. In a one-minute talk, summarize the theory and the evidence for it. For help in starting this activity, visit PHSchool.com, **Web Code mfd-0306.**

CHAPTER 4

The Thirteen English Colonies

1630–1750

1 The New England Colonies
2 The Middle Colonies
3 The Southern Colonies
4 Roots of Self-Government
5 Life in the Colonies

Puritan settlers building homes

Collar given by Quakers to Native Americans

AMERICAN EVENTS

1630 Puritans from England set up the Massachusetts Bay Colony.

1675 Metacom leads fight against settlers in New England.

1682 William Penn founds the colony of Pennsylvania.

1630 1660 1690

WORLD EVENTS

1660 ▲ English Parliament passes a stronger version of the Navigation Act.

1689 ▲ William and Mary sign the English Bill of Rights.

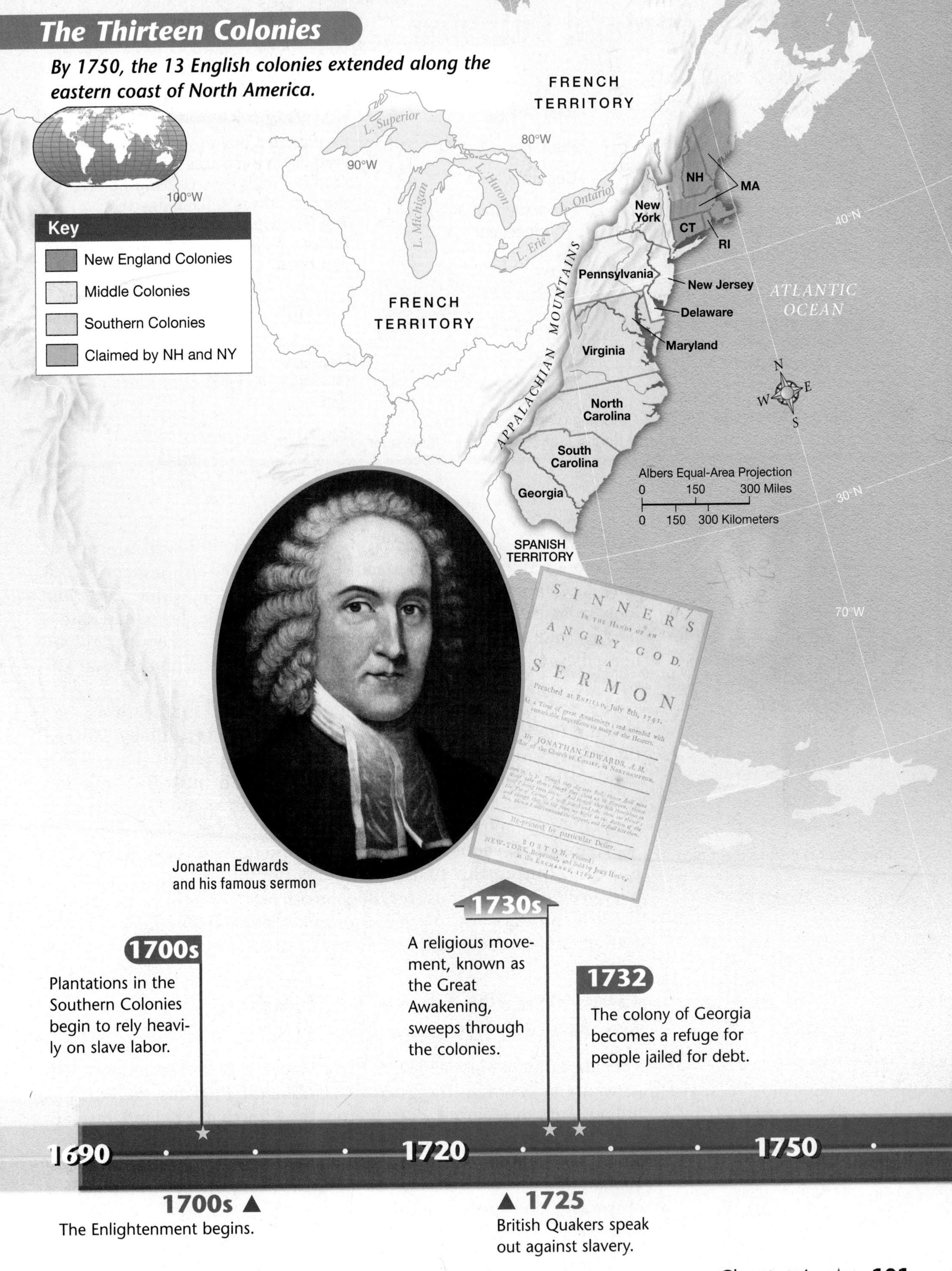

Jonathan Edwards and his famous sermon

1 The New England Colonies

Prepare to Read

Objectives

In this section, you will

- List the reasons the Puritans decided to leave England.
- Identify problems in the Massachusetts colony that caused people to leave.
- Explain why the Puritans and Native Americans fought.
- Summarize why towns and villages were important in New England.

Key Terms

Puritans

General Court

Fundamental Orders of Connecticut

religious tolerance

Sabbath

town meeting

Target Reading Skill

Sequence Copy this chart. As you read, fill in the boxes with the name of each New England Colony, the date it was settled, and why. The first two boxes have been started for you. Add as many lines as you need.

COLONY	DATE SETTLED	REASONS FOR SETTLEMENT
• Plymouth • Massachusetts Bay	• 1620 • 1630	• •

Main Idea The New England Colonies were founded by reformers and developed around tightly knit towns and villages.

Powdered wig from the 1700s

Setting the Scene Boston merchant Samuel Sewall frowned as he greeted Mr. Hayward, an acquaintance. Hayward had cut off his long gray hair and was wearing a full wig of dark hair that made him look younger! Sewall protested that in the Bible, Jesus had said a person cannot "make one's Hair white or black." Hayward gulped nervously. He claimed that his doctors had advised him to wear the wig.

By the time Sewall recorded this story in 1685, Boston had become the busiest town in the Massachusetts Bay Colony. Most of the colony's founders were no longer living. Yet, Sewall shared their ideals. He looked to the Bible to guide him in matters large and small—even the treatment of one's hair. Sewall wanted his colony to be a "holy commonwealth" that followed the laws of God.

Religion played a large part in the founding of colonies in New England. During the 1630s, thousands of English settlers came to live around Massachusetts Bay, north of Plymouth. Gradually, English settlers built towns and farms throughout the region. These settlements shared a distinctive way of life.

The Puritans Leave England for Massachusetts

The migration to Massachusetts Bay during the 1630s was led by a religious group known as the **Puritans.** Unlike the Pilgrims, the Puritans did not want to separate entirely from the Church of England. Instead, they hoped to reform the church by introducing simpler forms of worship. They wanted to do away with many practices inherited from the Roman Catholic Church, such as organ music, finely decorated houses of worship, and special clothing for priests.

Leaving England During "Evil Times"

The Puritans were a powerful group in England. Although some were small farmers, many were well-educated and successful merchants or landowners.

Charles I, who became king in 1625, disapproved of the Puritans and their ideas. He canceled Puritan business charters and even had a few Puritans jailed.

By 1629, some Puritan leaders were convinced that England had fallen on "evil and declining times." They persuaded royal officials to grant them a charter to form the Massachusetts Bay Company. The company's bold plan was to build a new society based on biblical laws and teachings. John Winthrop, a lawyer and a devout Puritan, believed that the new colony would set an example to the world.

Some settlers joined the Massachusetts colonists for economic rather than religious reasons. In wealthy English families, the oldest son usually inherited his father's estate. With little hope of owning land, younger sons sought opportunity elsewhere. They were attracted to Massachusetts Bay because it offered cheap land or a chance to start a business.

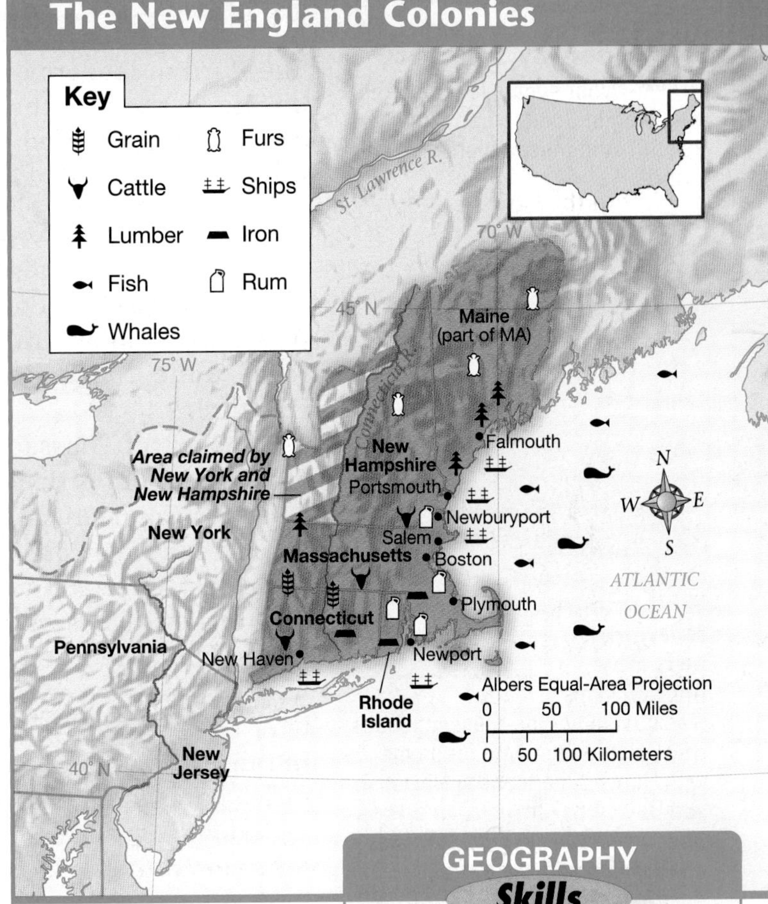

GEOGRAPHY Skills

The New England colonies were among the first English settlements in North America. Major economic activities in the region included shipbuilding, fishing, and fur trapping.

1. **Location** On the map, locate: **(a)** Massachusetts, **(b)** Connecticut, **(c)** Rhode Island, **(d)** New Hampshire, **(e)** Boston, **(f)** Plymouth.
2. **Interaction** In which colonies did settlers mine iron ore?
3. **Critical Thinking Analyzing Information** How did New England's geography encourage the growth of shipbuilding?

Governing the Colony In 1629, the Puritans sent a small advance party to North America. John Winthrop and a party of more than 1,000 arrived the following year. Winthrop was chosen first governor of the Massachusetts Bay Colony.

Once ashore, Winthrop set an example for others. Although he was governor, he worked hard to build a home, clear land, and plant crops.

There was discontent among some colonists, though. Under the charter, only stockholders who had invested money in the Massachusetts Bay Company had the right to vote. Most settlers, however, were not stockholders. They resented taxes and laws passed by a government in which they had no say.

Winthrop and other stockholders saw that the colony would run more smoothly if a greater number of settlers could take part. At the same time, Puritan leaders wished to keep non-Puritans out of the government. As a result, they granted the right to vote for governor to all men who were church members. Later, male church members also elected representatives to an assembly called the **General Court.**

Under the leadership of Winthrop and other Puritans, the Massachusetts Bay Colony prospered. Between 1629 and 1640, some 15,000 men, women, and children journeyed from England to Massachusetts. This movement of people is known as the Great Migration. Many of the newcomers settled in Boston, which grew into the colony's largest town.

Identify Sequence (Target Skill) What events led up to the founding of Connecticut? Rhode Island? Add these colonies to your chart.

Problems in Massachusetts Bay

The Puritan leaders did not like anyone to question their religious beliefs or the way the colony was governed. Usually, discontented colonists were forced to leave. Some colonists who left Massachusetts founded other colonies in New England.

Thomas Hooker Founds Connecticut In May 1636, a Puritan minister named Thomas Hooker led about 100 settlers out of Massachusetts Bay. Pushing west, they drove their cattle, goats, and pigs along Indian trails that cut through the forests. When they reached the Connecticut River, they built a town, which they called Hartford.

Hooker left Massachusetts Bay because he believed that the governor and other officials had too much power. He wanted to set up a colony in Connecticut with strict limits on government.

The settlers wrote a plan of government called the **Fundamental Orders of Connecticut** in 1639. It created a government much like that of Massachusetts. There were, however, two important differences. First, the Fundamental Orders gave the vote to all men who were property owners, including those who were not church members. Second, the Fundamental Orders limited the governor's power. In this way, the Fundamental Orders expanded the idea of representative government in the English colonies.

Connecticut became a separate colony in 1662, with a new charter granted by the king of England. By then, 15 towns were thriving along the Connecticut River.

Viewing History

Roger Williams in Narragansett Bay

Rhode Island

After Williams was cast out of the Massachusetts Bay Colony, he stayed for a time with Native Americans in Narragansett Bay. **Drawing Inferences** ***How would you describe Williams's relationship with the Native Americans?***

Roger Williams Settles Rhode Island Another Puritan who challenged the leaders of Massachusetts Bay was Roger Williams. A young minister in the village of Salem, Williams was gentle and good-natured. William Bradford described him as "zealous but very unsettled in judgment." Some Puritan leaders probably agreed with this. Most people, including Governor Winthrop, liked him. Williams's ideas, however, alarmed Puritan leaders.

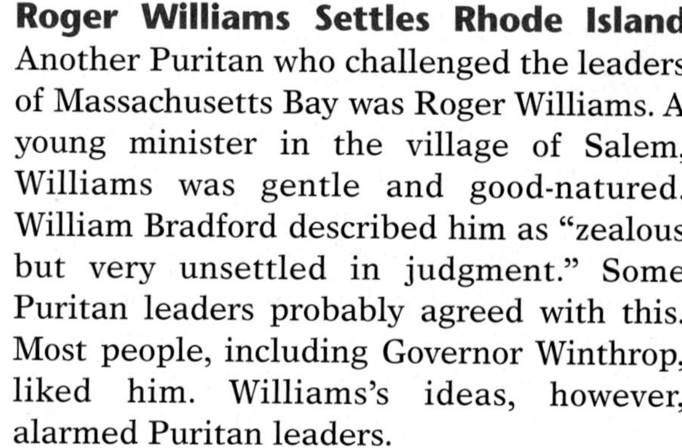

Williams believed that the Puritan church in Massachusetts had too much power. In Williams's view, the business of church and state should be completely separate since concern with political affairs would corrupt the church. The role of the state, said Williams, was to maintain order and peace. It should not support a particular church. Finally, Williams did not believe that the Puritan leaders had the right to force people to attend religious services.

Williams also believed in religious tolerance. **Religious tolerance** means a willingness to let others practice their own beliefs.

In Puritan Massachusetts, non-Puritans were not allowed to worship freely.

Puritan leaders viewed Williams as a dangerous troublemaker. In 1635, the General Court ordered him to leave Massachusetts. Fearing that the court would send him back to England, Williams fled to Narragansett Bay, where he spent the winter with Indians. In the spring of 1636, the Indians sold him land for a settlement. After a few years, the settlement became the English colony of Rhode Island.

In Rhode Island, Williams put into practice his ideas about tolerance. He allowed complete freedom of religion for all Protestants, Jews, and Catholics.* He did not set up a state church or require settlers to attend church services. He also gave all white men the right to vote. Before long, settlers who disliked the strict Puritan rule of Massachusetts flocked to Providence and other towns in Rhode Island.

Anne Hutchinson Speaks Out Among those who fled to Rhode Island was Anne Hutchinson. A devout Puritan, Hutchinson regularly attended church services in Boston, where she first lived. After church, she and her friends gathered at her home to discuss the minister's sermon. Often, she seemed to question some of the minister's teachings. Hutchinson was very persuasive and neighbors flocked to hear her.

Puritan leaders grew angry. They believed that Hutchinson's opinions were full of religious errors. Even worse, they said, a woman did not have the right to explain God's law. In November 1637, Hutchinson was ordered to appear before the Massachusetts General Court.

At her trial, Hutchinson answered the questions put to her by Governor Winthrop and other members of the court. Each time, her answers revealed weaknesses in their arguments. They could not prove that she had broken any Puritan laws or that she had disobeyed any religious teachings.

Then, after two long days of hostile questioning, Hutchinson made a serious mistake. She told the court that God spoke directly to her, "By the voice of His own spirit to my soul." Members of the court were shocked. Puritans believed that God spoke only through the Bible, not directly to individuals. The court ordered her out of the colony.

In 1638, Hutchinson, along with her family and some friends, went to Rhode Island. The Puritan leaders had won their case. For later Americans, however, Hutchinson became an important symbol of the struggle for religious freedom.

Viewing History

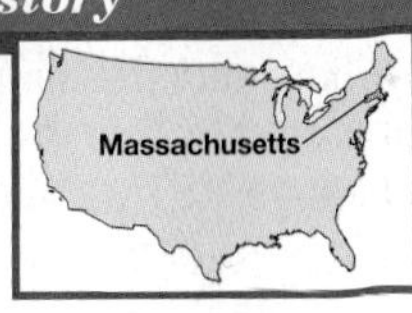

Anne Hutchinson Known in the colony as a "woman of ready wit with a bold spirit," Hutchinson won the respect of Puritan leaders at first. However, they soon saw her as a troublemaker. Here, she defends herself before the General Court.
Making Decisions ***Do you think Hutchinson was a "bold spirit"? Explain.***

*In 1763, Jewish settlers in Rhode Island built Touro Synagogue, the first Jewish house of worship in North America. It still stands today.

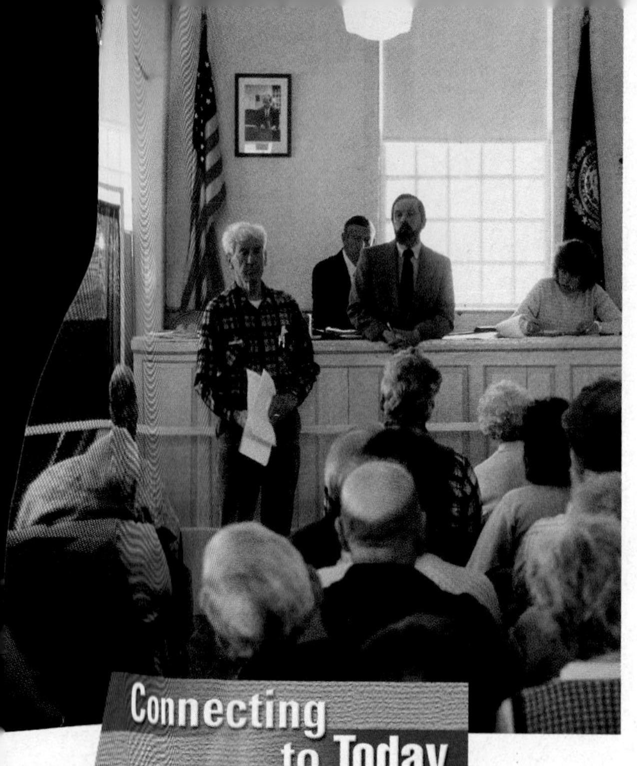

Connecting to Today

Democracy in Action

In New England and some other states, town meetings still occur. Citizens discuss and vote on important issues, such as town laws or how to use the town's money.

Today, new technology is giving a whole new meaning to town meetings. In "electronic town meetings" (ETM), televisions, telephones, or computers link people from distant locations and provide instant voting results. Experts give background talks on an issue. Citizens ask questions, speak their minds, and then vote. The way in which citizens conduct their meetings is different from the way it was in colonial times. However, the citizens' desire to make their voices heard is the same.

What issues might you like to see addressed by a town meeting in your community?

Puritans at War With Native Americans

From Massachusetts Bay, settlers fanned out across New England. Some built trading and fishing villages along the coast north of Boston. In 1680, the king made these coastal settlements into a separate colony called New Hampshire.

The first meetings between English settlers and Native Americans did not foreshadow the conflict that would eventually occur between them. Some colonial leaders such as William Penn and Roger Williams tried to treat Native Americans fairly.

As more colonists settled in New England, they began to take over more Native American lands. By 1670, nearly 45,000 English settlers were living in the towns in New England. As a result, fighting broke out between white settlers and Indian nations of the region.

The largest conflict came in 1675. Metacom, also known by his English name, King Phillip, was chief of the Wampanoag Indians. He watched for years as English towns were built on Wampanoag lands. "I am resolved not to see the day when I have no country," he told an English friend. Metacom's people attacked villages throughout New England. Other Indian groups, from Rhode Island to Maine, soon allied themselves with the Wampanoags. They were determined to drive the English settlers off their land. Metacom and his allies destroyed 12 towns and killed more than 600 European settlers.

After more than a year of fighting, however, Metacom was captured and killed. The English sold his family and about 1,000 other Indians into slavery in the West Indies. Other Indians were forced from their homelands.

The pattern of English expansion followed by war was repeated between colonists and Indians throughout the colonies. It would continue for many years to come.

Life in New England Towns and Villages

Puritans believed that people should worship and tend to local matters as a community. As a result, New England became a land of tightly knit towns and villages.

At the center of each village was the common, an open field where cattle grazed. Nearby stood the meetinghouse, where Puritans worshiped and held town meetings.

Religion and Family The Puritans took their **Sabbath,** or holy day of rest, very seriously. On Sundays, no one was allowed to play games or visit taverns to joke, talk, and drink. The law required all citizens to attend Sunday church services, which would last all day.

During the 1600s, women sat on one side of the church and men on the other. Blacks and Indians stood in a balcony at the back. Children had separate pews, where an adult watched over them.

Government At **town meetings,** settlers discussed and voted on many issues. What roads should be built? How much should the schoolmaster be paid? Town meetings gave New Englanders a chance to speak their minds. This early experience encouraged the growth of democratic ideas in New England.

Puritan laws were strict. About 15 crimes carried the death penalty. One crime punishable by death was witchcraft. In 1692, Puritans in Salem Village executed 20 men and women as witches.

Economy New England was a difficult land for colonists. The rocky soil was poor for farming. After a time, however, Native Americans taught English settlers how to grow many crops, such as Indian corn, pumpkins, squash, and beans.

Although the soil was poor, the forests were full of riches. Settlers hunted wild turkey and deer. Settlers also cut down trees and floated them to sawmills near ports such as Boston, Massachusetts, or Portsmouth, New Hampshire. These cities grew into major shipbuilding centers.

Other New Englanders fished for cod and halibut. In the 1600s, people began to hunt whales. Whales supplied oil for lamps and other products. In the 1700s and 1800s, whaling grew into a big business.

Decline of the Puritans During the 1700s, the Puritan tradition declined. Fewer families left England for religious reasons. Ministers had less influence on the way colonies were governed. Nevertheless, the Puritans had stamped New England with their distinctive customs and their dream of a religious society.

★ ★ ★ Section 1 Assessment ★ ★ ★

Recall

1. **Identify** Explain the significance of **(a)** Puritans, **(b)** John Winthrop, **(c)** General Court, **(d)** Thomas Hooker, **(e)** Fundamental Orders of Connecticut, **(f)** Roger Williams, **(g)** Anne Hutchinson, **(h)** Metacom.
2. **Define** **(a)** religious tolerance, **(b)** Sabbath, **(c)** town meeting.

Comprehension

3. Why did the Puritans settle the Massachusetts Bay Colony?
4. Why did Thomas Hooker leave the colony?
5. Discuss how the settlement affected Native Americans.
6. What was the purpose of the town meeting?

Critical Thinking and Writing

7. **Exploring the Main Idea** Review the Main Idea statement at the beginning of this section. Then, write a paragraph about how religion and politics affected the development of the New England Colonies.
8. **Drawing Conclusions** The way in which the Puritans governed the Massachusetts Bay Colony led to its success. List arguments to support this viewpoint. Then, list arguments that do not support this statement.

Activity

Writing a Persuasive Letter You have followed Roger Williams to Rhode Island. Write a letter persuading some friends from Massachusetts to join you.

2 The Middle Colonies

Prepare to Read

Objectives

In this section, you will

- Explain why the colony of New Netherland became the colony of New York.
- Identify why New Jersey separated from New York.
- Describe how Pennsylvania was founded.
- Summarize life in the Middle Colonies.

Key Terms

patroon

proprietary colony

royal colony

Quakers

Pennsylvania Dutch

cash crop

Target Reading Skill

Main Idea Copy the concept web below. As you read, fill in the blank ovals with important facts about the settlement of the Middle Colonies. Add as many ovals as you need.

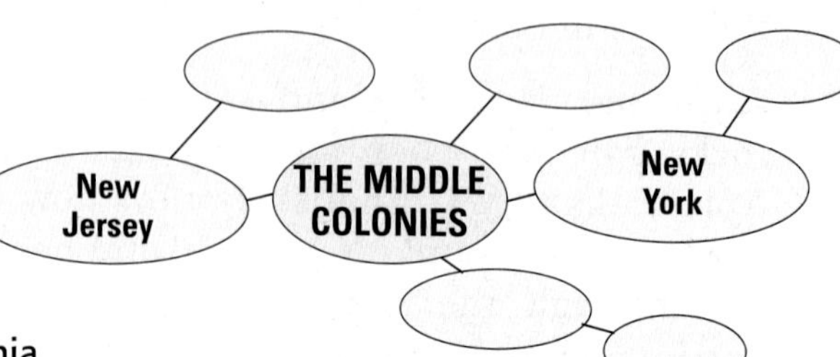

Main Idea The Middle Colonies attracted a wide variety of immigrants who settled on farms and in the cities of Philadelphia and New York.

A chair from colonial Philadelphia

Setting the Scene A doctor from the colony of Maryland traveled north to Philadelphia in the summer of 1744. Dr. Hamilton kept his eyes open to see how the customs in that city differed from those of Maryland. Merchants opened for business much earlier, he discovered: at five in the morning. For dinner at a tavern, Hamilton sat around a single large table with 24 other diners. Unfortunately, the "great hall [was] well stocked with flies," he complained.

However, what most surprised Hamilton was the variety of people at the table:

> "I dined at a tavern with a very mixed company of different nations and religions. There were Scots, English, Dutch, Germans, and Irish. There were Roman Catholics, Church [of England] men, Presbyterians, Quakers, . . . Moravians . . . and one Jew."
>
> —Alexander Hamilton, *Itinerarium,* 1744

By 1700, England had four colonies in the region south of New England. These colonies became known as the Middle Colonies because they were located between New England and the Southern Colonies. As Dr. Hamilton observed, the Middle Colonies had a much greater mix of people than either New England or the Southern Colonies.

New Netherland Becomes New York

As you have read, the Dutch set up the colony of New Netherland along the Hudson River. In the colony's early years, settlers traded with Indians for furs and built the settlement of New Amsterdam into a thriving port. Since beaver skins were very valuable, most people came to the colonies to trade furs.

To encourage farming in New Netherland, Dutch officials granted large parcels of land to a few rich families. A single land grant could stretch for miles. Indeed, one grant was as big as Rhode Island! Owners of these huge estates were called **patroons.** In return for the grant, each patroon promised to settle at least 50 European farm families on the land. Few farmers wanted to work for the patroons, however. Patroons had great power and could charge whatever rents they pleased.

Most settlers lived in the trading center of New Amsterdam. They came from all over Europe. Many were attracted by the chance to practice their religion freely. African slaves were in demand as well. In the early years they made up more than a quarter of the population of the town.

Dutch colonists were mainly Protestants who belonged to the Dutch Reformed Church. Still, they permitted members of other religions—including Roman Catholics, French Protestants, and Jews—to buy land. "People do not seem concerned what religion their neighbor is," wrote a shocked visitor from Virginia. "Indeed, they do not seem to care if he has any religion at all."

By 1664, the rivalry between England and the Netherlands for trade and colonies was at its height. In August of that year, English warships entered New Amsterdam's harbor. Peter Stuyvesant (STI vuh sehnt), the governor of New Netherland, swore to defend the city. However, he had few weapons and little gunpowder. Also, Stuyvesant had made himself so unpopular with his harsh rule and heavy taxes that the colonists refused to help him. In the end, he surrendered without firing a shot.

King Charles II of England then gave New Netherland to his brother, the Duke of York. He renamed the colony New York in the duke's honor.

New Jersey Separates From New York

At the time of the English takeover, New York stretched as far south as the Delaware River. The Duke of York decided that the colony was too big to govern easily. He gave some of the land to friends, Lord Berkeley and Sir George Carteret. They set up a proprietary (proh PRI uh tehr ee) colony, which they called New Jersey, in 1664.

In setting up a **proprietary colony,** the king gave land to one or more people in return for a yearly payment. These proprietors were free to divide the land and rent it to others. They made laws for the colony but had to respect the rights of colonists under English law.

Like New York, New Jersey had fertile farmland and a wealth of other resources that attracted people from many lands. Settlers came from Finland, Ireland, Scotland, Germany, and Sweden. There were also English and Dutch settlers who moved there from the colony of New York. In addition, some New England colonists, hoping to find better farmland, chose to relocate to New Jersey.

In 1702, New Jersey became a **royal colony,** which is a colony under the direct control of the English crown. The colony's charter protected religious freedom and the rights of an assembly that voted on local matters.

An American Profile

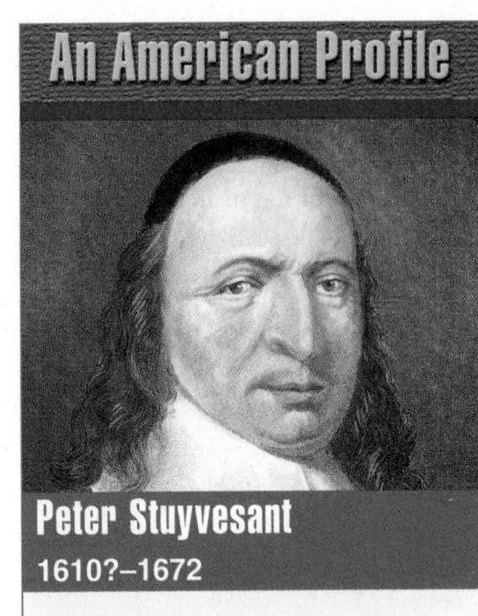

Peter Stuyvesant

1610?–1672

When Peter Stuyvesant arrived in New Amsterdam in 1647, the town was in chaos. "I shall govern you as a father his children," he told the colonists. On his orders, roaming pigs were fenced in. Outdoor toilets were removed from public streets. A new police force patrolled the town after dark. With his big sword, heavy mustache, and silver-tipped wooden leg, Stuyvesant was a commanding sight. Many colonists disliked him. They said he dressed like a one-legged peacock and that he ruled them like the czar of Russia. Even so, Stuyvesant restored law and order in New Amsterdam.

How does your town or county protect the health and safety of its citizens?

Identify Supporting Details

List the subheads under "The Founding of Pennsylvania." As you read, list one or two facts about each subhead.

The Founding of Pennsylvania

West of New Jersey, William Penn founded the colony of Pennsylvania in 1681. Penn came from a wealthy English family and was a personal friend of King Charles II. At age 22, however, Penn shocked family and friends by joining the **Quakers,** one of the most despised religious groups in England.

The Quakers Like Pilgrims and Puritans, Quakers were Protestant reformers. Their reforms went further than those of other groups, however. Quakers believed that all people—men and women, nobles and commoners—were equal in God's sight. They allowed women to preach in public and refused to bow or remove their hats in the presence of nobles. Quakers spoke out against all war and refused to serve in the army.

To most English people, Quaker beliefs seemed wicked. In both England and New England, Quakers were arrested, fined, or even hanged for their ideas. Penn became convinced that the Quakers must leave England. He turned to the king for help.

Charles II issued a royal charter naming Penn proprietor of a large tract of land in North America. The king named the new colony Pennsylvania, or Penn's woodlands.

A Policy of Fairness Penn thought of his colony as a "holy experiment." He wanted it to be a model of religious freedom, peace, and Christian living. Protestants, Catholics, and Jews went to Pennsylvania to escape persecution. Later, English officials forced Penn to turn away Catholic and Jewish settlers.

Penn's Quaker beliefs led him to speak out for fair treatment of Native Americans. Penn believed that the land in North America belonged to the Indians. He insisted that settlers should pay for the land. Native Americans respected him for this policy. As a result, Pennsylvania colonists enjoyed many years of peace with their Indian neighbors. One settler remarked, "as Penn treated the Indians with extraordinary humanity, they became civil and loving to us."

The Colony Grows Penn sent pamphlets describing his colony all over Europe. Soon, settlers from England, Scotland, Wales, the Netherlands, France, and Germany began to cross the Atlantic Ocean to Pennsylvania.

Among the new arrivals were large numbers of German-speaking Protestants. They became known as **Pennsylvania Dutch** because people could not pronounce the word Deutsch (DOICH), which means German. African slaves were also brought to Pennsylvania. They made up about one third of all new arrivals to the colony between 1730 and 1750. Most stayed in Philadelphia, working as laborers.

Penn carefully planned a capital city along the Delaware River. He named it Philadelphia, a Greek word meaning "brotherly love." Philadelphia grew quickly. By 1710, a visitor wrote that it was "the most noble, large, and well-built city I have seen."

Delaware For a time, Pennsylvania included some lands along the lower Delaware River. The region was known as Pennsylvania's Lower Counties.

Primary Source

A Letter to the Native Americans

Before he would allow people to settle his colony, William Penn insisted on establishing good relations with the Native Americans. He wrote this letter:

"The king of the country where I live hath given me a great province, but I desire to enjoy it with your love and consent, that we may always live together as neighbors and friends, else what would the great God say to us, who hath made us not to devour and destroy one another, but live soberly and kindly together in the world. . . ."

—William Penn, Letter to the Indians, 1681

Analyzing Primary Sources
How does Penn explain his belief about living peacefully with Native Americans?

Settlers in the Lower Counties did not want to send delegates to a distant assembly in Philadelphia. In 1701, Penn allowed them to elect their own assembly. Later, in 1704, the Lower Counties would break away to form the colony of Delaware.

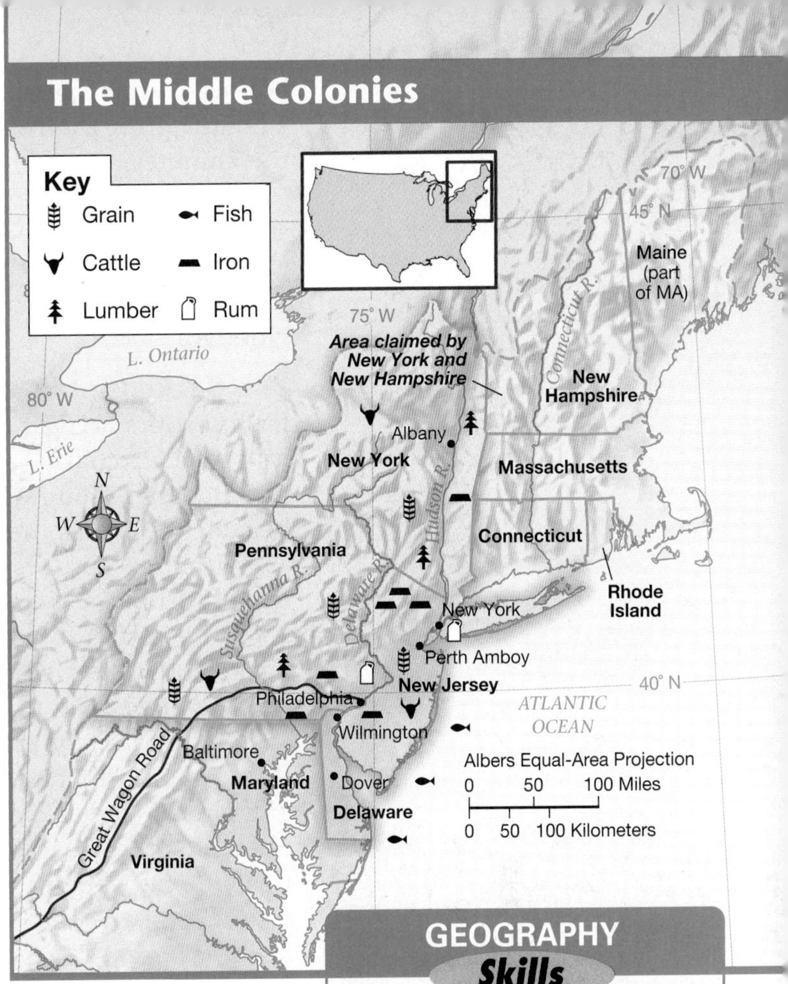

Life in the Middle Colonies

The majority of the people made their living by farming. Farmers found more favorable conditions in the Middle Colonies than in New England. The broad Hudson and Delaware river valleys were rich and fertile. Winters were milder than in New England, and the growing season lasted longer.

A Thriving Economy in the Eastern Counties On such promising land, farmers in the eastern counties of the Middle Colonies cleared their fields. They raised wheat, barley, and rye. These were **cash crops,** or crops that are sold for money at market. In fact, the Middle Colonies exported so much grain that they became known as the Breadbasket Colonies.

Farmers of the Middle Colonies also raised herds of cattle and pigs. Every year, they sent tons of beef, pork, and butter to the ports of New York and Philadelphia. From there, the goods went by ship to New England and the South or to the West Indies, England, and other parts of Europe.

Farms in the Middle Colonies were generally larger than those in New England. Landowners hired workers to help with the planting, harvesting, and other tasks. Enslaved African Americans worked on a few large farms. However, most workers were farmhands who worked alongside the families that owned the land.

Aside from farmers, there were also skilled artisans in the Middle Colonies. Encouraged by William Penn, skilled German craftsworkers set up shop in Pennsylvania. In time, the colony became a center of manufacturing and crafts. One visitor reported that workshops turned out "hardware, clocks, watches, locks, guns, flints, glass, stoneware, nails, [and] paper."

Settlers in the Delaware River valley profited from the region's rich deposits of iron ore. Heating the ore in furnaces, they purified it and then hammered it into nails, tools, and parts for guns.

Middle Colony Homes Because houses tended to be far apart in the Middle Colonies, towns were less important than in New England. Counties, rather than villages, became centers of local government.

The different groups who settled the Middle Colonies had their own favorite ways of building. Swedish settlers introduced log cabins to the Americas. The Dutch used red bricks to build narrow, high-walled

The Middle Colonies

GEOGRAPHY *Skills*

The Middle Colonies were located to the south and west of New England and north of the Southern Colonies.

1. **Location** On the map, locate: **(a)** New York, **(b)** New Jersey, **(c)** Pennsylvania, **(d)** Delaware, **(e)** Hudson River, **(f)** Philadelphia, **(g)** Great Wagon Road.
2. **Movement** Identify two ways settlers could have traveled inland from the Atlantic coast.
3. **Critical Thinking Analyzing Information** Based on the map, why do you think Philadelphia would become a major trading center?

houses. German settlers developed a wood-burning stove that heated a home better than a fireplace, which let blasts of cold air leak down the chimney.

Everyone in a household had a job to do. Households were self-sufficient, which meant that everything needed for survival—food, clothing, and any other items—was made at home. As one farmer said, "Nothing to wear, eat, or drink was purchased, as my farm provided all."

The Backcountry In the 1700s, thousands of German and Scotch-Irish settlers arrived in Philadelphia. From there, they traveled west into the backcountry, the area of land along the eastern slopes of the Appalachian Mountains. Settlers followed an old Iroquois trail that became known as the Great Wagon Road.

Although settlers planned to follow farming methods they had used in Europe, they found the challenge of farming the backcountry more difficult than they had thought it would be. To farm the backcountry, settlers had to clear thick forests. From Indians, settlers learned how to use knots from pine trees as candles to light their homes. They made wooden dishes from logs, gathered honey from hollows in trees, and hunted wild animals for food. German gunsmiths developed a lightweight rifle for use in forests. Sharpshooters boasted that the "Pennsylvania rifle" could hit a rattlesnake between the eyes at 100 yards.

Many of the settlers who arrived in the backcountry moved onto Indian lands. "The Indians . . . are alarmed at the swarm of strangers," one Pennsylvania official reported. "We are afraid of a [fight] between them for the [colonists] are very rough to them." On more than one occasion, disputes between settlers and Indians resulted in violence.

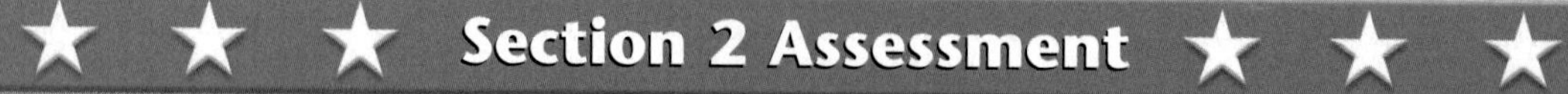

Section 2 Assessment

Recall

1. **Identify** Explain the significance of **(a)** Peter Stuyvesant, **(b)** William Penn, **(c)** Quakers, **(d)** Pennsylvania Dutch.
2. **Define** **(a)** patroon, **(b)** proprietary colony, **(c)** royal colony, **(d)** cash crop.

Comprehension

3. How did New Netherland become New York?
4. Why did New Jersey become a proprietary colony?
5. Why did the Quakers settle Pennsylvania?
6. How did life in the Middle Colonies differ from life in the backcountry?

Critical Thinking and Writing

7. **Exploring the Main Idea** Review the Main Idea statement at the beginning of this section. Then, write a paragraph explaining why settlers were attracted to the Middle Colonies.
8. **Comparing** **(a)** How was Penn's "holy experiment" like the Puritan idea of setting an example for the world? **(b)** How was it different?

ACTIVITY

Connecting to Today
Descendants of the Pennsylvania Dutch still live in Pennsylvania today. Use the Internet to find out about the Pennsylvania Dutch. Write a brief report or create a short Powerpoint presentation describing how and where they live. For help in completing the activity, visit PHSchool.com, **Web Code mfd-0401.**

3 The Southern Colonies

Prepare to Read

Objectives

In this section, you will
- Explain Maryland's religious beginnings.
- Describe how the Carolinas and Georgia were founded.
- Identify two ways of life that developed in the Southern Colonies.
- Summarize slave trade growth in the 1700s.

Key Terms

Mason-Dixon Line
Act of Toleration
Bacon's Rebellion
indigo
debtor
slave code
racism

Target Reading Skill

Cause and Effect Copy the chart below. As you read, complete the chart to show the causes that led to the founding of the Southern Colonies. Add as many boxes as you need.

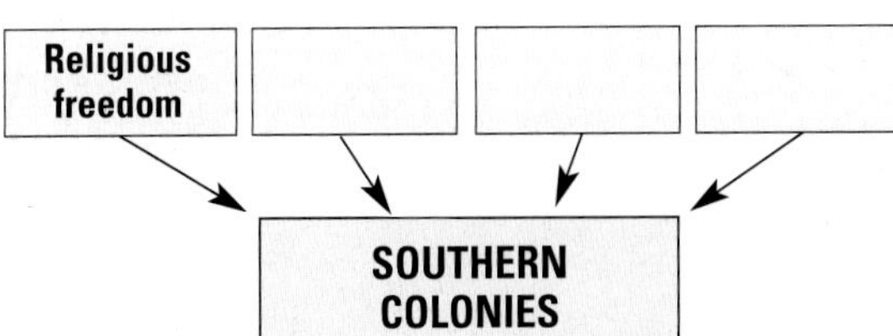

Main Idea The large tobacco and rice plantations of the Tidewater region contrasted with the settlements of hunters and farmers in the backcountry.

Setting the Scene In 1763, two English surveyors, Charles Mason and Jeremiah Dixon, began a remarkable journey that lasted nearly four years. Their mission was to survey the 244-mile boundary between Pennsylvania and Maryland.

Mason and Dixon used surveyors' instruments and long chains to map their line. As they went, they carefully laid stone markers on the border between the two colonies. If the line crossed a river, they stretched chains across to measure. If the line went up hills or through swamps, Mason and Dixon followed. More than once, fierce thunderstorms swirled around them:

> "The Lightning . . . continued [in] streams or streaks, from the Cloud to the ground all round us; about 5 minutes before the hurricane of wind and Rain; the Cloud from the Western part of the Mountain put on the most Dreadful appearance I ever saw . . ."
>
> —Charles Mason *Journal,* August 4, 1766

Charles Mason and Jeremiah Dixon

The **Mason-Dixon Line** was more than just the boundary between Pennsylvania and Maryland. It also divided the Middle Colonies from the Southern Colonies. South of the Mason-Dixon Line, the Southern Colonies developed a way of life different in many ways from that of the other English colonies.

Lord Baltimore's Colony of Maryland

In 1632, Sir George Calvert persuaded King Charles I to grant him land for a colony in the Americas. Calvert had ruined his career in Protestant England by becoming a Roman Catholic. Now, he planned to build a colony where Catholics could practice their religion freely.

He named the colony Maryland in honor of Queen Henrietta Maria, the king's wife.

Calvert died before his colony could get underway. His son Cecil, Lord Baltimore, pushed on with the project.

Settling the Colony In the spring of 1634, about 200 colonists landed along the upper Chesapeake Bay, across from England's first southern colony, Virginia. Maryland was truly a land of plenty. Chesapeake Bay was full of fish, oysters, and crabs. Across the bay, Virginians were already growing tobacco for profit. Maryland's new settlers hoped to do the same.

Remembering the early problems at Jamestown, the newcomers avoided the swampy lowlands. They built their first town, St. Mary's, in a drier location.

As proprietor of the colony, Lord Baltimore appointed a governor and a council of advisers. He gave colonists a role in government by creating an elected assembly. Eager to attract settlers to Maryland, Lord Baltimore made generous land grants to anyone who brought over servants, women, and children.

A few women took advantage of Lord Baltimore's offer of land. Two sisters, Margaret and Mary Brent, arrived in Maryland in 1638 with nine male servants. In time, they set up two plantations of about 1,000 acres each. Later, Margaret Brent helped prevent a rebellion among the governor's soldiers. The Maryland assembly praised her efforts, saying that "the colony's safety at any time [was better] in her hands than in any man's."

Religious Tolerance To make sure Maryland continued to grow, Lord Baltimore welcomed Protestants as well as Catholics to the colony.

Later, Lord Baltimore came to fear that Protestants might try to deprive Catholics of their right to worship freely. In 1649, he asked the assembly to pass an **Act of Toleration.** The law provided religious freedom for all Christians. As in many colonies, this freedom did not extend to Jews.

Bacon's Rebellion Meanwhile, English settlers continued to arrive in Virginia, attracted by the promise of profits from tobacco. Wealthy planters, however, controlled the best lands near the coast. Newcomers had to push farther inland, onto Indian lands.

As in New England, conflicts over land led to fighting between some white settlers and Indians. After several bloody clashes, settlers called on the governor to take action against Native Americans. The governor refused. He was unwilling to act, in part because he profited from his own fur trade with Indians. Frontier settlers were furious.

Finally, in 1676, Nathaniel Bacon, an ambitious young planter, organized angry men and women on the frontier. He raided Native American villages, regardless of whether the Indians there had been friendly to the colonists or not. Then, he led his followers to Jamestown and burned the capital.

The uprising, known as **Bacon's Rebellion,** lasted only a short time. When Bacon died suddenly, the revolt fell apart. The governor hanged 23 of Bacon's followers. Still, he could not stop English settlers from moving onto Indian lands along the frontier.

The Carolinas

South of Virginia and Maryland, English colonists settled in a region which they called the Carolinas. In 1663, a group of eight English nobles received a grant of land from King Charles II. Settlement took place in two separate areas, one in the north and the other in the south.

In the northern part of the Carolinas, settlers were mostly poor tobacco farmers who had drifted south from Virginia. They tended to have small farms. Eventually, in 1712, the colony became known as North Carolina.

Farther south, the group of eight English nobles set up a larger colony. The largest settlement, Charles Town, sprang up where the Ashley and Cooper rivers met. Later, Charles Town's name was shortened to Charleston. The colony became known as South Carolina in 1719.

Most early settlers in Charleston were English people who had been living in Barbados, a British colony in the Caribbean. Later, other immigrants arrived, including Germans, Swiss, French Protestants, and Spanish Jews.

Rise of Plantation Slavery Around 1685, a few planters discovered that rice grew well in the swampy lowlands along the coast. However, they were unable to grow rich crops until slaves from rice-growing areas of Africa arrived in the colony. Before long, Carolina rice was a profitable crop traded around the world. Settlers in southern Carolina later learned to raise **indigo,** a plant used to make a valuable blue dye.

Carolina planters needed large numbers of workers to grow rice. At first, they tried to enslave local Indians; however, many Indians died of disease or mistreatment, while others escaped into the forests.

Planters then turned to slaves from Africa. By 1700, most people coming to Charleston were African men and women brought against their will. Soon, African Americans in South Carolina outnumbered European Americans by more than two to one. On the mainland of North America, South Carolina was the only English colony where African Americans made up the majority of the population.

Georgia

The last of England's 13 colonies was carved out of the southern part of South Carolina. James Oglethorpe, a respected English soldier and energetic reformer, founded Georgia in 1732. He wanted the new colony to be a

GEOGRAPHY *Skills*

The five Southern Colonies stretched along the Atlantic coast from Maryland to Georgia. Farm products and lumber were important to the economy of the region.

1. **Location** On the map, locate: **(a)** Maryland, **(b)** Virginia, **(c)** North Carolina, **(d)** South Carolina, **(e)** Georgia, **(f)** Chesapeake Bay, **(g)** Charles Town.
2. **Place** Describe the area where cattle herding took place.
3. **Critical Thinking Comparing** Compare this map to the maps on pages 103 and 111. **(a)** What crops were grown only in the Southern Colonies? **(b)** Why do you think such products were not grown farther north?

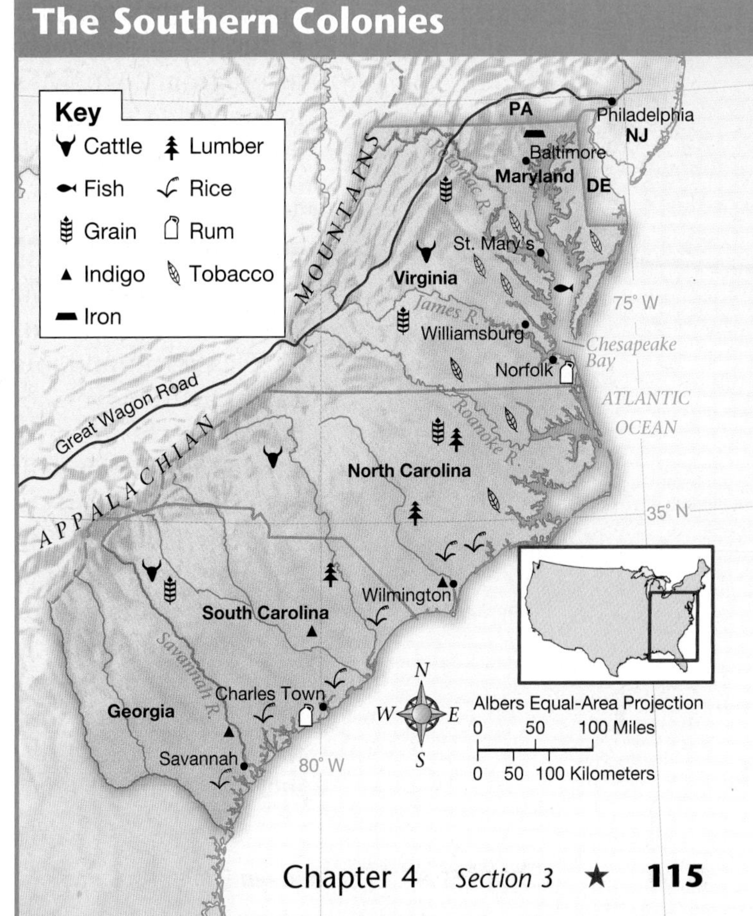

Recognizing Multiple Causes

A cause makes something happen. Why did James Oglethorpe found Georgia?

place where **debtors,** or people who owed money they could not pay back, could make a fresh start.

Under English law, the government could imprison debtors until they paid what they owed. If they ever got out of jail, debtors often had no money and no place to live. Oglethorpe offered to pay for debtors and other poor people to travel to Georgia. "In America," he said, "there are enough fertile lands to feed all the poor of England."

In 1733, Oglethorpe and 120 colonists built the colony's first settlement at Savannah, above the Savannah River. Oglethorpe set strict rules for the colony. Farms could be no bigger than 500 acres, and slavery was forbidden.

At first, Georgia grew slowly. Later, however, Oglethorpe changed the rules to allow large plantations and slave labor. After that, the colony grew more quickly.

Two Ways of Life

Today, we often think of the colonial South as a land where wealthy planters lived in elegant homes, with large numbers of enslaved African Americans toiling in the fields. In fact, this picture is only partly true. As the Southern Colonies grew, two distinct ways of life emerged—one along the Atlantic coast and another in the backcountry.

Tidewater Plantations The Southern Colonies enjoyed warmer weather and a longer growing season than the colonies to the north. Virginia, Maryland, and parts of North Carolina all became major tobacco-growing areas. Settlers in South Carolina and Georgia raised rice and indigo.

Colonists soon found that it was most profitable to raise tobacco and rice on large plantations. As you recall, a plantation is a large estate farmed by many workers. On these southern plantations, anywhere from 20 to 100 slaves did most of the work. Most slaves worked in the fields. Others were skilled workers, such as carpenters, barrel makers, or blacksmiths. Still other slaves worked in the main house as cooks, servants, or housekeepers.

The earliest planters settled along rivers and creeks of the coastal plain. Because the land was washed by ocean tides, the region was known as the Tidewater. The Tidewater's gentle slopes and rivers offered rich farmland for plantations.

Farther inland, planters settled along rivers. Rivers provided an easy way to move goods to market. Planters loaded crops onto ships bound for the West Indies and Europe. On the return trip, the ships carried English manufactured goods and other luxuries for planters and their families.

Most Tidewater plantations had their own docks along the river, and merchant ships picked up crops and delivered goods directly to them. For this reason, few large seaport cities developed in the Southern Colonies.

Only a small percentage of white southerners owned large plantations. Yet, planters set the style of southern living. Life centered around the Great House. There, the planter's family lived in elegant quarters, including a parlor for visitors, a dining room, and guest bedrooms.

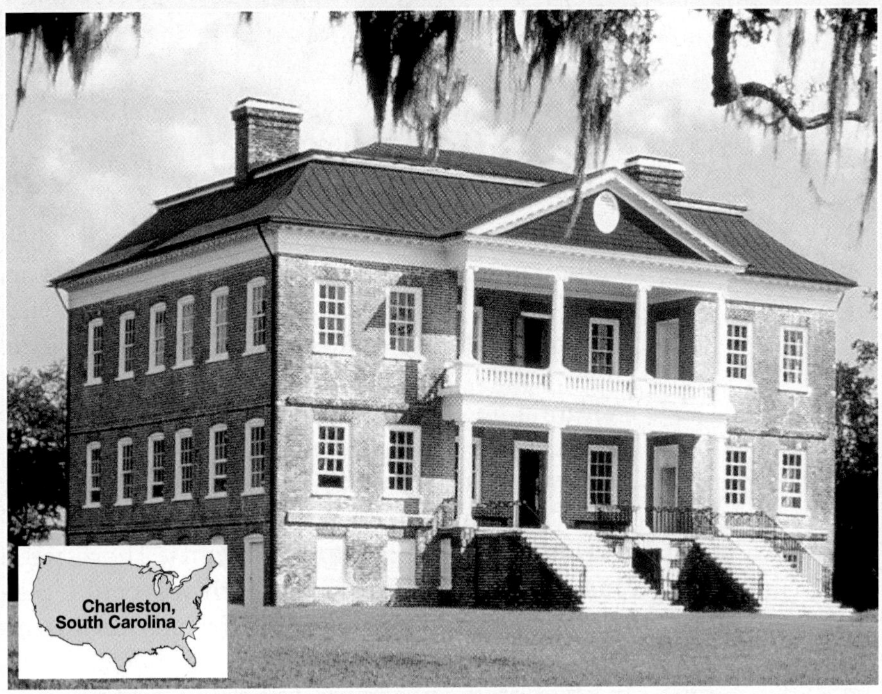

Drayton Hall

By the 1700s, there were plantations in South Carolina that produced cash crops such as rice, tobacco, and indigo. One plantation in Charleston, South Carolina, was Drayton Hall. Completed in 1742, it is one of the oldest surviving plantation houses in the South.

Virtual Field Trip For an interactive look at the Drayton Hall, visit PHSchool.com, **Web Code mfd-0402.**

During the growing season, planters decided which fields to plant, what crops to grow, and when to harvest the crops. Planters' wives kept the household running smoothly. They directed house slaves and made sure daily tasks were done, such as milking cows.

Enslaved Africans played a crucial role on many plantations. They used farming skills they had brought from West Africa. With their help, English settlers learned how to grow rice. Africans also knew how to use wild plants unfamiliar to the English. They made water buckets out of gourds, and they used palmetto leaves to make fans, brooms, and baskets.

The Backcountry South West of the Tidewater, life was very different. Here, at the base of the Appalachians, rolling hills and thick forests covered the land. As in the Middle Colonies, this inland area was called the backcountry. Attracted by rich soil, settlers followed the Great Wagon Road into the backcountry of Maryland, Virginia, and the Carolinas.

The backcountry was more democratic than the Tidewater. Settlers there were more likely to treat one another as equals. Men tended smaller fields of tobacco or garden crops such as beans, corn, or peas. They also hunted game. Largely self-sufficient, these farmers provided all the food they needed. Surplus goods were sold at local markets. Women cooked meals and fashioned simple, rugged clothing out of wool or deerskins. Another major difference between the backcountry and the Tidewater was slavery. Few enslaved Africans worked on the smaller farms in the backcountry.

The hardships of backcountry life brought settlers closer together. Families gathered to husk corn or help one another build barns. Spread out along the edge of the Appalachians, these hardy settlers felled trees, grew crops, and changed the face of the land.

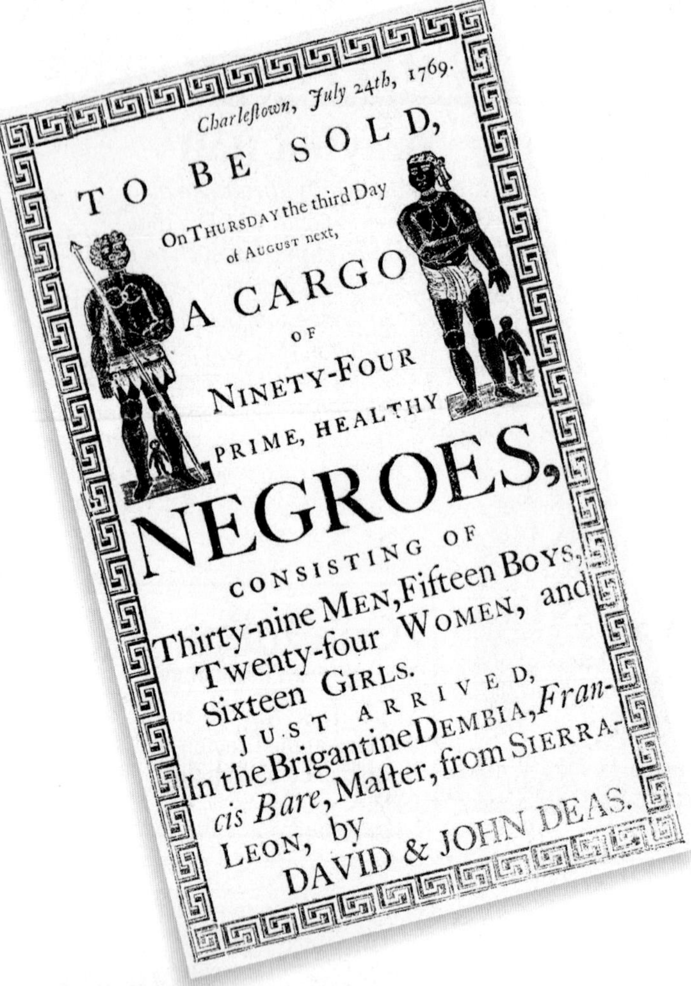

Growth of Slavery and the Slave Trade

In the early years, Africans in the English colonies included free people and servants as well as slaves. Indeed, during the 1600s, even Africans who were enslaved enjoyed some freedom. The first enslaved Africans arrived in Virginia in 1619. However, for the next fifty years, since the African population was small, the status of Africans in the colony was not clearly established. Some Africans were enslaved and some became servants. There were instances where enslaved Africans could purchase their freedom. Several Africans during the 1600s, such as Anthony Johnson, became successful property owners. In South Carolina some enslaved Africans worked without supervision as cowboys, herding cattle to market.

By 1700, plantations in the Southern Colonies had come to rely on slave labor. After a time, slaves made up the majority of the population in South Carolina and Georgia. Slaves cleared the land, worked the crops, and tended the livestock. In order to maintain the supply of slaves, southern planters relied on a system of slave trading that stretched halfway across the globe.

Viewing History

The Sale of Africans The selling of Africans as slaves was legal in the colonies. In this advertisement, the details of the sale are listed. By the late 1700s, nearly 500,000 enslaved Africans lived in the Southern Colonies.

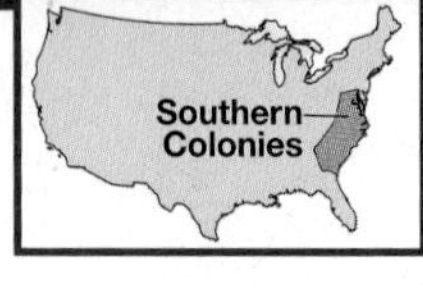

Analyzing Information
Where did the slaves advertised on the poster come from?

Slavery in Africa In Africa, as elsewhere around the world, slavery had been part of the social and economic system since ancient times. Usually, slaves were people who had been captured in war. Slaves were part of a community and were often treated as servants rather than property. In Africa, traders often transported and sold slaves as laborers. Muslim merchants also carried African slaves into Europe and the Middle East.

Over a period of less than 400 years, as the transatlantic slave trade grew, millions of Africans were enslaved. Slave traders from many Western European nations set up posts along the West African coast. They offered guns and other goods in exchange for slaves. As the demand for slaves increased, Africans who lived along the coast made raids into the interior, seeking captives to sell to the Europeans. They marched their captives to the coast. There, the slaves were loaded aboard European ships headed for the Americas.

The Middle Passage In the 1700s, English sailors began referring to the passage of slave ships west across the Atlantic Ocean as the Middle Passage. Below the decks of the slave ships, slaves were crammed tightly together on shelves. One observer noted that they were "chained to each other hand and foot, and stowed so close, that they were not allowed above a foot and a half for each in breadth." The captives were allowed above deck to eat and exercise in the fresh air only once or twice a day.

Many enslaved Africans resisted, but only a few escaped. Some fought for their freedom during the trip. They would stage a mutiny or revolt. The slave traders lived in constant fear of this and were heavily armed. Other slaves resisted by refusing to eat or even jumping overboard to avoid a life of slavery.

Records of slave ships show that about 10 percent of Africans loaded aboard a ship for passage to the Americas died during the voyage. Many died of illnesses that spread rapidly in the filthy, crowded conditions inside a ship's hold. Others died of mistreatment. The Atlantic slave trade would last about 400 years. During that time, it may have caused the deaths of as many as 2 to 3 million Africans.

Limiting Rights As the importance of slavery increased, greater limits were placed on the rights of slaves. Colonists passed laws that set out rules for slaves' behavior and denied slaves their basic rights. These **slave codes** treated enslaved Africans not as human beings but as property.

Most English colonists did not question the justice of owning slaves. They believed that black Africans were inferior to white Europeans. The belief that one race is superior to another is called **racism.** Some colonists believed that they were helping slaves by introducing them to Christianity.

A handful of colonists spoke out against the evils of slavery. In 1688, Quakers in Germantown, Pennsylvania, became the first group of colonists to call for an end to slavery.

Primary Source

Surviving the Middle Passage

Olaudah Equiano (oh LAW dah ehk wee AH noh), an enslaved African, recalled an incident from his trip on a slave ship:

"One day . . . two of my wearied countrymen who were chained together. . . jumped into the sea; immediately another . . . followed their example . . . . Two of the wretches were drowned, but [the ship's crew] got the other, and afterwards flogged him unmercifully for thus attempting to prefer death to slavery."

—Olaudah Equiano, *The Interesting Narrative of the Life of Olaudah Equiano,* 1789

Analyzing Primary Sources

How does Equiano use language to express his feelings about the Middle Passage?

★ ★ ★ Section 3 Assessment ★ ★ ★

Recall

1. **Identify** Explain the significance of **(a)** Mason-Dixon Line, **(b)** Lord Baltimore, **(c)** Act of Toleration, **(d)** Bacon's Rebellion, **(e)** James Oglethorpe.
2. **Define** **(a)** indigo, **(b)** debtor, **(c)** slave code, **(d)** racism.

Comprehension

3. Why did Lord Baltimore set up the colony of Maryland?
4. Why was Georgia called a "haven for debtors"?
5. How was life in the Tidewater different from life in the backcountry South?
6. What role did Africans play in the economy of the Southern Colonies by 1700?

Critical Thinking and Writing

7. **Exploring the Main Idea** Review the Main Idea statement at the beginning of this section. List the reasons why you think tensions might have developed between the backcountry and the Tidewater.
8. **Analyzing Information** Review the discussion of religious tolerance. Did Maryland's Act of Toleration provide true religious tolerance? Write your answer in a paragraph.

Activity

Creating Flashcards

Do you get confused about the 13 English colonies? Use the text, including the maps and charts, to create 13 flashcards. On one side, write the name of a colony. On the other, write three facts about that colony. You may later use these cards for review.

4 Roots of Self-Government

Prepare to Read

Objectives

In this section, you will
- Summarize why England wanted to regulate colonial trade.
- Describe colonial governments.
- Explain how the liberties of the colonists were limited.

Key Terms

mercantilism
export
import
Navigation Acts
Yankee
triangular trade
legislature
Glorious Revolution
bill of rights
English Bill of Rights

Target Reading Skill

Clarifying Meaning As you read, prepare an outline of this section. Use roman numerals to indicate the major headings, capital letters for subheadings, and numbers for the supporting details. The sample below will help you get started.

I. **England Regulates Trade**
  A.
    1.
    2.
II. **Trade in Rum and Slaves**
  A.
  B.
  C.
III. **Colonial Government**

Main Idea During the late 1600s and 1700s, England regulated colonial trade, while colonial legislatures passed laws.

Horse-drawn carriage

Setting the Scene Young Stephen Lamb hardly had time to look up before it was too late. A horse-drawn cart raced by, and the next instant Stephen was pulled beneath the wheels. One of Boston's newspapers reported the sad news: "A Child of about Five Years old, at the South End of the Town, was run over by a Cart, and died immediately after."

The streets in colonial cities like Boston had become busy—and sometimes dangerous—by the early 1700s. Farmers drove cattle, pigs, and sheep to market along narrow cobblestone streets. New York merchants complained that "Mischievous Mastiffs, Bull Doggs and Other Useless Dogs" chased their cattle and horses. Philadelphia spaced wooden posts along both sides of its main streets. The posts protected pedestrians from the "excessive Galloping, Trotting & Pacing of Horses."

Colonial city streets were becoming hazardous because there was so much activity. By the 1700s, trade flourished all along the Atlantic coast. As trade increased, England began to take a new interest in its colonies.

England Regulates Trade

Like other European nations at the time, England believed that its colonies should benefit the home country. This belief was part of an economic theory known as **mercantilism** (MER kuhn tihl ihz uhm). According to this theory, a nation became strong by keeping strict control over its trade. As one English gentleman put it, "Whosoever commands the trade of the world commands the riches of the world."

Mercantilists thought that a country should export more than it imported. **Exports** are goods sent to markets outside a country. **Imports** are goods brought into a country. If England sold more goods abroad, gold would flow into the home country as payment for those exports.

Beginning in the 1650s, the English Parliament passed a series of Navigation Acts that regulated trade between England and its colonies. The purpose of these laws was to ensure that only England benefited from colonial trade.

Under the new laws, only colonial or English ships could carry goods to and from the colonies. The Navigation Acts also listed certain products, such as tobacco and cotton, that colonial merchants could ship only to England. In this way, Parliament created jobs for English workers who cut and rolled tobacco or spun cotton into cloth.

The Navigation Acts helped the colonies as well as England. For example, the law encouraged colonists to build their own ships. As a result, New England became a prosperous shipbuilding center. Also, because of the acts, colonial merchants did not have to compete with foreign merchants because they were sure of having a market for their goods in England.

Still, many colonists resented the Navigation Acts. In their view, the laws favored English merchants. Colonial merchants often ignored the Navigation Acts or found ways to get around them.

Viewing History

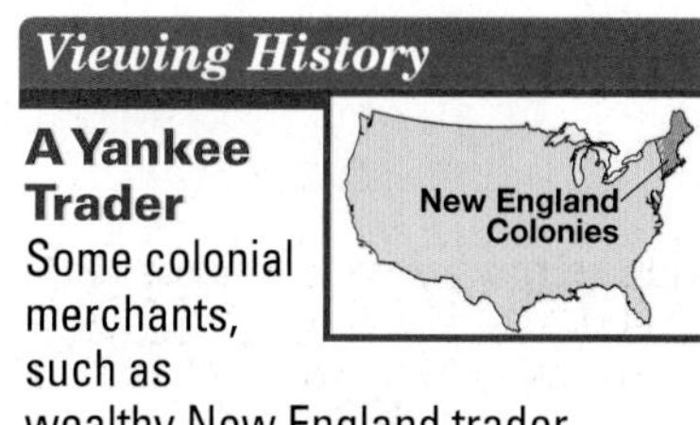

A Yankee Trader Some colonial merchants, such as wealthy New England trader Moses Marcy, benefited from the Navigation Acts. **Drawing Inferences** ***How can you tell that Moses Marcy is successful?***

Trade in Rum and Slaves

The colonies produced a wide variety of goods, and merchant ships sailed up and down the Atlantic coast. Merchants from New England dominated colonial trade. They were known as Yankees, a nickname that implied they were clever and hard-working. Yankee traders earned a reputation for profiting from any deal.

Colonial merchants developed many trade routes. One route was known as the triangular trade because the three legs of the route formed a triangle. On the first leg, ships from New England carried fish, lumber, and other goods to the West Indies. There, Yankee traders bought molasses—a dark-brown syrup made from sugar cane—and sugar. The ships then sailed back to New England, where colonists used the molasses and sugar to make rum.

On the second leg of the journey, ships carried rum, guns, gunpowder, cloth, and tools from New England to West Africa. In Africa, Yankee merchants traded these goods for slaves. On the final leg, ships carried enslaved Africans to the West Indies. With the profits from selling the enslaved Africans, traders bought more molasses.

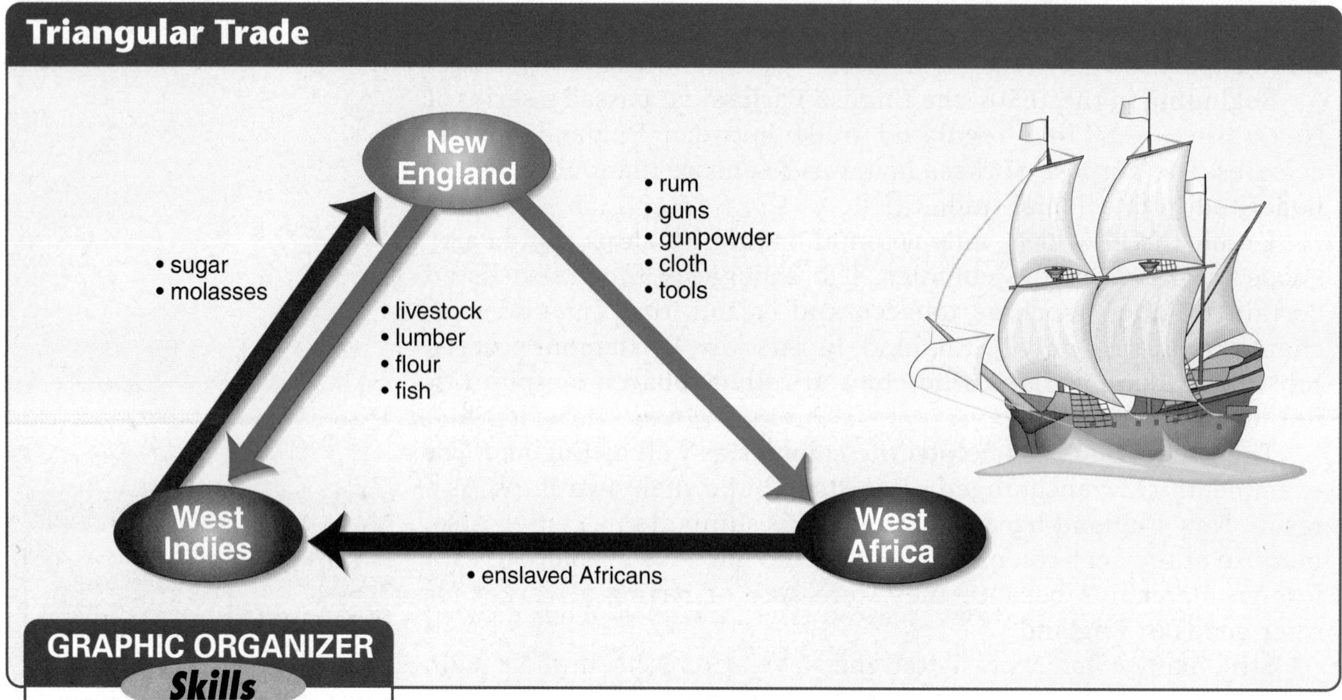

GRAPHIC ORGANIZER *Skills*

Colonists traded with the West Indies, Africa, and Europe in a route known as the triangular trade.

1. **Comprehension**
   (a) What did American ships bring to Africa?
   (b) Where were enslaved African Americans traded for molasses?
2. **Critical Thinking Making Decisions**
   How did New England benefit from the slave trade?

Economics $

Many New England merchants grew wealthy from the triangular trade. In doing so, they often disobeyed the Navigation Acts. Traders were supposed to buy sugar and molasses only from English colonies in the West Indies. However, the demand for molasses was so high that New Englanders smuggled in cargoes from the Dutch, French, and Spanish West Indies, too. Bribes made customs officials look the other way.

Colonial Government

Although each colony developed its own government, the governments had much in common. A governor directed the colony's affairs and enforced the laws. Most governors were appointed, either by the king or by the colony's proprietor. In Rhode Island and Connecticut, however, colonists elected their own governors.

Elected Assemblies Each colony also had a **legislature.** A legislature is a group of people who have the power to make laws. In most colonies, the legislature had an upper house and a lower house. The upper house was made up of advisers appointed by the governor.

The lower house was an elected assembly. It approved laws and protected the rights of citizens. Just as important, it had the right to approve any taxes the governor asked for. This "power of the purse," or right to raise or spend money, was an important check on the governor's power. Any governor who ignored the assembly risked losing his salary.

The Right to Vote Each colony had its own rules about who could vote. By the 1720s, however, all the colonies had laws that restricted the right to vote to white Christian men over the age of 21. In some colonies, only Protestants or members of a particular church could vote. All voters had to own property. Colonial leaders believed that only property owners knew what was best for a colony.

A Bill of Rights Colonists took great pride in their elected assemblies. They also valued the rights that the Magna Carta gave them as English subjects.

Colonists won still more rights as a result of the **Glorious Revolution** of 1688. Parliament removed King James II from the throne and asked William and Mary of the Netherlands to rule. In return for Parliament's support, William and Mary signed the English Bill of Rights in 1689. A **bill of rights** is a written list of freedoms the government promises to protect.

The **English Bill of Rights** protected the rights of individuals and gave anyone accused of a crime the right to a trial by jury. Just as important, the English Bill of Rights said that a ruler could not raise taxes or an army without the approval of Parliament.

Limits on Liberties

English colonists in the Americas enjoyed more freedoms than did the English themselves. However, the rights of English citizens did not extend to all colonists. Women had more rights in the colonies but far fewer rights than did free, white males. A woman's father or husband was supposed to protect her. A married woman could not start her own business or sign a contract unless her husband approved it.

In most colonies, unmarried women and widows had more rights than married women. They could make contracts and sue in court. In Maryland and the Carolinas, women settlers who headed families could buy land on the same terms as men.

Africans and Native Americans in the colonies had almost no rights. While so many colonists enjoyed English liberties, most Africans were bound in slavery. The conflict between liberty and slavery would not be resolved until the 1860s.

Target Skill **Summarize** Summarize the paragraphs under "Limits on Liberties." Add this information to your outline.

★ ★ ★ Section 4 Assessment ★ ★ ★

Recall

1. **Identify** Explain the significance of **(a)** Navigation Acts, **(b)** Yankee, **(c)** Glorious Revolution, **(d)** English Bill of Rights.
2. **Define** **(a)** mercantilism, **(b)** export, **(c)** import, **(d)** triangular trade, **(e)** legislature, **(f)** bill of rights.

Comprehension

3. List two ways in which the Navigation Acts benefited **(a)** England **(b)** the colonies.
4. How were colonial governments organized?
5. Which colonists had the right to vote?

Critical Thinking and Writing

6. **Exploring the Main Idea** Review the Main Idea statement at the beginning of this section. Then, write a paragraph in which you analyze how colonial legislatures reflected the tradition of self-rule.
7. **Making Predictions** How do you think the Navigation Acts might affect future relations between England and the colonies? Write your answer in a paragraph.

Activity

Start a Dialogue **You are a New England merchant who meets with another colonial merchant. Write a conversation you might have about trade in the colonies. Consider the Navigation Acts and triangular trade.**

Summarizing

SKILLS FOR LIFE

What were the sources of the English colonists' ideas about self-government? As you read different references to learn about these roots, you'll find it helpful to summarize information.

A document deeply rooted in the English concept of representative government is the Magna Carta signed by King John in 1215. These excerpts are from this important document.

(12) No [tax] may be levied in our kingdom without its general consent, unless it is for the ransom of our person, to make our eldest son a knight, and (once) to marry our eldest daughter. For these purposes only a reasonable [tax] may be levied.

(14) To obtain the general consent of the realm for the assessment of a [tax]—except in the three cases specified above—we will cause the archbishops, bishops, abbots, earls, and greater barons to be summoned individually by letter. To those who hold lands directly of us we will cause a general summons to be issued, through the sheriffs and other officials, to come together on a fixed day (of which at least forty days notice shall be given) and at a fixed place. In all letters of summons, the cause of the summons will be stated. When a summons has been issued, the business appointed for the day shall go forward in accordance with the resolution of those present, even if not all those who were summoned have appeared.

—The Magna Carta, 1215

King John signing the Magna Carta

Learn the Skill *To summarize information, use the following steps:*

1. **Identify the main idea.** The main idea of a passage explains its purpose. Usually, the main idea is presented in the first sentence of the passage.
2. **Look for details.** These include facts, reasons, explanations, examples, and descriptions that expand the main idea.
3. **Restate the main idea.** Put the main idea in your own words.
4. **Choose important details.** Select the most significant details to include in your summary. Remember, a summary should be brief and to the point.

Practice the Skill *Answer the following questions about the passages above:*

1. Which sentence contains the main point of these passages?
2. **(a)** What three exceptions are given? **(b)** Who has to approve the assessment of a tax? **(c)** Identify another detail about approving taxes.
3. Restate the main idea in your own words.
4. Complete your summary by adding two important details to go with your main idea statement.

Apply the Skill *See the Chapter Review and Assessment.*

5 Life in the Colonies

Prepare to Read

Objectives

In this section, you will
- List the class differences that existed in colonial society.
- Summarize how the Great Awakening affected the colonies.
- Describe education for colonial children.
- Explain how the colonies were affected by the spread of new ideas.

Key Terms

gentry
middle class
indentured servant
Great Awakening
public school
tutor
apprentice
dame school
Enlightenment
libel

Target Reading Skill

Cause and Effect Copy the cause-and-effect chart at right. As you read, complete the chart to show the effect of different factors in shaping life in the colonies. Add as many entries as you need.

CAUSES
1. Puritan belief in education
2.
3.

LIFE IN THE COLONIES

EFFECTS
1. Public school system in New England
2.
3.

Main Idea During the 1700s, England's 13 colonies became societies with their own ideas and traditions.

Setting the Scene On a warm May day in the 1750s, a parade made its way down a main street in Newport, Rhode Island. Most of the city's Africans had turned out for a holiday known as Negro Election Day. Dressed in their finest clothes, enslaved and free Africans alike sang and marched. One resident recalled:

> "All the various languages of Africa, mixed with broken . . . English, filled the air, accompanied with the music of the fiddle, tambourine, the banjo [and African] drum."
>
> —Henry Bull, *Memoir of Rhode Island,* 1837

African drum

Similar parades took place throughout New England. Each year, at about the time white New Englanders voted for their colonial government, Africans elected a leader of their community. The winner's job was to settle disputes that arose among black townspeople during the year.

Negro Election Day was a truly American custom, blending traditions from Africa and England. As the American colonies grew in the 1700s, they became more than rough settlements. Gradually, old customs and ideas were being shaped into a new culture that was distinctly American.

Colonial Society

For the most part, colonists enjoyed more social equality than people in England, where a person's opportunities in life were largely determined by birth. Still, class differences existed. Like Europeans, colonial Americans thought it was only natural that some people rank more highly than others. A person's birth and wealth still determined his or her social status.

The Gentry and the Middle Class At the top of society stood the **gentry.** The gentry included wealthy planters, merchants, ministers, successful lawyers, and royal officials. They could afford to dress in the latest fashions from London.

Below the gentry were the **middle class.** The middle class included farmers who worked their own land, skilled craftsworkers, and some tradespeople. Nearly three quarters of all white colonists belonged to the middle class. They prospered because land in the colonies was plentiful and easy to buy.

Primary Source

An Indentured Servant

This is a contract Richard Garfford entered into with Thomas Workman. Garfford wanted to become an indentured servant:

"The Condition of this obligation is such that . . . Richard Garfford . . . shall well and truly deliver or cause to be delivered [to] . . . Thomas Workman . . . in Virginia a sound and able man servant between Eighteen and 25 years of age that shall have [four] years to serve at the least, and that [when] the first second or third ship . . . [arrives] in the Port of James Ariver in Virginia from London, that then the bond above [will] be [void] . . ."

—Richard Garfford, 1654

Analyzing Primary Sources
What kind of worker is Thomas Workman looking for?

Indentured Servants The lowest social class included hired farmhands, indentured servants, and slaves. **Indentured servants** signed contracts to work without wages for a period of four to seven years for anyone who would pay their ocean passage to the Americas. When their term of service was completed, indentured servants received "freedom dues": a set of clothes, tools, and 50 acres of land. Because there were so few European women in the colonies, female indentured servants often shortened their terms of service by marrying.

Thousands of men, women, and children came to North America as indentured servants. After completing their terms, some became successful and rose into the middle class.

Women's Work in the Colonies From New Hampshire to Georgia, colonial women performed many of the same tasks. A wife took care of her household, husband, and family. By the kitchen fire, she cooked the family's meals. She milked cows, watched the children, and made clothing.

In the backcountry, wives and husbands often worked side by side in the fields at harvest time. With so much to be done, no one worried whether harvesting was proper "woman's work." One surprised visitor described a backcountry woman's activities: "She will carry a gunn in the woods and kill deer, turkeys &c., shoot down wild cattle, catch and tye hoggs, knock down [cattle] with an ax, and perform the most manfull Exercises as well as most men."

In cities, women sometimes worked outside the home. A young single woman from a poorer family might work for one of the gentry as a maid, a cook, or a nurse. Other women were midwives, who delivered babies. Still others sewed fine hats or dresses to be sold to women who could afford them. Learning such skills often required years of training.

Some women learned trades from their fathers, brothers, or husbands. They worked as butchers, shoemakers, or silversmiths. Quite a few women became printers. A woman might take over her husband's business when he died.

Identify Causes and Effects

What influence did African culture have on colonial society? Add this information to your chart.

African Cultural Influences By the mid-1700s, the culture of Africans in the colonies varied greatly. On rice plantations in South Carolina, slaves saw few white colonists. As a result, African customs remained strong. For example, parents often chose African names for their children, such as Quosh or Juba or Cuff. In some coastal areas, African Americans spoke a distinctive combination of English and West African languages known as Gullah.

In Charleston and other South Carolina port towns, many African Americans worked along the docks, making rope or barrels or helping to build ships. Skilled craftsworkers made fine wooden cabinets or silver plates and utensils. Many of their designs reflected African artistic styles. Although most Africans in these towns were enslaved, many opened their own shops or stalls in the market. Some used their earnings to buy their own and their family's freedom.

In Virginia and Maryland, Africans were less isolated from white farmers and planters. Even so, many African customs survived. For instance, mourners took part in a ceremony to speed a dead man's spirit to his home, which they believed was in Africa.

In the Middle Colonies and New England, the African population increased during the 1700s. As you have read, customs like Negro Election Day became a part of colonial life, especially in cities.

The Great Awakening

In the 1730s and 1740s, a religious movement known as the Great Awakening swept through the colonies. Its drama and emotion touched women and men of all backgrounds and classes.

Powerful Preachers A New England preacher, Jonathan Edwards, helped set off the Great Awakening. In powerful sermons, Edwards called on colonists, especially young people, to examine their lives. He preached of the sweetness and beauty of God. At the same time, he warned listeners to heed the Bible's teachings. Otherwise, they would be "sinners in the hands of an angry God," headed for the fiery torments of hell.

In 1739, when an English minister named George Whitefield arrived in the colonies, the movement spread like wildfire. Whitefield drew huge crowds to outdoor meetings. An enthusiastic and energetic preacher, his voice would ring with feeling as he called on sinners to repent. After hearing Whitefield speak, Jonathan Edwards's wife reported, "I have seen upwards of a thousand people hang on his words with breathless silence, broken only by an occasional half-suppressed sob."

Viewing History

George Whitefield George Whitefield was the most popular preacher of the Great Awakening. Nathan Cole, who attended one of Whitefield's sermons said "[he] appeared almost angelical before thousands of people with a bold, [fearless] countenance."

The English Colonies

Synthesizing Information ***Why did some American preachers oppose preachers like Whitefield?***

Impact of the Great Awakening The Great Awakening aroused bitter debate. People who supported the movement often split away from their old churches to form new ones. Opponents warned that the movement was too emotional. Still, the growth of so many new churches forced colonists to become more tolerant of people with different beliefs.

The Great Awakening contributed in another way to the spread of democratic feelings in the colonies. Many of the new preachers were not as well educated as most ministers. They argued that formal training was less important than a heart filled with the holy spirit. Such teachings encouraged a spirit of independence. Many believers felt more free to challenge authority when their liberties were at stake. People began to think differently about their political rights and their governments. They felt if they could figure out how to worship on their own, then they could govern themselves. Eventually, many of these colonists would challenge British authority.

Education in the Colonies

Among the colonists, New Englanders were the most concerned about education. Puritans taught that all people had a duty to study the Bible. If colonists did not learn to read, how would they fulfill this duty?

New England In 1642, the Massachusetts assembly passed a law ordering all parents to teach their children "to read and understand the principles of religion." They also required all towns with 50 or more families to hire a schoolteacher. Towns with 100 or more families also had to set up a grammar school to prepare boys for college.

In this way, Massachusetts set up the first **public schools,** or schools supported by taxes. Public schools allowed both rich and poor children to receive an education.

The first New England schools had only one room for students of all ages. Parents paid the schoolteacher with corn, peas, or other foods. Each child was expected to bring a share of wood to burn in the stove. Students who forgot would find themselves seated in the coldest corner of the room!

Middle and Southern Colonies In the Middle Colonies, churches and individual families set up private schools. Because pupils paid to attend, only wealthy families could afford to educate their children.

In the Southern Colonies, people lived too far from one another to bring children together in one school building. Some planters engaged **tutors,** or private teachers. The wealthiest planters sent their sons to school in England. As a rule, slaves were denied education of any kind.

Apprenticeships and Dame Schools Boys whose parents wished them to learn a trade or craft served as **apprentices** (uh PREHN tihs ehz). An apprentice worked for a master to learn a trade or a craft. For example, when a boy reached the age of 12 or 13, his parents might apprentice him to a master glassmaker. The young apprentice lived in the glassmaker's home for six or seven years while learning the craft. The glassmaker gave the boy food and clothing. He was also supposed to teach his apprentice how to read and write and provide him with religious training.

In return, the apprentice worked without pay in the glassmaker's shop and learned the skills he needed to set up his own shop. Boys were apprenticed in many trades, including papermaking and printing, and tanning (making leather).

In New England, most schools accepted only boys. However, some girls attended **dame schools,** or private schools run by women in their own homes. Other girls, though, usually learned skills from their mothers, who taught them to spin wool, weave, and embroider. A few learned to read and write.

Spread of Ideas

During the 1600s, European scientists began to use reason and logic instead of superstition to understand the world. They developed theories, and then performed experiments to test them. In doing so,

LINKING PAST AND PRESENT

▲ Past

▲ Present

they discovered many of the laws of nature. The English scientist Isaac Newton, for example, explained the law of gravity.

The Enlightenment Spreads European thinkers of the late 1600s and 1700s believed that reason and scientific methods could be applied to the study of society. They tried to discover the natural laws that governed human behavior. Because these thinkers believed in the light of human reason, the movement that they started is known as the **Enlightenment.** John Locke, an English philosopher, wrote works that were widely read in the colonies. He said people could gain knowledge of the world by observing and by experimenting.

In the 13 colonies, the Enlightenment spread among better educated colonists. They included wealthy merchants, lawyers, ministers, and others who had the leisure to read the latest books from Europe. Urban craftsmen also heard and discussed these ideas.

Benjamin Franklin The best example of the Enlightenment spirit in the 13 colonies was Benjamin Franklin. Franklin was born in 1706, the son of a poor Boston soap and candle maker. Although he had only two years of formal schooling, he used his spare time to study literature, mathematics, and foreign languages.

At age 17, Franklin made his way to Philadelphia. There, he built up a successful printing business. His most popular publication was *Poor Richard's Almanack.* Published yearly, it contained useful information and clever quotes, such as "Early to bed, early to rise, makes a man healthy, wealthy, and wise."

Viewing History

School Days

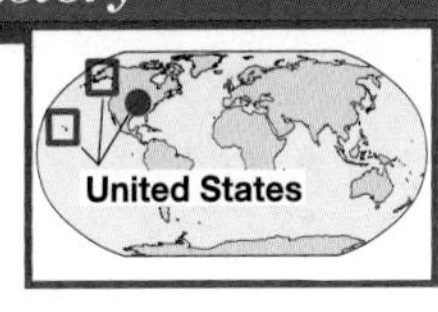

Students in colonial times attended one-room schools. Usually, they studied subjects that would help them in their daily lives. Today, students attend schools that offer many subjects and the latest technology. Sometimes, students study in special classrooms, such as computer rooms like the one shown here.

Applying Information

(a) How has public education changed since colonial times? (b) How is it the same?

Like other Enlightenment thinkers, Franklin wanted to use reason to improve the world around him. He invented practical devices such as a lightning rod, a smokeless fireplace, and bifocal glasses. As a community leader, Franklin persuaded Philadelphia officials to pave streets, organize a fire company, and set up the first lending library in the Americas. Franklin's inventions and his public service earned him worldwide fame.

Colonial Cities While most colonists lived on farms, towns and cities strongly influenced colonial life. Through the great ports of Philadelphia, New York, Boston, and Charleston, merchants shipped products overseas. Towns and cities also served as the center of a busy trade between the coast and the growing backcountry.

Culture flourished in the cities. By the mid-1700s, many colonial cities had their own theaters. City dwellers found entertainment at singing societies, traveling circuses, carnivals, and horse races.

In 1704, John Campbell founded the *Boston News-Letter,* the first regular weekly newspaper in the English colonies. Within 50 years, each of the colonies, except New Jersey and Delaware, had at least one weekly paper.

The Trial of John Peter Zenger The growth of colonial newspapers led to a dispute over freedom of the press. John Peter Zenger published the *Weekly Journal* in New York City. In 1734, he was arrested for publishing stories that criticized the governor. Zenger was put on trial for libel—the act of publishing a statement that may unjustly damage a person's reputation. Zenger's lawyer argued that, since the stories were true, his client had not committed libel. The jury agreed and freed Zenger. At the time, the case did not attract a great deal of attention. However, freedom of the press would become recognized as a basic American right.

Section 5 Assessment

Recall

1. **Identify** Explain the significance of **(a)** Great Awakening, **(b)** Jonathan Edwards, **(c)** George Whitefield, **(d)** Enlightenment, **(e)** Benjamin Franklin, **(f)** John Peter Zenger.
2. **Define** **(a)** gentry, **(b)** middle class, **(c)** indentured servant, **(d)** public school, **(e)** tutor, **(f)** apprentice, **(g)** dame school, **(h)** libel.

Comprehension

3. What social classes existed in the colonies?
4. How did the Great Awakening affect religion in the colonies?
5. Why did the Puritans support public education?
6. In what ways did Benjamin Franklin's ideas reflect the ideas of the Enlightenment?

Critical Thinking and Writing

7. **Exploring the Main Idea** Review the Main Idea statement at the beginning of this section. Then, make a list of five statements that support the main idea.
8. **Drawing Inferences** Why do you think there was greater social equality in the colonies than in England?

ACTIVITY

Go Online
PHSchool.com

Preparing a Skit
Use the Internet to find out more about the John Peter Zenger trial. Then, prepare a class skit of the trial. For help in completing the activity, visit PHSchool.com, **Web Code mfd-0403.**

Benjamin Franklin, Scientist and Inventor

In his day, Benjamin Franklin was a well-known journalist and diplomat. He was also well known for his scientific experiments and inventions.

Benjamin Franklin

Bifocals

After he turned forty, the nearsighted Franklin needed a second pair of glasses for reading. He invented bifocals. Now, he could see objects far away and read—all without changing glasses. Every major optical store still sells bifocals.

Odometer

When he was postmaster, Franklin had to map the mailing routes for surrounding towns. He came up with a simple odometer for his carriage. It counted the number of times the wheels of his wagon rotated on a trip. Today, odometers are used in cars to measure mileage.

Electricity Experiments

Franklin was curious about electricity. In some of his experiments, he used a vacuum pump (shown here). An experiment he tried in 1752 gave him the idea for a lightning rod. Variations of this device protect homes and buildings from lightning to this day.

Activity

Make a list of at least three inventions that you think would make people's lives easier, healthier, or just more fun. For each of your ideas, explain how you think it might work, whom it would benefit, and if you think it will ever be used.

CHAPTER 4

Review and Assessment

CHAPTER SUMMARY

Section 1
Political and religious reformers settled the New England colonies. Life in the region centered around small towns and villages. Tensions between settlers and Native Americans led to war.

Section 2
A variety of immigrants populated the five Middle Colonies. Skilled artisans and farmers contributed to a thriving economy in this region.

Section 3
The Southern Colonies developed two ways of life—one along the Atlantic coast and one in the backcountry. Slavery became part of the fabric of the economy of the Southern Colonies.

Section 4
Although England controlled the economy of its colonies, self-government emerged over time in the English settlements. Legislatures, the right to vote, and a bill of rights were features of many colonies.

Section 5
The 13 colonies developed their own ideas and traditions during the eighteenth century. Both the Great Awakening and the Enlightenment had a profound impact on the English colonies.

Interactive Textbook

For additional review and enrichment activities, see the interactive version of *The American Nation,* available on the Web and on CD-ROM.

Chapter Self-Test For practice test questions for Chapter 4, visit PHSchool.com, **Web Code mfa-0404.**

Building Vocabulary

Review the chapter vocabulary words listed below. Then, use the words and their definitions to create a matching quiz. Exchange quizzes with another student. Check each other's answers when you are finished.

1. **religious tolerance**
2. **town meeting**
3. **royal colony**
4. **cash crop**
5. **indigo**
6. **mercantilism**
7. **import**
8. **bill of rights**
9. **apprentice**
10. **libel**

Reviewing Key Facts

11. What caused conflicts between the New England colonists and the Native Americans? (Section 1)
12. What policies did William Penn follow in the Pennsylvania Colony? (Section 2)
13. What events caused Nathaniel Bacon and his followers to rebel in 1676? (Section 3)
14. How did England's belief in mercantilism affect the colonies? (Section 4)
15. How did cities influence colonial life? (Section 5)

Critical Thinking and Writing

16. **Connecting to Geography: Location** Analyze how location influenced a colony's economy.
17. **Comparing** Discuss the differences between the Southern plantations and the farms in the Middle and New England Colonies.
18. **Analyzing Information** Explain how each of the following individuals contributed to the growth of self-government: **(a)** John Winthrop, **(b)** Thomas Hooker, **(c)** Lord Baltimore.
19. **Synthesizing Information** Why do you think the colonists were open to the ideas of the Enlightenment?
20. **Linking Past and Present** What rights and freedoms enjoyed by Americans today had their beginnings in colonial times?

Skills Assessment

Analyzing Primary Sources

In the trial of John Peter Zenger, his lawyer Andrew Hamilton gave a speech to the jury defending Zenger. Read the excerpt, and then answer the questions.

> "... the question before the court and you gentlemen of the jury, is not of small nor private concern. It is not the cause of the poor printer . . . it may in its consequence affect every freeman that lives under a British Government on the main of America. It is the best cause. It is the cause of liberty; and I make no doubt but your upright conduct, this day, will . . . entitle you to the love and esteem of your fellow citizens. . . ."
>
> —Andrew Hamilton, speech before the jury in the Zenger trial, New York, 1735

21. According to Hamilton, what is the main issue in the Zenger case?

- **A.** the cause of liberty
- **B.** the power of the British government
- **C.** the cause of printers
- **D.** the importance of "upright conduct"

22. Hamilton probably feels that the jury's verdict

- **A.** will have very little impact on society.
- **B.** can be ignored.
- **C.** will be overturned on appeal.
- **D.** is very important.

Applying Your Skills

Summarizing

Read the following passage about river trade in colonial Virginia. Answer the questions.

An early Tye River Scottish tobacco planter, Parson Robert Rose, was one of the first to use the Indian dugout canoe to carry his hogsheads [of tobacco] to the Richmond market, but found them neither large enough nor stable enough to carry much cargo. By the mid 1740s, Parson Rose . . . devised a method of lashing two canoes together with a sawn board platform in between which enabled him to carry up to nine hogshead at a time down the James . . . Hogsheads could now be transported downriver . . . to the market in Richmond.

—Dian McNaught, "The Early Virginia River Trade of the 1700s"

23. What is the main idea of this passage?

- **A.** Indian dugout canoes are sturdy.
- **B.** Hogsheads are durable holding devices.
- **C.** Double dugout canoes are best for carrying goods.
- **D.** Parson Rose was a wealthy planter.

24. **(a)** What details in the passage support the main idea? **(b)** Write a summary of the paragraph.

Activities

Connecting With... Culture

Making a Chart Make a chart that describes the lifestyle in the colonies. Write the names of the colonial regions—New England, Middle Colonies, and Southern Colonies—at the top of the chart. The left column should include: Geography, Economy, Government, Education, Region, Population Density. You may add other categories.

Connecting to Today

A Comparison Report Use the Internet to research facts about past and present-day immigration. Compare the challenges faced by immigrants coming to the United States today with those of the English colonists in the 1600s and early 1700s. Work with a partner to complete your report. For help in starting this activity, visit PHSchool.com, **Web Code mfd-0405.**

TEST PREPARATION

1 Which of the following is not an example of a primary source?

A An entry from Christopher Columbus's journal

B The cargo list of a colonial slave ship

C A modern biography of Benjamin Franklin

D The Fundamental Orders of Connecticut

Use the map and your knowledge of social studies to answer the following question.

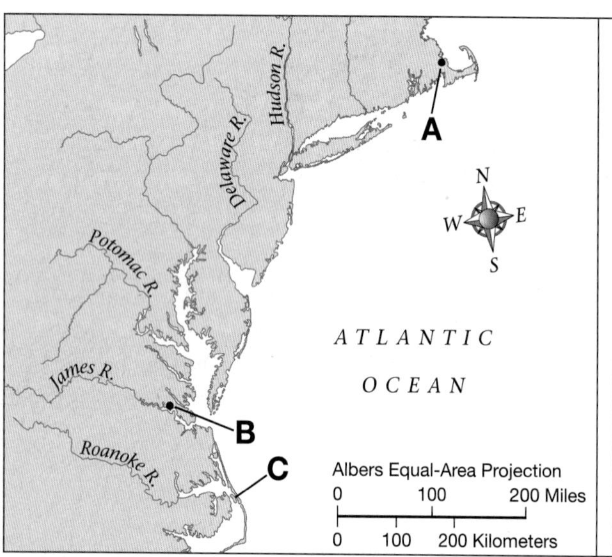

2 In what sequence were the three English colonies shown on the map settled?

A A, B, C

B C, B, A

C B, A, C

D B, C, A

3 The Navigation Acts were linked to which economic system?

A Mercantilism

B Feudalism

C Encomienda system

D Free enterprise

4 "Nomadic bands learned to make the most of limited resources." This statement best applies to Native Americans living in which region?

A Eastern Woodlands

B Arctic

C Southeast

D Pacific Northwest

Use the quotation and your knowledge of social studies to answer the following question.

> "There has been a great lasting change in this town in many respects. There has been vastly more religion kept up. . . . There has also been an evident change with respect to a charitable spirit to the poor."

5 What event or development is described in this passage?

A The founding of Pennsylvania

B The signing of the Mayflower Compact

C The Enlightenment

D The Great Awakening

6 How was the founding of the Virginia House of Burgesses similar to the signing of the Mayflower Compact?

A Both strengthened the English Parliament's control over the colonies.

B Both gave settlers the right to establish colonies.

C Both contributed to the development of representative democracy.

D Both created elected legislatures.

7 Which kind of thematic map would you use to find out how much of your state is made up of farmland?

A A political map

B A climate map

C A land use map

D A population density map

8 Which of the following individuals is best known for helping the spread of new ideas in Europe?

A Prince Henry of Portugal

B Johannes Gutenberg

C Augustus Caesar

D Martin Luther

Use the chart <u>and</u> your knowledge of social studies to answer the following question.

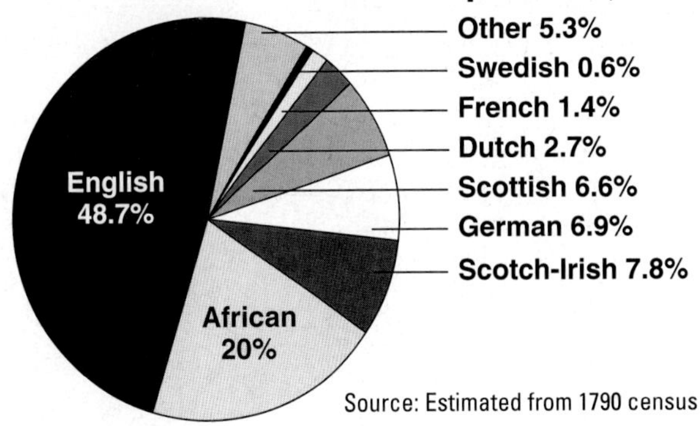

9 What valid conclusion about the colonial population can you draw from this pie chart?

A More people in the colonies were of English descent than all other European nationalities combined.

B Slaves made up 20 percent of the colonial population.

C The Dutch population lived entirely in New York.

D One out of every ten colonists was of either German or French background.

Writing Practice

10 **(a)** What are the major elements of the free enterprise system? **(b)** Describe some of the benefits of free enterprise. Use at least one example from modern life.

11 Trace the development of religious freedom in the 13 colonies. Describe at least three milestones. Then, make two generalizations about the roots of religious freedom.

Unit 2

The Revolutionary Era

UNIT OUTLINE

Chapter 5
Crisis in the Colonies (1745–1775)

Chapter 6
The American Revolution (1775–1783)

Chapter 7
Creating a Republic (1776–1790)

The Constitution of the United States

Chapter 8
Government, Citizenship, and the Constitution (1787–Present)

Revolutionary Turning Point
General George Washington looks determined to win an American victory in Emanuel Leutze's ***Washington Crossing the Delaware.***

“If we separate from Britain, what code of laws will be established? How shall we be governed so as to retain our liberties?”

—Abigail Adams, wife of John Adams (1775)

CHAPTER 5

Crisis in the Colonies

1745–1775

1 The French and Indian War
2 Turmoil Over Taxation
3 From Protest to Revolution

British capture Quebec

AMERICAN EVENTS

1740s
The first migration of settlers across the Appalachian Mountains sets off conflicts with the Indians of the Ohio River Valley.

1754
The Albany Congress proposes to unite the British colonies. However, the proposal is rejected by all the colonies.

1759
British forces climb to the Plains of Abraham and capture Quebec, the capital of New France.

1740 1750 1760

WORLD EVENTS

▲ 1748
Britain and France fight for control of trade in India.

▲ 1756
Seven Years' War begins in Europe between France and Britain.

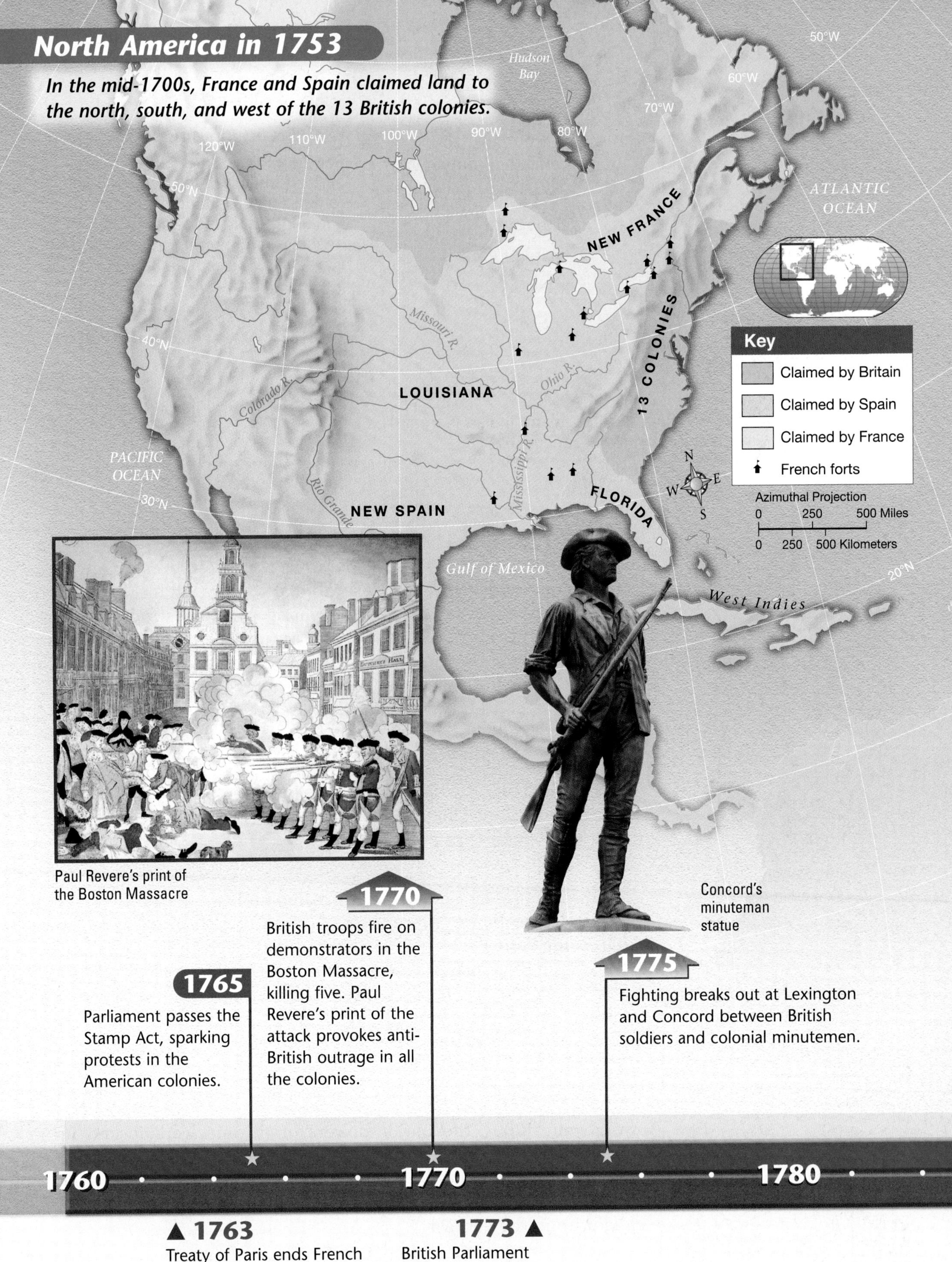

Paul Revere's print of the Boston Massacre

Concord's minuteman statue

1765
Parliament passes the Stamp Act, sparking protests in the American colonies.

1770
British troops fire on demonstrators in the Boston Massacre, killing five. Paul Revere's print of the attack provokes anti-British outrage in all the colonies.

1775
Fighting breaks out at Lexington and Concord between British soldiers and colonial minutemen.

1760 · 1770 · 1780

▲ 1763
Treaty of Paris ends French power in North America.

1773 ▲
British Parliament passes the Tea Act.

1 The French and Indian War

Prepare to Read

Objectives

In this section, you will
- Explain why war began in North America.
- Describe how mistakes led to British defeats early in the war.
- Identify what turned the tide of war in Britain's favor.
- Explain how British troops defeated French troops.

Key Terms

French and Indian War
Albany Plan of Union
Plains of Abraham
Treaty of Paris

Target Reading Skill

Reading Process As you read, prepare an outline of this section. Use roman numerals to indicate major headings, capital letters for subheadings, and numbers for supporting details. The sample below will get you started.

I. European Rivals in North America
 A.
 B.
II. The French and Indian War Begins
III. The Albany Congress

Main Idea Britain's victory in the French and Indian War marked the end of the French empire in North America.

George Washington as a young officer

Setting the Scene When Captain Daniel Joncaire sat down to dinner on December 4, 1753, he wasn't expecting company. The weather was cold, rainy, and miserable at the French fort near Lake Erie. To Joncaire's surprise, a tall young stranger strode into the room. He introduced himself as Major George Washington. Washington had traveled several hundred miles from Virginia to deliver a letter to the French.

Joncaire politely invited Washington to dine. As they ate, the captain boasted that France was determined to control the Ohio River Valley. Washington reported:

> "He told me, That it was their absolute Design to take possession of the Ohio [River], and by God they would do it."
>
> —George Washington, in his journal

Joncaire's remark made Washington pause. The letter he was carrying from Virginia's governor warned the French to get out of the Ohio River Valley! For years, tensions had been building between France and England. At stake was more than control of the Ohio River Valley. The two rivals wanted to drive each other out of North America. In the end, the issue was decided by war. And Washington was the man who struck the first blow.

European Rivals in North America

By the mid-1700s, the major powers of Europe were locked in a worldwide struggle for empire. England, France, Spain, and the Netherlands competed for trade and colonies in far-flung corners of the globe. The English colonies in North America soon became caught up in the contest.

The most serious threat came from France. It claimed a vast area that stretched from the St. Lawrence River west to the Great Lakes and south to the Gulf of Mexico. To protect their land claims, the French built an extensive system of forts. These forts blocked the English colonies from expanding to the west.

Conflict in the Ohio Valley At first, most English settlers were content to remain along the Atlantic coast. By the 1740s, however, traders were crossing the Appalachian Mountains in search of furs. Pushing into the Ohio Valley, they tried to take over the profitable French trade with the Indians.

France was determined to stop the English from expanding westward. The Ohio River was especially important to the French because it provided a vital link between their lands in Canada and their settlements along the Mississippi River.

Viewing History

A Pioneer Home

After clearing the woods, pioneer families built their log cabins and set out to harvest the riches of the land. This romantic view of a pioneer homestead was created more than 100 years after pioneers started crossing the Appalachian Mountains.

Identifying Points of View ***Do you think the artist admired the early pioneers? Explain your answer. How does he show his point of view?***

Native Americans Choose Sides Native Americans had hunted animals and grown crops in the Ohio Valley for centuries. They did not want to give up the land to European settlers, French or English. One Native American protested to an English trader, "You and the French are like the two edges of a pair of shears. And we are the cloth which is to be cut to pieces between them."

Still, the growing conflict between England and France was too dangerous to ignore. Some Native Americans decided that the only way to protect their way of life was to take sides in the struggle.

The French expected the Indians to side with them. Most French in North America were trappers and traders. Generally, they did not destroy Indian hunting grounds by clearing forests for farms. Also, many French trappers married Native American women and adopted their ways. As a result, France had built strong alliances with such Native American groups as the Algonquins and the Hurons.

Many English settlers were farmers. These settlers usually ignored Indian rights by felling trees and clearing land for crops. In the end, though, Britain managed to convince the powerful Iroquois nations to join with them. The British alliance was attractive to the Iroquois because they were old enemies of the Algonquin and the Huron peoples.

An English trader and official, William Johnson, helped gain Iroquois support for England. The Iroquois respected Johnson. He was one of the few English settlers who had an Indian wife, Molly Brant. She was the sister of the Mohawk chief Thayendanegea, known to the English as Joseph Brant. Both Joseph and Molly Brant became valuable allies for the English. The English also won Native American allies in the Ohio Valley by charging lower prices than the French for trade goods.

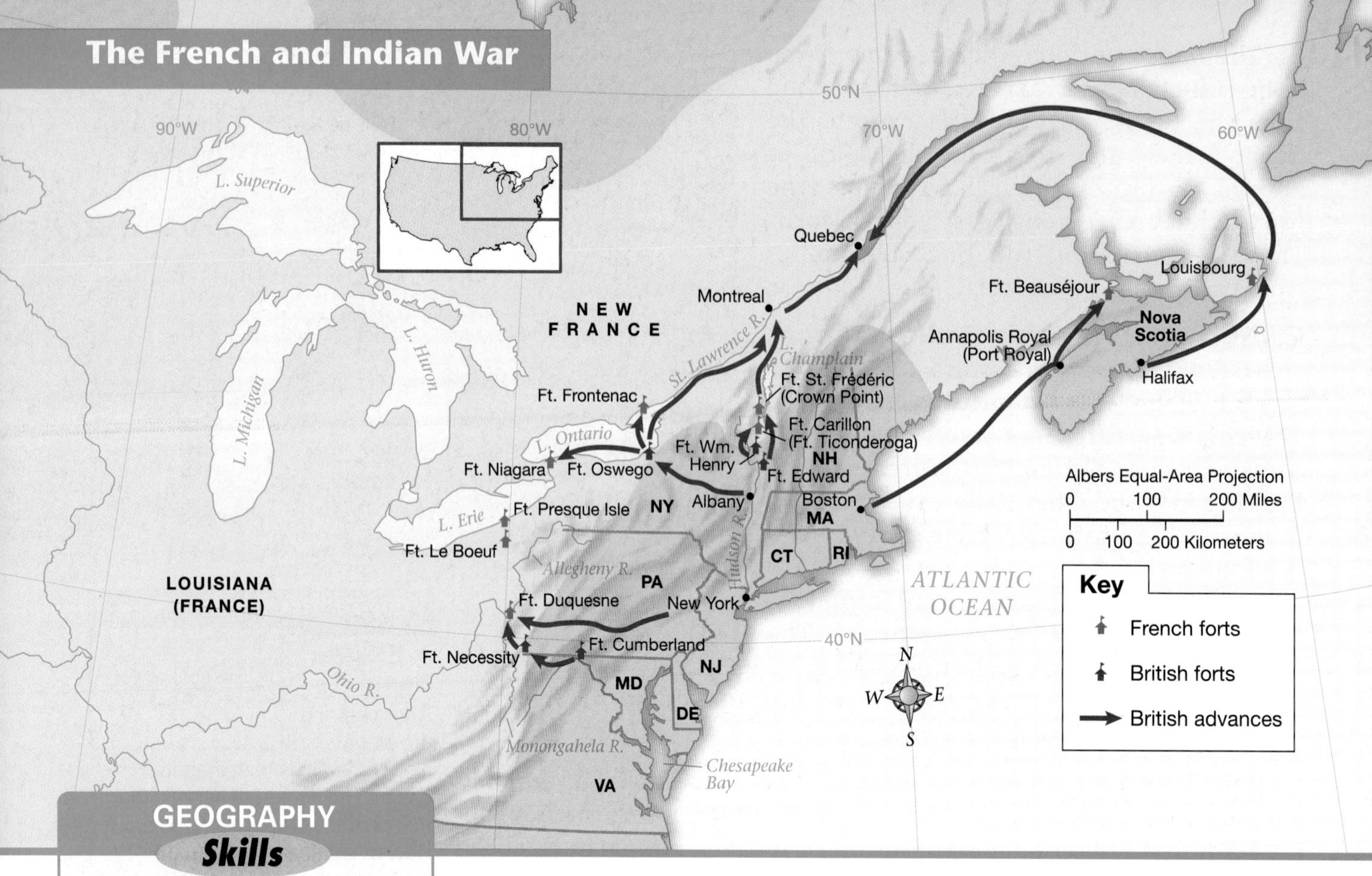

GEOGRAPHY *Skills*

During the French and Indian War, Britain and France battled for control of North America. The conflict began in the Ohio River Valley.

1. **Location** On the map locate **(a)** Fort Necessity, **(b)** Fort Duquesne, **(c)** Louisbourg, **(d)** Albany.
2. **Movement** About how many miles did advancing British forces travel from Louisbourg to Quebec?
3. **Critical Thinking Analyzing Information** How were the causes of the French and Indian War related to events during the Age of Exploration?

The French and Indian War Begins

Three times between 1689 and 1748, France and Great Britain* fought for power in Europe and North America. Each war ended with an uneasy peace.

In 1754, fighting broke out for a fourth time. English settlers called the conflict the **French and Indian War** because it pitted them against France and its Native American allies. Once again, the Ohio River Valley was at the center of the dispute. There, the opening shots of the war were fired by soldiers led by George Washington.

A Bold Young Leader Washington was only 22 years old in 1754. He had grown up on a plantation in Virginia, the son of wealthy parents. Gifted at mathematics, he began working as a land surveyor at the age of 15. His job took him to frontier lands in western Virginia.

After Washington returned from his first visit to the French, the governor of Virginia sent him west again. This time Washington's assignment was to build a fort where the Monongahela and Allegheny rivers meet to form the Ohio River.

Washington led 150 men into the Ohio country in April 1754. Along the way, he heard that the French had just completed Fort

*In 1707, England and Scotland were officially joined into the United Kingdom of Great Britain. After that date, the terms *Great Britain* and *British* were used to describe the country and its people. However, the terms *England* and *English* were still used throughout much of the 1700s.

Duquesne (doo KAYN) at the very spot where Washington hoped to build his fort.

Conflict at Fort Necessity Determined to carry out his orders, Washington hurried on. Indian allies revealed that French scouts were camped in the woods ahead. Marching quietly through the night, Washington launched a surprise attack and scattered the French.

His success was brief, however. Hearing that the French were about to counterattack, Washington and his men quickly threw up a makeshift stockade. They named it Fort Necessity. A force of 700 French and Indians surrounded the fort. Badly outnumbered, the Virginians surrendered. The French then released Washington, and he returned home.

British officials recognized the significance of Washington's skirmish. "The volley fired by this young Virginian in the forests of America," a British writer noted, "has set the world in flames."

Set a Purpose for Reading

When you set a purpose for reading, you give yourself a focus. As you read about Washington and Fort Necessity, think about the meaning of the British writer's comment. Why did he say that Washington had "set the world in flames"?

The Albany Congress

While Washington was defending Fort Necessity, delegates from seven colonies gathered in Albany, New York. One purpose of the meeting was to cement the alliance with the Iroquois. Another goal was to plan a united colonial defense.

The delegates in Albany knew that the colonists had to work together to defeat the French. Benjamin Franklin, the delegate from Pennsylvania, proposed the **Albany Plan of Union.** The plan was an attempt to create "one general government" for the 13 colonies. It called for a Grand Council made up of representatives from each colony. The council would make laws, raise taxes, and set up the defense of the colonies.

The delegates voted to accept the Plan of Union. However, when the plan was submitted to the colonial assemblies, not one approved it. None of the colonies wanted to give up any of its powers to a central council. A disappointed Benjamin Franklin expressed his frustration at the failure of his plan:

> "Everyone cries a union is necessary. But when they come to the manner and form of the union, their weak noodles are perfectly distracted."
>
> —Benjamin Franklin, in a letter to Governor William Shirley, 1755

Primary Source

Battle in the Wilderness

Early in the war, a small force of Native Americans and French routed an army led by Edward Braddock. George Washington later wrote of the defeat:

"The Virginia troops showed a good deal of bravery, and were near all killed. For I believe out of three companies that were there, there are scarce 30 men left alive. . . . The general [Braddock] was wounded; of which he died three days after. Sir Peter Halket was killed in the field, where died many other brave officers. I luckily escaped without a wound, though I had four bullets through my coat and two horses shot under me."

—George Washington in a letter to his mother, July 18, 1755

Analyzing Primary Sources

How did the battle build Washington's reputation among his fellow colonists?

A String of British Defeats

In 1755, General Edward Braddock led British and colonial troops in an attack against Fort Duquesne. Braddock was a stubborn man who had little experience at fighting in the forests of North America. Still, the general boasted that he would sweep the French from the Ohio Valley.

Disaster for Braddock Braddock's men moved slowly and noisily through the forests. Although warned of danger by Washington and by Indian scouts, Braddock pushed ahead.

As the British neared Fort Duquesne, the French and their Indian allies launched a surprise attack. Sharpshooters hid in the forest and picked off British soldiers, whose bright red uniforms made easy targets.

Braddock himself had five horses shot out from under him before he fell, fatally wounded. Almost half the British were killed or wounded. Washington, too, was nearly killed.

Further British Setbacks During the next two years, the war continued to go badly for the British. British attacks against several French forts failed. Meanwhile, the French won important victories, capturing Fort Oswego on Lake Ontario and Fort William Henry on Lake George. All these defeats put a serious strain on the alliances with Native Americans who had been counting on the British to protect them from the French.

The Tide of Battle Turns

In 1757, William Pitt became the new head of the British government. Pitt made it his first job to win the war in North America. Once that goal was achieved, he argued, the British would be free to focus on victory in other parts of the world. So Pitt sent Britain's best generals to North America. To encourage the colonists to support the war, he promised large payments for military services and supplies.

Under Pitt's leadership, the tide of battle turned. In 1758, Major General Jeffrey Amherst captured Louisbourg, the most important fort in French Canada. That year, the British also seized Fort Duquesne, which they renamed Fort Pitt after the British leader. The city of Pittsburgh later grew up on the site of Fort Pitt.

The Fall of New France

The British enjoyed even greater success in 1759. By summer, they had pushed the French from Fort Niagara, Crown Point, and Fort Ticonderoga (ty kahn duh ROH guh). Next, Pitt sent General James Wolfe to take Quebec, capital of New France.

Battle for Quebec Quebec was vital to the defense of New France. Without Quebec, the French could not supply their forts farther up the St. Lawrence River. Quebec was well defended, though. The city sat on the edge of the **Plains of Abraham,** on top of a steep cliff high above the St. Lawrence. An able French general, the Marquis de Montcalm, was prepared to fight off any British attack.

General Wolfe devised a bold plan to capture Quebec. He knew that Montcalm had only a few soldiers guarding the cliff because the French thought that it was too steep to climb. Late at night, Wolfe ordered

GEOGRAPHY Skills

The Treaty of Paris ended the French and Indian War and greatly changed the map of North America.

1. **Location** On the map, locate **(a)** the 13 colonies, **(b)** Louisiana, **(c)** New Spain.
2. **Region** Which countries shared control of North America after 1763?
3. **Critical Thinking Comparing** Compare this map to the map at the beginning of the chapter. What effect did the Treaty of Paris have on French power in North America?

North America in 1763

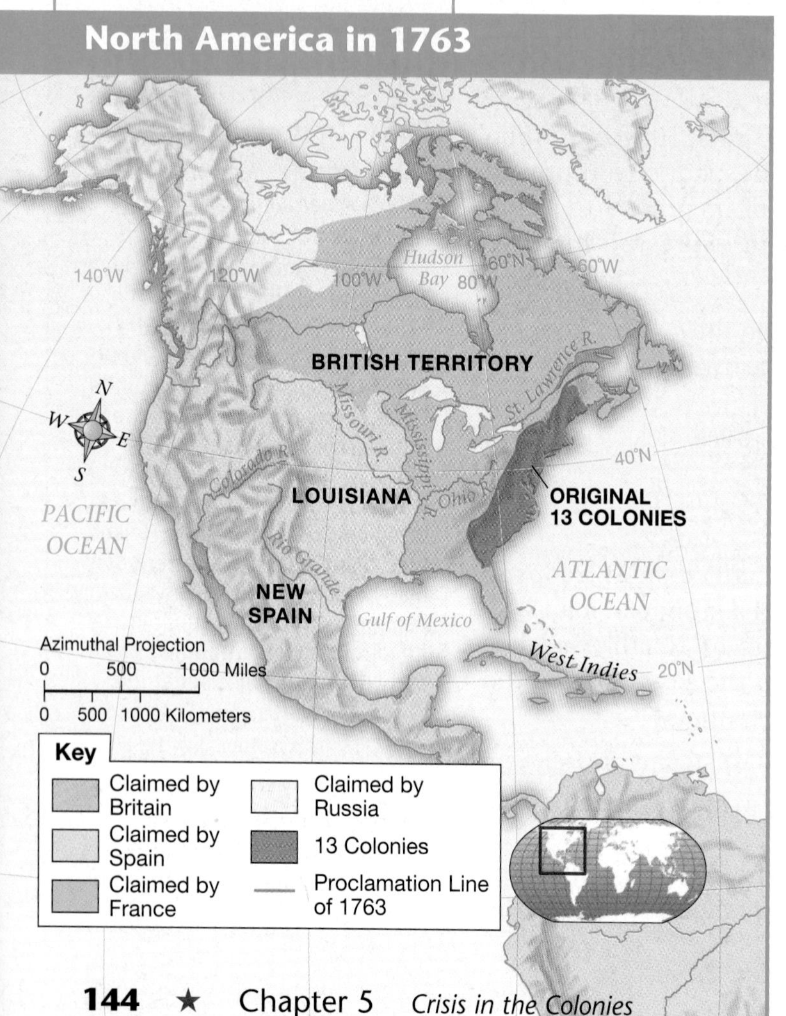

British troops to row quietly in small boats to the foot of the cliff. In the dark, the soldiers swarmed ashore, climbed up the cliff, and assembled at the top.

The next morning, Montcalm awakened to a surprise. A force of 4,000 British troops was drawn up and ready for battle on the Plains of Abraham.

Quickly, Montcalm marched his own troops out to join in battle. By the time the fierce fighting was over, both Montcalm and Wolfe lay dead. Moments before Wolfe died, a soldier gave him the news that the British had won. Wolfe is said to have whispered, "Now, God be praised, I will die in peace." On September 18, 1759, Quebec surrendered to the British.

Treaty of Paris The fall of Quebec sealed the fate of New France, though fighting dragged on in Europe for several more years. Finally, in 1763, Britain and France signed the Treaty of Paris, bringing the long conflict to an end.

The Treaty of Paris marked the end of French power in North America. By its terms, Britain gained Canada and all French lands east of the Mississippi River except New Orleans. France was allowed to keep only two islands in the Gulf of St. Lawrence and its prosperous sugar-growing islands in the West Indies. Spain, which had entered the war on the French side in 1762, gave up Florida to Britain. In return, Spain received all French land west of the Mississippi. In addition, Spain gained the vital port city of New Orleans. Spain retained control of its vast empire in Central America and South America.

After years of fighting, peace returned to North America. Yet, in a few short years, a new conflict would break out. This time, the struggle would pit Britain against its own 13 colonies.

Section 1 Assessment

Recall

1. **Identify** Explain the significance of **(a)** George Washington, **(b)** Joseph Brant, **(c)** French and Indian War, **(d)** Benjamin Franklin, **(e)** Albany Plan of Union, **(f)** Edward Braddock, **(g)** William Pitt, **(h)** Plains of Abraham, **(i)** Treaty of Paris.

Comprehension

2. Why did France and Britain go to war in 1754?
3. How did defeat and disunity hurt the early British war effort?
4. What events turned the tide of battle after William Pitt became head of the British government?
5. How did the battle of Quebec lead to the fall of New France to the British?

Critical Thinking and Writing

6. **Exploring the Main Idea** Review the Main Idea statement at the beginning of this section. Write a paragraph explaining how Britain's victory in the French and Indian War made it the most powerful force in North America.
7. **Analyzing Ideas (a)** List two ways in which the Albany Plan of Union would have helped the colonies fight the French. **(b)** Why did the colonists reject the Plan of Union?

ACTIVITY

Writing a Skit
Use the Internet to find resources describing the strategies of Generals Wolfe and Montcalm at Quebec. Then, prepare a five-minute skit about an imaginary meeting between the two generals. For help in completing the activity, visit PHSchool.com, **Web Code mfd-0501.**

2 Turmoil Over Taxation

Prepare to Read

Objectives

In this section, you will
- Describe how Britain tried to ease growing tensions on the American frontier.
- List the ways colonists reacted to new taxes imposed by Parliament.
- Identify new colonial leaders.
- Explain the events that led to the Boston Massacre.

Key Terms

Pontiac's War
Proclamation of 1763
Stamp Act
petition
boycott
repeal
Townshend Acts
writ of assistance
Boston Massacre
committee of correspondence

Target Reading Skill

Main Idea Copy the concept web below. As you read the section, fill in the blank ovals with important facts that led to the conflict between Britain and its American colonies. Add as many ovals as you need.

Main Idea Many colonists opposed Parliament's attempts to tighten control over Britain's North American empire.

A tax stamp

Setting the Scene The lieutenant governor of Massachusetts, Thomas Hutchinson, was at supper with his children in Boston when an out-of-breath messenger arrived. A mob was coming for Hutchinson, he warned. "I directed my children to fly to a secure place," Hutchinson recalled. Then, he fled to a neighbor's house.

> "I had been there but a few minutes before the hellish crew fell upon my house with the Rage of devils and in a moment with axes split down the doors and entered. . . ."
>
> —Thomas Hutchinson, lieutenant governor of Massachusetts, 1765

The furious mob went to work. It smashed windows and broke down walls. It ripped up Hutchinson's garden and chopped down his trees. The entire house would have been demolished except that daylight came before the job could be finished. "Such ruins were never seen in America," Hutchinson mourned.

How could such a riot take place? Only two years earlier, in 1763, British colonists had celebrated Britain's victory over France. They lit bonfires and set church bells ringing. Now, some of these same people were destroying the homes of royal officials. In truth, the riots of 1765 were only the beginning of a growing dispute.

New Troubles on the Frontier

By 1760, the British and their Indian allies had driven France from the Ohio Valley. Their troubles in the region were not over, however. For many years, fur traders had sent back glowing reports of the land beyond the Appalachian Mountains. With the French gone, British colonists eagerly headed west to claim the lands for themselves.

Clashes With Native Americans Many Native American nations lived in the Ohio Valley. They included the Senecas, Delawares, Shawnees, Ottawas, Miamis, and Hurons. As British settlers moved into the valley, they often clashed with these Native Americans.

In 1762, the British sent Lord Jeffrey Amherst to the frontier to keep order. French traders had always treated Native Americans as friends, holding feasts for them and giving them presents. Amherst refused to do this. Instead, he raised the price of goods traded to Indians. Also, unlike the French, Amherst allowed settlers to build farms and forts on Indian lands.

Angry Native Americans found a leader in Pontiac, an Ottawa chief who had fought on the French side. An English trader remarked that Pontiac "commands more respect amongst these nations than any Indian I ever saw." In April 1763, Pontiac spoke out against the British, calling them "dogs dressed in red, who have come to rob [us] of [our] hunting grounds and drive away the game."

War on the Frontier Soon after, Pontiac led an attack on British troops at Fort Detroit. A number of other Indian nations joined him. In a few short months, they captured most British forts in the Ohio country. British and colonial troops then struck back and regained much of what they had lost.

Pontiac's War, as it came to be called, did not last long. In October 1763, the French told Pontiac that they had signed the Treaty of Paris. Because the treaty marked the end of French power in North America, the Indians could no longer hope for French aid against the British. One by one, the Indian nations stopped fighting and returned home.

Viewing History

Pontiac's War

Area of Pontiac's War

At councils throughout the West, the Ottawa chief Pontiac urged Native Americans to rise up against the British. Despite a hard-fought struggle, Indian forces were unable to drive settlers out of the Ohio Valley. **Evaluating Information** ***How did Native American leaders of the Ohio River Valley accept Pontiac's message?***

Proclamation of 1763

Pontiac's War convinced British officials that they should stop British subjects from settling on the western frontier. To do this, the government issued the Proclamation of 1763. The proclamation drew an imaginary line along the crest of the Appalachian Mountains. Colonists were forbidden to settle west of the line. All settlers already west of the line were "to remove themselves" at once.

The proclamation was meant to protect Indians in the western lands. To enforce it, Britain sent 10,000 troops to the colonies. Few troops went to the frontier, however. Most stayed in cities along the Atlantic coast.

The proclamation angered colonists. Some colonies, including New York, Pennsylvania, and Virginia, claimed lands in the west. Also, colonists now had to pay for the additional British troops that had been sent to enforce the proclamation. In the end, many settlers simply ignored the proclamation and moved west anyway.

Crisis on the Frontier

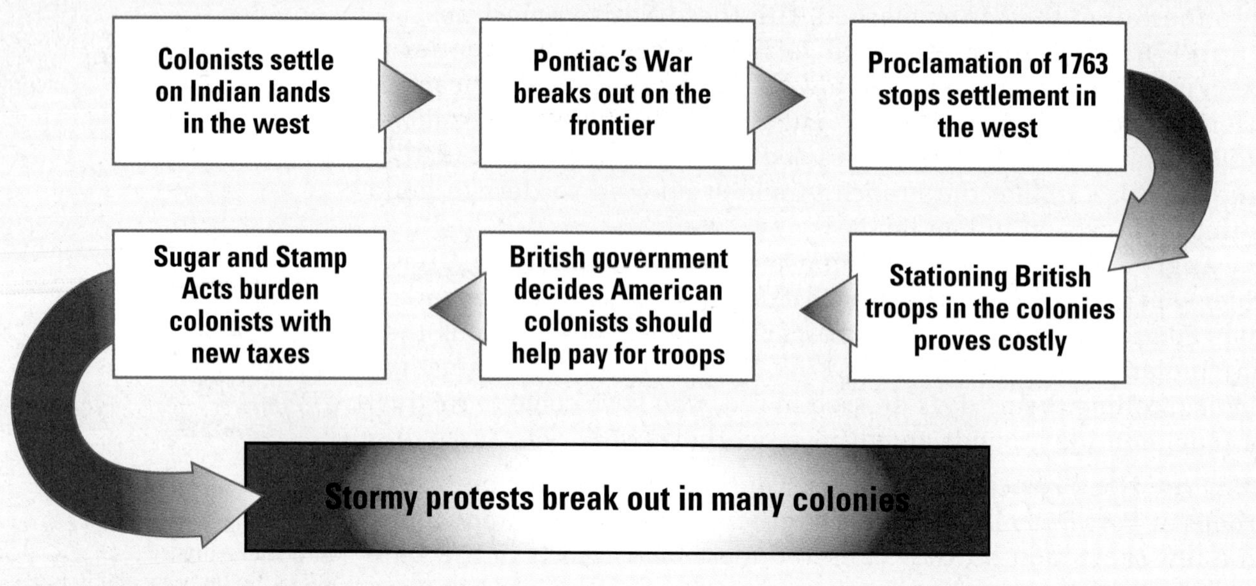

Colonists settle on Indian lands in the west → Pontiac's War breaks out on the frontier → Proclamation of 1763 stops settlement in the west → Stationing British troops in the colonies proves costly → British government decides American colonists should help pay for troops → Sugar and Stamp Acts burden colonists with new taxes → Stormy protests break out in many colonies

GRAPHIC ORGANIZER *Skills*

Events on the western frontier created pressures that led to conflict in all the colonies.

1. **Comprehension** **(a)** How did the Proclamation of 1763 affect settlement in the west? **(b)** Why did the British decide that American colonists should help pay for the troops it was stationing in the colonies?
2. **Critical Thinking** **Applying Information** Which do you think caused a greater uproar among colonists of the coastal cities, the Proclamation of 1763 or the Sugar Act? Explain your answer.

One colonist who defied the Proclamation of 1763 was Daniel Boone. In 1767, Boone visited Kentucky, west of the Appalachians. In 1769, he began what became a two-year journey of exploration through Kentucky. He traveled as far as the Falls of the Ohio, the site of the present-day city of Louisville. Later, he led settlers through the Cumberland Gap along an old Indian path. During his travels, Boone fought a number of battles against the Indians and was taken captive for a short period.

Britain Imposes New Taxes

The French and Indian War plunged Britain deeply into debt. As a result, the taxes paid by citizens in Britain rose sharply. The British prime minister, George Grenville, decided that colonists in North America should help share the burden. In a mercantilist system, colonies were expected to serve the colonial power. Grenville reasoned that the colonists would not oppose small tax increases.

Sugar Act In 1764, Grenville asked Parliament to approve the Sugar Act, which put a new tax on molasses. Molasses, you will recall, was a valuable item in the triangular trade.

The Sugar Act replaced an earlier tax, which had been so high that any merchant who paid it would have been driven out of business. As a result, most colonial merchants simply avoided the tax by smuggling molasses into the colonies. Often, they bribed tax collectors to look the other way. The Sugar Act of 1764 lowered the tax. At the same time, the law made it easier for British officials to bring colonial smugglers to trial. Grenville made it clear that he expected the new tax to be paid.

Stamp Act Grenville also persuaded Parliament to pass the Stamp Act of 1765. The act placed new duties on legal documents such as wills, diplomas, and marriage papers. It also taxed newspapers, almanacs, playing cards, and even dice.

All items named in the law had to carry a stamp showing that the tax had been paid. Stamp taxes were used in Britain and other countries to raise money. However, Britain had never required American colonists to pay such a tax.

Viewing History

Protesting the Stamp Act

The Stamp Act created a storm of opposition in the colonies. Colonists expressed their opposition to the tax in many ways, including this message on a teapot.

Linking Past and Present

How do people today display their support or opposition to a political issue?

Protesting the Stamp Act

When British officials tried to enforce the Stamp Act, they met with stormy protests from colonists. Lieutenant Governor Hutchinson in Massachusetts was not the only official to feel the anger of a mob. Some colonists threw rocks at agents trying to collect the unpopular tax. Others tarred and feathered the agents. In addition to riots in Boston, other disturbances broke out in New York City, Newport, and Charleston. In New York City, rioters destroyed the home of a British official who had said he would "cram the stamps down American throats" at the point of his sword.

The fury of the colonists shocked the British. After all, Britain had spent a great deal of money to protect the colonies against the French. The British at home were paying much higher taxes than the colonists. Why, British officials asked, were colonists so angry about the Stamp Act? As one English letter-writer commented,

> "Our Colonies must be the biggest Beggars in the World, if such small Duties appear to be intolerable Burdens in their Eyes."
>
> —"Pacificus," Maryland *Gazette*, March 20, 1766

"No Taxation Without Representation!" Colonists replied that the Stamp Act taxes were unjust. The taxes, they claimed, went against the principle that there should be no taxation without representation. That principle was rooted in English traditions dating back to the Magna Carta.

Colonists insisted that only they or their elected representatives had the right to pass taxes. Since the colonists did not elect representatives to Parliament, Parliament had no right to tax them. The colonists were willing to pay taxes—but only if the taxes were passed by their own colonial legislatures.

Uniting in Peaceful Protest The Stamp Act crisis united colonists from New Hampshire to Georgia. Critics of the law called for delegates from every colony to meet in New York City. There, a congress would form to consider actions against the hated Stamp Act.

In October 1765, nine colonies sent delegates to what became known as the Stamp Act Congress. The delegates drew up petitions to King George III and to Parliament. A **petition** is a formal written request to someone in authority, signed by a group of people. In these petitions, the delegates rejected the Stamp Act and asserted that Parliament had no right to tax the colonies. Parliament paid little attention.

The colonists took other steps to change the law. They joined together to boycott British goods. To **boycott** means to refuse to buy certain goods and services. The boycott of British goods took its toll. Trade fell off by 14 percent. British merchants complained that they were facing ruin. So, too, did British workers who made goods for the colonies.

Finally, in 1766, Parliament **repealed,** or canceled, the Stamp Act. At the same time, however, it passed a law asserting that Parliament had the right to raise taxes in "all cases whatsoever."

Target Skill **Identify Supporting Details**

What details in the subsection "The Townshend Acts" tell you about the conflict between Britain and the colonies? Add these details to your concept web.

The Townshend Acts

In May 1767, Parliament reopened the debate over taxing the colonies. In a fierce exchange, George Grenville, now a member of Parliament, clashed with Charles Townshend, the official in charge of the British treasury. "You are cowards, you are afraid of the Americans, you dare not tax America!" Grenville shouted.

"Fear? Cowards?" Townshend snapped back. "I dare tax America!"

The next month, Parliament passed the **Townshend Acts,** which taxed goods such as glass, paper, paint, lead, and tea. The taxes were low, but colonists still objected. The principle was the same: Parliament did not have the right to tax them without their consent.

Searching Without a Reason The Townshend Acts also set up new ways to collect taxes. Customs officials were sent to American ports with orders to stop smuggling. Using legal documents known as **writs of assistance,** the officers would be allowed to inspect a ship's cargo without giving a reason.

Colonists protested that the writs of assistance violated their rights as British citizens. Under British law, a government official could not search a person's property without a good reason for suspecting that the person had committed a crime. Colonists angrily cited the words of James Otis of Massachusetts. Arguing against a British attempt to impose writs of assistance six years earlier, he had said:

> "Now, one of the most essential branches of English liberty is the freedom of one's house. A man's house is his castle; and while he is quiet, he is as well guarded as a prince in his castle. This writ, if it should be declared legal, would totally destroy this privilege. Customhouse officers may enter our houses when they please . . . break locks, bars, and everything in their way. . . ."
>
> —James Otis, February 24, 1761

Colonial Protests Widen Colonists responded swiftly and strongly to the Townshend Acts. From north to south, colonial merchants and planters signed agreements promising to stop importing goods taxed by the Townshend Acts. The colonists hoped that the new boycott would win repeal of the Townshend Acts.

To protest British policies, some angry colonists formed the Sons of Liberty. From Boston to Charleston, Sons of Liberty staged mock hangings of cloth or straw effigies, or likenesses, dressed as British

LINKING PAST AND PRESENT

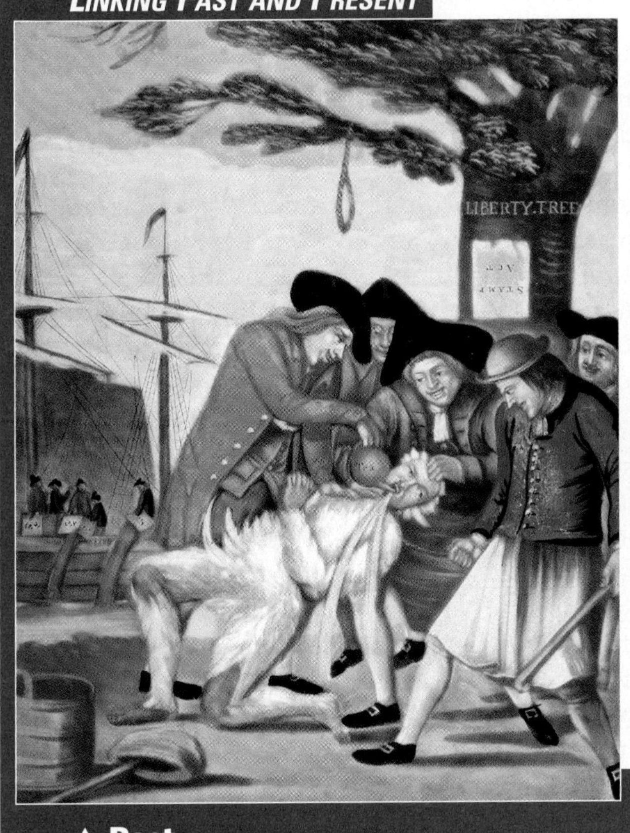

▲ Past

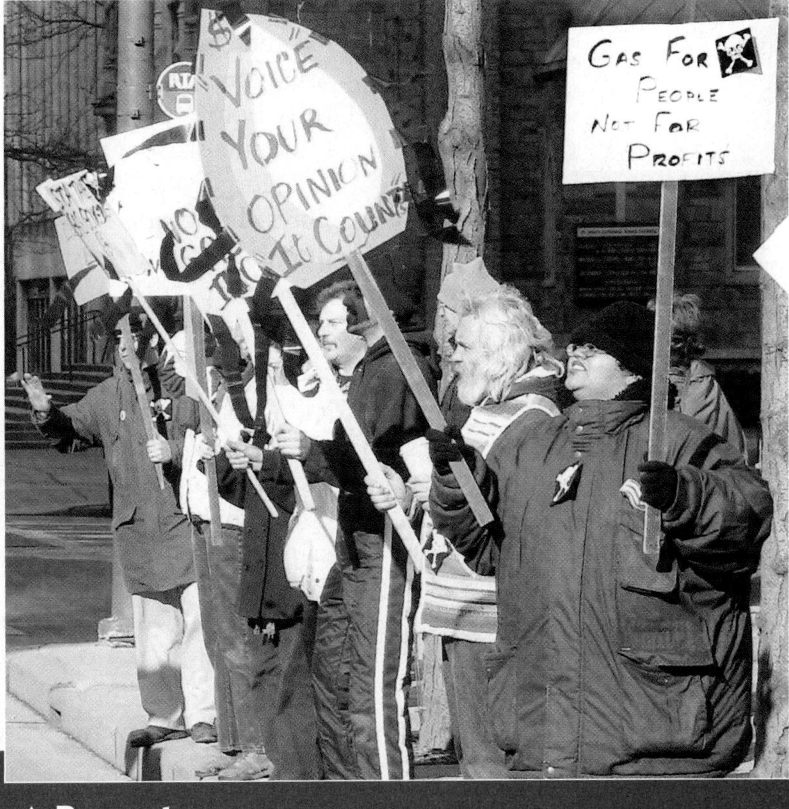

▲ Present

officials. The hangings were meant to show tax collectors what might happen to them if they tried to collect the unpopular taxes.

Some women joined the Daughters of Liberty. They paraded, signed petitions, and organized a boycott of fine British cloth. They urged colonial women to raise more sheep, prepare more wool, and spin and weave their own cloth. A slogan of the Daughters of Liberty declared, "It is better to wear a Homespun coat than to lose our Liberty."

Some Sons and Daughters of Liberty also used other methods to support their cause. They visited merchants and urged them to boycott British imports. A few even threatened people who continued to buy British goods.

Viewing History

Demonstrations Then and Now

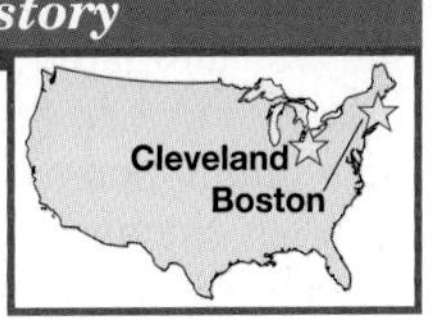

Colonial demonstrations over taxes imposed by the British could get pretty nasty, as when protestors tarred and feathered a tax collector and poured tea down his throat. The recent demonstration at right is more peaceful, but also deals with a controversial issue. **Drawing Inferences** ***Why do issues such as taxes and gas prices bring out strong emotions?***

New Colonial Leaders

As the struggle over taxes continued, new leaders emerged in all the colonies. Men and women in New England and Virginia were especially active in the colonial cause.

In Massachusetts Samuel Adams of Boston stood firmly against Britain. Sam Adams seemed an unlikely leader. He was a failure in business and a poor public speaker. Often, he wore a red suit and a cheap gray wig for which people poked fun at him. Still, Adams loved politics. He always attended Boston town meetings and Sons of Liberty rallies. Adams's real talent was organizing people. He worked behind the scenes, arranging protests and stirring public support.

Sam's cousin John was another important Massachusetts leader. John Adams had been a schoolteacher before becoming a skilled lawyer. Adams longed for fame and could often be difficult. Still, he was more cautious than his cousin Sam. He weighed evidence carefully before taking any actions. His knowledge of British law earned him much respect.

Mercy Otis Warren also aided the colonial cause. Warren wrote plays that made fun of British officials. The plays were published in newspapers and widely read in the colonies. Warren formed a close friendship with Abigail Adams, the wife of John Adams. The two women used their pens to spur the colonists to action. They also called for greater rights for women in the colonies.

An American Profile

Mercy Otis Warren
1728–1814

Like most young women in the American colonies, Mercy Otis Warren received no formal schooling. She managed to educate herself, however, and like her brother, James Otis, became dedicated to the cause of freedom.

She was infuriated when James Otis was struck on the head by a British officer and suffered permanent brain damage. Warren used her writing skills to stir feelings against the British. In plays like *The Blockheads,* she ridiculed British officials. Her home became a meeting place for colonists who opposed British policies.

How do writers influence public opinion today?

In Virginia Virginia contributed many leaders to the struggle against taxes. In the House of Burgesses, George Washington joined other Virginians to protest the Townshend Acts.

A young lawyer, Patrick Henry, became well known as a vocal critic of British policies. His speeches in the House of Burgesses moved listeners to both tears and anger. Once, Henry attacked Britain with such fury that some listeners cried out, "Treason!" Henry boldly replied, "If this be treason, make the most of it!" Henry's words moved a young listener, Thomas Jefferson. At the time, Jefferson was a 22-year-old law student.

The Boston Massacre

Port cities like Boston and New York were centers of protest. In New York, a dispute arose over the Quartering Act. Under that law, colonists had to provide housing, candles, bedding, and beverages to soldiers stationed in the colonies. When the New York assembly refused to obey the law, Britain dismissed the assembly in 1767.

Britain also sent two regiments to Boston to protect customs officers from local citizens. To many Bostonians, the soldiers were a daily reminder that Britain was trying to bully them into paying unjust taxes. When British soldiers walked along the streets of Boston, they risked insults or even beatings. A serious clash was not long in coming.

A Bloody Night On the night of March 5, 1770, a crowd gathered outside the Boston customs house. Colonists shouted insults at the "lobsterbacks," as they called the redcoated British who guarded the building. Then the Boston crowd began to throw snowballs, oyster shells, and chunks of ice at the soldiers.

The crowd grew larger and rowdier. Suddenly, the soldiers panicked. They fired into the crowd. When the smoke from the musket volley cleared, five people lay dead or dying. Among the first to die were Samuel Maverick, a 17-year-old white youth, and Crispus Attucks, an African American sailor.

Colonists were quick to protest the incident, which they called the **Boston Massacre.** A Boston silversmith named Paul Revere fanned anti-British feeling with an engraving that showed British soldiers firing on unarmed colonists. Sam Adams wrote letters to other colonists to build outrage about the shooting.

The soldiers were arrested and tried in court. John Adams agreed to defend them, saying that they deserved a fair trial. He wanted to show the world that the colonists believed in justice, even if the British government did not. At the trial, Adams argued that the crowd had provoked the soldiers. His arguments convinced the jury. In the end, the heaviest punishment any soldier received was a branding on the hand.

Samuel Adams later expanded on the idea of a letter-writing campaign by forming a **committee of correspondence.** Members of the committee regularly wrote letters and pamphlets reporting to other colonies on events in Massachusetts. Within three months, there were 80 committees organized in Massachusetts. Before long, committees of correspondence became a major tool of protest in every colony.

A Temporary Calm By chance, on the very day of the Boston Massacre, a bill was introduced into Parliament to repeal most of the Townshend Acts. British merchants, harmed by the American boycott of British goods, had again pressured Parliament to end the taxes. The Quartering Act was repealed and most of the taxes that had angered the Americans were ended. However, King George III asked Parliament to retain the tax on tea. "There must always be one tax to keep up the right [to tax]," he argued. Parliament agreed.

News of the repeal delighted the colonists. Most people dismissed the remaining tax on tea as unimportant and ended their boycott of British goods. For a few years, calm returned. Yet the basic issue—Britain's power to tax the colonies—remained unsettled. The debate over taxes had forced the colonists to begin thinking more carefully about their political rights.

Recall

1. **Identify** Explain the significance of **(a)** Pontiac's War, **(b)** Proclamation of 1763, **(c)** Stamp Act, **(d)** Townshend Acts, **(e)** writ of assistance, **(f)** Boston Massacre, **(g)** committee of correspondence.
2. **Define** **(a)** petition, **(b)** boycott, **(c)** repeal.

Comprehension

3. How did Pontiac's War and the Proclamation of 1763 grow out of the migration of colonists?
4. Why did colonists oppose the Stamp Act and the Townshend Acts?
5. Name some of the new leaders who protested British policy.
6. What role did the Townshend Acts play in the events that led to the Boston Massacre?

Critical Thinking and Writing

7. **Exploring the Main Idea** Review the Main Idea statement at the beginning of this section. Then, write a letter to a newspaper explaining why colonists object to the new taxes.
8. **Supporting a Point of View** Write a position paper explaining how British policies spurred the growth of representative government during the colonial period.

Activity

Go Online PHSchool.com

Connecting to Today

Use the Internet to find out more about Paul Revere's engraving of the Boston Massacre and other protest art in American history. For help in completing the activity, visit PHSchool.com, **Web Code mfd-0502.**

The Economic Effects of the Stamp Act

Much of the opposition to the Stamp Act in the colonies focused on whether Americans could be taxed by a parliament in which they were not represented. Yet, the Stamp Act also stirred opposition because of its economic effects.

Fast Facts

1. Britain believed that the tax would cover 20 percent of the cost of keeping an army in North America.
2. Samuel Adams, one of the most outspoken opponents of the Stamp Act, had once been a tax collector.

Fighting Back

The Stamp Act placed a tax on almost every business record, such as invoices, bills, and receipts. It took effect at a time when economies were slumping following the French and Indian War. Businesses were hurt when the British Army stopped buying food and clothing in the colonies.

Not surprisingly, the opposition to the Stamp Act was led by the very people who were most affected by it—shippers, manufacturers, merchants, lawyers, journalists, and clergy. They faced a major loss of income because they expected many Americans to resist buying stamps.

To protest, many American merchants stopped trading with Britain. This led British business leaders to voice serious opposition to the Stamp Act. As a result, Parliament repealed the Stamp Act in March 1766.

New Yorkers protest the Stamp Act

English Exports to the 13 Colonies

Pounds Sterling (in thousands): 1,500; 1,750; 2,000; 2,250

Year: 1763; 1764; 1765; 1766; 1767

Source: *Historical Statistics of the United States*

English exports fell soon after Americans began the boycott.

Activity

You are the editor of a London newspaper. Write a one-paragraph editorial either supporting or opposing the Stamp Act. Give reasons for your point of view.

3 From Protest to Revolution

Prepare to Read

Objectives

In this section, you will
- Explain how a dispute over tea led to tension between the colonists and Britain.
- Describe how Parliament struck back at Boston.
- Identify the reasons fighting broke out at Lexington and Concord.

Key Terms

Tea Act
Boston Tea Party
Intolerable Acts
Quebec Act
First Continental Congress
militia
minuteman
battles of Lexington and Concord

Target Reading Skill

Sequence Copy this flowchart. As you read, fill in the boxes with some of the major events described in this section that led from the dispute over taxes on tea to fighting at Lexington and Concord.

British East India Company has millions of pounds of unsold tea in its warehouses.
↓
[ ]
↓
Fighting breaks out at Lexington and Concord.

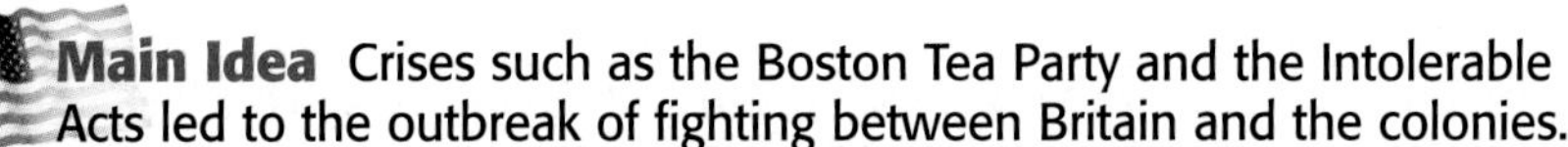

Main Idea Crises such as the Boston Tea Party and the Intolerable Acts led to the outbreak of fighting between Britain and the colonies.

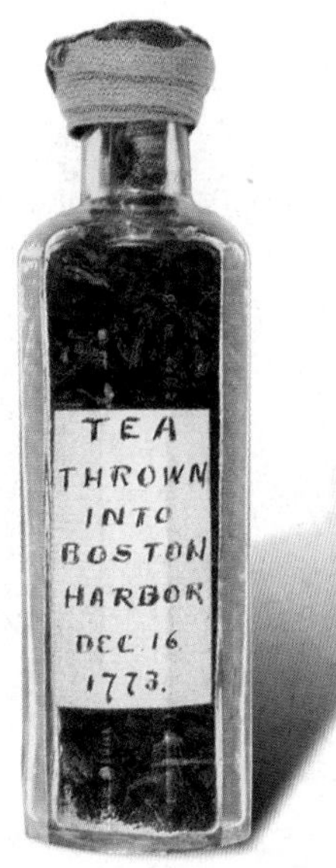

Colonial tea jar

Setting the Scene All day, the men collected burnt cork and coal dust. As dusk approached, they began to gather in small groups. In twos and threes, they met in homes across Boston. It was December 16, 1773. Outside, a cold drizzle was falling. Inside, by warm fires, the men were smearing coal dust and cork on their faces. Then, they threw blankets over their shoulders, trying to disguise themselves as Indians.

George Hewes, a shoemaker, waited with some of the others for a signal from a packed town meeting. By the time the signal came, the rain had stopped and night had fallen. As Hewes recalled:

> “When I first appeared in the street after being disguised, I fell in with many who were dressed, equipped and painted as I was, and . . . marched in order to the place of our destination.”
>
> —George Hewes, *Recollections,* 1834

That place was Griffin's Wharf, and the painted “Indians” were after tea. By 1773, the quarrel between Britain and the 13 colonies had erupted again over taxes. Only, this time colonists began to think the unthinkable. Perhaps the time had come to reject British rule and declare independence.

A Dispute Over Tea

Tea was tremendously popular in the colonies. By 1770, at least one million Americans brewed tea twice a day. People “would rather go without their dinners than without a dish of tea,” a visitor to the colonies noted.

Parliament Passes the Tea Act Most of the tea was brought to the colonies by the British East India Company. The company bought tea in southern Asia, shipped it to the colonies, and then sold it to colonial tea merchants. The merchants then sold the tea to the colonists. To make a profit, the merchants sold the tea at a higher price than they had paid for it.

In the 1770s, however, the British East India Company found itself in deep financial trouble. The British Parliament had kept a tax on tea as a symbol of its right to tax the colonies. The tax was a small one, but colonists resented it. Many of them refused to buy British tea. As a result, more than 15 million pounds of tea sat unsold in British warehouses.

Parliament tried to help the British East India Company by passing the **Tea Act** of 1773. The act let the company bypass the tea merchants and sell directly to colonists. Although colonists would still have to pay the tea tax, they would not have to pay the higher price charged by tea merchants. As a result, the tea itself would cost less than ever before. Parliament hoped this would encourage Americans to buy more British tea.

To the surprise of Parliament, colonists protested the Tea Act. American tea merchants were angry because they had been cut out of the tea trade. They believed that forcing Americans to buy tea through the British East India Company violated the Americans right to conduct free enterprise.

Even tea drinkers, who would have benefited from the law, scorned the Tea Act. They believed that it was a British trick to make them accept Parliament's right to tax the colonies.

A New Boycott Once again, colonists responded to the new tax with a boycott. A Philadelphia poet, Hannah Griffitts, urged American women to:

> “Stand firmly resolved and bid Grenville to see
> That rather than freedom we part with our tea,
> And well as we love the dear drink when a-dry,
> As American patriots our taste we deny.”
>
> —Hannah Griffitts in Milcah Martha Moore, *Commonplace Book,* 1773

Daughters of Liberty and women like Griffitts led the boycott. They served coffee or made "liberty tea" from raspberry leaves. At some ports, Sons of Liberty enforced the boycott by keeping the British East India Company from unloading cargoes of tea.

Boston Tea Party Three ships loaded with tea reached Boston harbor in late November 1773. The colonial governor of Massachusetts, Thomas Hutchinson, insisted that they unload their cargo as usual.

Sam Adams and the Sons of Liberty had other plans. On the night of December 16, they met in Old South Meetinghouse. They sent a message to the governor, demanding that the ships leave the harbor. When the governor rejected the demand, Adams stood up and declared, "This meeting can do nothing further to save the country."

Adams's words seemed to be a signal. As if on cue, a group of men in Indian disguises burst into the meetinghouse. From the gallery above, voices cried, "Boston harbor a teapot tonight! The Mohawks are come!"

An American Profile

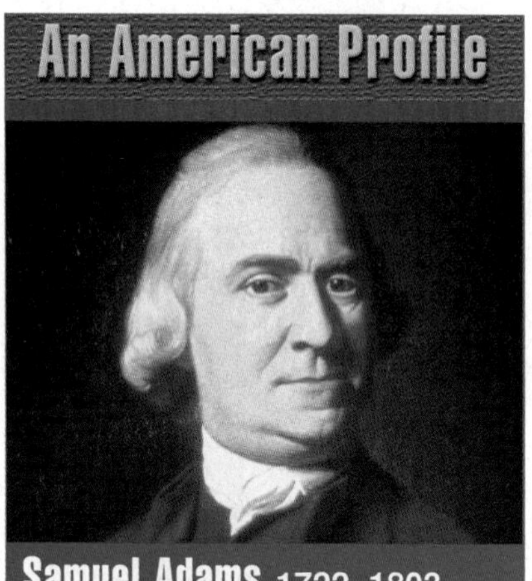

Samuel Adams 1722–1803

Sam Adams was not afraid of a little controversy. For example, when he was a student at Harvard University, Sam read his graduation paper to a large audience that included the governor of Massachusetts. Sam's subject, disobeying the law, deeply disturbed the governor. Sam argued that when a law was morally wrong, a person was entitled to break the law. This belief paved the way for his challenge to British authority.

Why might Sam Adams's graduation paper have disturbed many people in his audience?

The disguised colonists left the meetinghouse and headed for the harbor. Others joined them along the way. Under a nearly full moon, the men boarded the ships, split open the tea chests, and dumped the tea into the harbor. By 10 P.M., the **Boston Tea Party,** as it was later called, was over. The contents of 342 chests of tea floated in Boston harbor. The next day, John Adams wrote about the event in his diary.

> "This destruction of the tea is so bold, so daring, so firm . . . it must have such important and lasting results that I can't help considering it a turning point in history."
>
> —Diary of John Adams, December 17, 1773

Viewing History

Boston Tea Party

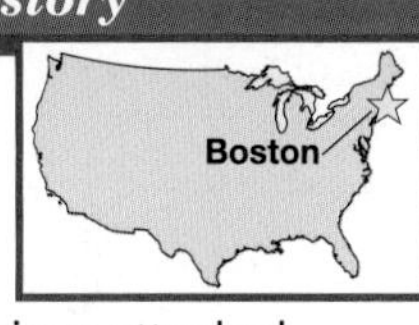

Disguised as Indians, some 50 or 60 Bostonians attacked British tea ships. A crowd watched as the colonists dumped tea into Boston harbor. British officials called the Boston Tea Party "the most wanton and unprovoked insult offered to the civil power that is recorded in history." At lower right is a tea chest. **Drawing Conclusions** ***Why did the colonists disguise themselves as Indians?***

Parliament Strikes Back

Colonists had mixed reactions to the Boston Tea Party. Some cheered it as a firm protest against unfair British laws. Others worried that it would encourage lawlessness in the colonies. Even those who condemned the Boston Tea Party, though, were shocked at Britain's harsh response to it.

Punishing Massachusetts The British were outraged by what they saw as Boston's lawless behavior. In 1774, Parliament, encouraged by King George III, acted to punish Massachusetts. Colonists called the four laws they passed the **Intolerable Acts** because they were so harsh.

Recognize Words That Signal Sequence

Target Skill

Signal words point out relationships among ideas or events. What words signal sequence in the first four paragraphs on this page? Can you find other signal words on this page?

First, Parliament shut down the port of Boston. No ship could enter or leave the harbor—not even a small boat. The harbor would remain closed until the colonists paid for the tea they had destroyed in the Boston Tea Party and repaid British officials, such as Thomas Hutchinson, for damage to personal property.

Second, Parliament forbade Massachusetts colonists to hold town meetings more than once a year without the governor's permission. In the past, colonists had called town meetings whenever they wished. All juries would now be selected by the king's officials, rather than be elected by citizens.

Third, Parliament allowed customs officers and other officials who might be charged with major crimes to be tried in Britain or Canada instead of in Massachusetts. Colonists protested. They argued that a dishonest official could break the law in the colonies and avoid punishment by being tried before a sympathetic jury.

Fourth, Parliament passed a new Quartering Act. No longer would redcoats camp in tents on Boston Common. Instead, colonists would have to house British soldiers in their homes when no other housing was available.

Quebec Act About the same time, Parliament also passed the **Quebec Act.** It set up a government for Canada and gave complete religious freedom to French Catholics. The Quebec Act also extended the borders of Quebec to include the landing between the Ohio and Missouri rivers. The act pleased French Canadians. But it angered the American colonists, because some of the colonies claimed ownership of these lands.

Other Colonies Support Boston The committees of correspondence spread news of the Intolerable Acts to other colonies. They warned that the people of Boston faced hunger while their port was closed. People from other colonies responded quickly. Carts rolled into the city with rice from South Carolina, corn from Virginia, and flour from Pennsylvania.

In the Virginia assembly, Thomas Jefferson suggested that a day be set aside to mark the shame of the Intolerable Acts. The royal governor of Virginia rejected the idea. The colonists went ahead anyway. On June 1, 1774, church bells tolled slowly. Merchants closed their shops. Many colonists prayed and fasted all day.

In September 1774, colonial leaders called a meeting in Philadelphia. Delegates from 12 colonies gathered in what became known as the **First Continental Congress.** Only Georgia did not send delegates.

After much debate, the delegates passed a resolution backing Massachusetts in its struggle. They agreed to boycott all British goods and to stop exporting goods to Britain until the Intolerable Acts were repealed. The delegates also urged each colony to set up and train its own militia (muh LIHSH uh). A **militia** is an army of citizens who serve as soldiers during an emergency.

Before leaving Philadelphia, the delegates agreed to meet again in May 1775. Little did they suspect that before then, an incident in Massachusetts would change the fate of the colonies forever.

Minute Man National Park

The battles at Lexington and Concord began the long struggle for independence of the 13 American colonies against Britain. Today, Minute Man National Historical Park in Massachusetts preserves the historic sites. Here, present-day Americans re-create the battle at the Concord Bridge.

Virtual Field Trip For an interactive look at Minute Man National Park, visit PHSchool.com, **Web Code mfd-0503.**

Lexington and Concord

In Massachusetts, colonists were already preparing to resist. Newspapers called on citizens to prevent what they called "the Massacre of American Liberty." Volunteers known as minutemen trained regularly. Minutemen got their name because they kept their muskets at hand and were prepared to fight at a minute's notice. In towns near Boston, minutemen collected weapons and gunpowder. Meanwhile, Britain built up its forces. More troops arrived in Boston, bringing the total number of British soldiers in that city to 4,000.

Early in 1775, General Thomas Gage, the British commander, sent scouts to towns near Boston. They reported that minutemen had a large store of arms in Concord, a village about 18 miles from Boston. Gage planned a surprise march to Concord to seize the arms.

Sounding the Alarm On April 18, about 700 British troops quietly left Boston in the darkness. Their goal was to seize the colonial arms. The Sons of Liberty were watching. As soon as the British set out, the Americans hung two lamps from the Old North Church in Boston. This signal meant that the redcoats were crossing the Charles River.

Colonists who were waiting across the Charles River saw the signal. Messengers mounted their horses and galloped through the night toward Concord. One midnight rider was Paul Revere. "The redcoats are coming! The redcoats are coming!" shouted Revere as he passed through each sleepy village along the way.

"The Shot Heard Round the World" At daybreak on April 19, the redcoats reached Lexington, a town near Concord. On the village green, some 70 minutemen were waiting, commanded by Captain John Parker. The British ordered the minutemen to go home.

Outnumbered, the colonists began to leave. Suddenly, a shot rang out through the chill morning air. No one knows who fired it. In the brief struggle that followed, eight colonists were killed.

The British pushed on to Concord. Finding no arms in the village, they turned back to Boston. On a bridge outside Concord, they met 300 minutemen. Again, fighting broke out. This time, the British were forced to retreat. As the redcoats withdrew, colonial sharpshooters took deadly aim at them from the woods and fields. Local women also fired at the British from their windows. By the time they reached Boston, the redcoats had lost 73 men. Another 200 British soldiers were wounded or missing.

News of the **battles of Lexington and Concord** spread swiftly. To many colonists, the fighting ended all hope of a peaceful settlement. Only war would decide the future of the 13 colonies.

More than 60 years after the battles of Lexington and Concord, a well-known New England writer, Ralph Waldo Emerson, wrote a poem honoring the minutemen. Emerson's "Concord Hymn" created a vivid picture of the clash at Concord. It begins:

> “By the rude bridge that arched the flood,
> Their flag to April's breeze unfurled,
> Here once the embattled farmers stood,
> And fired the shot heard round the world.”
>
> —Ralph Waldo Emerson, "Concord Hymn," 1837

The "embattled farmers" faced six long years of fighting. At war's end, though, the 13 colonies would be a new, independent nation.

Section 3 Assessment

Recall

1. **Identify** Explain the significance of **(a)** Tea Act, **(b)** Samuel Adams, **(c)** Boston Tea Party, **(d)** Intolerable Acts, **(e)** Quebec Act, **(f)** First Continental Congress, **(g)** minuteman, **(h)** Lexington and Concord.
2. **Define** militia.

Comprehension

3. Why did the Tea Act anger many people in the colonies?
4. Describe two of the Intolerable Acts.
5. Explain why fighting broke out at Lexington and Concord in 1775.

Critical Thinking and Writing

6. **Exploring the Main Idea** Review the Main Idea statement at the beginning of this section. Then, draw a flowchart showing the connection between the Boston Tea Party and the fighting at Lexington and Concord.
7. **Analyzing Information** You are a concerned citizen of Boston in 1775. Write a letter to the editor of your newspaper analyzing the political and economic causes of the American Revolution.

Activity

Composing a Catchy Tune **You are a colonist in Boston in 1773. You are so angry at British actions that you are composing a ditty—a catchy tune—to encourage other colonists to boycott British goods. Take any tune you know and write eight lines of lyrics that will support a boycott.**

Identifying Causes and Effects

The events that shape history don't just happen. They are related to earlier events. To understand historical events, it is important to recognize their causes. It also is important to recognize the effects of the events—what resulted because the event happened.

Cause *and* Effect

Causes

- Parliament passes the Townshend Acts
- Parliament repeals the Townshend Acts but later passes a new tax, the Tea Act
- The colonies oppose the tax by boycotting tea
- The British ship tea to Boston harbor

THE BOSTON TEA PARTY

Effects

- Parliament passes the Intolerable Acts to punish Massachusetts
- Other colonies back Massachusetts in its struggle against Britain
- Massachusetts minutemen clash with British soldiers at Lexington and Concord

Learn the Skill *To learn to analyze a cause-and-effect chart, use the following steps:*

1. **Look at the headings.** The headings on the chart indicate which statements are the causes of an event and which statements are the results of it.
2. **Read the causes.** These statements give reasons why a particular event occurred. Some events have one cause. Others have many.
3. **Identify the effects.** These statements tell what happened because of the event. Very important events may have effects in many different areas.
4. **Make connections.** Think about why certain causes led to the event and why the event in turn had the results it did. Remember that an event will be both cause and effect. It may flow out of a previous event while itself creating many results.

Practice the Skill *Answer the following questions about the chart above.*

1. **(a)** What event do the causes on this chart lead to? **(b)** If you could add to the chart, under which heading would you put the outbreak of the French and Indian War?
2. Give two reasons for the Boston Tea Party.
3. Give two effects of the Boston Tea Party.
4. **(a)** Why did the tea shipped to Boston harbor lead to the Boston Tea Party? **(b)** How was the clash at Lexington and Concord a result of the Boston Tea Party?

Apply the Skill *See the Chapter Review and Assessment.*

CHAPTER

5 Review and Assessment

CHAPTER SUMMARY

Section 1

The French and Indian War marked the end of the French empire in North America. In the treaty that ended the war, Britain gained control of Canada and lands east of the Mississippi River, except New Orleans.

Section 2

Many colonists opposed Parliament's attempts to tighten control over the colonies. Colonists met Britain's efforts to tax the colonies with protests. Rising tensions resulted in the Boston Massacre in March 1770.

Section 3

Crises such as the Boston Tea Party and the Intolerable Acts increased the gulf between Britain and the colonies. Unified against Britain, the colonies sent delegates to the First Continental Congress. In 1775, fighting broke out in Lexington and Concord.

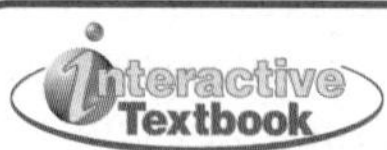

For additional review and enrichment activities, see the interactive version of *The American Nation,* available on the Web and on CD-ROM.

Chapter Self-Test For practice test questions for Chapter 5, visit PHSchool.com, **Web Code mfa-0504.**

Building Vocabulary

Write sentences using the vocabulary words below. Leave blanks where the vocabulary words go. Exchange your sentences with a classmate, and fill in the blanks in each other's sentences.

1. **petition**
2. **boycott**
3. **repeal**
4. **militia**
5. **minuteman**
6. **French and Indian War**
7. **Albany Plan of Union**
8. **Pontiac's War**
9. **Proclamation of 1763**
10. **writ of assistance**

Reviewing Key Facts

11. What were the main results of the Treaty of Paris of 1763? (Section 1)
12. What role did Sam Adams play in aiding the colonial cause? (Section 2)
13. How did the Intolerable Acts unite people in the American colonies? (Section 3)

Critical Thinking and Writing

14. **Analyzing Primary Sources** Review the statement made by a Native American to an English trader: "You and the French are like the two edges of a pair of shears. And we are the cloth which is to be cut to pieces between them." **(a)** Write a paragraph explaining what the speaker meant by these words. **(b)** Do you think he believed that Native Americans could hold out against the British and French? Write a paragraph explaining your answer.
15. **Drawing Conclusions** List three ways your life might be different if France, not Britain, had won the French and Indian War.
16. **Ranking** List the events described in Sections 2 and 3. Then, rank them in the order of their importance in bringing about war between the American colonies and Britain. Put the most important event at the top of the list and the least important event at the bottom.

17. **Connecting to Geography: Place** Describe how the geographic setting influenced the way the battles of Lexington and Concord were fought.

Skills Assessment

Analyzing Primary Sources

Read this selection from Patrick Henry's speech and answer the questions that follow:

> "... The war is inevitable—and let it come! I repeat, sir, let it come. . . . The next gale that sweeps from the north will bring to our ears the clash of resounding arms! Our brethren are already in the field! Why stand we here idle? What is it that gentlemen wish? What would they have? Is life so dear, or peace so sweet, as to be purchased at the price of liberty and slavery? Forbid it, Almighty God! I know not what course others may take; but as for me, give me liberty or give me death."
>
> —From a speech by Patrick Henry, March 23, 1775

18. When Henry says, " . . . let it come! I repeat, sir, let it come," to what is he referring?
- **A.** the Boston Massacre
- **B.** the French and Indian War
- **C.** war with Britain
- **D.** war with Spain

19. Who are the "brethren . . . already in the field"?
- **A.** British soldiers
- **B.** minutemen
- **C.** Native American allies
- **D.** French soldiers

Applying Your Skills

Identifying Causes and Effects

The French and Indian War

Causes
- British colonists settle on lands claimed by France
- France and Britain involved in a worldwide struggle for empire

THE FRENCH AND INDIAN WAR

Effects
- Britain left with a large debt
- Colonists begin settling in Ohio River Valley

20. What was Britain's financial situation after the French and Indian War?
- **A.** It was in debt.
- **B.** It was extremely prosperous.
- **C.** It had so much money it was able to lend some to hard-pressed colonies.
- **D.** It had to pay large amounts of money to France.

21. How did the French and Indian War lead to the Proclamation of 1763?

Activities

Connecting With . . . Culture

Write a Poem At the end of this chapter, you read a portion of Emerson's "Concord Hymn," which celebrates the minutemen at Concord Bridge. Another famous poem about this period is Henry Wadsworth Longfellow's "Paul Revere's Ride." It begins "Listen, my children, and you shall hear / Of the midnight ride of Paul Revere." Pick another event covered in this chapter and write a short poem about it. The poem should convey a sense of the emotions of the time. It need not be longer than eight lines.

Creating a Database

Collecting Information About Colonial Leaders
Use the Internet to research the colonial leaders mentioned in this chapter. Find the following information: date of birth, date of death, home state/colony, major event involved in. Use the computer to list the information on a chart. Then, sort the information by (1) alphabetized last name, (2) date of birth, and (3) home state/colony. For help in starting this activity, visit PHSchool.com, **Web Code mfd-0506.**

Johnny Tremain

Esther Forbes

Introduction ***Johnny Tremain*** **is a work of historical fiction, a novel that uses actual people, places, and events to tell a fictional story. The author, Esther Forbes, wrote both real histories and historical fiction. The selection below begins as Boston is facing punishment by Britain for the Boston Tea Party.**

Vocabulary Before you read the selection, find the meanings of these words in a dictionary: **paroxysm, indifferent, submission, gesticulating, wharfingers, tethered, flintlocks, impartially, filching, misdemeanor.**

Esther Forbes (1891–1967)

When that bill [for the Tea Party] came . . . , it was so much heavier than anyone expected, Boston was thrown into a paroxysm of anger and despair. There had been many a moderate man who had thought the Tea Party a bit lawless and was now ready to vote payment for the tea. But when these men heard how cruelly the Town was to be punished, they swore it would never be paid for. And those other thirteen colonies. Up to this time many of them had had little interest in Boston's struggles. Now they were united as never before. The punishment united the often jealous, often indifferent, separate colonies, as the Tea Party itself had not.

Sam Adams was so happy his hands shook worse than ever.

For it had been voted in far-off London that the port of Boston should be closed—not one ship might enter, not one ship might leave the port, except only His Majesty's warships and transports, until the tea was paid for. Boston was to be starved into submission.

On that day, that first of June, 1774, Johnny and Rab, like almost all the other citizens, did no work, but wandered from place to place over the town. People were standing in angry knots talking, gesticulating, swearing that yes, they would starve, they would go down to ruin rather than give in now. Even many of the Tories were talking like that, for the punishment fell equally heavily upon the King's most loyal subjects in Boston and the very "Indians" who had tossed the tea overboard. This closing of the port of Boston was indeed tyranny; this was oppression; this was the last straw upon the back of many a moderate man.

The boys strolled the waterfront. Here, on Long Wharf, merchants' counting houses were closed and shuttered, sail lofts deserted, the riggers and porters stood idle. Overnight, hundreds of such, and sailors and ropemakers, wharfingers and dock hands, had been thrown out of work. The great ships of Boston, which had been bringing wealth for over a hundred years, were idle at their berths. No one might come and go. . . .

June was ending and the boys stood about the Common watching the soldiers of the First Brigade camped there under Earl Percy. Row upon row of identical tents, cook fires, tethered horses of officers, camp followers, stacked muskets, the quick, smart pacing of sentries. All was neat and orderly.

Muskets. It was the muskets which interested Rab the most. Already on every village green throughout New England, men and boys were drilling in defiance of the King's orders. They said they were afraid of an attack from the French. These men had no uniforms. They came from the fields and farms in the very clothes they used for plowing. That was all right. But the weapons they brought to their drilling were not. Many had ancient flintlocks, old squirrel guns, handed down for generations. Rab, for instance, all that spring had been going to Lexington once or twice a week to drill with his fellow townsmen. But he could not beg nor buy a decent gun. . . .

Rab, so concerned over a gun as he was, did an uncharacteristic, foolish thing. The two boys were standing close to a stack of muskets. As Rab explained to Johnny their good points, he put out a hand and touched the lock on one.

Without even showing bad temper, almost impartially, a mounted officer sitting on his horse close by [and] chatting with a couple of Boston's Tory girls, swung about and struck Rab a heavy blow on the side of his head with the flat of his sword. Then he went on flirting with the girls as though nothing had happened. Rab never knew what hit him. . . .

A gray, older man, a medical officer, approached, called for water, sponged Rab's face for him, and said he was coming to. Johnny was not to worry.

"What was he doing?"

"Just looking at a gun."

"Touching it?"

"Well. . . yes."

British soldiers entering Boston

"And only got hit over the head? He got off easy. Filching a soldier's arms is a serious misdemeanor. Wonder Lieutenant Bragg didn't kill him."

Rab said thickly, "I hadn't thought to filch it! Not a bad idea. Guess I'll. . . guess I'll. . ." He was still groggy from the blow. "If ever I get a chance I'll. . . ."

The medical man only laughed at him.

Analyzing Literature

1. When Johnny and Rab strolled along the waterfront, they found that people were
   - **A** ready to give in to the British.
   - **B** saying they would starve rather than give in to the British.
   - **C** so busy with their jobs they took little notice of British actions.
   - **D** agreeing with the British.
2. How would you describe the attitude of the British medical officer toward Rab and Johnny?
   - **A** Angry
   - **B** Uncaring
   - **C** Sympathetic
   - **D** Nervous
3. **Critical Thinking and Writing** **Drawing Inferences** **(a)** What do the actions of the British officer, Lieutenant Bragg, suggest about his attitude toward the colonists? **(b)** In what ways do you think the medical officer agreed with Lieutenant Bragg? In what ways do you think he disagreed with Bragg?

CHAPTER 6

The American Revolution

1775–1783

1. Fighting Begins in the North
2. The Colonies Declare Independence
3. Struggles in the Middle States
4. Fighting for Liberty on Many Fronts
5. Winning the War in the South

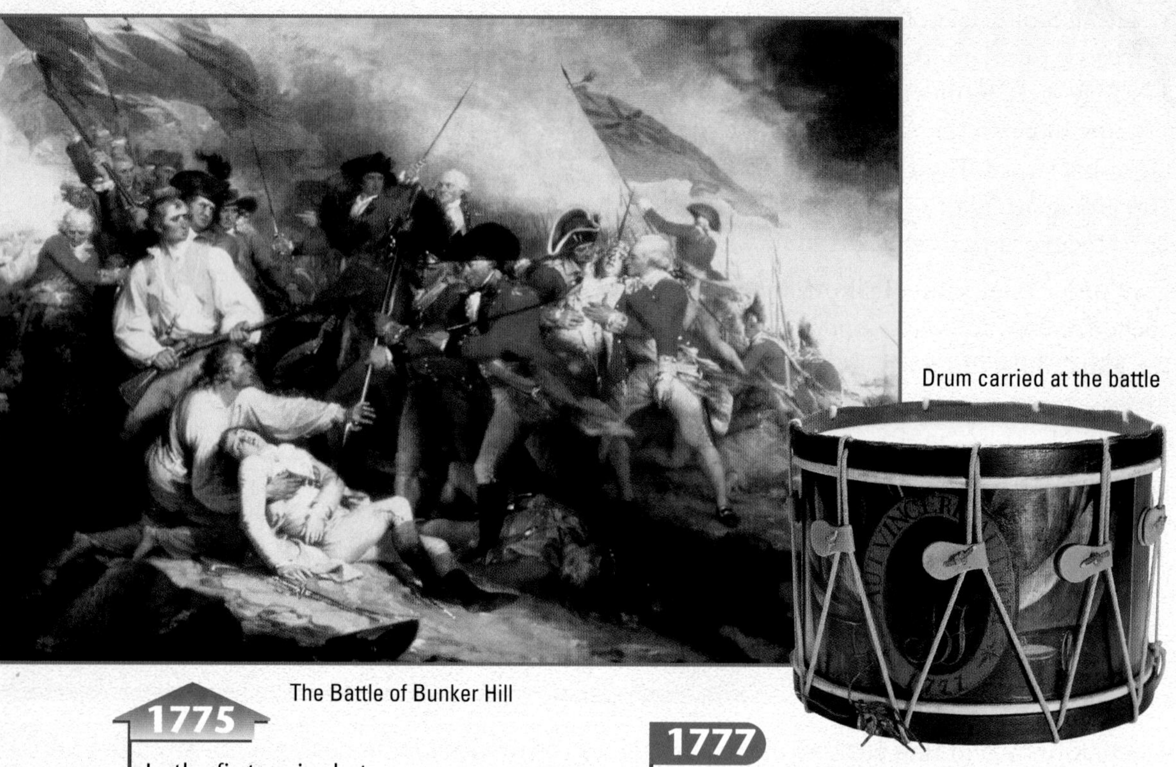

The Battle of Bunker Hill

Drum carried at the battle

AMERICAN EVENTS

1775 In the first major battle of the American Revolution, the colonists face the British at Bunker Hill.

1777 The American victory at the Battle of Saratoga is the turning point of the war. After this victory, the French decide to join the Americans in their fight against the British.

1775 · 1777 · 1779

WORLD EVENTS

1778 ▲ France recognizes American independence.

1779 ▲ Spain enters the war against Britain.

Turning Points in the Revolution

In spite of early defeats in the war, the Americans scored victories that renewed their hopes for winning independence.

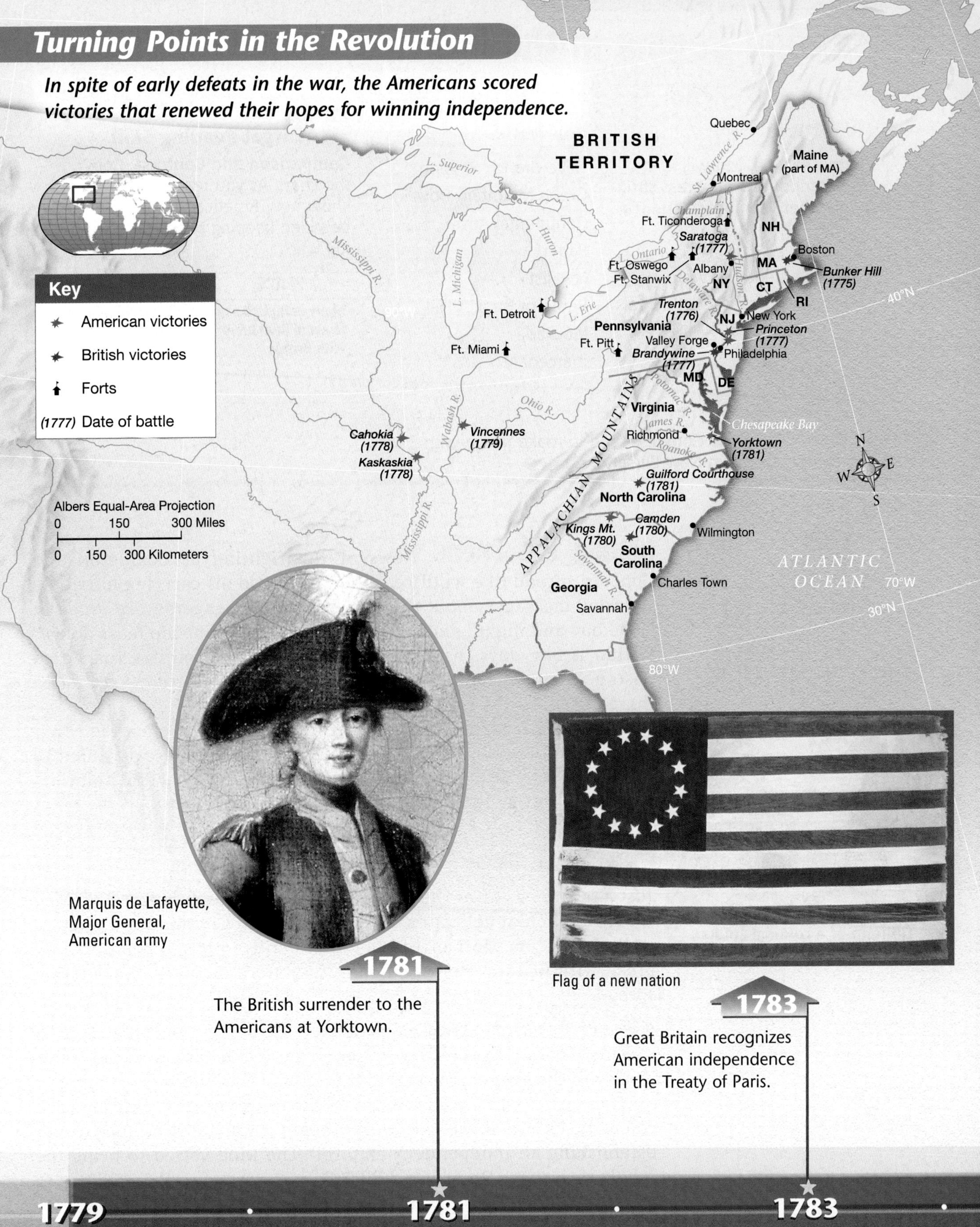

Marquis de Lafayette, Major General, American army

Flag of a new nation

1781 The British surrender to the Americans at Yorktown.

1783 Great Britain recognizes American independence in the Treaty of Paris.

▲ 1780
Tupac Armaru, a descendant of the Incas, leads a revolt against Spain.

1 Fighting Begins in the North

Prepare to Read

Objectives

In this section, you will

- Describe how Congress struggled between peace and war with Britain.
- List the advantages each side had as it entered the war.
- Explain how the Continental Army gained control of Boston.

Key Terms

Olive Branch Petition
Green Mountain Boys
Continental Army
Patriot
Loyalist
Battle of Bunker Hill
blockade
mercenary

Target Reading Skill

Comparison and Contrast Copy the chart. As you read, add facts to show how Americans struggled between keeping peace and waging war.

PEACE	WAR
• Many colonists hope to avoid final break with Britain • •	• Green Mountain Boys capture Fort Ticonderoga • •

Main Idea Even while Congress tried to make peace with Britain, fighting began in New England.

Uniform of a colonial soldier

Setting the Scene News of the fighting at Lexington and Concord spread like wildfire. Riders galloped off carrying hurriedly scrawled messages about the battles. The messengers were urged to "ride day and night" and spread the news "without the least delay." Within a few days, between 10,000 and 15,000 militia rushed to Boston. They surrounded the city and the British troops stationed there.

The sudden arrival of rebellious colonists was a clear sign that the quarrel between Britain and its American colonies was about to blaze into war. Still, many colonists hoped for a peaceful solution. Was there no way to heal relations with Britain?

Peace or War?

Just a few weeks after the battles at Lexington and Concord, on May 10, 1775, colonial delegates met at the Second Continental Congress in Philadelphia. Most of the delegates still hoped to avoid a final break with Britain. However, while they were meeting, the fighting spread.

A Peace Petition After much debate, the delegates sent a petition to King George. In the **Olive Branch Petition,** they declared their loyalty to the king and asked him to repeal the Intolerable Acts.

George III was furious when he heard about the petition. The colonists, he raged, were trying to begin a war "for the purpose of establishing an independent empire!" The king vowed to bring the rebels to justice. He ordered 20,000 more troops to the colonies to crush the revolt.

Congress did not learn of the king's response until months later. But even before the petition was sent, leaders like John and Sam Adams were convinced that war could not be avoided.

Rebels Take Ticonderoga Ethan Allen, a Vermont blacksmith, did not wait for Congress to act. Allen decided to lead a band of Vermonters, known as the **Green Mountain Boys,** in a surprise attack on Fort Ticonderoga, located at the southern tip of Lake Champlain. (See the map on page 170.) Allen knew that the fort held cannons that the colonists could use.

In early May, the Green Mountain Boys crept quietly through the morning mists to Fort Ticonderoga. They quickly overpowered the guard on duty and entered the fort. Allen rushed to the room where the British commander slept. "Come out, you old rat!" he shouted. The commander demanded to know by whose authority Allen acted. "In the name of the Great Jehovah and the Continental Congress!" Allen replied.

The British commander surrendered Ticonderoga. With the fort, the Green Mountain Boys won a valuable supply of cannons and gunpowder. Allen's success also gave Americans control of a key route into Canada.

Setting Up an Army In the meantime, the Second Continental Congress had to decide what to do about the makeshift army gathering around Boston. In June, delegates took the bold step of setting up the **Continental Army.** They appointed George Washington of Virginia as commander.

Washington knew that he would be fighting against one of the world's toughest armies. Still, he was willing to do his best. He set off at once to take charge of the forces around Boston.

Target Skill

Identify Contrasts

How did the Green Mountain Boys differ from the delegates who signed the Olive Branch Petition? In which categories on your chart would you place each group?

Viewing History

Rebels Take Fort Ticonderoga

Fort Ticonderoga

In May 1775, Ethan Allen and the Green Mountain Boys made a bold attack on Fort Ticonderoga. In this painting, Allen demands that the British commander surrender the fort. **Applying Information** ***Why was Fort Ticonderoga an important prize?***

Advantages of the Opposing Sides

The colonists who favored war against Britain called themselves **Patriots.** They thought British rule was harsh and unjust. About one third of the colonists were Patriots, one third were Loyalists, and one third did not take sides.

Patriots The Patriots entered the war with many disadvantages. Colonial forces were poorly organized and untrained. They had few cannons, little gunpowder, and no navy. Also, few colonists were willing to enlist in the Continental Army for long terms of service. They preferred to fight near home, as part of a local militia.

Yet, the Patriots also had advantages. Many Patriots owned rifles and were good shots. Their leader, George Washington, developed into a brilliant commander. Furthermore, Patriots were determined to fight to defend their homes and property. Reuben Stebbins of Massachusetts was

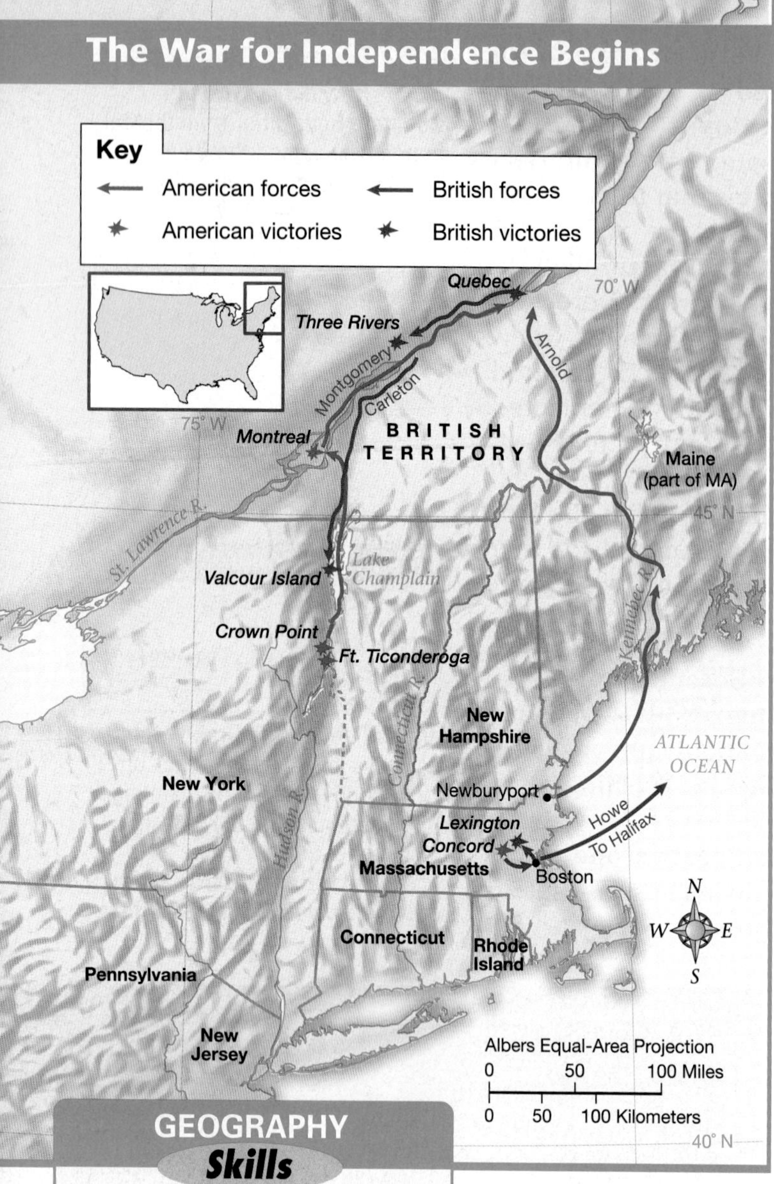

GEOGRAPHY *Skills*

At the beginning of the War for Independence, most of the fighting took place in the northern colonies and in Canada.

1. **Location** On the map, locate **(a)** Lexington, **(b)** Concord, **(c)** Boston, **(d)** Fort Ticonderoga, **(e)** Quebec.
2. **Movement** **(a)** Describe Arnold's route to Canada. **(b)** Describe Montgomery's route from Crown Point to Quebec.
3. **Critical Thinking** **Making Decisions** Based on the map, which American commander would have a harder time reaching Quebec? Explain.

typical of many patriotic farmers. When the British approached, he rode off to battle. "We'll see who's going t'own this farm!" he cried.

The British The British were a powerful foe. They had highly trained, experienced troops. Their navy was the best in the world. In addition, many colonists supported the British.

Still, Britain faced problems. Its armies were 3,000 miles from home. News and supplies took months to travel from Britain to North America. Also, British soldiers risked attacks by colonists once they marched out of the cities into the countryside.

Loyalists American colonists who remained loyal to Britain were known as **Loyalists.** They included wealthy merchants and former officials of the royal government. However, some farmers and craftsworkers were also Loyalists. There were more Loyalists in the Middle Colonies and the South than in New England.

Loyalists faced hard times during the war. Patriots tarred and feathered people known to favor the British. Many Loyalists fled to England or Canada. Others found shelter in cities controlled by the British. Those who fled lost their homes, stores, and farms.

The Fight for Boston

During the first year of conflict, much of the fighting centered around Boston. About 6,000 British troops were stationed there. Colonial militia surrounded the city and prevented the British from marching out.

Battle of Bunker Hill Even before Washington reached Boston, the Patriots took action. On June 16, 1775, Colonel William Prescott led 1,200 minutemen up Bunker Hill, across the river from Boston. From there, they could fire on British ships in Boston harbor. Prescott, however, noticed that nearby Breed's Hill was an even better position. He ordered his men to move there.

At sunrise, the British general, William Howe, spotted the Americans. He ferried about 2,400 redcoats across the harbor to attack the rebels' position. As the British approached, the Patriots held their fire.

When the Americans finally fired, the British were forced to retreat. A second British attack was also turned back. On the third try, the British pushed over the top. They took both Bunker Hill and Breed's Hill, but they paid a high price for their victory. More than

1,000 redcoats lay dead or wounded. American losses numbered only about 400.

The **Battle of Bunker Hill** was the first major battle of the Revolution. It proved that the Americans could fight bravely. It also showed that the British would not be easy to defeat.

The British Leave Boston When Washington reached Boston a few weeks after the Battle of Bunker Hill, he found about 16,000 troops camped in huts and tents at the edge of the city.

General Washington quickly began to turn raw recruits into a trained army. His job was especially difficult because soldiers from different colonies mistrusted one another. "Connecticut wants no Massachusetts men in her corps," he wrote. And "Massachusetts thinks there is no necessity for a Rhode Islander to be introduced into her [ranks]." However, Washington won the loyalty of his troops. They, in turn, learned to take orders and work together.

In January 1776, Washington had a stroke of good fortune. The cannons that the Green Mountain Boys had captured at Fort Ticonderoga arrived in Boston. Soldiers had dragged them across the mountains from Fort Ticonderoga. Washington had the cannons placed on Dorchester Heights, overlooking the harbor.

Once General Howe saw the American cannons in place, he knew that he could not hold Boston. In March 1776, he and his troops sailed from Boston to Halifax, Canada. About 1,000 American Loyalists went with them.

Although the British left New England, they did not give up. King George III ordered a blockade of all colonial ports. A **blockade** is the shutting of a port to keep people or supplies from moving in or out. The king also used **mercenaries,** or troops for hire, from Germany to help fight the colonists.

★ ★ ★ Section 1 Assessment ★ ★ ★

Recall

1. **Identify** Explain the significance of **(a)** King George III, **(b)** Olive Branch Petition, **(c)** Green Mountain Boys, **(d)** Continental Army, **(e)** George Washington, **(f)** Patriot, **(g)** Loyalist, **(h)** Battle of Bunker Hill.
2. **Define** **(a)** blockade, **(b)** mercenary.

Comprehension

3. **(a)** What steps did the Continental Congress take to pursue peace with Britain? **(b)** What steps did the Congress take to pursue war with Britain?
4. **(a)** What advantages did the Patriots have as the war began? **(b)** What advantages did the British have?
5. How did Washington force the British to leave Boston?

Critical Thinking and Writing

6. **Exploring the Main Idea** Review the Main Idea statement at the beginning of this section. Then, write a letter to Congress explaining why you think war can or cannot be avoided.
7. **Drawing Inferences** Why did some Loyalists feel they had to go with the British to Canada?

ACTIVITY

Writing a Diary Entry

You have George Washington's job at the beginning of the war. Write several diary entries describing the task you face as commander of the Continental Army.

Identifying Points of View

When reading about a historical event, it is important to keep in mind that people wrote about an event from different points of view.

Ann Hulton was a Loyalist who lived with her brother in Boston just before the Revolution. His job was to collect taxes for the British. In this letter, Hulton describes an attack by a mob:

"You will be surprised to hear how we were obliged to take refuge on board the *Romney* man of war lying in Boston Harbor. Mrs. Burch at whose house I was, had frequently been alarmed with the Sons of Liberty surrounding her house with most hideous howlings. . . . She had been exposed since her arrival and threatened with greater violence. She had removed her most valuable [possessions] and held herself in readiness to depart at an hour's notice. The occasion soon happened . . . we soon found that the mobs here are very different from those in Old England . . . these Sons of Violence after attacking houses, breaking windows, beating, stoning and bruising several gentlemen belonging to the Customs, the Collector mortally and burning his boat. . . . All was ended with a speech from one of the leaders, concluding thus, 'We will defend our Liberties and property, by the Strength of our Arm and the Help of our God. . . .' This is a specimen of the Sons of Liberty, of whom no doubt you have heard, and will hear more. . . ."

—Ann Hulton, in a letter written June 30, 1768

This engraving shows boys laughing at a Loyalist.

Learn the Skill *Use these steps to identify points of view:*

1. **Identify the source.** If you know the background of the writer, you can evaluate that person's attitude.
2. **Note the frame of reference.** The place, time, and circumstances can make a difference.
3. **Find main ideas.** What is the main point that the writer or speaker is making?
4. **Look for emotionally charged words.** How information is presented affects the point of view.
5. **Identify points of view.** How does the writer or speaker feel?

Practice the Skill *Use the introduction and the letter to answer the following questions:*

1. How do you know that Ann Hulton was writing to a Loyalist?
2. **(a)** Where did the event described take place? **(b)** How would you characterize the event?
3. Restate the main point of the letter.
4. Identify three emotionally charged words used in the letter.
5. **(a)** What is the writer's point of view? **(b)** Explain how you can tell.

Apply the Skill *See the Chapter Review and Assessment.*

2 The Colonies Declare Independence

Prepare to Read

Objectives

In this section, you will
- Describe the impact of *Common Sense.*
- List the steps Congress took to declare independence.
- Summarize the main ideas of the Declaration of Independence.

Key Terms

Common Sense
traitor
Declaration of Independence
preamble
natural rights

Target Reading Skill

Clarifying Meaning Copy the concept web. As you read, fill in the blank ovals with information about the creation and contents of the Declaration of Independence. Add as many ovals as you need.

DECLARATION OF INDEPENDENCE
Thomas Jefferson writes the Declaration
Preamble
Part 1

Main Idea In July 1776, the colonies declared independence from Britain.

Setting the Scene Dr. Benjamin Rush of Philadelphia looked down at the manuscript in his hand. A line referring to King George as "the royal brute of Great Britain" seemed to leap off the page. Apparently, that was only the beginning! Would any printer dare to publish such a document?

Rush had asked his friend Thomas Paine to write an essay urging the colonies to declare independence. By the winter of 1775, the Patriots had been fighting Britain for months. Yet, many colonists were still reluctant to cut their ties with Britain. In a fiery pamphlet, Paine told these colonists that it was time to make the break. He called the pamphlet **Common Sense.**

Thomas Paine

When *Common Sense* appeared in January 1776, curious readers snatched up copies. In six months, more than 500,000 were sold. "*Common Sense* is working a powerful change in the minds of men," George Washington observed.

Urged on by Paine and other radicals—people who want to make drastic changes in society—the colonists were beginning to think the unthinkable. They were thinking of creating a nation of their own.

Common Sense

By 1776, many colonists had come to believe that Parliament did not have the right to make laws for the 13 colonies. After all, they argued, the colonists had their own elected legislatures. At the same time, however, most colonists still felt a bond of loyalty to Britain. They especially felt that they owed allegiance to the king.

In *Common Sense,* Thomas Paine set out to change the colonists' attitudes toward Britain and the king. Colonists, he said, did not owe loyalty to George III or any other monarch. The very idea of having kings and queens was wrong, he said.

> ❝ In England a King hath little more to do than to make war and give away [jobs]; which in plain terms, is

Viewing History

Signing the Declaration

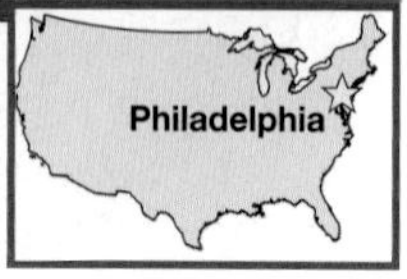

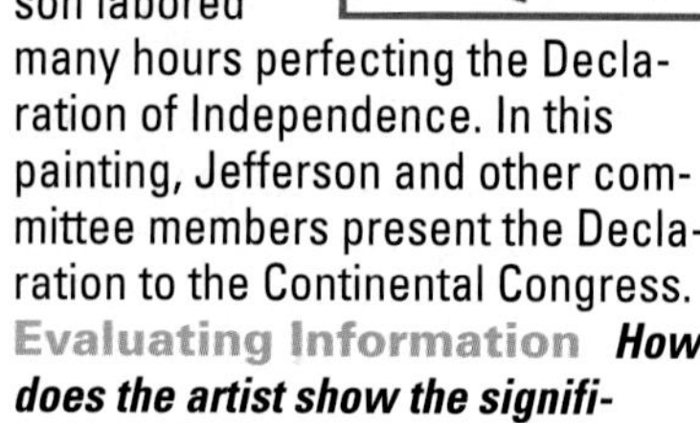

Thomas Jefferson labored many hours perfecting the Declaration of Independence. In this painting, Jefferson and other committee members present the Declaration to the Continental Congress. **Evaluating Information** ***How does the artist show the significance of the meeting?***

to impoverish the nation. . . . Of more worth is one honest man to society and in the sight of God, than all the crowned ruffians that ever lived. ❞

—Thomas Paine, *Common Sense,* 1776

The colonists did not owe anything to Britain, either, Paine went on. If the British had helped the colonists, they had done so for their own profit. It could only hurt the colonists to remain under British rule. "Everything that is right or reasonable pleads for separation," he concluded. " 'Tis time to part."

Congress Votes for Independence

Common Sense sold many colonists on the idea of independence. It also deeply impressed many members of the Continental Congress. Richard Henry Lee of Virginia wrote to Washington, "I am now convinced . . . of the necessity for separation." In June 1776, Lee arose in Congress to introduce a resolution in favor of independence:

❝ *Resolved,* That these United Colonies are and of right ought to be, free and independent States, that they are absolved from all allegiance to the British Crown, and that all political connection between them and the State of Great Britain is, and ought to be, totally dissolved. ❞

—Richard Henry Lee, Resolution at the Second Continental Congress, June 7, 1776

Making the Break The delegates faced a difficult decision. There could be no turning back once they declared independence. If they fell into British hands, they would be hanged as traitors. A **traitor** is a person who betrays his or her country.

After long debate, the Congress took a fateful step. They appointed a committee to draw up a formal declaration of independence. The committee included John Adams, Benjamin Franklin, Thomas Jefferson, Robert Livingston, and Roger Sherman. Their job was to tell the world why the colonies were breaking away from Britain.

The committee asked Thomas Jefferson to write the document. Jefferson was one of the youngest delegates. He was a quiet man who spoke little at formal meetings. Among friends, however, he liked to sprawl in a chair with his long legs stretched out and talk for hours. His ability to write clearly and gracefully had earned him great respect.

Signing the Document In late June, Jefferson completed the declaration, and it was read to the Congress. On July 2, the Continental Congress voted that the 13 colonies were "free and independent States." After polishing Jefferson's language, the delegates adopted the document on the night of July 4, 1776. They then ordered the **Declaration of Independence** to be printed.

John Hancock, president of the Continental Congress, signed the Declaration first. He penned his signature boldly, in large, clear letters. "There," he said, "I guess King George will be able to read that."

Copies of the Declaration were distributed throughout the colonies. Patriots greeted the news of independence with joyous—and sometimes rowdy—celebrations. In New York, colonists tore down a statue of King George III. In Boston, the sound of cannons could be heard for hours.

Primary Source

"Remember the Ladies"

While John Adams served as a delegate in the second Continental Congress, his wife, Abigail, wrote him the following letter:

"I long to hear that you have independence. And . . . in the new Code of Laws which I suppose it will be necessary for you to make I desire you would Remember the Ladies, and be more generous and favourable to them than your ancestors. Do not put such unlimited power into the hands of the Husbands. . . . If particular care and attention is not paid to the Ladies we are determined to foment a Rebellion, and will not hold ourselves bound by any Laws in which we have no voice, or Representation."

—Abigail Adams, letter to John Adams, March 31, 1776

Analyzing Primary Sources

How did Abigail Adams use arguments for independence made by Patriots to promote greater rights for women?

The Declaration of Independence

The Declaration of Independence consists of a **preamble,** or introduction, followed by three main parts.*

Natural Rights The first section of the Declaration stresses the idea of **natural rights,** or rights that belong to all people from birth. In bold, ringing words, Jefferson wrote:

> "We hold these truths to be self-evident, that all men are created equal; that they are endowed by their Creator with certain unalienable rights; that among these are life, liberty, and the pursuit of happiness."

According to the Declaration of Independence, people form governments in order to protect their natural rights and liberties. Governments can exist only if they have the "consent of the governed." If a government fails to protect the rights of its citizens, then it is the people's "right [and] duty, to throw off such government, and to provide new guards for their future security."

*The complete Declaration of Independence is printed at the end of this section on pages 177–180.

British Wrongs The second part of the Declaration lists the wrongs that led the Americans to break away from Britain. Jefferson condemned King George III for disbanding colonial legislatures and for sending troops to the colonies in peacetime. He complained about limits on trade and about taxes imposed without the consent of the people.

Jefferson listed many other wrongs to show why the colonists had the right to rebel. He also pointed out that the colonies had petitioned the king to correct these injustices. Yet, the injustices remained. A ruler who treated his subjects in this manner, he boldly concluded, is a tyrant and not fit to rule:

> ❝ In every state of these oppressions, we have petitioned for redress in the most humble terms; our repeated petitions have been answered only by repeated injury. A prince whose character is thus marked by every act which may define a tyrant is unfit to be the ruler of a free people. ❞

Target Skill — Summarize
Write a paragraph that summarizes the three major parts of the Declaration of Independence.

Independence The last part of the Declaration announces that the colonies are the United States of America. All political ties with Britain have been cut. As a free and independent nation, the United States has the full power to "levy war, conclude peace, contract alliances, establish commerce, and to do all other acts and things which independent states may of right do."

The signers close the declaration with a solemn pledge:

> ❝ And, for the support of this declaration, with a firm reliance on the protection of Divine Providence, we mutually pledge to each other our lives, our fortunes, and our sacred honor. ❞

★ ★ ★ Section 2 Assessment ★ ★ ★

Recall

1. **Identify** Explain the significance of **(a)** Thomas Paine, **(b)** *Common Sense,* **(c)** Richard Henry Lee, **(d)** Thomas Jefferson, **(e)** Declaration of Independence.
2. **Define** **(a)** traitor, **(b)** preamble, **(c)** natural rights.

Comprehension

3. What arguments did Thomas Paine use in *Common Sense* to persuade the colonists to declare independence?
4. What actions did Congress take to make the final break with Britain?
5. Describe the main parts of the Declaration of Independence.

Critical Thinking and Writing

6. **Exploring the Main Idea** Review the Main Idea statement at the beginning of this section. Explain the arguments that the colonies used for declaring independence from Britain.
7. **Analyzing Primary Sources** Review the excerpt from Thomas Paine's *Common Sense* that appears on pages 173–174. Explain the meaning of this excerpt in your own words.

Activity

Connecting to Today
Use the Internet to visit the exhibition of the original Declaration of Independence in Washington, D.C. Prepare a guided tour of the exhibit. Include information about the meaning of the document to Americans today. For help in completing the activity, visit PHSchool.com, **Web Code mfd-0601.**

The Declaration of Independence

On June 7, 1776, the Continental Congress approved the resolution that "these United Colonies are, and of right ought to be, free and independent States." Congress then appointed a committee to write a declaration of independence. The committee members were John Adams, Benjamin Franklin, Robert Livingston, Roger Sherman, and Thomas Jefferson.

Jefferson actually wrote the Declaration, but he got advice from the others. On July 2, Congress discussed the Declaration and made some changes. On July 4, 1776, it adopted the Declaration of Independence in its final form.

The Declaration is printed in black. The headings have been added to show the parts of the Declaration. They are not part of the original text. Annotations, or explanations, are on the white side of the page. Difficult words are defined.

When in the course of human events it becomes necessary for one people to dissolve the political bands which have connected them with another and to assume, among the powers of the earth, the separate and equal station to which the laws of nature and of nature's God entitle them, a decent respect to the opinions of mankind requires that they should declare the causes which impel them to the separation.

dissolve: break ***powers of the earth:*** other nations ***station:*** place ***impel:*** force

The colonists feel that they must explain to the world the reasons why they are breaking away from England.

The Purpose of Government Is to Protect Basic Rights

We hold these truths to be self-evident, that all men are created equal; that they are endowed by their Creator with certain unalienable rights; that among these are life, liberty, and the pursuit of happiness. That, to secure these rights, governments are instituted among men, deriving their just powers from the consent of the governed; that, whenever any form of government becomes destructive of these ends, it is the right of the people to alter or to abolish it, and to institute a new government, laying its foundation on such principles and organizing its powers in such form, as to them shall seem most likely to effect their safety and happiness. Prudence, indeed, will dictate that governments long established should not be changed for light and transient causes; and, accordingly, all experience hath shown that mankind are more disposed to suffer, while evils are sufferable, than to right themselves by abolishing the forms to which they are accustomed. But when a long train of abuses and usurpations, pursuing invariably the same object, evinces a design to reduce them under absolute despotism, it is their right, it is their duty, to throw off such government and to provide new guards for their future security. Such has been the patient sufferance of these colonies, and such is now the necessity which constrains them to alter their former systems of government. The history of the present King of Great Britain is a history of repeated injuries and usurpations, all having, in direct object, the establishment of an absolute tyranny over these States. To prove this, let facts be submitted to a candid world:

endowed: given ***unalienable rights:*** so basic that they cannot be taken away ***secure:*** protect ***instituted:*** set up ***deriving:*** getting ***alter:*** change ***effect:*** bring about

People set up governments to protect their basic rights. Governments get their power from the consent of the governed. If a government takes away the basic rights of the people, the people have the right to change the government.

prudence: wisdom ***transient:*** temporary, passing ***disposed:*** likely

usurpations: taking and using powers that do not belong to a person ***invariably:*** always ***evinces a design to reduce them under absolute despotism:*** makes a clear plan to put them under complete and unjust control ***sufferance:*** endurance

constrains: forces ***absolute tyranny:*** harsh and unjust government ***candid:*** free from prejudice

People do not readily change governments. But they are forced to do so when a government becomes tyrannical. King George III has a long record of abusing his power.

Wrongs Done by the King

assent: approval ***relinquish:*** give up ***inestimable:*** too great a value to be measured ***formidable:*** causing fear

This part of the Declaration spells out three sets of wrongs that led the colonists to break with Britain.

The first set of wrongs is the king's unjust use of power. The king refused to approve laws that are needed. He has tried to control the colonial legislatures.

He has refused his assent to laws the most wholesome and necessary for the public good.

He has forbidden his governors to pass laws of immediate and pressing importance, unless suspended in their operation till his assent should be obtained; and, when so suspended, he has utterly neglected to attend to them.

He has refused to pass other laws for the accommodation of the large districts of people, unless those people would relinquish the right of representation in the legislature; a right inestimable to them and formidable to tyrants only.

depository: storehouse ***fatiguing:*** tiring out ***compliance:*** giving in ***dissolved:*** broken up ***annihilation:*** total destruction ***convulsions:*** disturbances

The king has tried to force colonial legislatures into doing his will by wearing them out. He has dissolved legislatures (such as those of Massachusetts).

He has called together legislative bodies at places unusual, uncomfortable, and distant from the depository of their public records, for the sole purpose of fatiguing them into compliance with his measures.

He has dissolved representative houses, repeatedly for opposing, with manly firmness, his invasions on the rights of the people.

He has refused, for a long time after such dissolutions, to cause others to be elected: whereby the legislative powers, incapable of annihilation, have returned to the people at large for their exercise; the state remaining, in the meantime, exposed to all the danger of invasion from without and convulsions within.

endeavored: tried ***obstructing:*** blocking ***naturalization:*** process of becoming a citizen ***migration:*** moving ***hither:*** here ***appropriations:*** grants ***obstructed the administration of justice:*** prevented justice from being done ***judiciary powers:*** system of law courts ***tenure:*** term (of office) ***erected:*** set up ***multitude:*** large number ***swarms:*** huge crowds ***harass:*** cause trouble ***render:*** make

Among other wrongs, he has refused to let settlers move west to take up new land. He has prevented justice from being done. Also, he has sent large numbers of customs officials to cause problems for the colonists.

He has endeavored to prevent the population of these States; for that purpose, obstructing the laws for naturalization of foreigners, refusing to pass others to encourage their migration hither, and raising the conditions of new appropriations of lands.

He has obstructed the administration of justice by refusing his assent to laws for establishing judiciary powers.

He has made judges dependent on his will alone for the tenure of their offices and the amount and payment of their salaries.

He has erected a multitude of new offices and sent hither swarms of officers to harass our people and eat out their substance.

He has kept among us, in time of peace, standing armies, without the consent of our legislatures.

He has affected to render the military independent of, and superior to, the civil power.

jurisdiction: authority ***quartering:*** housing ***mock:*** false

The king has joined with others, meaning Parliament, to make laws for the colonies. The Declaration then lists the second set of wrongs—unjust acts of Parliament.

He has combined with others to subject us to a jurisdiction foreign to our Constitution and unacknowledged by our laws, giving his assent to their acts of pretended legislation:

For quartering large bodies of armed troops among us;

For protecting them by a mock trial from punishment for any murders which they should commit on the inhabitants of these States;

For cutting off our trade with all parts of the world;

For imposing taxes on us without our consent;

For depriving us, in many cases, of the benefit of trial by jury;

For transporting us beyond seas to be tried for pretended offences;

For abolishing the free system of English laws in a neighboring province, establishing therein an arbitrary government, and enlarging its boundaries, so as to render it at once an example and fit instrument for introducing the same absolute rule into these colonies;

For taking away our charters, abolishing our most valuable laws, and altering, fundamentally, the powers of our governments;

For suspending our own legislatures and declaring themselves invested with power to legislate for us in all cases whatsoever.

He has abdicated government here by declaring us out of his protection and waging war against us.

He has plundered our seas, ravaged our coasts, burnt our towns, and destroyed the lives of our people.

He is, at this time, transporting large armies of foreign mercenaries to complete the works of death, desolation, and tyranny already begun with circumstances of cruelty and perfidy scarcely paralleled in the most barbarous ages, and totally unworthy the head of a civilized nation.

He has constrained our fellow citizens, taken captive on the high seas, to bear arms against their country, to become the executioners of their friends and brethren, or to fall themselves by their hands.

He has excited domestic insurrections amongst us and has endeavored to bring on the inhabitants of our frontiers, the merciless Indian savages, whose known rule of warfare is an undistinguished destruction of all ages, sexes, and conditions.

In every state of these oppressions, we have petitioned for redress in the most humble terms; our repeated petitions have been answered only by repeated injury. A prince whose character is thus marked by every act which may define a tyrant is unfit to be the ruler of a free people.

Nor have we been wanting in attention to our British brethren. We have warned them, from time to time, of attempts made by their legislature to extend an unwarrantable jurisdiction over us. We have reminded them of the circumstances of our emigration and settlement here. We have appealed to their native justice and magnanimity, and we have conjured them, by the ties of our common kindred, to disavow these usurpations, which would inevitably interrupt our connections and correspondence. They, too, have been deaf to the voice of justice and consanguinity. We must, therefore, acquiesce in the necessity which denounces our separation, and hold them, as we hold the rest of mankind, enemies in war, in peace, friends.

imposing: forcing ***depriving:*** taking away ***transporting us beyond seas:*** sending colonists to England for trial ***neighboring province:*** Quebec ***arbitrary government:*** unjust rule ***fit instrument:*** suitable tool ***invested with power:*** having the power

During the years leading up to 1776, the colonists claimed that Parliament had no right to make laws for them because they were not represented in Parliament. Here, the colonists object to recent laws of Parliament, such as the Quartering Act and the blockade of colonial ports, which cut off their trade. They also object to Parliament's claim that it had the right to tax them without their consent.

abdicated: given up ***plundered:*** robbed ***ravaged:*** attacked ***mercenaries:*** hired soldiers ***desolation:*** misery ***perfidy:*** falseness ***barbarous:*** uncivilized ***constrained:*** forced ***brethren:*** brothers ***domestic insurrections:*** internal revolts

Here, the Declaration lists the third set of wrongs—warlike acts of the king. Instead of listening to the colonists, the king has made war on them. He has hired soldiers to fight in America.

oppressions: harsh rule ***petitioned:*** asked ***redress:*** relief ***unwarrantable jurisdiction over:*** unfair authority ***magnanimity:*** generosity ***conjured:*** called upon ***common kindred:*** relatives ***disavow:*** turn away from ***consanguinity:*** blood relationships, kinship ***acquiesce:*** agree ***denounces:*** speaks out against

During this time, colonists have repeatedly asked for relief. But their requests have brought only more suffering. They have appealed to the British people but received no help. So they are forced to separate.

Colonies Declare Independence

appealing: calling on ***rectitude of our intentions:*** moral rightness of our plans ***absolved from all allegiance:*** freed from loyalty ***levy war:*** declare war ***contract alliances:*** make treaties

As the representatives of the United States, they declare that the colonies are free and independent states.

The states need no longer be loyal to the British king. They are an independent nation that can make war and sign treaties.

Relying on help from Divine Providence, the signers of the Declaration promise their lives, money, and honor to fight for independence.

We, therefore, the representatives of the United States of America, in general Congress assembled, appealing to the Supreme Judge of the world for the rectitude of our intentions, do, in the name and by the authority of the good people of these colonies, solemnly publish and declare, that these united colonies are, and of right ought to be, free and independent states: that they are absolved from all allegiance to the British Crown, and that all political connection between them and the state of Great Britain is, and ought to be, totally dissolved; and that, as free and independent states, they have full power to levy war, conclude peace, contract alliances, establish commerce, and to do all other acts and things which independent states may of right do. And, for the support of this declaration, with a firm reliance on the protection of Divine Providence, we mutually pledge to each other our lives, our fortunes, and our sacred honor.

Signers of the Declaration of Independence

John Hancock, President

Charles Thomson, Secretary

New Hampshire
Josiah Bartlett
William Whipple
Matthew Thornton

Massachusetts
Samuel Adams
John Adams
Robert Treat Paine
Elbridge Gerry

Rhode Island
Stephen Hopkins
William Ellery

Connecticut
Roger Sherman
Samuel Huntington
William Williams
Oliver Wolcott

Delaware
Caesar Rodney
George Read
Thomas McKean

New York
William Floyd
Philip Livingston
Francis Lewis
Lewis Morris

New Jersey
Richard Stockton
John Witherspoon
Francis Hopkinson
John Hart
Abraham Clark

Georgia
Button Gwinnett
Lyman Hall
George Walton

Maryland
Samuel Chase
William Paca
Thomas Stone
Charles Carroll

North Carolina
William Hooper
Joseph Hewes
John Penn

Virginia
George Wythe
Richard Henry Lee
Thomas Jefferson
Benjamin Harrison
Thomas Nelson, Jr.
Francis Lightfoot Lee
Carter Braxton

South Carolina
Edward Rutledge
Thomas Heyward, Jr.
Thomas Lynch, Jr.
Arthur Middleton

Pennsylvania
Robert Morris
Benjamin Rush
Benjamin Franklin
John Morton
George Clymer
James Smith
George Taylor
James Wilson
George Ross

3 Struggles in the Middle States

Prepare to Read

Objectives

In this section, you will
- List the battles fought in New York and New Jersey.
- Explain how the Battle of Saratoga marked a turning point in the war.
- Describe the conditions at Valley Forge.

Key Terms

Battle of Long Island
Battle of Trenton
Battle of Saratoga
ally
cavalry
Valley Forge

Target Reading Skill

Sequence Copy the flowchart. As you read, fill in the boxes with the major events of the struggles in the Middle States.

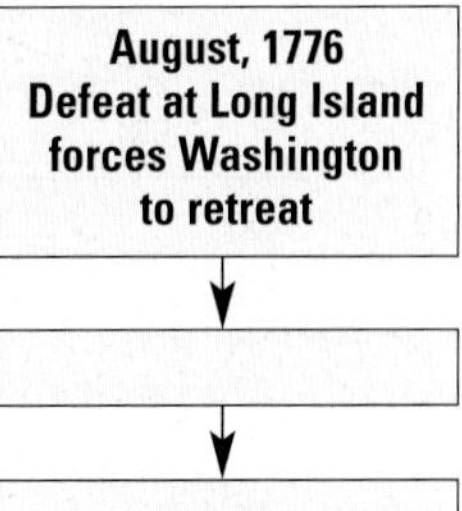

Main Idea After a series of Patriot defeats, an American victory at Saratoga marked a major turning point in the Revolution.

Setting the Scene Early one morning in June 1776, Daniel McCurtin glanced out his window at New York harbor. He was amazed to see "something resembling a wood of pine trees trimmed." He watched the forest move across the water. Then, he understood. The trees were the masts of ships!

> "I could not believe my eyes . . . the whole bay was full of shipping as ever it could be. I declare that I thought all London was afloat."
>
> —George F. Scheer and Hugh F. Rankin, *Rebels and Redcoats*

McCurtin had witnessed the arrival of a large British fleet in New York. Aboard the ships were General Howe and thousands of redcoats. Thus began a new stage in the war. Previously, most of the fighting of the American Revolution had taken place in New England. In mid-1776, the heavy fighting shifted to the Middle States. There, the Continental Army suffered through the worst days of the war.

A British redcoat

The British Take New York

Washington, expecting Howe's attack, had led his forces south from Boston to New York City. His army, however, was no match for the British. Howe had about 34,000 troops and 10,000 sailors. He also had ships to ferry them ashore. Washington had fewer than 20,000 poorly trained troops. Worse, he had no navy.

In August, Howe's army landed on Long Island. In the **Battle of Long Island,** more than 1,400 Americans were killed, wounded, or captured. The rest retreated to Manhattan. The British pursued. To avoid capture, Washington hurried north.

Throughout the autumn, Washington fought a series of battles with Howe's army. In November, he crossed the Hudson River into

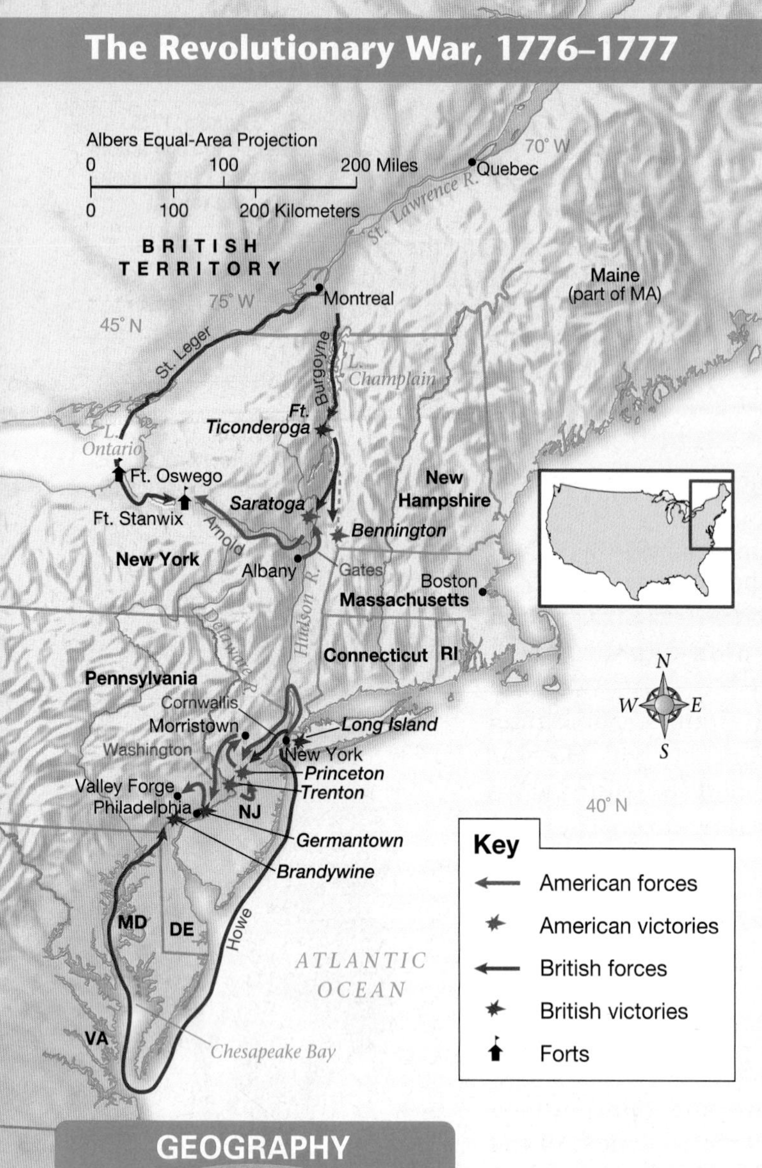

GEOGRAPHY *Skills*

In 1776 and 1777, the Americans and British battled over a large area. The American victory at Saratoga marked a major turning point in the war.

1. **Location** On the map, locate **(a)** Long Island, **(b)** New York City, **(c)** Trenton, **(d)** Hudson River, **(e)** Saratoga, **(f)** Valley Forge.
2. **Movement** How did the British use sea power to help them capture Philadelphia?
3. **Critical Thinking Applying Information** How did Burgoyne and St. Leger use geography to help move their armies quickly toward Albany?

New Jersey. Chased by the British, the Americans retreated across the Delaware River into Pennsylvania.

During the campaign for New York, Washington needed information about Howe's forces. Nathan Hale, a young Connecticut officer, volunteered to go behind British lines. On his way back with the information, Hale was seized by the British and searched. Hidden in the soles of his shoes was information about British troop movements.

There was no trial. Howe ordered Hale to be hanged the next morning. As Hale walked to the gallows, he is said to have declared: "I only regret that I have but one life to lose for my country."

Washington Turns Retreat Into Victory in New Jersey

Months of hard campaigning took a toll on the Continental Army. In December 1776, Washington described his troops as sick, dirty, and "so thinly clad as to be unfit for service." Every day, soldiers deserted. Washington wrote to his brother: "I am wearied to death. I think the game is pretty near up."

Washington decided on a bold move: a surprise attack on Trenton. On Christmas night, he secretly led his troops across the icy Delaware River. Soldiers shivered as spray from the river froze on their faces. Once ashore, they marched through swirling snow. Some had no shoes. They tied rags around their feet. "Soldiers, keep by your officers," Washington urged.

Early on December 26, the Americans surprised the Hessian troops guarding Trenton and took most of them prisoner. The Hessians were soldiers from Germany. An American summed up the **Battle of Trenton:** "Hessian population of Trenton at 8 A.M.—1,408 men and 39 officers; Hessian population at 9 A.M.—0."

British General Charles Cornwallis set out at once to retake Trenton and to capture Washington. Late on January 2, 1777, he saw the lights of Washington's campfires. "At last we have run down the old fox," he said, "and we will bag him in the morning."

Washington fooled Cornwallis. He left the fires burning and slipped behind British lines to attack a British force that was marching toward Princeton. There, the Continental Army won another victory. From Princeton, Washington moved to Morristown, where the army would spend the winter. The victories at Trenton and Princeton gave the Americans new hope.

A Turning Point in the War

Identifying Sequence

Read the paragraphs that appear below "A Turning Point in the War." Identify the important events and note them on your flowchart.

In London, British officials were dismayed by the army's failure to crush the rebels. Early in 1777, General John Burgoyne (buhr GOIN) presented a new plan for victory. If British troops cut off New England from the other colonies, he argued, the war would soon be over.

Burgoyne's Plan Burgoyne wanted three British armies to march on Albany, New York, from different directions. They would crush American forces there. Once they controlled the Hudson River, the British could stop the flow of soldiers and supplies from New England to Washington's army.

Burgoyne's plan called for General Howe to march on Albany from New York City. George III, however, wanted Howe to capture Philadelphia first.

In July 1777, Howe sailed from New York to Chesapeake Bay, where he began his march on Philadelphia. Howe captured Philadelphia, defeating the Americans at the battles of Brandywine and Germantown. But instead of moving toward Albany to meet Burgoyne as planned, he retired to comfortable quarters in Philadelphia for the winter. For his part, Washington retreated to Valley Forge, Pennsylvania.

Meanwhile, British armies under Burgoyne and Barry St. Leger (lay ZHAIR) marched from Canada toward Albany. St. Leger tried to take Fort Stanwix. However, a strong American army, led by Benedict Arnold, drove him back.

Victory at Saratoga Only Burgoyne was left to march on Albany. His army moved slowly because it had many heavy baggage carts to drag through the woods. To slow Burgoyne further, Patriots cut down trees and dammed up streams to block the route.

Despite these obstacles, Burgoyne recaptured Fort Ticonderoga. He then sent troops into Vermont to find food and horses. There, Patriots attacked the redcoats. At the Battle of Bennington, they wounded or captured nearly 1,000 British.

Burgoyne's troubles grew. The Green Mountain Boys hurried into New York to help American forces there. At the village of Saratoga, the Americans surrounded the British. When Burgoyne tried to break free, the Americans beat him back. Realizing that he was trapped, Burgoyne surrendered his entire army to the Americans on October 17, 1777.

The American victory at the **Battle of Saratoga** was a major turning point in the war. It ended the British threat to New England. It boosted American spirits at a time when Washington's army was suffering defeats. Most important, it convinced France to become an ally of the United States. Nations that are **allies** work together to achieve a common goal.

Aid From Europe The Continental Congress had long hoped for French aid. In 1776, the Congress had sent Benjamin Franklin to Paris to persuade Louis XVI, the French king, to give the Americans weapons and other badly needed supplies. In addition, the Congress wanted France to declare war on Britain.

France Enters the War

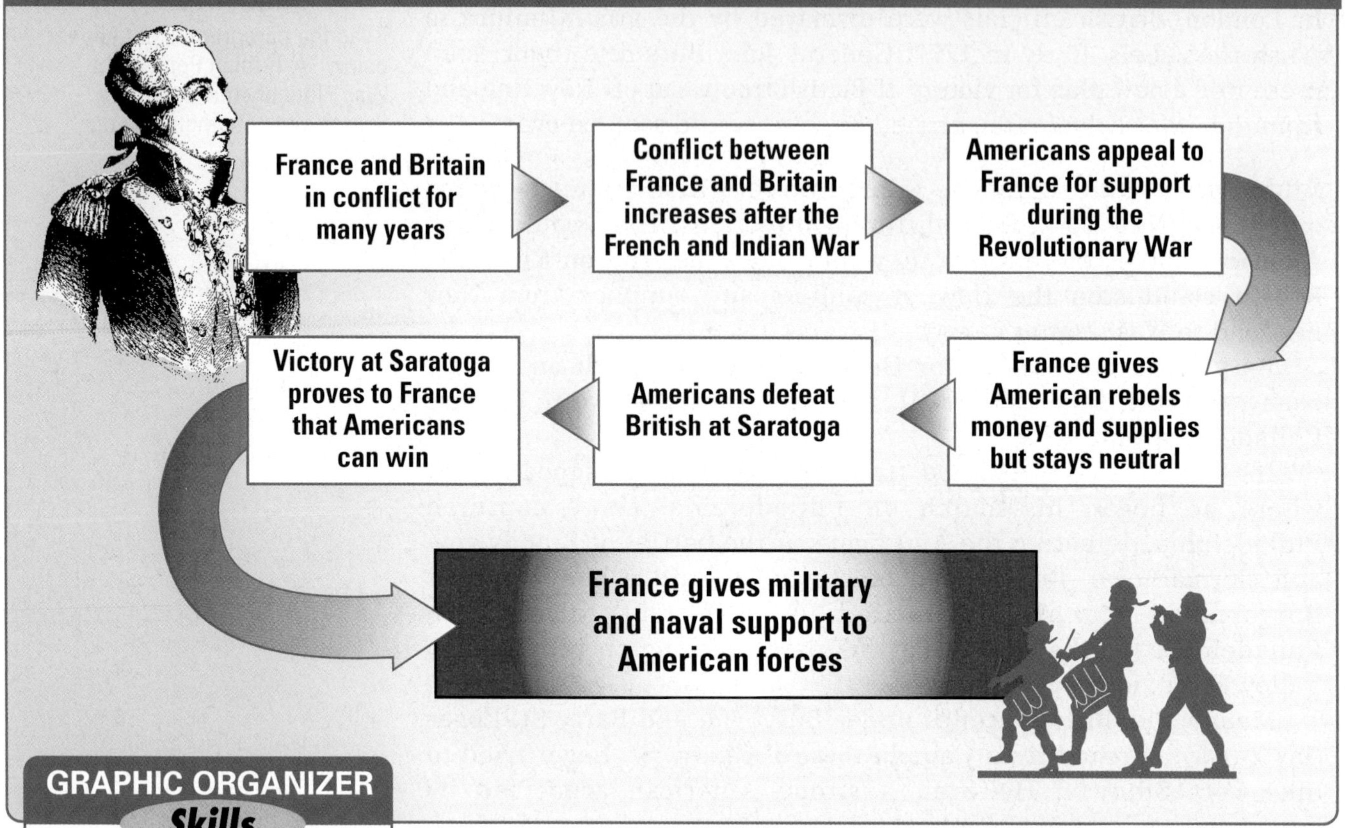

France and Britain in conflict for many years → Conflict between France and Britain increases after the French and Indian War → Americans appeal to France for support during the Revolutionary War → France gives American rebels money and supplies but stays neutral → Americans defeat British at Saratoga → Victory at Saratoga proves to France that Americans can win → France gives military and naval support to American forces

GRAPHIC ORGANIZER *Skills*

The American defeat of the British at Saratoga was a turning point in the war.

1. **Comprehension** What happened between France and Britain after the French and Indian War?
2. **Critical Thinking Making Decisions** What do you think France hoped to gain by helping the Americans?

The French were eager to defeat Britain, but they were also cautious. France was still angry about its defeat at British hands in the French and Indian War. However, Louis XVI did not want to help the Americans openly unless he was sure that they could win.

The American victory at Saratoga convinced France that the United States could stand up to Britain. In February 1778, France became the first nation to sign a treaty with the United States. It recognized the new nation and agreed to provide military aid. Later, the Netherlands and Spain also joined in the war against Britain. France, the Netherlands, and Spain all provided loans to the United States.

Even before European nations agreed to help the United States, individual volunteers had been coming from Europe to join the American cause. Some became leading officers in the American army.

The Marquis de Lafayette (lah fee EHT), a young French noble, brought trained soldiers to help the Patriot cause. Lafayette, who fought at Brandywine, became one of Washington's most trusted friends.

From the German state of Prussia came Friedrich von Steuben (STOO buhn), who helped train Washington's troops to march and drill. Von Steuben had served in the Prussian army, which was considered the best in Europe.

Two Polish officers also joined the Americans. Thaddeus Kosciusko (kahs ee UHS koh), an engineer, helped build forts and other defenses. Casimir Pulaski trained **cavalry,** or troops on horseback.

The Hardships of Valley Forge

The victory at Saratoga and the promise of help from Europe boosted American morale. Even so, Washington's Continental Army had to face hard times as it suffered through the long, cold winter of 1777–1778 at a makeshift camp at Valley Forge.

Conditions at Valley Forge were terrible. Soldiers shivered in damp, drafty huts. Many slept on the frozen ground. Some soldiers stood guard wrapped only in blankets. Others had no shoes, so they wrapped bits of cloth around their feet. As the bitter winter wore on, soldiers suffered from frostbite and disease. An army surgeon from Connecticut wrote about his hardships:

> "I am sick—discontented—and out of humor. Poor food—hard lodging—cold weather—fatigue—nasty clothes—nasty cookery . . . a pox on my bad luck! There comes a bowl of beef soup, full of burnt leaves and dirt. . . . Away with it, boys!—I'll live like the chameleon upon air."
>
> —Albigence Waldo, *Diary,* December 14, 1777

As news of the suffering at Valley Forge spread, Patriots from around the nation sent help. Women collected food, medicine, warm clothes, and ammunition for the army. Some women, like Martha Washington, wife of the commander, went to Valley Forge to help the sick and wounded.

The arrival of desperately needed supplies was soon followed by warmer weather. The drills of Baron von Steuben helped the Continentals to march and fight with a new skill. By the spring of 1778, the army at Valley Forge was more hopeful. Washington could not know it at the time, but the Patriots' bleakest hour had passed.

Section 3 Assessment

Recall

1. **Identify** Explain the significance of **(a)** Battle of Long Island, **(b)** Nathan Hale, **(c)** Battle of Trenton, **(d)** General John Burgoyne, **(e)** Battle of Saratoga, **(f)** Marquis de Lafayette, **(g)** Friedrich von Steuben, **(h)** Thaddeus Kosciusko, **(i)** Valley Forge.
2. **Define (a)** ally, **(b)** cavalry.

Comprehension

3. How did Washington turn retreat into victory in New Jersey?
4. Explain the results of the Battle of Saratoga.
5. How did the Continental Army come through the terrible winter at Valley Forge with new hope?

Critical Thinking and Writing

6. **Exploring the Main Idea** Review the Main Idea statement at the beginning of this section. Then, write a newspaper article celebrating the victory at Saratoga. Why was it a turning point?
7. **Analyzing Information** Why do you think people from other lands, such as Lafayette and Pulaski, were willing to risk their lives to help the American cause?

Activity

Creating a Dramatic Scene **Write a scene in which Benjamin Franklin meets with the French King Louis XVI to convince him to support the Continental Army. Focus on how France and the Continental Army would benefit from such an alliance.**

4 Fighting for Liberty on Many Fronts

Prepare to Read

Objectives

In this section, you will

- Describe the role of women in the war.
- List the choices African Americans had during the American Revolution.
- Explain how the war was fought on the frontier and at sea.

Target Reading Skill

Cause and Effect Copy the cause chart below. As you read, fill in the chart to show how the cause of fighting for independence united different groups of colonists. Add as many boxes as you need.

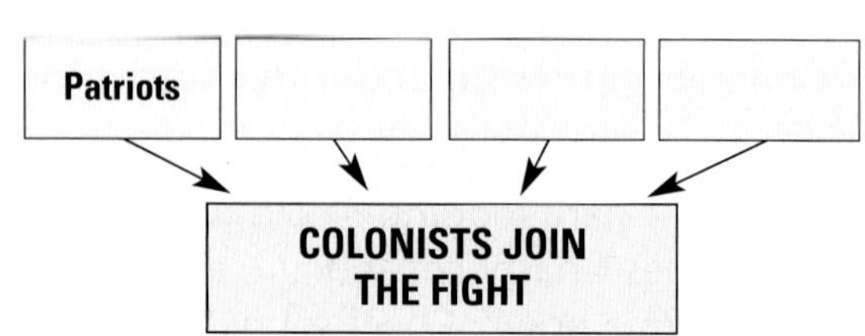

Main Idea During the Revolution, Americans fought for liberty on many fronts and in many ways.

An African American sailor

Setting the Scene Ten years before the Revolution, white colonists in Charleston protested the Stamp Act. "Liberty! Liberty and stamped paper!" they cried as they paraded around the homes of British officials. Shortly after, a group of African Americans held their own parade. To the amazement of white colonists, the marchers chanted the same cry: "Liberty! Liberty!"

Many African Americans believed that the ideal of liberty applied to them just as it did to whites. In Massachusetts, a group of slaves presented petitions to the governor, asking for their freedom. One slave compared the situation of whites and African Americans:

> "You [white colonists] are taxed without your consent, because you are not represented in parliament. I grant that [is] a grievance . . . [But] pray, sir, . . . are not your hearts also hard, when you hold [Africans] in slavery who are entitled to liberty by the law of nature, equal as yourselves?"
>
> —Letter to a Boston newspaper *The Massachusetts Spy*, February 10, 1774

As the fighting continued, Americans worked for liberty in many ways and on many fronts. Sailors, as well as soldiers, fought in the various battles of the war. Women and African Americans took part too.

Women Take Part in the War

When men went off to fight in the Revolution, women took on added work at home. Some planted and harvested the crops. Others made shoes and wove cloth for blankets and uniforms. One woman, called "Handy Betsy the Blacksmith," was known for making cannons and guns for the army.

Helping the Army Many women joined their husbands at the front. They cared for the wounded, washed clothes, and cooked. Martha Washington joined her husband whenever she could.

Some women achieved lasting fame for their wartime service. Betsy Ross of Philadelphia sewed flags for Washington's army. Legend claims that she made the first American flag of stars and stripes.

A few women even took part in battle. During the Battle of Monmouth in 1778, Mary Ludwig Hays carried water to her husband and other soldiers. The soldiers called her Molly Pitcher. When her husband was wounded, she took his place, loading and firing the cannon.

New Attitudes As women participated in the war, they began to think differently about their rights. Those women who had taken charge of farms or their husbands' businesses became more confident and willing to speak out.

Most men in Congress did not agree that women should be treated equally. Still, the Revolution established important ideals of liberty and equality. In later years, these ideals of the Revolution would encourage women to campaign for equal treatment—and eventually to win it.

African Americans Face Hard Choices

By 1776, more than a half million African Americans lived in the colonies. At first, the Continental Congress refused to let African Americans, whether free or enslaved, join the army. Some members doubted the loyalty of armed African Americans. The British, however, offered freedom to some male slaves who would serve the king. Washington feared that this would greatly increase the ranks of the British army. In response, Washington changed his policy and asked Congress to allow free African Americans to enlist.

Joining the Fight About 5,000 African Americans from all the colonies, except South Carolina, served in the army. Another 2,000 served in the navy which, from the start, allowed African Americans to join. At least nine black minutemen saw action at Lexington and Concord. One of them, Prince Estabrook, was wounded. Two others, Peter Salem and Salem Poor, went on to fight bravely at Bunker Hill.

Some African Americans formed special regiments. Others served in white regiments as drummers, fifers, spies, and guides. Saul Matthews and James Armistead were among those African Americans who served as spies. Whites recognized the courage of their African American comrades. As one eyewitness recalled, "Three times in succession, [African Americans] were attacked . . . by [British troops] and three times did they successfully repel the assault and . . . preserve our army from capture. . . ."

Viewing History

James Armistead

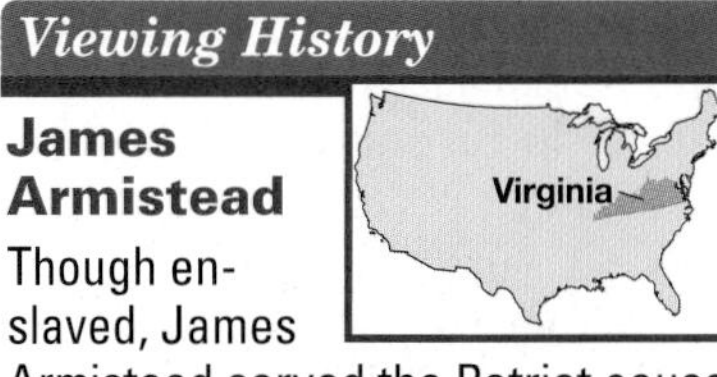

Though enslaved, James Armistead served the Patriot cause as a spy. Under the direction of General Lafayette, Armistead was a volunteer in British army camps. The information he gained contributed to the American victory at Yorktown. **Drawing Inferences** ***Why do you think Armistead later decided to change his name to Lafayette?***

Understand Effects Why do you think some slaves offered their services to the British? Why did others fight for the Revolution?

Enslaved African Americans faced difficult choices. If they joined the American army or continued to work on Patriot plantations, the British might capture and sell them. If they tried to flee to the British army to gain freedom, they risked being hanged by angry Patriots.

Hoping for Freedom Yet, many slaves did flee their masters, especially those who lived near the coast, where the British navy patrolled. One British captain reported that "near 500" runaway slaves offered their services to him. Toward the end of the war, several thousand slaves sought freedom by following British troops through the Carolinas.

Black Patriots hoped that the Revolution would bring an end to slavery. After all, the Declaration of Independence proclaimed that "all men are created equal." Some white leaders also hoped the war would end slavery. James Otis wrote that "the colonists are by the law of nature free born, as indeed all men are, white or black." Quakers in particular spoke out strongly against slavery.

By the 1770s, slavery was declining in the North, where a number of free African Americans lived. During the American Revolution, several states moved to make slavery illegal, including Massachusetts, New Hampshire, and Pennsylvania. Other states also began to debate the slavery issue.

GEOGRAPHY Skills

American, British, and Native American forces fought for control of lands in the West.

1. **Location** On the map, locate **(a)** Kaskaskia, **(b)** Vincennes, **(c)** Ohio River, **(d)** Fort Detroit.
2. **Place** What was the importance of the place where Fort Pitt was built?
3. **Critical Thinking Applying Information** Why did many Native Americans ally themselves with the British?

The War on the Western Frontier

As the war spread to Indian lands in the West, the Americans and British both tried to win the support of Indian tribes. In the end, the British were more successful. They convinced many Native Americans that a Patriot victory would mean more white settlers crossing the Appalachians and taking Indian lands.

Indian Allies of the British In the South, the British gained the support of the Cherokees, Creeks, Choctaws, and Chickasaws. The British encouraged the Cherokees to attack dozens of settlements on the southern frontier. Only after hard fighting were Patriot militia able to drive the Native Americans into the mountains.

Fighting was equally fierce on the northern frontier. In 1778, Iroquois forces led by the Mohawk leader Joseph Brant joined with Loyalists in raiding settlements in Pennsylvania and New York. The next year, Patriots struck back by destroying dozens of Iroquois villages.

Victory at Vincennes Farther west, in 1778, George Rogers Clark led Virginia frontier fighters against the British in the

The War in the West

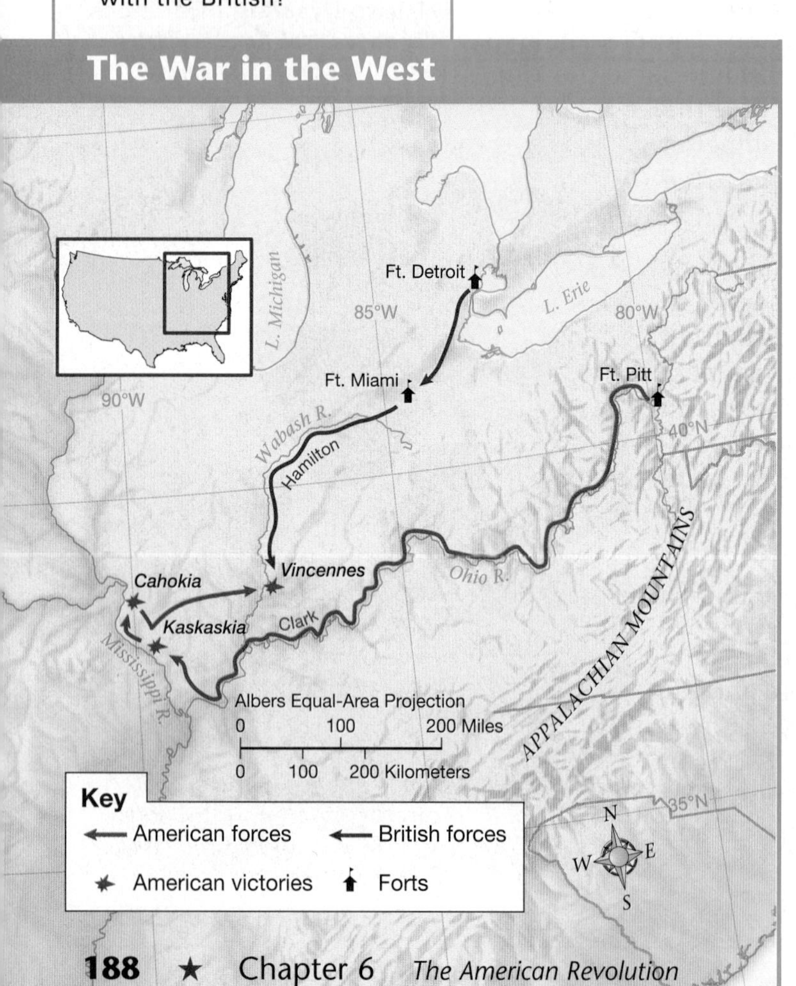

Ohio Valley. With help from Miami Indians, Clark captured the British forts at Kaskaskia and Cahokia.

Clark then plotted a surprise attack on the British fort at Vincennes. When Clark's small force reached the fort, they spread out through the woods to make their numbers appear greater than they really were. The British commander thought it was useless to fight so many Americans. He surrendered Vincennes in February 1779.

Spanish Aid On the southwestern frontier, Americans received help from New Spain. In the early years of the war, Spain was neutral. However, Bernardo de Gálvez, governor of Spanish Louisiana, favored the Patriots. He secretly supplied medicine, cloth, muskets, and gunpowder to the Americans.

When Spain entered the war against Britain in 1779, Gálvez took a more active role. He seized British forts along the Mississippi River and the Gulf of Mexico. He also drove the British out of West Florida. The city of Galveston, in Texas, is named after this courageous leader.

Fighting at Sea

At sea, the Americans could do little against the powerful British navy. British ships blockaded American ports. From time to time, however, a bold American captain captured a British ship.

The greatest American sea victory took place in September 1779 in Britain's backyard, on the North Sea. After a hard-fought battle, Captain John Paul Jones, captured the powerful British warship *Serapis.*

Raids on the high seas and along the frontiers kept many Americans on the alert. However, the war between the Americans and Great Britain would be settled by battles in the South.

An American Profile

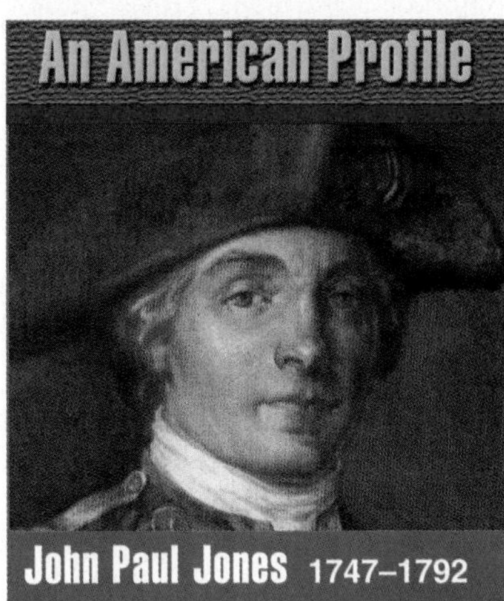

John Paul Jones 1747–1792

John Paul Jones was the first lieutenant commissioned in the Continental Navy. He showed his daring by sailing into British waters to raid enemy merchant ships. On September 23, 1779, Jones, at the helm of *Bonhomme Richard,* attacked the clearly superior British warship *Serapis* in the North Sea. The *Richard* was badly damaged in the first few minutes of battle. With their ship sinking beneath them, Jones and his men fought on. But the *Serapis* was also hurt. At last, the British captain of the *Serapis* lowered his flag and surrendered.

How did John Paul Jones help the Patriot cause?

 **Section 4 Assessment**  

Recall

1. **Identify** Explain the significance of **(a)** Mary Ludwig Hays, **(b)** Peter Salem, **(c)** George Rogers Clark, **(d)** Bernardo de Gálvez, **(e)** John Paul Jones.

Comprehension

2. How did the war change many women's attitudes?
3. **(a)** Why did some slaves escape to the British? **(b)** Why did African American Patriots hope that the Revolution would end slavery?
4. Why was John Paul Jones a hero to Americans?

Critical Thinking and Writing

5. **Exploring the Main Idea** Review the Main Idea statement at the beginning of this section. List three ways in which Americans fought for liberty during the Revolution.
6. **Identifying Causes and Effects** Read the following two statements. Decide which is the cause and which is the effect: **(a)** Many Native Americans sided with the British. **(b)** During the Revolution, settlers continued to push west of the Appalachians. Write a paragraph explaining the importance of the effect on the war.

Activity

Making an Almanac
Use the Internet to research women who took part in the Revolution. Among the women you might research are Margaret Corbin and Deborah Sampson. Use what you find to draw up a Who's Who of Women During the Revolution. For help in completing the activity, visit PHSchool.com, **Web Code mfd-0602.**

Women in the Revolution

Many women patriots of the Revolution performed courageous deeds. They were spies and couriers, and disguised as men, enlisted in the army. Many women, just as courageous, fought for the cause on the home front.

Sybil Ludington Sometimes called the "female Paul Revere," Sybil Ludington was just 16 years old when on a chilly April night in 1777 she mounted her horse, Star, to gallop through the countryside and call the militia to report. The British were attacking, and there was no one to call the men to arms but Sybil.

Deborah Sampson When young Robert Shurtleff was wounded, he deliberately concealed his leg wound. But when he came down with yellow fever and was taken to a hospital, the truth was discovered: "He" was really Deborah Sampson, a woman in disguise! Instead of being punished for her deception, Deborah earned respect from her comrades. She received an honorable discharge.

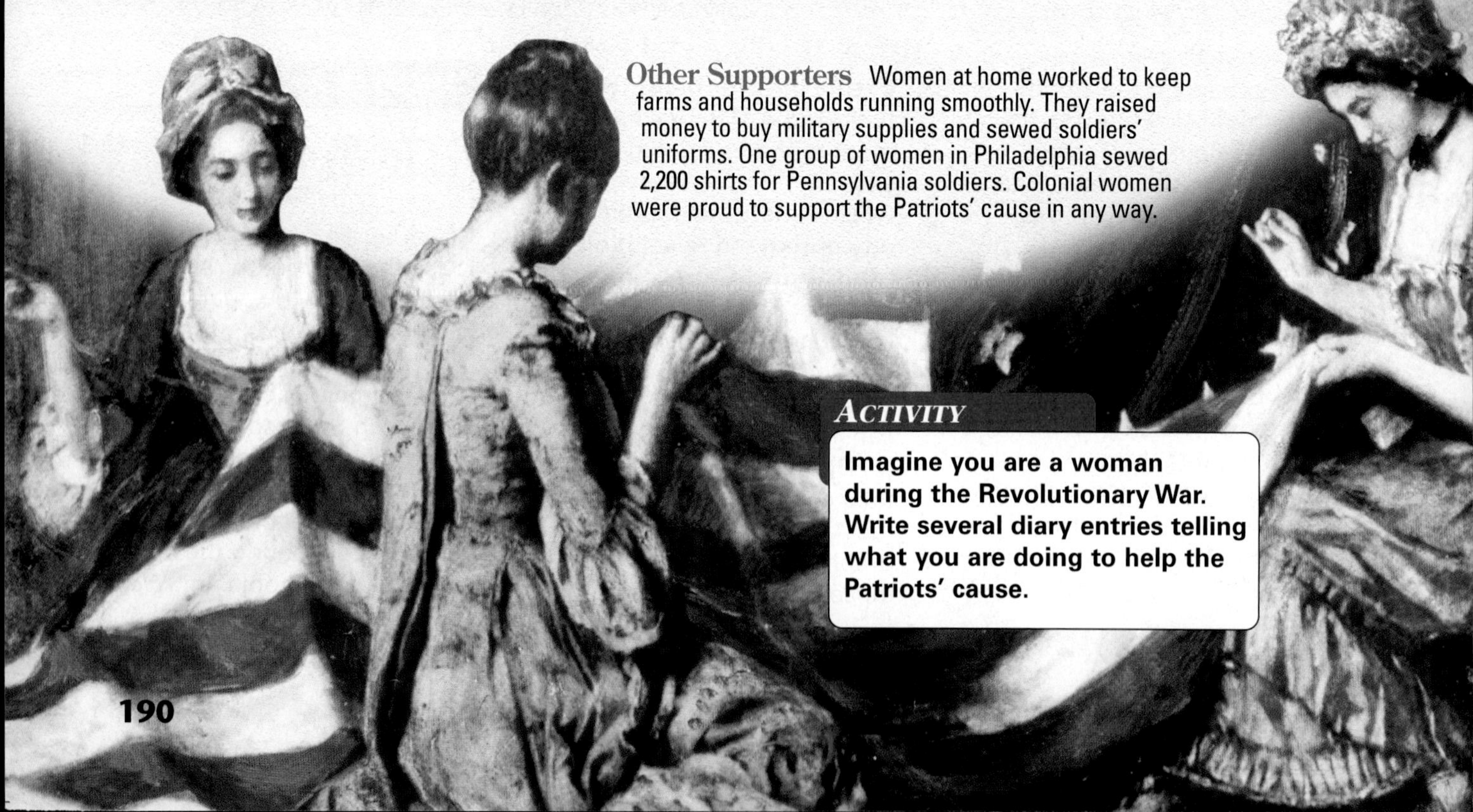

Other Supporters Women at home worked to keep farms and households running smoothly. They raised money to buy military supplies and sewed soldiers' uniforms. One group of women in Philadelphia sewed 2,200 shirts for Pennsylvania soldiers. Colonial women were proud to support the Patriots' cause in any way.

Activity

Imagine you are a woman during the Revolutionary War. Write several diary entries telling what you are doing to help the Patriots' cause.

5 Winning the War in the South

Prepare to Read

Objectives

In this section, you will

- Explain why Britain decided to start fighting in the South.
- Describe the British defeat at Yorktown.
- List the terms of the Treaty of Paris.
- Explain why the Americans won the war.

Key Terms

Battle of Cowpens
guerrilla
siege
Battle of Yorktown
Treaty of Paris
ratify

Target Reading Skill

Main Idea As you read, prepare an outline of the section. Use roman numerals to indicate major headings, capital letters for subheadings, and numbers for supporting details.

I. Fighting in the South
A. Patriots versus Loyalists
1. Patriots and Loyalists launch raids
2.
B. Green and Morgan help turn the tide
1.
2.
C.
II. Victory at Yorktown
A.
B.

Main Idea After the British surrendered at Yorktown, Britain recognized the United States as an independent country.

Setting the Scene When he was only 16 years old, Thomas Young set out with about 900 other Patriots to capture Kings Mountain in South Carolina. Although they were barefoot, they moved quickly up the wooded hillside, shouldering their old muskets. They were determined to take the mountain from the Loyalists who were dug in at the top.

Whooping and shouting, Young and his comrades dashed from tree to tree, dodging bullets as they fired back. Suddenly, Thomas heard the frantic cry, "Colonel Williams is shot!"

> ❝ I ran to his assistance for I loved him as a father. . . . He revived, and his first words were, 'For God's sake boys, don't give up the hill!'❞
>
> —Thomas Young, Memoir, *The Orion*

Colonial soldiers received badges of honor for acts of bravery

The Patriots captured Kings Mountain on October 7, 1780. The victory was an important sign. Britain had decided to make the South the key to winning the war. The American victory at Kings Mountain showed that Britain's new strategy might not work.

Fighting in the South

The South became the main battleground of the war in 1778. Sir Henry Clinton, the new British commander-in-chief, knew that many Loyalists lived in the southern backcountry. He hoped that if British troops marched through the South, Loyalists would join them.

At first, Clinton's plan seemed to work. In short order, beginning in December 1778, the British seized Savannah in Georgia and Charleston and Camden in South Carolina. "I have almost ceased to hope," wrote Washington when he learned of the defeats.

Patriots versus Loyalists In the Carolina backcountry, Patriots and Loyalists launched violent raids against one another. Both sides

The War Ends in the South

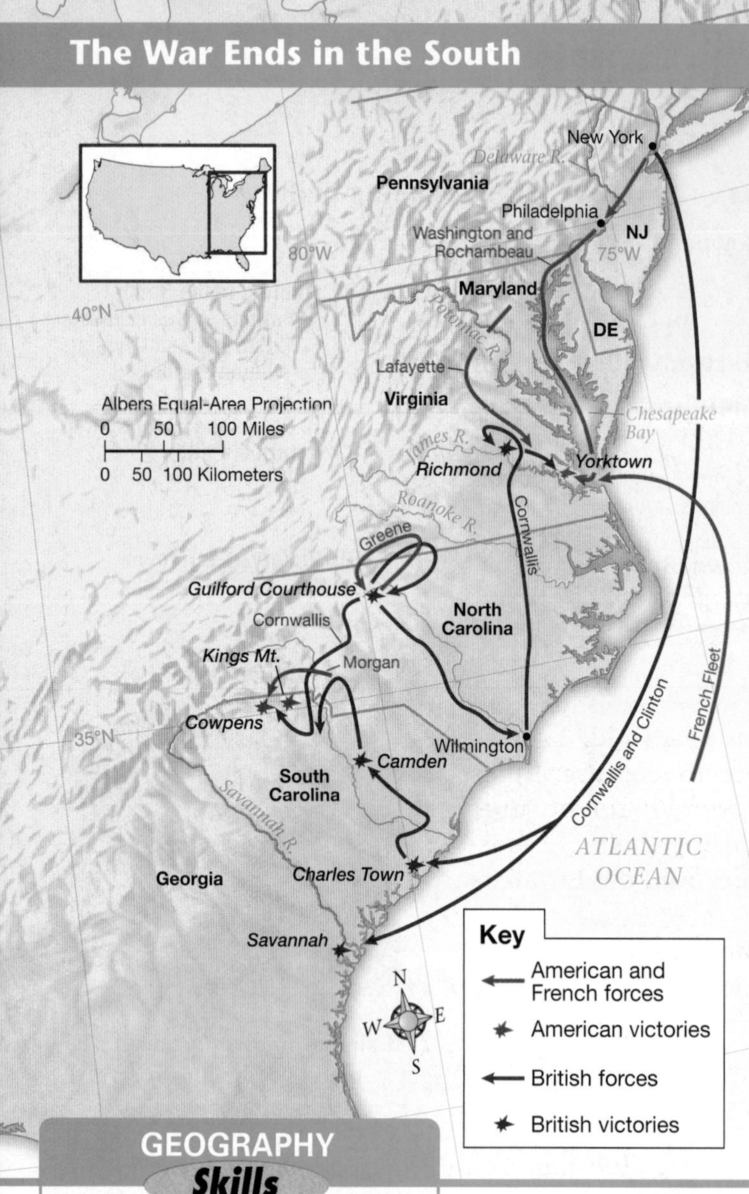

GEOGRAPHY Skills

The war ended in the South. After a string of defeats, the Americans gradually gained the upper hand. The last major battle was the American victory at Yorktown.

1. **Location** On the map, locate **(a)** Savannah, **(b)** Kings Mountain, **(c)** Guilford Courthouse, **(d)** Chesapeake Bay, **(e)** Yorktown.
2. **Region** Did the British have greater control over coastal or inland regions of the South?
3. **Critical Thinking Drawing Conclusions** Why was it a mistake for Cornwallis to retreat to the Yorktown peninsula?

burned farms, killed civilians, and sometimes even tortured prisoners.

After 1780, attacks by British troops and Loyalist militia became especially cruel. As a result, more settlers began to side with the Patriots. As one Loyalist admitted, "Great Britain has now a hundred enemies, where it had one before."

Greene and Morgan Help Turn the Tide After the victory at Kings Mountain, two able American generals helped turn the tide against the main British army, led by General Charles Cornwallis. They were Nathanael Greene of Rhode Island and Daniel Morgan of Virginia.

General Greene's ability as a military leader was perhaps second only to Washington's. In 1780, Greene took command of the Continental Army in the South. Using his knowledge of local geography, Greene engaged the British only on ground that put them at a disadvantage. General Cornwallis wore out his soldiers trying to catch Greene's army.

In January 1781, General Morgan won an important victory at Cowpens, South Carolina. Morgan used a clever tactic to defeat the British. He divided his soldiers into a front line and a rear line. He ordered the front line to retreat after firing just two volleys. The British, thinking the Americans were retreating, charged forward—straight into the fire of Morgan's second rank. In this way, the Americans won the **Battle of Cowpens.**

Greene and Morgan combined their armies when they fought Cornwallis at Guilford Courthouse, near present-day Greensboro, North Carolina. The battle was one of the bloodiest of the war. Although the Americans retreated, the British sustained great losses.

Hit and Run Known as the Swamp Fox, Francis Marion of South Carolina added to British frustrations. He led a small band of militia, who often slept by day and traveled by night. His soldiers used **guerrilla**, or **hit-and-run, tactics** to harass the British. Marion's band appeared suddenly out of the swamps, attacked quickly, and retreated swiftly back into the swamps.

Victory at Yorktown

Cornwallis abandoned his plan to take the Carolinas. In the spring of 1781, he moved his troops north into Virginia. He planned to conquer Virginia and cut off the Americans' supply routes to the South.

An American Traitor The British had achieved some success in Virginia, even before the arrival of Cornwallis. Benedict Arnold, formerly one of the Americans' best generals, was now leading British troops. Arnold captured and burned the capital city of Richmond. His forces also raided and burned other towns.

Arnold had turned traitor to the American cause in September 1780, while commanding West Point, a key fort in New York. The ambitious general was angry because he felt that he had not received enough credit for his victories. He also needed money. Arnold secretly agreed to turn over West Point to the British. The plot was uncovered by a Patriot patrol, but Arnold escaped to join the British.

Arnold's treason and his raids on towns in Connecticut and Virginia enraged the Patriots. Thomas Jefferson, governor of Virginia, offered a sizable reward for his capture. Washington ordered Arnold to be hanged. However, he was never captured.

Battle at Yorktown Cornwallis hoped to meet with the same kind of success in Virginia that Arnold had achieved. At first, things went well. Cornwallis sent Loyalist troops to attack Charlottesville, where the Virginia legislature was meeting. Governor Thomas Jefferson and other officials had to flee.

American troops under Lafayette fought back by staging raids against the British. Lafayette did not have enough troops to fight a major battle. Still, his strategy kept Cornwallis at bay.

Then, Cornwallis made a mistake. He disregarded an order from Sir Henry Clinton to send part of his army to New York. Instead, he retreated to Yorktown peninsula, a strip of land jutting into Chesapeake Bay. He felt confident that British ships could supply his army from the sea.

Washington saw an opportunity to trap Cornwallis on the Yorktown peninsula. He marched his Continental troops south from New York. With the Americans were French soldiers under the Comte de Rochambeau (roh shahm BOH). The combined army rushed to join Lafayette in Virginia.

Meanwhile, a French fleet under Admiral de Grasse was also heading toward Virginia. Once in Chesapeake Bay, De Grasse's fleet closed the trap. Cornwallis was cut off. He could not get supplies. He could not escape by land or by sea.

The British Surrender By the end of September, more than 16,000 American and French troops laid siege to Cornwallis's army of fewer than 8,000. A **siege** occurs when an army surrounds and blockades an enemy position in an attempt to capture it. Day after day, American and French artillery pounded the British.

For several weeks, Cornwallis held out. Finally, with casualties mounting and his supplies running low, the general decided that the situation was hopeless. The British had lost the **Battle of Yorktown.**

On October 19, 1781, the British surrendered their weapons. The French and the Americans lined up in two facing columns. As the defeated redcoats marched between the victorious troops, a British army band played the tune "The World Turned Upside Down."

Geography and History

Britain's Dilemma

Because they controlled the seas, the British could land and establish bases almost anywhere along the American coast. The navigable rivers that flowed inland from the coast provided convenient invasion routes into the interior.

To win the war, the British Army had to move away from these coastal bases and rivers. Yet when it did so, it opened its lines of communications and supply to constant attack. British armies nearly always met defeat when they moved away from the areas where they could be supplied by ships from the homeland. These problems, a British colonel noted in 1777, had "absolutely prevented us this whole war from going fifteen miles from a navigable river."

Why did the British face problems when they moved away from the coast?

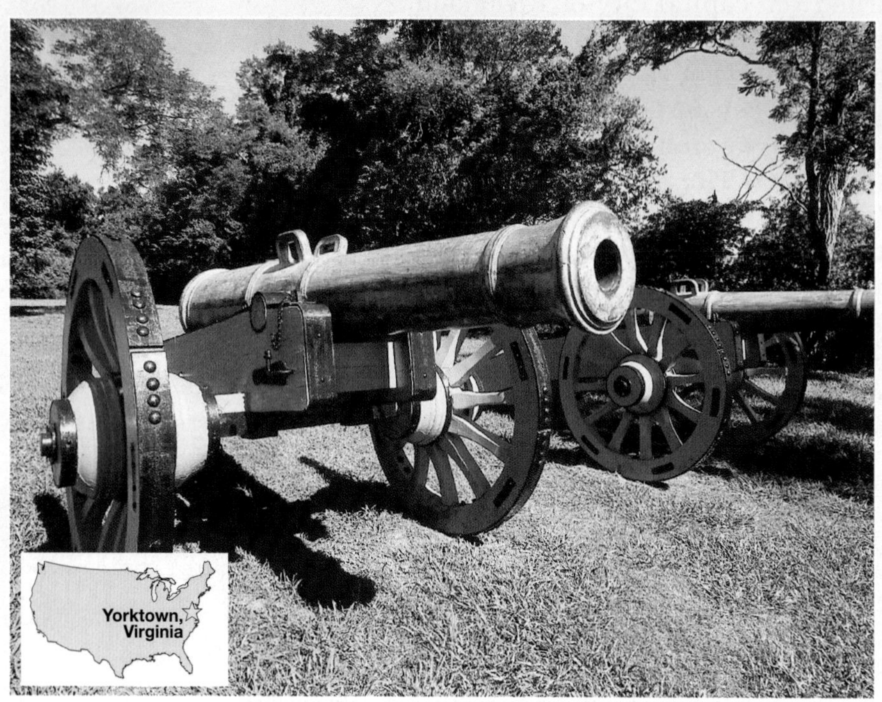

Yorktown

October 17, 1781, marked the end of a long battle between the American army and powerful Great Britain. The Yorktown victory led to peace talks, which began in Paris in 1782. The next year, the representatives from the new nation and Great Britain signed the Treaty of Paris. The battle site of Yorktown is part of the Colonial National Historic Park.

Virtual Field Trip For an interactive look at Yorktown, visit PHSchool.com, **Web Code mfd-0603.**

The Peace Treaty

In London, the defeat shocked the British. "It is all over," cried the British prime minister, Lord North. Discouraged, he agreed to peace talks.

The talks began in Paris in 1782. Congress sent Benjamin Franklin and John Adams, along with John Jay of New York and Henry Laurens of South Carolina, to work out a treaty. Because Britain was eager to end the war, the Americans got most of what they wanted.

Under the Treaty of Paris, the British recognized the United States as an independent nation. It extended from the Atlantic Ocean to the Mississippi River. The northern border of the United States stopped at the Great Lakes. The southern border stopped at Florida, which was returned to Spain.

For their part, the Americans agreed to ask the state legislatures to pay Loyalists for property they had lost in the war. In the end, however, most states ignored Loyalist claims.

On April 15, 1783, Congress ratified, or approved, the Treaty of Paris. It was almost eight years to the day since the battles of Lexington and Concord.

Why the Americans Won

Geography played an important role in the American victory. The British had to send soldiers and supplies to a war that was several thousand miles from home. They also had to fight an enemy that was spread over a wide area. For their part, the Americans were familiar with the local geography. They knew the best routes and the best places to fight.

Identify Supporting Details

What details in this paragraph tell why the Americans won the war? Add these details to your outline.

Foreign Help Help from other nations was crucial to the American cause. Spanish forces attacked the British along the Gulf of Mexico and in the Mississippi Valley. French money helped pay for supplies, and French military aid provided vital support to American troops. Without French soldiers and warships, for example, the Americans might not have won the Battle of Yorktown.

Americans' Growing Patriotism The Americans' patriotic spirit and fighting skills were another key to their victory. Despite early setbacks, the Patriots battled on. Gradually, Washington's inexperienced troops learned how to drill, how to march, and how to fight. Perhaps most important was Washington himself. By the end of the war, the general's leadership and military skills were respected by Americans and British alike.

Washington's Farewell In December 1783, General Washington bid farewell to his officers at Fraunces Tavern in New York City. Colonel Benjamin Tallmadge recalled the event:

> "Such a scene of sorrow and weeping I had never before witnessed. . . . We were then about to part from the man who had conducted us through a long and bloody war, and under whose conduct the glory and independence of our country had been achieved."
>
> —Benjamin Tallmadge, *Memoir*

All along Washington's route home to Virginia, crowds cheered their hero. The new nation faced difficult days ahead. In time, Americans would call on Washington to lead them once again.

★ ★ ★ Section 5 Assessment ★ ★ ★

Recall

1. **Identify** Explain the significance of **(a)** Henry Clinton, **(b)** Charles Cornwallis, **(c)** Nathanael Greene, **(d)** Daniel Morgan, **(e)** Battle of Cowpens, **(f)** Francis Marion, **(g)** Benedict Arnold, **(h)** Comte de Rochambeau, **(i)** Battle of Yorktown, **(j)** Treaty of Paris.
2. **Define** **(a)** guerrilla, **(b)** siege, **(c)** ratify.

Comprehension

3. Why did the South become the main battleground of the war in 1778?
4. Why was Cornwallis forced to surrender at Yorktown?
5. Describe the major points of the Treaty of Paris.
6. Give three reasons why the Americans defeated the British in the Revolution.

Critical Thinking and Writing

7. **Exploring the Main Idea** Review the Main Idea statement at the beginning of this section. Then, create a timeline of the major events at the end of the war, beginning with the Battle of Kings Mountain and ending with the Treaty of Paris.
8. **Making Predictions** Suppose that Britain had won the war. What might have been the effects of a British victory?

ACTIVITY

Writing a Letter You are General Cornwallis. In a letter to George III, describe the events at Yorktown.

CHAPTER 6
Review and Assessment

CHAPTER SUMMARY

Section 1
Fighting broke out in New England even while Congress tried to make peace with Britain. The opening battles indicated that the war would not be easily won by either side.

Section 2
Thomas Paine's *Common Sense* persuaded many colonists to support independence. In July 1776, the colonies declared independence from Britain.

Section 3
After a series of defeats, an American victory at Saratoga marked a major turning point in the Revolution. The victory convinced several European nations to aid the Americans.

Section 4
During the Revolution, women such as Martha Washington and Mary Ludwig Hays contributed to the American war effort. Free and enslaved African Americans made decisions to join American or British forces.

Section 5
In October 1781, the British surrendered at Yorktown. In the 1783 Treaty of Paris, Britain recognized United States independence.

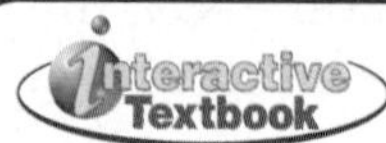

For additional review and enrichment activities, see the interactive version of *The American Nation,* available on the Web and on CD-ROM.

Chapter Self-Test For practice test questions for Chapter 6, visit PHSchool.com, **Web Code mfa-0604.**

Building Vocabulary

Use the chapter vocabulary words listed below to create a crossword puzzle. Exchange puzzles with a classmate. Complete the puzzles, and then check each other's answers.

1. **blockade**
2. **mercenary**
3. **traitor**
4. **preamble**
5. **natural rights**
6. **ally**
7. **cavalry**
8. **guerrilla**
9. **siege**
10. **ratify**

Reviewing Key Facts

11. What did the Battle of Bunker Hill show about each side in the conflict? (Section 1)
12. Describe three ideas contained in the Declaration of Independence. (Section 2)
13. When did France decide to help the Americans? (Section 3)
14. How did African Americans support the Patriot cause? (Section 4)
15. List the terms of the Treaty of Paris. (Section 5)

Critical Thinking and Writing

16. **Analyzing Primary Sources** According to the Declaration of Independence, when do people have a right and duty to rebel against their government?
17. **Identifying Causes and Effects (a)** Apply absolute chronology by placing the following events in order: **(1)** British defeat at Yorktown, **(2)** American victory at Saratoga, **(3)** French entry into the war against Britain, **(4)** signing of the Treaty of Paris. **(b)** Explain how each event caused the following event.
18. **Connecting to Geography: Place** How did the Patriots' knowledge of local geography help them to defeat the British?
19. **Synthesizing Information** What were the three biggest mistakes of British political and military leaders between 1775 and 1783? Explain.
20. **Linking Past and Present** Today, the United States and Britain are close allies. Why do you think the two nations now have close ties?

Skills Assessment

Analyzing Primary Sources

Thomas Paine had retreated with Washington's army through New Jersey. Seated by a campfire and using a drum for a desk, he wrote *The Crisis*. Read the following excerpt. Then, answer the questions:

> “These are the times that try men's souls. The summer soldier and the sunshine patriot will, in this crisis, shrink from the service of his country; but he that stands it now deserves the love and thanks of man and woman. Tyranny . . . is not easily conquered; yet we have this consolation with us . . . the harder the conflict, the more glorious the triumph.”
>
> Thomas Paine, *The Crisis*, 1776

21. The terms "summer soldier" and "sunshine patriot" refer to people who
- **A.** support the Revolution in all times.
- **B.** support the Revolution in good times but refuse to support it in hard times.
- **C.** fought at Princeton and Trenton.
- **D.** fought only in warm weather.

22. Based on the excerpt, what tyranny is Paine speaking of?
- **A.** American generals' treatment of their troops
- **B.** the treatment of African Americans
- **C.** the terms of the Treaty of Paris
- **D.** Britain's harsh rule over the colonies

Applying Your Skills

Identifying Points of View

THE HORSE AMERICA, *throwing his Master.*

This cartoon was published in 1779. Read the caption. Then, answer the questions.

23. How would you describe the event shown?
- **A.** The colonies are at peace with Britain.
- **B.** The colonies want independence.
- **C.** Britain won the war.
- **D.** The colonies are at war with France.

24. How does the cartoonist feel about the Patriot cause? Explain.

Activities

Connecting With . . . Geography

On a large sheet of paper, draw an outline map of the United States. On the map, show the sites of major battles of the American Revolution. Mark each site with a symbol to show who won. For each battle, include a text box giving one or two important facts about it.

Connecting to Today

Conducting an Interview During the Revolution, African Americans fought in special regiments. Use the Internet to research significant contributions of African Americans to the United States military since then. Prepare a short fictional interview with the group or person that you have researched. For help in starting this activity, visit PHSchool.com, **Web Code mfd-0605.**

CHAPTER 7

Creating a Republic

1776–1790

1 A Loose Confederation
2 The Constitutional Convention
3 Ideas Behind the Constitution
4 Ratification and the Bill of Rights

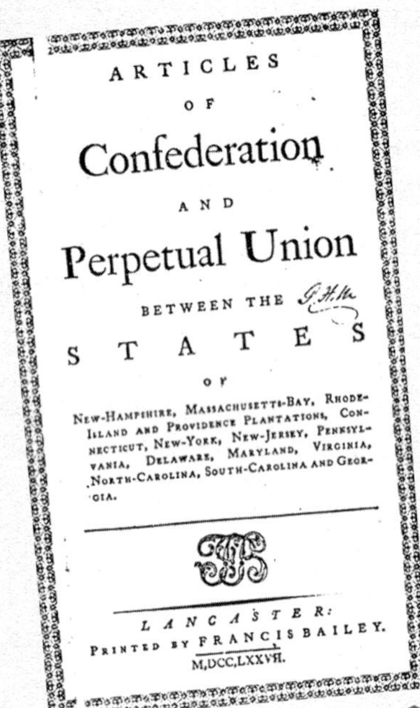

ARTICLES OF Confederation AND Perpetual Union BETWEEN THE STATES OF New-Hampshire, Massachusetts-Bay, Rhode-Island and Providence Plantations, Connecticut, New-York, New-Jersey, Pennsylvania, Delaware, Maryland, Virginia, North-Carolina, South-Carolina and Georgia.

LANCASTER: Printed by Francis Bailey. M,DCC,LXXVII.

Articles of Confederation

Surveyors (right) and surveying compass (left)

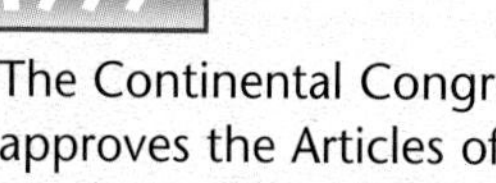

1777 The Continental Congress approves the Articles of Confederation. The Articles create a loose association of states.

1785 Congress passes the Land Ordinance of 1785. It sets up a system for surveying and settling the Northwest Territory between the Mississippi and Ohio Rivers.

1781 The Articles of Confederation take effect.

AMERICAN EVENTS

Presidential Terms:

1775 · 1780 · 1785

WORLD EVENTS

▲ **1776** Adam Smith publishes *The Wealth of Nations.*

▲ **1781** The Emperor of Austria grants religious toleration.

Ratifying the Constitution

A new, united nation took shape as each of the 13 original states in turn ratified, or approved, the Constitution.

Claimed by Great Britain and the United States
BRITISH TERRITORY
(claimed by NY & NH)
Maine (part of Mass.)
New Hampshire (June 21, 1788)
Massachusetts (Feb. 6, 1788)
New York (July 26, 1788)
Rhode Island (May 29, 1790)
Connecticut (Jan. 9, 1788)
Pennsylvania (Dec. 12, 1787)
New Jersey (Dec. 18, 1787)
Delaware (Dec. 7, 1787)
Maryland (Apr. 28, 1788)
Virginia (June 25, 1788)
North Carolina (Nov. 21, 1789)
South Carolina (May 23, 1788)
Georgia (Jan. 2, 1788)
NORTHWEST TERRITORY
SPANISH LOUISIANA
SPANISH FLORIDA
L. Superior
L. Michigan
L. Huron
L. Ontario
L. Erie
St. Lawrence R.
Mississippi R.
Missouri R.
Ohio R.
Wabash R.
Chesapeake Bay
ATLANTIC OCEAN
60°W
40°N
30°N
70°W
80°W
90°W
N E S W

Key
(Dec. 7, 1787) Date of ratification

Albers Equal-Area Projection
0 150 300 Miles
0 150 300 Kilometers

Writing of the Constitution

1787
The Constitutional Convention meets in Philadelphia. The new Constitution creates a stronger central government.

1789
The first election under the new Constitution takes place.

1791
The Bill of Rights is added to the Constitution to protect individual liberties.

George Washington 1789–1797

1785 · 1790 · 1795

1789 ▲
The French Revolution begins.

1793 ▲
The Emperor of China rejects British trade.

1 A Loose Confederation

Prepare to Read

Objectives

In this section, you will
- Explain why state governments wrote constitutions.
- List the weaknesses of the Articles of Confederation.
- Describe the process the Articles created for admitting new states.
- Explain why many Americans called for changes in the Articles.

Key Terms

constitution
bill of rights
Articles of Confederation
cede
currency
Land Ordinance of 1785
Northwest Ordinance
depression
Shays' Rebellion

Target Reading Skill

Reading Process As you read, prepare an outline of this section. Use roman numerals to indicate the major headings, capital letters for the subheadings, and numbers for the supporting details. The sample at right will help you get started.

I. The States Write Constitutions
  A. Type of government
    1. Legislature
    2.
  B.
II. The Articles of Confederation
  A. Limited power
    1.
    2.
  B.

Main Idea The Articles of Confederation created a weak central government and a loose alliance of independent states.

Thomas Jefferson

Setting the Scene In 1775, Thomas Jefferson rode 300 miles from Virginia to attend the Continental Congress in Philadelphia. The roads were so poorly marked that Jefferson got lost twice. The only way he could get back on the path was to hire guides.

The ties uniting the 13 states often seemed as hard to find as the roads linking them. The Declaration of Independence had created a new nation. But the former colonies had little experience working together. Many Americans wondered if they could create a central government that would unite the states effectively.

The States Write Constitutions

In forming a government, most states wrote constitutions. A **constitution** is a document that sets out the laws, principles, organization, and processes of a government. States wrote constitutions for two reasons. First, a written constitution would spell out the rights of all citizens. Second, it would limit the power of government.

Virginia's constitution included a **bill of rights,** or list of freedoms that the government promises to protect. Virginia's bill of rights guaranteed trial by jury, freedom of religion, and freedom of the press. Several other states followed Virginia's lead. For example, the Massachusetts state constitution guaranteed people:

> "... the right of enjoying and defending their lives and liberties; that of acquiring, possessing, and protecting property; in [short], that of seeking and obtaining their safety and happiness."
>
> —Massachusetts Constitution of 1780

The new state governments were somewhat similar to the colonial governments in structure. The states divided power between an executive and a legislature. The legislature was elected by the voters to pass laws. Every state but Pennsylvania had a governor to execute, or carry out, the laws.

Under the state constitutions, more people had the right to vote than in colonial times. To vote, a citizen had to be white, male, and over age 21. He had to own a certain amount of property or pay a certain amount of taxes. For a time, some women in New Jersey could vote. In a few states, free African American men who owned property could vote.

The Articles of Confederation

As citizens formed state governments, the Continental Congress was drafting a plan for the nation as a whole. Delegates believed that the colonies needed to be united by a national government in order to win independence.

It was hard to write a constitution that all states would approve. They were reluctant to give up power to a central government. Few Americans saw themselves as citizens of one nation. Instead, they felt loyal to their own states. Also, people feared replacing the "tyranny" of British rule with another strong government.

After much debate, the Continental Congress approved the first American constitution in 1777. The **Articles of Confederation** created a very loose alliance of 13 independent states.

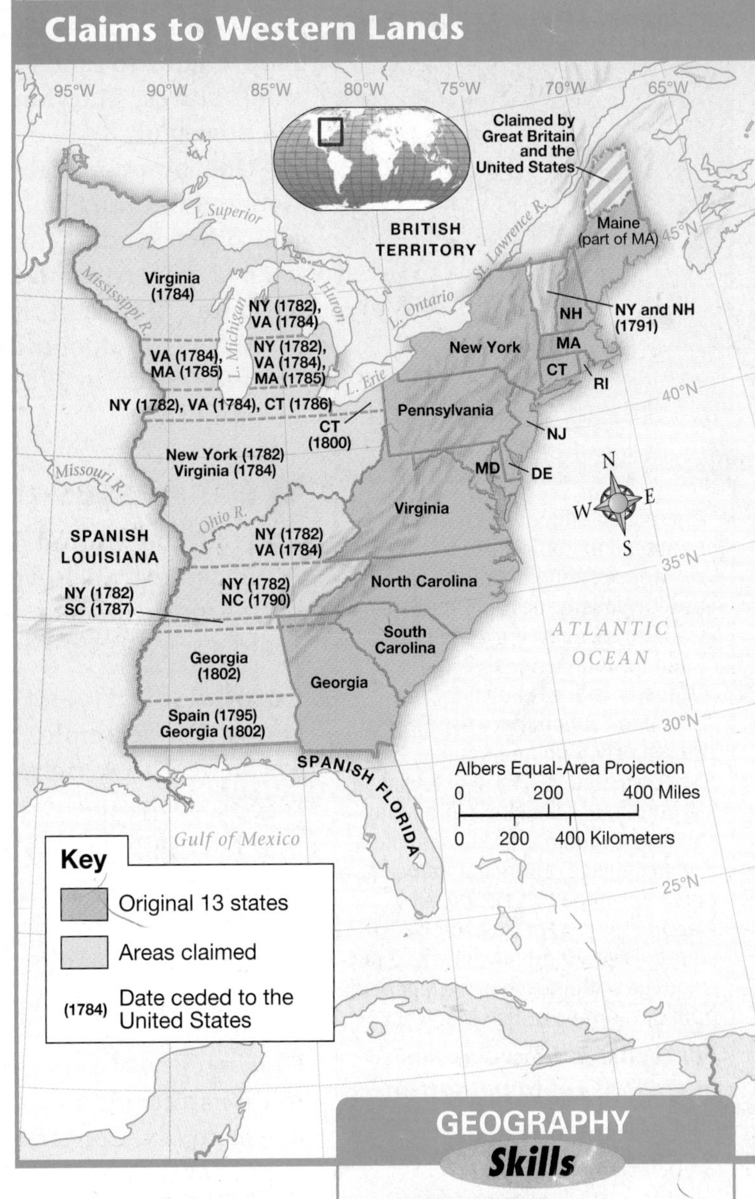

GEOGRAPHY Skills

By 1783, several states claimed land west of the Appalachians.

1. **Location** On the map, locate western lands claimed by **(a)** Virginia, **(b)** New York, **(c)** Massachusetts, **(d)** Spain.
2. **Region** Which states had no western land claims?
3. **Critical Thinking Making Predictions** Based on this map, how might western land claims threaten national unity?

Limited Powers Under the Articles of Confederation, the states sent delegates to Congress. Each state had one vote. Congress could declare war, appoint military officers, and coin money. It was also responsible for foreign affairs.

Still, compared to the states, Congress had very limited powers. Congress could pass laws, but nine states had to approve a law before it could go into effect. Congress could not regulate trade between states or between states and foreign countries. Nor did it have the power to tax. To raise money, Congress had to ask the states for it or borrow it. No state could be forced to contribute funds.

The Articles included no president to execute laws. It was up to the states to enforce the laws passed by Congress. There was also no system of courts to settle conflicts between states.

Dispute Over Western Lands A dispute arose even before the Articles of Confederation went into effect. Maryland refused to ratify

An American Profile

Noah Webster 1758–1843

"A national language is a bond of national union," wrote Noah Webster. A schoolteacher and patriot, Webster devoted much of his life to trying to unify the new nation through language.

Webster is best known for his *American Dictionary of the English Language,* which he began in 1807 and completed in 1828. It established the practice of dividing words into phonetic syllables. It also simplified British spelling, changing *colour* to *color, develope* to *develop,* and *waggon* to *wagon.* Webster declared, "We Americans must rid our language of the oddities we inherited from our former British Masters."

For Webster, how was language related to patriotism?

Set a Purpose When you set a purpose for reading, you give yourself a focus. If your purpose is to learn about the Articles of Confederation, how do the paragraphs under "Weaknesses of the Confederation" help you meet your goal? Add this information to your outline.

the Articles unless Virginia and other states **ceded,** or gave up, their claims to lands west of the Appalachian Mountains. Like other small states, Maryland feared that "landed" states would become too powerful.

One by one, the states agreed to cede their western claims to Congress. Finally, only Virginia held out. However, Thomas Jefferson and other leading Virginians recognized the great need to form a central government. They persuaded state lawmakers to give up Virginia's claims in the West.

With its demands met, Maryland ratified the Articles of Confederation in 1781. The new American government could at last go into effect.

Weaknesses of the Confederation

By 1783, the United States had won its independence. Yet, the end of the American Revolution did not solve the confederation's troubles. Americans had reason to doubt whether "these United States" could survive.

Conflicts Between States Disputes continued to arise among states. For example, both New Hampshire and New York claimed Vermont. The Articles did not give the central government power to resolve such conflicts. Noah Webster, a teacher from New England, saw the problem clearly:

> "So long as any individual state has power to defeat the measures of the other twelve, our pretended union is but a name, and our confederation, a cobweb."
>
> —Noah Webster, *Sketches of American Policy*

Money Problems After the Revolution, the United States owed millions of dollars to individuals and foreign nations. Without the power to tax, Congress had no way to repay these debts. It asked the states for money, but the states often refused.

During the Revolution, the Continental Congress had solved the problem of raising funds by printing paper **currency,** or money. However, the Continental dollar had little value because it was not backed by gold or silver.* Before long, Americans began to describe any useless thing as "not worth a Continental."

As Continental dollars became nearly worthless, states printed their own currency. This caused confusion. How much was a North Carolina dollar worth? Was a Virginia dollar as valuable as a Maryland dollar? Most states refused to accept the money of others. As a result, trade became very difficult.

Other Nations Take Advantage Foreign countries took advantage of the confederation's weakness. Ignoring the Treaty of Paris, Britain refused to withdraw its troops from the Ohio Valley. Spain

*In a stable economy, currency has value because the government keeps reserves of gold or silver. Coins and paper money represent a portion of this reserve. Today, the United States government keeps its gold reserves in underground vaults at Fort Knox, Kentucky.

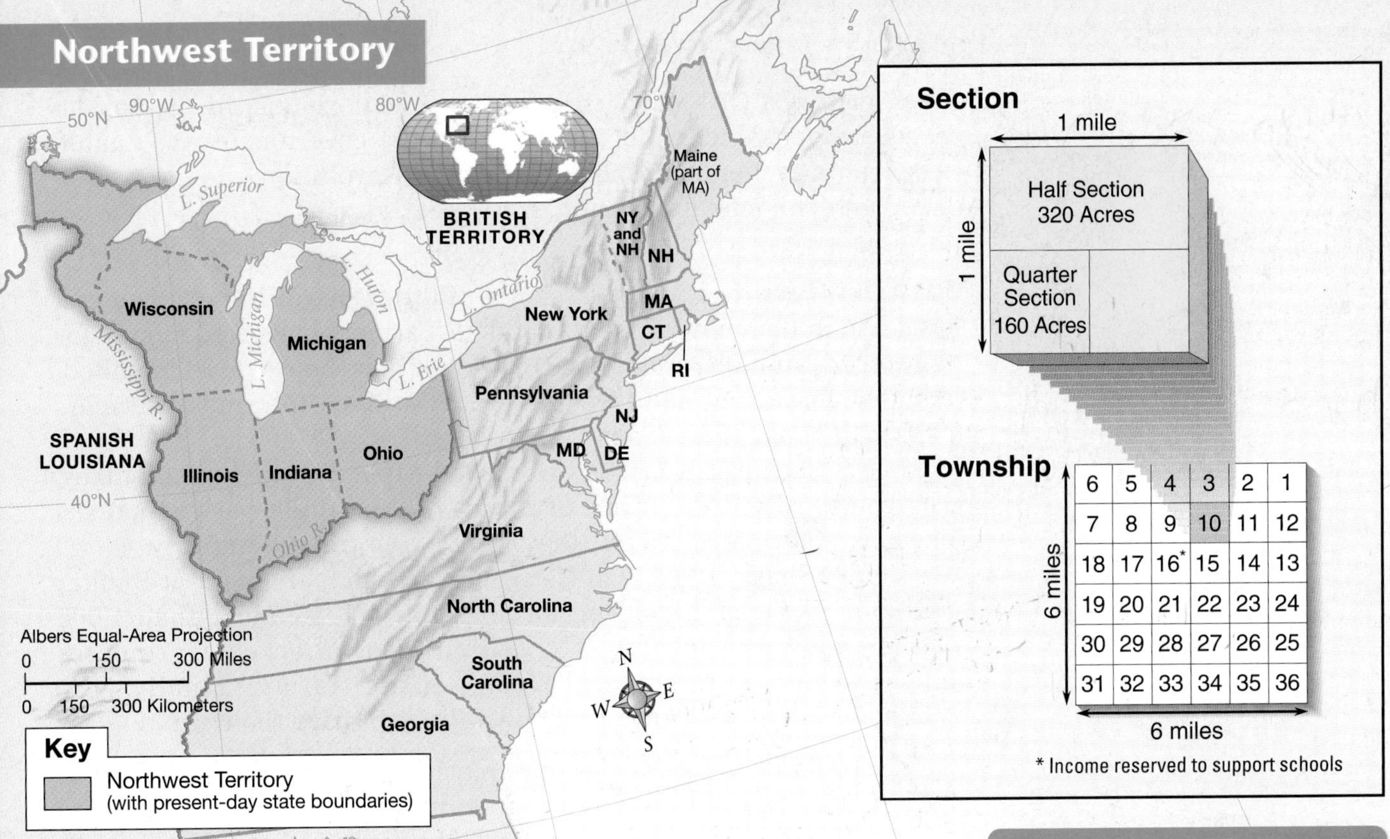

GEOGRAPHY *Skills*

Under the Articles of Confederation, Congress set up a system for settling and governing the Northwest Territory.

1. **Location** On the map, locate **(a)** Ohio, **(b)** Michigan, **(c)** Indiana, **(d)** Illinois, **(e)** Wisconsin.
2. **Place** What was the size of a township? A section?
3. **Critical Thinking Synthesizing Information** Did Indiana have public education when it became a state in 1816? Explain.

closed its port in New Orleans to American shipping. This was a serious blow to western farmers, who depended on the port to ship their products to the East.

Admitting New States

Despite its troubles, Congress did pass important laws about how to govern the Northwest Territory. These lands lay north of the Ohio River and east of the Mississippi. The laws established how territories would be governed and how they could become states.

The **Land Ordinance of 1785** set up a system for settling the Northwest Territory. The law called for the territory to be surveyed and divided into townships. Each township would then be further divided into 36 sections of 1 square mile each. Congress planned to sell sections to settlers for $640 apiece. One section in every township was set aside to support public schools.

In 1787, Congress passed the **Northwest Ordinance.** It set up a government for the Northwest Territory, guaranteed basic rights to settlers, and outlawed slavery there. It also provided for the vast region to be divided into separate territories in the future.

The Northwest Ordinance provided a way to admit new states to the nation. Once a territory had a population of 60,000 free settlers, it could ask Congress to be admitted as a new state. Each new state would be "on an equal footing with the original states in all respects whatsoever." In time, the states of Ohio, Indiana, Illinois, Michigan, and Wisconsin were created from the Northwest Territory.

A Call for Change

The Northwest Ordinance was the finest achievement of the national government under the Articles. Still, the government was unable to solve its economic problems. After the Revolution, the nation suffered an economic depression. A **depression** is a period when business activity slows, prices and wages fall, and unemployment rises.

Farmers Revolt The depression hit farmers hard. The war had created a high demand for farm products. Farmers borrowed money for land, seed, animals, and tools. However, when the Revolution ended, demand for farm goods went down. As prices fell, many farmers could not repay their loans.

In Massachusetts, matters worsened when the state raised taxes. The courts seized the farms of those who could not pay their taxes or loans. Angry farmers felt they were being treated unfairly.

Daniel Shays, a Massachusetts farmer who had fought at Bunker Hill and Saratoga, organized an uprising in 1786. More than 1,000 farmers took part in **Shays' Rebellion.** They attacked courthouses and prevented the state from seizing farms. Finally, the Massachusetts legislature sent the militia to drive them off.

A Convention Is Called Many Americans saw Shays' Rebellion as a sign that the Articles of Confederation did not work. Warned George Washington, "I predict the worst consequences from a half-starved, limping government, always moving upon crutches and tottering at every step."

To avert a crisis, leaders from several states called for a convention to revise the Articles of Confederation. They met in Philadelphia in May 1787. In the end, however, this convention would create an entirely new framework of government.

Section 1 Assessment

Recall

1. **Identify** Explain the significance of **(a)** Articles of Confederation, **(b)** Land Ordinance of 1785, **(c)** Northwest Ordinance, **(d)** Shays' Rebellion.
2. **Define** **(a)** constitution, **(b)** bill of rights, **(c)** execute, **(d)** cede, **(e)** currency, **(f)** depression.

Comprehension

3. What kind of governments did state constitutions create?
4. Describe two weaknesses of the Articles of Confederation.
5. Explain the process by which a territory became a state.
6. How did many Americans react to Shays' Rebellion?

Critical Thinking and Writing

7. **Exploring the Main Idea** Review the Main Idea statement at the beginning of this section. Then, list two arguments in favor of creating a stronger central government.
8. **Solving Problems** Choose one of the problems the nation faced in 1787. Then, write a letter to a delegate to the upcoming Philadelphia Convention. Suggest one idea to solve that problem.

ACTIVITY

Connecting to Today
Use the Internet to look at your state constitution. Write a paragraph summarizing one of the following: **(a)** powers of the governor and state legislature; **(b)** requirements for voting; **(c)** what rights are guaranteed. For help in completing the activity, visit PHSchool.com, **Web Code mfd-0701.**

Settling the Western Frontier

Migration into the Northwest Territory was slow at first. Clarksville, the first American town to be set up in the territory, had only 40 settlers in 1793. In time, more and more Americans endured hardship and danger to make the journey west.

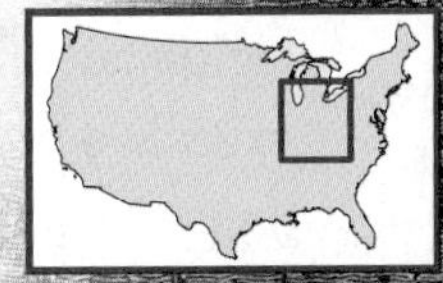

Why did people go west? Reports like this one certainly attracted eager and adventurous Americans:

> "The toils of agriculture will here be rewarded with a greater variety of valuable productions, than in any part of America. The advantages of almost every climate are here blended together; every considerable commodity that is [grown] in any part of the United States is here produced in the greatest plenty and perfection. The high and dry lands are of a deep, rich soil—producing, in abundance, wheat, rye, Indian corn, buck wheat, oats, barley, flax. . . ."
>
> —Manasseh Cutler, *The First Map and Description of Ohio, 1787*

After 1780, pioneers from the east floated down the Ohio River in large, flat-bottomed rafts such as these. Settlers sweated and strained as they propelled the boats with long barge poles. Down river, families dismantled the rafts, using the planks to build wilderness homes.

All settlers did their part to clear land and build homes in the thick forest. Families then outfitted their log cabins with the necessities they had brought on their raft—from rifles and seed to pots and the family Bible.

ACTIVITY

Based on the pictures and reading here, write a letter from a settler in the Northwest Territory to a friend back east. Explain how you feel about living on the frontier and what you hope the future will bring.

2 The Constitutional Convention

Prepare to Read

Objectives

In this section, you will
- Identify the leaders of the Constitutional Convention.
- Explain the main differences between the two rival plans for the new Constitution.
- Describe the compromises the delegates had to reach before the Constitution could be signed.

Key Terms

Constitutional Convention
Virginia Plan
legislative branch
executive branch
judicial branch
New Jersey Plan
compromise
Great Compromise
Three-Fifths Compromise

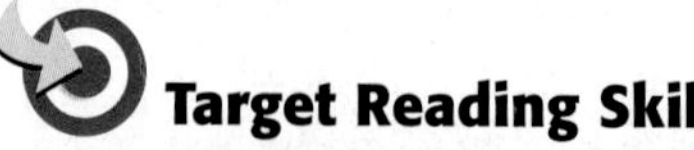

Target Reading Skill

Comparison and Contrast Copy the table below. As you read, complete the table with information about rival plans proposed at the Constitutional Convention.

VIRGINIA PLAN	NEW JERSEY PLAN	GREAT COMPROMISE
• • Favored large states • •	• Proposed by Paterson • • •	• Proposed by Sherman • • •

Main Idea Delegates to the Constitutional Convention of 1787 had to compromise on key issues in order to complete a new constitution.

The Liberty Bell at the State House

Setting the Scene An air of mystery hung over the State House in Philadelphia. All through the hot summer of 1787, the nation's great leaders passed in and out of the doors. Guards allowed only the delegates to enter. The windows remained closed, to keep passersby from overhearing any debates.

Like other Philadelphians, Susannah Dillwyn was curious and excited. She wrote to her father, "There is now sitting in this city a grand convention, who are to form some new system of government or mend the old one."

What would the convention decide? Rumors buzzed. Wrote Dillwyn, "They say it depends entirely upon their pleasure whether we shall in the future have a congress." For almost four months, Americans waited to learn the fate of their infant republic.

The Delegates to the Convention

The **Constitutional Convention** opened on May 25, 1787. Its goal was to revise the Articles of Confederation. Every state except Rhode Island sent representatives.

An Amazing Assembly The convention's 55 delegates were a remarkable group. Eight of them had signed the Declaration of Independence, including the oldest, Benjamin Franklin. At age 81, Franklin was wise in the ways of government and human nature. George Washington was a representative from Virginia. Washington was so well respected that the delegates at once elected him president of the Convention.

Still, most of the delegates represented a new generation of American leaders. Nearly half were young men in their thirties, including Alexander Hamilton of New York. During the Revolution,

Independence Hall

To many, the birthplace of the United States is the old Pennsylvania State House in Philadelphia, known today as Independence Hall. Here, independence was declared, the Articles of Confederation were approved, and the Constitution was debated and signed. Enter the chamber today and you can almost see patriots like Washington, Madison, Franklin, and Hamilton forging a new nation.

Virtual Field Trip For an interactive look at Independence Hall, visit PHSchool.com, **Web Code mfd-0702.**

Hamilton had served for a time as Washington's private secretary. Hamilton despised the Articles of Confederation. "The nation," he wrote, "is sick and wants powerful remedies." The powerful remedy he prescribed was a strong central government.

James Madison Perhaps the best-prepared delegate was 36-year-old James Madison of Virginia. For months, he had been reading books on history, politics, and commerce. He arrived in Philadelphia with a case bulging with volumes of research.

Madison was quiet and rather shy. Still, his keen intelligence and his ideas about how to structure a democratic government strongly influenced the other delegates. Today, Madison is often called the "Father of the Constitution."

Secret Debates When the Convention began, the delegates decided to keep their talks secret. They wanted to speak their minds freely and be able to explore issues without pressures from outside.

The closed windows helped keep the debates secret, but they made the room very hot. New Englanders in their woolen suits suffered terribly in the summer heat. Southerners, with clothing more suited to warm temperatures, were less bothered.

Two Rival Plans

Soon after the meeting began, the delegates realized they would have to do more than simply revise the Articles of Confederation. They chose instead to write an entirely new constitution for the

Compare and Contrast

How did the Virginia Plan differ from the New Jersey Plan? How were the plans similar?

nation. They disagreed, however, about what form the new national government should take.

The Virginia Plan Edmund Randolph and James Madison, both from Virginia, proposed a plan for the new government. This **Virginia Plan** called for a strong national government with three branches. The **legislative branch** would pass the laws. The **executive branch** would carry out the laws. The **judicial branch,** or system of courts, would decide if laws were carried out fairly.

According to the Virginia Plan, the legislature would consist of two houses. Seats would be awarded on the basis of population. Thus, in both houses, larger states would have more representatives than smaller ones. Under the Articles of Confederation, each state, regardless of population, only had one vote in Congress.

The New Jersey Plan Small states opposed the Virginia Plan. They feared that the large states could easily outvote them in Congress. Supporters of the Virginia Plan replied that it was only fair for a state with more people to have more representatives.

After two weeks of debate, William Paterson of New Jersey presented a plan that had the support of the small states. Like the Virginia Plan, the **New Jersey Plan** called for three branches of government. However, it provided for a legislature that had only one house. Each state, regardless of its population, would have one vote in the legislature.

An American Profile

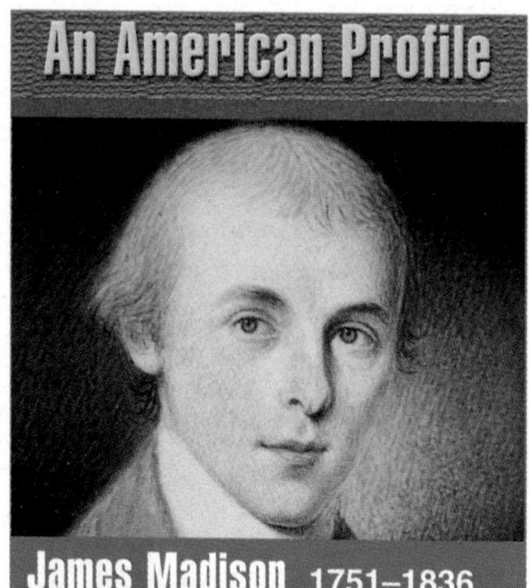

James Madison 1751–1836

Someone once said that James Madison looked "no bigger than a half a piece of soap." If so, looks were deceiving. By the age of 25, Madison was a skilled politician and a learned scholar.

Madison kept a close record of the debates at the Constitutional Convention. He chose a seat directly in front of the president's chair. "I was not absent a single day," he said. Unpublished for more than 50 years, Madison's notebooks are now our main source of information about the birth of the Constitution.

Why do you think Madison did not publish his notebooks immediately?

The Great Compromise

For a while, no agreement could be reached. With tempers flaring, it seemed that the Convention would fall apart without adopting any plan. Finally, Roger Sherman of Connecticut worked out a compromise that he hoped would satisfy both the large and small states. A **compromise** is a settlement in which each side gives up some of its demands in order to reach an agreement.

Sherman's compromise called for the creation of a two-house legislature. Members of the lower house, known as the House of Representatives, would be elected by popular vote. As the larger states wished, seats in the lower house would be awarded to each state according to its population.

Members of the upper house, called the Senate, would be chosen by state legislatures. Each state, no matter what its size, would have two senators. This part of Sherman's compromise appealed to the smaller states.

On July 16, the delegates narrowly approved Sherman's plan. It became known as the **Great Compromise.** Each side gave up some demands to achieve unity.

Northern and Southern States Compromise

Just as there were disagreements between large states and small states, there were also disagreements between northern states and southern states. The most serious disagreements concerned the issue of slavery. Would slaves be counted as part of a state's population?

Would the slave trade continue to bring enslaved Africans into the United States?

The Three-Fifths Compromise Southerners wanted to include slaves in the population count even though they would not let slaves vote. If slaves were counted, southern states would have more representatives in the House of Representatives. Northerners objected. They argued that, since slaves could not vote, they should not be counted when assigning representatives.

Once again, the delegates compromised. They agreed that three fifths of the slaves in any state would be counted. In other words, if a state had 5,000 slaves, 3,000 of them would be included in the state's population count. This agreement became known as the **Three-Fifths Compromise.**

The Slave Trade There was another disagreement over slavery. By 1787, some northern states had banned the slave trade within their borders. Delegates from these states urged that the slave trade be banned in the entire nation. Southerners warned that such a ban would ruin their economy.

In the end, northern and southern states compromised once more. Northerners agreed that Congress could not outlaw the slave trade for at least 20 years. After that, Congress could regulate the slave trade if it wished. Northerners also agreed that no state could stop a fugitive slave from being returned to an owner who claimed that slave.

Viewing History

Signing the Constitution

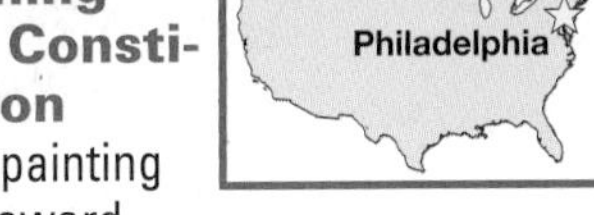

This painting by Howard Chandler Christy shows the signing of the Constitution on September 17, 1787. Some of the same men had signed the Declaration of Independence 11 years earlier. **Evaluating Information** ***How would you describe the way Washington is portrayed? Why do you think Christy painted him this way?***

James Madison
Roger Sherman
Benjamin Franklin
George Washington

Signing the Constitution

As the long, hot summer drew to a close, the weary delegates struggled with one difficult question after another. How many years should the President, head of the executive branch, serve? How should the system of federal courts be organized? Would members of Congress be paid?

Finally, on September 17, 1787, the Constitution was ready to be signed. Its opening lines, or Preamble, expressed the goals of the framers: "We the People of the United States, in order to form a more perfect union . . ."

Gathering for the last time, delegates listened quietly as Benjamin Franklin rose to speak. He pleaded that the document be accepted:

> "I doubt . . . whether any other Convention . . . may be able to make a better Constitution. . . . I cannot help expressing a wish, that every member of the Convention who may still have objections to it, would with me, on this occasion, doubt a little of his own infallibility, and . . . put his name to this instrument."
>
> —Benjamin Franklin, *Records of the Federal Convention of 1787*

One by one, delegates came forward to sign the document. All but three of the delegates remaining in Philadelphia did so. Edmund Randolph and George Mason of Virginia, along with Elbridge Gerry of Massachusetts, refused to sign. They feared that the new Constitution gave too much power to the national government.

The Constitution called upon each state to hold a convention to approve or reject the plan for the new government. Once nine states endorsed it, the Constitution would go into effect.

★ ★ ★ Section 2 Assessment ★ ★ ★

Recall

1. **Identify** Explain the significance of **(a)** Constitutional Convention, **(b)** James Madison, **(c)** Virginia Plan, **(d)** New Jersey Plan, **(e)** Roger Sherman, **(f)** Great Compromise, **(g)** Three-Fifths Compromise.
2. **Define** **(a)** legislative branch, **(b)** executive branch, **(c)** judicial branch, **(d)** compromise.

Comprehension

3. In what way did the delegates to the 1787 Convention represent a new generation of American leaders?
4. **(a)** Why did small states oppose the Virginia Plan? **(b)** How was this conflict resolved?
5. What compromises did the North and South reach?

Critical Thinking and Writing

6. **Exploring the Main Idea** Review the Main Idea statement at the beginning of this section. Then, list two or three things you think might have happened if the delegates had been unable to compromise.
7. **Drawing Inferences** Some historians call slavery the "unfinished business" of the 1787 Convention. Write a paragraph explaining why.

ACTIVITY

Drawing a Political Cartoon **Draw a political cartoon analyzing the conflict between the large and small states at the Constitutional Convention. Identify in which state your cartoon might have appeared. Select a viewpoint, either in favor of the larger states, in favor of the smaller states, or in favor of compromise.**

3 Ideas Behind the Constitution

Prepare to Read

Objectives

In this section, you will
- Explain what American leaders learned from studying ancient Rome.
- Identify the traditions of freedom that Americans inherited from Great Britain and from their own colonial past.
- Explain how Enlightenment ideas shaped the development of the Constitution.

Key Terms

Founding Fathers

republic

dictatorship

Magna Carta

English Bill of Rights

habeas corpus

separation of powers

Target Reading Skill

Main Idea Copy the concept web below. As you read, add ovals and fill them in with ideas that influenced the Constitution.

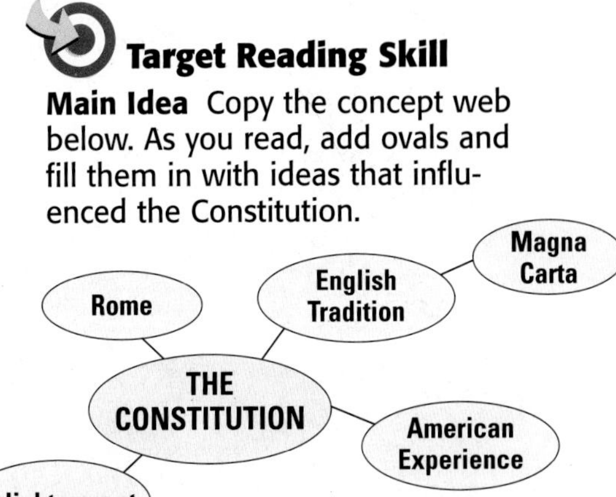

Main Idea The Constitution reflects ancient traditions, Enlightenment ideas, and Americans' experience.

Setting the Scene Serving as the ambassador to France, Thomas Jefferson did not attend the Constitutional Convention. James Madison, however, kept in touch with his friend in Paris. As Madison prepared for the convention, he asked Jefferson to send whatever books "may throw light" on various governments.

Jefferson sent not five or ten books but hundreds. Some discussed the laws of nations. Others were biographies of important leaders. A French encyclopedia alone came to 37 volumes. In gratitude, Madison shipped Jefferson unusual American plants to show the French. (Jefferson had also asked for a live opossum, but that, alas, Madison could not manage!)

Today, we often refer to Madison, Jefferson, and other leaders who laid the groundwork for the United States as the **Founding Fathers.** These patriots were well aware that their nation was embarking on a bold experiment. Still, they did not have to invent a government from scratch.

French encyclopedia

The Lessons of Rome's Republic

Long before the Revolution, John Adams called on Americans to investigate how governments worked:

> "Let us . . . search into the spirit of the British constitution; read the histories of ancient ages; contemplate the great examples of Greece and Rome; [and] set before us the conduct of our own British ancestors. . . ."
>
> —John Adams, *Dissertation on the Canon and Feudal Law*

The delegates to the Constitutional Convention followed this advice. They wanted to create a **republic,** a government in which citizens rule themselves through elected representatives. Few

Viewing History

Respect for the Ancient World

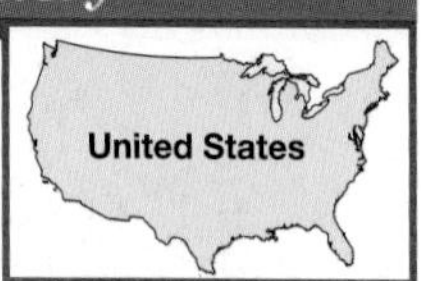

Even the arts reflected the respect that Americans felt for ancient Greece and Rome. Roman domes and Greek pillars influenced Thomas Jefferson's design for his home, Monticello (above). The bust (left) shows Benjamin Franklin dressed in a Roman toga. **Linking Past and Present** ***What kinds of buildings today have similarities to Monticello?***

republics in the history of the world had survived very long. In order to create one that would last, American leaders looked first to the ancient examples of Greece and, especially, Rome.

The Roman Example Americans greatly admired the Roman Republic. General Charles Lee, one of George Washington's commanders, commented, "I used to regret not being thrown into the World in the glorious [era] of the Romans."

Independence and public service were virtues that the Founding Fathers saw in the citizens of Rome. Roman citizens were willing to serve in public office, not for money, but because they were devoted to their republic. American colonists admired Rome so much that when they debated politics in the newspapers, they often signed their opinions with Roman names like Cincinnatus or Cicero.

The Roman Warning At the same time, the Founding Fathers saw the collapse of Rome's republic as a warning to the United States. No republic could survive unless its citizens remained independent and devoted to public service. Under the ruler Caesar Augustus, Rome eventually became a **dictatorship,** a government in which one person or a small group holds complete authority. The leaders of the American Revolution believed that Romans stumbled once they began to value luxury and comfort more than independence.

Historians today admit that the Founding Fathers somewhat exaggerated the virtues of Rome's republic. Yet, the lessons they learned still have force. Republics do not always die because they are invaded from outside. Without educated and dedicated citizens, republics can decay from within.

Britain's Traditions of Freedom

Greece and Rome were not the only examples of democratic government. Despite their quarrel with Great Britain, leaders of the Revolution valued British traditions of freedom.

Magna Carta As you learned in Chapter 3, King John of England signed the Magna Carta in 1215. The Magna Carta contained two basic ideas that helped to shape both British and American government. First, it made it clear that English monarchs themselves had to obey the law. King John agreed not to raise taxes without first consulting the Great Council of nobles and church officials. Eventually, the Great Council grew into the British Parliament.

Just as important, the Magna Carta stated that English nobles had certain rights—rights that were later extended to other classes of people as well. These included rights to private property and the right to trial by jury.

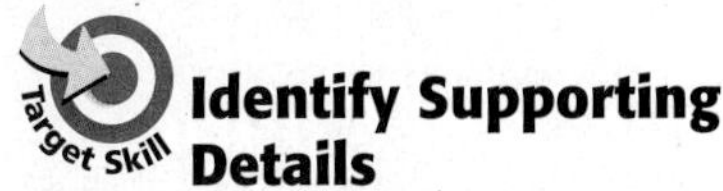

Identify Supporting Details

What details in the first two paragraphs on this page tell which English traditions influenced the Constitution? Add these details to your concept web.

English Bill of Rights In 1689, the English Bill of Rights went further in protecting the rights of citizens. The document said that parliamentary elections should be held regularly. It upheld the right to a trial by jury and allowed citizens to bear arms. It also affirmed the right of habeas corpus, the idea that no person could be held in prison without first being charged with a specific crime.

The American Experience

Americans enjoyed a long tradition of representative government. The Virginia colonists set up the House of Burgesses. Eventually, each British colony elected its own legislature.

A Constitutional Tradition Americans were also used to relying on written documents that clearly identified the powers and limits of government. The Mayflower Compact, written in 1620, was the first document of self-government in North America. Each of the 13 colonies had a written charter granted by the monarch or by Parliament.

The Revolutionary Era The framers of the Constitution also drew on their own experiences. The Founding Fathers bitterly remembered their grievances against the English king. In writing the Constitution, they sought to prevent such abuses.

For example, the Declaration of Independence accused the king of placing military power above civilian authority. The Constitution made the elected President "Commander in Chief of the Army and Navy . . . and of the militia of the several states." The Declaration protested that the king had made judges "dependent on his will alone." The Constitution set up a court system independent of the President and legislature.

The framers were very familiar with the workings of the Second Continental Congress, the Articles of Confederation, and their own state governments. Much that went into the Constitution came either from the Articles or from the state constitutions.

Teachings of the Enlightenment

The Constitution was also based on the ideas of the European Enlightenment. As you read in Chapter 4, Enlightenment thinkers believed that people could improve society through the use of reason. Many of the Constitution's framers had read the works of Enlightenment thinkers.

Primary Source

The Spirit of the Laws

Baron de Montesquieu's ideas about government had a strong influence on American thinkers. Here, Montesquieu discusses separation of powers:

"There is no liberty, if the judiciary power be not separated from the legislative and executive. Were it joined . . . to the executive power, the judge might behave with violence and oppression. There would be an end of everything, were the same man or the same body, whether of the nobles or of the people, to exercise those three powers, that of enacting laws, that of executing the public laws, and of trying the causes of individuals."

—Baron de Montesquieu, *The Spirit of the Laws*

Analyzing Primary Sources

What does Montesquieu say would result if judges also had the power to make and carry out laws?

Locke and Natural Rights The English writer John Locke published *Two Treatises of Government* in 1690. In it, he stated two important ideas. First, Locke declared that all people had natural rights to life, liberty, and property. Second, he suggested that government is an agreement between the ruler and the ruled. The ruler must enforce the laws and protect the people. If a ruler violates the people's natural rights, the people have a right to rebel.

Locke's ideas were popular among Americans. The framers of the Constitution wanted to protect people's natural rights and limit the power of government. They saw the Constitution as a contract between the people and their government.

Montesquieu and the Separation of Powers The French Enlightenment thinker Baron de Montesquieu (MOHN tehs kyoo) influenced American ideas of how a government should be constructed. In his 1748 book *The Spirit of the Laws,* Montesquieu stressed the importance of the rule of law. The powers of government, he said, should be clearly defined and divided up. He suggested that three separate branches be created: the legislative, executive, and judicial. This idea, known as the **separation of powers,** was designed to keep any person or group from gaining too much power. In the next chapter, you will see how the Constitution established separation of powers in the United States government.

From Out of the Old, the New The Founding Fathers drew on many traditions. In the end, though, the new system of government was not quite like anything that came before it.

When John Adams received the news from Philadelphia, he wrote, "As we say at sea, huzza for the new world and farewell to the old one!" He called the Constitution "the greatest single effort of national deliberation that the world has ever seen."

★ ★ ★ Section 3 Assessment ★ ★ ★

Recall

1. **Identify** Explain the significance of **(a)** Founding Fathers, **(b)** Magna Carta, **(c)** English Bill of Rights, **(d)** John Locke, **(e)** Baron de Montesquieu.
2. **Define** **(a)** republic, **(b)** dictatorship, **(c)** habeas corpus, **(d)** separation of powers.

Comprehension

3. How did the Roman republic provide both an example and a warning to Americans?
4. Identify two ways the Constitution addressed grievances listed in the Declaration of Independence.
5. What ideas did Americans adopt from John Locke?

Critical Thinking and Writing

6. **Exploring the Main Idea** Review the Main Idea statement at the beginning of this section. Then, write a letter from Madison to Jefferson discussing why American leaders looked to the past.
7. **Applying Information** The Magna Carta states, "Neither we nor our [representatives] shall take . . . wood which is not ours, against the will of the owner of that wood." Write a paragraph explaining how this principle applies to the United States.

ACTIVITY

Giving a Talk

Use the Internet to find quotations from an Enlightenment writer such as Locke, Montesquieu, or Voltaire. Choose one quotation and give a one-minute talk explaining how it relates to American ideals and principles. For help in completing the activity, visit PHSchool.com, **Web Code mfd-0703.**

4 Ratification and the Bill of Rights

Prepare to Read

Objectives

In this section, you will
- List the key issues in the constitutional debate.
- Explain how the Constitution was finally ratified.
- Describe how the Bill of Rights was added to the Constitution.

Key Terms

Federalists

Antifederalists

The Federalist Papers

amend

Bill of Rights

Target Reading Skill

Sequence Copy this flowchart. As you read, fill in the boxes with the major events relating to the ratification of the Constitution. The first and last boxes have been completed to help you get started. Add as many boxes as you need.

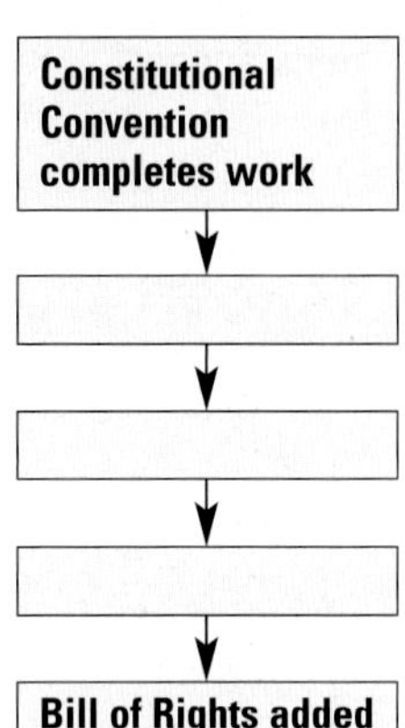

Main Idea After heated debates, the 13 states voted one by one to approve the new Constitution.

Setting the Scene Across the nation, Americans discussed the new Constitution. The Boston *Daily Advertiser* called for citizens to debate the new plan in the pages of its newspaper:

> “Come on brother scribblers, 'tis idle to lag!
> The Convention has let the cat out of the bag.”
>
> —quoted in *Miracle at Philadelphia* (Bowen)

The Constitutional Convention had done its work. Now, in the fall of 1787, the debates began. Each state had to decide whether or not to ratify the new framework of government.

Printing press

Federalists Debate Antifederalists

The framers of the Constitution sent the document to Congress, along with a letter from George Washington. Washington warmly approved the document, predicting that the Constitution would "promote the lasting welfare of that country so dear to us all."

The framers had set up a process for the states to approve the new government. At least 9 of the 13 states had to ratify the Constitution before it could go into effect. In 1787 and 1788, voters in each state elected delegates to special state conventions. These delegates would decide whether or not to ratify the Constitution.

The Federalist Position In every state, heated debates took place. Supporters of the Constitution called themselves **Federalists** because they favored a strong federal, or national, government. They called people who opposed the Constitution **Antifederalists.**

Federalists argued that the Articles of Confederation left too much power with the individual states. This imbalance produced a dangerously weak central government. Disputes among the states, Federalists said, made it too difficult for the government to function.

Federalists believed that the Constitution gave the national government the authority it needed to function effectively. At the same

Understand Sequence

Where on the flowchart will the Federalist and Antifederalist positions appear?

Connecting to Today

A Coin for Every State

Delaware, the second smallest state in the nation, enjoys one big honor no other state can match. It has the right to call itself "The First State." On December 7, 1787, Delaware became the first state to ratify the Constitution.

Delaware again led the way more than 200 years later. The United States mint began to issue a series of special quarters honoring the 50 states. The "heads" side of each coin carries the familiar image of George Washington. The "tails" side displays a different design for each state, in the order they ratified the Constitution or joined the Union. The Delaware quarter was issued on January 1, 1999. The final coins—honoring Alaska and Hawaii—are scheduled to be released in 2008.

Why do you think many people are eager to collect all 50 state quarters?

time, they said, the Constitution still protected the rights and powers of the individual states.

Federalists James Madison, Alexander Hamilton, and John Jay wrote a series of essays, known today as the ***Federalist Papers.*** Their purpose was to explain and defend the Constitution. They used pen names, but most people knew who they were. Today, the *Federalist Papers* remains one of the best discussions of the political theory behind the American system of government.

The Antifederalist Position Antifederalists felt that the Constitution made the national government too strong and left the states too weak. They also thought that the Constitution gave the President too much power. Patrick Henry of Virginia protested:

> "This Constitution is said to have beautiful features, but . . . they appear to me horribly frightful. . . . Your President may become king . . . If your American chief be a man of ambition and abilities, how easy is it for him to render himself absolute!"
>
> —Patrick Henry, Speech to the Virginia Convention, June 1788

Most people expected George Washington to be elected President. Antifederalists admired Washington, but they warned that future Presidents might lack Washington's honor and skill. For this reason, they said, the office should not be too powerful.

Key Issue: Need for a Bill of Rights

The chief objection of Antifederalists was that the Constitution had no bill of rights. Americans, they said, had just fought a revolution to protect their freedoms. A bill of rights was needed to protect such basic liberties as freedom of speech and religion.

One of the strongest supporters of a bill of rights was George Mason of Virginia. In 1776, Mason had written the bill of rights for Virginia's constitution. After the Constitutional Convention refused to include a bill of rights, Mason joined the Antifederalists.

Federalists replied that it was impossible to list all the natural rights of people. Besides, they said, the Constitution protected citizens well enough as it was. Antifederalists responded that unless rights were spelled out, they could be too easily ignored.

The States Vote to Ratify

One by one, the states voted. Delaware led the way, ratifying on December 7, 1787. Pennsylvania and New Jersey soon followed.

New England Approves Massachusetts was the first key battleground. There, the old patriots Sam Adams and John Hancock held back their support. The delay seemed "very ominous," wrote Madison. Finally, Adams and Hancock convinced the state convention to recommend adding a bill of rights to the Constitution.

Still the debate continued. "Some gentlemen say, don't be in a hurry . . . don't take a leap in the dark," a Federalist farmer told his fellow delegates. "I say . . . gather fruit when it is ripe." In February 1788, Massachusetts became the sixth state to ratify.

In June, New Hampshire joined ranks as the ninth state. The new government could now go into effect. Still, the nation's unity remained in doubt. New York and Virginia, two of the largest states, had not yet ratified the plan. In both states, Federalists and Antifederalists were closely matched.

Last Holdouts In Virginia, Patrick Henry, George Mason, and Governor Edmund Randolph led the opposition. Still a spellbinding speaker, Henry at one point spoke for seven hours. Soft-spoken, James Madison could not match Henry's dramatic style. Yet his arguments in favor of the Constitution were always clear, patient, and to the point.

The tide finally turned when Governor Randolph changed his mind. He gave his support when the Federalists promised to support a bill of rights. Virginia voted to ratify in late June.

In New York, the struggle went on for another month. In July 1788, the state convention voted to ratify. North Carolina followed in November 1789. Only Rhode Island, which had refused to send delegates to the Constitutional Convention, remained. On May 29, 1790, Rhode Island became the last state to ratify.

The Nation Celebrates Throughout the land, Americans celebrated the news that the Constitution was ratified. The city of Philadelphia set its festival for July 4, 1788.

A festive parade filed along Market Street, led by soldiers who had fought in the Revolution. Thousands cheered as six colorfully outfitted horses pulled a blue carriage shaped like an eagle. Thirteen stars and stripes were painted on the front, and the Constitution was raised proudly above it. Benjamin Rush, a Philadelphia doctor and strong supporter of the Constitution, wrote to a friend, "'Tis done. We have become a nation."

Adding a Bill of Rights

Americans voted in the first election under the Constitution in January 1789. As expected, George Washington was elected President, while John Adams was chosen as Vice President.

The first Congress met in New York City, which was chosen as the nation's first capital. Congress quickly turned its attention to adding a bill of rights to the Constitution. As you have read, several states had agreed to ratify the Constitution only on the condition that a bill of rights be added.

Cause *and* Effect

Causes

- Articles of Confederation creates weak national government
- Trade and money problems arise between states
- Foreign nations take advantage of weak government
- Shays' Rebellion breaks out
- Convention meets to revise Articles of Confederation

THE WRITING OF THE CONSTITUTION

Effects

- New government includes President and two-house legislature
- Power is divided between national and state governments
- Compromises allow slavery to continue
- States debate and ratify Constitution
- Bill of Rights is added

Effects Today

- United States is world's oldest continuing constitutional democracy
- Debate about federal versus state power continues
- Amendments extend rights to more citizens
- New democracies look to the Constitution as a model

GRAPHIC ORGANIZER Skills

The long-term impact of the Constitutional Convention reached far beyond its original goals.

1. **Comprehension** Why is Shays' Rebellion listed as a cause?
2. **Critical Thinking Linking Past and Present** Why do you think new nations see the United States Constitution as a model?

Proposed and Ratified The framers had established a way to amend, or change, the Constitution. They did not want people to make changes lightly, however. Thus, they made the process of amending the Constitution fairly difficult. (You will read more about the amendment process in Chapter 8.)

In 1789, the first Congress proposed a set of twelve amendments, written by James Madison. As required by the Constitution, the amendments then went to the states. By December 1791, three fourths of the states had ratified 10 of the 12 amendments. These 10 amendments became known as the Bill of Rights.

The Bill of Rights James Madison insisted that the Bill of Rights does not give Americans any rights. The rights listed, he said, are natural rights that belong to all human beings. The Bill of Rights simply prevents the government from taking these rights away.

Some of the first 10 amendments were intended to prevent the kind of abuse Americans had suffered under English rule. For example, the Declaration of Independence had condemned the king for forcing colonists to quarter troops in their homes and for suspending trial by jury. The Third Amendment forbids the government to quarter troops in citizens' homes without their consent. The Sixth and Seventh Amendments guarantee the right to trial by jury.

Other amendments protected individual rights as many states had already done. In 1786, the Virginia Statute of Religious Freedom stated that "No man shall be compelled to frequent or support any religious worship . . . or otherwise suffer, on account of his religious opinions or belief." Religious freedom became the very first right listed in the First Amendment. (You will read more about the freedoms protected by the Bill of Rights in Chapter 8.)

With the Bill of Rights in place, the new framework of government was complete. Over time, the Constitution became a living document that grew and changed along with the nation.

Section 4 Assessment

Recall

1. **Identify** Explain the significance of **(a)** Federalists, **(b)** Antifederalists, **(c)** *The Federalist Papers,* **(d)** George Mason, **(e)** Bill of Rights.
2. **Define** amend.

Comprehension

3. **(a)** Why did Federalists support the Constitution? **(b)** Why did Antifederalists oppose it?
4. Describe the ratification debate in one battleground state.
5. Why did the new government quickly take steps to amend the Constitution?

Critical Thinking and Writing

6. **Exploring the Main Idea** Review the Main Idea statement at the beginning of this section. Then, write a paragraph explaining what you think was the single most important reason in favor of ratifying the Constitution.
7. **Drawing Conclusions** Analyze the views of George Mason and Alexander Hamilton about the Bill of Rights. Explain how the influence of both shaped the Bill of Rights as it now exists.

Activity

Planning a Celebration **You are an official in an American city or village in 1789. With a group of classmates, create a plan for your own celebration of the ratification of the Constitution. Make a list of activities you would include. If you like, you may also design a banner, prepare a short speech, or select music.**

Analyzing Primary Sources

Why did the Antifederalists oppose the new Constitution? To gain an accurate understanding of past events, it is often helpful to analyze the words of those who were present when the events took place.

Patrick Henry, a fiery patriot and a firm Antifederalist, spoke against the ratification of the Constitution to the delegates at the Virginia state convention:

Patrick Henry

"You ought to be extremely cautious, watchful, jealous of your liberty; for instead of securing your rights, you may lose them forever. If a wrong step be now made, the republic may be lost forever. If this new government will not come up to the expectation of the people, and they shall be disappointed, their liberty will be lost, and tyranny must and will arise. I repeat it again, and I beg gentlemen to consider that a wrong step made now will plunge us into misery, and our republic will be lost. . . .

And here I would make this inquiry of those worthy characters who composed a part of the late federal Convention. . . . I have the highest veneration for those gentlemen; but, sir, give me leave to demand: What right had they to say, 'We, the people'? My political curiosity, exclusive of my anxious [concern] for the public welfare, leads me to ask: Who authorized them to speak the language of, 'We, the people,' instead of, 'We, the states'?"

—Patrick Henry, Speech at the Virginia Convention, June 1788

Learn the Skill *To analyze a primary source, use the following steps:*

1. **Identify the writer.** Knowing the source of a document helps you evaluate the writer's information and point of view.
2. **Identify the context.** When was the document written? What was its purpose?
3. **Identify the main idea.** What is the main idea of the document?
4. **Look for words that indicate the point of view.** Emotional words can be a clue to the writer's feelings about the subject matter.
5. **Analyze.** What conclusions can you reach about the writer and the information given?

Practice the Skill *Answer the following questions about the document above:*

1. What do you know about Patrick Henry and his political views?
2. What was Henry's purpose in giving the speech?
3. In this excerpt, what are Henry's main objections to the new Constitution?
4. **(a)** What words indicate that Henry has strong feelings about the Constitution? **(b)** Describe his attitude toward the framers.
5. Analyze Henry's view of the relationship of the central government to the states.

Apply the Skill *See the Chapter Review and Assessment.*

CHAPTER 7
Review and Assessment

Chapter Summary

Section 1
The Articles of Confederation created a weak central government and loose alliance of independent states. These weaknesses and an economic depression led to calls for change.

Section 2
Delegates to the Constitutional Convention had to compromise to create a new constitution. After compromising on a number of key issues, delegates signed the Constitution.

Section 3
The U.S. Constitution draws on many ideas. These include Greek and Roman traditions, British traditions, Enlightenment ideas, and the unique American experience.

Section 4
After heated debates, the 13 states voted to approve the new Constitution. The first ten amendments to the Constitution make up the Bill of Rights. These amendments protect personal liberties and the natural rights of citizens.

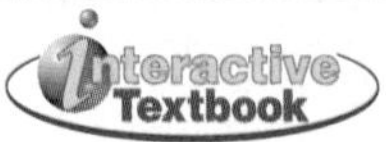

For additional review and enrichment activities, see the interactive version of *The American Nation,* available on the Web and on CD-ROM.

Chapter Self-Test For practice test questions for Chapter 7, visit PHSchool.com, **Web Code mfa-0704.**

Building Vocabulary

Review the meaning of the chapter vocabulary words listed below. Then, write a sentence for each word in which you define the word and describe its relation to the writing of the Constitution.

1. **constitution**
2. **bill of rights**
3. **depression**
4. **legislative branch**
5. **executive branch**
6. **judicial branch**
7. **compromise**
8. **republic**
9. **habeas corpus**
10. **separation of powers**

Reviewing Key Facts

11. Summarize the strengths and weaknesses of the Articles of Confederation. (Section 1)
12. What kind of legislature did the Constitution create? Why? (Section 2)
13. How did the Constitution build on the earlier experience of Americans? (Section 3)
14. Identify one way Antifederalists influenced the Constitution. (Section 4)

Critical Thinking and Writing

15. Connecting to Geography: **Regions** Review the map Claims to Western Lands in Section 1. **(a)** Describe the region that was considered "the West" in the 1780s. **(b)** Write a paragraph describing what would have happened if Virginia had won all of its land claims.
16. **Analyzing Information** Choose one issue at the Philadelphia Convention of 1787. Describe what each side won and gave up. Was the issue resolved successfully? Explain.
17. **Applying Information** Review the opening lines of the Declaration of Independence in Chapter 6. Copy two sentences or phrases that reflect the ideas of John Locke. Explain how they show that Locke influenced Jefferson.
18. **Supporting a Point of View** When the Constitution was ratified, Benjamin Rush commented, "We have become a nation." List three reasons to support Rush's comment. Explain in what way the United States was not a "nation" before the Constitution.

SKILLS ASSESSMENT

Analyzing Primary Sources

The cartoon below appeared in an American newspaper in 1788. Look at the cartoon and answer the questions that follow:

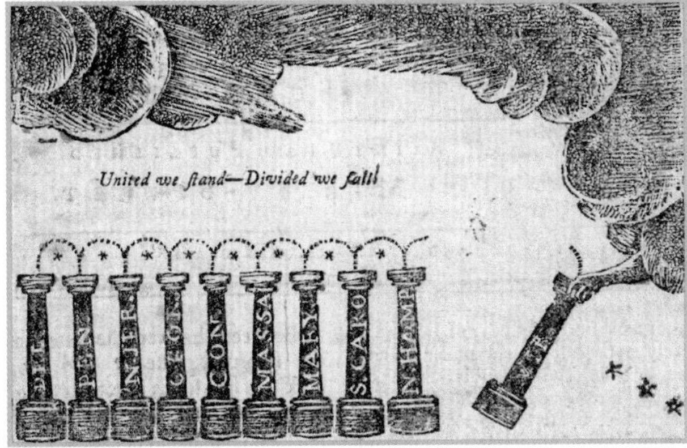

19. The subject of this cartoon is the
- **A.** American Revolution.
- **B.** Great Compromise.
- **C.** great power of state governments.
- **D.** ratification of the Constitution.

20. What do the pillars represent?
- **A.** the states
- **B.** articles of the Constitution
- **C.** U.S. expansion west
- **D.** presidential candidates

APPLYING YOUR SKILLS

Analyzing a Primary Source

In this letter, George Washington discusses the weaknesses of the early government. Read the excerpt and answer the questions that follow:

> “I am told that even respectable characters speak of a monarchical form of government without horror. . . . What a triumph for the advocates of [tyranny] to find that we are incapable of governing ourselves, and that systems founded on the basis of equal liberty are merely ideal and [false]! Would to God that wise measures be taken in time to avert the consequences.”
>
> —George Washington, Letter to John Jay, August 1, 1786

21. Washington is disturbed because
- **A.** the Constitution has no bill of rights.
- **B.** the Articles of Confederation have no executive.
- **C.** some Americans want a monarchy.
- **D.** a government based on equal liberty can never succeed.

22. How does this letter help explain why Washington agreed to serve as president of the Constitutional Convention?

ACTIVITIES

Connecting With . . . Government and Citizenship

Making a Chart With a partner, review the Declaration of Independence printed in Chapter 6. Identify the list of grievances against the king of England. Then, skim the Constitution and Bill of Rights, which appear at the end of this chapter. Make a chart showing how specific grievances in the Declaration were addressed in the Constitution. Include at least five grievances.

Connecting to Today

Exploring American Symbols In 1782, Congress declared the bald eagle to be an official symbol of the new nation. Use the Internet to find out more about another familiar American symbol. Prepare a three-minute report on the meaning of that symbol. For help in starting this activity, visit PHSchool.com, **Web Code mfd-0705.**

Creating a Database

A Constitutional Convention Information Bank With the class, create an information bank on the delegates to the Constitutional Convention. Use the Internet to find information about one delegate. Prepare a fact sheet showing his background, the state he represented, and his position on a key issue. Combine your fact sheet with those of the rest of the class. For help in starting this activity, visit PHSchool.com, **Web Code mfd-0706.**

The Constitution at a Glance

Original Constitution

Preamble

Article

1 The Legislative Branch
2 The Executive Branch
3 The Judicial Branch
4 Relations Among the States
5 Amending the Constitution
6 National Supremacy
7 Ratification

Amendments

Bill of Rights

1 Freedoms of Religion, Speech, Press, Assembly, and Petition
2 Right to Bear Arms
3 Lodging Troops in Private Homes
4 Search and Seizure
5 Rights of the Accused
6 Right to Speedy Trial by Jury
7 Jury Trial in Civil Cases
8 Bail and Punishment
9 Powers Reserved to the People
10 Powers Reserved to the States

Additional Amendments

11 Suits Against States
12 Election of President and Vice-President
13 Abolition of Slavery
14 Rights of Citizens
15 Voting Rights
16 The Income Tax
17 Direct Election of Senators
18 Prohibition of Alcoholic Beverages
19 Women's Suffrage
20 Presidential Terms, Sessions of Congress
21 Repeal of Prohibition
22 Limit on Number of President's Terms
23 Presidential Electors for District of Columbia
24 Abolition of Poll Tax in National Elections
25 Presidential Succession and Disability
26 Voting Age
27 Congressional Pay Increases

The Constitution of the United States of America

The Constitution is printed in black. The titles of articles, sections, and clauses are not part of the original document. They have been added here to help you find information in the Constitution. Some words or lines are crossed out because they have been changed by amendments or no longer apply. Annotations, or explanations, are on the tan side of the page. Difficult words are defined.

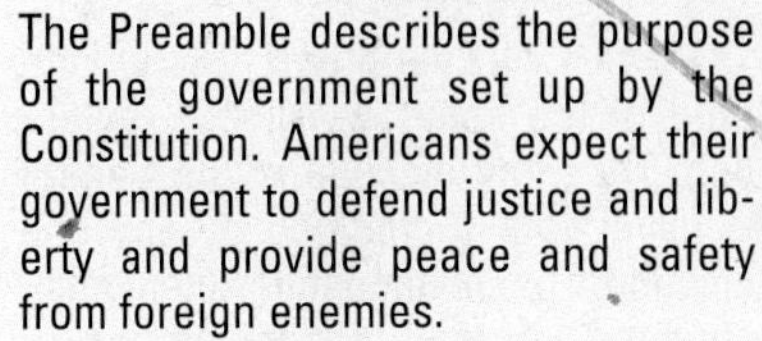

Preamble

We the people of the United States, in order to form a more perfect Union, establish justice, insure domestic tranquillity, provide for the common defense, promote the general welfare, and secure the blessings of liberty to ourselves and our posterity, do ordain and establish this Constitution for the United States of America.

The Preamble describes the purpose of the government set up by the Constitution. Americans expect their government to defend justice and liberty and provide peace and safety from foreign enemies.

Article 1. The Legislative Branch

Section 1. A Two-House Legislature

All legislative powers herein granted shall be vested in a Congress of the United States, which shall consist of a Senate and House of Representatives.

The Constitution gives Congress the power to make laws. Congress is divided into the Senate and the House of Representatives.

Section 2. House of Representatives

1. **Election of Members** The House of Representatives shall be composed of members chosen every second year by the people of the several states, and the electors in each state shall have the qualifications requisite for electors of the most numerous branch of the state legislature.

2. **Qualifications** No person shall be a Representative who shall not have attained to the age of twenty-five years, and been seven years a citizen of the United States, and who shall not, when elected, be an inhabitant of that state in which he shall be chosen.

3. **Determining Representation** Representatives ~~and direct taxes~~ shall be apportioned among the several states which may be included within this Union, according to their respective numbers ~~which shall be determined by adding to the whole number of free persons, including those bound to service for a term of years, and excluding Indians not taxed, three fifths of all other persons.~~ The actual enumeration shall be made within three years after the first meeting of the Congress of the United States, and within every subsequent term of ten years, in such manner as they shall by law direct. The number of Representatives shall not exceed one for every 30,000, but each state shall have at least one Representative; ~~and until such enumeration shall be made, the state of New Hampshire shall be entitled to choose three; Massachusetts, eight; Rhode Island and Providence Plantations, one; Connecticut, five; New York, six; New Jersey, four; Pennsylvania, eight; Delaware, one; Maryland, six; Virginia, ten; North Carolina, five; South Carolina, five; and Georgia, three.~~

Clause 1 ***Electors*** refers to voters. Members of the House of Representatives are elected every two years. Any citizen allowed to vote for members of the larger house of the state legislature can also vote for members of the House.

Clause 2 A member of the House of Representatives must be at least 25 years old, an American citizen for 7 years, and a resident of the state he or she represents.

Clause 3 The number of representatives each state elects is based on its population. An ***enumeration,*** or census, must be taken every 10 years to determine population. Today, the number of representatives in the House is fixed at 435.

This is the famous Three-Fifths Compromise worked out at the Constitutional Convention. ***Persons bound to service*** meant indentured servants. ***All other persons*** meant slaves. All free people in a state were counted. However, only three fifths of the slaves were included in the population count. This three-fifths clause became meaningless when slaves were freed in 1865 by the Thirteenth Amendment.

Clause 4 ***Executive authority*** means the governor of a state. If a member of the House leaves office before his or her term ends, the governor must call a special election to fill the seat.

4. **Filling Vacancies** When vacancies happen in the representation from any state, the executive authority thereof shall issue writs of election to fill such vacancies.

Clause 5 The House elects a speaker. Today, the speaker is usually chosen by the party that has a majority in the House. Also, only the House has the power to ***impeach,*** or accuse, a federal official of wrongdoing.

5. **Selection of Officers; Power of Impeachment** The House of Representatives shall choose their Speaker and other officers; and shall have the sole power of impeachment.

Section 3. The Senate

Clause 1 Each state has two senators, who serve for six-year terms. The Seventeenth Amendment changed the way senators were elected.

1. **Selection of Members** The Senate of the United States shall be composed of two Senators from each state ~~chosen by the legislature thereof~~, for six years, and each Senator shall have one vote.

Clause 2 Every two years, one third of the senators run for reelection. Thus, the makeup of the Senate is never totally changed by any one election. The Seventeenth Amendment changed the way that ***vacancies,*** or empty seats, are filled. Today, the governor of a state must choose a senator to fill a vacancy that occurs between elections.

2. **Alternating Terms; Filling Vacancies** Immediately after they shall be assembled in consequence of the first election, they shall be divided as equally as may be into three classes. ~~The seats of the Senators of the first class shall be vacated at the expiration of the second year, of the second class at the expiration of the fourth year, and of the third class at the expiration of the sixth year,~~ so that one-third may be chosen every second year; ~~and if vacancies happen by resignation, or otherwise, during the recess of the legislature of any state, the executive thereof may make temporary appointments until the next meeting of the legislature, which shall then fill such vacancies.~~

Clause 3 A senator must be at least 30 years old, an American citizen for 9 years, and a resident of the state he or she represents.

3. **Qualifications** No person shall be a Senator who shall not have attained to the age of thirty years, and been nine years a citizen of the United States, and who shall not, when elected, be an inhabitant of that state for which he shall be chosen.

Clause 4 The Vice President presides over Senate meetings, but he or she can vote only to break a tie.

4. **President of the Senate** The Vice-President of the United States shall be president of the Senate, but shall have no vote, unless they be equally divided.

Clause 5 ***Pro tempore*** means "temporary." The Senate chooses a member to serve as president *pro tempore* when the Vice President is absent.

5. **Election of Senate Officers** The Senate shall choose their other officers, and also a president *pro tempore,* in the absence of the Vice-President, or when he shall exercise the office of the President of the United States.

Clause 6 The Senate acts as a jury if the House impeaches a federal official. The Chief Justice of the Supreme Court presides if the President is on trial. Two thirds of all senators present must vote for ***conviction,*** or a finding of guilty. No President has ever been convicted, though the House impeached President Andrew Johnson in 1868 and President Bill Clinton in 1998. In 1974, President Richard Nixon resigned before he could be impeached.

6. **Impeachment Trials** The Senate shall have the sole power to try all impeachments. When sitting for that purpose, they shall be on oath or affirmation. When the President of the United States is tried, the Chief Justice shall preside; and no person shall be convicted without the concurrence of two-thirds of the members present.

Clause 7 If an official is found guilty by the Senate, he or she can be removed from office and barred from holding federal office in the future. These are the only punishments the Senate can impose. However, the convicted official can still be tried in a criminal court.

7. **Penalties Upon Conviction** Judgment in cases of impeachment shall not extend further than to removal from office, and disqualification to hold and enjoy any office of honor, trust, or profit under the United States; but the party convicted shall nevertheless be liable and subject to indictment, trial, judgment, and punishment, according to law.

Section 4. Elections and Meetings

1. **Election of Congress** The times, places, and manner of holding elections for Senators and Representatives shall be prescribed in each state by the legislature thereof; but the Congress may at any time by law make or alter such regulations, except as to the places of choosing Senators.

Clause 1 Each state legislature can decide when and how congressional elections take place, but Congress can overrule these decisions. In 1842, Congress required each state to set up congressional districts with one representative elected from each district. In 1872, Congress decided that congressional elections must be held in every state on the same date in even-numbered years.

2. **Annual Sessions** The Congress shall assemble at least once in every year, ~~and such meeting shall be on the first Monday in December, unless they shall by law appoint a different day.~~

Clause 2 Congress must meet at least once a year. The Twentieth Amendment moved the opening date of Congress to January 3.

Section 5. Rules for the Conduct of Business

1. **Organization** Each house shall be the judge of the elections, returns, and qualifications of its own members, and a majority of each shall constitute a quorum to do business; but a smaller number may adjourn from day to day, and may be authorized to compel the attendance of absent members, in such manner, and under such penalties, as each house may provide.

Clause 1 Each house decides whether a member has the qualifications for office set by the Constitution. A ***quorum*** is the smallest number of members who must be present for business to be conducted. Each house can set its own rules about absent members.

2. **Procedures** Each house may determine the rules of its proceedings, punish its members for disorderly behavior, and with the concurrence of two-thirds, expel a member.

Clause 2 Each house can make rules for the conduct of members. It can only expel a member by a two-thirds vote.

3. **A Written Record** Each house shall keep a journal of its proceedings, and from time to time publish the same, excepting such parts as may in their judgment require secrecy; and the yeas and nays of the members of either house on any question shall, at the desire of one-fifth of those present, be entered on the journal.

Clause 3 Each house keeps a record of its meetings. *The Congressional Record* is published every day with excerpts from speeches made in each house. It also records the votes of each member.

4. **Rules for Adjournment** Neither house, during the session of Congress, shall, without the consent of the other, adjourn for more than three days, nor to any other place than that in which the two houses shall be sitting.

Clause 4 Neither house can ***adjourn,*** or stop meeting, for more than three days unless the other house approves. Both houses of Congress must meet in the same city.

Section 6. Privileges and Restrictions

1. **Salaries and Immunities** The Senators and Representatives shall receive a compensation for their services, to be ascertained by law and paid out of the Treasury of the United States. They shall in all cases, except treason, felony, and breach of the peace, be privileged from arrest during their attendance at the session of their respective houses, and in going to and returning from the same; and for any speech or debate in either house, they shall not be questioned in any other place.

Clause 1 ***Compensation*** means "salary." Congress decides the salary for its members. While Congress is in session, a member is free from arrest in civil cases and cannot be sued for anything he or she says on the floor of Congress. This allows for freedom of debate. However, a member can be arrested for a criminal offense.

2. **Restrictions on Other Employment** No Senator or Representative shall, during the time for which he was elected, be appointed to any civil office under the authority of the United States, which shall have been created, or the emoluments whereof shall have been increased, during such time; and no person holding any office under the United States shall be a member of either house during his continuance in office.

Clause 2 ***Emolument*** also means "salary." A member of Congress cannot hold another federal office during his or her term. A former member of Congress cannot hold an office created while he or she was in Congress. An official in another branch of government cannot serve at the same time in Congress. This strengthens the separation of powers.

Section 7. Law-Making Process

Clause 1 ***Revenue*** is money raised by the government through taxes. Tax bills must be introduced in the House. The Senate, however, can make changes in tax bills. This clause protects the principle that people can be taxed only with their consent.

Clause 2 A ***bill,*** or proposed law, that is passed by a majority of the House and Senate is sent to the President. If the President signs the bill, it becomes law.

A bill can also become law without the President's signature. The President can refuse to act on a bill. If Congress is in session at the time, the bill becomes law 10 days after the President receives it.

The President can ***veto,*** or reject, a bill by sending it back to the house where it was introduced. Or if the President refuses to act on a bill and Congress adjourns within 10 days, then the bill dies. This way of killing a bill without taking action is called the ***pocket veto.***

Congress can override the President's veto if each house of Congress passes the bill again by a two-thirds vote. This clause is an important part of the system of checks and balances.

1. **Tax Bills** All bills for raising revenue shall originate in the House of Representatives; but the Senate may propose or concur with amendments as on other bills.

2. **How a Bill Becomes a Law** Every bill which shall have passed the House of Representatives and the Senate shall, before it become a law, be presented to the President of the United States; if he approve, he shall sign it, but if not, he shall return it, with his objections, to that house in which it shall have originated, who shall enter the objections at large on their journal, and proceed to reconsider it. If after such reconsideration two-thirds of that house shall agree to pass the bill, it shall be sent, together with the objections, to the other house, by which it shall likewise be reconsidered, and, if approved by two-thirds of that house, it shall become a law. But in all such cases the votes of both houses shall be determined by yeas and nays, and the names of the persons voting for and against the bill shall be entered on the journal of each house respectively. If any bill shall not be returned by the President within ten days (Sundays excepted) after it shall have been presented to him, the same bill shall be a law, in like manner as if he had signed it, unless the Congress by their adjournment prevent its return, in which case it shall not be a law.

How a Bill Becomes a Law

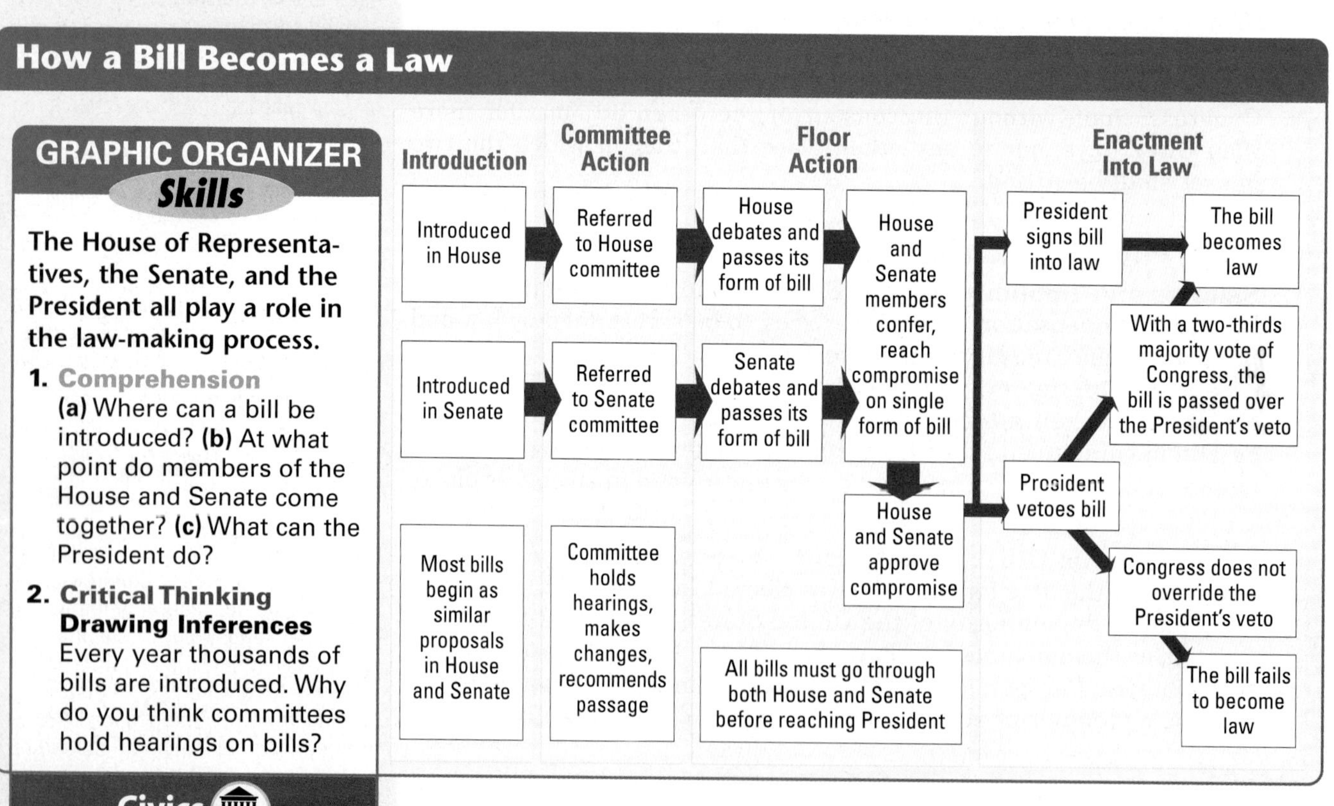

GRAPHIC ORGANIZER *Skills*

The House of Representatives, the Senate, and the President all play a role in the law-making process.

1. **Comprehension** **(a)** Where can a bill be introduced? **(b)** At what point do members of the House and Senate come together? **(c)** What can the President do?
2. **Critical Thinking Drawing Inferences** Every year thousands of bills are introduced. Why do you think committees hold hearings on bills?

Civics

3. **Resolutions Passed by Congress** Every order, resolution, or vote to which the concurrence of the Senate and House of Representatives may be necessary (except on a question of adjournment) shall be presented to the President of the United States; and before the same shall take effect, shall be approved by him, or being disapproved by him, shall be repassed by two-thirds of the Senate and House of Representatives, according to the rules and limitations prescribed in the case of a bill.

Clause 3 Congress can pass resolutions or orders that have the same force as laws. Any such resolution or order must be signed by the President (except on questions of adjournment). This clause prevents Congress from bypassing the President simply by calling a bill by another name.

Section 8. Powers Delegated to Congress

The Congress shall have the power

1. **Taxes** To lay and collect taxes, duties, imposts, and excises, to pay the debts and provide for the common defense and general welfare of the United States; but all duties, imposts, and excises shall be uniform throughout the United States;

Clause 1 ***Duties*** are tariffs. ***Imposts*** are taxes in general. ***Excises*** are taxes on the production or sale of certain goods. Congress has the power to tax and spend tax money. Taxes must be the same in all parts of the country.

2. **Borrowing** To borrow money on the credit of the United States;

Clause 2 Congress can borrow money for the United States. The government often borrows money by selling ***bonds,*** or certificates that promise to pay the holder a certain sum of money on a certain date.

3. **Commerce** To regulate commerce with foreign nations, and among the several states, and with the Indian tribes;

Clause 3 Only Congress has the power to regulate foreign and ***interstate trade,*** or trade between states. The Constitution recognizes four sovereign governments: the federal government, state governments, American Indian Tribal governments, and foreign nations.

4. **Naturalization; Bankruptcy** To establish a uniform rule of naturalization, and uniform laws on the subject of bankruptcies throughout the United States;

Clause 4 ***Naturalization*** is the process whereby a foreigner becomes a citizen. ***Bankruptcy*** is the condition in which a person or business cannot pay its debts. Congress has the power to pass laws on these two issues.

5. **Coins; Weights; Measures** To coin money, regulate the value thereof, and of foreign coin, and fix the standard of weights and measures;

Clause 5 Congress has the power to coin money and set its value. Congress has set up the National Bureau of Standards to regulate weights and measures.

6. **Counterfeiting** To provide for the punishment of counterfeiting the securities and current coin of the United States;

Clause 6 ***Counterfeiting*** is the making of imitation money. ***Securities*** are bonds. Congress can make laws to punish counterfeiters.

7. **Post Offices** To establish post offices and post roads;

Clause 7 Congress has the power to set up and control the delivery of mail.

8. **Copyrights; Patents** To promote the progress of science and useful arts by securing for limited times to authors and inventors the exclusive right to their respective writings and discoveries;

Clause 8 Congress may pass copyright and patent laws. A ***copyright*** protects an author. A ***patent*** makes an inventor the sole owner of his or her work for a limited time.

9. **Federal Courts** To constitute tribunals inferior to the Supreme Court;

Clause 9 Congress has the power to set up ***inferior,*** or lower, federal courts under the Supreme Court.

10. **Piracy** To define and punish piracies and felonies committed on the high seas and offenses against the law of nations;

Clause 10 Congress can punish ***piracy,*** or the robbing of ships at sea.

Clause 11 Only Congress can declare war. Declarations of war are granted at the request of the President. ***Letters of marque and reprisal*** were documents allowing merchant ships to arm themselves. They are no longer issued.

11. Declarations of War To declare war, ~~grant letters of marque and reprisal,~~ and make rules concerning captures on land and water;

Clauses 12, 13, 14 These clauses place the army and navy under the control of Congress. Congress decides on the size of, and the amount of money to spend on, the armed forces. It also has the power to write rules governing the armed forces.

12. Army To raise and support armies, but no appropriation of money to that use shall be for a longer term than two years;

13. Navy To provide and maintain a navy;

14. Rules for the Military To make rules for the government and regulation of the land and naval forces;

Clauses 15, 16 The ***militia*** is a body of citizen soldiers. Congress can call up the militia to put down rebellions or fight foreign invaders. Each state has its own militia, today called the National Guard. Normally, the militia is under the command of a state's governor. However, it can be placed under the command of the President.

15. Militia To provide for calling forth the militia to execute the laws of the Union, suppress insurrections, and repel invasions;

16. Rules for the Militia To provide for organizing, arming, and disciplining the militia, and for governing such part of them as may be employed in the service of the United States, reserving to the states, respectively, the appointment of the officers, and the authority of training the militia according to the discipline prescribed by Congress;

Clause 17 Congress controls the district around the national capital. In 1790, Congress made Washington, D.C., the nation's capital. In 1973, it gave residents of the District the right to elect local officials.

17. National Capital To exercise exclusive legislation in all cases whatsoever, over such district (not exceeding ten miles square) as may, by cession of particular states, and the acceptance of Congress, become the seat of government of the United States, and to exercise like authority over all places purchased by the consent of the legislature of the state in which the same shall be, for the erection of forts, magazines, arsenals, dock-yards, and other needful buildings;—and

Clause 18 Clauses 1–17 list the powers delegated to Congress. The framers added Clause 18 so that Congress could make laws as needed to carry out the first 17 clauses. Clause 18 is sometimes called the elastic clause because it lets Congress stretch the meaning of its power.

18. Necessary Laws To make all laws which shall be necessary and proper for carrying into execution the foregoing powers, and all other powers vested by this Constitution in the government of the United States, or in any department or officer thereof.

Section 9. Powers Denied to the Federal Government

Clause 1 ***Such persons*** refers to slaves. This clause resulted from a compromise between the supporters and the opponents of the slave trade. In 1808, as soon as Congress was permitted to abolish the slave trade, it did so. The import tax was never imposed.

1. The Slave Trade ~~The migration or importation of such persons as any of the states now existing shall think proper to admit shall not be prohibited by the Congress prior to the year 1808; but a tax or duty may be imposed on such importation, not exceeding $10 for each person.~~

Clause 2 A ***writ of habeas corpus*** is a court order requiring government officials to bring a prisoner to court and explain why he or she is being held. A writ of habeas corpus protects people from unlawful imprisonment. This right cannot be suspended except in times of rebellion or invasion.

2. Writ of Habeas Corpus The privilege of the writ of habeas corpus shall not be suspended, unless when in cases of rebellion or invasion the public safety may require it.

3. **Bills of Attainder and *Ex Post Facto* Laws** No bill of attainder or *ex post facto* law shall be passed.

Clause 3 A ***bill of attainder*** is a law declaring that a person is guilty of a particular crime. An ***ex post facto law*** punishes an act which was not illegal when it was committed. Congress cannot pass such laws.

4. **Apportionment of Direct Taxes** ~~No capitation or other direct tax shall be laid, unless in proportion to the census or enumeration herein before directed to be taken.~~

Clause 4 A ***capitation tax*** is a tax placed directly on each person. ***Direct taxes*** are taxes on people or on land. They can be passed only if they are divided among the states according to population. The Sixteenth Amendment allowed Congress to tax income without regard to the population of the states.

5. **Taxes on Exports** No tax or duty shall be laid on articles exported from any state.

Clause 5 This clause forbids Congress to tax exports. Southerners insisted on this clause because their economy depended on exports.

6. **Special Preference for Trade** No preference shall be given any regulation of commerce or revenue to the ports of one state over those of another; nor shall vessels bound to, or from, one state, be obliged to enter, clear, or pay duties in another.

Clause 6 Congress cannot make laws that favor one state over another in commerce. Also, states cannot place tariffs on interstate trade.

7. **Spending** No money shall be drawn from the Treasury, but in consequence of appropriations made by law; and a regular statement and account of the receipts and expenditures of all public money shall be published from time to time.

Clause 7 The federal government cannot spend money unless Congress ***appropriates*** it, or passes a law allowing it. The government must publish a statement showing how it spends public funds.

8. **Creation of Titles of Nobility** No title of nobility shall be granted by the United States; and no person holding any office of profit or trust under them, shall, without the consent of the Congress, accept of any present, emolument, office, or title, of any kind whatever, from any king, prince, or foreign state.

Clause 8 The government cannot award titles of nobility, such as Duke or Duchess. Americans cannot accept titles of nobility from foreign governments without the consent of Congress.

Section 10. Powers Denied to the States

1. **Unconditional Prohibitions** No state shall enter into any treaty, alliance, or confederation; grant letters of marque and reprisal; coin money; emit bills of credit; make anything but gold and silver coin a tender in payment of debts; pass any bill of attainder, *ex post facto* law, or law impairing the obligation of contracts, or grant any title of nobility.

Clause 1 The writers of the Constitution did not want the states to act like separate nations. So, they prohibited states from making treaties or coining money. Some powers denied to the federal government are also denied to the states. For example, states cannot pass *ex post facto laws.*

2. **Powers Conditionally Denied** No state shall, without the consent of the Congress, lay any imposts or duties on imports or exports, except what may be absolutely necessary for executing its inspection laws; and the net produce of all duties and imposts, laid by any state on imports or exports, shall be for the use of the Treasury of the United States; and all such laws shall be subject to the revision and control of the Congress.

3. **Other Denied Powers** No state shall, without the consent of Congress, lay any duty of tonnage, keep troops, or ships of war in time of peace, enter into any agreement or compact with another state, or with a foreign power, or engage in war, unless actually invaded, or in such imminent danger as will not admit of delay.

Clauses 2, 3 Powers listed here are forbidden to the states, but Congress can lift these prohibitions by passing laws that give these powers to the states.

Clause 2 forbids states from taxing imports and exports without the consent of Congress. States may charge inspection fees on goods entering the states. Any profit from these fees must be turned over to the United States Treasury.

Clause 3 forbids states from keeping an army or navy without the consent of Congress. States cannot make treaties or declare war unless an enemy invades or is about to invade.

Article 2. The Executive Branch

Section 1. President and Vice-President

Clause 1 The President is responsible for ***executing,*** or carrying out, laws passed by Congress.

1. **Chief Executive** The executive power shall be vested in a President of the United States of America. He shall hold his office during the term of four years, and together with the Vice-President, chosen for the same term, be elected as follows:

Clauses 2, 3 Some writers of the Constitution were afraid to allow the people to elect the President directly. Therefore, the Constitutional Convention set up the electoral college. Clause 2 directs each state to choose electors, or delegates to the electoral college, to vote for President. A state's electoral vote is equal to the combined number of senators and representatives. Each state may decide how to choose its electors. Members of Congress and federal officeholders may not serve as electors. This much of the original electoral college system is still in effect.

Clause 3 called upon each elector to vote for two candidates. The candidate who received a majority of the electoral votes would become President. The runner-up would become Vice President. If no candidate won a majority, the House would choose the President. The Senate would choose the Vice President.

The election of 1800 showed a problem with the original electoral college system. Thomas Jefferson was the Republican candidate for President, and Aaron Burr was the Republican candidate for Vice President. In the electoral college, the vote ended in a tie. The election was finally decided in the House, where Jefferson was chosen President. The Twelfth Amendment changed the electoral college system so that this could not happen again.

2. **Selection of Electors** Each state shall appoint, in such manner as the legislature thereof may direct, a number of electors, equal to the whole number of Senators and Representatives to which the state may be entitled in the Congress; but no Senator or Representative, or person holding an office or trust or profit under the United States, shall be appointed an elector.

3. **Electoral College Procedures** ~~The electors shall meet in their respective states, and vote by ballot for two persons, of whom one at least shall not be an inhabitant of the same state with themselves. And they shall make a list of all the persons voted for, and of the number of votes for each; which list they shall sign and certify, and transmit sealed to the seat of the government of the United States, directed to the president of the Senate. The president of the Senate shall, in the presence of the Senate and House of Representatives, open all the certificates, and the votes shall then be counted. The person having the greatest number of votes shall be President, if such number be a majority of the whole number of electors appointed; and if there be more than one who have such majority, and have an equal number of votes, then the House of Representatives shall immediately choose by ballot one of them for President; and if no person have a majority, then from the five highest on the list the said House shall in like manner choose the President. But in choosing the President the votes shall be taken by states, the representation from each state having one vote. A quorum for this purpose shall consist of a member or members from two thirds of the states, and a majority of all the states shall be necessary to a choice. In every case, after the choice of the President, the person having the greatest number of votes of the electors shall be the Vice President. But if there should remain two or more who have equal votes, the Senate shall choose from them by ballot the Vice President.~~

Clause 4 By a law passed in 1792, electors are chosen on the Tuesday after the first Monday of November every four years. Electors from each state meet to vote in December.

Today, voters in each state choose ***slates***, or groups, of electors who are pledged to a candidate for President. The candidate for President who wins the popular vote in each state wins that state's electoral vote.

4. **Time of Elections** The Congress may determine the time of choosing the electors, and the day on which they shall give their votes; which day shall be the same throughout the United States.

5. **Qualifications for President** No person except a natural-born citizen ~~or a citizen of the United States, at the time of the adoption of this Constitution,~~ shall be eligible to the office of the President; neither shall any person be eligible to that office who shall not have attained to the age of thirty-five years, and been fourteen years a resident within the United States.

Clause 5 The President must be a citizen of the United States from birth, at least 35 years old, and a resident of the country for 14 years. The first seven Presidents of the United States were born under British rule, but they were allowed to hold office because they were citizens at the time the Constitution was adopted.

6. **Presidential Succession** In case of the removal of the President from office, or of his death, resignation, or inability to discharge the powers and duties of the said office, the same shall devolve on the Vice-President, and the Congress may by law provide for the case of removal, death, resignation, or inability, both of the President and Vice-President, declaring what officer shall then act as President, and such officer shall act accordingly, until the disability be removed, or a President shall be elected.

Clause 6 The powers of the President pass to the Vice President if the President leaves office or cannot discharge his or her duties. The wording of this clause caused confusion the first time a President died in office. When President William Henry Harrison died, it was uncertain whether Vice President John Tyler should remain Vice President and act as President or whether he should be sworn in as President. Tyler persuaded a federal judge to swear him in. So he set the precedent that the Vice President assumes the office of President when it becomes vacant. The Twenty-fifth Amendment clarified this clause.

7. **Salary** The President shall, at stated times, receive for his services, a compensation, which shall neither be increased nor diminished during the period for which he shall have been elected, and he shall not receive within that period any other emolument from the United States, or any of them.

Clause 7 The President is paid a salary. It cannot be raised or lowered during his or her term of office. The President is not allowed to hold any other federal or state position while in office. Today, the President's salary is $200,000 a year.

8. **Oath of Office** Before he enter on the execution of his office, he shall take the following oath or affirmation:—"I do solemnly swear (or affirm) that I will faithfully execute the office of President of the United States, and will to the best of my ability, preserve, protect, and defend the Constitution of the United States."

Clause 8 Before taking office, the President must promise to protect and defend the Constitution. Usually, the Chief Justice of the Supreme Court gives the oath of office to the President.

Section 2. Powers of the President

1. **Commander in Chief of the Armed Forces** The President shall be Commander in Chief of the Army and Navy of the United States, and of the militia of the several states, when called into the actual service of the United States; he may require the opinion, in writing, of the principal officer in each of the executive departments, upon any subject relating to the duties of their respective offices, and he shall have power to grant reprieves and pardons for offenses against the United States, except in cases of impeachment.

Clause 1 The President is head of the armed forces and the state militias when they are called into national service. So, the military is under ***civilian***, or nonmilitary, control.

The President can get advice from the heads of executive departments. In most cases, the President has the power to grant a reprieve or pardon. A ***reprieve*** suspends punishment ordered by law. A ***pardon*** prevents prosecution for a crime or overrides the judgment of a court.

Clause 2 The President has the power to make treaties with other nations. Under the system of checks and balances, all treaties must be approved by two thirds of the Senate. Today, the President also makes agreements with foreign governments. These executive agreements do not need Senate approval.

The President has the power to appoint ambassadors to foreign countries and to appoint other high officials. The Senate must ***confirm***, or approve, these appointments.

2. **Making Treaties and Nominations** He shall have power, by and with the advice and consent of the Senate, to make treaties, provided two-thirds of the Senators present concur; and he shall nominate, and by and with the advice and consent of the Senate, shall appoint ambassadors, other public ministers and consuls, judges of the Supreme Court, and all other officers of the United States, whose appointments are not herein otherwise provided for, and which shall be established by law; but the Congress may by law vest the appointment of such inferior officers, as they think proper, in the President alone, in the courts of law, or in the heads of departments.

Clause 3 If the Senate is in ***recess,*** or not meeting, the President may fill vacant government posts by making temporary appointments.

3. **Temporary Appointments** The President shall have power to fill up all vacancies that may happen during the recess of the Senate, by granting commissions which shall expire at the end of their next session.

The President must give Congress a report on the condition of the nation every year. This report is now called the State of the Union Address. Since 1913, the President has given this speech in person each January.

The President can call a special session of Congress and can adjourn Congress if necessary. The President has the power to receive, or recognize, foreign ambassadors.

The President must carry out the laws. Today, many government agencies oversee the execution of laws.

Section 3. Duties

He shall from time to time give to the Congress information of the state of the Union, and recommend to their consideration such measures as he shall judge necessary and expedient; he may, on extraordinary occasions, convene both houses, or either of them, and in case of disagreement between them, with respect to the time of adjournment, he may adjourn them to such time as he shall think proper; he shall receive ambassadors and other public ministers; he shall take care that the laws be faithfully executed, and shall commission all the officers of the United States.

Civil officers include federal judges and members of the Cabinet. ***High crimes*** are major crimes. ***Misdemeanors*** are lesser crimes. The President, Vice President, and others can be forced out of office if impeached and found guilty of certain crimes.

Section 4. Impeachment and Removal From Office

The President, Vice-President, and all civil officers of the United States, shall be removed from office on impeachment for, and conviction of, treason, bribery, or other high crimes or misdemeanors.

Article 3. The Judicial Branch

Judicial power is the right of the courts to decide legal cases. The Constitution creates the Supreme Court but lets Congress decide the size of the Supreme Court. Congress has the power to set up inferior, or lower, courts. The Judiciary Act of 1789 set up district and circuit courts, or courts of appeal. Today, there are 94 district courts and 13 courts of appeal. All federal judges serve for life.

Section 1. Federal Courts

The judicial power of the United States shall be vested in one Supreme Court, and in such inferior courts as the Congress may from time to time ordain and establish. The judges, both of the Supreme and inferior courts, shall hold their offices during good behavior, and shall, at stated times, receive for their services a compensation, which shall not be diminished during their continuance in office.

Separation of Powers

Legislative Branch
(Congress)

Passes Laws
- Can override President's veto
- Approves treaties and presidential appointments
- Can impeach and remove President and other high officials
- Creates lower federal courts
- Appropriates money
- Prints and coins money
- Raises and supports the armed forces
- Can declare war
- Regulates foreign and interstate trade

Executive Branch
(President)

Carries Out Laws
- Proposes laws
- Can veto laws
- Negotiates foreign treaties
- Serves as commander in chief of the armed forces
- Appoints federal judges, ambassadors, and other high officials
- Can grant pardons to federal offenders

Judicial Branch
(Supreme Court and Other Federal Courts)

Interprets Laws
- Can declare laws unconstitutional
- Can declare executive actions unconstitutional

GRAPHIC ORGANIZER *Skills*

The Constitution set up three branches of government. Each branch has its own powers.

1. **Comprehension** **(a)** Who heads the executive branch? **(b)** What is the role of the legislative branch?
2. **Critical Thinking** **Analyzing Information** Based on this chart, what is the relationship between the judicial branch and the legislative branch?

Civics

Section 2. Jurisdiction of Federal Courts

1. **Scope of Judicial Power** The judicial power shall extend to all cases, in law and equity, arising under this Constitution, the laws of the United States, and treaties made or which shall be made, under their authority; to all cases affecting ambassadors, other public ministers and consuls; to all cases of admiralty and maritime jurisdiction; to controversies to which the United States shall be a party; to controversies between two or more states; ~~between a state and citizens of another state;~~ between citizens of the same state claiming lands under grants of different states, and between a state or the citizens thereof, and foreign states, citizens, or subjects.

Clause 1 ***Jurisdiction*** refers to the right of a court to hear a case. Federal courts have jurisdiction over cases that involve the Constitution, federal laws, treaties, foreign ambassadors and diplomats, naval and maritime laws, disagreements between states or between citizens from different states, and disputes between a state or citizen and a foreign state or citizen.

In *Marbury* v. *Madison,* the Supreme Court established the right to judge whether or not a law is constitutional.

2. **The Supreme Court** In all cases affecting ambassadors, other public ministers and consuls, and those in which a state shall be a party, the Supreme Court shall have original jurisdiction. In all the other cases before mentioned, the Supreme Court shall have appellate jurisdiction, both as to law and fact, with such exceptions, and under such regulations as the Congress shall make.

Clause 2 ***Original jurisdiction*** means the power of a court to hear a case where it first arises. The Supreme Court has original jurisdiction over only a few cases, such as those involving foreign diplomats. More often, the Supreme Court acts as an appellate court. An ***appellate court*** does not decide guilt. It decides whether the lower court trial was properly conducted and reviews the lower court's decision.

Clause 3 This clause guarantees the right to a jury trial for anyone accused of a federal crime. The only exceptions are impeachment cases. The trial must be held in the state where the crime was committed.

3. **Trial by Jury** The trial of all crimes, except in cases of impeachment, shall be by jury; and such trial shall be held in the state where the said crimes shall have been committed; but when not committed within any state, the trial shall be at such place or places as the Congress may by law have directed.

Section 3. Treason

Clause 1 Treason is clearly defined. An ***overt act*** is an actual action. A person cannot be convicted of treason for what he or she thinks. A person can be convicted of treason only if he or she confesses or two witnesses testify to it.

1. **Definition** Treason against the United States shall consist only in levying war against them, or in adhering to their enemies, giving them aid and comfort. No person shall be convicted of treason unless on the testimony of two witnesses to the same overt act, or on confession in open court.

Clause 2 Congress has the power to set the punishment for traitors. Congress may not punish the children of convicted traitors by taking away their civil rights or property.

2. **Punishment** The Congress shall have power to declare the punishment of treason, but no attainder of treason shall work corruption of blood or forfeiture except during the life of the person attainted.

Article 4. Relations Among the States

Section 1. Official Records and Acts

Each state must recognize the official acts and records of any other state. For example, each state must recognize marriage certificates issued by another state. Congress can pass laws to ensure this.

Full faith and credit shall be given in each state to the public acts, records, and judicial proceedings of every other state. And the Congress may by general laws prescribe the manner in which such acts, records, and proceedings shall be proved, and the effect thereof.

Section 2. Privileges of Citizens

Clause 1 All states must treat citizens of another state in the same way it treats its own citizens. However, the courts have allowed states to give residents certain privileges, such as lower tuition rates.

1. **Privileges** The citizens of each state shall be entitled to all privileges and immunities of citizens in the several states.

Clause 2 ***Extradition*** means the act of returning a suspected criminal or escaped prisoner to a state where he or she is wanted. State governors must return a suspect. However, the Supreme Court has ruled that governors cannot be forced to do so if they feel that justice will not be done.

2. **Extradition** A person charged in any state with treason, felony, or other crime, who shall flee from justice, and be found in another state, shall on demand of the executive authority of the state from which he fled, be delivered up, to be removed to the state having jurisdiction of the crime.

Clause 3 ***Persons held to service or labor*** refers to slaves or indentured servants. This clause required states to return runaway slaves to their owners. The Thirteenth Amendment replaces this clause.

3. **Return of Fugitive Slaves** ~~No person held to service or labor in one state, under the laws thereof, escaping into another, shall in consequence of any law or regulation therein, be discharged from such service or labor, but shall be delivered up on claim of the party to whom such service or labor may be due.~~

Section 3. New States and Territories

Clause 1 Congress has the power to admit new states to the Union. Existing states cannot be split up or joined together to form new states unless both Congress and the state legislatures approve. New states are equal to all other states.

1. **New States** New states may be admitted by the Congress into this Union; but no new state shall be formed or erected within the jurisdiction of any other state; nor any state be formed by the junction of two of more states, or parts of states, without the consent of the legislatures of the states concerned as well as of the Congress.

Clause 2 Congress can make rules for managing and governing land owned by the United States. This includes territories not organized into states, such as Puerto Rico, and federal lands within a state.

2. **Federal Lands** The Congress shall have power to dispose of and make all needful rules and regulations respecting the territory or other property belonging to the United States; and nothing in this Constitution shall be so construed as to prejudice any claims of the United States, or of any particular state.

The Federal System

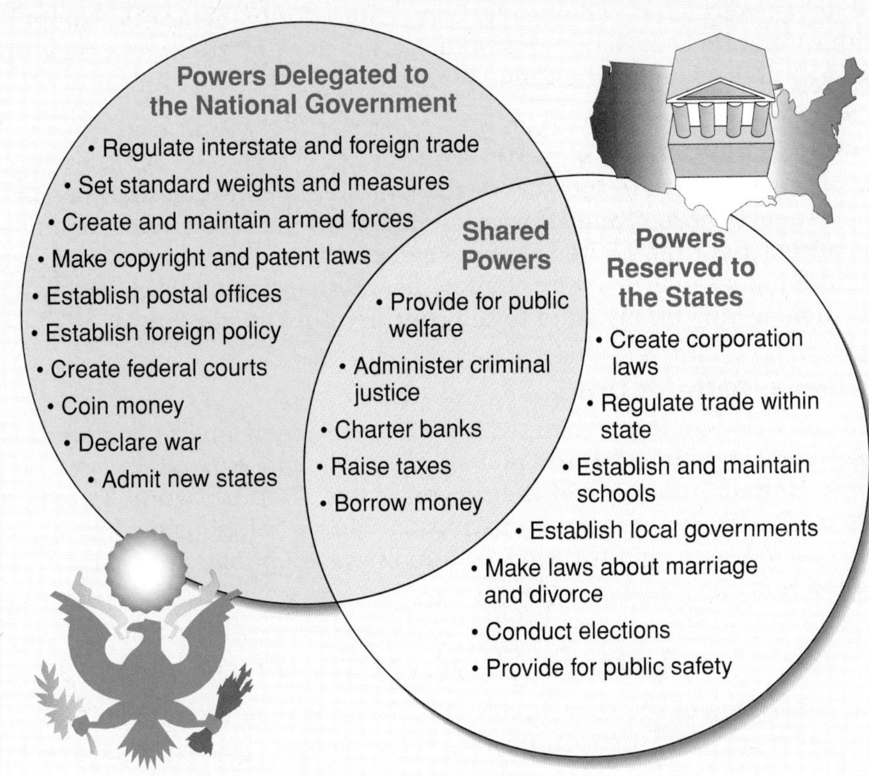

GRAPHIC ORGANIZER *Skills*

Federalism is the distribution of power between the national government and the state governments.

1. **Comprehension**
   (a) Name two powers reserved to the states.
   (b) Name two powers shared by the national and state governments.
2. **Critical Thinking**
   Applying Information
   Why do you think the power to create and maintain the armed forces was delegated to the national government?

Civics

Section 4. Guarantees to the States

The United States shall guarantee to every state in this Union a republican form of government, and shall protect each of them against invasion; and on application of the legislature, or of the executive (when the legislature cannot be convened) against domestic violence.

In a ***republic***, voters choose representatives to govern them. The federal government must protect the states from foreign invasion and from ***domestic***, or internal, disorder if asked to do so by a state.

Article 5. Amending the Constitution

The Congress, whenever two-thirds of both houses shall deem it necessary, shall propose amendments to this Constitution, or, on the application of the legislatures of two-thirds of the several states, shall call a convention for proposing amendments, which, in either case, shall be valid to all intents and purposes, as part of this Constitution, when ratified by the legislatures of three-fourths of the several states, or by conventions in three-fourths thereof, as the one or the other mode of ratification may be proposed by the Congress; provided that ~~no amendments which may be made prior to the year 1808 shall in any manner affect the first and fourth clauses in the Ninth Section of the First Article; and that~~ no state, without its consent, shall be deprived of its equal suffrage in the Senate.

The Constitution can be ***amended***, or changed, if necessary. An amendment can be proposed by (1) a two-thirds vote of both houses of Congress or (2) a national convention called by Congress at the request of two thirds of the state legislatures. (This second method has never been used.) An amendment must be ***ratified***, or approved, by (1) three fourths of the state legislatures or (2) special conventions in three fourths of the states. Congress decides which method will be used.

Article 6. National Supremacy

The United States government promised to pay all debts and honor all agreements made under the Articles of Confederation.

Section 1. Prior Public Debts

All debts contracted and engagements entered into, before the adoption of this Constitution, shall be as valid against the United States under this Constitution, as under the Confederation.

The Constitution, federal laws, and treaties that the Senate has ratified are the supreme, or highest, law of the land. Thus, they outweigh state laws. A state judge must overturn a state law that conflicts with the Constitution or with a federal law.

Section 2. Supreme Law of the Land

This Constitution, and the laws of the United States which shall be made in pursuance thereof, and all treaties made, or which shall be made, under the authority of the United States, shall be the supreme law of the land; and the judges in every state shall be bound thereby, anything in the constitution or laws of any state to the contrary notwithstanding.

State and federal officeholders take an oath, or solemn promise, to support the Constitution. However, this clause forbids the use of religious tests for officeholders. During the colonial period, every colony except Rhode Island required a religious test for officeholders.

Section 3. Oaths of Office

The Senators and Representatives before mentioned, and the members of the several state legislatures, and all executive and judicial officers, both of the United States and of the several states, shall be bound by oath or affirmation, to support this Constitution; but no religious test shall ever be required as a qualification to any office or public trust under the United States.

Article 7. Ratification

During 1787 and 1788, states held special conventions. By October 1788, the required nine states had ratified the Constitution.

The ratification of the conventions of nine states shall be sufficient for the establishment of the Constitution between the states so ratifying the same.

Done in convention, by the unanimous consent of the states present, the seventeenth day of September, in the year of our Lord one thousand seven hundred and eighty-seven, and of the independence of the United States of America the twelfth. In Witness *whereof, we have hereunto subscribed our names.*

Attest: William Jackson
Secretary

George Washington
President and deputy from Virginia

New Hampshire
John Langdon
Nicholas Gilman

Massachussetts
Nathaniel Gorham
Rufus King

Connecticut
William Samuel Johnson
Roger Sherman

New York
Alexander Hamilton

New Jersey
William Livingston
David Brearley
William Paterson
Jonathan Dayton

Pennsylvania
Benjamin Franklin
Thomas Mifflin
Robert Morris
George Clymer
Thomas FitzSimons
Jared Ingersoll
James Wilson
Gouverneur Morris

Delaware
George Read
Gunning Bedford, Jr.
John Dickinson
Richard Bassett
Jacob Broom

Maryland
James McHenry
Dan of St. Thomas Jennifer
Daniel Carroll

Virginia
John Blair
James Madison, Jr.

North Carolina
William Blount
Richard Dobbs Spaight
Hugh Williamson

South Carolina
John Rutledge
Charles Cotesworth Pinckney
Charles Pinckney
Pierce Butler

Georgia
William Few
Abraham Baldwin

Amendments to the Constitution

Amendment 1

Freedoms of Religion, Speech, Press, Assembly, and Petition

Congress shall make no law respecting an establishment of religion, or prohibiting the free exercise thereof; or abridging the freedom of speech, or of the press; or the right of the people peaceably to assemble, and to petition the government for a redress of grievances.

Congress cannot set up an established, or official, church or religion for the nation. During the colonial period, most colonies had established churches. However, the authors of the First Amendment wanted to keep government and religion separate.

Congress may not ***abridge***, or limit, the freedom to speak and write freely. The government may not censor, or review, books and newspapers before they are printed. This amendment also protects the right to assemble, or hold public meetings. ***Petition*** means "ask." ***Redress*** means "to correct." ***Grievances*** are wrongs. The people have the right to ask the government for wrongs to be corrected.

Amendment 2

Right to Bear Arms

A well-regulated militia, being necessary to the security of a free state, the right of the people to keep and bear arms shall not be infringed.

Each state has the right to maintain a ***militia,*** an armed force for its own protection. Today, the militia is the National Guard. The national government and the states can and do regulate the private ownership and use of firearms.

Amendment 3

Lodging Troops in Private Homes

No soldier shall, in time of peace, be quartered in any house, without the consent of the owner; nor in time of war, but in a manner to be prescribed by law.

During the colonial period, the British quartered, or housed, soldiers in private homes without the permission of the owners. This amendment limits the government's right to use private homes to house soldiers.

Amendment 4

Search and Seizure

The right of the people to be secure in their persons, houses, papers, and effects, against unreasonable searches and seizures, shall not be violated; and no warrants shall issue but upon probable cause, supported by oath or affirmation, and particularly describing the place to be searched, and the persons or things to be seized.

This amendment protects Americans from unreasonable searches and seizures. Search and seizure are permitted only if a judge has issued a ***warrant,*** or written court order. A warrant is issued only if there is probable cause. This means an officer must show that it is probable, or likely, that the search will produce evidence of a crime. A search warrant must name the exact place to be searched and the things to be seized. In some cases, courts have ruled that searches can take place without a warrant. For example, police may search a person who is under arrest. However, evidence found during an unlawful search cannot be used in a trial.

Amendment 5

Rights of the Accused

No person shall be held to answer for a capital, or otherwise infamous, crime, unless on a presentment or indictment of a grand jury, except in cases arising in the land or naval forces, or in the militia, when in actual service in time of war or public danger; nor shall any person be subject for the same offense to be twice put in jeopardy of life and limb; nor shall be compelled, in any criminal case, to be a witness against himself; nor be deprived of life, liberty, or property, without due process of law; nor shall private property be taken for public use, without just compensation.

This amendment protects the rights of the accused. ***Capital crimes*** are those that can be punished with death. ***Infamous crimes*** are those that can be punished with prison or loss of rights. The federal government must obtain an ***indictment,*** or formal accusation, from a ***grand jury*** to prosecute anyone for such crimes. A grand jury is a panel of between 12 and 23 citizens who decide if the government has enough evidence to justify a trial. This procedure prevents prosecution with little or no evidence of guilt. (Soldiers and the militia in wartime are not covered by this rule.)

Double jeopardy is forbidden. This means that a person cannot be tried twice for the same crime—unless a court sets aside a conviction because of a legal error. A person on trial cannot be forced to testify, or give evidence, against himself or herself. A person accused of a crime is entitled to ***due process of law,*** or a fair hearing or trial. Finally, the government cannot seize private property for public use without paying the owner a fair price for it.

Amendment 6

Right to Speedy Trial by Jury

In all criminal prosecutions, the accused shall enjoy the right to a speedy and public trial, by an impartial jury of the state and district wherein the crime shall have been committed, which district shall have been previously ascertained by law, and to be informed of the nature and cause of the accusation; to be confronted with the witnesses against him; to have compulsory process for obtaining witnesses in his favor, and to have the assistance of counsel for his defense.

In criminal cases, the jury must be ***impartial,*** or not favor either side. The accused is guaranteed the right to a trial by jury. The trial must be speedy. If the government purposely postpones the trial so that it becomes hard for the person to get a fair hearing, the charge may be dismissed. The accused must be told the charges against him or her and be allowed to question prosecution witnesses. Witnesses who can help the accused can be ordered to appear in court.

The accused must be allowed a lawyer. Since 1942, the federal government has been required to provide a lawyer if the accused cannot afford one. In 1963, the Supreme Court decided that states must also provide lawyers for a defendant too poor to pay for one.

Amendment 7

Jury Trial in Civil Cases

In suits at common law, where the value in controversy shall exceed $20, the right of trial by jury shall be preserved, and no fact tried by a jury shall be otherwise re-examined in any court of the United States than according to the rules of the common law.

Common law refers to rules of law established by judges in past cases. This amendment guarantees the right to a jury trial in lawsuits where the sum of money at stake is more than $20. An appeals court cannot change a verdict because it disagrees with the decision of the jury. It can set aside a verdict only if legal errors made the trial unfair.

Amendment 8

Bail and Punishment

Excessive bail shall not be required, nor excessive fines imposed, nor cruel and unusual punishments inflicted.

Bail is money the accused leaves with the court as a pledge to appear for trial. If the accused does not appear for trial, the court keeps the money. ***Excessive*** means too high. This amendment forbids courts to set unreasonably high bail. The amount of bail usually depends on the seriousness of the charge and whether the accused is likely to appear for the trial. The amendment also forbids cruel and unusual punishments such as mental and physical abuse.

Amendment 9

Powers Reserved to the People

The enumeration in the Constitution, of certain rights, shall not be construed to deny or disparage others retained by the people.

People have rights not listed in the Constitution. This amendment was added because some people feared that the Bill of Rights would be used to limit rights to those actually listed.

Amendment 10

Powers Reserved to the States

The powers not delegated to the United States by the Constitution, nor prohibited by it to the states, are reserved to the states respectively, or to the people.

This amendment limits the power of the federal government. Powers that are not given to the federal government belong to the states. The powers reserved to the states are not listed in the Constitution.

Amendment 11

Suits Against States

Passed by Congress on March 4, 1794. Ratified on January 23, 1795.

The judicial power of the United States shall not be construed to extend to any suit in law or equity, commenced or prosecuted against one of the United States, by citizens of another state, or by citizens or subjects of any foreign state.

This amendment changed part of Article 3, Section 2, Clause 1. As a result, a private citizen from one state cannot sue the government of another state in federal court. However, a citizen can sue a state government in a state court.

Amendment 12

Election of President and Vice-President

Passed by Congress on December 9, 1803. Ratified on June 15, 1804.

The electors shall meet in their respective states, and vote by ballot for President and Vice-President, one of whom, at least, shall not be an inhabitant of the same state with themselves; they shall name in their ballots the person voted for as President, and in distinct ballots the person voted for as Vice-President, and they shall make distinct lists of all persons voted for as President, and of all persons voted for as Vice-President, and of the number of votes for each, which lists they shall sign and certify, and transmit, sealed, to the seat of government of the United States, directed to the President of the Senate; the President of the Senate shall, in the presence of the Senate and House of Representatives, open all the certificates and the votes shall then be counted; the person having the greatest number of votes for President shall be the President, if such number be a majority of the whole number of electors appointed; and if no person have such majority, then from the persons having the highest numbers not exceeding three on the list of those voted for as President, the House of Representatives shall choose immediately, by ballot, the President. But in choosing the President, the votes shall be taken by the states, the representation from each state having one vote; a quorum for this purpose shall consist of a member or members from two-thirds of the states, and a majority of all the states shall be necessary to a choice. And if the House of Representatives shall not choose a President whenever the right of choice shall devolve upon them, before the fourth day of March next following, then the Vice-President shall act as President, as in the case of the death or other constitutional disability of the President. The person having the greatest number of votes as Vice-President, shall be the Vice-President, if such number be a majority of the whole

This amendment changed the way the electoral college voted. Before the amendment was adopted, each elector simply voted for two people. The candidate with the most votes became President. The runner-up became Vice President. In the election of 1800, however, a tie vote resulted between Thomas Jefferson and Aaron Burr.

In such a case, the Constitution required the House of Representatives to elect the President. Federalists had a majority in the House. They tried to keep Jefferson out of office by voting for Burr. It took 35 ballots in the House before Jefferson was elected President.

To keep this from happening again, the Twelfth Amendment was passed and ratified in time for the election of 1804.

This amendment provides that each elector choose one candidate for President and one candidate for Vice President. If no candidate for President receives a majority of electoral votes, the House of Representatives chooses the President. If no candidate for Vice President receives a majority, the Senate elects the Vice President. The Vice President must be a person who is eligible to be President.

This system is still in use today. However, it is possible for a candidate to win the popular vote and lose in the electoral college. This happened in 1876 and again in 2000.

number of electors appointed, and if no person have a majority, then, from the two highest numbers on the list, the Senate shall choose the Vice-President; a quorum for the purpose shall consist of two-thirds of the whole number of Senators, and a majority of the whole number shall be necessary to a choice. But no person constitutionally ineligible to the office of President shall be eligible to that of Vice-President of the United States.

Amendment 13

Abolition of Slavery

Passed by Congress on January 31, 1865. Ratified on December 6, 1865.

The Emancipation Proclamation (1863) freed slaves only in areas controlled by the Confederacy. This amendment freed all slaves. It also forbids ***involuntary servitude,*** or labor done against one's will. However, it does not prevent prison wardens from making prisoners work.

Section 2 says that Congress can pass laws to carry out this amendment.

Section 1. Neither slavery nor involuntary servitude, except as a punishment for crime whereof the party shall have been duly convicted, shall exist within the United States, or any place subject to their jurisdiction.

Section 2. Congress shall have power to enforce this article by appropriate legislation.

Amendment 14

Rights of Citizens

Passed by Congress on June 13, 1866. Ratified on July 9, 1868.

Section 1 defines citizenship for the first time in the Constitution, and it extends citizenship to blacks. It also prohibits states from denying the rights and privileges of citizenship to any citizen. This section also forbids states to deny due process of law.

Section 1 guarantees all citizens "equal protection under the law." For a long time, however, the Fourteenth Amendment did not protect blacks from discrimination. After Reconstruction, separate facilities for blacks and whites sprang up. In 1954, the Supreme Court ruled that separate facilities for blacks and whites were by their nature unequal. This ruling, in the case of *Brown* v. *Board of Education,* made school segregation illegal.

Section 1. Citizenship All persons born or naturalized in the United States and subject to the jurisdiction thereof, are citizens of the United States and of the state wherein they reside. No state shall make or enforce any law which shall abridge the privileges or immunities of citizens of the United States; nor shall any state deprive any person of life, liberty, or property, without due process of law; nor deny to any person within its jurisdiction the equal protection of the laws.

Section 2 replaced the three-fifths clause. It provides that representation in the House of Representatives is decided on the basis of the number of people in the state. It also provides that states which deny the vote to male citizens over age 21 will be punished by losing part of their representation in the House. This provision has never been enforced.

Despite this clause, black citizens were often prevented from voting. In the 1960s, federal laws were passed to end voting discrimination.

Section 2. Apportionment of Representatives Representatives shall be apportioned among the several states according to their respective numbers, counting the whole number of persons in each state, excluding Indians not taxed. But when the right to vote at any election for the choice of electors for President and Vice-President of the United States, Representatives in Congress, the executive and judicial officers of a state, or the members of the legislature thereof, is denied to any of the male inhabitants of such state, being twenty-one years of age and citizens of the United States, or in any way abridged, except for participation in rebellion, or other crime, the basis of representation therein shall be reduced in the proportion which the number of such male citizens shall bear to the whole number of male citizens twenty-one years of age in such state.

This section prohibited people who had been federal or state officials before the Civil War and joined the Confederate cause from serving again as government officials. In 1872, Congress restored the rights of former Confederate officials.

Section 3. Former Confederate Officials No person shall be a Senator or Representative in Congress, or elector of President and Vice-President, or hold any office, civil or military, under the United States, or under any state, who, having previously taken an oath, as a member of Congress, or as an officer of the United

States, or as a member of any state legislature, or as an executive or judicial officer of any state, to support the Constitution of the United States, shall have engaged in insurrection or rebellion against the same, or given aid or comfort to the enemies thereof. But Congress may, by vote of two-thirds of each house, remove such disability.

Section 4. Government Debt The validity of the public debt of the United States, authorized by law, including debts incurred for payment of pensions and bounties for services in suppressing insurrection or rebellion, shall not be questioned. But neither the United States nor any state shall assume or pay any debt or obligation incurred in aid of insurrection or rebellion against the United States or any claim for the loss or emancipation of any slave; but all such debts, obligations, and claims shall be held illegal and void.

This section recognized that the United States must repay its debts from the Civil War. However, it forbade the repayment of debts of the Confederacy. This meant that people who had loaned money to the Confederacy would not be repaid. Also, states were not allowed to pay former slave owners for the loss of slaves.

Section 5. Enforcement The Congress shall have power to enforce, by appropriate legislation, the provisions of this article.

Congress can pass laws to carry out this amendment.

Amendment 15

Voting Rights

Passed by Congress on February 26, 1869. Ratified on February 2, 1870.

Section 1. Extending the Right to Vote The right of citizens of the United States to vote shall not be denied or abridged by the United States or any state on account of race, color, or previous condition of servitude.

Previous condition of servitude refers to slavery. This amendment gave blacks, both former slaves and free blacks, the right to vote. In the late 1800s, southern states used grandfather clauses, literacy tests, and poll taxes to keep blacks from voting.

Section 2. Enforcement The Congress shall have power to enforce this article by appropriate legislation.

Congress can pass laws to carry out this amendment. The Twenty-fourth Amendment barred the use of poll taxes in national elections. The Voting Rights Act of 1965 gave federal officials the power to register voters in places where there was voting discrimination.

Amendment 16

The Income Tax

Passed by Congress on July 12, 1909. Ratified on February 3, 1913.

The Congress shall have power to lay and collect taxes on incomes, from whatever source derived, without apportionment among the several states, and without regard to any census or enumeration.

Congress has the power to collect taxes on people's income. An income tax can be collected without regard to a state's population. This amendment changed Article 1, Section 9, Clause 4.

Amendment 17

Direct Election of Senators

Passed by Congress on May 13, 1912. Ratified on April 8, 1913.

Section 1. Method of Election The Senate of the United States shall be composed of two Senators from each state, elected by the people thereof, for six years; and each Senator shall have one vote. The electors in each state shall have the qualifications requisite for electors of the most numerous branch of the state legislatures.

This amendment replaced Article 1, Section 3, Clause 1. Before it was adopted, state legislatures chose senators. This amendment provides that senators are directly elected by the people of each state.

Section 2. Vacancies When vacancies happen in the representation of any state in the Senate, the executive authority of such state shall issue writs of election to fill such vacancies: *Provided* that the legislature of any state may empower the executive thereof to make temporary appointments until the people fill the vacancies by election as the legislature may direct.

When a Senate seat becomes vacant, the governor of the state must order an election to fill the seat. The state legislature can give the governor power to fill the seat until an election is held.

Section 3. Exception ~~This amendment shall not be so construed as to affect the election or term of any Senator chosen before it becomes valid as part of the Constitution.~~

Senators who had already been elected by the state legislatures were not affected by this amendment.

Amendment 18

Prohibition of Alcoholic Beverages

Passed by Congress on December 18, 1917. Ratified on January 16, 1919.

Section 1. Ban on Alcohol ~~After one year from the ratification of this article the manufacture, sale, or transportation of intoxicating liquors within, the importation thereof into, or the exportation thereof from, the United States and all territory subject to the jurisdiction thereof for beverage purposes is hereby prohibited.~~

This amendment, known as ***Prohibition,*** banned the making, selling, or transporting of alcoholic beverages in the United States. Later, the Twenty-first Amendment ***repealed,*** or canceled, this amendment.

Section 2. Enforcement ~~The Congress and the several states shall have concurrent power to enforce this article by appropriate legislation.~~

Both the states and the federal government had the power to pass laws to enforce this amendment.

Section 3. Method of Ratification ~~This article shall be inoperative unless it shall have been ratified as an amendment to the Constitution by the legislatures of the several states, as provided in the Constitution, within seven years from the date of the submission hereof to the states by the Congress.~~

This amendment had to be approved within seven years. The Eighteenth Amendment was the first amendment to include a time limit for ratification.

Amendment 19

Women's Suffrage

Passed by Congress on June 4, 1919. Ratified on August 18, 1920.

Section 1. The Right to Vote The right of citizens of the United States to vote shall not be denied or abridged by the United States or by any state on account of sex.

Neither the federal government nor state governments can deny the right to vote on account of sex. Thus, women won ***suffrage,*** or the right to vote. Before 1920, some states had allowed women to vote in state elections.

Section 2. Enforcement Congress shall have power to enforce this article by appropriate legislation.

Congress can pass laws to carry out this amendment.

Amendment 20

Presidential Terms; Sessions of Congress

Passed by Congress on March 2, 1932. Ratified on January 23, 1933.

Section 1. Beginning of Term The terms of the President and Vice-President shall end at noon on the 20th day of January, and the terms of Senators and Representatives at noon on the 3rd day of January, of the years in which such terms would have ended if this article had not been ratified; and the terms of their successors shall then begin.

The date for the President and Vice President to take office is January 20. Members of Congress begin their terms of office on January 3. Before this amendment was adopted, these terms of office began on March 4.

Section 2. Congressional Sessions The Congress shall assemble at least once in every year, and such meeting shall begin at noon on the 3rd day of January, unless they shall by law appoint a different day.

Congress must meet at least once a year. The new session of Congress begins on January 3. Before this amendment, members of Congress who had been defeated in November continued to hold office until the following March. Such members were known as ***lame ducks.***

Section 3. Presidential Succession If at the time fixed for the beginning of the term of the President, the President-elect shall have died, the Vice-President-elect shall become President. If a President shall not have been chosen before the time fixed for the beginning of his term, or if the President-elect shall have failed to qualify, then the Vice-President-elect shall act as President until a President shall have qualified; and the Congress may by law

By Section 3, if the President-elect dies before taking office, the Vice President–elect becomes President. If no President has been chosen by January 20 or if the elected candidate fails to qualify for office, the Vice President–elect acts as President, but only until a qualified President is chosen.

provide for the case wherein neither a President-elect nor a Vice-President-elect shall have qualified, declaring who shall then act as President, or the manner in which one who is to act shall be selected, and such person shall act accordingly until a President or Vice-President shall have qualified.

Finally, Congress can choose a person to act as President if neither the President-elect nor Vice President-elect is qualified to take office.

Section 4. Elections Decided by Congress The Congress may by law provide for the case of the death of any of the persons from whom the House of Representatives may choose a President whenever the right of choice shall have devolved upon them, and for the case of the death of any of the persons from whom the Senate may choose a Vice-President whenever the right of choice shall have devolved upon them.

Congress can pass laws in cases where a presidential candidate dies while an election is being decided in the House. Congress has similar power in cases where a candidate for Vice President dies while an election is being decided in the Senate.

Section 5. Date of Effect ~~Sections 1 and 2 shall take effect on the 15th day of October following the ratification of this article.~~

Section 5 sets the date for the amendment to become effective.

Section 6. Ratification Period ~~This article shall be inoperative unless it shall have been ratified as an amendment to the Constitution by the legislatures of three-fourths of the several states within seven years from the date of its submission.~~

Section 6 sets a time limit for ratification.

Amendment 21

Repeal of Prohibition

Passed by Congress on February 20, 1933. Ratified on December 5, 1933.

Section 1. Repeal of National Prohibition The eighteenth article of amendment to the Constitution of the United States is hereby repealed.

The Eighteenth Amendment is repealed, making it legal to make and sell alcoholic beverages. Prohibition ended December 5, 1933.

Section 2. State Laws The transportation or importation into any state, territory, or possession of the United States for delivery or use therein of intoxicating liquors, in violation of the laws thereof, is hereby prohibited.

Each state was free to ban the making and selling of alcoholic drink within its borders. This section makes bringing liquor into a "dry" state a federal offense.

Section 3. Ratification Period ~~This article shall be inoperative unless it shall have been ratified as an amendment to the Constitution by conventions in the several states, as provided in the Constitution, within seven years from the date of the submission hereof to the states by the Congress.~~

Special state conventions were called to ratify this amendment. This is the only time an amendment was ratified by state conventions rather than state legislatures.

Amendment 22

Limit on Number of President's Terms

Passed by Congress on March 12, 1947. Ratified on March 1, 1951.

Section 1. Two-Term Limit No person shall be elected to the office of the President more than twice, and no person who has held the office of President, or acted as President, for more than two years of a term to which some other person was elected President shall be elected to the office of the President more than once. ~~But this Article shall not apply to any person holding the office of President when this Article was proposed by the Congress, and shall not prevent any person who may be holding the office of President, or acting as President, during the term within which this Article becomes operative from holding the office of President or acting as President during the remainder of such term.~~

Before Franklin Roosevelt became President, no President served more than two terms in office. Roosevelt broke with this custom and was elected to four terms. This amendment provides that no President may serve more than two terms. A President who has already served more than half of someone else's term can serve only one more full term. However, the amendment did not apply to Harry Truman, who had become President after Franklin Roosevelt's death in 1945.

A seven-year time limit is set for ratification.

Section 2. Ratification Period ~~This Article shall be inoperative unless it shall have been ratified as an amendment to the Constitution by the legislatures of three-fourths of the several states within seven years from the date of its submission to the states by the Congress.~~

Amendment 23

Presidential Electors for District of Columbia

Passed by Congress on June 16, 1960. Ratified on April 3, 1961.

This amendment gives residents of Washington, D.C., the right to vote in presidential elections. Until this amendment was adopted, people living in Washington, D.C., could not vote for President because the Constitution had made no provision for choosing electors from the nation's capital. Washington, D.C., has three electoral votes.

Section 1. Determining the Number of Electors The District constituting the seat of Government of the United States shall appoint in such manner as the Congress may direct: A number of electors of President and Vice-President equal to the whole number of Senators and Representatives in Congress to which the District would be entitled if it were a State, but in no event more than the least populous State; they shall be in addition to those appointed by the States, but they shall be considered, for the purposes of the election of President and Vice-President, to be electors appointed by a State; and they shall meet in the District and perform such duties as provided by the twelfth article of amendment.

Congress can pass laws to carry out this amendment.

Section 2. Enforcement The Congress shall have power to enforce this article by appropriate legislation.

Amendment 24

Abolition of Poll Tax in National Elections

Passed by Congress on August 27, 1962. Ratified on January 23, 1964.

A ***poll tax*** is a tax on voters. This amendment bans poll taxes in national elections. Some states used poll taxes to keep blacks from voting. In 1966, the Supreme Court struck down poll taxes in state elections, also.

Section 1. Poll Tax Banned The right of citizens of the United States to vote in any primary or other election for President or Vice-President, for electors for President or Vice-President, or for Senator or Representative in Congress, shall not be denied or abridged by the United States or any state by reason of failure to pay any poll tax or other tax.

Congress can pass laws to carry out this amendment.

Section 2. Enforcement The Congress shall have the power to enforce this article by appropriate legislation.

Amendment 25

Presidential Succession and Disability

Passed by Congress on July 6, 1965. Ratified on February 11, 1967.

If the President dies or resigns, the Vice President becomes President. This section clarifies Article 2, Section 1, Clause 6.

Section 1. President's Death or Resignation In case of the removal of the President from office or his death or resignation, the Vice-President shall become President.

When a Vice President takes over the office of President, he or she appoints a Vice President who must be approved by a majority vote of both houses of Congress. This section was first applied after Vice President Spiro Agnew resigned in 1973. President Richard Nixon appointed Gerald Ford as Vice President.

Section 2. Vacancies in Vice-Presidency Whenever there is a vacancy in the office of the Vice-President, the President shall nominate a Vice-President who shall take the office upon confirmation by a majority vote of both houses of Congress.

Section 3. Disability of the President Whenever the President transmits to the President *pro tempore* of the Senate and the Speaker of the House of Representatives his written declaration that he is unable to discharge the powers and duties of his office, and until he transmits to them a written declaration to the contrary, such powers and duties shall be discharged by the Vice-President as Acting President.

If the President declares in writing that he or she is unable to perform the duties of office, the Vice President serves as Acting President until the President recovers.

Section 4. Whenever the Vice-President and a majority of either the principal officers of the executive departments or of such other body as Congress may by law provide, transmit to the President *pro tempore* of the Senate and the Speaker of the House of Representatives their written declaration that the President is unable to discharge the powers and duties of his office, the Vice-President shall immediately assume the powers and duties of the office as Acting President.

Thereafter, when the President transmits to the President *pro tempore* of the Senate and the Speaker of the House of Representatives his written declaration that no inability exists, he shall resume the powers and duties of his office unless the Vice-President and a majority of either the principal officers of the executive department or of such other body as Congress may by law provide, transmit within four days to the President *as* of the Senate and the Speaker of the House of Representatives their written declaration that the President is unable to discharge the powers and duties of his office. Thereupon Congress shall decide the issue, assembling within 48 hours for that purpose if not in session. If the Congress, within 21 days after receipt of the latter written declaration, or, if Congress is not in session, within 21 days after Congress is required to assemble, determines by two-thirds vote of both houses that the President is unable to discharge the powers and duties of his office, the Vice-President shall continue to discharge the same as Acting President; otherwise, the President shall assume the powers and duties of his office.

Two Presidents, Woodrow Wilson and Dwight Eisenhower, have fallen gravely ill while in office. The Constitution contained no provision for this kind of emergency.

Section 3 provided that the President can inform Congress that he or she is too sick to perform the duties of office. However, if the President is unconscious or refuses to admit to a disabling illness, Section 4 provides that the Vice President and Cabinet may declare the President disabled. The Vice President becomes Acting President until the President can return to the duties of office. In case of a disagreement between the President and the Vice President and Cabinet over the President's ability to perform the duties of office, Congress must decide the issue. A two-thirds vote of both houses is needed to decide that the President is disabled or unable to fulfill the duties of office.

Amendment 26

Voting Age

Passed by Congress on March 23, 1971. Ratified on July 1, 1971.

Section 1. Lowering of Voting Age The right of citizens of the United States, who are 18 years of age or older, to vote shall not be denied or abridged by the United States or any state on account of age.

In 1970, Congress passed a law allowing 18-year-olds to vote. However, the Supreme Court decided that Congress could not set a minimum age for state elections. So this amendment was passed and ratified.

Section 2. Enforcement The Congress shall have the power to enforce this article by appropriate legislation.

Congress can pass laws to carry out this amendment.

Amendment 27

Congressional Pay Increases

Proposed by Congress on September 25, 1789. Ratified on May 7, 1992.

No law varying the compensation for the services of the Senators and Representatives shall take effect, until an election of Representatives shall have intervened.

If members of Congress vote themselves a pay increase, it cannot go into effect until after the next congressional election.

CHAPTER 8

Government, Citizenship, and the Constitution

1787–PRESENT

1 Goals and Principles of the Constitution
2 How the Federal Government Works
3 Changing the Constitution
4 State and Local Governments
5 Rights and Responsibilities of Citizenship

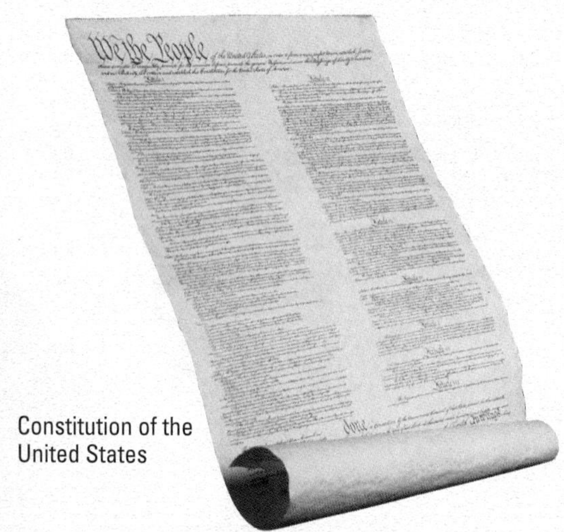

Constitution of the United States

African American man voting for the first time

AMERICAN EVENTS

1787 The Constitution is written. It will serve as the framework of the United States government up to the present.

1830 In most states, white men over 21 can vote.

1870 As a result of the Fifteenth Amendment, African American men win the vote.

1780 · 1840 · 1900

WORLD EVENTS

▲ 1791 French constitution sets up a limited monarchy.

▲ 1821 Mexico wins independence from Spain.

1893 ▲ New Zealand extends the vote to women.

The Electoral College

To become President, a candidate must win the majority of electoral votes.

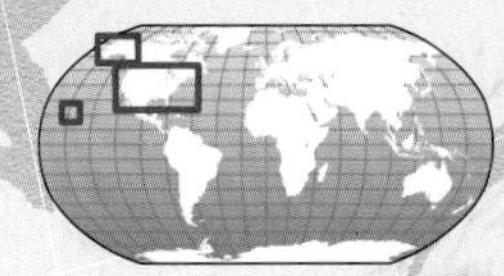

Women's suffrage banner

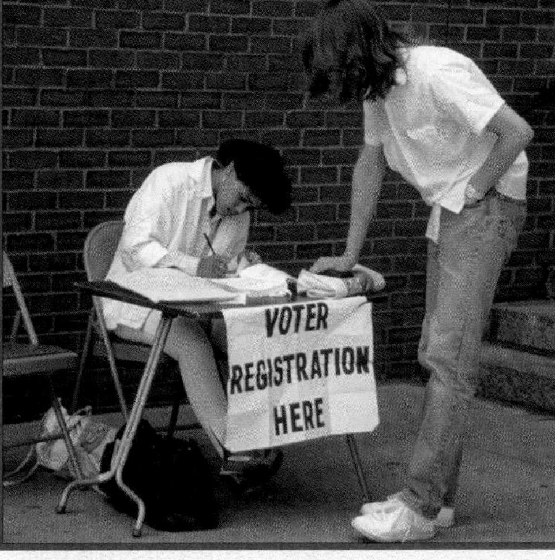

Voter registration drive

1920

The Nineteenth Amendment guarantees the right to vote to women.

1951

The Twenty-second Amendment limits the President to two terms.

1971

The Twenty-sixth Amendment extends the right to vote to Americans 18–21 years of age.

1900 • • • **1960** • • • **PRESENT** • •

1947 ▲

Japan adopts a democratic constitution.

1994 ▲

South Africa holds free multiracial elections.

1 Goals and Principles of the Constitution

Prepare to Read

Objectives

In this section, you will
- Explain how the Preamble defines the basic goals of the Constitution.
- Identify the framework of government established by the Constitution.
- Name the seven basic principles of American government.

Key Terms

Preamble
domestic tranquillity
civilian
general welfare
liberty
Articles
popular sovereignty
limited government
checks and balances
federalism

Target Reading Skill

Reading Process Copy the concept web below. As you read, add ovals and fill them in with goals and principles of the Constitution.

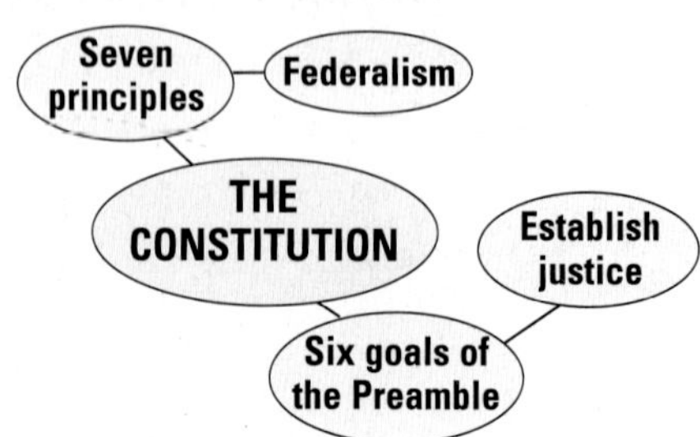

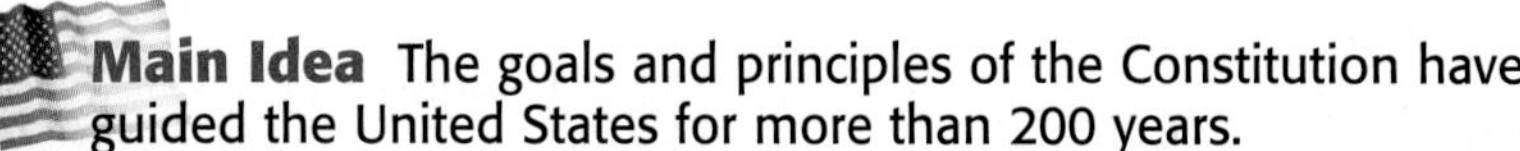

Main Idea The goals and principles of the Constitution have guided the United States for more than 200 years.

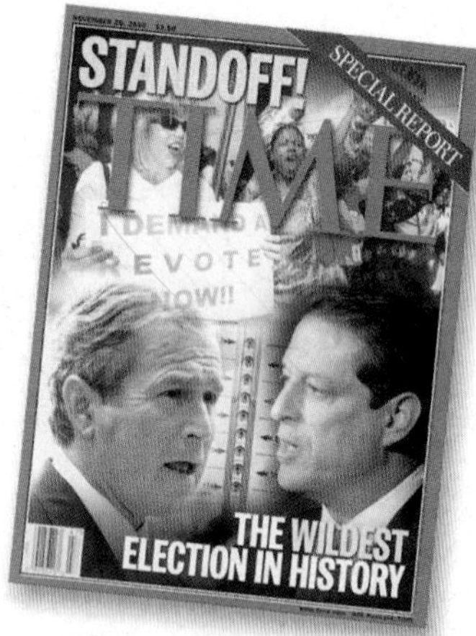

2000 election magazine cover

Setting the Scene On Election Day, 2000, some 100 million Americans voted for a new President. But they learned the next morning that the election was not over. Across the nation, the vote was split almost down the middle. Neither the Democratic candidate, Albert Gore, nor the Republican candidate, George W. Bush, had the 270 electoral votes needed to become President. The result would depend on the vote in Florida—a race that was too close to call!

For 36 days, Americans watched and argued as the candidates battled for Florida's 25 electoral votes. Teams of lawyers, local election officials, state legislators, and state and federal judges all became involved in the battle. At last, a ruling by the Supreme Court of the United States allowed Bush to claim victory. Gore offered his opponent best wishes for a successful presidency.

The election of 2000 raised some troubling issues. In the end, though, the election showed the strength of our constitutional system. The electoral battle was fierce but not violent. The candidates fought bitterly to win, but they fought in the courts, not in the streets. As in the past, in a time of crisis Americans relied on the system established by their Constitution.

The Preamble Sets Goals

The Constitution is divided into three main parts: the **Preamble,** or opening statement, the Articles, and the Amendments. The Preamble defines six goals:

> “We the people of the United States, in order to form a more perfect Union, establish justice, insure domestic tranquillity, provide for the common defense, promote the general welfare, and secure the blessings of liberty to

ourselves and our posterity, do ordain and establish this Constitution for the United States of America. ❞

—Preamble to the Constitution

To Form a More Perfect Union When the Constitution was written, the states saw themselves almost as separate nations. The framers wanted to work together as a unified nation. Fortunately for us, they achieved this goal. Think of what it would be like if you had to exchange your money every time you visited another state!

To Establish Justice The framers knew the nation needed a uniform system to settle legal disputes. Today, the American justice system requires that the law be applied fairly to every American, regardless of race, religion, gender, or country of origin.

To Insure Domestic Tranquillity Under the Constitution, the national government has the power to insure domestic tranquillity, or peace and order at home. Have you seen reports of the National Guard providing assistance in a disaster area? By such actions, the government works to insure domestic tranquillity.

To Provide for the Common Defense Every country has a duty to protect its citizens against foreign attack. The framers of the Constitution gave the national government the power to raise armies and navies. At the same time, they placed the military under civilian, or nonmilitary, control.

To Promote the General Welfare The Constitution set out to give the national government the means to promote the general welfare, or the well-being of all its citizens. For example, today the National Institutes of Health leads the fight against many diseases.

To Secure the Blessings of Liberty During the Revolution, the colonists fought and died for liberty, or freedom. It is no surprise that the framers made liberty a major goal of the Constitution. Over the years, amendments to the Constitution have extended the "blessings of liberty" to more and more Americans.

Viewing History

Working to Fulfill the Constitution

United States

Every day, hundreds of Americans like these work to fulfill the goals set out in the Constitution. **Applying Information** ***Which of the goals set out in the Preamble is associated with each of the people shown here?***

Articles and Amendments

The main body of the Constitution is a short document, divided into seven sections called Articles. Together, they establish the framework for our government.

The Articles The first three Articles describe the three branches of the national government: legislative, executive, and judicial. Article I establishes the powers of and limits on Congress. Articles II and III do the same for the President and the courts.

Article IV deals with relations between the states. It requires states to honor one another's laws and legal decisions. It also sets out a system for admitting new states. Article V provides a process to amend the Constitution.

Article VI states that the Constitution is the "supreme law of the land." This means that states may not make laws that violate the Constitution. If a state law conflicts with a federal law, the federal

System of Checks and Balances

Executive Branch (President carries out laws)	**Checks on the Legislative Branch** • Can propose laws • Can veto laws • Can call special sessions of Congress • Makes appointments • Negotiates foreign treaties	**Checks on the Judicial Branch** • Appoints federal judges • Can grant pardons to federal offenders
Legislative Branch (Congress makes laws) 	**Checks on the Executive Branch** • Can override President's veto • Confirms executive appointments • Ratifies treaties • Can declare war • Appropriates money • Can impeach and remove President	**Checks on the Judicial Branch** • Creates lower federal courts • Can impeach and remove judges • Can propose amendments to overrule judicial decisions • Approves appointments of federal judges
Judicial Branch (Supreme Court interprets laws) 	**Check on the Executive Branch** • Can declare executive actions unconstitutional	**Check on the Legislative Branch** • Can declare acts of Congress unconstitutional

CHART *Skills*

Through checks and balances, each branch of the government limits the power of the other two.

1. **Comprehension** Identify two ways in which the President can check Congress.
2. **Critical Thinking Ranking** What do you think is the most important check Congress has on the President? Explain.

Civics 

law prevails. The final article, Article VII, sets up a procedure for the states to ratify the Constitution.

Amendments In more than 200 years, only 27 formal changes have been made to the Constitution. The first ten amendments, known as the Bill of Rights, were added in 1791. In Section 3, you will read how other amendments have changed the working of the government or extended rights to more Americans.

Seven Basic Principles

The Constitution rests on seven basic principles. They are popular sovereignty, limited government, separation of powers, federalism, checks and balances, republicanism, and individual rights.

Target Skill — Set a Purpose Check to see whether you understand how the ideas of popular sovereignty and limited government differ from monarchy.

Popular Sovereignty The framers of the Constitution lived at a time when monarchs claimed that their power came from God. The Preamble, with its talk of "We the people," reflects a revolutionary new idea: that a government gets its authority from the people. This principle, known as **popular sovereignty,** states that the people have the right to alter or abolish their government.

Limited Government The colonists had lived under the harsh rule of a king. To avoid such tyranny in their new government, the framers made limited government a principle of the Constitution. In a **limited government,** the government has only the powers that the Constitution gives it. Just as important, everyone from you to the President must obey the law.

Separation of Powers To further limit government power, the framers provided for separation of powers. The Constitution divides the government into three branches. Congress, or the legislative branch, makes the laws. The executive branch, headed by the President, carries out the laws. The judicial branch, composed of the courts, explains and interprets the laws.

Checks and Balances A system of checks and balances safeguards against abuse of power. Each branch of government has the power to check, or limit, the actions of the other two. (You will read more about checks and balances in Section Two.)

Federalism The Constitution also establishes the principle of federalism, or division of power between the federal government and the states. Among the powers the Constitution gives the federal government are the power to coin money, declare war, and regulate trade between the states. States regulate trade within their own borders, make rules for state elections, and establish schools. Some powers are shared between the federal government and the states. (See the chart on page 235.) Powers not clearly given to the federal government belong to the states.

Republicanism The Constitution provides for a republican form of government. Instead of taking part directly in government, citizens elect representatives to carry out their will. Once in office, representatives vote according to their own judgment. However, they must remain open to the opinions of the people they represent. For that reason, members of Congress maintain offices in their home districts, and often Web sites as well.

Individual Rights The Constitution protects individual rights, such as freedom of speech, freedom of religion, and the right to trial by jury. You will read more about the rights protected by the Constitution later in this chapter.

Primary Source

Limits on Individual Rights

Although the Constitution protects individual rights, these rights are not unlimited. Here, Oliver Wendell Holmes, Jr., a justice of the Supreme Court, talks about the limits on free speech:

"The character of every act depends upon the circumstances in which it is done. The most [strict] protection of free speech would not protect a man in falsely shouting fire in a theatre and causing a panic. . . . The question in every case is whether the words used are used in such circumstances and are of such a nature as to create a clear and present danger that they will bring about the [real] evils that Congress has a right to prevent."

—Oliver Wendell Holmes, Jr.,
Schenck v. *United States*, 1919

Analyzing Primary Sources

What do you think Holmes meant by "a clear and present danger"?

★ ★ ★ Section 1 Assessment ★ ★ ★

Recall

1. **Identify** Explain the significance of **(a)** Preamble, **(b)** Articles.
2. **Define** **(a)** domestic tranquility, **(b)** civilian, **(c)** general welfare, **(d)** liberty, **(e)** popular sovereignty, **(f)** limited government, **(g)** checks and balances, **(h)** federalism.

Comprehension

3. Identify the six goals of the Constitution.
4. What system is established in Articles I, II, and III?
5. List the seven basic principles behind the Constitution.

Critical Thinking and Writing

6. **Exploring the Main Idea** Review the Main Idea statement at the beginning of this section. Then, choose three principles of the Constitution. Analyze the meaning of each, and list two ways in which you can see that principle at work today.
7. **Ranking** Which of the goals set out in the Preamble do you think is most important? Write a paragraph explaining why.

Activity

Designing a Poster

With a partner, design a poster as part of a display celebrating the Constitution. The poster should highlight one of the six goals or seven principles described in this section. Use a combination of words and pictures to create your poster.

2 How the Federal Government Works

Prepare to Read

Objectives

In this section, you will
- List the powers of the legislative branch.
- Identify the roles the President fills as head of the executive branch.
- Describe how the judicial branch is organized.
- Explain how each branch of government can check the powers of the others.

Key Terms

House of Representatives
Senate
bill
electoral college
Supreme Court
appeal
unconstitutional
veto
override
impeach

Target Reading Skill

Main Idea Copy the table below. As you read, complete the table with information about the three branches of the federal government.

LEGISLATIVE	EXECUTIVE	JUDICIAL
• Congress • Makes laws	• President •	• •

Main Idea The United States government is divided into three branches with separate roles and responsibilities.

Great Seal of the United States

Setting the Scene Tonight, the vast chamber of the House of Representatives is packed to capacity. Applause begins as the President of the United States enters the room and steps to the podium. Behind the President sit the Vice President and the Speaker of the House. In the audience are many of the most powerful people in the nation—members of Congress, justices of the Supreme Court, Cabinet secretaries. At home, millions of Americans tune in on their television sets. The State of the Union Address is about to begin.

In delivering this speech each January, the President fulfills a duty spelled out in the Constitution: "He shall from time to time give to the Congress information of the state of the Union, and recommend to their consideration such measures as he shall judge necessary and expedient." The State of the Union Address also gives Americans a rare chance to see leaders of the legislative, executive, and judicial branches in one place at one time. Our government depends on these three branches working together.

The Legislative Branch

The first and longest article of the Constitution deals with the legislative, or lawmaking, branch. Article I sets up the Congress to make the nation's laws. Congress is made up of two bodies: the House of Representatives and the Senate.

House of Representatives The larger of the two bodies is the **House of Representatives,** which currently has 435 members. Representation in the House is based on population, with larger states having more representatives than smaller states. Every state has at least one representative.

Federal Officeholders

Office	Number	Term	Selection	Requirements
Representative	At least 1 per state; based on population	2 years	Elected by voters of congressional district	Age 25 or over Citizen for 7 years Resident of state in which elected
Senator	2 per state	6 years	Original Constitution—elected by state legislature Amendment 17—elected by voters	Age 30 or over Citizen for 9 years Resident of state in which elected
President and Vice President	1	4 years	Elected by electoral college	Age 35 or over Natural-born citizen Resident of United States for 14 years
Supreme Court Justice	9	Life	Appointed by President Approved by Senate	No requirements in Constitution

CHART *Skills*

The Constitution details the length of term, method of selection, and requirements for officeholders in the three branches of government.

1. **Comprehension** **(a)** At what age can you be elected to the Senate? The House of Representatives? **(b)** How long may a Supreme Court Justice remain in office?
2. **Critical Thinking Drawing Inferences** Why are the requirements for President and Vice President the same?

Civics

Representatives are elected by the people of their district for two-year terms. As a result, the entire House is up for election every other year. Representatives may run for reelection as many times as they want.

The leader of the House is called the Speaker. The Speaker of the House is one of the most powerful people in the federal government. The Speaker regulates debates and controls the agenda. If the President dies or leaves office, the Speaker of the House is next in line after the Vice President to become President.

The Senate Unlike the House, the Senate is based on equal representation, with two senators for each state. Senators are elected to six-year terms. Their terms overlap, however, so that one third of the members come up for election every two years. This way, there is always a majority of experienced senators.

Not all of the Founding Fathers trusted the judgment of the common people. As a result, they called for senators to be chosen by state legislatures. Over the years, the nation slowly became more democratic. The Seventeenth Amendment, ratified in 1913, provided that senators be directly elected by the people, like members of the House.

The Vice President of the United States is president of the Senate. The Vice President presides over the Senate and casts a vote when there is a tie. The Vice President cannot, however, take part in Senate debates. When the Vice President is absent, the president pro tempore, or temporary president, presides.

Powers of Congress The most important power of Congress is the power to make the nation's laws. All laws start as proposals called bills. A new bill may be introduced in either the House or the Senate. However, an appropriations bill, which is a bill designed to raise money for the government, must be introduced in the House. After a bill is introduced, it is debated. If both houses vote to approve the bill, it is then sent to the President, who must sign it before it becomes a law. (See the chart on page 226 to see the steps a bill must follow in order to become a law.)

The Constitution gives Congress many other powers besides lawmaking. Article I, Section 8, lists most of the powers of Congress. They include the power to levy, or collect, taxes and to borrow money. Congress also has the power to coin money, to establish post offices, to fix standard weights and measures, and to declare war.

The Elastic Clause Not all the powers of Congress are specifically listed. Article I, Section 8, Clause 18, states that Congress can "make all laws which shall be necessary and proper" for carrying out its specific duties. This clause is known as the elastic clause because it enables Congress to stretch its powers to deal with the changing needs of the nation.

Americans have long debated the true meaning of the elastic clause. What did the framers mean by the words *necessary* and *proper?* For example, early leaders debated whether the elastic clause gave Congress the right to set up a national bank, even though the Constitution does not specifically give Congress that power. Today, some Americans still worry that Congress might use the clause to abuse its powers.

Committees The first Congress, meeting from 1789 to 1791, considered a total of 31 new bills. Today, more than 10,000 bills are introduced in Congress each year. Clearly, it would be impossible for every member of Congress to give each new bill careful study. To deal with this problem, Congress relies on committees.

Both the House and the Senate have permanent, or standing, committees. Each committee deals with a specific topic, such as agriculture, banking, business, defense, education, science, or transportation. Members who have served in Congress the longest are usually appointed to the most important committees.

Congress may sometimes create joint committees made up of both Senate and House members. One of the most important kinds of joint committees is the conference committee. Its task is to settle differences between House and Senate versions of the same bill.

The Executive Branch

Article II of the Constitution sets up an executive branch to carry out the laws and run the affairs of the national government. The President is the head of the executive branch. Other members include the Vice President, the Cabinet, and the many departments and agencies that help them in their work.

Roles of the President You are probably more familiar with the President than with any other government leader. You see him on television climbing in and out of airplanes, greeting foreign leaders, or making speeches. Yet, many Americans do not know exactly what the President does.

The White House

No building is more a symbol of the United States than the White House, official home of the President. Originally called the "Presidential Palace," it got its white coat of paint after being burned during the War of 1812. Here, Presidents meet with leaders of Congress and host grand dinners for foreign leaders. The front lawn is also the site of an annual Easter egg roll for local children!

Virtual Field Trip For an interactive look at the White House, visit PHSchool.com, **Web Code mfd-0801.**

The framers thought that Congress would be the most important branch of government. Thus, while the Constitution is very specific about the role of the legislature, it offers fewer details about the powers of the President. Beginning with George Washington, Presidents have often taken those actions they thought necessary to carry out the job. In this way, they have shaped the job of President to meet the nation's changing needs.

The President is our highest elected official and, along with the Vice President, the only one who represents all Americans. As head of the executive branch, the President has the duty to carry out the nation's laws. The President directs foreign policy and has the power to make treaties with other nations and to appoint ambassadors.

The President is Commander in Chief of the armed forces. (Only Congress, however, has the power to declare war.) As the nation's chief legislator, the President suggests new laws and works for their passage. The President can grant pardons and call special sessions of Congress. The President is also the living symbol of the nation. Presidents welcome foreign leaders, make speeches to commemorate national holidays, and give medals to national heroes.

Electing the President The President is elected for a four-year term. As a result of the Twenty-second Amendment, adopted in 1951, no President may be elected to more than two complete terms.

The framers set up a complex system for electing the President, known as the electoral college. When Americans vote for President, they do not vote directly for the candidate of their choice. Rather, they

Identify Supporting Details

Why do you think the framers of the Constitution set a specific term of office for the President? Add information about the President's term of office to your chart.

Federal Court System

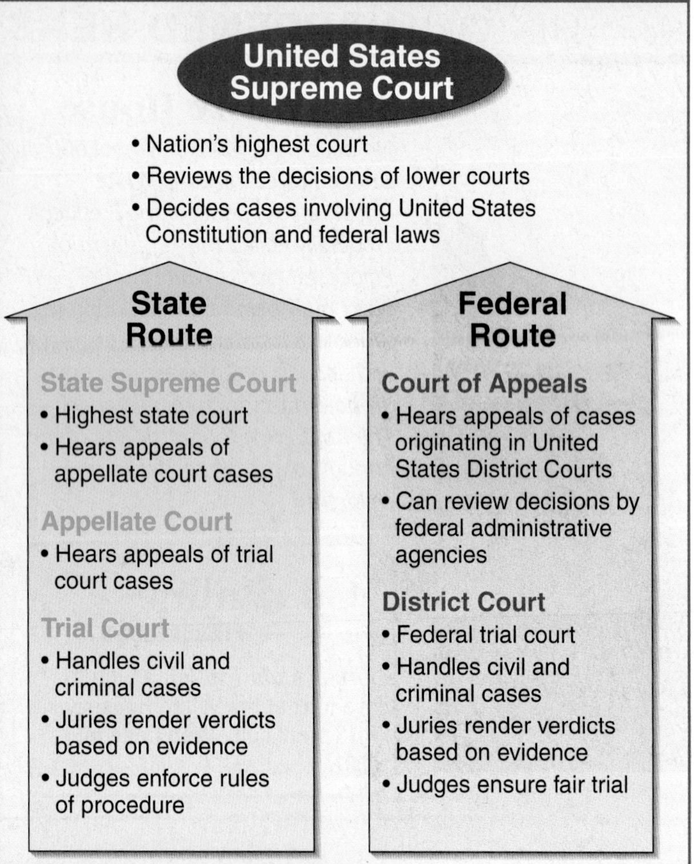

United States Supreme Court

- Nation's highest court
- Reviews the decisions of lower courts
- Decides cases involving United States Constitution and federal laws

State Route

State Supreme Court
- Highest state court
- Hears appeals of appellate court cases

Appellate Court
- Hears appeals of trial court cases

Trial Court
- Handles civil and criminal cases
- Juries render verdicts based on evidence
- Judges enforce rules of procedure

Federal Route

Court of Appeals
- Hears appeals of cases originating in United States District Courts
- Can review decisions by federal administrative agencies

District Court
- Federal trial court
- Handles civil and criminal cases
- Juries render verdicts based on evidence
- Judges ensure fair trial

CHART *Skills*

Cases may come before the Supreme Court either through federal courts or through state courts.

1. **Comprehension** Describe the steps by which a case might travel from a state trial court to the Supreme Court.
2. **Critical Thinking Drawing Conclusions** Why do you think relatively few cases come before the Supreme Court?

Civics

vote for a group of electors who are pledged to the candidate. The number of a state's electors depends on the number of its Senators and Representatives. No state has fewer than three electors.

A few weeks after Election Day, the electors meet in each state to cast their votes for President. In most states, the candidate with the majority of the popular vote receives all that state's electoral votes. The candidate who receives a majority of the electoral votes nationwide becomes President.

Because of the "winner-take-all" nature of the electoral college, a candidate can lose the popular vote nationwide but still be elected President. This has happened four times. Today, some people favor replacing the electoral college with a system that directly elects the President by popular vote. Others oppose any change, pointing out that the system has served the nation well for over 200 years.

The Judicial Branch

The Constitution establishes a **Supreme Court** and authorizes Congress to establish any other courts that are needed. Under the Judiciary Act of 1789, Congress set up the system of federal courts that is still in place today.

Lower Courts Most federal cases begin in district courts. Evidence is presented during trials, and a jury or a judge decides the facts of the case. A party that disagrees with the decision of the judge or jury may **appeal** it, that is, ask that the decision be reviewed by a higher court. The next level of courts is the appellate court, or court of appeal. Appellate court judges review decisions of district courts to decide whether the lower court judges interpreted and applied the law correctly.

Supreme Court At the top of the American judicial system is the Supreme Court. The Court is made up of a Chief Justice and eight Associate Justices. The President appoints the justices, but Congress must approve the appointments. Justices serve for life.

The main job of the Supreme Court is to serve as the nation's final court of appeals. It hears cases that have been tried and appealed in lower courts. Because its decisions are final, the Supreme Court is called "the court of last resort."

The Supreme Court hears and decides fewer than 100 cases each year. Most of the cases are appeals from lower courts that involve federal laws. After hearing oral arguments, the justices vote. Decisions rest on a majority vote of at least five justices.

The greatest power of the Supreme Court is the power to decide what the Constitution means. In the words of Chief Justice Charles Evans Hughes, "The Constitution is what the judges say it is." Early on, the Court asserted the right to declare whether acts of the President or laws passed by Congress are **unconstitutional,** that is, not allowed under the Constitution.

Checks and Balances

The framers hoped that the separation of powers among three branches would prevent the rise of an all-powerful leader who would rob the people of their liberty. But how could the framers prevent one of the branches from abusing its power? To answer this problem, they set up a system of checks and balances.

The system of checks and balances allows each of the three branches of government to check, or limit, the power of the other two. The President, for example, can check the actions of Congress by **vetoing,** or rejecting, bills that Congress has passed. Congress can check the President by **overriding,** or overruling, the veto. Congress must also approve presidential appointments and ratify treaties made by the President. The Supreme Court can check both the President and Congress by declaring laws unconstitutional.

Congress's most extreme check on the President is its power to remove the President from office. To do this, the House of Representatives must **impeach,** or bring charges of serious wrong-doing against, the President. The Senate then conducts a trial. If two thirds of the senators vote to convict, the President must leave office. Throughout our history, only two Presidents—Andrew Johnson and Bill Clinton—have been impeached by the House. Neither was convicted by the Senate.

An American Profile

Sandra Day O'Connor
born 1930

Sandra Day O'Connor graduated with honors from law school but then had trouble finding work at a leading law firm. "None had ever hired a woman as a lawyer," she recalled, "and they were not prepared to do so." Still, she worked her way up to the top. In 1981, she became the first woman to serve on the Supreme Court.

As a justice, O'Connor earned a reputation for sticking closely to the facts and the law in making her decisions. She received many letters from young girls saying they wanted to be just like her.

Why do you think many girls have admired O'Connor?

Section 2 Assessment

Recall

1. **Identify** Explain the significance of **(a)** House of Representatives, **(b)** Senate, **(c)** electoral college, **(d)** Supreme Court.
2. **Define** **(a)** bill, **(b)** appeal, **(c)** unconstitutional, **(d)** veto, **(e)** override, **(f)** impeach.

Comprehension

3. What is the most important power given to Congress?
4. Describe two powers or roles of the President.
5. What is the main job of the Supreme Court?
6. **(a)** Describe one way the President can check the power of Congress. **(b)** Describe one way Congress can check the power of the President.

Critical Thinking and Writing

7. **Exploring the Main Idea** Review the Main Idea statement at the beginning of this section. Then, write a paragraph summarizing the reasons that the Constitution separated the government into branches.
8. **Supporting a Point of View** Write a letter to the editor of your local newspaper explaining whether or not you think the electoral college should be retained.

Activity

Reviewing a Web Site
Use the Internet to find the Web site of your own Senator or Representative. Write a review of the Web site describing the kind of information that is available and how useful it is. For help in completing the activity, visit PHSchool.com, **Web Code mfd-0802.**

Interpreting Bar and Line Graphs

Graphs are visual presentations of data organized so that you can see information at a glance. Two types of graphs that show changes over time are bar graphs and line graphs.

A bar graph shows statistics in the form of bars at regular time intervals.

A line graph shows statistics as connected points. The line that connects the points shows a pattern over time.

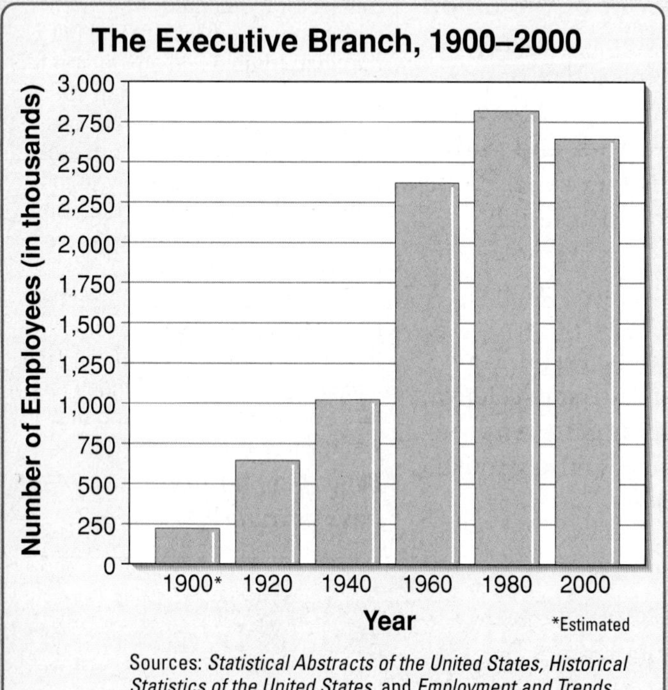

Sources: *Statistical Abstracts of the United States, Historical Statistics of the United States,* and *Employment and Trends*

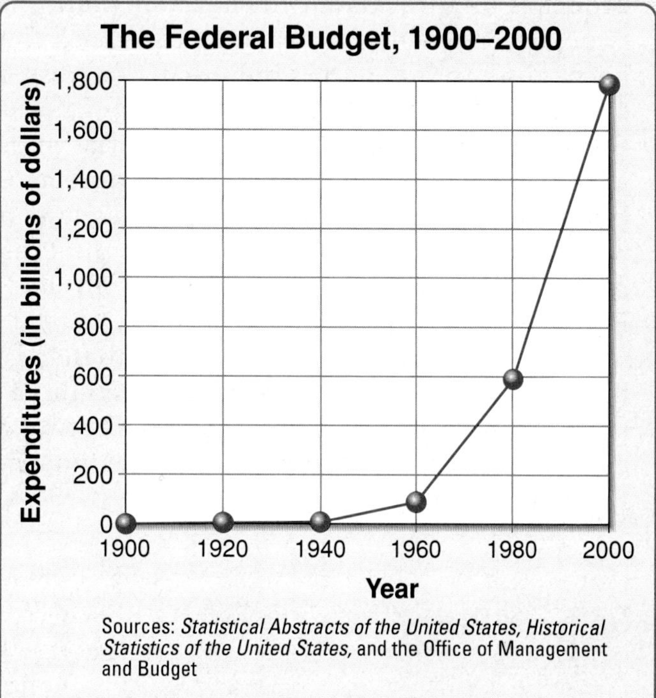

Sources: *Statistical Abstracts of the United States, Historical Statistics of the United States,* and the Office of Management and Budget

Learn the Skill *To review how to read line and bar graphs, use the following steps:*

1. **Read the title.** The title identifies the basic information shown on a graph.
2. **Read the graph labels.** Both the horizontal axis and the vertical axis of a graph have labels that give more specific information about the data. When you read a graph, check the intervals between the dates or other statistics.
3. **Read the statistics on the graph.** Find the points where the horizontal axis meets the vertical axis.
4. **Interpret the statistics.** Draw conclusions or make predictions about the data given on the graph.

Practice the Skill *Use the graphs above to answer the following questions:*

1. **(a)** What is the subject of the bar graph? **(b)** What does the line graph show?
2. **(a)** What years do both graphs show? **(b)** Which graph shows the number of employees?
3. **(a)** In what year were there about one million employees in the executive branch? **(b)** What was the federal budget in 1960? **(c)** During what years did the budget increase the most?
4. Make one generalization about the federal government based on these two graphs.

Apply the Skill *See the Chapter Review and Assessment.*

3 Changing the Constitution

Prepare to Read

Objectives

In this section, you will
- Describe how to amend the Constitution.
- Name the rights that the Bill of Rights protects.
- Explain how later amendments expanded democratic rights.

Key Terms

First Amendment

Second Amendment

incriminate

civil

Civil War Amendments

Nineteenth Amendment

Twenty-sixth Amendment

Target Reading Skill

Sequence Copy this chart. As you read, fill in the boxes with information about constitutional amendments discussed in this section.

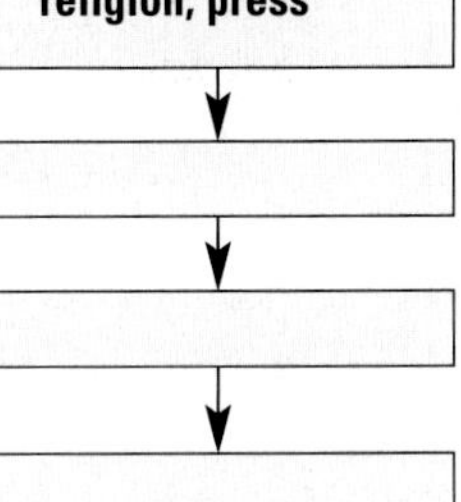

Main Idea The amendment process has made the Constitution a living document that reflects changing times.

Setting the Scene "My faith in the Constitution is whole, it is complete, it is total." The speaker was Barbara Jordan, the first African American elected to Congress from Texas. In her rich voice, Jordan reminded her listeners of the first words of the Constitution:

> "When that document was completed, on the seventeenth of September in 1787, I was not included in that *We, the people.* . . . But through the process of amendment, interpretation, and court decision I have finally been included in *We, the people.*"
>
> —Barbara Jordan, testimony before the House Judiciary Committee, July 25, 1974

Barbara Jordan

Jordan lived in a different world from that of the framers of the Constitution. They did not know *how* the nation would change. But they knew it *would* change and that the Constitution would have to change with it. The formal amendment process that they designed has helped make the Constitution a living document.

The Amendment Process

The framers did not want to make it too easy for Americans to change the Constitution. As a result, they created a complex amendment process. (See the chart on the next page.) The process may take months, or even years, to complete.

Article V outlines two ways to propose an amendment. An amendment may be proposed by two thirds of both the House and the Senate, or by a national convention called by Congress at the request of two thirds of the state legislatures. The second method has never been used.

An amendment may also be ratified in one of two ways. An amendment may be approved by the legislatures of three fourths of

Methods of Amending the Constitution

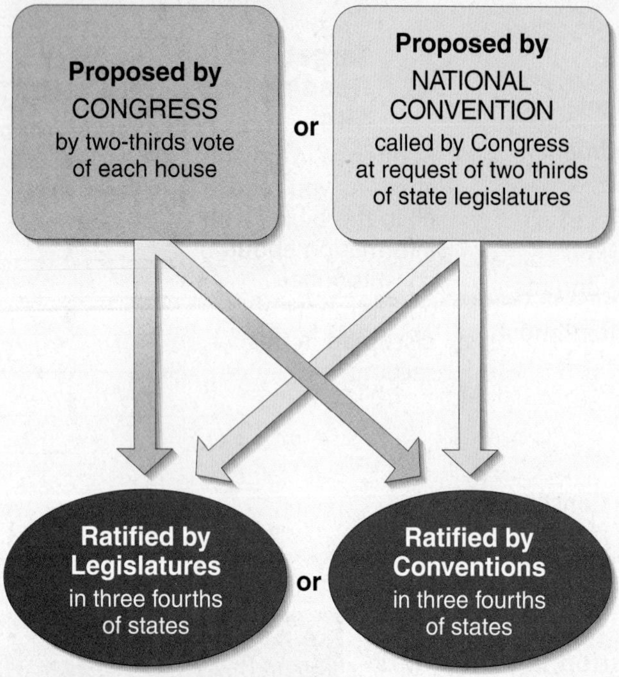

Proposed by CONGRESS by two-thirds vote of each house

or

Proposed by NATIONAL CONVENTION called by Congress at request of two thirds of state legislatures

Ratified by Legislatures in three fourths of states

or

Ratified by Conventions in three fourths of states

GRAPHIC ORGANIZER *Skills*

The amendment process requires two steps: proposal and ratification.

1. **Comprehension** **(a)** Can an amendment proposed by Congress be ratified by state conventions? **(b)** Can an amendment proposed by a national convention be ratified by state legislatures?
2. **Critical Thinking Evaluating Information** Which method of proposing an amendment seems more difficult? Explain.

the states. Every amendment but the Twenty-first was ratified using this method. In the second method, an amendment may be approved by special conventions in three fourths of the states.

The Bill of Rights

As one of its first acts, the new Congress drafted a series of amendments in 1789 and sent them to the states for approval. In 1791, the Bill of Rights, the first ten amendments, became part of the Constitution.

Protecting Individual Liberties The **First Amendment** safeguards basic individual liberties. It protects freedom of religion, speech, and the press. It also guarantees the right to assemble peacefully and to petition the government to change its policies.

Because of the First Amendment, you cannot be arrested for criticizing a government official. You can attend the house of worship of your choice or none at all. You can read newspapers that do not represent the views of an official party. Still, there are limits on the First Amendment. For example, the government can limit free speech if there is "a clear and present danger," such as in time of war.

Protecting Against Abuse of Power The next three amendments reflect the colonists' experiences under British rule. (See Chapter 5.) The **Second Amendment** states, "A well-regulated militia being necessary to the security of a free state, the right of the people to keep and bear arms shall not be infringed." The Third Amendment says that Congress may not force citizens to put up troops in their homes. The Fourth Amendment protects Americans from unlawful searches of home or property.

Since early times, Americans have debated the exact meaning of the Second Amendment. Some experts believe that it guarantees individuals a basic right to bear arms. Others argue that it simply guarantees the individual states the right to maintain a militia. Gun control is one of the most complex and controversial constitutional issues facing Americans today.

Protecting Rights of the Accused The Fifth through Eighth amendments deal with the rights of people accused of crimes. The Fifth Amendment states that people cannot be forced to incriminate, or give evidence against, themselves. The Sixth Amendment guarantees the right to a speedy and public trial by an impartial, or fair, jury. It also states that people accused of crimes have the right to know the charges against them, as well as the right to confront the person making the charges.

The Seventh Amendment provides for juries for civil, or non-criminal, trials. The Eighth Amendment forbids judges from ordering excessive bail or fines or "cruel and unusual punishments."

Amendments Nine and Ten Some Americans had opposed adding a Bill of Rights. They argued that, if specific rights were listed in the Constitution, Americans might lose other rights that were not listed. The Ninth Amendment solved that problem. It makes clear that a citizen's rights are not limited to those listed in the Constitution.

The Tenth Amendment reaffirmed the framers' plan to create a limited federal government. It states that all powers not given to the national government or denied to the states are reserved for the states or for the people.

Later Amendments

Since the addition of the Bill of Rights, the Constitution has been amended only 17 times. Many later amendments reflect changing attitudes about equality and the expansion of democracy.

The Thirteenth, Fourteenth, and Fifteenth amendments are known as the Civil War Amendments. The Thirteenth Amendment abolished slavery. The Fourteenth Amendment guaranteed citizenship to former slaves. The Fifteenth Amendment declared that states may not deny the vote to any citizen on the basis of "race, color, or previous condition of servitude." This guaranteed African American men the right to vote.

Other amendments further expanded voting rights. The Nineteenth Amendment, ratified in 1920, gave women the right to vote. Women achieved this victory after more than 70 years of struggle. In 1971, changing attitudes toward the rights and responsibilities of young people gave birth to the Twenty-sixth Amendment. It lowered the minimum voting age from 21 to 18.

Target Skill **Identify Sequence** When did the amendments discussed in this subsection take place? Where should you place them on your chart?

★ ★ ★ Section 3 Assessment ★ ★ ★

Recall

1. **Identify** Explain the significance of (a) First Amendment, (b) Second Amendment, (c) Civil War Amendments, (d) Nineteenth Amendment, (e) Twenty-sixth Amendment.
2. **Define** (a) incriminate, (b) civil.

Comprehension

3. How can an amendment to the Constitution be ratified?
4. Summarize the rights protected by the Bill of Rights.
5. How did later amendments reflect changing ideas about equality?

Critical Thinking and Writing

6. **Exploring the Main Idea** Review the Main Idea statement at the beginning of this section. Then, write a sentence giving your own definition of the term "living document."
7. **Drawing Conclusions** Why do you think the Bill of Rights carefully spells out the rights of people accused of crimes?

ACTIVITY

Prepare a Dialogue
With a partner, act out a scene between two students. One of you is an American. The other has fled from a country that does not protect freedom of speech, the press, or religion. Discuss the importance of these freedoms to Americans.

4 State and Local Governments

Prepare to Read

Objectives

In this section, you will
- Compare state constitutions to the national Constitution.
- Summarize the services that state governments provide.
- Describe how local governments affect our daily lives.

Key Terms

constitutional initiative

infrastructure

local government

Target Reading Skill

Comparison and Contrast Copy this incomplete Venn diagram. As you read, write key services provided by state and local governments. Include shared services in the overlapping section.

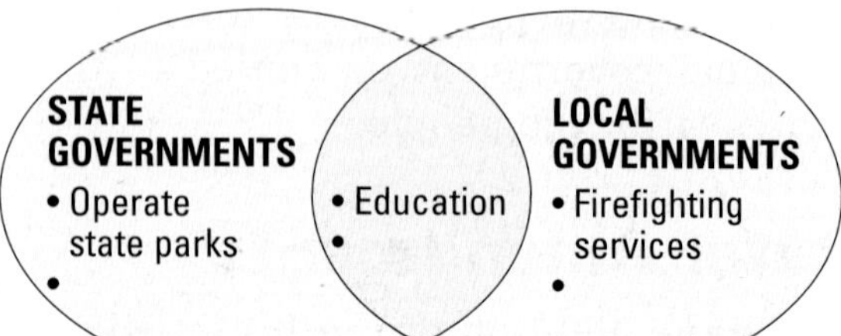

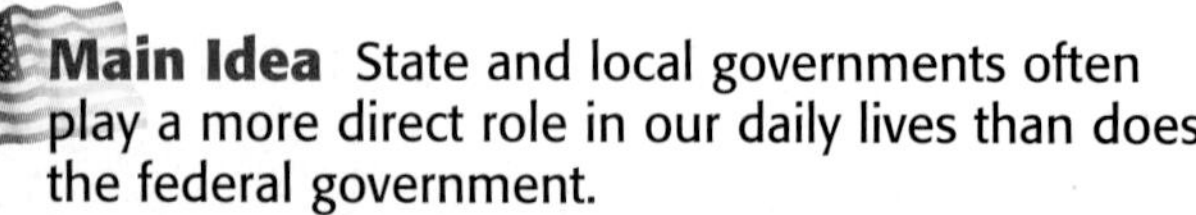

Main Idea State and local governments often play a more direct role in our daily lives than does the federal government.

Visitors at the Bronx Zoo

Setting the Scene In the Bronx, New York, more families wanted to enjoy the area's most popular attraction: the Bronx Zoo, the largest zoo in the United States. A state senator introduced a law allowing local families free admission to the zoo one day a week.

In Oxnard, California, the Police Commissioner learned that 20 percent of all 9-1-1 emergency calls—many of them false alarms—were being made by children. To solve the problem, he got together with state education officials to create "9-1-1 for Kids." This program educates young children on what to do in a real emergency.

In Bexar County, Texas, parents needed help getting their children to school. Local officials banded together to start a program called SchoolPool. It identifies parents who live near one another and provides information about driving duties. Besides helping busy parents, the program reduced the number of cars on local roads.

When we hear the word *government,* most of us think first of the national government in Washington, D.C. Yet, day to day, state and local governments often have a more direct impact on our lives.

State Constitutions

The Constitution divides power between the federal government and the states. The federal government deals with national issues. The states have the power to meet more local needs.

A Frame of Government Each of the 50 states has a constitution that sets forth the principles and framework of its government. Although constitutions vary from state to state, they must all conform to the Constitution of the United States. If a conflict arises, the national Constitution—the "supreme law of the land"—prevails.

Most state constitutions resemble the national Constitution in form. They start with a preamble stating their goals and include a bill of rights guaranteeing individual liberties. State constitutions tend to be longer and more detailed than the national Constitution. Many include provisions on finance, education, and other matters.

State constitutions set up a government with three branches. The powers of the legislative, executive, and judicial branches on the state level are similar to those of the national government.

Changing Constitutions State constitutions can be changed in several ways. In the most common method, amendments are proposed by the state legislature and approved by the people in an election.

In almost one half of the states, citizens can act directly to change the constitution. In a process known as the **constitutional initiative,** sponsors of an amendment gather signatures on a petition. When the required number of signatures is attained, the petition goes to the legislature or to the voters for approval.

Finally, a state can rewrite its constitution. With the approval of the legislature or the people, the state may call a constitutional convention. The new constitution is then submitted to the people.

States Provide Services

State governments provide a wide range of services. They maintain law and order, enforce criminal law, protect property, and regulate business. They also supervise public education, provide public health and welfare programs, build and maintain highways, operate state parks and forests, and regulate use of state-owned land.

The states, not the federal government, have the main responsibility for public education in the United States. Most students attend schools paid for and overseen by the state. The state sets general standards for schools and establishes a recommended course of study. It also sets requirements for promotion and graduation.

Each state must build and maintain its own **infrastructure,** or system of roads, bridges, and tunnels. State departments or agencies manage more than 3,000 state parks and recreation areas. To help maintain high standards, state governments license the professionals who serve you, such as doctors, lawyers, and teachers. When you are old enough to drive, the state will test you and, if you pass, give you a license. State police keep highways safe and protect us against criminal acts.

Local Governments

The Constitution defines the powers of the federal and state governments. But it does not mention **local government,** that is, government on the county, parish, city, town, village, or district level. Local governments are created

Viewing History

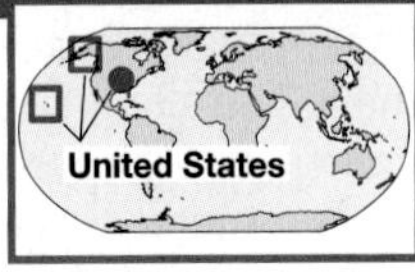

Firefighter in Action Maintaining fire departments is one of the responsibilities of local governments. Some communities hire professional firefighters. Others rely on highly trained volunteers. **Drawing Conclusions** ***In addition to training, what other costs would be necessary for a community to support a fire department?***

Connecting to Today

Parks for the People

When he planned the city of Philadelphia, William Penn hoped to build "a green country town." So, he set aside some areas as parks. In the 1800s, Philadelphia kept Penn's vision alive by adding a long park along one of its rivers. Today, the bustling city of Philadelphia has 4,400 acres of parkland.

Philadelphians use these parks in many ways. Runners, bikers, and in-line skaters swiftly move along paved paths. Families hold reunions in picnic areas. Art lovers visit the museum, and music lovers enjoy an outdoor music hall. People of all ages enjoy seeing the animals at the zoo. Philadelphia's vibrant parks are just one example of the many services that local governments provide for people.

What recreational activities does your local government provide?

Target Skill — Identify Contrasts How do the responsibilities of local governments differ from those of state governments?

entirely by the states and have only those powers and functions that states give them.

Local governments have perhaps the greatest impact on our daily lives. At the same time, it is on the local level that citizens have the greatest opportunity to influence government.

Local Governments and Education The service that local governments spend the most money on is education. While state governments set standards for schools, it is the cities or school districts that actually run them. Local school boards build schools and hire teachers and staff. They also have a strong say in which courses will be taught. However, school officials must make all decisions within the guidelines set by state law.

Education is one area of local government where citizens exert a great deal of control. Local residents may give up part of their time to serve on local school boards. In most communities, voters have the right to approve or turn down the annual school budget.

Other Services Local governments provide a variety of other services. They hire or support firefighters, police, and garbage collectors. Local governments provide sewers and water, maintain local roads and hospitals, and conduct safety inspections of buildings and restaurants. In many cases, water and sewage treatment plants are owned and run by local governments. Other communities hire private companies to supply local needs.

Over the years, Americans have looked to local government for more than basic services. Today, most local governments provide libraries and parks and other cultural and recreational facilities. In larger cities, citizens expect their local governments to support airports, sports arenas, and civic centers. San Francisco, for example, maintains a busy airport, a major-league baseball stadium, several major museums, a world-class zoo, and a leading convention center.

★ ★ ★ Section 4 Assessment ★ ★ ★

Recall

1. **Define** **(a)** constitutional initiative, **(b)** infrastructure, **(c)** local government.

Comprehension

2. **(a)** Describe one way in which state constitutions are similar to the United States Constitution. **(b)** Describe one way in which they are different.
3. Identify two services performed by state governments.
4. How do local governments support education?

Critical Thinking and Writing

5. **Exploring the Main Idea** Review the Main Idea statement at the beginning of this section. Then, rank in order what you consider to be the five most important services you get from your state and local governments.
6. **Drawing Inferences** Why do you think state constitutions tend to be longer than the United States Constitution?

ACTIVITY

Connecting to Today

Use the Internet to find the Web site of your state or local historical society. Review the Web site and discuss why maintaining local history is an important service. For help in completing the activity, visit PHSchool.com, **Web Code mfd-0803**.

5 Rights and Responsibilities of Citizenship

Prepare to Read

Objectives

In this section, you will
- Explain what makes a person a citizen of the United States.
- Identify how Americans can develop democratic values.
- Describe the responsibilities of citizenship.

Key Terms

citizen
naturalize
immigrant
resident alien
civic virtue
patriotism
jury duty

Target Reading Skill

Clarifying Meaning As you read, prepare an outline of this section. Use roman numerals to indicate the major headings, capital letters for the subheadings, and numbers for the supporting details.

I. What Is a Citizen?
   A. Definition of citizenship
      1. Born in United States
      2.
   B. Becoming a citizen
      1.
      2.
   C.
II. Civic Virtue and Democratic Values
   A.
   B.

Main Idea Being an American citizen brings both rights and responsibilities.

David Levitt

Setting the Scene While he was in middle school, David Levitt of Seminole, Florida, read about an organization that collected left-over food from restaurants and donated it to the needy. This gave Levitt an idea. Why not start a similar program in his community?

He started by asking his principal if the school could donate left-over cafeteria food. Levitt went on to present his idea to the school board. A year later, at his bar mitzvah, he collected 500 pounds of canned goods from his guests. In time, the food program expanded across Florida and led to passage of a new state law.

Florida governor Jeb Bush called David Levitt a "big-hearted . . . young man blessed with a strong desire to help others." But Levitt insisted that all young people had the power to get things done:

> "You have to use your age as an advantage. In government, adults face people who complain and ask for things. It's such a change of pace to hear someone say, 'We can do this.'"
>
> —David Levitt, quoted in *American Profile* (Schantz-Feld)

The framers of the Constitution planned our government carefully. Yet, a good constitution alone is not enough. To safeguard our democracy, each of us must exercise our rights and fulfill our responsibilities as citizens.

What Is a Citizen?

A **citizen** is a person who owes loyalty to a particular nation and is entitled to all its rights and protections. To be a citizen of the United States, you must fulfill one of three requirements:

- You were born in the United States (or at least one parent is a citizen of the United States).
- You were **naturalized,** that is, you have completed the official legal process for becoming a citizen.

- You were 18 or younger when your parents were naturalized.

Becoming a Citizen Throughout American history, many millions of immigrants have become naturalized citizens. An **immigrant** is a person who enters another country in order to settle there. To illustrate the naturalization process, we will look at one immigrant's story.

At age 15, Carla Rojas came to the United States from Argentina. Her mother returned home two years later, but Rojas decided to remain. After submitting numerous documents and photographs and attending several interviews, she received permission to remain in the country as a **resident alien,** or noncitizen living in the country.

After a required five-year waiting period, Carla submitted an application for citizenship. She had to take a test to show that she was comfortable with the English language and that she was familiar with American history and government. She also had to show that she was of "good moral character." Then, a naturalization examiner interviewed her about her reasons for becoming a citizen.

At last, Rojas stood before a judge and took the oath that confirmed her as an American citizen:

> "I hereby declare, on oath, that . . . I will support and defend the Constitution and laws of the United States against all enemies . . . that I will bear true faith and allegiance to the same . . . so help me God."
>
> —Oath of Allegiance to the United States

A naturalized citizen enjoys every right of a natural-born citizen except one. Only natural-born citizens may serve as President or Vice President.

Rights and Responsibilities All American citizens have equal rights under the law. As Americans, you have the right to speak freely, to worship as you choose, to vote, and to serve on juries. These rights are not based on inherited wealth or family connections. They are yours because you are a citizen.

Still, nothing is free. As you will see, if we want to enjoy the rights of citizenship, we must also accept its responsibilities.

An American Profile

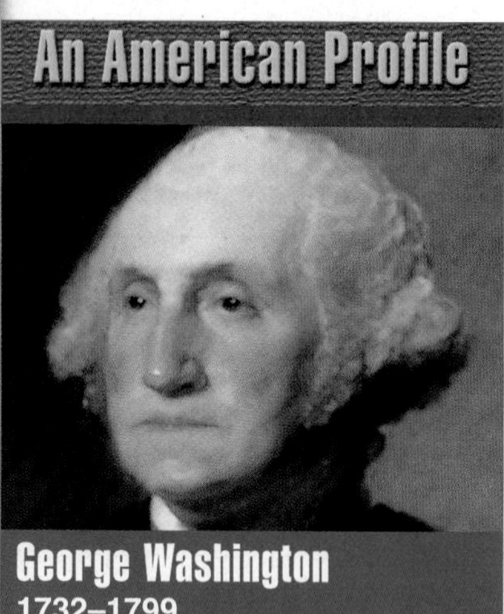

George Washington
1732–1799

Several times in his life, George Washington set aside his hopes for a quiet life to serve his country.

After winning the battle of Yorktown in 1781, Washington ached to return home. Still, he led the army until a peace treaty was signed two years later. In 1787, though ill, he yielded to friends who urged him to attend the Constitutional Convention. After his first term as President, Washington sought to retire. Once again, Washington was persuaded to stay on to keep the young republic stable. After his second term, Washington finally retired. He died two years later.

Why do many people point to Washington as an example of civic virtue?

Civic Virtue and Democratic Values

The Founding Fathers admired **civic virtue,** that is, the willingness to work for the good of the nation or community even at great sacrifice. They looked to Roman models such as Cincinnatus, who, it was said, gave up a peaceful life on his farm when called upon to lead Rome. Again and again, leaders such as Washington and Jefferson put the common good ahead of their own wishes.

Still, you do not have to go to such lengths to be a good citizen. At home, at school, and in the community, you can work to develop the values that are the foundation of our democratic system. Among these basic values are honesty and compassion. Others include patriotism, respect, responsibility, and courage.

A key democratic value is **patriotism,** or a feeling of love and devotion toward one's country. A sense of patriotism inspires

"Maybe I ought to listen. This is the year I start voting."

POLITICAL CARTOON *Skills*

Young Voters
Voting is one of the main responsibilities of citizenship. This cartoon appeared in 1960, a presidential election year.

1. **Comprehension** Describe what is going on in this cartoon.
2. **Understanding Main Ideas** What point does the cartoon make about staying informed?
3. **Critical Thinking Supporting a Point of View** Based on this cartoon, would you call this young man a good citizen? Explain.

Civics 

Americans to serve their nation. It also encourages us to fulfill the ideals set forth in the Declaration of Independence, the Constitution, and the Bill of Rights.

As citizens, we must respect ourselves, our families, our neighbors, and the other members of our community. Respect may also involve objects or ideas. For example, a good citizen respects the property of others and the laws of the nation.

Responsibility may be both personal and public. We must accept responsibility for ourselves and the consequences of our actions. For example, parents have a duty to support their families and teach their children. As a student, you have a responsibility to learn.

Courage may be either physical or moral. Soldiers, police, or firefighters display physical courage when they risk their lives for the good of others. Moral courage enables us to do the right thing even when it is unpopular, difficult, or dangerous. Americans such as George Washington, Abraham Lincoln, Susan B. Anthony, and Martin Luther King, Jr., faced risks in order to defend their democratic values.

Responsibilities of a Citizen

As citizens, we must accept our own civic responsibilities. Only if government and citizens work together can we meet our needs as a democratic society.

Voting As citizens of a republic, we have the right to select the people who will represent us in government. But if that right is to have any meaning, then we must fulfill our responsibility to vote. A good citizen studies the candidates and the issues in order to make responsible choices.

Target Skill — Paraphrase When you paraphrase, you restate what you have read in your own words. Paraphrase the information about the responsibilities of a citizen. Add this information to your outline.

Obeying the Laws In the Constitution, "we the people" give the government the power to make laws for us. Thus, we have a duty to obey the nation's laws. We have thousands of laws that keep us from hurting one another, regulate contracts, or protect citizens' rights. No one can know them all, but you must know and obey the laws that affect your life and actions.

Defending the Nation Americans have the duty to help defend the nation against threats to its peace or security. At age 18, all men must register for the draft. In time of war, the government may call them to serve in the armed forces. Many young citizens feel the duty to enlist in the military without being called.

Serving on a Jury The Bill of Rights guarantees the right to trial by jury. In turn, every citizen has the responsibility to serve on a jury when called. **Jury duty** is a serious matter. Jurors must take time out from their work and personal lives to decide the fate of others.

Serving the Community Many Americans use their time and skills to improve their communities or to help others. As you read, David Levitt was in middle school when he started a program to help the needy in his Florida community. Many young people participate in walk-a-thons or bike-a-thons for charity. Others volunteer in hospitals or fire departments. When terrorist attacks hit New York City and Washington, D.C., in September 2001, millions of citizens aided in rescue efforts, donated blood, or contributed money and supplies.

Being Informed Thomas Jefferson observed, "If a nation expects to be ignorant and free . . . it expects what never was and never will be." You cannot protect your rights as a citizen unless you know what they are. It is your responsibility to be informed. You can watch television news programs and read newspapers, magazines, or government pamphlets. Your work in school will help you become educated about our history, our government, and the workings of our society.

Section 5 Assessment

Recall

1. **Define** **(a)** citizen, **(b)** naturalize, **(c)** immigrant, **(d)** resident alien, **(e)** civic virtue, **(f)** patriotism, **(g)** jury duty.

Comprehension

2. How may a person become an American citizen?
3. List four values that citizens in a democratic society need.
4. Describe two responsibilities of citizenship.

Critical Thinking and Writing

5. **Exploring the Main Idea** Review the Main Idea statement at the beginning of this section. Then, write a paragraph analyzing how rights and responsibilities help define our identity as Americans.
6. **Making Decisions** You are a resident alien who has decided to apply for citizenship. Write a letter to a family member in your native country explaining why you reached that decision.

Activity

Preparing a Questionnaire With a partner, prepare a questionnaire titled "Are You a Responsible Citizen?" Questions may cover responsibility to oneself, to one's family, to the community, and to the nation. Include seven to ten questions.

Becoming an American Citizen

Becoming an American citizen is not easy. But for many immigrants, the benefits of freedom and opportunity make it worth the effort.

Steps to Citizenship

1. Establish five-year residency.

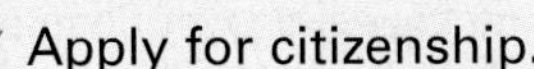
2. Apply for citizenship.
   - Submit application and fee
   - Get fingerprinted for background check

3. Go through the interview process.
   - Take English and civics tests
   - Answer questions about background and character

4. Take Oath of Allegiance

Could you pass the citizenship test? See how many of the following typical test questions you can answer correctly.

1. How many stripes are there on our flag?
2. What country did we fight during the Revolutionary War?
3. Who elects the President of the United States?
4. What are the duties of the Supreme Court?
5. What are the three branches of our government?
6. How many Senators are there in Congress?
7. For how long do we elect each senator?
8. Who said, "Give me liberty or give me death"?
9. How many terms can the President serve?
10. Who is the Commander in Chief of the United States military?

Activity

The citizenship test includes about a dozen questions selected from a master list of one hundred. What questions, aside from those listed here, do you think would be important to ask a future citizen? Make a list of at least five questions, and provide the answers.

CHAPTER 8

Review and Assessment

Chapter Summary

Section 1
The ideals expressed in the U.S. Constitution have guided the nation for more than 200 years. The Preamble sets goals, while the first three articles set up the framework for government.

Section 2
The U.S. government is divided into three branches: the legislative, executive, and judicial branches. Each branch has separate roles and responsibilities.

Section 3
The U.S. Constitution can be amended. The first ten amendments are the Bill of Rights. There have been 27 amendments to the Constitution.

Section 4
State and local governments provide many services on which we rely. In fact, state and local governments often play a more direct role in our daily lives than does the federal government.

Section 5
Being a U.S. citizen brings both rights and responsibilities. These include voting, obeying laws, and defending the country.

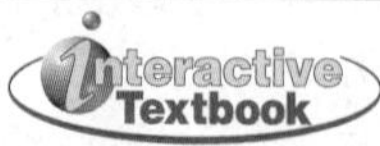

For additional review and enrichment activities, see the interactive version of *The American Nation,* available on the Web and on CD-ROM.

Chapter Self-Test For practice test questions for Chapter 8, visit PHSchool.com, **Web Code mfa-0804.**

Building Vocabulary

Use the chapter vocabulary words listed below to create a crossword puzzle. Exchange puzzles with a classmate. Complete the puzzles, and then check each other's answers.

1. **liberty**
2. **popular sovereignty**
3. **checks and balances**
4. **federalism**
5. **bill**
6. **veto**
7. **citizen**
8. **naturalize**
9. **civic virtue**
10. **patriotism**

Reviewing Key Facts

11. What is limited government? (Section 1)
12. How does the electoral college work? (Section 2)
13. In what two ways can a constitutional amendment be proposed? (Section 3)
14. How are local governments created? (Section 4)
15. Summarize the steps of the naturalization process. (Section 5)

Critical Thinking and Writing

16. **Contrasting** **(a)** How does our republican system differ from a system where all citizens participate directly in government? **(b)** Write a sentence explaining why you think the framers chose a republican system.
17. **Supporting a Point of View** Your local newspaper has printed an editorial arguing that the process of amending the Constitution should be simplified. Write a letter to the editor agreeing or disagreeing with this position.
18. **Connecting to Geography: Movement** Locate the Mississippi River on a map of the United States. Do you think the federal government or the state governments would be primarily responsible for laws regarding shipping along the Mississippi? Write a paragraph explaining the reason for your answer.
19. **Finding the Main Idea** A popular saying states, "Your right to swing your fist ends where my nose begins." Write a sentence restating the main idea of this saying in your own words.

Skills Assessment

Analyzing Primary Sources

General John A. Wickham, Jr., served as Chief of Staff for the United States Army. Here, he talks about what military service means to him:

> "The history of the Army is intertwined with the history of our Constitution. Before our young nation could even be in a position to draft a constitution, her freedom had to be won. It was won with the courage and blood of the first American soldiers. Once our liberty was secured, these same soldiers became the citizens upon whose commitment and hard work a great nation would be built."
>
> —John A. Wickham, Jr., in *Collected Works of the Thirtieth Chief of Staff,* United States Army

20. According to Wickham, which of the following qualities do soldiers and citizens need?
- **A.** courage and commitment
- **B.** popular sovereignty
- **C.** patriotism and naturalization
- **D.** pacifism and liberty

21. Which of the following statements accurately reflects Wickham's point of view?
- **A.** No Army was needed after the Revolution.
- **B.** Before the Constitution could be written, American soldiers had to win the war.
- **C.** Soldiers do not make good citizens.
- **D.** Only soldiers should be naturalized.

Applying Your Skills

Interpreting Bar and Line Graphs

Look at the bar graph below, and answer the questions that follow.

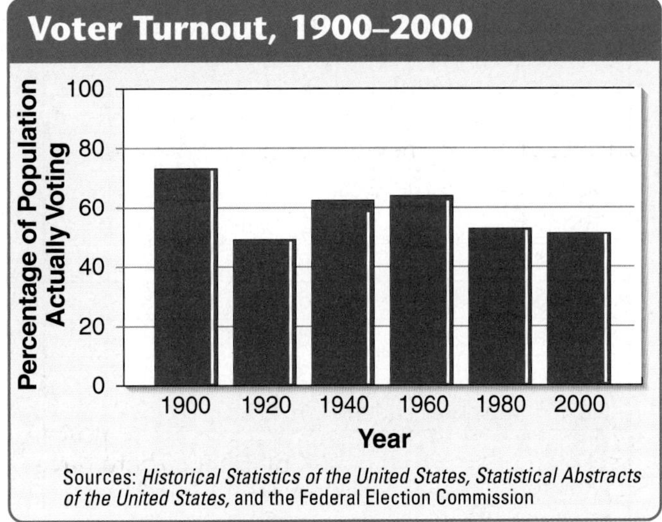

22. Which statement about voter turnout does this graph support?
- **A.** Voter turnout steadily declined after 1900.
- **B.** Voter turnout steadily rose after 1920.
- **C.** Voter turnout varied in the 1900s.
- **D.** Most Americans do not vote.

23. List three factors that you think might lead to an increase in voter turnout.

Activities

Connecting With . . . Government and Citizenship

Creating an Election Chart Look at the electoral college map at the beginning of this chapter. Suppose there is a presidential election between Smith and Jones. Smith wins 18 states: Alabama, Arizona, Arkansas, California, Florida, Georgia, Illinois, Kentucky, Louisiana, Michigan, Missouri, New Mexico, North Carolina, South Carolina, Tennessee, Texas, Virginia, and Wyoming. Jones wins the other 32 states plus the District of Columbia. Create a two-column chart showing the electoral votes for each candidate. Then, determine the winner of the election.

Connecting to Today

Giving a News Report Use the Internet to find a recent court case that involves the freedoms protected by the Bill of Rights. Deliver to the class a one- to two-minute summary of that case. For help in starting this activity, visit PHSchool.com, **Web Code mfd-0805.**

TEST PREPARATION

Use the table and your knowledge of social studies to answer the following question.

Ratification of the Constitution

STATE	DATE	VOTE
Delaware	Dec. 7, 1787	30–9
Pennsylvania	Dec. 12, 1787	46–23
New Jersey	Dec. 18, 1787	38–0
Georgia	Jan. 2, 1788	26–0
Connecticut	Jan. 9, 1788	128–40
Massachusetts	Feb. 6, 1788	187–168
Maryland	Apr. 28, 1788	63–11
South Carolina	May 23, 1788	149–73
New Hampshire	June 21, 1788	57–47
Virginia	June 25, 1788	89–79
New York	July 26, 1788	30–27
North Carolina	Nov. 21, 1789	194–77
Rhode Island	May 29, 1790	34–32

1 Which conclusion about the ratification of the Constitution is supported by this table?

- **A** Antifederalist influence was strong in Georgia.
- **B** Federalists faced little opposition in New England.
- **C** Antifederalist influence was stronger in New York than in New Jersey.
- **D** The Constitution could go into effect by June 1, 1788.

2 Which statement best summarizes the main idea of Thomas Paine's *Common Sense*?

- **A** The colonists must make one last effort to reconcile with the king.
- **B** The best strategy for winning the war would be for Americans to seek help from France.
- **C** At this time, Washington and the army need the full support of all Patriots.
- **D** Separation from England is the most logical course for the American colonies.

3 How did the French and Indian War lead to the American Revolution?

- **A** The British king encouraged colonists to settle on lands won from France.
- **B** The British government taxed the colonists to help pay for the war.
- **C** The French encouraged American colonists to seek independence from Britain.
- **D** After the war, more British troops were permanently stationed in the colonies.

4 Which is not a power of Congress under the Constitution?

- **A** Declaring war
- **B** Ratifying constitutional amendments
- **C** Removing a President from office
- **D** Regulating foreign trade

Use the quotation and your knowledge of social studies to answer the following question.

Constitution of the United States, Article I, Section 1

"The House of Representatives shall be composed of members chosen every second year by the people of the several states. . . ."

5 Which principle of the Constitution is primarily reflected in the passage above?

- **A** Republicanism
- **B** Federalism
- **C** Checks and balances
- **D** Individual rights

6 In which of the following pairs was the first event an immediate cause of the second?

A Intolerable Acts; Boston Tea Party

B Battle of Saratoga; French aid to colonies

C Declaration of Independence; Battle of Lexington

D Stamp Act; Shays' Rebellion

Use the map and your knowledge of social studies to answer the following question.

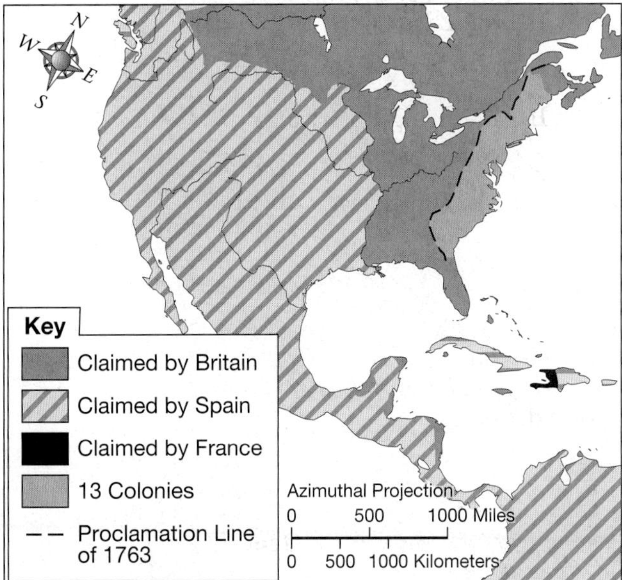

7 How would a map showing the same area 10 years earlier have looked different?

A The original 13 colonies would have taken up a larger area.

B British land claims would have taken up a larger area.

C French land claims would have taken up a larger area.

D The map would have looked about the same.

8 Which of these grievances against England listed in the Declaration of Independence was later addressed in the Bill of Rights?

A ". . . imposing taxes on us without our consent"

B ". . . depriving us, in many cases, of the benefit of trial by jury"

C ". . . cutting off our trade with all parts of the world"

D ". . . suspending our own legislatures"

9 The dispute between large states and small states at the Constitutional Convention largely concerned what subject?

A Legislative branch of government

B Executive branch of government

C Judicial branch of government

D Checks and balances among the three branches of government

Writing Practice

10 Compare the advantages and disadvantages of the Americans and the British during the American Revolution. Then, explain why the United States won the war.

11 Choose one of the following principles of the Constitution: republicanism, checks and balances, federalism, separation of powers, popular sovereignty, or individual rights. Explain its meaning, why the framers valued that principle, and how it affects American government and society.

Unit 3 The Early Republic

UNIT OUTLINE

Life on the Canals
The building of canals like the one shown in ***Junction of the Erie and Northern (Champlain) Canals*** by John Hill helped spur economic growth during the early 1800s.

“We have learned to love our country . . . because the sweat of our fathers’ brows has subdued its soil . . . because it embraces our fathers and mothers.”

—John Thornton Kirkland, Boston minister (1798)

CHAPTER 9

Launching the New Government

1789–1800

Washington's inaugural flag, 1789

Map of the new capital city

Benjamin Banneker

AMERICAN EVENTS

1789 George Washington is inaugurated as the first President of the United States.

1791 Benjamin Banneker helps lay out the District of Columbia, the nation's new capital.

1793 Washington issues the Neutrality Proclamation to prevent the United States from being dragged into a European war.

Presidential Terms: George Washington 1789–1797

1788 · 1791 · 1794

WORLD EVENTS

▲ 1789 The French Revolution begins.

1793 ▲ French radicals execute the king and queen of France.

Where Americans Lived, 1800

In the early years of the United States, most Americans lived along the eastern coastal plain.

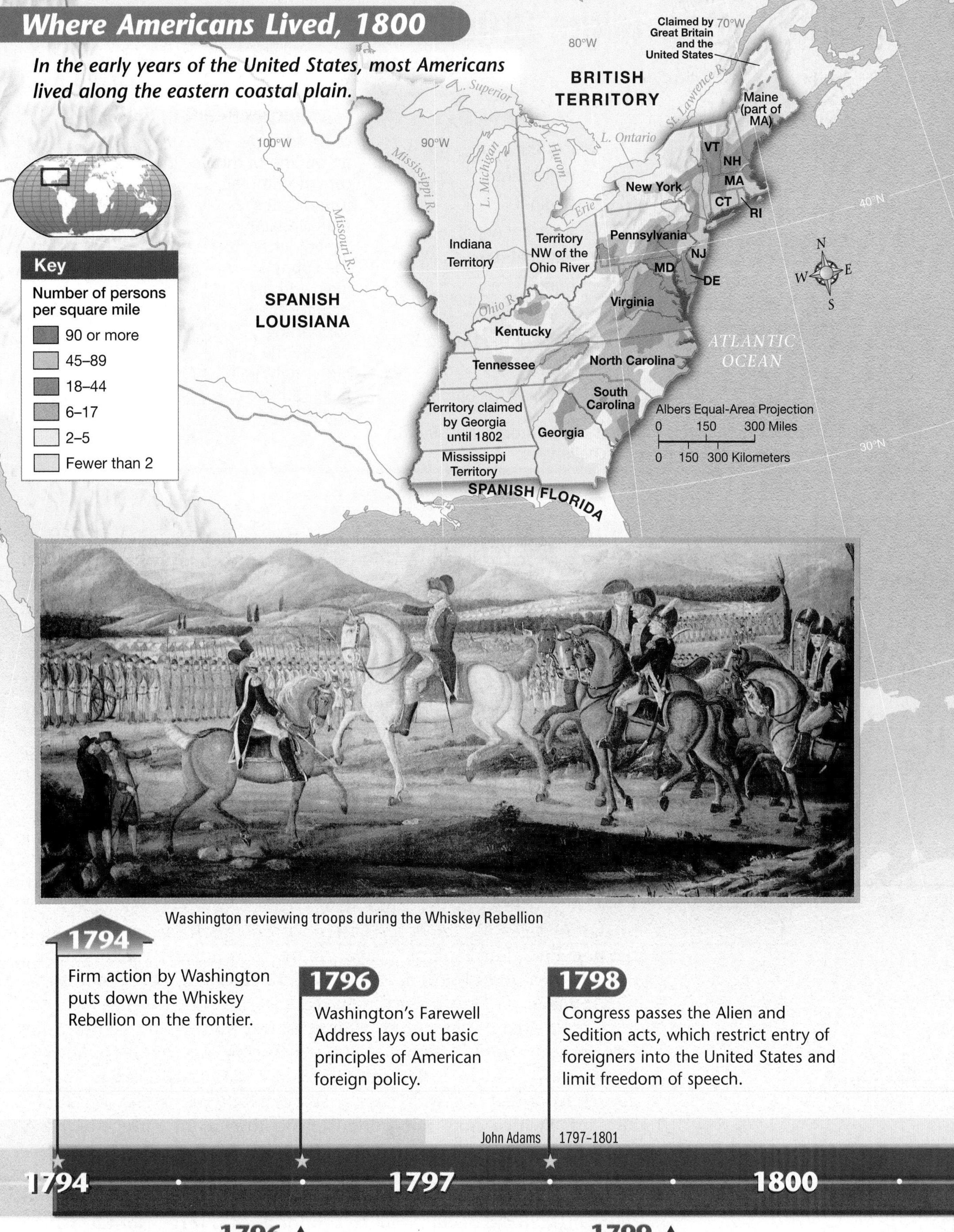

Washington reviewing troops during the Whiskey Rebellion

1794 Firm action by Washington puts down the Whiskey Rebellion on the frontier.

1796 Washington's Farewell Address lays out basic principles of American foreign policy.

1798 Congress passes the Alien and Sedition acts, which restrict entry of foreigners into the United States and limit freedom of speech.

John Adams 1797-1801

1794 · 1797 · 1800

1796 ▲ Emperor Qianlong ends his 60-year reign in China by resigning from office.

1799 ▲ Napoleon Bonaparte seizes power in France.

1 Washington Takes Office

Prepare to Read

Objectives

In this section, you will

- Describe the steps Washington took to make the new government work.
- Explain Hamilton's plan to reduce the nation's debt and build the economy.
- List the causes and results of the Whiskey Rebellion.

Key Terms

inauguration
precedent
Cabinet
Judiciary Act
national debt
bond
speculator
Bank of the United States
tariff
Whiskey Rebellion

Target Reading Skill

Main Idea As you read, prepare an outline of this section. Use roman numerals to indicate the major headings, capital letters for the subheadings, and numbers for the supporting details. The sample at right will help you get started.

I. Washington's First Steps
A. The first Cabinet
B.
II. Reducing the Nation's Debt
A. Hamilton's plan
1.
2.
B.
C.
III. Plans to Build the Economy
IV.

Main Idea As the nation's first President, George Washington faced many economic and political challenges.

Washington's first inaugural

Setting the Scene When the new Congress met in 1789, it debated a curious question. How should people address the President? Some members of Congress favored the simple title "President Washington." Others urged a more dignified title, such as "His Highness the President of the United States and Protector of the Rights of the Same."

Washington soon let Congress know that he preferred "President of the United States." By choosing that simple title, he rejected the grandeur and power linked to European monarchs. With that decision, as with many others, Washington set an example for later Presidents.

Washington's First Steps

George Washington was inaugurated in New York City on April 30, 1789. A presidential **inauguration** is the ceremony in which the President officially takes the oath of office. A witness reported that the new President looked "grave, almost to sadness." Washington, no doubt, felt a great burden. He knew that Americans were looking to him to make the new government work.

As the first President, Washington was setting an example for future generations. Although the Constitution provided a framework for the new government, it did not explain how the President should govern from day to day. "There is scarcely any part of my conduct," he said, "which may not hereafter be drawn into precedent." A **precedent** (PREHS uh dehnt) is an act or a decision that sets an example for others to follow.

Washington set an important precedent at the end of his second term. In 1796, he decided not to run for a third term. Not until 1940 did any President seek a third term.

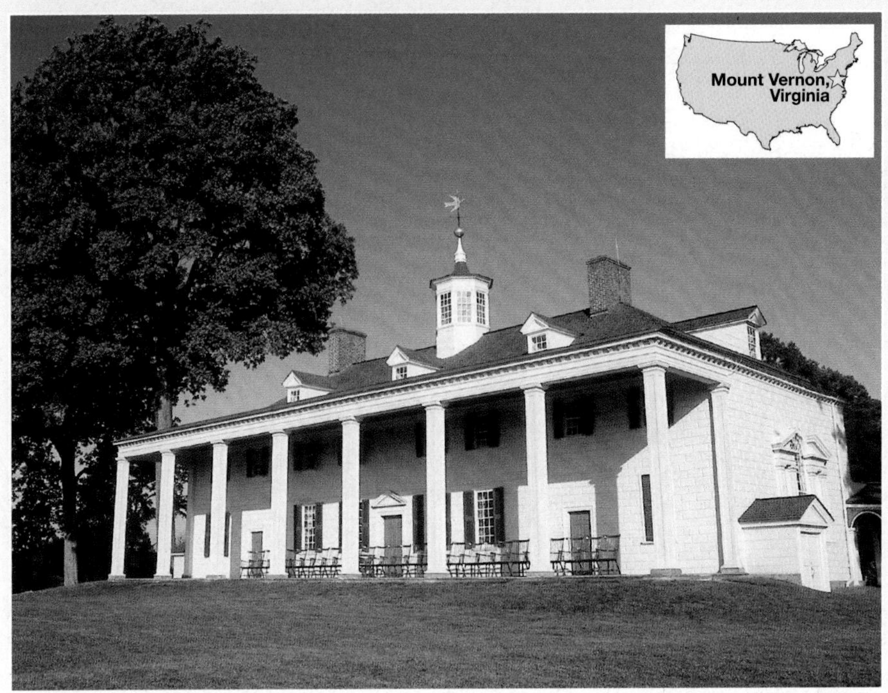

Mount Vernon

Mount Vernon was George Washington's home for more than 45 years. He had a deep affection for the place. "I can truly say I had rather be at home at Mount Vernon with a friend or two about me than to be attended at the seat of the government by the officers of State and the representatives of every power in Europe." Today, more than a million people a year visit the estate.

Virtual Field Trip For an interactive look at Mount Vernon, visit PHSchool.com, **Web Code mfd-0901.**

The First Cabinet The Constitution said little about how the executive branch should be organized. It was clear, however, that the President needed talented people to help him carry out his duties.

In 1789, the first Congress created five executive departments. They were the departments of State, Treasury, and War and the offices of Attorney General and Postmaster General. The heads of these departments made up the President's **Cabinet.** Members of the Cabinet gave Washington advice and were responsible for directing their departments.

Washington set a precedent by choosing well-known leaders to serve in his Cabinet. The two most influential were the Secretary of State, Thomas Jefferson, and the Secretary of the Treasury, Alexander Hamilton.

The Federal Court System The Constitution called for a Supreme Court. Congress, however, had to set up the federal court system. In 1789, Congress passed the **Judiciary Act.** It called for the Supreme Court to consist of one Chief Justice and five Associate Justices.* Washington named John Jay the first Chief Justice of the United States.

The Judiciary Act also set up a system of district courts and circuit courts across the nation. Decisions made in these lower courts could be appealed to the Supreme Court, the highest court in the land.

* Today, the Supreme Court has a Chief Justice and eight Associate Justices.

Money Problems of the New Nation, 1789–1791

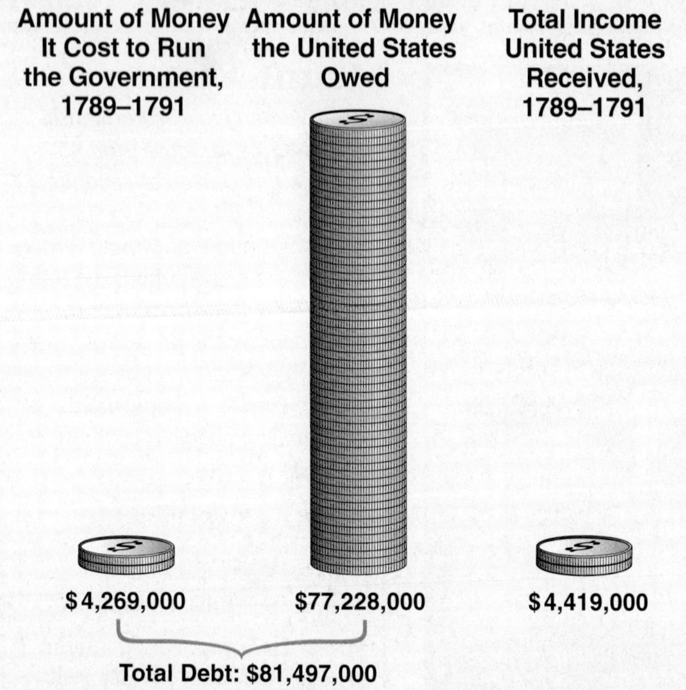

Amount of Money It Cost to Run the Government, 1789–1791	Amount of Money the United States Owed	Total Income United States Received, 1789–1791
$4,269,000	$77,228,000	$4,419,000

Total Debt: $81,497,000

Source: *Historical Statistics of the United States*

NO TAX

DOWN TAX

CHART *Skills*

The U.S. government had far greater expenses than income and desperately needed money. The solution: Congress raised taxes, which led to a rebellion on the frontier (right).

1. **Comprehension**
   (a) What was the government's total income between 1789 and 1791?
   (b) What were its total expenses during that period?
2. **Critical Thinking Applying Information**
   Does the chart provide information suggesting the government should raise or lower taxes? Explain.

Reducing the Nation's Debt

As Secretary of the Treasury, Alexander Hamilton faced many problems. Among the most pressing was the large national debt. The **national debt** is the total amount of money that a government owes to others.

During the Revolution, both the national government and individual states had desperately needed money. They had borrowed heavily from foreign countries and ordinary citizens to pay soldiers and buy supplies. Then, as now, governments borrowed money by issuing bonds. A **bond** is a certificate that promises to repay the money loaned, plus interest, on a certain date. For example, if a person pays $100 for a bond, the government agrees to pay back $100 plus interest by a certain time.

Hamilton's Plan Hamilton called for the government to repay both federal and state debts. He wanted the government to buy up all the bonds issued by both the national and state governments before 1789. He then planned to issue new bonds to pay off the old debts. As the economy improved, the government would then be able to pay off the new bonds. Many people, including bankers and investors, welcomed Hamilton's plan. Others attacked it.

Debating Hamilton's Plan James Madison led the opposition. Madison argued that Hamilton's plan would reward speculators. A **speculator** is someone who invests in a risky venture in the hope of making a large profit.

During the Revolution, the government had issued bonds to soldiers and citizens who supplied goods. Many of these bondholders needed cash to survive. So, they sold their bonds to speculators. Speculators bought bonds worth one dollar for only 10 or 15 cents. If the government paid off the old bonds in full, speculators stood to make fortunes. Madison thought that speculators did not deserve to make such profits.

Hamilton replied that the United States must repay its debts in full. Otherwise, he said, it risked losing the trust of investors in the future. The support of investors, he argued, was crucial to building the new nation's economy. After much debate, Congress approved full repayment of the national debt.

As a southerner, James Madison also led the fight against the other part of Hamilton's plan, the repaying of state debts. By 1789, most southern states had paid off their debts from the Revolution. They thought that other states should do the same. As a result, they bitterly opposed Hamilton's plan.

Identify Supporting Details

Which details in the first two paragraphs on this page describe the debate over Hamilton's plan to reduce the national debt? Add these details to your outline.

Hamilton's Compromise In the end, Hamilton proposed a compromise. Many southerners wanted the nation's capital to be located in the South. Hamilton offered to support that goal if southerners agreed to his plan to repay state debts.

Madison and others accepted the compromise. In July 1790, Congress voted to repay state debts and to build a new capital city. The new capital would not be part of any state. Instead, it would be built on land along the Potomac River between Virginia and Maryland. Congress called the area the District of Columbia. Today, it is known as Washington, D.C. Plans called for the new capital to be ready by 1800. Meanwhile, the nation's capital was moved from New York to Philadelphia.

Geography and History

Building the Nation's New Capital

The location of the nation's new capital was at a crossroads between the North and the South. Pierre L'Enfant, the city's first designer, drew up ambitious plans for the new capital. L'Enfant's assistant, Benjamin Banneker, then helped lay out the wide streets and the mile-long avenue—today's Pennsylvania Avenue. The city was built on tobacco fields, marshes, woodlands, and pastures. For years, residents faced severe problems from mud, insects, and malaria. Even after John Adams moved into the White House in 1800, a nearby creek often flooded Pennsylvania Avenue, and pigs roamed among the half-finished buildings and tree stumps.

What geographic challenges did planners face in building Washington, D.C.?

Plans to Build the Economy

Hamilton's next challenge was to strengthen the faltering national economy. His economic plan was designed to help both agriculture and industry.

Hamilton called on Congress to set up a national bank. In 1791, Congress created the **Bank of the United States.** The government deposited money from taxes in the Bank. In turn, the Bank issued paper money to pay the government's bills and to make loans to farmers and businesses. Through these loans, the Bank encouraged economic growth.

To help American manufacturers, Hamilton asked Congress to pass a **tariff,** or **tax,** on foreign goods brought into the country. He wanted a high tariff, to make imported goods more expensive than American-made goods. A tariff meant to protect local industry from foreign competition is called a protective tariff.

In the North, where there were more and more factories, many people supported Hamilton's plan. Southern farmers, however, bought many imported goods. They opposed a protective tariff that would make imports more expensive.

In the end, Congress did pass a tariff, but it was much lower than the protective tariff Hamilton wanted.

The Whiskey Rebellion

To raise money for the Treasury, Congress approved a tax on all liquor made and sold in the United States. Hamilton wanted this tax to raise money for the Treasury. Instead, the new tax sparked a rebellion that tested the strength of the new government.

A Hated Tax Like many Americans, backcountry farmers grew corn. However, corn was bulky and hard to haul over rough roads. Instead, farmers converted their corn into whiskey. Barrels of whiskey could be shipped more easily to markets in the East.

Backcountry farmers hated the tax on whiskey. Many refused to pay it. They compared it to the taxes Britain had forced on the colonies.

In 1794, when officials in western Pennsylvania tried to collect the tax, farmers rebelled. Thousands marched in protest through the streets of Pittsburgh. They sang Revolutionary songs and tarred and feathered the tax collectors.

A Show of Strength Washington responded quickly. He called up the militia and dispatched them to Pennsylvania. When the rebels heard that thousands of troops were marching against them, they fled back to their farms. Hamilton wanted the leaders of the rebellion executed, but Washington disagreed and pardoned them. He believed that the government had shown its strength to all. Now, it was time to show mercy.

The **Whiskey Rebellion** tested the will of the new government. Washington's quick response proved to Americans that their new government would act firmly in times of crisis. The President also showed those who disagreed with the government that violence would not be tolerated.

★ ★ ★ Section 1 Assessment ★ ★ ★

Recall

1. **Identify** Explain the significance of **(a)** Judiciary Act, **(b)** Bank of the United States, **(c)** Whiskey Rebellion.
2. **Define** **(a)** inauguration, **(b)** precedent, **(c)** Cabinet, **(d)** national debt, **(e)** bond, **(f)** speculator, **(g)** tariff.

Comprehension

3. Describe two steps that George Washington took as President to organize the new government.
4. What were three features of Alexander Hamilton's plan to lower the national debt and strengthen the economy?
5. How did the Whiskey Rebellion reveal George Washington's concern with national security?

Critical Thinking and Writing

6. **Exploring the Main Idea** Review the Main Idea statement at the beginning of this section. Then, write five statements of fact that support the main idea.
7. **Supporting a Point of View** Hamilton and Madison disagreed about paying off bonds issued during the Revolution. Suppose that you had to defend one side. Write a statement explaining which side you support in that debate and why.

ACTIVITY

Go Online
PHSchool.com

Connecting to Today
Use the Internet to find the names of the current Cabinet departments and the person who runs each today. Make a chart listing each department and its head. Then, summarize its main functions. For help in completing the activity, visit PHSchool.com, **Web Code mfd-0902.**

Connecting With... Culture

EARLY AMERICAN *Folk Art*

Early American folk artists were rarely trained in art. They were usually house painters, carpenters, cabinetmakers, blacksmiths, sailors, farmers, and homemakers. They believed that what they were creating would be used, not left to sit in museums.

Whirligigs, or wind toys, were made as outdoor decorations, usually carved of wood. The wind caused the arms of a whirligig, such as those of this swordsman from the 1800s, to turn.

This 1730 painting of a child named Susanna Truax was created by an unknown artist who painted it on a mattress cover.

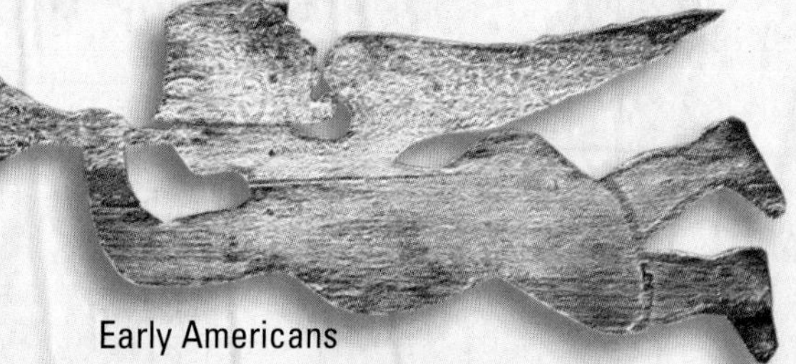

Early Americans used much imagination in creating weather vanes. This "trumpeting angel" weather vane was made of sheet iron around 1800.

Shipping was an important industry in the new nation, and ship carvers created figureheads and other parts of a ship. This figurehead was carved in the early 1800s, probably for a small ship.

ACTIVITY

Design your own piece of folk art. Think of an object that you see or use every day—a storage chest, a pencil sharpener, a tablecloth, or some other object. Then, sketch a design for it that expresses some emotion or patriotic feeling.

2 Creating a Foreign Policy

Prepare to Read

Objectives

In this section, you will
- Describe American opinions of the French Revolution.
- Explain why Washington wanted the nation to remain neutral in foreign affairs.
- Describe why it was difficult for the United States to remain neutral.

Key Terms

French Revolution

foreign policy

neutral

Neutrality Proclamation

Jay's Treaty

Farewell Address

Target Reading Skill

Clarifying Meaning Copy the concept web below. As you read, fill in each blank oval with events and developments that affected President Washington's foreign policy. Add as many ovals as you need.

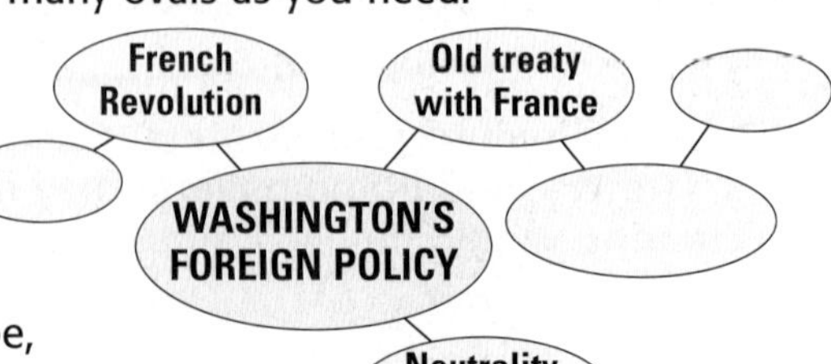

Main Idea As the French Revolution and wars raged in Europe, President Washington steered a neutral course in foreign affairs.

The guillotine: death machine of the French Revolution

Setting the Scene Late in 1789, French ships arrived in American ports with startling news. On July 14, an angry mob in Paris, France, had destroyed the Bastille (bahs TEEL), an ancient fort that was used as a prison. The attack on the Bastille was an early event in the **French Revolution.** Before long, the revolution would topple the monarch and lead to the execution of thousands of ordinary French citizens.

The French Revolution broke out a few years after Americans had won their independence. Like Americans, the French fought for liberty and equality. As the French Revolution grew more violent, however, it deepened political divisions within the United States.

Responses to the French Revolution

The French had many reasons to rebel against their king, Louis XVI. The peasants and the middle class paid heavy taxes, while nobles paid none. Reformers wanted a constitution to limit the king's power and protect basic rights, as the American Constitution did.

American Support At first, most Americans supported the French Revolution. They knew what it meant to struggle for liberty. Then, too, France had been their first ally. Also, many Americans admired the Marquis de Lafayette, a leading French reformer, who had fought with them in the American Revolution.

In 1793, however, the French Revolution turned more and more violent. Radical reformers gained power. They beheaded the king and later the queen. During the Reign of Terror, tens of thousands of ordinary French citizens were executed.

Violence Stirs Division The violence in France divided Americans. Some, like Thomas Jefferson, continued to support the French. He condemned the executions of the king and queen. Still, he felt that the French had the right to use violence to win freedom.

Alexander Hamilton, John Adams, and others strongly disagreed. One could no more create democracy through widespread violence, claimed Adams, "than a snowball can exist in the streets of Philadelphia under a burning sun."

The United States Remains Neutral

The French Revolution frightened most European rulers and nobles. They wanted to prevent revolutionary ideas from spreading to their lands. Europe was soon plunged into a string of wars that lasted on and off for more than 20 years.

A Difficult Decision Faced with war in Europe, President Washington had to decide on a foreign policy. **Foreign policy** refers to the actions that a nation takes in relation to other nations. During the American Revolution, the United States and France had signed a treaty that made the two countries allies. Now, France wanted to use American ports to supply its ships and launch attacks on British ships. Washington worried that the United States could not honor its treaty with France and still remain neutral in the European conflict. **Neutral** means not taking sides in a conflict.

Divisions in the Cabinet The issue of the treaty deepened the divisions within Washington's Cabinet. Hamilton pointed out that the United States had signed the treaty with Louis XVI. With the king dead, he argued, the treaty was no longer valid. Jefferson, a supporter of France, urged strict acceptance of the treaty.

After much debate, Washington issued the **Neutrality Proclamation** in April 1793. It stated that the United States would not support either side in the war. Further, it forbade Americans from aiding either Britain or France.

The Neutrality Proclamation was a defeat for Jefferson. This and other defeats eventually led Jefferson to leave the Cabinet.

Viewing History

On the March

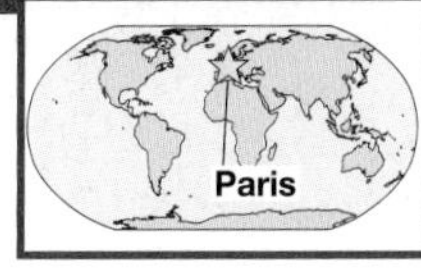

At the start of the French Revolution, famine gripped Paris. Thousands of angry women marched on the palace of the king shouting "Bread, Bread." **Drawing Conclusions** ***Why might women such as these expect Americans to support their revolution?***

Paraphrase Paraphrase the information about Jay's Treaty. Add this information to your concept web.

Struggling to Remain Neutral

Declaring neutrality was easier than enforcing it. Americans wanted to trade with both Britain and France. However, those warring nations seized American cargoes headed for each other's ports.

Jay's Treaty In 1793, the British captured more than 250 American ships trading in the French West Indies. Some Americans called for war. Washington, however, knew that the United States was too weak to fight. He sent Chief Justice John Jay to Britain for talks.

Jay negotiated an agreement that called for Britain to pay damages for the seized American ships. Britain also agreed to give up the forts it still held in the West. Meanwhile, Americans had to pay debts long owed to British merchants.

Jay's Treaty sparked loud protests because it did nothing to protect the rights of neutral American ships. After furious debate, the Senate finally approved the treaty in 1795.

Washington Retires Before retiring in 1796, George Washington published his **Farewell Address.** In it, he advised Americans against becoming involved in European affairs:

> "Tis our true policy to steer clear of permanent Alliances, with any portion of the foreign World. . . . The great rule of conduct for us, in regard to foreign nations is . . . to have with them as little political connection as possible."
>
> —George Washington, Farewell Address, 1796

Washington did not oppose foreign trade, but he did reject alliances that could drag the country into war. His advice guided American foreign policy for many years.

Section 2 Assessment

Recall

1. **Identify** Explain the significance of **(a)** French Revolution, **(b)** Neutrality Proclamation, **(c)** Jay's Treaty, **(d)** Farewell Address.
2. **Define** **(a)** foreign policy, **(b)** neutral.

Comprehension

3. Why did the French Revolution divide Americans?
4. Describe two actions that Washington took to avoid war.
5. What problems did the United States have remaining neutral when France and Britain went to war?

Critical Thinking and Writing

6. **Finding the Main Idea** Review the Main Idea statement at the beginning of this section. Then, list two threats to American neutrality during the 1790s. Explain how Washington responded to each.
7. **Identifying Points of View** Writing about the French Revolution, Thomas Jefferson said that he was willing to see "half the earth devastated" in order to win the "liberty of the whole." **(a)** Restate Jefferson's main idea in your own words. **(b)** What does this idea tell you about Jefferson's values?

Activity

Giving an Introduction
President Washington has decided to give his Farewell Address in your school auditorium. You have been asked to introduce him. Prepare a two-minute introduction, mentioning what you consider to be Washington's greatest achievements.

3 Political Parties Emerge

Prepare to Read

Objectives

In this section, you will
- Explain why many Americans distrusted the idea of political parties.
- Contrast the views of Hamilton and Jefferson.
- Explain why political parties developed.
- Describe how the election of 1796 increased political tensions.

Key Terms

faction
unconstitutional
Democratic Republican
Federalist

Target Reading Skill

Comparison and Contrast Copy the table below. As you read, fill in each column with the views of Hamilton and Jefferson. Add as many rows as you need.

HAMILTON'S VIEWS	JEFFERSON'S VIEWS
• Admired British economy; favored manufacturing, trade, cities	•
•	• Wanted to keep federal government small
•	•

Main Idea During the 1790s, two political parties were formed: the Federalists and the Republicans.

Setting the Scene When George Washington took office in 1789, the United States had no political parties. In fact, most American leaders disliked even the idea of parties. "If I could not go to heaven but with a party," said Thomas Jefferson, "I would not go at all."

Early on, though, political disagreements divided Americans. "Men who have been [friends] all their lives," noted Jefferson, "cross streets to avoid meeting, and turn their heads another way, lest they should be obliged to touch their hats." Before Washington left office in 1797, two rival political parties had emerged to compete for power.

E pluribus unum

A Distrust of Political Parties

Americans had reason to distrust political parties. They had seen how **factions,** or opposing groups within parties, worked in Britain. There, members of factions often plotted to win government favors and bribes. Many were more interested in personal gain than in the public good.

Americans also saw political parties as a threat to national unity. They agreed with George Washington, who warned Americans that parties would lead to "jealousies and false alarms."

Despite the President's warning, factions grew up around two members of his Cabinet, Alexander Hamilton and Thomas Jefferson. The two men differed in background, looks, and personality as well as in politics. Born in the West Indies, Hamilton had worked his way up from poverty. He dressed in fine clothes and spoke forcefully. Energetic, brilliant, and restless, Hamilton enjoyed political debate.

Jefferson was tall and lanky. Although he was a wealthy Virginia planter, he dressed and spoke informally. One senator recalled:

> “His clothes seem too small for him. He sits in a lounging manner, on one hip commonly, and with one of his shoulders elevated much above the other. His face has a sunny aspect. His whole figure has a loose, shackling air. . . . [His conversation] was loose and rambling; and yet he scattered information wherever he went.”
>
> —*The Diary of William Maclay and Other Notes on Senate Debates*

An American Profile

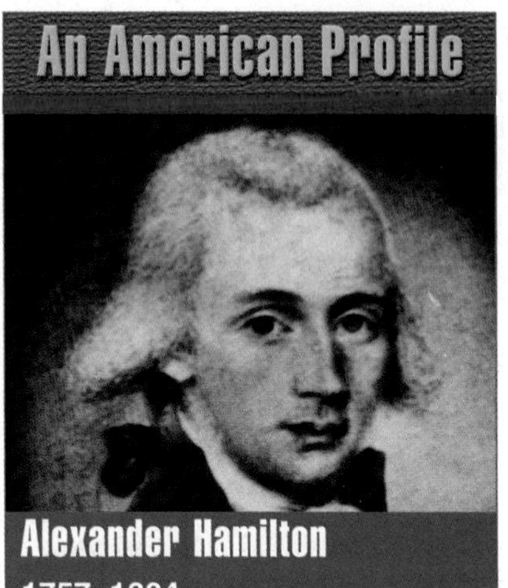

Alexander Hamilton
1757–1804

When Alexander Hamilton was about eight years old, his father abandoned his family. A few years later, Alexander's mother died. Despite these early losses, the boy worked hard to succeed. He studied his mother's books. At the age of 11, Alexander became an apprentice to a local merchant. He quickly rose to become manager. Impressed by his talents, his employer paid for Alexander to be educated in New York. There the 19-year-old college student wrote three pamphlets supporting the Patriot cause. Readers were startled to learn that the author was such a young man.

How might Hamilton's early life have helped prepare him for government service?

Differing Views

Hamilton and Jefferson disagreed on many issues. Their quarrels were rooted in their different views about what was best for the new nation.

Manufacturing or Farming The two leaders differed on economic policy. Hamilton wanted the United States to model itself on Britain. The government, he thought, should encourage manufacturing and trade. He also favored the growth of cities and the merchant class.

Jefferson thought that farmers, rather than merchants, were the backbone of the new nation. “Cultivators of the earth,” he wrote, “are the most valuable citizens.” He feared that a manufacturing economy would corrupt the United States by concentrating power in the hands of a small group of wealthy Americans.

Federal or State Power Hamilton and Jefferson also disagreed about the power of the federal government. Hamilton wanted the federal government to have greater power than state governments. A strong federal government, he argued, was needed to increase commerce. It would also be able to restrain mob violence like that of the Whiskey Rebellion.

In contrast, Jefferson wanted as small a federal government as possible, in order to protect individual freedom. He feared that a strong federal government might take over powers that the Constitution gave to the states.

Strict or Loose Interpretation of the Constitution Jefferson and Hamilton also clashed over the Bank of the United States. Jefferson worried that a national bank would give too much power to wealthy investors who would help run it and to the government.

Jefferson opposed the law setting up the bank. He claimed that it was **unconstitutional,** or not permitted by the Constitution. Nowhere did the Constitution give Congress the power to create a Bank, he argued. For Jefferson, any power not specifically given to the federal government belonged to the states.

Hamilton did not agree with Jefferson's strict interpretation of the Constitution. He preferred a looser interpretation. The Constitution gave Congress the power to make all laws “necessary and proper” to carry out its duties. Hamilton argued that the Bank was necessary for the government to collect taxes and pay its bills.

Federalists vs. Republicans

FEDERALISTS		REPUBLICANS
1 Were led by Alexander Hamilton		1 Were led by Thomas Jefferson
2 Believed wealthy and well educated should lead nation		2 Believed people should have political power
3 Favored strong central government		3 Favored strong state governments
4 Emphasized manufacturing, shipping, and trade	VS.	4 Emphasized agriculture
5 Favored loose interpretation of Constitution		5 Favored strict interpretation of Constitution
6 Were pro-British		6 Were pro-French
7 Favored national bank		7 Opposed national bank
8 Favored protective tariff		8 Opposed protective tariff

GRAPHIC ORGANIZER *Skills*

By the late 1790s, there were two political parties in the United States: the Federalist party and the Republican party.

1. **Comprehension** Describe two ways in which the Republicans and the Federalists differed on economic issues.
2. **Critical Thinking Analyzing Primary Sources** "The average person is far too ignorant to make wise political decisions." Do you think a Republican or a Federalist would be more likely to agree with this statement? Explain your answer.

Britain or France Finally, the two leaders disagreed over foreign policy. Hamilton wanted close ties with Britain, a major trading partner. Jefferson favored France, the first ally of the United States.

Development of Political Parties

At first, Hamilton and Jefferson clashed in private. Then, as Congress began to pass many of Hamilton's programs, Jefferson and James Madison decided to organize supporters of their views.

The two men moved cautiously at first. In 1791, they went to New York, telling people that they wanted to study its wildlife. In fact, Jefferson was interested in nature. Their main goal, though, was to meet with leading New York politicians like Governor George Clinton and Aaron Burr, a fierce critic of Hamilton. Jefferson asked them to help defeat Hamilton's program by convincing New Yorkers to vote for Jefferson's supporters.

Republicans and Federalists Soon, leaders in other states were organizing to support either Hamilton or Jefferson. Jefferson's supporters called themselves **Democratic Republicans,** often shortened to Republicans.* This group included small farmers, artisans, and some wealthy planters.

Hamilton and his supporters were called **Federalists** because they wanted a strong federal government. Federalists drew support mainly from merchants and manufacturers in such cities as Boston and New York. They also had the backing of some southern planters.

Newspapers Take Sides In the late 1700s, the number of American newspapers more than doubled. This growth met a

Identify Contrasts As you read, check to see if you understand the major differences between the Republicans and the Federalists.

*Jefferson's Republican party was not the same as today's Republican party. In fact, his party later grew into the Democratic party.

Primary Source

A Newspaper Attack

Philip Freneau's Republican newspaper, the National Gazette, *launched bitter attacks on Hamilton's economic policies—such as this anonymous letter:*

"It is a Fact that money set aside to the sinking of the debt has been laid out, not so as most to sink the debt, but so as to help gamblers in the funds.

It is a Fact that a Bank law has given a reward of from four to five million dollars to men in great part of the same description.

It is a Fact that a share of this bounty went immediately into the pockets of the very men most active and forward in granting it."

—Letter to Philip Freneau, Editor, *National Gazette,* October 20, 1792

Analyzing Primary Sources

In your own words, describe the "facts" that the writer cites. Based on your reading of the chapter, are the "facts" true, false, or exaggerated?

demand for information. A European visitor was surprised that so many Americans could read. "The common people . . . all read and write, and understand arithmetic," he reported, and "almost every little town now furnishes a circulating library."

As party rivalry grew, newspapers took sides. In the *Gazette of the United States,* publisher John Fenno backed Hamilton and the Federalists. Jefferson's friend Philip Freneau (frih NOH) started a rival paper, the *National Gazette,* which supported Republicans.

Newspapers had great influence on public opinion. In stinging language, they raged against political opponents. Often, articles mixed rumor and opinion with facts. Emotional attacks and counterattacks fanned the flames of party rivalry.

Election of 1796

Political parties played a large role in the election of George Washington's successor. In 1796, Republicans backed Thomas Jefferson for President and Aaron Burr for Vice President. Federalists supported John Adams for President and Thomas Pinckney for Vice President.

The election had an unexpected outcome. Under the Constitution, the person with the most electoral votes became President. The candidate with the next highest total was made Vice President. John Adams, a Federalist, won office as President. The leader of the Republicans, Thomas Jefferson, came in second and became Vice President.

Having the President and Vice President from opposing parties further increased political tensions. John Adams took office in March 1797 as the nation's second President. Events soon deepened the distrust between him and Jefferson.

★ ★ ★ Section 3 Assessment ★ ★ ★

Recall

1. **Identify** Explain the significance of **(a)** Democratic Republican, **(b)** Federalist.
2. **Define (a)** faction, **(b)** unconstitutional.

Comprehension

3. What reasons did Americans have to distrust political parties?
4. List two issues on which Thomas Jefferson and Alexander Hamilton disagreed and describe their points of view.
5. Explain why political parties emerged in the 1790s.
6. What role did political parties play in the election of 1796?

Critical Thinking and Writing

7. **Exploring the Main Idea** Review the Main Idea statement at the beginning of this section. Then, write a letter to the editor supporting either the Republicans or the Federalists in the election of 1796.
8. **Supporting a Point of View** Whose political ideas do you favor, Jefferson's or Hamilton's? Explain your answer.

Activity

Writing Newspaper Headlines You are the publisher of either the *Gazette of the United States* or the *National Gazette.* Write three headlines about the election of 1796. Be sure that your headlines express the point of view of your newspaper.

4 The Second President

Prepare to Read

Objectives

In this section, you will
- Summarize how John Adams handled the conflict with France.
- Explain why the Federalist party split.
- Describe how the Alien and Sedition acts raised the issue of the rights of states.
- Identify the role Congress played in the election of 1800.

Key Terms

XYZ Affair
frigate
Alien and Sedition acts
sedition
nullify
Kentucky and Virginia resolutions
states' rights

Target Reading Skill

Sequence As you read, complete this table describing the major events of John Adams's presidency. Add as many rows as needed to complete the table.

CONFLICT WITH FRANCE	ALIEN AND SEDITION ACTS	ELECTION OF 1800
• French seize U.S. ships	•	•

Main Idea As President, John Adams pursued policies that made the Federalists increasingly unpopular.

Setting the Scene John Adams was very different from George Washington. Washington was tall and dignified. Adams was short and a bit pudgy. Washington spoke little and chose his words carefully. Adams was outspoken. He said what he believed, and he held strong beliefs. Jefferson recalled how Adams sometimes became so angry during an argument that he ended up "dashing and trampling his wig on the floor."

Despite his temper, Adams was an honest and able leader. As President, he tried to act in the best interests of the nation, even when he knew his actions could hurt him politically. More than once, Adams stood up to public opinion or the leaders of his party.

Adams as President

Conflict With France

No sooner had Adams taken office than he faced a crisis with France. The French objected to Jay's Treaty because they felt that it favored Britain. In 1797, French ships began to seize American ships in the West Indies, as the British had done.

Once again, Americans called for war, this time against France. To avoid war, Adams sent diplomats to Paris to discuss the rights of neutral nations.

The French foreign minister, Charles Maurice de Talleyrand, did not deal directly with the Americans. Instead, he sent three agents to offer the Americans a deal. Before Talleyrand would even begin talks, the agents said, he wanted $250,000 for himself and a $10 million loan to France. "Not a sixpence!" replied one of the Americans angrily.

The diplomats informed Adams about the offer. He then told Congress. Adams did not reveal the names of the French agents, referring to them only as X, Y, and Z.

POLITICAL CARTOON *Skills*

The XYZ Affair
The French demand for tribute outraged Americans. In the cartoon, a five-headed monster demands a bribe from three Americans. They respond: "Cease bawling, Monster. We will not give you sixpence!"

1. **Comprehension** **(a)** Who does the monster represent? **(b)** Who are the three people at left?
2. **Understanding Main Ideas** How does the cartoonist show that the XYZ Affair stirred strong feelings?
3. **Critical Thinking Identifying Points of View** What details in the cartoon show the cartoonist's dislike of the French Revolution?

Many Americans were outraged when they heard about the **XYZ Affair** in 1798. They took up the slogan, "Millions for defense, but not one cent for tribute!" They were willing to spend money to defend their country, but they would not pay a bribe to another nation.

The XYZ Affair ignited war fever in the United States. Despite strong pressure, Adams refused to ask Congress to declare war on France. Like Washington, he wanted to keep the country out of European affairs. However, he could not ignore French attacks on American ships, so he strengthened the navy by building **frigates,** fast-sailing ships with many guns. That move helped convince France to stop attacking American ships.

The Federalist Party Splits

Led by Hamilton, many Federalists criticized Adams. They hoped a war would weaken the Republicans, who supported France. War would also force the nation to build its military forces. A strong military would increase federal power, a key Federalist goal.

Although Adams was a Federalist, he resisted Hamilton's pressure for war. Their disagreement created a split in the Federalist party.

Over Hamilton's opposition, Adams again sent diplomats to France. When they arrived, they found an ambitious young army officer, Napoleon Bonaparte, in charge. Napoleon was planning for war against several European powers. Thus, he had no time for a war with the United States. He signed an agreement to stop seizing American ships.

Like Washington, Adams kept the nation out of war. His success, however, cost him the support of many Federalists and weakened the party for the election of 1800.

Alien and Sedition Acts

In 1798, during the crisis with France, Federalists pushed several laws through Congress. These laws were known as the **Alien and Sedition acts.**

Under the Alien Act, the President could expel any alien, or foreigner, thought to be dangerous to the country. Another law made it harder for immigrants to become citizens. Before 1798, white immigrants could become citizens after living in the United States for five years. The new law made immigrants wait 14 years. The Federalists passed this act because many recent immigrants supported Jefferson and the Republicans. The act would keep these immigrants from voting for years.

Republicans grew even angrier when Congress passed the Sedition Act. **Sedition** means stirring up rebellion against a government. Under this law, citizens could be fined or jailed if they criticized the government or its officials. In fact, several Republican newspaper editors, and even members of Congress, were fined and jailed for expressing their opinions.

Republicans protested that the Sedition Act violated the Constitution. The First Amendment, they argued, protected freedom of speech and of the press. Jefferson warned that the new laws threatened American liberties:

> "They have brought into the lower house a sedition bill, which . . . undertakes to make printing certain matters criminal . . . Indeed this bill & the alien bill both are so [against] the Constitution as to show they mean to pay no respect to it."
>
> —*The Writings of Thomas Jefferson,* 1798

Target Skill: Identify Sequence What events resulted from the Alien and Sedition acts? Add this information to your chart.

The Rights of States

Vice President Jefferson bitterly opposed the Alien and Sedition acts. He could not ask the courts for help because the Federalists controlled them. So, he urged the states to take strong action against the acts. He argued that the states had the right to **nullify,** or cancel, a law passed by the federal government. In this way, states could resist the power of the federal government.

With help from Jefferson and Madison, Kentucky and Virginia passed resolutions in 1798 and 1799. The **Kentucky and Virginia resolutions** claimed that each state "has an equal right to judge for itself" whether a law is constitutional. If a state decides a law is unconstitutional, said the resolutions, it has the power to nullify that law within its borders.

The Kentucky and Virginia resolutions raised the issue of **states' rights.** Did the federal government have only those powers that were listed in the Constitution? If so, the states possessed all other powers—for example, the power to declare a federal law unconstitutional? Within a few years, the Alien and Sedition acts were changed or dropped. Still, the issue of a state's right to nullify federal laws would come up again.

Primary Source

The Virginia Resolution

The Virginia Resolution was a protest against the Alien and Sedition acts passed by Congress: "[Virginia protests] against the . . . alarming infractions of the Constitution, . . . the first of which exercises a power no where delegated to the federal government, . . . and the other of which acts, exercises in like manner, a power which . . . [violates] that right of freely examining public characters and measures, and of free communication among the people . . . which has ever been justly deemed, the only [effective] guardian of every other right."

Analyzing Primary Sources

What right is "the only [effective] guardian of every other right"?

Election of 1800

By 1800, the war cry against France was fading. As the election neared, Republicans focused on two issues. First, they attacked the Federalists for raising taxes to prepare for war. Second, they opposed the unpopular Alien and Sedition acts.

Republicans backed Thomas Jefferson for President and Aaron Burr for Vice President. Despite the bitter split in the Federalist party, John Adams was again named its candidate.

Deadlock In the race for the presidency, Republicans won the popular vote. However, when the electoral college voted, Jefferson and Burr each received 73 votes. At the time, the electoral college did not vote separately for President and Vice President. Each Republican elector cast one vote for Jefferson and one vote for Burr.

Under the Constitution, if no candidate wins the electoral vote, the House of Representatives decides the election. Only after four days and 36 votes was the tie finally broken. The House chose Jefferson as President. Burr became Vice President.

Soon after, Congress passed the Twelfth Amendment. It required electors to vote separately for President and Vice President. The states ratified the amendment in 1804.

The election of 1800 set an important precedent. From then until today, power has passed peacefully from one party to another.

The Federalist Era Ends After 1800, the Federalist party slowly declined. Federalists won fewer seats in Congress. In 1804, the party was greatly weakened after its leader, Alexander Hamilton, was killed in a duel with Aaron Burr. Despite its early decline, the Federalist party did help shape the new nation. Even Republican Presidents kept most of Hamilton's economic programs.

Section 4 Assessment

Recall

1. **Identify** Explain the significance of **(a)** XYZ Affair, **(b)** Alien and Sedition acts, **(c)** Kentucky and Virginia resolutions.
2. **Define** **(a)** frigate, **(b)** sedition, **(c)** nullify, **(d)** states' rights.

Comprehension

3. How did President Adams deal with the French seizure of American ships?
4. Why did Adams lose the support of many Federalists?
5. Why did Thomas Jefferson and the Republicans oppose the Alien and Sedition acts?
6. Why did Congress have to settle the election of 1800?

Critical Thinking and Writing

7. **Finding the Main Idea** Review the Main Idea statement at the beginning of this section. Then, write a paragraph explaining why the Federalists lost popular support during Adams's presidency.
8. **Applying Information** How did the Kentucky and Virginia resolutions reflect Jefferson's view of government?

Activity

Creating a Timeline

Use the Internet to discover the many ways in which John Adams served his country. Use the information you find to make a timeline of Adams's life. For help in completing the activity, visit PHSchool.com, **Web Code mfd-0903.**

Drawing Inferences

As you study history, you are constantly interpreting what you read. Sometimes, you make *inferences.* This involves adding what you already know to ideas that are implied but not directly stated in the text. By making inferences, you can more fully understand what you read and can analyze different points of view.

Read this passage comparing John Adams with George Washington:

George Washington and John Adams were a study in contrasts. Washington was tall and dignified, and because he was a general, his officers addressed him as "Excellency." Adams was short and a bit pudgy. His rivals referred to him as "His Rotundity."

Washington spoke little and chose his words carefully, but John Adams could never do the same. He said what he believed, and he held strong beliefs. At times, his anger led him to trample his wig on the floor. Still, Adams was an honest and able leader who always tried to act in the nation's best interests.

Learn the Skill *To make inferences, use the following steps:*

1. **Identify main ideas.** What is the main point being made in the passage?
2. **Note stated facts and opinions.** What information is directly stated?
3. **Identify unstated ideas.** What ideas or information are suggested but not directly stated in the passage?
4. **Add what you know.** What details can you fill in from your own knowledge or experience to make inferences about the text?
5. **Identify the point of view.** Based on the inferences you made, what does the writer or speaker feel or believe about this topic?

Practice the Skill *Answer the following questions about the passage above:*

1. **(a)** How did his officers address Washington? **(b)** What did the rivals of Adams call him?
2. **(a)** Find a sentence that directly states a fact. **(b)** Find a sentence that directly states an opinion.
3. What does the passage suggest about how Adams was viewed by others?
4. How could always speaking one's mind create problems for a President?
5. What does the writer infer about Adams's leadership qualities?

Apply the Skill *See the Chapter Review and Assessment.*

CHAPTER 9

Review and Assessment

Chapter Summary

Section 1
George Washington was America's first President. He faced many challenges, including how to organize the new government and build a strong economy.

Section 2
As the French Revolution and wars raged in Europe, President Washington steered a neutral course in foreign affairs. In his Farewell Address, Washington advised Americans to remain neutral.

Section 3
During the 1790s, two political parties were formed: the Federalists and the Republicans. Alexander Hamilton led the Federalists. Thomas Jefferson led the Republicans.

Section 4
As President, John Adams pursued policies that made the Federalists increasingly unpopular. Some of Adams's decisions split the Federalist party. In 1800, Thomas Jefferson was elected President.

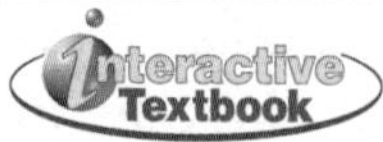

For additional review and enrichment activities, see the interactive version of *The American Nation,* available on the Web and on CD-ROM.

Chapter Self-Test For practice test questions for Chapter 9, visit PHSchool.com, **Web Code mfa-0904.**

Building Vocabulary

Use the chapter vocabulary words listed below to create a crossword puzzle. Exchange puzzles with a classmate. Complete the puzzles, and then check each other's answers.

1. **inauguration**
2. **precedent**
3. **bond**
4. **tariff**
5. **foreign policy**
6. **faction**
7. **unconstitutional**
8. **frigate**
9. **sedition**
10. **nullify**

Reviewing Key Facts

11. Describe how the Judiciary Act provided the framework for the nation's court system. (Section 1)
12. What advice did George Washington give in his Farewell Address? (Section 2)
13. Name three differences between the Federalists and the Republicans. (Section 3)
14. How was the Sedition Act used to silence Republicans? (Section 4)

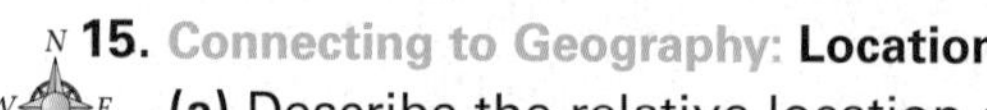

Critical Thinking and Writing

15. Connecting to Geography: **Location** (a) Describe the relative location of the United States in regard to Europe. (b) How did location help the United States "steer clear of permanent alliances" with European nations for many years? (c) How did location make the possession of a strong navy important to the United States?
16. **Summarizing** Summarize arguments for and against protective tariffs and a national banking system.
17. **Ranking** (a) List the disagreements that divided Jefferson and Hamilton. (b) In your opinion, which of these disagreements was the most serious? Explain.
18. **Analyzing Information** Write a paragraph explaining how the Twelfth Amendment helped prevent deadlocks like the one that took place in the election of 1800.

Skills Assessment
Analyzing Primary Sources

George Washington was the focus of attention when he arrived in New York in 1789 for his first inauguration.

19. In the painting, you can identify George Washington
- **A.** in the bow of the boat, tipping his hat.
- **B.** as the first person rowing the boat.
- **C.** on shore waiting to greet the boat.
- **D.** nearest the shelter on the boat.

20. The mood of the painting can be described as
- **A.** somber.
- **B.** joyful.
- **C.** angry.
- **D.** unpatriotic.

Applying Your Skills
Drawing Inferences

Read this passage from your textbook, and then answer the questions below:

> When George Washington took office in 1789, the United States had no political parties. . . . Early on, though, political disagreements divided Americans. "Men who have been [friends] all their lives," noted Jefferson, "cross streets to avoid meeting, and turn their heads another way, lest they should be obliged to touch their hats." Before Washington left office in 1797, two rival political parties had emerged. . . .

21. The author does not say why the men avoid meeting, but a reader can infer that
- **A.** the men have quarreled over finances.
- **B.** religion is starting to divide the nation.
- **C.** old wounds from the American Revolution are still open.
- **D.** the men support different political parties.

22. If the men were forced to meet, what do you think they would talk about? Explain your reasoning.

Activities

Connecting With . . .
Government and Citizenship

Creating a Line Graph The chart below shows the change in the number of people serving in the navy. **(a)** Use the data to describe what happened to the United States Navy between 1798 and 1801. **(b)** Use the figures below to create a line graph.

YEAR	NUMBER OF PEOPLE
1798	1,856
1799	2,200
1800	5,400
1801	2,700

Source: *Historical Statistics of the United States*

Connecting to Today

Making a Database Use the Internet to find information about the Federal Reserve Bank. Then, make a database that includes the main functions of the Federal Reserve Bank and the location of the 12 regional reserve banks. For help in starting this activity, visit PHSchool.com, **Web Code mfd-0905.**

The Patriots

Sidney Kingsley

Introduction **Sidney Kingsley was a leading American playwright of the first part of the twentieth century. Many of his plays dealt with serious social issues. His 1943 play, *The Patriots,* focuses on major problems facing the nation's first leaders. In this scene, Jefferson has just told Hamilton that he has accepted the position of secretary of state in President Washington's Cabinet.**

Vocabulary Before you read the selection, find the meanings of these words in a dictionary: **in concert, chaos, galling, promissory, secede.**

Sidney Kingsley (1906–1995)

HAMILTON: My congratulations. We must work in concert.

JEFFERSON: I'm such a stranger here, I shall lean on you.

HAMILTON: No, I'm afraid—it's—I who need your help. [*Suddenly agitated, emotional*] Mr. Jefferson, it's enough to make any man who loves America want to cry. Forgive me! I really shouldn't burden you with this. It's a matter of my own department.

JEFFERSON: If I can be of any assistance . . . ?

HAMILTON: It's often been remarked that it's given to this country here to prove once and for all whether men can govern themselves by reason, or whether they must forever rely on the accident of tyranny. An interesting thought, Mr. Jefferson.

JEFFERSON: God, yes. We live in an era perhaps the most important in all history.

HAMILTON: An interesting thought! An awful thought! For if it is true, then we dare not fail.

JEFFERSON: No.

HAMILTON: But we are failing. The machinery is already breaking down. [*He snaps his fingers.*] We haven't that much foreign credit. The paper money issued by States is worthless. We are in financial chaos. [*He paces to and fro.*] The galling part is I have a remedy at hand. The solution is so simple. A nation's credit, like a merchant's, depends on paying its promissory notes in full. I propose to pay a hundred cents on the dollar for all the paper money issued by the States. Our credit would be restored instantaneously.

JEFFERSON: [*Worried*] Mr. Madison spoke to me very briefly of your bill last night. It seems there's been some speculation in this paper, and he fears . . .

HAMILTON: Madison! I loved that man. I thought so high of that man. I swear I wouldn't have taken this office—except I counted on his support. And now, he's turned against me.

JEFFERSON: Mr. Madison has a good opinion of your talents. But this speculation . . .

HAMILTON: I don't want his good opinion. I want his support. Will you use your influence?

JEFFERSON: You understand I've been away six years. I've gotten out of touch here. I'll need time to study the facts.

HAMILTON: There is no time.

JEFFERSON: Well, three or four weeks.

HAMILTON: Three or four . . . ? For God's sake, man, can't you understand what I'm trying to tell you? The North is about to secede!

JEFFERSON: Secede?

HAMILTON: Hasn't the President told you?

JEFFERSON: No.

HAMILTON: Unless my bill is passed there is every prospect the Union will dissolve.

JEFFERSON: I'm aware there's a great deal of tension here, but . . .

HAMILTON: Walk in on a session of Congress tomorrow.

JEFFERSON: I see evils on both sides. [*A long pause*] However, it seems to me—if the Union is at stake—reasonable men sitting about a table discussing this coolly should arrive at some compromise. [*He comes to a sudden decision.*] Have dinner with me tomorrow night.

HAMILTON: Delighted.

JEFFERSON: I'll invite a friend or two.

HAMILTON: Mr. Madison?

JEFFERSON: I can't promise anything. He's bitterly opposed to your plan.

HAMILTON: I have a way to sweeten the pill. The cost of living in New York has become so unreasonable there's talk of moving the capital.

JEFFERSON: Yes.

HAMILTON: It's already been promised temporarily to Philadelphia. Give me my bill and I can promise Madison the nation's capital will go to the South. Permanently. I was born in the West Indies—I have no local preference. However, for the sake of the Great Man, I'd like to see it go to Virginia.

JEFFERSON: [*Pause*] Well, I'll bring you together, and sit at the table to see you don't shoot each other.

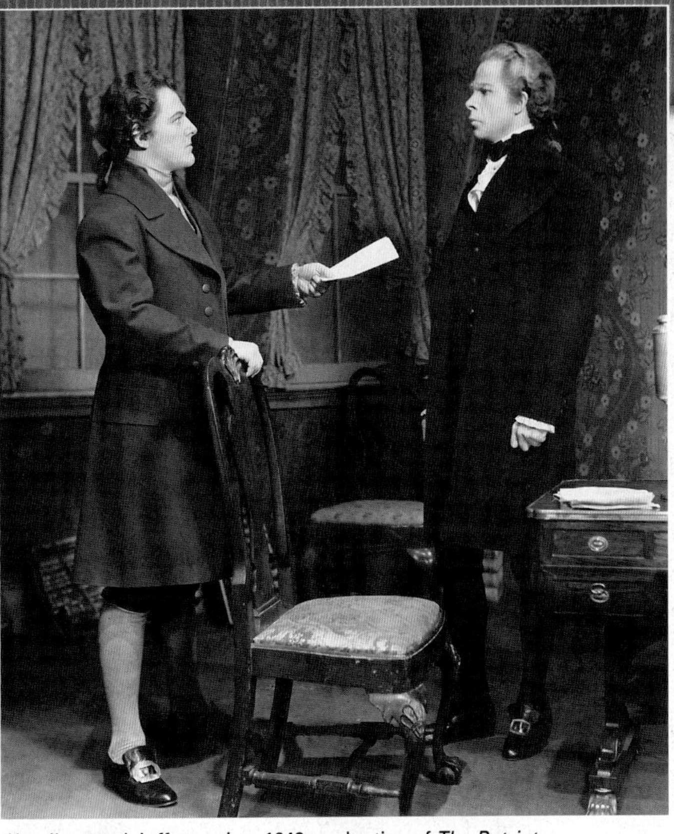

Hamilton and Jefferson in a 1943 production of *The Patriots*

HAMILTON: [*Laughs*] Fair enough.

JEFFERSON [*Takes out his fan-shaped notebook, jots down the appointment*] You see, Colonel Hamilton, we must never permit ourselves to despair of the republic.

HAMILTON: My dear Jefferson, if I haven't despaired of this republic till now, it's because of my nature, not my judgment. [JEFFERSON *laughs.*]

Analyzing Literature

1. When Hamilton asks whether men "must forever rely on the accident of tyranny," he is referring to

A breaking the traditions of the Roman Republic

B relying on rule by a hereditary monarch

C relying on accidents and assassination to replace unpopular government leaders

D a new emphasis on frontier democracy

2. When Hamilton says "for the sake of the Great Man," he is referring to

A George Washington

B King George III

C Thomas Jefferson

D James Madison

3. **Critical Thinking and Writing** **Making Predictions** **(a)** Based on your reading of Chapter 9, what do you think will happen to the proposal to build the new nation's capital? **(b)** What do you think will happen to the working relationship between Hamilton and Jefferson?

CHAPTER 10

The Age of Jefferson

1801–1816

Thomas Jefferson

Lewis and Clark with Native American translator Sacagawea

AMERICAN EVENTS

1801 Thomas Jefferson becomes President. Jefferson seeks to reduce the power of the federal government.

1803 The United States purchases Louisiana from France. The next year, Jefferson sends Lewis and Clark to explore the Louisiana Purchase.

1807 The Embargo Act halts American overseas trade.

Presidential Terms: Thomas Jefferson 1801–1809

1800 · 1804 · 1808

WORLD EVENTS

1804 ▲ Haiti declares independence from France.

▲ **1805** British and French navies clash at the Battle of Trafalgar.

The Louisiana Purchase, 1803

President Thomas Jefferson bought the territory of Louisiana from France, doubling the size of the United States.

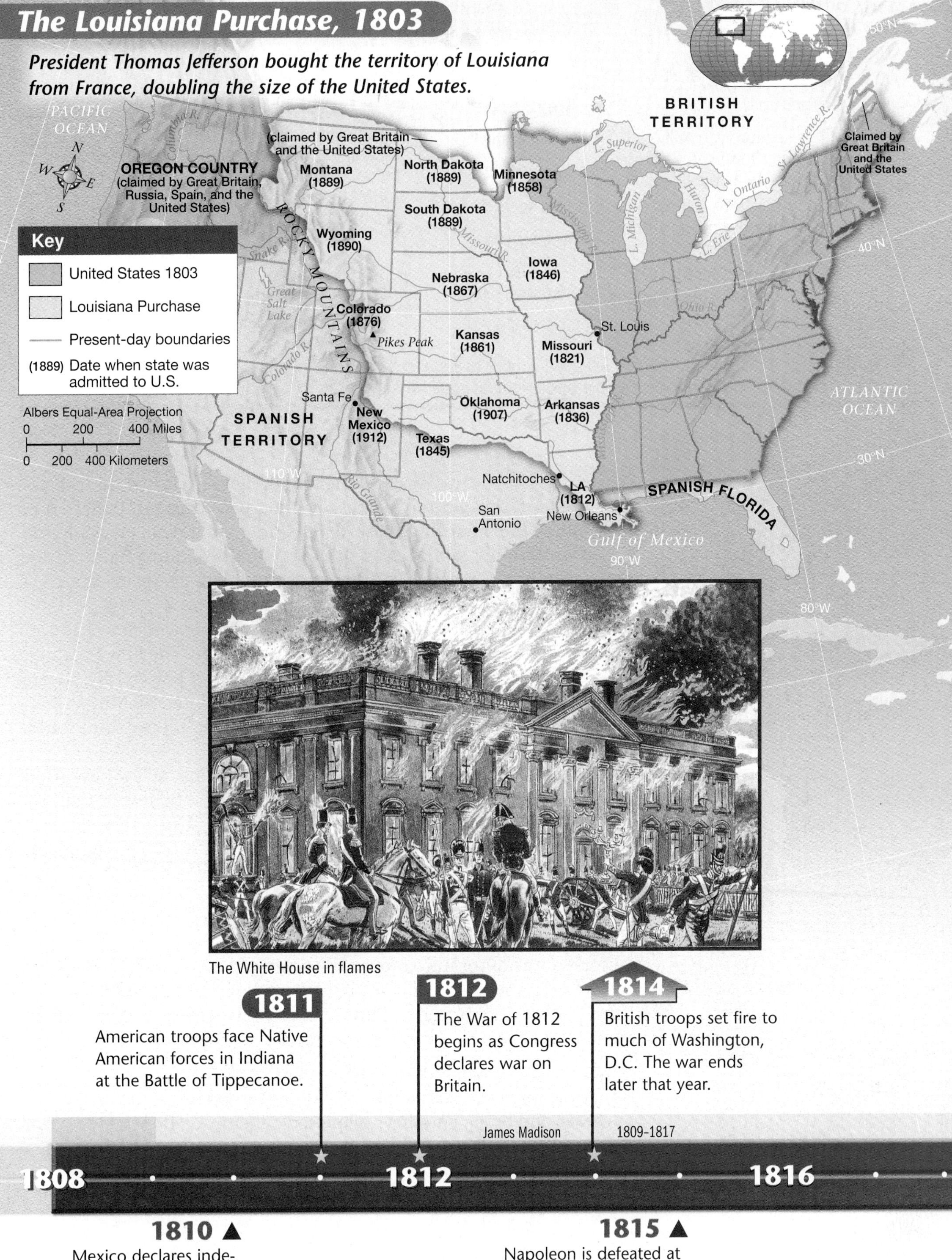

The White House in flames

1811
American troops face Native American forces in Indiana at the Battle of Tippecanoe.

1812
The War of 1812 begins as Congress declares war on Britain.

1814
British troops set fire to much of Washington, D.C. The war ends later that year.

James Madison 1809-1817

1808 1812 1816

1810
Mexico declares independence from Spain.

1815
Napoleon is defeated at the Battle of Waterloo.

1 A Republican Takes Office

Prepare to Read

Objectives

In this section, you will
- Describe Jefferson's democratic style as president.
- List the actions Jefferson took to reduce the power of the federal government.
- Explain how Chief Justice John Marshall strengthened the Supreme Court.

Key Terms

democratic

laissez faire

free market

Marbury v. *Madison*

judicial review

Target Reading Skill

Comparison and Contrast Copy this incomplete Venn diagram. As you read, fill in key facts about Thomas Jefferson and John Marshall. Write common characteristics in the overlapping section.

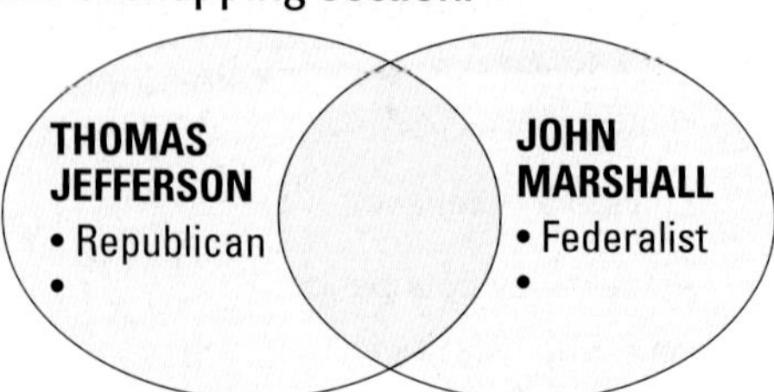

Main Idea As President, Thomas Jefferson sought to set a democratic tone and to reduce the role of the federal government.

Banner celebrating Jefferson's inauguration

Setting the Scene The morning Thomas Jefferson became President of the United States, he ate breakfast at Conrad and McMunn's, the boardinghouse where he was staying. Washington, D.C., the nation's capital, was so new that the Capitol Building was still unfinished. Even so, Congress assembled there on March 4, 1801, to witness Jefferson's inauguration.

Jefferson wanted his inauguration to be simple, not showy. Rather than riding in a carriage to the Capitol, he walked. The new President gave a speech at the ceremony, but in a voice so low, hardly anyone could hear him. Then, he walked back to Conrad and McMunn's for a quiet dinner. When he entered, only one of his fellow diners even bothered to stand and offer Jefferson a chair.

Jefferson deliberately made his inauguration a low-key affair. Although he came from a wealthy family, he believed that the nation's strength came from ordinary people, such as farmers. As President, he rejected most Federalist ideas and turned the nation in a new direction.

Jefferson's Democratic Style

Jefferson was determined to make the government more democratic. **Democratic** means ensuring that all people have the same rights. Years before, in a letter to James Madison, he stressed that each citizen should play a part in a democracy:

> "Educate and inform the whole mass of the people. Enable them to see that it is their interest to preserve peace and order, and they will preserve them. . . . They are the only [ones to rely on] for the preservation of our liberty."
>
> —Thomas Jefferson, letter to James Madison, 1787

Jefferson's personal style matched his democratic beliefs. The new President preferred quiet dinners to the formal parties that George Washington and John Adams had given. He wore casual clothes and greeted people by shaking hands instead of bowing. With his informal manner, Jefferson showed that the President was an ordinary citizen.

Some Federalists were worried about Jefferson's democratic beliefs. They knew that he supported the French Revolution and they feared that he might bring revolutionary change to the United States. They were also afraid that he might punish Federalists who had used the Alien and Sedition acts to jail Republicans.

In his inaugural address, Jefferson tried to calm Federalists' fears. He promised that, although the Republicans were in the majority, he would not treat the Federalists harshly. "The minority possess their equal rights, which equal laws must protect," he told the nation. He called for an end to the political disputes of the past few years. "We are all Republicans, we are all Federalists," the President concluded.

A Smaller Role for the Federal Government

Jefferson had no plan to punish Federalists. He did, however, want to change their policies. In his view, the Federalists had made the national government too large and too powerful.

New Economic Policies One way Jefferson wanted to lessen government power was by reducing the federal budget. Such budget cuts would also keep the federal debt low. His Secretary of the Treasury, Albert Gallatin (GAHL uh tin), helped him achieve this goal. A financial wizard, Gallatin reduced government spending through careful management.

Jefferson believed in an economic idea known as **laissez faire** (lehs ay FAYR), a French term meaning "let alone." The idea of laissez faire was promoted by the Scottish economist Adam Smith. In his book *The Wealth of Nations,* Smith argued in favor of a **free market** where goods and services are exchanged with little regulation. Free competition, Smith said, would benefit everyone, not just the wealthy.

Laissez faire economists believed that government should play as small a role as possible in economic affairs. Laissez faire was very different from the Federalist idea of government. Alexander Hamilton, you recall, wanted government to promote trade and manufacturing.

Goals and Policies of Jefferson

Policies
- Tries to cut federal budget and reduce federal debt
- Promotes laissez-faire policies in economic affairs
- Decreases the size of government departments
- Reduces the size of the army and navy
- Asks Congress to repeal the whiskey tax

GOAL
- Reduce size of government
- Reconcile party differences

Policies
- Retains the Bank of the United States
- Continues to pay off state debts using federal moneys
- Allows many Federalists to keep their government jobs

GRAPHIC ORGANIZER *Skills*

Jefferson set the nation in a new direction, but kept some existing policies.

1. **Comprehension** Identify two ways Jefferson continued Federalist policies.
2. **Critical Thinking Linking Past and Present** Which of the goals and policies shown here might still be issues today? Why?

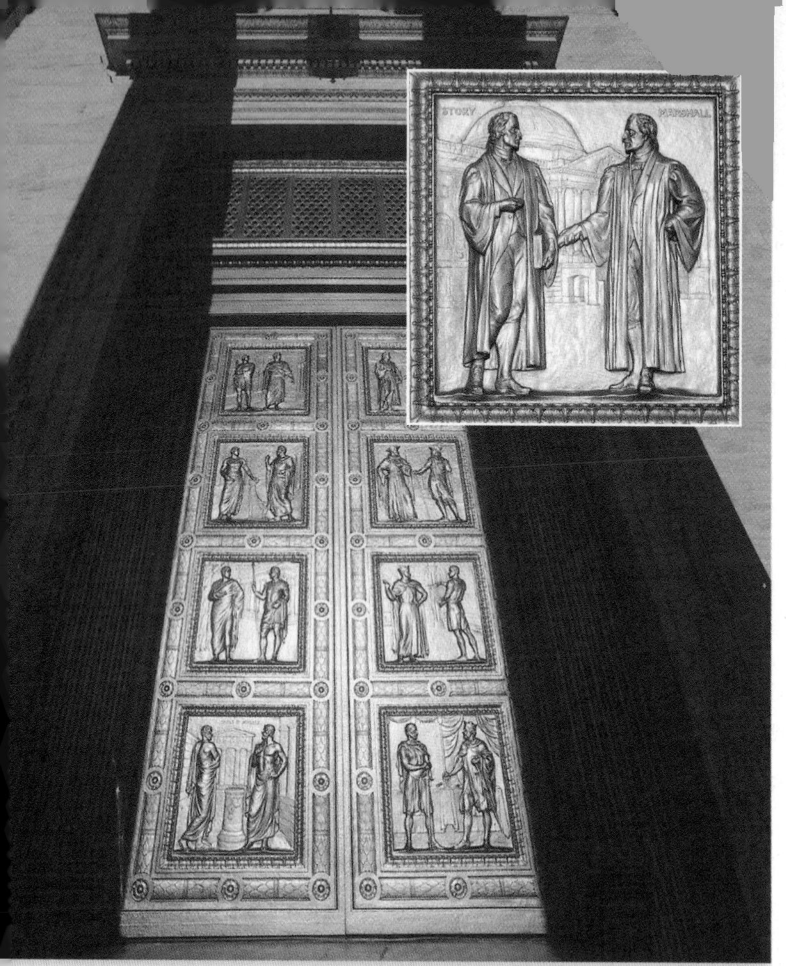

A Less Active Government Jefferson believed that the government should protect the rights of its citizens. Beyond that, he wanted the federal government to take a less active role in governing the nation. He decreased the size of government departments and cut the federal budget. With the approval of Congress, he reduced the size of the army and navy. He also asked Congress to repeal the unpopular whiskey tax.

The Sedition Act expired the day before Jefferson took office. Jefferson hated the law, and he pardoned those who were in jail because of it. He also asked Congress to restore the law allowing foreign-born people to become citizens after only a five-year waiting period.

Federalist Policies Remain Jefferson did not discard all Federalist programs. On the advice of Albert Gallatin, he kept the Bank of the United States. The federal government also continued to pay off state debts, which it had taken over while Washington was President. In addition, Jefferson let many Federalists keep their government jobs.

Viewing History

Chief Justice John Marshall

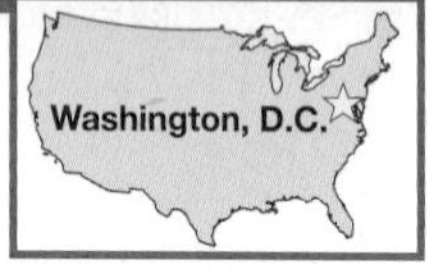

Today, these 20-foot-tall bronze doors lead into the Supreme Court chambers. The carved panels stand for important moments in legal history—including John Marshall delivering the decision in *Marbury* v. *Madison* (inset).

Applying Information ***Why do you think the sculptor included* Marbury *v.* Madison *as an important moment?***

Strengthening the Supreme Court

The election of 1800 gave Republicans control of Congress. Federalists, however, remained powerful in the courts.

Several months passed between Jefferson's election and his inauguration. In that time, Federalists in the old Congress passed a law increasing the number of federal judges. President Adams then appointed Federalists to fill these new judicial positions.

One of the judges that Adams appointed was John Marshall, the Chief Justice of the Supreme Court. Like Jefferson, Marshall was a rich Virginia planter with a brilliant mind. Unlike Jefferson, however, Marshall was a staunch Federalist. He wanted to make the federal government stronger.

The framers of the Constitution expected the courts to balance the powers of the President and Congress. However, John Marshall found the courts to be much weaker than the other branches of government. In his view, it was not clear what powers the federal courts had.

Marbury* v. *Madison In 1803, Marshall decided a case that increased the power of the Supreme Court. The case involved William Marbury, one of the judges appointed by Adams. Adams made the appointment on his last night as President. The Republicans refused to accept this "midnight judge." They accused Federalists of using unfair tactics to keep control of the courts. Jefferson ordered Secretary of State James Madison not to deliver the official papers confirming Marbury's appointment.

Target Skill **Compare and Contrast**

How was John Marshall different from Thomas Jefferson? What did they have in common? Add these observations to your Venn diagram.

Marbury sued Madison. According to the Judiciary Act of 1789, only the Supreme Court could decide a case that was brought against a federal official. Therefore, the case of ***Marbury* v. *Madison*** was tried before the Supreme Court.

An Important Precedent The Supreme Court ruled against Marbury. Chief Justice Marshall wrote the decision, stating that the Judiciary Act was unconstitutional. The Constitution, Marshall argued, did not give the Supreme Court the right to decide cases brought against federal officials. Therefore, Congress could not give the Court that power simply by passing the Judiciary Act.

The Supreme Court's decision in *Marbury* v. *Madison* set an important precedent. It gave the Supreme Court the power to decide whether laws passed by Congress were constitutional and to reject laws that it considered to be unconstitutional. This power of the Court is called **judicial review.**

Jefferson was displeased with the decision. True, Marshall had ruled against Marbury, the Federalist judge. But Marshall's decision gave more power to the Supreme Court, where Federalists were still strong. Jefferson also argued that the decision upset the balance of power among the three branches of government:

> "The opinion which gives to the judges the right to decide what laws are constitutional and what not, not only for themselves . . . but for the Legislature and Executive also . . . would make the Judiciary a [tyrannical] branch."
>
> —Thomas Jefferson, letter to Abigail Adams, 1804

In the end, the President and Congress accepted the right of the Court to overturn laws. Today, judicial review remains one of the most important powers of the Supreme Court.

Connecting to Today

The Supreme Court

Under the strong hand of John Marshall, the Supreme Court increased its power. Today, as in Marshall's time, the justices base their decisions on the Constitution, as well as on past decisions. They may overturn a law because it violates the Constitution. They may reverse decisions by lower courts that did not apply the Constitution correctly.

Today, the Court faces questions that Marshall could not have imagined. How does freedom of speech apply to the Internet? Can members of a school athletic team be required to submit to random drug tests? Can a state government release information contained in a driver's license? Such decisions reach into the lives of every American.

Why do Supreme Court decisions have a wider effect than decisions by state courts?

★ ★ ★ Section 1 Assessment ★ ★ ★

Recall

1. **Identify** Explain the significance of **(a)** Albert Gallatin, **(b)** John Marshall, **(c)** *Marbury* v. *Madison.*
2. **Define** **(a)** democratic, **(b)** laissez faire, **(c)** free market, **(d)** judicial review.

Comprehension

3. **(a)** How did Jefferson's actions as President reflect his democratic beliefs? **(b)** Why did his beliefs worry Federalists?
4. Describe three steps that Jefferson took to reduce the power of the federal government.
5. What important precedent did John Marshall set in the case of *Marbury* v. *Madison*?

Critical Thinking and Writing

6. **Exploring the Main Idea** Review the Main Idea statement at the beginning of this section. Then, write an outline for a speech Jefferson might have given to explain his goals.
7. **Supporting a Point of View** Write a paragraph explaining whether or not you think judicial review upsets the balance of power in the government.

Activity

Connecting to Today
Use the Internet to find out about a current law that affects the goods Americans buy. Summarize the law, and explain what a laissez faire economist would think of it. For help in completing the activity, visit PHSchool.com, **Web Code mfd-1001.**

2 The Louisiana Purchase

Prepare to Read

Objectives

In this section, you will
- Explain why control of the Mississippi River was important to the United States.
- Describe how the United States purchased Louisiana.
- List the results of the explorations of Lewis and Clark and of Zebulon Pike.

Key Terms

Pinckney Treaty
Louisiana Purchase
expedition
continental divide

Target Reading Skill

Sequence Copy this flowchart. As you read, fill in the boxes with events that led up to the Lewis and Clark expedition. Two boxes have been completed to help you get started. Add as many boxes as you need.

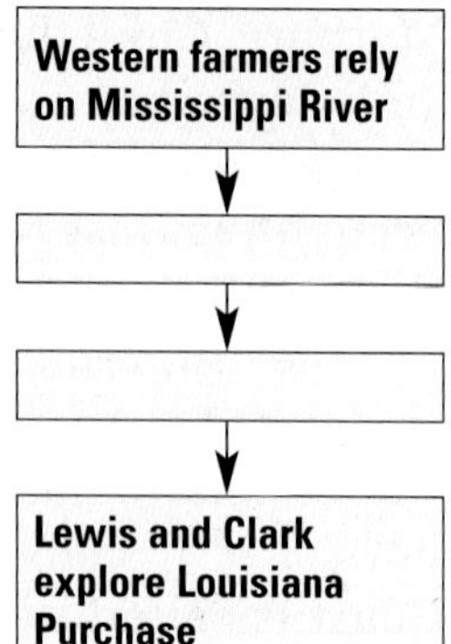

Main Idea In 1803, the United States purchased the territory of Louisiana from France, doubling the size of the nation.

William Clark's journal

Setting the Scene In Jefferson's day, riders of the "post" usually traveled on horseback, carrying mail in saddlebags. But the parcels arriving at the White House this particular day must have required a whole cart. Jefferson eagerly opened package after package, to find a remarkable assortment of goods.

The smaller items included more than a hundred plants, a tin box full of insects, and mineral specimens. Skeletons of pronghorned antelope and the horns of a mountain ram took up more room. There was even live cargo—a prairie dog and a magpie!

Almost two years earlier, the United States had purchased from France vast lands west of the Mississippi River. Jefferson then sent Meriwether Lewis and William Clark to explore the territory. The President carefully examined their reports and packages, and later read their detailed journals. All this evidence confirmed Jefferson's belief that the new lands were a valuable addition to the nation.

Control of the Mississippi

By 1800, almost one million Americans lived between the Appalachian Mountains and the Mississippi River. Most were farmers. With few roads west of the Appalachians, western farmers relied on the Mississippi to ship their wheat and corn. First, they sent their produce down the river to the city of New Orleans. From there, oceangoing ships carried the produce to ports along the Atlantic coast.

Identify Sequence When did the United States and Spain sign the Pinckney Treaty? What happened in 1800 to change the terms of the treaty? Add these events to your flowchart.

Spain, which controlled New Orleans, sometimes threatened to close the port to Americans. In 1795, President Washington sent Thomas Pinckney to find a way to keep the vital port open. In the **Pinckney Treaty,** Spain agreed to let Americans ship their goods down the Mississippi and store them in New Orleans.

For a time, Americans shipped their goods through New Orleans peacefully. In 1800, however, Spain signed a treaty giving Louisiana back to France. President Jefferson was alarmed. He knew that the

French ruler, Napoleon Bonaparte, had already set out to conquer Europe. Would he now try to build an empire in North America?

Jefferson had reason to worry. Napoleon wanted to grow food in Louisiana and ship it to French islands in the West Indies. However, events in Haiti, a French colony in the Caribbean, soon ruined Napoleon's plan. Inspired by the French Revolution, enslaved Africans in Haiti decided to fight for their liberty. Toussaint L'Ouverture (too SAN loo vehr TYOOR) led the revolt. By 1801, Toussaint and his followers had nearly forced the French out of Haiti.

Napoleon sent troops to retake Haiti. Although the French captured Toussaint, they did not regain control of the island. In 1804, Haitians declared their independence.

The United States Buys Louisiana

Meanwhile, Jefferson decided to try to buy New Orleans. He wanted to be sure that American farmers would always be able to ship their goods through the port. The President sent Robert Livingston and James Monroe to buy New Orleans and West Florida from Napoleon. Jefferson said they could offer as much as $10 million.

A Surprise Offer Livingston and Monroe negotiated with Talleyrand, the French foreign minister. At first, Talleyrand showed little interest in their offer. However, losing Haiti caused Napoleon to give up his plan for an empire in the Americas. He also needed money to pay for his costly wars in Europe. Suddenly, Talleyrand asked Livingston if the United States wanted to buy all of Louisiana, not just New Orleans.

The question surprised Livingston. He offered $4 million. "Too low," replied Talleyrand. "Reflect and see me tomorrow."

Livingston and Monroe carefully debated the matter. They had no authority to buy all of Louisiana. However, they knew that Jefferson wanted control of the Mississippi. They agreed to pay the French $15 million for Louisiana. "This is the noblest work of our whole lives," declared Livingston when he signed the treaty. "From this day the United States take their place among the powers of the first rank."

Was the Purchase Constitutional? Jefferson hailed the news from France. Still, he was not sure whether the President had the power to purchase Louisiana. He had always insisted that the federal government had only those powers spelled out in the Constitution. The document said nothing about a President having the power to buy land.

Viewing History

Celebrating the Louisiana Purchase

This painting depicts a ceremony held in New Orleans on December 20, 1803. The French flag has been lowered and the American flag is being raised. **Evaluating Information** ***What would you need to know to decide if this painting is accurate?***

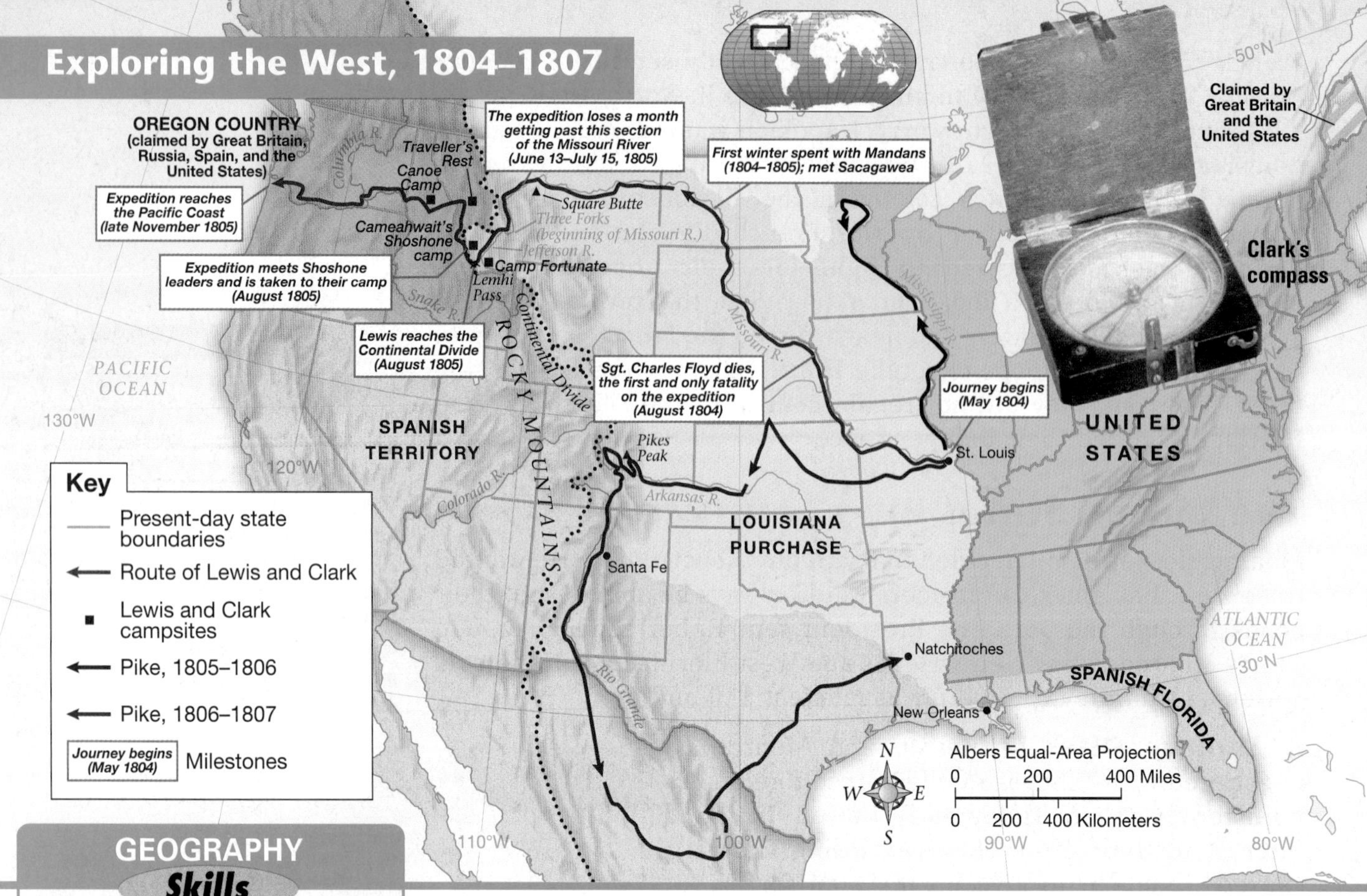

GEOGRAPHY Skills

The explorations of Lewis and Clark and of Zebulon Pike helped Americans learn more about the West.

1. **Location** On the map, locate **(a)** Louisiana Purchase, **(b)** Mississippi River, **(c)** St. Louis, **(d)** Rocky Mountains, **(e)** Pikes Peak.
2. **Movement** Along which rivers did Lewis and Clark travel in order to reach the Pacific Ocean?
3. **Critical Thinking Making Predictions** Based on this map, how might westward expansion lead to conflict with other nations?

In the end, Jefferson decided that he did have the authority to buy Louisiana. The Constitution, he reasoned, allowed the President to make treaties. At his request, the Senate approved the treaty, and the **Louisiana Purchase** went into effect. In 1803, the United States took control of the vast lands west of the Mississippi. With one stroke, the size of the nation had doubled.

Planning an Expedition Few Americans knew anything about the Louisiana territory. In 1803, Congress provided money for a team of explorers to study the new lands. Jefferson chose Meriwether Lewis, his private secretary, to head the **expedition,** or long voyage of exploration. Lewis asked William Clark to go with him.

Jefferson asked Lewis and Clark to map a route to the Pacific Ocean. He also told them to study the geography of the territory, including:

> ❝ . . . climate as characterized by the thermometer, by the proportion of rainy, cloudy, and clear days, by lightning, hail, snow, ice . . . the dates at which particular plants put forth or lose their flower, or leaf, times of appearance of particular birds, reptiles or insects. ❞
>
> —Thomas Jefferson, letter to Meriwether Lewis, 1803

Jefferson also instructed Lewis and Clark to learn about the Indian nations who lived in the Louisiana Purchase. These Native Americans carried on a busy trade with English, French, and Spanish merchants. Jefferson hoped that the Indians might trade with American merchants instead. Therefore, he urged Lewis and Clark to tell the Indians of "our wish to be neighborly, friendly, and useful to them."

The Lewis and Clark Expedition

Dozens of adventurous young men eagerly competed to join the expedition. Lewis and Clark judged volunteers on the basis of their character, strength, hunting skills, and ability to survive in the wilderness. In the end, about 50 men made up the "Corps of Discovery." The party also included York, an enslaved African American who had been Clark's companion since boyhood.

In May 1804, Lewis and Clark started up the Missouri River from St. Louis. At first, the expedition's boats made slow progress against the Missouri's swift current. One night, the current tore away the riverbank where they were camping. The party had to scramble into the boats to avoid being swept downstream.

Across the Plains Lewis and Clark marveled at the broad, grassy plains that stretched "as far as the eye can reach." Everywhere, they saw "immense herds of buffalo, deer, elk, and antelope."

As they traveled across the plains, the expedition met people of various Indian nations. Lewis and Clark had brought many gifts for Native Americans. They carried "peace medals" stamped with the United States seal. They also brought mirrors, beads, knives, blankets, and thousands of sewing needles and fishhooks.

During the first winter, Lewis and Clark stayed with the Mandans in present-day North Dakota. The explorers planned to continue up the Missouri in the spring. However, they worried about how they would cross the steep Rocky Mountains.

Also staying with the Mandans was an Indian woman named Sacagawea (sahk uh guh WEE uh). Sacagawea belonged to the Shoshone (shoh SHOH nee) people, who lived in the Rockies. She and her French Canadian husband agreed to accompany Lewis and Clark as translators.

Over the Rockies In early spring, the party set out. In the foothills of the Rockies, the landscape and wildlife changed. Bighorn sheep ran along the high hills. The thorns of prickly pear cactus jabbed the explorers' moccasins. Once, a grizzly bear chased Lewis while he was exploring alone.

Finally, Lewis and Clark met some Shoshones. One of them was Sacagawea's brother, whom she had not seen for many years. Upon seeing her own people, wrote Clark, she began to "dance and show every mark of the most extravagant joy." The Shoshones supplied the expedition with food and horses. They also advised Lewis and Clark about the best route to take over the Rockies.

In the Rocky Mountains, Lewis and Clark crossed the Continental Divide. A **continental divide** is a mountain ridge that separates river systems flowing toward opposite sides of a continent. In North America, some rivers flow east from the Rockies into the Mississippi, which drains into the Gulf of Mexico. Other rivers flow west from the Rockies and empty into the Pacific Ocean.

An American Profile

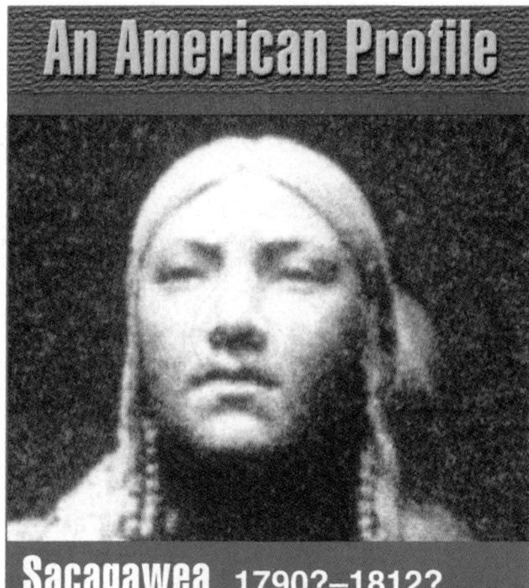

Sacagawea 1790?–1812?

Sacagawea proved invaluable to the Lewis and Clark expedition. Because she knew about the healing qualities of plants and herbs, the expedition relied on her for medical help. The presence of Sacagawea and her baby showed Indians in the area that the party was friendly. As Clark noted, "a woman with a party of men is a token of peace." She helped win the needed gift of horses from her people, the Shoshone. After the journey was completed, Clark wrote that she "deserved a greater reward . . . than we had in our power to give her."

Why would the presence of a woman and baby be seen as a sign of peace?

To the Pacific After building canoes, Lewis and Clark's party floated toward the Columbia River into the Pacific Northwest. Finally, on November 7, 1805, Clark wrote in his journal, "Great joy in camp. We are in view of the ocean, this great Pacific Ocean which we have been so long anxious to see." Lewis and Clark had reached their goal.

The return trip to St. Louis took another year. In 1806, Americans celebrated the return of Lewis and Clark. The explorers brought back much useful information about the Louisiana Purchase.

Pike Explores the West

Before Lewis and Clark returned, another explorer set out from St. Louis. From 1805 to 1807, Zebulon Pike explored the upper Mississippi River, the Arkansas River, and parts of present-day Colorado and New Mexico. In November 1806, Pike viewed a mountain peak rising above the Colorado plains. Today, this mountain is known as Pikes Peak.

Continuing southward, Pike entered into Spanish territory. Spanish troops soon arrested Pike and his men and took them into Mexico. The Americans were later escorted through Texas back into the United States. The Spanish took Pike's maps and journals, but he was able to hide one map in the barrel of his gun. His report on the expedition greatly expanded Americans' knowledge about the Southwest.

The journeys of Pike and Lewis and Clark excited Americans. However, settlers did not move into the rugged western lands for a number of years. As you will read, they first settled the region closest to the Mississippi River. Soon, the territory around New Orleans had a large enough population of American citizens for the settlers to apply for statehood. In 1812, this territory entered the Union as the state of Louisiana.

★ ★ ★ Section 2 Assessment ★ ★ ★

Recall

1. **Identify** Explain the significance of **(a)** Pinckney Treaty, **(b)** Napoleon Bonaparte, **(c)** Toussaint L'Ouverture, **(d)** Louisiana Purchase, **(e)** Lewis and Clark, **(f)** Sacagawea, **(g)** Zebulon Pike.
2. **Define** **(a)** expedition, **(b)** continental divide.

Comprehension

3. Why did Jefferson seek to control the Mississippi River?
4. Why did the French offer to sell Louisiana to the United States?
5. Identify two goals and one result of the Lewis and Clark expedition.

Critical Thinking and Writing

6. **Exploring the Main Idea** Review the Main Idea statement at the beginning of this section. Then, list three ways in which the United States might be different today if Jefferson had not bought Louisiana in 1803.
7. **Making Decisions** If you had been a Shoshone or Mandan leader, would you have decided to help Lewis and Clark? Explain your reasons.

ACTIVITY

Writing a Journal You are a member of Lewis and Clark's "Corps of Discovery." Write three journal entries describing what you feel as you explore the territory and meet the Native Americans who live there.

American Wildlife

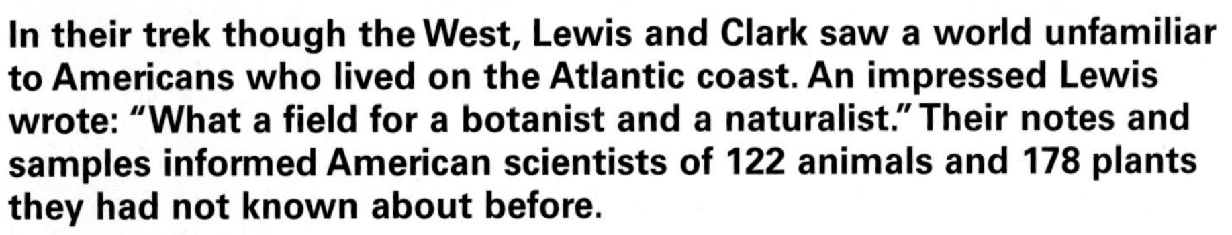

In their trek though the West, Lewis and Clark saw a world unfamiliar to Americans who lived on the Atlantic coast. An impressed Lewis wrote: "What a field for a botanist and a naturalist." Their notes and samples informed American scientists of 122 animals and 178 plants they had not known about before.

The only animals named for the explorers are this woodpecker (left) named for Lewis and this nutcracker (right) named for Clark.

At the expedition's winter quarters on the Pacific coast, Indians caught a 2-foot, 8-inch long coho salmon. Lewis sketched and described the fish in his journal.

In Nebraska, Lewis first saw these "barking squirrels." Another member of the expedition gave them the name they have today—prairie dogs.

Native Americans had warned the explorers about the fierce grizzly bear. Lewis wrote that the explorers were "anxious to meet them." After being chased up a tree by a grizzly, Lewis wrote "I find the curiosity of our party is pretty well satisfied with respect to this animal."

Activity

With the class or in a small group, brainstorm a list of the wildlife native to your area. Choose one animal from the list. Prepare an entry for a visitor's guide describing that animal and how it reflects the local geography.

3 New Threats From Overseas

Prepare to Read

Objectives

In this section, you will
- List the benefits and risks of overseas trade.
- Describe how the British and French violated the neutrality of American ships.
- Explain why Jefferson decided to impose an embargo.

Key Terms

tribute
impressment
embargo
Embargo Act
smuggling
Nonintercourse Act

Target Reading Skill

Clarifying Meaning As you read, prepare an outline of this section. Use roman numerals to indicate the major headings, capital letters for the subheadings, and numbers for the supporting details. The sample at right will help you get started.

I. Trading Around the World
  A. Yankee traders
    1. China trade
    2.
  B.
    1.
    2.
II. American Neutrality Is Violated
  A.
  B.

Main Idea As Great Britain went to war against France, both sides ignored the claim of the United States that American ships were neutral.

British seize American sailors

Setting the Scene It was along the coast of India that Jacob Nagle saw his chance to escape. An American sailor, Nagle had been forced to work on a British ship. He and three shipmates jumped into a small boat and rowed away as fast as they could.

The surf and wind made it difficult to reach shore before dark. Finally, Nagle and his mates rowed to another ship instead. Unfortunately, officers from their own ship were lying in wait. "Not suspecting, we asked for some water," Nagle later recalled:

> "The captain said if we would come up, he would give us some [drink]. . . . As soon as we got on the quarter deck they all surrounded us and the second mate clapped a pistol to my breast. 'If you move an inch, I will blow your brains out.' "
>
> —Jacob Nagle, *The Nagle Journal: A Diary of the Life of Jacob Nagle, Sailor, From the Year 1775 to 1841*

In the early 1800s, the British navy forced thousands of American sailors to serve on their ships. This was only one of many dangers that Americans faced as their sea trade began to thrive.

Trading Around the World

After the Revolution, American overseas trade grew rapidly. Ships sailed from New England on voyages that sometimes lasted three years.

Yankee Traders Wherever they went, Yankee captains kept a sharp lookout for new goods and new markets. Clever traders sawed winter ice from New England ponds into blocks, packed it in sawdust, and carried it to India. There, they traded the ice for silk and spices. In 1784, the *Empress of China* became the first American ship to trade with China. New England merchants quickly built up a profitable China trade.

More than 10 years before Lewis and Clark, Yankee merchants sailed up the Pacific coast of North America. So many traders from Boston visited the Pacific Northwest that Indians there called every white man "Boston." Traders bought furs from Native Americans and sold them for large profits in China.

Conflict With the Barbary States Traders ran great risks, especially in the Mediterranean Sea. Pirates from the Barbary States, the nations along the coast of North Africa, attacked passing vessels. To protect American ships, the United States paid a yearly **tribute,** or bribe, to rulers of Barbary States such as Tripoli.

In 1801, Tripoli increased its demands. When Jefferson refused to pay, Tripoli declared war on the United States. Jefferson then ordered the navy to blockade the port of Tripoli.

During the blockade, the American ship *Philadelphia* ran aground near Tripoli. Pirates boarded the ship and hauled the crew off to prison. The pirates planned to use the *Philadelphia* to attack other ships. To prevent this, American naval officer Stephen Decatur and his crew quietly sailed into Tripoli harbor by night. They then set the captured American ship on fire.

In the meantime, American marines landed on the coast of North Africa. They marched 500 miles to launch a surprise attack on Tripoli. In 1805, the ruler of Tripoli signed a treaty promising not to interfere with American ships.

Viewing History

Trading in China

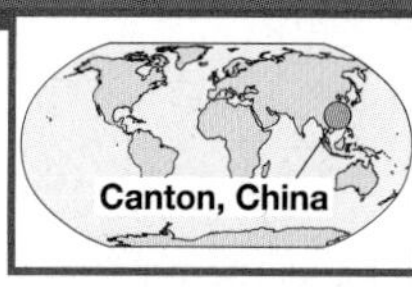

Chinese tea and fine dishes, or china, fetched high prices in the United States. Still, China permitted foreigners to trade in just a few ports, such as Canton (below). **Drawing Conclusions** ***How would you describe the china shown here? Why do you think Americans were willing to pay high prices for such goods?***

American Neutrality Is Violated

American ships faced another problem. Britain and France went to war again in 1803. At first, Americans profited from the conflict. British and French ships were too busy fighting to engage in trade. American merchants eagerly traded with both sides. As profits increased, Americans hurried to build new ships.

Neither Britain nor France wanted the United States to sell supplies to its enemy. As in the 1790s, they ignored American claims of neutrality. Napoleon seized American ships bound for England. At the same time, the British stopped Yankee traders on their way to France. Between 1805 and 1807, hundreds of American ships were captured.

Needing more sailors, the British navy stepped up **impressment,** the practice of forcing people into service. In Britain, impressment gangs raided English villages and took young men to serve in the navy. On the seas, British ships stopped American vessels, seizing any British sailors serving on American ships. Many American-born sailors were also impressed. Furious Americans clamored for war.

Jefferson Tries an Embargo

Jefferson knew that the small American fleet was no match for the powerful British navy. Like Washington and Adams, he sought to avoid war.

A Total Ban Jefferson hoped that an American **embargo,** or ban on trade, would hurt France and Britain by cutting off needed supplies. "Our trade is the most powerful weapon we can use in our defense," one Republican newspaper wrote. In 1807, Jefferson persuaded Congress to impose a total embargo on foreign trade.

The **Embargo Act** did hurt Britain and France. But it hurt Americans even more. Supplies of imports such as sugar, tea, and molasses were cut off. Exports dropped by more than $80 million in one year. Docks in the South were piled high with cotton and tobacco. The Embargo Act hurt New England merchants most of all.

Merchants protested loudly against the embargo. Some turned to **smuggling,** importing or exporting goods in violation of trade laws. Jefferson began using the navy and federal troops to enforce the embargo. On the border between New York and Canada, some smugglers engaged in skirmishes with federal troops.

Target Skill: Summarize Write two or three sentences explaining the purpose of the Embargo Act and its effects on Britain, France, and the United States. Add these details to your outline.

A Limited Ban In 1809, Jefferson admitted that the Embargo Act had failed. Congress replaced it with the milder **Nonintercourse Act.** It allowed Americans to carry on trade with all nations except Britain and France.

The embargo was the most unpopular measure of Jefferson's presidency. Still, Republicans remained strong. Following President Washington's precedent, Jefferson refused to run for a third term. Republican James Madison easily won the 1808 presidential election. Madison hoped that Britain and France would soon agree to respect American neutrality.

★ ★ ★ Section 3 Assessment ★ ★ ★

Recall

1. **Identify** Explain the significance of **(a)** *Empress of China,* **(b)** Stephen Decatur, **(c)** Embargo Act, **(d)** Nonintercourse Act.
2. **Define** **(a)** tribute, **(b)** impressment, **(c)** embargo, **(d)** smuggling.

Comprehension

3. How did increased overseas trade lead to conflict with the Barbary States?
4. Why did Britain and France begin to seize American ships after 1803?
5. **(a)** What was the goal of the Embargo Act? **(b)** Why did it fail?

Critical Thinking and Writing

6. **Exploring the Main Idea** Review the Main Idea statement at the beginning of this section. Then, list as many ways as you can think of that a war between two foreign powers can affect a neutral nation.
7. **Making Predictions** Write a paragraph explaining what you think President Madison might do if Britain and France continue to violate American neutrality.

ACTIVITY

Go Online
PHSchool.com

Creating an Advertisement
Use the Internet to find out what goods were traded in China in the early 1800s. Create an advertisement offering American goods to Chinese merchants or Chinese goods to Americans. For help in completing the activity, visit PHSchool.com, **Web Code mfd-1002.**

Synthesizing Information

How did Jefferson's attempt to maintain American neutrality affect the nation's economy? As you learn about history, you will often use evidence from many types of sources. To get the most from these sources, you need to synthesize—that is, put different pieces of information together to form conclusions. To start this lesson, read the excerpt below and study the graph to the right.

A New Englander sent a letter to President Jefferson about the Embargo Act. It began with these words:

> "You Infernal Villain:
>
> How much longer are you going to keep this [cursed] Embargo on to starve us poor people? . . . One of my children has already starved to death of which I [am] ashamed and declared that it died of apoplexy. . . . I am a Federalist."
>
> —quoted in *A Diplomatic History of the American People* (Bailey)

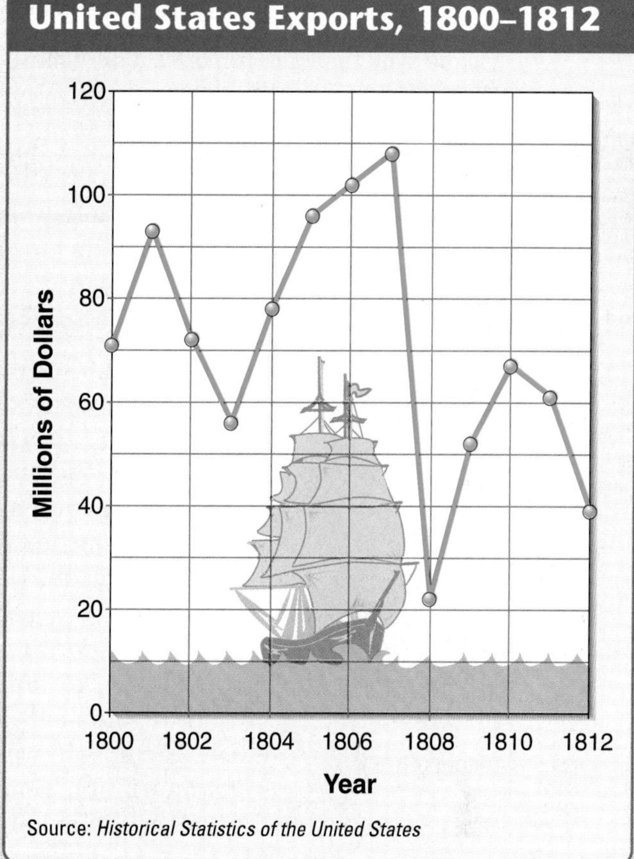

Learn the Skill *To synthesize information, use the following steps:*

1. **Identify the sources.** Knowing the background of a writer or the source of a graph helps you evaluate the information.
2. **Identify key facts and ideas.** What are the main points being made?
3. **Analyze the evidence.** Examine and compare the different kinds of evidence—graphs, pictures, text, primary sources—you are using.
4. **Draw conclusions.** Use the different pieces of evidence to form conclusions.

Practice the Skill *Use the letter, the graph, and what you have read in Section 3 to answer the following questions:*

1. **(a)** Who wrote the letter? **(b)** How did the writer feel about the embargo? **(c)** What is the source of the graph information?
2. **(a)** Restate the main point of the letter. **(b)** Describe the changes in the value of exports shown on the graph.
3. **(a)** Based on your reading, why did American exports fall sharply in 1807? **(b)** How does the graph explain the letter writer's point of view?
4. Based on the evidence, draw one conclusion about American trade in the early 1800s.

Apply the Skill *See the Chapter Review and Assessment.*

4 The Road to War

Prepare to Read

Objectives

In this section, you will
- Explain why conflicts between white settlers and Native Americans increased during the early 1800s.
- Identify the goal of Tecumseh's Native American confederation.
- Describe why the War Hawks pushed for war against Britain.

Key Terms

Treaty of Greenville

confederation

Battle of Tippecanoe

War Hawks

nationalism

Target Reading Skill

Cause and Effect Copy the chart below. As you read, complete the chart by filling in some of the causes that led Congress to declare war. Add as many boxes as you need.

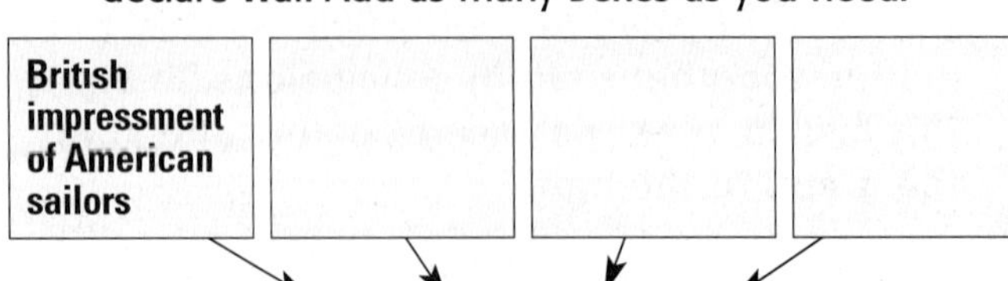

Main Idea Conflicts with Native Americans in the West and with the British at sea led to the War of 1812.

Tecumseh

Setting the Scene August 1810: William Henry Harrison, governor of the Indiana Territory, was ready to welcome an Indian delegation. Under a canopy, government officials sat and waited.

At last, the leader of the Indian delegation approached. His name was Tecumseh (tih KUHM suh). Behind him stood 30 members of the Shawnee nation.

"Your father requests you to sit by his side," Harrison's assistant told Tecumseh. He meant Harrison was a chief, a "white father."

Scornfully, Tecumseh pointed to the sky. "My father! The Great Spirit is my father! The earth is my mother. . . . Houses are made for white men to hold councils in. Indians hold theirs in open air." He and his men sat down where they were.

Tecumseh was determined to push back white settlers from Indian lands. Soon, the United States was fighting on two fronts—against Tecumseh's Indian allies and against Great Britain.

Conflict With Native Americans

About 900,000 white settlers moved west of the Appalachians between 1790 and 1810. Native Americans resented these newcomers, who built farms on Indian lands and hunted the animals Indians needed for food. The settlers ignored treaties that the United States had signed with Indian nations of the region.

Fighting often broke out between the Native Americans and settlers. Isolated acts of violence led to larger acts of revenge. As both sides killed innocent people, warfare spread. In Ohio, Little Turtle of the Miamis and Blue Jacket of the Shawnees organized Indian resistance in 1791. Armed with British muskets and gunpowder, the Indians drove white settlers from the area.

President Washington sent General Anthony Wayne into Ohio in 1794. Native American forces gathered at a place called Fallen Timbers. They thought that Wayne would have trouble fighting there because fallen trees covered the land. But Wayne's well-trained army pushed through the tangle of logs and defeated the Indians.

In 1795, leaders of the Miamis and other Indian nations signed the Treaty of Greenville. They gave up land that would later become part of Ohio. In return, they received $20,000 and the promise of more money if they kept the peace.

Tecumseh's Confederation

Ohio joined the Union in 1803. By then, white settlers were pushing beyond Ohio into the Indiana Territory. Angry Native Americans vowed to keep settlers from taking more Indian land. They included two Shawnee leaders: Tecumseh and his brother Tenskwatawa (tehn SKWAH tuh wuh), a religious leader also called the Prophet.

Unity and Old Ways The Prophet and Tecumseh taught that white customs corrupted the Indian way of life. They said that many Indians depended on white trade goods, such as muskets, cloth, cooking pots, and whiskey. They believed that by returning to the old ways, Indians could gain the power to resist white invaders.

In 1808, the Prophet built a village for his followers along Tippecanoe Creek in Indiana Territory. Indians from lands as far away as Missouri, Iowa, and Minnesota traveled to Prophetstown to hear his message.

Tecumseh worked to organize Indian nations into a confederation, or league. He called for unity against settlers:

> “The whites have driven us from the great salt water, forced us over the mountains. . . . The way, the only way, to check and stop this evil is for all red men to unite in claiming a common equal right in the land.”
>
> —Tecumseh, quoted in *Tecumseh: Vision of Glory* (Tucker)

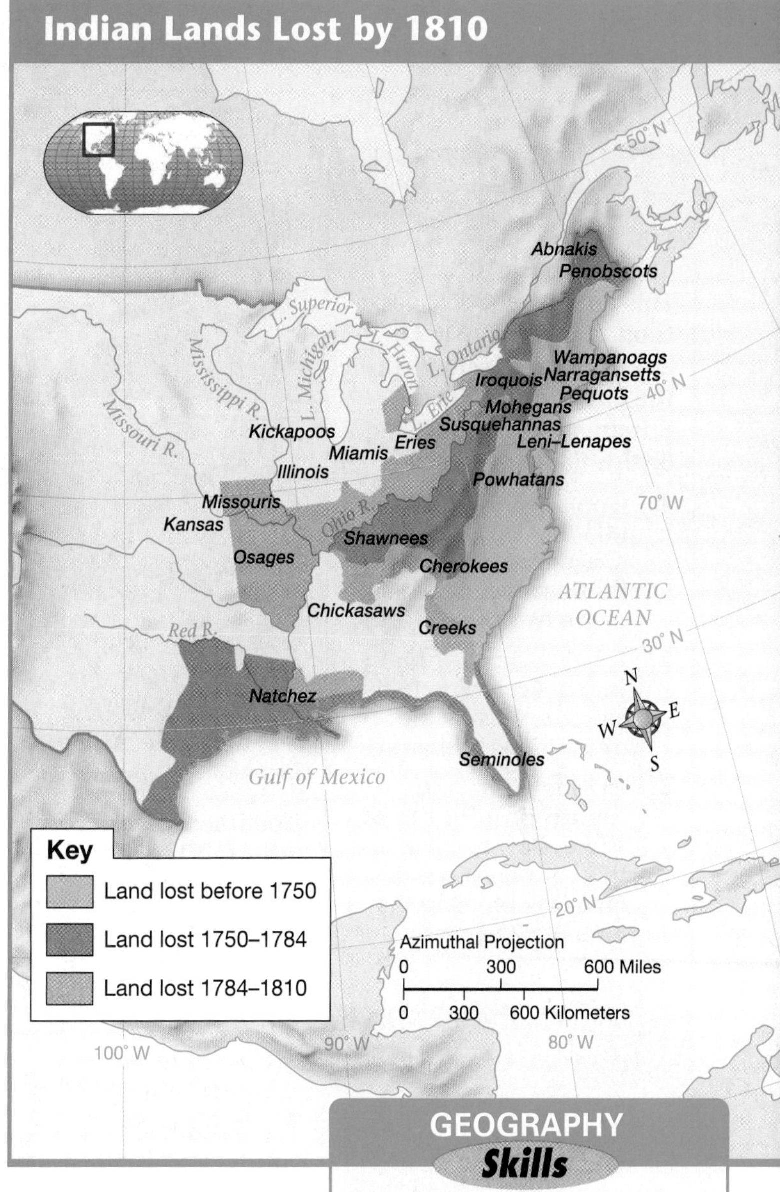

GEOGRAPHY *Skills*

As settlers moved west, they settled on Native American lands.

1. **Location** On the map, locate the original lands of the **(a)** Iroquois, **(b)** Miamis, **(c)** Shawnees.
2. **Regions** When did Indian nations west of the Ohio River begin to lose land?
3. **Critical Thinking Drawing Inferences** Why do you think many of the lands lost by Indians were located along rivers?

Tecumseh impressed white leaders. Governor William Henry Harrison grudgingly admitted, “He is one of those uncommon geniuses which spring up occasionally to produce revolutions and overturn the established order of things.”

Showdown at Tippecanoe Rivalries among Native American nations kept Tecumseh from uniting all Indians east of the Mississippi River. Still, white settlers were alarmed at his success.

In 1811, Harrison marched 1,000 soldiers against Prophetstown on the Tippecanoe Creek. The Prophet was in charge because

POLITICAL CARTOON *Skills*

The Embargo Continues This famous political cartoon appeared in 1811, after Congress renewed the embargo against Britain. (The ship is flying a British flag.)

1. **Comprehension** **(a)** What is Ograbme spelled backward? **(b)** Describe the actions of the two speakers.
2. **Understanding Main Ideas** According to the cartoon, what is the effect of the embargo?
3. **Critical Thinking Identifying Points of View** Do you think that this cartoonist was in favor of enforcing the embargo? Explain.

Tecumseh was away trying to organize Indians in the South. The Prophet led a surprise night attack on Harrison's troops. Both sides suffered heavy losses in the **Battle of Tippecanoe.** In the end, Harrison's troops defeated the Prophet's forces and destroyed Prophetstown. Whites celebrated the battle as a major victory. Still, Tecumseh and his followers continued to resist white settlement.

A Push Toward War

Fighting with Native Americans hurt relations between the United States and Britain. The British were supplying guns and ammunition to the Native Americans on the frontier. They also encouraged Indians to attack United States settlements.

Meanwhile, the continuing ban on trade with Britain and France was due to expire. Congress then authorized President Madison to make a tantalizing offer. If either the British or French stopped seizing American ships, the United States would halt trade with the other nation. Napoleon quickly announced that France would respect American neutrality. As promised, the United States continued trade with France, but stopped all shipments to Britain.

Understanding Multiple Causes

As you read, look for the three main arguments that the War Hawks used to push for war against Britain. Add this information to your chart.

The War Hawks While Madison did not want war, other Americans were not as cautious. Except in New England, where many merchants wanted to restore trade with Britain, anti-British feeling ran strong. Members of Congress from the South and the West called for war. They were known as **War Hawks.**

War Hawks were stirred by a strong sense of **nationalism,** or devotion to one's country. War Hawks felt that Britain was treating the United States as if it were still a British colony. They were willing to fight a war to defend American rights.

The most outspoken War Hawk was Henry Clay of Kentucky. Clay wanted to punish Britain for seizing American ships. He also hoped to conquer Canada. "The militia of Kentucky are alone [able] to place Montreal and Upper Canada at your feet," Clay boasted to Congress.

War Hawks saw other advantages of war with Britain. If Americans went to war with Britain, War Hawks said, the United States could seize Florida from Britain's ally, Spain. They also pointed out that Britain was arming Native Americans on the frontier and encouraging them to attack settlers. The War Hawks felt that winning a war against Britain would bring lasting safety to settlers on the frontier.

Congress Declares War The United States and Britain drifted closer to war. The British continued to board American ships and impress American seamen. To cut off American trade with France, British warships blockaded some American ports. In May 1811, near New York Harbor, a brief battle broke out between an American frigate and a British warship. The Americans crippled the British ship and left 32 British sailors dead or wounded.

The War Hawks urged Congress to prepare for war. Others in Congress disagreed. John Randolph of Virginia warned that the people of the United States would "not submit to be taxed for this war of conquest and dominion." Representatives of New England were especially concerned. They feared that the British navy would attack New England seaports.

At last, President Madison gave in to war fever. In June 1812, he asked Congress to declare war on Britain. The House and Senate both voted in favor of war. Americans would soon learn, though, that declaring war was easier than winning.

Primary Source

A War Hawk Speaks

Felix Grundy of Tennessee was one of the most outspoken War Hawks in Congress. In December 1811, he gave an emotional speech on the benefits of war:

"This war, if carried on successfully, will have its advantages. We shall drive the British from our continent—they will no longer have an opportunity of intriguing with our Indian neighbors . . . . That nation will lose her Canadian trade, and by having no resting place in this country, her means of annoying us will be diminished. . . . I therefore feel anxious not only to add the Floridas to the South, but the Canadas to the North of this empire."

—Felix Grundy, *Annals of the Congress of the United States, 12th Congress, First Session*

Analyzing Primary Sources

How does Grundy's speech reflect a sense of nationalism?

Section 4 Assessment

Recall

1. **Identify** Explain the significance of **(a)** Treaty of Greenville, **(b)** Tecumseh, **(c)** the Prophet, **(d)** William Henry Harrison, **(e)** Battle of Tippecanoe, **(f)** War Hawks, **(g)** Henry Clay.
2. **Define** **(a)** confederation, **(b)** nationalism.

Comprehension

3. Why did war break out between Indians and white settlers in Ohio?
4. Why did Tecumseh want to unite Indian nations?
5. Identify three reasons why the War Hawks wanted Congress to declare war on Britain.

Critical Thinking and Writing

6. **Exploring the Main Idea** Review the Main Idea statement at the beginning of this section. Then, write a paragraph explaining how the Battle of Tippecanoe helped to pave the way for the coming war between Britain and the United States.
7. **Supporting a Point of View** Write an outline for a speech Tecumseh or the Prophet might have given to persuade Native Americans to join his league. Include at least two different reasons.

Activity

Drawing a Political Cartoon **Draw a political cartoon that might have appeared in a War Hawk newspaper in 1812. Your cartoon should express one of the reasons that you favor a declaration of war against Britain. Use human figures to represent the United States and Britain.**

5 The War of 1812

Prepare to Read

Objectives

In this section, you will

- Describe how the United States was not ready for war.
- List the successes Americans had in the West.
- Describe the progression of the final battles of the war.
- Explain why New Englanders protested the war.

Key Terms

Battle of Lake Erie

Battle of New Orleans

Hartford Convention

Treaty of Ghent

Target Reading Skill

Reading Process Copy the concept web below. As you read, fill in blank ovals with important facts about the War of 1812. Add as many ovals as you need.

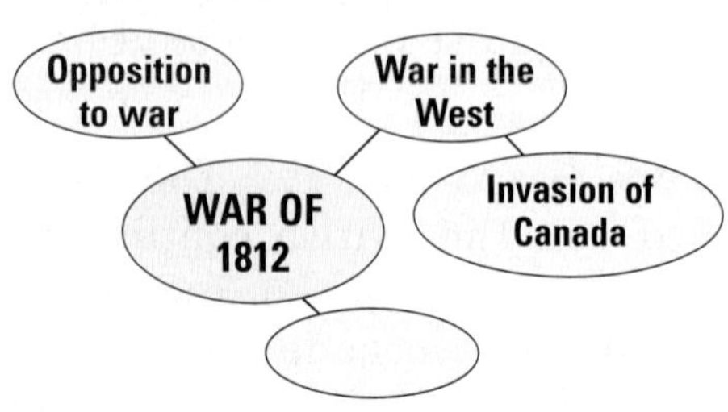

Main Idea Although neither nation won the War of 1812, Americans proved that their republic would remain independent.

Soldier's uniform of 1812

Setting the Scene Many Americans welcomed the news of war with Britain. In some cities, they fired cannons and guns and danced in the streets. A Republican newspaper published this poem:

> ❝ Since war is the word, let us strain every nerve
> To save our America, her glory increase;
> So shoulder your firelock, your country preserve,
> For the hotter the war, boys, the quicker the peace. ❞
>
> —War poem, quoted in *The Oxford History of the American People* (Morison)

Other Americans were less enthusiastic. New Englanders, especially, talked scornfully of "Mr. Madison's War." In fact, before the war ended, some New Englanders would threaten to leave the Union.

Early Days of the War

The American declaration of war took the British by surprise. They were locked in a bitter struggle with Napoleon and could not spare troops to fight the United States. As the war began, however, the United States faced difficulties of its own.

Unprepared for War The United States was not ready for war. Because Jefferson had reduced spending on defense, the navy had only 16 ships to meet the huge British fleet. The army was small and ill equipped, and many of the officers knew little about warfare. "The state of the Army," said a member of Congress, "is enough to make any man who has the smallest love of country wish to get rid of it."

Since there were few regular troops, the government relied on volunteers. Congress voted to give them a bounty of cash and land. The money was equal to about a year's salary for most workers. Attracted by the high pay and the chance to own their own farms, young men eagerly enlisted. They were poorly trained, however, with little experience in battle. Many deserted after a few months.

USS *Constitution*

The USS Constitution *is affectionately known as "Old Ironsides." During the War of 1812, British cannonballs bounced off her thick wooden hull. Later, a public outcry saved the old ship from being scrapped. Today, if you visit Boston, you can step aboard the restored "Old Ironsides." In the nearby museum, you can relive naval history by hoisting a sail or firing a cannon.*

Virtual Field Trip For an interactive look at the *Constitution,* visit PHSchool.com, **Web Code mfd-1003.**

Fighting at Sea The British navy blockaded American ports to stop American trade. Though unable to break the blockade, several American sea captains won stunning victories.

One famous battle took place early in the war, in August 1812. As he was sailing near Newfoundland, Isaac Hull, captain of the USS *Constitution,* spotted the British ship HMS *Guerrière* (gai ree AIR). For nearly an hour, the two ships jockeyed for position. At last, the guns of the *Constitution* roared into action. They tore holes in the sides of the *Guerrière* and shot off both masts. Stunned, the British captain had no choice but to surrender.

American sea captains won other victories at sea. These victories cheered Americans but did little to win the war.

War in the West

One goal of the War Hawks was to conquer Canada. They were convinced that Canadians would welcome the chance to throw off British rule and join the United States.

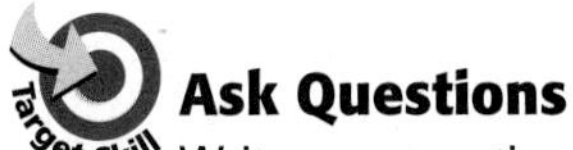

Ask Questions Write one question relating to each subheading under the heading "War in the West." As you read, look for the answers to your questions. Add facts from the answers to your concept web.

Invasion of Canada General William Hull moved American troops into Canada from Detroit. The Canadians had only a few untrained troops to ward off the invasion. However, they were led by a clever British general, Isaac Brock.

Brock paraded his soldiers in red coats to make it appear that experienced British troops were helping the Canadians. He also led Americans to think that a large number of Indians were fighting

An American Profile

Oliver Hazard Perry

1785–1819

At age 14, Oliver Hazard Perry joined the United States Navy. He spent the rest of his life there.

At the Battle of Lake Erie, Perry's ship, the USS *Lawrence,* drew most of the British fire in the early hours of the battle. When the *Lawrence* could no longer fight, Perry took down his ship's flag. He then rowed a mile—while under fire—to reach another American ship. Raising his flag again, he fought on to victory.

Perry was hailed across the country as a hero. Today, the U.S. Naval Academy treasures his battle flag from Lake Erie.

Why did Americans consider Perry a hero?

alongside the Canadians. Brock's scare tactics worked. Hull retreated from Canada. Other attempts to invade Canada also failed.

Battle of Lake Erie In 1813, the Americans set out to win control of Lake Erie. Captain Oliver Hazard Perry had no fleet, so he designed and built his own ships. In September 1813, he sailed his tiny fleet against the British.

During the Battle of Lake Erie, the British battered Perry's own ship and left it helpless. Perry rowed over to another American ship and continued to fight. Finally, the Americans won the battle. Captain Perry wrote his message of victory on the back of an envelope: "We have met the enemy and they are ours."

Native American Losses After losing control of Lake Erie, the British and their ally Tecumseh retreated from Detroit into Canada. General William Henry Harrison, veteran of Tippecanoe, pursued them. The Americans won a decisive victory at the Battle of the Thames. Tecumseh died in the fighting. Without Tecumseh's leadership, the Indian confederation soon fell apart.

Still, the Creeks continued their fight against the settlers in the South. Andrew Jackson, a Tennessee officer, took command of American troops in the Creek War. In 1814, with the help of the Cherokees, Jackson won a crushing victory at the Battle of Horseshoe Bend. The leader of the Creeks walked alone into Jackson's camp to surrender. "Your people have destroyed my nation," he said.

Final Battles

In 1814, Britain and its allies defeated France. With the war in Europe over, Britain could send more troops and ships against the United States.

The British Burn Washington In August 1814, British ships sailed into Chesapeake Bay and landed an invasion force about 30 miles from Washington, D.C. American troops met the British at Bladensburg, Maryland. As President Madison watched, the battle-hardened British quickly scattered the untrained Americans. The British met little further resistance on their march to the capital.

In the White House, First Lady Dolley Madison waited for her husband to return. Hastily, she scrawled a note to her sister:

> ❝ Will you believe it, my sister? We have had a battle or skirmish near Bladensburg and here I am still within sound of the cannon! Mr. Madison comes not. May God protect us. Two messengers covered with dust come bid me fly. But here I mean to wait for him. ❞
>
> —Dolley Madison, *Memoirs and Letters of Dolley Madison*

Soon after, British troops marched into the capital. Dolley Madison gathered up important papers of the President and a portrait of George Washington. Then, she fled south. She was not there to see the British set fire to the White House and other buildings.

From Washington, the British marched north toward the city of Baltimore. The key to Baltimore's defense was Fort McHenry. From

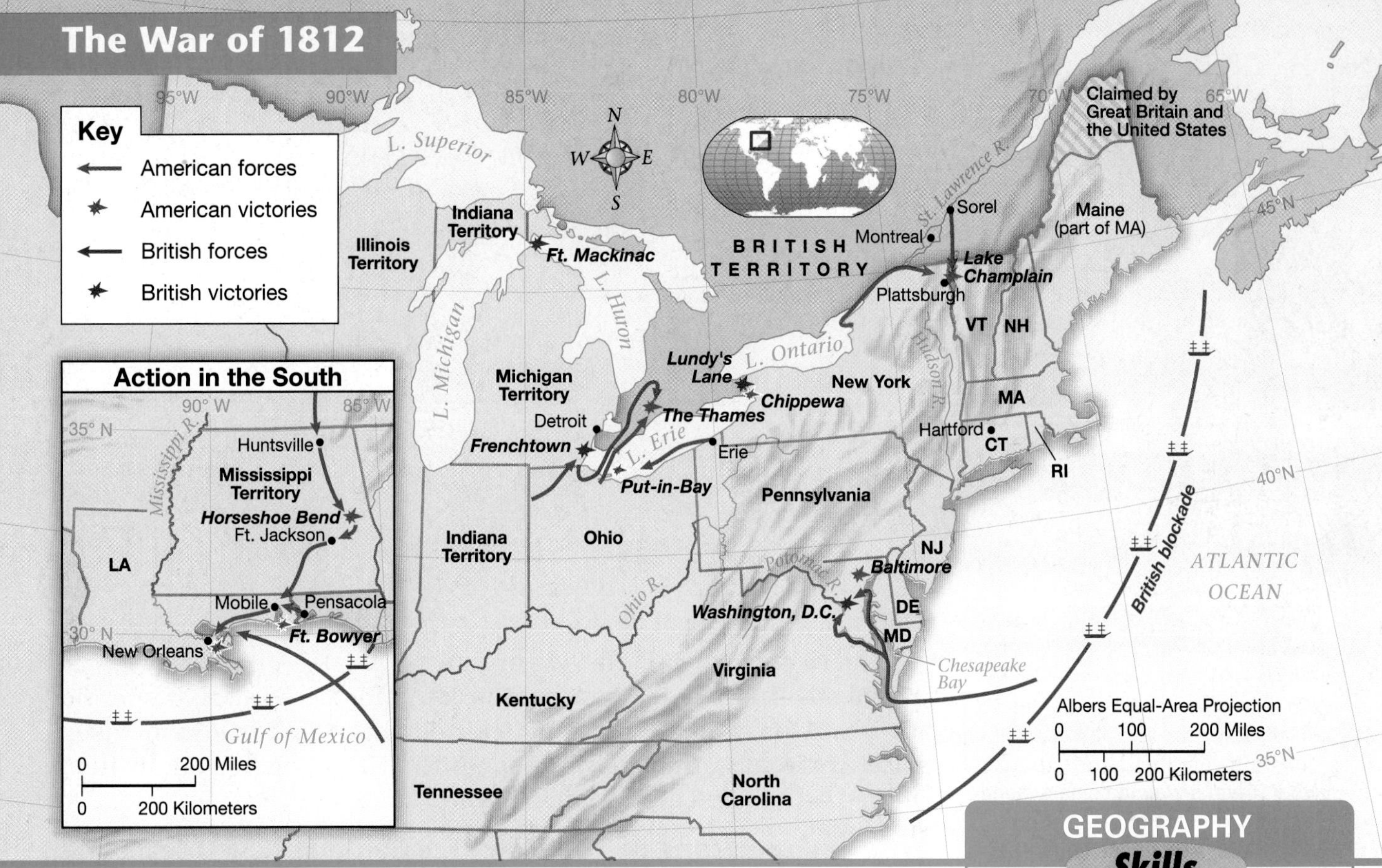

GEOGRAPHY *Skills*

The War of 1812 was fought along several fronts.

1. **Location** On the map, locate the following: **(a)** Lake Erie, **(b)** Horseshoe Bend, **(c)** Baltimore, **(d)** New Orleans.
2. **Movement** Describe the American route from Huntsville to New Orleans.
3. **Critical Thinking Drawing Conclusions** Based on the map, do you think the British blockade had a serious impact on Americans? Explain.

the evening of September 13 until dawn on September 14, British rockets bombarded the harbor.

When the early morning fog lifted, the "broad stripes and bright stars" of the American flag still waved over Fort McHenry. The British withdrew. Francis Scott Key, a young American lawyer who witnessed the battle, wrote a poem about it. Soon, "The Star-Spangled Banner" was published and set to music. Today, it is the national anthem of the United States.

Battle of New Orleans In late 1814, the British prepared to attack New Orleans. From there, they hoped to sail up the Mississippi. However, Andrew Jackson was waiting. Jackson had turned his frontier fighters into a strong army. He took Pensacola in Spanish Florida to keep the British from using it as a base. He then marched through Mobile and set up camp in New Orleans.

Jackson's force included thousands of frontiersmen and Choctaw Indians. The Choctaws were longtime rivals of the northern Indian nations who had been allied with the British. Many of Jackson's troops were expert riflemen. Citizens of New Orleans also joined the army to defend their city from the British. Among the volunteers were hundreds of African Americans.

The American soldiers dug trenches to defend themselves. On January 8, 1815, the British attacked. Again and again, British soldiers marched toward the American trenches. More than 2,000 British fell under the deadly fire of American sharpshooters and, especially, American cannons. Only seven Americans died.

Viewing History

Battle of New Orleans

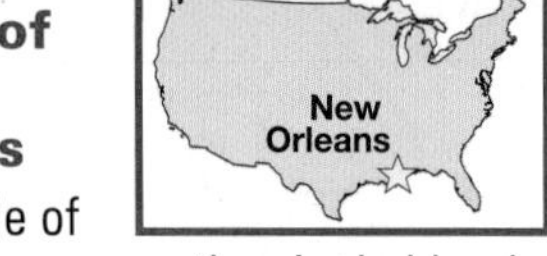

The Battle of New Orleans was the single bloodiest engagement of the War of 1812. Here, Americans under the command of Andrew Jackson fire at advancing British soldiers.

Analyzing Information ***How does this painting show the varied makeup of Jackson's troops?***

Americans cheered the victory at the **Battle of New Orleans.** Overnight, Andrew Jackson became a national hero. His fame did not dim even when Americans learned that the battle had taken place two weeks after the war ended. The United States and Britain had already signed a treaty in Europe.

African Americans in the War The Battle of New Orleans was not the only place where black and white soldiers fought side by side. Throughout the War of 1812, African Americans joined in defending the nation against the British.

Following the British attacks on Washington and Baltimore, African American volunteers helped defend Philadelphia against a possible British attack. Bishop Richard Allen and the Reverend Absalom Jones recruited more than 2,000 men to help build Philadelphia's fortifications. The state of New York organized two regiments of black volunteers to serve in the army.

African Americans also served with distinction in the United States Navy. They helped win the Battle of Lake Erie as well as other naval battles. Commander Nathaniel Shaler praised one particular black sailor who was killed in battle:

> "He fell near me, and several times requested to be thrown overboard, saying he was only in the way of others. When America has such [sailors], she has little to fear from the tyrants of the ocean."
>
> —Nathaniel Shaler, letter to his agent, January 1, 1813

Protest and Peace

In the early 1800s, news took weeks to cross the Atlantic Ocean. By late 1814, Americans knew that peace talks had begun, but they did not know if they would succeed or how long they would last. As Jackson was preparing to fight the British at New Orleans, New Englanders were meeting to protest "Mr. Madison's War."

New Englanders Protest The British blockade had hurt New England's sea trade. Also, many New Englanders feared that the United States might win land in Florida and Canada. If new states were carved out of these lands, the South and the West would become more influential than New England.

Delegates from around New England met in Hartford, Connecticut, in December 1814. Most were Federalists. They disliked the Republican President and the war. The delegates to the Hartford Convention threatened to leave the Union if the war continued.

Then, while the delegates debated what to do, news of the peace treaty arrived. The Hartford Convention ended quickly. With the war over, the protest was meaningless. In the end, the threat of secession further weakened the dying Federalist party.

"Nothing Was Settled" A peace treaty was signed in the city of Ghent, Belgium, on December 24, 1814. John Quincy Adams, one of the American delegates, summed up the Treaty of Ghent in one sentence: "Nothing was adjusted, nothing was settled."

Britain and the United States agreed to restore prewar conditions. The treaty said nothing about impressment or neutrality. These issues had faded due to the end of the wars in Europe. Other issues were settled later. In 1818, for example, the two nations settled a dispute over the border between Canada and the United States.

Looking back, some Americans felt that the War of 1812 had been a mistake. Others argued that Europe would now treat the young republic with more respect. The victories of heroes like Oliver Hazard Perry, William Henry Harrison, and Andrew Jackson gave Americans new pride in their country. As one Republican leader remarked, "The people are now more American. They feel and act more as a nation."

Section 5 Assessment

Recall

1. **Identify** Explain the significance of **(a)** Oliver Hazard Perry, **(b)** Battle of Lake Erie, **(c)** Andrew Jackson, **(d)** Dolley Madison, **(e)** Battle of New Orleans, **(f)** Hartford Convention, **(g)** Treaty of Ghent.

Comprehension

2. What military problems did the United States face at the start of the war?
3. How did the death of Tecumseh affect the war in the West?
4. How did Andrew Jackson achieve victory in the Battle of New Orleans?
5. Why did New Englanders threaten to leave the Union?

Critical Thinking and Writing

6. **Exploring the Main Idea** Review the Main Idea statement at the beginning of this section. Then, list two reasons supporting and two reasons opposing John Quincy Adams's statement, "Nothing was adjusted, nothing was settled."
7. **Drawing Conclusions** Both William Henry Harrison and Andrew Jackson later became President. Write a paragraph explaining why war heroes often make attractive political candidates.

Activity

Writing a Song **Like Francis Scott Key, you are a witness to one of the major conflicts of the War of 1812. With a partner, write a song or poem describing your feelings about the events going on around you.**

CHAPTER 10 Review and Assessment

Chapter Summary

Section 1
As President, Thomas Jefferson's goals included reducing the role of the federal government. *Marbury* v. *Madison* gave the Supreme Court the power of judicial review.

Section 2
In 1803, the United States purchased the Louisiana territory from France, doubling the size of the nation and giving it control of the Mississippi River. Lewis and Clark explored the Louisiana territory.

Section 3
As Great Britain went to war against France, both sides ignored U.S. neutrality. When France and Britain seized American ships, Jefferson imposed an embargo on the two nations.

Section 4
Tecumseh tried to unite several Indian nations to oppose the spread of white settlers west. Conflicts with Native Americans in the West and with the British at sea led to the War of 1812.

Section 5
Neither Great Britain nor the United States won the War of 1812. However, Americans proved that their republic would remain independent.

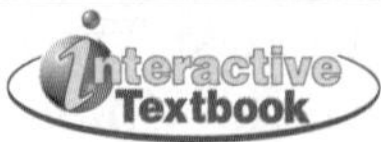

For additional review and enrichment activities, see the interactive version of *The American Nation,* available on the Web and on CD-ROM.

Chapter Self-Test For practice test questions for Chapter 10, visit PHSchool.com, **Web Code mfa-1004.**

Building Vocabulary

Review the chapter vocabulary words listed below. Then, use the words and their definitions to create a matching quiz. Exchange quizzes with another student. Check each other's answers.

1. **democratic**
2. **laissez faire**
3. **free market**
4. **judicial review**
5. **expedition**
6. **continental divide**
7. **impressment**
8. **embargo**
9. **confederation**
10. **nationalism**

Reviewing Key Facts

11. Describe two ways that Jefferson reversed Federalist policies. (Section 1)
12. Why did Jefferson decide that the Louisiana Purchase was constitutional? (Section 2)
13. How did Americans react to the British practice of impressment? (Section 3)
14. What were the results of the battles of Fallen Timbers and Tippecanoe? (Section 4)
15. What role did African American soldiers play in the War of 1812? (Section 5)

Critical Thinking and Writing

16. **Applying Information** In 1787, Jefferson stated, "The policy of the American government is to leave their citizens free, neither restraining nor aiding them in their pursuits." **(a)** Restate Jefferson's main point in your own words. **(b)** List two ways in which Jefferson's economic policies reflected this idea.
17. **Connecting to Geography: Place** Jefferson had Lewis and Clark take detailed notes about the Louisiana Purchase. Make a list of at least five geographic features, such as climate or plant life. For each item on your list, write a sentence explaining why information about this feature might be important for future settlers.
18. **Ranking** List the reasons the War Hawks wanted to go to war with Britain. Circle the reason you think is most valid, and underline the reason you think is least valid. Write a sentence explaining your ranking.

Skills Assessment

Analyzing Primary Sources

In 1812, a New York newspaper printed an editorial in favor of war with Britain. Nicholas Smyth of Boston wrote this reply. Read the excerpt and answer the questions that follow:

> "We hear from the halls of Congress the cry 'On to Canada!' It is the fur dealer and the land speculator who want war, but it is we of New England who will pay the price. If war comes, it is our seaports that will be blockaded; it is our cities that will be destroyed. The War Hawks of Tennessee and Kentucky are safe. I doubt if the English navy can reach them."
>
> —Nicholas Smyth, Records of the House Foreign Affairs Committee

19. According to Smyth, who is in favor of conquering Canada?
- **A.** people from New England
- **B.** people from Great Britain
- **C.** shipbuilders and loggers
- **D.** fur dealers and land speculators

20. What does Smyth say will happen if war comes?
- **A.** New England's cities will be destroyed.
- **B.** America will conquer Canada.
- **C.** Tennessee and Kentucky will lose power in Congress.
- **D.** The western states will leave the Union.

Applying Your Skills

Synthesizing Information

War of 1812 Vote in House of Representatives

REGIONS	FOR WAR	AGAINST WAR
New England	12	20
Middle States	21	18
The South	37	11
The West	9	0
Total	79	49

Source: Thomas A. Bailey, *A Diplomatic History of the American People*

This table shows the war vote in the House of Representatives in 1812. Look at the table and compare it to the letter at left.

21. Based on the table, which is a true statement?
- **A.** New England was largely in favor of war.
- **B.** The West was largely in favor of war.
- **C.** The war had overwhelming support.
- **D.** Regional differences played no role.

22. How did the vote in Congress reflect the concerns expressed in Smyth's letter?

Activities

Connecting With . . .

Government and Citizenship

Giving a Talk Give a one-minute talk based on one of the following quotations from Thomas Jefferson. Explain what Jefferson meant and how that idea still applies today.

- "The minority possess their equal rights, which equal laws must protect."
- "No government can continue good, but under the control of the people."
- "Whenever the people are well-informed, they can be trusted with their own government."

Connecting to Today

Preparing a Report Use the Internet to find out about one of the Indian nations shown on the map in Section 4. Prepare a report showing where they live today and how they maintain their traditions. For help in starting this activity, visit PHSchool.com, **Web Code mfd-1005.**

CHAPTER 11

The Nation Grows and Prospers

1790–1825

1. The Industrial Revolution
2. Americans Move Westward
3. Unity and Division
4. New Nations in the Americas

Slater's Mill

One of Fulton's early steamboats

1793

Samuel Slater builds a textile mill in Pawtucket, Rhode Island. It is the first successful textile mill in the United States.

1790s

The Lancaster Road improves travel between Philadelphia and central Pennsylvania.

Early 1800s

Development of the steam-powered boat creates a new age of steamboat travel on the major rivers of the United States.

AMERICAN EVENTS

Presidential Terms: George Washington 1789–1797 | John Adams 1797–1801 | Thomas Jefferson 1801–1809 | James Madison 1809–1817

1790 · 1800 · 1810

WORLD EVENTS

▲ **1791**

Enslaved plantation workers in Haiti revolt against their French masters.

▲ **1802**

Britain passes a law limiting child labor.

Early Roads West

In the early 1800s, new roads linked the East to settlements in the West.

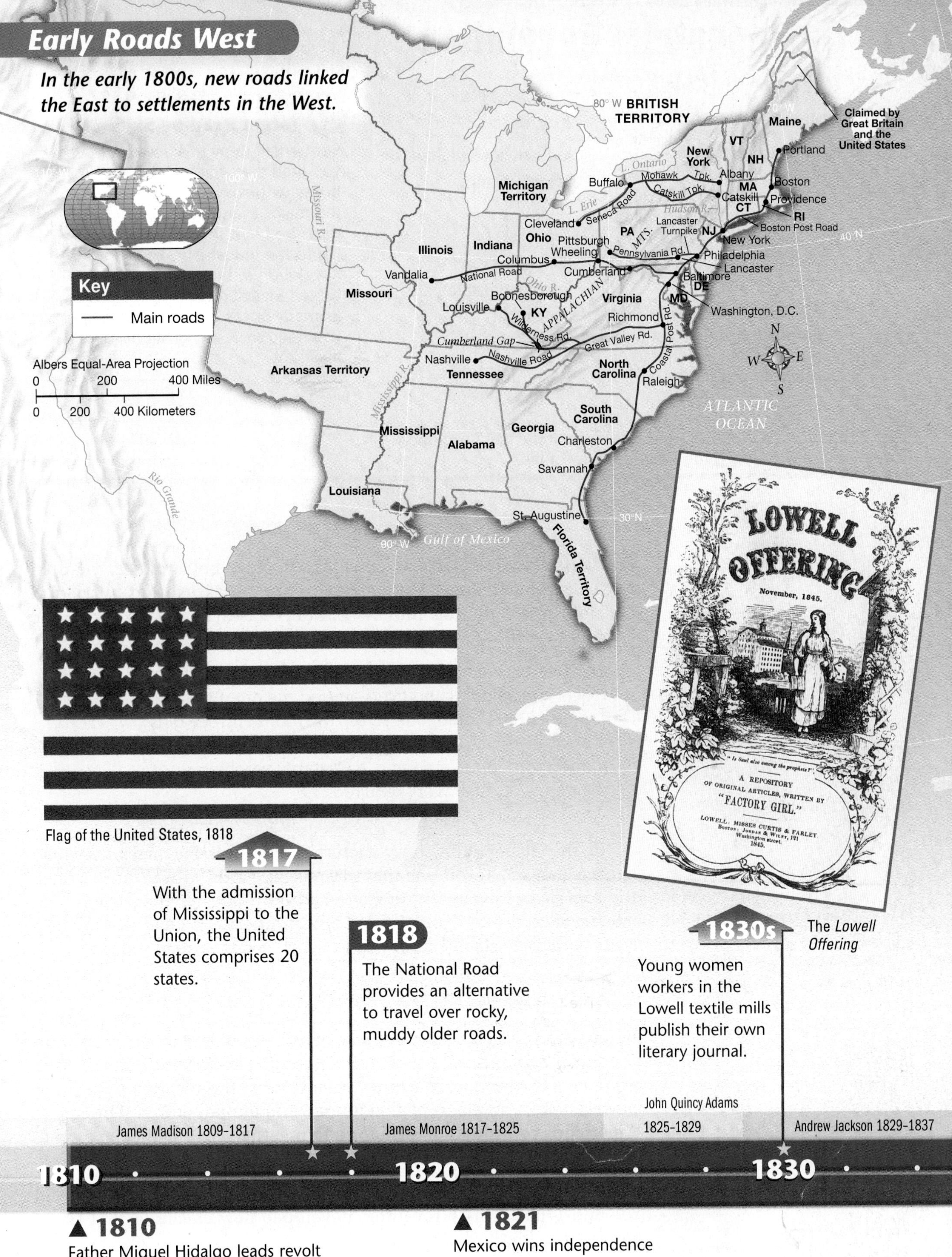

Flag of the United States, 1818

1817
With the admission of Mississippi to the Union, the United States comprises 20 states.

1818
The National Road provides an alternative to travel over rocky, muddy older roads.

The *Lowell Offering*

1830s
Young women workers in the Lowell textile mills publish their own literary journal.

James Madison 1809–1817 | James Monroe 1817–1825 | John Quincy Adams 1825–1829 | Andrew Jackson 1829–1837

1810 · 1820 · 1830

▲ 1810
Father Miguel Hidalgo leads revolt against Spanish rule in Mexico.

▲ 1821
Mexico wins independence from Spain.

1 The Industrial Revolution

Prepare to Read

Objectives

In this section, you will
- Identify the Industrial Revolution and explain its effects on the United States.
- Explain why Lowell, Massachusetts, was called a model factory town.
- Describe life in early factories.
- Summarize the impact the Industrial Revolution had on American cities.

Key Terms

Industrial Revolution
spinning jenny
capital
capitalist
factory system
interchangeable parts
Lowell girl
urbanization

Target Reading Skill

Sequence Copy this flowchart. As you read the section, fill in the boxes with some of the major events described in it that led to the Industrial Revolution in the United States. Add as many boxes as you need to finish the flowchart.

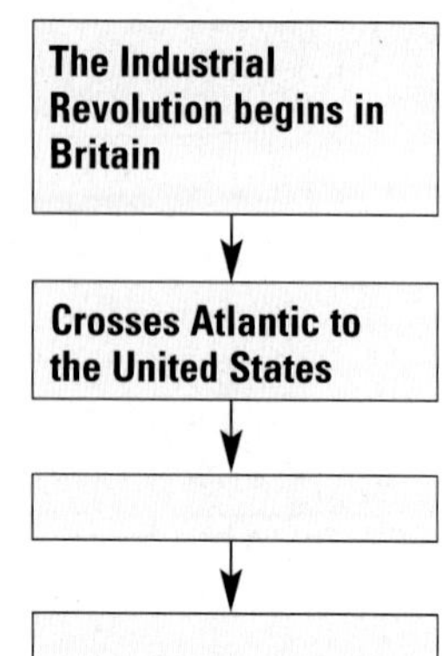

Main Idea During the early 1800s, the Industrial Revolution dramatically changed the American way of life.

Lucy Larcom

Setting the Scene At dawn, the factory bell woke 11-year-old Lucy Larcom. Rising quickly, she ate her breakfast and hurried to her job at a spinning mill in Lowell, Massachusetts. Years later, Larcom described her workplace:

> "The buzzing and hissing and whizzing of pulleys and rollers and spindles and flyers around me often grew tiresome. . . . I could look across the room and see girls moving backward and forward among the spinning frames, sometimes stooping, sometimes reaching up their arms, as their work required."
>
> —Lucy Larcom, *Among Lowell Mill-Girls: A Reminiscence,* 1881

In the early 1800s, busy factories and whirring machinery had become part of a revolution that was reaching the United States. Unlike the American Revolution, this one had no battles or fixed dates. The new revolution—the **Industrial Revolution**—was a long, slow process that completely changed the way in which goods were produced.

The Industrial Revolution Begins

Before the 1800s, most Americans were farmers and most goods were produced by hand. As a result of the Industrial Revolution, this situation slowly changed. Machines replaced hand tools. New sources of power, such as steam, replaced human and animal power. While most Americans continued to farm for a living, the economy began a gradual shift toward manufacturing.

New Technology The Industrial Revolution started in Britain in the mid-1700s. British inventors developed new machines that transformed the textile industry.

Viewing History

Changing Landscape

The Industrial Revolution changed the face of the nation. In this painting, the artist shows an early factory among the church spires and green fields of a New England town. **Identifying Points of View** ***What do you think is the point of view of the artist toward the changing face of the village? Explain.***

Since the Middle Ages, workers had used spinning wheels to make thread. A spinning wheel, however, could spin only one thread at a time. In 1764, James Hargreaves developed the **spinning jenny,** a machine that could spin several threads at once. Other inventions speeded up the process of weaving thread into cloth. In the 1780s, Edmund Cartwright built a loom powered by water. It allowed a worker to produce a great deal more cloth in a day than was possible before.

The Factory System New inventions led to a new system of producing goods. Before the Industrial Revolution, most spinning and weaving took place in the home. Large machines however, had to be housed in large mills near rivers. Water flowing downstream or over a waterfall turned a wheel that produced the power to run the machines.

To set up and operate a spinning mill required large amounts of **capital,** or money. Capitalists supplied this money. A **capitalist** is a person who invests in a business in order to make a profit. Capitalists built factories and hired workers to run the machines.

The new **factory system** brought workers and machinery together in one place to produce goods. Factory workers earned daily or weekly wages. They had to work a set number of hours each day.

A Revolution Crosses the Atlantic

Britain wanted to keep its new technology secret. It did not want rival nations to copy the new machines. Therefore, the British Parliament passed a law forbidding anyone to take plans of the new machinery out of the country.

Slater Breaks the Law Samuel Slater soon proved that this law could not be enforced. Slater was a skilled mechanic in a British textile mill. When he heard that Americans were offering large rewards for plans of British factories, he decided to leave Britain. In 1789,

Identify Sequence What events noted on this page contributed to the rise of the Industrial Revolution in the United States? Add these events to your flowchart.

Slater boarded a ship bound for New York City. He knew that British officials searched the baggage of passengers sailing to the United States. To avoid getting caught, he memorized the design of the machines in the mill.

The First American Mill Slater soon visited Moses Brown, a Quaker capitalist who had a mill in Pawtucket, Rhode Island. The mill was not doing well because its machinery constantly broke down. Slater set to work on improving the machinery. By 1793, in Pawtucket, he built what became the first successful textile mill in the United States that was powered by water. Slater's wife, Hannah Slater, contributed to the success of the mill. She discovered how to make thread stronger so that it would not snap on the spindles.

Slater's factory was a huge success. Before long, other American manufacturers began using his ideas.

Interchangeable Parts American manufacturers benefited from the pioneering work of American inventor Eli Whitney. Earlier, skilled workers made goods by hand. For example, gunsmiths spent days making the barrel, stock, and trigger for a single musket. Because the parts were handmade, each musket differed a bit from every other musket. If a part broke, a gunsmith had to make a new part to fit that particular gun.

Whitney wanted to speed up the making of guns by having machines manufacture each part. All machine-made parts would be alike—for example, one trigger would be identical to another. **Interchangeable parts** would save time and money.

Because the government bought many guns, Whitney went to Washington, D.C., to try to sell his idea. At first, officials laughed at his plan. Carefully, Whitney sorted parts for 10 muskets into separate piles. He then asked an official to choose one part from each pile. In minutes, the first musket was assembled. Whitney repeated the process until 10 muskets were complete.

The idea of interchangeable parts spread rapidly. Inventors designed machines to produce interchangeable parts for clocks, locks, and many other goods. With such machines, small workshops grew into factories.

Lowell, Massachusetts: A Model Factory Town

The War of 1812 provided a boost to American industries. The British blockade cut Americans off from their supply of foreign goods. As a result, they had to produce more goods themselves.

The Lowell Mills During the war, Francis Cabot Lowell, a Boston merchant, found a way to improve on British textile mills. In Britain, one factory spun thread and a second factory wove it into cloth. Why not, Lowell wondered, combine spinning and weaving under one roof? The new mill that he built in Waltham, Massachusetts, had all the machines needed to turn raw cotton into finished cloth.

After Lowell's death, his partners took on a more ambitious project. They built an entire factory town and named it after him. In

1821, Lowell, Massachusetts, was a village of five farm families. By 1836, it boasted more than 10,000 people. Visitors to Lowell described it as a model community composed of "small wooden houses, painted white, with green blinds, very neat, very snug, very nicely carpeted."

"Lowell Girls" To work in their new mills, the company hired young women from nearby farms. The **Lowell girls,** as they came to be called, usually worked for a few years in the mills before returning home to marry. Most sent their wages home to their families.

At first, parents hesitated to let their daughters work in the mills. To reassure parents, the company built boardinghouses. The company also made rules to protect the young women.

Although factory work was often tedious and hard, many women valued the economic freedom they got from working in the mills. One worker wrote her sister Sarah back on a farm in New Hampshire:

> "Since I have wrote you, another pay day has come around. I earned 14 dollars and a half . . . I like it well as ever and Sarah don't I feel independent of everyone!"
>
> — from *Lowell Offering: Writings by New England Mill Women*

Viewing History

Inside a Textile Mill

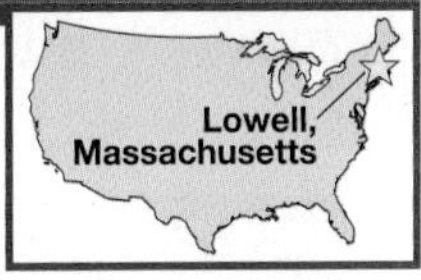

Work in the textile mills in the early 1800s was hard. Workers faced long hours on their feet amid the noisy machines. Yet, the mills were generally clean and orderly.

Analyzing Primary Sources

What clues does the picture give to conditions in this mill?

Daily Life During the Industrial Revolution

In Lowell and elsewhere, mill owners hired mostly women and children. They did this because they could pay women and children half of what they would have had to pay men.

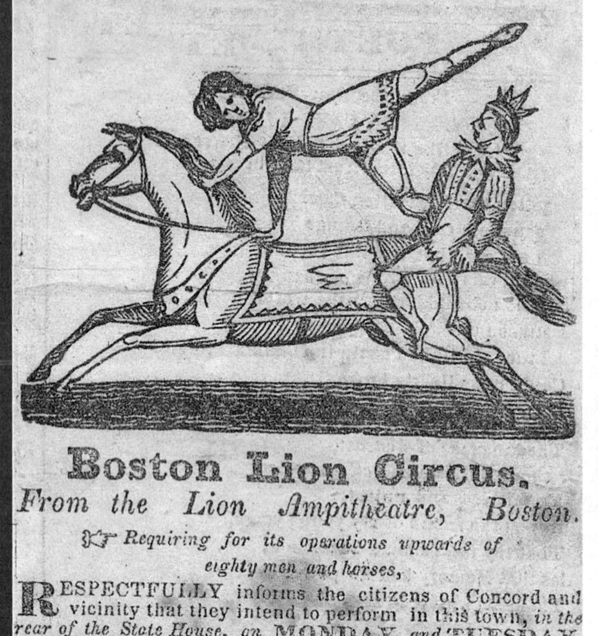

▲ Past

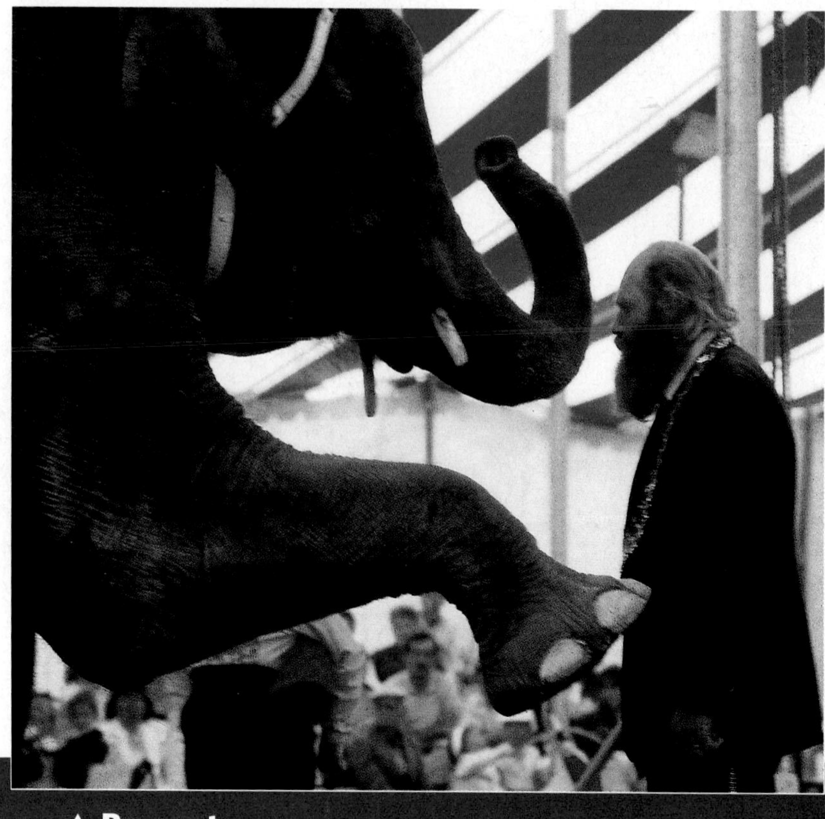

▲ Present

Viewing History

Circuses Then and Now

Concord, Massachusetts

From Roman times to the present, circuses have been one of the world's most popular forms of family entertainment. The world has changed dramatically, but trained animals continue to delight and enthrall us. At left, a poster from the early 1800s promises trick riders and a "wonderful variety of feats, many of which have never before been attempted on this side of the Atlantic."

Linking Past and Present

Why have circuses maintained their popularity for so many years?

Child Labor Boys and girls as young as seven worked in factories. Small children were especially useful in textile mills because they could squeeze around the large machines to change spindles.

Today, most Americans look upon child labor as cruel. Yet in the 1800s, farm children also worked hard. Most people did not see much difference between children working in a factory or on a farm. Often, a child's wages were needed to help support the family.

Long Hours Working hours in the mills were long—12 hours a day, 6 days a week. True, farmers also put in long hours. However, farmers worked shorter hours in winter. Mill workers, in contrast, worked nearly the same hours all year round.

In the early 1800s, conditions in American mills were generally much better than in most factories in Europe. As industries grew, however, competition increased and employers took less interest in the welfare of their workers. In later chapters, you will read how working conditions grew worse.

Changes in Home Life The Industrial Revolution had a great impact on home life. As the factory system spread, more family members left the home to earn a living.

These changes affected ideas about the role of women. In poorer families, women often had to go out to work. In wealthier families, husbands supported the family while wives stayed at home. For many husbands, having a wife who stayed at home became a sign of success.

Growing Cities

In 1800, the vast majority of Americans lived in rural areas. During the Industrial Revolution, many people left farms to work in factories. Older cities expanded rapidly, while new cities sprang up around factories. This movement of the population from farms to cities is called **urbanization.**

Urbanization was a steady but gradual process. In 1800, only 6 percent of the nation's population lived in urban areas. By 1850, the number had risen to 15 percent. Not until 1920 did more Americans live in cities than on farms.

By today's standards, these early cities were small. A person could walk from one end of any American city to the other in as little as 30 minutes. Buildings were only a few stories tall. As the factory system spread, the nation's cities grew.

Hazards Growing cities had many problems. Dirt and gravel streets turned into mudholes when it rained. Cities had no sewers, and people threw garbage into the streets. A visitor to New York reported that "The streets are filthy, and the stranger is not a little surprised to meet the hogs walking about in them, for the purpose of devouring the vegetables and trash thrown into the gutter."

Under these conditions, disease spread easily. Epidemics of influenza and cholera (KAHL er uh) raged through cities, killing hundreds.

Attractions Cities had attractions, too. Theaters, museums, and circuses created an air of excitement. In cities, people could shop in fine stores that sold the latest fashions from Europe. Some offered modern "ready-to-wear" clothing. While most women continued to sew their own clothes, many enjoyed visiting hat shops, china shops, shoe stores, and "fancy-goods" stores.

★ ★ ★ Section 1 Assessment ★ ★ ★

Recall

1. **Identify** Explain the significance of **(a)** Industrial Revolution, **(b)** Samuel Slater, **(c)** Eli Whitney, **(d)** Lowell girl.
2. **Define** **(a)** spinning jenny, **(b)** capital, **(c)** capitalist, **(d)** factory system, **(e)** interchangeable parts, **(f)** urbanization.

Comprehension

3. How did the Industrial Revolution begin in the United States?
4. What was unusual about the factory town of Lowell, Massachusetts?
5. What were conditions like for workers during the early Industrial Revolution?
6. Describe three ways in which American cities were changed by the early Industrial Revolution.

Critical Thinking and Writing

7. **Exploring the Main Idea** Review the Main Idea statement at the beginning of the section. Then, list three examples of changes in the way Americans lived and worked that were a result of the Industrial Revolution.
8. **Drawing Conclusions** Make a list of the reasons why both inventors and capitalists were needed to bring about the Industrial Revolution.

Activity

Use the Internet to learn more about life for the "Lowell girls" of the early 1800s. Then, suppose that you are a worker at the mill, and compose a diary entry describing a typical day. For help in completing the activity, visit PHSchool.com, **Web Code mfd-1101.**

How a Textile Mill Worked

New technology, like that used by Samuel Slater's mill, helped spark the Industrial Revolution. The diagram shows how rapidly moving water turned a water wheel. The wheel produced the power to run the machines.

Samuel Slater

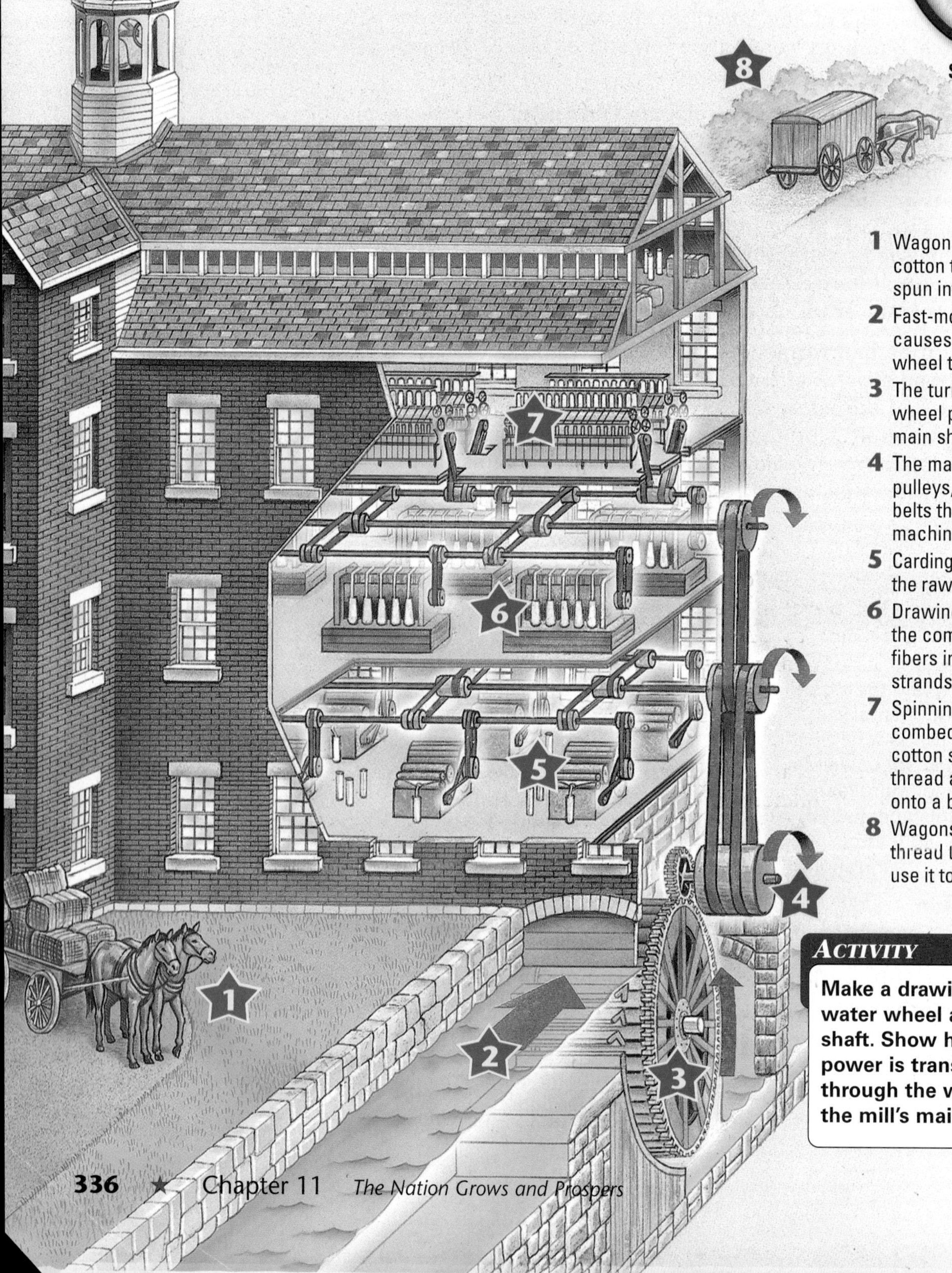

1 Wagons bring raw cotton to the mill to be spun into thread.
2 Fast-moving water causes the water wheel to turn.
3 The turning water wheel powers the mill's main shaft.
4 The main shaft drives pulleys, which turn belts that drive the mill machinery.
5 Carding machines comb the raw cotton fiber.
6 Drawing machines pull the combed cotton fibers into ropelike strands.
7 Spinning frames twist combed and drawn cotton strands into thread and wind them onto a bobbin.
8 Wagons carry spun thread to weavers, who use it to make cloth.

ACTIVITY

Make a drawing of the mill's water wheel and main mill shaft. Show how water power is transmitted through the water wheel to the mill's main shaft.

2 Americans Move Westward

Prepare to Read

Objectives

In this section, you will
- Describe how settlers traveled west.
- List the steps Americans took to improve their roads.
- Explain how steamboats and canals improved transportation for Americans.

Key Terms

flatboat
turnpike
Lancaster Turnpike
corduroy road
National Road
Clermont
Erie Canal

Target Reading Skill

Reading Process As you read, complete this table listing important developments in transportation in the United States at the beginning of the 1800s. Add as many rows as you need.

TRAVELING WEST	IMPROVING ROAD TRANSPORTATION	NEW STEAMBOATS AND CANALS
• Roads to the West • Travel by flatboat	•	•

Main Idea Improvements in transportation in the first half of the 1800s helped make it easier to move people and goods in the expanding nation.

Setting the Scene The stagecoach was bogged down in the spring mud, its big wheels sunk up to the axles. The passengers stood by the side of the road while the stage driver urged his horses to pull the coach out of the mud. Suddenly, one traveler spotted a beautiful fur cap lying in the middle of a huge mudhole just ahead. He had to have that cap!

The traveler stepped through the mud until at last he snatched up the hat. To his surprise, he saw a man's head *underneath*—a man buried in the mud! "Come help pull this fellow out!" called the traveler to his friends. The man in the mud shook his head. "Just leave me alone, stranger," he said. "I have a good horse under me, and have just found bottom."

Americans during the 1830s loved to tell this tall tale. The story was so popular because travel in the United States was often difficult. As the young nation grew, Americans saw an urgent need to improve transportation, both on water and over land.

A necessary stop

Traveling West

Settlers had been moving steadily westward since the 1600s. In the early 1800s, the stream of pioneers turned into a flood. By 1820, so many people had moved west that the population in some of the original 13 states had actually declined!

Western Routes Settlers took a number of routes west. One well-traveled path was the Great Wagon Road across Pennsylvania. It dated back to colonial days. Some settlers then continued south and west along the trail opened by Daniel Boone before the Revolution. Known as the Wilderness Road, it led through the Cumberland Gap into Kentucky.

Other settlers pushed west to Pittsburgh. There, they loaded their animals and wagons onto **flatboats,** or flat-bottom boats, and journeyed down the Ohio River into Indiana, Kentucky, and Illinois.

Conner Prairie Village

Conner Prairie is a center for entertainment and education focusing on the lives and times of western settlers in the early 1800s. It consists of five historic areas, including the re-created 1836 village of Prairietown. Another site is the Lenape (luh-NAH-pay) Indian Camp and McKinnen's Trading Post, shown here. The historic areas are set on a 210-acre woodland site.

Virtual Field Trip For an interactive look at the Conner Prairie Village, visit PHSchool.com, **Web Code mfd-1102.**

Flatboats were well suited to the shallow waters of the Ohio. Even when carrying heavy cargoes, these barges rode high in the water.

Pioneers from Georgia and South Carolina followed other trails west to Alabama, Mississippi, and Louisiana. Enslaved African Americans helped to carve plantations in the rich, fertile soil of these territories.

People from New England, New York, and Pennsylvania pushed into the Northwest Territory. Some settlers traveled west from Albany, New York, along the Mohawk River and across the Appalachians. Many then sailed across Lake Erie into Ohio.

New States Before long, some western territories had populations large enough to apply for statehood. Between 1792 and 1819, eight states joined the Union: Kentucky (1792), Tennessee (1796), Ohio (1803), Louisiana (1812), Indiana (1816), Mississippi (1817), Illinois (1818), and Alabama (1819).

Target Skill **Ask Questions** As you read the next two sections, turn each blue heading into a question. Then, read to find the answers to these questions. Use the answers to fill in your table.

Improvements to Roads

Settlers faced difficult journeys to the West. Many roads were narrow trails, barely wide enough for a single wagon. Trails often plunged through muddy swamps. Tree stumps stuck up through the road and often broke the wagon axles of careless travelers. The nation badly needed better roads.

Turnpikes and Corduroy Roads In the United States, as in Europe, private companies built gravel and stone roads. To pay for these roads, the companies collected tolls from travelers. At various points along the road, a pike, or pole, blocked the road. After a wagon driver had paid a toll, the pike keeper turned the pole aside to let the wagon pass. As a result, these toll roads were called **turnpikes.**

Probably the best road in the United States was the **Lancaster Turnpike.** Built in the 1790s by a private company, the road linked Philadelphia and Lancaster, Pennsylvania. Because the road was set on a bed of gravel, water drained off quickly. For a smooth ride, the road was topped with flat stones.

Other roads were more primitive. In swampy areas, roads were made of logs. These roads were known as **corduroy roads** because the lines of logs looked like corduroy cloth. Corduroy roads kept wagons from sinking into the mud, but they made for a very noisy and bumpy ride.

The National Road Some states set aside money to improve roads or build new ones. In 1806, for the first time, Congress approved funds for a national road-building project. The **National Road** was to run from Cumberland, Maryland, to Wheeling, in western Virginia.

Work on the National Road began in 1811. Because of the War of 1812, it was not completed until 1818. Later, the road was extended into Illinois. As each new section of road was built, settlers eagerly used it to drive their wagons west.

Steam Transport

Whenever possible, travelers and freight haulers used river transportation. Floating downstream on a flatboat was both faster and more comfortable than bumping along rutted roads. It also cost less.

Yet, river travel had its own problems. Moving upstream was difficult. People used paddles or long poles to push boats against the current. Sometimes, they hauled boats from the shore with ropes. Both methods were slow. A boat could travel downstream from Pittsburgh to New Orleans in about six weeks. However, the return trip upstream took at least 17 weeks!

Fitch and Fulton A new invention, the steam engine, opened a new era in river travel. In 1787, John Fitch showed members of the Constitutional Convention how a steam engine could power a boat. He then opened a ferry service on the Delaware River. However, few people used the ferry, and Fitch went out of business.

Inventor Robert Fulton may have seen Fitch's steamboat in Philadelphia. In 1807, Fulton launched his own steamboat, the *Clermont,* on the Hudson River. On its first run, the *Clermont* carried passengers from New York City to Albany and back. The 300-mile trip took just 62 hours—a record at the time.

The Age of Steamboats Fulton's success ushered in the age of steamboats. Soon, steamboats were ferrying passengers up and down the Atlantic coast. More important, steamboats revolutionized travel in the West. Besides carrying people, steamboats on the Mississippi, Ohio, and Missouri rivers gave farmers and merchants a cheap means of moving goods.

Primary Source

An English Traveler's View of American Travel

Road travel in the early 1800s had many hardships. An English visitor reports on the physical hardships and the cultural divide that separated her from the Americans:

"Bones of me! What a road! Even my father's solid proportions . . . were jerked up to the roof and down again every three minutes. Our companions . . . laughed and talked [constantly], the young ladies, at the very top of their voices, and with the national nasal twang. . . . The few cottages and farmhouses which we passed reminded me of similar dwellings in France and Ireland. . . . The farms had the same desolate, untidy, untended look. . . ."

—Journal of Frances Anne (Fanny) Kemble Butler

Analyzing Primary Sources

What is Frances Kemble's attitude toward the Americans whom she meets? Explain your answer.

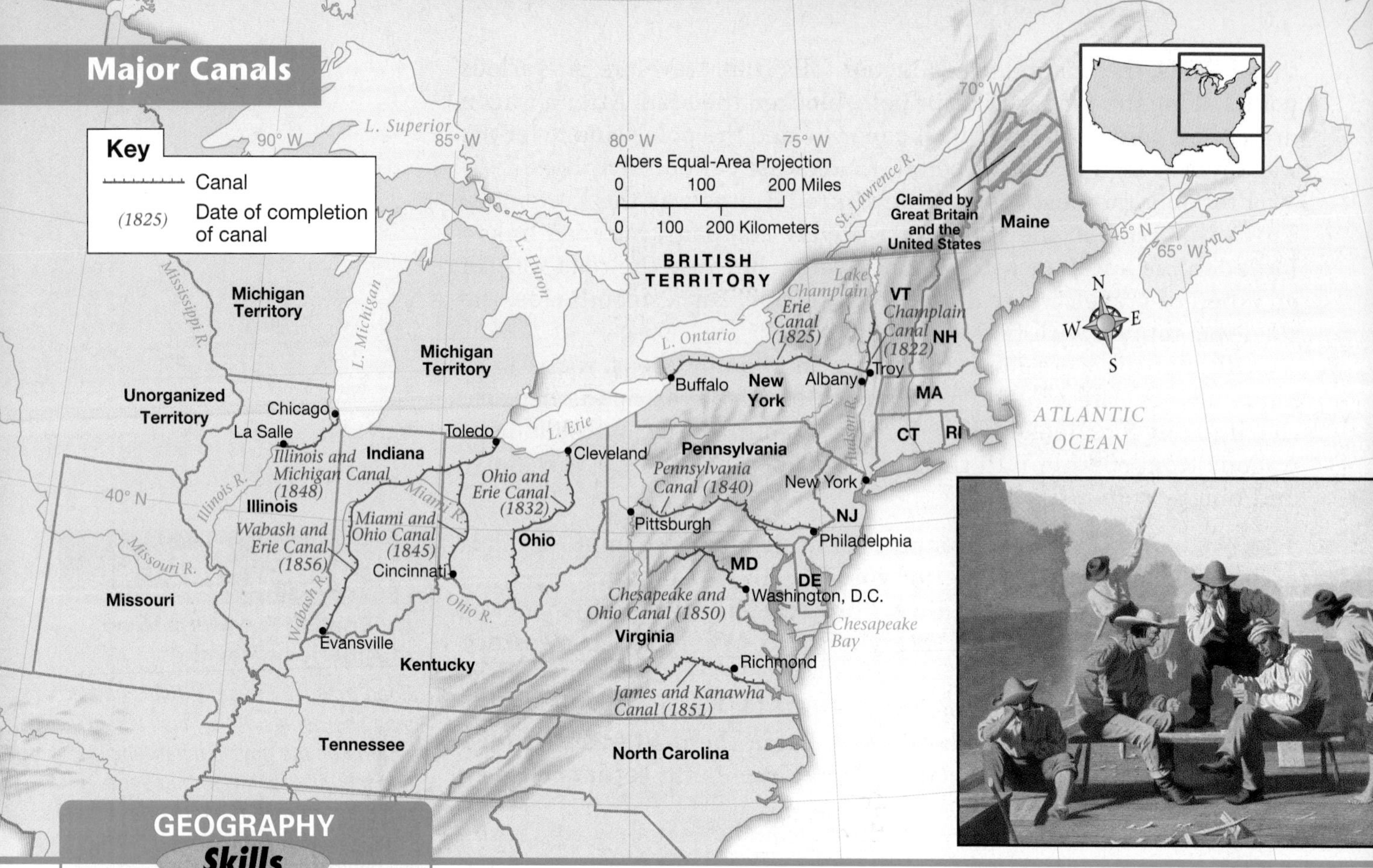

GEOGRAPHY Skills

The success of the Erie Canal, completed in 1825, set off an age of canal building. The painting by George Caleb Bingham shows boatsmen relaxing after a long workday.

1. **Location** On the map, locate **(a)** New York City, **(b)** Troy, **(c)** Buffalo, **(d)** Lake Erie, **(e)** Erie Canal.
2. **Movement** What two bodies of water were linked by the Illinois and Michigan Canal?
3. **Critical Thinking Applying Information** Use the map to trace an all-water route from Evansville, Indiana, to New York City.

Because western rivers were shallow, Henry Shreve designed a flat-bottomed steamboat. It could carry heavy loads without getting stuck on sandbars.

Still, steamboat travel could be dangerous. Sparks from smokestacks could cause fires. As steamboat captains raced each other along the river, high-pressure boilers sometimes exploded. Between 1811 and 1851, 44 steamboats collided, 166 burned, and more than 200 exploded.

The Canal Boom

Steamboats and better roads brought many improvements. But they did not help western farmers get their goods directly to markets in the East. To meet this need, Americans dug canals. A canal is an artificial channel filled with water that allows boats to cross a stretch of land.

The earliest American canals were no more than a few miles long. Some provided routes around waterfalls on a river. Other canals linked rivers to nearby lakes. By the early 1800s, however, Americans were building longer canals.

Building the Erie Canal Some New Yorkers had a bold idea. They wanted to build a canal linking the Great Lakes with the Mohawk and Hudson rivers. The **Erie Canal** would let western farmers ship their goods to the port of New York. It would also bring business to towns along the route.

To many people, the idea of such a canal seemed far-fetched. When Thomas Jefferson heard of the plan, he exclaimed:

> "Why, sir, you talk of making a canal 350 miles through the wilderness—it is little short of madness to think of it at this day!"
>
> —Thomas Jefferson to Joshua Forman of New York, 1809

New York's governor DeWitt Clinton ignored such criticism. He persuaded state lawmakers to provide money for the Erie Canal. Scoffers referred to the project as "Clinton's Ditch."

Work on the Erie Canal began in 1817. At first, thousands of workers dug the waterway by hand. To speed up progress, inventors developed new equipment. One machine, a stump-puller, could pull out nearly 40 tree stumps a day. In two places, the canal had to cross over rivers. Workers built stone bridges to carry the canal over the rivers.

An Instant Success By 1825, the immense job was finished. On opening day of the Erie Canal, a cannon fired a volley in Buffalo, New York. When the sound got to the next town along the route, that town, too, fired a cannon. Town after town fired cannons—all the way to New York City. The thunderous salute took 80 minutes to complete.

The Erie Canal was an instant success. The cost of shipping goods dropped to about one tenth of what it had been before the canal was built. The canal also helped to make New York City a center of commerce.

The success of the Erie Canal led other states to build canals. These canals created vital economic links between western farms and eastern cities.

Section 2 Assessment

Recall

1. **Identify** Explain the significance of **(a)** Lancaster Turnpike, **(b)** National Road, **(c)** John Fitch, **(d)** Robert Fulton, **(e)** *Clermont,* **(f)** Henry Shreve, **(g)** DeWitt Clinton, **(h)** Erie Canal.
2. **Define** **(a)** flatboat, **(b)** turnpike, **(c)** corduroy road.

Comprehension

3. What routes did settlers use to reach the West in the early 1800s?
4. Describe two ways in which road transportation improved in the early 1800s.
5. What role did the steamboat play in the growing nation?

Critical Thinking and Writing

6. **Exploring the Main Idea** Review the Main Idea statement at the beginning of this section. Then, write an imaginary diary entry of a trip along the National Road that explains how the road has made travel easier.
7. **Identifying Alternatives** Examine the maps in this chapter. Then, describe two ways a farmer might have shipped a cargo of grain from Cleveland, Ohio, to New York City. Explain the advantages of each route.

Activity

Writing a Newspaper Story **Review the chapter's description of opening day on the Erie Canal. Write a newspaper story reporting on that first day. Write a newspaper-style headline and a lead sentence that covers the *who, what, when, where,* and *why* of the event.**

3 Unity and Division

Prepare to Read

Objectives

In this section, you will
- Discuss sectionalism's impact in the Era of Good Feelings.
- Explain how Congress helped industry after the war ended.
- Describe Henry Clay's American System.
- Explain how the Supreme Court gave more power to the federal government.

Key Terms

sectionalism
American System
internal improvements
McCulloch v. *Maryland*
Gibbons v. *Ogden*
interstate commerce

Target Reading Skill

Main Idea As you read, prepare an outline of this section. Use roman numerals to indicate the major headings of this section, capital letters for the subheadings, and numbers for the supporting details. The sample at right will help you get started.

I. An Era of Good Feelings
II. Three Sectional Leaders
  A. Calhoun of the South
    1.
    2.
  B. Webster of the North
    1.
    2.
  C.
    1.
    2.
III. Helping American Businesses Grow

Main Idea Despite some tensions between different sections, the nation enjoyed an "era of good feelings" after the War of 1812.

The Fourth of July in 1819

Setting the Scene In Charleston, a cook named Abigail Jones put her advertisement in the newspaper early. Turtle meat would be available for sale on July 4 only. When Americans celebrated the Fourth of July in the early 1800s, turtle soup was one of the two most popular holiday foods.

What was the other? For a hot summer holiday like the Fourth, Americans loved the rare treat of ice cream. In Boston, a Mr. Shindles advertised "iced creams, of the best quality" in four flavors. At Vauxhall Gardens in Charleston, sellers warned people to come early, before all the ice cream was eaten.

After the War of 1812, Fourth of July celebrations became more popular than ever. Americans were proud of their country. They were especially proud that the nation was growing rapidly. Improved transportation allowed the opening of new lands to settlers. New industries were appearing. In Congress, a new generation of political leaders sought to direct this expansion.

An Era of Good Feelings

In 1816, the Republican candidate for President, James Monroe, easily defeated the Federalist, Senator Rufus King of New York. The election showed how seriously the Federalist party had declined in popularity. Many Federalists had joined the Republican party and voted for Monroe.

Monroe was the last Revolutionary War officer to become President. He was almost 60 years old when he took office, and he still followed the fashions of the late 1700s. He wore a powdered wig at a time when young men were wearing their hair loose. While other Americans wore long trousers, he still wore breeches and long stockings.

Americans were fond of his old-fashioned ways. In 1817, he made a goodwill tour of the country. In Boston, crowds cheered Monroe enthusiastically. Boston newspapers expressed surprise at this warm welcome for a Republican from Virginia. After all, Boston had long been a Federalist stronghold.

Monroe hoped to create a new sense of national unity. One newspaper wrote that the United States was entering an "era of good feelings." By the time Monroe ran for a second term in 1820, no candidate opposed him. The Federalist party had disappeared.

Three Sectional Leaders

While conflict between political parties declined, disputes between different sections of the nation sharpened. In Congress, three ambitious young men took center stage. All three would play key roles in Congress for more than 30 years, as well as serving in other offices. Each represented a different section of the country.

Calhoun of the South John C. Calhoun spoke for the South. He had grown up on a frontier farm in South Carolina. Calhoun's immense energy and striking features earned him the nickname "young Hercules." He was slim and handsome, with deep-set eyes and a high forehead. His way of speaking was so intense that it sometimes made people uncomfortable to be in his presence.

Calhoun had supported the War of 1812. Like many southerners, he was a firm defender of slavery. In general, he opposed policies that would strengthen the power of the federal government.

Webster of the North Daniel Webster of New Hampshire was perhaps the most skillful public speaker of his time. With eyes flashing and shoulders thrown back, Webster was an impressive sight when he stood up to speak in Congress. An observer described him as a "great cannon loaded to the lips."

Like many New Englanders, Webster had opposed the War of 1812. He even refused to vote for taxes to pay for the war effort. After the war, he wanted the federal government to take a larger role in building the nation's economy. Unlike Calhoun, Webster thought that slavery was evil.

Clay of the West Henry Clay spoke for the West. You have already met Clay as a leader of the War Hawks, who pushed for war against Britain in 1812.

Clay was born in Virginia but moved to Kentucky when he was 20. As a young lawyer, he was once fined for brawling with an opponent. Usually, however, he charmed both friends and rivals. Supporters called him "Gallant Harry of the West." Like Webster, Clay strongly favored a more active role for the central government in promoting the country's growth.

An American Profile

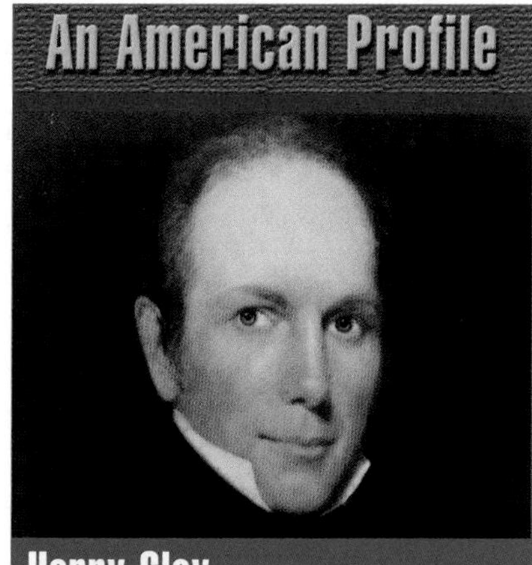

Henry Clay 1777–1852

During his long service to his country, Henry Clay was a firm defender of the Union. Clay helped to guide his country through some of its most difficult crises. Three times he helped resolve bitter disputes that threatened to tear the nation apart.

One office that eluded him was the presidency. He was defeated three times in efforts to become President. Yet, he was proud that he had held to his principles. Once, when asked if he was bitter about his failure to become President, he responded: "No. I had rather be right than be President."

Name two qualities that Clay demonstrated during his career in public service.

Helping American Businesses Grow

After the War of 1812, leaders like Calhoun, Webster, and Clay had to deal with serious economic issues. Despite the nation's great physical growth and the soaring spirits of its people, the United States economy faced severe problems. This was due in part to the lack of a national bank.

The charter that had set up the Bank of the United States ran out in 1811. Without the Bank to lend money and regulate the nation's money supply, the economy suffered. State banks made loans and issued money. However, they often put too much money into circulation. With so much money available to spend, prices rose rapidly.

In the nation's early years, Republicans like Jefferson and Madison had opposed a national bank. By 1816, however, many Republicans believed that a bank was needed. They supported a law to charter the second Bank of the United States. By lending money and restoring order to the nation's money supply, the Bank helped American businesses grow.

Target Skill: Identify Supporting Details What details in this subsection explain the relationship between the money supply and the Bank of the United States? Add these details to your outline.

Protection From Foreign Competition Another economic problem facing the nation was foreign competition, especially from Britain. In the early 1800s, the Embargo Act and then the War of 1812 kept most British goods out of the United States. In response, ambitious American business leaders like Francis Cabot Lowell established their own mills and factories. As a result, American industry grew quickly until 1815.

A Flood of British Goods With the end of the War of 1812, British goods again poured into the United States. Because the British had a head start in industrializing, they could make and sell goods more cheaply than Americans could. Most British factory buildings and machines were older and had already been paid for. In contrast, Americans still had to pay for their new factory buildings.

Sometimes, British manufacturers sold cloth in the United States for less than it cost to make. British manufacturers hoped to put American rivals out of business. Then, the British planned to raise prices.

Congress Passes a Protective Tariff The British plan caused dozens of New England businesses to fail. Angry owners asked Congress to place a protective tariff on all goods imported from Europe. As you have read, the purpose of a protective tariff is to protect a country's industries from foreign competition.

Viewing History

Cheapened Money

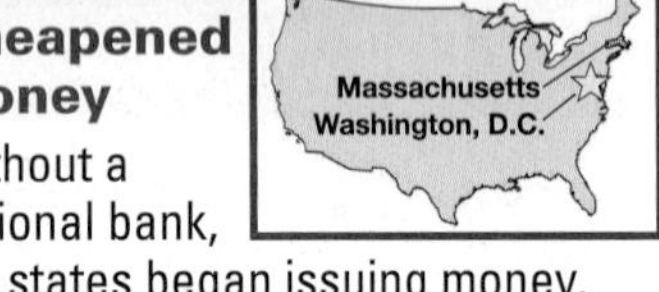

Without a national bank, the states began issuing money, like this one-dollar bank note issued by the state of Massachusetts. With so much money being issued, the value of the money declined. **Analyzing Primary Sources** ***What do the illustrations on the money show about the changing nature of work at the time?***

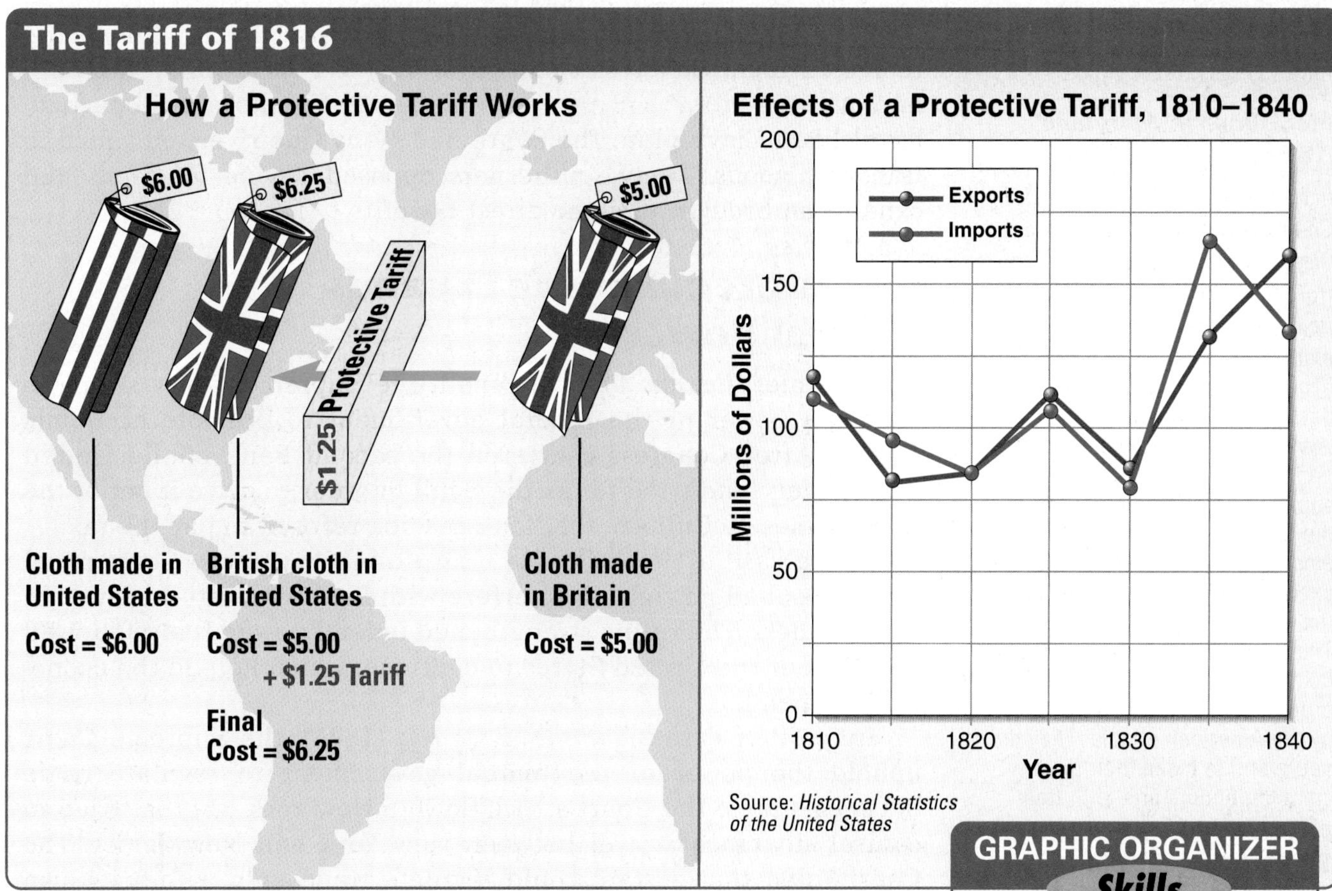

Congress responded by passing the Tariff of 1816. It greatly raised tariffs on imports. This increase made imported goods far more expensive than similar American-made goods. Higher tariffs led to angry protests from southerners. Southerners had built few factories. As a result, they did not benefit from the tariff. Also, southerners bought many British goods. The new tariff drove up the price of British-made goods. Southerners complained that the tariff made northern manufacturers rich at the expense of the South.

Clay's American System

The bitter dispute over tariffs reflected the growth of sectionalism. **Sectionalism** is loyalty to one's state or section rather than to the nation as a whole. Americans identified themselves as southerners, northerners, or westerners. In Congress, representatives from different sections often clashed.

Henry Clay wanted to promote economic growth for all sections. His program, known as the **American System,** called for high tariffs on imports, which would help northern factories. With wealth from industry, Clay believed, northerners would have the money to buy farm products from the West and the South. High tariffs would also reduce American dependence on foreign goods.

Clay also urged Congress to use money from tariffs to build roads, bridges, and canals. A better transportation system, he believed, would make it easier and cheaper for farmers in the West and the South to ship goods to city markets.

GRAPHIC ORGANIZER *Skills*

In 1816, Congress passed a protective tariff to help American factory owners.

1. **Comprehension** **(a)** According to the chart (above, left) how did the protective tariff affect the price of a bolt of cloth? **(b)** In which years on the graph (above, right) did United States exports exceed imports?
2. **Critical Thinking Identifying Causes and Effects** The Tariff of 1816 was followed by additional tariffs in 1824 and 1828. When did United States foreign trade begin to recover from these tariffs?

Economics $

Primary Source

***McCulloch* v. *Maryland* (1819)**

In McCulloch *v.* Maryland *(1819) Chief Justice John Marshall ruled that no state has the right to control any federal organization within its borders. Here is a passage explaining his reasoning:*

"The American people have declared their Constitution and the laws . . . to be supreme, but this principle would transfer the supremacy, in fact, to the States. If the States may tax one [body], employed by the government in the execution of its powers, they may tax any and every other [body]. They may tax the mail; they may tax the mint; they may tax judicial process. . . . This was not intended by the American people. They did not [want] to make their government dependent on the States."

Analyzing Primary Sources

What does Marshall suggest may happen if the states can tax federal banks?

Clay's American System never fully went into effect. While tariffs remained high, Congress spent little on **internal improvements**—improvements for roads, bridges, and canals. Southerners in particular disliked Clay's plan. The South had many fine rivers on which to transport goods. Many southerners opposed paying for roads and canals that brought them no direct benefits.

The Supreme Court Expands Federal Power

Under Chief Justice John Marshall, the Supreme Court strengthened the power of the federal government to promote economic growth. After Congress chartered the second Bank of the United States, Maryland tried to tax the Bank in order to drive it out of the state. James McCulloch, the Bank cashier, refused to pay the tax.

In the case of ***McCulloch* v. *Maryland*** (1819), the Court ruled that states had no right to interfere with federal institutions within their borders. The ruling strengthened federal power. It also allowed the Bank of the United States to continue, which helped the economy to expand.

In another case, ***Gibbons* v. *Ogden*** (1824), the Supreme Court upheld the power of the federal government to regulate trade between states. The Court struck down a New York law that tried to control steamboat travel between New York and New Jersey. The Court ruled that a state could regulate trade only within its own borders. Only the federal government had the power to regulate **interstate commerce,** or trade between different states. This decision helped the national economy by making it easier for the government to regulate trade.

★ ★ ★ Section 3 Assessment ★ ★ ★

Recall

1. **Identify** Explain the significance of **(a)** American System, **(b)** *McCulloch* v. *Maryland,* **(c)** *Gibbons* v. *Ogden.*
2. **Define** **(a)** sectionalism, **(b)** internal improvements, **(c)** interstate commerce.

Comprehension

3. How did Calhoun, Webster, and Clay each represent the views of his own section?
4. How did protective tariffs help American industry after the War of 1812?
5. Why did southerners oppose Clay's American System?
6. How did Supreme Court rulings give the federal government greater power?

Critical Thinking and Writing

7. **Exploring the Main Idea** Review the Main Idea statement at the beginning of this section. Then, describe one result of the Era of Good Feelings.
8. **Analyzing Primary Sources** In 1816, a member of Congress said, "It is unjust to aggravate the burdens of the people [to favor] the manufacturers." Do you think the speaker was from the North or the South? Explain.

ACTIVITY

Chairing a Debate It is 1825, and you are chairing a three-way debate between Calhoun, Webster, and Clay. Part of your responsibility is to introduce each debater. Write a one-paragraph introduction for each person. Then, work with a partner to practice giving the introduction.

Comparing and Contrasting

In what ways were the interests of Americans in the three regions of their country alike or different? As you learn about history, you often need to compare and contrast information to understand how the similarities and differences affected events. A graphic organizer is often helpful in comparing and contrasting information.

The Beginning of Sectionalism

Similarities

- Each region had a bright, young leader who represented its interests in the United States Congress.
- Each leader wanted to protect his region's economy.

North	South	West
• Economy: Textile mills and new factories • Spokesperson: Daniel Webster • Favored Tariff of 1816 because it kept Europeans from selling their goods at a lower price than that of American goods	• Economy: Agricultural with few factories • Spokesperson: John C. Calhoun • Opposed Tariff of 1816 because it raised prices on European goods that the South favored and forced Southerners to buy costly American-made goods	• Economy: Small farms • Spokesperson: Henry Clay • Wanted economic growth for all sections; supported tariff in belief that if North were protected, it would buy products from South and West and that the United States should reduce its dependence on foreign goods • Wanted internal improvements such as better transportation in the United States

Learn the Skill *To compare and contrast information, use the following steps:*

1. **Read the title and headings.** These name the subject and tell what is being compared and contrasted.
2. **Identify similarities.** In what ways are the things being compared alike?
3. **Identify differences.** What contrasts or differences are given?
4. **Analyze the information.** What issues or problems might the differences cause?

Practice the Skill *Answer the following questions about the graphic organizer above:*

1. What are the three sections being compared?
2. What did all three regions of the nation have in common?
3. **(a)** How did the economy of the North differ from that of the South? **(b)** Why did southerners see the Tariff of 1816 as harmful to them? **(c)** What was Henry Clay's view of protective tariffs?
4. What issues do you think developed from these regional differences?

Apply the Skill *See the Chapter Review and Assessment.*

4 New Nations in the Americas

Prepare to Read

Objectives

In this section, you will

- Explain how Latin American nations won independence and became republics.
- Describe how the United States gained Florida.
- Explain the purpose of the Monroe Doctrine.

Key Terms

creole

Republic of Great Colombia

United Provinces of Central America

Negro Fort

Monroe Doctrine

intervention

Target Reading Skill

Cause and Effect As you read, complete the following chart to show some of the events that led to the Monroe Doctrine. Add as many boxes as you need.

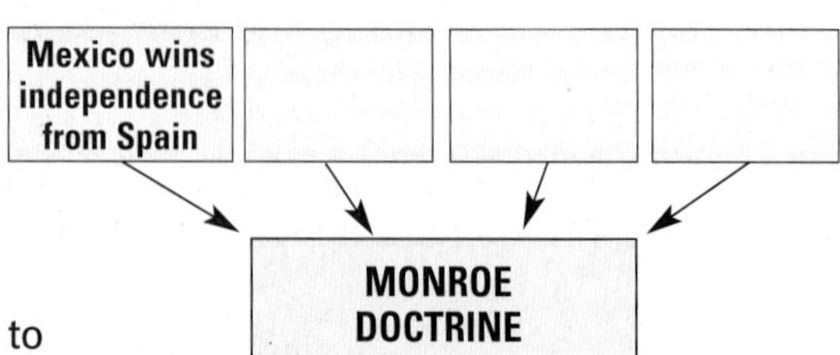

Main Idea The United States issued the Monroe Doctrine to discourage Europe from interfering in Latin America's affairs.

Father Hidalgo speaks

Setting the Scene On a quiet Sunday in September 1810, the church bell rang in the Mexican village of Dolores. In the square, Indians gathered around the village priest, Miguel Hidalgo (mee GEHL ee DAHL goh).

Hidalgo issued a bold call for Indians to join the struggle to make Mexico independent. No one knows the exact words Hidalgo used, but these are the words that have been passed down:

> "My children. . . . Will you be free? Will you recover the lands stolen 300 years ago from your forefathers by the hated Spaniards? We must act at once!"
>
> —Father Miguel Hidalgo y Costilla, "Cry of Dolores" speech, September 16, 1810

Thousands of Mexicans rallied to Father Hidalgo's call for freedom.

Like Mexico, other Spanish colonies were reacting to the call for freedom from Spain. In most parts of Latin America,* people in the early 1800s fought wars for independence. As new nations emerged, President Monroe formed a bold new foreign policy. His goal was to keep Europeans from using the fighting as an excuse to create new colonies in the Americas.

Revolution in Latin America

By 1810, many people in Spain's American colonies were eager for independence. They had many reasons to be unhappy. Most people, even wealthy creoles, had little or no say in government. In Latin America, the term **creole** described people born to Spanish parents there. They demanded a role in government. Opposition to Spain was also growing among Indians. Harsh rules kept Indians forever in

---

* Latin America refers to the Western Hemisphere region in which Latin-based languages, such as Spanish, French, and Portuguese, are spoken. It includes Mexico, Central America, South America, and the West Indies.

debt. All over Latin America, people were eager to be free of the Spanish.

Mexican Independence As you have read, Miguel Hidalgo sounded the call for Mexican independence in 1810. Rebel forces won control of several provinces before Father Hidalgo was captured. In 1811, he was executed.

Another priest, José Morelos (hoh ZAY moh RAY lohs), took up the fight. Because he called for a program to give land to peasants, wealthy creoles opposed him. Before long, Morelos, too, was captured and killed by the Spanish.

Slowly, creoles began to join the revolutionary movement. In 1821, revolutionary forces led by creoles won control of Mexico. A few years later, Mexico became a republic with its own constitution.

The Liberator In South America, too, a series of revolutions freed colonies from Spanish rule. The best-known revolutionary leader was Simón Bolívar (see MOHN boh LEE vahr). He became known as The Liberator for his role in the Latin American wars of independence.

Bolívar came from a wealthy creole family in Venezuela. As a young man, he took up the cause of Venezuelan independence. Bolívar promised, "I will never allow my hands to be idle, nor my soul to rest until I have broken the shackles which chain us to Spain."

Bolívar rose to become a leader of the rebel forces. In a bold move, he led an army from Venezuela over the high Andes Mountains into Colombia. There, Bolívar took the Spanish forces by surprise and defeated them in 1819.

Soon after, Bolívar became president of the independent **Republic of Great Colombia.** It included the present-day nations of Venezuela, Colombia, Ecuador, and Panama.

Other New Nations Other independent nations emerged in Latin America. José de San Martín (san mahr TEEN) led Argentina to freedom in 1816. He then helped the people of Chile, Peru, and Ecuador win independence.

In 1821, the peoples of Central America declared independence from Spain. Two years later, they formed the **United Provinces of Central America.** It included the present-day nations of Nicaragua, Costa Rica, El Salvador, Honduras, and Guatemala. By 1825, Spain had lost all its colonies in Latin America except Puerto Rico and Cuba.

The Portuguese colony of Brazil won independence peacefully. When Brazilian revolutionaries demanded independence, Prince Pedro, son of the Portuguese king, joined their cause. He became emperor of the new independent nation of Brazil.

New Nations in Latin America

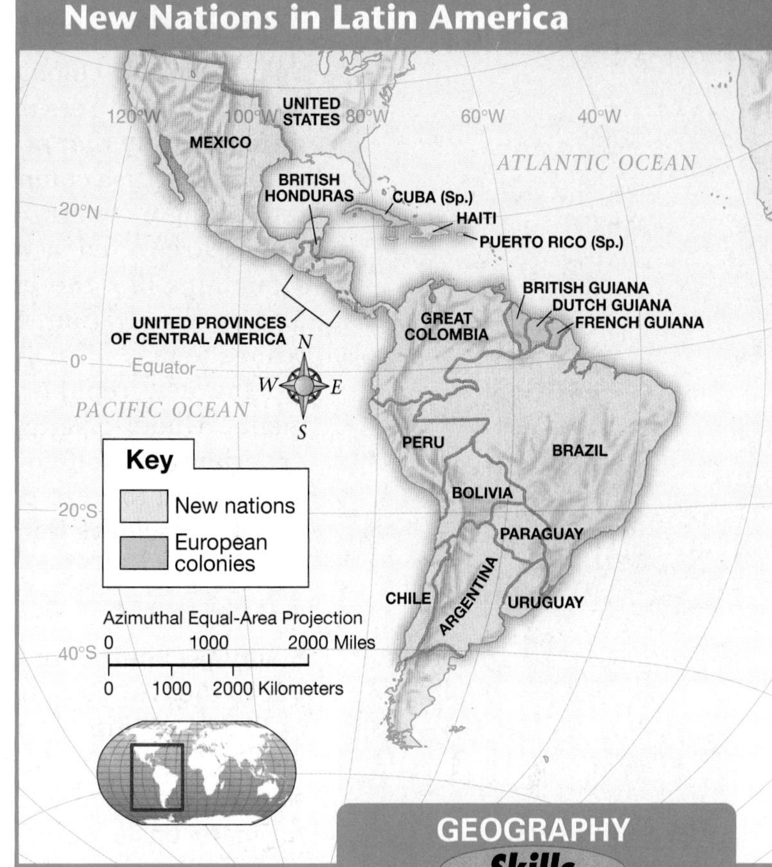

GEOGRAPHY *Skills*

Wars of independence led to the creation of many new countries in Latin America.

1. **Location** On the map, locate **(a)** Mexico, **(b)** Great Colombia, **(c)** United Provinces of Central America, **(d)** Brazil, **(e)** Argentina, **(f)** Chile, **(g)** Bolivia.
2. **Region** What parts of Latin America remained European colonies?
3. **Critical Thinking Applying Information** Use the world map in the Reference Section to identify the modern nations that were eventually carved out of Great Colombia.

The New Republics

Spain's former colonies modeled their constitutions on that of the United States. Yet, their experience after independence was very different from that of their neighbor to the north. Unlike the people of the 13 British colonies, the peoples of Latin America did not unite into a single country. In part, geography made unity difficult. Latin America covered a much larger area than the English colonies. Mountains like the high, rugged Andes acted as barriers to travel and communication. Also, the Spanish colonies were spread out over a huge area.

The new republics had a hard time setting up stable governments. Under Spanish rule, the colonists had gained little or no experience in self-government. Powerful leaders took advantage of the turmoil to seize control. As a result, the new nations were often unable to achieve democratic rule.

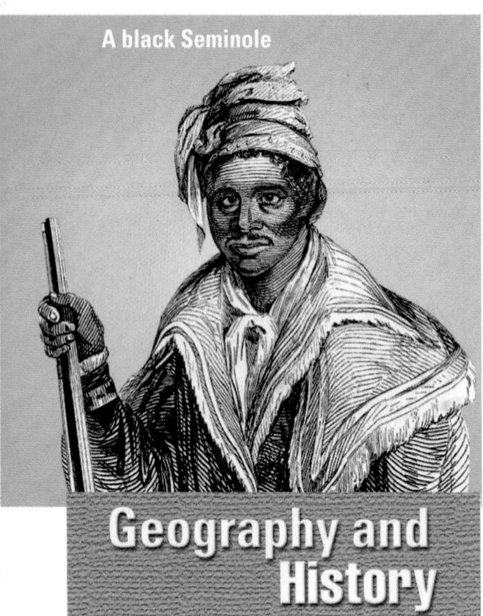
A black Seminole

Geography and History

The Negro Fort

The Negro Fort was built along the Apalachicola River, in the Spanish territory of Florida, about 60 miles from Georgia. At its height, some 1,000 African Americans farmed along the river. They worried Georgia planters, who feared they would encourage slaves to revolt.

The fort sat on a hill surrounded on three sides by forests and swamps. The weak side lay along the river. In early skirmishes against the Americans, the defenders beat their land forces. Then, the Americans launched an all-out attack by land and river. Gunboats bombarding the fort hit the room where gunpowder was stored. The explosion destroyed the fort, killing most of the inhabitants. The survivors were returned to slavery.

How might the defenders of the Negro Fort have inspired enslaved African Americans in the United States?

The United States Gains Florida

Spain lost another one of its colonies, Florida—not to independence, but to the United States. Many Americans wanted to gain possession of Florida. White southerners were especially worried about disturbances across the border. Creek and Seminole Indians in Florida sometimes raided settlements in Georgia. Also, Florida was a refuge for many enslaved African Americans.

"Black Seminoles" Since the 1700s, Spanish officials had protected slaves who had fled from plantations in Georgia and South Carolina. Seminole Indians allowed African Americans to live near their villages. In return, these "black Seminoles" gave the Indians a share of the crops they raised. The black Seminoles adopted many Indian customs.

One settlement on the Apalachicola River known as the Negro Fort contained about 1,000 African Americans. General Andrew Jackson demanded that Spain demolish the Negro Fort. (See Geography and History feature on this page.) When the Spanish governor refused, the United States invaded Florida and destroyed the fort.

Spain Gives Up Florida In 1818, Jackson again headed to Florida with a force of more than 3,000 soldiers. Spain protested but did little else. It was busy fighting rebels in Latin America and could not risk war with the United States.

In the end, Spain agreed to peace talks. Secretary of State John Quincy Adams worked out a treaty with Spain. In it, Spain agreed to give Florida to the United States in exchange for $5 million. The Adams-Onís (oh NEES) Treaty took effect in 1821.

The Monroe Doctrine

Americans cheered as Latin American nations won independence. The actions of European powers, however, worried Secretary Adams and President Monroe. In 1815, Prussia, France, Russia, and Austria formed an alliance aimed at crushing any revolution that sprang up in Europe. They seemed ready to help Spain regain its colonies in Latin America. In addition, Russia claimed lands on the Pacific coast of North America.

The British, too, worried about other European nations meddling in the Western Hemisphere. They feared that their profitable trade would be hurt if Spain regained control of its former colonies. Thus, they suggested that the United States and Britain issue a joint statement guaranteeing the freedom of the new nations of Latin America.

Monroe decided to act independently of Britain. In a message to Congress in 1823, he made a bold foreign policy statement, known as the **Monroe Doctrine.** Monroe declared that the United States would not interfere in the affairs of European nations or existing colonies of the European nations. At the same time, he warned European nations not to attempt to regain control of the newly independent nations of Latin America.

The Monroe Doctrine stated that the United States would oppose any attempt to build new colonies in the Americas. Monroe's message showed that the United States was determined to keep European powers out of the Western Hemisphere.

The United States did not have the military power to enforce the Monroe Doctrine. Britain, however, supported the statement. With its strong navy, it could stop Europeans from building new colonies in the Americas.

As the United States became stronger, the Monroe Doctrine grew in importance. On several occasions, the United States successfully challenged European **intervention,** or direct involvement, in Latin America. In the early 1900s, Presidents also used the Monroe Doctrine to justify sending troops to Caribbean nations. Thus, Monroe's bold statement helped shape United States foreign policy for more than 100 years.

Recognizing Multiple Causes

A cause makes something happen. What were some of the causes of the Monroe Doctrine? Add these causes to your chart.

★ ★ ★ Section 4 Assessment ★ ★ ★

Recall

1. **Identify** Explain the significance of **(a)** Republic of Great Colombia, **(b)** United Provinces of Central America, **(c)** Negro Fort, **(d)** Monroe Doctrine.
2. **Define** **(a)** creole, **(b)** intervention.

Comprehension

3. How did revolutions change Latin America?
4. How did the United States acquire Florida?
5. Why was the Monroe Doctrine issued?

Critical Thinking and Writing

6. **Exploring the Main Idea** Review the Main Idea statement at the beginning of this section. Then, list as many ways as you can think of in which the Western Hemisphere might be different today if the United States had not issued the Monroe Doctrine.
7. **Analyzing Information** What parts of the United States Constitution do you think most appealed to people in other nations?

ACTIVITY

Connecting to Today

The role of the Monroe Doctrine is still debated today. Use the Internet to discover opinions on the Monroe Doctrine. Then, answer the question, Do you think the Monroe Doctrine is still important today? For help in completing the activity, visit PHSchool.com, **Web Code mfd-1103.**

CHAPTER

11 Review and Assessment

Chapter Summary

Section 1
The Industrial Revolution began in Great Britain but spread to the United States. It caused a great deal of change in how Americans worked and lived during the first half of the 1800s.

Section 2
Improvements in roads, the development of steam engines, and digging canals helped to move people and goods westward.

Section 3
Sectional tensions grew between the North, the South, and the West during the early 1800s. Congress began passing laws to help U.S. business grow.

Section 4
By 1825, most nations in Latin America had won independence. The United States issued the Monroe Doctrine to discourage Europe from intervening in the affairs of Latin American nations.

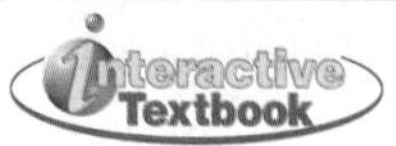

For additional review and enrichment activities, see the interactive version of *The American Nation,* available on the Web and on CD-ROM.

Chapter Self-Test For practice test questions for Chapter 11, visit PHSchool.com, **Web Code mfa-1104.**

Building Vocabulary

Write sentences using the chapter vocabulary words listed below, leaving blanks where the vocabulary words should go. Exchange your sentences with another student, and fill in the blanks in each other's sentences.

1. **spinning jenny**
2. **capital**
3. **capitalist**
4. **urbanization**
5. **flatboat**
6. **turnpike**
7. **corduroy road**
8. **sectionalism**
9. **creole**
10. **intervention**

Reviewing Key Facts

11. How did Samuel Slater bring the Industrial Revolution to the United States? (Section 1)
12. Describe three ways in which transportation improved in the early 1800s. (Section 2)
13. Why did southerners oppose the protective tariff while northern manufacturers supported it? (Section 3)
14. Why was British support of the Monroe Doctrine important to its success? (Section 4)

Critical Thinking and Writing

15. **Linking Past and Present** **(a)** Make a list of the ways in which the cities of today are like the cities of the early 1800s. **(b)** Make a list of the ways in which they are different.
16. **Connecting to Geography: Regions** **(a)** Make a list of the physical and economic differences between the North, South, and West. **(b)** Analyze how these differences affected the political views of people in the regions.
17. **Identifying Causes and Effects** **(a)** Which came first: the War of 1812 or the innovations of Francis Cabot Lowell? **(b)** Analyze the relationship between the War of 1812 and economic change in the United States.
18. **Analyzing Information** How did steam power help change the way goods were manufactured?

SKILLS ASSESSMENT

Analyzing Primary Sources

In 1831, a young Frenchman named Alexis de Tocqueville (TOHK vihl) made a nine-month tour of the United States. Tocqueville later described what he admired about the young nation.

> "Of all the countries in the world, America is that in which the spread of ideas and of human industry is most continual and most rapid. . . . The American . . . is less afraid than any other inhabitant of the globe to risk what he has gained in the hope of a better future. . . . There is not a country in the world where man . . . feels with more pride that he can fashion the universe to please himself."
>
> —Alexis de Tocqueville, *Democracy in America,* 1835

19. According to Tocqueville, new ideas in the United States

- **A.** cannot thrive in the new country.
- **B.** do not exist because inventors copy European ideas.
- **C.** do not occur very often.
- **D.** are encouraged to flourish.

20. Based on this quote, what are the qualities Tocqueville admires about Americans?

- **A.** their willingness to take risks
- **B.** their willingness to expand their territory
- **C.** their ability to beat Britain in war
- **D.** their democratic government

APPLYING YOUR SKILLS

Comparing and Contrasting

A Venn diagram is a useful way of showing similarities and differences between two people or groups. Study the Venn diagram below, and then answer the questions.

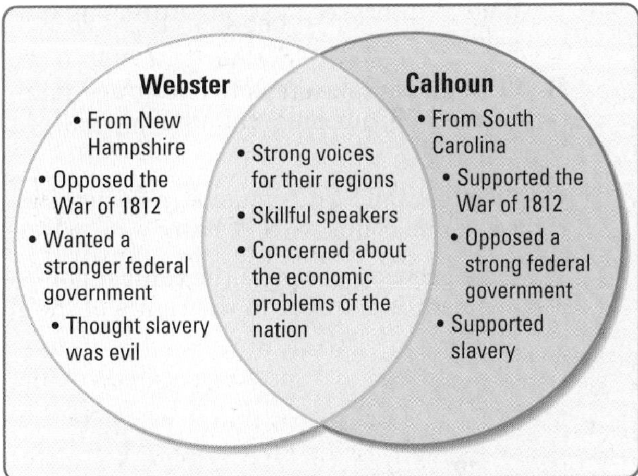

21. Which of the following characteristics did Webster and Calhoun share?

- **A.** They were both from South Carolina.
- **B.** They both supported the War of 1812.
- **C.** They were both concerned about the economic problems of the nation.
- **D.** They both hated slavery.

22. Based on this diagram, on what issues might you expect Calhoun to clash most seriously with Webster?

ACTIVITIES

Connecting With . . .

Science and Technology

Creating a Time Capsule It is December 31, 1825, and you are creating a time capsule to be buried on the lawn of the White House in Washington, D.C. The time capsule will celebrate the previous 35 years of change in the nation's transportation system. Write an imaginary news story with its own headline about one of the events discussed in this chapter. Use the library and Internet resources to write short biographies of some of the most important people who participated in this change.

Creating a Database

Independence for Latin America Use the Internet to find sites relating to the struggles of Latin Americans for independence. Then, create a database that compares the road to independence of the various countries of Latin America. Include such categories as leaders and dates that independence was won. For help in starting this activity, visit PHSchool.com, **Web Code mfd-1106.**

TEST PREPARATION

1 Which of the following statements best reflects a key belief of the Democratic Republican Party?

A "The Supreme Court must have the freedom to interpret the Constitution as it sees fit."

B "Unless we take steps to encourage manufacturing, our national economy will fail."

C "The United States must strengthen its economic bonds with Britain."

D "The growing power of the central government is a threat to the rights of the states."

Use the quotation and your knowledge of social studies to answer the following question.

George Washington's Farewell Address, 1796
"The great rule of conduct for us, in regard to foreign nations, is . . . to have with them as little political connection as possible."

2 The statement above expresses Washington's support for what policy?

A Imposing a trade embargo

B Forming an alliance with France

C Maintaining neutrality

D Increasing the size of the navy

3 Which of the following did the most to establish the principle of judicial review?

A The Bill of Rights

B The Judiciary Act of 1789

C *Marbury* v. *Madison*

D *McCulloch* v. *Maryland*

4 Which of the following was not part of Alexander Hamilton's economic plan for the nation?

A High tariffs

B Payment of state debts

C Laissez faire economics

D A national bank

Use the map and your knowledge of social studies to answer the following question.

The Louisiana Purchase, 1803

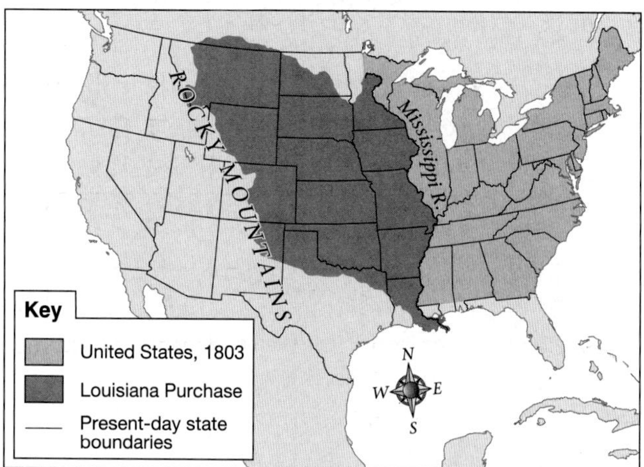

5 Which statement is best supported by the map?

A As a result of the Louisiana Purchase, the United States expanded to the Pacific Ocean.

B Half of all current states were part of the Louisiana Purchase.

C The Mississippi River formed most of the eastern border of the Louisiana Purchase.

D The Louisiana Purchase gave the United States control of the Rocky Mountains.

6 Which of the following actions would President Monroe have viewed as a violation of the Monroe Doctrine?

A Spain invades Portugal.

B Spain retakes Mexico.

C Spain refuses to sell Florida.

D Simón Bolívar declares himself king of Venezuela.

Use the graph and your knowledge of social studies to answer the following question.

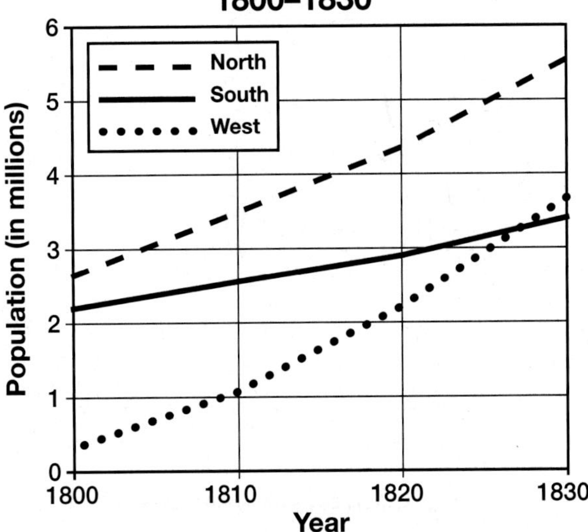

Source: *Historical Statistics of the United States*

7 Which generalization about the period from 1800–1830 is supported by the graph?

A The West had a larger population than the South.

B The population of the South declined.

C The West grew at a faster rate than the North.

D All three regions grew at an equal rate.

8 Which group would have been most likely to support the aims of the War Hawks?

A New England merchants

B Settlers on the western frontier

C Members of Tecumseh's federation

D Delegates to the Hartford Convention

9 Which of the following is the best example of the impact of geography on the Industrial Revolution?

A The location of the first American textile mill

B The invention of interchangeable parts

C The use of child labor

D The combination of spinning and weaving in a single factory

Writing Practice

10 "The first five Presidents provided models of bold leadership and creative thinking." Using at least two different Presidents, give three examples that support this statement.

11 Trace the development of American foreign policy from Washington to Monroe. Choose what you think were the three most important policies or events involving foreign nations. Describe the key issues and the course followed by the President. Then, make two generalizations about foreign policy in this period.

Unit 4 An Era of Expansion

UNIT OUTLINE

Chapter 12
The Jacksonian Era (1824–1840)

Chapter 13
Westward Expansion (1820–1860)

Chapter 14
North and South (1820–1860)

Chapter 15
Reform and a New American Culture (1820–1860)

The Nation Grows
In Oscar E. Berninghaus's ***Westward Ho!***, a long line of wagons carries settlers west.

"Our population is rolling toward the shores of the Pacific. . . . It will soon . . . reach the Rocky Mountains and be ready to pour into the Oregon territory."

—John C. Calhoun, South Carolina Senator (1843)

CHAPTER 12

The Jacksonian Era

1824–1840

Discussing politics

Cherokees on the Trail of Tears

1820s

A growing spirit of equality spreads through the nation. As President, Andrew Jackson supports the interests of the common people.

1830

Congress passes the Indian Removal Act, which forces Native Americans to move west of the Mississippi.

AMERICAN EVENTS

Presidential Terms: John Quincy Adams 1825–1829 | Andrew Jackson 1829–1837

1824 · 1828 · 1832

WORLD EVENTS

▲ **1824**
Simón Bolívar becomes dictator of Peru.

▲ **1829**
The Swiss adopt universal male suffrage.

The Election of 1824

Andrew Jackson received the most popular votes in the 1824 election but not a majority of the electoral votes. The election was decided in the House of Representatives.

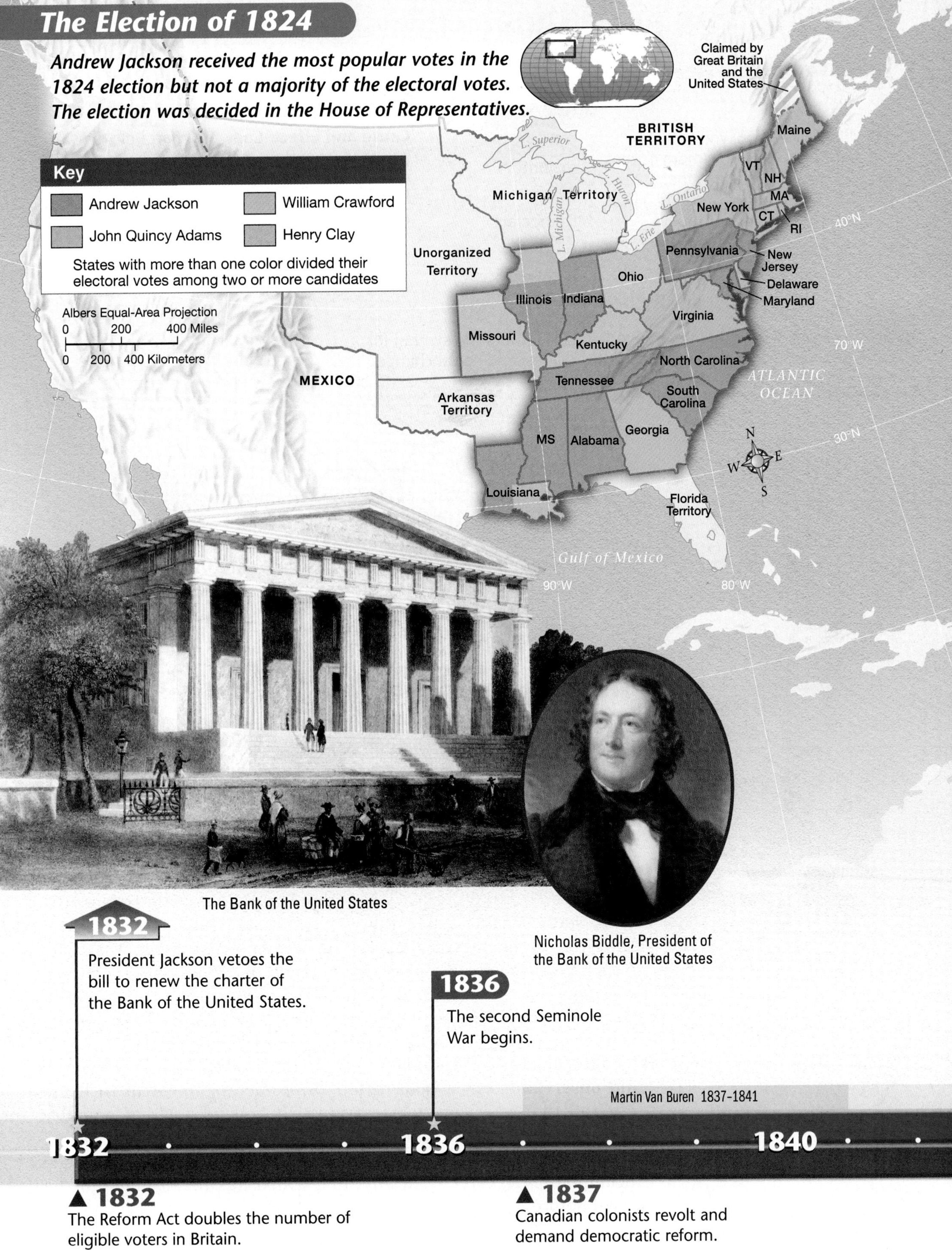

The Bank of the United States

Nicholas Biddle, President of the Bank of the United States

1832
President Jackson vetoes the bill to renew the charter of the Bank of the United States.

1836
The second Seminole War begins.

▲ 1832
The Reform Act doubles the number of eligible voters in Britain.

▲ 1837
Canadian colonists revolt and demand democratic reform.

1 A New Era in Politics

Prepare to Read

Objectives

In this section, you will
- Summarize how more citizens gained suffrage in the 1820s.
- Explain the dispute over the 1824 election.
- Describe why President Adams was unpopular.
- List the new political parties.

Key Terms

suffrage
majority
Whigs
Democrats
caucus
nominating convention

Target Reading Skill

Cause and Effect Copy the chart below. As you read, complete the chart to show some of the developments that caused changes in political parties in the 1820s. Add as many boxes as you need.

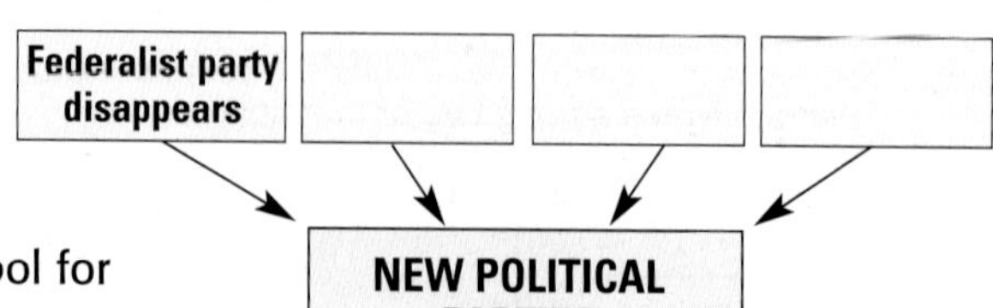

Main Idea As President, Andrew Jackson became the symbol for the new democratic spirit that brought political and social changes to the nation.

Statue of Andrew Jackson

Setting the Scene Harry Ward, a New England teacher, made a visit to Cincinnati, Ohio, during the 1824 presidential election campaign. Writing to a friend, he described how Ohioans felt about Andrew Jackson, who was running for President. Jackson's supporters, he observed were "Strange! Wild! Infatuated! All for Jackson!"

On election day, more people voted for Andrew Jackson than for any of the other candidates. Oddly enough, Jackson did not become President that year.

Growing Spirit of Equality

The spirit of democracy, which was changing the political system, affected American ideas about social classes. Most Americans did not feel that the rich deserved special respect.

Wealthy European visitors to the United States were surprised that American servants expected to be treated as equals. Others were amazed that butlers and maids refused to be summoned with bells, as in Europe.

Alexis de Tocqueville A visitor from France, Alexis de Tocqueville (TOHK veel) became especially well known for his observations on American Democracy. He arrived in the United States in 1831. The French government had sent him to study the American prison system. For several months, Tocqueville toured much of the United States. However, he observed much more than prisons. He observed a society that was becoming more and more democratic.

After his return to France, Tocqueville recorded his experiences and observations in a book titled *Democracy in America.* In it, he admired the American democratic spirit and its goals of equality and freedom. He found the results of the "revolution taking place" in America while "still far from coming to an end" were "already incomparably greater than anything which has taken place in the world before."

More Voters During the 1820s, more people gained **suffrage,** or the right to vote. Others, however, were denied full participation in the growing democracy.

The United States was growing rapidly. New states were joining the Union, and there were many citizens eager to participate in elections. Some of the first states to give voting privileges to white males without property were in the West. In these states, any white man over age 21 could vote.

Reformers in the East worked to expand suffrage. By the 1830s, most eastern states dropped the requirement that voters own land. In this way, many craftsworkers and shopkeepers won the right to vote.

Throughout the country, growing numbers of Americans exercised their right to vote. Before 1828, the turnout of eligible voters was never more than 27 percent. That low percentage rose to nearly 58 percent in the election of 1828. By 1840, voter turnout was nearly 80 percent.

Limits on Suffrage Despite the nation's growing democratic spirit, a great many Americans did not have the right to vote. They included women, Native Americans, and the vast majority of African Americans. Slaves had no political rights at all.

As more white men were winning suffrage, free African Americans were losing it. In the early years of the nation, most northern states had allowed free African American men to vote. In the 1820s, many of these states took away that right. By 1830, only a few New England states permitted African American men to vote on equal terms with white men. In New York, African American men had to own property in order to vote. White men did not.

The Disputed Election of 1824

There were four candidates for President in 1824. All four were members of the old Republican party. However, each had support in different parts of the country. John Quincy Adams was strong in New England. Henry Clay and Andrew Jackson had support in the West. William Crawford was favored in the South. However, he became too ill to campaign.

The Candidates John Quincy Adams of Massachusetts was the son of Abigail and John Adams, the second President. A graduate of Harvard University, the younger Adams had served as Secretary of State and helped end the War of 1812. People admired Adams for his intelligence and high morals. Adams, however, was uncomfortable campaigning among the common people. In fact, to most people he seemed hard and cold.

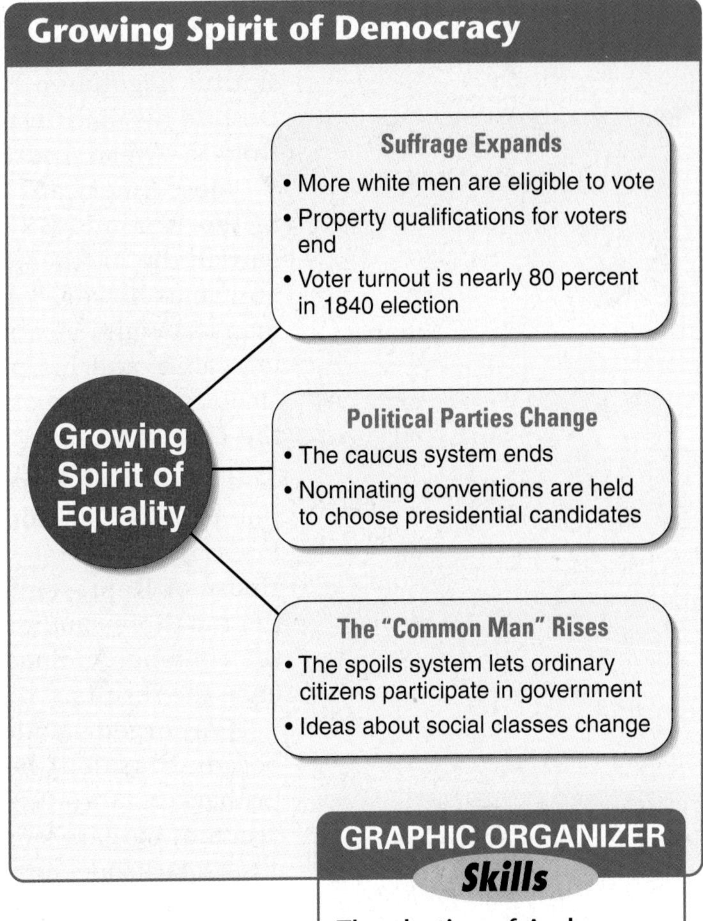

GRAPHIC ORGANIZER *Skills*

The election of Andrew Jackson in 1828 marked a change in ideas about democracy.

1. **Comprehension** How were candidates chosen for office?
2. **Critical Thinking Supporting a Point of View** Do you think the growing spirit of democracy helped Jackson in the 1828 election? Explain.

Civics 

A Kentuckian, Henry Clay was a shrewd politician who became Speaker of the House of Representatives. In Congress, Clay was a skillful negotiator. He worked out several important compromises. Despite his abilities, Clay was less popular than the other candidate from the West, Andrew Jackson.

Most Americans knew Andrew Jackson for his military victories in the War of 1812. He was the "Hero of New Orleans." He also earned the nickname "Old Hickory" after a soldier said that he was "tough as hickory." Although he was a landowner and a slave owner, many saw him as a man of the people. Jackson had been born in a log cabin, and his parents were poor farmers. He was admired by small farmers and others who felt left out of the growing economy in the United States.

The "Corrupt Bargain" No clear winner emerged from the election of 1824. Jackson won the popular vote, but no candidate won a **majority,** or more than half, of the electoral votes. As a result, the House of Representatives had to choose the President from among the top three candidates. Because he finished fourth, Clay was out of the running. As Speaker of the House, though, he was able to influence the results.

Clay urged members of the House to vote for Adams. After Adams became President, he named Clay his Secretary of State. Jackson and his backers were furious. They accused Adams and Clay of making a "corrupt bargain" and stealing the election from Jackson.

As Jackson was riding home to Tennessee, he met an old friend. "Well, General," said the friend, "we did all we could for you here, but the rascals at Washington cheated you out of it."

"Indeed, my old friend," replied Jackson, "there was cheating and corruption and bribery, too."

The charges were not true, however. The election was decided as the Constitution stated. Still, the anger of Jackson and his supporters seriously hampered President Adams's efforts to unify the nation.

An Unpopular President

Adams knew that the election had angered many Americans. To "bring the whole people together," he pushed for a program of economic growth through internal improvements. His plan backfired, however, and opposition to him grew.

Promoting Economic Growth Similar to Alexander Hamilton and Henry Clay, Adams thought that the federal government should promote economic growth. He called for the government to pay for new roads and canals. These internal improvements would help farmers to transport goods to market.

Adams also favored projects to promote the arts and the sciences. He suggested building a national university and an observatory from which astronomers could study the stars.

Most Americans objected to spending money on such programs. They feared that the federal government would become too powerful. Congress approved money for a national road and some canals but turned down most of Adams's other programs.

Connecting to Today

Promoting Science

John Quincy Adams failed to win popular support for his plan to promote the arts and sciences. Today, however, the federal government funds art programs and scientific research. Here are two of the science projects the government supports:

Robofly Scientists developed a pair of robotic wings that helped them learn how insects such as flies and bees can hover and perform amazing flying maneuvers.

What ancient people ate Scientists have found stone tools that are about 2.5 million years old. Now, they are searching for fossil animal bones that show tool cut marks. Such marks would prove that ancient ancestors used these tools to cut meat.

Why do you think some people still oppose such programs?

A Bitter Campaign In 1828, Adams faced an uphill battle for reelection. This time, Andrew Jackson was Adams's only opponent.

The campaign was a bitter contest. The focus was not on issues, but on the candidates' personalities. Jackson supporters, however, renewed charges that Adams made a "corrupt bargain" after the 1824 election. But they also attacked Adams as an aristocrat, or member of the upper class. Adams supporters replied with similar attacks. They called Jackson a dangerous "military chieftain." If Jackson became President, they warned, he could become a dictator like Napoleon Bonaparte of France.

Jackson won the election easily. His supporters cheered the outcome as a victory for common people. For the first time, the politics of the common people were important. By common people, they meant farmers in the West and South and city workers in the East.

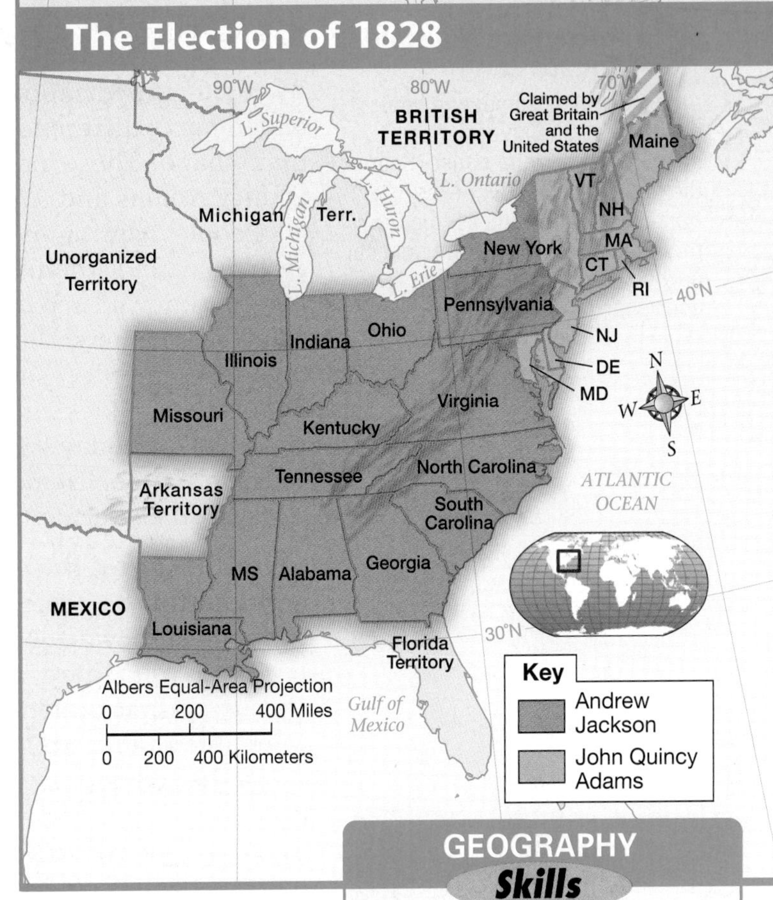

GEOGRAPHY *Skills*

In the election of 1828, Andrew Jackson defeated John Quincy Adams. Unlike in the election of 1824, Jackson was a decisive winner in 1828.

1. **Location** On the map, locate **(a)** Massachusetts, **(b)** Kentucky, **(c)** Tennessee.
2. **Place** In which section of the country did Adams have the most support?
3. **Critical Thinking Applying Information** Which of the two candidates would probably have won Florida and Arkansas if they had been states in 1828? Explain.

Jacksonian Democracy Andrew Jackson's inauguration in 1829 reflected the growing spirit of democracy. The spread of political power to more people was part of what became known as Jacksonian democracy.

Jackson was also the first westerner to occupy the White House. His election represented the beginning of a shift of political power to the West.

As Jackson traveled to Washington to be inaugurated, large crowds cheered him along the way. For the first time, thousands of ordinary people flooded the capital to watch the President take the oath of office. After Jackson was sworn in, the crowd followed the new President to a reception at the White House. One onlooker described the scene with amazement:

> "Country men, farmers, gentlemen, mounted and dismounted, boys, women and children, black and white. Carriages, wagons, and carts all pursuing [Jackson] to the President's house."
>
> —Margaret Bayard Smith, *The First Forty Years of Washington Society*

The crowds were so huge, the observer continued, that the President was "almost suffocated and torn to pieces by the people in their eagerness to shake hands."

Jackson's critics said the scene showed that "King Mob" was ruling the nation. Amos Kendall, a loyal Jackson supporter, viewed the inauguration celebration in a more positive way: "It was a proud day for the people. General Jackson is their own President."

Target Skill: Recognize Multiple Causes

A cause makes something happen. Sometimes an effect can have more than one cause. Read the paragraphs under "New Political Parties" and list the factors that led to changes in political parties. Add this information to your chart.

New Political Parties

By 1820, the disappearance of the Federalist party temporarily ended party differences. In the 1830s, however, new political parties took shape. These parties grew out of the conflict between John Quincy Adams and Andrew Jackson.

People who supported Adams and his programs for national growth called themselves National Republicans. In 1834, they became known as **Whigs.** Whigs wanted the federal government to spur the economy. Those who supported the Whigs included eastern business people, some southern planters, and many former Federalists. Jackson and his supporters called themselves **Democrats.** Today's Democratic party traces its roots to Andrew Jackson's time. Democrats included frontier farmers, as well as workers in eastern cities.

New Ways to Choose Candidates The two new political parties developed more democratic ways to choose candidates for President. In the past, powerful members of each party held a **caucus,** or private meeting. There, they chose their candidate. Critics called the caucus system undemocratic because only a few powerful people were able to take part in it.

In the 1830s, each party began to hold a **nominating convention,** where delegates from all the states chose the party's candidate for President. Party leaders might still dominate a particular convention, but the people could now have some influence in the nominating process. Also, state nominating conventions encouraged citizen participation in elections. Once citizens learned about the events of the convention, they would work for their party's choices. Today, the major political parties still hold conventions.

★ ★ ★ Section 1 Assessment ★ ★ ★

Recall

1. **Identify** Explain the significance of **(a)** Alexis de Tocqueville, **(b)** John Quincy Adams, **(c)** Whigs, **(d)** Democrats.
2. **Define** **(a)** suffrage, **(b)** majority, **(c)** caucus, **(d)** nominating convention.

Comprehension

3. How did political parties reflect the growing spirit of equality?
4. Why did Andrew Jackson feel that the election of 1824 was unfair?
5. What programs did Adams propose that made him unpopular?

Critical Thinking and Writing

6. **Exploring the Main Idea** Review the Main Idea statement at the beginning of this section. Then, write a paragraph explaining how a Jackson supporter might respond to this question: "Does a man become wiser, stronger, or more virtuous and patriotic because he has a fine house?"
7. **Supporting a Point of View** Write a paragraph in which you agree or disagree with John Quincy Adams's position that government should spend money to support the arts and sciences. Explain your answer.

ACTIVITY

Writing a Dialogue
Write a dialogue in which John Quincy Adams and Andrew Jackson discuss the election of 1824.

2 Jackson in the White House

Prepare to Read

Objectives

In this section, you will
- List the qualities that helped Andrew Jackson succeed.
- Explain the spoils system.
- Summarize why President Jackson fought the Bank of the United States.

Key Terms

spoils system

"kitchen cabinet"

Target Reading Skill

Sequence Copy this flowchart. As you read, fill in the boxes with the events that led to the closing of the Bank of the United States in 1836. The first and last boxes have been completed for you. Add as many boxes as you need.

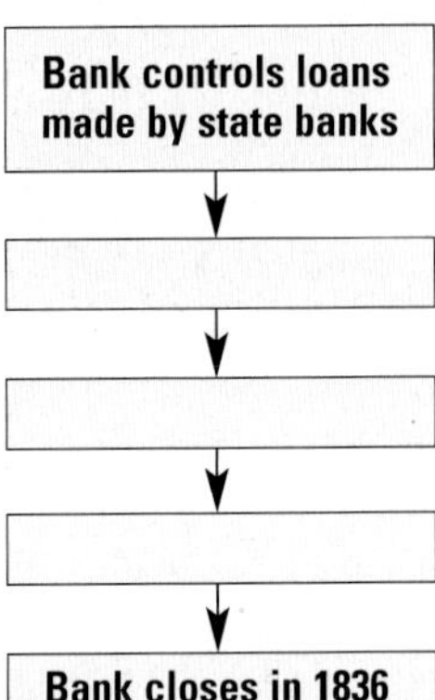

Main Idea President Jackson showed the strength of his will in his fight with the Bank of the United States.

Setting the Scene During the 1828 election campaign, many stories about Andrew Jackson spread. One recalled his days as a judge in Tennessee. A frontiersman named Russell Bean was supposed to appear before Jackson's court, but he refused to come inside. Jackson came roaring out of the courthouse. "Surrender, you infernal villain," he shouted, "or I'll blow you through." Bean looked into Jackson's blazing eyes and quietly surrendered. The iron will that made Russell Bean surrender also made Jackson a powerful President.

Andrew Jackson confronts Russell Bean

Andrew Jackson

Like many who admired him, Jackson was born in a log cabin on the frontier. His parents had left Ireland to settle in the Carolinas. Both died before Jackson was 15. Young Andrew had to grow up quickly.

A Self-made Man Although he was lean, he was a strong fighter. A friend who wrestled with him recalled, "I could throw him three times out of four, but he would never stay throwed."

Always determined, Jackson showed his toughness at 13 when he joined the Patriots during the American Revolution. He was captured by the British. When a British officer ordered the young prisoner to clean his boots, Jackson refused. The officer took a sword and slashed the boy's hand and face. The memory of that attack stayed with Jackson for the rest of his life.

After the Revolution, Jackson studied law in North Carolina. Later, he moved to Tennessee and set up a successful law practice. He became very wealthy by buying and selling land in Georgia and Alabama. While still in his twenties, he was elected to Congress.

Jackson won national fame for his achievements during the War of 1812. He led American forces to a major victory over the British at the Battle of New Orleans. He also defeated the Creek Indians and forced them to give up vast amounts of land in Georgia and Alabama.

A Man of Many Qualities Andrew Jackson was a complex person. He had led a violent and adventurous life. He was quick to lose his temper, and he dealt with his enemies harshly. When he became President, his opponents sarcastically called him "King Andrew." Jackson intended to be a strong president by expanding the powers of the presidency.

At the same time, Jackson's supporters admired his ability to inspire and lead others. They considered him a man of his word and a champion of the common people.

To the Creek Indians, however, Jackson was an enemy who showed no mercy. After defeating them in battle during the War of 1812, Jackson threatened to kill their leaders if they did not give up lands guaranteed them by earlier treaties. As a result, the Creeks had no affection for Jackson. Their name for him was "Sharp Knife."

The Spoils System

In 1828, President Jackson knew that Americans wanted change. "The people expected reform," he said. "This was the cry from Maine to Louisiana."

Reward for Victory After taking office, Jackson fired many government employees. He replaced them with his own supporters. Most other Presidents had done the same, but Jackson did it on a larger scale. He dismissed more than 200 previous presidential appointees.

Critics accused Jackson of rewarding Democrats who had helped elect him instead of choosing qualified men. Jackson replied that he was serving democracy by letting more citizens take part in government. According to Jackson, this would prevent a small group of wealthy men from controlling the government. He felt that ordinary Americans could fill government jobs. "The duties of all public officers are . . . so plain and simple that men of intelligence may readily qualify themselves for their performance," he said.

A Jackson supporter explained the system another way. "To the victor belong the spoils," he declared. Spoils are profits or benefits. From then on, the practice of rewarding supporters with government jobs became known as the **spoils system.**

The "Kitchen Cabinet" Jackson rewarded a number of his supporters with Cabinet jobs. However, few of them were qualified for the positions. Only Secretary of State Martin Van Buren was truly qualified for his position.

As a result, Jackson seldom met with his official Cabinet. Instead, he relied on a group of unofficial advisers. They included Democratic leaders and newspaper editors. These men had a good sense of the nation's mood. Because Jackson met with them in the White House kitchen, the group became known as the **"kitchen cabinet."**

Target Skill — Identify Sequence After you read "The Bank War," make sure you understand the issues involved in the Bank dispute. Add these issues to your chart in chronological order.

The Bank War

President Jackson waged war on the Bank of the United States. Like many westerners, he thought that it was too powerful.

POLITICAL CARTOON *Skills*

Andrew Jackson Battles the Bank of the United States In this cartoon, President Jackson battles the Bank of the United States and its branches (represented by the multiple heads).

1. **Comprehension** Read the cane Jackson is holding. What does it say?
2. **Understanding Main Ideas** How does Jackson fight the Bank?
3. **Critical Thinking Identifying Bias** How do you think the cartoonist felt about the Bank of the United States?

Civics 

Mr. Biddle's Bank The Bank of the United States had been a subject of dispute since its early days. The Bank had great power because it controlled loans made by state banks. When the Bank's directors thought that state banks were making too many loans, they limited the amount these banks could lend. The cutbacks angered farmers and merchants who borrowed money to buy land or finance new businesses.

President Jackson and other leading Democrats saw the Bank as undemocratic. Although Congress created the Bank, it was run by private bankers. Jackson condemned these men as agents of "special privilege" who grew rich with public funds. He especially disliked Nicholas Biddle, president of the Bank since 1823.

Biddle came from a wealthy Philadelphia family. He was well qualified to run the bank, but he was also arrogant and vain. Jackson felt that Biddle used the Bank to benefit only the rich. He also resented Biddle's influence over certain members of Congress.

The War Begins Biddle and other Whigs worried that the President might try to destroy the Bank. Two Whig senators, Henry Clay and Daniel Webster, thought of a way to save the Bank and defeat Jackson at the same time.

The Bank's charter was not due for renewal by Congress until 1836. However, Clay and Webster wanted to make the Bank an issue in the 1832 election. They persuaded Biddle to apply for renewal early.

The Whigs believed that most Americans supported the Bank of the United States. If Jackson vetoed the bill to renew the charter, they felt sure that he would anger voters and lose the election. Clay pushed the charter renewal bill through Congress in 1832. Jackson was sick in bed when he heard that Congress had renewed the Bank's charter. "The Bank . . . is trying to kill me," Jackson fumed, "but I will kill it!"

Jackson's Veto In an angry message to Congress, Jackson vetoed the Bank bill. He gave two reasons for his veto. First, he declared the Bank unconstitutional, even though the Supreme Court had ruled in the Bank's favor. Jackson believed that only states, not the federal government, had the right to charter banks. Second, Jackson felt that the Bank helped aristocrats at the expense of the common people. He warned:

> "When the laws undertake . . . to make the rich richer and the potent more powerful, the humble members of the society—the farmers, mechanics, and laborers—who have neither the time nor the means of [getting] like favors for themselves . . . have a right to complain of the injustice of their government."
>
> —Andrew Jackson, Veto Message, July 10, 1832

As planned, the Whigs made the Bank a major issue in the election of 1832. They chose Henry Clay as their candidate to run against Andrew Jackson. The counted votes showed that Jackson had won a stunning election victory. The common people had surprised the Whigs by supporting Jackson and rejecting the Bank of the United States.

The Bank Closes Without a new charter, the Bank would have to close in 1836. Jackson refused to wait. He ordered Secretary of the Treasury Roger Taney to stop putting government money in the Bank. Instead, Taney deposited federal money in state banks. They became known as pet banks because Taney and his friends controlled many of them. The loss of federal money crippled the Bank of the United States. Its closing in 1836 contributed to an economic crisis.

★ ★ ★ Section 2 Assessment ★ ★ ★

Recall

1. **Identify** Explain the significance of **(a)** "King Andrew," **(b)** Nicholas Biddle.
2. **Define (a)** spoils system, **(b)** "kitchen cabinet."

Comprehension

3. Why was Andrew Jackson called a self-made man?
4. Explain the impact of Andrew Jackson's election on the spoils system.
5. Why did Jackson veto the bill to extend the charter of the Bank of the United States?

Critical Thinking and Writing

6. **Exploring the Main Idea** Review the Main Idea statement at the beginning of this section. Then, analyze the characteristics that made Andrew Jackson a strong leader.
7. **Evaluating Information** Why might one argue that Jackson was not serving democracy with the spoils system? Write your answer in a paragraph.

Activity

Connecting to Today

In the 1800s, the Bank of the United States loaned money to banks and individuals. Today, the Federal Reserve Bank is the central bank of the United States. Use the Internet to find out how the Federal Reserve system works. Then, list four facts about it. For help in completing the activity, visit PHSchool.com, **Web Code mfd-1201.**

Distinguishing Facts From Opinions

To understand history, it is important to be able to distinguish facts from opinions. A fact is something that can be proved or observed. An opinion is a judgment that reflects someone's feelings or beliefs. An opinion is not necessarily true.

In the following letter, Andrew Jackson writes about his political supporters:

> “The most disagreeable duty I have to perform is the removals and appointments to office. It appears that all who possess office do so as a result of political reward. Thousands who are pressing for office do it upon the ground that they are starving, and say that their families will perish unless they can be relieved by receiving some political office.
>
> These hungry office-seekers, as well as those who are now in office, are dangerous contestants for the public purse. When it is so easy for men seeking these offices to get good recommendations, it requires the greatest skill and judgement to pick men of honesty and integrity.
>
> We have, as you shall see from the newspapers, begun to reform. We are trying to remove those with no ability from office and expose to view the corruption of some of the office-holders appointed by the previous administration.”
>
> —Andrew Jackson

Learn the Skill *To distinguish fact from opinion, use the following steps:*

1. **Identify the facts.** What information could be proved or observed in some way?
2. **Distinguish facts from opinions.** Look for phrases such as "I think," "I believe," or "I feel" and for emotion-packed words, which may signal opinions.
3. **Note how facts and opinions are mixed.** A combination of facts and opinions in a statement can be a clue to the writer's point of view. Are opinions supported by facts?
4. **Identify points of view.** How does the writer feel about this topic?

Practice the Skill *Use the letter to answer the following questions:*

1. **(a)** Identify one fact in this letter. **(b)** Explain how the fact could be proved.
2. **(a)** Identify two opinions in this letter. **(b)** Identify three emotion-packed words used by Jackson.
3. Reread the first sentence. **(a)** What part is fact? **(b)** What part is opinion?
4. How would you describe Jackson's point of view?

Apply the Skill *See the Chapter Review and Assessment.*

3 A New Crisis

Prepare to Read

Objectives

In this section, you will
- Explain how the tariff crisis led to the Nullification Act.
- Summarize why Native Americans were forced off their land.
- List the economic problems Martin Van Buren faced.
- Describe the campaigns of 1840.

Key Terms

states' rights
nullification
Nullification Act
Indian Removal Act
Trail of Tears
Seminole War
depression
mudslinging

Target Reading Skill

Main Idea Copy the concept web below. As you read, fill in the blank ovals with events that were influenced by the struggle over states' rights. Add as many ovals as you need.

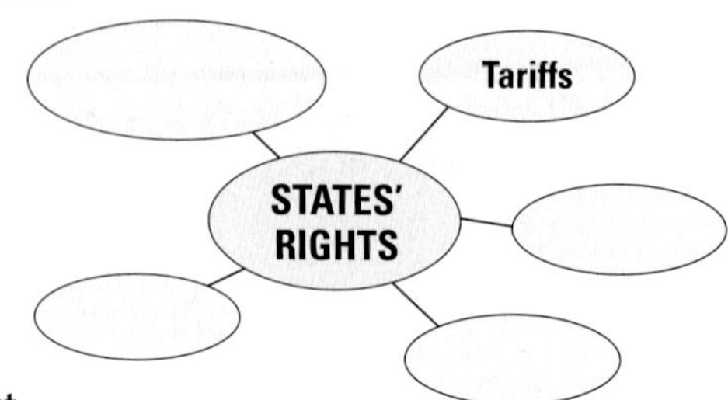

Main Idea The states' rights issue led President Jackson to insist that a state cannot defy federal law, but Jackson defied federal law by removing Native Americans from their homes.

John C. Calhoun

Andrew Jackson

Setting the Scene They had once been friends and allies. They were still the President and Vice President of the United States. Now, however, Andrew Jackson and John C. Calhoun were about to become fierce opponents. The issue that led them to quarrel was **states' rights,** or the right of states to limit the power of the federal government.

In 1830, the two men attended a dinner on the anniversary of Thomas Jefferson's birthday. Several guests made toasts in favor of states' rights. The room fell silent as the President rose. Old Hickory raised his glass, looked straight at the Vice President, and said "Our Federal Union—it must be preserved." Calhoun returned Jackson's stare. "The Union!" he returned, his glass trembling in his hand. "Next to our liberty, most dear."

During Andrew Jackson's presidency, the debate over states' rights affected two important issues. One was the tariff question. The second was the rights of Native Americans to lands they had been guaranteed in treaties.

A Crisis Over Tariffs

In 1828, Congress passed the highest tariff in the history of the nation. Southerners called it the Tariff of Abominations. An abomination is something that is hated.

Just like earlier tariffs, the new law, which was passed before Andrew Jackson's first term, protected manufacturers from foreign competition. Most manufacturers lived in the North. Southern planters, however, were hurt by the tariff. They sold their cotton in Europe and bought European goods in return. The high tariff meant that southerners had to pay more for these imports. Many people thought the tariff was unconstitutional.

Calhoun Versus Webster A leader in the South's fight against the tariff was Vice President John C. Calhoun. Calhoun claimed that a state had the right to nullify, or cancel, a federal law that it considered to be unconstitutional. This idea is called **nullification.** Calhoun supported states' rights. He argued that the states had final authority because they had created the national government.

Daniel Webster disagreed. He made a speech in 1830 before the Senate attacking the idea of nullification. The Constitution, he said, united the American people, not just the states. If states had the right to nullify federal laws, the nation would fall apart. Because Calhoun strongly disagreed with Jackson, he resigned from the office of Vice President. He was then elected as a senator from South Carolina. The debate over states' rights would continue for years.

Identify Supporting Details

What details in this paragraph further explain the issue of states' rights? Add these details to your concept web.

The Nullification Crisis Anger against the tariff increased in the South. Congress passed a new tariff in 1832 that lowered the rate slightly. South Carolina was not satisfied. It passed the **Nullification Act,** declaring the new tariff illegal. It also threatened to secede, or withdraw, from the Union if challenged. Jackson was furious. He knew that nullification could lead to civil war.

Publicly, the President supported a lower compromise tariff proposed by Henry Clay. Jackson also asked Congress to pass the Force Bill. It allowed him to use the army, if necessary, to enforce the tariff.

Faced with Jackson's firm stand, no other state chose to support South Carolina. Calhoun supported the compromise tariff that Clay had proposed. South Carolina repealed the Nullification Act, and the Nullification Crisis passed. However, tensions between the North and South would increase in the years ahead.

An American Profile

Sequoyah 1775?–1843

To the Cherokee Sequoyah, written words were power. He knew that white people collected and passed on knowledge with writing. Sequoyah wanted the same for his own people. In 1809 he began developing a writing system for the Cherokees. In his system, each symbol represented a syllable of the spoken Cherokee language.

Sequoyah's system was easy to learn, and it caught on quickly. Cherokees were soon writing and publishing books and newspapers in their own language and teaching the writing system in their schools.

Why do you think Sequoyah believed a writing system could help keep his people independent?

Tragedy for Native Americans

Jackson took a firm stand on another key issue. It affected the fate of Native Americans. Since the early colonial era, white settlers had forced Native Americans off their land. Indian leaders like Pontiac and Tecumseh had failed to stop the invasion of white settlers.

Indian Nations in the Southeast The Creek, Choctaw, Chickasaw, Cherokee, and Seminole lived in the Southeast. Many hoped to live in peace with their white neighbors. However, their fertile land was attractive to white settlers because it was ideal for growing cotton.

At Jackson's urging, the government set aside lands beyond the Mississippi River and then persuaded or forced Indians to move there. Jackson believed that this policy would provide land for white settlers as well as protect Native Americans from destruction.

Few Indians wanted to move. Some tribes, like the Cherokee nation, had adapted customs in order to preserve their way of life. They created a legal system and government that blended European and Cherokee traditions. Others, like the Choctaw, believed they would be spared the move because they had sided with the United States during the War of 1812.

In 1821, Sequoyah (sih KWOY uh) created a written alphabet for his people. Using Sequoyah's letters, Cherokee children learned to read and write. The Cherokees also published a newspaper.

AmericanHeritage M A G A Z I N E

HISTORY **HAPPENED HERE**

Martin Van Buren Historic Site

While serving as President in 1839, Van Buren purchased the estate that would become his retirement home. Located near his birthplace, Kinderhook, the estate was named Lindenwald. During his stay there, the estate grew to 226 acres and became a profitable farm. Much of the estate remains as it was during Van Buren's lifetime.

Virtual Field Trip For an interactive look at the Van Buren Historic Site, visit PHSchool.com, **Web Code mfd-1202.**

A Legal Battle Georgia claimed the right to make laws for the Cherokee nation in 1828. The Cherokees went to court pointing to treaties with the federal government that protected their rights and property. The Cherokee case reached the Supreme Court. In the 1832 case of *Worcester* v. *Georgia,* Chief Justice John Marshall declared Georgia's action unconstitutional and stated that Native Americans were protected by the U.S. Constitution.

However, President Jackson refused to enforce the Court's decision. In the Nullification Crisis, Jackson defended the power of the federal government. In the Cherokee case, he backed states' rights. He said that the federal government could not stop Georgia from extending its authority over Cherokee lands.

Forced to Leave Jackson supporters in Congress pushed through the **Indian Removal Act** in 1830. It forced many Native Americans to move west of the Mississippi. Whites did not mind turning land over to Indians that they thought was a vast desert. In 1838, the United States Army drove more than 15,000 Cherokees westward. The Cherokees trekked hundreds of miles over a period of several months. Thousands perished during the march, mostly children and the elderly. The Cherokees' long, sorrowful journey west became known as the **Trail of Tears.**

The Seminoles Resist In Florida, the Seminole Indians resisted removal. Led by Chief Osceola (ahs ee oh luh), they began fighting the United States Army in 1817. This conflict, known as the first

Seminole War, ended in 1818. The second Seminole War lasted from 1835 to 1842. It was the costliest war waged by the government to gain Indian lands.

In the end, after a third war ending in 1858, the Seminoles were defeated. The government forced the Seminole leaders and most of their people to leave Florida.

Indian Removal in the Old Northwest Further north, Native Americans were also facing pressure from expanding white settlements. As the white population expanded, groups of Sauk and Fox Indians were forced from their homes in Illinois across the Mississippi River. In 1832, a large band of Sauk and Fox returned to Illinois under the leadership of a warrior named Black Hawk.

Tensions rose sharply between Native Americans and settlers. In one confrontation, panicky settlers killed two Indians who had come to discuss peace. The Native Americans then defeated a band of settlers and retreated into what is today Wisconsin.

A force made up of U.S. Army troops and volunteer militia set out after the Indians. After months of searching, the Americans located the Native Americans and defeated them at the battle of Bad Axe. Many women and children were killed during the battle. Black Hawk soon surrendered, and the Native American resistance collapsed.

Martin Van Buren and Hard Times

Andrew Jackson left office after two terms. Americans then elected Martin Van Buren President. Although Van Buren did not have Jackson's popularity, he was clever and intelligent. As President, however, Van Buren needed more than sharp political instincts.

The Panic of 1837 Two months after taking office, Van Buren faced the worst economic crisis the nation had known. After the Bank of the United States closed, state banks could lend money without limit. To meet the demand for loans, state banks printed more and more paper money. Often, the paper money was not backed by gold or silver.

Before leaving office, Jackson was alarmed at the wild speculation in land. To slow it down, he ordered that anyone buying public land had to pay for it with gold or silver. Speculators and others rushed to state banks to exchange their paper money for gold and silver. Many banks did not have enough gold and silver and were forced to close.

Economic Depression The nation soon plunged into a deep economic **depression,** a period when business declines and many people lose their jobs. The depression lasted three years. In the worst days, 90 percent of the nation's factories were closed. Thousands of people were out of work.

Many Americans blamed Van Buren and his policies for the economic depression. Van Buren believed in laissez faire—the idea that government should play as small a role as possible in the economy. As the depression wore on, Van Buren became increasingly unpopular.

Primary Source

Van Buren Opposes Handouts

Van Buren had scarcely taken office before he was faced with the depression of 1837. His critics blamed his administration for the failing economy, calling it "Van Ruin's Depression." In the following excerpt, Van Buren defends his plan for helping the economy:

"The framers of our excellent Constitution, and the people who approved it . . . acted at a time on a sounder principle. They judged that the less government interferes with private interests, the better for the general prosperity. It is not [the government's] purpose to make men rich, or to repair . . . losses not [received] in the public service. "

—President Martin Van Buren, Letter to Congress, 1837

Analyzing Primary Sources

According to Van Buren, what is the relationship between citizens and the federal government?

Campaigns of 1840

Although Van Buren lost support, the Democrats chose him to run for reelection in 1840. The Whigs chose William Henry Harrison of Ohio. Harrison was known as the hero of the Battle of Tippecanoe. To run for Vice President, the Whigs chose John Tyler.

To appeal to voters, the Whigs focused on Harrison's war record. "Tippecanoe and Tyler too" became their campaign slogan. The Whigs created an image for Harrison as a "man of the people." They presented him as a humble farmer and boasted that he had been born in a log cabin. Harrison was actually a wealthy, educated man who, at the time of the campaign, lived in a large mansion.

A New Sort of Politics The campaigns of 1840 reflected a new sort of politics. Harrison traveled across the land, making speeches and greeting voters. Both parties competed for votes with rallies, banquets, and entertainment.

In their campaigns, both Whigs and Democrats engaged in **mudslinging,** or the use of insults to attack an opponent's reputation. They used name-calling, half-truths, and lies to win votes.

Whigs in the White House Harrison won the election of 1840. The Whigs' program included creating a new Bank of the United States, improving roads and canals, and demanding a high tariff.

However, Whig hopes were dashed when, soon after taking office, President Harrison died of pneumonia. John Tyler became President.

President Tyler failed to live up to Whig expectations. A former Democrat, he opposed some Whig plans for developing the economy. When the Whigs in Congress passed a bill to recharter the Bank of the United States, Tyler vetoed it. In response, most of Tyler's Cabinet resigned. The Whigs threw Tyler out of their party.

★ ★ ★ Section 3 Assessment ★ ★ ★

Recall

1. **Identify** Explain the significance of **(a)** Nullification Act, **(b)** Indian Removal Act, **(c)** Trail of Tears, **(d)** Seminole War.
2. **Define** **(a)** states' rights, **(b)** nullification, **(c)** depression, **(d)** mudslinging.

Comprehension

3. Why did South Carolina pass the Nullification Act?
4. How did the Indian Removal Act affect Native Americans?
5. What hardships did citizens face during the Panic of 1837?
6. Describe some of the campaign tactics Democrats and Whigs used in the election of 1840.

Critical Thinking and Writing

7. **Exploring the Main Idea** Review the Main Idea statement at the beginning of this section. Then, answer the following question in a paragraph. Why do you think Andrew Jackson supported states' rights in the case of the Native Americans but not in the Nullification Crisis?
8. **Solving Problems** What do you think President Van Buren could have done to ease the economic crisis in 1837?

ACTIVITY

Go Online
PHSchool.com

The Banana Wars

Tariffs are still part of domestic and international trade. Use the Internet to find out about the recent banana wars between the United States and Europe. Prepare a brief oral report about the dispute. For help in completing the activity, visit PHSchool.com, **Web Code mfd-1203.**

The LOG CABIN Campaign

In *The Log Cabin Minstrel,* William Henry Harrison is portrayed as a poor farmer who "lives at his cabin, enjoying crackers, hard cider and cheese," while President Van Buren "drank up the milk of the Treasury Cow."

William Henry Harrison

Harrison Song

Tune: "Yankee Doodle"
When our frontiers were drench'd in tears,
Their cabins sack'd and gory,
He struck the blow, chastis'd the foe,
And conquer'd peace with glory.

Then join the throng and swell the song,
Extend the circle wider;
and let us on for HARRISON,
"Log Cabin and Hard Cider."

With HARRISON, our country's one,
No treachery can divide her,
The thing is done with "HARRISON,
Log Cabin and Hard Cider."

Come farmers all, attend the call,
'Tis working like a charmer,
Hitch on the team, and start for him,
For he's a *brother farmer.*

His cabin's fit, and snug and neat,
And full and free his larder,
And though his cider may be hard,
The times are vastly harder.

The South and West will stand the test,
In spite of every spoiler,
And we'll engage to seal the pledge
For HARRISON and TYLER.

—from *The Log Cabin Minstrel,* 1840

Fast Facts

- *The Log Cabin Minstrel* or *Tippecanoe Songster* was compiled in 1840 by the Roxbury, Massachusetts, Democratic Whig Association, and sold for 12 cents per copy.
- More people voted in 1840 than in any previous presidential election.

Activity

Prepare for a class discussion about the way in which political campaigns are conducted today. How can this affect voter turnout and the results of an election?

CHAPTER 12

Review and Assessment

Chapter Summary

Section 1
Andrew Jackson's victory in the presidential election signaled the birth of a democratic spirit that brought political and social changes to the nation. New political parties emerged during Jackson's presidency.

Section 2
Jackson was criticized for introducing the spoils system while serving as President. During his eight years in office, Jackson succeeded in closing the Bank of the United States.

Section 3
Jackson supported states in their attempts to relocate Native Americans, but he opposed states' rights during the Nullification Crisis. An economic crisis hit the country after Jackson left office.

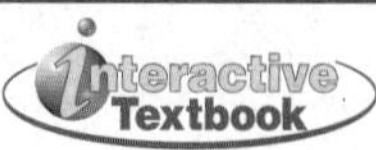

For additional review and enrichment activities, see the interactive version of *The American Nation,* available on the Web and on CD-ROM.

Chapter Self-Test For practice test questions for Chapter 12, visit PHSchool.com, **Web Code mfa-1204.**

Building Vocabulary

Use the chapter vocabulary words listed below to create a crossword puzzle. Exchange puzzles with a classmate. Complete the puzzles, and then check each other's answers.

1. **suffrage**
2. **Whigs**
3. **caucus**
4. **spoils system**
5. **"kitchen cabinet"**
6. **states' rights**
7. **nullification**
8. **Indian Removal Act**
9. **depression**
10. **mudslinging**

Reviewing Key Facts

11. How was a winner selected in the election of 1824? Explain. [Section 1]
12. What role did each of the following play in the struggle over the Bank of the United States? **(a)** Nicholas Biddle **(b)** Henry Clay **(c)** Andrew Jackson [Section 2]
13. What were the causes of the Panic of 1837? [Section 3]

Critical Thinking and Writing

14. **Supporting a Point of View** Andrew Jackson said "The President is the direct representative of the people." During his time in office, did Jackson's actions uphold his statement? Write a paragraph in which you agree or disagree.
15. **Analyzing Information** The new voter group in the 1820s consisted of white men who did not own property. Consider the elections of 1828 and 1840. **(a)** How did Jackson appeal to this group in 1828? **(b)** How did the campaign of 1840 appeal to this group?
16. **Connecting to Geography: Regions** Analyze how the different economic interests of the North and the South influenced their views on the tariff of 1828.
17. **Evaluating Information** Do election campaigns today resemble the election campaign of 1840? Why or why not?

Skills Assessment

Analyzing Primary Sources

Davy Crockett, the frontiersman from Tennessee, served as a member of the Tennessee State legislature from 1821 to 1825. In the following excerpt, he offers advice to those seeking public office.

> “Get up on all occasions, and sometimes on no occasion at all, and make long-winded speeches, though composed of nothing else than wind. Talk of your devotion to your country, your modesty . . . or on any such fanciful subject. Rail against taxes of all kinds, officeholders, and bad harvest weather. . . . To be sure, you run the risk of being considered . . . an empty barrel. But never mind that; you will find enough of the same [company] to keep you in favor.”
>
> —Davy Crockett, *Advice to Politicians,* 1833

18. What advice does Crockett give to a person seeking public office?
- **A.** Do not talk in public.
- **B.** Worry about your image.
- **C.** Criticize taxes.
- **D.** Become a farmer.

19. What opinion might some people have after listening to a politician?
- **A.** They have no strong opinion.
- **B.** Some politicians say nothing of substance.
- **C.** Politicians are always well informed.
- **D.** Politicians tend to be shy.

Applying Your Skills

Distinguishing Facts From Opinions

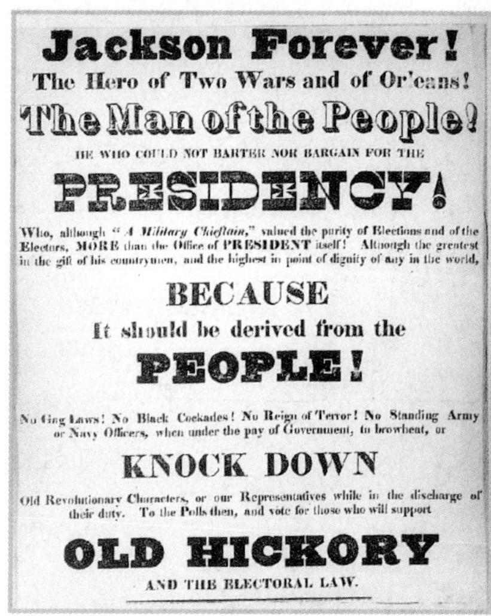

This is an 1828 election poster that praises Jackson's conduct during the election of 1824. Read the poster. Then, answer the following questions:

20. One fact stated on the poster is
- **A.** Jackson is a man of the people.
- **B.** An election should be derived from the people.
- **C.** Jackson was a hero of two wars.
- **D.** Jackson supports electoral law.

21. What point of view do Jackson's supporters want the public to have?

Activities

Connecting With . . . Government and Citizenship

Researching a Campaign Symbol The use of a donkey as the official campaign symbol for the Democratic party began during Andrew Jackson's campaign for election in 1828. Use the Internet to research the history of this campaign symbol and symbols of other political parties. Present the information you find in an illustrated chart.

An Illustrated Report

Researching de Tocqueville Use the Internet to find out more about Alexis de Tocqueville and his visit to the United States in 1831. Choose an event he wrote about. Describe how it reflected American life at that time. Add illustrations to your report. For help in starting this activity, visit PHSchool.com, **Web Code mfd-1206.**

CHAPTER 13

Westward Expansion

1820–1860

1 Oregon Country
2 The Republic of Texas
3 California and the Southwest
4 The Mexican War
5 Americans Rush West

Mountain man Jim Beckwourth

Defending the Alamo

AMERICAN EVENTS

1820s The era of the mountain men is at its height. Mountain men such as Jim Beckwourth open trails through the Rockies into Oregon and California.

1830 Joseph Smith founds the Mormon Church in Fayette, New York.

1836 Texans defend the Alamo during the Texas War of Independence.

Presidential Terms: James Monroe 1817–1825 | John Quincy Adams 1825–1829 | Andrew Jackson 1829–1837 | Martin Van Buren 1837–1841

1820 · 1830 · 1840

WORLD EVENTS

▲ **1821** Mexico wins independence from Spain.

▲ **1830** Mexico bars any additional emigration from the United States to Texas.

Growth of the United States to 1853

By 1848, the United States stretched all the way from the Atlantic Ocean to the Pacific Ocean.

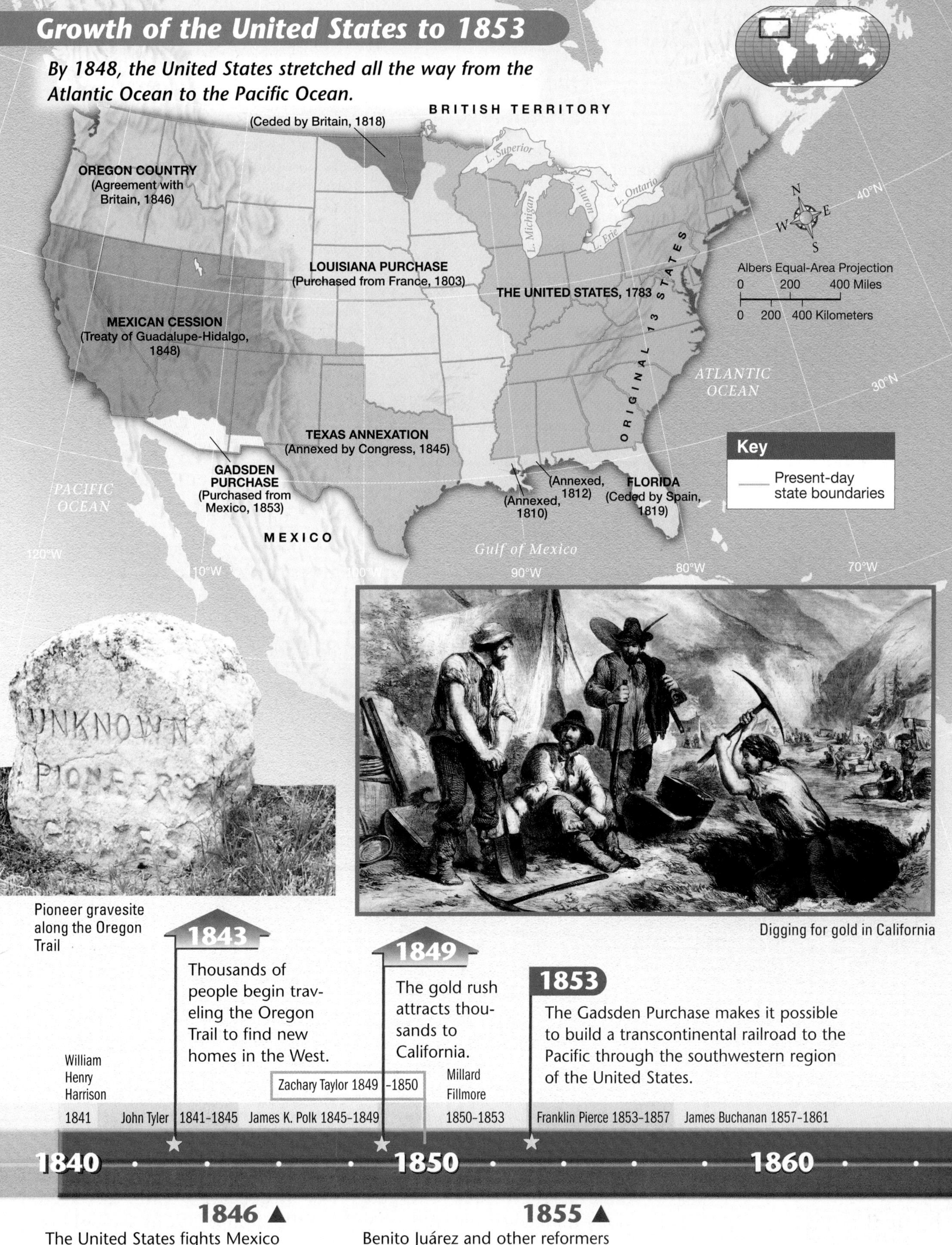

Pioneer gravesite along the Oregon Trail

Digging for gold in California

1843 Thousands of people begin traveling the Oregon Trail to find new homes in the West.

1849 The gold rush attracts thousands to California.

1853 The Gadsden Purchase makes it possible to build a transcontinental railroad to the Pacific through the southwestern region of the United States.

William Henry Harrison 1841 | John Tyler 1841–1845 | James K. Polk 1845–1849 | Zachary Taylor 1849–1850 | Millard Fillmore 1850–1853 | Franklin Pierce 1853–1857 | James Buchanan 1857–1861

1840 · 1850 · 1860

1846 ▲ The United States fights Mexico during the Mexican War.

1855 ▲ Benito Juárez and other reformers seize power in Mexico.

1 Oregon Country

Prepare to Read

Objectives

In this section, you will
- Explain the appeal of Oregon and the Far West.
- Summarize how mountain men helped explore the Far West.
- Describe the role missionaries played in Oregon.
- Identify the hardships faced on wagon trains to the West.

Key Terms

Oregon Country
mountain man
rugged individualist
rendezvous
Oregon Trail

Target Reading Skill

Reading Process As you read, prepare an outline of this section. Use roman numerals to indicate the major headings, capital letters for the subheadings, and numbers for the supporting details.

I. The Lure of Oregon
  A. Land and climate
    1.
    2.
  B. Competing claims
    1.
    2.
II. Fur Trappers in the Far West
  A. Lives filled with danger
    1.
    2.
  B.

Main Idea By the 1840s, thousands of pioneers were following in the footsteps of fur traders and missionaries to settle in Oregon Country.

Traveling the trail

Setting the Scene Young John Johnson and Jane Jones fell in love as their families were moving west by wagon train. John's parents did not like the match, so they left the wagon train. John and Jane, though, secretly promised to leave letters for each other on the buffalo skulls that dotted the trail. They signed their letters "Laurie." For the next month, Jane later told John "not a day passed . . . but what I have found a letter signed by Laurie so I knew just where you were and was sure we would overtake you."

The Johnson and Jones families were among thousands of people who traveled to Oregon in the mid-1800s. In 1820, Oregon had seemed a distant and dangerous place. Yet, by the early 1850s, large numbers of pioneers were heading across the Great Plains to the Far West. Their presence would support the claims of the United States to Oregon and put the nation into conflict with Great Britain.

The Lure of Oregon

By the 1820s, white settlers had occupied much of the land between the Appalachians and the Mississippi River. Families in search of good farmland kept moving farther west. Few, however, settled on the Great Plains between the Mississippi and the Rockies. The plains were considered too dry to support settlement. Instead, settlers headed to lands in the Far West.

Americans first heard about the area known as Oregon Country in the early 1800s. **Oregon Country** was a huge region west of the Rocky Mountains. Today, it includes Oregon, Washington, Idaho, and parts of Wyoming, Montana, and western Canada.

Land and Climate The geography of Oregon Country is varied. Along the Pacific coast, the soil is fertile. Temperatures are mild all year round, and rainfall is plentiful. Early white settlers found fine farmland in the valley of the Willamette River and the lowlands around Puget Sound.

Farther inland, dense forests covered the coastal mountain range. Beavers and other fur-bearing animals roamed these forests and the Rocky Mountains to the east. For this reason, fur trappers were the first whites to head into Oregon Country.

Not all of Oregon Country attracted Americans. Between the coastal mountains and the Rockies is a barren and dry plateau. This region was home to neither fur trappers nor farmers.

Competing Claims In the early 1800s, four countries claimed Oregon. They were the United States, Great Britain, Spain, and Russia. Of course, Native American groups had lived there for centuries. However, the United States and European nations gave little thought to Indian rights.

In 1818, the United States and Britain agreed to occupy Oregon jointly. Citizens of each nation would have equal rights in Oregon. Spain and Russia had few settlers there, so they withdrew their claims to Oregon Country.

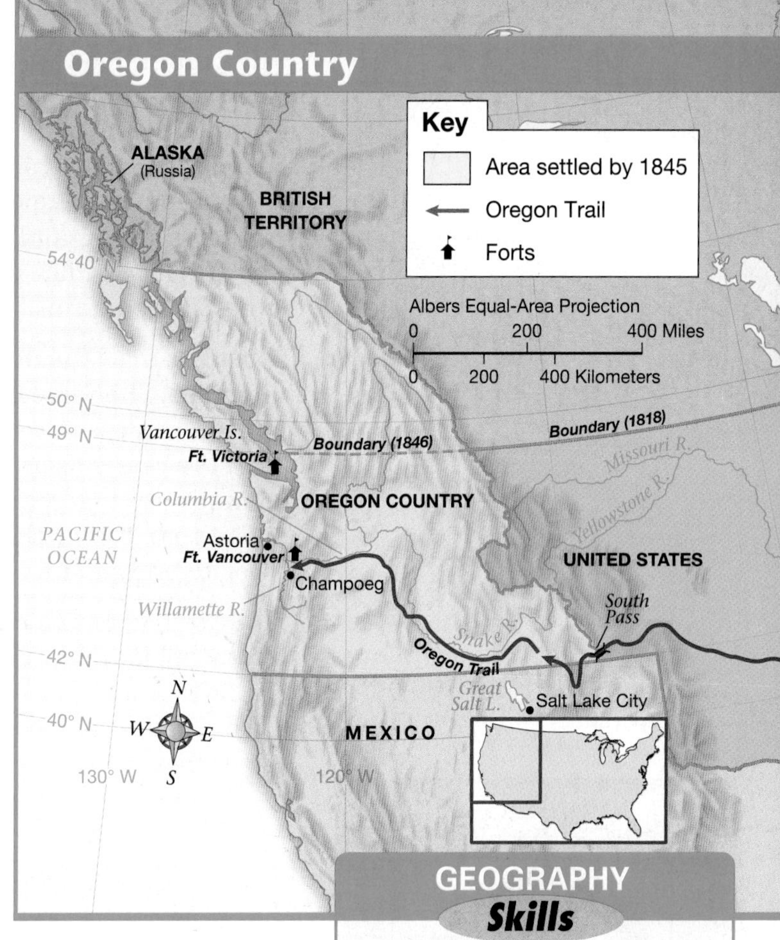

GEOGRAPHY Skills

Oregon Country was the first area in the far west to draw settlers from the United States.

1. **Location** On the map, locate **(a)** Oregon Country, **(b)** British territory, **(c)** Willamette River, **(d)** South Pass.
2. **Region** What line of latitude marked the northern boundary of Oregon Country after 1846?
3. **Critical Thinking Drawing Inferences** Why do you think the Oregon Trail often followed the course of a river?

Fur Trappers in the Far West

At first, only a handful of Europeans or Americans traveled to Oregon Country. Most were fur traders. Since furs could be sold for huge profits in China, merchants from New England stopped along the Oregon coast before crossing the Pacific. In fact, so many Yankee traders visited Oregon to buy furs that, in some areas, the Indian name for a white man was "Boston."

Only a few hardy trappers actually settled in Oregon. These adventurous men hiked through the region's vast forests, trapping animals and living off the land. They were known as **mountain men.**

Mountain men were admired as **rugged individualists,** people who follow their own independent course in life. Even their colorful appearance set them apart from ordinary society. Their shirts and trousers were made of animal hides and decorated with porcupine quills. Their hair reached to their shoulders. Pistols and tomahawks hung from their belts.

Lives Filled With Danger Mountain men could make fine profits selling their furs. They led dangerous lives, however. The long, cold winters demanded special survival skills. In the forests, mountain men had to watch out for bears, wildcats, or other animals that might attack.

In winter, food was scarce. Faced with starvation, a hungry trapper would eat almost anything. "I have held my hands in an anthill until they were covered with ants, then greedily licked them off," one mountain man recalled.

Trappers often spent winters in Native American villages. They learned trapping and hunting skills from Indians. Some mountain men married Indian women who helped the newcomers survive in the harsh mountains.

Trading Furs During the fall and spring, mountain men tended their traps. Then in July, they tramped out of the wilderness to meet with fur traders. They headed to a place chosen the year before, called the rendezvous (RAHN day voo). **Rendezvous** is a French word meaning "get-together."

The first day of the rendezvous was a time for entertainment. A visitor to one rendezvous captured the excitement:

> "[The mountain men] engaged in contests of skill at running, jumping, wrestling, shooting with the rifle, and running horses. . . . They sang, they laughed, they whooped; they tried to out-brag and out-lie each other in stories of their adventures."
>
> —Washington Irving, *The Adventures of Captain Bonneville, U.S.A., in the Rocky Mountains and the Far West,* 1837

Soon enough, trappers and traders settled down to bargain. As long as beaver hats were in demand in the East and in Europe, mountain men got a good price for their furs.

By the late 1830s, however, the fur trade was dying. Trappers had killed too many beavers, and the animals had become scarce. Also, beaver hats went out of style. Even so, the mountain men found new uses for their skills. Some began to lead settlers across rugged mountain trails into Oregon.

Exploring New Lands

In their search for furs, mountain men explored many parts of the West. They followed Indian trails through passes in the Rocky Mountains. Later, they showed these trails to settlers heading west.

Jedediah Smith led settlers across the Rockies through South Pass, in present-day Wyoming. Manuel Lisa, a Latino fur trader, led a trip up the Missouri River in 1807. He founded Fort Manuel, the first outpost on the upper Missouri.

James Beckwourth, an African American, traveled west from Virginia to escape slavery. He was accepted as a chief by the Crow Indians. As a guide, Beckwourth discovered a mountain pass through the Sierra Nevadas that later became a major route to California.

Missionaries in Oregon

The first white Americans to settle permanently in Oregon Country were missionaries. Among them were Marcus and Narcissa Whitman. The couple married in 1836 and set out for Oregon, where they planned to convert local Native Americans to Christianity.

An American Profile

Narcissa Whitman
1808–1847

Marcus and Narcissa Whitman arrived in Oregon after a seven-month journey. In Oregon, Narcissa's life proved harsh and lonely. Marcus was often away for weeks, working among the Indians. Narcissa desperately missed her family back East. Sending or receiving letters, however, was difficult. Often she had to wait a whole year for letters to arrive from home.

Soon after reaching Oregon, Narcissa gave birth to a baby girl. Tragically, her daughter drowned at the age of two.

Why do you think Narcissa did not just give up and return home?

The Whitmans built their mission near the Columbia River and began to work with Cayuse (KI oos) Indians, setting up a mission school and a clinic. Soon, other missionaries and settlers joined them.

Missionaries like the Whitmans helped stir up interest in Oregon Country. Eager to have others join them, the missionaries sent back glowing reports about the land. People throughout the nation read these reports. By 1840, more and more Americans were making the long and difficult journey to Oregon.

As settlers spread onto Cayuse lands, conflicts arose. Worse, the newcomers carried diseases that often killed the Indians.

In 1847, tragedy struck. A measles outbreak among the settlers spread to the Cayuses. Many Cayuse children died. Blaming the settlers, a band of angry Indians attacked the mission, killing the Whitmans and 12 others.

Wagon Trains West

Despite the killings, other pioneers boldly set out for Oregon. They were attracted by tales of wheat that grew taller than a man and turnips five feet around. Stories like these touched off a race to get to Oregon. Americans called it "Oregon fever."

As Oregon fever spread, pioneers clogged the trails west. Beginning in 1843, wagon trains left every spring for Oregon. They followed a route called the **Oregon Trail.**

Families planning to go west met at Independence, Missouri, in the early spring. By mid-April, the prairie outside Independence was packed with people and wagons. Somehow, the pioneers formed themselves into wagon trains. Each group elected leaders to make decisions along the way.

The Oregon-bound pioneers hurried to leave Independence in May. Timing was important. Travelers had to reach Oregon by early October before the snow fell in the mountains. This meant that pioneers had to cover 2,000 miles in five months. In the 1840s, traveling 15 miles a day was considered making good time!

Life on the Trail On the trail, families woke at dawn to a bugle blast. Everyone had a job to do. Girls helped their mothers prepare food. Men and boys harnessed the horses and oxen. By 6 A.M., the cry of "Wagons Ho!" rang across the plains.

The wagon train stopped for a brief noonday meal. Then, it returned to the trail until 6 or 7 P.M. At night, wagons drew up into a circle to keep the cattle from wandering.

Viewing History

On the Trail

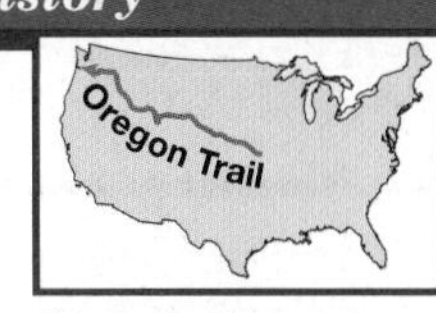

People and wagon trains crowded the trails to the West in the 1840s. Here, families struggle to drive their animals just a few miles farther before darkness. At the bottom of the picture is a trunk that one woman used to get her precious china to the West. **Making Generalizations** ***Based on these pictures, make a generalization about the character of the people who journeyed along the Oregon Trail.***

Most pioneer families started the journey with a large amount of gear. As they crossed rivers and scaled mountains, they discarded belongings to lighten their wagons.

The trail west held many dangers. During the spring, travelers risked drowning as they floated their wagons across rain-swollen rivers. In summer, they faced blistering heat on the treeless plains. Early snows could block passes through the mountains. Getting the heavy wagons past these obstacles was hard work.

The biggest threat was sickness. Cholera and other diseases could wipe out whole wagon trains. Because the travelers lived so close together, diseases spread quickly.

Trading With Native Americans As they moved toward the Rockies, pioneers often saw Indians. Many Native Americans traded with the wagon trains. Hungry pioneers were grateful for the food that the Indians sold in return for clothing and tools. A traveler noted:

Target Skill: Use Prior Knowledge As you read this quotation, think about how the description of pioneers and Native Americans differs from what has often been portrayed in movies.

> "Whenever we camp near any Indian village, we are no sooner stopped than a whole crowd may be seen coming galloping into our camp. The [women] do all the swapping."
>
> —John S. Unruh, quoted in *The Plains Across: The Overland Emigrants and the Trans-Mississippi West, 1840–1860*

Oregon at Last! Despite the many hardships, more than 50,000 people reached Oregon between 1840 and 1860. Their wagon wheels cut so deeply into the plains that the ruts can still be seen today.

By the 1840s, Americans outnumbered the British in Oregon. As you have read, the two nations had agreed to occupy Oregon jointly. Now, many Americans wanted Oregon for the United States alone.

★ ★ ★ Section 1 Assessment ★ ★ ★

Recall

1. **Identify** Explain the significance of **(a)** Oregon Country, **(b)** James Beckwourth, **(c)** Oregon Trail.
2. **Define** **(a)** mountain man, **(b)** rugged individualist, **(c)** rendezvous.

Comprehension

3. Why were trappers and settlers attracted to Oregon Country?
4. How did mountain men contribute to the settlement of the Far West?
5. How did missionaries like the Whitmans attract other people to settle in Oregon?
6. Describe two difficulties that settlers faced on the Oregon Trail.

Critical Thinking and Writing

7. **Exploring the Main Idea** Review the Main Idea statement at the beginning of this section. Then, write a letter that a missionary might have sent East encouraging people to settle in the Oregon Country.
8. **Linking Past and Present** **(a)** What qualities helped the settlers survive the Oregon Trail? **(b)** Do you think such qualities are still important today? Write a paragraph explaining your answers.

Activity

Writing a Diary
Use the Internet to find out more about the life of the mountain men. Then, use the information to write two or three diary entries describing the way of life of an imaginary mountain man. For help in completing the activity, visit PHSchool.com, **Web Code mfd-1301.**

2 The Republic of Texas

Prepare to Read

Objectives

In this section, you will
- Summarize why Americans in Texas conflicted with Mexico.
- Explain how Texas gained independence.
- Describe how the Alamo affected Texans.
- Identify the challenges the Lone Star Republic faced.

Key Terms

dictator
Tejano
Alamo
siege
Battle of San Jacinto
Lone Star Republic
annex

Target Reading Skill

Cause and Effect As you read, complete the following chart to show some of the causes that led Texans to declare independence from Mexico.

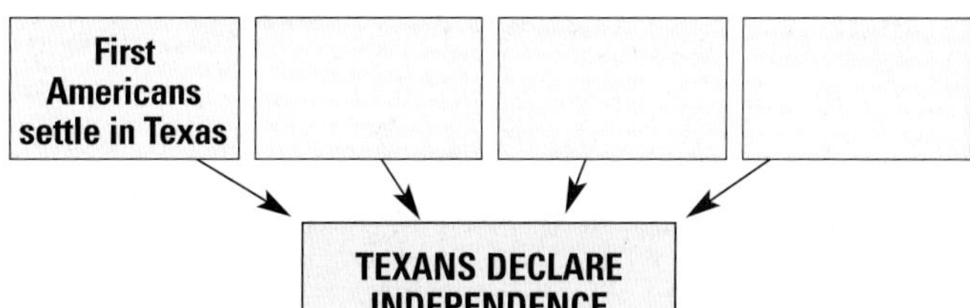

Main Idea In 1835, American settlers in Texas revolted against Mexican rule and in 1836, set up the republic of Texas.

Setting the Scene News of fighting in Texas spread to the United States in late 1835. People heard how Americans in Texas were rebelling against Mexico. "I was at Chicago, Illinois, practicing medicine," recalled Joseph Barnard, a young doctor, "when the news of the Texan revolt from Mexico reached our ears." The news inspired him. The Texans, he wrote, "were in arms for a cause that I had always been taught to consider sacred, . . . Republican principles and popular institutions. They had entered into the contest with spirit and were carrying it on with vigor."

Along with hundreds of other Americans, Dr. Barnard made his way to Texas. There, he fought alongside other American settlers eager to win independence.

Fighting for independence

Americans in Mexican Texas

In the early 1800s, American farmers, especially from the South, looked eagerly at the vast region called Texas. At the time, Texas was part of the Spanish colony of Mexico.

At first, Spain refused to let Americans settle in Texas. Then in 1821, Spain gave Moses Austin a land grant there. Although Austin died before he could set up a colony, his son, Stephen, took over.

Before Stephen Austin could establish his colony, Mexico won independence from Spain. Austin went to Mexico City to make sure that the new government supported the land grant. The new leaders agreed to let Austin bring settlers to Texas. Mexico wanted settlers to develop the land and control Indian attacks. At the time, only about 4,000 Mexicans lived in Texas.

Austin gathered about 300 families to move to Texas. Starting in 1821, they began settling the colony. Many settlers came from the cotton country of the Southeast. Some built large cotton plantations and brought in slaves to work the land.

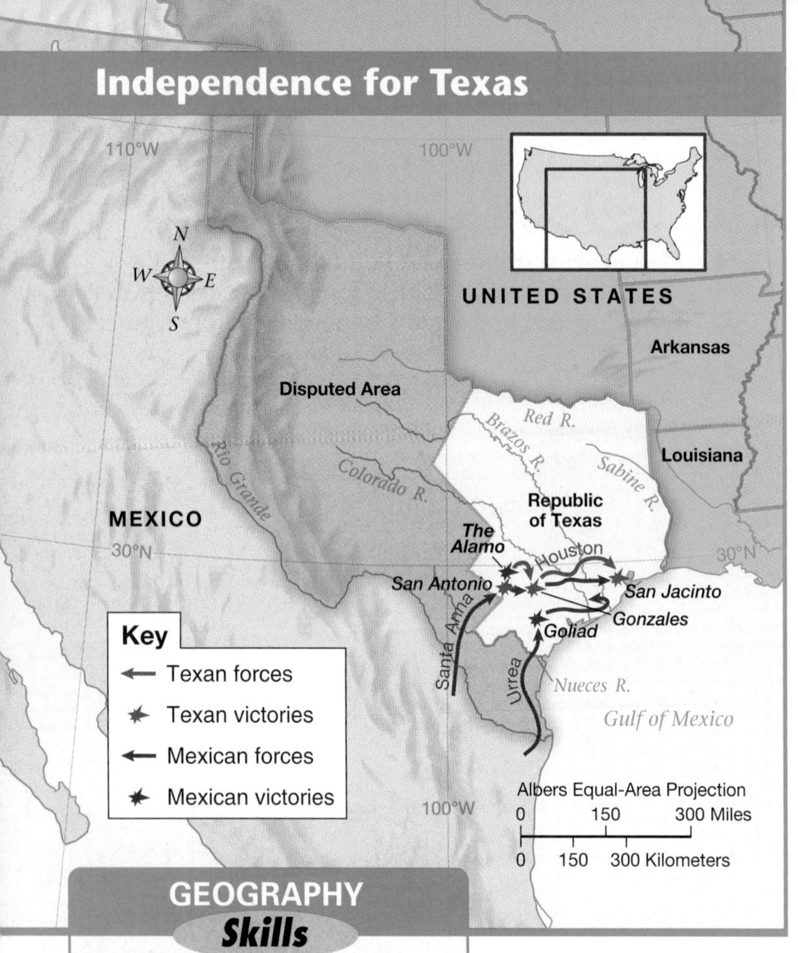

GEOGRAPHY Skills

After a brief but bloody war, Texas gained its independence from Mexico.

1. **Location** On the map, locate **(a)** Rio Grande, **(b)** Nueces River, **(c)** Gonzales, **(d)** San Antonio, **(e)** the Alamo, **(f)** Goliad, **(g)** San Jacinto.
2. **Movement** **(a)** Where did Santa Anna's army first fight the Texans? **(b)** Describe the movement of Mexican and Texan forces after the Alamo.
3. **Critical Thinking Comparing** Refer to the political map of the United States in the Reference Section. How do the boundaries of the Republic of Texas compare with the boundaries of Texas today?

As Austin's colony grew and succeeded, Mexico gave land grants to other people. Some were from Mexico, but the largest number came from the United States. By 1830, about 20,000 Americans had moved to Texas.

Conflict With Mexico

In return for land, Austin and the original American settlers agreed to become Mexican citizens and to worship in the Roman Catholic Church. Later American settlers, however, felt no loyalty to Mexico. They spoke little or no Spanish. Most were Protestant. These and other differences led to conflict between the settlers and the Mexican government.

Mexico Fears Losing Texas In 1830, Mexico barred any more Americans from settling in Texas. Mexico feared that the Americans would try to make Texas a part of the United States. It had good reason to fear this possibility. The United States had already tried twice to buy Texas.

To assert its authority, Mexico began to enforce laws that had long been ignored. One was the law requiring Texans to promise to worship in the Catholic Church. Another law banned slavery in Texas. American settlers resented these laws. Their anger grew when Mexico sent troops to enforce its will.

In 1833, General Antonio López de Santa Anna gained power in Mexico. Two years later, he threw out the Mexican constitution and became a dictator. A **dictator** is a ruler with absolute power and authority. Rumors spread that Santa Anna intended to drive the Americans out of Texas.

Texans Take Action With Santa Anna in power, Americans in Texas felt that the time had come for action. They had the support of many **Tejanos** (teh HAH nohs), people of Mexican descent born in in Texas. Tejanos did not necessarily want independence from Mexico. They did, however, want to be rid of the dictator, Santa Anna.

In October 1835, Texans in the town of Gonzales (gahn ZAH lehs) clashed with Mexican troops. They forced the troops to withdraw. Inspired by that victory, Stephen Austin vowed to "see Texas forever free from Mexican domination." Two months later, Texans occupied the city of San Antonio. Determined to stamp out the rebellion, Santa Anna marched north with a large army.

While Santa Anna was on the move, a group of Texans declared independence for the Republic of Texas on March 2, 1836. Sam Houston was given command of the army. Volunteers from the United States and from other nations, along with African Americans and Tejanos, joined the fight for Texan independence.

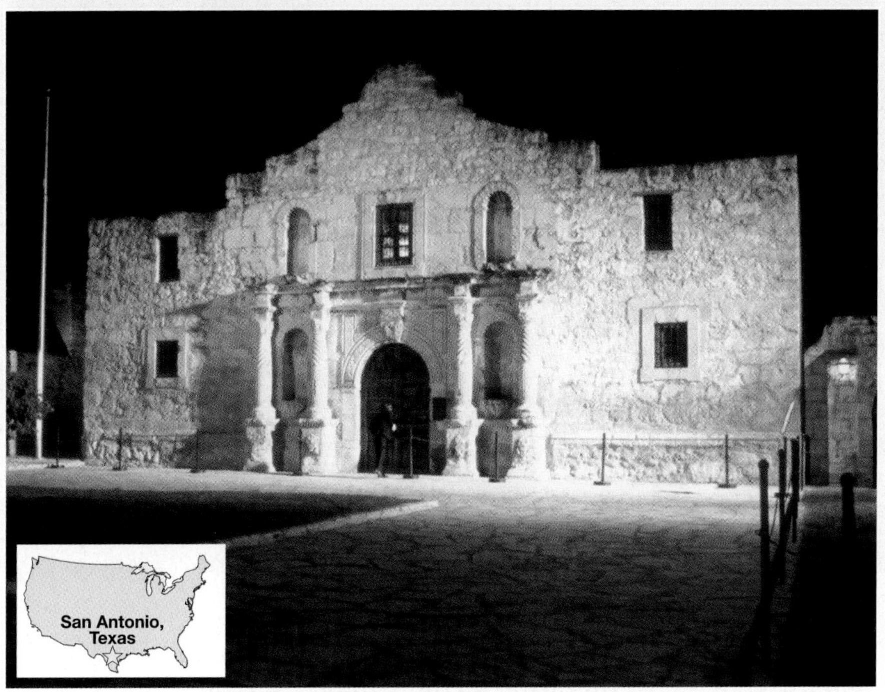

The Alamo

Each year, millions of tourists visit the Alamo in San Antonio, Texas. Few of them realize just how close the building came to collapsing into ruin. After 1836, the Alamo was used as a warehouse and a general store. Since 1905, however, the Alamo has been managed by the Daughters of the Republic of Texas. Three buildings house exhibits on Texas's struggle for independence.

Virtual Field Trip For an interactive look at the Alamo, visit PHSchool.com, **Web Code mfd-1302.**

Siege at the Alamo

By the time Santa Anna reached San Antonio, the Texans had taken up positions in an old Spanish mission called the Alamo. There they waited for the Mexican attack.

Against Great Odds The Texans were poorly equipped. Their supplies of ammunition, food, water, and medicine were low. Only about 150 Texans faced a force of 6,000 Mexican troops!

Inside the mission, young William B. Travis was in command. Among the volunteers at the Alamo were the famous frontiersmen Jim Bowie and Davy Crockett. Several Tejano families, two Texan women, and two young male slaves were also there.

"Victory or Death!" On February 23, 1836, Mexican troops began the siege of the Alamo. In a **siege,** enemy forces try to capture a city or fort, often by surrounding and bombarding it. The Texan defenders bravely held out as cannon pounded the walls. Still, Travis knew that without help, the defenders were doomed. He sent a messenger through the Mexican lines with a letter addressed "to the People of Texas and all the Americans in the World":

> ❝ *I shall never surrender or retreat.*
>
> I call on you in the name of Liberty, of patriotism, and of everything dear to the American character to come to our aid with all [speed]. . . . *Victory or Death!* ❞
>
> —William B. Travis, Letter, February 24, 1836

Target Skill — Recognize Multiple Causes

A cause makes something happen. Sometimes an effect can have more than one cause. Read the subsections "Siege at the Alamo" and "Texan Independence" to discover the connection between the Alamo and the independence of Texas. Add this information to your chart.

Santa Anna

Sam Houston

Viewing History

Winning Texas Independence

Sam Houston was wounded in the leg during the Battle of San Jacinto. Despite tremendous pain and a boot full of blood, Houston fought on to victory. This painting shows Houston accepting the surrender of the Mexican commander Santa Anna. The flag is that of the Lone Star Republic. **Drawing Conclusions** ***Why was San Jacinto a turning point in Texas history?***

Travis also sent scouts to find more volunteers and food. About 40 men managed to slip through enemy lines and join the fighters in the Alamo. Still, no large force arrived.

For 12 days, the Mexican bombardment continued. At dawn on March 6, Mexican cannons shattered the mission walls. Santa Anna now launched an all-out attack. Thousands of Mexican soldiers poured over the broken walls, shouting "Viva Santa Anna!" Attackers and defenders battled in hand-to-hand combat. In the end, about 180 Texans and almost 1,500 Mexicans lay dead. Most of the handful of Texan survivors were executed.

Texan Independence

The fall of the Alamo ignited cries for revenge. Texan fury grew a few weeks later, when Mexican troops killed several hundred soldiers fighting for the Texan cause after they had surrendered at Goliad. News of these events inspired new volunteers to join the Texan forces. Many came from the United States. Houston worked hard to turn the volunteers into an effective army. The Texans were eager to attack, but Houston held them back until the time was right.

Houston soon found the chance to attack Santa Anna. Scouts reported that the Mexican general and his army were camped near the San Jacinto (juh SIN toh) River. On the afternoon of April 21, 1836, the Texans caught their enemies by surprise. With cries of "Remember the Alamo!" and "Remember Goliad!" Texans charged into battle.

The **Battle of San Jacinto** lasted only 18 minutes. Although the Texans were outnumbered, they killed 630 Mexicans and captured 700 more. The next day, they captured Santa Anna, forcing him to sign a treaty granting Texas independence.

The Lone Star Republic

In battle, Texans had carried a flag with a single white star. After winning independence, they nicknamed their nation the Lone Star Republic. They wrote a constitution using the United States Constitution as a model. In September 1836, voters elected Sam Houston president of the Republic of Texas.

The new country faced several serious problems. First, the government of Mexico refused to accept the treaty that Santa Anna had signed. For Mexicans, Texas was still a part of their country. Second, Texas was nearly bankrupt. Third, Comanches and other Indian groups threatened to attack small Texan communities. Most Texans thought that the best way to solve their problems was to become part of the United States.

In the United States, people were divided about whether to annex, or add on, Texas. The arguments reflected sectional divisions in the country. White southerners generally favored the idea. Many northerners opposed it. At issue was slavery.

By the 1830s, antislavery feeling was growing in the North. Because many Texans owned slaves, northerners feared that Texas would join the Union as a slave-owning state. In addition, President Andrew Jackson worried that annexing Texas would lead to war with Mexico. As a result, Congress refused to annex Texas.

For the next nine years, leaders of the Lone Star Republic worked to attract new settlers. The new Texas government encouraged immigration by offering settlers free land. During the Panic of 1837, thousands of Americans moved to Texas. Settlers also arrived from Germany and Switzerland. They helped the new nation grow and prosper. By the 1840s, about 140,000 people lived in Texas, including many African Americans and some Mexicans.

★ ★ ★ Section 2 Assessment ★ ★ ★

Recall

1. **Identify** Explain the significance of **(a)** Stephen Austin, **(b)** Antonio López de Santa Anna, **(c)** Tejano, **(d)** Sam Houston, **(e)** Alamo, **(f)** William B. Travis, **(g)** Battle of San Jacinto, **(h)** Lone Star Republic.
2. **Define** **(a)** dictator, **(b)** siege, **(c)** annex.

Comprehension

3. Describe two causes of the conflict between American settlers and Mexico.
4. How did the fighting at the Alamo inspire Texans to win their independence?
5. Why did Texas not join the United States after San Jacinto?
6. Explain two problems that Texans tried to solve after winning independence.

Critical Thinking and Writing

7. **Exploring the Main Idea** Review the Main Idea statement at the beginning of this section. Then, write at least five headlines to mark events described in this section.
8. **Supporting a Point of View** As a Texan in 1838, you must vote to support or to oppose Texas's annexation by the United States. Write a position paper stating your opinion.

Activity

Connecting to Today

Use the Internet to find out what programs are underway today to preserve the Alamo. Then, write a paragraph that describes these efforts. For help in completing the activity, visit PHSchool.com, **Web Code mfd-1303.**

Determining Patterns and Distributions on Maps

Maps can help to make clear much of the information that historians collect. For example, a distribution map shows how people or things are spread over an area. A distribution map is a kind of thematic map—a map that presents certain themes. The theme of this map is settlement patterns in the newly formed Republic of Texas.

Patterns of Settlement, 1836

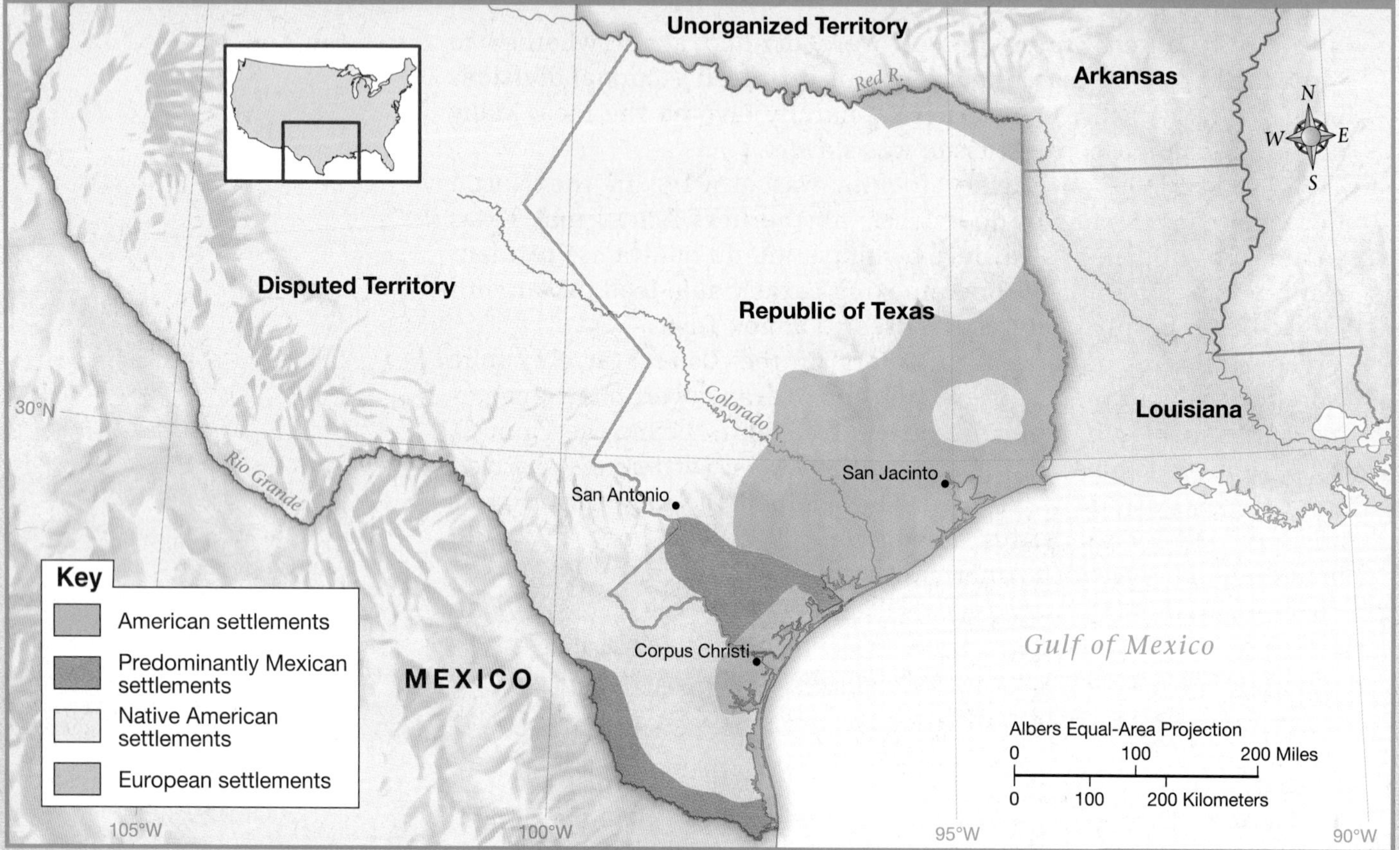

Unorganized Territory
Arkansas
Red R.
N
W
E
S
Disputed Territory
Republic of Texas
Louisiana
30°N
Colorado R.
Rio Grande
San Jacinto
San Antonio
Corpus Christi
MEXICO
Gulf of Mexico

Key
- American settlements
- Predominantly Mexican settlements
- Native American settlements
- European settlements

Albers Equal-Area Projection
0 100 200 Miles
0 100 200 Kilometers
105°W
100°W
95°W
90°W

Learn the Skill *To determine patterns and distribution on a map, use the following steps:*

1. **Read the title.** A map title provides a summary of the information shown on the map. In the case of a distribution map, the title should provide information about where people or things are located.
2. **Study the map key.** The key, or legend, tells what the different symbols on the map represent.
3. **Determine patterns.** Note which groups dominate in different areas.
4. **Analyze the information.** Put together what the map shows and what you already know about the subject to draw conclusions or make predictions.

Practice the Skill *Answer the following questions based on the map above:*

1. What is the title of the map?
2. **(a)** What color indicates Native American settlements on the map? **(b)** How are American settlements shown?
3. **(a)** Where were the Mexican settlements? **(b)** What was the smallest settlement in terms of area in 1836?
4. Analyze the reasons why people settled in Texas where they did by 1836.

Apply the Skill *See the Chapter Review and Assessment.*

3 California and the Southwest

Prepare to Read

Objectives

In this section, you will
- Explain why Americans took an interest in the New Mexico Territory.
- Describe life for Native Americans on California's missions and ranches.
- Summarize why many Americans supported the idea of westward expansion.

Key Terms

New Mexico Territory
Santa Fe Trail
self-sufficient
vaquero
Manifest Destiny

Target Reading Skill

Comparison and Contrast Copy this incomplete Venn diagram. As you read, write key facts about the Southwest and California in the 1840s in the appropriate sections.

SOUTHWEST	Both	CALIFORNIA
• Includes all or parts of Arizona, New Mexico, Nevada, Utah, Colorado • Santa Fe is capital • •	• Settled by the Spanish • •	• Region of contrasts in land, climate, and rainfall • •

Main Idea As Americans learned more about California and the Southwest in the 1840s, many came to think that the United States should expand its borders to the Pacific Ocean.

Setting the Scene Richard Henry Dana reached California after 150 days at sea. His ship had sailed from Boston around the tip of South America. One "fine Saturday afternoon," Dana and his crewmates sailed into Monterey Bay. "Everything was as green as nature could make it—the grass, the leaves, and all; the birds were singing in the woods and great numbers of wild fowl were flying over our heads. . . . The Mexican flag was flying from the little square Presidio, and the drums and trumpets of the soldiers . . . sounded over the water and gave life to the scene."

Life in Old California

Dana wrote about his experiences in the book *Two Years Before the Mast,* which appeared in 1840. Dana's book contains a detailed description of life on the California coast. In it, Dana gives close attention to the daily lives of the peoples of California: Latino, Native American, and European.

At the time, California belonged to Mexico. With the help of books like *Two Years Before the Mast,* however, many Americans began to think that the United States should take control of all the lands between the Atlantic and Pacific oceans.

New Mexico Territory

In the early 1840s, Mexico ruled not only California but all of the Southwest. The Southwest included most of present-day Arizona and New Mexico, all of Nevada and Utah, and parts of Colorado. This huge region was called **New Mexico Territory.**

Much of the Southwest is hot and dry with deserts and mountains. In some areas, thick grasses grow. Before the Spanish arrived, the Zuñi (ZOON yee) and other Indians farmed using irrigation. Other Native Americans, such as the Apaches, lived mainly by hunting.

The Spanish explorer Juan de Oñate (ohn YAH tay) claimed the region for Spain in 1598. In the early 1600s, the Spanish built Santa Fe and made it the capital of the territory. In time, Santa Fe grew into a busy trading town.

Spain, however, would not let Americans settle in Santa Fe or anywhere else in New Mexico. Only after Mexico became independent in 1821 were Americans welcome there. William Becknell, a merchant and adventurer, was the first American to head for Santa Fe. In 1821, he led some traders from Franklin, Missouri, across the plains to the New Mexico town. Other Americans soon followed Becknell's route. It became known as the **Santa Fe Trail.**

Compare and Contrast

As you read the subsection "California's Missions and Ranches," note the similarities and differences between California and the Southwest. Add this information to your Venn diagram.

California's Missions and Ranches

California, too, was ruled first by Spain and then by Mexico. Spanish explorers had reached California in 1542, long before the English settled in Jamestown. Spanish and Native American cultures shaped life in California.

A String of Missions As you have read, Spanish soldiers and missionaries built the first European settlements in California. In 1769, Captain Gaspar de Portolá led an expedition up the Pacific coast. With him was Father Junípero Serra (hoo NEE peh roh SEHR rah). Father Serra built his first mission at San Diego. Later he and other missionaries set up a string of 21 missions along the California coast.

Each mission included a church and the surrounding land. Each became **self-sufficient,** producing enough for its own needs. Spanish soldiers built forts near the missions. The missions supplied meat, grain, and other foods to the forts.

California Missions and Ranches Before the Spanish arrived, California Indians lived in small, scattered groups. As a result, they had little success resisting the Spanish soldiers who forced them to work on mission lands.

Native Americans herded sheep and cattle and raised crops for the missions. In return, they lived at the missions and learned about the Roman Catholic faith. Many missionaries were dedicated to converting the Indians to Christianity. However, mission life was hard. Thousands of Native Americans died from overwork and diseases.

In the 1820s, newly independent Mexico decided that California's economy was growing too slowly. Hoping to speed up growth, the government took land from the missions and gave it to wealthy individuals. These people set up huge cattle ranches in California.

Native Americans did most of the work on the ranches, tending cattle and other animals. A new culture developed on the ranches—the culture of the **vaqueros.** Vaqueros were the Indian and Mexican cowhands who worked on the ranches. They were excellent riders and ropers, and their traditions strongly influenced later cowhands.

Primary Source

A Vaquero Roundup

Many of our traditions of cattle herding began with the vaqueros, Latino ranch hands in the Southwest and California. In this selection, a rancher describes some of the skills of the vaqueros:

"It was my good fortune to be taken on [a roundup]. . . . Even on the ground covered with grass, a huge cloud of dust envelopes everything, and nothing is heard but the thundering bank ahead. This is kept up for two or three hours, when the horsemen managed to get into the center of the flying herd. When the dust finally cleared, here and there over the plains could be seen colts and young mares, their forelegs tied to prevent them from escaping, which the vaqueros had lassoed . . ."

—Ygnacio Pedro Villegas, *Roundup*, 1895

Analyzing Primary Sources

What is Villegas's (vee YAY gahs) attitude toward the vaqueros?

Support for Expansion

In the mid-1840s, only about 700 people from the United States lived in California. Every year, however, more Americans began moving west. On several occasions, the United States government offered to buy California from Mexico. Some officials were eager to gain control of the ports at San Francisco and San Diego.

The Idea of Manifest Destiny There was another reason for wanting to purchase California. Many Americans saw their nation and its democratic government as the best in the world. They believed that Americans had the right and the duty to spread their culture across the continent all the way to the Pacific Ocean.

In the 1840s, a newspaper in New York called this belief **Manifest Destiny.** Manifest means clear or obvious. Destiny means something that is sure to happen. Americans who believed in Manifest Destiny thought that expansion would also open new opportunities for the United States economy.

Manifest Destiny had a negative side. Many white Americans believed that they were superior to Native Americans and Mexicans. They used this belief to justify taking lands belonging to people whom they considered inferior.

Election of 1844 Manifest Destiny played a role in the election of 1844. The Whigs nominated Henry Clay for President. Clay was a well-known national leader. The Democrats chose a little-known candidate, James K. Polk.

Voters soon labeled Polk the candidate who favored expansion. Polk wanted to add Texas and Oregon to the United States. Clay, on the other hand, opposed the annexation of Texas.

The Democrats made Oregon a campaign issue. Britain and the United States held Oregon jointly. Polk demanded the whole region as far north as latitude 54°40'N. "Fifty-four forty or fight!" became the Democrats' campaign cry. On election day, Americans showed their support for expansion by choosing James Polk President.

An American Profile

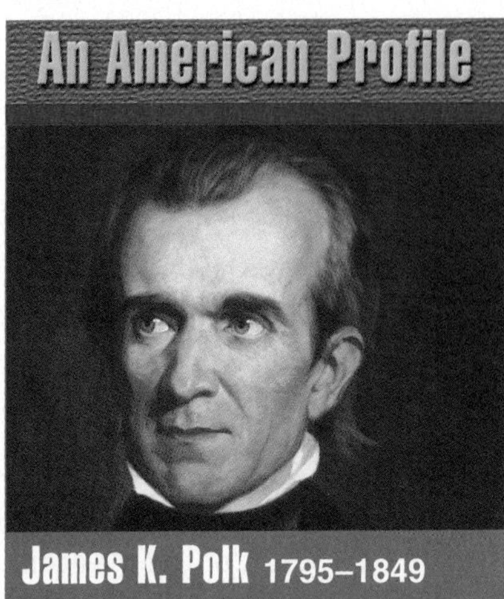

James K. Polk 1795–1849

It is easy to forget just how hard life could be 200 years ago. Consider this: As a teenager, James Polk suffered from severe stomach pains. A doctor discovered gallstones and recommended surgery. Anesthesia was unknown at the time. In 1812, when he was 17, Polk was strapped to a table and operated on while he was awake.

James Polk was a very determined person. Although he had little formal education, he mastered Latin and Greek, graduated with honors from the University of North Carolina, and became a lawyer.

What qualities did Polk show in early life that might serve him well as President?

★ ★ ★ Section 3 Assessment ★ ★ ★

Recall

1. **Identify** Explain the significance of **(a)** New Mexico Territory, **(b)** William Becknell, **(c)** Santa Fe Trail, **(d)** Junípero Serra, **(e)** Manifest Destiny, **(f)** James K. Polk.
2. **Define** **(a)** self-sufficient, **(b)** vaquero.

Comprehension

3. Why were Americans attracted to the New Mexico Territory?
4. How did mission and ranch life affect Native Americans in California?
5. Why did many Americans feel strongly about expansion to the Pacific Ocean?

Critical Thinking and Writing

6. **Exploring the Main Idea** Review the Main Idea statement at the beginning of this section. Then, write a newspaper editorial that might have appeared in the 1840s for or against expansion.
7. **Supporting a Point of View** You are a supporter of one of the major candidates for President in the election of 1844. Write a paragraph stating whether you support Polk or Clay. Give reasons to support your choice.

Activity

Drawing a Political Cartoon **Draw a political cartoon about Manifest Destiny from the point of view of the people of the Southwest.**

4 The Mexican War

Prepare to Read

Objectives

In this section, you will
- Explain how the United States gained Oregon and Texas.
- List the causes and results of the Mexican War.
- Name the new lands the United States acquired as a result of the Mexican War.
- Describe how a mix of cultures shaped California and the Southwest.

Key Terms

Bear Flag Republic

Chapultepec

Treaty of Guadalupe-Hidalgo

cede

Mexican Cession

Gadsden Purchase

Target Reading Skill

Cause and Effect As you read, complete the following chart to show some of the causes and effects of the Mexican War.

CAUSES

1. **United States annexes Texas**
2.
3.

MEXICAN WAR

EFFECTS

1. **Treaty of Guadalupe-Hidalgo**
2. **United States acquires vast new lands**
3.

Main Idea As a result of the Mexican War, the United States expanded its borders to the Pacific Ocean.

Wartime spirit

Setting the Scene American troops marched off to war with Mexico in 1846. Many of them proudly sang new words to the popular tune "Yankee Doodle": "They attacked our men upon our land, / And crossed our river too, sir. / Now show them all with sword in hand / What yankee boys can do, sir."

The bloody Mexican War would last 20 months. When it ended, the United States had expanded its borders to the Pacific Ocean. In the end, the war helped the United States achieve its dream of Manifest Destiny.

War Clouds Over Oregon and Texas

James K. Polk took office in March 1845 on a wave of support for expansion. Acting on his campaign promise, Polk took steps to gain control of Oregon. That move brought close the possibility of war with Britain.

Dividing Oregon Polk did not really want to fight Britain. Instead, in 1846, he agreed to a compromise. Oregon was divided at latitude 49°N. Britain got the lands north of the line, and the United States got the lands south of the line.

The United States named its lands the Oregon Territory. Later, the states of Oregon (1859), Washington (1889), and Idaho (1890) were carved out of the Oregon Territory.

Annexing Texas Texas proved a more difficult problem. As you have read, the United States at first had refused to annex Texas. Then, in 1844, Texan president Sam Houston signed a treaty of annexation with the United States. However, the Senate again refused to ratify the treaty. Senators feared that annexing Texas would cause a war with Mexico.

Sam Houston would not give up. To pressure the United States to annex Texas, he pretended that Texas might ally itself with Britain. The trick worked. Americans did not want Britain to gain a foothold in Texas. In 1845, Congress passed a joint resolution admitting Texas to the Union.

The United States and Mexico Clash

The annexation of Texas outraged Mexicans. They had never accepted Texan independence. They also worried that Americans might encourage rebellions in California and New Mexico as they had in Texas.

At the same time, Americans resented Mexico. They were annoyed when Mexico rejected President Polk's offer of $30 million to buy California and New Mexico. Many Americans felt that Mexico stood in the way of Manifest Destiny.

War Begins A border dispute finally sparked war. Both the United States and Mexico claimed control over the land between the Rio Grande and the Nueces (noo AY says) River. In January 1846, Polk ordered General Zachary Taylor to set up posts in the disputed area. (See the map above.) Polk knew that the move might lead to war. In April 1846, Mexican troops crossed the Rio Grande and clashed with the Americans. Soldiers on both sides were killed.

When Polk heard about the fighting, he asked Congress to declare war. "Mexico," he said, "has passed the boundary of the United States, has invaded our territory, and shed American blood upon American soil." At Polk's urging, Congress declared war on Mexico.

Americans Respond Americans were divided over the war. Many people in the South and West were eager to fight, hoping to win new lands. Some northerners, however, opposed the war. They saw it as a southern plot to add slave states to the Union. The writer Henry David Thoreau refused to pay taxes because he thought the war was unjust. For this, Thoreau was arrested and imprisoned. Still, the war was generally popular. When the army called for volunteers, thousands of young recruits flocked to the cause. A large number came from the South and West.

GEOGRAPHY *Skills*

Fighting along a disputed border between Texas and Mexico triggered the Mexican War.

1. **Location** On the map, locate **(a)** Rio Grande, **(b)** Nueces River, **(c)** Buena Vista, **(d)** Veracruz, **(e)** Mexico City.
2. **Movement** Describe the movements of each of the following American commanders: **(a)** Winfield Scott, **(b)** Stephen Kearny, **(c)** John C. Frémont.
3. **Critical Thinking Drawing Inferences** Based on the map, was sea power important to the United States in the Mexican War? Explain.

Fighting in Mexico

During the Mexican War, the United States attacked on several fronts at once. President Polk hoped this strategy would win a quick victory. General Taylor crossed the Rio Grande into northern Mexico.

Viewing History

Battle at Buena Vista

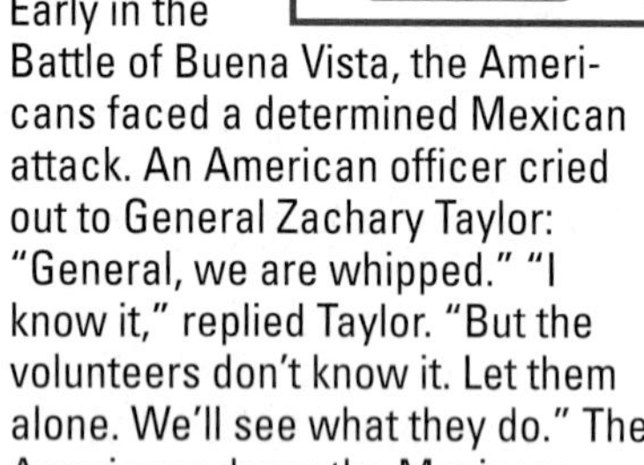

Early in the Battle of Buena Vista, the Americans faced a determined Mexican attack. An American officer cried out to General Zachary Taylor: "General, we are whipped." "I know it," replied Taylor. "But the volunteers don't know it. Let them alone. We'll see what they do." The Americans drove the Mexicans back and won the battle. In this picture, Taylor, at center, gives instructions to his artillery. **Drawing Inferences** ***Do you think Taylor really believed that his forces were "whipped"?***

In February 1847, he met Mexican General Santa Anna at the Battle of Buena Vista. The Americans were outnumbered more than two to one but were better armed and led. After fierce fighting, they forced Santa Anna to retreat.

Meanwhile, a second army under General Winfield Scott landed at Mexico's port of Veracruz. After a long battle, the Americans took the city. Scott then headed toward Mexico City, the capital.

Revolt in California A third army, led by General Stephen Kearny, captured Santa Fe without firing a shot. Kearny hurried on to San Diego. After several battles, he won control of southern California early in 1847.

Even before hearing of the war, Americans in northern California had begun a revolt against Mexican rule. The rebels declared California an independent republic on June 14, 1846. They nicknamed their new nation the **Bear Flag Republic.**

Led by a young American officer, John C. Frémont (FREE mont), rebel forces then drove the Mexican troops out of northern California. Frémont later joined forces with United States troops.

The Final Battle By 1847, the United States controlled all of New Mexico and California. General Scott, meanwhile, had reached Mexico City. There, his forces faced fierce resistance.

Young Mexican soldiers made a heroic stand at **Chapultepec** (chah POOL tuh pehk), a fort just outside the capital. Today, Mexicans honor those young soldiers as heroes.

Target Skill

Understand Effects An effect is what happens as a result of a specific cause or factor. Read the subsection "Peace Brings New Lands" to learn about the effects of the Mexican War. Add the information to your chart.

Peace Brings New Lands

With Mexico City in American hands, the Mexican government moved to make peace. In 1848, it signed the **Treaty of Guadalupe-Hidalgo** (gwah duh LOOP ay ih DAHL goh). Mexico had to **cede,** or give up, all of California and New Mexico to the United States. These lands were called the **Mexican Cession.** In return, the United States paid Mexico $15 million and agreed to respect the rights of Spanish-speaking people in the Mexican Cession.

A few years later in 1853, the United States paid Mexico $10 million for a strip of land in present-day Arizona and New Mexico. The Americans needed the land to complete a railroad. The land was called the **Gadsden Purchase.** With the Gadsden Purchase, many Americans felt that their dream of Manifest Destiny had been fulfilled.

Viewing History

The Bear Flag

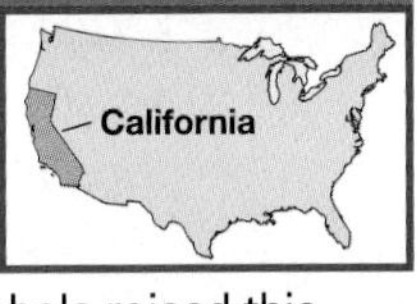

As a symbol of their freedom, the California rebels raised this "Bear Flag." It remains California's state flag today. **Analyzing Primary Sources** ***(a) Why do you think the flag makers put a single star on the flag? (b) Why do you suppose they chose a grizzly bear as their main symbol?***

A Mix of Cultures

After 1848, English-speaking settlers flocked to the Southwest. They brought their own culture, including ideas about democracy. Still, the newcomers had much to learn from earlier residents. Mexican Americans taught them how to mine silver and irrigate crops. Many Spanish and Native American words—such as stampede, buffalo, tortilla, soda, and tornado—were added to the English language.

The newcomers often treated Mexican Americans and Native Americans poorly. Earlier residents tried hard to protect their traditions and rights. However, when Mexican Americans went to court to defend their property, they often lost their cases. Mariano Vallejo (vah YAY hoh), whose family had settled in California long before the Mexican War wrote that American settlers "took advantage of laws which they understood, but which were new to the Spaniards."

In the Southwest, however, Americans kept some Mexican laws. One law said that a husband and wife owned property jointly. In the rest of the United States, married women could not own property. Another Mexican law prevented landowners from cutting off water to their neighbors. This law was especially important in the desert Southwest, where water was scarce.

★ ★ ★ Section 4 Assessment ★ ★ ★

Recall

1. **Identify** Explain the significance of **(a)** Zachary Taylor, **(b)** Winfield Scott, **(c)** Stephen Kearny, **(d)** Bear Flag Republic, **(e)** John C. Frémont, **(f)** Chapultepec, **(g)** Treaty of Guadalupe-Hidalgo, **(h)** Mexican Cession, **(i)** Gadsden Purchase.
2. **Define** cede.

Comprehension

3. Describe how the United States gained **(a)** Oregon, **(b)** Texas.
4. Describe two causes of the Mexican War.
5. What new lands were added to the United States as a result of the Mexican War?
6. Name three groups whose cultures influenced California and the Southwest, and describe some of their influences.

Critical Thinking and Writing

7. **Exploring the Main Idea** Review the Main Idea statement at the beginning of this section. Then, write a paragraph or two summarizing how the Mexican War helped the United States expand.
8. **Identifying Alternatives** Do you think the United States could have avoided going to war with Mexico in 1846? Explain.

ACTIVITY

Mental Mapping **Study the map showing war with Mexico on page 395. On a piece of paper, draw your own sketch map of the region. Label the major bodies of water and the routes of U.S. and Mexican forces. Show the location of U.S. victories and forts. Use colors to outline and shade each country and area.**

5 Americans Rush West

Prepare to Read

Objectives

In this section, you will

- Explain why the Mormons moved to Utah.
- Describe how the gold rush affected life in California.
- Summarize why California developed such a diverse population.

Key Terms

Mormons
Nauvoo
refuge
Sutter's Mill
forty-niner
vigilante
lynch

Target Reading Skill

Cause and Effect As you read, complete the following chart to show the effects of the gold rush on California.

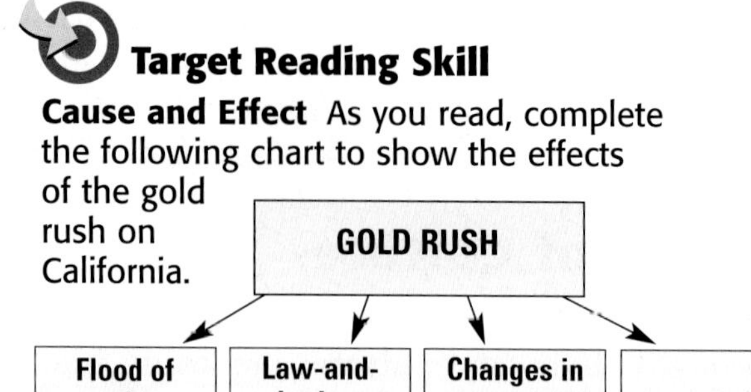

Main Idea In the late 1840s, thousands of Americans headed west, including the Mormons who went to Utah and the forty-niners who headed to California.

Entering the new land

Setting the Scene In 1848, exciting news reached the people of Toishan in southern China. Mountains of gold had been discovered across the Pacific Ocean, in a place called California. The gold was there just for the digging!

At the time, strict laws forbade Chinese citizens from leaving the country. Anyone caught leaving could be beheaded. Still, tens of thousands of Chinese risked their lives to sail across the Pacific to California. There, they joined the flood of people arriving from Europe, South America, and other parts of the United States. All were eager to find gold.

Gold was not the only attraction of the West. By 1848, California, New Mexico Territory, Oregon Country, and Texas had all been added to the United States. Pioneers set out hoping to make new lives. There, they put their hopes and dreams into building homes and working to make a living.

Mormons Settle in Utah

The largest group of settlers to move into the Mexican Cession were the Mormons. Mormons belonged to the Church of Jesus Christ of Latter-Day Saints. The church was founded by Joseph Smith in 1830. Smith, a farmer in upstate New York, attracted many followers to his faith.

Troubles With Neighbors Smith was an energetic, popular man. His teachings, however, angered many non-Mormons. For example, Mormons at first believed that property should be owned in common. Smith also said that a man could have more than one wife. Angry neighbors forced the Mormons to leave New York.

The Mormons moved west to Ohio. There, too, they faced opposition. From Ohio, they went to Missouri and then to Illinois. In the 1840s, the Mormons built a community called Nauvoo on the banks of the Mississippi River in Illinois. Once again, the Mormons and their neighbors clashed. In 1844, an angry mob killed Joseph Smith. The Mormons then chose Brigham Young as their new leader.

Young realized that the Mormons needed to find a **refuge,** a place where they would be safe from persecution. He had read about a valley between the Rocky Mountains and the Great Salt Lake in Utah. Young hoped that this isolated valley might make a good home for the Mormons.

A Difficult Journey To move 15,000 men, women, and children from Illinois to Utah was an awesome challenge. Relying on religious faith and careful planning, Brigham Young achieved his goal. In 1847, Young led an advance party into the valley of the Great Salt Lake. Later, waves of Mormon families followed. For several years, Mormon wagon trains struggled across the plains and over the Rockies to Utah. When they ran short of wagons or their oxen died, the families made the long trip pulling their gear in handcarts.

Life in the Desert In Utah, the Mormons had to learn how to survive in the desert climate. Harsh as the environment was, Young was convinced that Utah was Zion, or the promised land for the Mormons:

> “We will raise our wheat, build our houses, fence our farms, plant our vineyards and orchards, and produce everything that will make our bodies comfortable and happy and in this manner we intend to build up Zion on the earth.”
>
> —Brigham Young, “Building Up and Adornment of Zion by the Saints,” February 23, 1862

To meet these goals, Young planned an irrigation system to bring water to farms. He also drew up plans for a large city, called Salt Lake City, to be built in the desert.

The Mormon settlements in Utah grew quickly. Like other white settlers, however, Mormons took over Native American land, usually paying nothing for it.

Congress recognized Brigham Young as governor of the Utah Territory in 1850. Later, as non-Mormons began moving into the area, trouble broke out. In time, though, peace was restored, and Utah became a state in 1896.

California Gold Rush

While the Mormons were making the long trek to Utah, thousands of other Americans were racing even farther west to California. The great attraction there was gold.

Cause *and* Effect

Causes

- Oregon has fertile land
- Texas is ideal for raising cattle and growing cotton
- Many Americans believe in Manifest Destiny
- Mormons seek a safe home
- Gold is discovered in California

WESTWARD MOVEMENT

Effects

- Texas wins war for independence
- United States annexes Texas
- Britain and United States divide Oregon
- United States defeats Mexico in war
- Cotton Kingdom spreads

Effects Today

- United States stretches from sea to sea
- California and Texas are the most populous states
- Mexican American culture enriches the United States

GRAPHIC ORGANIZER *Skills*

Westward movement increased at a tremendous rate in the mid-1800s.

1. **Comprehension** List two attractions that drew Americans to the West.
2. **Critical Thinking Drawing Conclusions** According to this chart, was Manifest Destiny successful? Explain.

Target Skill **Understand Effects** Skim the subheadings in this section. Then, predict how the gold rush would affect the population in the West. Read to learn new information about population change in the West.

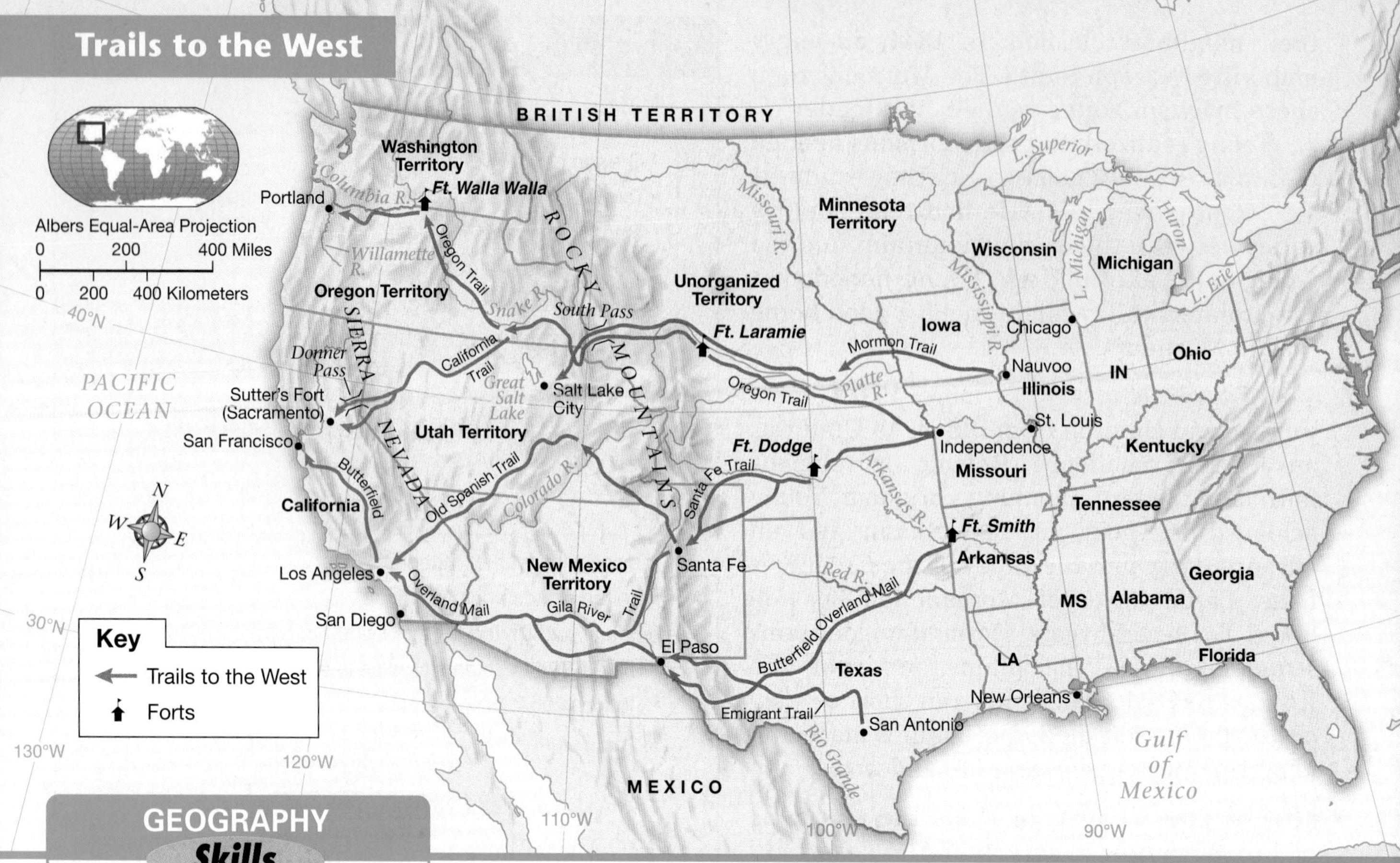

GEOGRAPHY Skills

In the 1800s, Americans followed a number of different trails to the West. Mountain passes allowed settlers to cross the Rockies and Sierra Nevada.

1. **Location** On the map, locate **(a)** Santa Fe, **(b)** Santa Fe Trail, **(c)** Sierra Nevada, **(d)** Rocky Mountains, **(e)** San Diego, **(f)** San Francisco, **(g)** Salt Lake City.
2. **Movement** Which trails ended in cities in California?
3. **Critical Thinking Applying Information** **(a)** What would be the best route for a pioneer family to take from Independence, Missouri, to Sutter's Fort, California? **(b)** What mountains would they have to cross? **(c)** In which community might they seek shelter along the way?

Sutter's Mill In 1848, John Sutter was having a sawmill built on the American River, north of Sacramento, California. Sutter had hired James Marshall to supervise the job. Early on January 24, Marshall set out to inspect a ditch his crew was digging. He later recalled the events of that day:

> ❝ It was a clear, cold morning; I shall never forget that morning. As I was taking my usual walk, . . . my eye was caught with the glimpse of something shining in the bottom of the ditch. There was about a foot of water running then. I reached my hand down and picked it up; it made my heart thump, for I was certain it was gold. ❞
>
> —James Marshall, quoted in *Hutchings' Illustrated California Magazine,* 1857–1858

At first, Sutter tried to keep the news a secret. His efforts failed. Within a few days, news reached San Francisco that gold had been found at **Sutter's Mill.** Carpenters threw down their saws. Bakers left bread in their ovens. Schools emptied as teachers and students joined the rush to the gold fields.

From San Francisco, the news spread across the United States and to the rest of the world. Thousands of Americans caught "gold fever." People from Europe, China, Australia, and South America joined in the great gold rush. More than 80,000 people made the long journey to California in 1849. They became known as **forty-niners.**

Working the Gold Fields At first, gold was easy to find near the surface of the Earth. Miners could dig it out with knives. Later on, miners found a better way to get the gold out of riverbeds. They loaded sand and gravel from the riverbed into a washing pan. Then, they held the pan under water, gently swirling it. The water washed away the gravel, leaving the heavier gold in the pan. This process was known as "panning for gold."

Very few miners actually struck it rich. Many went broke trying to make their fortunes in the gold fields. Still, although many miners left the gold fields, they stayed in California. In time, they found jobs or took up farming.

Women joined the gold rush, too. Some staked claims and mined for gold. Others took advantage of economic opportunities in the mining camps. Women ran boardinghouses, took in laundry, sewed for the miners, and opened bakeries.

A New State The gold rush brought big changes to California. Almost overnight, San Francisco grew from a sleepy town to a bustling city as newcomers poured in from all over the world. In the gold fields, towns sprang up just as quickly.

Greed led some forty-niners into crime. Murders and robberies plagued many mining camps. As the crime wave grew, miners and even some city-dwellers formed vigilance committees. **Vigilantes** (vihj uh LAN teez), or self-appointed law enforcers, dealt out punishment even though they had no legal right to do so. Sometimes, a person accused of a crime was **lynched**—hanged without a legal trial.

Californians soon realized that they needed a strong government to stop such lawlessness. In 1849, they drafted a state constitution. They then asked to be admitted to the Union. Their request caused an uproar in the United States. Many people wanted to know whether the new state would allow slavery. As you will read, after a heated debate, California was admitted to the Union in 1850 as a free state.

A Diverse Population

The gold rush changed California in many ways. It brought diverse groups of people to the West. Most of the newcomers were white Americans. However, California's mining camps included runaway slaves from the South, Native Americans, and New Englanders. There were also people from Hawaii, China, Peru, Chile, France, Germany, Italy, Ireland, and Australia.

Mexican Americans and Indians Before the gold rush, California's population included large numbers of Mexicans. Due to the efforts of people such as José Carrillo (cah REE yoh), much of their culture was preserved. Carillo came from an old California family. In part through his efforts, the state's first constitution was written in both Spanish and English. Despite such efforts, many Mexican Americans faced serious hardships. During the 1850s and 1860s, many lost land that their families had owned for generations.

Native Americans fared even worse. Many were driven off the lands where they lived. Without any means to earn a living, large

Connecting to Today

California's Water Wars

Pioneer settlers in California sometimes fought over water rights. Although tempers have cooled since then, control of water still creates conflict in California.

Today, farmers, city dwellers, and environmentalists compete for the state's limited water resources. Farmers use 80 percent of the state's water to grow crops and support the economy. Cities want more water to supply a growing population. Environmental groups want to cut water usage to preserve rivers and wetlands and the plants and animals that depend on them.

These three groups have to compete to achieve their goals. In the long run, however, they will have to work together if California is to make the best use of its limited water resources.

Describe one thing people in California can do to solve the state's water problems.

numbers died of starvation or diseases brought by the newcomers. Still others were murdered.

In 1850, about 100,000 Indians lived in California. By the 1870s, the state's Indian population had dropped to 17,000.

Chinese Americans Attracted by the tales of a "mountain of gold," thousands of Chinese sailed across the Pacific to California. At first, the Chinese were welcomed because California needed workers. When the Chinese staked claims in the gold fields, however, white miners often drove them off.

Chinese Americans and, later, other immigrants from Asia, faced prejudice in California. Despite the harsh treatment, many Chinese Americans stayed in California. They helped the state to grow. They drained swamplands and dug irrigation systems to turn dry land into fertile farmland. They also helped build the railroads that linked California with other parts of the country.

African Americans Free blacks, too, joined the gold rush in California, hoping to strike it rich. Some became well-off. In fact, by the 1850s, California had the richest African American population of any state. Yet, African Americans faced discrimination and were denied certain rights. For example, under California law, African Americans and other minorities were denied the right to testify against whites in court. After a long struggle, African Americans won this right in 1863.

In spite of these problems, California continued to grow and prosper. Settlers from other states and immigrants from all over the world kept arriving. With their diverse backgrounds, the newcomers added to California's unique culture. By 1860, the state's population was about 300,000.

★ ★ ★ Section 5 Assessment ★ ★ ★

Recall

1. **Identify** Explain the significance of **(a)** Mormons, **(b)** Joseph Smith, **(c)** Nauvoo, **(d)** Brigham Young, **(e)** Sutter's Mill.
2. **Define** **(a)** refuge, **(b)** forty-niner, **(c)** vigilante, **(d)** lynch.

Comprehension

3. Why did Brigham Young decide to lead the Mormons to Utah?
4. Describe two effects of the gold rush on California.
5. How did California's population become so diverse?

Critical Thinking and Writing

6. **Exploring the Main Idea** Review the Main Idea statement at the beginning of this section. Then, write at least two paragraphs describing how settlers in California and Utah modified their environment.
7. **Linking Past and Present** California is still a diverse land. In the 1990s, almost 30 percent of immigrants to the United States settled in California. Most came from Asia. **(a)** Why do you think California still attracts many immigrants? **(b)** Why might many Asian immigrants settle in California?

Activity

Visualizing the Gold Rush
Use the Internet to learn more about the California gold rush. Look for photos and paintings. Then, describe life in: **(a)** the gold fields, **(b)** a gold-rush city. For help in completing the activity, visit PHSchool.com, **Web Code mfd-1304.**

Connecting With... Economics

Women and the California Gold Rush

Women as well as men had the vision and willpower to make a profit in the mining towns of the California gold rush. One enterprising woman was Luzena Stanley Wilson, who in 1849 arrived at the gold mines near Sacramento with her husband and two sons. At first, the Wilsons built and ran a hotel in Sacramento, but lost it in a flood. Then, the family moved to Nevada City, where Luzena started a new business.

Miners' tools

"I determined to set up [another] hotel. So I bought two boards from a precious pile belonging to a man who was building the second wooden house in town. With my own hands I chopped stakes, drove them into the ground, and set up my table. I bought provisions at a neighboring store, and when my husband came back at night he found, mid the weird light of the pine torches, twenty miners eating at my table. Each man as he rose put a dollar in my hand and said I might count him as a permanent customer. I called my hotel 'El Dorado.'

"From the first day it was well patronized, and I shortly after took my husband into partnership."

Working a claim

ACTIVITY

Luzena Wilson wanted to run her own business. What were the advantages of running her own business? Divide a piece of paper into two columns, "Advantages" and "Disadvantages." List four items in each column.

CHAPTER 13

Review and Assessment

Chapter Summary

Section 1
In the early 1800s, fur trappers hunted the rich forests of Oregon Country. By the 1840s, missionaries and pioneers arrived to settle the region.

Section 2
The presence of a growing number of Americans in Texas led to tension with Mexico. After revolting, the settlers won a short war against Mexico. The victors established the independent republic of Texas.

Section 3
Spain built missions along the West coast of North America. Later, Mexico controlled the New Mexico Territory and California. Many Americans moved into this area, driven there by the idea of Manifest Destiny.

Section 4
A compromise with Britain gave the United States the Oregon Territory. The United States annexed Texas, and it took control of California and most of the Southwest after its victory in the Mexican War.

Section 5
In the late 1840s, the Mormons moved to Utah to escape religious persecution. Thousands of other Americans were drawn to California by the gold rush, thus turning California into a land of diverse peoples.

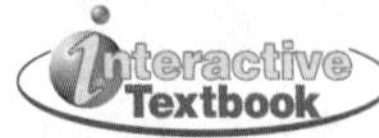

For additional review and enrichment activities, see the interactive version of *The American Nation,* available on the Web and on CD-ROM.

Chapter Self-Test For practice test questions for Chapter 13, visit PHSchool.com, **Web Code mfa-1305.**

Building Vocabulary

Review the chapter vocabulary words listed below. Then, use the words and their definitions to create a matching quiz. Exchange quizzes with another student.

1. **mountain man**
2. **rendezvous**
3. **dictator**
4. **siege**
5. **annex**
6. **cede**
7. **forty-niner**
8. **vigilante**

Reviewing Key Facts

9. Describe the life of the mountain men in Oregon Country. (Section 1)
10. How did Texans force Santa Anna to grant Texas independence? (Section 2)
11. Why was the idea of Manifest Destiny important to many Americans? (Section 3)
12. How did the Treaty of Guadalupe-Hidalgo affect the United States? (Section 4)
13. Why did California try to become a state in 1849? (Section 5)

Critical Thinking and Writing

14. **Analyzing Information** Analyze the relationship between Manifest Destiny and the westward growth of the United States.
15. **Understanding Causes and Effects** Write a paragraph explaining one result of the battle of San Jacinto.
16. **Drawing Conclusions** Explain how the Alamo was both a defeat and a victory for Texas.
17. **Connecting to Geography: Regions** Use the map at the beginning of this chapter that shows the growth of the United States to 1853. **(a)** List three of today's states that were added to the United States between 1820 and 1860. **(b)** How did westward expansion change the borders of the United States?

Skills Assessment

Analyzing Primary Sources

Read this excerpt from President Polk's speech asking for a declaration of war, and then answer the questions that follow:

> “[Mexico] has invaded our territory and shed American blood upon the American soil. She has proclaimed that hostilities have commenced, and that the two nations are now at war. As war exists, and, [despite] all our efforts to avoid it, exists by the act of Mexico herself, we are called upon by every consideration of duty and patriotism to [clear] . . . the honor, the rights, and the interests of our country.”
>
> —James K. Polk, Message to Congress, May 11, 1846

18. Whom does Polk blame for the fighting?
   A. France
   B. Spain
   C. Mexico
   D. the United States

19. According to Polk, the United States and Mexico are already at war because
   A. Congress had declared war right before his speech.
   B. of Mexico's actions.
   C. Manifest Destiny holds that peace between the two nations is impossible.
   D. negotiations to avoid war have failed.

Applying Your Skills

Determining Patterns and Distributions on Maps

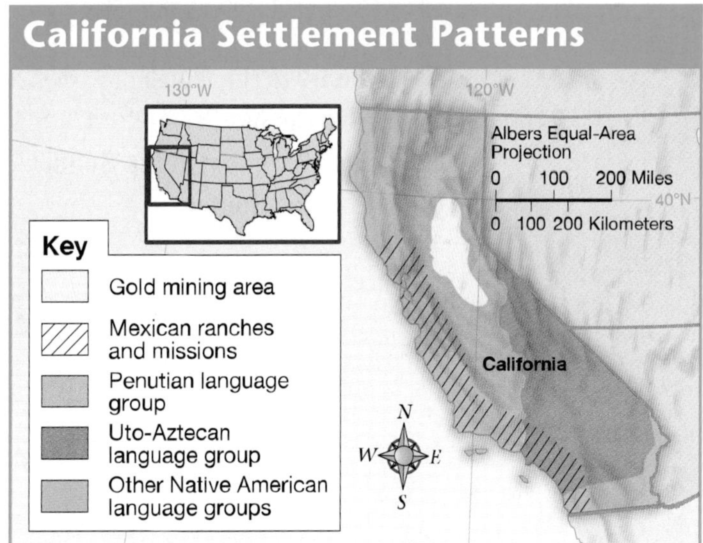

20. Which of the following regions covers the smallest land area?
   A. areas where the main language is Penutian
   B. areas where the main language is English
   C. areas where the main language is Uto-Aztecan
   D. areas where the main language is Spanish

21. **(a)** Which of the regions on the map is the most recently established? **(b)** Does this map show conditions in 1800? 1825? 1850? Explain your answer.

Activities

Connecting With . . . Geography

Describing Expansion Locate the following places on the map on the chapter-opening page: **1.** Louisiana Purchase, **2.** Gadsden Purchase, **3.** Oregon Country, **4.** Mexican Cession. After locating these places, describe at least four steps by which the United States expanded its borders from the Mississippi River to the Pacific Ocean.

Connecting to Today

Transferring Information Use the Internet to find the Census Bureau's estimate of the Hispanic population of the United States today. Then, use the Bureau's historical statistics to create a chart showing how that population has grown since the 1850 census. For help in starting this activity, visit PHSchool.com, **Web Code mfd-1306.**

Writing a Journal Entry

Examining the Texan Struggle for Independence Use the Internet to find sites that offer eyewitness accounts of the Texas war for independence. Choose one eyewitness account and identify the author's point of view. Then, write a journal entry that tells of the person's experiences. For help in starting this activity, visit PHSchool.com, **Web Code mfd-1307.**

CHAPTER 14

North and South

1820–1860

A railroad advertisement

Cotton press used to make cotton bales

AMERICAN EVENTS

1820s Skilled workers begin to organize unions.

1830 The growth of railroads changes the way goods are shipped. With railroads, goods can be shipped quickly and cheaply.

1840s The invention of the cotton gin increases the production of cotton. The cotton boom increases the spread of slavery.

Presidential Terms: James Monroe 1817–1825 | John Quincy Adams 1825–1829 | Andrew Jackson 1829–1837 | Martin Van Buren 1837–1841

1820 · 1830 · 1840

WORLD EVENTS

1829 ▲ A steam-powered locomotive in England travels 30 miles per hour.

1840 ▲ The World Anti-Slavery Convention is held in Great Britain.

Products of the North and South

By the mid-1800s, industry was growing in the North. In the South, the economy was agricultural.

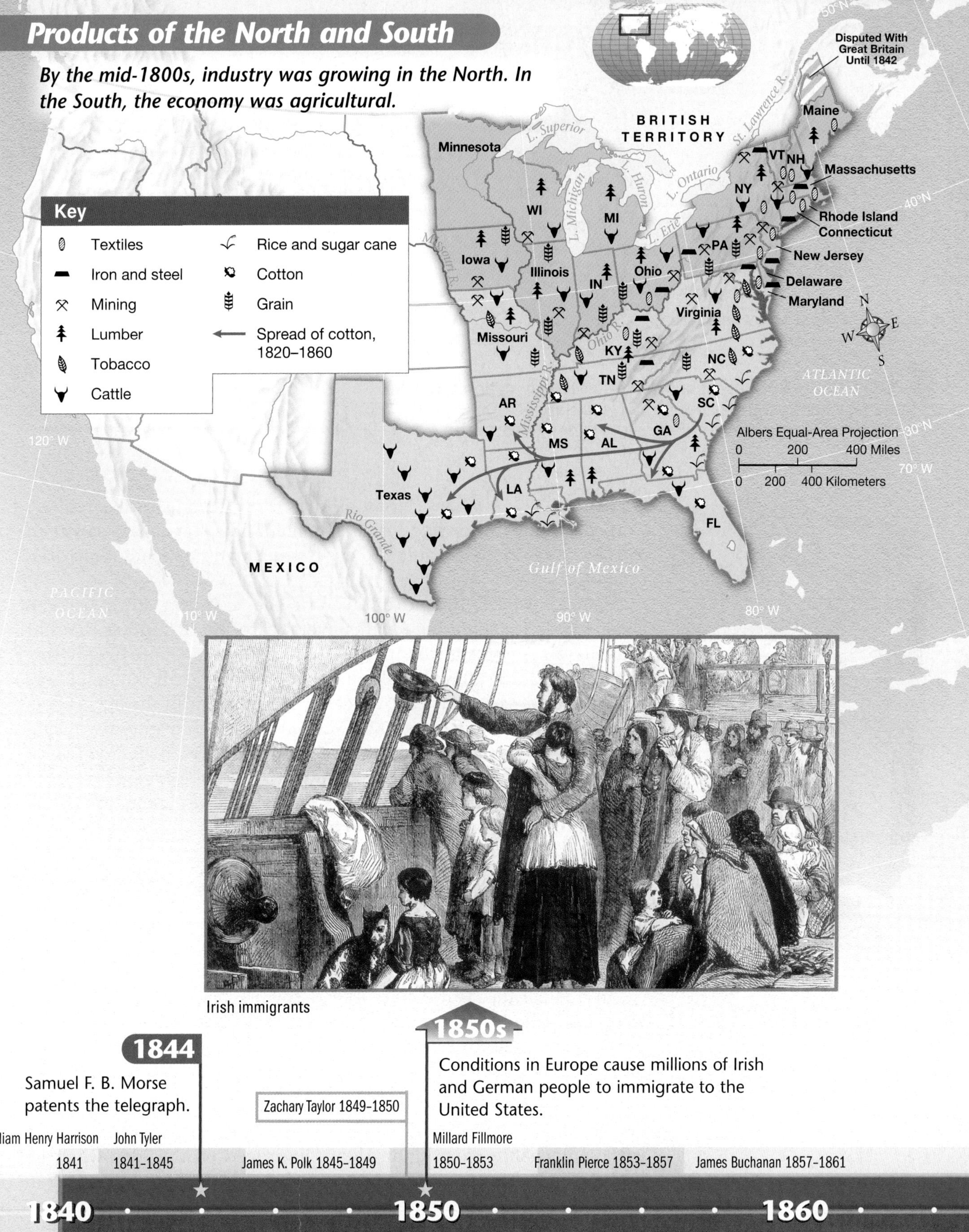

Irish immigrants

1844
Samuel F. B. Morse patents the telegraph.

1850s
Conditions in Europe cause millions of Irish and German people to immigrate to the United States.

William Henry Harrison 1841	John Tyler 1841–1845	James K. Polk 1845–1849	Zachary Taylor 1849–1850	Millard Fillmore 1850–1853	Franklin Pierce 1853–1857	James Buchanan 1857–1861

1840 · 1850 · 1860

▲ 1848
In revolutions in Germany, rebels demand national unity and social and economic reforms.

1 Industry in the North

Prepare to Read

Objectives

In this section, you will
- Summarize how new inventions changed manufacturing and farming in the North.
- Identify the difficulties faced by the first railroads.
- Explain how railroads and clipper ships helped the northern economy.

Key Terms

telegraph

locomotive

clipper ship

Target Reading Skill

Cause and Effect Copy the chart below. As you read, complete the chart to show the causes that led to a change in manufacturing in the North. Add as many boxes as you need.

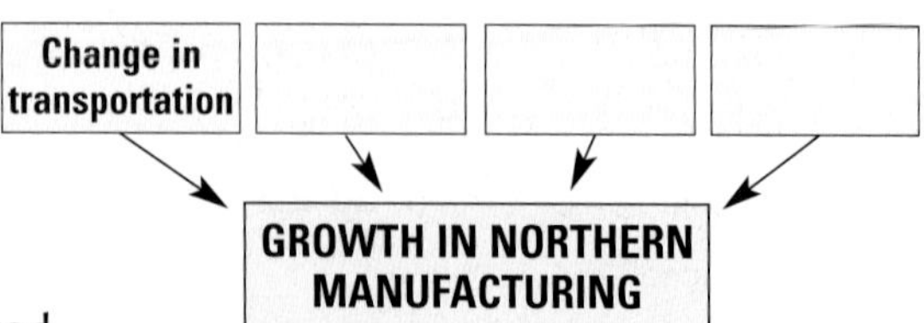

Main Idea New inventions and faster transportation changed the way goods were manufactured and shipped.

A cast-iron stove from the 1800s

Setting the Scene Susan Blunt's New Hampshire neighbors were suspicious when she brought home a new stove in the autumn of 1838. Was she really going to cook meals on it, instead of over the kitchen fire?

Soon, however, the advantages of the cast-iron stove became clear. Instead of hanging kettles over a fire, Blunt tended them at waist height, on the stove top. The oven heated food more evenly, too. In the end, Susan Blunt recalled: "In a year or two all the neighbors had one, after they saw that we came out all right in the spring."

Susan Blunt's cast-iron stove was only one sign of the way northern factories were changing the lives of ordinary people. Northern industry grew steadily in the mid-1800s. Most northerners still lived on farms. However, more and more of the northern economy began to depend on manufacturing and trade.

New Inventions

The 1800s brought a flood of new inventions in the North. "In Massachusetts and Connecticut," a European visitor exclaimed, "there is not a laborer who has not invented a machine or a tool."

In 1846, Elias Howe patented a sewing machine. A few years later, Isaac Singer improved on Howe's machine. Soon, clothing makers bought hundreds of the new sewing machines. Workers could now make dozens of shirts in the time it took a tailor to sew one by hand.

Farm Machines Some new inventions made work easier for farmers. In 1825, Jethro Wood began the manufacture of an iron plow with replaceable parts. John Deere improved on the idea when he invented a lightweight steel plow. Earlier plows made of heavy iron or wood had to be pulled by slow-moving oxen. A horse could pull a steel plow through a field more quickly.

In 1847, Cyrus McCormick opened a factory in Chicago that produced mechanical reapers. The reaper was a horse-drawn machine that mowed wheat and other grains. McCormick's reaper could do the work of five people using hand tools.

Other farm machines followed. There was a mechanical drill to plant grain, a threshing machine to beat grain from its husk and a horse-drawn hay rake. These machines helped farmers raise more grain with fewer hands. As a result, thousands of farmworkers left the countryside. Some went west to start farms of their own. Others found jobs in new factories in northern cities.

The Telegraph Samuel F. B. Morse received a patent for a "talking wire," or **telegraph** in 1844. The telegraph was a device that sent electrical signals along a wire. The signals were based on a code of dots, dashes, and spaces. Later, this system of dots and dashes became known as the Morse code.

Congress gave Morse funds to run wire from Washington, D.C., to Baltimore. On May 24, 1844, Morse set up his telegraph in the Supreme Court chamber in Washington. As a crowd of onlookers watched, Morse tapped out a short message: "What hath God wrought!" A few seconds later, the operator in Baltimore tapped back the same message. The telegraph worked!

Morse's invention was an instant success. Telegraph companies sprang up everywhere. Thousands of miles of wire soon stretched across the country. As a result of the telegraph, news could now travel long distances in a matter of minutes.

The telegraph helped many businesses to thrive. Merchants and farmers could have quick access to information about supply, demand, and prices of goods in different areas of the country. For example, western farmers might learn of a wheat shortage in New York and ship their grain east to meet the demand.

Viewing History

Elias Howe and the Sewing Machine

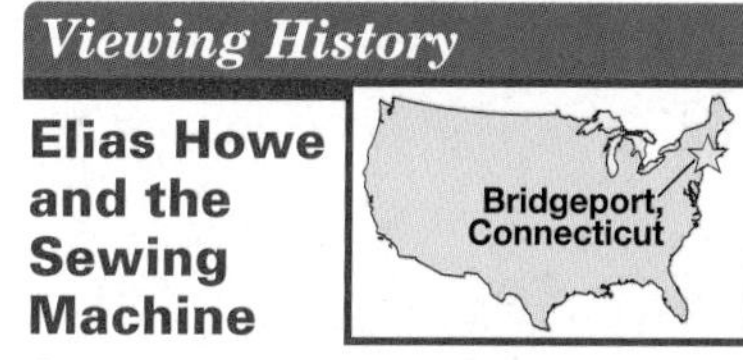

Once clothing manufacturers started using Elias Howe's invention, the time it took to make a shirt was reduced from 14 hours to little more than one hour. **Drawing Conclusions** ***Why would tailors be unhappy with Howe's invention?***

The First Railroads

At first, railroads were used to provide transportation to canals. In time, however, the railroad became a more practical means of transportation. The first railroads were built in the early 1800s. Horses or mules pulled cars along wooden rails covered with strips of iron. Then, in 1829, an English family developed a steam-powered **locomotive** engine to pull rail cars. The engine, called the Rocket, barreled along at 30 miles per hour.

Early Difficulties Not all Americans welcomed the new railroads. Workers who moved freight on horse-drawn wagons feared that they would lose their jobs. People who invested in canals worried that competition from the railroads might cause them to lose their investments.

There were problems with the early railroads. They were not always safe or reliable. Soft roadbeds and weak bridges often led to accidents. Locomotives often broke down. Even when they worked, their smokestacks belched thick black smoke and hot embers. The embers sometimes burned holes in passengers' clothing or set nearby buildings on fire.

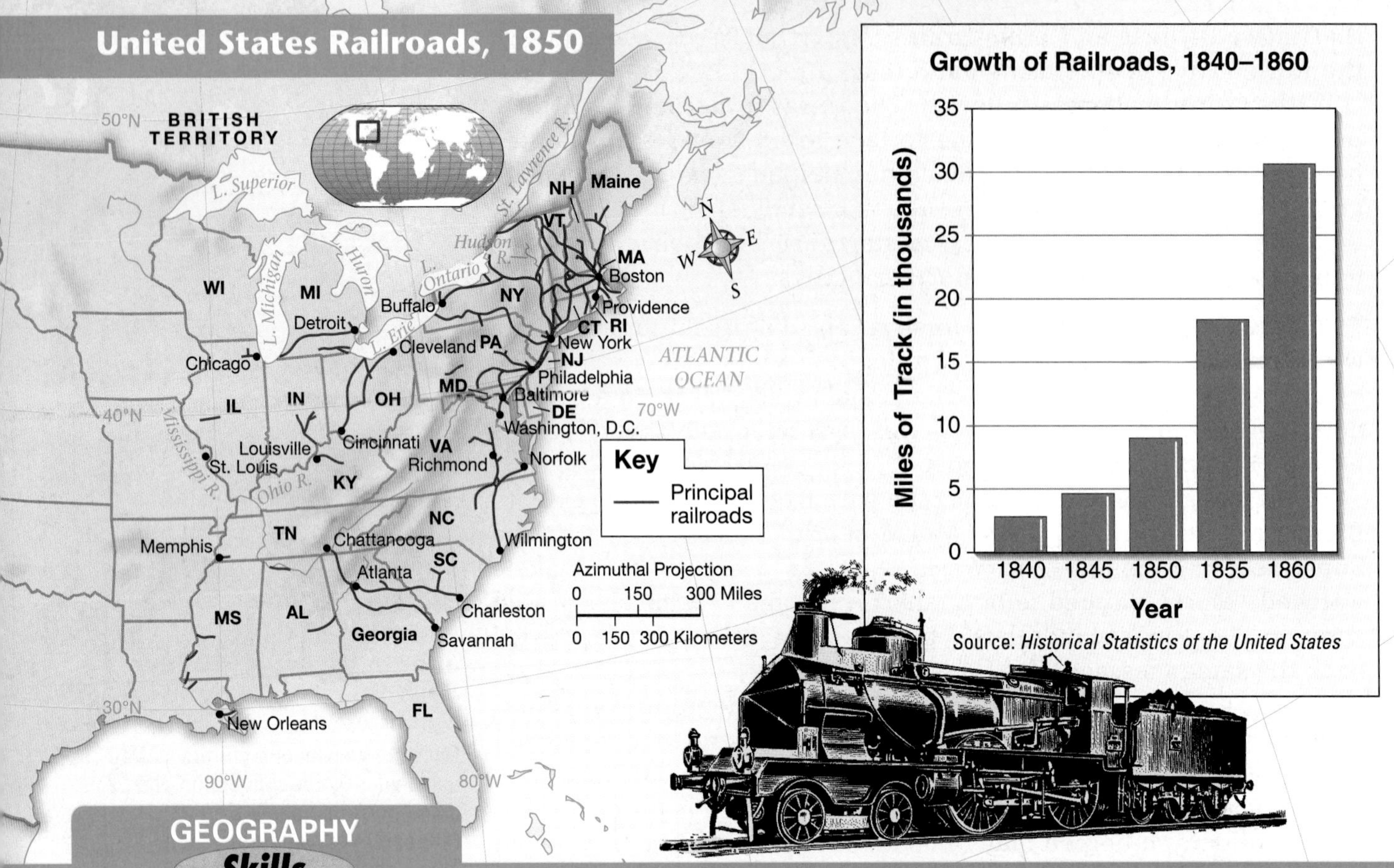

GEOGRAPHY *Skills*

There were about 23 miles of railroad tracks in 1830. From 1840 to 1860, railroad construction increased greatly. Goods could be transported more quickly by rail than by canals, and railroads were in service all year-round.

1. **Location** On the map, locate **(a)** New York, **(b)** Lake Erie, **(c)** Chicago, **(d)** Mississippi River, **(e)** Wisconsin.
2. **Movement** How many principal railroads ran through Atlanta?
3. **Critical Thinking Applying Information** What area of the country had the most railroad mileage? Explain.

Part of the problem was the way in which railroads were built. Often, instead of two tracks being laid—one for each direction—only one was set. This increased the likelihood of a collision.

A Railroad Boom Gradually, railroad builders overcame problems and removed obstacles. Engineers learned to build sturdier bridges and solid roadbeds. They replaced wooden rails with iron rails. Such improvements made railroad travel safer and faster.

By the 1850s, railroads crisscrossed the nation. The major lines were concentrated in the North and West. New York, Chicago, and Cincinnati became major rail centers. The South had much less track than the North.

Yankee Clippers

Railroads increased commerce within the United States. At the same time, trade also increased between the United States and other nations. At seaports in the Northeast, captains loaded their ships with cotton, fur, wheat, lumber, and tobacco. Then, they sailed to other parts of the world.

Speed was the key to successful trade at sea. In 1845, an American named John Griffiths launched the *Rainbow,* the first of the **clipper ships.** These sleek vessels had tall masts and huge sails that caught every gust of wind. Their narrow hulls clipped swiftly through the water.

In the 1840s, American clipper ships broke every speed record. One clipper sped from New York to Hong Kong in 81 days, flying past older ships that took five months to reach China. The speed of the clippers helped the United States win a large share of the world's sea trade in the 1840s and 1850s.

The golden age of the clipper ship was brief. In the 1850s, Britain launched the first oceangoing iron steamships. These sturdy vessels carried more cargo and traveled even faster than clippers.

The Northern Economy Expands

By the 1830s, factories began to use steam power instead of water power. Machines that were driven by steam were powerful and cheap to run. Also, factories that used steam power could be built almost anywhere, not just along the banks of swift-flowing rivers. As a result, American industry expanded rapidly.

Recognize Multiple Causes

Which factors causing the expansion of the northern economy are discussed in this subsection? Add this information to your chart.

At the same time, new machines made it possible to produce more goods at a lower cost. These more affordable goods attracted eager buyers. Families no longer had to make clothing and other goods in their homes. Instead, they could buy factory-made products.

Railroads allowed factory owners to transport large amounts of raw materials and finished goods cheaply and quickly. Also, as railroads stretched across the nation, they linked distant towns with cities and factories. These towns became new markets for factory goods.

The growth of railroads also affected northern farming. Railroads brought cheap grain and other foods from the West to New England. New England farmers could not compete with this new source of cheap foods. Many left their farms to find new jobs as factory workers, store clerks, and sailors.

★ ★ ★ Section 1 Assessment ★ ★ ★

Recall

1. **Identify** Explain the significance of **(a)** Elias Howe, **(b)** John Deere, **(c)** Cyrus McCormick, **(d)** Samuel F. B. Morse, **(e)** John Griffiths.
2. **Define** **(a)** telegraph, **(b)** locomotive, **(c)** clipper ship.

Comprehension

3. What new inventions made work easier for farmers?
4. Why was safety a major concern with the first railroads?
5. How did steam power and railroads change the northern economy?

Critical Thinking and Writing

6. **Exploring the Main Idea** Review the Main Idea statement at the beginning of this section. Then, write a paragraph about how the new inventions affected the rapid growth of factories in the North.
7. **Understanding Cause and Effect** How do you think life might have changed in a small Ohio town after a railroad linked it to New York City in 1840?

Activity

Creating an Advertisement **It is the mid-1800s. Create an advertisement poster urging people to buy or use one of the inventions of the period. Use both words and pictures to make your advertisement persuasive.**

The Telegraph

Like the Internet today, the telegraph had a revolutionary effect on communication. Before the telegraph, messages were hand carried. With the telegraph, people could communicate across great distances almost instantly.

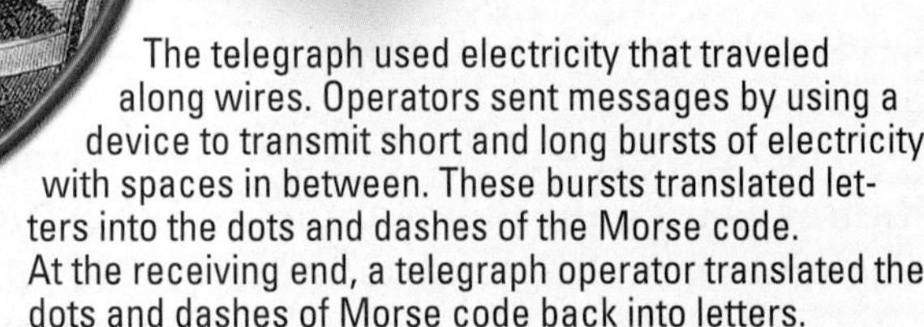

The telegraph used electricity that traveled along wires. Operators sent messages by using a device to transmit short and long bursts of electricity with spaces in between. These bursts translated letters into the dots and dashes of the Morse code. At the receiving end, a telegraph operator translated the dots and dashes of Morse code back into letters.

In 1861, transcontinental telegraph lines were erected along the route of the Pony Express. The Pony Express had operated between St. Joseph, Missouri, and Sacramento, California. Riding relays of fast horses, Pony Express riders could deliver a letter from point to point in ten days or less. Once the telegraph lines were completed, the Pony Express was no longer needed.

ACTIVITY

Working with a partner, create your own Morse code. Then, use it to write a brief message from one to the other.

2 Life in the North

Prepare to Read

Objectives

In this section, you will
- Describe factory conditions in the 1840s.
- Identify what factory workers hoped to accomplish by joining together.
- Describe the new immigrants.
- Explain how free African Americans were treated in the North.

Key Terms

artisan

trade union

strike

famine

nativist

Know-Nothing party

discrimination

Target Reading Skill

Main Idea As you read, prepare an outline of this section. Use roman numerals to indicate the major headings of this section, capital letters for the subheadings, and numbers for the supporting details.

I. Factory Conditions Become Worse
   A. A change in values
      1. Factory workers feel differently about their jobs
      2.
   B. Families in factories
      1.
      2.
   C. Hazards at work
      1.
      2.

Main Idea Industry in the North changed with the arrival of new immigrants and the efforts of factory workers to improve their working conditions.

Setting the Scene Alzina Parsons never forgot her thirteenth birthday. The day began as usual, with work in the local spinning mill. Suddenly, Alzina cried out. She had caught her hand in the spinning machine, badly mangling her fingers. The foreman summoned the factory doctor. He cut off one of the injured fingers and sent the girl back to work.

Twenty years earlier, such an incident probably would not have occurred. Factory work was hard, but mill owners treated workers like human beings. By the 1840s, however, there was an oversupply of workers. Many factory owners now treated workers like machines.

Factory workers

Factory Conditions Become Worse

Factories of the 1840s and 1850s were very different from the mills of the early 1800s. The factories were larger, and they used steam-powered machines. Laborers worked longer hours for lower wages. Usually, workers lived in dark, dingy houses in the shadow of the factory.

A Change in Values The emphasis on mass production changed the way workers felt about their jobs. Before the growth of factories, skilled workers, or **artisans,** were proud of the goods they made. The factory owner, however, was more interested in how much could be produced than in how well it was made. Workers could not be creative. Furthermore, unlike the artisan who could have his own business, the factory worker was not likely to rise to a management position.

Families in Factories As the need for workers increased, entire families labored in factories. In some cases, a family agreed to work for one year. If even one family member broke the contract, the entire family might be fired.

The factory day began when a whistle sounded at 4 A.M. The entire family—father, mother, and children—headed off to work. Many factories, at that time, employed young children. The workday did not end until 7:30 P.M., when a final whistle sent the workers home.

Hazards at Work Factory workers faced discomfort and danger. Few factories had windows or heating systems. In summer, the heat and humidity inside the factory were stifling. In winter, the extreme cold contributed to frequent sickness.

Factory machines had no safety devices, and accidents were common. There were no laws regulating factory conditions, and injured workers often lost their jobs.

Workers Join Together

Poor working conditions and low wages led workers to organize. The first workers to organize were artisans.

Trade Unions and Strikes In the 1820s and 1830s, artisans in each trade united to form **trade unions.** The unions called for a shorter workday, higher wages, and better working conditions. Sometimes, unions went on strike to gain their demands. In a **strike,** union workers refuse to do their jobs.

At the time, strikes were illegal in many parts of the United States. Strikers faced fines or jail sentences. Employers often fired strike leaders.

Progress for Artisans Slowly, however, workers made progress. In 1840, President Van Buren approved a ten-hour workday for government employees. Workers celebrated another victory in 1842 when a Massachusetts court declared that they had the right to strike.

Artisans won better pay because factory owners needed their skills. Unskilled workers, however, were unable to bargain for better wages since their jobs required little or no training. Because these workers were easy to replace, employers did not listen to their demands.

Women Workers Organize The success of trade unions encouraged other workers to organize. Workers in New England textile mills were especially eager to protest cuts in wages and unfair work rules. Many of these workers were women.

Women workers faced special problems. First, they had always earned less money than men did. Second, most union leaders did not want women in their ranks. Like many people at the time, they believed that women should not work outside the home. In fact, the goal of many unions was to raise men's wages so that their wives could leave their factory jobs.

Despite these problems, women workers organized. They staged several strikes at Lowell, Massachusetts, in the 1830s. In the 1840s, Sarah Bagley organized the Lowell Female Labor Reform Association. The group petitioned the state legislature for a ten-hour workday.

An American Profile

Sarah Bagley 1806–1870?

Sarah Bagley had left her New Hampshire home to work in the textile mills of Lowell, Massachusetts. Over the years, her health—like that of other workers—suffered. She decided to do something about it.

In 1844, Bagley began to organize women workers. About 500 formed a group called the Lowell Female Labor Reform Association—the first American organization of working women. As the group's president, she testified to the Massachusetts legislature about working in the mills. She spoke out against the long workdays and short meal breaks. Bagley also traveled to other factory towns and urged women workers there to organize. She wrote articles promoting workers' rights.

By 1846, the state legislature had still refused to act. Bagley left the mills and entered a new industry, becoming the first woman telegraph operator.

In what way was Bagley a pioneer?

A New Wave of Immigrants

By the late 1840s, many factory workers in the North were immigrants. An immigrant is a person who enters a new country in order to settle there. In the 1840s and 1850s, about 4 million immigrants arrived in the United States. Among them were immigrants from Great Britain who came to the United States to earn higher wages. There was a greater demand for skilled machinists, carpenters, and miners.

From Ireland and Germany In the 1840s, a disease destroyed the potato crop in Ireland, which was the main food of the poor people. Other crops, such as wheat and oats, were not affected. At the time, Ireland was under British rule and most Irish crops were exported to Great Britain. When a large part of the potato crop was lost to disease, British landowners continued to ship the wheat and oats to England. There was little left for the Irish to eat. This situation caused a **famine**, or severe food shortage. Thousands of people died of starvation. Nearly as many died from disease. Between 1845 and 1860, over 1.5 million Irish fled to the United States.

Meanwhile, many Germans were also arriving in the United States. Harsh weather conditions from 1829 to 1830 resulted in severe food shortages. By 1832, more than 10,000 Germans were coming to the United States in a single year. In 1848, revolutions had broken out in several parts of Germany. The rebels fought for democratic reforms. When the revolts failed, thousands had to flee. Many other German immigrants came simply to make a better life for themselves. Between 1848 and 1860, nearly one million Germans arrived in the United States.

Enriching the Nation Immigrants supplied much of the labor that helped the nation's economy grow. Although most of the Irish immigrants had been farmers, few had money to buy farmland. Many settled in the northern cities where low-paying factory jobs were available. Other Irish workers helped build many new canals and railroads. Irish women often worked as servants in private homes.

Immigrants from Germany often had enough money to move west and buy good farmland. Others were artisans and merchants. Towns of the Midwest such as St. Louis, Milwaukee, and Cincinnati had German grocers, butchers, and bakers.

A small minority of the immigrants from Germany were Jewish. German Jews began immigrating to the United States in the 1820s. By the early 1860s, there were about 150 communities in the United States with large Jewish populations.

Sources of Immigration, 1820–1860

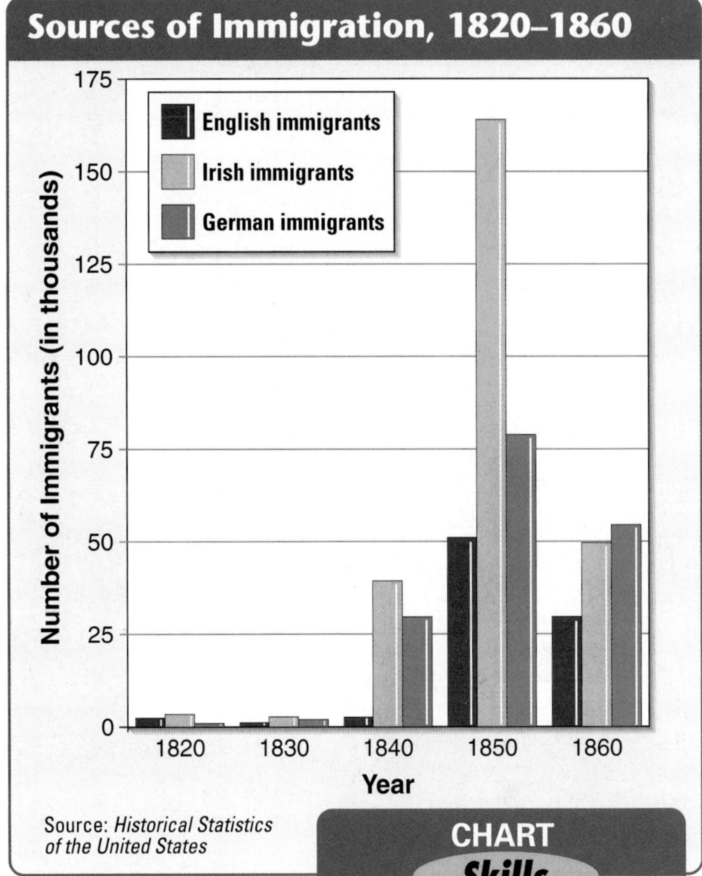

Source: *Historical Statistics of the United States*

CHART *Skills*

Throughout the 1800s, immigrants from Great Britain, Ireland, and Germany came to the United States. From 1840 to 1850, the numbers increased as more immigrants wanted to escape the political and economic difficulties in Europe.

1. **Comprehension**
   (a) About how many more Irish immigrants arrived in 1850 than did in 1860?
   (b) In 1860, how many more German immigrants than Irish immigrants arrived?
2. **Critical Thinking Synthesizing Information** Why do you think fewer immigrants came from Great Britain than from Ireland and Germany during the 1800s?

Civics 

American Heritage MAGAZINE HISTORY **HAPPENED HERE**

Portsmouth Black Heritage Trail

The first known African to arrive in Portsmouth, New Hampshire, landed in 1645 at a wharf (shown here) near what is now Prescott Park. For the next 350 years, African Americans, both enslaved and tree, would be part of this seacoast town. Visitors can tour the communities where Portsmouth's African American population lived, worked, and served their town and state.

Virtual Field Trip For an interactive look at the Black Heritage Trail, visit PHSchool.com, **Web Code mfd-1401.**

Identify Supporting Details

Which details in the paragraphs on this page reveal how some Americans felt about new immigrants? Add these details to your outline.

A Reaction Against Immigrants Not everyone welcomed the flood of immigrants. One group of Americans, called **nativists,** wanted to preserve the country for native-born, white citizens. Using the slogan "Americans must rule America," they called for laws to limit immigration. They also wanted to keep immigrants from voting until they had lived in the United States for 21 years. At the time, newcomers could vote after only 5 years in the country.

Some nativists protested that newcomers "stole" jobs from native-born Americans because they worked for lower pay. Furthermore, when workers went out on strike, factory owners often hired immigrant workers to replace them. Many distrusted the different language, customs, and dress of the immigrants. Others blamed immigrants for the rise in crime in the growing cities. Still others mistrusted Irish newcomers because many of them were Catholics. Until the 1840s, the majority of immigrants from Europe had been Protestants.

By the 1850s, hostility to immigrants was so strong that nativists formed a new political party. Members of the party were anti-Catholic and anti-immigrant. Many meetings and rituals of the party were kept secret. It was called the **Know-Nothing party** because members answered, "I know nothing," when asked about the party. The message of the party did gain supporters. In 1856, the Know-Nothing candidate for President won 21 percent of the popular vote. Soon after, however, the party died out. Still, many Americans continued to blame the nation's problems on immigrants.

African Americans in the North

During the nation's early years, slavery was legal in the North. By the early 1800s, however, all the northern states had outlawed slavery. As a result, thousands of free African Americans lived in the North.

Denied Equal Rights Free African Americans in the North faced discrimination. **Discrimination** is a policy or an attitude that denies equal rights to certain groups of people. As one writer pointed out, African Americans were denied "the ballot-box, the jury box, the halls of the legislature, the army, the public lands, the school, and the church."

Even skilled African Americans had trouble finding good jobs. One black carpenter was turned away by every furniture maker in Cincinnati. At last, a shop owner hired him. However, when he entered the shop, the other carpenters dropped their tools. Either he must leave or they would, they declared. Similar experiences occurred throughout the North. In addition, African Americans faced competition from immigrants who settled in northern cities.

Some Success Despite such obstacles, some African Americans achieved notable success in business. William Whipper grew wealthy as the owner of a lumberyard in Pennsylvania. He devoted much of his time and money to help bring an end to slavery. Henry Boyd operated a profitable furniture company in Cincinnati.

African Americans made strides in other areas as well. Henry Blair invented a corn planter and a cottonseed planter. In 1845, Macon Allen became the first African American licensed to practice law in the United States. After graduating from Bowdoin College in Maine, John Russwurm became one of the editors of *Freedom's Journal,* the first African American newspaper.

★ ★ ★ Section 2 Assessment ★ ★ ★

Recall

1. **Identify** Explain the significance of **(a)** Sarah Bagley, **(b)** Know-Nothing party, **(c)** William Whipper, **(d)** Henry Boyd, **(e)** Macon Allen, **(f)** John Russwurm.
2. **Define** **(a)** artisan, **(b)** trade union, **(c)** strike, **(d)** famine, **(e)** nativist, **(f)** discrimination.

Comprehension

3. Describe factory conditions in the 1840s.
4. How did factory workers improve working conditions?
5. Why did German and Irish immigrants come to the United States in the mid-1800s?
6. **(a)** How did discrimination affect free African Americans in the North? **(b)** What successes did they have?

Critical Thinking

7. **Exploring the Main Idea** Review the Main Idea statement at the beginning of this section. Then, prepare a cause-and-effect chart about the effects of immigration on the United States from 1820 to 1860. The first entry in the "Causes" box can be "Famine in Ireland."
8. **Making Inferences** How would a nativist define a "real" American?

ACTIVITY

Delivering a Speech
You are a worker in a northern factory. Prepare a speech urging other workers to strike. Deliver your finished speech to the class.

3 Cotton Kingdom in the South

Prepare to Read

Objectives

In this section, you will
- Identify how the cotton gin improved cotton production in the South.
- Explain how the South became an agricultural economy.
- Describe the ways in which the South was dependent on the North.

Key Terms

boom

cultivate

Target Reading Skill

Clarifying Meaning Copy the concept web below. As you read, fill in the blank ovals with important facts about the southern economy in the 1800s. Add as many ovals as you need.

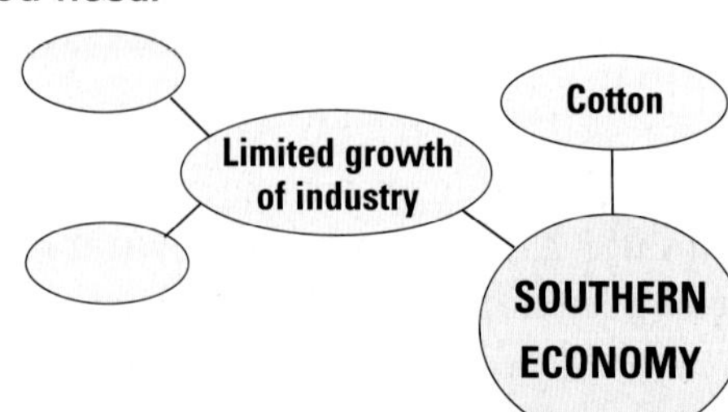

Main Idea Cotton was the leading crop in the agricultural economy of the South.

A cotton plant

Setting the Scene An Englishman, Basil Hall, traveled through much of the South aboard a riverboat in 1827. He complained that the southerners he met were interested in only one thing—cotton:

> "All day and almost all night long, the captain, pilot, crew and passengers were talking of nothing else; and sometimes our ears were so wearied with the sound of cotton! cotton! cotton! that we gladly hailed fresh . . . company in hopes of some change—but alas! . . . 'What's cotton at?' was the first eager inquiry."
>
> —Basil Hall, *Travels in North America in the Years 1827 and 1828*

Cotton became even more important to the South in the years after Hall's visit. It was so profitable, southerners did not even feel a need to invest in factories. Even though southerners grew other crops, cotton remained the region's leading export. Cotton plantations—and the slave system on which they depended—shaped the way of life in the South.

Cotton Gin, Cotton Boom

The Industrial Revolution greatly increased the demand for southern cotton. Textile mills in the North and in Britain needed more and more cotton to make cloth. At first, southern planters could not meet the demand. They could grow plenty of cotton because the South's soil and climate were ideal. However, removing the seeds from the cotton by hand was a slow process. Planters needed a better way to clean cotton.

Eli Whitney's Invention Eli Whitney, a young Connecticut schoolteacher, was traveling to Georgia in 1793. He was going to be a tutor on a plantation. At that time, there were few public schools in the South. When Whitney learned of the planters' problem, he decided to build a machine to clean cotton.

In only 10 days, Whitney came up with a model. His cotton engine, or gin, had two rollers with thin wire teeth. When cotton was swept between the rollers, the teeth separated the seeds from the fibers.

The simple cotton gin had an enormous effect on the southern economy. A single worker using a gin could do the work of 50 people cleaning cotton by hand. Because of the gin, planters could now grow cotton at a huge profit.

Cotton Kingdom and Slavery The cotton gin led to a boom, or swift growth, in cotton production. In 1792, planters grew only 6,000 bales of cotton a year. By 1850, the figure was over 2 million bales.

Planters soon learned that soil wore out if planted with cotton year after year. They needed new land to cultivate, or prepare for planting. After the War of 1812, cotton planters began to move west.

By the 1850s, there were cotton plantations extending in a wide band from South Carolina through Alabama and Mississippi to Texas. This area of the South became known as the Cotton Kingdom.

Tragically, as the Cotton Kingdom spread, so did slavery. Even though cotton could now be cleaned by machine, it still had to be planted and picked by hand. The result was a cruel cycle in which the work of slaves brought profits to planters, who then used the profits to buy more land and more slaves.

An Agricultural Economy

Cotton was the South's most profitable cash crop. However, the best conditions for growing cotton could be found mostly in the southernmost portion of the region. In other areas of the South, rice, sugar cane, and tobacco were major crops. In addition, southerners raised much of the nation's livestock.

Rice was an important crop along the coasts of South Carolina and Georgia. Sugar cane was important in Louisiana and Texas. Growing rice and sugar cane required expensive irrigation and drainage systems. Cane growers also needed costly machinery to grind their harvest. Small-scale farmers could not afford such expensive equipment, however. As a result, the plantation system dominated sugar and rice production just as it did cotton production.

Tobacco had been an export of the South since 1619, and it continued to be planted in Virginia, North Carolina, and Kentucky. However, in the early 1800s, the large tobacco plantations of colonial days had given way to small tobacco farms. On these farms, a few field hands tended five or six acres of tobacco.

In addition to the major cash crops of cotton, rice, sugar, and tobacco, the South also led the nation in livestock production. Southern livestock owners profited from hogs, oxen, horses, mules, and beef cattle. Much of this livestock was raised in areas that were unsuitable for growing crops, such as the pine woods of North Carolina. Kentucky developed a rural economy that included the breeding of horses.

Primary Source

The Cotton Gin

Thomas Jefferson was secretary of state and inspector of patents in 1793. He received a request for a patent from a schoolteacher named Eli Whitney. Interested in learning more about it, Jefferson asked Whitney the following questions:

"Has the machine been thoroughly tried in the ginning of cotton, or is it as yet but a machine in theory? What quantity of cotton has it cleaned on an average of several days, worked by hand, and by how many hands? . . . Favorable answers to these questions would induce me to engage one of them to be forwarded to Richmond for me."

—Thomas Jefferson, from "That With This Ginn," 1793

Analyzing Primary Sources

Why do you think Jefferson was interested in the cotton gin?

Cotton Production and Slavery

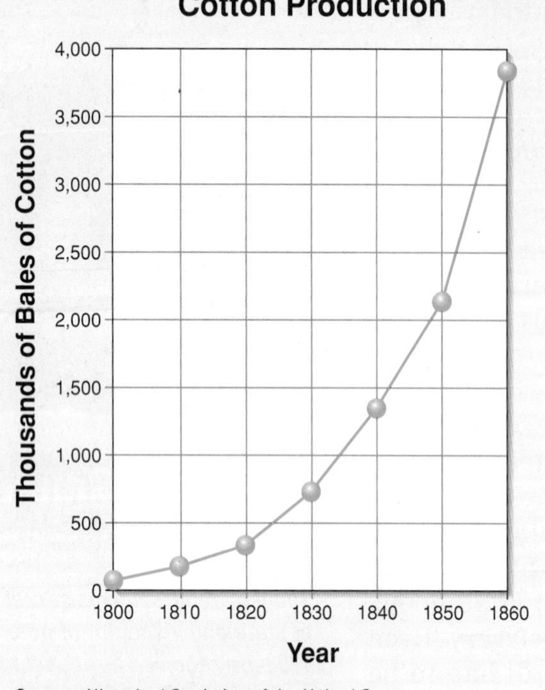

Source: *Historical Statistics of the United States*

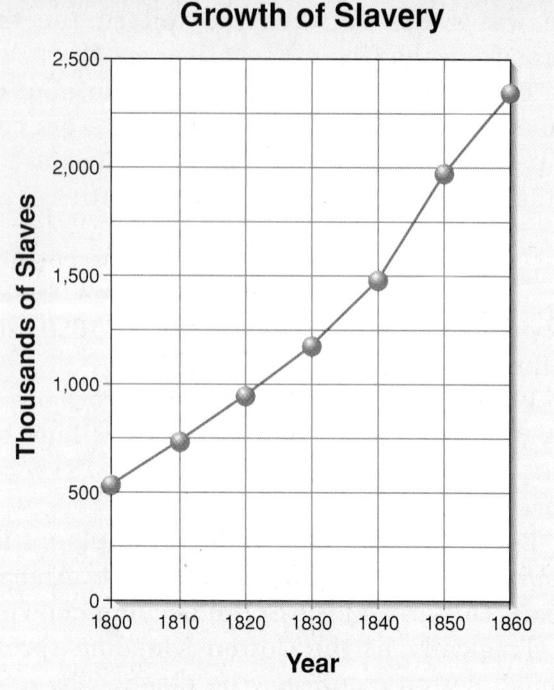

Source: *Historical Statistics of the United States*

GRAPH Skills

As cotton production increased in the South, so did the number of enslaved African Americans.

1. **Comprehension** **(a)** How many more bales of cotton were produced in 1850 than in 1820? **(b)** In which decade did the number of slaves increase the most?
2. **Critical Thinking Making Predictions** In what way do you think ending slavery would affect the southern economy?

Limited Industry Most of the industry in the South remained small and existed only to meet the needs of a farming society. Agricultural tools such as cotton gins, planters, and plows were manufactured. Factories also made goods such as ironware, hoes, and materials made of hemp, which were used to make bags for holding bales of cotton. Cheap cotton cloth was made for use in slaves' clothing. Some southerners wanted to encourage the growth of industry in the South. William Gregg, for example, modeled his cotton mill in South Carolina on the mills in Lowell, Massachusetts. Gregg built houses and gardens for his workers and schools for their children.

The South also developed a few other successful industries. In Richmond, Virginia, for example, the Tredegar Iron Works turned out railroad equipment, machinery, tools, and cannons. Flour milling was another important southern industry.

Even so, the South lagged behind the North in manufacturing. Rich planters preferred to invest their money in land and slaves rather than in factories.

Slavery also reduced the need for southern industry. In the North, most people had enough money to buy factory goods. In the South, however, millions of slaves could not buy anything. As a result, the demand for manufactured goods in the South was not as great as it was in the North.

Southern Cities Although the South was mainly rural, there were some cities. The major ones were New Orleans, Louisiana; Charleston, South Carolina; and Richmond, Virginia. These cities had the same problems as northern cities, including poor housing and poor sanitation.

Fewer than 8 percent of white southerners lived in towns of more than 4,000 people. However, many free African Americans lived in towns and cities.

Economically Dependent

With little industry of its own, the South came to depend more and more on the North and on Europe. Southern planters often borrowed money from northern banks in order to expand their plantations. They also purchased much of their furniture, farm tools, and machines from northern or European factories.

Reread
Reread this quote to make sure you understand how the writer's description shows the South's dependence on the North. Add this information to your concept web.

Many southerners resented this situation. One southerner described a burial to show how the South depended on the North for many goods in the 1850s:

> "The grave was dug through solid marble, but the marble headstone came from Vermont. It was in a pine wilderness but the pine coffin came from Cincinnati. An iron mountain overshadowed it but the coffin nails and the screws and the shovel came from Pittsburgh. . . . A hickory grove grew nearby, but the pick and shovel handles came from New York. . . . That country, so rich in underdeveloped resources, furnished nothing for the funeral except the corpse and the hole in the ground."
>
> —Henry Grady, Speech to the Bay Street Club, Boston, 1889

Still, most southerners were proud of the booming cotton industry in their region. As long as cotton remained king, southerners believed, they could look to the future with confidence.

★ ★ ★ Section 3 Assessment ★ ★ ★

Recall

1. **Identify** Explain the significance of **(a)** Eli Whitney, **(b)** Cotton Kingdom, **(c)** William Gregg.
2. **Define** **(a)** boom, **(b)** cultivate.

Comprehension

3. How did the cotton gin lead to the spread of slavery?
4. Explain the importance of cotton as a cash crop in the southern economy.
5. Why was there limited growth of industry in the South?

Critical Thinking and Writing

6. **Exploring the Main Idea** Review the Main Idea statement at the beginning of this section. Then, list the positive and negative effects of cotton production on life in the South.
7. **Drawing Conclusions** Although most southerners owned no slaves, many defended slavery. Why do you think this was so?

ACTIVITY

Connecting to Today
Today, cotton is still widely used in fabrics. Use the Internet to find out more about cotton. Write a brief report with interesting cotton facts. For help in completing the activity, visit PHSchool.com, **Web Code mfd-1402**.

4 Life in the South

Prepare to Read

Objectives

In this section, you will
- Name the groups of white southerners that made up southern society.
- Describe how free African Americans and enslaved African Americans were treated.
- Explain how African Americans resisted slavery.

Key Terms

"cottonocracy"

slave codes

extended family

Target Reading Skill

Comparison and Contrast Copy this table. As you read, complete the table with information about the white southerners and the African American southerners. The first entry is done for you.

WHITE SOUTHERNERS	AFRICAN AMERICAN SOUTHERNERS
• Rich southern planter • Owned slaves •	• •

Main Idea Most white southerners were not plantation owners; however, the plantation system and slavery were at the center of southern life.

Katie Darling

Setting the Scene In 1937, at the age of 88, Katie Darling recalled her life growing up as an enslaved person in East Texas:

> "Miss Stella, my young mistress, got all our ages down in a Bible, that is how I knows I was born in 1849. . . . Mammy died in slavery, and Pappy run away. . . . By the time I was big enough to tote a cow pail they put me to milking. Master had over a hundred head of cows and most of the time me and Violet, another house girl, did all the milking. We was up before five. By five we better be in that cow pen. We better milk all of them cows too or they'd bull-whip us."
>
> —Katie Darling, Interview, August 2, 1937

With her brothers and sisters, Darling worked from dawn to dusk and often on Sundays. She was only one of millions of African Americans throughout the South who suffered the anguish of slavery.

White Southerners

The Old South is often pictured as a land of vast plantations worked by hundreds of slaves. Such grand estates did exist in the South. However, most white southerners were not rich planters. In fact, most whites owned no slaves at all.

The "Cottonocracy" A planter was someone who owned at least 20 slaves. In 1860, only one white southerner in 30 belonged to a planter family. An even smaller number—less than 1 percent—owned 50 or more slaves. These wealthy families were called the **"cottonocracy"** because they made huge amounts of money from cotton. Though few in number, their views and way of life dominated the South.

The richest planters built elegant homes and filled them with expensive furniture from Europe. They entertained lavishly. They tried to dress and behave like European nobility.

Because of their wealth and influence, many planters became political leaders. They devoted many hours to local, state, and national politics. Planters hired overseers to run day-to-day affairs on their plantations and to manage the work of slaves.

Small Farmers About 75 percent of southern whites were small farmers. These "plain folk" owned the land they farmed. They might also own one or two slaves. Unlike planters, plain folk worked with their slaves in the fields.

Among small farmers, helping each other was an important duty. "People who lived miles apart counted themselves as neighbors," wrote a farmer in Mississippi. "And in case of sorrow or sickness, there was no limit to the service neighbors provided."

Poor Whites Lower on the social ladder was a small group of poor whites. They did not own the land they farmed. Instead, they rented it, often paying the owner with part of their crop. Many barely made a living.

Poor whites often lived in the hilly, wooded areas of the South. They planted crops such as corn, potatoes, and other vegetables. They also herded cattle and pigs. Poor whites had hard lives, but they enjoyed rights that were denied to all African Americans, enslaved or free.

African American Southerners

Both free and enslaved African Americans lived in the South. Although free under the law, free African Americans faced harsh discrimination. Enslaved African Americans had no rights at all.

Free African Americans Most free African Americans were descendants of slaves freed during and after the American Revolution. Others had bought their freedom. In 1860, over 200,000 free blacks lived in the South. Most lived in Maryland and Delaware, where slavery was in decline. Others lived in cities such as New Orleans, Richmond, and Charleston.

Slave owners did not like free African Americans living in the South. They feared that free African Americans set a bad example, encouraging slaves to rebel. Also, slave owners justified slavery by claiming that African Americans could not take care of themselves. Free African American workers proved this idea wrong.

To discourage free African Americans, southern states passed laws that made life even harder for them. Free African Americans were not allowed to vote or travel. In some southern states, they either had to move out of the state or allow themselves to be enslaved.

Despite these limits, free African Americans were able to make a life for themselves. Some even made valuable contributions to southern life. For example, Norbert Rillieux (RIHL yoo) invented a machine that revolutionized the way sugar was refined. Another inventor, Henry Blair, patented a seed planter.

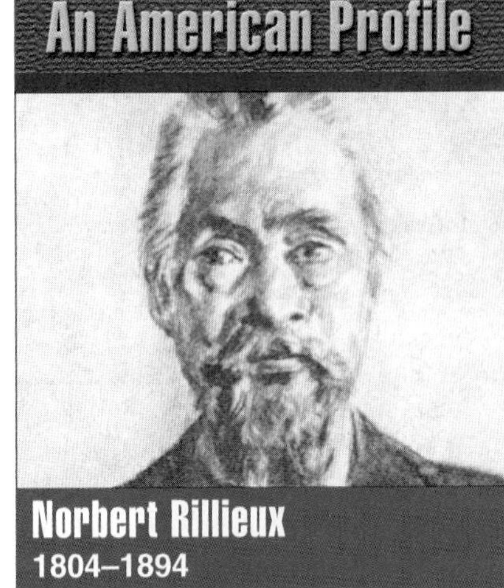

An American Profile

Norbert Rillieux
1804–1894

In the early 1800s, sugar was refined by boiling sugar cane in huge vats. Moving the hot liquid between vats was dangerous.

Norbert Rillieux invented a machine that cooked the sugar in closed vats under low air pressure. Since pipes moved the liquid from one vat to another, there was no danger to workers. Rillieux's machine made better sugar, too. The method quickly spread across Louisiana and to Mexico and Cuba. Factories today use essentially the same technique. Rillieux also invented a machine that improved the processing of sugar from sugar beets.

Was Rillieux's method less or more costly to operate than the old technique? Why?

Identify Contrasts How was life in the South different for free African Americans than it was for whites? How did white southerners make life difficult for free African Americans? Add this information to your table.

Enslaved African Americans By 1860, enslaved African Americans made up one third of the South's population. Most worked as field hands on cotton plantations. Both men and women cleared new land and planted and harvested crops. Children helped by pulling weeds, collecting wood, and carrying water to the field hands. By the time they were teenagers, they worked between 12 and 14 hours a day.

On large plantations, some African Americans became skilled workers, such as carpenters and blacksmiths. A few worked in cities and lived almost as if they were free. Their earnings, however, belonged to their owners.

Viewing History

Two Ways of Life

Wealthy southern planters lived in large, beautiful homes with many slaves and acres of fertile land. More typical of the South during the 1800s was the small farmer who lived in a modest home and worked hard to make a living. Most white farmers did not have slaves. **Synthesizing Information** ***Why do you think rich planters thought of themselves as aristocrats?***

Life Without Freedom

The life of enslaved African Americans was determined by strict laws and the practices of individual slave owners. Conditions varied from plantation to plantation. Some owners made sure their slaves had clean cabins, decent food, and warm clothes. Other planters spent as little as possible on their slaves.

Slave Codes Southern states passed laws known as slave codes to keep slaves from either running away or rebelling. Under the codes, enslaved African Americans were forbidden to gather in groups of more than three. They could not leave their owner's land without a written pass. They were not allowed to own guns.

Slave codes also made it a crime for slaves to learn how to read and write. Owners hoped that this law would make it hard for African Americans to escape slavery. They reasoned that uneducated runaway slaves would not be able to use maps or read train schedules. They would not be able to find their way north.

Some laws were meant to protect slaves, but only from the worst forms of abuse. However, enslaved African Americans did not have the right to testify in court. As a result, they were not able to bring charges against owners who abused them.

Enslaved African Americans had only one real protection against mistreatment. Owners looked on their slaves as valuable property. Most slave owners wanted to keep this human property healthy and productive.

Hard Work Even the kindest owners insisted that their slaves work long, hard days. Slaves worked from "can see to can't see," or from dawn to dusk, up to 16 hours a day. Frederick Douglass, who escaped slavery, recalled his life under one harsh master:

> "We were worked in all weathers. It was never too hot or too cold; it could never rain, blow, hail, or snow too hard for us to work in the field. Work, work, work. . . . The longest days were too short for him and the shortest nights too long for him."
>
> —Frederick Douglass, *Narrative of the Life of Frederick Douglass, An American Slave*

Southern Society in 1860

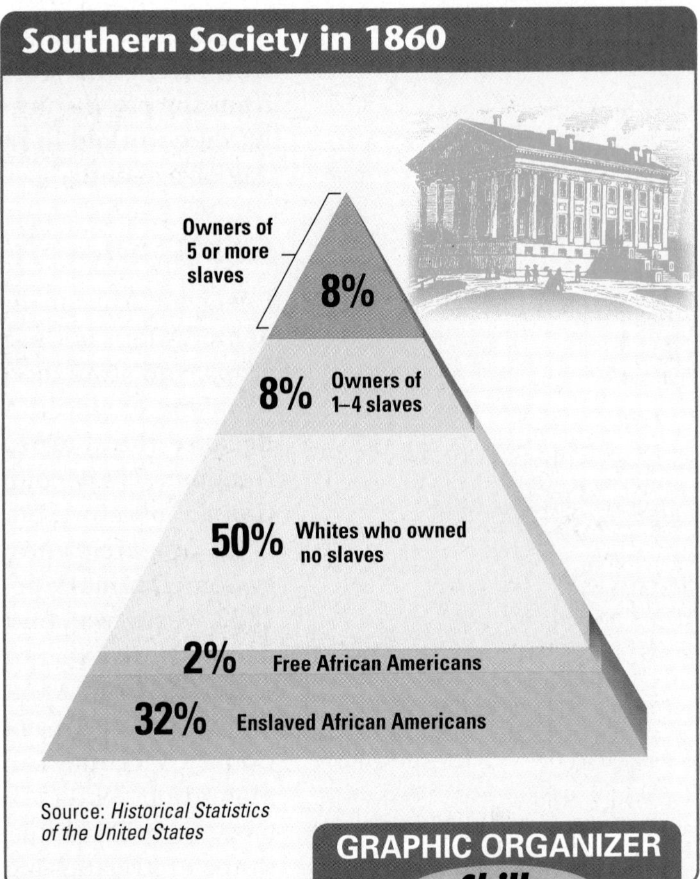

Source: *Historical Statistics of the United States*

GRAPHIC ORGANIZER *Skills*

This social pyramid represents the structure of southern society in 1860. At the top are wealthy and powerful planters. At the bottom are millions of enslaved African Americans.

1. **Comprehension** Which group in southern society was most numerous?
2. **Critical Thinking Analyzing Information** How did the social structure of the South reflect the importance of slavery?

Economics $

Family Life It was hard for enslaved African Americans to keep their families together. Southern laws did not recognize slave marriages or slave families. As a result, owners could sell a husband and wife to different buyers. Children were often taken from their parents and sold.

On large plantations, many enslaved families did manage to stay together. For those African Americans, the family was a source of strength, pride, and love. Grandparents, parents, children, aunts, uncles, and cousins formed a close-knit group. This idea of an **extended family** had its roots in Africa.

Enslaved African Americans preserved other traditions as well. Parents taught their children traditional African stories and songs. They used folk tales to pass on African history and moral beliefs.

Religion Offers Hope By the 1800s, many enslaved African Americans were devout Christians. Planters often allowed white ministers to preach to their slaves. African Americans also had their own preachers and beliefs.

Religion helped African Americans cope with the harshness of slave life. Bible stories about how the ancient Hebrews had escaped from slavery inspired a new type of religious song called a spiritual. As they worked in the fields, slaves would often sing about a coming day of freedom.

Resistance Against Slavery

Enslaved African Americans struck back against the system that denied them both freedom and wages. Some broke tools, destroyed crops, and stole food.

Many enslaved African Americans tried to escape to the North. Because the journey was long and dangerous, very few made it to freedom. Every county had slave patrols and sheriffs ready to question an unknown black person.

A few African Americans used violence to resist the brutal slave system. Denmark Vesey, a free African American, planned a revolt in 1822. Vesey was betrayed before the revolt began. He and 35 other people were executed.

In 1831, an African American preacher named Nat Turner led a major revolt. An enslaved worker on a plantation in Southampton County, Virginia, Turner believed his mission was to take revenge on plantation owners. Turner led his followers through Virginia, killing more than 57 whites. For nearly two months terrified whites hunted the countryside looking for Turner. They killed many innocent African Americans before catching and hanging him.

Nat Turner's revolt increased southern fears of an uprising of enslaved African Americans. Revolts were rare, however. Since whites were cautious and well armed, a revolt by African Americans had almost no chance of success.

★ ★ ★ Section 4 Assessment ★ ★ ★

Recall

1. **Identify** Explain the significance of **(a)** Norbert Rillieux, **(b)** Henry Blair, **(c)** Denmark Vesey, **(d)** Nat Turner.
2. **Define** **(a)** "cottonocracy," **(b)** slave codes, **(c)** extended family.

Comprehension

3. Describe the way of life of each of the following groups in the South: **(a)** rich planters, **(b)** small farmers, **(c)** poor whites.
4. How did laws restrict the freedom of both free and enslaved African Americans?
5. In what ways did enslaved African Americans struggle against slavery?

Critical Thinking and Writing

6. **Exploring the Main Idea** Review the Main Idea statement at the beginning of this section. Then, write a paragraph discussing the importance of plantations in the southern economy.
7. **Synthesizing Information** Few southerners were planters. Why do you think this small group was able to dominate the political and social life of the South?

Activity

Go Online
PHSchool.com

Learning More About Spirituals

During slavery, African American spirituals were passed on by word of mouth. Use the Internet to learn the words to a spiritual sung during the 1800s. Explain what the words mean. For help in completing the activity, visit PHSchool.com, **Web Code mfd-1403.**

Making Generalizations

You can extend your understanding of how new technology affected American life by making generalizations. Making generalizations means taking a number of examples and facts and arriving at a general statement.

This passage tells about the daguerreotype, an image printed on a chemically treated copper plate, and developed by a Frenchman named Louis Daguerre in 1839:

In 1847, two Americans began a collaboration that would advance science on several fronts. The men were John A. Whipple, a photographer, and William Cranch Bond, an astronomer who headed the Harvard College Observatory. Whipple had already developed a technique for making paper prints from the daguerreotype images. Bond had just acquired the world's largest telescope. The collaborators' goal was to photograph the sky through the telescope. Although their first attempts were unsuccessful, Whipple and Bond finally produced the first astronomical daguerreotype—an image of the star Vega. This was soon followed by pictures of the moon. Bond and Whipple then toured Europe to great acclaim, distributing copies of the exciting new images to observatories on the continent.

The chart shows how to organize facts to make a generalization based on the passage.

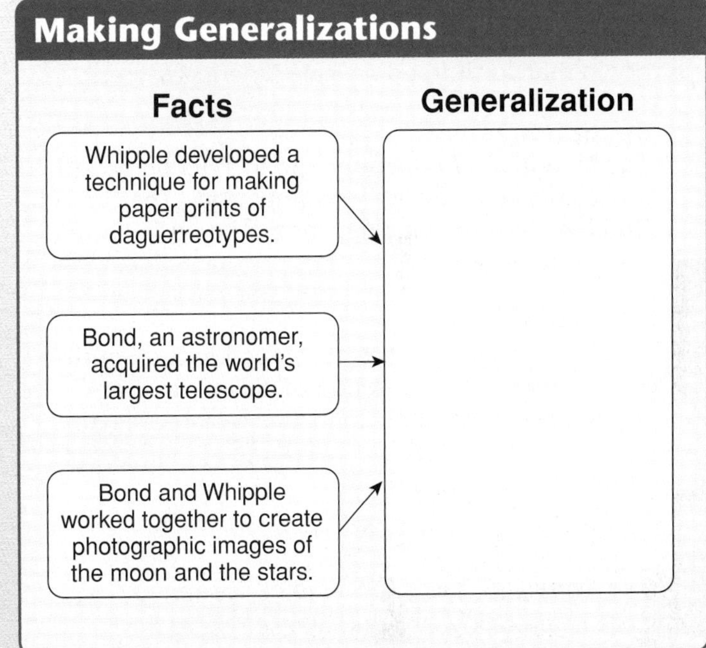

Learn the Skill *To make generalizations, use the following steps:*

1. **Identify the main idea and details.** What information is being given?
2. **Compile a list of relevant facts.** You may find that not every fact given is necessary for a generalization.
3. **Find a common element.** Look for a single feature that is true of all the facts you have listed.
4. **Make a generalization.** Make a general statement based on the facts. Accurate generalizations often include words such as *many, most, often, usually, some, few,* and *sometimes.* Faulty generalizations may include words such as *all, none, always, never,* or *every.*

Practice the Skill *Answer the following questions about the passage and chart:*

1. What is the subject of the passage?
2. **(a)** Identify a fact that is not relevant to those listed on the chart. **(b)** Identify a relevant fact that fits with those given on the chart.
3. How are the facts on the chart related?
4. Write a generalization based on the facts. Use a clue word.

Apply the Skill *See the Chapter Review and Assessment.*

CHAPTER 14

Review and Assessment

Chapter Summary

Section 1
A flood of new inventions in the 1800s aided the growth of industry in the North. Railroads and clipper ships increased both domestic and international commerce.

Section 2
Workers formed unions to battle poor conditions in northern factories. Nativists tried to keep immigrants out of the United States. The end of slavery in the North freed African Americans there.

Section 3
The invention of the cotton gin in 1793 helped to make cotton the South's leading crop. The South's economy was dependent on agriculture, not industry.

Section 4
The "cottonocracy" that developed in the South strengthened the institution of slavery in that region. Some African Americans resisted slavery.

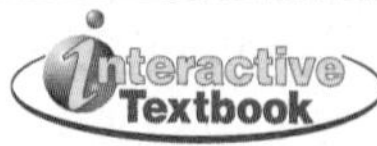

For additional review and enrichment activities, see the interactive version of *The American Nation,* available on the Web and on CD-ROM.

Chapter Self-Test For practice test questions for Chapter 14, visit PHSchool.com, **Web Code mfa-1404.**

Building Vocabulary

Write sentences using the chapter vocabulary words listed below, leaving blanks where the vocabulary words would go. Exchange your sentences with another student and fill in the blanks in each other's sentences.

1. **telegraph**
2. **locomotive**
3. **clipper ship**
4. **trade union**
5. **strike**
6. **nativist**
7. **discrimination**
8. **"cottonocracy"**
9. **slave codes**
10. **extended family**

Reviewing Key Facts

11. Describe three inventions that caused the North's economy to expand. (Section 1)
12. Give two reasons for Irish and German immigration to the United States in the 1840s and 1850s. (Section 2)
13. Explain how the cotton gin changed life in the South. (Section 3)
14. Discuss the difference between the planter and the small farmer. (Section 4)

Critical Thinking and Writing

15. **Comparing** Compare two inventions that you think had the greatest impact on American life during the mid-1800s. Explain your answer.
16. **Evaluating Information** Why is transportation important to economic progress?
17. **Analyzing Information** How did the political, social, and economic situation of free African Americans and enslaved African Americans differ?
18. Connecting to Geography: **Regions** Make a comparison chart that shows how economic differences affected life in the North and in the South.

SKILLS ASSESSMENT

Analyzing Primary Sources

Frederick Law Olmsted, who often wrote about social issues, gives his view on poor white women working in the South. Read the excerpt. Then, answer the questions that follow:

> " Poor white girls never hired themselves out to do servants' work, but they would come and help another white woman with her sewing or quilting, and take wages for it. . . . That their condition is not as unfortunate by any means as that of Negroes, however, is most obvious, since among them, people may sometimes elevate themselves to positions and habits of usefulness and respectability. "
>
> —Frederick Law Olmsted, *A Journey in the Seaboard Slave States,* 1856

19. According to Olmsted, poor white girls
- **A.** never hired themselves out as servants.
- **B.** competed with African American women for the same jobs.
- **C.** were worse off than African American women.
- **D.** could do nothing to improve their lives.

20. Why do you think poor white girls would refuse to be hired as servants?
- **A.** They didn't like their bosses.
- **B.** The work was "beneath" them.
- **C.** It would take too long to travel to the job.
- **D.** They would have to leave their homes.

APPLYING YOUR SKILLS

Making Generalizations

Read the following passage about steamboats. Then, answer the questions that follow:

> " The western steamboat carried both freight and passengers; but it won its greatest fame as a way to travel. The most luxurious boats, called 'floating palaces,' offered accommodations far beyond the experience of the average American. Steamboats also provided the cheapest form of inland transportation before the Civil War.
>
> Despite the discomforts of swarming mosquitoes, heat from the boilers, and noisy engines at all hours of the night, observers agreed that journeying by steamboat was far more pleasant than taking a stagecoach, the principal alternative in the West before 1850. "
>
> —Davidson, et al., *Nation of Nations*

21. What is the main idea of the passage?
- **A.** Steamboat travel was costly.
- **B.** Steamboats are the best way to travel.
- **C.** Steamboats carried freight and people.
- **D.** Steamboat travel was comfortable.

22. Make a generalization based on the passage.

ACTIVITIES

Connecting With . . . Culture

Understanding the Nation in the 1800s Read the following quotations. Determine which person or event is being referred to. Then, write a brief paragraph describing how each person or event affected American society.

"The roads, the canals, and the mails play [an important] part in the prosperity of the Union. . . ."

"I thank God I am not property now, but am regarded as a man like yourself. . . ."

Becoming a Citizen

A Citizenship Pamphlet Immigrants in the mid-1800s had to live in the United States for five years before gaining voting privileges. Use the Internet to find out how immigrants can become citizens today. Present the information in a pamphlet. For help in starting this activity, visit PHSchool.com, **Web Code mfd-1406.**

Incidents in the Life of a Slave Girl

Harriet A. Jacobs

Harriet Jacobs

Introduction **Born in Edenton, North Carolina, in the early 1800s, Harriet Jacobs did not realize she was a slave until she was six years old. When Jacobs was 11, her mistress died and she was sent to a new master, Dr. James Norcom. Jacobs found her new situation at the Norcom household unbearable. In 1835, she escaped from Norcom and went into hiding in her hometown. For seven years, she hid in the cramped space of an attic in her grandmother's house. The following selection describes her life in the attic.**

Vocabulary Before you read the selection, find the meanings of these words in a dictionary: **benumb, delirious, stupefy, kindle.**

I suffered much more during the second winter than I did during the first. My limbs were benumbed by inaction, and the cold filled them with cramp. I had a very painful sensation of coldness in my head; even my face and tongue stiffened, and I lost the power of speech. Of course it was impossible, under the circumstances, to summon any physician. My brother William came and did all he could for me. Uncle Philip also watched tenderly over me; and poor grandmother crept up and down to inquire whether there were any signs of returning life. I was restored to full consciousness by the dashing of cold water on my face, and found myself leaning against my brother's arm, while he bent over me with streaming eyes. He afterwards told me he thought I was dying, for I had been in an unconscious state for sixteen hours. I next became delirious, and was in great danger of betraying myself and my friends. To prevent this, they stupefied me with drugs. I remained in bed for six weeks, weary in body and sick at heart. How to get medical advice was the question. William finally went to a Thompsonian doctor, and described himself as having all my pains and aches. He returned with herbs, roots, and ointment. He was especially charged to rub on the ointment by a fire, but how could a fire be made in my little den? Charcoal in a furnace was tried, but there was no outlet for the gas, and it nearly cost my life. Afterwards coals, already kindled, were brought up in an iron pan, and placed on bricks. I was so weak, and it was so long since I had enjoyed the warmth of a fire, that those few coals actually made me weep. I think the medicines did me some good; but my recovery was very slow. Dark thoughts passed through my mind as I lay there day after day. I tried to be thankful for my little cell, dismal as it was, and even to love it, as part of the price I had paid for the redemption of my children. Sometimes I thought God was a compassionate Father, who would forgive my sins for the sake of my sufferings. At other times, it seemed to me there was no justice or mercy in the divine government. I asked why the curse of slavery was permitted to exist, and why I had been so persecuted and wronged from youth upward. These things took the shape of mystery, which is to this day not so clear to my soul as I trust it will be hereafter.

In the midst of my illness, grandmother broke down under the weight of anxiety and

This house was a "station" where runaway slaves could hide.

toil. The idea of losing her, who had always been my best friend and a mother to my children, was the sorest trial I had yet had. O, how earnestly I prayed that she might recover! How hard it seemed, that I could not tend upon her, who had so long and so tenderly watched over me!

One day the screams of a child nerved me with strength to crawl to my peeping-hole, and I saw my son covered with blood. A fierce dog, usually chained, had seized and bitten him. A doctor was sent for, and I heard the groans and screams of my child while the wounds were being sewed up. O, what torture to a mother's heart, to listen to this and be unable to go to him!

But childhood is like a day in spring, alternately shower and sunshine. Before long Benny was bright and lively, threatening the destruction of the dog; and great was his delight when the doctor told him the next day that the dog had bitten another boy and been shot. Benny recovered from his wounds; but it was long before he could walk.

Analyzing Literature

1. What hardships did Harriet endure the second winter in the attic?

- **A** She was always hungry and lonely.
- **B** Her body was stiff from cold and she could not talk.
- **C** The attic was too warm and she could not communicate with anyone.
- **D** She was not able to let anyone know that she was ill.

2. How did Harriet's brother help her?

- **A** He helped her send messages to the doctor.
- **B** He sealed the cracks in the walls of the attic.
- **C** He managed to bring her ointments.
- **D** He brought her children to the attic.

3. **Critical Thinking** **Drawing Inferences** What inner conflicts does Harriet experience?

CHAPTER 15

Reform and a New American Culture

1820–1860

1 The Reforming Spirit
2 Opposing Slavery
3 A Call for Women's Rights
4 American Art and Literature

Religious revival meeting

William Lloyd Garrison and his antislavery vow

AMERICAN EVENTS

Early 1800s The Second Great Awakening sweeps the nation. At outdoor revival meetings, converts promise to reform their lives.

1831 William Lloyd Garrison begins publishing his antislavery newspaper, *The Liberator.*

1837 Horace Mann pushes for education reform in Massachusetts.

Presidential Terms: James Monroe 1817–1825 | John Quincy Adams 1825–1829 | Andrew Jackson 1829–1837 | Martin Van Buren 1837–1841

1820 · 1830 · 1840

WORLD EVENTS

▲ **1822** Liberia is founded in western Africa.

1837 ▲ First kindergarten opens in Germany.

The Underground Railroad

Some reformers helped enslaved African Americans escape to the North or Canada by a route known as the Underground Railroad.

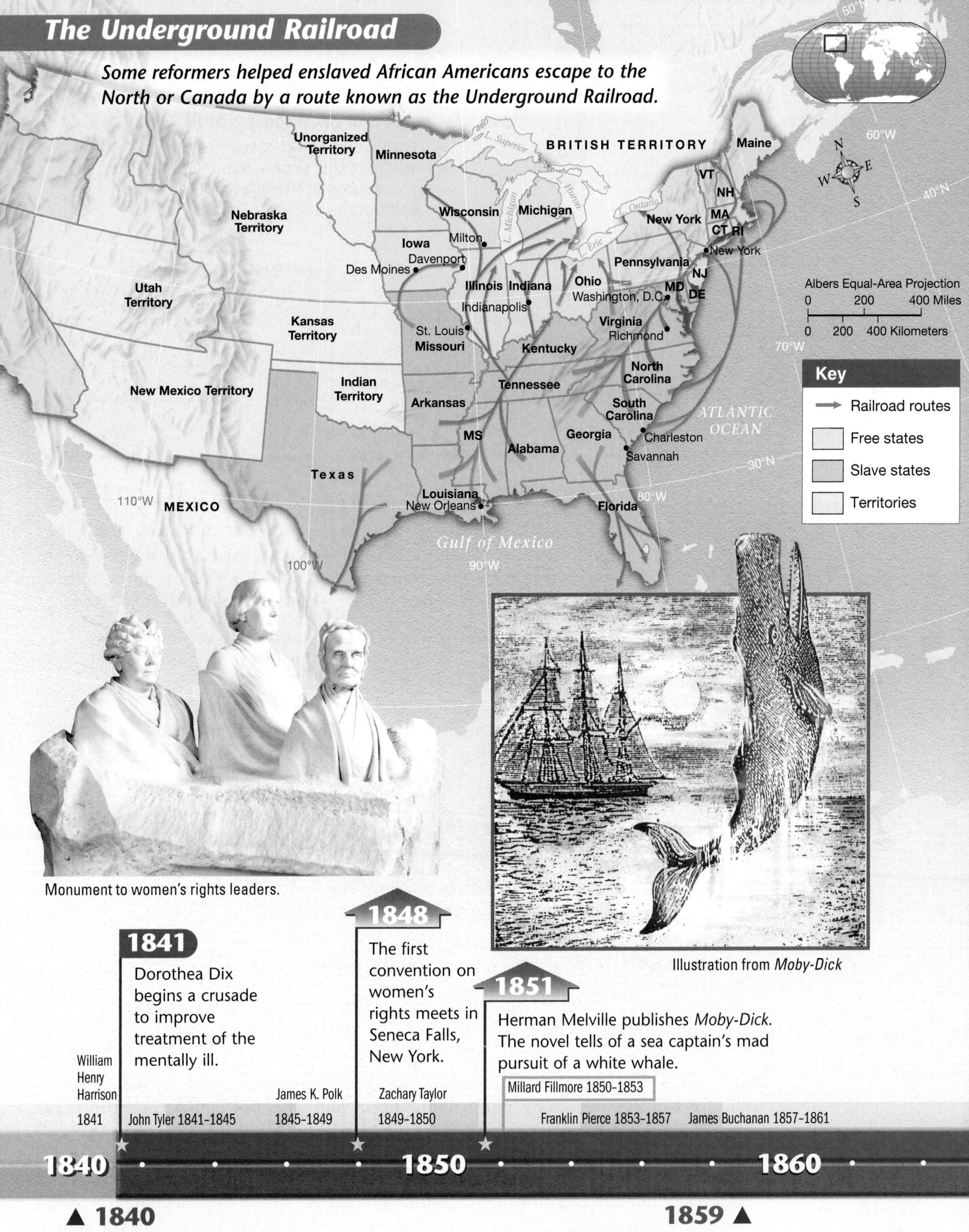

Monument to women's rights leaders.

Illustration from *Moby-Dick*

1841 Dorothea Dix begins a crusade to improve treatment of the mentally ill.

1848 The first convention on women's rights meets in Seneca Falls, New York.

1851 Herman Melville publishes *Moby-Dick*. The novel tells of a sea captain's mad pursuit of a white whale.

William Henry Harrison 1841 | John Tyler 1841–1845 | James K. Polk 1845–1849 | Zachary Taylor 1849–1850 | Millard Fillmore 1850–1853 | Franklin Pierce 1853–1857 | James Buchanan 1857–1861

1840 • 1850 • 1860

▲ 1840 World Antislavery Convention opens in London.

1859 ▲ Charles Dickens publishes *A Tale of Two Cities*.

1 The Reforming Spirit

Prepare to Read

Objectives

In this section, you will

- Explain how political and religious ideals provided inspiration for reform.
- Summarize reforms sought for criminals and the mentally ill.
- Identify the goals of the temperance movement.
- Describe how reformers improved education.

Key Terms

social reform
predestination
Second Great Awakening
revival
debtor
temperance movement

Target Reading Skill

Cause and Effect Copy the chart below. As you read this section, complete the chart to show some of the effects of the reforming spirit of the 1800s.

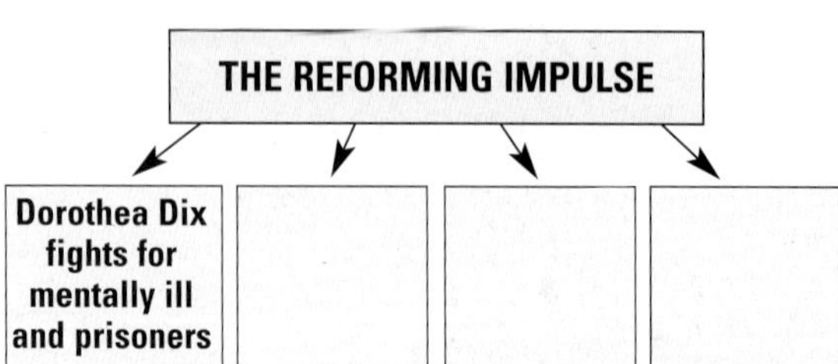

Main Idea Between 1820 and 1860, a wide variety of reform movements sprang up to improve conditions in the United States.

Caves at Newgate prison

Setting the Scene Two reporters entered the small, ordinary-looking brick hut. Opening a trapdoor in the floor, they peered down the dark shaft of an abandoned copper mine. Nervously, they climbed 50 feet down an old wooden ladder until they reached the bottom:

> “Lighting the candles . . . I led the way down a series of stone steps. . . . The roof was very low, and the candle gave so little light, that I was compelled to feel my way forward with my walking-stick. . . . [I] groped forward twenty or thirty feet into the caverns . . . where the prisoners used to sleep.”
>
> —quoted in Phelps, *Newgate of Connecticut*

Years earlier, these cramped caves had served as Connecticut's state prison, Newgate. It was shut down in 1827.

In the mid-1800s, some Americans began to condemn the way prisoners were treated. Prison reform was just one of many movements that sprang up to cure the nation's ills.

The Reforming Impulse

The impulse toward social reform had both political and religious roots. **Social reform** is an organized attempt to improve what is unjust or imperfect in society.

Political Ideals As you have read, during the Jackson era, politics was becoming more democratic. More people could vote and take part in government than ever before.

Still, some critics said American society was not democratic enough. They pointed to the promise of liberty and equality expressed in the Declaration of Independence. A true democracy, they argued, would not allow slavery. Others asked why women had fewer rights than men. By changing such injustices, reformers hoped to move the nation closer to its political ideals.

The Second Great Awakening During the colonial era, many American Protestants believed in **predestination.** According to this idea, God decided in advance which people would attain salvation after death. This belief led many people to worry that they could do nothing to be saved.

In the early 1800s, a dynamic religious movement known as the **Second Great Awakening** swept the nation. Its leaders stressed free will rather than predestination. They taught that individuals could choose to save their souls by their own actions.

To stir religious feelings, preachers held **revivals,** huge outdoor meetings. Revivals might last for days and attract thousands of people. A witness recalled the excitement of a revival at Cane Ridge, Kentucky:

> “The vast sea of human beings seemed to be agitated as if by storm. I counted seven ministers all preaching at once. . . . Some of the people were singing, others praying, some crying for mercy.”
>
> —James B. Finley, *Autobiography*

One leader of the Second Great Awakening was a minister named Charles Grandison Finney. A powerful speaker, Finney taught that individual salvation was the first step toward "the complete reformation of the whole world." Such teachings inspired new efforts to improve society.

Roots of Reform

The Reform Movement

Political Origins	Religious Influences
• The ideals of liberty and equality in the Declaration of Independence inspire people to try to improve society • During Jackson era, more people can vote than ever before • Critics say slavery and other injustices violate democratic ideals	• Second Great Awakening stresses free will rather than predestination • Revivals encourage people to reform their lives • Finney teaches that individual salvation is the first step to the reform of a society

GRAPHIC ORGANIZER *Skills*

Both political and religious ideas inspired Americans to work for reform.

1. **Comprehension** Identify one political change in the country that encouraged reform.
2. **Critical Thinking Identifying Causes and Effects** Why might a belief in free will inspire a spirit of reform?

Hospital and Prison Reform

One of the most vigorous social reformers was Dorothea Dix, a Boston schoolteacher. She turned her attention to what one minister called the "outsiders" in society: criminals and the mentally ill.

Reforms for the Mentally Ill In 1841, Dix visited a jail for women near Boston. She was outraged to discover that some of the prisoners were not criminals, but mentally ill. Dix demanded to know why these women were locked in small, dark, unheated cells. The jailer replied that "lunatics" did not feel the cold.

During the next 18 months, Dix visited every jail, poorhouse, and hospital in Massachusetts. Her shocking reports helped persuade state legislators to fund a new mental hospital:

> “I proceed, gentlemen, briefly to call your attention to the present state of Insane Persons confined . . . in cages, closets, cellars, stalls, pens! Chained, naked, beaten with rods, and lashed into obedience.”
>
> —Dorothea Dix, "Memorial to the State Legislators of Massachusetts"

Dix went on to inspect jails as far away as Louisiana and Illinois. Her reports persuaded most legislatures to treat the mentally ill as patients, not criminals.

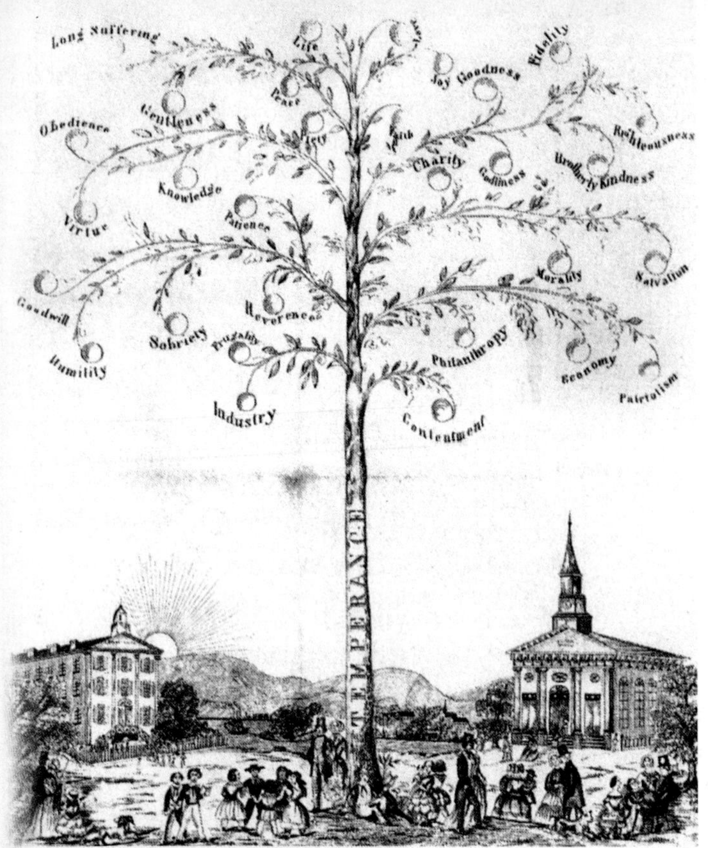

POLITICAL CARTOON *Skills*

A Call for Temperance **Temperance leaders believed a ban on alcoholic beverages would benefit society. This cartoon appeared in 1855.**

1. **Comprehension** What object in this cartoon symbolizes temperance?
2. **Understanding Main Ideas** According to the cartoon, what are some of the ways temperance would benefit society?
3. **Critical Thinking Drawing Inferences** Why do you think the cartoonist included a school and a church?

Prison Reform Dix also joined a growing movement to improve conditions in prisons. Men, women, and children were often crammed together in cold, damp rooms. When food supplies were low, prisoners went hungry—unless they had money to buy meals from jailers.

Five out of six people in northern jails were **debtors,** or people who could not pay money they owed. While behind bars, debtors had no way to earn money to pay back their debts. As a result, many debtors remained in prison for years.

Dix and others called for changes in the prison system. As a result, some states built prisons with only one or two inmates to a cell. Cruel punishments were banned, and people convicted of minor crimes received shorter sentences. Slowly, states stopped treating debtors as criminals.

The Temperance Movement

Alcohol abuse was widespread in the early 1800s. At political rallies, weddings, and funerals, men, women, and sometimes even children drank heavily. Men could buy whiskey in candy stores or barbershops.

The **temperance movement,** a campaign against alcohol abuse, took shape in the late 1820s. Women often took a leading role in the battle. They knew that "demon rum" could lead to wife beating, child abuse, and the breakup of families.

Some temperance groups urged people to drink less. Others sought to end drinking altogether. They won a major victory in 1851, when Maine banned the sale of alcohol. Eight other states passed "Maine laws." Most states later repealed the laws, but the temperance crusade would gain new strength in the late 1800s.

Improving Education

In 1800, few American children attended school. Massachusetts was the only state that required free public schools supported by the community. Teachers were poorly trained and ill paid. Students of all ages crowded together in a single room.

As more men won the right to vote, reformers acted to improve education. They argued that a republic required educated citizens.

Growth of Public Schools New York State took the lead in improving public education. In 1814, the state passed a law requiring local governments to set up tax-supported school districts.

Horace Mann became head of the Massachusetts board of education in 1837. He hounded legislators to provide more money for education. Under his leadership, Massachusetts built new schools, extended the school year, and raised teachers' pay. The state also opened three colleges to train teachers.

Other states followed the lead of Massachusetts and New York. By the 1850s, most northern states had set up free tax-supported elementary schools. Schools in the South improved more slowly. In both the North and the South, schooling usually ended in the eighth grade. There were few public high schools.

Understand Effects Read the paragraphs in the subsection "Improving Education." Explain the changes reformers made to education in the 1800s. Add this information to your chart.

Education for African Americans In most areas, African Americans had little chance to attend school. A few cities, like Boston and New York, set up separate schools for black students. However, these schools received less money than schools for white students did. In the North, African American men and women often opened their own schools to educate their children.

Some attempts to educate African Americans met with hostility. In the 1830s, Prudence Crandall, a Connecticut Quaker, began a school for African American girls. Crandall continued to teach even as rocks smashed through the window. Finally, a mob broke in one night and destroyed the school.

Despite such obstacles, some African Americans went on to attend private colleges such as Harvard, Dartmouth, and Oberlin. In 1854, Pennsylvania chartered the first college for African American men.

Educating People With Disabilities Some reformers improved education for people with disabilities. In 1817, Thomas Gallaudet (gal uh DEHT) set up a school for the deaf in Hartford, Connecticut.

Samuel Gridley Howe founded the first American school for the blind in 1832. Howe used a system of raised letters to enable students to read with their fingers. One of Howe's pupils, Laura Bridgman, was the first deaf and blind student to receive a formal education.

★ ★ ★ Section 1 Assessment ★ ★ ★

Recall

1. **Identify** Explain the significance of **(a)** Second Great Awakening, **(b)** Charles Grandison Finney, **(c)** Dorothea Dix, **(d)** Horace Mann, **(e)** Thomas Gallaudet, **(f)** Samuel Gridley Howe, **(g)** Laura Bridgman.
2. **Define** **(a)** social reform, **(b)** predestination, **(c)** revival, **(d)** debtor, **(e)** temperance movement.

Comprehension

3. Why did the reforming spirit grow in the 1800s?
4. How did Dorothea Dix help improve treatment of the mentally ill?
5. Why did many women join the temperance movement?
6. Describe two educational reforms of the mid-1800s.

Critical Thinking and Writing

7. **Exploring the Main Idea** Review the Main Idea statement at the beginning of this section. Then, write a paragraph evaluating the possible impact of one reform movement on American society.
8. **Linking Past and Present** List two ways that religious groups promote social reform in the United States today.

ACTIVITY

Go Online PHSchool.com

Connecting to Today

Many organizations today combat alcohol or drug abuse. Use the Internet to find out about one such organization. Report to the class on its goals and methods. For help in completing the activity, visit PHSchool.com, **Web Code mfd-1501**.

An American Classroom

In colonial times, many schoolhouses were one-room log cabins with paper covering a few small windows. They were often supported by churches or private charities. But by the mid-1800s, all northern states began supporting public education. What were these early classrooms like?

Fast Facts

- Girls and boys were usually taught together in elementary school. In high school, however, they were often separated.
- New technologies, such as the invention of the steel pen and the blackboard, changed classrooms in the 1800s.
- Physical punishment was common in schoolrooms. A popular saying advised, "Spare the rod and spoil the child."

Public schools taught large numbers of students from different backgrounds. Students wrote their lessons on slate boards. Memorization and recitation were common. Here, students "toe the line"—standing behind a line on the floor as they recite their daily lessons.

In elementary schools, students learned their lessons from picture books called primers. These pages from an 1845 primer combine lessons in arithmetic, reading, and history.

Activity

With a partner, design two pages for a modern primer for elementary-school students. Use the one shown at left as a model. Include illustrations and a variety of subjects.

2 Opposing Slavery

Prepare to Read

Objectives

In this section, you will

- Explain how the antislavery movement began and grew.
- Describe the Underground Railroad.
- Identify why so many white northerners and southerners opposed abolition.

Key Terms

American Colonization Society

abolitionist

The Liberator

Underground Railroad

Target Reading Skill

Reading Process As you read, prepare an outline of this section. Use roman numerals for the major headings, capital letters for the subheadings, and numbers for the supporting details.

I. Roots of the Antislavery Movement
  A. Early efforts
    1. Quakers protest
    2.
  B. Colonization movement
    1.
    2.
II. The Abolitionist Movement Grows
  A.
  B.

Main Idea In the 1830s and 1840s, reformers became more active in calling for an end to slavery in the United States.

Setting the Scene As the spirit of reform spread, many young people joined antislavery efforts. In Providence, Rhode Island, white and black girls met together every week, starting in 1834. As they sewed, one member would read aloud from an antislavery newspaper. By selling their needlework, the girls raised $90 for the antislavery cause in a single year.

The idea quickly spread. In Albany, New York, black students pledged six cents a month. Members of the Pittsburgh Juvenile Society pledged a "cent a week."

Today, a penny a week doesn't seem like much. But it was a great deal for a boy or girl whose family was lucky to earn fifty or a hundred dollars for the entire year. The spread of such organizations showed that in the North, many black and white Americans had come to believe that slavery must end.

Antislavery medallion

Roots of the Antislavery Movement

In the Declaration of Independence, Thomas Jefferson had written that "all men are created equal." Yet many Americans, including Jefferson himself, did not believe that this statement applied to enslaved African Americans. In the 1800s, a growing number of reformers began to think differently.

Early Efforts Religious beliefs led some Americans to oppose slavery. Since colonial times, Quakers had taught that it was a sin for one human being to own another. All people, they said, were equal in the sight of God. Later, during the Second Great Awakening, ministers like Charles Grandison Finney called on Christians to join a crusade to stamp out slavery.

In the North, slavery gradually came to an end. By 1804, all the states from Pennsylvania through New England had promised to free their slaves over time. Still, there were only 50,000 slaves in the North in 1800, compared with nearly one million in the South.

Colonization Movement The American Colonization Society proposed to end slavery by setting up an independent colony in Africa for freed slaves. In 1822, President Monroe helped the society found the nation of Liberia in western Africa.

Some African Americans favored colonization, believing that they would never have equal rights in the United States. Most, however, opposed the movement. Nearly all, enslaved or free, had been born in the United States. They wanted to stay in their homeland. In the end, only a few thousand African Americans settled in Liberia.

The Abolitionist Movement Grows

A growing number of reformers, known as **abolitionists,** wanted to end slavery completely in the United States. Some abolitionists favored a gradual end to slavery. They expected slavery to die out if it was kept out of the western territories. Other abolitionists demanded that slavery end everywhere, at once.

African American Abolitionists Free African Americans played a key role in the abolitionist movement. Some tried to end slavery through lawsuits and petitions. In the 1820s, Samuel Cornish and John Russwurm set up an abolitionist newspaper, *Freedom's Journal.* They hoped to turn public opinion against slavery by printing stories about the brutal treatment of enslaved African Americans.

Other African American abolitionists called for stronger measures. In *An Appeal to the Colored Citizens of the World,* David Walker encouraged enslaved African Americans to free themselves by any means necessary. Walker's friend Maria Stewart also spoke out against slavery. Stewart was the first American woman to make public political speeches.

Frederick Douglass The best-known African American abolitionist was Frederick Douglass. Douglass was born into slavery in Maryland. As a child, he defied the slave codes by learning to read.

Douglass escaped in 1838 and made his way to New England. One day at an antislavery meeting, he felt a powerful urge to speak. Rising to his feet, he talked about the sorrows of slavery and the meaning of freedom. The audience was moved to tears. Soon, Douglass was lecturing across the United States and Britain. In 1847, he began publishing an antislavery newspaper, the *North Star.*

William Lloyd Garrison The most outspoken white abolitionist was a fiery young man named William Lloyd Garrison. To Garrison, slavery was an evil to be ended immediately. In 1831, Garrison launched *The Liberator,* the most influential antislavery newspaper. On the first page of the first issue, Garrison revealed his commitment:

> “I will be as harsh as truth, and as uncompromising as justice. . . . I am in earnest. . . . I will not excuse—I will not retreat a single inch—and I WILL BE HEARD.”
>
> —William Lloyd Garrison, *The Liberator,* January 1831

A year later, Garrison helped to found the New England Anti-Slavery Society. Members included Theodore Weld, a young minister

An American Profile

Frederick Douglass
1817–1895

Even while he was still enslaved, Frederick Douglass bravely fought slavery. He suffered beatings for resisting commands and was once jailed for trying to escape. Even after he finally did escape, Douglass was in constant danger of being recaptured and returned to the South. Despite the risk, he did not hesitate to speak out against slavery.

In 1845, Douglass wrote his autobiography. Fearing for Douglass's life, an abolitionist friend warned him not to publish it. Douglass did so anyway. Two years later, friends raised money to buy Douglass his freedom at last.

What risks did Frederick Douglass take by publishing his autobiography?

Bethel AME Church

Founded in 1816, the African Methodist Episcopal Church was a center of African American life. The Bethel AME Church in the African American community of Springtown, New Jersey, became a key station on the Underground Railroad. Harriet Tubman herself often led runaways from Maryland and Delaware there to spend a safe night on their way to freedom.

Virtual Field Trip For an interactive look at the Underground Railroad, visit PHSchool.com, **Web Code mfd-1502.**

and follower of Charles Grandison Finney. Weld brought the energy of a religious revival to antislavery meetings.

The Grimké Sisters Angelina and Sarah Grimké were the daughters of a South Carolina slaveholder. Hating slavery, they moved to Philadelphia to work for abolition. Their lectures drew large crowds.

Some people, including other abolitionists, objected to women speaking out in public. "Whatsoever it is morally right for a man to do," replied Sarah Grimké, "it is morally right for a woman to do." As you will see, this belief helped spark a crusade for women's rights.

The Underground Railroad

Some abolitionists formed the **Underground Railroad.** It was not a real railroad, but a network of black and white abolitionists who secretly helped slaves escape to freedom in the North or Canada.

"Conductors" guided runaways to "stations" where they could spend the night. Some stations were homes of abolitionists. Others were churches or even caves. Conductors sometimes hid runaways under loads of hay in wagons with false bottoms.

One daring conductor, Harriet Tubman, had escaped slavery herself. Risking her freedom and her life, Tubman returned to the South 19 times. She led more than 300 slaves, including her parents, to freedom. Admirers called Tubman the "Black Moses" after the biblical leader who led the Israelites out of slavery in Egypt. Slave owners offered a $40,000 reward for her capture.

Predict

Target Skill Before you read this section, predict the reactions of northerners and southerners to the abolitionist movement. Then, read to see whether your predictions were correct.

Opposition to Abolition

By the mid-1800s, slavery existed only in the South. Still, abolitionists like Douglass and Garrison made enemies in the North as well.

Reaction in the North Northern mill owners, bankers, and merchants depended on cotton from the South. They saw attacks on slavery as a threat to their livelihood. Some northern workers also opposed abolition. They feared that African Americans might come north and take their jobs by working for low pay.

In northern cities, mobs sometimes broke up antislavery meetings or attacked homes of abolitionists. At times, the attacks backfired and won support for the abolitionists. One night, a Boston mob dragged William Lloyd Garrison through the streets at the end of a rope. A witness wrote, "I am an abolitionist from this very moment."

Reaction in the South Most white southerners were disturbed by the growing abolitionist movement. They accused abolitionists of preaching violence. Many southerners blamed Nat Turner's rebellion on William Lloyd Garrison, who had founded *The Liberator* only a few months earlier. David Walker's call for a slave revolt seemed to confirm the worst fears of southerners.

Slave owners responded to the abolitionist crusade by defending slavery even more. If slaves were treated well, wrote one slave owner, they would "love their master and serve him . . . faithfully." Others argued that slaves were better off than northern workers who labored long hours in dusty, airless factories.

Even some southerners who owned no slaves defended slavery. To them, slavery was essential to the southern economy. Many southerners believed northern support for the antislavery movement was stronger than it really was. They began to fear that northerners wanted to destroy their way of life.

Section 2 Assessment

Recall

1. **Identify** Explain the significance of **(a)** American Colonization Society, **(b)** David Walker, **(c)** Frederick Douglass, **(d)** William Lloyd Garrison, **(e)** *The Liberator,* **(f)** Grimké sisters, **(g)** Underground Railroad, **(h)** Harriet Tubman.
2. **Define** abolitionist.

Comprehension

3. Describe two ways reformers fought against slavery.
4. How did the Underground Railroad work?
5. **(a)** Why did some northerners oppose abolition? **(b)** Describe two effects of the abolitionist movement in the South.

Critical Thinking and Writing

6. **Exploring the Main Idea** Review the Main Idea statement at the beginning of this section. Then, write a paragraph explaining what you think was the most powerful reason for ending slavery.
7. **Identifying Alternatives** Some abolitionists favored a gradual end to slavery rather than immediate abolition. List two possible arguments for and two possible arguments against this position.

ACTIVITY

Sending a Secret Message You are a conductor on the Underground Railroad. You have a cousin in New Jersey whose home you want to use as a station. Write a letter describing what your cousin will need to do. Include a map showing the route you will be taking. (See the map at the beginning of this chapter.)

Making Decisions

We make decisions all the time, but some are much more difficult than others. One way to learn decision-making skills is to look at the choices that others have made. What would you have decided if you had been living as a slave and had seen the chance to escape?

James Adams escaped from a plantation in Virginia as a teenager. Years later, he described the journey:

> "After crossing the road, we came out from the mountains to a level cleared place of farms and houses. Then we were afraid, and put ourselves on guard, resolving to travel by night. . . . We would follow a road until it bent away from the north; then we would leave it and go by the compass. This caused us to meet many rivers and streams where there were no bridges; some we could wade over, and some we crossed by swimming. . . . Our feet were now sore with long travelling."
>
> —James Adams, quoted in *The Underground Railroad* (Hansen)

A table like this one can help you weigh the pros and cons of a decision.

PROS AND CONS OF ESCAPING SLAVERY	
Arguments For	**Arguments Against**
becoming free	being caught, punished, or killed
escaping hardship	undergoing a dangerous trip
escaping abuse	leaving family behind

Reward poster for runaway slave

Learn the Skill *To learn decision-making skills, use the following steps:*

1. **Identify the problem.** What is the issue you want to resolve or the goal you want to achieve?
2. **Identify the facts.** Gather enough information to make an informed decision.
3. **List options.** What choices of action are there?
4. **Predict consequences.** What are the pros and cons of each alternative?
5. **Make a decision.** Choose a course of action based on the facts and evidence you have found.

Practice the Skill *Use the passage, poster, and table above to answer the following questions:*

1. What was James Adams's goal?
2. **(a)** What benefits did the Underground Railroad offer? **(b)** What were two dangers that people faced when escaping?
3. What alternatives did enslaved people have?
4. Identify two possible consequences of trying to escape.
5. What decision would you have made about escaping? Give reasons for your answer.

Apply the Skill *See the Chapter Review and Assessment.*

3 A Call for Women's Rights

Prepare to Read

Objectives

In this section, you will
- Explain why some women called for equal rights in the 1800s.
- List the goals that were set at the Seneca Falls Convention.
- Summarize how women won new educational opportunities.

Key Terms

Seneca Falls Convention

women's rights movement

Target Reading Skill

Sequence Copy this flowchart. As you read, fill in the boxes with information about the development of the women's rights movement. Two boxes have been begun to help you get started.

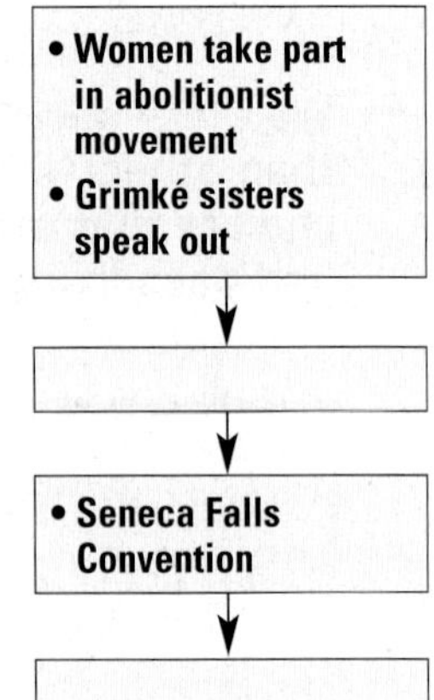

Main Idea The abolitionist movement helped spark a new reform movement that sought equality for women.

Sarah and Angelina Grimké

Setting the Scene As you have read, Sarah and Angelina Grimké became powerful speakers against slavery. However, their bold activities shocked many people, including some male abolitionists. Many ministers refused to let the Grimkés speak in their churches. One minister did allow them to speak—but left as soon as he introduced them. He announced that he would rather rob a chicken coop than hear a woman speaking in public.

A friend of the Grimkés made fun of such attitudes in a poem:

> ❝ They've taken a notion to speak for themselves,
> . . . And are wielding the tongue and the pen;
> They've mounted the rostrum; the [quarrelsome] elves!
> . . . And—oh horrid!—are talking to men! ❞
>
> —Maria Chapman, "The Times That Try Men's Souls"

More determined than ever, the Grimkés continued their crusade. "Can you not see," Angelina asked one abolitionist, "that woman could do and would do a hundred times more for the slave, if she were not fettered?" Now, however, the Grimkés had a second topic to lecture about: women's rights.

Seeking Equal Rights

Women had few political or legal rights in the mid-1800s. They could not vote or hold office. When a woman married, her husband became owner of all her property. If a woman worked outside the home, her wages belonged to her husband. A husband also had the right to hit his wife as long as he did not seriously injure her.

Many women, like the Grimkés, had joined the abolitionist movement. As these women worked to end slavery, they became aware that they lacked full social and political rights themselves. Both black and white abolitionists, men and women, joined the struggle for women's rights.

Sojourner Truth One of the most effective women's rights leaders was born into slavery in New York. Her original name was Isabella. After gaining freedom, she came to believe that God wanted her to fight slavery. Vowing to sojourn, or travel, across the land speaking the truth, she took the name Sojourner Truth.

Truth was a spellbinding speaker. Her exact words were rarely written down. However, her message spread by word of mouth. According to one witness, Truth ridiculed the idea that women were inferior to men by nature:

> “I have as much muscle as any man, and can do as much work as any man. I have plowed and reaped and husked and chopped and mowed, and can any man do more than that?”
>
> —Sojourner Truth, speech at Akron women's rights convention, 1851

Mott and Stanton Other abolitionists also turned to the cause of women's rights. The two most influential were Lucretia Mott and Elizabeth Cady Stanton. Lucretia Mott was a Quaker and the mother of five children. A quiet speaker, she won the respect of many listeners with her persuasive logic. Mott also used her organizing skills to set up petition drives across the North.

Elizabeth Cady Stanton was the daughter of a New York judge. As a child, she was an excellent student and an athlete. However, her father gave her little encouragement. Stanton later remarked that her "father would have felt a proper pride had I been a man."

In 1840, Stanton and Mott joined a group of Americans at a World Antislavery Convention in London. However, convention officials refused to let women take an active part in the proceedings. Female delegates were even forced to sit behind a curtain, hidden from view. After returning home, Mott and Stanton took up the cause of women's rights with new energy.

An American Profile

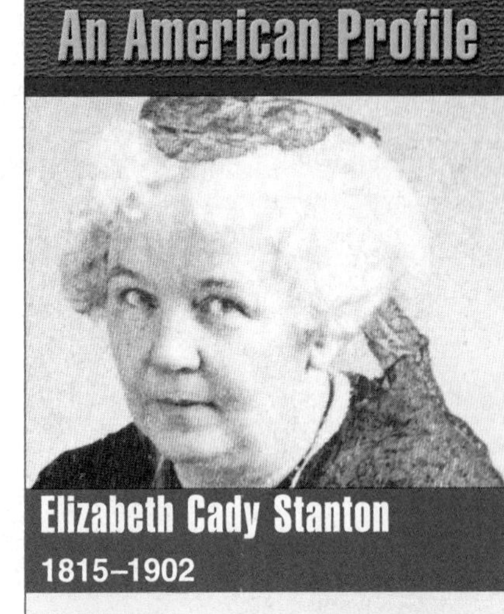

Elizabeth Cady Stanton
1815–1902

Elizabeth Cady's first memory was of adult visitors sympathizing with her parents on the birth of her younger sister. Another girl! Witty, energetic Elizabeth was viewed as a rebellious daughter who loved riding horses, detested sewing, and enjoyed spending time in her father's law office. There, the clerks teased her by reading aloud laws that denied basic rights to women.

In 1839, Cady met abolitionist Henry Stanton. At their wedding ceremony, the couple removed the word "obey" from their vows. Elizabeth Cady Stanton chose to obey only her sense of right and wrong.

How did her childhood experiences influence Stanton's career?

Seneca Falls Convention

Even in London, Mott and Stanton had begun thinking about holding a convention to draw attention to the problems women faced. "The men . . . had [shown] a great need for some education on that question," Stanton later recalled. The meeting finally took place in 1848 in Seneca Falls, New York.

"Women Are Created Equal" About 200 women and 40 men attended the **Seneca Falls Convention.** The delegates approved a *Declaration of Sentiments,* modeled on the Declaration of Independence. It proclaimed, "We hold these truths to be self-evident: that all men and women are created equal."

The women and men at Seneca Falls voted for resolutions that demanded equality for women at work, at school, and at church. Only one resolution met with any opposition at the convention. It demanded that women be allowed to vote. Even the bold reformers at Seneca Falls hesitated to take this step. In the end, the resolution narrowly passed.

Linking Past and Present

▲ Past

▲ Present

Viewing History

Reforming Fashions

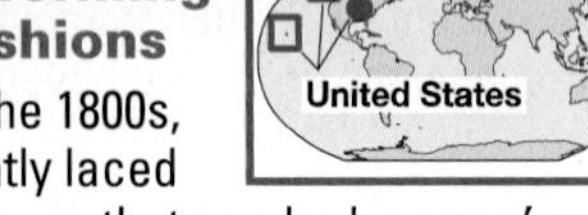

In the 1800s, tightly laced dresses that crushed women's rib cages often caused them to faint. Journalist Amelia Bloomer promoted a new fashion: loose-fitting trousers. Many Americans objected to these "bloomers" (left). Today, Amelia Bloomer would be pleased to see that women wear comfortable clothes every day.

Linking Past and Present
Do changing fashions ever cause controversy today? Give examples.

A Long Struggle The Seneca Falls Convention marked the start of an organized campaign for equal rights, or the **women's rights movement.** Other leaders took up the struggle. Susan B. Anthony built a close working partnership with Elizabeth Cady Stanton. While Stanton usually had to stay at home with her seven children, Anthony was free to travel across the country. Anthony was a tireless speaker. Even when audiences heckled her and threw eggs, she always finished her speech.

In the years after 1848, women worked for change in many areas. They won additional legal rights in some states. For example, New York passed laws allowing married women to keep their own property and wages. Still, many men and women opposed the women's rights movement. The struggle for equal rights would last many years.

New Opportunities in Education

The women at Seneca Falls believed that education was a key to equality. Elizabeth Cady Stanton said:

> ❝ The girl must be allowed to romp and play, climb, skate, and swim. Her clothing must be more like those of the boy—strong, loose-fitting garments, thick boots. . . . She must be taught to look forward to a life of self-dependence and, like the boy, prepare herself for some [profitable] trade profession. ❞
>
> —Elizabeth Cady Stanton, Letter, 1851

Such an idea was startling in the early 1800s. Women from poor families had little hope of learning even to read. Middle-class girls who went to school learned dancing and drawing rather than science or mathematics. After all, people argued, women were expected to care for their families. Why did they need an education?

Identify Sequence What events led to more educational opportunities for girls and women? Put these events on your flowchart.

Schools for Women Reformers worked to improve education for women. Emma Willard opened a high school for girls in Troy, New York. Here, young women studied "men's" subjects, such as mathematics and physics.

Mary Lyon opened Mount Holyoke Female Seminary in Massachusetts in 1837. She did not call the school a college because many people thought it was wrong for women to attend college. In fact, however, Mount Holyoke was the first women's college in the United States.

New Careers At about this time, a few men's colleges began to admit women. As their education improved, women found jobs teaching, especially in grade schools.

A few women entered fields such as medicine. Elizabeth Blackwell attended medical school at Geneva College in New York. To the surprise of school officials, she graduated first in her class. Women had provided medical care since colonial times, but Blackwell was the first woman in the United States to earn a medical degree. She later helped found the nation's first medical school for women.

Women made their mark in other fields as well. Maria Mitchell was a noted astronomer. Sarah Josepha Hale edited *Godey's Lady's Book*, an influential magazine for women. Antoinette Blackwell became the first American woman ordained a minister. She also campaigned for abolitionism, temperance, and women's right to vote.

★ ★ ★ Section 3 Assessment ★ ★ ★

Recall

1. **Identify** Explain the significance of **(a)** Sojourner Truth, **(b)** Elizabeth Cady Stanton, **(c)** Seneca Falls Convention, **(d)** Emma Willard, **(e)** Elizabeth Blackwell.
2. **Define** women's rights movement.

Comprehension

3. What legal rights did women lack in the early 1800s?
4. **(a)** Why did Mott and Stanton organize a women's rights convention? **(b)** Describe two resolutions passed by the convention.
5. How did reformers change education for women?

Critical Thinking and Writing

6. **Exploring the Main Idea** Review the Main Idea statement at the beginning of this section. Then, write a sentence summarizing the link between the abolitionist and women's rights movements.
7. **Making Predictions** How do you think the growth of educational opportunities in the mid-1800s would affect the future of the women's rights movement later in the century? Write a paragraph explaining the reasons for your prediction.

ACTIVITY

Designing a Banner
With a partner, design a banner to be displayed at the Seneca Falls Convention. Make a clever and attractive design that expresses the feelings of early women's rights crusaders. Include a brief slogan.

4 American Art and Literature

Prepare to Read

Objectives

In this section, you will
- Describe the new style of American painting.
- Summarize themes that American writers explored.
- Identify why the "inner light" was important to Emerson and Thoreau.

Key Terms

Hudson River School

transcendentalist

individualism

civil disobedience

Target Reading Skill

Main Idea Copy the concept web below. As you read, fill in the blank ovals with information about American art and literature. Add as many ovals as you need.

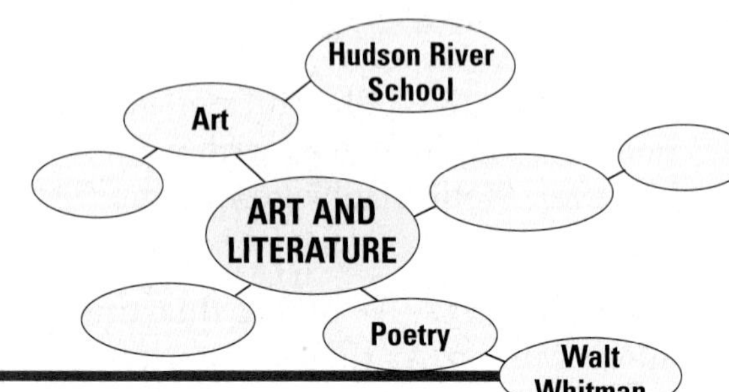

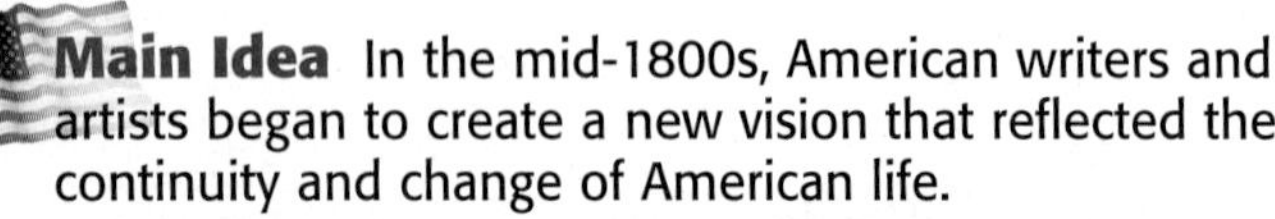

Main Idea In the mid-1800s, American writers and artists began to create a new vision that reflected the continuity and change of American life.

Painter's easel and equipment

Setting the Scene In 1820, a Scottish minister named Sydney Smith deplored what he saw as a lack of culture in the United States:

> "In the four quarters of the globe, who reads an American book? Or goes to an American play? Or looks at an American picture or statue? What does the world yet owe to Americans?"
>
> —Sydney Smith, *The Edinburgh Review*

Even as Smith wrote these words, American artists and writers were breaking free of European traditions to create a unique American vision. At the same time, their work expressed universal themes—such as the love of nature or the desire for liberty—that appealed to audiences far beyond the United States.

American Painters

Before 1800, most American painters studied in Europe. Benjamin West of Philadelphia was appointed historical painter to King George III. Many American painters journeyed to London to study with West. Two of them, Charles Willson Peale and Gilbert Stuart, later painted famous portraits of George Washington.

By the mid-1800s, American artists began to develop their own style. The first group to do so became known as the **Hudson River School.** Artists such as Thomas Cole and Asher B. Durand painted vivid landscapes of New York's Hudson River region. African American artist Robert S. Duncanson reflected the style of the Hudson River School.

Other artists painted scenes of hard-working country people. George Caleb Bingham of Missouri created a timeless picture of frontier life along the rivers that feed the great Mississippi. George Catlin and Alfred Jacob Miller traveled to the Far West to record the daily life of Indians on the Great Plains and in the Rockies.

The Poetry of Democracy

Henry Wadsworth Longfellow was the favorite poet of Americans in the mid-1800s. Longfellow based many poems on events from the past. "Paul Revere's Ride" honored the Revolutionary War hero. "The Song of Hiawatha" idealized Native American life.

Other poets spoke out on social issues. John Greenleaf Whittier, a Quaker from Massachusetts, and Frances Watkins Harper, an African American woman from Maryland, used their pens to make readers aware of the evils of slavery.

Walt Whitman published only one book of poems, *Leaves of Grass.* However, he added to it over a period of 27 years. Whitman had great faith in the common people. His poetry celebrated democracy. He wrote proudly of being part of a "nation of many nations":

> "At home on the hills of Vermont or in the
> woods of Maine, or the Texan ranch,
> Comrade of Californians, comrade of free
> North-Westerners. . . .
> Of every hue and caste am I, of every rank
> and religion."
>
> —Walt Whitman, *Song of Myself*

Viewing History

Hudson River School

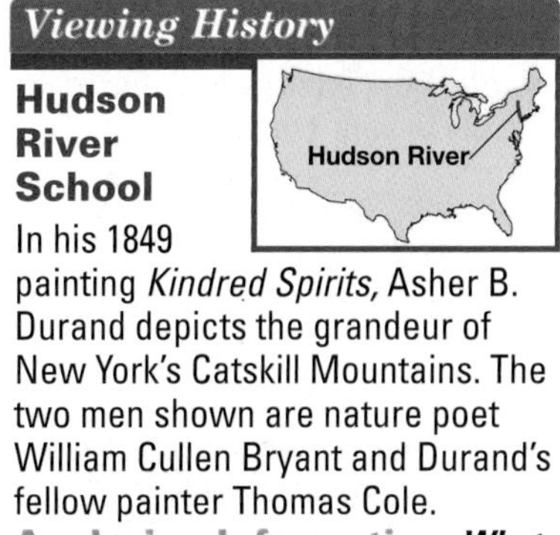

In his 1849 painting *Kindred Spirits,* Asher B. Durand depicts the grandeur of New York's Catskill Mountains. The two men shown are nature poet William Cullen Bryant and Durand's fellow painter Thomas Cole. **Analyzing Information** ***What kinds of emotions might a painting like this stir?***

Only seven of Emily Dickinson's more than 1,700 poems were published in her lifetime. A shy woman who rarely left her home, Dickinson called her poetry "my letter to the world / That never wrote to me." Today, she is recognized as one of the nation's greatest poets.

Novels and Stories

Like painters, early American writers also depended on Europe for their ideas and inspiration. In the 1820s, however, a new crop of writers began to write stories with American themes.

Two Early Writers One of the most popular American writers was Washington Irving, a New Yorker. Irving first became known for *The Sketch Book,* a collection of tales published in 1820. Two of his best-loved tales are "Rip Van Winkle" and "The Legend of Sleepy Hollow."

The exciting novels of James Fenimore Cooper were also set in the American past. In *The Deerslayer* and *The Last of the Mohicans,* Cooper created Natty Bumppo, a heroic model of a strong, solitary frontiersman. The novels gave an idealized view of relations between whites and Native Americans on the frontier.

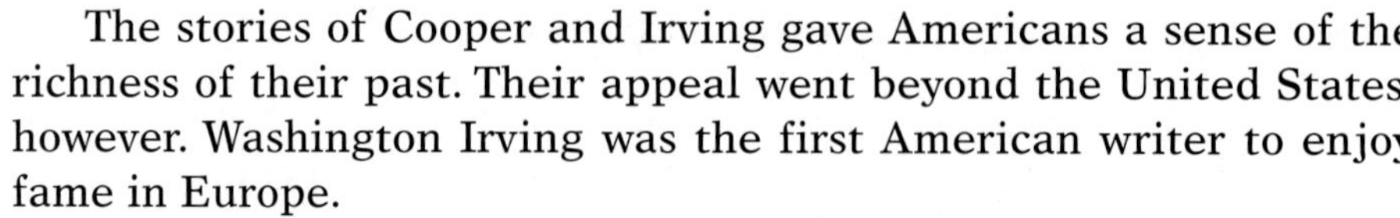

The stories of Cooper and Irving gave Americans a sense of the richness of their past. Their appeal went beyond the United States, however. Washington Irving was the first American writer to enjoy fame in Europe.

Later Writers In 1851, Herman Melville published *Moby-Dick.* The novel tells the story of Ahab, the crazed captain of a whaling ship. Ahab vows revenge on the white whale that years earlier bit off his leg. *Moby-Dick* had only limited success when it was first published. Today, however, critics rank it among the finest American novels.

Target Skill: Identify Supporting Details

Which details in this paragraph give examples of the types of novels written during the mid-nineteenth century? Add these details to your concept web.

Nathaniel Hawthorne often drew on the history of New England in his novels and short stories. In *The Scarlet Letter,* published in 1850, Hawthorne explored Puritan notions of sin and salvation. The novel shows how a young man is consumed by guilt when he tries to hide his wrongdoing from the world.

Edgar Allan Poe became famous for his many tales of horror. His short story "The Tell-Tale Heart" is about a murderer, driven mad by guilt, who imagines he can hear his victim's heartbeat. Poe is also known as the "father of the detective story" for his mystery stories, such as "The Murders in the Rue Morgue."

William Wells Brown was the first African American to earn his living as a writer. He published *Clotel,* a novel about slave life, in 1853. Brown also wrote a play inspired by his own experiences as a fugitive slave and a conductor on the Underground Railroad. His lectures and readings drew large audiences in Europe as well as throughout the North.

Viewing History

Sleepy Hollow "The Legend of Sleepy Hollow," by Washington Irving, remains one of the most popular American stories. This modern statue depicts the Headless Horseman that terrified schoolteacher Ichabod Crane. **Linking Past and Present** ***Why do you think this story is so popular?***

Women Writers Many best-selling novels of the period were written by women. Some novels told about young women who gained wealth and happiness through honesty and self-sacrifice. Others showed the hardships faced by widows and orphans.

Few of these novels are read today. However, writers like Catherine Sedgwick and Fanny Fern earned far more than Hawthorne or Melville. Hawthorne complained about the success of a "mob of scribbling women."

The "Inner Light"

In New England, a small but influential group of writers and thinkers emerged. They called themselves **transcendentalists** because they believed that the most important truths in life transcended, or went beyond, human reason. Transcendentalists valued the spark of deeply felt emotions more than reason. They believed that each individual should live up to the divine possibilities within. This belief influenced many transcendentalists to support social reform.

Emerson The leading transcendentalist was Ralph Waldo Emerson. Emerson was the most popular essayist and lecturer of his day. Audiences flocked to hear him talk on subjects such as self-reliance and character. Emerson believed that the human spirit was reflected in nature. Civilization might provide material wealth, he said, but nature exhibited higher values that came from God.

In his essays and lectures, Emerson stressed **individualism,** or the importance of each individual. Each person, Emerson said, has an "inner light." He urged people to use this inner light to guide their lives and improve society. "Trust thyself," he wrote. "Every heart vibrates to that iron string."

Thoreau Henry David Thoreau (thuh ROW), Emerson's friend and neighbor, believed that the growth of industry and the rise of cities were ruining the nation. He urged people to live as simply and as close to nature as possible. In *Walden,* his best-known work, Thoreau describes spending a year alone in a cabin on Walden Pond in Massachusetts.

Like Emerson, Thoreau believed that each individual must decide what is right or wrong. "If a man does not keep pace with his companions," he wrote, in *Walden*, "perhaps it is because he hears a different drummer. Let him step to the music he hears."

Thoreau's "different drummer" told him that slavery was wrong. He argued in favor of **civil disobedience,** the idea that people have a right to disobey unjust laws if their consciences demand it. He once went to jail for refusing to pay taxes to support the Mexican War, which he felt promoted slavery. Thoreau's writings on civil disobedience and nonviolence later influenced Mohandas Gandhi and Martin Luther King, Jr.

Primary Source

Civil Disobedience

In his famous essay "Civil Disobedience," Henry David Thoreau discussed his refusal to pay taxes to support the Mexican War:

"I have paid no poll tax for six years. I was put into a jail once on this account, for one night; and, as I stood considering the walls of solid stone, two or three feet thick, the door of wood and iron, a foot thick, and the iron grating which strained the light, I could not help being struck with the foolishness of that institution which treated me as if I were mere flesh and blood and bones, to be locked up. . . . I was not born to be forced. I will breathe after my own fashion. Let us see who is the strongest."

—Henry David Thoreau, "Civil Disobedience"

Analyzing Primary Sources

How does this passage show Thoreau's belief in the individual conscience?

★ ★ ★ Section 4 Assessment ★ ★ ★

Recall

1. **Identify** Explain the significance of **(a)** Hudson River School, **(b)** Emily Dickinson, **(c)** Washington Irving, **(d)** Herman Melville, **(e)** William Wells Brown, **(f)** Ralph Waldo Emerson, **(g)** Henry David Thoreau.
2. **Define** **(a)** transcendentalist, **(b)** individualism, **(c)** civil disobedience.

Comprehension

3. How did American painting change in the mid-1800s?
4. Describe the themes explored by two of the following: **(a)** Henry Wadsworth Longfellow, **(b)** Walt Whitman, **(c)** James Fenimore Cooper, **(d)** Nathaniel Hawthorne.
5. Identify the reasons for and the impact of Thoreau's idea of civil disobedience.

Critical Thinking and Writing

6. **Exploring the Main Idea** Review the Main Idea statement at the beginning of this section. Then, analyze how the work of one writer reflected continuity or change in American life.
7. **Drawing Conclusions** List two themes expressed by American writers. For each one, give reasons why it was also meaningful to audiences outside the United States.

ACTIVITY

Writing a Museum Guide

Use the Internet to find other examples of American painting from 1800–1865. Choose one work, and write a description that might appear in a museum guide. Include the title, artist, and date, as well as a description of the subject matter. For help in completing the activity, visit PHSchool.com, **Web Code mfd-1503.**

CHAPTER 15

Review and Assessment

Chapter Summary

Section 1
A reforming impulse led to the Second Great Awakening. It also produced leaders who attacked problems in hospitals, prisons, politics, and education. The temperance movement battled alcohol abuse.

Section 2
The abolitionist movement arose in the North. The Underground Railroad helped slaves escape to freedom. Southerners opposed the abolitionists.

Section 3
The women's rights movement was born at the Seneca Falls Convention of 1848. New educational and career opportunities opened for women in the 1800s.

Section 4
A first wave of U.S. painters, poets, and writers with an American-inspired vision emerged in the 1800s. New England transcendentalists gave birth to two new ideas: individualism and civil disobedience.

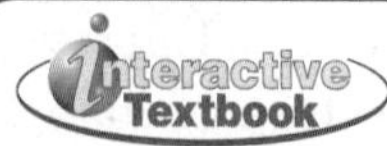

For additional review and enrichment activities, see the interactive version of *The American Nation,* available on the Web and on CD-ROM.

Chapter Self-Test For practice test questions for Chapter 15, visit PHSchool.com, **Web Code mfa-1504.**

Building Vocabulary

Use the chapter vocabulary words listed below to create a crossword puzzle. Exchange puzzles with a classmate. Complete the puzzles, and then check each other's answers.

1. **social reform**
2. **predestination**
3. **revival**
4. **debtor**
5. **abolitionist**
6. **Underground Railroad**
7. **women's rights movement**
8. **individualism**

Reviewing Key Facts

9. What were the effects of the Second Great Awakening? (Section 1)
10. How did public education improve in the early 1800s? (Section 1)
11. How did abolitionists achieve their goals? (Section 2)
12. What ideas were contained in the Seneca Falls Declaration of Sentiments? (Section 3)
13. Identify two writers who explored the American past in their work. (Section 4)

Critical Thinking and Writing

14. **Drawing Inferences** In his *Appeal to the Colored Citizens of the World,* David Walker wrote that "all men are created equal; that they are endowed by their Creator with certain inalienable rights." **(a)** From which document did Walker borrow this idea? **(b)** Write a paragraph explaining why he included this phrase.
15. **Comparing** Compare the abolitionist movement and the women's rights movement in terms of causes and impact.
16. **Connecting to Geography: Place** Look at the painting from the Hudson River School in Section 4. Write down five adjectives that describe the geographic setting of the painting. Then, list five places or types of landform found in the United States that you think would attract landscape painters.
17. **Synthesizing Information** Write a paragraph explaining how the Second Great Awakening, the educational reform movement, and the work of Emerson and Thoreau all stressed the importance of the individual.

Skills Assessment

Analyzing Primary Sources

At an 1852 abolitionist meeting in Rochester, New York, Frederick Douglass denounced the continuing slave trade in the United States:

> “Fellow citizens, this murderous traffic is, today, in active operation in this boasted republic. In the solitude of my spirit, I see clouds of dust raised on the highways of the South; I see the bleeding footsteps; I hear the doleful [sad] wail of fettered humanity on the way to the slave markets where victims are to be sold like horse, sheep, and swine. . . . My soul sickens at the sight.”
>
> —Frederick Douglass, "What, to the Slave, Is the Fourth of July?"

18. What emotion is Douglass trying to stir up?
- **A.** joy
- **B.** complacency
- **C.** outrage
- **D.** despair

19. What point is Douglass making by using the phrase *boasted republic?*
- **A.** The United States should be proud of its plentiful livestock.
- **B.** The United States leads the way in opposing murder.
- **C.** The United States is home to brave individuals who carry on despite their hardships.
- **D.** The existence of slavery undermines the U.S. boast that the nation is a land of the free.

Applying Your Skills

Making Decisions

ARGUMENTS FOR	ARGUMENTS AGAINST
A. Men, women, and children live in poor conditions	**C.** Cost of building new prisons is too high
B. Eighth Amendment prohibits "cruel and unusual" punishment	**D.** Tax money should be used to benefit law-abiding citizens

You are a state legislator trying to decide whether to use state money to build new prisons. Copy the table above. Add any arguments for or against. Then, answer the following questions:

20. Argument B is most closely linked to
- **A.** Second Great Awakening
- **B.** Declaration of Independence
- **C.** Bill of Rights
- **D.** Economics

21. Would you have voted in favor of funding new prisons? Explain your decision.

Activities

Connecting With . . . Culture

Writing a Song With a group of students, write a marching song that might have been used at one of the following events: a temperance rally, an abolitionist meeting, a march for women's rights. Use a familiar tune, or write your own. Write words. Include a refrain, or repeated phrase, that emphasizes the main goal of the song. Gather musical instruments, and perform the song in class.

Researching

Preparing a Biographical Sketch Use the Internet to find information on one of the following women: Antoinette Blackwell, Sara Josepha Hale, Emily Blackwell, Elizabeth Blackwell, Amelia Bloomer, Myra Bradwell, Margaret Fuller, Mary Ann Cary, Maria Mitchell, or Lucy Stone. Write a brief sketch explaining her contribution to women's rights. Include a timeline of major events in her life. For help in starting this activity, visit PHSchool.com, **Web Code mfd-1506.**

TEST PREPARATION

1 "Individual reform is the first step toward social reform." This statement represents a key idea of what reform movement?

A The Second Great Awakening

B The temperance movement

C The abolitionist movement

D The women's rights movement

Use the quotation and your knowledge of social studies to answer the following question.

> **Daniel Webster, Reply to Robert Hayne, 1830** (adapted)
>
> "While the people choose to maintain the Constitution as it is, while they are satisfied with it, and refuse to change it, who has given, or who can give, to the state legislatures a right to alter it?"

2 What idea or policy is the subject of Webster's speech?

A Nullification

B Manifest Destiny

C Federalism

D Civil disobedience

3 What was one result of the rise of the Cotton Kingdom?

A Slavery began to decline.

B The South developed an industrial economy.

C Eli Whitney invented the cotton gin.

D Large planters gained political influence.

Use the map and your knowledge of social studies to answer the following question.

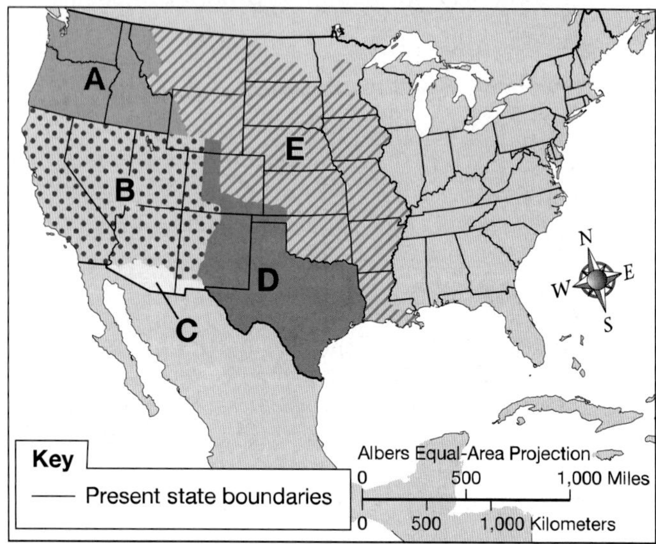

4 Which two areas shown on this map did the United States acquire by the same method?

A A and B

B C and E

C B and D

D C and D

5 How were the works of James Fenimore Cooper similar to those of Henry Wadsworth Longfellow?

A Both were best known for their poetry.

B Both used their pens to oppose slavery.

C Both explored historical subjects in their work.

D Both were transcendentalists.

6 Which statement is true of both Texas and California?

A It was admitted to the Union as a slave state.

B American settlers there rebelled against Mexican rule.

C It became part of the United States as a result of the Mexican War.

D Its annexation was an important issue in the election of 1844.

Use the graph <u>and</u> your knowledge of social studies to answer the following question.

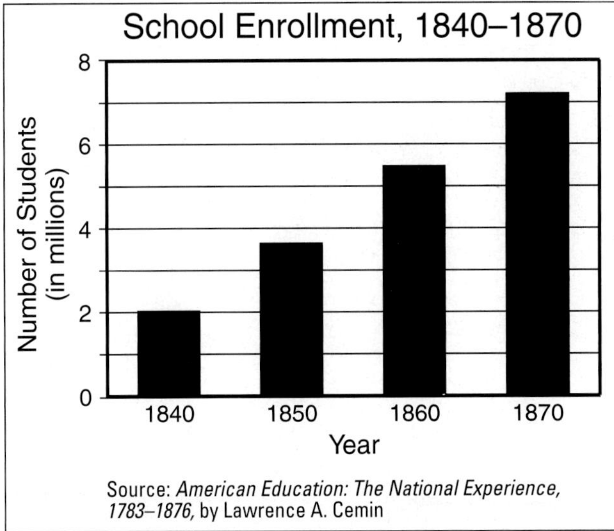

Source: *American Education: The National Experience, 1783–1876,* by Lawrence A. Cemin

7 The trend shown on this graph is most closely related to what development?

A The expansion of voting rights

B Increased immigration from Ireland

C The abolitionist movement

D The rise of the Hudson River School

8 Which slogan best reflects the main beliefs of the Know-Nothing party?

A "Fifty-four forty or fight!"

B "America for Americans!"

C "To the victor go the spoils!"

D "Stamp out demon rum!"

9 Which was one result of Andrew Jackson's Native American policy?

A The Seminole nation was completely destroyed.

B The United States annexed Florida and Texas.

C Few Native Americans remained east of the Mississippi.

D War broke out between the United States Army and the Cherokees.

Writing Practice

10 Describe and evaluate one political, one social, and one economic effect of westward expansion.

11 Analyze the impact of transportation systems on the nation. Choose at least two advances in transportation and explain how each one affected the growth, development, or urbanization of the United States.

Unit 5 Division and Reunion

UNIT OUTLINE

The Soldiers of the Civil War
In ***A Rainy Day in Camp*** by Winslow Homer, Civil War soldiers find time to gather around a campfire.

"Union! I can more easily conceive of the Lion and Lambs lying down together, than of a union of the North and South."

—Sarah Chase, Massachusetts teacher in the South (1866)

CHAPTER 16

Slavery Divides the Nation

1820–1861

1 Slavery in the Territories
2 The Compromise of 1850
3 The Crisis Deepens
4 The Republican Party Emerges
5 A Nation Divides

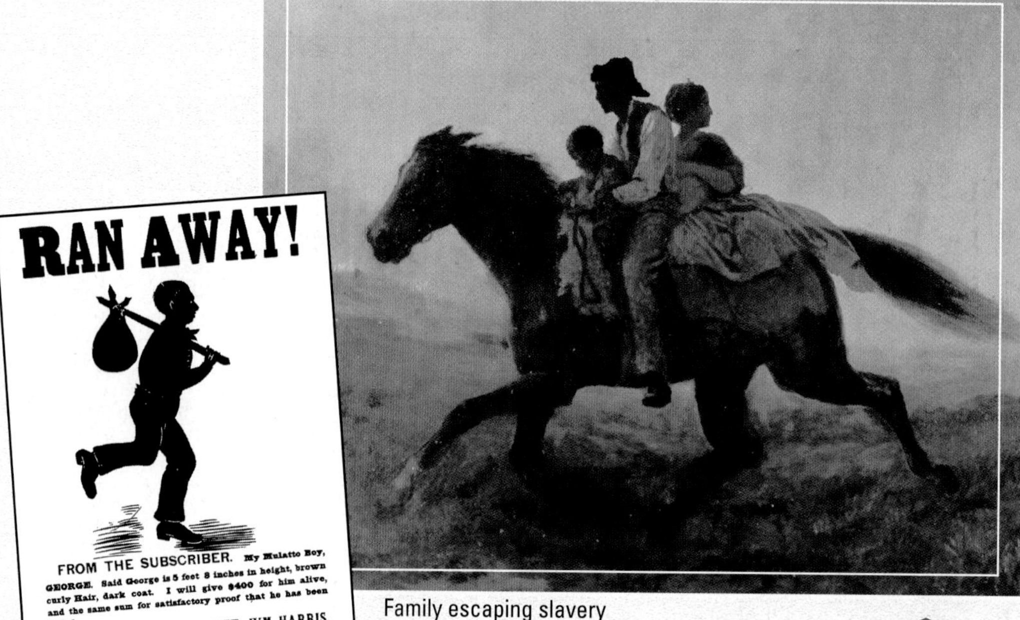

Fugitive slave poster

Family escaping slavery

AMERICAN EVENTS

1820 The Missouri Compromise maintains the balance of free and slave states in the Union.

John Quincy Adams	1825–1829
Andrew Jackson	1829–1837
Martin Van Buren	1837–1841
William Henry Harrison	1841

1848 The Free-Soil party is formed to oppose the extension of slavery in the West.

1850 Congress passes the Compromise of 1850. One new law requires all Americans to help recapture fugitive slaves.

Presidential Terms: James Monroe 1817–1825 | John Tyler 1841–1845 | James K. Polk 1845–1849 | Zachary Taylor 1849–1850

1820 · 1845 · 1850

WORLD EVENTS

▲ 1833 Slavery is abolished in the British Empire.

1850 ▲ Civil war breaks out in China.

Slave and Free States, 1850

As new states entered the Union, the balance between slave and free states became harder to maintain.

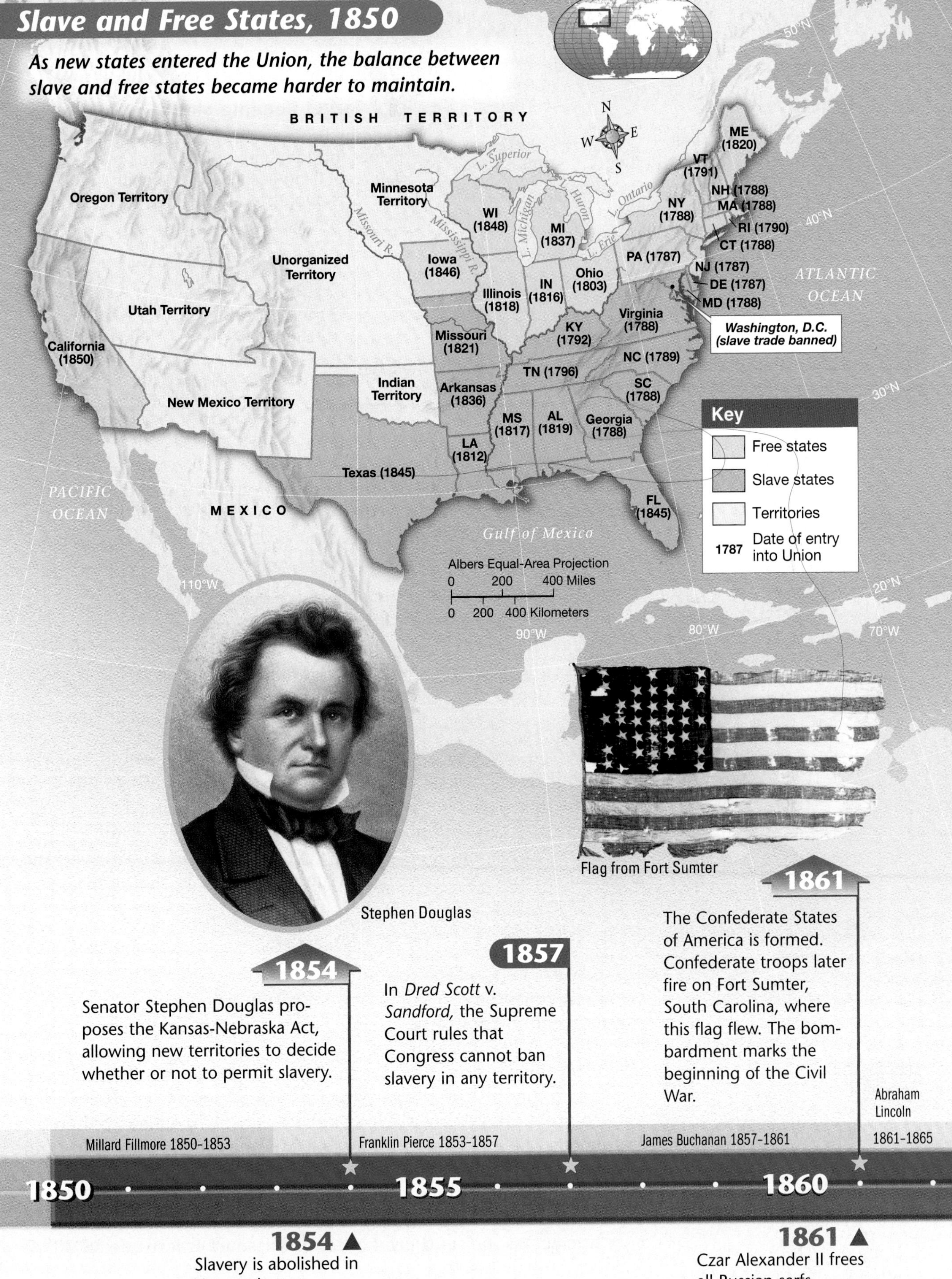

Stephen Douglas

Flag from Fort Sumter

1854 Senator Stephen Douglas proposes the Kansas-Nebraska Act, allowing new territories to decide whether or not to permit slavery.

1857 In *Dred Scott* v. *Sandford,* the Supreme Court rules that Congress cannot ban slavery in any territory.

1861 The Confederate States of America is formed. Confederate troops later fire on Fort Sumter, South Carolina, where this flag flew. The bombardment marks the beginning of the Civil War.

Millard Fillmore 1850–1853 | Franklin Pierce 1853–1857 | James Buchanan 1857–1861 | Abraham Lincoln 1861–1865

1850 · 1855 · 1860

1854 ▲ Slavery is abolished in Venezuela.

1861 ▲ Czar Alexander II frees all Russian serfs.

1 Slavery in the Territories

Prepare to Read

Objectives

In this section, you will
- Describe the purpose of the Missouri Compromise.
- Explain why conflict arose over the issue of slavery in the western territories.
- Identify why the Free-Soil party was founded.

Key Terms

Missouri Compromise

Wilmot Proviso

popular sovereignty

Free-Soil party

Target Reading Skill

Reading Process Copy the concept web below. Include three or four blank ovals. As you read, fill in each blank oval with important facts about slavery in the territories.

Main Idea The Missouri Compromise attempted to settle the issue of whether slavery should be allowed in the western territories.

Jefferson at 78

Setting the Scene When he reached his seventies, Thomas Jefferson vowed "never to write, talk, or even think of politics." Still, in 1820 at the age of 77, he broke this vow. Jefferson voiced alarm at the fierce debate going on in Congress:

> "This momentous question, like a fire bell in the night, awakened and filled me with terror. I considered it at once as the [funeral bells] of the Union. . . . We have the wolf by the ears, and we can neither hold him, nor safely let him go."
>
> —Thomas Jefferson, Letter to John Holmes, April 22, 1820

Jefferson knew the "wolf," or the issue of slavery, could tear the North and South apart. As settlers moved west, Congress faced an agonizing decision. Should it ban slavery in the territories and later admit them to the Union as free states? Or should it permit slavery in the territories and later admit them as slave states? This was the critical question that filled Jefferson with terror in the night.

The Missouri Compromise

There were 11 free states and 11 slave states in 1819. That year, Congress considered Missouri's application to join the Union as a slave state. Immediately, a crisis erupted. Missouri's admission would give the South a majority in the Senate. Determined not to lose power, northerners opposed letting Missouri enter as a slave state.

The argument lasted many months. Finally, Senator Henry Clay made a proposal. During the long debate, Maine had also applied for statehood. Clay suggested admitting Missouri as a slave state and Maine as a free state. His plan, called the **Missouri Compromise,** kept the number of slave and free states equal.

As part of the Missouri Compromise, Congress drew an imaginary line across the southern border of Missouri at latitude 36°30′ N.

Slavery was permitted in the part of the Louisiana Purchase south of that line. It was banned north of the Missouri Compromise line. The only exception to this was Missouri itself.

Slavery in the West

The Missouri Compromise applied only to the Louisiana Purchase. In 1848, the Mexican War added vast western lands to the United States. Once again, the question of slavery in the territories arose.

Wilmot Proviso Many northerners feared that the South would extend slavery into the West. David Wilmot, a member of Congress from Pennsylvania, called for a law to ban slavery in any territories won from Mexico. Southern leaders angrily opposed this **Wilmot Proviso.** They said that Congress had no right to ban slavery in the West.

The House passed the Wilmot Proviso in 1846, but the Senate defeated it. As a result, Americans continued to argue about slavery in the West even while their army fought in Mexico.

Opposing Views As the debate heated up, people found it hard not to take sides. Abolitionists wanted slavery banned throughout the country. They insisted that slavery was morally wrong.

Southern slaveholders thought that slavery should be allowed in any territory. They also demanded that slaves who escaped to the North be returned to them. Even white southerners who did not own slaves generally agreed with these ideas.

Between these two extreme views were more moderate positions. Some moderates argued that the Missouri Compromise line should be extended across the Mexican Cession to the Pacific. Any new state north of the line would be a free state. Any new state south of the line could

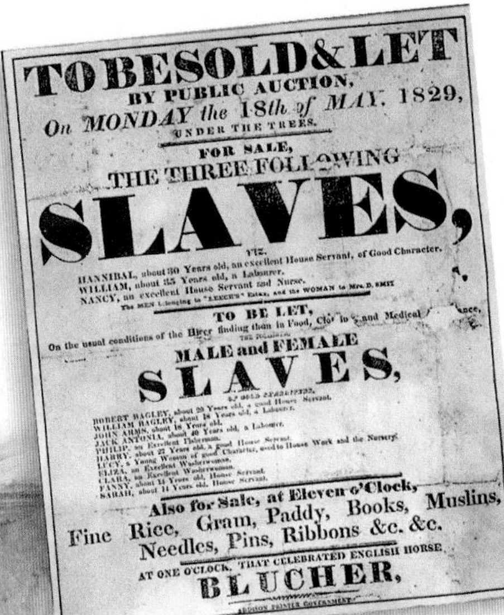

Viewing History

A Family for Sale

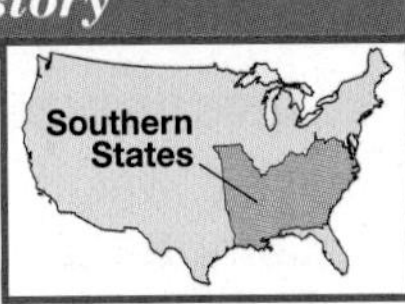

As Americans debated the issue of slavery, slave auctions continued in the South. The family members on the auction block here might never see each other again. **Drawing Inferences** ***What do the poster (above) and the painting (left) suggest about the attitude of slaveholders toward slaves?***

allow slavery. Other moderates supported the idea of **popular sovereignty,** or the right of people to create their government. Under popular sovereignty, voters in a new territory would decide for themselves whether or not to allow slavery.

The Free-Soil Party

The debate over slavery led to the birth of a new political party. By 1848, many northern Democrats and Whigs opposed the spread of slavery. However, the leaders of both parties refused to take a stand. They did not want to lose any southern votes. Some also feared that the slavery issue would split the nation.

In 1848, antislavery members of both parties met in Buffalo, New York. There, they founded the **Free-Soil party.** The main goal of the Free-Soil party was to keep slavery out of the western territories. Only a few Free-Soilers were abolitionists who wanted to end slavery in the South.

In the 1848 presidential campaign, Free-Soilers named former President Martin Van Buren as their candidate. Democrats chose Lewis Cass of Michigan. The Whigs selected Zachary Taylor, a hero of the Mexican War.

For the first time, slavery was an important election issue. Van Buren called for a ban on slavery in the Mexican Cession. Cass supported popular sovereignty. Taylor did not speak on the issue. However, because he was a slave owner from Louisiana, many southern voters assumed that he supported slavery.

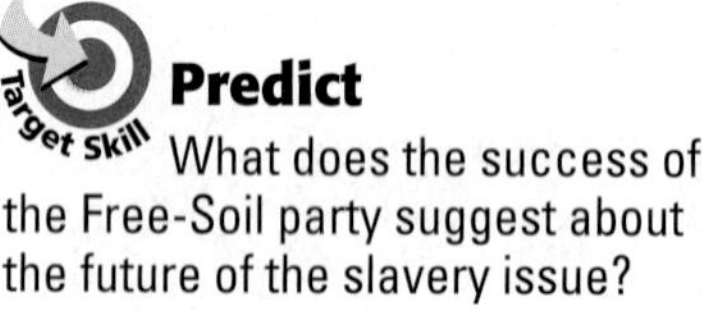

Predict What does the success of the Free-Soil party suggest about the future of the slavery issue?

Zachary Taylor won the election. Still, Van Buren took 10 percent of the popular vote, and 13 other Free-Soil candidates won seats in Congress. The success of the new Free-Soil party showed that slavery had become a national issue.

★ ★ ★ Section 1 Assessment ★ ★ ★

Recall

1. **Identify** Explain the significance of **(a)** Missouri Compromise, **(b)** Wilmot Proviso, **(c)** Free-Soil party, **(d)** Zachary Taylor.
2. **Define** popular sovereignty.

Comprehension

3. What was the Missouri Compromise?
4. Describe three conflicting views on slavery in the West.
5. Why did voters leave the Whig and Democratic parties to join the Free-Soil party in 1848?

Critical Thinking and Writing

6. **Exploring the Main Idea** Review the Main Idea statement at the beginning of this section. Then, write a paragraph explaining whether the Missouri Compromise settled the issue of slavery in the western territories.
7. **Drawing Conclusions** The goals of the Free-Soil party pleased some northerners but not others. Write a paragraph explaining why some northerners were pleased and others displeased by the Free-Soil party.

Activity

Drawing a Political Cartoon With a partner, plan and sketch a political cartoon about the issue of slavery in the western territories. Assume one of the opposing viewpoints described in this section: southern slaveholder, abolitionist, supporter of extending the Missouri Compromise line across the country, or supporter of popular sovereignty. Then, create a cartoon that represents your point of view.

2 The Compromise of 1850

Prepare to Read

Objectives

In this section, you will
- Explain why the slavery debate erupted again in 1850.
- Describe the impact of the Compromise of 1850.
- Summarize how *Uncle Tom's Cabin* affected attitudes toward slavery.

Key Terms

secede

fugitive

civil war

Compromise of 1850

Fugitive Slave Act

Uncle Tom's Cabin

Target Reading Skill

Cause and Effect As you read, complete the chart at right to show some of the causes and effects of the Compromise of 1850.

CAUSES
1. California seeks statehood
2.
3.

COMPROMISE OF 1850

EFFECTS
1. North reacts to Fugitive Slave Act
2.
3.

Main Idea The Compromise of 1850, which was supposed to save the Union, only inflamed tensions.

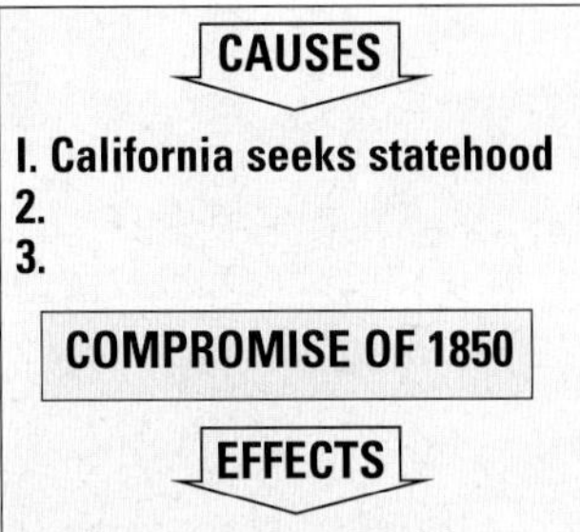

Violence threatens in the Senate

Setting the Scene Tempers in Congress had reached the boiling point. California had applied to be admitted to the Union as a free state in 1850. Senator Thomas Hart Benton of Missouri supported California's request. He denounced Senator Henry Foote of Mississippi for opposing California's admission.

In response, Senator Foote rose angrily, picked up a pistol, and aimed it at Benton. As other senators watched in horror, Benton turned toward Foote and roared, "Let him fire. Stand out of the way and let the assassin fire!"

No blood was shed in the Senate that day. However, even as Congress tried to reach a new compromise, many Americans began to fear that a peaceful solution to the slavery issue was impossible.

The Slavery Debate Erupts Again

For a time after the Missouri Compromise, both slave and free states entered the Union peacefully. However, when California requested admission to the Union as a free state in 1850, the balance of power in the Senate was once again threatened.

California's Impact In 1849, there were 15 slave states and 15 free states in the nation. If California entered the union as a free state, the balance of power would be broken. Furthermore, it seemed quite possible that Oregon, Utah, and New Mexico might also join the Union as free states.

Many southerners feared that the South would be hopelessly outvoted in the Senate. Some even suggested that southern states might want to **secede,** or remove themselves, from the United States. Northern congressmen, meanwhile, argued that California should enter the Union as a free state because most of the territory lay north of the Missouri Compromise line.

It was clear that the nation faced a crisis. Many in Congress looked to Senator Henry Clay for a solution.

Daniel Webster

Henry Clay

John C. Calhoun

Balance of Free and Slave States

Free States	Slave States
California (1850)	
Wisconsin (1848)	Texas (1845)
Iowa (1846)	Florida (1845)
Michigan (1837)	Arkansas (1836)
Maine (1820)	Missouri (1821)
Illinois (1818)	Alabama (1819)
Indiana (1816)	Mississippi (1817)
Ohio (1803)	Louisiana (1812)
Vermont (1791)	Tennessee (1796)
Rhode Island	Kentucky (1792)
New York	Virginia
New Hampshire	North Carolina
Massachusetts	South Carolina
Connecticut	Maryland
New Jersey	Georgia
Pennsylvania	Delaware

Original 13 states

Viewing History

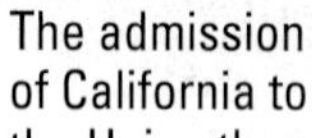

Crisis in the Senate

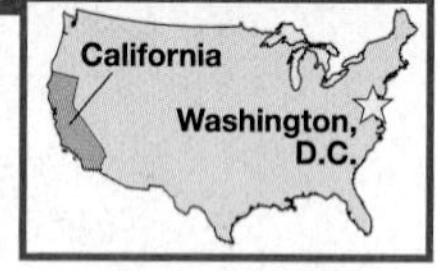

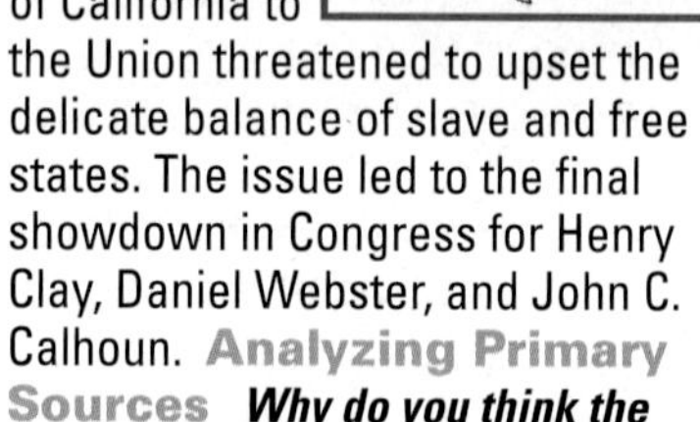

The admission of California to the Union threatened to upset the delicate balance of slave and free states. The issue led to the final showdown in Congress for Henry Clay, Daniel Webster, and John C. Calhoun. **Analyzing Primary Sources** ***Why do you think the gallery was filled with spectators to hear this debate?***

Clay vs. Calhoun Clay had won the nickname "the Great Compromiser" for working out the Missouri Compromise. Now, nearly 30 years later, the 73-year-old Clay was frail and ill. Still, he pleaded for the North and South to reach an agreement. If they failed to do so, Clay warned, the nation could break apart.

Senator John C. Calhoun of South Carolina replied to Clay. Calhoun was dying of tuberculosis and could not speak loudly enough to address the Senate. He stared defiantly at his northern foes while Senator James Mason of Virginia read his speech.

Calhoun refused to compromise. He insisted that slavery be allowed in the western territories. In addition, Calhoun demanded that **fugitive,** or runaway, slaves be returned to their owners. He wanted northerners to admit that southern slaveholders had the right to reclaim their "property."

If the North rejected the South's demands, Calhoun told the Senate, "let the states . . . agree to part in peace. If you are unwilling that we should part in peace, tell us so, and we shall know what to do." Everyone knew what Calhoun meant. If an agreement could not be reached, the South would use force to leave the Union.

Webster Calls for Unity Daniel Webster of Massachusetts spoke next. He supported Clay's plea to save the Union. Webster stated his position clearly:

> ❝ I speak today not as a Massachusetts man, nor as a northern man, but as an American. . . . I speak today for the preservation of the Union. . . . There can be no such thing as a peaceable secession. ❞
>
> —Daniel Webster, Speech in the U.S. Senate, July 17, 1850

Webster feared that the states could not separate without starting a bloody civil war. A **civil war** is a war between people of the same country.

Like many northerners, Webster viewed slavery as evil. The breakup of the United States, however, he believed was worse. To save the Union, Webster was willing to compromise. He would support southern demands that northerners be forced to return fugitive slaves.

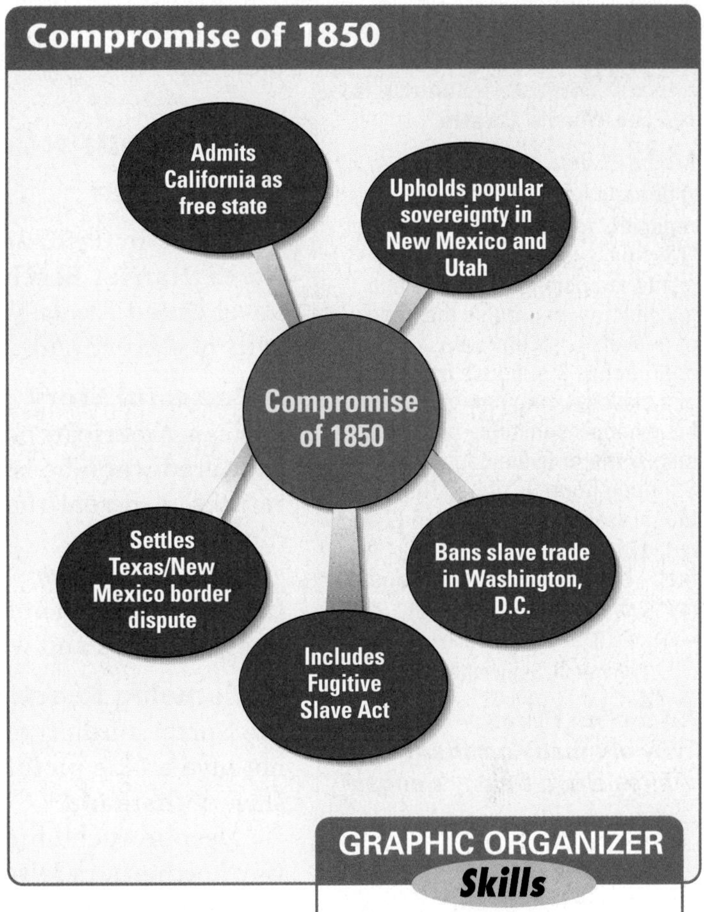

GRAPHIC ORGANIZER *Skills*

The Compromise of 1850 was a desperate attempt to save the Union.

1. **Comprehension** Which parts of the Compromise would have been favored by the South?
2. **Critical Thinking Identifying Points of View** Would an abolitionist approve of the Compromise of 1850? Why or why not?

Compromise of 1850

In 1850, as the debate raged, Calhoun died. His last words reportedly were "The South! The poor South! God knows what will become of her now!" President Taylor also died in 1850. The new President was Millard Fillmore. Unlike Taylor, he supported Clay's compromise plan.

The Compromise Passes Henry Clay gave more than 70 speeches in favor of a compromise. At last, however, he became too sick to continue. Stephen Douglas, of Illinois, took up the fight for him and guided Clay's plan, the **Compromise of 1850,** through Congress.

The Compromise of 1850 had five parts. First, it allowed California to enter the Union as a free state. Second, it divided the rest of the Mexican Cession into the territories of New Mexico and Utah. Voters in each would decide the slavery question according to popular sovereignty. Third, it ended the slave trade in Washington, D.C., the nation's capital. Congress, however, declared that it had no power to ban the slave trade between slave states. Fourth, it included a strict fugitive slave law. Fifth, it settled a border dispute between Texas and New Mexico.

Fugitive Slave Act The **Fugitive Slave Act** of 1850 required all citizens to help catch runaway slaves. People who let fugitives escape could be fined $1,000 and jailed. The new law also set up special courts to handle the cases of runaways. Suspects were not allowed a jury trial. Judges received $10 for sending an accused runaway to the South but only $5 for setting someone free. Lured by the extra money, some judges sent African Americans to the South whether or not they were runaways.

Identify Causes and Effects

Which factors on this page were effects of the Compromise of 1850? Add these to your chart.

Reaction The Fugitive Slave Act enraged antislavery northerners. By forcing them to catch runaways, the law made northerners feel as if they were part of the slave system. In several northern cities, crowds tried to rescue fugitive slaves from their captors.

Despite the compromise, tensions remained high because neither side got everything that it wanted. The new Fugitive Slave Act was especially hard for northerners to accept. Each time the act was enforced, it convinced more northerners that slavery was immoral and evil.

Primary Source

A Free Man's Castle

Martin R. Delany, an African American newspaper editor, responds to the Fugitive Slave Act:
"My house is my castle; in that castle are none but my wife and my children, as free as the angels of heaven. . . . If any man approaches that house in search of a slave—I care not who he may be, whether constable or sheriff, magistrate or even judge of the Supreme Court . . . if he crosses the threshold of my door, and I do not lay him a lifeless corpse at my feet, I hope the grave may refuse my body a resting place."

—Martin R. Delany, speech given in Pittsburgh, September 30, 1850

Analyzing Primary Sources
Why did many northern whites share Delany's anger?

Uncle Tom's Cabin: An Antislavery Bestseller

An event in 1852 added to the growing antislavery mood of the North. Harriet Beecher Stowe, a New England woman, published a novel called ***Uncle Tom's Cabin.*** Stowe wrote the novel to show the evils of slavery and the injustice of the Fugitive Slave Act.

A Powerful Story Stowe told the story of Uncle Tom, an enslaved African American noted for his kindness and piety. Tom's world is shattered when he is bought by the brutal Simon Legree. When Tom refuses to reveal the whereabouts of two runaways, Legree whips him to death.

Uncle Tom's Cabin had wide appeal among northern readers. The first printing sold out in just two days. Eventually, the book sold millions of copies and was translated into dozens of languages.

Nationwide Reaction Although *Uncle Tom's Cabin* was popular in the North, southerners objected to the book. They claimed that it did not give a true picture of slave life. Indeed, Stowe had seen little of slavery firsthand.

Despite such objections, *Uncle Tom's Cabin* helped to change the way northerners felt about slavery. No longer could they ignore slavery as a political problem for Congress to settle. More and more northerners now saw slavery as a moral problem facing every American. For this reason, *Uncle Tom's Cabin* was one of the most important books in American history.

Section 2 Assessment

Recall

1. **Identify** Explain the significance of **(a)** Stephen Douglas, **(b)** Compromise of 1850, **(c)** Fugitive Slave Act, **(d)** Harriet Beecher Stowe, **(e)** *Uncle Tom's Cabin.*
2. **Define** **(a)** secede, **(b)** fugitive, **(c)** civil war.

Comprehension

3. How did the issue of admitting California to the Union in 1850 again raise the debate over slavery?
4. How did Americans respond to the Compromise of 1850?
5. What was the impact of *Uncle Tom's Cabin?*

Critical Thinking and Writing

6. **Exploring the Main Idea** Review the Main Idea statement at the beginning of this section. Then, write a letter to a newspaper editor explaining whether you think the Compromise of 1850 was a success or a failure. Give reasons for your answer.
7. **Summarizing** For each of the following leaders, write one sentence summarizing his attitude toward the need for a compromise in 1850: **(a)** Calhoun, **(b)** Webster, **(c)** Clay.

Activity

Making a Decision **You are a northerner during the 1850s. There is a knock at your door. It's a fugitive slave! Will you help the runaway, or will you turn the person in to the authorities? Write a brief statement explaining the reasons for your decision.**

Connecting With... **Culture**

Uncle Tom's Cabin

Harriet Beecher Stowe saw the horrors of slavery while living in Cincinnati. Across the Ohio River was Kentucky, a slave state. Her hatred of slavery led her to write *Uncle Tom's Cabin.* The novel had an impact that lasted long after slavery ended.

Harriet Beecher Stowe

Uncle Tom Defies Simon Legree

"Well, Tom!" said Legree, walking up and seizing him grimly by the collar of his coat, and speaking through his teeth, in a paroxysm of determined rage, "do you know I've made up my mind to KILL you?"

"It's very likely, Mas'r," said Tom, calmly.

"I have," said Legree, with grim terrible calmness, "done—just—that—thing, Tom, unless you tell me what you know about these yer gals!"

Tom stood silent.

"D'ye hear?" said Legree, stamping with a roar like that of an incensed lion. "Speak!"

"I han't got nothing to tell, Mas'r," said Tom with a slow, firm deliberate utterance.

"Do you dare to tell me, ye old black Christian, ye don't know?"...

"I know, Mas'r; but I can't tell anything. I can die!"

— Harriet Beecher Stowe,
Uncle Tom's Cabin, Chapter 40

Fast Facts

- The character of Tom was inspired by Josiah Henson, a Methodist preacher who had escaped slavery.
- Some southerners wrote "anti-Tom" novels to defend slavery.
- The first movie of *Uncle Tom's Cabin* was made in 1903.

In this poster for a stage version of *Uncle Tom's Cabin,* the fugitive slave Eliza flees across an icy river.

Simon Legree and Uncle Tom

ACTIVITY

You are hosting a dinner honoring Harriet Beecher Stowe. Prepare a brief speech introducing Stowe. Explain how her book reflects divisions in the United States.

3 The Crisis Deepens

Prepare to Read

Objectives

In this section, you will
- Identify the goal of the Kansas-Nebraska Act.
- Explain why violence erupted in Kansas and in the Senate.
- Summarize the impact of the Dred Scott case on the nation.

Key Terms

Kansas-Nebraska Act

Border Ruffians

guerrilla warfare

lawsuit

Dred Scott v. *Sandford*

Target Reading Skill

Cause and Effect As you read, complete the following chart to show some of the causes that directly led the United States to become a more divided nation.

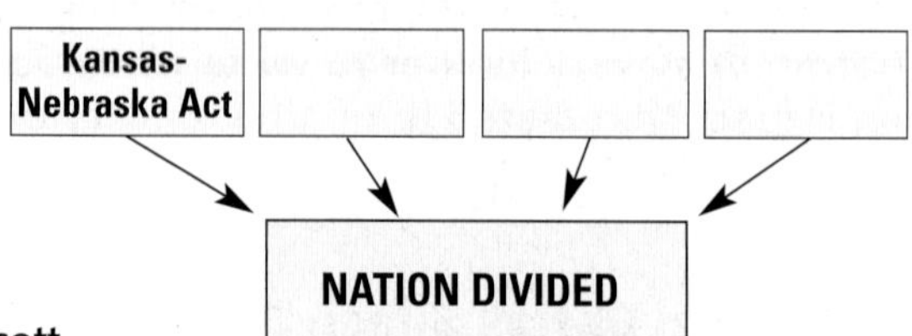

Main Idea In the 1850s, violence in Kansas and the Dred Scott decision inflamed tensions over slavery.

An election in Kansas

Setting the Scene Americans had hoped that the Compromise of 1850 would end the debate over slavery in the West. Before long, though, proslavery and antislavery forces were battling for control of the territory of Kansas. An observer described election day in one Kansas district in 1855:

> “On the morning of the election, before the polls were opened, some 300 or 400 Missourians and others were collected in the yard . . . where the election was to be held, armed with bowie-knives, revolvers, and clubs. They said they came to vote, and whip the . . . Yankees, and would vote without being sworn. Some said they came to have a fight, and wanted one.”
>
> —Report of the Congressional Committee, July 1, 1856

Hearing of events in Kansas, Abraham Lincoln, then a young lawyer in Illinois, predicted that “the contest will come to blows, and bloodshed.” Once again, the issue of slavery in the territories divided the nation.

Kansas-Nebraska Act

The Compromise of 1850 dealt mainly with lands that were part of the Mexican Cession. It did not resolve the issue of slavery in lands that had been part of the Louisiana Purchase. In January 1854, Senator Stephen Douglas introduced a bill to set up a government for the Nebraska Territory. This territory stretched from Texas north to Canada, and from Missouri west to the Rockies.

Douglas knew that white southerners did not want to add another free state to the Union. He proposed that the Nebraska Territory be divided into two territories, Kansas and Nebraska. The settlers living in each territory would then be able to decide the issue of slavery by popular sovereignty. Douglas's bill was known as the **Kansas-Nebraska Act.**

Support for the Act The Kansas-Nebraska Act seemed fair to many people. After all, the Compromise of 1850 had applied popular sovereignty in New Mexico and Utah. Southern leaders especially supported the Kansas-Nebraska Act. They were sure that slave owners from neighboring Missouri would move with their slaves across the border into Kansas. In time, they hoped, Kansas would become a slave state.

President Franklin Pierce, a Democrat elected in 1852, also supported the bill. With the President's help, Douglas pushed the Kansas-Nebraska Act through Congress. He did not realize it at the time, but he had lit a fire under a powder keg.

Northern Outrage Many northerners were unhappy with the new law. The Missouri Compromise had already banned slavery in Kansas and Nebraska, they insisted. In effect, the Kansas-Nebraska Act would repeal the Missouri Compromise.

The northern reaction to the Kansas-Nebraska Act was swift and angry. Opponents of slavery called the act a "criminal betrayal of precious rights." Slavery could now spread to areas that had been free for more than 30 years. Some northerners protested by openly challenging the Fugitive Slave Act.

The Crisis Turns Violent

Kansas now became a testing ground for popular sovereignty. Stephen Douglas hoped that settlers would decide the slavery issue peacefully on election day. Instead, proslavery and antislavery forces sent settlers to Kansas to fight for control of the territory.

GEOGRAPHY *Skills*

The issue of whether to allow slavery in the territories created tension between the North and the South.

1. **Location** On the map, locate **(a)** Missouri Compromise Line, **(b)** Kansas Territory, **(c)** Nebraska Territory.
2. **Region** **(a)** Which territories were open to slavery after 1854? **(b)** Which territories were closed to slavery?
3. **Critical Thinking** **Making Predictions** How would the balance of power in the Senate change if western territories became slave states?

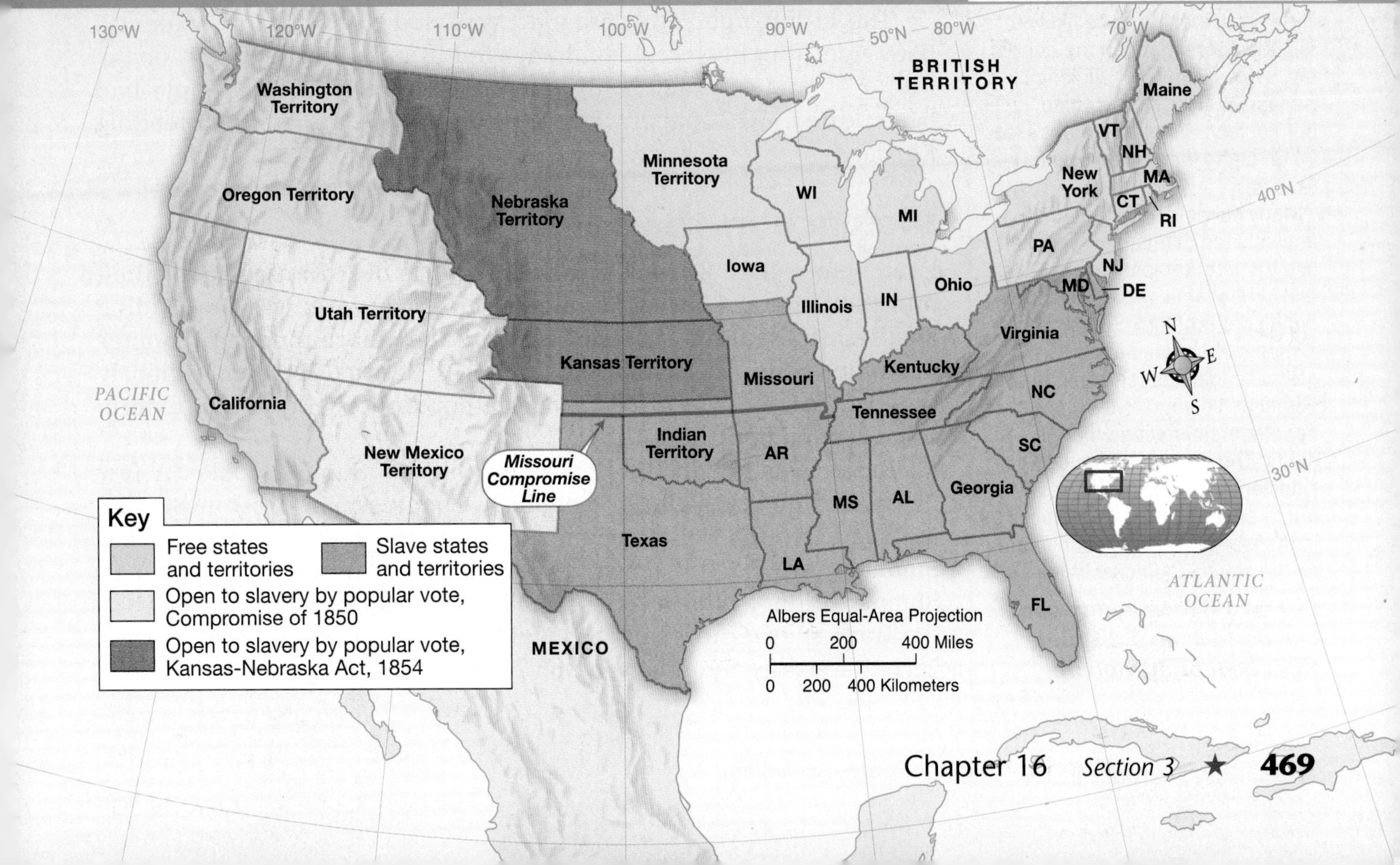

Most of the new arrivals were farmers from neighboring states. Their main interest in moving to Kansas was to acquire cheap land. Few of these settlers owned slaves. At the same time, abolitionists brought in more than 1,000 settlers from New England.

Proslavery settlers moved into Kansas as well. They wanted to make sure that antislavery forces did not overrun the territory. Proslavery bands from Missouri often rode across the border. These **Border Ruffians,** as they were called, battled the antislavery forces in Kansas.

Two Governments In 1855, Kansas held elections to choose lawmakers. Hundreds of Border Ruffians crossed into Kansas and voted illegally. They helped to elect a proslavery legislature.

The new legislature quickly passed laws to support slavery. One law said that people could be put to death for helping slaves escape. Another made speaking out against slavery a crime punishable by two years of hard labor.

Antislavery settlers refused to accept these laws. They elected their own governor and legislature. With two rival governments, Kansas was in chaos. Armed gangs roamed the territory looking for trouble.

"Bleeding Kansas" A band of proslavery men raided the town of Lawrence, an antislavery stronghold, in 1856. The attackers destroyed homes and smashed the press of a Free-Soil newspaper.

John Brown, an abolitionist, decided to strike back. Brown had moved to Kansas to help make it a free state. He claimed that God had sent him to punish supporters of slavery.

Brown rode with his four sons and two other men to the town of Pottawatomie (paht uh WAHT uh mee) Creek. In the middle of the night, they dragged five proslavery settlers from their beds and murdered them.

The killings at Pottawatomie Creek led to even more violence. Both sides fought fiercely and engaged in **guerrilla warfare,** or the use of hit-and-run tactics. By late 1856, more than 200 people had been killed. Newspapers started calling the territory "Bleeding Kansas."

Violence in the Senate

Even before John Brown's attack, the battle over Kansas had spilled into the Senate. Charles Sumner of Massachusetts was the leading abolitionist senator. In one speech, the sharp-tongued Sumner denounced the proslavery legislature of Kansas. He then viciously criticized his southern foes, singling out Andrew Butler, an elderly senator from South Carolina.

Butler was not in the Senate on the day Sumner spoke. A few days later, however, Butler's nephew, Congressman Preston Brooks, marched into the Senate chamber. Using a heavy cane, Brooks beat Sumner until he fell down, bloody and unconscious, to the floor. Sumner did not fully recover from the beating for three years.

Many southerners felt that Sumner got what he deserved for his verbal abuse of another senator. Hundreds of people sent canes to

Connecting to Today

Stopping the Violence

Today, you would not be likely to see a physical fight on the floor of the Senate. However, violence remains a disturbing problem in our society. We all know of cases when angry words had tragic results.

Many schools have launched antiviolence campaigns. Students use the Internet, posters, essays, and school activities to call attention to the problem. Some schools also use "peer mediation" programs to find peaceful solutions to conflicts. Volunteers train to act as negotiators between other students. The mediator listens to both sides and tries to get them to reach an agreement. In schools, as in the world, communication can be the key to ending violence.

List two things young people can do to keep a dispute from becoming violent.

Brooks to show their support. To northerners, however, the brutal act was more evidence that slavery led to violence.

The Dred Scott Case

With Congress in an uproar, many Americans looked to the Supreme Court to settle the slavery issue and restore peace. In 1857, the Court ruled on a case that involved an enslaved person named Dred Scott. Instead of bringing harmony, however, the Court's decision further divided the North and the South.

Dred Scott had been enslaved for many years in Missouri. Later, he moved with his owner to Illinois and then to the Wisconsin Territory, where slavery was not allowed. After they returned to Missouri, Scott's owner died. Antislavery lawyers helped Scott to file a **lawsuit,** a legal case brought to settle a dispute between people or groups. Scott's lawyers argued that, because Scott had lived in a free territory, he had become a free man.

The Supreme Court's Decision In time, the case reached the Supreme Court as *Dred Scott* v. *Sandford.* The Court's decision shocked and dismayed Americans who opposed slavery. First, the Court ruled that Scott could not file a lawsuit because, as an enslaved person, he was not a citizen. Also, the Court's written decision clearly stated that slaves were considered to be property.

The Court's ruling did not stop there. Instead, the Justices went on to make a sweeping decision about the larger issue of slavery in

Viewing History

Bleeding Kansas

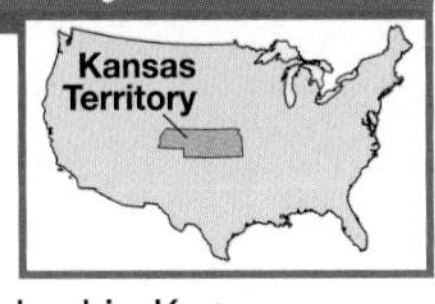

In 1856, the slavery issue sparked bloodshed in Kansas. Here, Border Ruffians attack antislavery settlers. Abolitionists like John Brown also committed acts of violence. **Identifying Bias** ***What details in the picture suggest that the artist favored the antislavery settlers?***

the territories. According to the Court, Congress did not have the power to outlaw slavery in any territory. The Court's ruling meant that the Missouri Compromise was unconstitutional.

Recognize Multiple Causes

Why did the Dred Scott decision drive the North and South apart? Add this information to your chart.

The Nation Reacts White southerners rejoiced at *Dred Scott* v. *Sandford.* It meant that slavery was legal in all the territories. This was just what white southerners had been demanding for years.

African Americans responded angrily to the Dred Scott decision. In the North, many held public meetings to condemn the ruling. At one meeting in Philadelphia, a speaker hoped that the ruling would lead more whites to "join with us in our efforts to recover the long lost boon of freedom."

White northerners were also shocked by the ruling. Many had hoped that slavery would eventually die out if it were restricted to the South. Now, however, slavery could spread throughout the West. Even northerners who disliked abolitionists felt that the ruling in *Dred Scott* v. *Sandford* was wrong. A newspaper in Cincinnati declared, "We are now one great . . . slaveholding community."

Abolitionist Frederick Douglass also spoke out against *Dred Scott* v. *Sandford*: "This infamous decision," he declared, "maintains that slaves . . . are property in the same sense that horses, sheep, and swine are property . . . that [people] of African descent are not and cannot be citizens of the United States." He told his listeners:

> ❝ All I ask of the American people is that they live up to the Constitution, adopt its principles, [take in] its spirit, and enforce its provisions. When this is done . . . liberty . . . will become the inheritance of all the inhabitants of this highly favored country. ❞
>
> —Frederick Douglass, *Collected Speeches,* 1857

Section 3 Assessment

Recall

1. **Identify** Explain the significance of **(a)** Kansas-Nebraska Act, **(b)** Franklin Pierce, **(c)** Border Ruffians, **(d)** Charles Sumner, **(e)** *Dred Scott* v. *Sandford.*
2. **Define** **(a)** guerrilla warfare, **(b)** lawsuit.

Comprehension

3. Why did Stephen Douglas propose the Kansas-Nebraska Act?
4. How did the Kansas-Nebraska Act lead to violence?
5. How did white southerners, African Americans, and white northerners react to the Dred Scott decision?

Critical Thinking and Writing

6. **Exploring the Main Idea** Review the Main Idea statement at the beginning of this section. Then, make a list of five statements from this section that support the main idea.
7. **Analyzing Primary Sources** After the Kansas-Nebraska Act was passed, Stephen Douglas stated: "The struggle for freedom was forever banished from the halls of Congress to the western plains." Rewrite Douglas's statement in your own words. Then, explain why you agree or disagree with it.

Activity

Connecting to Today

Use the Internet to find out more about a recent Supreme Court decision involving the rights of workers, minorities, or students. Write a brief summary describing both sides of the issue and what the court decided. For help in completing the activity, visit PHSchool.com, **Web Code mfd-1601.**

4 The Republican Party Emerges

Prepare to Read

Objectives

In this section, you will
- Explain why the Republican party was founded.
- Explain the rapid emergence of Abraham Lincoln as a Republican leader.
- Describe the reaction to John Brown's raid on Harpers Ferry.

Key Terms

Republican party
arsenal
treason
martyr

Target Reading Skill

Comparison and Contrast As you read, complete this table listing the conflicting views of Abraham Lincoln and Stephen Douglas.

LINCOLN'S VIEWS	DOUGLAS'S VIEWS
• Slavery was morally wrong • •	• • Western territories should decide slavery issue by popular sovereignty •

Main Idea Abraham Lincoln emerged as a leader of the new Republican party, which was dedicated to halting the spread of slavery.

Setting the Scene The tall lawyer stood before a political convention in Springfield, Illinois. People in the packed hall listened carefully as he addressed the number one issue of the day—slavery:

> "A house divided against itself cannot stand. I believe this government cannot endure permanently half slave and half free. I do not expect the Union to be dissolved—I do not expect the house to fall—but I do expect it will cease to be divided. It will become all one thing, or all the other."
>
> —Abraham Lincoln, Speech, June 16, 1858

Figure of Abraham Lincoln

Few people outside of Illinois had heard of Abraham Lincoln. Yet, his speech became famous. Many northerners were soon repeating his prediction about the "house divided." Lincoln and the new party he represented—the **Republican party**—moved to the forefront of the debate over slavery.

The Republican Party

By the mid-1850s, people who opposed slavery in the territories sought a new political voice. Neither Whigs nor Democrats, they argued, would take a strong stand against slavery. "We have submitted to slavery long enough," an Ohio Democrat declared.

A group of Free-Soilers, northern Democrats, and antislavery Whigs gathered in Michigan in 1854. There they formed the Republican party. Its main goal was to keep slavery out of the western territories. A few Republicans were abolitionists. They hoped to end slavery in the South as well. Most Republicans, however, wanted only to stop the spread of slavery.

The new party grew quickly. By 1856, it was ready to challenge the older parties for power. Republicans selected John C. Frémont to run for President. Frémont was a frontiersman who had fought for

POLITICAL CARTOON *Skills*

The Election of 1856 In this 1856 cartoon, Millard Fillmore steps in between John C. Frémont (left) and James Buchanan (right).

1. **Comprehension** What accusations do Frémont and Buchanan make against one another?
2. **Finding the Main Idea** How does the cartoonist show that the slavery issue stirred strong feelings?
3. **Critical Thinking Identifying Points of View** Which candidate do you think the cartoonist favored? Explain.

Civics 

California's independence. He had little political experience, but he opposed the spread of slavery.

Frémont's main opponent was Democrat James Buchanan of Pennsylvania. Many Democrats saw Buchanan as a "northern man with southern principles." They hoped that he would attract voters in both the North and the South. Former President Millard Fillmore also ran as the candidate of the American, or "Know-Nothing," party. A strong supporter of the Union, Fillmore feared that a Republican victory would split the nation apart.

Buchanan won the election with support from a large majority of southerners and many northerners. Still, the Republicans made a strong showing in the election. Without the support of a single southern state, Frémont won one third of the popular vote. Southerners worried that their influence in the national government was fading.

Abe Lincoln of Illinois

The next test for the Republican party came in 1858 in Illinois. Abraham Lincoln, a Republican, challenged Democrat Stephen Douglas for his seat in the Senate. Because most Americans expected Douglas to run for President in 1860, the race captured the attention of the whole nation.

From the Backwoods of Kentucky Abraham Lincoln was born on the Kentucky frontier. Like many frontier people, his parents moved often to find better land. The family lived in Indiana and later in Illinois. As a child, Lincoln spent only a year in school. Still, he taught himself to read, poring over his books by firelight.

After Lincoln left home, he opened a store in Illinois. There, he studied law on his own and launched a career in politics. He served eight years in the state legislature and one term in Congress. Bitterly opposed to the Kansas-Nebraska Act, he decided to run for the Senate in 1858.

When the race began, Lincoln was not a national figure. Still, people in Illinois knew him well and liked him. To them, he was "just folks"—someone who enjoyed picnics, wrestling contests, and all their favorite pastimes. His honesty, wit, and plain-spoken manner made him a good speaker.

Compare and Contrast

Read the paragraphs following "Lincoln-Douglas Debates." How did Douglas and Lincoln differ on the issue of slavery? Add this information to your chart.

Lincoln-Douglas Debates During the Senate campaign, Lincoln challenged Douglas to a series of debates. Douglas was not eager to accept, but he did. During the campaign, the two debated seven times. Slavery was the important issue.

Douglas wanted to settle the slavery question by popular sovereignty. He personally disliked slavery, but stated that he did not care whether people in the territories voted "down or up" for it.

Lincoln, like nearly all whites of his day, did not believe in "perfect equality" between blacks and whites. He did, however, believe that slavery was wrong:

> " There is no reason in the world why the negro is not entitled to all the natural rights [listed] in the Declaration of Independence, the right to life, liberty, and the pursuit of happiness. . . . In the right to eat the bread, without the leave of anybody else, which his own hand earns, he is my equal and the equal of Judge Douglas, and the equal of every living man. "
>
> —Abraham Lincoln, Speech at Ottawa, Illinois, August 21, 1858

Since slavery was a "moral, social, and political wrong," said Lincoln, Douglas and other Americans should not treat it as an unimportant question to be voted "down or up." Lincoln was totally opposed to slavery in the territories. Still, he was not an abolitionist. He had no wish to interfere with slavery in the states where it already existed.

A Leader Emerges Week after week, both men spoke nearly every day to large crowds. Newspapers reprinted their campaign speeches. The more northerners read Lincoln's words, the more they thought about the injustice of slavery.

In the end, Douglas won the election by a slim margin. Still, Lincoln was a winner, too. He was now known throughout the country. Two years later, the two rivals would again meet face to face—both seeking the office of President.

Primary Source

Douglas Debates Lincoln

In his first debate with Lincoln, Stephen Douglas defended the principle of popular sovereignty: "We have settled the slavery question as far as we are concerned; we have prohibited it in Illinois forever, . . . but when we settled it for ourselves, we exhausted all our power over that subject. We must leave each and every other state to decide for itself the same question. . . . Now, my friends, if we will only act conscientiously and rigidly upon this great principle of popular sovereignty, we will continue at peace, one with another."

—Stephen Douglas, Speech at Ottawa, Illinois, August 21, 1858

Analyzing Primary Sources

How might an abolitionist respond to Douglas?

John Brown's Raid

In the meantime, more bloodshed inflamed divisions between the North and the South. In 1859, the radical abolitionist John Brown carried his antislavery campaign from Kansas to the East. He led a group of followers, including five African Americans, to the town of Harpers Ferry, Virginia.

There, Brown planned to raid a federal **arsenal,** or gun warehouse. He thought that enslaved African Americans would flock to him at the arsenal. He would then give them weapons and lead them in a revolt.

Sentenced to Death Brown quickly gained control of the arsenal. No slave uprising took place, however. Instead, troops under the command of Robert E. Lee killed ten raiders and captured Brown.

Most people, in both the North and the South, thought that Brown's plan to lead a slave revolt was insane. After all, there were few enslaved African Americans in Harpers Ferry. Furthermore, after seizing the arsenal, Brown did nothing further to encourage a slave revolt. At his trial, however, Brown seemed perfectly sane. He sat quietly as the court found him guilty of murder and **treason,** or actions against one's country. Before hearing his sentence, he gave a moving defense of his actions. He showed no emotion as he was sentenced to death.

Hero or Villain? Because he conducted himself with such dignity during his trial, John Brown became a hero to many northerners. Some considered him a **martyr** because he was willing to give up his life for his beliefs. On the morning he was hanged, church bells rang solemnly throughout the North. In years to come, New Englanders would sing a popular song with the chorus: "John Brown's body lies a mold'ring in the grave, but his soul is marching on."

To white southerners, the northern response to John Brown's death was outrageous. People were singing the praises of a man who had tried to lead a slave revolt! Many southerners became convinced that the North wanted to destroy slavery—and the South along with it. The nation was poised for a violent clash.

Section 4 Assessment

Recall

1. **Identify** Explain the significance of **(a)** Republican party, **(b)** John C. Frémont, **(c)** James Buchanan, **(d)** Abraham Lincoln, **(e)** Harpers Ferry.
2. **Define** **(a)** arsenal, **(b)** treason, **(c)** martyr.

Comprehension

3. What issue led to the founding of the Republican party?
4. How did Abraham Lincoln emerge as a Republican leader?
5. How did northerners and southerners respond to John Brown's raid?

Critical Thinking and Writing

6. **Exploring the Main Idea** Review the Main Idea statement at the beginning of this section. Then, write a paragraph explaining how the views of the Republican party differed from the views of earlier parties.
7. **Supporting a Point of View** Lincoln said the nation could not "endure permanently half slave and half free." Do you agree that slavery was too important an issue to allow differences among the states? Write a paragraph explaining the reasons for your opinion.

ACTIVITY

Writing a Profile

Use the Internet to find out more about the Lincoln-Douglas debates. Use the information to prepare a profile of either Douglas or Lincoln for a TV news report on the debates. For help in completing the activity, visit PHSchool.com, **Web Code mfd-1602.**

Identifying Bias

SKILLS FOR LIFE

Was John Brown a hero or a villain? That depends on your point of view. To evaluate historical evidence correctly, you must be able to identify *bias*, strong beliefs that prejudice someone's point of view.

A North Carolina newspaper ran this editorial after the execution of John Brown:

The Execution of Brown

"We give to-day full accounts of the scenes attending the execution of the traitor, murderer, and thief, John Brown. He died, as he lived, a hardened criminal. [When] his wretched confederates shall have paid the penalty of their crimes, we hope that their allies and sympathizers at the North will realize the fact that the South has the power to protect her soil and property, and will exercise it in spite of all the measures which can be leveled at her by the abolitionists and their [supporters]."

—Raleigh, North Carolina, *Register*, December 9, 1859

In this abolitionist painting, John Brown pauses on his way to his execution to kiss an enslaved woman's baby.

Learn the Skill *To identify bias, use the following steps:*

1. **Identify the sources.** Knowing a person's background helps you evaluate that person's attitudes.
2. **Identify main ideas.** What is the main point that is being made?
3. **Distinguish facts from opinions.** Remember, facts are statements that can be proven, while opinions are someone's beliefs.
4. **Look for emotion-packed words or images.** How information is presented is an important clue to the point of view.
5. **Identify bias.** How do the writer's or artist's feelings and beliefs affect his or her presentation?

Practice the Skill *Answer the following questions about the editorial and picture above:*

1. Where was the newspaper published?
2. What are the points of view of the editorial and the painting?
3. **(a)** Which statements made by the writer can be proven as facts? **(b)** Which are opinions?
4. **(a)** Evaluate the language the writer uses to describe John Brown. **(b)** What emotions do the images in the painting create?
5. **(a)** What bias does the editorial show? **(b)** What bias does the painting show?

Apply the Skill *See the Chapter Review and Assessment.*

5 A Nation Divides

Prepare to Read

Objectives

In this section, you will

- Explain how the 1860 election reflected sectional divisions.
- Describe how the South reacted to the election results.
- Identify how the Civil War began in 1861.

Key Term

unamendable

Target Reading Skill

Main Idea As you read, prepare an outline of this section. Use roman numerals to indicate the major headings, capital letters for the subheadings, and numbers for the supporting details.

I. The Election of 1860
A. Candidates and political parties
1.
2.
3.
4.
B. Results of the election
1.
2.
II. The South Reacts
A. Secession
1.
2.

Main Idea The election of Abraham Lincoln as President in 1860 led a number of southern states to secede from the Union.

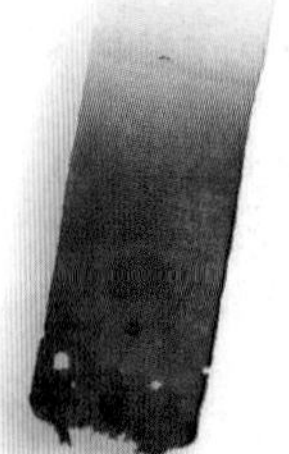

Lincoln campaign badge

Setting the Scene Thousands of people swarmed into Chicago, Illinois, for the 1860 Republican national convention. They filled all of the city's 42 hotels. When beds ran out, people slept on billiard tables. All were there to find out one thing: Who would win the Republican nomination for President—William Seward of New York or Abraham Lincoln of Illinois?

On the third day of the convention, a delegate rushed to the roof of the hall. There, a man stood waiting next to a cannon. "Fire the salute," ordered the delegate. "Old Abe is nominated!" Amid the celebration, though, a delegate from Kentucky struck a somber note. "Gentlemen, we are on the brink of a great civil war."

The Election of 1860

The Democrats held their convention in Charleston, South Carolina. Southerners wanted the party to support slavery in the territories. However, northern Democrats refused to do so. In the end, the party split in two. Northern Democrats chose Stephen Douglas to run for President. Southern Democrats picked John Breckinridge of Kentucky.

Some Americans tried to heal the split between the North and the South by forming a new party. The Constitutional Union party chose John Bell of Tennessee to run for President. Bell was a moderate who wanted to keep the Union together. He got support only in a few southern states that were still seeking a compromise.

Douglas was sure that Lincoln would win. However, he believed that Democrats "must try to save the Union." He urged southerners to stay with the Union, no matter who was elected.

When the votes were counted, Lincoln had carried the North and won the election. Southern votes did not affect the outcome at all. Lincoln's name was not even on the ballot in 10 southern states. Northerners outnumbered southerners and outvoted them.

The South Reacts

Lincoln's election brought a strong reaction in the South. A South Carolina woman described how the news was received:

> “The excitement was very great. Everybody was talking at the same time. One . . . more moved than the others, stood up saying . . . 'No more vain regrets—sad forebodings are useless. The stake is life or death—.'”
>
> —Mary Boykin Chesnut, *A Diary From Dixie*, 1860

To many southerners, Lincoln's election meant that the South no longer had a voice in national government. They believed that the President and Congress were now set against their interests—especially slavery. Even before the election, South Carolina's governor had written to other southern governors. If Lincoln won, he wrote, it would be their duty to leave the Union.

Secession Senator John Crittenden of Kentucky made a last effort to save the Union. In December 1860, he introduced a bill to extend the Missouri Compromise line to the Pacific. Crittenden also proposed an amendment to the Constitution that was **unamendable**, one that could not be changed. Such an amendment would guarantee forever the right to hold slaves in states south of the compromise line.

The compromise bill received little support. Slavery in the West was no longer the issue. Many southerners believed that the North had put an abolitionist in the White House. They felt that secession was their only choice. Most Republicans also were unwilling to surrender what they had won in the national election.

GEOGRAPHY *Skills*

Abraham Lincoln won the election of 1860 with less than 40 percent of the popular vote.

1. **Location** On the map, locate **(a)** Kentucky, **(b)** Illinois, **(c)** South Carolina.
2. **Region** **(a)** Which political party did the northern states support? **(b)** Which party did most southern states support?
3. **Critical Thinking Drawing Conclusions** Did the results of the popular vote weaken or strengthen Lincoln's chances of effectively leading the nation? Explain.

Election of 1860

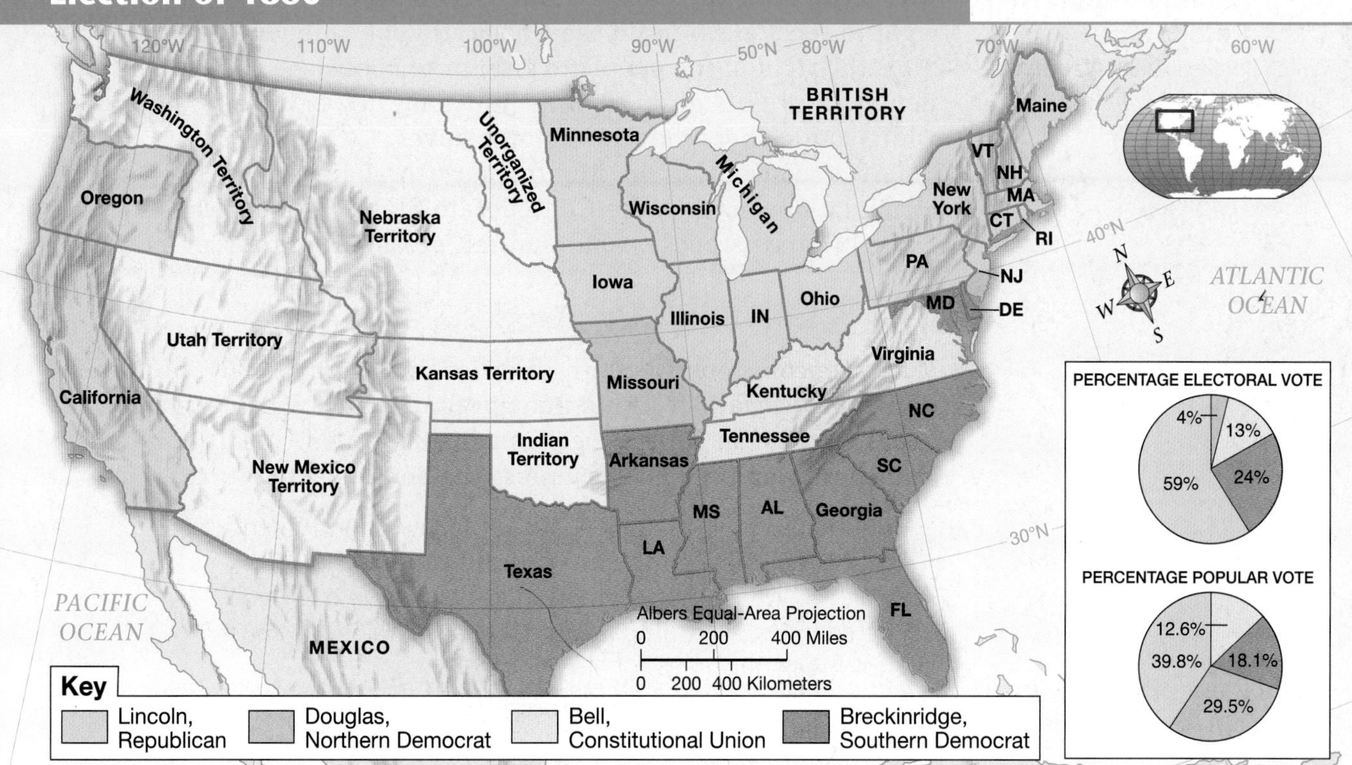

AmericanHeritage MAGAZINE

HISTORY **HAPPENED HERE**

Fort Sumter

The Civil War began in 1861 when Confederate forces bombarded and captured Fort Sumter in Charleston Harbor, South Carolina. Later in the war, Union gunships reduced Sumter to rubble. The fort was rebuilt, and it remained part of the seacoast defenses until 1947. Today, Fort Sumter is a national monument. Tour boats to the fort leave regularly from downtown Charleston.

Virtual Field Trip For an interactive look at Fort Sumter, visit PHSchool.com, **Web Code mfd-1603.**

On December 20, 1860, South Carolina became the first state to secede. By late February, 1861, Alabama, Florida, Georgia, Louisiana, Mississippi, and Texas had also seceded.

Identify Supporting Details

Which details explain why the South believed it had the right to secede from the Union? Add these details to your outline.

The Confederacy Most southerners believed that they had every right to secede. After all, the Declaration of Independence said that "it is the right of the people to alter or to abolish" a government that denies the rights of its citizens. Lincoln, they believed, would deny white southerners the right to own slaves.

At a convention in Montgomery, Alabama, the seven states formed a new nation, the Confederate States of America. Jefferson Davis of Mississippi became the first president of the Confederacy.

The Civil War Begins

When Lincoln took the oath of office on March 4, 1861, he faced a dangerous situation. In his inaugural address, Lincoln warned that "no state . . . can lawfully get out of the Union." Still, he pledged that there would be no war unless the South started it:

> ❝ In YOUR hands, my dissatisfied fellow-countrymen, and not in MINE, is the momentous issue of civil war. . . . We are not enemies, but friends. We must not be enemies. Though passion may have strained, it must not break our bonds of affection. ❞
>
> — Abraham Lincoln, First Inaugural Address

Lincoln's Difficult Decision Jefferson Davis, however, had already ordered Confederate forces to begin seizing federal forts in the South. President Lincoln faced a difficult decision. Should he let the Confederates take over federal property? If he did, he would seem to be admitting that states had the right to leave the Union. On the other hand, if he sent troops to hold the forts, he might start a civil war. He might also lose the support of the eight slave states that had not seceded from the Union.

In April, the Confederacy forced Lincoln to make up his mind. By then, Confederate troops controlled nearly all forts, post offices, and other federal buildings in the South. The Union held only three forts off the Florida coast and Fort Sumter in South Carolina. Fort Sumter was important to the Confederacy because it guarded Charleston Harbor.

Bombardment of Fort Sumter President Lincoln learned that food supplies at Fort Sumter were running low. He notified the governor of South Carolina that he was going to ship food to the fort. Lincoln promised not to send troops or weapons.

The Confederates, however, felt that they could not leave the fort in Union hands. On April 11, 1861, they demanded that Fort Sumter surrender. Major Robert Anderson, the Union commander, refused to give in until he had run out of food or was ordered to surrender by the United States government. Confederate guns then opened fire. The Union troops quickly ran out of ammunition. On April 13, Anderson surrendered the fort.

When Confederate troops shelled Fort Sumter, people in Charleston gathered on their rooftops to watch. To many, it was like a fireworks show. No one knew that the fireworks marked the start of a civil war that would last four terrible years.

An American Profile

Jefferson Davis
1808–1889

After service in the Mexican War, Jefferson Davis became a United States Senator from Mississippi. Here, he championed states' rights. Then, as secretary of war, he influenced President Pierce to sign the Kansas-Nebraska Act. But Davis opposed splitting the Union. As tensions grew between the South and the North, he urged southern states not to secede.

They disregarded his advice. When Mississippi left the Union in 1861, Davis left the Senate and became president of the Confederacy.

Why do you think Jefferson Davis opposed secession?

Section 5 Assessment

Recall

1. **Identify** Explain the significance of **(a)** John Breckinridge, **(b)** John Bell, **(c)** John Crittenden, **(d)** Jefferson Davis.
2. **Define** unamendable.

Comprehension

3. How did the four candidates for President in 1860 reflect the nation's sectional differences?
4. Why did many southerners support secession after Lincoln won the presidency in 1860?
5. What happened at Fort Sumter in 1861 to begin the Civil War?

Critical Thinking and Writing

6. **Exploring the Main Idea** Review the Main idea statement at the beginning of this section. Then, write a newspaper editorial about Lincoln's election that might have appeared in a southern newspaper in November 1860.
7. **Solving Problems** Write an outline for a compromise plan that tries to save the Union in 1861. Your plan should offer advantages to both the North and the South.

Activity

Planning a Political Campaign **You are a political campaign manager in 1860. Write a campaign slogan for each of the four candidates in the presidential election of 1860. Or, choose one of the candidates and design a campaign poster for that candidate.**

CHAPTER 16

Review and Assessment

Chapter Summary

Section 1
The Missouri Compromise addressed slavery in the Louisiana Purchase. The issue was unresolved in lands that were part of the Mexican Cession. Abolitionists founded the Free-Soil party.

Section 2
The balance of power between North and South came to the forefront again when western territories applied for statehood. The Compromise of 1850 failed to completely satisfy either side. Tensions continued to build.

Section 3
Popular sovereignty did not solve the slavery issue in the new territories. Proslavery and antislavery forces clashed violently in Kansas. The Dred Scott case further divided North and South.

Section 4
During the 1858 Illinois Senate race, veteran politician Stephan Douglas and newcomer Abraham Lincoln debated the slavery issue. John Brown's raid drove the North and South farther apart.

Section 5
Seven southern states seceded from the Union after Abraham Lincoln was elected President. The Confederacy's attack on Fort Sumter marked the beginning of the Civil War.

For additional review and enrichment activities, see the interactive version of *The American Nation,* available on the Web and on CD-ROM.

Chapter Self-Test For practice test questions for Chapter 16, visit PHSchool.com, **Web Code mfa-1604.**

Building Vocabulary

Review the chapter vocabulary words listed below. Then, use the words and their definitions to create a matching quiz. Exchange quizzes with another student. Check each other's answers when you are finished.

1. **popular sovereignty**
2. **fugitive**
3. **civil war**
4. **guerrilla warfare**
5. **lawsuit**
6. **arsenal**
7. **treason**
8. **martyr**
9. **Missouri Compromise**
10. **Kansas-Nebraska Act**

Reviewing Key Facts

11. Describe three positions on slavery held by Americans in the 1840s. (Section 1)
12. What were the five parts of the Compromise of 1850? (Section 2)
13. How did Kansas gain the nickname "Bleeding Kansas"? (Section 3)
14. What groups combined to form the Republican party? (Section 4)
15. Why did South Carolina secede from the Union? (Section 5)

Critical Thinking and Writing

16. **Connecting to Geography: Regions** Study the map of the election of 1860 in Section 5. **(a)** From which regions did Lincoln draw his support? **(b)** Does the map show from what regions Douglas drew most of his support? Why or why not?
17. **Supporting a Point of View** Write two brief statements summarizing one argument for and one argument against Daniel Webster's support of the Fugitive Slave Act.
18. **Identifying Causes and Effects** **(a)** List two causes for the split in the Democratic party in the 1860 election. **(b)** List two effects of the election.

Skills Assessment

Analyzing Primary Sources

Look at this drawing that appeared in northern newspapers in 1856.

19. The beating of Charles Sumner by Preston Brooks resulted in
   A. northern support of slavery.
   B. southern support of abolition.
   C. dismissal of both men from the Senate.
   D. a wider rift between North and South.

20. What was the national mood in 1856?
   A. Most Americans supported slavery.
   B. Many Americans felt strongly about slavery.
   C. Americans did not care about slavery.
   D. Most Americans were abolitionists.

Applying Your Skills

Identifying Bias

The election of 1860 outraged white southerners. They were especially upset that a President had been elected without any southern electoral votes. According to an Augusta, Georgia, newspaper editor, the Republican party:

> “stands forth today, hideous, revolting, loathsome, a menace not only to the Union of these states, but to Society, to Liberty, and to Law. It has drawn to it the corrupt, the vile, and [immoral], the [wasteful], the lawless. . . . It is a fiend, the type of lawless Democracy, a law unto itself, its only Lord King Numbers, its decrees but the will of a wild mob.”
>
> —Augusta, Georgia, *Chronicle,* November 1860, quoted in "Michael Holt, the Political Crisis of the 1850s"

21. Which of the following titles best reflects the viewpoint of the editorial writer?
   A. A Tribute to the Republicans
   B. A Loathsome Menace
   C. Separation of Powers
   D. Dangers of the Party System

22. What does this editorial tell you about the state of relations between the North and the South in November 1860?

Activities

Connecting With . . . Economics

Transferring Information to Charts By 1861, the North had 65 percent of the farmland, 71 percent of the railroad track, 85 percent of the factories, 92 percent of the industrial workers, and 63 percent of the population of the United States. Create a series of pie charts comparing the resources of the North and the South.

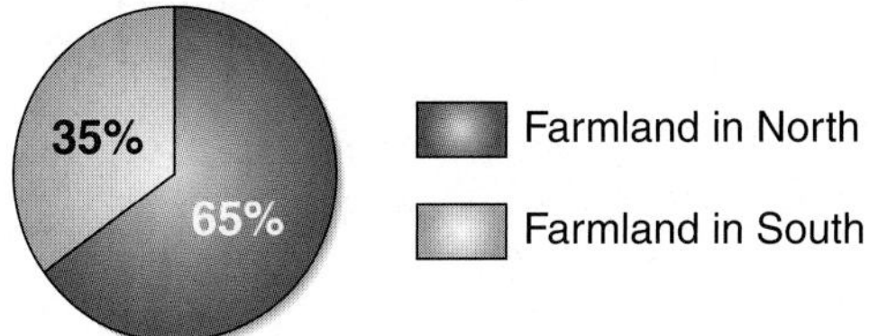

Researching a Biography

Ranking Lincoln Web Sites Use the Internet to find sites relating to Abraham Lincoln. Write a report listing the resources you found on these sites that make them valuable for a Lincoln biography. List five sites, and rank them in order of usefulness. For help in starting this activity, visit PHSchool.com, **Web Code mfd-1606.**

CHAPTER 17

The Civil War

1861–1865

1 The Conflict Takes Shape
2 No Easy Victory
3 A Promise of Freedom
4 Hardships of War
5 The War Ends

The Battle of Bull Run

AMERICAN EVENTS

1861 The first major battle of the war takes place at Bull Run on July 21.

1862 Union gunboats capture New Orleans and Memphis.

1863 The Battle of Gettysburg ends the Confederate drive into the North.

Presidential Terms: Abraham Lincoln 1861–1865

1861 · 1862 · 1863

WORLD EVENTS

▲ **1861** The Russian czar frees the serfs.

▲ **1862** Great Britain refuses to recognize the Confederacy.

Choosing Sides

In April 1861, eight slave states were still in the Union. These states would have to decide whether to remain in the Union or join the Confederacy.

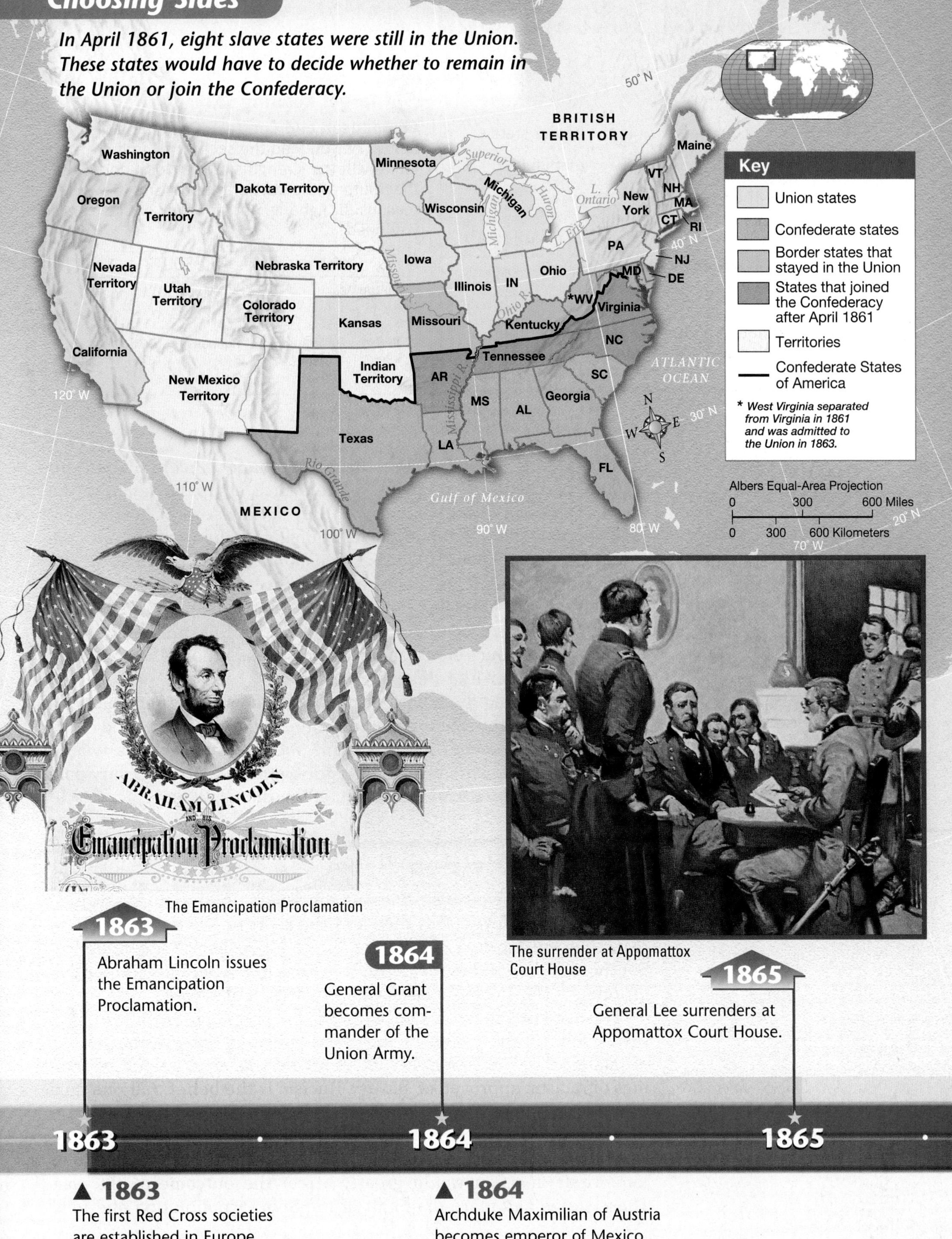

The Emancipation Proclamation

The surrender at Appomattox Court House

1863
Abraham Lincoln issues the Emancipation Proclamation.

1864
General Grant becomes commander of the Union Army.

1865
General Lee surrenders at Appomattox Court House.

1863 • **1864** • **1865** •

▲ 1863
The first Red Cross societies are established in Europe.

▲ 1864
Archduke Maximilian of Austria becomes emperor of Mexico.

1 The Conflict Takes Shape

Prepare to Read

Objectives

In this section, you will
- Explain the issues that divided the nation.
- Describe the strengths and weaknesses of the North and the South.
- Identify the leaders of each side in the war.

Key Terms

border state

martial law

Target Reading Skill

Comparison and Contrast Copy the table below. As you read the section, fill in the table with the strengths of the North and the South at the start of the war and their reasons for fighting. Add as many entries as you need.

NORTH	SOUTH
Strengths	**Strengths**
•	•
•	•
Reasons for fighting	**Reasons for fighting**
•	•
•	•

Main Idea Although both sides believed that their cause was just, the North had important advantages at the start of the war.

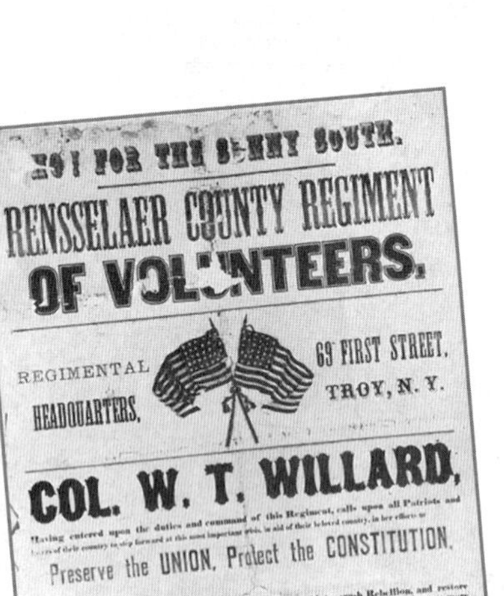

A poster calling for volunteers

Setting the Scene President Abraham Lincoln called for 75,000 volunteers to serve as soldiers in a campaign against the South. The term of enlistment was only 90 days—most northerners believed that the war would be over quickly. In the words of one confident Union supporter, "We shall crush out this rebellion as an elephant would trample on a mouse."

Southerners were just as convinced that a Confederate victory would be quick. A Confederate in North Carolina predicted, "Just throw three or four [bomb]shells among those blue-bellied Yankees and they'll scatter like sheep."

With flags held high, both northerners and southerners marched off to war. Most felt certain that a single, gallant battle would bring a quick end to the conflict. Few suspected that the Civil War would last four terrible years. By the time the fighting was over, every part of American society would be affected by the Civil War.

A Nation Divided

When the war began, each side was convinced that its cause was just. Southerners believed that they had the right to leave the Union. In fact, they called the conflict the War for Southern Independence. Southerners wanted independence so that they could keep their traditional way of life—including the institution of slavery.

Northerners, meanwhile, believed that they had to fight to save the Union. At the outset of the war, abolishing slavery was not an official goal of the North. In fact, many northerners, guided by feelings of racism, approved of slavery. Racism is the belief that one race is by nature superior to another.

In April 1861, eight slave states were still in the Union. As the war began, they had to make the difficult decision of which side to join. Their decision would greatly affect the outcome of the war. These states had more than half of the South's population and food crops. In addition, many of the South's factories were in these states.

Four of these states—Virginia,* North Carolina, Tennessee, and Arkansas—quickly joined the Confederacy. However, after some wavering between the North and South, the four **border states**—Kentucky, Missouri, Maryland, and Delaware—decided to remain in the Union. Maryland was especially critical to the Union cause since it bordered the nation's capital at Washington, D.C.

Still, there were some citizens of the border states who supported the South. In April 1861, pro-Confederate mobs attacked Union troops in Baltimore, Maryland. In response, President Lincoln declared **martial law,** or rule by the army instead of the elected government. Many people who sided with the South were arrested.

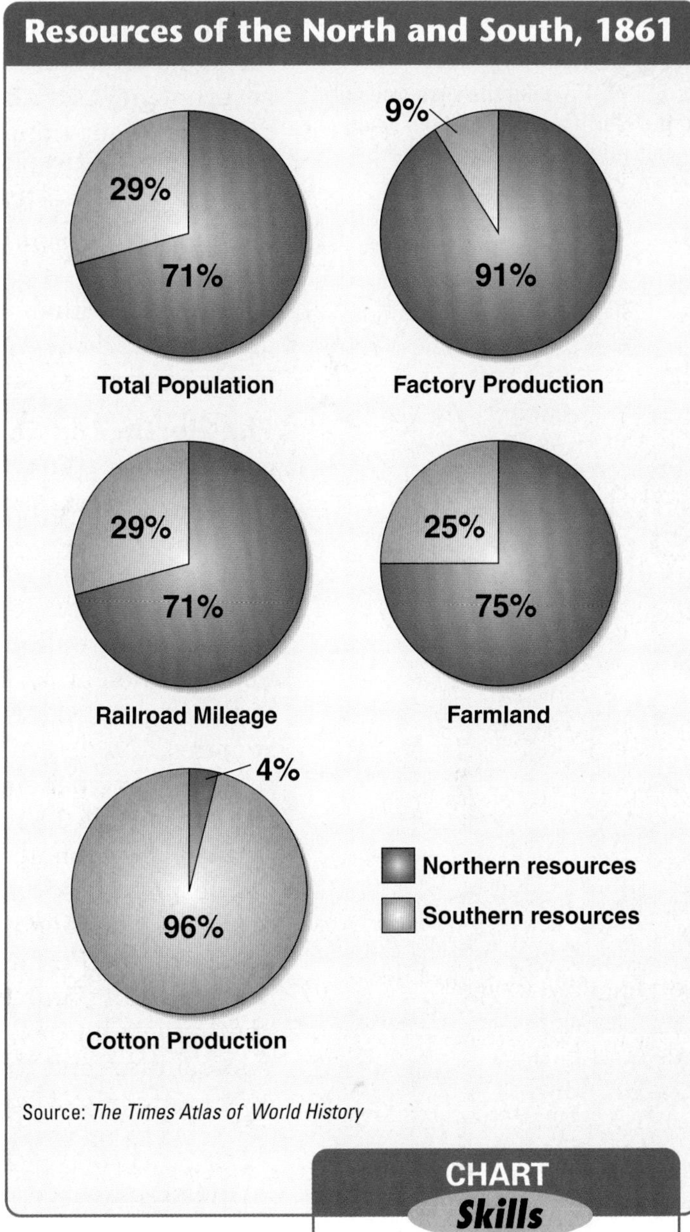

CHART *Skills*

As the Civil War began, the North had a number of economic advantages over the South.

1. **Comprehension** **(a)** How much farmland did each side have? **(b)** What percentage of the nation's factories did the South have?
2. **Critical Thinking Making Predictions** **(a)** Which side had more railroad track? **(b)** How would this affect the war?

Economics

Strengths and Weaknesses

Both sides in the conflict had strengths and weaknesses as the war began. The South had the strong advantage of fighting a defensive war. "We seek no conquest," said Confederate President Jefferson Davis. "All we ask is to be let alone." If the North did not move its forces into the South, the Confederacy would remain a separate country.

The South White southerners believed that they were fighting a war for independence, similar to the American Revolution. Defending their homeland and their way of life gave them a strong reason to fight. "Our men must prevail in combat," one Confederate said, "or they will lose their property, country, freedom—in short, everything."

Confederate soldiers also enjoyed an advantage because they knew the southern countryside better. Friendly civilians often guided soldiers along obscure roads that did not appear on maps. Much of the South was wooded, too. Confederate forces used the woods for cover as they defended themselves against invading Union troops.

The South, however, had serious economic weaknesses. It had few factories to produce weapons and other vital supplies. It also had few railroads to move troops and supplies. The railroads that it did have often did not connect to one another. Tracks simply ran between two points and then stopped.

*In western Virginia, where there were few slave owners, many people supported the Union. When Virginia seceded, westerners formed their own government. West Virginia became a state of the Union in 1863.

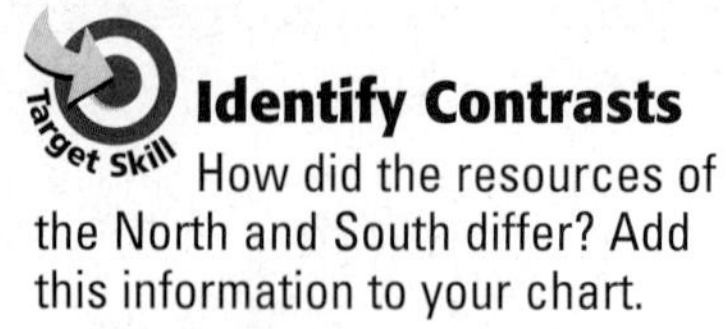

Identify Contrasts How did the resources of the North and South differ? Add this information to your chart.

The South also had political problems. The Confederate constitution favored states' rights and limited the authority of the central government. As a result, the Confederate government often found it difficult to get things done. On one occasion, for example, the governor of Georgia insisted that only Georgian officers should command Georgian troops.

Finally, the South had a small population. Only about 9 million people lived in the Confederacy, compared with 22 million in the Union. More than one third of the southern population were enslaved African Americans. As a result, the South did not have enough people to serve as soldiers and to support the war effort.

The North The North had almost four times as many free citizens as the South. Thus, it had a large source of volunteers. It also had many people to grow food and to work in factories making supplies.

Industry was the North's greatest resource. Before the war, northern factories produced more than 90 percent of the nation's manufactured goods. Once the war began, these factories quickly began making guns, bullets, cannons, boots, uniforms, and other supplies for the Union army. In addition, the North had more than 70 percent of the nation's rail lines, which it used to transport both troops and supplies.

The North benefited from a strong navy and a large fleet of trading ships. With few warships and only a small merchant fleet, the South was unable to compete with the North at sea.

Despite these advantages, the North faced a difficult military challenge. To bring the South back into the Union, northern soldiers had to conquer a huge area. Instead of defending their homes, they were invading unfamiliar land. As Union armies marched into the South, their lines of supply would be much longer than those of the Confederates and thus more open to attack.

The War's Leaders

Leadership was a crucial factor in the Civil War. President Jefferson Davis of the Confederacy, President Abraham Lincoln of the Union, and military leaders on both sides played key roles in determining the war's outcome.

President Jefferson Davis Many people thought that Davis was a stronger leader than Lincoln. Davis's experience prepared him for the position. However, he did not want it. As one observer stated:

> “Mr. Davis's military instincts still predominate, and his eager wish was to have joined the army instead of being elected President.”
>
> —Arthur James Freemantle, from *The Freemantle Diary*

Davis had attended the United States Military Academy at West Point. He had served as an officer in the Mexican War. Later, he served as Secretary of War under President Franklin Pierce. Furthermore, Davis was widely respected for his honesty and courage.

Davis, however, did not like to turn over to others the details of military planning. As a result, he spent much time worrying about small matters and arguing with his advisers.

President Abraham Lincoln At first, some northerners had doubts about Abraham Lincoln's ability to lead. He did not have much experience in national politics or military matters. However, Lincoln proved to be a patient but strong leader and a fine war planner.

Day by day, Lincoln gained the respect of those around him. Many liked his sense of humor. They noted that Lincoln even accepted criticism with a smile. When Secretary of War Edwin Stanton called Lincoln a fool, Lincoln commented, "Did Stanton say I was a fool? Then I must be one, for Stanton is generally right and he always says what he means."

Military Leaders As the war began, army officers in the South had to decide whether to stay in the Union army and fight against their home states, or join the Confederate forces.

Robert E. Lee of Virginia faced this dilemma when Lincoln asked him to command the Union army. He explains in a letter to a friend:

> "If Virginia stands by the old Union, so will I. But if she secedes . . . , then I will still follow my native State with my sword and, if need be, with my life."
>
> —Robert E. Lee, quoted in Carl Sandburg, *Abraham Lincoln*

Virginia did secede and Lee refused Lincoln's offer. Later, Lee became commander of the Confederate army.

Many of the army's best officers served the Confederacy. As a result, President Lincoln had trouble finding generals to match those of the South.

An American Profile

Robert E. Lee 1807–1870

Robert E. Lee came from a distinguished Virginia family. After graduating with honors from West Point, he served in the Army Corps of Engineers. During the Mexican War, his superior officer described him as "the very best soldier I ever saw in the field." Despite that, Lee hated the horror of war.

When the Civil War broke out, Lee was torn between the Union and his home state of Virginia. In the end, he chose Virginia. "I have not been able to make up my mind to raise my hand against my relatives, my children, my home," he said.

Why did Lee choose to side with the Confederacy?

 Section 1 Assessment  

Recall

1. **Identify** Explain the significance of **(a)** Abraham Lincoln, **(b)** Jefferson Davis, **(c)** Robert E. Lee.
2. **Define** **(a)** border state, **(b)** martial law.

Comprehension

3. What were the goals of each side as the war began?
4. Describe two advantages that the North had over the South at the start of the Civil War.
5. Describe one strength and one weakness of **(a)** President Abraham Lincoln, **(b)** President Jefferson Davis.

Critical Thinking and Writing

6. **Exploring the Main Idea** Review the Main Idea statement at the beginning of this section. Then, list five statements from the section that support the main idea.
7. **Making Decisions** Imagine that you are an army officer from the South at the beginning of the war. Would you side with the Union or with the Confederacy? Give at least two reasons for your decision.

Activity

Analyzing a Chart
Study the chart on page 487. Then, use the information on the chart to write a report analyzing the strengths and weaknesses of each side at the start of the Civil War. Based on your analysis, which side do you think will win the war? Explain.

2 No Easy Victory

Prepare to Read

Objectives

In this section, you will
- Describe the strategies each side adopted to win the war.
- Explain how early encounters dispelled hopes for a quick end to the war.
- Identify the victories of the Confederates.
- List the victories of the Union.

Key Terms

Battle of Bull Run
Virginia
Monitor
Battle of Antietam
Battle of Fredericksburg
Battle of Chancellorsville
Battle of Shiloh

Target Reading Skill

Main Idea As you read, prepare an outline of the section. Use roman numerals to indicate major headings, capital letters for subheadings, and numbers for supporting details.

I. Strategies for Victory
  A. Union plans
    1.
    2.
    3.
  B. Confederate plans
    1.
    2.
II. Early Encounters

Main Idea Despite hopes for a quick victory, both northerners and southerners soon learned that they were in for a long, difficult struggle.

Bullet caught in a shoulder plate

Setting the Scene At first, the armies of the North and the South marched proudly off to war. Each side expected a quick and painless victory. The reality of war soon shattered this expectation. Over and over, soldiers wrote home describing the awful face of battle:

> "I never saw so many broken down and exhausted men in all my life. I was sick as a horse, and as wet with blood and sweat as I could be. . . . Our tongues were parched and cracked for water, and our faces blackened with powder and smoke."
>
> —quoted by Shelby Foote in *The Civil War: A Narrative*

It soon became clear that there would be no quick end to the struggle. Both sides began to dig in for a long, difficult war.

Strategies for Victory

The North and South had different strategies for victory. The Union planned an aggressive campaign against the South. The South, meanwhile, planned to hold tight until the North lost the will to fight.

Union Plans First, the Union planned to use its navy to blockade southern ports. This would cut off the South's supply of manufactured goods from Europe.

In the East, Union generals aimed to seize Richmond, Virginia, the Confederate capital. They thought that they might end the war quickly by capturing the Confederate government.

In the West, the Union planned to seize control of the Mississippi River. This would prevent the South from using the river to supply its troops. It would also separate Arkansas, Texas, and Louisiana from the rest of the Confederacy.

Confederate Plans The South's strategy was simpler: The Confederate army would fight a defensive war until northerners tired of fighting. If the war became unpopular in the North, President Lincoln would have to stop the war and recognize the South's independence.

The Confederacy counted on European money and supplies to help fight the war. Southern cotton was important to the textile mills of England and other countries. Southerners were confident that Europeans would recognize the Confederacy as an independent nation and continue to buy southern cotton for their factories.

Early Encounters

"Forward to Richmond! Forward to Richmond!" Every day for more than a month, the influential *New York Tribune* blazed this war cry across its front page. At last, responding to popular pressure, President Lincoln ordered an attack.

Battle of Bull Run On July 21, 1861, Union troops set out from Washington, D.C., for Richmond, about 100 miles away. Hundreds of Washingtonians, in a festive mood, rode out along with them to watch the battle.

The Union troops had not gone far when they met up with Confederate soldiers. A battle quickly followed. It took place near a small Virginia stream known as Bull Run.

At first, Union forces succeeded in breaking up Confederate battle lines. "The war is over!" yelled some soldiers from Massachusetts. But General Thomas Jackson rallied the Virginia troops on a nearby hill. "Look!" cried a Confederate officer to his men, "There is Jackson standing like a stone wall! Rally behind the Virginians!" From that day on, the general was known as "Stonewall" Jackson.

In the end, it was the Union troops who panicked and ran. "Off they went," reported one observer, "across fields, toward the woods, anywhere, everywhere, to escape." For most of the soldiers, the retreat did not stop until they reached Washington, D.C.

The **Battle of Bull Run** showed both the Union and the Confederacy that their soldiers needed training. It also showed that the war would be long and bloody.

Caution, Delay, and Retreat After the shocking disaster at Bull Run, President Lincoln appointed General George McClellan as commander of the Union army of the East, known as the Army of the Potomac. McClellan, a superb organizer, transformed inexperienced recruits into an army of trained soldiers prepared for battle.

GEOGRAPHY Skills

Early in the war, Union armies were unsuccessful in their attempts to capture Richmond, the Confederate capital.

1. **Location** On the map, locate **(a)** Washington, D.C., **(b)** Richmond, **(c)** Bull Run, **(d)** Chancellorsville.
2. **Movement** Describe the route that General McClellan took when he tried to capture Richmond in 1862.
3. **Critical Thinking Making Decisions** Do you think that the Confederacy made a wise decision in locating its capital at Richmond? Explain.

The Civil War in the East

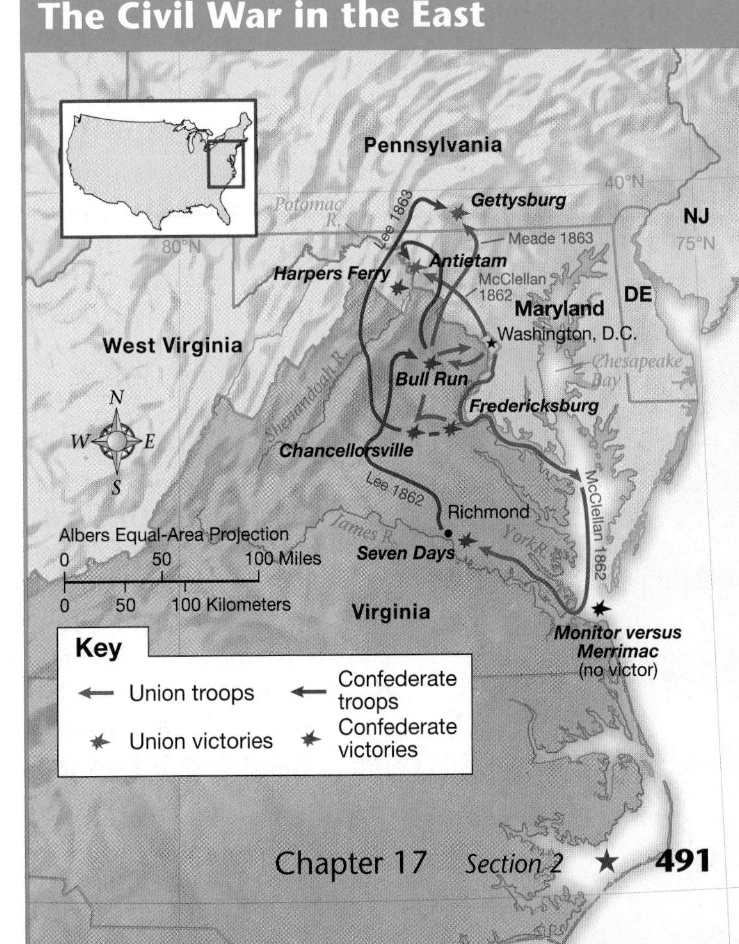

McClellan, however, was very cautious. He delayed leading his troops into battle. Newspapers reported "all quiet along the Potomac" so often that the phrase became a national joke. Finally, President Lincoln lost patience. "If General McClellan does not want to use the army," the President snapped, "I would like to borrow it."

At last, in March 1862, McClellan and most of his troops left Washington and sailed down the Potomac River. After landing south of Richmond, McClellan began inching slowly toward the Confederate capital.

Learning of the Union approach, General Robert E. Lee launched a series of counterattacks. At the same time, Lee sent General Stonewall Jackson north to threaten Washington. As a result, Lincoln was prevented from sending the rest of the Union army to help McClellan. Cautious as usual, McClellan abandoned the attack and retreated.

Identify Supporting Details

Which details in the paragraphs under "Naval Action" explain why ironclad ships were important? Add this information to your outline.

Naval Action Early in the war, Union ships blockaded southern ports. At first, some small, fast ships slipped through the blockade. These "blockade runners" brought everything from matches to guns to the Confederacy.

In time, however, the blockade became more effective. Trade through southern ports dropped by more than 90 percent. The South desperately needed a way to break the Union blockade. One method it tried was the ironclad ship.

Confederates took over an abandoned Union warship, the USS *Merrimack*. They covered it with iron plates and renamed it the ***Virginia***. On its first day out in March 1862, the *Virginia* destroyed two Union ships and drove three more aground. Union cannonballs bounced harmlessly off the *Virginia's* metal skin.

The Union countered with its own ironclad, the ***Monitor***. The two ships clashed in the waters off Hampton Roads, Virginia. Despite an exhausting battle, neither vessel seriously damaged the other, and both withdrew. Two months later Confederates had to sink the *Virginia* when the Union captured Norfolk. The Union eventually built more than 50 ironclads.

Ironclad ships changed naval warfare. However, the South was never again able to mount a serious attack against the Union navy. The Union blockade held throughout the war.

Antietam In September 1862, General Lee took the offensive and marched his troops north into Maryland. He believed that a southern victory on northern soil would be a great blow to northern morale.

Luck was against Lee, however. At an abandoned Confederate campsite, a Union officer found a copy of Lee's battle plan. It was wrapped around three cigars, left behind by a careless general. General McClellan was overjoyed to have the information. "If I cannot whip 'Bobbie Lee,' I will be willing to go home," he boasted.

However, McClellan was slow to act. Finally, after a few days, he attacked Lee's main force at Antietam (an TEE tuhm) on September 17. In the day-long battle that followed, more than 23,000 Union and Confederate soldiers were killed or wounded.

Antietam National Battlefield

On September 17, 1862, Union and Confederate troops faced one another at Antietam Creek near Sharpsburg, Maryland.

Today, 103 monuments at Antietam honor those who fought there. Most of the monuments were built by Civil War veterans. The barrels of 500 cannons, which were used in the Civil War, are on the battlefield. These mark the location of artillery during the battle.

Virtual Field Trip For an interactive look at the Antietam battle site, visit PHSchool.com, **Web Code mfd-1701.**

On the night of September 18, Lee ordered his troops to slip back into Virginia. The Confederates breathed a sigh of relief when they saw that McClellan was not pursuing them.

Neither side was a clear winner at the **Battle of Antietam.** The North was able to claim victory, though, because Lee had ordered his forces to withdraw. As a result, northern morale increased. Still, President Lincoln was keenly disappointed. General McClellan had failed to follow up his victory by pursuing the Confederates. In November, Lincoln appointed General Ambrose Burnside to replace McClellan as commander of the Army of the Potomac.

Confederate Victories in the East

Two stunning victories for the Confederacy came in late 1862 and 1863. In December 1862, Union forces set out once again toward Richmond.

Meeting Burnside's army outside Fredericksburg, Virginia, Lee's forces dug into the crest of a hill. There, in a strong defensive position, Confederate guns mowed down wave after wave of charging Union troops. The **Battle of Fredericksburg** was one of the Union's worst defeats. (See page 495.)

Half a year later, in May 1863, Lee, aided by Stonewall Jackson, again outmaneuvered Union forces. The **Battle of Chancellorsville** took place on thickly wooded ground near Chancellorsville, Virginia. Lee and Jackson defeated the Union troops in three days. Victory came at a high price for the South, however. During the battle, nervous

An American Profile

Ulysses S. Grant 1822–1885

General Ulysses S. Grant's troops had the Confederates surrounded at Fort Donelson. Confederate General Simon Bolivar Buckner wanted to discuss terms of surrender.

Grant's response was to the point: "No terms except an unconditional and immediate surrender can be accepted." Buckner immediately surrendered the fort. Grant's victory caused great celebration in the North. It also earned him the nickname "Unconditional Surrender" Grant.

What characteristics did Grant reveal by his actions at Fort Donelson?

Confederate sentries fired at what they thought was an approaching Union soldier. The "Union soldier" was General Stonewall Jackson. Several days later, Jackson died as a result of his injuries.

Union Victories in the West

In the West, Union forces met with better success. As you have read, the Union strategy was to seize control of the Mississippi River. General Ulysses S. Grant began moving toward that goal. In February 1862, Grant attacked and captured Fort Henry and Fort Donelson in Tennessee. These Confederate forts guarded two important tributaries of the Mississippi.

Grant now pushed south to Shiloh, a village on the Tennessee River. There, on April 6, he was surprised by Confederate forces. By the end of the day, the Confederates had driven the Union troops back toward the river.

Grant now showed the toughness and determination that would enable him to win many battles in the future. That night, one of Grant's soldiers approached him. The officer thought Union forces should retreat. But, seeing Grant's stubborn face, the officer only said, "Well, Grant, we've had the devil's own day, haven't we?"

"Yes," Grant replied. "Lick 'em tomorrow, though."

And they did. With the aid of reinforcements, Grant beat back the Confederates and won the **Battle of Shiloh.** It was, however, one of the bloodiest encounters of the Civil War.

While Grant was fighting at Shiloh, the Union navy moved to gain control of the Mississippi River. In April 1862, Union gunboats captured New Orleans. Other ships seized Memphis, Tennessee. By capturing these two cities, the Union controlled both ends of the Mississippi. The South could no longer use the river as a supply line.

★ ★ ★ Section 2 Assessment ★ ★ ★

Recall

1. **Identify** Explain the significance of **(a)** Stonewall Jackson, **(b)** Battle of Bull Run, **(c)** George McClellan, **(d)** *Virginia,* **(e)** *Monitor,* **(f)** Battle of Antietam, **(g)** Battle of Fredericksburg, **(h)** Battle of Chancellorsville, **(i)** Ulysses S. Grant, **(j)** Battle of Shiloh.

Comprehension

2. Describe **(a)** the North's three-part plan for defeating the South, **(b)** the South's plan to defeat the North.
3. What did both sides learn from the Battle of Bull Run?
4. Why was the Confederate victory at Fredericksburg critical?
5. How did Union victories at New Orleans and Memphis affect the South?

Critical Thinking and Writing

6. **Exploring the Main Idea** Review the Main Idea statement at the beginning of this section. Make a list of five events and their results during the first two years of the war.
7. **Analyzing Ideas** Analyze the meaning of this statement: "The South could win the war by not losing, but the North could win only by winning."

ACTIVITY

Go Online
PHSchool.com

Connecting to Today

Both the Union and Confederate navies developed ironclad ships during the Civil War. Use the Internet to research technological advances in modern naval vessels. Prepare an oral class presentation including pictures. For help in completing the activity, visit PHSchool.com, **Web Code mfd-1702.**

Connecting With... **Geography**

The Battle of Fredericksburg

Fredericksburg, Virginia, was located between Washington, D.C., and Richmond, the Confederate capital. Taking Fredericksburg was a step toward capturing Richmond.

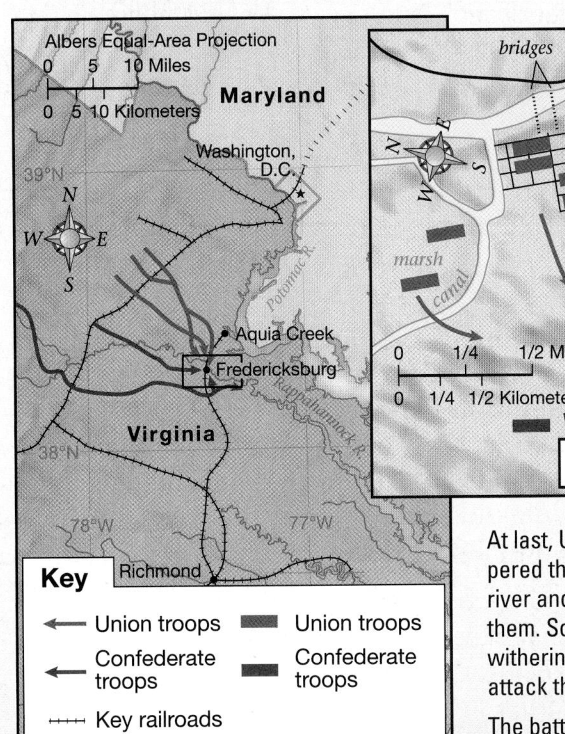

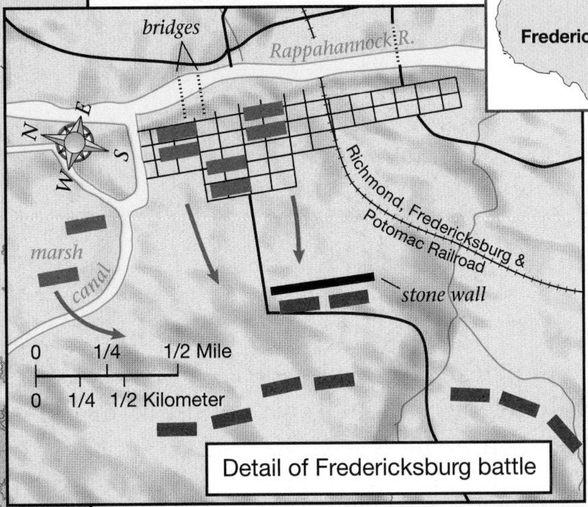

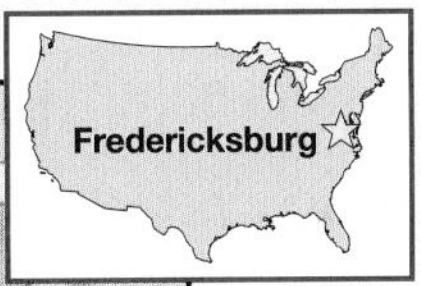

In the fall of 1862, General Ambrose Burnside began moving his Union army toward Fredericksburg. They were stopped by the Rappahannock River. While the Union troops waited for engineers to bridge the river, General Robert E. Lee's Confederate forces occupied the city and the high ground behind it. They took up a strong position, overlooking a large, open field.

At last, Union bridge builders set to work, but Confederate snipers peppered them with gunfire. Finally, though, the Union army got across the river and, on December 13, launched an attack. The terrain was against them. Some troops had to cross 400 yards of open ground in the face of withering fire. Others, running into a canal and a marsh, were forced to attack the Confederate line at its strongest point—the top of a hill.

The battle was a disaster for the Union army. For hours, soldiers marched up the hill only to be mowed down by gunfire. Finally, Burnside halted the attack. His army had lost 13,000 men, compared with only 5,000 for Lee's.

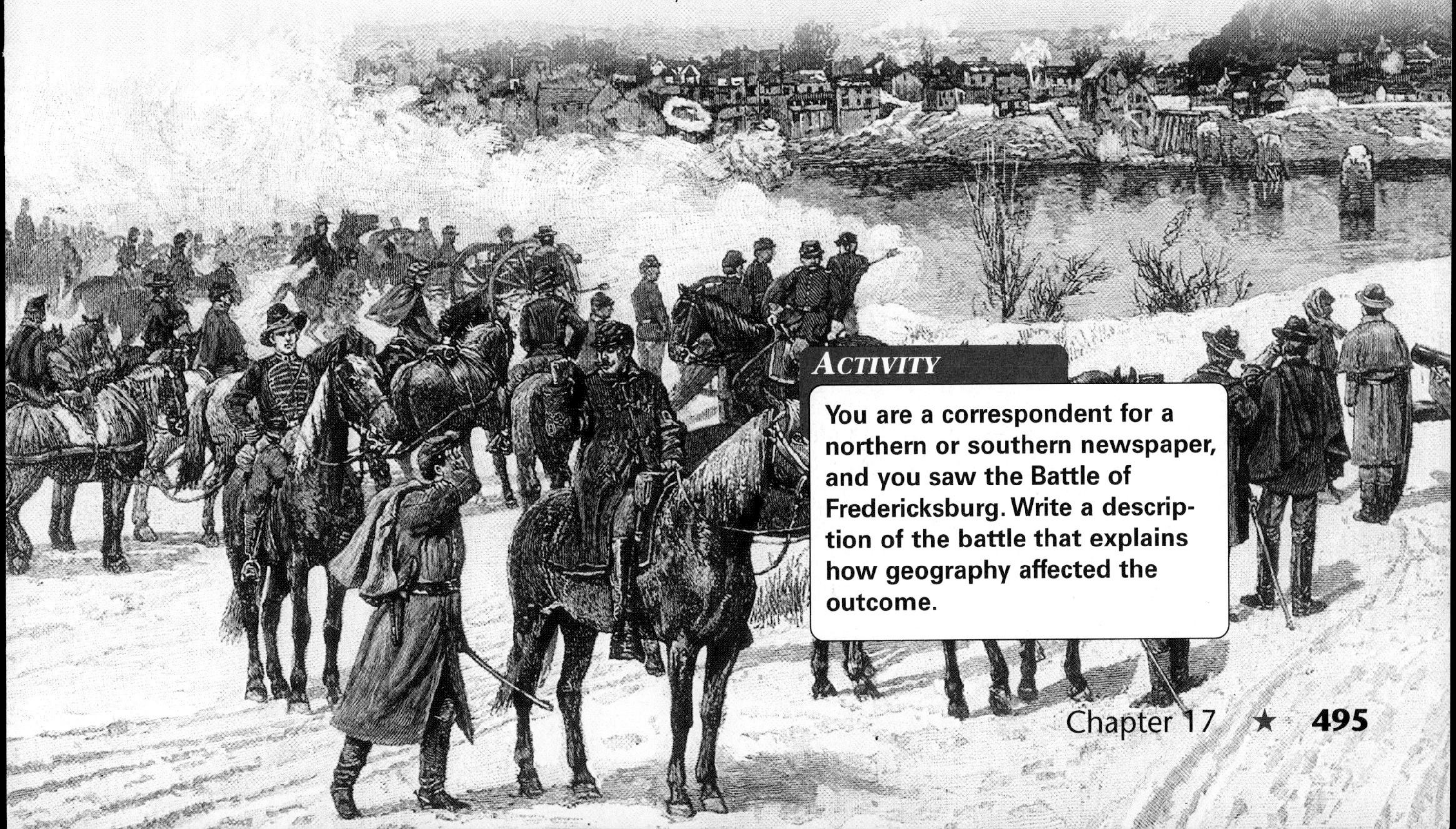

ACTIVITY

You are a correspondent for a northern or southern newspaper, and you saw the Battle of Fredericksburg. Write a description of the battle that explains how geography affected the outcome.

3 A Promise of Freedom

Prepare to Read

Objectives

In this section, you will
- Identify Lincoln's primary goal in the war.
- Describe the effects of the Emancipation Proclamation.
- Explain African Americans' contribution to the war effort both in the Union army and behind Confederate lines.

Key Terms

emancipate

Emancipation Proclamation

54th Massachusetts Regiment

Fort Wagner

Target Reading Skill

Cause and Effect Copy the chart. As you read, complete the chart to show the causes and effects of the Emancipation Proclamation.

CAUSES
1.
2. Lincoln wanted to weaken the Confederacy's ability to fight

EMANCIPATION PROCLAMATION

EFFECTS
1. Union fighting to end slavery
2.

Main Idea By issuing the Emancipation Proclamation, Lincoln expanded the goals of the war to include the ending of slavery.

African American soldier

Setting the Scene John Finnely heard the news first thing in the morning: Ten slaves had run off the night before. Finnely, a twelve-year-old slave on a plantation in Alabama, had a pretty good idea where the escapees had gone. Most certainly, they had headed for Union troops camped a few miles to the north—and freedom.

Finnely, too, began to "think and think 'bout gittin' freedom." At last, with a mixture of hope and fear, he decided to make the break:

> "I makes up my mind to go and I leaves with a chunk of meat and cornbread . . . half skeert to death. I sure have my eyes open and my ears forward, watchin' for the [Confederate slave patrols]. I step off the road in the night, at the sight of anything, and in the day I take to the woods."
>
> —John Finnely, quoted in *Remembering Slavery*

At first, the Civil War was not a war against slavery. But as thousands of slaves like John Finnely rushed into the arms of Union troops with the hope of freedom, some northerners began to rethink the aims of the war.

Lincoln's Goal

The Civil War began as a war to restore the Union, not to end slavery. President Lincoln made this point clear in a letter that was widely distributed:

> "If I could save the Union without freeing any slave, I would do it; and if I could save it by freeing all the slaves, I would do it; and if I could do it by freeing some and leaving others alone, I would also do that."
>
> —Abraham Lincoln, August 22, 1862, quoted in Carl Sandburg, *Abraham Lincoln*

Lincoln had a reason for handling the slavery issue cautiously. As you have read, four slave states remained in the Union. The President did not want to do anything that might cause these states to shift their loyalty to the Confederacy. The resources of the border states might allow the South to turn the tide of the war.

The Emancipation Proclamation

By mid-1862, Lincoln came to believe that he could save the Union only by broadening the goals of the war. He decided to **emancipate,** or **free,** enslaved African Americans living in the Confederacy. In the four loyal slave states, however, slaves would not be freed. Nor would slaves be freed in Confederate lands that had already been captured by the Union, such as the city of New Orleans.

Motives and Timing Lincoln had practical reasons for his emancipation plan. At the start of the Civil War, more than 3 million slaves labored for the Confederacy. They helped grow the food that fed Confederate soldiers. They also worked in iron and lead mines that were vital to the South's war effort. Some served as nurses and cooks for the army. Lincoln knew that emancipation would weaken the Confederacy's ability to carry on the war.

However, Lincoln did not want to anger slave owners in the Union. Also, he knew that many northerners opposed freedom for enslaved African Americans. Lincoln hoped to introduce the idea of emancipation slowly, by limiting it to territory controlled by the Confederacy.

The President had another motive. As you read in Chapter 16, Lincoln believed that slavery was wrong. When he felt that he could act to free slaves without threatening the Union, he did so.

Lincoln was concerned about the timing of his announcement. The war was not going well for the Union. He did not want Americans to think he was freeing slaves as a desperate effort to save a losing cause. He waited for a victory to announce his plan.

On September 22, 1862, following the Union victory at Antietam, Lincoln issued a preliminary proclamation. He issued the formal **Emancipation Proclamation** on January 1, 1863.

Impact of the Proclamation Because the rebelling states were not under Union control, no slaves actually gained their freedom on January 1, 1863. Still, the Emancipation Proclamation changed the purpose of the war. Now, Union troops were fighting to end slavery as well as to save the Union.

The opponents of slavery greeted the proclamation with joy. In Boston, African American abolitionist Frederick Douglass witnessed one of the many emotional celebrations that took place:

> “The effect of this announcement was startling . . . and the scene was wild and grand. . . . My old friend Rue, a Negro preacher, . . . expressed the heartfelt emotion of the hour, when he led all voices in the anthem, 'Sound the loud timbrel o'er Egypt's dark sea, Jehovah hath triumphed, his people are free!'”
>
> —Frederick Douglass, *Life and Times of Frederick Douglass*

Primary Source

The Emancipation Proclamation

On January 1, 1863, President Lincoln issued the Emancipation Proclamation. The document declared the following:

"On the 1st day of January, in the year of our Lord 1863, all persons held as slaves within any state or . . . part of a state [whose] people . . . shall then be in rebellion against the United States, shall be then, thenceforward, and forever free."

Analyzing Primary Sources

Were all enslaved African Americans freed? Explain.

Target Skill — Understand Effects Which effects of the Emancipation Proclamation are discussed in this paragraph? Add these to your chart.

Viewing History

Assault on Fort Wagner

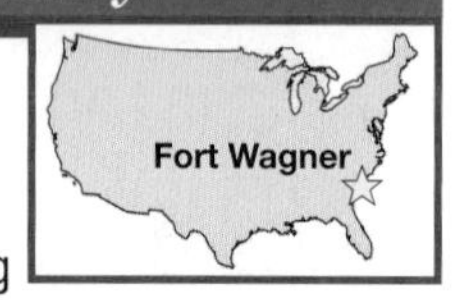

In this painting by Tom Lovell, African American soldiers of the 54th Massachusetts Regiment charge Confederate troops at Fort Wagner. Nearly half the regiment died in the failed attack, including the regiment's commander, Colonel Robert Gould Shaw. **Applying Information** ***Why did African Americans have their own regiments?***

In the South, Lincoln's proclamation was seen as a "fiend's act" that destroyed expensive property. The proclamation won the sympathy of Europeans, especially workers. As a result, it became less likely that Britain or any other European country would come to the aid of the South.

African American Contributions

When the war began, thousands of free blacks volunteered to fight for the Union. At first, federal law forbade African Americans to serve as soldiers. When Congress repealed that law in 1862, however, both free African Americans and escaped slaves enlisted in the Union army.

In the Union Army The army assigned African American volunteers to all-black units, commanded by white officers. At first, the black troops served only as laborers. They performed noncombat duties such as building roads and guarding supplies. Black troops received only half the pay of white soldiers.

African American soldiers protested against this policy of discrimination that denied them the same treatment as other soldiers. Gradually, conditions changed. By 1863, African American troops were fighting in major battles against the Confederates. In 1864, the United States War Department announced that all soldiers would receive equal pay. By the end of the war, about 200,000 African Americans had fought for the Union. Nearly 40,000 lost their lives.

Acts of Bravery One of the most famous African American units in the Union army was the **54th Massachusetts Regiment.** The 54th accepted African Americans from all across the North. Frederick Douglass helped recruit troops for the regiment, and two of his sons served in it.

On July 18, 1863, the 54th Massachusetts Regiment led an attack on **Fort Wagner** near Charleston, South Carolina. Under heavy fire, troops fought their way into the fort before being forced to withdraw. In the desperate fighting, almost half the regiment was killed.

The courage of the 54th Massachusetts and other regiments helped to win respect for African American soldiers. Sergeant William Carney of the 54th Massachusetts was the first of 16 African American soldiers to win the Medal of Honor in the Civil War. Such soldiers had "proved themselves among the bravest of the brave," Secretary of War Edwin Stanton told Lincoln.

Behind Confederate Lines Despite the Emancipation Proclamation, African Americans still worked in the South as slaves on plantations. However, many slaves slowed down their work or refused to work at all. In this way, they hoped to weaken the South's war effort. They knew that when victorious Union troops arrived in their area, they would be free.

Thousands of enslaved African Americans took direct action to free themselves. Whenever a Union army appeared, slaves from all over the area would flee their former masters. They crossed the Union lines to freedom. By the end of the war, about one fourth of the South's enslaved population had escaped to freedom.

★ ★ ★ Section 3 Assessment ★ ★ ★

Recall

1. **Identify** Explain the significance of **(a)** Emancipation Proclamation, **(b)** 54th Massachusetts Regiment, **(c)** Fort Wagner.
2. **Define** emancipate.

Comprehension

3. Why was President Lincoln cautious about making the abolition of slavery a goal of the war?
4. How did the Emancipation Proclamation affect the status of enslaved African Americans?
5. How did enslaved African Americans help to hurt the Confederate war effort?

Critical Thinking and Writing

6. **Exploring the Main Idea** Review the Main Idea statement at the beginning of this section. Write a newspaper article explaining why Lincoln issued the Emancipation Proclamation.
7. **Analyzing Primary Sources** In 1861, Frederick Douglass said, "This is no time to fight with one hand when both hands are needed. This is no time to fight with only your white hand, and allow your black hand to remain tied!" **(a)** What did Douglass mean by this statement? **(b)** Did the United States Congress agree with Douglass? Explain.

Activity

Writing a Poem **A monument is being built to honor the courageous African American soldiers of the Civil War. Write a poem to be inscribed on the monument, mentioning some of the facts you learned in this section.**

4 Hardships of War

Prepare to Read

Objectives

In this section, you will
- Describe conditions for Confederate and Union soldiers.
- Explain what problems each side faced at home.
- Summarize how the war affected the economies of the North and the South.
- Identify the role women played in the war.

Key Terms

Copperhead
draft
habeas corpus
income tax
inflation
profiteer

Target Reading Skill

Comparison and Contrast Copy this incomplete Venn diagram. As you read, fill in key facts about conditions in the North and South during the Civil War. Write common characteristics in the overlapping section.

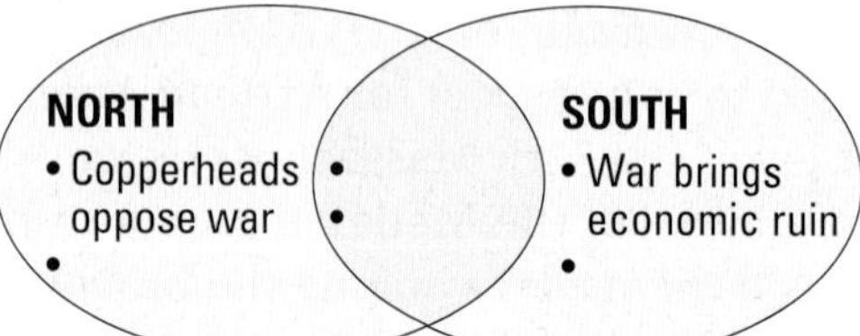

Main Idea The demands of the war hurt civilians as well as soldiers on both sides, but the problems were worse in the Confederate States.

Homecoming

Setting the Scene John Jones knew that he was not alone in the hardships he experienced. All he had to do was look around in the Confederate capital of Richmond. Some of the city's residents, he noted, looked "like vagabonds . . . gaunt and pale with hunger." As for his own family:

> "My daughter's cat is staggering today, for want of animal food. Sometimes I fancy I stagger myself. We do not average two ounces of meat daily; and some do not get any for several days together."
>
> —John B. Jones, *A Rebel War Clerk's Diary*

The Civil War caused hardships not only for soldiers but for people at home as well. Southerners were especially hard hit, because most of the fighting took place in the South. But for both North and South, the war affected every area of life.

The Hard Life of Soldiers

On both sides, most soldiers were under the age of 21. War, however, quickly turned gentle boys into tough men. Soldiers drilled and marched for long hours. They slept on the ground even in rain and snow. In combat, boys of 18 learned to stand firm as cannon blasts shook the earth and bullets whizzed past their ears.

As the death toll rose, the age restrictions for soldiers were relaxed. The South drafted boys as young as 17 and men as old as 50.

New technology added to the horror of war. Cone-shaped bullets made rifles twice as accurate. Improved cannons hurled exploding shells several miles. The new weapons had deadly results. In most battles, one fourth or more of the soldiers were killed or wounded.

Sick and wounded soldiers faced other horrors. Medical care on the battlefield was crude. Surgeons routinely amputated injured arms and legs. At the time, doctors did not know how germs cause infection and disease. As a result, minor wounds often became infected. In addition, poor sanitary conditions in the army camps allowed disease to spread rapidly. Diseases such as pneumonia and malaria killed more men than guns or cannons did.

On both sides, prisoners of war faced horrifying conditions. At Andersonville, a prison camp in Georgia, many Union prisoners died of disease or starvation.

The difficult life of soldiers led many to desert. One out of every seven Union soldiers and one out of every nine Confederate soldiers deserted.

Opposition to War in the North

Some northerners opposed using force to keep the South in the Union. Supporters of the war called these people **Copperheads,** after the poisonous snake. Other northerners supported the war but opposed the way Lincoln was conducting it.

The Draft Law As the war dragged on, public support dwindled. When the war began, the North offered men money to enlist. However, some men abused the system. They would sign up, collect the money, and then desert. Soon, however, there was a shortage of volunteers to serve in the Union army.

Viewing History

Battlefield Medicine

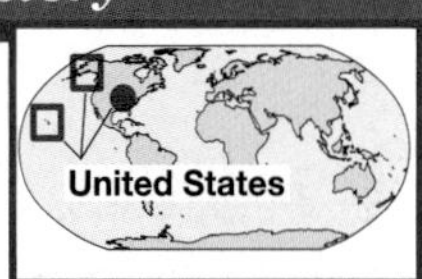

Improved weapons during the Civil War made the injuries suffered by soldiers worse. Soldiers hit with the Minié ball suffered severe bone damage. Shown at left are the tools used by surgeons to amputate the limb. Unlike today, surgeons at that time worked without gloves, antiseptic, or masks. Now, there are better ways to care for wounds and, as shown at right, improved surgical procedures. **Drawing Conclusions** ***How has technology been an advantage and a disadvantage in war?***

LINKING PAST AND PRESENT

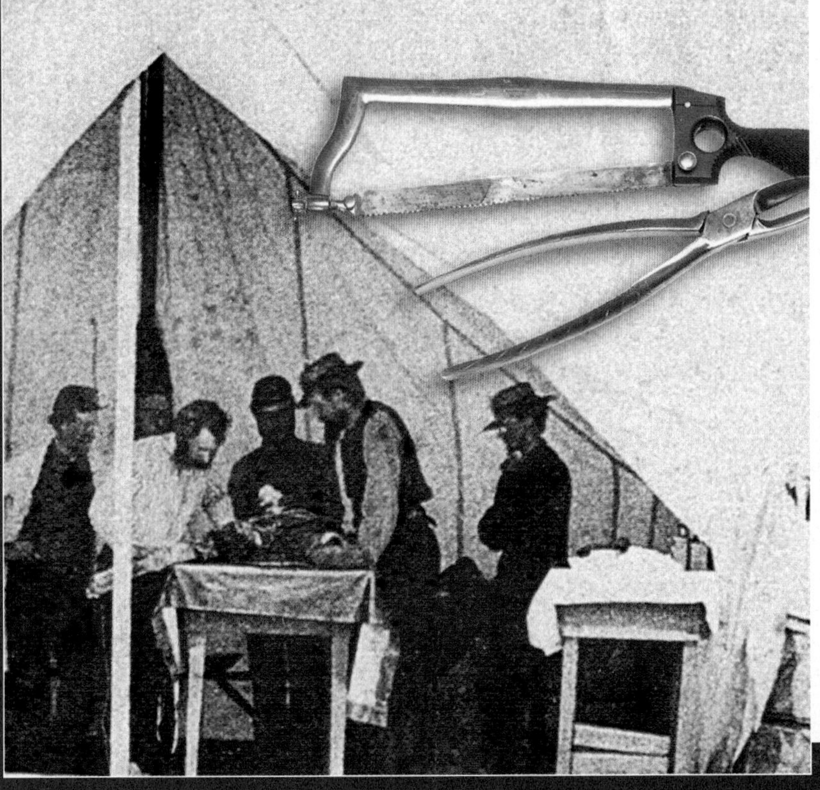

▲ **Past**

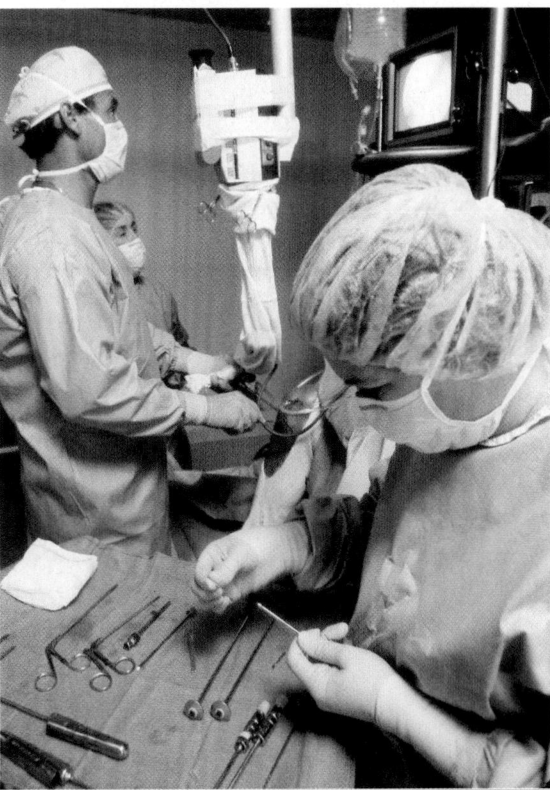

▲ **Present**

Congress passed a **draft** law in 1863. It required all able-bodied males between the ages of 20 and 45 to serve in the military if they were called. Under the law, a man could avoid the draft by paying the government $300 or by hiring someone to serve in his place. This angered many people, who began to see the Civil War as "a rich man's war and a poor man's fight."

Riots in the Cities Opposition to the draft law led to riots in several northern cities. The law had gone into effect soon after Lincoln issued the Emancipation Proclamation. Some white northerners, especially recent immigrants in the cities, believed that they were being forced to fight to end slavery. They also worried that they would have to compete with free African Americans for jobs.

The worst riot took place in New York City during July 1863. For four days, white workers attacked free blacks. Rioters also attacked rich New Yorkers who had paid to avoid serving in the army. At least 74 people were killed during the riot.

President Lincoln moved to stop the riots and other "disloyal practices." Several times, he suspended **habeas corpus** (HAY bee uhs KOR puhs), the right to be charged or have a hearing before being jailed. Lincoln argued that the Constitution allowed him to deny people their rights "when in the cases of rebellion or invasion, the public safety may require it." The President also said that those arrested could be tried under the stricter rules of a military court. Eventually, nearly 14,000 people were arrested. However, most were never charged with a specific crime or brought to trial.

Problems in the South

President Davis, meanwhile, struggled to create a strong federal government for the Confederacy. Many southerners firmly believed in states' rights. They resisted paying taxes to a central government. At one point, Georgia even threatened to secede from the Confederacy!

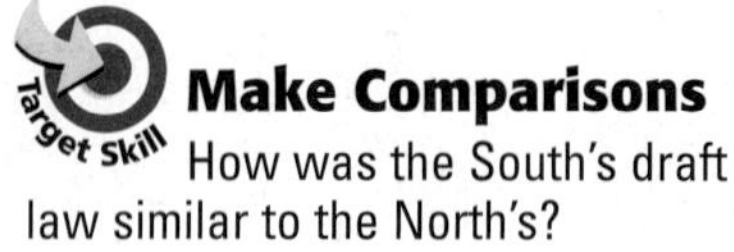

Make Comparisons How was the South's draft law similar to the North's?

Like the North, the South was forced to pass a draft law to fill its army. However, men who owned or supervised more than 20 slaves did not have to serve. Southern farmers who had few or no slaves resented this law.

Near the end of the war, the South no longer had enough white men to fill the ranks. Robert E. Lee urged that enslaved African Americans be allowed to serve as soldiers. Desperate, the Confederate congress finally agreed. The war ended, however, before any enslaved people put on Confederate uniforms.

The Northern Economy

The Civil War cost far more than any previous war. The Union had to use several strategies to raise money. In some ways, however, war helped the North's economy.

Taxation and Inflation To pay for the war, Congress established the nation's first **income tax,** or tax on people's earnings, in 1861. A new agency, the Internal Revenue Bureau, oversaw the collection process. The Union also issued bonds worth millions of dollars. Still, taxes and bonds did not raise enough money. To get the funds it needed, the North printed more than $400 million in paper money.

As the money supply increased, each dollar was worth less. In response, businesses charged more for their goods. The North was experiencing **inflation,** a rise in prices and a decrease in the value of money. During the war, prices for goods nearly doubled in the North.

Economic Benefits The war helped the North's economy in several ways. Since many farmers went off to fight, there was a greater need for machines to plant and harvest crops. The purchase of reapers rose to nearly 165,000 during the war. As a result, farm production actually went up during the war.

The wartime demand for clothing, shoes, guns, and other goods helped many northern industries. Some manufacturers made fortunes by profiteering. **Profiteers** charged excessive prices for goods that the government desperately needed for the war.

Cause *and* Effect

Causes

- Issue of slavery in the territories divides the North and South
- Abolitionists want slavery to end
- South fears it will lose power in the national government
- Southern states secede after Lincoln's election
- Confederates bombard Fort Sumter

THE CIVIL WAR

Effects

- Lincoln issues the Emancipation Proclamation
- Northern economy booms
- South loses its cotton trade with Britain
- Total war destroys the South's economy
- Hundreds of thousands of Americans killed

Effects Today

- Disagreements over states' rights persist
- African Americans have equal protection under the Constitution
- Millions of Americans visit Civil War battlefields each year

GRAPHIC ORGANIZER *Skills*

The Civil War was a major turning point in the history of the United States.

1. **Comprehension** How did the war affect the northern and southern economies?
2. **Critical Thinking Identifying Causes and Effects** Describe another cause or effect that could be added to this chart.

The Southern Economy

For the South, war brought economic ruin. The South had to struggle with the cost of the war, the loss of the cotton trade, and severe shortages brought on by the Union blockade.

The Economy Suffers To raise money, the Confederacy imposed an income tax and a tax-in-kind. The tax-in-kind required farmers to turn over one tenth of their crops to the government. The government took crops because it knew that southern farmers had little money.

Like the North, the South printed paper money. It printed so much that wild inflation set in. By 1865, one Confederate dollar was worth only two cents in gold. Prices were especially high in Richmond, where a barrel of flour was $275 in early 1864, potatoes were $25 a bushel, and butter was $15 a pound.

The war did serious damage to the cotton trade, the South's main source of income. Early in the war, President Davis halted cotton shipments to Britain. He hoped to force Britain to side with the South in return for renewed shipments of cotton. The tactic backfired. Britain simply bought more cotton from Egypt and India. Davis succeeded only in cutting the South's income.

Effects of the Blockade The Union blockade created severe shortages in the South. Confederate armies sometimes had to wait weeks for supplies of food and clothing. With few factories of its own, the South bought many of its weapons in Europe. However, the blockade cut off most deliveries from across the Atlantic. To acquire goods, the government began building and running factories. Private manufacturers were offered contracts and draft exemptions for their workers if they started making war goods.

For civilians, the blockade brought food shortages. The production of food became critical to the economy. Many plantations switched from growing cotton to raising grain and livestock, or animals raised for food. In some states, cotton production was limited.

Women in the War

Women of both the North and the South played vital roles during the war. As men left for the battlefields, women took jobs in industry and on farms.

Women's aid societies helped supply the troops with food, bedding, clothing, and medicine. Throughout the North, women held fairs and other fundraising events to pay for supplies.

Nursing the Wounded Women on both sides worked as nurses. At first, doctors were unwilling to permit even trained nurses to work in military hospitals. When wounded men began to swamp army hospitals, however, this attitude soon changed. In fact, women performed so well that nursing became an accepted occupation for women after the war.

Dorothea Dix, famous for her work reforming prisons and mental hospitals, and Clara Barton, who later founded the American Red Cross, both became nurses for the Union army. Sojourner Truth, the African American antislavery leader, worked in Union hospitals and in camps for freed slaves. In the South, Sally Tompkins set up a hospital in Richmond, Virginia.

★ ★ ★ Section 4 Assessment ★ ★ ★

Recall

1. **Identify** Explain the significance of **(a)** Copperhead, **(b)** Dorothea Dix, **(c)** Clara Barton, **(d)** Sojourner Truth, **(e)** Sally Tompkins.
2. **Define** **(a)** draft, **(b)** habeas corpus, **(c)** income tax, **(d)** inflation, **(e)** profiteer.

Comprehension

3. Describe three hardships faced by soldiers during the Civil War.
4. **(a)** Why did some northerners oppose the war? **(b)** How did the blockade affect the southern economy?
5. Describe three ways in which women contributed to the war effort.

Critical Thinking and Writing

6. **Exploring the Main Idea** Review the Main Idea statement at the beginning of this section. Then, write a diary entry describing conditions in the South during the later days of the Civil War.
7. **Linking Past and Present** **(a)** What advances in technology made Civil War battles deadly? **(b)** In what ways would war today be even more deadly?

ACTIVITY

Go Online
PHSchool.com

Writing a Report

Use the Internet to find out more about Civil War medicine. Among the topics you might research are nurses, surgeons, field hospitals, battle wounds, and disease. Then, write a report about battlefield medicine during the Civil War. For help in completing the activity, visit PHSchool.com, **Web Code mfd-1703.**

5 The War Ends

Prepare to Read

Objectives

In this section, you will
- Explain why the Union victories at Vicksburg and Gettysburg were important.
- Describe Grant's plan for ending the war.
- Identify Lincoln's hopes for the Union after his reelection.
- Summarize why the Civil War was a major turning point in U.S. history.

Key Terms

siege
Battle of Gettysburg
Pickett's Charge
Gettysburg Address
total war
Appomattox Court House

Target Reading Skill

Sequence Copy the flowchart. As you read the section, fill in the boxes with information about the conclusion of the war.

Vicksburg
- **Grant makes many attempts to capture**
- **Grant has brilliant plan**
-

↓

Gettysburg
-
-

↓

[ ]

↓

[ ]

Main Idea Under the leadership of General Ulysses S. Grant, Union armies used their resources and manpower to defeat the Confederacy.

Setting the Scene To General Ulysses S. Grant, every problem had a solution. For example, he needed telegraph lines to coordinate the march of his Union troops into the South. So, he had them strung as his troops advanced. Some of Grant's operators even learned to receive messages without a telegraph station. Touching the ends of the bare wires to their tongues, these resourceful men picked up the faint spark of the Morse Code signals.

In 1864, President Lincoln had appointed Ulysses S. Grant commander in chief of the Union army. "The art of war is simple," Grant said. "Find out where your enemy is, get at him as soon as you can and strike him as hard as you can, and keep moving on." It seemed the President had finally found the general who could lead the Union to victory.

Civil War soldier on a telegraph pole

The Fall of Vicksburg

As you have read, Confederate armies won major battles at Fredericksburg in December 1862 and at Chancellorsville in May 1863. These were gloomy days for the North. Then, in July 1863, the tide of war turned against the South as Union forces won major victories in both the East and the West.

In the West, Union triumph came along the Mississippi River. The Union, which had captured New Orleans and Memphis, already controlled both ends of the Mississippi River. Still, the Confederates held Vicksburg, Mississippi. Vicksburg sat on a cliff high above the river.

Early in 1863, Grant's forces tried again and again to seize Vicksburg. The Confederates held out bravely. At last, Grant devised a brilliant plan. Marching his troops inland, he launched a surprise attack on Jackson, Mississippi. Then, he turned west and attacked Vicksburg from the rear. (See the map on page 507.)

Geography and History

The Vicksburg Campaign

Set on high bluffs overlooking the Mississippi River, Vicksburg was a major strategic target during the Civil War. If Union forces captured Vicksburg, they would control the river and split the Confederacy into two parts. "Vicksburg is the key!" said President Lincoln.

The swamps, rivers, and bluffs around Vicksburg made a direct attack almost impossible. At the same time, Confederate artillery, perched high above the Mississippi, could easily blast Union ships attempting to sail past the city.

In the end, General Grant determined that the only way to subdue Vicksburg was to lay siege to the city. After 48 days of being cut off from all supplies and of constant hammering by cannon fire, the Confederates finally surrendered.

Analyze the effect of geography on the Battle of Vicksburg.

For more than six weeks, Grant's forces lay siege to Vicksburg. A **siege** is a military encirclement of an enemy position and blockading or bombarding it in order to force it to surrender. Finally, on July 4, 1863, the Confederates surrendered Vicksburg.

On July 9, Union forces also captured Port Hudson, Louisiana. The entire Mississippi was now under Union control. The Confederacy was split into two parts. Texas, Arkansas, and Louisiana were cut off from the rest of the Confederate states.

Union Victory at Gettysburg

Meanwhile, in the East, after his victory at Chancellorsville, General Lee moved his army north into Pennsylvania. He hoped to take the Yankees by surprise. If he succeeded in Pennsylvania, Lee planned to swing south and capture Washington, D.C.

On June 30, 1863, a Union force under General George C. Meade met part of Lee's army at the small town of Gettysburg, Pennsylvania. Both sides quickly sent in reinforcements. The three-day **Battle of Gettysburg** that followed was one of the most important battles of the Civil War.

On the first day of battle, July 1, the Confederates drove the Union forces out of Gettysburg. The Yankees, however, took up strong positions on Cemetery Ridge, overlooking the town.

The next day, Lee ordered an attack on both ends of the Union line. Southern troops fought hard, but the Union army was well prepared for Lee's offensive. At the end of a day of savage fighting, Lee's forces had suffered heavy casualties but failed to dislodge the Union army from its strong position.

Pickett's Charge Despite his losses, Lee decided to attack again. He wanted to "create a panic and virtually destroy the [Union] army." On July 3, he ordered General George Pickett to lead 15,000 men in a daring charge against the center of the Union line. To reach their target, Pickett's men would have to march 1,000 yards across open ground and climb up a steep slope within clear view of the enemy.

This last attack led by Pickett is known as **Pickett's Charge.** Pickett gave the order to charge. As the men rushed forward, Union guns opened fire. Row after row of soldiers fell to the ground, dead. The battle noise, one soldier recalled, was "strange and terrible, a sound that came from thousands of human throats . . . like a vast mournful roar."

Pickett's Charge failed. The steady barrage of bullets and shells kept all but a few Confederate soldiers from reaching the Union lines. The next day, a Union officer trying to ride over the battlefield could not because "the dead and wounded lay too thick to guide a horse through them."

As the survivors limped back, Lee rode among them. "It's all my fault," he admitted humbly. Lee had no choice but to retreat. After they were defeated at Gettysburg, the Confederates would never invade the North again.

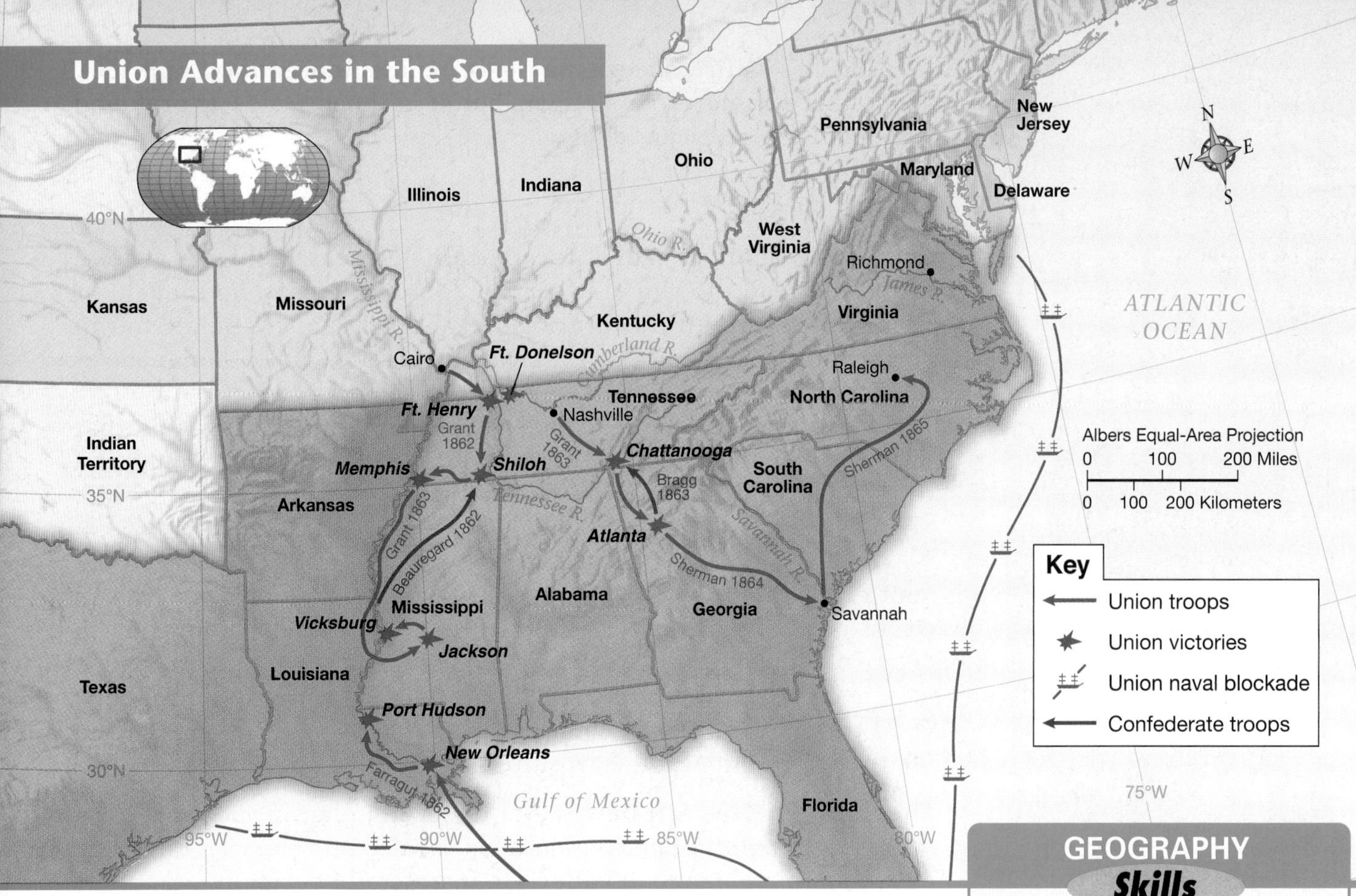

GEOGRAPHY Skills

As the Civil War dragged on, Union armies advanced deeper and deeper into the South. General Sherman marched his troops through Georgia and the Carolinas.

1. **Location** On the map, locate **(a)** Vicksburg, **(b)** Atlanta, **(c)** Savannah.
2. **Place** What three Confederate states were cut off from the rest of the Confederacy after Union forces gained control of the Mississippi River?
3. **Critical Thinking Applying Information** Based on the map, why would the South suffer more damage than the North—no matter who won the war?

General Meade was proud of the victory. Lincoln, however, was disappointed. He felt that the Union army had once again allowed the Confederate troops to get away.

The Union victories at Vicksburg and Gettysburg marked the turning point of the Civil War. It seemed just a matter of time before the Confederacy would fall. However, the South was still determined to fight. The war would last another two years.

The Gettysburg Address

The Battle of Gettysburg left more than 50,000 dead or wounded. On November 19, 1863, there was a ceremony to dedicate a cemetery to the memory of those soldiers who died in the battle. President Lincoln attended the ceremony. He delivered a speech now known as the **Gettysburg Address.** Lincoln said that the Civil War was a test of whether or not a democratic nation could survive. He reminded Americans that their nation was founded on the belief that "all men are created equal." Lincoln told the audience:

> "We here highly resolve that these dead shall not have died in vain—that this nation, under God, shall have a new birth of freedom—and that government of the people, by the people, for the people, shall not perish from the earth."
>
> —Abraham Lincoln, Gettysburg Address, November 19, 1863

Lincoln's entire speech was only ten sentences long and took about three minutes to deliver, but it is honored as a profound statement of American ideals.

Grant's Plan for Total War

Since the beginning of the war, Lincoln had searched for a general who could lead the Union to victory. More and more, he thought of Ulysses S. Grant. After capturing Vicksburg, Grant continued to win battles in the West. In 1864, Lincoln appointed him commander of the Union forces.

Some questioned the choice, but President Lincoln felt that "Unconditional Surrender" Grant was the general who would end the war in the Union's favor. "I can't spare this man," Lincoln said. "He fights."

Grant had a plan for ending the war. He wanted to destroy the South's ability to fight. To achieve this, Grant ordered his generals to wage **total war** against the South. He wanted the Union army to destroy food, equipment, and anything else they found that might be useful to the enemy. In the past, war had been restricted to soldiers. Total war, however, did not make any distinctions. Civilians in the South suffered the same hardships as the army.

Target Skill: Identify Sequence As you read, look for specific examples of Grant's strategy for waging total war. Add these to your flowchart.

Sheridan in the Shenandoah To set his plan in motion, Grant sent General Philip Sheridan and his cavalry into the rich farmland of Virginia's Shenandoah Valley. He instructed Sheridan:

> "Leave nothing to invite the enemy to return. Destroy whatever cannot be consumed. Let the valley be left so that crows flying over it will have to carry their rations along with them."
>
> —Ulysses S. Grant, quoted in Bruce Catton, *Grant Takes Command*

Sheridan obeyed. In the summer and fall of 1864, he marched through the valley, destroying farms and livestock. During the campaign, Sheridan's troops burned 2,000 barns filled with grain. There was nothing left for Lee's troops or for southern civilians.

Sherman's March to the Sea Grant also ordered General William Tecumseh Sherman to capture Atlanta, Georgia, and then march to the Atlantic coast. Like Sheridan, Sherman had orders to destroy everything useful to the South.

Sherman's troops captured Atlanta in September 1864. They began their campaign by turning the people of Atlanta out of their homes and burning a large part of the city. Then, Sherman began his "march to the sea."

As they marched through Georgia, Sherman's troops ripped up railroad tracks, built bonfires from the ties, then heated and twisted the rails. They killed livestock and tore up fields. They burned barns, homes, bridges, and factories.

Lincoln Is Reelected

Lincoln ran for reelection in 1864. At first, his defeat seemed, in his own words, "exceedingly probable." Before the capture of Atlanta,

Union chances for victory looked bleak. Lincoln knew that many northerners were unhappy with his handling of the war. He thought that this might cost him the election.

The Democrats nominated General George McClellan to oppose Lincoln. They adopted a resolution demanding the immediate "cessation of hostilities" against the South. Although he had commanded the Union army, McClellan was willing to compromise with the Confederacy. If peace could be achieved, he was ready to restore slavery.

Then, in September, Sherman took Atlanta, and the North rallied around Lincoln. Sheridan's smashing victories in the Shenandoah Valley in October further increased Lincoln's popular support. In the election in November, the vote was close, but Lincoln remained President.

In his second Inaugural Address, Lincoln looked forward to the coming of peace:

> "With malice toward none, with charity for all . . . let us strive . . . to bind up the nation's wounds . . . to do all which may achieve a just and a lasting peace among ourselves and with all nations."
>
> —Abraham Lincoln, Second Inaugural Address

The Final Battles

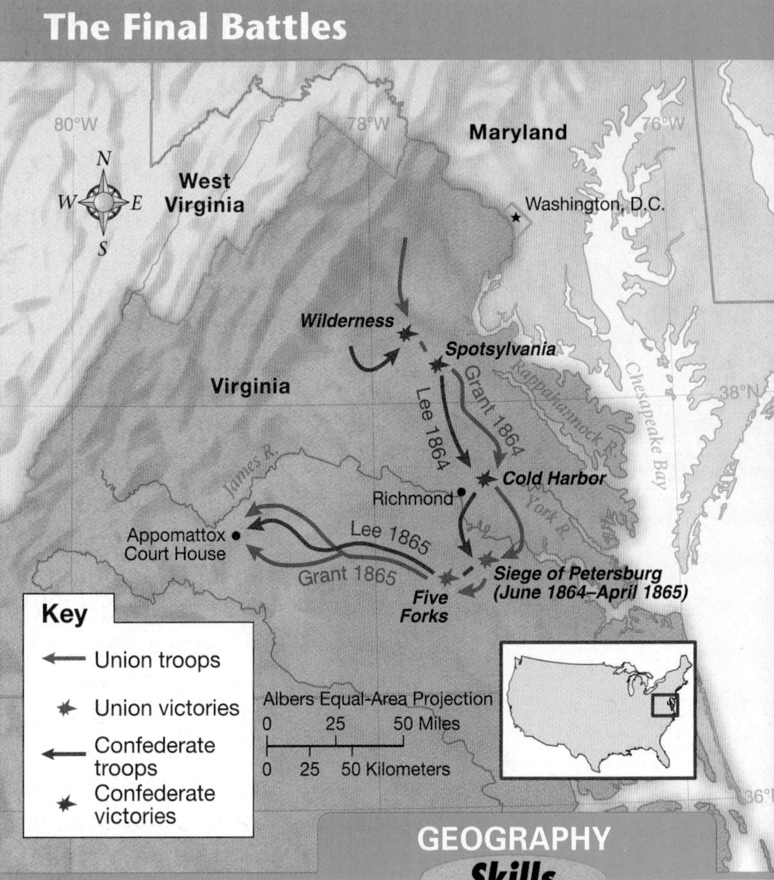

GEOGRAPHY Skills

The final battles of the Civil War pitted Grant against Lee in Virginia. Finally, on April 9, 1865, Lee surrendered at Appomattox Court House.

1. **Location** On the map, locate **(a)** Richmond, **(b)** Petersburg, **(c)** Appomattox Court House.
2. **Place** Where did Grant lay siege to Lee's forces for nine months?
3. **Critical Thinking Applying Information** Which battle took place first: Cold Harbor or Spotsylvania? Explain.

The Civil War Ends

Grant had begun a drive to capture Richmond in May 1864. Throughout the spring and summer, he and Lee fought a series of costly battles.

Northerners read with horror that 60,000 men were killed or wounded in a single month at the battles of the Wilderness, Spotsylvania, and Cold Harbor. Still, Grant pressed on. He knew that the Union could replace men and supplies. The South could not.

Lee dug in at Petersburg, near Richmond. Here, Grant kept Lee under siege for nine months. At last, with a fresh supply of troops, Grant took Petersburg on April 2, 1865. The same day, Richmond fell.

Lee and his army withdrew to a small Virginia town called **Appomattox Court House.** There, a week later, they were trapped by Union troops. Lee knew that his men would be slaughtered if he kept fighting. On April 9, 1865, Lee surrendered.

At Appomattox Court House, Grant offered generous terms of surrender to the defeated Confederate army. Soldiers were required to turn over their rifles, but officers were allowed to keep their pistols. Soldiers who had horses could keep them. Grant knew that southerners would need the animals for spring plowing. Finally, ordered Grant, "each officer and man will be allowed to return to his home, not to be disturbed by the United States authorities."

As the Confederates surrendered, Union soldiers began to cheer. Grant ordered them to be silent. "The war is over," he said. "The rebels are our countrymen again."

A Turning Point in American History

The toll of the Civil War was immense. More than 360,000 Union soldiers and 250,000 Confederate soldiers lost their lives. No war has ever resulted in more American deaths. In dollars, the war's cost was about 20 billion. That was more than 11 times the entire amount spent by the federal government between 1789 and 1861!

The Civil War was a major turning point in American history. The balance of power was changed. The Democratic party lost its influence and the Republicans were in a commanding position. No longer would Americans speak of the nation as a confederation of states. Before the war, Americans referred to "*these* United States." After, they began speaking of "*the* United States." The idea that each state might secede, if it chose, was dead. As a result, the power of the federal government grew.

The war also put an end to slavery in the United States. For years, Americans had debated whether slavery could exist in a nation dedicated to the ideals of liberty and equality. By the war's end, millions of African Americans had gained their freedom. Millions more Americans, both North and South, began to think about what it meant to be free and equal.

To be sure, a long and difficult struggle for equality lay ahead. Yet, Lincoln's words at Gettysburg were prophetic: "We here highly resolve . . . that this nation, under God, shall have a new birth of freedom." From out of a cruel, bitter, often heart-rending war, the United States did indeed emerge a stronger, freer nation.

Recall

1. **Identify** Explain the significance of **(a)** Battle of Gettysburg, **(b)** Pickett's Charge, **(c)** Gettysburg Address, **(d)** Ulysses S. Grant, **(e)** William Tecumseh Sherman, **(f)** Appomattox Court House.
2. **Define** **(a)** siege, **(b)** total war.

Comprehension

3. Which Union victories were a turning point?
4. What was Grant's plan for ending the war?
5. What ideals did Lincoln express in the Gettysburg Address and his Second Inaugural Address?
6. How did the Civil War change the United States?

Critical Thinking and Writing

7. **Exploring the Main Idea** Review the Main Idea statement at the beginning of this section. Then, make a list of the major events of the years 1863–1865 of the Civil War. Indicate the importance of each.
8. **Supporting a Point of View** Some people believe that Grant's decision to wage total war on the South was wrong because it caused great suffering among civilians. Do you agree or disagree? Explain.

ACTIVITY

Writing a Speech

Suppose that you are President of the United States at the end of the Civil War. Write a speech summarizing the important events of the war and explaining what you believe the Union victory accomplished.

Analyzing Photographs

When the Civil War began, photography was just beginning. Pioneer photographers shouldered their bulky cameras and followed armies into battle. The result was the first detailed photographic record of a war.

These Civil War photographs, like all photographs, are valuable primary source documents. Just as with other primary sources, however, we must learn to evaluate them for accuracy and bias.

In this photograph, a family gathers at a Union Army camp in 1862.

Learn the Skill *To analyze a photograph, use the following steps:*

1. **Identify the subject.** What does the photograph show?
2. **Look for details.** What evidence does the photograph include about people, daily life, the weather, events, or the environment?
3. **Analyze the photographer's intent.** Why did the photographer take this picture? How did the photographer feel about the subject?
4. **Draw conclusions.** What can you learn from this photograph? How does it add to your understanding of history?

Practice the Skill *Answer the following questions about the photograph above:*

1. **(a)** Who are the people in the photograph? **(b)** Where are they?
2. **(a)** What tools, utensils, and furniture do you see? **(b)** Where are the people living? **(c)** What other details do you see?
3. **(a)** Why do you think the photographer took this picture? **(b)** How do you think the photographer felt about families and war?
4. What did you learn from this photograph?

Apply the Skill *See the Chapter Review and Assessment.*

CHAPTER 17

Review and Assessment

Chapter Summary

Section 1
At the start of the Civil War, both the North and the South had strengths and weaknesses. The North, however, had a larger population and industries that could make war supplies.

Section 2
The Union and Confederacy had different plans for winning the war. Early on, the Confederacy won some important eastern battles, but the Union had victories in the west.

Section 3
Lincoln issued the Emancipation Proclamation, which freed slaves in Confederate states under Union control. African American soldiers and civilians played an important role in the war.

Section 4
New technologies added to the horror of war. On both sides civilians and soldiers suffered. The southern economy fell into ruin. Many women contributed to the war effort.

Section 5
Grant's plan for total war produced a string of important Union victories. Lincoln was reelected in 1864. The war's end in 1865 represented a turning point in American history.

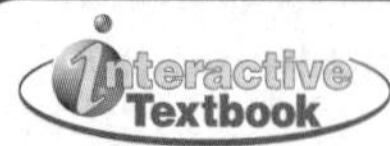

For additional review and enrichment activities, see the interactive version of *The American Nation,* available on the Web and on CD-ROM.

Chapter Self-Test For practice test questions for Chapter 17, visit PHSchool.com, **Web Code mfa-1704.**

Building Vocabulary

Review the meaning of the vocabulary words listed below. Then, write a sentence for each word in which you define the word and describe its relationship to the Civil War.

1. **border state**
2. **martial law**
3. **emancipate**
4. **draft**
5. **habeas corpus**
6. **inflation**
7. **profiteer**
8. **total war**

Reviewing Key Facts

9. Why did each side go to war? (Section 1)
10. Why was President Lincoln unhappy with General McClellan? (Section 2)
11. **(a)** What did the Emancipation Proclamation provide? **(b)** How did it change the nature of the war? (Section 3)
12. **(a)** Why did some northerners object to the draft law? **(b)** What was the response to the draft law in the South? (Section 4)
13. How did the Union wage total war on the South in 1864 and 1865? (Section 5)

Critical Thinking and Writing

14. **Making Generalizations** Make a generalization about the strengths and weaknesses of the North and South at the start of the war. List three facts to support your generalization.
15. **Summarizing** Write one or two sentences summarizing Lincoln's attitudes toward slavery and the war.
16. **Making Comparisons** How did the North's General Grant and the South's General Lee compare as military leaders?
17. **Connecting to Geography: Movement** Describe the effects of the Union blockade of southern ports.
18. **Synthesizing Information** Review the excerpt from Lincoln's Second Inaugural Address on page 509. How did Grant's treatment of the defeated Confederate army at Appomattox Court House reflect the ideas in the Inaugural Address?

Skills Assessment

Analyzing Primary Sources

The Union blockade caused great difficulty for southern families. Dr. Paul Barringer recalls how his family managed.

> “Almost at once we began to feel the pinch of war. White sugar disappeared immediately; . . . there was no sugar for the table. There was, however, an unlimited quantity of sorghum syrup, and around the barrels of sorghum, a thick crust of brown sugar often formed. This was carefully scraped off to be served with coffee and berries, the fluid product going to the slaves.”
>
> —Dr. Paul B. Barringer, *The Natural Bent: The Memories of Dr. Paul Barringer*

19. According to Barringer, how soon were southerners affected by the blockade?
- **A.** about one year later
- **B.** almost at once
- **C.** right after South Carolina seceded
- **D.** before Lincoln's inauguration in March 1861

20. What substitute was used for white sugar?
- **A.** berries
- **B.** a pinch of table salt
- **C.** liquid sorghum syrup
- **D.** brown sugar

Applying Your Skills

Analyzing Photographs

Mathew Brady took this picture of Abraham Lincoln and his son, Tad, in 1864. Look at the picture. Then, answer the questions that follow.

21. What details are emphasized in the photograph?
- **A.** Lincoln's position in the chair.
- **B.** His son's lack of interest in the book.
- **C.** The concentration of Lincoln and his son.
- **D.** Tad's hand resting on his father's chair.

22. What can you learn about Lincoln from this photograph?

Activities

Connecting With . . . Economics

Making a Chart You are the graphic illustrator for an economics magazine. Create a flowchart to illustrate how the high cost of the Civil War led to inflation.

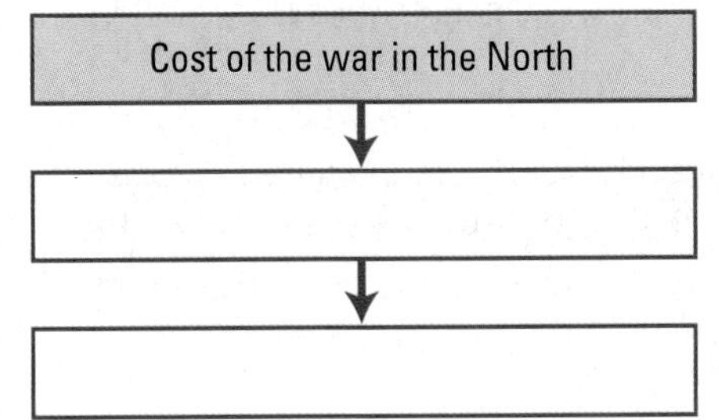

Connecting to Today

Planning a TV Documentary The Civil War ended slavery for African Americans. Use the Internet to find out how African Americans fight for equality today. Use what you learn to write an outline for a TV documentary on the person of your choice. For help in starting this activity, visit PHSchool.com, **Web Code mfd-1705.**

Researching Civil War Photos

Creating a Photo Essay Photographers like Mathew Brady took thousands of pictures documenting the Civil War. Use the Internet to find photographs taken of the war. Then, download selected pictures to create a photo essay of the war. For help in starting this activity, visit PHSchool.com, **Web Code mfd-1706**.

CHAPTER 18

Reconstruction and the Changing South

1863–1896

Reward poster (left) and chair in which Lincoln was shot (right)

Thaddeus Stevens

AMERICAN EVENTS

1863 President Abraham Lincoln proposes a mild Reconstruction plan for readmitting southern states after the Civil War.

1865 Lincoln is assassinated five days after the war ends. As the nation mourns, the issue of readmitting southern states remains unresolved.

1867 Radical Reconstruction begins. Republican leaders in Congress like Thaddeus Stevens call for harsh measures against the South.

Presidential Terms: Abraham Lincoln 1861–1865; Andrew Johnson 1865–1869; Ulysses S. Grant 1869–1877

1860 · 1865 · 1870

WORLD EVENTS

1867 ▲ The Dominion of Canada is formed.

1870 ▲ Italy becomes a unified nation.

The South After the Civil War

One by one, southern states rejoined the Union after the Civil War.

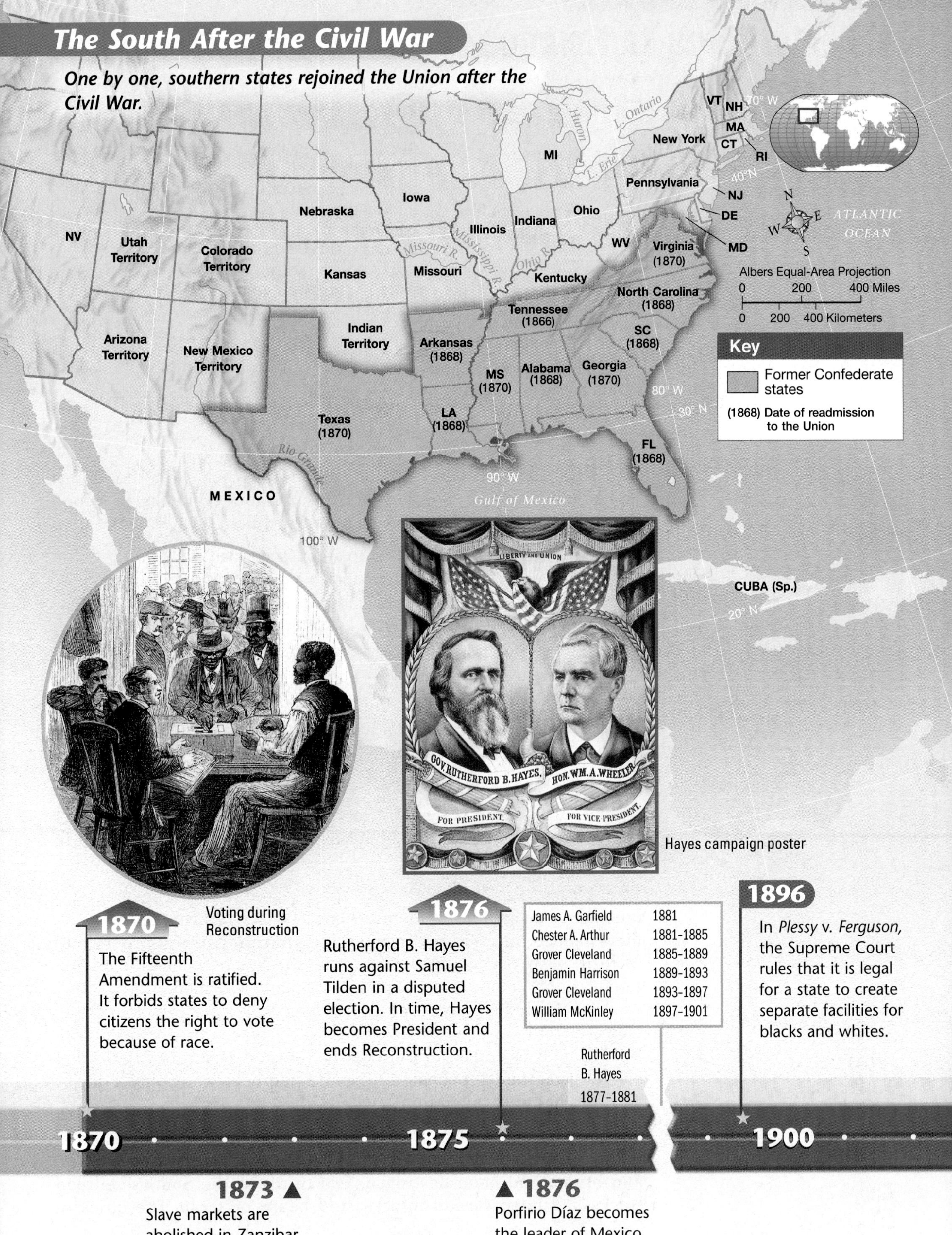

Voting during Reconstruction

Hayes campaign poster

1870

The Fifteenth Amendment is ratified. It forbids states to deny citizens the right to vote because of race.

1876

Rutherford B. Hayes runs against Samuel Tilden in a disputed election. In time, Hayes becomes President and ends Reconstruction.

James A. Garfield	1881
Chester A. Arthur	1881-1885
Grover Cleveland	1885-1889
Benjamin Harrison	1889-1893
Grover Cleveland	1893-1897
William McKinley	1897-1901

Rutherford B. Hayes 1877-1881

1896

In *Plessy* v. *Ferguson,* the Supreme Court rules that it is legal for a state to create separate facilities for blacks and whites.

1870 · · · 1875 · · · 1900 · ·

1873 ▲

Slave markets are abolished in Zanzibar.

▲ 1876

Porfirio Díaz becomes the leader of Mexico.

1 Early Steps to Reunion

Prepare to Read

Objectives

In this section, you will
- Describe the nation's postwar problems.
- List the early steps that were taken toward Reconstruction.
- Explain how the assassination of Lincoln and the inauguration of a new President led to conflict.

Key Terms

freedmen
Reconstruction
Ten Percent Plan
amnesty
Wade-Davis Bill
Freedmen's Bureau
Thirteenth Amendment

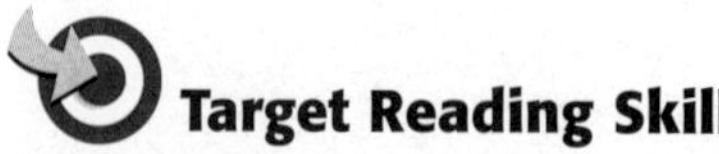

Target Reading Skill

Sequence Copy this flowchart. As you read, fill in the boxes with information about the early years of Reconstruction. Two boxes have been completed to help you get started.

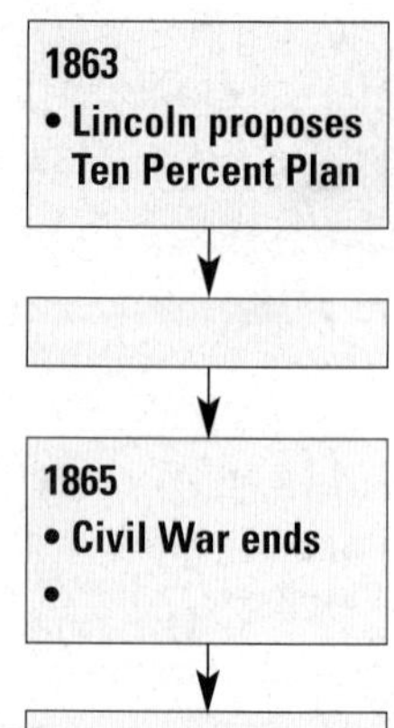

Main Idea After the Civil War, the country had to repair the damage done by the fighting and find a way to rebuild.

Ruined plantation house

Setting the Scene At the end of the Civil War, the future looked bleak to many southerners. Susan Dabney Smedes described the scene facing her father, once a wealthy planter:

> "My father had come home to a house stripped of nearly every article of furniture and to a plantation stripped of the means of cultivating . . . it. A few mules and one cow were all that were left of the stock."
>
> —Susan Dabney Smedes, *Memorials of a Southern Planter*

Across the South, cities and farms lay in ruins. All southerners, black or white, faced an unfamiliar new world. At the same time, a shattered nation had to find a way to become whole again.

Postwar Problems

After four years of war, both northerners and southerners had to adjust to a changed world. The adjustment was far more difficult in the South.

The Victorious North Despite their victory, northerners faced a number of economic problems. Some 800,000 returning Union soldiers needed jobs. The government was canceling its war orders, and factories were laying off workers. Still, the North's economic disruption was only temporary. Boom times quickly returned.

The North lost more soldiers in the war than the South did. However, only a few battles had taken place on northern soil. Northern farms and cities were hardly touched. One returning Union soldier remarked, "It seemed . . . as if I had been away only a day or two, and had just taken up . . . where I had left off."

The Defeated South Confederate soldiers had little chance of taking up where they had left off. In some areas, every house, barn, and bridge had been destroyed. Two thirds of the South's railroad tracks had been turned into twisted heaps of scrap. The cities of

Columbia, Richmond, and Atlanta had been leveled.

The war wrecked the South's financial system. After the war, Confederate money was worthless. People who had loaned money to the Confederacy were never repaid. Many southern banks closed, and depositors lost their savings.

The war changed southern society forever. Almost overnight, there was a new class of nearly four million people known as **freedmen**—men and women who had been slaves. Under slavery, they had been forbidden to own property and to learn to read and write. What would become of them? How could the South cope with this sudden, drastic change?

Early Steps Toward Reconstruction

President Lincoln was worried about **Reconstruction,** or the rebuilding of the South. He wanted to make it fairly easy for southerners to rejoin the Union. The sooner the nation was reunited, Lincoln believed, the faster the South would be able to rebuild.

Lincoln's Reconstruction Plan As early as 1863, Lincoln outlined his **Ten Percent Plan** for Reconstruction. Under this plan, a southern state could form a new government after 10 percent of its voters swore an oath of loyalty to the United States. The new government had to abolish slavery. Voters could then elect members of Congress and take part in the national government once again.

Lincoln's plan also offered **amnesty,** or a government pardon, to Confederates who swore loyalty to the Union. Amnesty would not apply to the former leaders of the Confederacy, however.

A Rival Proposal Many Republicans in Congress felt that the Ten Percent Plan was too generous toward the South. In 1864, they passed the **Wade-Davis Bill,** a rival plan for Reconstruction. It required a majority of white men in each southern state to swear loyalty to the Union. It also denied the right to vote or hold office to anyone who had volunteered to fight for the Confederacy. Lincoln refused to sign the Wade-Davis Bill because he felt it was too harsh.

The Freedmen's Bureau Congress and the President did agree on one proposal. One month before Lee surrendered, Congress passed a bill creating the **Freedmen's Bureau,** a government agency to help former slaves. Lincoln signed the bill.

The Freedmen's Bureau gave food and clothing to former slaves. It also tried to find jobs for freedmen. The bureau helped poor whites as well. It provided medical care for more than one million people.

Viewing History

Richmond in Ruins

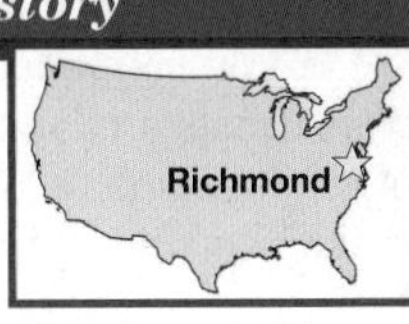

After the Civil War, some of the South's most important cities lay in ruins. This picture shows the devastation in Richmond, Virginia. **Drawing Conclusions** ***What effect do you think this kind of devastation had on southerners?***

Ford's Theatre

On April 14, 1865, John Wilkes Booth crept into Abraham Lincoln's box at Ford's Theatre. As the President watched the comedy Our American Cousin, *Booth shot him. Today, park rangers at the restored theatre recount the story of the tragic assassination. You can visit a museum devoted to Lincoln's death—and even attend a play.*

Virtual Field Trip For an interactive look at Ford's Theatre, visit PHSchool.com, **Web Code mfd-1801.**

Target Skill: Identify Sequence As you read, identify the major goals and accomplishments of the Freedmen's Bureau. Add these items to your flowchart.

One of the bureau's most important tasks was to set up schools for freedmen. Most of the teachers were volunteers, often women, from the North. Grandparents and grandchildren sat side by side in the classroom. Charlotte Forten, an African American volunteer from Philadelphia, wrote:

> “It is wonderful how a people who have been so long crushed to the earth . . . can have so great a desire for knowledge, and such a capacity for attaining it.”
>
> —Charlotte Forten, article in the *Atlantic Monthly*

The Freedmen's Bureau laid the foundation for the South's public school system. It also created colleges for African Americans, including Howard, Morehouse, and Fisk. Many of the graduates of these schools became teachers themselves. By the 1870s, African Americans were teaching in grade schools throughout the South.

Lincoln Is Assassinated

President Lincoln hoped to persuade Congress to accept his Reconstruction plan. However, he never got the chance.

On April 14, 1865, just five days after Lee's surrender, the President attended a play at Ford's Theatre in Washington, D.C. A popular actor from the South, John Wilkes Booth, crept into the President's box and shot Lincoln in the head. Lincoln died the next morning. Booth was later caught and killed in a barn outside the city.

The nation was plunged into grief. Millions who had been celebrating the war's end now mourned Lincoln's death. "Now he belongs to the ages," commented Secretary of War Edwin Stanton.

The New President

Vice President Andrew Johnson was now President. Johnson had represented Tennessee in Congress. When his state seceded, Johnson had remained loyal to the Union.

Johnson's Plan Republicans in Congress believed Johnson would support a strict Reconstruction plan. But his plan was much milder than expected. It called for a majority of voters in each southern state to pledge loyalty to the United States. Each state also had to ratify the **Thirteenth Amendment,** which Congress had approved in January 1865. It banned slavery throughout the nation. (As you read, the Emancipation Proclamation did not free slaves in states loyal to the Union.)

Congress Rebels The southern states quickly met Johnson's conditions. As a result, the President approved their new state governments in late 1865. Voters in the South then elected representatives to Congress. Many of those elected had held office in the Confederacy. For example, Alexander Stephens, the former vice president of the Confederacy, was elected senator from Georgia.

Republicans in Congress were outraged. The men who had led the South out of the Union were being elected to the House and Senate. Also, no southern state allowed African Americans to vote.

When the new Congress met, Republicans refused to let southern representatives take their seats. Instead, they set up a Joint Committee on Reconstruction to form a new plan for the South. The stage was set for a showdown between Congress and the President.

Connecting to Today

Involuntary Servitude

The Thirteenth Amendment banned not only slavery but also "involuntary servitude" anywhere in the United States. Today, this provision helps the government combat new forms of forced labor.

In one case, farm workers were smuggled into the United States in a van. During the three-day trip, they were not allowed to leave the van even for food or bathroom breaks. Then, they were forced by threats of violence to work for their captors to pay off their smuggling fees. The youngest of the victims was 13 years old. In 2000, new laws made it unlawful to hold a person in a "condition of slavery." The government set up a National Worker Exploitation Complaint Line to report such violations of the Thirteenth Amendment.

Why do you think Congress wanted the Thirteenth Amendment to apply to all people, not just citizens?

★ ★ ★ Section 1 Assessment ★ ★ ★

Recall

1. **Identify** Explain the significance of **(a)** Reconstruction, **(b)** Ten Percent Plan, **(c)** Wade-Davis Bill, **(d)** Freedmen's Bureau, **(e)** John Wilkes Booth, **(f)** Andrew Johnson, **(g)** Thirteenth Amendment.
2. **Define (a)** freedmen, **(b)** amnesty.

Comprehension

3. Describe two problems faced by the South after the Civil War.
4. What early Reconstruction measure did Lincoln and Congress agree upon?
5. Why did Republicans in Congress oppose Johnson's Reconstruction plan?

Critical Thinking and Writing

6. **Exploring the Main Idea** Review the Main Idea statement at the beginning of this section. Then, write a letter to President Lincoln supporting or opposing his Reconstruction plan.
7. **Drawing Inferences** One teacher said that freedmen "will starve themselves in order to send their children to school." Write a paragraph explaining why you think education meant so much to the freedmen.

ACTIVITY

Conducting an Interview
Use the Internet to find out more about the assassination of Lincoln. With a partner, act out an interview between a reporter and a witness to the event. For help in completing the activity, visit PHSchool.com, **Web Code mfd-1802.**

Solving Problems

Learning how to solve problems is an important skill for both citizens and government leaders. Just as the solutions to problems of the past affect the present, the solutions you choose today will have consequences in the future.

African American writer W.E.B. DuBois described some of the problems faced by the Freedmen's Bureau:

> "Here, at a stroke of the pen, was erected a government of millions of men,—and not ordinary men, either, but black men [weakened] by a peculiarly complete system of slavery, centuries old; and now, suddenly, violently, they come into a new birthright, at a time of war and passion, in the midst of the stricken, embittered population of their former masters. Any man might well have hesitated to assume charge of such a work, with vast responsibilities, indefinite powers, and limited resources . . . for Congress had appropriated no money for salaries and expenses."
>
> —W.E.B. DuBois, "The Freedmen's Bureau"

As it set up new schools throughout the South, the Freedmen's Bureau faced the problem of finding enough teachers for so many eager new students.

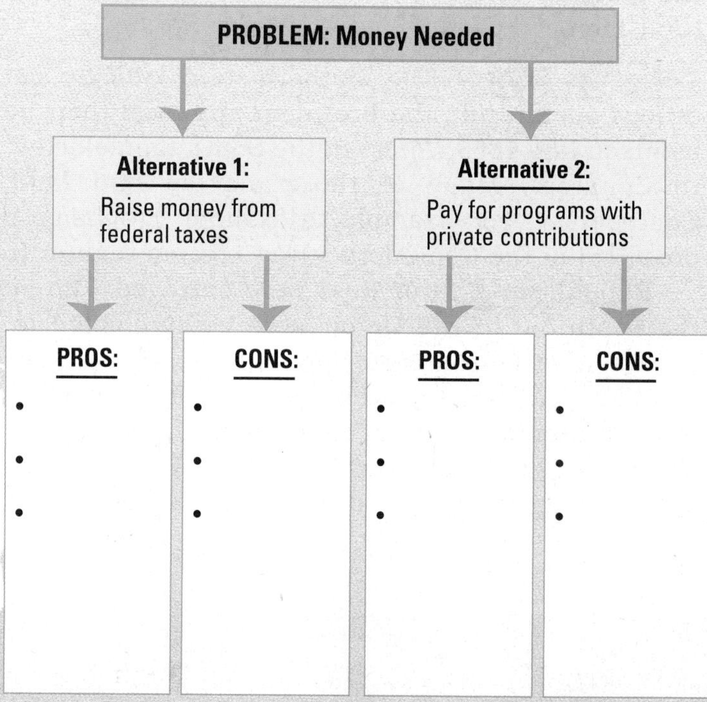

Learn the Skill *To learn problem-solving skills, use the following steps:*

1. **Identify the problem.** State the problem you want to solve as simply and completely as possible.
2. **List possible solutions.** There is usually more than one way to solve a problem. Identify your alternatives.
3. **Review the alternatives.** What resources would be needed to implement the solution? What would the consequences be?
4. **Choose a course of action.** Decide how you will resolve the problem.

Practice the Skill *Use the information above to answer the following questions:*

1. According to DuBois what was one problem that the Freedmen's Bureau faced?
2. **(a)** What two alternatives are shown on the chart? **(b)** Can you think of a third alternative? Explain.
3. **(a)** What might be some of the pros and cons of Alternative 1? **(b)** What might be some of the pros and cons of Alternative 2?
4. What solution to the problem would you have favored? Why?

Apply the Skill *See the Chapter Review and Assessment.*

2 Radical Reconstruction

Prepare to Read

Objectives

In this section, you will

- Describe how Congress reacted to the passage of black codes in the South.
- Explain how Radical Republicans gained power in Congress.
- Identify why President Johnson was impeached.

Key Terms

black codes

Radical Republican

Fourteenth Amendment

Radical Reconstruction

Reconstruction Act

impeach

Fifteenth Amendment

Target Reading Skill

Cause and Effect Copy the chart below. As you read, complete the chart to show some of the effects of the rise of Radical Republicans in Congress. Add as many boxes as you need.

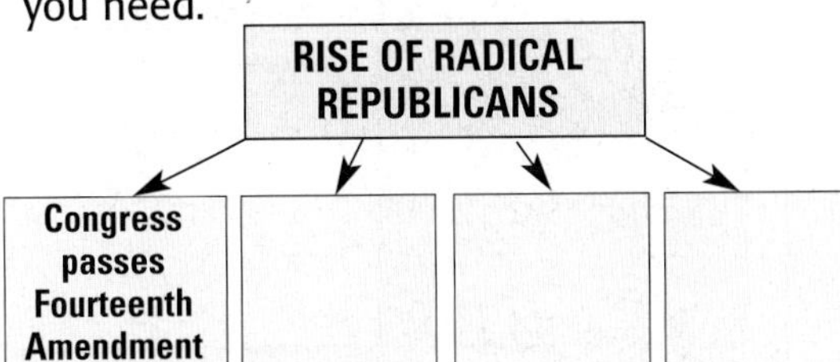

Main Idea Angered by the South's response to President Johnson's Reconstruction program, Republicans in Congress put in place a harsher plan.

Setting the Scene In New Orleans, Confederate flags were being sold in the streets. In Mississippi, the governor refused to fly the American flag over the state capitol. Many southerners were singing, "I'm a good old rebel, that's what I am / And I don't want no pardon for anything I done." Hearing such reports in 1866, Republicans decided to take harsh measures against the South.

Confederate flag

Black Codes Anger Congress

After the war, most southern states promptly ratified the Thirteenth Amendment. However, southern legislatures also passed **black codes,** laws that severely limited the rights of freedmen.

Rights and Restrictions The black codes did grant some rights. For example, African Americans could marry legally and own some kinds of property. Still, the codes were clearly meant to keep freedmen from gaining political or economic power.

Black codes forbade freedmen to vote, own guns, or serve on juries. In some states, African Americans were permitted to work only as servants or farm laborers. In others, they had to sign contracts for a year's work. Those without contracts could be arrested and sentenced to work on a plantation.

Congress Reacts Republicans charged that Johnson's lenient Reconstruction plan had encouraged southern legislatures to pass the black codes. Republicans were also outraged by reports of violence against freedmen. In 1866, angry whites burned homes, churches, and schoolhouses in a black section of Memphis, Tennessee. More than 40 African Americans were killed. Similar riots broke out in New Orleans when freedmen met to support the right to vote.

A report by the Joint Committee on Reconstruction accused the South of trying to "preserve slavery . . . as long as possible." When

Rival Plans for Reconstruction

Plan	Ten Percent Plan	Wade-Davis Bill	Johnson Plan	Reconstruction Act
Proposed by	President Abraham Lincoln (1863)	Republicans in Congress (1864)	President Andrew Johnson (1865)	Radical Republicans (1867)
Conditions for Former Confederate States to Rejoin Union	• 10 percent of voters must swear loyalty to Union • Must abolish slavery	• Majority of white men must swear loyalty • Former Confederate volunteers cannot vote or hold office	• Majority of white men must swear loyalty • Must ratify Thirteenth Amendment • Former Confederate officials may vote and hold office	• Must disband state governments • Must write new constitutions • Must ratify Fourteenth Amendment • African American men must be allowed to vote

GRAPHIC ORGANIZER *Skills*

In the early years of Reconstruction, federal leaders debated several plans for readmitting southern states to the Union.

1. **Comprehension**
(a) Identify one similarity between the Wade-Davis Bill and President Johnson's plan. (b) Identify one difference.
2. **Critical Thinking**
Evaluating Information Which of the plans shown here seems to be the harshest toward the South? Explain.

President Johnson ignored the report, members of Congress called **Radical Republicans** vowed to take control of Reconstruction.

Rise of the Radicals

The Radicals were led by Thaddeus Stevens of Pennsylvania in the House and Charles Sumner of Massachusetts in the Senate. Radical Republicans had two main goals. First, they wanted to break the power of wealthy planters who had long ruled the South. Second, they wanted to ensure that freedmen received the right to vote.

Republican Control Radicals needed the support of moderate Republicans, the largest group in Congress. Moderates and Radicals disagreed on many issues, but they shared a strong political motive. Most southerners were Democrats. With southerners barred from Congress, Republicans could control both houses.

To combat the black codes, Congress passed the Civil Rights Act in April 1866. It gave citizenship to African Americans. When Johnson vetoed the bill, Congress overrode the veto.

Fourteenth Amendment Republicans feared that the Supreme Court might use its power of judicial review to declare the Civil Rights Act unconstitutional. In the Dred Scott decision of 1857, the Court had ruled that African Americans were not citizens. To avoid a similar ruling, Republicans proposed the **Fourteenth Amendment.** It defined citizens as "all persons born or naturalized in the United States." (The amendment did not apply to most Native Americans.) It guaranteed citizens "equal protection of the laws" and forbade states to "deprive any person of life, liberty, or property without due process of law." Thus, states could not legally discriminate against a citizen on unreasonable grounds, such as race.

Under the Fourteenth Amendment, any state that denied any male citizen age 21 or older the right to vote would have its representation in Congress reduced. Republicans believed that freedmen would be able to defend their rights if they could vote.

Republicans hoped the amendment would secure basic political rights for African Americans in the South. That goal would take a century to achieve. In the 1950s, the Fourteenth Amendment became a powerful tool in the struggle for citizenship rights.

Radicals in Power

President Johnson encouraged former Confederate states to reject the Fourteenth Amendment. He also decided to make the amendment an issue in the 1866 congressional elections.

Election of 1866 Across the North, Johnson urged voters to reject the Radicals. When a heckler yelled for Johnson to hang Jefferson Davis, Johnson shouted, "Why not hang Thad Stevens?" Many northerners criticized the President for losing his temper.

In July, white mobs in New Orleans killed 34 African Americans. The violence convinced many northerners that stronger measures were needed. In the end, the elections were a disaster for Johnson. Republicans won majorities in both houses of Congress.

The Radical Program In 1867, Republicans in Congress prepared to take charge of Reconstruction. With huge majorities in both houses, Congress could easily override a veto. The period that followed is often called **Radical Reconstruction.**

Congress passed the first **Reconstruction Act** in March 1867. It threw out the state governments that had refused to ratify the Fourteenth Amendment—all the former Confederate states except Tennessee. The act also divided the South into five military districts. Army commanders were given broad powers to enforce Reconstruction. Many southerners bitterly resented the imposition of military rule.

To rejoin the Union, former Confederate states had to write new constitutions and ratify the Fourteenth Amendment. The Reconstruction Act also required that southern states allow African Americans to vote.

With the new constitutions in place, reconstructed states held elections to set up new state governments. Former Confederate officials were barred from voting. Many other white southerners stayed away from the polls in protest. Protected by the army, freedmen proudly exercised their new right to vote. As a result, Republicans gained control of all of the new southern state governments.

Impeachment and a New President

Congress passed other Reconstruction acts over Johnson's veto. As President, Johnson had a duty to execute the new laws. However, Johnson did what he could to limit their effect. He fired several military commanders who supported Radical Reconstruction. Republicans in Congress decided to remove Johnson from office.

Trial On February 24, 1868, the House of Representatives voted to **impeach,** or bring formal charges against, Johnson. According to the Constitution, the House may impeach a President for "treason,

Primary Source

The Impeachment of Andrew Johnson

At the impeachment trial of President Johnson, Senator James Grimes of Iowa voted against conviction. Here, he explains why:

"Nor can I suffer my judgment of the law governing this case to be influenced by political considerations. I cannot agree to destroy the harmonious working of the Constitution for the sake of getting rid of an unacceptable President. Whatever may be my opinion of [Johnson], I cannot consent to trifle with the high office he holds. I can do nothing which, by implication, may be [seen as] an approval of impeachment as a part of future political machinery."

—James Grimes, quoted in *Trial of Andrew Johnson* (Poore)

Analyzing Primary Sources

Write a sentence summarizing the main reason that Grimes voted against the removal of President Johnson.

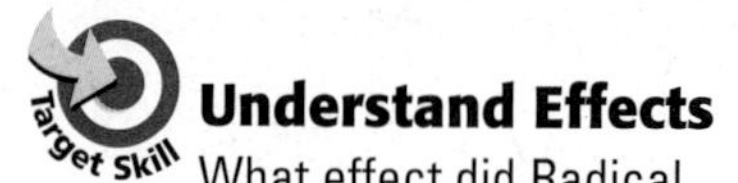

Understand Effects What effect did Radical Republicans have on the presidency of Andrew Johnson? Add this information to your chart.

bribery, or other high crimes and misdemeanors." The President is removed from office if found guilty by two thirds of the Senate.

During Johnson's trial, it became clear that he was not guilty of high crimes and misdemeanors. Even Charles Sumner, Johnson's bitter foe, admitted that the charges were "political in character."

Despite intense pressure, seven Republican senators refused to vote for conviction. The Constitution, they said, did not allow Congress to remove a President just because they disagreed with him. In the end, the vote was 35 to 19—one vote shy of the two thirds needed to convict.

A New President Johnson served out the few remaining months of his term. In 1868, Republicans nominated the Union's greatest war hero, Ulysses S. Grant, for President.

By election day, most southern states had rejoined the Union. As Congress demanded, the southern governments allowed African American men to vote. About 500,000 blacks voted—nearly all of them for Grant. He easily won the election.

Fifteenth Amendment In 1869, Congress proposed the **Fifteenth Amendment.** It forbade any state to deny any citizen the right to vote because of "race, color, or previous condition of servitude."

Republicans had moral and political reasons for supporting the Fifteenth Amendment. They remembered the great sacrifices made by African American soldiers in the Civil War. They also felt it was wrong to let African Americans vote in the South but not in the North. In addition, Republicans knew that if African Americans could vote in the North, they would help Republicans win elections there.

The Fifteenth Amendment was ratified in 1870. At last, all African American men over age 21 had the right to vote.

Section 2 Assessment

Recall

1. **Identify** Explain the significance of **(a)** Radical Republicans, **(b)** Thaddeus Stevens, **(c)** Charles Sumner, **(d)** Fourteenth Amendment, **(e)** Radical Reconstruction, **(f)** Reconstruction Act, **(g)** Fifteenth Amendment.
2. **Define** **(a)** black codes, **(b)** impeach.

Comprehension

3. Why did the black codes anger Republicans in Congress?
4. How did Radical Republicans win control of Congress?
5. Why did Congress impeach President Johnson?

Critical Thinking and Writing

6. **Exploring the Main Idea** Review the Main Idea statement at the beginning of this section. Then, write two sentences evaluating the Reconstruction Act—one from Andrew Johnson's viewpoint, the other from a Radical Republican's viewpoint.
7. **Supporting a Point of View** Write a note from one member of Congress to another explaining why you think the Fourteenth or Fifteenth Amendment is necessary.

Activity

Drawing a Political Cartoon **Draw a political cartoon that might have appeared during the congressional elections of 1866. Your cartoon should express a point of view about the conflict between Radical Republicans and the President over control of Reconstruction.**

The Power of the Fourteenth Amendment

The Fourteenth Amendment was originally intended to grant citizenship to former slaves and to ensure their rights. As society changed, the Court's interpretation of the Fourteenth Amendment changed as well.

"...No State shall make or enforce any law which shall abridge the privileges or immunities of citizens of the United States; nor shall any State deprive any person of life, liberty, or property, without due process of law; nor deny to any person within its jurisdiction the equal protection of the laws."
—Fourteenth Amendment

1905

Lochner v. *New York*

The Supreme Court strikes down a law regulating working hours. The Court rules that **equal protection** means that employers have the right to make contracts with workers freely. This ruling is later reversed.

1954

Brown v. *Board of Education of Topeka*

The Supreme Court rules that having separate schools for white and black students discriminates against African Americans and is a violation of **equal protection.** The ruling ends school segregation and becomes a landmark in the fight for equal rights.

1963

Gideon v. *Wainwright*

The Supreme Court rules that **due process** means that all people accused of a crime have the right to an attorney. If a person cannot afford an attorney, the state must provide one for her or him.

1971

Reed v. *Reed*

The Supreme Court strikes down an Idaho law giving men automatic preference over women in certain situations. The Court rules that **equal protection** means that men and women must be treated equally before the law.

ACTIVITY

The Fourteenth Amendment has affected every citizen's life in some way. List two ways in which your life has been or might be affected by the Fourteenth Amendment.

3 The South Under Reconstruction

Prepare to Read

Objectives

In this section, you will
- Identify new forces in southern politics.
- Describe how southern Conservatives resisted Reconstruction.
- List the challenges facing Reconstruction governments.
- Explain why sharecropping led to a cycle of poverty.

Key Terms

scalawag
carpetbagger
Conservatives
Ku Klux Klan
sharecropper

Target Reading Skill

Clarifying Meaning As you read, prepare an outline of this section. Use roman numerals to indicate the major headings, capital letters for the subheadings, and numbers for the supporting details.

I. New Forces in Southern Politics
A. White southern Republicans
1. Opposed secession
2.
B. Northerners
1.
2.
C.
II. Conservatives Resist
A.
B.

Main Idea Reconstruction governments tried to rebuild the South despite sometimes fierce opposition.

Meeting of a southern legislature

Setting the Scene White superintendents in Virginia's tobacco factories were puzzled. Suddenly, many of their black workers were absent from their jobs. White households experienced the same problem. With their servants missing, they were forced "to cook their own dinners or content themselves with a cold lunch."

What was going on? In 1867, as southern states began writing new constitutions, African American delegates took an active part. On days when important issues were debated, freedmen from all around flocked to watch. In Alabama, a political convention of freedmen declared, "We claim exactly the same rights, privileges and immunities as are enjoyed by white men."

Before the Civil War, a small group of rich planters had dominated southern politics. During Reconstruction, however, new groups tried to reshape southern politics.

New Forces in Southern Politics

The state governments created during Radical Reconstruction were different from any governments the South had known before. The old leaders had lost much of their influence. Three groups stepped in to replace them.

White Southern Republicans Some white southerners supported the new Republican governments. Many were businesspeople who had opposed secession in 1860. They wanted to forget the war and get on with rebuilding the South.

Many whites in the South felt that any southerner who helped the Republicans was a traitor. They called the white southern Republicans **scalawags,** a word used for small, scruffy horses.

Northerners Northerners who came to the South after the war were another important force. White southerners accused the new arrivals of hoping to get rich from the South's misery. Southerners claimed that these northerners were in such a hurry they had time only to fling a few clothes into cheap suitcases, or carpetbags. As a result, they became known as **carpetbaggers.**

In fact, northerners went south for various reasons. A few did hope to profit as the South was being rebuilt. Many more, however, were Union soldiers who had grown to love the South's rich land. Others, both white and black, were teachers, ministers, and reformers who sincerely wanted to help the freedmen.

African Americans African Americans were the third major new group in southern politics. Before the war, they had no voice in southern government. During Reconstruction, they not only voted in large numbers, but they also ran for and were elected to public office in the South. African Americans became sheriffs, mayors, and legislators in the new state and local governments. Sixteen African Americans were elected to Congress between 1869 and 1880.

Two African Americans, both representing Mississippi, served in the Senate. Hiram Revels, a clergyman and teacher, became the nation's first black senator in 1870. He completed the unfinished term of former Confederate president Jefferson Davis. In 1874, Blanche K. Bruce became the first African American to serve a full term in the Senate.

Freedmen had less political influence than many whites claimed, however. Only in South Carolina did African Americans win a majority in one house of the state legislature. No state elected a black governor.

Conservatives Resist

Most white southerners who had held power before the Civil War resisted Reconstruction. These **Conservatives** resented the changes imposed by Congress and enforced by the military. They wanted the South to change as little as possible. Conservatives were willing to let African Americans vote and hold a few offices. Still, they were determined that real power would remain in the hands of whites.

A few wealthy planters tried to force African Americans back onto plantations. Many small farmers and laborers wanted the government to take action against freedmen, who now competed with them for land and power.

Most of these white southerners were Democrats. They declared war on anyone who cooperated with the Republicans. "This is a white man's country," declared one southern senator, "and white men must govern it."

Spreading Terror Some white southerners formed secret societies to help them regain power. The most dangerous was the **Ku Klux Klan,** or KKK. The Klan worked to keep African Americans and white Republicans out of office.

Dressed in white robes and hoods to hide their identities, Klansmen rode at night to the homes of African American voters, shouting threats and burning wooden crosses. When threats did not work, the Klan turned to violence. Klan members murdered hundreds of African Americans and their white allies.

An American Profile

Hiram Revels 1822–1901

Hiram Revels was born to free parents in North Carolina. Yet, he had to learn to read in secret because the law banned education for free blacks as well as slaves. Moving north, he became a minister and educator with the African Methodist Episcopal Church. He recalled, "I was imprisoned in Missouri in 1854, for preaching the gospel to Negroes, though I was never subjected to violence." During the Civil War, he helped recruit the first two black regiments in Maryland. This life of service paved the way for Revels to become the first African American in the Senate.

How might his previous experience have prepared Hiram Revels for service in the Senate?

POLITICAL CARTOON *Skills*

The Ku Klux Klan
The KKK used terror and violence to keep African Americans from voting. Northern cartoonist Thomas Nast attacked the Klan and other secret societies in this cartoon.

1. **Comprehension** Identify two Klan activities shown in this cartoon.
2. **Understanding Main Ideas** How does Nast show the impact of the Ku Klux Klan and similar groups on African Americans?
3. **Critical Thinking Identifying a Point of View** What details in this cartoon show Nast's view of the Ku Klux Klan?

Congress Responds Many moderate southerners condemned the violence of the Klan. Yet, they could do little to stop the Klan's reign of terror. Freedmen turned to the federal government for help. In Kentucky, African American voters wrote to Congress:

> ❝ We believe you are not familiar with the Ku Klux Klan's riding nightly over the country spreading terror wherever they go by robbing, whipping, and killing our people without provocation. ❞
>
> — Records of the U.S. Senate, April 11, 1871

In 1870, Congress made it a crime to use force to keep people from voting. Although Klan activities decreased, the threat of violence remained. Some African Americans continued to vote and hold office, but others were frightened away from the ballot box.

The Challenge of Rebuilding

Despite political problems, Reconstruction governments tried to rebuild the South. They built public schools for both black and white children. Many states gave women the right to own property. In addition, Reconstruction governments rebuilt railroads, telegraph lines, bridges, and roads. Between 1865 and 1879, the South put down 7,000 miles of railroad track.

Rebuilding cost money. Before the war, southerners paid low taxes. Reconstruction governments raised taxes sharply. This created discontent among many southern whites.

Southerners were further angered by widespread corruption in the Reconstruction governments. One state legislature, for example, voted $1,000 to cover a member's bet on a horse race. Other items billed to the state included hams, perfume, and a coffin.

Corruption was not limited to the South. After the Civil War, dishonesty plagued northern governments, as well. Most southern officeholders, however, served their states honestly.

A Cycle of Poverty

In the first months after the war, freedmen left the plantations on which they had lived and worked. They found few opportunities, however.

Paraphrasing Paraphrasing can help you understand what you read. When you paraphrase, you restate what you have read in your own words. Paraphrase the paragraphs under "A Cycle of Poverty." Add the information to your outline.

"Nothing but Freedom" Some Radical Republicans talked about giving each freedman "40 acres and a mule." Thaddeus Stevens suggested breaking up big plantations and distributing the land. Most Americans opposed the plan, however. In the end, former slaves received—in the words of a freedman—"nothing but freedom."

Through hard work or good luck, some freedmen were able to become landowners. Most, however, had little choice but to return to where they had lived in slavery. At the same time, some large planters found themselves with land but nobody to work it.

Sharecropping During Reconstruction, many freedmen and poor whites went to work on the large plantations. These sharecroppers rented and farmed a plot of land. Planters provided seed, fertilizer, and tools in return for a share of the crop at harvest time. To many freedmen, sharecropping offered a measure of independence. Many hoped to own their own land one day.

In fact, most sharecroppers and small landowners became locked in a cycle of poverty. Each spring, they received supplies on credit. In the fall, they had to repay what they had borrowed. If the harvest did not cover what they owed, they sank deeper into debt. Many farmers lost their land and became sharecroppers themselves.

★ ★ ★ Section 3 Assessment ★ ★ ★

Recall

1. **Identify** Explain the significance of **(a)** Hiram Revels, **(b)** Blanche K. Bruce, **(c)** Conservatives, **(d)** Ku Klux Klan.
2. **Define** **(a)** scalawag, **(b)** carpetbagger, **(c)** sharecropper.

Comprehension

3. What role did freedmen play in Reconstruction governments?
4. What was the goal of groups like the Ku Klux Klan?
5. Describe two economic problems faced by Reconstruction governments in the South.
6. Why did many farmers become sharecroppers?

Critical Thinking and Writing

7. **Exploring the Main Idea** Review the Main Idea statement at the beginning of this section. Then, list two accomplishments of Reconstruction governments. Evaluate the impact of each on the South.
8. **Making Decisions** If you had been an African American during Reconstruction, would you have tried to vote despite threats? Write a paragraph explaining your reasons.

Activity

Writing a Welcoming Speech **You are a Republican member of Congress in 1870. You have been asked to write a brief speech welcoming one of the first African Americans elected to the House of Representatives. Your speech should highlight the importance of this occasion.**

4 The End of Reconstruction

Prepare to Read

Objectives

In this section, you will
- List the events that led to the end of Reconstruction.
- Explain how the rights of African Americans were restricted in the South after Reconstruction.
- Identify industries that flourished in the "New South."

Key Terms

poll tax
literacy test
grandfather clause
segregation
Jim Crow laws
Plessy v. *Ferguson*
"New South"

Target Reading Skill

Main Idea Copy the concept web below. As you read, fill in the blank ovals with information about the aftermath of Reconstruction. Add as many ovals as you need.

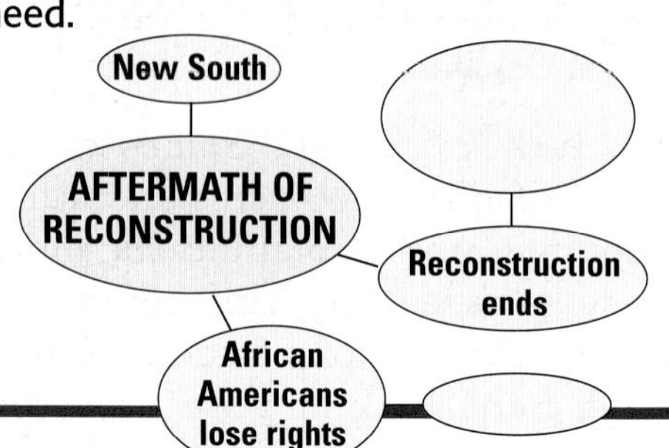

Main Idea When the North lost interest in protecting the goals of Reconstruction, the era came to an end.

Frederick Douglass

Setting the Scene Americans flocked to the great Centennial Exposition held in Philadelphia in 1876. Fairgoers gazed at the latest wonders of modern industry—the elevator, a giant steam engine, and the telephone ("Of what use is such an invention?" asked the New York *Tribune*).

At the opening ceremony, Frederick Douglass was invited to sit on the platform. But when the famed abolitionist tried to take his place, a policeman barred the way. The officer could not believe that a black man belonged on stage. Finally, a United States Senator persuaded the policeman to let Douglass pass.

By 1876, Americans were looking ahead to a bright future. Eager to put the past behind them, many northerners lost interest in Reconstruction. For African Americans in the South, the end of Reconstruction meant a slow erosion of their hard-won rights.

The End of Reconstruction

By the 1870s, Radical Republicans were losing power. Many northerners grew weary of trying to reform the South. It was time to let southerners run their own governments, they said—even if it meant that African Americans in the South might lose their rights.

Radicals in Decline Disclosure of widespread corruption also hurt Republicans. President Grant had appointed many friends to government offices. Some used their position to steal large sums of money from the government. Grant won reelection in 1872, but many northerners lost faith in Republicans and their policies.

Congress passed the Amnesty Act in 1872. It restored the right to vote to nearly all white southerners. They voted solidly Democratic. At the same time, threats of violence kept many African Americans from voting. By 1876, only three southern states—South Carolina, Florida, and Tennessee—remained under Republican control.

Election of 1876 The end of Reconstruction came with the election of 1876. The Democrats nominated Samuel Tilden, governor of New York, for President. The Republicans chose Ohio governor Rutherford B. Hayes. Both candidates vowed to fight corruption.

Tilden won the popular vote. However, he had only 184 electoral votes, one short of the number needed to win. The outcome of the election hung on 20 disputed votes. All but one came from the three southern states still controlled by Republicans.

As inauguration day drew near, the nation still had no one to swear in as President. Congress set up a special commission to settle the crisis. The commission, made up mostly of Republicans, decided to give all the disputed electoral votes to Hayes.

Southern Democrats could have fought the decision. Hayes, however, had privately agreed to end Reconstruction. Once in office, he removed all remaining federal troops from Louisiana, South Carolina, and Florida. Reconstruction was over.

Impact of Reconstruction Reconstruction had a deep and lasting impact on southern politics. White southerners had bitter memories of Radical Republican policies and military rule. For the next hundred years, the South remained a stronghold of the Democratic party. At the same time, black southerners steadily lost most of their political rights.

Restricted Rights

As Conservatives tightened their grip on southern governments, states found new ways to keep African Americans from exercising their rights. Many of these laws restricted the right to vote.

GEOGRAPHY *Skills*

The 1876 presidential election hinged on the disputed votes of three southern states. Although Samuel Tilden won the popular vote, Rutherford B. Hayes was declared the winner of the election.

1. **Location** On the map, locate **(a)** Florida, **(b)** Louisiana, **(c)** South Carolina.
2. **Regions** Which candidate carried the southern states where the vote was not disputed?
3. **Critical Thinking Drawing Inferences** Based on this map, do you think the Civil War ended sectionalism in the United States? Explain.

Election of 1876

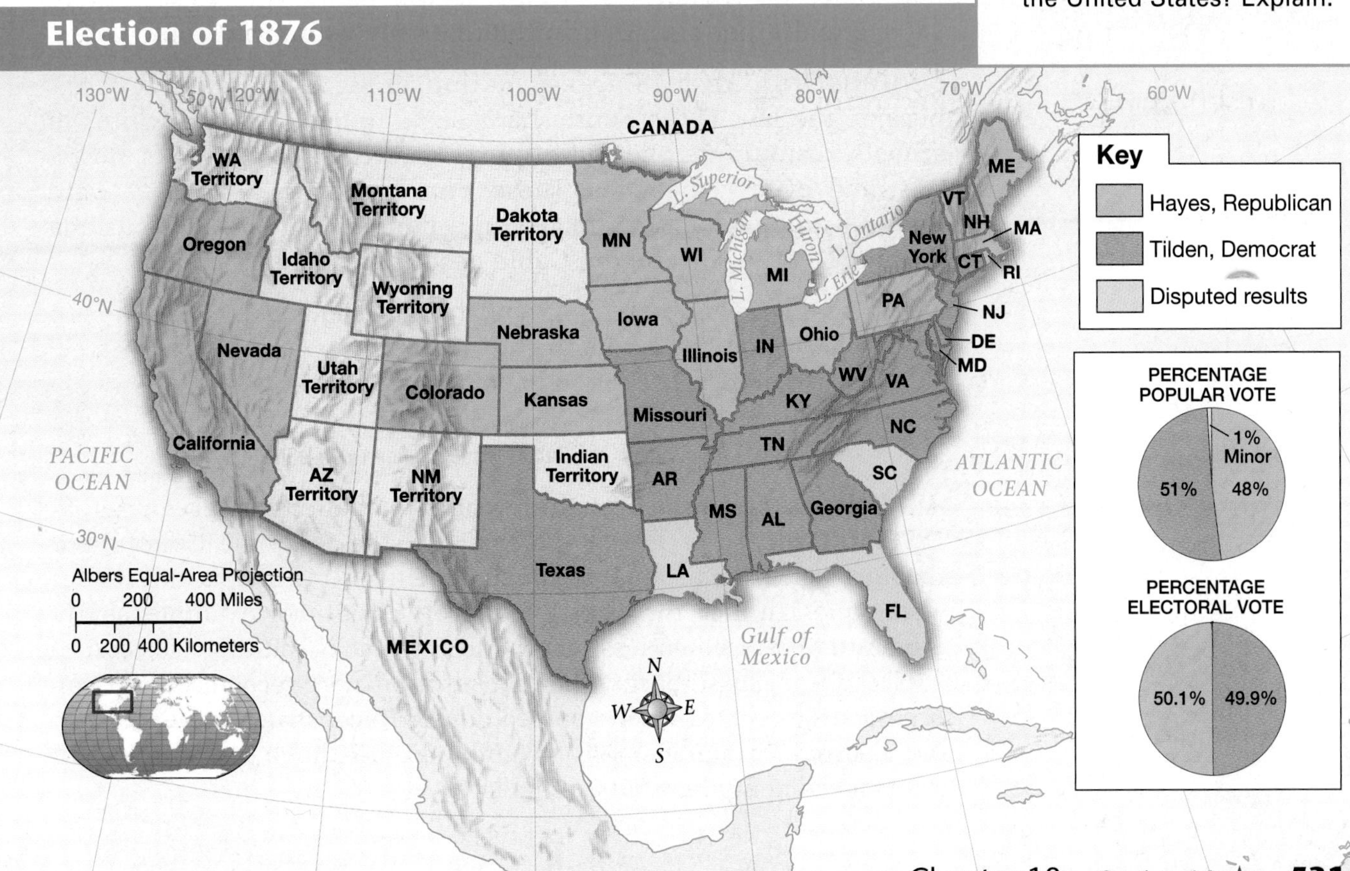

Viewing History

A Port in the New South

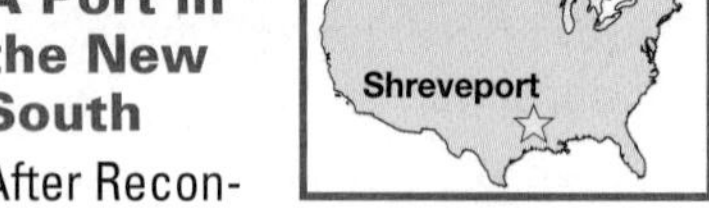

After Reconstruction, the economy of the South slowly began to recover. This print, made in the 1870s, shows the port of Shreveport, Louisiana. **Analyzing Information** ***How does this picture suggest that the South was recovering from the effects of the war?***

Voting Restrictions Over time, many southern states passed **poll taxes,** requiring voters to pay a fee each time they voted. As a result, poor freedmen could rarely afford to vote. States also imposed **literacy tests** that required voters to read and explain a section of the Constitution. Since most freedmen had little education, such tests kept them away from the polls.

Many poor whites could not pass the literacy test. To increase the number of white voters, states passed **grandfather clauses.** These laws stated that if a voter's father or grandfather had been eligible to vote on January 1, 1867, the voter did not have to take a literacy test. Since no African Americans in the South could vote before 1868, grandfather clauses ensured that only white men could vote.

Segregation After 1877, **segregation,** or legal separation of races, became the law of the South. Laws separated blacks and whites in schools, restaurants, theaters, trains, streetcars, playgrounds, hospitals, and even cemeteries. These **Jim Crow laws,** as they were known, trapped southern blacks in a hopeless situation. Louisiana novelist George Washington Cable described segregation as:

> ❝ A system of oppression so rank that nothing could make it seem small except the fact that [African Americans] had already been ground under it for a century and a half. ❞
>
> George Washington Cable, "The Freedman's Case in Equity"

African Americans brought lawsuits to challenge segregation. In 1896, in the case of ***Plessy* v. *Ferguson,*** the Supreme Court ruled that segregation was legal so long as facilities for blacks and whites were equal. In fact, facilities were rarely equal. For example, southern states spent much less on schools for blacks than for whites.

Despite such setbacks, the Constitution now recognized African Americans as citizens. Laws passed during Reconstruction—especially the Fourteenth Amendment—would become the basis of the civil rights movement almost 100 years later.

Industry in the "New South"

During Reconstruction, the South made some progress toward rebuilding its economy. Cotton production, long the basis of the South's economy, slowly recovered. By 1880, planters were growing as much cotton as they had in 1860.

A new generation of southern leaders worked to expand the economy. In stirring speeches, Atlanta journalist Henry Grady described a "New South" that used its vast natural resources to build up its own industry instead of depending on the North.

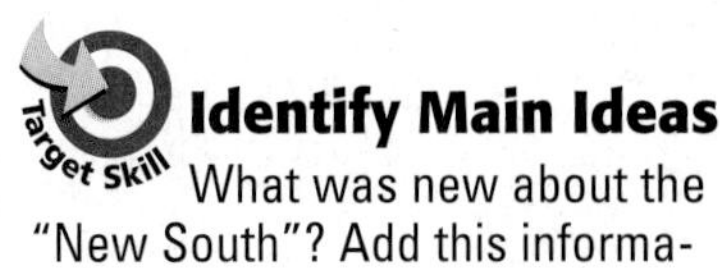

Identify Main Ideas What was new about the "New South"? Add this information to your concept web.

Agricultural Resources In 1880, the entire South still produced fewer finished textiles than Massachusetts. In the next decade, more and more communities started building textile mills to turn cotton into cloth.

The tobacco industry also grew. In North Carolina, James Duke used new machinery to revolutionize the manufacture of tobacco products. Duke's American Tobacco Company eventually controlled 90 percent of the nation's tobacco industry.

New Industries The South also tapped its mineral resources. With its large deposits of iron ore and coal, Alabama became a center of the steel industry. Oil refineries sprang up in Louisiana and Texas. Other states produced copper, granite, and marble.

By the 1890s, many northern forests had been cut down. The southern yellow pine competed with the northwestern white pine as a lumber source. Southern factories turned out cypress shingles and hardwood furniture.

The South had developed a more balanced economy by 1900. "We find a South wide awake with business," wrote a visitor, "eagerly laying lines of communication, rapidly opening mines, building furnaces, foundries, and all sorts of shops." Still, the South could not keep up with even more rapid growth in the North and the West.

★ ★ ★ Section 4 Assessment ★ ★ ★

Recall

1. **Identify** Explain the significance of **(a)** Rutherford B. Hayes, **(b)** Jim Crow laws, **(c)** *Plessy* v. *Ferguson,* **(d)** Henry Grady, **(e)** "New South," **(f)** James Duke.
2. **Define** **(a)** poll tax, **(b)** literacy test, **(c)** grandfather clause, **(d)** segregation.

Comprehension

3. Why did the Radical Republicans lose their power?
4. Describe two ways in which African Americans in the South lost political rights.
5. How did the southern economy change after Reconstruction?

Critical Thinking and Writing

6. **Exploring the Main Idea** Review the Main Idea statement at the beginning of this section. Then, evaluate the ways in which Reconstruction was both a success and a failure.
7. **Making Predictions** Write a paragraph predicting how the Supreme Court decision in *Plessy* v. *Ferguson* might affect later efforts by African Americans to achieve equality.

ACTIVITY

Go Online PHSchool.com

Connecting to Today
Choose one of the former Confederate states. Then, use the Internet to find out what the major industries and resources of that state are. Use this information to create a chart. For help in completing the activity, visit PHSchool.com, **Web Code mfd-1803.**

CHAPTER 18

Review and Assessment

Chapter Summary

Section 1
The South had a more difficult time recovering from the Civil War than the North. Lincoln's Reconstruction plan met with some resistance. Andrew Johnson became President after Lincoln's assassination.

Section 2
The South's black codes restricted the rights of freed African Americans. Congress responded by passing harsh Reconstruction measures. President Johnson survived an impeachment attempt.

Section 3
Southern and northern groups competed to control the South in the postwar period. The effort to rebuild the South created a cycle of poverty that affected freed African Americans and poor whites.

Section 4
Reconstruction did little to improve the condition of freed African Americans. However, new industries helped to improve the economy of the South.

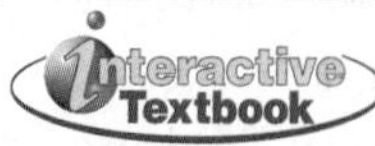

For additional review and enrichment activities, see the interactive version of *The American Nation*, available on the Web and on CD-ROM.

Chapter Self-Test For practice test questions for Chapter 18, visit PHSchool.com, **Web Code mfa-1804.**

Building Vocabulary

Review the meaning of the chapter vocabulary words listed below. Then, write a sentence for each word in which you define the word and describe its relation to the postwar South.

1. **freedmen**
2. **amnesty**
3. **black codes**
4. **scalawag**
5. **carpetbagger**
6. **sharecropper**
7. **poll tax**
8. **literacy test**
9. **grandfather clause**
10. **segregation**

Reviewing Key Facts

11. Describe Lincoln's plan for Reconstruction. (Section 1)
12. Describe two accomplishments of the Freedmen's Bureau. (Section 1)
13. What did the Fifteenth Amendment state? (Section 2)
14. Why did many northerners go to the South during Reconstruction? (Section 3)
15. What were the results of the presidential election of 1876? (Section 4)

Critical Thinking and Writing

16. **Drawing Conclusions** If Abraham Lincoln had lived, do you think he would have supported Radical Reconstruction? Write a paragraph explaining your answer and giving reasons.
17. **Supporting a Point of View** Do you think former Confederate officeholders should have been barred from serving in Congress? Write a position statement giving reasons for your point of view.
18. **Identifying Causes and Effects** Analyze the causes and effects of the passage of the Fourteenth Amendment.
19. **Linking Past and Present** **(a)** What action did the federal government take to stop violence by groups like the Ku Klux Klan? **(b)** List two ways governments and individuals work to end hate crimes today.
20. **Connecting to Geography: Place** Analyze the effect of geographic factors on the rise of the "New South." List at least three specific examples.

Skills Assessment

Analyzing Primary Sources

In an 1876 speech, Senator Blanche K. Bruce of Mississippi discussed the hopes that African Americans had for the future:

> “Although many of us are uneducated in the schools, we are informed and advised as to our duties to the government, our state, and ourselves. . . . With scrupulous respect for the rights of others, and with the hopefulness of political youth, we are determined that the great government that gave us liberty and rendered its gift valuable by giving us the ballot shall not find us wanting in a sufficient response to any demand that humanity or patriotism may make upon us.”
>
> —Blanche K. Bruce, Record of the 44th Congress, 1876

21. According to Bruce, what is African Americans' most important duty?
- **A.** to go to school in order to get an education
- **B.** to remain politically youthful
- **C.** to do what patriotism demands
- **D.** to cherish the gift of the vote

22. What government actions does Bruce praise?
- **A.** keeping African Americans informed
- **B.** giving African Americans their freedom and the right to vote
- **C.** trying to keep African Americans hopeful that their condition will improve in the future
- **D.** opening new schools in African American neighborhoods

Applying Your Skills

Solving Problems

Examine the chart below, and answer the questions that follow.

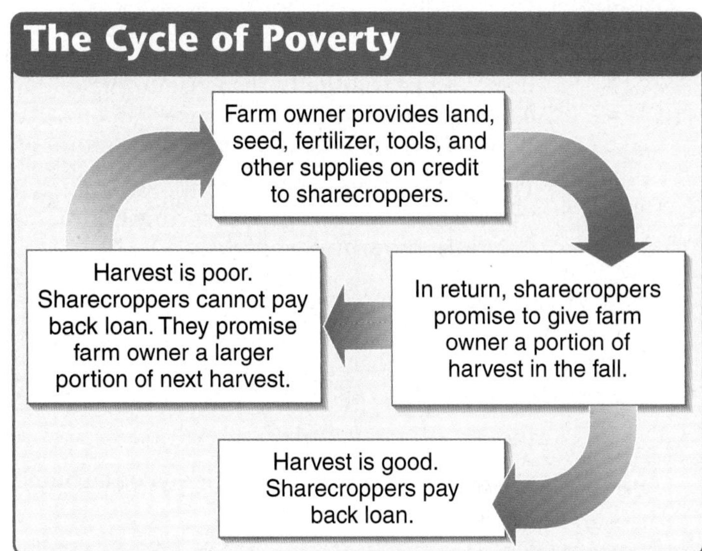

23. What problem is the main topic of this chart?
- **A.** Poor harvest
- **B.** Scarcity of supplies
- **C.** Sharecroppers' rising debt
- **D.** Inability to get credit

24. Suggest and evaluate one possible solution to the problem shown on the chart.

Activities

Connecting With . . . Government and Citizenship

Creating a Poster Choose one of the three Civil War amendments to the Constitution discussed in this chapter. With a partner, create a poster that expresses the key ideas of that amendment and its importance to Americans. Include both images and words. You may include modern images that reflect the importance of the amendment today.

Connecting to Today

Giving a Report Use the Internet to find out about the nation's Historically Black Colleges and Universities (HBCUs). Report to the class on the location, history, and current goals of one of these schools. For help in starting this activity, visit PHSchool.com, **Web Code mfd-1805.**

Leaves of Grass

Walt Whitman

Walt Whitman

Introduction **One of the best-loved of all American poets, Walt Whitman served as a Union nurse in the Civil War. The following poems were written in response to the end of the war and the death of Abraham Lincoln. In the most famous, "O Captain! My Captain!" Whitman compares Lincoln to the captain of a ship.**

Vocabulary Before you read the selections, find the meanings of these words in a dictionary: **reconciliation, carnage, incessantly, exulting, mournful, ceaseless.**

Reconciliation

Word over all, beautiful as the sky,
Beautiful that war and all its deeds of carnage must in time be utterly lost,
That the hands of the sisters Death and Night incessantly softly wash again, and ever, this soil'd world;
For my enemy is dead, a man divine as myself is dead,
I look where he lies white-faced and still in the coffin—I draw near,
Bend down and touch lightly with my lips the white face in the coffin.

O Captain! My Captain!

O Captain! My Captain! our fearful trip is done,
Our ship has weather'd every rack,* the prize we sought is won,
The port is near, the bells I hear, the people all exulting,
While follow eyes the steady keel, the vessel grim and daring;
But O heart! heart! heart!
O the bleeding drops of red,
Where on the deck my Captain lies,
Fallen cold and dead.

O Captain! My Captain! rise up and hear the bells;
Rise up—for you the flag is flung—for you the bugle trills,
For you bouquets and ribbon'd wreaths—for you the shores a-crowding,
For you they call, the swaying mass, their eager faces turning;
Here Captain! dear father!
This arm beneath your head!
It is some dream that on the deck
You've fallen cold and dead.

My Captain does not answer, his lips are pale and still,
My father does not feel my arm, he has no pulse nor will,
The ship is anchor'd safe and sound, its voyage closed and done,
From fearful trip the victor ship comes in with object won;
Exult O shores, and ring O bells!
But I with mournful tread,
Walk the deck my Captain lies,
Fallen cold and dead.

*__rack:__ storm

HUSH'D BE THE CAMPS TO-DAY (MAY 4, 1865)

Hush'd be the camps to-day,
And soldiers let us drape our war-worn weapons,
And each with musing soul retire to celebrate
Our dear commander's death.

No more for him life's stormy conflicts,
Nor victory, nor defeat—no more time's dark events,
Charging like ceaseless clouds across the sky.

But sing poet in our name,
Sing of the love we bore him—because you, dweller in camps, know it truly.

As they invault the coffin there,
Sing—as they close the doors of earth upon him—one verse,
For the heavy hearts of soldiers.

Statue at the Lincoln Memorial

Analyzing Literature

1. In "Reconciliation," how would you describe the speaker's attitude toward the enemy?
   - **A** Triumphant
   - **B** Forgiving
   - **C** Vengeful
   - **D** Fearful

2. In "Oh Captain! My Captain!" the people are rejoicing because
   - **A** Lincoln is dead
   - **B** Lincoln has issued the Emancipation Proclamation
   - **C** the Union has been preserved
   - **D** the South has been destroyed

3. **Critical Thinking and Writing** **Applying Information** How does Whitman's depiction of Abraham Lincoln reflect what you have learned about his role as a leader during the Civil War? Refer to at least two lines from Whitman's poems.

TEST PREPARATION

Use the map <u>and</u> your knowledge of social studies to answer the following question.

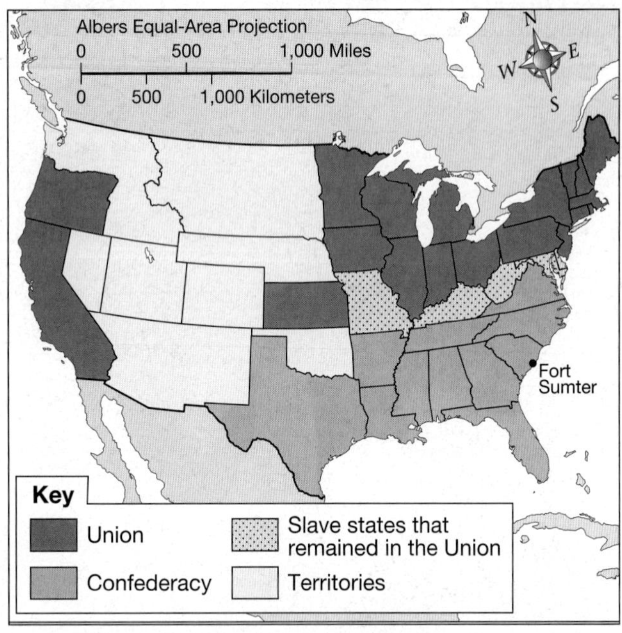

1 Which conclusion can you draw from this map?

A More people lived in the Union than in the Confederacy.

B The Confederacy occupied most of the Atlantic Coast.

C Most of the fighting in the Civil War took place in the South.

D All slave states seceded from the Union.

2 Which of the following was not a goal of Radical Reconstruction?

A Break the power of southern planters

B Guarantee the vote to freedmen

C End slavery

D Strengthen Republican control of Congress

3 In which of the following pairs was the first event a cause of the second?

A Fort Sumter is fired upon; South Carolina secedes

B California applies for statehood; Compromise of 1850 passed

C Fighting erupts in Kansas; Kansas-Nebraska Act passed

D John Brown leads raid on Harpers Ferry; Republican party is formed

4 What was one major effect of the Emancipation Proclamation?

A It immediately freed slaves in the North.

B It immediately freed slaves in the South.

C It allowed African Americans to enlist in the Union army.

D It increased support for the Union cause in Europe.

5 With which of these statements would both Abraham Lincoln and Stephen Douglas have agreed?

A "The Kansas-Nebraska Act will help save the Union."

B "The Union must be preserved."

C "The people of each state have the right to decide whether to allow slavery."

D "The nation cannot survive half-slave, half-free."

Use the statements below and your knowledge of social studies to answer the following question.

- "All persons formerly held as slaves shall have the right to own, sell, purchase, and inherit property."
- "No one other than white men shall be permitted to serve on juries, hold office, or vote in any election."

6 Where would you be most likely to find *both* of the above statements?

A The Wade-Davis Bill

B The Reconstruction Act

C One of the black codes

D The Supreme Court decision in *Plessy* v. *Ferguson*

7 Which of the following individuals would have been most likely to agree with the Dred Scott decision?

A Harriet Beecher Stowe

B Frederick Douglass

C John C. Calhoun

D John Brown

8 Which of the following explained which people were considered to be American citizens?

A Thirteenth Amendment

B Fourteenth Amendment

C Fifteenth Amendment

D Gettysburg Address

Use the table and your knowledge of social studies to answer the following question.

Casualties of Selected Civil War Battles

Battle Site	Union Casualties	Confederate Casualties
Gettysburg	23,053	28,063
Antietam	12,410	10,316
Shiloh	13,047	10,694
Fredericksburg	12,653	5,309

Source: *The Civil War,* Time-Life Books

9 Which battle had the largest percentage of Union casualties?

A Antietam

B Gettysburg

C Shiloh

D Fredericksburg

Writing Practice

10 "Slavery was the chief cause of the Civil War." Agree or disagree with this statement. Give reasons for your answer.

11 Describe one social, one political, and one economic effect of the Civil War on the South. Explain which effect you think had the greatest impact.

Unit 6

Transforming the Nation

UNIT OUTLINE

An American Steel Mill
The manufacture of stronger steel, as shown in Peter Kroyer's ***The Biermeister and Main Steel Forge,*** helped spark rapid industrial growth.

"The manufacturers of this country, with our wonderful stores of raw materials at hand, [have] become the successful rivals . . . of any country that desires to compete with them."

—Carroll D. Wright, United States labor commissioner (1882)

CHAPTER 19

The New West

1865–1914

1 Indian Peoples of the Great Plains
2 Mining and Railroading
3 The Cattle Kingdom
4 Indian Peoples in Retreat
5 Farming

Battle at Little Bighorn

Sioux warrior's bow and arrow case

AMERICAN EVENTS

1869 The first transcontinental railroad is completed.

1876 The Lakota Sioux, Arapahos, and Cheyenne, led by Chief Crazy Horse, defeat General Custer at the Battle of Little Bighorn.

1887 The Dawes Act encourages Native Americans to become farmers.

Presidential Terms: Andrew Johnson 1865-1869; Ulysses S. Grant 1869-1877; Rutherford B. Hayes 1877-1881; James A. Garfield 1881; Chester A. Arthur 1881-1885; Grover Cleveland 1885-1889

1860 — 1875 — 1890

WORLD EVENTS

1869 ▲ The Suez Canal opens in Egypt.

1885 ▲ The first transcontinental railroad is completed in Canada.

New States in the West

As settlers flooded into the West, towns and cities quickly grew. Between 1865 and 1914, eight western territories became states.

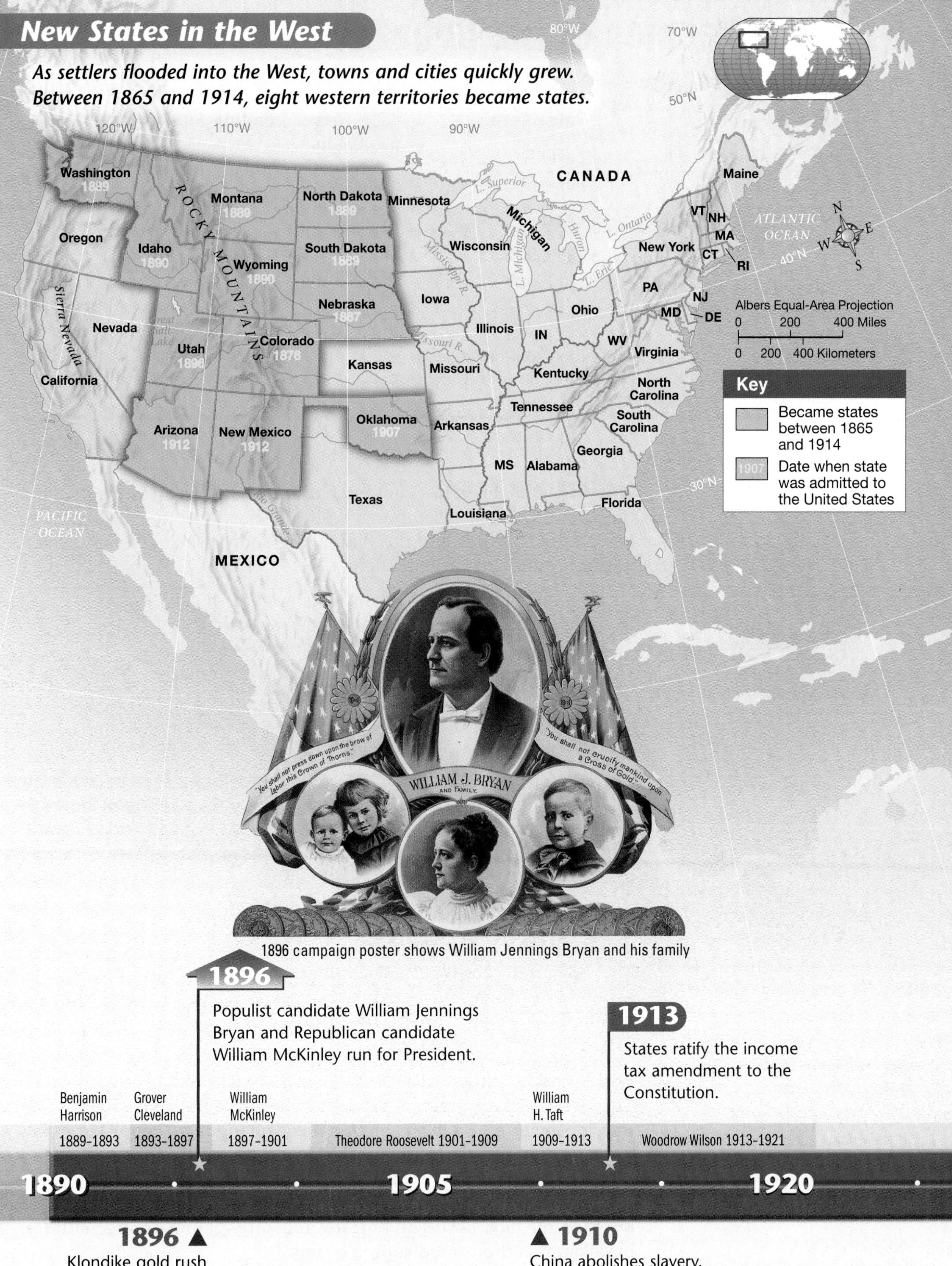

1896 campaign poster shows William Jennings Bryan and his family

1 Indian Peoples of the Great Plains

Prepare to Read

Objectives

In this section, you will
- Describe the life of the Plains Indians.
- Explain why the Plains Indians followed buffalo.
- Identify how the rules of men and women differed in the Plains Indian society.

Key Terms

tepee

travois

corral

jerky

Target Reading Skill

Reading Process As you read, prepare an outline of this section. Use roman numerals to indicate the major headings, capital letters for the subheadings, and numbers for the supporting details.

I. The Plains Indians
- **A. Life on the Plains**
  - **1. Different cultures**
  - **2.**
- **B. The arrival of horses**
  - **1.**
  - **2.**

II. Following the Buffalo

Main Idea Different Indian peoples lived on the Great Plains, and many relied on the horse and the buffalo as they developed their varied cultures and traditions.

Kiowa warrior's shield

Setting the Scene Looking back years later, Old Lady Horse of the Kiowa nation remembered well her childhood days when huge herds of buffalo roamed the Plains. The Kiowa, she explained, could not have survived without them:

> "Everything the Kiowas had came from the buffalo. Their tipis were made of buffalo hides, so were their clothes and moccasins. They ate buffalo meat. Their containers were made of hide, or of bladders or stomachs. The buffalo were the life of the Kiowas."
>
> —Old Lady Horse, quoted in Alice Marriott and Carol K. Rachlin, *American Indian Mythology*

Indian peoples had been living for centuries on the Great Plains. The many uses of the buffalo provide just one example of how the Indians adapted their ways of life to the region. They created well-ordered societies that divided work between men and women and made the most of the resources on hand.

The Plains Indians

Many different Native American nations lived on the Great Plains. A number of them, such as the Arikaras, had lived on the Plains for hundreds of years. Others, like the Lakotas, did not move to the Plains until the early 1700s.

Life on the Plains Plains Indians had rich and varied cultures. They were skilled artists. They also had well-organized religions and warrior societies. Each nation had its own language. People from different nations used sign language to talk to one another.

At one time, most Plains Indians were farmers who lived in semi-permanent villages. From there, they sent out hunting parties that pursued on foot herds of buffalo and other animals. Agriculture, however, was their main source of food.

The Arrival of Horses During the 1600s, the Plains Indians' way of life changed as they learned about horses from neighboring tribes.

The Spanish had brought horses to the Americas in the late 1400s. At first, Indians were not allowed to own horses, but they did learn how to care for and how to ride them. After the Pueblo Indians revolted against the Spaniards in 1680, the Pueblos were left with thousands of horses. They started trading these horses to neighboring tribes. Eventually, the horses reached the tribes of the northern plains.

Plains Indians used horses while hunting. They also used horses when moving their villages and going on raids.

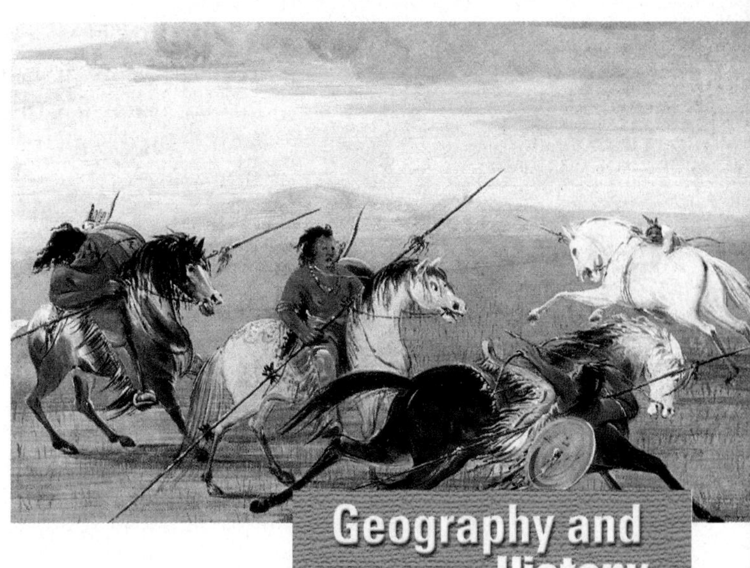

Following the Buffalo

The buffalo served as a living grocery store for Plains Indians. After acquiring horses, they followed the huge herds that had roamed their homeland for centuries. They began to live in **tepees** (TEE pees), or tents made by stretching buffalo skins on tall poles. The tepees could easily be carried on a **travois** (truh VOI), or sled pulled by a dog or horse.

The migration of the Plains Indians mirrored the movement of the buffalo. In winter, small groups of buffalo moved to protected valleys and forests. In summer, huge buffalo herds gathered on the Plains where the grass was plentiful. In the same way, Plains Indians spent the winter in small bands and gathered in large groups during the summers.

The Buffalo Hunt There were different ways to hunt buffalo. Before horses came to the Plains, a group of hunters would shout and wave colored robes at the buffalo. The hunters would gradually drive a herd of buffalo into a **corral,** or enclosure. There they killed the trapped buffalo. When the hunt was over, the women and children joined the hunters in cutting up the buffalo and taking it back to camp. Once they had horses, hunters would ride the horses right into the herd and kill the buffalo with bows and arrows.

Uses of the Buffalo Although the Plains Indians also hunted deer and elk, they depended on the buffalo for food, clothing, and shelter. Buffalo meat, rich in protein, was a main item of the Indians' diet. Women cut up and dried the meat on racks. The dried meat was called **jerky.**

Women also tanned buffalo hides to make sleeping robes and tepee covers. They wove buffalo fur into coarse, warm cloth. The cloth was used as an outer covering for a tepee.

Tradition and Ceremony Many Native American groups met on the Plains. They hunted together and attended special events.

Summer gatherings were the time for councils. At the councils, the elders were consulted about the problems that affected the whole nation.

Geography and History

Wild Horses in the West

At the first sight of horses, the Plains Indians believed them to be mysterious, magical animals. They called them "sacred dogs." These "sacred dogs" forever changed the life of Plains Indians. Before the horse, tribes lived at the edge of the plains, venturing out to hunt buffalo on foot during the summer. Horses made them mobile, allowing them to live on the Plains year round and to follow the buffalo herds. The Comanches, one of the first tribes to ride horses, became skilled and feared warriors who moved swiftly over long distances. With horses, the Comanches could expand their territory and defend it from neighboring tribes. A man on foot was no match for the "sacred dog."

Why did the Plains Indians refer to horses as "sacred dogs"?

The most important religious ceremony was the Sun Dance. Hundreds of people attended the four-day ceremony to thank the Great Spirit for blessings, good hunts, and help in times of trouble. Sun Dancers also asked the Great Spirit for good fortune in the coming year.

Target Skill: Ask Questions What questions would you have asked the Plains Indians about the roles of men and women?

The Roles of Women and Men

Women and men usually had specific roles in Indian society. In some tribes, women helped men with the hunting and governing. A Blackfoot woman, Running Eagle, led many hunting parties herself.

The Role of Women Women oversaw life in the home. They gathered food and prepared meals for their families. The women not only made the tepees, but they were also responsible for raising and taking down tepees. Women cared for the children and, along with the men, passed along the traditions of their people.

Women also engaged in many crafts. They made the baskets and blankets. Their work often showed great artistic skill and design. In fact, a woman's ability in crafts established her rank in society.

The Role of Men The men of the Plains Indians had important responsibilities too. They hunted and protected the women, children, and the elders. They passed on their valuable skills and knowledge to the boys. They supervised the spiritual life of the community by leading religious ceremonies.

Another important responsibility of the men was to provide military leadership. They waged war to defend or extend territory, to gain horses and other riches, or to seek revenge. More than anything else, however, men waged war to protect their people and to prove their bravery and ability. The most successful warriors gained great respect from the members of their nation.

★ ★ ★ Section 1 Assessment ★ ★ ★

Recall

1. **Define** **(a)** tepee, **(b)** travois, **(c)** corral, **(d)** jerky.

Comprehension

2. How did the arrival of the horse change the life of the Plains Indians?
3. Why did the Plains Indians depend on the buffalo?
4. **(a)** What were the responsibilities of women in the society? **(b)** What were the responsibilities of men?

Critical Thinking and Writing

5. **Exploring the Main Idea** Review the Main Idea statement at the beginning of this section. Then, write a paragraph describing how the dependence on buffalo hunting affected the lives of the men and the women.
6. **Making Generalizations** Based on what you know about the Sun Dance ceremony, what were some religious beliefs of the Plains Indians?

Activity

Go Online PHSchool.com

Connecting to Today

The buffalo was important to the Plains Indians. Use the Internet to find out about the status of the buffalo today. Work with a partner to prepare a museum exhibit about the buffalo in the past and today. For help in completing the activity, visit PHSchool.com, **Web Code mfd-1901**.

2 Mining and Railroading

Prepare to Read

Objectives

In this section, you will
- Describe how the boom in gold and silver changed the West.
- Identify problems that arose on the mining frontier.
- Explain how railroads helped the West develop.

Key Terms

lode

vigilante

transcontinental railroad

subsidy

Target Reading Skill

Sequence Copy this flowchart. As you read, fill in the boxes with some of the events that led up to completion of the first transcontinental railroad. The first and last boxes have been filled in to help you get started.

Mining towns need supplies
↓
[ ]
↓
[ ]
↓
Transcontinental railroad is completed in 1869

Main Idea A mining boom changed the West, bringing people and a new means of transportation to the region.

Setting the Scene Late in 1859, a pack train of 80 mules made its way across the Sierra Nevada mountains into California. The mules bore tons of silver ore fresh from a new strike in the Washoe Valley east of the Sierras. At $5,000 a ton, this single load was enough to make a man rich beyond his dreams. Later, glittering white bars of silver made from the ore were put on exhibit in the window of a San Francisco bank. Passersby gazed in amazement at the sight of so much wealth.

The lure of instant riches drew tens of thousands west. Miners came from all over the globe to strike it rich in the new West.

Men with a pile of silver bars

A Boom in Gold and Silver

The western mining boom had begun with the California gold rush of 1849. When the gold rush ended, miners looked for new opportunities. A mere rumor sent them racing east in search of new strikes.

The Comstock Lode Two prospectors struck gold in the Sierra Nevada in 1859. Then, another miner, Henry Comstock, appeared. "The land is mine," he cried, demanding to be made a partner. From then on, Comstock boasted about "his" mine. The strike became known as the Comstock Lode. A **lode** is a rich vein of gold or silver.

Comstock and his partners often complained about the heavy blue sand that was mixed in with the gold. It clogged the devices used for separating out the gold and made the gold hard to reach. When Mexican miners took the "danged blue stuff" to an expert in California, tests showed that it was loaded with silver. Comstock had stumbled onto one of the richest silver mines in the world.

Miners moved into many other areas of the West. Some found valuable ore in Montana and Idaho. Others struck it rich in Colorado. In the 1870s, miners discovered gold in the Black Hills of South Dakota. In the late 1890s, thousands rushed north to Alaska after major gold strikes were made there.

From Boomtown to Ghost Town Gold and silver strikes attracted thousands of prospectors. Towns sprang up almost overnight near all the major mining sites.

First, miners built a tent city near the diggings. Then, people came to supply the miners' needs. Traders brought mule teams loaded with tools, food, and clothing. Merchants hauled in wagonloads of supplies and set up stores.

Soon, wood-frame houses, hotels, restaurants, and stores replaced the tents. For example, it took less than a year for the mining camp at the Comstock Lode to become the boomtown of Virginia City, Nevada.

Most settlers in the boomtowns of the mining frontier were men. However, enterprising women also found ways to profit. Some women ran boardinghouses and laundries. Others opened restaurants, where miners gladly paid high prices for home-cooked meals.

Many boomtowns lasted for only a few years. When the gold or silver ore was gone, the miners moved away. Without the miners for customers, businesses often had to close. In this way, a boomtown could quickly go bust and turn into a ghost town.

Still, some boomtowns survived and prospered even after the mines shut down. In these towns, miners stayed and found new ways to make a living.

Problems Along the Mining Frontier

The surge of miners in the West created problems, as did the arrival of cattle ranchers and homesteaders. Mines and towns polluted clear mountain streams. Miners cut down forests to get wood for buildings. They also forced Native Americans from the land.

GEOGRAPHY *Skills*

The discovery of gold, the Homestead Act, and the arrival of railroad builders, ranchers, and other settlers contributed to the population growth of the West.

1. **Location** On the map, locate **(a)** Comstock Lode, **(b)** Central Pacific Railroad, **(c)** Promontory, **(d)** Chisholm Trail.
2. **Interaction** How did mining affect nearby soil, water, and other natural resources?
3. **Critical Thinking Applying Information** How do you think the railroad lines affected the cattle ranchers in Colorado?

The Changing West

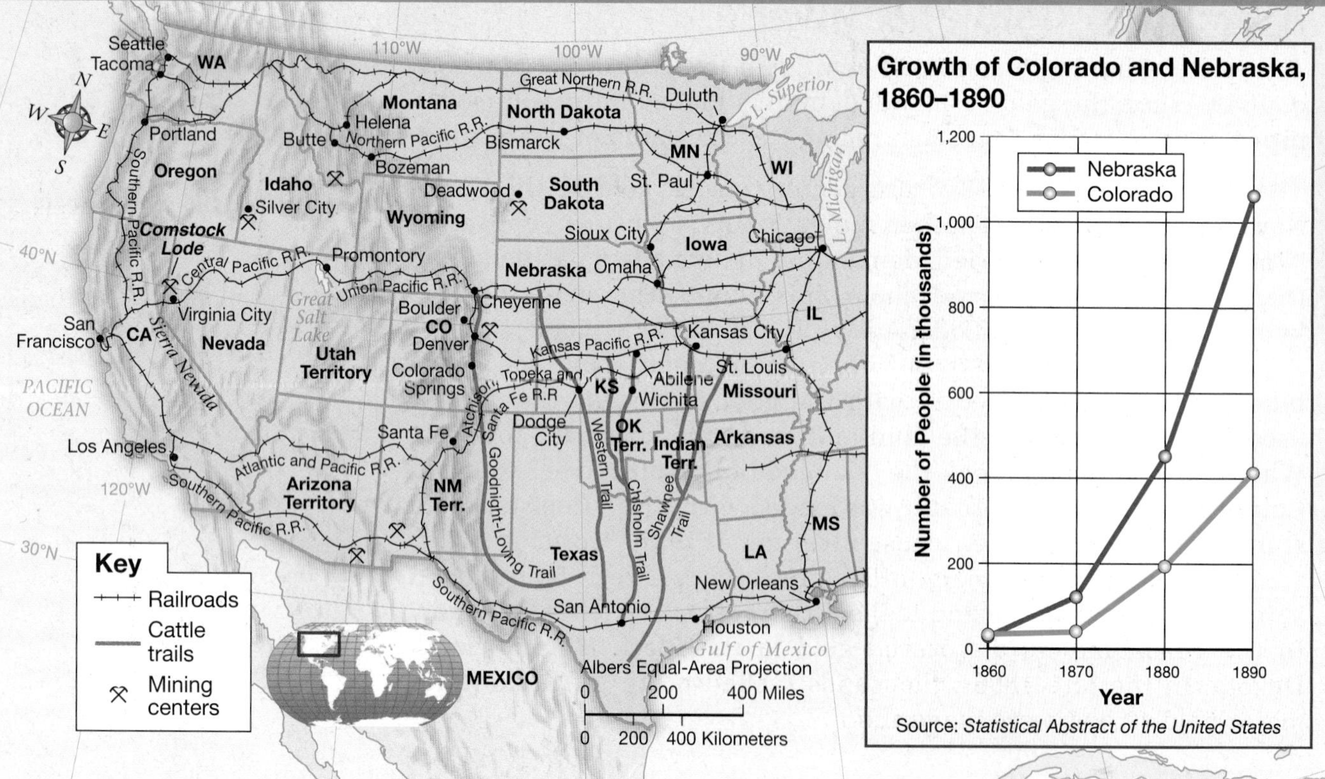

Foreign miners were often treated unfairly. In many camps, mobs drove Mexicans from their claims. Chinese miners were heavily taxed or forced to work claims abandoned by others.

Few miners ever got rich. Much of the gold and silver lay deep underground. It could be reached only with costly machinery. Eventually, most mining in the West was taken over by large companies that could afford to buy this equipment. Furthermore, independent prospectors like Henry Comstock largely disappeared. They were replaced by paid laborers who worked for the large companies.

Territorial Government Lawlessness and disorder often accompanied the rapid growth of a town. Stories have exaggerated the number of fights and killings that took place in these towns, but some towns actually were violent places. In response, miners sometimes resorted to organizing groups of **vigilantes,** or self-appointed law enforcers. Vigilantes tracked down outlaws and punished them, usually without trials. A common punishment was lynching.

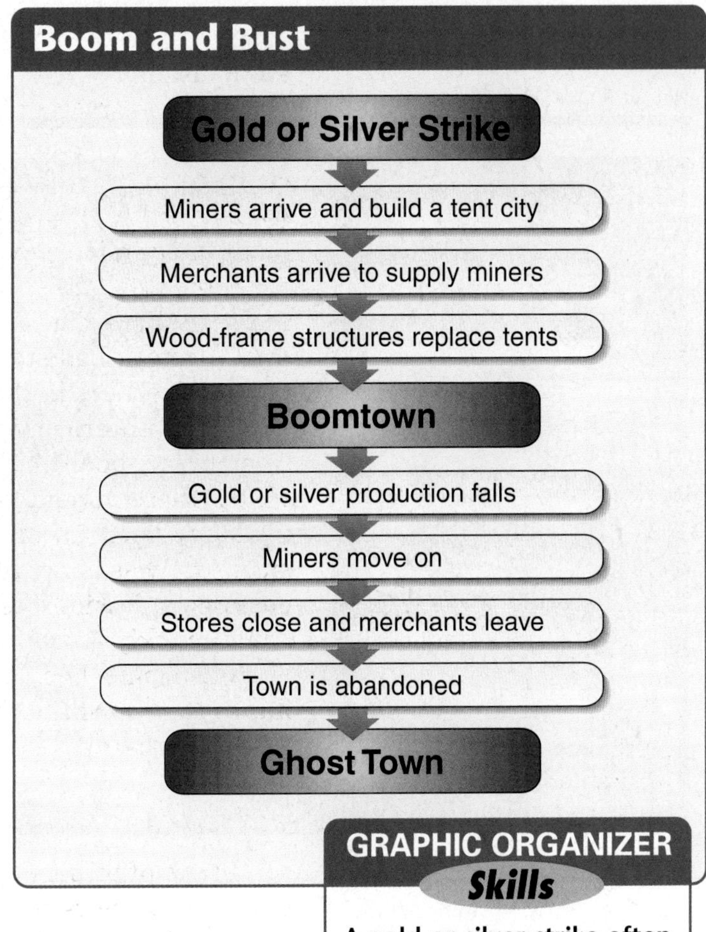

GRAPHIC ORGANIZER *Skills*

A gold or silver strike often led to the building of a boomtown. However, many boomtowns quickly became ghost towns.

1. **Comprehension (a)** Why did merchants often follow miners? **(b)** What caused large numbers of miners to suddenly leave a boomtown?
2. **Critical Thinking Analyzing Information** Based on this chart and on the map on page 548, why do you think there are more ghost towns today in Idaho than there are in Texas?

Economics $

Occasionally, vigilante groups did not form to fight crime. At least one San Francisco group organized to take political control of the city.

Informal methods of governing gradually gave way to more formal arrangements. In 1861, Colorado, Dakota, and Nevada were organized into territories. Idaho and Arizona followed in 1863 and Montana, in 1864. The process of permanent settlement and government had begun.

The Railroads

To the Indians, the railroad was a terrifying monster, an "iron horse" belching black smoke and moving at stunning speeds. However, for the people of mining towns, railroads meant supplies, new townsfolk, and a rapid means of transporting their gold and silver. The West needed a transportation system that could carry heavy loads over great distances at a cost low enough to guarantee a profit. It is no wonder, then, that railroad companies raced to lay track to the mines and boomtowns.

A Transcontinental Railroad In 1863, two companies began a race to build the first transcontinental railroad. A **transcontinental railroad** is one that stretches across a continent from coast to coast. The Union Pacific Railroad started building a rail line westward from Omaha, Nebraska. The Central Pacific Railroad began in Sacramento, California, and built eastward. A local paper reported:

Garnet, Montana

Bustling boomtowns became abandoned ghost towns once the mines no longer yielded gold or silver. Garnet, Montana, now a ghost town, was founded in 1895 and swelled to nearly 1,000 people by 1898. Aside from the saloons found in all boomtowns, Garnet also had a school, barbershops, a union hall, and a doctor's office. It even claimed to have a low crime rate. By 1905, the population had fallen to 150.

Virtual Field Trip For an interactive look at Garnet, Montana, visit PHSchool.com, **Web Code mfd-1902.**

> “ With rites appropriate to the occasion . . . ground was formally broken at noon for the commencement of the Central Pacific Railroad—the California link of the continental chain that is to unite American communities now divided by thousands of miles of trackless wilderness. ”
>
> —Sacramento *Union*, January 8, 1863

Target Skill **Identify Sequence** Which events in this paragraph contributed to the construction of the transcontinental railroad? Add these to your flowchart.

The federal government helped the railroad companies because it felt that rail lines in the West would benefit the entire nation. The government's aid came in the form of subsidies. A **subsidy** is financial aid or a land grant from the government. Congress lent money to the railroad companies and gave them land. For every mile of track completed, the railroad companies received twenty sections of land in the states along the route and forty sections per mile in the territories. By the time the Central Pacific and Union Pacific railroads were completed, they had received about 45 million acres of land. Often, both business and government ignored the fact that Native Americans lived on the land.

Working on the Railroad Both companies had trouble getting workers. Labor was scarce during the Civil War. Also, the work was backbreaking and dangerous and the pay was low.

The railroad companies hired immigrant workers, who accepted low wages. The Central Pacific brought in thousands of workers from China. The Union Pacific hired newcomers from Ireland. African Americans and Mexican Americans also worked for each line.

The workers faced a daunting task. The Central Pacific had to carve a path through the rugged Sierra Nevada. The Union Pacific had to cut through the towering Rocky Mountains. Snowstorms and avalanches killed workers and slowed progress. At times, crews cutting tunnels through rock advanced only a few inches a day.

Railroads Promote Growth The Central Pacific and Union Pacific met at Promontory, Utah, on May 10, 1869. Leland Stanford, president of the Central Pacific, dropped a solid-gold spike into a pre-drilled hole in the rail. In doing so, he joined the two tracks and united the country. The nation's first transcontinental railroad was complete.

With the Civil War fresh in their minds, people cheered this new symbol of unity. The words that were engraved on the golden spike expressed their feelings:

> "May God continue the unity of our Country as the Railroad unites the two great Oceans of the world."

Before long, other major rail lines linked the West and the East. The railroads brought growth and new settlement all across the West. They enabled people, supplies, and mail to move quickly and cheaply across the plains and mountains. Wherever rail lines went, settlements sprang up along the tracks. The largest towns and cities developed where major railroad lines met. Cities where sea and land transportation met, such as Seattle, San Francisco, and Los Angeles, experienced huge population growth with the coming of the Southern Pacific and Santa Fe railroads. Western cities, such as Denver, Cheyenne, and Wichita, grew when railroads were joined to the great cattle trails.

Because of their rapid growth, western territories began to apply for statehood. Nevada became a state in 1864; Colorado, in 1876; North Dakota, South Dakota, Montana, and Washington, in 1889; Idaho and Wyoming in 1890.

Primary Source

Roughing It

In 1861, Mark Twain traveled west to prospect for gold. Here he describes some of the hardships of the journey:

"On the nineteenth day, we crossed the Great American Desert—forty memorable miles of bottomless sand. . . . We worked our passage most of the way across. That is to say, we got out and walked. It was a dreary pull and a long thirsty one, for we had no water. From one extremity of this desert to the other, the road was white with the bones of oxen and horses. . . . we could have walked forty miles and set our feet on a bone every step! The desert was one [large] graveyard. And the log-chains, wagon tyres, and rotting wrecks of vehicles were almost as thick as the bones."

Analyzing Primary Sources

Why do you think Twain and the other prospectors were willing to endure such hardships?

★ ★ ★ Section 2 Assessment ★ ★ ★

Recall

1. **Identify** Explain the significance of **(a)** Comstock Lode, **(b)** Union Pacific Railroad, **(c)** Central Pacific Railroad, **(d)** Leland Stanford.
2. **Define** **(a)** lode, **(b)** vigilante, **(c)** transcontinental railroad, **(d)** subsidy.

Comprehension

3. How did mining encourage the growth of towns in the West?
4. Describe three problems that occurred in mining towns.
5. How did railroads change the West?

Critical Thinking and Writing

6. **Exploring the Main Idea** Review the Main Idea statement at the beginning of this section. Then, prepare a cause-and-effect chart that gives information on how mining changed the West. The first "cause" entry can be: Silver discovered in Sierra Nevada in 1859. The first "effect" entry can be: Huge numbers of people rush to Nevada.
7. **Linking Past and Present** Are railroads as important today as they were in the late 1800s? Explain.

Activity

Writing a Speech **You are a railroad official in 1869. Write a short speech to celebrate the completion of the first transcontinental railroad. In your speech, explain how you think the railroad will benefit the entire nation.**

3 The Cattle Kingdom

Prepare to Read

Objectives

In this section, you will
- Identify the Cattle Kingdom.
- Describe the life of a cowhand.
- Explain why cow towns were important during the cattle boom.

Key Terms

cattle drive

vaquero

cow town

Target Reading Skill

Cause and Effect Copy the chart below. As you read, complete the chart to show other causes that led to the end of the Cattle Kingdom. Add as many boxes as you need.

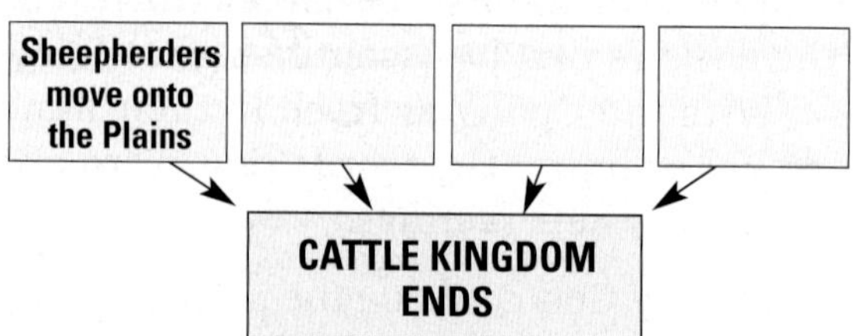

Main Idea Cattle ranching boomed on the open range in the 1870s, producing a Cattle Kingdom of ranchers, cowboys, cattle drives, and cow towns.

A pair of spurs

Setting the Scene Andy Adams was a cattleman on a "long drive" from Texas to the rail stations in the North. Adams reported that the cattle had been under the blistering sun for three days. Crazed with thirst, the steers were out of control. Then, Adams made a terrible discovery:

> ❝ In a number of instances wild steers deliberately walked against our horses, and then for the first time a fact dawned on us that chilled the marrow in our bones—the herd was going blind. ❞
>
> —Andy Adams, *The Log of a Cowboy,* 1903

There was little for the cowhands to do now. "Nothing short of water would stop the herd and we rode aside and let them pass," Adams explained. Eventually the herd found water, and with it "their eyesight would gradually return."

In the 1860s a new group of Americans began arriving on the Plains. Along with miners, these newcomers created a new way of life on the Great Plains.

Creating a Cattle Kingdom

Before the arrival of settlers from the United States, the Spanish, and then the Mexicans, set up cattle ranches in the Southwest. Over the years, strays from these ranches, along with American breeds, grew into large herds of wild cattle. These wild cattle were known as longhorns. They roamed freely across the grassy plains of Texas.

After the Civil War, the demand for beef increased. People in the growing cities in the East needed more meat. Miners, railroad crews, farmers, and growing communities in the West added to the demand. The Texas longhorns were perfect for the commercial market. They could travel far on little water, and they required no winter feeding.

Cattle Drives In response, Texas ranchers began rounding up herds of longhorns. They drove the animals hundreds of miles north to railroad lines in Kansas and Missouri on trips called **cattle drives.**

The Chisholm Trail Jesse Chisholm blazed one of the most famous cattle trails. Chisholm was half Scottish and half Cherokee. In the late 1860s, he began hauling goods by wagon between Texas and the Kansas Pacific Railroad. His route crossed rivers at the best places and passed by water holes. Ranchers began using the Chisholm Trail in 1867. Within five years, more than one million cattle had walked the road.

The Life of a Cowhand

Ranchers employed cowhands to tend their cattle and drive herds to market. These hard workers rode alongside the huge herds in good and bad weather. They kept the cattle moving and rounded up strays. After the Civil War, veterans of the Confederate Army made up the majority of the cowhands who worked in Texas. However, it is estimated that nearly one in three cowhands was either Mexican American or African American. Some cowhands dreamed of setting aside enough money to start a herd of their own. Most, in the end, just worked to earn wages.

Spanish Heritage American cowhands learned much about riding, roping, and branding from Spanish and Mexican vaqueros (vah KYEHR ohs). **Vaqueros** were skilled riders who herded cattle on ranches in Mexico, California, and the Southwest.

The gear used by American cowhands was modeled on the tools of the vaquero. Cowhands used the leather lariat to catch cattle and horses. "Lariat" comes from the Spanish word for rope. Cowhands wore wide-brimmed hats like the Spanish *sombrero.* Their leather leggings, called "chaps," were modeled on Spanish *chaparreras* (chap ah RAY rahs). Chaps protected a rider's legs from the thorny plants that grow in the Southwest.

On the Trail A cattle drive was hot, dirty, tiring, and often boring work. A cowboy's day could last for nearly 18 hours. The work was so strenuous that cowhands usually brought a number of horses so that each day a fresh one would be available. Cowhands worked in all kinds of weather and faced many dangers, including prairie dog holes, rattlesnakes, and fierce thunderstorms. They had to prevent nervous cattle from drowning while crossing a fast-flowing river. They had to fight raging grass fires. They also faced attacks from cattle thieves who roamed the countryside.

One of the cowhand's worst fears on a cattle drive was a stampede. A clap of thunder or a gunshot could set thousands of longhorns off at a run. Cowhands had to avoid the crush of hoofs and horns while attempting to turn the stampeding herd in a wide circle.

Most cowhands did not work for themselves. Instead, they were hired hands for the owners of large ranches. For all their hard work, cowhands were fed, housed, and lucky to earn $1 a day! Even in the 1870s, this was low pay.

LINKING PAST AND PRESENT

▲ Past

▲ Present

Viewing History

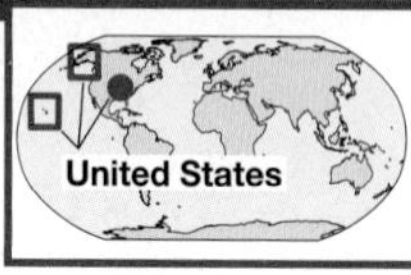

Western Clothing A cowhand, as shown above, dressed for his job. Spurs on boots, leather leggings, tall hats, and neckerchiefs were essential for hot, dry cattle trails. Today, western clothing, such as the hat, blue jeans, western boots, and belt buckle shown here, is fashionable rather than functional. **Applying Information** ***What workers today wear special clothing for their jobs?***

The Cow Towns

Cattle drives ended in **cow towns** that had sprung up along the railroad lines. The Chisholm Trail, for example, ended in Abilene, Kansas. Other cow towns in Kansas were Wichita, Caldwell, and Dodge City. In cow towns, cattle were held in great pens until they could be loaded into railroad cars and shipped to markets in the East.

In Abilene and other busy cow towns, dance halls, saloons, hotels, and restaurants catered to the cowhands. Sheriffs often had a hard time keeping the peace. Some cowhands spent wild nights drinking, dancing, and gambling.

Cow towns also attracted settlers who wanted to build stable communities where families could thrive. Doctors, barbers, artisans, bankers, and merchants helped to turn cow towns into communities.

The main street of a town was where people conducted business. Almost every town had a general store that sold groceries, tools, clothing, and all sorts of other goods. The general store also served as a social center where people could talk and exchange the latest news. As a town grew, drugstores, hardware stores, and even ice-cream parlors lined its main street.

Religion also played an important role for the townspeople. Throughout the West, places of worship grew in number and membership. They served as spiritual and social centers and as symbols of progress and stability. "A church does as much to build up a town as a school, a railroad, or a fair," noted one New Mexico newspaper.

The Cattle Boom

In the 1870s, ranching spread north from Texas and across the grassy Plains. Soon, cattle grazed from Kansas to present-day Montana. Ranchers had built a Cattle Kingdom in the West. They came to expect high profits. Millions of dollars poured into the West from people in the East and in foreign countries who wanted to earn money from the cattle boom. However, the boom did not last.

Recognize Multiple Causes

Which factors leading to the end of the Cattle Kingdom are discussed on this page? Add these factors to your chart.

The Open Range Ranchers let their cattle run wild on the open range. To identify cattle, each ranch had its own brand that was burned into a cow's hide.

Sometimes, there were conflicts on the range. When sheepherders moved onto the Plains, ranchers tried to drive them out. The ranchers complained that sheep nibbled the grass so low that cattle could not eat it. To protect the range, which they saw as their own, ranchers sometimes attacked sheepherders and their flocks.

The End of the Cattle Kingdom In the 1870s, farmers began moving onto the range. They fenced their fields with barbed wire, which kept cattle and sheep from pushing over fences and trampling plowed fields. As more farmers bought land, the open range began to disappear. Large grants of land to the railroads also limited it.

Nature imposed limits on the cattle boom. After a time, there just was not enough grass to feed all the cattle that lived on the plains. The need to buy feed and land pushed up the costs. Diseases such as "Texas fever" sometimes destroyed entire herds. Then, the bitterly cold winters of 1886 and 1887 killed entire herds of cattle. In the summer, severe heat and drought dried up water holes and scorched the grasslands.

Cattle owners began to buy land and fence it in. Soon, farmers and ranchers divided the open range into a patchwork of large fenced plots. The days of the Cattle Kingdom were over.

★ ★ ★ Section 3 Assessment ★ ★ ★

Recall

1. **Identify** Explain the significance of **(a)** Chisholm Trail, **(b)** Cattle Kingdom.
2. **Define** **(a)** cattle drive, **(b)** vaquero, **(c)** cow town.

Comprehension

3. How did the Cattle Kingdom begin?
4. Describe the life of a cowhand.
5. Why did cow towns develop?

Critical Thinking and Writing

6. **Exploring the Main Idea** Review the Main Idea statement at the beginning of this section. Then, write several paragraphs describing the cattle industry in the 1870s and 1880s.
7. **Analyzing Information** How do you think the growth of the Cattle Kingdom affected the Plains Indians? Explain.

ACTIVITY

Connecting to Today

Where do boomtowns exist today? Use the Internet to find out about boomtowns such as those in Silicon Valley. How do they compare with earlier boomtowns? Write a brief report. For help in completing the activity, visit PHSchool.com, **Web Code mfd-1903.**

Evaluating Written Sources

What was the "Old West" really like? As you have learned, historical evidence comes from many sources. Evaluating the validity of written sources is important in putting together a picture of the past.

In his novel *The Big Sky,* the newspaperman and author A. B. Guthrie, Jr. (1901–1991) wrote the following description of life in the West in the 1800s. *The Big Sky* was published in 1947:

> "This was the way to live. . . . A body got so's he felt everything was kin to him, the earth and sky and buffalo and beaver and the yellow moon at night. It was better than being walled in by a house, better than breathing in spoiled air and feeling caged like a varmint."

The following passage was written by Teddy Blue Abbott, a famous cowboy in the 1880s. Here, he describes a blizzard in Montana in 1887. Abbott's account was published in 1939 in a book called *We Pointed Them North: Recollections of a Cowpuncher.*

> "The cattle drifted down on all the rivers. . . . On the Missouri we lost I don't know how many that way. They would walk out on the ice and the ones behind would push the front ones in. The cowpunchers worked like slaves to move them back in the hills, but as all the outfits cut their forces down every winter, they were shorthanded. No one knows how they worked but themselves. They saved thousands of cattle. Think of riding all day in a blinding snow storm, the temperature fifty and sixty below zero, and no dinner."

Learn the Skill *To evaluate written sources, use the following steps:*

1. **Identify the sources.** Knowing the background of a writer helps you evaluate that person's account.
2. **Note the context.** When was the account written? In what form did it appear? What was the purpose of the account?
3. **Analyze the point of view.** What is the message? How does the writer feel about the subject?
4. **Evaluate the validity of the material.** How true is this account? Why do you think so?

Practice the Skill *Answer the following questions about the passages above:*

1. **(a)** Who was A. B. Guthrie? **(b)** Who was Teddy Blue Abbott? **(c)** Which passage is from a firsthand account?
2. **(a)** When did each account appear? **(b)** In what form did it appear? **(c)** What was the purpose of each account?
3. **(a)** What message does Guthrie's passage give? **(b)** What is the message in Abbott's account? **(c)** How does each writer feel about his subject?
4. Which account is more accurate? Why do you think so?

Apply the Skill *See the Chapter Review and Assessment.*

4 Indian Peoples in Retreat

Prepare to Read

Objectives

In this section, you will
- Identify promises made to Native Americans.
- Describe why the Indian way of life ended.
- Explain why reformers failed.

Key Term

reservation

Target Reading Skill

Main Idea Copy the concept web below. As you read, fill in the blank ovals with events that show the effects of western settlement on Native American life. Add as many ovals as you need.

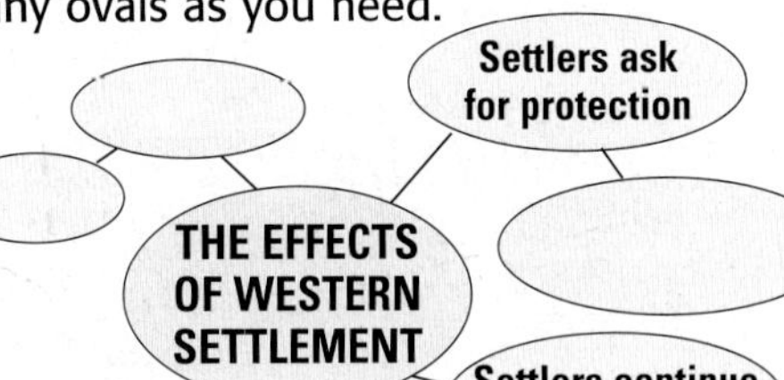

Main Idea Despite government promises to protect their land, Indian peoples found their way of life threatened as white settlers invaded their territory.

Sitting Bull

Setting the Scene In 1883, Sitting Bull, a Lakota war chief and holy man, addressed a group of senators from Washington.

> " If a man loses anything and goes back and looks carefully for it he will find it, and that is what the Indians are doing now when they ask you to give them the things that were promised them in the past. And I do not think they should be treated like beasts, and that is the reason I have grown up with the feelings I have. "
>
> —Tatanka Iyotanka (Sitting Bull), Report to the Senate Committee, 1883

As settlers moved into the West after the Civil War, the government promised to protect Indian hunting grounds. However, the government soon broke its promises, as more settlers pushed westward. When Indians resisted white settlement, wars erupted. The result was tragedy for the Indian peoples.

Promises Made and Broken

Conflict began as early as the 1840s, when settlers and miners began to cross Indian hunting grounds. The settlers and miners asked for government protection from the Indians.

Fort Laramie Treaty The government built a string of forts to protect settlers and miners. In 1851, federal government officials met with Indian nations near Fort Laramie in Wyoming. The officials asked each nation to keep to a limited area. In return, they promised money, domestic animals, agricultural tools, and other goods. Officials told the Native Americans that the lands that were reserved for them would be theirs forever.

Native American leaders agreed to the terms of the Fort Laramie Treaty. However, in 1858, gold was discovered at Pikes Peak in Colorado. A wave of miners rushed to land that the government had promised to the Cheyennes and Arapahos. Federal officials forced

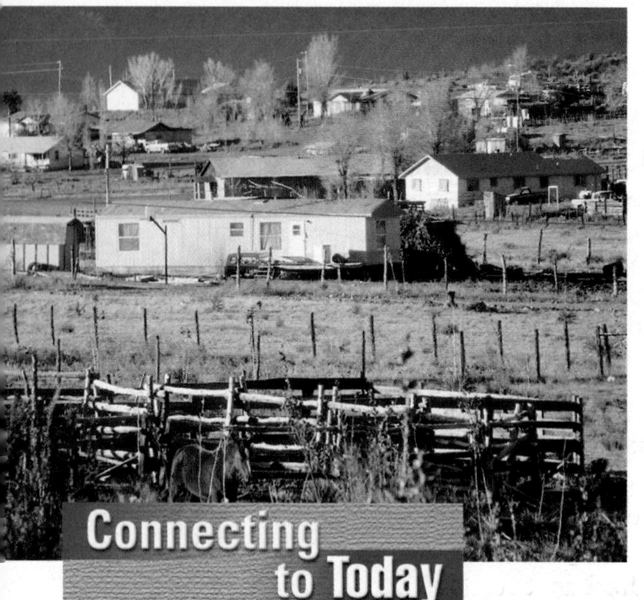

Connecting to Today

Housing on Indian Reservations

Since the late 1800s, many Native Americans in the West have lived a dreary existence on reservations. Today, one of the biggest problems on the reservations is housing. Homes are crowded and often lack adequate plumbing. Older people, especially, have been known to freeze to death in the cold, drafty shacks. The government is trying to help by offering home mortgage loans. Other help comes from the Red Feather Development Group, which teaches the straw-bale construction technique. This is an efficient and economical method of building. The first home, built on the Crow Reservation, is now a model for buildings being constructed by Native Americans on other reservations in the West.

How can the new building technique help the housing problem?

Indian leaders to sign a new treaty giving up the land around Pikes Peak. Some Native Americans refused to accept the agreement. They attacked white settlers.

The Chivington Massacre The settlers struck back. In 1864, Colonel John Chivington led his militia against a Cheyenne village whose leaders had come to a fort asking for protection. When Chivington attacked, the Indians raised both a white flag of surrender and the flag of the United States. Chivington ignored the flags. He ordered his men to destroy the village and take no prisoners. In the Chivington Massacre, the militia slaughtered more than 200 men, women, and children.

People throughout the United States were outraged at the brutality and the bloodshed. "When the white man comes in my country he leaves a trail of blood behind him," said Lakota War Chief Red Cloud. Across the Plains, soldiers and Indians went to war.

Learning "American" Ways In 1867, federal officials established a peace commission to end the wars on the Plains so that settlers would be safe. The commission urged Native Americans to settle down and live as white farmers did. It also urged them to send their children to white schools to learn "American" ways.

Forced Onto Reservations In 1867, the Kiowas, Comanches, and other southern Plains Indians signed a new treaty with the government. They promised to move to Indian Territory in present-day Oklahoma. The soil there was poor. Also, most Plains Indians were hunters, not farmers. The Indians did not like the treaty but knew they had no choice.

The Lakotas and Arapahos of the northern Plains also signed a treaty. They agreed to live on **reservations** in present-day South Dakota. A reservation is a limited area set aside for Native Americans.

End of the Buffalo

The Plains Indians suffered from lost battles and broken treaties. Even worse for them, however, was the destruction of the buffalo.

The decline of the buffalo began before the arrival of white settlers. Herds of buffalo lived in areas east of the Mississippi and west of the Rockies. However, with disease, drought, and destruction of the areas in which they lived, the herds were slowly growing smaller. As the market demand for buffalo robes increased during the 1830s and 1840s, professional buffalo hunters killed more buffalo. In addition, buffalo hunting became a pleasure sport where railroads cut through the areas in which buffalo lived. Indian people themselves learned to hunt more efficiently. Some Indian tribes, such as the Pawnees, continued to hunt buffalo even though they recognized that the number of buffalo was decreasing. The buffalo hunt was a part of their culture that they did not want to give up. As the buffalo disappeared, so did the Plains Indians' way of life.

Identify Supporting Details

What role did the buffalo play in Native American culture? How did western settlement affect the buffalo? Add this information to your concept web.

The War for the West

Settlers and miners continued to move into the West. They wanted more and more land for themselves. Even on reservations, the Indians were not left in peace.

Custer's Last Stand In 1874, prospectors found gold in the Black Hills region of the Lakota, or Sioux, reservation. Thousands of miners rushed to the area. Led by Sitting Bull, Crazy Horse, and other Lakota chiefs, the Indians fought back in what became known as the Sioux War of 1876.

In June 1876, Colonel George A. Custer led a column of soldiers into the Little Bighorn Valley. They were sent by the federal government to protect the miners. A group of 600 men under Custer's command prepared to attack. Indian scouts warned Custer that there were many Lakotas and Cheyennes camped ahead. Nearly 2,000 warriors awaited Custer and his men. Custer divided his troops and attacked with only 225 men. Custer and all his men died in the Battle of Little Bighorn.

The Indian victory at the Little Bighorn was short-lived. The army soon defeated the Lakotas and Cheyennes. Then, Congress ordered that no food rations be distributed to the Indians until they agreed to the government's demands. To avoid starvation, the Lakotas gave up most claims to the Black Hills and other territory. In this way, they surrendered about one third of the lands that the United States government had guaranteed them with the Fort Laramie Treaty.

Sitting Bull and Crazy Horse had taken their few remaining followers to Canada. Eventually, both men returned.

Chief Joseph Flees The Nez Percé lived in the Snake River valley, at the place where Oregon, Washington, and Idaho meet. In 1855, some Nez Percé signed a treaty with the United States government in which they relinquished part of their land.

In the 1860s, gold strikes brought miners onto Nez Percé land. The government ordered the Nez Percés to move to a reservation in Idaho. Those who had not signed the treaty refused. Led by Chief Joseph, about 500 Nez Percés fled north to Canada. Army troops followed close behind.

In the months that followed, the Nez Percés fought off or eluded pursuing army units. Finally, after a tragic journey of more than 1,000 miles, Chief Joseph decided that he must surrender. Of the approximately 800 Nez Percés who had set out with him, fewer than 450 remained.

The Apache Wars In the arid lands of the Southwest, the Apaches fiercely resisted the loss of their lands. One leader, Geronimo, continued fighting the longest. In 1876, he assumed leadership of a band of Apache warriors when the government tried to force his people onto a reservation.

Geronimo waged war off and on for the next 10 years. From Mexico, he led frequent raids into Arizona and New Mexico. His surrender in 1886 marked the end of formal warfare between Indians and whites.

An American Profile

Geronimo (1829–1909)

Geronimo was an Apache warrior, revered for his wisdom. He was also one of the fiercest and most courageous warriors the United States army ever pursued. When his family was killed by whites, Geronimo vowed vengeance and led his band of warriors in fierce raids against whites. More than once, he was captured, only to escape. In the last campaign, his small, ragged band was pursued by over 5,000 United States troops. Finally, in 1886, Geronimo was forced to surrender.

Why was Geronimo willing to fight against such great odds to remain free?

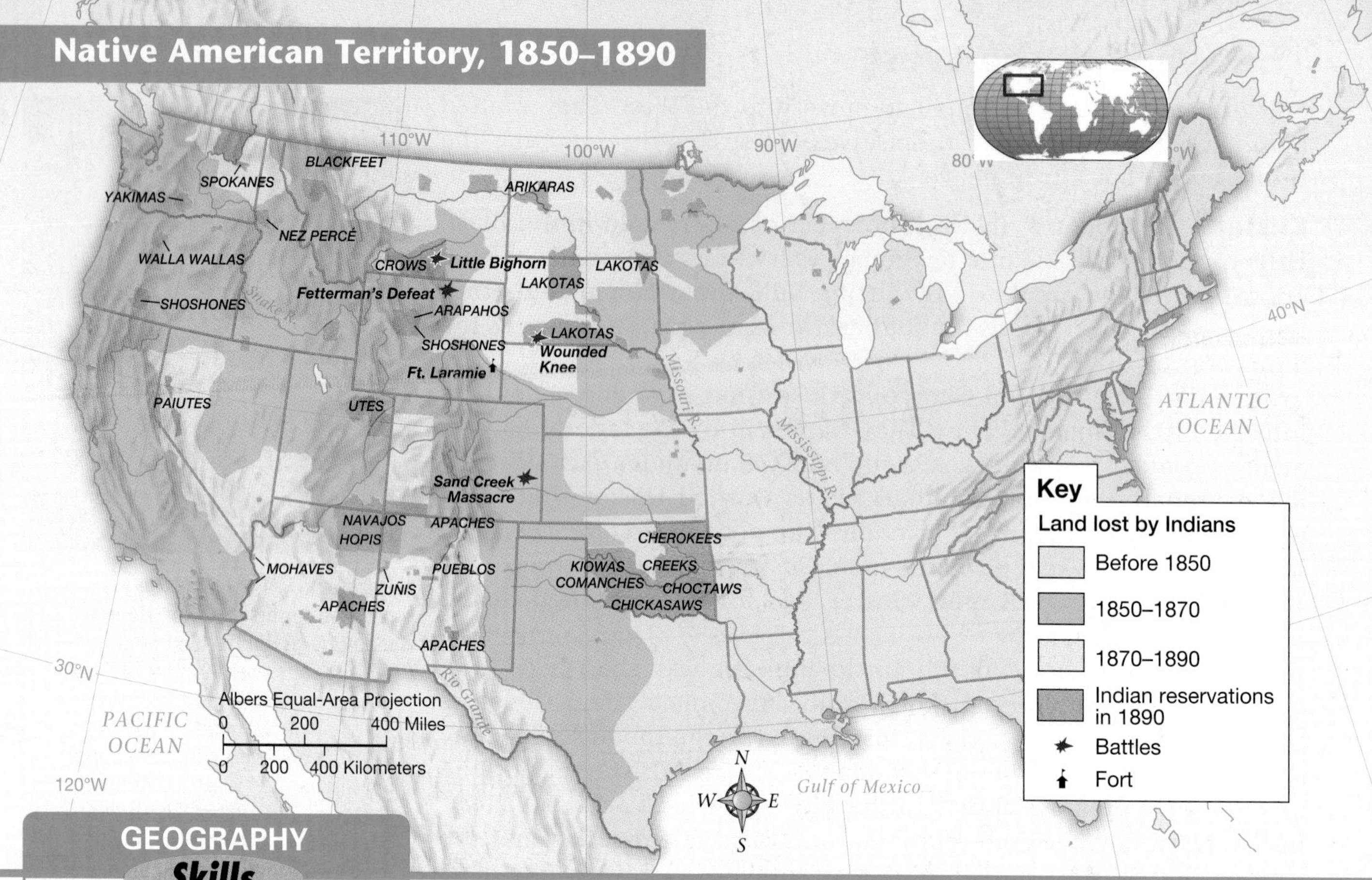

GEOGRAPHY *Skills*

Fighting between Native Americans and the United States government went on for years, until most Indians were forced onto reservations.

1. **Location** On the map, locate **(a)** Fort Laramie, **(b)** Little Bighorn, **(c)** Apache reservations, **(d)** Wounded Knee.
2. **Region** In which areas of the country did Native Americans still retain much of their land in 1870?
3. **Critical Thinking Drawing Inferences** Why do you think the Apaches of the desert Southwest were one of the last Indian nations to lose their land?

The Indian Way of Life Ends

Many Indians longed for their lost way of life. On the reservations, the Lakotas and other Plains Indians turned to a religious ceremony called the Ghost Dance. It celebrated the time when Native Americans lived freely on the Plains.

The Ghost Dance In 1889, word spread that a prophet named Wovoka had appeared among the Paiute people of the southern Plains. Wovoka said that the Great Spirit would make a new world for his people, free from whites and filled with plenty. To bring about this new world, all the Indians had to do was to dance the Ghost Dance.

In their ceremonies, Ghost Dancers joined hands in a large circle in which they danced, chanted, and prayed. As they danced, some felt a "growing happiness." Others saw a glowing vision of a new world.

Settlers React Many settlers grew alarmed. The Ghost Dancers, they said, were preparing for war. The settlers persuaded the government to outlaw the Ghost Dance.

In December 1890, police officers entered a Lakota reservation to arrest Sitting Bull, who had returned from Canada and was living on the reservation. They claimed that he was spreading the Ghost Dance among the Lakotas. In the struggle that followed, Sitting Bull was accidentally shot and killed.

Massacre at Wounded Knee Upset by Sitting Bull's death, groups of Lakotas fled the reservations. Army troops pursued them to Wounded Knee Creek, in present-day South Dakota. On December 29, the Indians were preparing to surrender. As nervous troops watched, the Indians began to give up their guns.

Suddenly, a shot rang out. The army opened fire. By the time the shooting stopped, nearly 300 Native American men, women, and children lay dead. About 25 soldiers had also died. The fighting at Wounded Knee marked the end of the Ghost Dance religion.

Reformers Fail

The Native Americans were no longer able to resist the government. During the late 1800s, more Indians were forced onto reservations.

Reformers Speak Out Many people, Indian and white, spoke out against the tragedy that was occurring. One reformer, Susette La Flesche, was the daughter of an Omaha chief. She wrote and lectured about the destruction of the Native American way of life.

Another reformer, Helen Hunt Jackson, published *A Century of Dishonor* in 1881. The book recounts the long history of broken treaties between the United States and the Native Americans.

A New Federal Policy Calls for reform led Congress to pass the Dawes Act in 1887. The act encouraged Native Americans to become farmers. Some tribal lands were divided up and given to individual Native American families.

The Dawes Act was unsuccessful. To Native Americans, land was an open place for riding and hunting. As a result, Indians often sold their shares of land to whites for low prices.

Life on the reservations changed Native American culture. The federal government took away the power of Indian leaders. In their place, it appointed government agents to make most decisions.

★ ★ ★ Section 4 Assessment ★ ★ ★

Recall

1. **Identify** Explain the significance of **(a)** Sitting Bull, **(b)** Fort Laramie Treaty, **(c)** Chivington Massacre, **(d)** Battle of Little Bighorn, **(e)** Chief Joseph, **(f)** Geronimo, **(g)** Ghost Dance, **(h)** Susette La Flesche, **(i)** Helen Hunt Jackson, **(j)** Dawes Act.

Comprehension

2. What promises to Native Americans did the government break?
3. How did the loss of the buffalo affect Native Americans?
4. Describe two conflicts between Native Americans and settlers.
5. How did reformers try to help Native Americans?

Critical Thinking and Writing

6. **Exploring the Main Idea** Review the Main Idea statement at the beginning of this section. Then, write a paragraph describing what you think the government could have done to avoid wars with the Native Americans in the West.
7. **Making Inferences** Why do you think the religious movement called the Ghost Dance became so popular among Native Americans?

Activity

Writing Editorials **As a reformer supporting the cause of Native Americans, you feel the Dawes Act is significant. Write an editorial giving your reasons for supporting it. Then, write an editorial that a Native American might have composed in response to the Dawes Act.**

5 Farming

Prepare to Read

Objectives

In this section, you will

- Explain why farmers and other settlers moved west.
- Describe the Oklahoma land rush.
- Identify why life was hard for Plains farmers.
- Summarize why the Populist party was formed.

Key Terms

sod house

sodbuster

cooperative

wholesale

inflation

Target Reading Skill

Comparison and Contrast Copy this incomplete Venn diagram. As you read, write key facts about the National Grange and the Farmers' Alliance. Write common characteristics in the overlapping section.

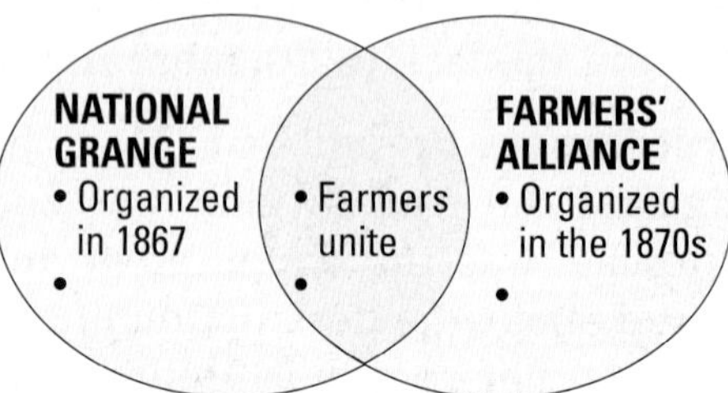

Main Idea The Homestead Act opened the West to farmers who struggled to survive the harsh environment of the Great Plains.

A farmer hoping for rain

Setting the Scene No matter what he did, W. M. Taylor could not get ahead. He planted his crops in the rich Nebraska soil and tended them carefully. Sometimes the weather or grasshoppers ruined his harvest. However, in 1891, it was a human agent that was destroying his livelihood. Wrote Taylor:

> "We are cursed, many of us financially, beyond redemption, not by the hot winds so much as by the swindling games of the bankers and money loaners, who have taken the money and are now after the property, leaving the farmer moneyless and homeless."
>
> —W. M. Taylor, Letter to Editor, *Farmers' Alliance*, January 10, 1891

Like the miners and ranchers who came before them, farmers faced many challenges, including deals with "bankers and money loaners" who charged high interest rates, then laid their own claims to the land of farmers who could not pay their debts.

Farmers Move West

Congress passed the Homestead Act in 1862. The law promised 160 acres of free land to anyone who paid a small filing fee and farmed it for five years.

Problems With Homesteading Many immigrants and easterners rushed to accept the offer of free land. They planted their 160 acres with wheat and corn. By 1900, half a million Americans had set up farms under the Homestead Act. Under the Homestead Act the land was free, but many people did not have the money to move west and start a farm. Also, only about 20 percent of the homestead land went directly to small farmers. Land-owning companies took large areas of land illegally and resold it to farmers at a high price.

Exodusters African Americans joined the rush for homestead land. The largest group moved west at the end of Reconstruction, when the freedoms blacks had gained after the Civil War were slipping away.

In 1879, a group of African Americans moved to Kansas. They called themselves Exodusters, after Exodus, the book of the Bible that tells about the Jews escaping from slavery in Egypt. Between 40,000 and 70,000 African Americans had moved to Kansas by 1881.

Los Mexicanos Easterners who moved to the Southwest met a large Spanish-speaking population there. As you recall, the United States had gained much of the Southwest through the Mexican War. Spanish-speaking southwesterners called themselves Mexicanos. White Americans who lived in the region were known as Anglos.

Most Mexicanos lived in small villages, where they farmed and raised sheep. A few wealthy Mexicanos were large landowners and merchants.

As more Anglos settled in the Southwest, they acquired the best jobs and land. Often, Mexicanos found themselves working as low-paid laborers on Anglo farms. In New Mexico, in the 1880s, angry farmers known as *Las Gorras Blancas,* or "White Caps," demanded fair treatment. Other Mexicanos in Arizona founded the Hispanic-American Alliance in 1894 to protect and fight for their rights.

The Oklahoma Land Rush

As settlers spread across the West, free land began to disappear. The last major land rush took place in Oklahoma. Several Indian nations

Viewing History

The Rush for Land

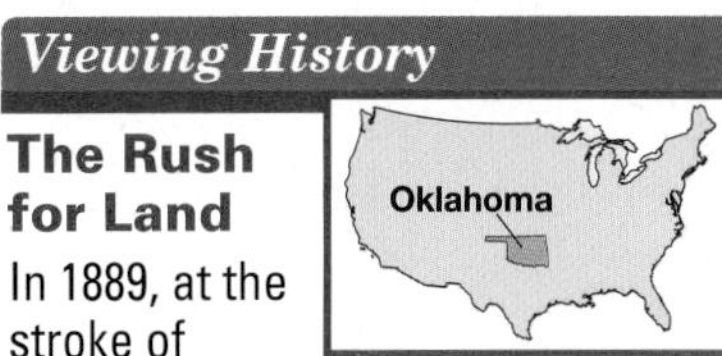

In 1889, at the stroke of noon, thousands of hopeful homesteaders rushed across the Oklahoma border to claim a piece of farmland. **Drawing Inferences** ***What type of people do you think these homesteaders were?***

lived there, but the government forced them to sell their land. The government then announced that farmers could claim free homesteads in Oklahoma. They could not stake their claims, however, until noon on April 22, 1889.

On the appointed day, as many as 100,000 land seekers lined up at the Oklahoma border. At noon, a gunshot rang out. The "boomers" charged into Oklahoma, but they found that others were already there. "Sooners" had sneaked into Oklahoma before the official opening and had staked out much of the best land.

Hard Life on the Plains

Farmers on the western plains faced many hardships. The first problem was shelter. Because wood was scarce on the Great Plains, many farmers built houses of sod—soil held together by grass roots. Rain was a serious problem for **sod houses.** One pioneer woman complained that her sod roof "leaked two days before a rain and for three days after."

Sodbusting The fertile soil of the Great Plains was covered with a layer of thick sod that could crack wood or iron plows. A new sodbusting plow made of steel reached the market by 1877. It enabled **sodbusters,** as Plains farmers were called, to cut through the sod to the soil below.

Technology helped farmers in other ways. On the Great Plains, water often lay hundreds of feet underground. Farmers built windmills to pump the water to the surface. New reapers, threshing machines, and binders helped farmers to harvest crops.

Surviving the Climate The dry climate was a constant threat. When too little rain fell, the crops shriveled and died. Dry weather also brought the threat of fire. A grass fire traveled "as fast as a horse could run."

The summers often brought swarms of grasshoppers that ate everything in their path—crops, food, tree bark, even clothing.

Pioneers dreaded the winters most. With few trees or hills to block the wind, icy gusts built huge snowdrifts. The deep snow buried farm animals and trapped families inside their homes.

Women on the Plains Women had to be strong to survive the hardships of life on the Great Plains. Since there were few stores, women made clothing, soap, candles, and other goods by hand. They also cooked and preserved food needed for the long winter.

Women served their communities in many ways. Most schoolteachers were women. When there were no doctors nearby, women treated the sick and injured.

Pioneer families usually lived miles apart. They relaxed by visiting with neighbors and gathering for church services. Picnics, dances, and weddings were eagerly awaited events.

More Crops, Less Money Despite the harsh conditions, farmers began to thrive in the West. Before long, they were selling huge amounts of wheat and corn in the nation's growing cities and even in Europe.

Then, farmers faced an unexpected problem. The more they harvested, the less they earned. In 1881, a bushel of wheat sold for $1.19. By 1894, the price had plunged to 49 cents. Western farmers were hurt most by low grain prices. They had borrowed money during good times to buy land and machinery. When wheat prices fell, they could not repay their debts.

Target Skill **Make Comparisons** What were the National Grange and the Farmers' Alliance positions on cooperatives and warehouses? Add this information to your Venn diagram.

Farmers Take Action

As early as the 1860s, farmers began to work together. They learned that they could improve their condition through economic cooperation and political action.

The Grange In 1867, farmers formed the National Grange. Grangers wanted to boost farm profits and reduce the rates that railroads charged for shipping grain.

Grangers helped farmers set up cooperatives. In a **cooperative** a group of farmers pooled their money to buy seeds and tools wholesale. **Wholesale** means buying or selling something in large quantities at lower prices. Grangers built cooperative warehouses so that farmers could store grain cheaply while waiting for better selling prices.

Leaders of the Grange urged farmers to use their vote. In 1873, western and southern Grangers pledged to vote only for candidates who supported their aims. They elected officials who understood the farmers' problems. As a result, several states passed laws limiting what could be charged for grain shipment and storage. Nevertheless, crop prices continued to drop. Farmers sank deeper into debt.

Farmers' Alliance Another group, the Farmers' Alliance, joined the struggle in the 1870s. Like the Grange, the Alliance set up cooperatives and warehouses. The Farmers' Alliance spread from Texas through the South and into the Plains states. Alliance leaders also tried to join with factory workers and miners who were angry about their treatment by employers.

Some women were active in the group. One of the most popular speakers was Kansas lawyer Mary Elizabeth Lease.

An American Profile

Mary Elizabeth Lease
(1853–1933)

Mary Elizabeth Lease's father and two brothers died in the Civil War. Since she held the Democratic party responsible for the war, she opposed the Democrats throughout her political career. Lease joined the Farmers' Alliance of the Populist Party. She quickly became its most influential speaker, making over 160 speeches for the 1890 campaign. One newspaper alleged that she told farmers in Kansas to "raise less corn and more hell." Lease also helped to defeat the Kansas senator, Democrat John Ingalls, a big victory for the Farmers' Alliance.

What did Mary Lease mean when she told the farmers to "raise less corn and more hell"?

The Populists

In 1892, farmers and labor unions joined together to form the Populist party. At their first national convention, the Populists demanded that the government help to raise farm prices and to regulate railroad rates. They also called for an income tax, an eight-hour workday, and limits on immigration.

Another Populist party demand was "free silver." Populists wanted all silver mined in the West to be coined into money. They said that farm prices dropped because there was not enough money in circulation. Free silver would increase the money supply and make it easier for farmers to repay their debts.

Eastern bankers and factory owners disagreed. They argued that increasing the money supply would cause **inflation,** or increased prices. Business people feared that inflation would wreck the

Primary Source

"The Cross of Gold"

On July 9, 1896, William Jennings Bryan spoke at the Democratic National Convention:

"You come to us and tell us that the great cities are in favor of the gold standard; we reply that the great cities rest upon our broad and fertile prairies. Burn down your cities and leave our farms, and your cities will spring up again . . . but destroy our farms and the grass will grow in the streets of every city in the country . . . we will answer [the] demand for a gold standard by saying . . . You shall not press down upon the brow of labor this crown of thorns, you shall not crucify mankind upon a cross of gold."

—William Jennings Bryan, speech to the Democratic National Convention, July 9, 1896

Analyzing Primary Sources

What does Bryan mean when he says that grass will grow in the cities if the farms are destroyed?

economy. They favored the gold standard with which the government backs every dollar with a certain amount of gold. Since the supply of gold is limited, there would be less money in circulation. Prices would drop.

Election of 1896 The Populist candidate for President in 1892 won one million votes. The next year, a severe depression brought the Populists new support. In 1894, they elected six senators and seven representatives to Congress.

The Populists looked toward the election of 1896 with high hopes. Their program had been endorsed by one of the great orators of the age: William Jennings Bryan.

A young Democratic congressman from Nebraska, Bryan was called the "Great Commoner" because he championed the cause of common people. Like the Populists, he believed that the nation needed to increase the supply of money. At the Democratic convention in 1896, Bryan made a powerful speech against the rich and for free silver.

Both Democrats and Populists supported Bryan for President. However, bankers and business people feared that Bryan would ruin the economy. They supported William McKinley, the Republican candidate.

Bryan narrowly lost the election of 1896. He carried the South and West, but McKinley won the heavily populated states of the East.

The End of the Populist Party The Populist party broke up after 1896. One reason was that the Democrats adopted several Populist causes. Also, prosperity returned in the late 1890s. People worried less about railroad rates and free silver.

★ ★ ★ Section 5 Assessment ★ ★ ★

Recall

1. **Identify** Explain the significance of **(a)** Homestead Act, **(b)** Exodusters, **(c)** Hispanic-American Alliance, **(d)** National Grange, **(e)** Farmers' Alliance, **(f)** Populist Party, **(g)** William Jennings Bryan, **(h)** William McKinley.
2. **Define** **(a)** sod house, **(b)** sodbuster, **(c)** cooperative, **(d)** wholesale, **(e)** inflation.

Comprehension

3. **(a)** What was the Homestead Act? **(b)** What was the Oklahoma land rush?
4. Describe the life of a Plains farmer.
5. How did the National Grange help farmers?
6. What was the purpose of the Populist party?

Critical Thinking and Writing

7. **Exploring the Main Idea** Review the Main Idea statement at the beginning of this section. Then, discuss the following questions: What geographic features of the Great Plains created a need for new kinds of machinery? How were these needs met?
8. **Analyzing Information** Discuss the reasons why the Populist party became popular.

ACTIVITY

Drawing a Political Cartoon **You are a cartoonist during the late 1800s. Draw a political cartoon to illustrate one of the problems that farmers faced during this period.**

Sodbusting on the Plains

The earliest settlers of the West quickly grabbed the fertile land near rivers and streams. Later homesteaders were forced to settle on outlying lands that had much less moisture. Out on the Great Plains, these settlers faced enormous challenges.

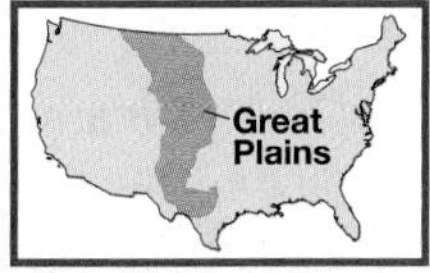

The Great Plains that were settled by homesteaders covered a huge portion of the middle part of the continent, as this map shows. The plains were covered with a variety of prairie grasses, the most common of which was buffalo grass. The grass was difficult to cut through. Its roots were densely intertwined. This was the sod that the farmers had to break up in order to plant their crops.

A sod house

Wood was scarce on the prairie, so the farmers invented a new kind of shelter: a sod house, or soddy. The long rows of sod turned over by the farmer's plow were cut into bricks with an ax. These blocks of sod were stacked in layers to make the walls. Timber—or twigs, branches, and bushes—was used to make a roof support, which was then covered with more sod. The dirt floor was packed down and smoothed. Settlers used dried buffalo chips as fuel to heat their homes.

A Plains farm family

Inside, the sod house was warm in winter and cool in summer. Occupants often had to deal with unwanted "guests," however, such as mice and—worst of all—prairie rattlesnakes. Outside, the family of settlers had to cope with insects—grasshoppers often invaded and ate entire crops. There was a lack of water, lack of schools and medical services, and above all, the terrible isolation of the western prairies. Despite all the difficulties, most sodbusters were determined to stay.

Activity

Suppose you could travel back in time to 1880 and visit a sodbuster family. You are able to take one modern invention with you to help make life easier for the farmer. Write a paragraph describing what item you would take and why.

CHAPTER 19

Review and Assessment

Chapter Summary

Section 1
The introduction of horses into North America transformed Plains Indian cultures, turning them into hunting societies. Men and women had clearly defined roles in Native American cultures in the West.

Section 2
Immigrants and people from other parts of the United States were drawn to the West by the discovery of gold and silver in the western territories and by the transcontinental railroad.

Section 3
The vast territory in the West became a Cattle Kingdom in the years after the Civil War. Cow towns and cattle drives were central features of this new culture.

Section 4
Native American groups slowly lost control of the West as a flood of new settlers came to their ancestral lands. This development put an end to the Indian way of life.

Section 5
Drawn by the promise of fertile land, many people came west, where they became farmers. These farmers joined together to form a cooperative, the Grange, and a new political party, the Populists.

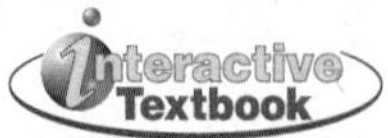

For additional review and enrichment activities, see the interactive version of *The American Nation,* available on the Web and on CD-ROM.

Chapter Self-Test For practice test questions for Chapter 19, visit PHSchool.com, **Web Code mfa-1904.**

Building Vocabulary

Review the meaning of the chapter vocabulary words listed below. Then, write a sentence for each word in which you define the word and describe its relation to the events that changed the West from 1865 to 1914.

1. **travois**
2. **lode**
3. **vigilante**
4. **transcontinental railroad**
5. **cattle drive**
6. **cow town**
7. **sod house**
8. **cooperative**
9. **wholesale**
10. **inflation**

Reviewing Key Facts

11. How did the Plains Indians rely on the horse and the buffalo? (Section 1)
12. Discuss the effects of mining on the West. (Section 2)
13. **(a)** What caused the cattle boom of the 1870s? **(b)** Why did the Cattle Kingdom end? (Section 3)
14. How did life change for the Plains Indians between the 1860s and the 1880s? (Section 4)
15. **(a)** What problems did farmers face? **(b)** How did farmers in the late 1800s unite? (Section 5)

Critical Thinking and Writing

16. **Connecting to Geography: Regions** Settlers crossing the Great Plains saw it as a vast land of grass. Yet, Native Americans survived on the Great Plains for nearly 200 years. Discuss the ways in which the geography of the region offered opportunities and challenges to the Native Americans and then to the new settlers.
17. **Drawing Inferences** Why do you think settlers stayed in spite of the hardships of life on the Great Plains?
18. **Applying Information** **(a)** What is inaccurate in the way movie westerns show the life of the American cowhand? **(b)** Why do you think the stories of cowhands live on today?

SKILLS ASSESSMENT

Analyzing Primary Sources

In 1890, Washington Gladden, a Congregational minister, spoke about the farmer.

> "The business of farming has become, for some reasons, extremely unprofitable. With the hardest work and with the sharpest economy, the average farmer is unable to make both ends meet; every year closes with debt, and the mortgage grows . . . The Labor Bureau of Connecticut . . . by an investigation of 693 representative farms, [shows] that the average annual reward of the farm proprietor of that state . . . is $181.31, while the average annual wage of the ordinary hired man is $368.36."
>
> —Washington Gladden, Congregational Minister, 1890

19. According to Gladden, a person can make the best living by working as
    - **A.** a Labor Bureau employee.
    - **B.** an ordinary hired man.
    - **C.** a farmer in Connecticut.
    - **D.** an economist.
20. How does Gladden feel about farming?
    - **A.** He thinks it is a noble calling.
    - **B.** He wishes he had become a farmer.
    - **C.** He thinks it involves a lot of hard work for little pay.
    - **D.** He has no strong feelings.

APPLYING YOUR SKILLS

Evaluating Written Sources

On April 22, 1889, Oklahoma was opened for settlement. Pioneers waited for the signal to start the race to stake their claims. Read the following passage and answer the questions.

> "Here was a contest in which thousands participated. Truly an historical event! We, . . . witnessed the spectacle. . . . Away dashed the thoroughbreds, the broncos, the pintos, and the mustangs at a breakneck pace across the prairie. . . . It was amazing to witness the recklessness of those cow-boy riders; they jumped obstacles; they leaped ditches; . . . and when they came to a ravine too wide to leap, down they would go with a rush, and up the other side with a spurt of energy. . . ."
>
> —Hamilton S. Wicks, "The Opening of Oklahoma," 1889

21. How would you describe the riders?
    - **A.** Eager but careful as they raced
    - **B.** Skilled riders who raced wildly
    - **C.** Skilled riders who jumped pools and fences
    - **D.** Eager but not skilled riders
22. How true is this account? Explain.

ACTIVITIES

Connecting With . . .

Government and Citizenship

Dangerous Jobs Workers who built the transcontinental railroad were subjected to hazardous conditions. Mining was another dangerous occupation. Should the government be responsible for imposing restrictions on dangerous occupations? Write your opinion in a persuasive essay.

Honoring Native Americans

Writing a Speech Use the Internet to find out about the large sculpture of Chief Crazy Horse that is being carved into a mountain near Custer, South Dakota. Then, write a speech that might be given at a ceremony honoring Chief Crazy Horse and other Native Americans. For help in starting this activity, visit PHSchool.com, **Web Code mfd-1906.**

Dragon's Gate

Laurence Yep

Laurence Yep

Introduction **When Charles Crocker, the head of the Central Pacific Railroad, needed workers, he at first dismissed the idea of using Chinese laborers. However, in the end, nearly 10,000 Chinese laborers picked and chipped a route for the transcontinental railroad through the Sierra Nevada. In *Dragon's Gate,* Laurence Yep uses the experience of the Chinese workers to tell the story of Otter, a Chinese boy who joins his father and uncle in California, where they are working as railroad laborers.**

Vocabulary Before you read the selection, find the meaning of these words in a dictionary: **pickax, goad.**

As we got ready to leave the next day, I said to Uncle Foxfire, "I want to use a pickax today." When he hesitated, I insisted. "I need to hit something."

Curly looked at me sympathetically. "He could use Doggy's today."

With a thoughtful nod, Uncle Foxfire got the pickax from the stack in the corner and handed it to me.

That day, I felt like I was marching with the others through the snow tunnels to a battle. Glancing around, I saw the same grim look on all the others' faces, and I realized they felt as much grief as I did and were determined to do something about it. Bright Star glanced at me and nodded as if he understood my thoughts. The loss of Doggy's music had bound us even more tightly together than the initial loss of his moon guitar.

Once we reached the tunnel, everyone sprang willingly into action. No one hesitated. No one held back or complained that someone else was doing more work. A few quick orders sent drill teams to the end under Father's command. The others began scraping and clawing at the rock while Uncle Foxfire tried again to teach me to use a pickax.

He swung it, twisting from the waist with his whole torso and shoulders, aiming a blow that would have crushed a water buffalo's skull. He did it effortlessly, ready to deliver one crushing blow after another for twelve hours if he had to. The pickax rang as it bit into the rock; and yet despite all the noise and the force, he hardly seemed to have scraped the rock at all.

Then he had me try the motion without the pickax, correcting a few things. When I finally picked up the pickax, it felt heavy as I lifted it over my shoulder and swung, trying to copy Uncle Foxfire. I let the motion itself bring the weight of my body into the blow. The pickax hit the wall with a clink. As before, my forearms felt numb.

"Good," Uncle Foxfire grunted. "Now get into a rhythm."

I swung the pickax again with all my strength; but the point hardly seemed to dent the hard granite.

"Hit it," Uncle Foxfire goaded me. "Don't pat it."

I aimed the pickax at the wall, and the point landed with a clank.

"I thought you were angry." He pretended to look disgusted.

"I am." This time when I hit the wall, I could feel the vibrations shake my whole body.

"Attack it," Uncle Foxfire urged. "Lazy monkey. Monkey! Monkey!"

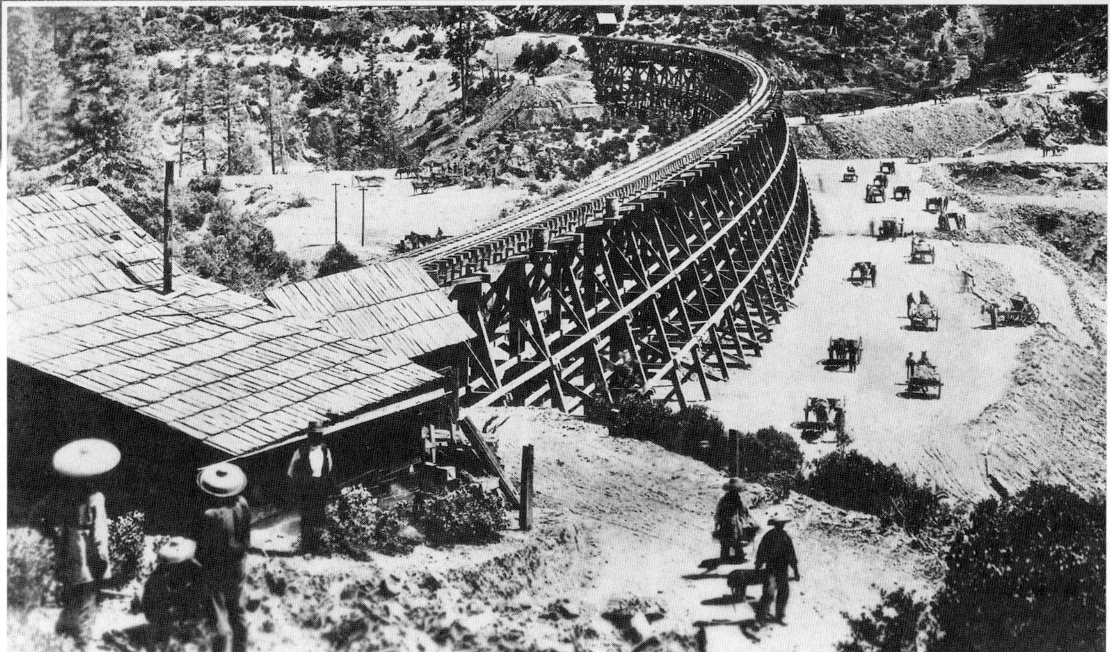

Chinese laborers working on the railroad

I could feel anger and fear swell up inside me and explode, and I began to pound the pickax in rhythm to his chant. I hated the slab of stone in front of me—hated it for being hard, hated it for being in the way of the westerners, hated it for making me come here to this crazy place, hated it for a lot of reasons that didn't make any real sense.

I hated the mountain for being so hard. I hated the pickax for not being sharper. My whole world narrowed to a sharp point. I wanted to drive it right through the heart of the Tiger.

Then, as if from a great distance, I heard Uncle Foxfire saying to me, "Easy. That's it. Get into a steady rhythm now." And I became aware of his hand on my shoulder.

I looked to the side. He smiled as if he knew just how much I'd needed to hit something. Then he stepped back so I could begin to swing the pickax in an easier, steadier rhythm. Each blow was still solid; but the stone was so hard, it felt like it was hammering back. . . .

Next to me, Uncle Foxfire had gotten a pickax and was swinging it just as hard. What had seemed like a wide enough space for one became very narrow as we swung our pickaxes in wide arcs that seemed just to miss one another.

Analyzing Literature

1. Why are the workers unhappy as they leave for the tunnel?

   A Their tools are too heavy.

   B They miss Doggy's music.

   C They are tired of marching.

   D They resent Doggy's presence.

2. How does Uncle Foxfire help Otter learn to use the pickax?

   A He guides Otter's arms and shoulders.

   B He quickly hands Otter the pickax.

   C He tries to make Otter angry.

   D He tells Otter to watch the other workers.

3. **Critical Thinking** **Drawing Conclusions** What does Otter experience as he works on the rock?

CHAPTER 20

Industrial Growth

1865–1914

1 Railroads Spur Industry
2 The Rise of Big Business
3 Inventions Change the Nation
4 The Rise of Organized Labor

Vanderbilt towering over his railroad empire

The Haymarket Riot

1869
Cornelius Vanderbilt gains control of the largest railroad empire in the United States.

1886
An explosion during a workers' protest in Chicago's Haymarket Square leads to a wave of antilabor feeling.

1890
Congress passes the Sherman Antitrust Act, which bans trusts and monopolies.

AMERICAN EVENTS

Presidential Terms:	Abraham Lincoln	Andrew Johnson	Ulysses S. Grant	Rutherford B. Hayes	James A. Garfield 1881	Chester A. Arthur	Grover Cleveland
	1861-1865	1865-1869	1869-1877	1877-1881		1881-1885	1885-1889

1860 · 1875 · 1890

WORLD EVENTS

▲ 1866
Swedish chemist Alfred Nobel invents dynamite.

▲ mid-1880s
Germany provides sickness, accident, and old age insurance.

Industrial Centers, 1865–1914

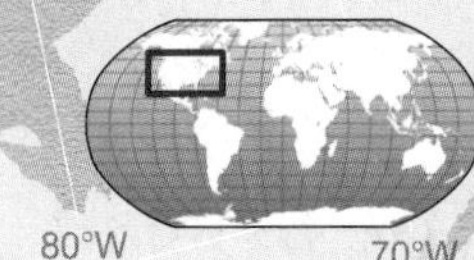

Large population centers grew up as American industry boomed.

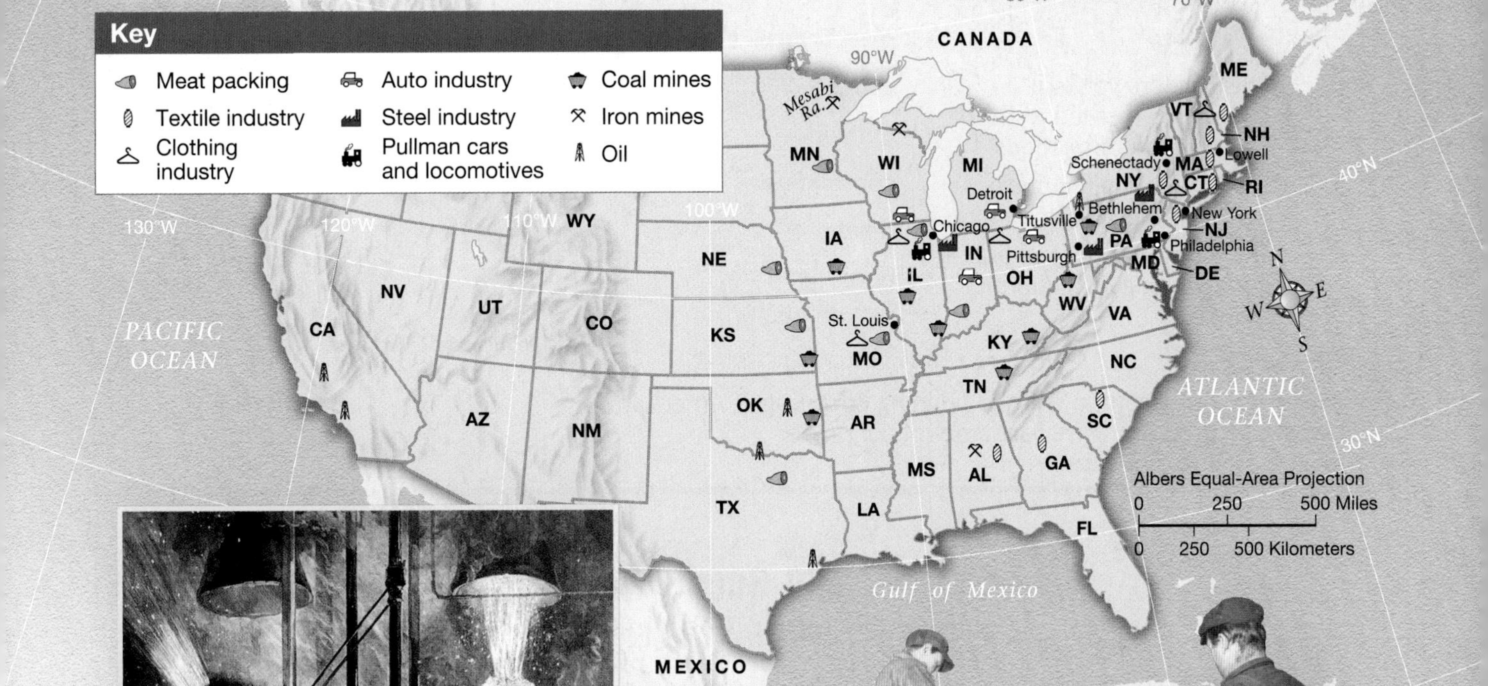

Key

- Meat packing
- Textile industry
- Clothing industry
- Auto industry
- Steel industry
- Pullman cars and locomotives
- Coal mines
- Iron mines
- Oil

Inside Carnegie's steelworks

On the Ford assembly line

1890 The huge Carnegie Steel Company produces more steel than does all of Britain.

1903 Orville Wright makes the first airplane flight.

1913 Henry Ford introduces the assembly line in his Highland Park, Michigan, automobile plant.

Benjamin Harrison	Grover Cleveland	William McKinley	Theodore Roosevelt	William Howard Taft	Woodrow Wilson 1913-1921
1889-1893	1893-1897	1897-1901	1901-1909	1909-1913	

1890 • • 1905 • • 1920 •

1900 ▲ The Labour party is founded in Britain.

1914 ▲ The Panama Canal opens, linking the Caribbean Sea with the Pacific Ocean.

1 Railroads Spur Industry

Prepare to Read

Objectives

In this section, you will
- List factors that led to the construction of railroads.
- Explain how railroad executives eliminated competition.
- Describe how railroad building encouraged economic growth.

Key Terms

gauge
network
consolidate
rebate
pool

Target Reading Skill

Main Idea Copy the concept web below. As you read, fill in the blank ovals with information about the age of railroad building after the Civil War.

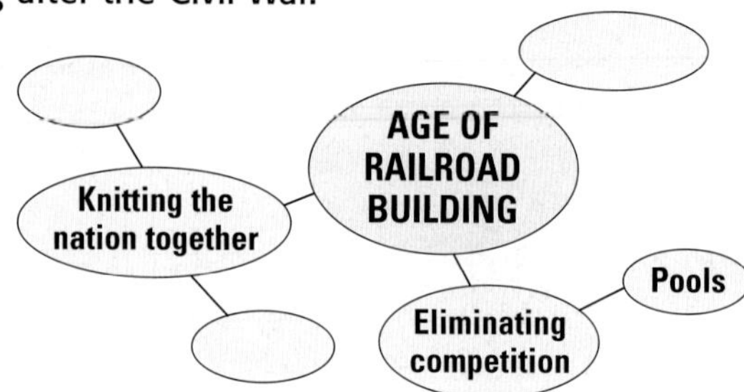

Main Idea A boom in railroad building encouraged American industry to grow but gave vast amounts of power to a few railroad owners.

William Vanderbilt

Setting the Scene William Vanderbilt knew how to make money. His father, Cornelius, had created a railroad empire worth millions. After the death of Cornelius, William doubled the family fortune. Cornelius had ruthlessly crushed competitors and ignored protests from the public. William followed much the same path. He kept his goal clear, telling reporters:

> "The railroads are not run for the benefit of the dear public. That cry is all nonsense. They are built for men who invest their money and expect to get a fair percentage on the same."
>
> —William H. Vanderbilt (to reporters), 1882

Railroad men like the Vanderbilts might ignore the public, but no one could ignore the vast changes that railroads had brought. The railroad was a breakthrough in transportation. For the first time, human beings could travel overland without relying on animals. Just as important, railroads were the single most significant spur to the amazing growth of industry in the United States.

A Network of Rails

The Civil War showed the importance of railroads. Railroads carried troops and supplies to the battlefields. They also moved raw materials to factories. After the war, railroad companies began to build new lines all over the country.

Knitting the Nation Together Early railroads were short lines that served local communities. Many lines ran for no more than 50 miles. When passengers and freight reached the end of one line, they had to move to a train on a different line to continue their journey.

Even if the lines had been connected, the problem would not have been eliminated. Different lines used tracks of different **gauges,** or widths. As a result, the trains from one line could not run on the tracks of another line. In general, the tracks of northern lines used different gauges from those of southern lines.

In 1886, railroads in the South decided to adopt the northern gauge. On May 30, southern railroads stopped running so that work could begin. Using crowbars and sledgehammers, crews worked from dawn to dusk to move the rails a few inches farther apart. When they had finished, some 13,000 miles of track had been changed.

Once the track was standardized, American railroads formed a **network,** or system of connected lines. The creation of a rail network brought benefits to shippers. Often, rail companies arranged for freight cars on one line to use the tracks of another. For example, goods loaded in Chicago could stay on the same car all the way to New York, instead of being transferred from one car to another. As a result, the shipper had to pay only one fare for the whole distance.

New rails knit the sprawling nation together. By 1900, there were more miles of tracks in the United States than in Europe and Russia combined.

Improving Rail Travel New inventions helped make railway travel safer and faster. On early trains, each railroad car had its own brakes and its own brake operator. If different cars stopped at different times, serious accidents could result. In 1869, George Westinghouse began selling his new air brake. Westinghouse's air brake allowed a locomotive engineer to stop all the railroad cars at once. The air brake increased safety and allowed for longer, faster trains.

Long distance travel also became more comfortable. In 1864, George Pullman designed a railroad sleeping car. Pullman cars had convertible berths for sleeping as well as lavatories. Rail lines also added dining cars. Porters, conductors, and waiters attended to the needs of passengers.

Consolidation Brings Efficiency As railroads grew, they looked for ways to operate more efficiently. Small lines were often costly to run, so many companies began to **consolidate,** or combine. Larger companies bought up smaller ones or forced them out of business. The Pennsylvania Railroad, for example, consolidated 73 companies into its system.

Tough-minded business people led the drive for consolidation. Cornelius Vanderbilt was among the most powerful of these leaders. The son of a poor farmer, Vanderbilt earned one fortune in steamship lines. He then began to buy up railroad lines in New York State.

Vanderbilt sometimes used ruthless tactics to force smaller owners to sell to him. In the early 1860s, he decided to buy the New York Central Railroad. The owners refused to sell. Vanderbilt then announced that New York Central passengers would not be allowed to transfer to his trains. With their passengers stranded and business dropping sharply, the New York Central owners gave in and sold their line to Vanderbilt.

Vanderbilt then bought up most of the lines between Chicago and Buffalo. By the time of his death in 1877, his companies controlled 4,500 miles of track and linked New York City to the Great Lakes region.

Geography and History

Why Are There Time Zones?

Our system of time zones is a result of the railroad boom of the late 1800s. At that time, many towns kept their own time. When the sun was highest over the town, it was noon. But 100 miles west, where the sun was still rising, the time was a few minutes before noon.Thus, for example, there were 27 local times in Illinois, 23 in Indiana, and 38 in Wisconsin.

To simplify train schedules, railroads established their own uniform time standard. On November 18, 1883, all railway clocks were set to the new standard. In 1918, Congress enacted the Standard Time Act, which was based on time zones in use by railroads.

Why was the old system of keeping time risky for railroad passengers?

POLITICAL CARTOON *Skills*

Farmers vs. Railroads

In this 1873 cartoon, Thomas Nast portrayed the railroad as a monster snaking through American farmland.

1. **Comprehension** Whom does the figure with the club represent?
2. **Finding the Main Idea** In the background, the monster has its coils wrapped around a building. What building is it? What point is Nast making?
3. **Critical Thinking Analyzing Primary Sources** What devices does Nast use to portray railroads as evil and farmers as good?

Civics 

Other consolidations were soon underway. Before long, the major railroads of the United States were organized into a number of systems directed by a handful of wealthy and powerful men.

Building New Lines Railroad builders raced to create thousands of miles of new tracks. In the years after completion of the first transcontinental rail line in 1869, Americans built three more. James Hill, a Canadian-born owner, finished the last major cross-country line in 1893. His Great Northern Railway wound from Duluth, Minnesota, to Everett, Washington.

Unlike other rail lines, the Great Northern was built without financial aid from Congress. To make his railroad succeed, Hill had to turn a profit from the start. He encouraged farmers and ranchers to move to the Northwest and settle near his railroad. He gave seed to farmers and helped them buy equipment. He imported special bulls in order to breed hardier cattle. Not only was Hill's policy generous, it also made good business sense.

Eliminating the Competition

With builders rushing to share in the profits of the railroad boom, overbuilding occurred. Soon, there were too many rail lines in some parts of the country. Between Atlanta and St. Louis, for example, 20 different lines competed for business. There was not nearly enough rail traffic to keep all these lines busy.

Rebates and Pools In the West, especially, there were too few people for the railroads to make a profit. Competition was fierce. Rate wars broke out as rival railroads slashed their fares to win customers. Usually, all the companies lost money as a result.

Often, railroads were forced to grant secret **rebates,** or discounts, to their biggest customers. This practice forced many small companies out of business. It also hurt small shippers, such as farmers, who still had to pay the full price.

Railroad owners soon realized that cutthroat competition was hurting even their large lines. They looked for ways to end the competition. One method was pooling. In a **pool,** several railroad companies agreed to divide up the business in an area. They then fixed their prices at a high level.

Extra Burdens for Farmers Railroad rebates and pools angered small farmers in the South and the West. Both practices kept shipping prices high for them. Indeed, rates were so high that at times farmers burned their crops for fuel rather than ship them to market.

As you have read in Chapter 19, many farmers joined the Populist party. Populists called for government regulation of rail rates. Some Populists even called for a government takeover of the railroads. Congress and several states passed laws regulating railroad companies. However, the laws did not end abuses. Railroad owners sometimes bribed officials to keep the laws from being enforced.

Railroads Fuel the Economy

Identify Main Ideas

As you read, look for the main ways in which the railroad "fueled" the economy.

Although railroads caused certain problems, they also made possible the rapid growth of industry after 1865. Building rail lines created thousands of jobs. Steelworkers turned millions of tons of iron into steel for tracks and engines. Lumberjacks cut down whole forests to supply wood for railroad ties. Miners sweated in dusty mine shafts digging coal to fuel railroad engines. The railroad companies themselves employed thousands of workers. They laid tracks, built trestles across rivers, carved tunnels through mountains, and built countless railroad stations.

The large railroads also pioneered new ways of managing business. Rail companies created special departments for shipping and accounting and for servicing equipment. Expert managers headed each department, while chains of command ensured that the organization ran smoothly. Other big businesses soon copied these management techniques.

Railroads opened every corner of the country to settlement and growth. They brought people together, especially in the West. New businesses sprang up, and towns sprouted where rail lines crossed. With rail lines in place, the United States was ready to become the greatest industrial nation the world had ever seen.

★ ★ ★ Section 1 Assessment ★ ★ ★

Recall

1. **Identify** Explain the significance of **(a)** William Vanderbilt, **(b)** George Westinghouse, **(c)** Cornelius Vanderbilt.
2. **Define** **(a)** gauge, **(b)** network, **(c)** consolidate, **(d)** rebate, **(e)** pool.

Comprehension

3. How did a broad network of railroads develop in the years after the Civil War?
4. What tactics did railroad owners use to eliminate competition?
5. How did American industry benefit from the widespread railroad building?

Critical Thinking and Writing

6. **Exploring the Main Idea** Review the Main Idea statement at the beginning of the section. Then, write at least four questions that you would ask a railroad owner or a western farmer to help decide whether the growth and consolidation of railroads were good for the country.
7. **Analyzing Information** After the Civil War, railroads consolidated as large railroad companies took over smaller ones. **(a)** What were the advantages of consolidation? **(b)** What were the disadvantages?

Activity

Go Online
PHSchool.com

Connecting to Today
Use the Internet to find out more about people who have built large business empires in recent years. Pick two or three people who have made a difference to the economy. Then, write a profile of one of them describing his or her accomplishments. For help in completing the activity, visit PHSchool.com, **Web Code mfd-2001.**

2 The Rise of Big Business

Prepare to Read

Objectives

In this section, you will
- Identify reasons for the growth of huge steel empires.
- List the benefits corporations and bankers provided to the growing economy.
- Explain how John D. Rockefeller amassed his huge oil holdings.
- Summarize the arguments for and against trusts.

Key Terms

Bessemer process
vertical integration
corporation
stock
dividend
trust
monopoly
free enterprise system
Sherman Antitrust Act

Target Reading Skill

Clarifying Meaning Copy the concept web below. Include three or four blank ovals. As you read, fill in each blank oval with a major development associated with the rise of big business during the late 1800s.

Main Idea As industry boomed, American businesses grew and developed new ways of organizing and limiting competition.

Steel-mill pollution

Setting the Scene In the spring of 1898, an Englishman named Charles Trevelyan visited Pittsburgh. Trevelyan found Pittsburgh to be a rough town dominated by the steel business.

> “A cloud of smoke hangs over it by day. The glow of scores of furnaces lights the riverbanks by night. It stands at the junction of two great rivers, the Monongahela which flows down today in a [slow] yellow stream, and the Allegheny which is blackish.”
>
> —Charles Philips Trevelyan, *Letters From North America and the Pacific,* April 15, 1898

Trevelyan met some of Pittsburgh's wealthiest people. He thought they were “a good breed and shrewd and friendly.”

Pittsburgh was one of many cities that drew its energy from business and industry in the late 1800s. Its wealthiest citizens were a new breed of American business leaders. They were bold, imaginative, sometimes generous, and sometimes ruthless. By the end of the 1800s, they had made their businesses big beyond imagining.

Growth of the Steel Industry

The growth of railroads after the Civil War spurred the growth of the steel industry. Early trains ran on iron rails that wore out quickly. Railroad owners knew that steel rails were much stronger and not as likely to rust as iron. Steel, however, was costly and difficult to make.

Making Steel a New Way In the 1850s, William Kelly in the United States and Henry Bessemer in England each discovered a new way to make steel. The **Bessemer process,** as it came to be called, enabled steel makers to produce strong steel at a lower cost. As a result, railroads began to lay steel rails.

Other industries also took advantage of the cheaper steel. Manufacturers made steel nails, screws, needles, and other items. Steel girders supported the great weight of the new "skyscrapers"—the new tall buildings going up in the cities.

Thriving Steel Mills Steel mills sprang up in cities throughout the midwest. Pittsburgh became the steel-making capital of the nation. Nearby coal mines and good transportation helped Pittsburgh's steel mills to thrive.

The boom in steel making brought jobs and prosperity to Pittsburgh and other steel towns. It also caused problems. The yellow-colored river that Charles Trevelyan saw on his visit to Pittsburgh in 1898 was the result of years of pouring industrial waste into waterways. Steel mills belched thick black smoke that turned the air gray. Soot blanketed houses, trees, and streets.

Andrew Carnegie's Steel Empire

Many Americans made fortunes in the steel industry. Richest of all was a Scottish immigrant, Andrew Carnegie. Carnegie's ideas about how to make money—and how to spend it—had a wide influence.

Controlling the Steel Industry During a visit to Britain, Carnegie had seen the Bessemer process in action. Returning to the United States, he borrowed money and began his own steel mill. Within a short time, Carnegie was earning huge profits. He used the money to buy out rivals. He also bought iron mines, railroad and steamship lines, and warehouses.

Soon, Carnegie controlled all phases of the steel industry—from mining iron ore to shipping finished steel. Gaining control of all the steps used to change raw materials into finished products is called **vertical integration.** Vertical integration gave Carnegie a great advantage over other steel producers. By 1900, Carnegie's steel mills were turning out more steel than was produced in all of Great Britain.

The "Gospel of Wealth" Like other business owners, Carnegie drove his workers hard. Still, he believed that the rich had a duty to help the poor and to improve society. He called this idea the "gospel of wealth." Carnegie gave millions of dollars to charities. After selling his steel empire in 1901, he spent his time and money helping people.

The Corporation and the Bankers

Before the railroad boom, nearly every American town had its own small factories. They produced goods for people in the area. By the late 1800s, however, big factories were producing goods more cheaply than small factories could. Railroads distributed these goods to nationwide markets. As demand for local goods fell, many small factories closed. Big factories then increased their output.

Expanding factories needed capital, or money, for investment. Factory owners used the capital to buy raw materials, pay workers, and cover shipping and advertising costs. To raise capital, Americans adopted new ways of organizing their businesses.

An American Profile

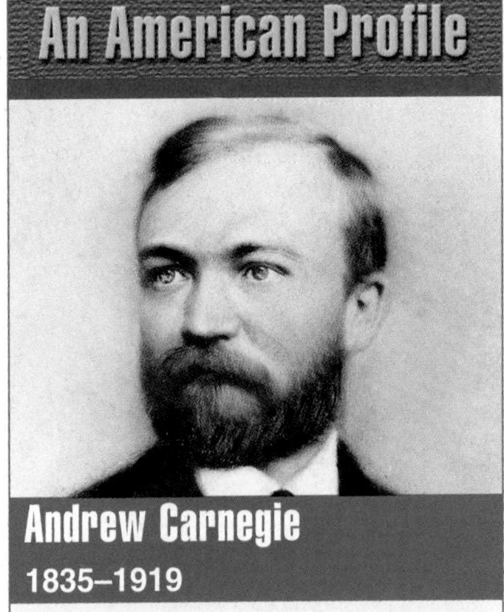

Andrew Carnegie
1835–1919

When Andrew Carnegie was 12, his family left Scotland to immigrate to the United States. He first worked in a cotton factory for $1.20 a week. Then, he worked as a telegram messenger. Carnegie worked long hours during the day and studied Morse code at night.

Luck favored Carnegie when Thomas Scott, superintendent of the Pennsylvania Railroad, hired the young man as his telegrapher. Scott introduced Carnegie to other industrial leaders and helped him invest his savings. Although Carnegie earned only a modest salary, shrewd investment made him a millionaire. By the 1890s, he was one of the world's richest men.

How did Carnegie take advantage of his good luck?

The Rise of the Corporation Many expanding businesses became corporations. A **corporation** is a business that is owned by investors. A corporation sells **stock,** or shares in the business, to investors, who are known as stockholders. The corporation can use the money invested by stockholders to build a new factory or buy new machines.

In return for their investment, stockholders hope to receive **dividends,** or shares of a corporation's profit. To protect their investment, stockholders elect a board of directors to run the corporation.

Stockholders face fewer risks than owners of private businesses do. If a private business goes bankrupt, the owner must pay all the debts of the business. By law, stockholders cannot be held responsible for a corporation's debts.

Summarize Read the paragraphs under the heading "Banks and Industry." Write a brief summary explaining how banks were linked with the development of big business. Add this information to your concept web.

Banks and Industry In the years after the Civil War, corporations attracted large amounts of capital from American investors. Corporations also borrowed millions of dollars from banks. These loans helped American industry grow at a rapid pace. At the same time, bankers made huge profits.

The most powerful banker of the late 1800s was J. Pierpont Morgan. Morgan's influence was not limited to banking. He used his banking profits to gain control of major corporations.

During economic hard times in the 1890s, Morgan and other bankers invested in the stock of troubled corporations. As large stockholders, they easily won seats on the boards of directors. They then adopted policies that reduced competition and ensured big profits. "I like a little competition, but I like combination more," Morgan used to say.

Between 1894 and 1898, Morgan gained control of most of the nation's major rail lines. He then began to buy up steel companies, including Carnegie Steel, and to merge them into a single large corporation. By 1901, Morgan had become head of the United States Steel Company. It was the first American business worth more than $1 billion.

Rockefeller's Oil Empire

Industry could not have expanded so quickly in the United States without the nation's rich supply of natural resources. Iron ore was plentiful, especially in the Mesabi Range of Minnesota. Pennsylvania, West Virginia, and the Rocky Mountains had large deposits of coal. The Rockies also contained minerals, such as gold, silver, and copper. Vast forests provided lumber for building.

In 1859, Americans discovered a valuable new resource: oil. Drillers near Titusville, Pennsylvania, made the nation's first oil strike. An oil boom quickly followed. Hundreds of prospectors rushed to western Pennsylvania ready to drill wells in search of oil.

Rockefeller and Standard Oil Among those who came to the Pennsylvania oil fields was young John D. Rockefeller. Rockefeller, however, did not rush to drill for oil. He knew that oil had little value until it was refined, or purified, to make kerosene. Kerosene was used as a fuel in stoves and lamps. So Rockefeller built an oil refinery.

Rockefeller believed that competition was wasteful. He used the profits from his refinery to buy up other refineries. He then combined the companies into the Standard Oil Company of Ohio.

Rockefeller was a shrewd businessman. He was always trying to improve the quality of his oil. He also did whatever he could to get rid of competition. Standard Oil slashed its prices to drive rivals out of business. It pressured its customers not to deal with other oil companies. It forced railroad companies eager for his business to grant rebates to Standard Oil. Lower shipping costs gave Rockefeller an important advantage over his competitors.

The Standard Oil Trust To tighten his hold over the oil industry, Rockefeller formed the Standard Oil trust in 1882. A **trust** is a group of corporations run by a single board of directors.

Stockholders in dozens of smaller oil companies turned over their stock to Standard Oil. In return, they got stock in the newly created trust. The trust paid the stockholders high dividends. However, the board of Standard Oil, headed by Rockefeller, managed all the companies that had previously been rivals.

The Standard Oil trust created a monopoly of the oil industry. A **monopoly** controls all or nearly all the business of an industry. The Standard Oil trust controlled 95 percent of all oil refining in the United States.

Other businesses followed Rockefeller's lead. They set up trusts and tried to build monopolies. By the 1890s, monopolies and trusts controlled some of the nation's most important industries.

The Case For and Against Trusts

Some Americans charged that the leaders of giant corporations were abusing the free enterprise system. In a **free enterprise system,** businesses are owned by private citizens. Owners decide what products to make, how much to produce, where to sell products, and what prices to charge. Companies compete to win customers by making the best product at the lowest price.

The Case Against Trusts Critics argued that trusts and monopolies reduced competition. Without competition, there was no reason for companies to keep prices low or to improve their products. It was also hard for new companies to compete with powerful trusts.

Critics were also upset about the political influence of trusts. Some people worried that millionaires were using their wealth to

Cause *and* Effect

Causes

- Railroad boom spurs business
- Businesses become corporations
- Nation has rich supply of natural resources
- New inventions make business more efficient

THE RISE OF INDUSTRY

Effects

- Steel and oil become giant industries
- Monopolies and trusts dominate important industries
- Factory workers face harsh conditions
- Membership in labor unions grows

Effects Today

- United States is world's leading economic power
- American corporations do business around the world
- Government laws regulate monopolies

GRAPHIC ORGANIZER *Skills*

American industry boomed after the Civil War. The effects of industrial growth are still being felt today.

1. **Comprehension** List two causes for the rise of industry.
2. **Critical Thinking Drawing Conclusions** Why do you think the government now tries to regulate monopolies?

Economics $

buy favors from elected officials. John Reagan, a member of Congress from Texas, said:

> “There were no beggars till Vanderbilts . . . shaped the actions of Congress and molded the purposes of government. Then the few became fabulously wealthy, the many wretchedly poor.”
>
> —John Reagan, *Austin Weekly Democratic Statesman*, 1877

Under pressure from the public, the government slowly moved toward controlling giant corporations. Congress approved the **Sherman Antitrust Act** in 1890, which banned the formation of trusts and monopolies. However, it was too weak to be effective. Some state governments passed laws to regulate business, but the corporations usually sidestepped them.

The Case for Trusts Naturally, some business leaders defended trusts. Andrew Carnegie published articles arguing that too much competition ruined businesses and put people out of work. In an article titled "Wealth and Its Uses," he wrote:

> “It will be a great mistake for the community to shoot the millionaires, for they are the bees that make the most honey, and contribute most to the hive even after they have gorged themselves full.”
>
> —Andrew Carnegie, "Wealth and Its Uses"

Defenders of big business argued that the growth of giant corporations brought lower production costs, lower prices, higher wages, and a better quality of life for millions of Americans. They pointed out that by 1900, Americans enjoyed the highest standard of living in the world.

★ ★ ★ Section 2 Assessment ★ ★ ★

Recall

1. **Identify** Explain the significance of **(a)** Andrew Carnegie, **(b)** Bessemer process, **(c)** John D. Rockefeller, **(d)** Sherman Antitrust Act.
2. **Define** **(a)** vertical integration, **(b)** corporation, **(c)** stock, **(d)** dividend, **(e)** trust, **(f)** monopoly, **(g)** free enterprise system.

Comprehension

3. Why did the steel industry grow so quickly after the Civil War?
4. How did corporations and banking help the United States economy to expand?
5. How did John D. Rockefeller monopolize the oil industry?
6. What arguments did supporters and opponents of trusts each use?

Critical Thinking and Writing

7. **Exploring the Main Idea** Review the Main Idea statement at the beginning of the section. Then, list the ways that the need for capital led to new ways of running businesses.
8. **Applying Information** Andrew Carnegie once said of people who held onto their fortunes, "The man who dies thus rich, dies disgraced." How did Carnegie follow this philosophy?

Activity

Creating an Advertisement **It is 1875, and you have been given the job of designing a one-page advertisement for the financial pages of a newspaper. The assignment: Explain the advantages of a corporation to a public that is not familiar with it. The goal: to get people to invest in corporations.**

Advertising in the Industrial Age

Although ads had appeared in newspapers since colonial times, there was a boom in advertising after 1870. The growth of industry and the expansion of railroads made it possible to sell goods all over the country. At first, there were few limits on what an ad could claim. Many promised happiness, popularity, and a life of ease—if only the consumer bought the product being advertised.

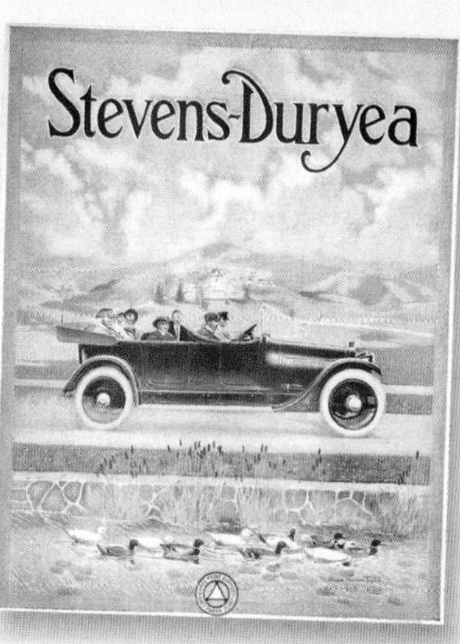

Elegance for the Wealthy

The Stevens-Duryea was so classy that its advertisement did not even need words. The spacious car and the well-dressed group of six adults—plus their chauffeur—said everything about luxury. The price for this 1914 model: $4,500 to $5,950—a huge amount for the times.

65 Cents Each!

That's what it cost for one of these 12-inch, double-sided records. The 1914 ad says: "If you think you have danced to the best dance music that your talking machine can produce, have your dealer play any one of these. Tangos, . . . One Steps and Turkey Trots, . . . Boston and Hesitation Waltzes. You will never be too tired when these waltzes are played."

Through the Wringer

Fashionable women tend to the laundry in this 1869 poster. It all seems very dignified in this spotless, well-stocked kitchen. However, before the days of electric-powered washing machines, doing the laundry was hard and messy work. Not a hint of this appears in the poster.

Activity

Ask your school media specialist for old magazines with advertisements. Select one ad and study it. To what emotion or hope does the ad appeal? Share your ideas with your classmates.

3 Inventions Change the Nation

Prepare to Read

Objectives

In this section, you will

- Identify the new devices that speeded up communications after the Civil War.
- Explain how Thomas Edison and other inventors brought new technologies to Americans at work and at home.
- Describe the changes the automobile and airplane made in American life.

Key Terms

patent

transatlantic

moving assembly line

mass production

Target Reading Skill

Reading Process As you read, complete this table listing the advances that transformed American life in the last half of the 1800s.

ADVANCES IN COMMUNICATION	ADVANCES IN TRAVEL	ADVANCES IN HOME AND OFFICE
• Transatlantic cable • •	• Air brakes • •	• Typewriters • •

Main Idea New technologies transformed American industry and life in the late 1800s.

An early washing machine

Setting the Scene The Patent Office had never seen a year like 1897. An average of nearly 60 **patents,** or licenses for new inventions, were being granted every day. By year's end, Americans had registered some 21,000 patents. This was more than the total recorded in the entire 1850s.

The United States had become a land of invention. Between 1870 and 1900, patent officers issued more than 500,000 new patents. Some went to lone inventors like William Blackstone of Indiana. In 1874, he built a machine that washed away dirt from clothes. It was the first washing machine designed for use in the home. Other inventors, like the legendary Thomas Edison, filed patent request after patent request with the government. Thousands of inventions poured from his laboratory.

A flood of invention swept the United States in the late 1800s. Some inventions helped industry to grow and become more efficient. Others made daily life easier in many American homes.

Speeding Up Communications

Better communication was vital to growing American businesses. Some remarkable new devices filled the need for faster communication. The telegraph, which had been in use since 1844, helped people around the nation stay in touch. For example, a steel maker in Pittsburgh could instantly order iron ore from a mine in Minnesota.

Communicating Across the Atlantic The telegraph speeded up communication within the United States. It still took weeks, however, for news from Europe to arrive by ship.

Cyrus Field had the idea of laying a cable under the ocean so that telegraph messages could go back and forth between North

A Time of Invention

INVENTOR	DATE	INVENTION
Elisha Otis	1852	Passenger elevator brake
George Pullman	1864	Sleeping car
George Westinghouse	1869	Air brake
Elijah McCoy	1872	Automatic engine-oiling machine
Andrew S. Hallidie	1873	Cable streetcar
Stephen Dudley Field	1874	Electric streetcar
Alexander Graham Bell	1876	Telephone
Thomas Alva Edison	1877	Phonograph
Anna Baldwin	1878	Milking machine
Thomas Alva Edison	1879	First practical incandescent light bulb
James Ritty	1879	Cash register
Jan E. Matzeliger	1883	Shoemaking machine
Lewis E. Waterman	1884	Fountain pen
Granville T. Woods	1887	Automatic air brake
Charles and J. Frank Duryea	1893	Gasoline-powered car
King C. Gillette	1895	Safety razor with throwaway blades
John Thurman	1899	Motor-driven vacuum cleaner
Leo H. Baekeland	1909	Improved plastic

A 1908 vacuum cleaner

GRAPHIC ORGANIZER *Skills*

New inventions transformed daily life in the United States. They also helped the American economy grow.

1. **Comprehension** **(a)** What did George Westinghouse invent? In what year? **(b)** Who improved on Westinghouse's invention? In what year?
2. **Critical Thinking Applying Information** Which of the inventions on the chart might be found in a home today?

America and Europe. He began working in 1854, making five attempts to lay the cable. Each time, the cable snapped. In 1858, two American ships managed to lay a cable between Ireland and Newfoundland. Field then arranged for Britain's Queen Victoria in London to send the first **transatlantic,** or across the Atlantic, message to President James Buchanan in Washington, D.C. For three weeks, Field was a hero. Then, the cable broke. But Field would not give up. In 1866, the ship *Great Eastern* succeeded in laying the cable. Field's transatlantic cable brought the United States and Europe closer together and made him famous. He marveled at his success:

> “In five months . . . the cable had been manufactured, shipped . . . stretched across the Atlantic, and was sending messages . . . swift as lightning from continent to continent.”
>
> —Cyrus Field, speech, 1866

Bell's "Talking Machine" The telegraph sent only dots and dashes over the wire. Several inventors were looking for a way to transmit voices. One of them was Alexander Graham Bell, a Scottish-born teacher of the deaf.

Bell had been working on his invention since 1865. In March 1876, he was ready to test his "talking machine." Bell sat in one room and spoke into his machine. His assistant, Thomas Watson, sat in another room with the receiver. "Mr. Watson, come here. I want to see you," Bell said. Watson heard the words faintly and rushed to

Bell's side. "Mr. Bell," he cried, "I heard every word you said!" The telephone worked.

Bell's telephone aroused little interest at first. Scientists praised the invention. Most people, however, saw it as a toy. Bell offered to sell the telephone to the Western Union Telegraph Company for $100,000. The company refused—a costly mistake. In the end, the telephone earned Bell millions.

Bell formed the Bell Telephone Company in 1877. By 1885, he had sold more than 300,000 phones, mostly to businesses. With the telephone, the pace of business speeded up even more. People no longer had to go to a telegraph office to send messages. Business people could find out about prices or supplies by picking up the telephone.

Edison: "The Wizard of Menlo Park"

In an age of invention, Thomas Edison was right at home. In 1876, he opened a research laboratory in Menlo Park, New Jersey. There, Edison boasted that he and his co-workers created a "minor" invention every 10 days and "a big thing every six months or so." By the end of his career, Edison had earned worldwide fame as the greatest inventor of the age.

Viewing History

Thomas Edison

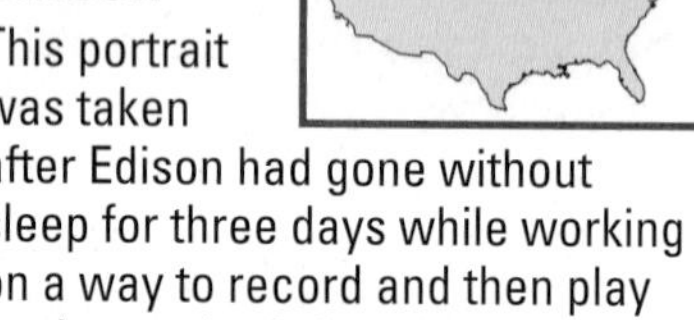

This portrait was taken after Edison had gone without sleep for three days while working on a way to record and then play back sounds. At last, he received his reward. He heard his own voice reciting "Mary Had a Little Lamb."

Supporting a Point of View ***How does Edison's experience illustrate his belief that genius is "one percent inspiration and ninety-nine percent perspiration"?***

Turning Invention Into a System The key to Edison's success lay in his approach. He turned inventing into a system. Teams of experts refined Edison's ideas and translated them into practical inventions. The work was long and grueling. "Genius," Edison said, "is one percent inspiration and ninety-nine percent perspiration."

The results were amazing. Edison became known as the "Wizard of Menlo Park" for inventing the light bulb, the phonograph, and hundreds of other devices.

One invention from Edison's laboratory launched a new industry: the movies. In 1893, Edison introduced his first machine for showing moving pictures. Viewers watched short films by looking through a peephole in a cabinet. Later, Edison developed a motion picture projector, making it possible for many people to watch a film at the same time. By 1908, thousands of silent-movie houses had opened in cities across the United States.

The Power of Electricity One of Edison's most important creations was the electric power plant. He built the first power plant in New York City in 1882 and wired the business district first in hopes of attracting investors. With the flip of a switch, Edison set the district ablaze with light.

Within a year, Edison's power plant was supplying electricity to homes as well as businesses. Soon, more power plants were built. Factories replaced steam-powered engines with safer, quieter, electric engines. Electric energy powered streetcars in cities and lighted countless homes. The modern age of electricity had begun.

Technology Takes Command

Almost every day, it seemed, American inventors were creating new devices. As technology took command, businesses became more efficient, and life became easier and more pleasant.

The Refrigerated Railroad Car In the 1880s, Gustavus Swift came up with an idea that transformed the American diet. Swift introduced refrigeration to the meatpacking industry. In the past, cattle, pigs, and chickens had been raised and sold locally. Meat spoiled quickly, so it could not be shipped over long distances.

Swift set up a meatpacking plant in Chicago, a railroad hub midway between the cattle ranches of the West and the cities of the East. Cattle were shipped by train to Chicago. At Swift's plant, the animals were slaughtered and carved up into sides of beef. The fresh beef was quickly loaded onto refrigerated railroad cars and carried to market. Even in summer, Swift sent fresh meat to eastern cities.

New Technologies at the Office and at Home New inventions also affected life at home and in the office. Christopher Sholes perfected the typewriter in 1868. This invention speeded up communication between businesses.

In 1888, George Eastman introduced the lightweight Kodak camera. No longer did photography require bulky equipment and chemicals. After 100 snaps of the shutter, the owner returned the camera to Kodak. The company developed the pictures and sent them back, along with a reloaded camera. Taking pictures became a popular pastime.

African American Inventors African Americans contributed to the flood of inventions. In 1872, Elijah McCoy created a special device that oiled engines automatically. It was widely used on railroad engines and in factories. Another inventor, Granville T. Woods, found a way to send telegraph messages between moving railroad trains.

Jan Matzeliger invented a machine that could perform almost all the steps in shoemaking that had previously been done by hand. Patented in 1883, Matzeliger's machine was eventually used in shoe factories across the country.

Many African American inventors had trouble getting patents for their inventions. Even so, in 1900, an assistant in the patent office compiled a list of patents issued to African American inventors. The list, together with drawings and plans of all the inventions, filled four huge volumes.

Target Skill **Ask Questions** Form a question from the heading "Technology Takes Command." Then, read to find the answer to your question.

Automobiles and the Assembly Line

No single person invented the automobile. Europeans had produced motorized vehicles as early as the 1860s. By 1890, France led the world in automaking. In the 1890s, several Americans began building cars. Still, only the wealthy could afford them.

Ford's Moving Assembly Line It was Henry Ford who made the auto a part of everyday American life. In 1913, Ford introduced the

Henry Ford Museum

Not far from his Detroit auto plant, Henry Ford built a place to display "every household article, every kind of vehicle, every sort of tool." Today at the Henry Ford Museum in Dearborn, Michigan, you can explore the world's largest transportation collection, from giant locomotives to classic cars.

Virtual Field Trip For an interactive look at the Henry Ford Museum, visit PHSchool.com, **Web Code mfd-2002.**

moving assembly line. With this method of production, workers stay in one place as products edge along on a moving belt. At Ford's auto plant, one group of workers would bolt seats onto a passing car frame, the next would add the roof, and so on. The assembly line greatly reduced the time needed to build a car. Other industries soon adopted the method.

Ford's assembly line allowed mass production of cars. **Mass production** means making large quantities of a product quickly and cheaply. Because of mass production, Ford could sell his cars at a lower price than other automakers.

Cars for the Public It took a number of years for the automobile to catch on. At first, most people laughed at it. Some thought the "horseless carriage" was a nuisance. Others thought it was dangerous. A backfiring auto engine could scare a horse right off the road. Towns and villages across the nation posted signs: "No horseless carriages allowed." In Tennessee, a person planning to drive a car had to advertise the fact a week ahead of time. This warning gave others time to prepare for the danger!

Over time, attitudes toward the automobile changed. No other means of travel offered such freedom. As prices dropped, more people could afford to buy cars. In 1900, only 8,000 Americans owned cars. By 1917, more than 4.5 million autos were chugging along American roads.

Automobiles were at first regarded as machines for men only. Automakers soon realized, however, that women could drive—and buy—cars. Companies began to direct advertisements to women, stressing the comfort and usefulness of automobiles. Driving gave women greater independence.

The First Flight

Meanwhile, two Ohio bicycle mechanics, Orville and Wilbur Wright, were experimenting with another new method of transportation: flying. The Wright brothers owned a bicycle shop in Dayton, Ohio. During the 1890s, they read about Europeans who were experimenting with glider planes. The brothers were soon caught up in the dream of flying.

After trying out hundreds of designs, the Wright brothers tested their first "flying machine" on December 17, 1903, at Kitty Hawk, North Carolina. Orville made the first flight. The plane, powered by a small gasoline engine, stayed in the air for 12 seconds and flew a distance of 120 feet. Orville flew three more times that day. His longest flight lasted 59 seconds.

Improvements came quickly after the first flight. By 1905, the Wrights had built a plane that could turn, make figure-eights, and remain in the air for up to half an hour.

Surprisingly, the first flights did not attract much interest. No one could see any practical use for the flying machine.

It was the United States military that first saw a use for airplanes. In 1908, the Wrights demonstrated how planes could fly over battlefields to locate enemy positions. Then, they produced an airplane for the military that could reach the amazing speed of 40 miles per hour!

In time, the airplane would achieve its vast potential. It would change the world by making travel quicker and trade easier.

★ ★ ★ Section 3 Assessment ★ ★ ★

Recall

1. **Identify** Explain the significance of **(a)** Cyrus Field, **(b)** Alexander Graham Bell, **(c)** Thomas Edison, **(d)** Gustavus Swift, **(e)** Elijah McCoy, **(f)** Henry Ford.
2. **Define** **(a)** patent, **(b)** transatlantic, **(c)** moving assembly line, **(d)** mass production.

Comprehension

3. How did the transatlantic cable and the telephone speed up communications?
4. Name five other inventions that changed the way Americans lived and worked in the late 1800s.
5. How did the auto and the airplane change American life?

Critical Thinking and Writing

6. **Exploring the Main Idea** Review the Main Idea statement at the beginning of the section. Then, make a list of the five most important inventions of this period. Rank the five inventions in order of importance, and write a paragraph explaining your choices.
7. **Drawing Conclusions** Why might inventors be more creative working in an invention factory, such as Edison's, than working on their own?

ACTIVITY

Inventions for the Twenty-first Century

Use the Internet to find Web sites that predict inventions likely to make an impact on American homes in 2050. Choose one invention, and write a description for a newspaper advertisement. For help in completing the activity, visit PHSchool.com, **Web Code mfd-2003.**

4 The Rise of Organized Labor

Prepare to Read

Objectives

In this section, you will
- Explain how workplace changes led to the rise of labor organizations.
- Describe the progress and problems that affected women in the workplace during the late 1800s.
- Identify why organized labor faced hard times after 1870.

Key Terms

sweatshop
Knights of Labor
strikebreaker
anarchist
Haymarket Riot
AFL
trade union
collective bargaining
ILGWU
Triangle Fire

Target Reading Skill

Main Idea As you read, prepare an outline of this section. Use roman numerals to indicate the major headings, capital letters for the subheadings, and numbers for the supporting details.

I. New Workplace
  A. Children at work
  B.
II. The Rise of Organized Labor
  A.
  B. Trouble in Haymarket Square

Main Idea As workers lost power over their working conditions, they began to organize into unions.

In the steel mills

Setting the Scene As James Davis looked back on his life, he recalled his youth working in a steel mill in the 1880s. Davis worked as a "puddler," the person who mixed the molten metals. Standing near white-hot furnaces, he learned to mix the right brew of metals at the right temperatures to produce fine steel. He noted with pride:

> "This process was handed down from father to son and in the course of time came to my father and so to me. None of us ever went to school and learned the chemistry of it from books. We learned the trick by doing it, standing with our faces in the scorching heat. . . ."
>
> —James Davis, *The Iron Puddler*, 1922

But machines were taking over what people had done in the past. Giant converters could automatically mix the metals, cook them at the right temperatures, and produce excellent steel. Skilled puddlers like Davis were being transformed into mere tenders of those machines.

The growth of these huge machine-driven factories affected all workers. By the late 1800s, a growing sense of powerlessness led workers to join together.

A New Workplace

Workers had to adjust to the new kinds of factories of the late 1800s. Before the Civil War, most factories were small and family run. Bosses knew their workers by name and chatted with them about their families. Because most workers had skills that the factory needed, they could bargain with the boss for wages.

By the 1880s, the relationship between worker and boss had changed. People worked all day tending machines in a large, crowded, noisy room. Because their skills were easily replaced, many workers were forced to work for low wages. In the garment trade and other industries, sweatshops became common. A **sweatshop** is a workplace where people labor long hours in poor conditions for low pay. Most sweatshop workers were young women, or children.

Children at Work The 1900 census reported nearly 2 million children under age 15 at work throughout the country. Boys and girls labored in hazardous textile mills, tobacco factories, and garment sweatshops. In coal mines, they picked stones out of the coal for 12 hours a day, 6 days a week. Working children had little time for schooling. Lack of education reduced their chance to build a better life as adults.

Hazards of Work Factories were filled with hazards. Lung-damaging dust filled the air of textile mills. Cave-ins and gas explosions plagued mines. In steel mills, vats of molten metal spilled without warning. Some workers had their health destroyed. Others were severely injured or killed in industrial accidents. In one year, 195 workers died in the steel mills of Pittsburgh.

The Rise of Organized Labor

Many workers found ways to fight back. Some workers slowed their work pace. Others went on strike. Strikes were usually informal, organized by workers in individual factories.

Sometimes, workers banded together to win better conditions. However, most early efforts to form unions failed.

Knights of Labor In 1869, workers formed the **Knights of Labor.** At first, the union was open to skilled workers only. The members held meetings in secret because employers fired workers who joined unions.

In 1879, the Knights of Labor elected Terence Powderly as their president. Powderly worked to strengthen the union by opening its membership to immigrants, African Americans, women, and unskilled workers.

Powderly did not believe in strikes. Rather, he relied on rallies and meetings to win public support. Goals of the Knights included a shorter workday, an end to child labor, and equal pay for men and women. Most important, Powderly wanted workers and employers to share ownership and profits.

In 1885, some members of the Knights of Labor launched a strike that forced the Missouri Pacific Railroad to restore wages that it had previously cut. The Knights did not officially support the strike. Still, workers everywhere saw the strike as a victory for the union. Membership soared to 700,000, including 60,000 African Americans.

Trouble in Haymarket Square The following year, the Knights of Labor ran into serious trouble. Workers at the McCormick Harvester Company in Chicago went on strike. Again, the Knights did not endorse the strike.

Like many companies at the time, the McCormick company hired **strikebreakers,** or replacements for striking workers. On

An American Profile

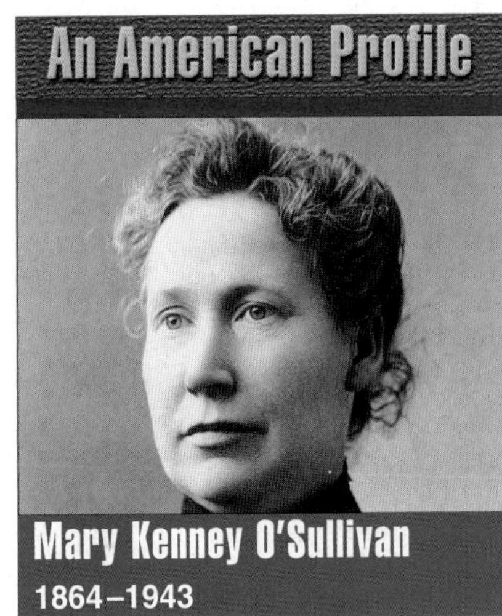

Mary Kenney O'Sullivan
1864–1943

Poverty forced Mary Kenney to leave school in Hannibal, Missouri, at the age of 14. She worked first as a dressmaker and later in a printing plant. Then, she moved to Chicago. Shocked by the city's sweatshops, child labor, and low wages, she helped form a women's bindery workers union. At the same time, she fought the terrible conditions in Chicago's slums. Kenney helped write a report for the state of Illinois exposing slum conditions.

In 1892, she became a union organizer. She kept up a hectic pace even after she married and raised three children.

How do you think Mary Kenney's early life affected her view of workers' rights?

Growth of Labor Unions

Thousands of Members: 0, 500, 1,000, 1,500, 2,000, 2,500, 3,000

Year: 1898, 1902, 1906, 1910, 1914

Source: *Historical Statistics of the United States*

CHART ***Skills***

A growing number of workers joined unions in the late 1800s and early 1900s.

1. **Comprehension**
   (a) How much did union membership increase between 1898 and 1914?
   (b) What years showed a decrease in membership?
2. **Critical Thinking Drawing Conclusions**
   In which time period on this chart do you think a recession hit the economy?

Economics $

May 3, 1886, workers clashed with strikebreakers outside the factory. Police opened fire, and four workers were killed.

The next day, thousands of workers gathered in Haymarket Square to protest the killings. The rally was led by **anarchists,** people who oppose all forms of organized government. Suddenly, a bomb exploded, killing seven police officers.

Eight anarchists were arrested for their part in the **Haymarket Riot,** as the incident was called. No real evidence linked these men to the bombing, but four were tried, convicted, and hanged. A wave of antilabor feeling swept the nation. Many Americans thought that the unions were controlled by anarchists. As a result, membership in the Knights of Labor dropped sharply.

American Federation of Labor

Despite the failure of the Knights of Labor, the labor movement continued to grow. In 1886, an immigrant cigar maker named Samuel Gompers organized a new union in Columbus, Ohio. The American Federation of Labor (**AFL**) was open to skilled workers only.

Workers did not join the AFL directly. Rather, they joined a **trade union,** a union of persons working in the same trade. For example, a typesetter joined a typesetter's union. The union then joined the AFL. Thus, the AFL was a large organization made up of many different unions.

Unlike the Knights of Labor, the AFL stressed practical goals. It focused on higher wages, shorter hours, and improved working conditions. It led the fight for **collective bargaining,** the right of unions to negotiate with management for workers as a group. The AFL also supported the use of strikes to achieve its goals.

Its practical approach helped the AFL become the most powerful labor organization in the nation. Between 1886 and 1910, membership in the AFL swelled from 150,000 to more than one and a half million. However, because African Americans, immigrants, and unskilled workers were barred from most trade unions, they could not join the AFL.

Identify Main Ideas

As you read, look for sentences that describe the conditions that women workers faced during this period.

Women at Work

By 1890, one million women worked in American factories. In the textile mills of New England and the tobacco factories of the South, women formed the majority of workers. In New York City, women outnumbered men in the garment industry.

During the 1800s, some women formed their own unions. A few, like the all-black Washerwomen's Association of Atlanta, struck for higher wages. None of these unions succeeded, however.

Mother Jones Organizes The best-known woman in the labor movement was Irish-born Mary Harris Jones, known as Mother Jones. Jones devoted much of her adult life to the cause of workers.

Jones spoke out about the hard lives of children in textile mills, "barefoot . . . reaching thin little hands into the machinery." By calling attention to such abuses, Mother Jones helped pave the way for reform.

Organizing Garment Workers In 1900, garment workers organized the International Ladies' Garment Workers Union (ILGWU). More than 20,000 women and men in the ILGWU walked off their jobs in 1909. After a few weeks, employers met union demands for better pay and shorter hours. The ILGWU became a key member of the AFL.

Despite the efforts of the ILGWU and other labor groups, most women with factory jobs did not join unions. They continued to work long hours for low pay. Many labored under unsafe conditions. Then, a tragic event focused attention on the dangers faced by women workers.

Tragedy at Triangle The workday was just ending on a cool March day in 1911, when a fire broke out in the Triangle Shirtwaist Factory, a sweatshop in New York City. Within minutes, the upper stories were ablaze. Hundreds of workers raced for the exits, only to find them locked. The company had locked the doors to keep workers at their jobs. In their panic, workers ran headlong into the doors, blocking them with their bodies.

Fire trucks arrived almost immediately, but their ladders could not reach the upper floors. One after another, workers trying to escape the flames leaped to their deaths. One reporter wrote:

> "As I looked up . . . there, at a window, a young man was helping girls to leap out. Suddenly one of them put her arms around him and kiss[ed] him. Then he held her into space and dropped her. He jumped next. Thud . . . dead. Thud . . . dead."
>
> —*The New York Times,* March 26, 1911

Nearly 150 people, mostly young women, lost their lives in the Triangle Fire. The deaths shocked the public. As a result, New York and other states approved new safety laws to help protect factory workers.

Hard Times for Organized Labor

The new era of industry led to vast economic growth. At the same time, it created economic strains. In the rush for profits, many industries expanded too fast. As goods flooded the market, prices dropped. To cover their losses, factory owners often fired workers. In time, factories geared up again, and the cycle was repeated.

The economy swung wildly between good times and bad. Between 1870 and 1900, two major depressions and three smaller recessions rocked the country. In such hard times, workers lost their jobs or faced pay cuts.

Primary Source

The Triangle Fire

The day after the fire, this story appeared in The New York Times*:*
"Cecilia Walker, 20 years old, . . . slid down the cable at the Washington Place elevator and escaped with burned hands and body bruises. She was on the eighth floor of the building when the fire started. Running over to the elevator shaft she rang for the car, but it did not come. As she passed the sixth floor sliding on the cable she became unconscious, . . . and does not know what happened until she reached St. Vincent's Hospital, where she is now.

"'A girl and I, . . . were on the eighth floor, and when I ran for the elevator shaft my girl friend started for the window on the Washington Street side. I looked around to call her but she had gone.'"

—*The New York Times,* March 26, 1911

Analyzing Primary Sources
How do you think the public reacted to stories of the fire?

Strike! During a severe depression in the 1870s, railroad workers were forced to take several cuts in pay. In July 1877, workers went on strike, shutting down rail lines across the country. Riots erupted in many cities as workers burned rail yards and ripped up track.

Violent strikes also broke out in the West. In the 1870s, miners in Idaho tried to shut down two large mines. In 1893, after another bitter strike, miners formed the Western Federation of Miners. This union gained great strength in the Rocky Mountain states. Between 1894 and 1904, it organized strike after strike.

Government Sides With Owners The federal government usually sided with factory owners. Several Presidents sent in troops to end strikes. Courts usually ruled against strikers, too.

In 1894, a Chicago court dealt a serious blow to unions. A year earlier, George Pullman had cut the pay of workers at his railroad car factory. Yet, he did not reduce the rents he charged them for company-owned houses. Workers walked off the job in protest.

A federal judge ordered the Pullman workers to stop their strike. Leaders of the strike were jailed for violating the Sherman Antitrust Act. This act had been meant to keep trusts from limiting free trade. The courts, however, said that the strikers were limiting free trade.

Slow Progress Union workers staged thousands of strikes during the late 1800s. However, few Americans supported the strikes. Many were afraid that unions were run by foreign-born radicals. Because unions were unpopular, owners felt free to try to crush them.

Workers did make some gains. Overall, wages rose slightly between 1870 and 1900. Still, union growth was slow. In 1910, only one worker in 20 belonged to a union. Some 30 years would pass before large numbers of unskilled workers were able to join unions.

★ ★ ★ Section 4 Assessment ★ ★ ★

Recall

1. **Identify** Explain the significance of **(a)** Knights of Labor, **(b)** Haymarket Riot, **(c)** American Federation of Labor, **(d)** ILGWU, **(e)** Triangle Fire.
2. **Define** **(a)** sweatshop, **(b)** strikebreaker, **(c)** anarchist, **(d)** trade union, **(e)** collective bargaining.

Comprehension

3. How did changing factory conditions promote the rise of labor unions in the late 1800s?
4. What advances did women make in the workplace, and what problems still remained in the late 1800s?
5. Why did the labor movement suffer a number of major defeats after 1870?

Critical Thinking and Writing

6. **Exploring the Main Idea** Review the Main Idea statement at the beginning of this section. Then, write five statements of fact that support the main idea.
7. **Making Generalizations** Why do you think that it often takes a tragedy to spur people to make reforms?

ACTIVITY

Creating Compound Words **During times of technological change, many new words are created. Some of them are compound words—words invented by combining two existing words. There are two examples of these words in the Key Terms for this section. Find these words and tell what they mean. Then, create five compound words of your own from the content of this chapter.**

Formulating Questions

You can increase your understanding of history by asking questions about what you see and read. Formulating, or drafting, questions is a critical-thinking process that helps you become a more effective learner. The better your questions, the more you will learn.

Child labor became a common practice in the United States during the 1800s. These photographs show boys and girls in work situations about a century ago.

Learn the Skill *To formulate questions, use the following steps:*

1. **Examine the material.** Ask basic questions to help summarize what you are seeing or reading. Formulate questions that begin with *who, what, when, where,* and *how much.*
2. **Think of analytical questions.** These are questions that reflect a thoughtful approach to the information. They might begin with *how* or *why.*
3. **Ask questions that evaluate.** These call for judgments and opinions based on evidence.
4. **Formulate hypothetical questions.** Hypothetical questions involve the word *if.* They suggest possible outcomes, such as *if this happens, would such and such occur?*

Practice the Skill *Answer the following questions about the photographs above:*

1. **(a)** What kind of work are the people in each photograph doing? **(b)** Ask and answer a basic question of your own.
2. **(a)** How are the people dressed? **(b)** Form an analytical question of your own.
3. **(a)** Are the working conditions healthful or harmful? Explain. **(b)** Create an evaluative question.
4. **(a)** If young people work and don't go to school, what might happen? **(b)** Ask and answer a hypothetical question about the workers.

Apply the Skill *See the Chapter Review and Assessment.*

CHAPTER 20

Review and Assessment

Chapter Summary

Section 1
In the decades after the completion of the transcontinental railroad, the railroads developed into a big business controlled by a few powerful men. The U.S. economy benefited from the railroads.

Section 2
The steel and oil industries emerged as powerful forces in the late 1800s. Corporations and trusts fueled the growth of some industries, but some business leaders developed giant monopolies that reduced competition.

Section 3
Alexander Bell, Thomas Edison, Henry Ford, and the Wright Brothers were just a few of the innovators and inventors whose work improved general living conditions near the end of the nineteenth century.

Section 4
Factory conditions grew worse as the nineteenth century wore on, leading to the emergence of organized labor. Unions achieved a mixed record in their fight to protect workers' rights.

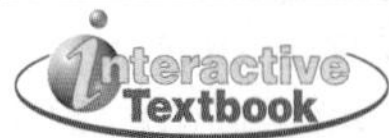

For additional review and enrichment activities, see the interactive version of *The American Nation,* available on the Web and on CD-ROM.

Chapter Self-Test For practice test questions for Chapter 20, visit PHSchool.com, **Web Code mfa-2004.**

Building Vocabulary

Write sentences that use the chapter vocabulary words listed below, leaving blanks where the vocabulary words would go. Exchange your sentences with another student, and fill in the blanks in each other's sentences.

1. **network**
2. **consolidate**
3. **rebate**
4. **corporation**
5. **stock**
6. **dividend**
7. **patent**
8. **transatlantic**
9. **strikebreaker**
10. **trade union**

Reviewing Key Facts

11. What methods did railroad companies use to limit competition? (Section 1)
12. What advantages did the corporation offer to investors? (Section 2)
13. What was the assembly line, and how did it transform manufacturing? (Section 3)
14. How was factory work in the late 1800s different from factory work before the Civil War? (Section 4)
15. How did the Triangle Fire influence public opinion? (Section 4)

Critical Thinking and Writing

16. **Connecting to Geography: Location** Study the map of industrial centers of the United States at the beginning of this chapter. Then, write a paragraph explaining why Pittsburgh's location helped it to become the steel-making capital of the United States.
17. **Identifying Causes and Effects** Suppose you were asked to create a graphic organizer in the shape of a pyramid showing the growth of American industry in the last half of the 1800s. At the bottom you plan to write three developments that caused this growth. What three developments would you choose?
18. **Summarizing** Summarize the arguments for and against monopolies and trusts.
19. **Identifying Bias** During the late 1800s, many people connected labor unions with violence and foreign influences. Why might people have associated these things with labor unions?

SKILLS ASSESSMENT

Analyzing Primary Sources

One of John D. Rockefeller's favorite sayings was "Every right implies a responsibility. Every opportunity, an obligation. Every possession, a duty." Late in life, Rockefeller wrote his only known poem. It summed up his approach to life so well that he had it printed on cards and distributed to many friends. It read:

> I was early taught to work as well as
> play;
>
> My life has been one long, happy
> holiday—
>
> Full of work, and full of play—
>
> I dropped the worry on the way—
>
> And God was good to me every day.
>
> —John D. Rockefeller, quoted in his obituary in *The New York Times*, May 24, 1937

20. According to Rockefeller, what was he taught early in life?
- **A.** how to worry
- **B.** the importance of long holidays
- **C.** how to become wealthy
- **D.** the importance of both work and play

21. What is the tone of Rockefeller's poem?
- **A.** sullen
- **B.** angry
- **C.** optimistic
- **D.** remorseful

APPLYING YOUR SKILLS

Formulating Questions

The cartoon above criticizes monopolies by showing Standard Oil as a huge octopus.

22. Which of the following is an analytical question you might ask the cartoonist?
- **A.** What is the building in the grip of the octopus?
- **B.** Why did you select the octopus as the main symbol of the cartoon?
- **C.** Who are the people at the bottom?
- **D.** When did you draw this cartoon?

23. Formulate an evaluative question about the cartoon.

ACTIVITIES

Connecting With . . . Economics

Advertising Catalog You work for the largest advertising agency in Chicago. Your boss has given you a challenging assignment: You are to create advertisements for a mail-order catalog that contains the new inventions discussed in this chapter. Write a one-paragraph description of the main features of three new inventions, and draw pictures for your ads. Then, organize your ads into a catalog.

Connecting to Today

Writing a Proposal Use the Internet to find sites dealing with the Rockefeller Foundation or the Carnegie Foundation for the Advancement of Teaching. Then, write a proposal for a project that you think deserves foundation support. For help in starting this activity, visit PHSchool.com, **Web Code mfd-2005.**

Collecting Data for a Project

Creating a Comic Strip Many of the business leaders who grew immensely wealthy during this period led fascinating and colorful lives. Use the Internet to find information about Jay Gould, Daniel Drew, William Vanderbilt, or Leland Stanford. Choose one of these people and draw a comic strip illustrating an interesting event in his life. For help in starting this activity, visit PHSchool.com, **Web Code mfd-2006.**

CHAPTER 21

A New Urban Culture

1865–1914

Mark Twain

The Statue of Liberty

AMERICAN EVENTS

1865 Mark Twain publishes "The Celebrated Jumping Frog of Calaveras County." Twain becomes one of the best-loved American writers.

1873 The first American kindergarten opens in St. Louis.

1886 The Statue of Liberty is dedicated in New York harbor. It becomes a symbol of welcome to new immigrants.

Presidential Terms:

Andrew Johnson	Ulysses S. Grant	Rutherford B. Hayes	James A. Garfield	Chester A. Arthur	Grover Cleveland
1865-1869	1869-1877	1877-1881	1881	1881-1885	1885-1889

1860 · 1875 · 1890

WORLD EVENTS 

▲ **1865** The Salvation Army is founded in London.

1881 ▲ The czar steps up persecution of Russian Jews.

Largest Cities in the United States, 1900

In 1900, there were 32 American cities with populations over 100,000—four times as many as before the Civil War.

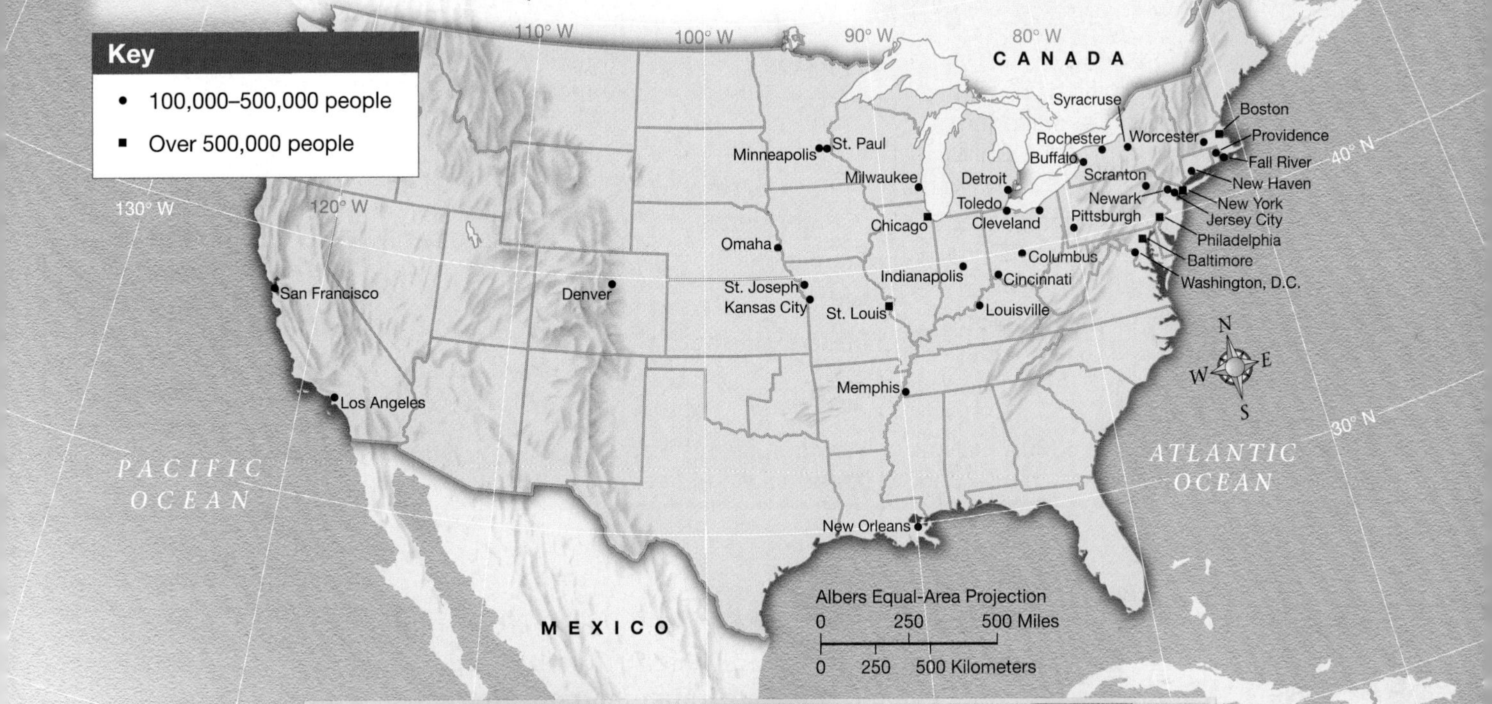

Key
- • 100,000–500,000 people
- ▪ Over 500,000 people

Boston subway station

1891
James Naismith invents basketball.

1897
The first subway system in the United States opens in Boston.

1910
Angel Island becomes processing center for Asian immigrants.

Benjamin Harrison	Grover Cleveland	William McKinley	Theodore Roosevelt	William H. Taft	Woodrow Wilson
1889–1893	1893–1897	1897–1901	1901–1909	1909–1913	1913–1921

1890 · · 1905 · · 1920 ·

▲ 1892
Arthur Conan Doyle publishes *Adventures of Sherlock Holmes.*

1910 ▲
The Mexican Revolution begins.

1 New Immigrants in a Promised Land

Prepare to Read

Objectives

In this section, you will
- Discuss why millions of immigrants decided to make the difficult journey to the United States.
- Describe the problems faced by the "new immigrants" in adapting to American life.
- Explain why some Americans were opposed to an increase in immigration.

Key Terms

push factor
pull factor
pogrom
steerage
Statue of Liberty
acculturation
nativist
Chinese Exclusion Act

Target Reading Skill

Sequence Copy this flowchart. As you read, fill in the boxes with stages in the process of immigration. The first box has been partly filled in.

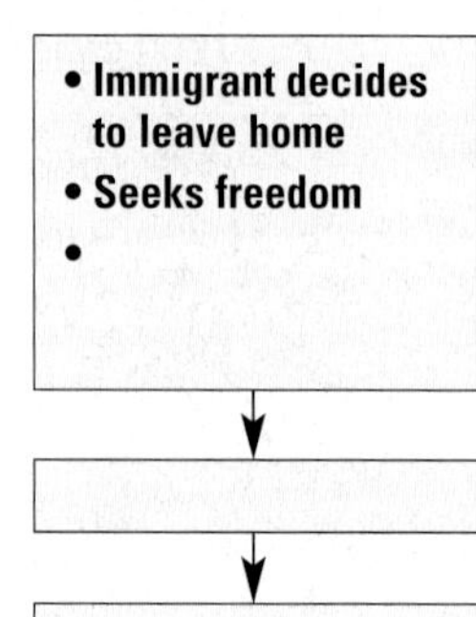

Main Idea In the late 1800s, millions of "new immigrants" came to the United States in search of economic opportunity and freedom.

Immigrants in New York

Setting the Scene For millions of immigrants, nothing quite matched their first sight of the "Promised Land"—America. Abraham Cahan, a Lithuanian-born journalist, wrote:

> "Imagine a new-born babe in possession of a fully developed intellect. Would it ever forget its entry into the world? Neither does the immigrant ever forget his entry into a country which is, to him, a new world . . . in which he expects to pass the rest of his life."
>
> —Abraham Cahan, *The Rise of David Levinsky*

Not all immigrants who came to the United States planned to remain. Pulled by the promise of work in industry, many hoped to make their fortunes and return home. But millions did end up staying. As new Americans, they helped to transform the nation.

Why Immigrants Came

Between 1865 and 1915, more than 25 million immigrants poured into the United States. They were part of a great network of some 60 million workers in search of jobs in industrial countries. As you have read, an industrial boom had created a huge need for workers.

Both push and pull factors played a part in this global migration. **Push factors** are conditions that drive people from their homes. **Pull factors** are conditions that attract immigrants to a new area.

Push Factors European immigrants were often small farmers or landless farmworkers. As European populations grew, land became scarce. Small farms could barely support the families that worked them. In some areas, new farm machines replaced farmworkers.

Political or religious persecution drove many people from their homes. In Russia, the czar supported **pogroms** (POH grahmz), or

Immigrants: Push and Pull Factors

Push Factors:	Pull Factors:
• Scarce land • Farm jobs lost to new machines • Political and religious persecution • Revolution • Poverty and hard lives	• Promise of freedom • Family or friends already settled in the United States • Factory jobs available

GRAPHIC ORGANIZER *Skills*

Push factors drove many people to leave their native countries. Pull factors drew them to the United States.

1. **Comprehension** Identify one push factor and one pull factor related to economics.
2. **Critical Thinking Linking Past and Present** Choose one push factor or pull factor listed here. Explain how that factor still brings immigrants to the United States.

organized attacks on Jewish villages. Persecution and violence also pushed Armenian Christians out of the Ottoman Empire (present-day Turkey).

Political unrest was another push factor. After 1910, a revolution erupted in Mexico. Thousands of Mexicans crossed the border into the southwestern United States.

Pull Factors Industrial jobs were the chief pull factor for immigrants. American factories needed labor. Factory owners sent agents to Europe and Asia to hire workers at low wages. Steamship companies offered low fares for the ocean crossing. Railroads posted notices in Europe advertising cheap land in the American West.

Often, one family member—usually a young, single male—made the trip. Once settled, he would send for family members to join him. As immigrants wrote home describing the "land of opportunity," they pulled other neighbors from the "old country." For example, one out of every ten Greeks immigrated to the United States in the late 1800s.

The promise of freedom was another pull factor. Many immigrants were eager to live in a land where police could not arrest or imprison you without a reason and where freedom of religion was guaranteed to all by the Bill of Rights.

A Difficult Journey

Leaving home required great courage. The voyage across the Atlantic or Pacific was often miserable. Most immigrants could afford only the cheapest berths. Shipowners jammed up to 2,000 people in steerage, the airless rooms below deck. On the return voyage, cattle or cargo filled the same spaces.

In such close quarters, disease spread rapidly. An outbreak of measles infected every child on one German immigrant ship. The dead were thrown into the water "like cattle," reported a horrified passenger.

Ellis Island

On tiny Ellis Island, millions of immigrants first set foot on American soil. Across the harbor was New York City, where many would soon make their homes. For years, Ellis Island was in disrepair. Now restored, the main building houses a museum of immigration. At the Ellis Island Web site, you can also search for individual immigrants by name.

Virtual Field Trip For an interactive look at Ellis Island, visit PHSchool.com, **Web Code mfd-2101.**

Identify Sequence (Target Skill) What stage in the process of immigration is described on this page? Add this information to your flowchart.

On the East Coast For most European immigrants, the voyage ended in New York City. Sailing into the harbor, they were greeted by the giant Statue of Liberty. Dedicated in 1886, it became a symbol of hope and freedom. A poem of welcome was carved on the base:

> "Give me your tired, your poor,
> Your huddled masses yearning to breathe free,
> The wretched refuse of your teeming shore.
> Send these, the homeless, tempest-tossed to me:
> I lift my lamp beside the golden door!"
>
> —Emma Lazarus, "The New Colossus"

In 1892, a new receiving station opened on Ellis Island. Here, immigrants had to face a dreaded medical inspection. Doctors watched newcomers climb a long flight of stairs. Anyone who limped or appeared out of breath might be stopped. Doctors also examined eyes, ears, and throats. The sick had to stay on Ellis Island until they got well. A small percentage who failed to regain full health were sent home.

With hundreds of immigrants to process each day, officials had only minutes to check each new arrival. To save time, they often changed names that they found hard to spell. Krzeznewski became Kramer. Smargiaso ended up as Smarga. Even the first name of one Italian immigrant was changed, from Bartolomeo to Bill.

Lucky immigrants went directly into the welcoming arms of friends and relatives. Many others stepped into a terrifying new land whose language and customs they did not know.

On the West Coast After 1910, many Asian immigrants were processed on Angel Island in San Francisco Bay. Because Americans wanted to discourage Asian immigration, new arrivals often faced long delays. One Chinese immigrant scratched these lines on the wall:

> "Imprisoned in the wooden building day after day,
> My freedom withheld; how can I bear to talk about it?"
>
> —Anonymous, quoted in *Strangers From a Different Shore* (Takaki)

Despite such obstacles, many Asians were able to make a home in the United States. Like European immigrants in the East, Asians on the West Coast faced a difficult adjustment.

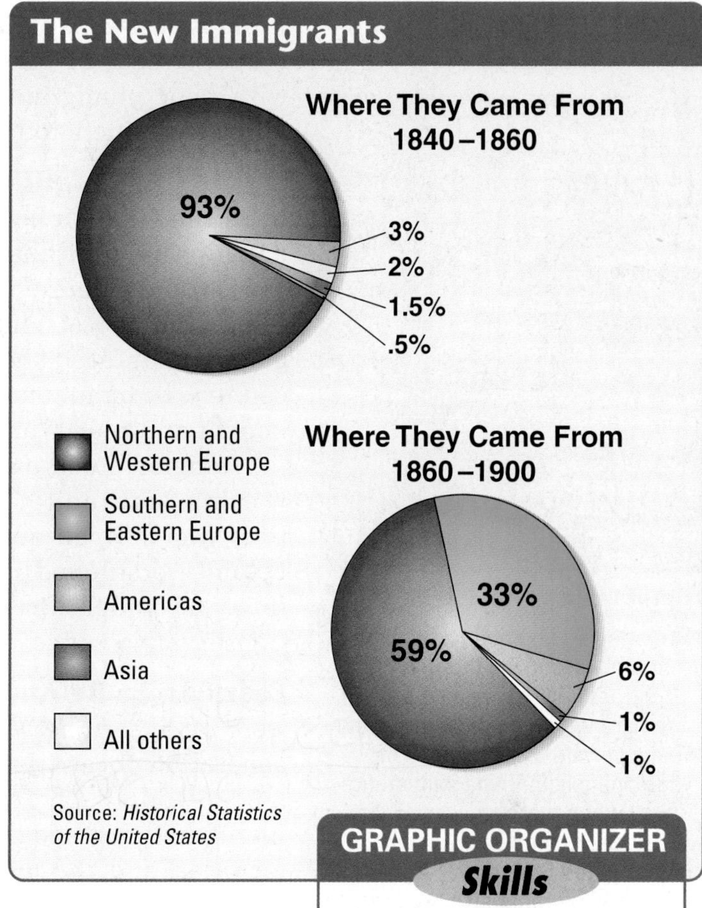

GRAPHIC ORGANIZER Skills

In the late 1800s, patterns of immigration to the United States began to shift.

1. **Comprehension** What percentage of immigrants came from Eastern and Southern Europe between 1840 and 1860? Between 1860 and 1900?
2. **Critical Thinking Drawing Inferences** Why would many immigrants who arrived between 1860 and 1900 find it harder to adapt than did earlier immigrants?

"Old" and "New" Immigrants

Immigration patterns changed in the late 1800s. Most earlier immigrants had been Protestants from Northern and Western Europe. Those from England and Ireland already spoke English. The early wave of English, Irish, Germans, and Scandinavians became known as "old immigrants." At first, Irish Catholics and other groups faced discrimination. In time, they were drawn into American life.

After 1885, millions of "new immigrants" arrived from Southern and Eastern Europe. They included Italians, Poles, Greeks, Russians, and Hungarians. On the West Coast, a smaller but growing number of Asian immigrants arrived, mostly from China and, later, from Japan. There were also a few immigrants from Korea, India, and the Philippines.

Few of these new immigrants spoke English. Many of the Europeans were Catholic, Jewish, or Eastern Orthodox. Immigrants from Asia might be Buddhist or Daoist. Set apart by language and religion, they found it harder to adapt to a new life.

Adapting to American Life

Many immigrants had heard stories that the streets in the United States were paved with gold. Once they arrived, they had to adjust to reality. "First," reported one immigrant, "the streets were not paved with gold. Second, they were not paved at all. Third, they expected me to pave them."

Newcomers immediately set out to find work. European peasants living off the land had had little need for money, but it took cash to survive in the United States. Through friends, relatives, labor contractors, and employment agencies, the new arrivals found jobs.

Most immigrants stayed in the cities where they landed. Cities were the seat of industrial work. City slums soon became packed with poor immigrants. By 1900, one neighborhood on New York's lower east side had become the most crowded place in the world.

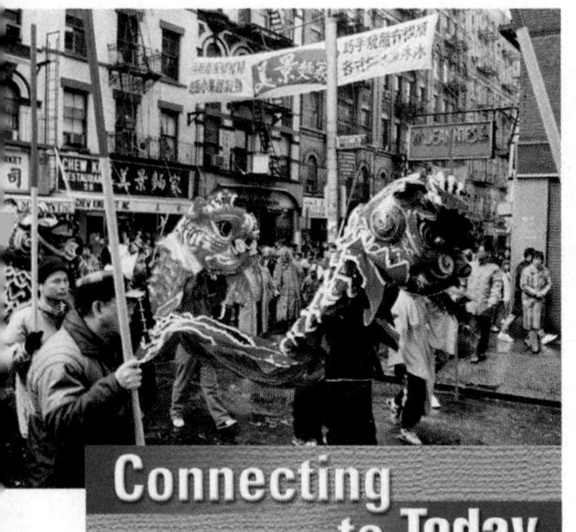

Connecting to Today

Celebrating Our Heritage

Firecrackers boom. Rockets flare. A dragon is snaking through the city streets! What is going on?

You are watching a Chinese New Year's parade. For hundreds of years, people in China shot off fireworks when the new year began. Today, the custom is alive and well in the United States.

Other immigrants also brought their holiday traditions to the United States. Irish Americans march in St. Patrick's Day parades. Italian Americans enjoy outdoor food festivals on the Feast of Saint Anthony. Mexican Americans mark Cinco de Mayo with parades, barbecues, and music. And you don't have to be Chinese, Irish, Italian, or Mexican to join in the fun.

In what other ways do Americans celebrate their ethnic heritage?

Immigrant Neighborhoods Immigrants eased into their new lives by settling in their own neighborhoods. Large American cities became patchworks of Italian, Irish, Polish, Hungarian, Greek, German, Jewish, and Chinese neighborhoods.

Within these neighborhoods, newcomers spoke their own language, celebrated special holidays, and prepared foods as in the old country. Italians joined clubs such as the Sons of Italy. Hungarians bought and read Hungarian newspapers.

Religion stood at the center of immigrant family life. Houses of worship both united and separated ethnic groups. Catholics from Italy worshipped in Italian neighborhood parishes. Those from Poland worshipped in Polish parishes. Jewish communities divided into the older Orthodox or Reform branches and the newer Conservative wing.

Learning to Be American As newcomers struggled to adjust, they were often torn between old traditions and American ways. The first generation to arrive acculturated. **Acculturation** is the process of holding on to older traditions while adapting to a new culture. Immigrants learned how to use American institutions such as schools, factories, and the political system. At the same time, they tried to keep their traditional religions, family structures, and community life.

In their effort to adapt, immigrants blended old and new ways. For example, some newcomers mixed their native tongues with English. Italians called the Fourth of July "Il Forte Gelato," a phrase that actually means "the great freeze." In El Paso, Texas, Mexican immigrants developed *Chuco,* a blend of English and Spanish.

Children adapted to the new culture more quickly than their parents. They learned English in school and then helped their families to speak it. Because children wanted to be seen as Americans, they often gave up customs that their parents honored. They played American games and dressed in American-style clothes.

Nativists Oppose Immigration

Even before the Civil War, Americans known as **nativists** sought to limit immigration and preserve the country for native-born white Protestants. As immigration boomed in the late 1800s, nativist feelings reached a new peak.

Nativists argued that immigrants would not fit into American culture because their languages, religions, and customs were too different. Many workers resented the new immigrants because they took jobs for low pay. Others feared them because they were different. One magazine described all immigrants as "long-haired, wild-eyed, bad-smelling, atheistic, reckless foreign wretches, who never did an honest hour's work in their lives."

Wherever new immigrants settled, nativist pressure grew. Nativists targeted Jews and Italians in the Northeast and Mexicans in the Southwest. On the West Coast, nativists worked to end immigration from China.

Chinese Exclusion Since the California Gold Rush, Chinese immigrants had helped build the West. Most lived in cities, in tight-knit communities called "Chinatowns." Others farmed for a living.

Most Americans did not understand Chinese customs. Also, some Chinese did not try to learn American ways. Like many other immigrants, they planned to stay only until they made a lot of money. They hoped to then return home, to live out their lives as rich and respected members of Chinese society. When that dream failed, many Chinese settled in the United States permanently.

As the numbers of Chinese grew, so did the prejudice and violence against them. Gangs attacked and sometimes killed Chinese people, especially during hard times.

Congress responded to this anti-Chinese feeling by passing the Chinese Exclusion Act in 1882. It barred Chinese laborers from entering the country. In addition, no Chinese person who left the United States could return.

The Chinese Exclusion Act was the first law to exclude a specific national group from immigrating to the United States. Congress renewed the original 10-year ban several times. It was finally repealed in 1943.

Restricting Immigration In 1887, nativists formed the American Protective Association. The group campaigned for laws to restrict immigration. Congress responded by passing a bill that denied entry to people who could not read their own language.

President Grover Cleveland vetoed the bill. It was wrong, he said, to keep out peasants just because they had never gone to school. Three later Presidents vetoed similar bills. Finally, in 1917, Congress overrode President Woodrow Wilson's veto, and the bill became law.

★ ★ ★ Section 1 Assessment ★ ★ ★

Recall

1. **Identify** Explain the significance of **(a)** Statue of Liberty, **(b)** Ellis Island, **(c)** Angel Island, **(d)** Chinese Exclusion Act.
2. **Define** **(a)** push factor, **(b)** pull factor, **(c)** pogrom, **(d)** steerage, **(e)** acculturation, **(f)** nativist.

Comprehension

3. Describe two push factors and two pull factors for immigration.
4. **(a)** Where did the new immigrants come from? **(b)** What problems did they face adjusting to life in the United States?
5. Why did nativists resent and distrust the new immigrants?

Critical Thinking and Writing

6. **Exploring the Main Idea** Review the Main Idea statement at the beginning of this section. Then, write a letter from an immigrant explaining your hopes and fears.
7. **Identifying Points of View** Write 2 or 3 sentences describing the process of acculturation from the viewpoint of immigrant parents. Then, write 2 or 3 sentences describing the same process from the children's viewpoint.

Activity

Go Online
PHSchool.com

Connecting to Today
Choose one of the groups of new immigrants mentioned in this section. Use the Internet to find out how that group helped shape modern American life and culture. Use your findings to give an oral report or create a poster. For help in completing the activity, visit PHSchool.com, **Web Code mfd-2102.**

2 An Age of Cities

Prepare to Read

Objectives

In this section, you will
- Explain why cities experienced a population explosion.
- Discuss how city settlement patterns changed.
- Describe how settlement house workers and other reformers worked to solve city problems.

Key Terms

urbanization
tenement
building code
Social Gospel
Salvation Army
Young Men's Hebrew Association
settlement house
Hull House

Target Reading Skill

Main Idea Copy the concept web below. As you read, fill in the blank ovals with information about the growth of American cities.

Main Idea Vast numbers of people migrated to cities, changing urban landscapes and creating new problems.

The Chicago Fire

Setting the Scene "The dogs of hell were upon the housetops . . . bounding from one to another," wrote Chicago journalist Horace White. He watched in horror as flames engulfed his city:

> "Billows of fire were rolling over the business palaces of the city and swallowing their contents. Walls were falling so fast that the quaking of the ground under our feet was scarcely noticed."
>
> —Horace White, Report to the *Cincinnati Commercial,* October 14, 1871

Fires were a constant danger in cities. Still, Americans agreed that they had never seen anything like the great Chicago Fire of 1871. Whipped by strong, dry winds, the blaze raced across the city, sometimes faster than a person could run. It killed nearly 300 people, left almost 100,000 homeless, and destroyed the entire downtown. Covered with factory grease and oil, even the Chicago River caught fire.

Yet, from the ashes, a new city rose. By the end of the century, Chicago was the fastest growing city in the world, with a population of over one million. Other American cities also underwent rapid population growth. For new and old Americans alike, the golden door of opportunity opened into the city.

Urban Populations Boom

"We cannot all live in cities," declared newspaper publisher Horace Greeley, "yet nearly all seem determined to do so." **Urbanization,** the movement of population from farms to cities, began slowly in the early 1800s. As the nation industrialized, the pace quickened. In 1860, only one American in five lived in a city. By 1890, one in three did.

Jobs drew people to cities. As industries grew, so did the need for workers. New city dwellers took jobs in steel mills, meatpacking plants, and garment factories. Others worked as salesclerks, waiters, barbers, bank tellers, and secretaries.

Immigrants and In-migrants The flood of immigrants swelled city populations. So, too, did migrations from farm to city within the country. As the frontier closed, fewer pioneers went west to homestead. In fact, many Americans left farms and migrated to cities to find a better life. One young woman summed up the feelings of many farmers toward their backbreaking work:

> "If I were offered a deed to the best farm . . . on the condition of going back to the country to live, I would not take it. I would rather face starvation in town."
>
> —quoted in *The Good Old Days—They Were Terrible!* (Bettmann)

African Americans Move to Cities African Americans, too, sought a better life in the cities. Most lived in the rural South. When hard times hit or prejudice led to violence, some headed to northern cities. By the 1890s, the south side of Chicago had a thriving African American community. Detroit, New York, Philadelphia, and other northern cities also had growing African American neighborhoods. The migration to the north began gradually, but increased rapidly after 1915.

As with overseas immigration, black migration usually began with one family member moving north. Later, relatives and friends followed. Like immigrants from rural areas in Europe, many African Americans faced the challenge of adjusting to urban life.

The Growth of Cities

Population Growth in Ten Selected Cities

City	Population in 1870	Population in 1900
New York	1,478,103	3,437,202
Chicago	298,977	1,698,575
Philadelphia	674,022	1,293,697
St. Louis	310,864	575,238
Boston	250,526	560,892
San Francisco	149,473	342,782
New Orleans	191,418	287,104
Denver	4,759	140,472
Los Angeles	5,728	104,266
Memphis	40,226	102,647

Rural and Urban Population in the United States, 1860–1920

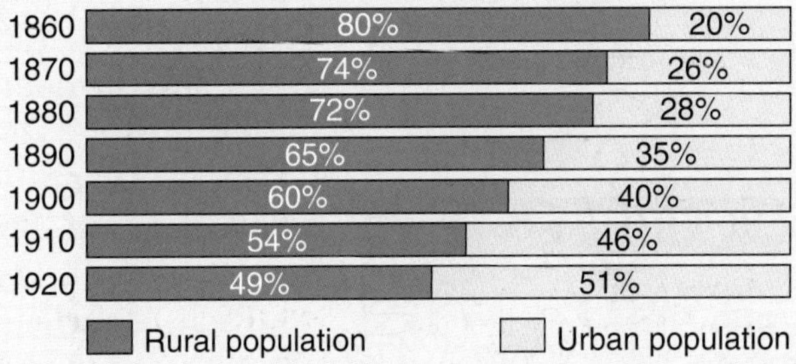

Year	Rural population	Urban population
1860	80%	20%
1870	74%	26%
1880	72%	28%
1890	65%	35%
1900	60%	40%
1910	54%	46%
1920	49%	51%

Sources: *Historical Statistics of the United States* and *Statistical Abstract of the United States*

GRAPHIC ORGANIZER *Skills*

The population of American cities grew rapidly after the Civil War.

1. **Comprehension** Between 1870 and 1900, which cities more than doubled in population?
2. **Critical Thinking Making Generalizations** Based on the bar graph, make one generalization about changes in the population of the United States.

Patterns of City Settlement

Cities grew outward from their old downtown sections. Before long, many cities took on a similar shape.

The Urban Poor Poor families crammed into the city's center, the oldest section. They struggled to survive in crowded slums. The streets were jammed with people, horses, pushcarts, and garbage.

Because space was so limited, builders devised a new kind of house to hold more people. They put up buildings six or seven stories high. They divided the buildings into small apartments, called **tenements.** Many tenements had no windows, heat, or indoor bathrooms. Often, 10 people shared a single room.

Crowding increased as factory owners moved into the city centers to take advantage of low rents and cheap labor. They took over buildings for use as factories, thus forcing more and more people into fewer and fewer apartments.

Typhoid and cholera raged through the tenements. Tuberculosis, a lung disease, was the biggest killer, accounting for thousands of deaths each year. Babies, especially, fell victim to disease. In one Chicago slum, around 1900, more than half of all babies died before they were one year old. Despite the poor conditions, the populations of slums grew rapidly.

The Urban Middle Class Beyond the slums stood the homes of the new middle class, including doctors, lawyers, business managers, skilled machinists, and office workers. Rows of neat houses lined tree-shaded streets. Here, disease broke out less frequently than in the slums.

Leisure activities gave middle-class people a sense of community and purpose. They joined clubs, singing societies, bowling leagues, and charitable organizations. As one writer said, the clubs "bring together many people who are striving upward, trying to uplift themselves."

The Rich On the outskirts of the city, behind brick walls or iron gates, lay the mansions of the very rich. In New York, huge homes dotted Fifth Avenue, which was then on the city's outskirts. In Chicago, 200 millionaires lived along the exclusive lakefront by the 1880s. In San Francisco, wealthy residents built their mansions nearer the center of the city, in the exclusive Nob Hill area.

Rich Americans modeled their lives on European royalty. They filled their mansions with priceless artwork and gave lavish parties. At one banquet, the host handed out cigarettes rolled in hundred-dollar bills.

Solving City Problems

As more and more people crowded into cities, problems grew. Garbage rotted in the streets. Factories polluted the air. Crime flourished. Thieves and pickpockets haunted lonely alleys, especially at night.

Viewing History

Lives of the Rich and Poor

These two photographs show the contrasting lives of families in New York City. The tenement family (left) lived near the center of the city. Wealthier families, like the one at right, lived closer to the outskirts.
Contrasting ***From these pictures, identify three differences between the lives of these two families.***

Tenement buildings were deathtraps if a fire broke out. News reporter Jacob Riis brought readers into the tenements in his startling expose, *How the Other Half Lives*. He wrote:

> "Step carefully over this baby—it is a baby, spite of its rags and dirt—under these iron bridges called fire-escapes, but loaded down . . . with broken household goods, with washtubs and barrels, over which no man could climb from a fire."
>
> —Jacob Riis, *How the Other Half Lives*

Identify Supporting Details

How did urban reform affect growing cities? Add this information to your concept web.

Urban Reforms By the 1880s, reformers pressured city governments for change. **Building codes** set standards for construction and safety. New buildings were required to have fire escapes and decent plumbing. Cities also hired workers to collect garbage and sweep the streets. To reduce pollution, zoning laws kept factories out of neighborhoods where people lived.

Safety improved when cities set up professional fire companies and police forces. Gas—and later electric—lights made streets less dangerous at night. As you will read, many cities built new systems of public transportation as well.

Pushed by reformers, city governments hired engineers and architects to design new water systems. New York City, for example, dug underground tunnels to the Catskill Mountains, 100 miles to the north. The tunnels brought a clean water supply to the city every day.

Religious Organizations Help the Poor Religious groups worked to ease the problems of the poor. The Catholic Church ministered to the needs of Irish, Polish, and Italian immigrants. An Italian-born nun, Mother Cabrini, helped found dozens of hospitals for the poor.

In cities, Protestant ministers began preaching a new **Social Gospel.** They called on their well-to-do members to do their duty as Christians by helping society's poor. One minister urged merchants and industrialists to pay their workers enough to enable them to marry and have families. He also proposed that they grant their workers a half day off on Saturdays.

In 1865, a Methodist minister named William Booth created the **Salvation Army** in London. It expanded to the United States by 1880. In addition to spreading Christian teachings, the Salvation Army offered food and shelter to the poor.

In Jewish neighborhoods, too, religious organizations provided community services. The first **Young Men's Hebrew Association** (YMHA) began in Baltimore in 1854. The YMHA provided social activities, encouraged good citizenship, and helped Jewish families preserve their culture. In the 1880s, the Young Women's Hebrew Association (YWHA) grew out of the YMHA.

The Settlement House Movement

Some people looked for ways to help the poor. By the late 1800s, individuals began to organize **settlement houses,** community centers that offered services to the poor. The leading figure of the settlement house movement was a Chicago woman named Jane Addams.

An American Profile

Jane Addams 1860–1935

Jane Addams developed her strong sense of duty early. Her father, a wealthy abolitionist, taught her that people should respect others and live moral lives. She also learned to value education. She wanted to become a doctor, but her own poor health ended that dream.

Recovering from an illness, Jane Addams traveled to Europe in 1888. There, she visited a settlement house in London. She and a friend decided to create such a place in Chicago. She devoted the rest of her life to making a better life for the poor.

How did Jane Addams's life reflect the values taught to her by her father?

Hull House Addams came from a well-to-do family but had strong convictions about helping the poor. After college, she moved into one of the poorest slums in Chicago. There, in an old mansion, she opened a settlement house, named **Hull House,** in 1889.

Other idealistic young women soon joined Addams. They took up residence in Hull House so that they could experience firsthand some of the hardships of the slum community in which they worked. These women dedicated their lives to service and to sacrifice—"like the early Christians," in the words of one volunteer.

Hull House volunteers offered a wide variety of services. To help immigrants acculturate, they taught classes in American government and the English language. Other volunteers gave instruction in health care or operated day nurseries for children whose mothers worked outside the home. In addition, Hull House provided recreational activities for young people, such as sports, a choral group, and a theater.

Over the years, the settlement house movement spread. By 1900, about 100 such centers had opened in cities across the United States.

Pressing for Reform Addams and her staff were an important influence in bringing about reform legislation. They studied the slum neighborhoods where they worked and lived. They realized that the problems were too big for any one person or group, and they urged the government to act.

Alice Hamilton, a Hull House doctor, campaigned for better health laws. Florence Kelley worked to ban child labor. Jane Addams herself believed that reform legislation would be speeded if women were allowed to vote. She joined the continuing campaign for women's suffrage.

★ ★ ★ Section 2 Assessment ★ ★ ★

Recall

1. **Identify** Explain the significance of **(a)** Mother Cabrini, **(b)** Social Gospel, **(c)** Salvation Army, **(d)** Young Men's Hebrew Association, **(e)** Jane Addams, **(f)** Hull House.
2. **Define** **(a)** urbanization, **(b)** tenement, **(c)** building code, **(d)** settlement house.

Comprehension

3. Why did American cities grow rapidly in the late 1800s?
4. Describe the settlement pattern of a typical American city.
5. **(a)** Identify two problems of growing cities. **(b)** How did reformers work to ease these problems?

Critical Thinking and Writing

6. **Exploring the Main Idea** Review the Main Idea statement at the beginning of this section. Then, draw a two-column chart. In the left column, list reasons for moving to the city from a poor farm. In the right column, list reasons for staying on the farm.
7. **Linking Past and Present** Write a paragraph comparing some of the problems faced by city dwellers in the late 1800s with problems faced by city dwellers today.

ACTIVITY

Writing a Proposal
You want to start a settlement house in a major American city in the late 1800s. Outline a proposal asking a wealthy contributor or a charity for funds to help you get started. Explain what services you plan to offer and how you will use the money.

Comparing Maps Over Time

History is the story of changes over time. By comparing maps from different time periods, you can see how historical changes affected a country, state, or city. The two maps below show settled areas (with at least one house per acre) in Kansas City, Missouri, at different times.

As a nation constantly on the move, Americans traveled West to build new lives. Small farm settlements became cities. Eventually, many cities—including Pittsburgh, Cincinnati, St. Louis, Louisville, Memphis, and St. Paul—appeared. Among the new crop of cities was the Town of Kansas, which became a city in 1853.

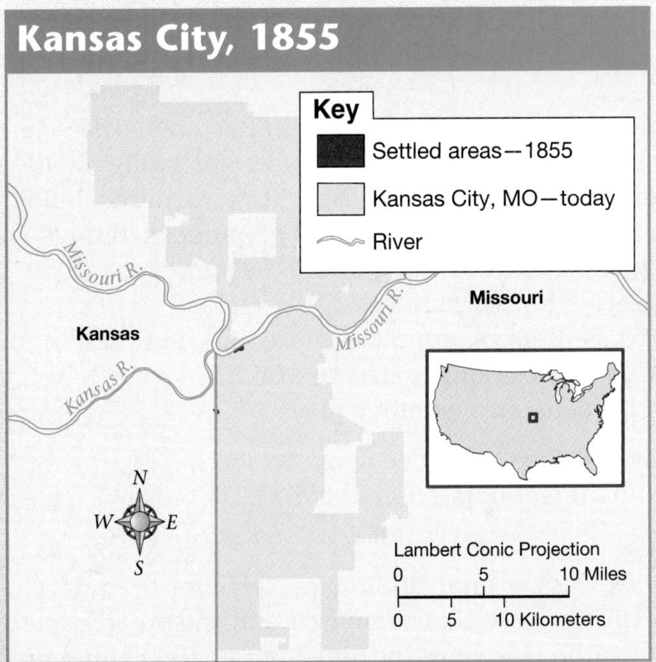

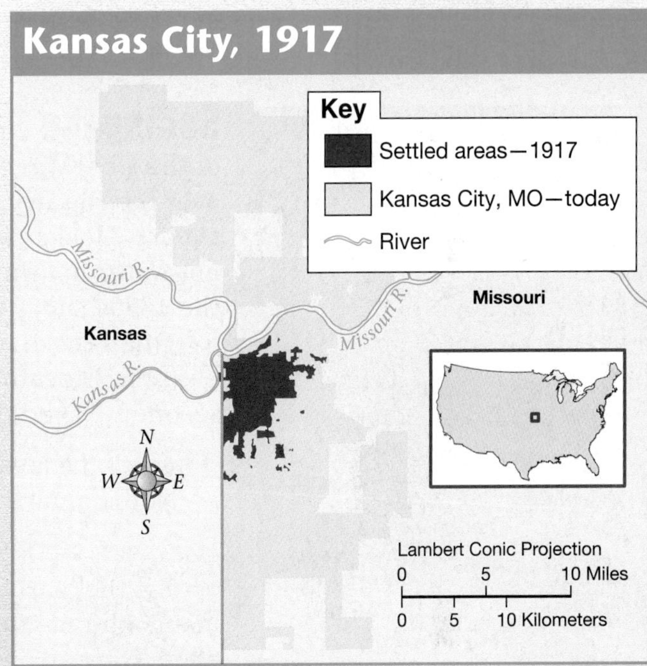

Learn the Skill *To learn to compare maps, use the following steps:*

1. **Check the subject and area shown on each map.** What do the title and labels tell you? Is the same area shown on each map?
2. **Study the map key.** Determine what symbols are used to present specific information.
3. **Compare the maps.** Use the data on the maps to make comparisons and note changes over time.
4. **Interpret the maps.** Think over what you already know about this period. Draw conclusions or make predictions.

Practice the Skill *Use the two maps above to answer the following questions:*

1. **(a)** What area is shown on both maps? Are they the same? **(b)** What is the date of each map?
2. **(a)** Do the two map keys give the same information? **(b)** What do their colors represent?
3. **(a)** Which were the settled areas in Kansas City in 1855? **(b)** How do the settled areas in 1917 differ from those in 1855?
4. **(a)** Based on the evidence shown on the maps, what conclusion can you reach about Kansas City during this time? **(b)** What changes would you expect to see on a later map of the same area?

Apply the Skill *See the Chapter Review and Assessment.*

3 Life in the Changing Cities

Prepare to Read

Objectives

In this section, you will
- Describe how the building boom affected city life.
- Explain why sports were so popular.
- List the forms of entertainment that city dwellers enjoyed.

Key Terms

skyscraper
suburb
department store
vaudeville
ragtime

Target Reading Skill

Reading Process Copy the table below. As you read, fill in the boxes with additional information about changes in city life.

CHANGING LANDSCAPE	NEW ACTIVITIES
• Skyscrapers • Streetcars • •	• Baseball • • •

Main Idea A building boom, new technology, and new leisure activities changed the way city dwellers lived.

Early elevator

Setting the Scene The first one appeared in Boston on the eve of the Civil War. Soon new "apartment hotels" were springing up all over the country. Some, like the Ansonia in New York, covered whole square blocks. They featured all the marvels of modern living—hot-water heating, kitchens, flush toilets, telephone service, and by the 1880s, electric lighting and appliances.

Of all these new conveniences, none was more amazing than the elevator. Elevators whisked residents to the top floors in a matter of seconds. Raved one character in a popular play:

> "It's the ideal way of living. All on one floor. No stairs. Nothing. All these apartment hotels have them."
>
> —William Dean Howells, *The Elevator*

By the early 1900s, less grand, one-room, "efficiency" apartments had begun to spring up in San Francisco and to spread eastward. New apartment buildings were but one sign of the changing landscape of American cities.

Target Skill — Use Prior Knowledge What other inventions from 1865–1915 have you learned about that might affect how people lived in cities?

A Building Boom

A building boom changed the face of American cities. Cities like Chicago and New York gradually began to run out of space in their downtown areas. Resourceful city planners and architects decided to build up instead of out.

Building Upward After fire leveled downtown Chicago in 1871, planners tried out many new ideas as they rebuilt the city. Using new technology, they designed **skyscrapers,** tall buildings with many floors supported by a lightweight steel frame. The first skyscraper, only nine stories tall, was built in Chicago in 1885. As technology improved, builders competed to raise taller and taller skyscrapers.

Newly invented electric elevators, like those installed in larger apartment buildings, carried residents and workers to upper floors.

Elevators moved so quickly, according to one rider, that "the passenger seems to feel his stomach pass into his shoes."

Moving People As skyscrapers crowded more people into smaller spaces, they added to a growing problem: traffic. Downtown streets were jammed with horse-drawn buses, carriages, and carts.

Electricity offered one solution. Frank Sprague, an engineer from Richmond, Virginia, designed the first electric streetcar system in 1887. Streetcars, or trolleys, were fast, clean, and quiet. Many trolley lines ran from the center of a city to the outlying countryside, creating the first suburbs. A **suburb** is a residential area on or near the outskirts of a city.

Other cities built steam-driven passenger trains on overhead tracks. In 1897, Boston built the first American subway, or underground electric railway. Subways and elevated railroads carried workers rapidly to and from their jobs.

Some cities needed ways to move masses of people across rivers or bays. In 1874, James B. Eads designed and built a three-arched bridge across the Mississippi River at St. Louis. The Eads Bridge was more than a quarter of a mile long. Nine years later, New York City completed the Brooklyn Bridge linking Manhattan Island and Brooklyn. Over a mile long, it contained a footpath and two railroad lines. The bridge was soon carrying 33 million people a year.

Public Parks While cities grew up and out, some planners wanted to preserve open spaces. They believed that open land would calm busy city dwellers.

In the 1850s, landscape architect Frederick Law Olmsted planned spacious Central Park in New York City. Other cities followed this model. They set aside land for public parks that contained zoos and gardens, so that city people could enjoy green grass and trees during their leisure time.

Shopping Shopping areas also got a new look. In the past, people had bought shoes in one store, socks in another, and dishes in a third. The new **department stores** sold all kinds of goods in different sections or departments.

In New York, R. H. Macy opened a nine-story department store in 1902. Its motto stated, "We sell goods cheaper than any house in the world." Soon, other cities had department stores. Shopping became a popular pastime. People browsed through each floor, looking at clothes, furniture, and jewelry. On the street, "window-shoppers" paused to view elaborate displays behind enormous new plate-glass windows.

Viewing History

A Street in Chicago

This photograph shows State Street in Chicago in the 1890s. Among the buildings shown here is Marshall Field's, Chicago's largest department store.

Applying Information ***Review the subsection A Building Boom. What other new features of cities can you identify in this photograph?***

Americans at Play

The rise of the factory split the worlds of work and play more sharply than ever. With less chance to socialize on the job, there was more interest in leisure. Sports provided a great escape from the pressures of work.

"Play Ball!" Baseball was the most popular sport in the nation. The game was first played in New York. During the Civil War, New York soldiers showed other Union troops how to play. By the 1870s, several cities had professional baseball teams and the first professional league was organized.

Early baseball was somewhat different from today's game. Pitchers threw underhanded. Catchers caught the ball after one bounce. Fielders did not wear gloves. As a result, high scores were common. One championship baseball game ended with a score of 103 to 8!

At first, African Americans played professional baseball. In time, though, the major leagues barred black players. In 1885, Frank Thompson organized a group of waiters into one of the first African American professional teams, the Cuban Giants of Long Island. They took the name "Cuban," not because they were from Cuba, but in hopes that all-white teams might be willing to play them.

Viewing History

The Days of Vaudeville

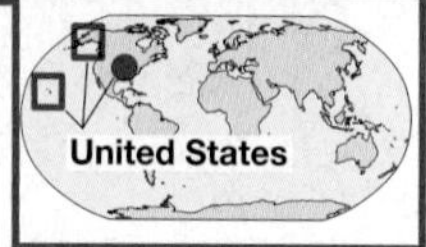

Audiences loved the ridiculous costumes and rowdy horseplay of comics such as Weber and Fields (top). A vaudeville program, or "bill," might also include a magician, an animal act, or even dancing "drummer girls" (bottom). **Drawing Conclusions** ***Why might sight gags and physical humor be popular with immigrant audiences?***

Football Football grew out of European soccer, which Americans had played since colonial times. Early football called for lots of muscle and little skill. On every play, the opposing teams crashed into each other like fighting rams. The quarterback ran or jumped over the tangle of bodies.

Players did not wear helmets and were often hurt. In 1908 alone, 33 college football players died from injuries. Some colleges banned the sport or drew up stricter rules of play for the game.

Basketball In 1891, James Naismith invented basketball. Naismith taught physical education at a Young Men's Christian Association (YMCA) in Springfield, Massachusetts. He wanted a sport that could be played indoors in winter. He nailed two bushel baskets to the gym walls. Players tried to throw a soccer ball into the baskets.

Basketball caught on quickly. It spread to other YMCAs and then to schools and colleges around the country.

A New World of Theater and Music

By the late 1800s, American cities supported a wide variety of cultural activities. Talented immigrants contributed to a new world of music and theater.

Music and other kinds of entertainment brought Americans together. People from different cultures sang the same songs and enjoyed the same shows. As railroads grew, circuses, acting companies, and "Wild West" shows toured the country. These traveling groups helped spread American culture beyond the cities to the small towns.

Variety Shows Many large cities organized symphony orchestras and opera companies. Generally, only the wealthy attended the symphony or the opera. For other city dwellers, an evening out often meant a trip to a vaudeville house. **Vaudeville** (VAWD vihl) was a variety show that included comedians, song-and-dance routines, and acrobats.

Vaudeville provided opportunities for people from many ethnic backgrounds, such as Irish American dancer-singer George M. Cohan and Jewish comedians like the Marx Brothers. Will Rogers, a performer of Cherokee descent, was one of the best-loved entertainers in the nation. Wearing a cowboy hat and twirling a rope, Rogers used gentle wit to comment on American life. "Everybody is ignorant," he said, "only on different subjects."

Popular Music Songwriters produced many popular tunes, such as "Shine On, Harvest Moon." Later, Thomas Edison's phonograph sparked a new industry. By 1900, millions of phonograph records had been sold.

Ragtime was a new kind of music with a lively, rhythmic sound. Scott Joplin, an African American composer, helped make ragtime popular. His "Maple Leaf Rag" was a nationwide hit.

In towns and cities, marching bands played the military music of John Philip Sousa. Sousa wrote more than 100 marches, including "The Stars and Stripes Forever." His marches became favorites at Fourth of July celebrations.

An American Profile

Scott Joplin 1868–1917

Growing up in Texas, Scott Joplin showed his musical talent at an early age. He was a fine singer and a skilled pianist. From his piano teacher, a German immigrant, Joplin learned to love classical music.

Joplin's popular rags combined bouncy ragtime rhythms with elements of European music. He wrote a textbook about ragtime, hoping that it would be recognized as a form of serious music. He even wrote ballets and operas, but they were rarely performed. Today, Joplin is most widely honored as the "King of Ragtime."

Why do you think Joplin wanted to use ragtime to write ballets and operas?

★ ★ ★ Section 3 Assessment ★ ★ ★

Recall

1. **Identify** Explain the significance of **(a)** Frank Sprague, **(b)** Frederick Law Olmsted, **(c)** R. H. Macy, **(d)** James Naismith, **(e)** Will Rogers, **(f)** Scott Joplin, **(g)** John Philip Sousa.
2. **Define** **(a)** skyscraper, **(b)** suburb, **(c)** department store, **(d)** vaudeville, **(e)** ragtime.

Comprehension

3. How did new technology change the face of American cities? Give three examples.
4. What sports became popular in the late 1800s?
5. How did entertainment unite Americans?

Critical Thinking and Writing

6. **Exploring the Main Idea** Review the Main Idea statement at the beginning of this section. Then, list what you think were the three most important developments mentioned in this section. Give reasons for your ranking.
7. **Identifying Causes and Effects** Write one sentence explaining the cause-and-effect relationship between population growth and the development of the skyscraper.

Activity

Designing a Poster

With a partner, create an illustrated poster advertising one of the following: the opening of a new subway or bridge, a new department store, a sporting event, a vaudeville show.

Connecting With... Culture

The Early Days of Baseball

As early as the American Revolution, George Washington's men played a game they called Base Ball. Not until 1834, however, did someone write a book of rules. At first, baseball was a hobby for those wealthy enough to have afternoons free. But by 1900, baseball had become "the national pastime."

Written in 1888, "Casey at the Bat" is one of the most popular American poems. It shows the devotion that fans felt toward home team heroes like the mighty Casey.

"Oh! Somewhere in this favored land the sun is shining bright;
The band is playing somewhere, and somewhere hearts are light.
And somewhere men are laughing, and somewhere children shout;
But there is no joy in Mudville—mighty Casey has Struck Out."

—Ernest Thayer, "Casey at the Bat"

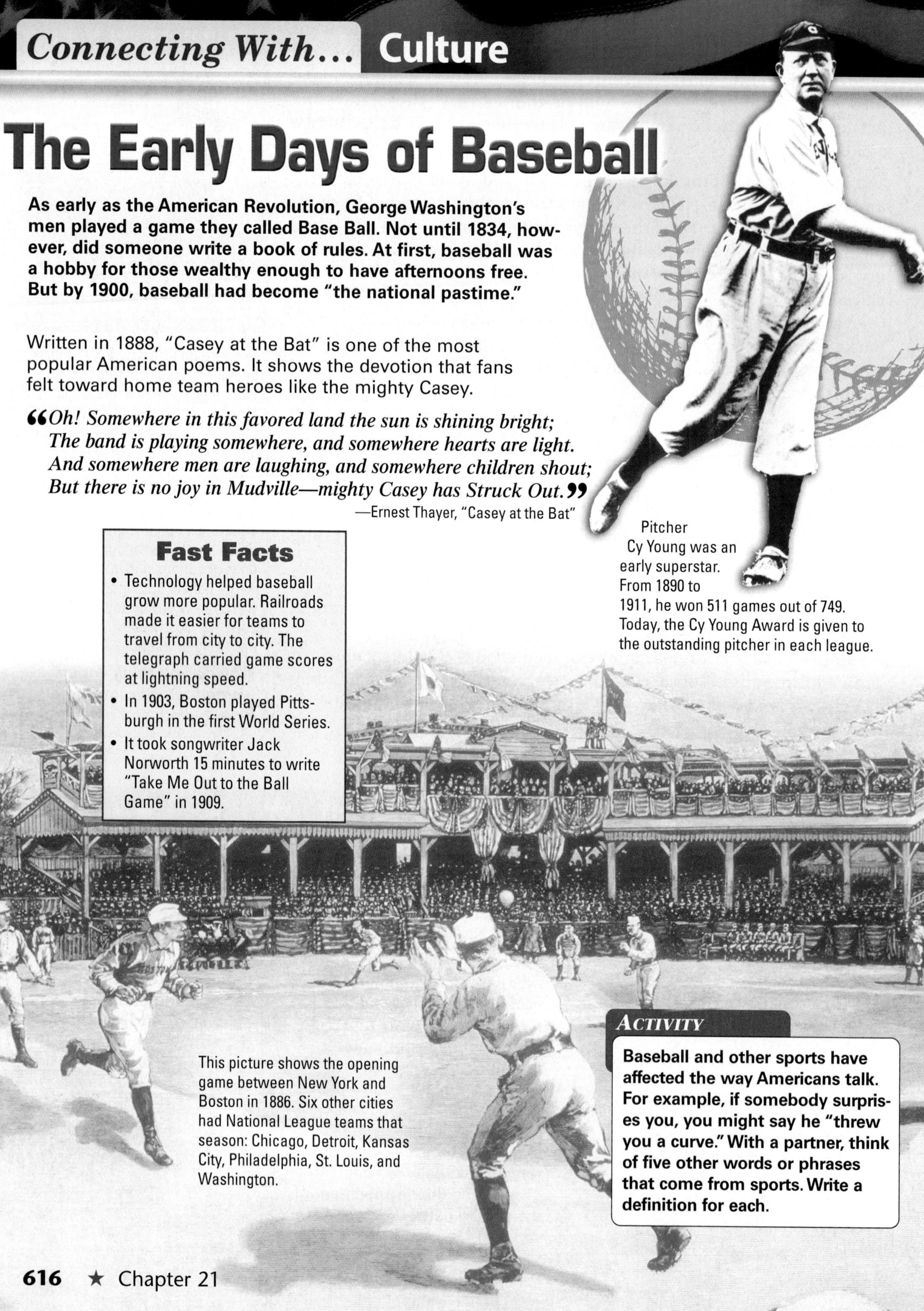

Pitcher Cy Young was an early superstar. From 1890 to 1911, he won 511 games out of 749. Today, the Cy Young Award is given to the outstanding pitcher in each league.

Fast Facts

- Technology helped baseball grow more popular. Railroads made it easier for teams to travel from city to city. The telegraph carried game scores at lightning speed.
- In 1903, Boston played Pittsburgh in the first World Series.
- It took songwriter Jack Norworth 15 minutes to write "Take Me Out to the Ball Game" in 1909.

This picture shows the opening game between New York and Boston in 1886. Six other cities had National League teams that season: Chicago, Detroit, Kansas City, Philadelphia, St. Louis, and Washington.

Activity

Baseball and other sports have affected the way Americans talk. For example, if somebody surprises you, you might say he "threw you a curve." With a partner, think of five other words or phrases that come from sports. Write a definition for each.

4 Public Education and American Culture

Prepare to Read

Objectives

In this section, you will
- Describe how public education grew after the Civil War.
- Identify changes in reading habits.
- Explain why writers and painters turned to everyday life for subjects.

Key Terms

compulsory education
parochial
Chautauqua Society
yellow journalism
dime novel
realist
local color

Target Reading Skill

Clarifying Meaning As you read, prepare an outline of this section. Use roman numerals to indicate the major headings, capital letters for the subheadings, and numbers for the supporting details.

I. Educating Americans
  A. Public schools
    1. First kindergartens
    2.
  B. The school day
    1.
    2.
II. Newspaper Boom
  A.
  B.

Main Idea The growth of public education was closely linked to other changes in American culture.

Setting the Scene The city of St. Louis tried a novel experiment in 1873. Following the lead of schools in Germany, the city opened the first American kindergarten. Children as young as three and four would be brought to school for part of the day. There, gentle teachers would help them to express themselves and learn to reason through songs, stories, and games. Educators believed that such creative play would give youngsters a head start on their education.

At the same time, children learned how to behave. Kindergartens taught cleanliness, politeness, and obedience. As public education spread, schools became centers of both learning and discipline.

Kindergarten class

Educating Americans

Before 1870, fewer than half of American children went to school. Many who did attended one-room schoolhouses, with only one teacher. Often, several students shared a single book.

Public Schools As industry grew, the nation needed an educated work force. As a result, states improved public schools at all levels. By 1900, there were 4,000 kindergartens across the nation.

In the North, most states passed **compulsory education** laws that required children to attend school, usually through sixth grade. In the South, which had no tradition of public schools, the Freedmen's Bureau had built grade schools for both African American and white students. By 1900, most southern schools were segregated.

In cities such as Boston and New York, public schools taught English to young immigrants. Children also learned about the duties and rights of citizens. In the 1880s, Catholics became worried that public schools stressed Protestant teachings. They opened their own **parochial,** or church-sponsored, schools.

The School Day The typical school day lasted from 8:00 A.M. to 4:00 P.M. Pupils learned the "three Rs": reading, 'riting, and 'rithmetic. Students memorized and recited passages from the most widely

Viewing History

A City Newsboy

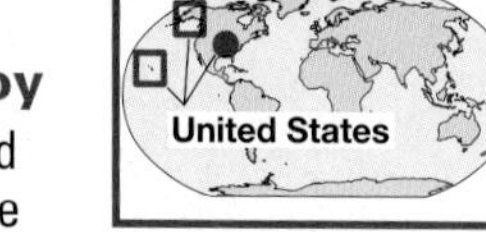

Introduced in 1895, the Yellow Kid (left) became the first popular comic strip character. Here, the Kid encourages other boys to sell the New York *Journal.* Drawing Conclusions ***Why might selling newspapers on the street be an appealing job for young city boys?***

used textbook, *McGuffey's Eclectic Reader.* With titles like "Waste Not, Want Not," the poems and stories taught not only reading but also religion, ethics, and values.

Schools emphasized discipline and obedience. Students had to sit upright in their seats, often with their hands folded in front of them. Punishment was swift and severe—a cuff on the head for whispering, or a paddling for arriving late.

Higher Learning After the Civil War, many cities and towns built public high schools. By 1900, there were 6,000 high schools in the country. Higher education also expanded. New private colleges for both women and men opened. Many states built universities that offered free or low-cost education.

To help meet the need for trained workers, the Chicago Manual Training School opened in 1884. It offered courses in "shop work," such as electricity and carpentry, as well as in a few academic subjects. Soon, most public schools in the nation had programs to prepare students for jobs in business and in industry.

Family Learning In 1874, a Methodist minister opened a summer school for Bible teachers along Lake Chautauqua in New York. The next year, the camp was opened to the general public. Mostly middle-class men and women of all ages gathered at Chautauqua each summer. In addition to receiving spiritual guidance, they enjoyed lectures about art, politics, philosophy, and other subjects.

In 1903, the Chautauqua Society began to send out traveling companies. Before long, Chautauquas were reaching as many as 5 million people in 10,000 American towns every year.

A Newspaper Boom

"Read all about it!" cried newsboys on city street corners. As education spread, people read more, especially newspapers. The number of newspapers grew dramatically. By 1900, half the newspapers in the world were printed in the United States.

The newspaper boom was linked to the growth of cities. In towns and villages, neighbors shared news face to face. In the crowded and busy cities, people needed newspapers to stay informed.

Newspapers reported on major events of the day. Most of them featured stories about local government, business, fashion, and sports. Many immigrants learned to read English by spelling their way through a daily paper. They also learned about American life.

Two Newspaper Giants Joseph Pulitzer, a Hungarian immigrant, created the first modern, mass-circulation newspaper. In 1883, Pulitzer bought the New York *World*. He set out to make it lively and "truly democratic." To win readers, Pulitzer slashed prices and added comic strips. Pictures and bold "scare" headlines attracted reader attention. The *World* splashed crimes and political scandals across its front page.

William Randolph Hearst challenged Pulitzer. Hearst's New York *Journal* began to outdo the *World* in presenting scandals, crime stories, and gossip. Critics complained that the papers offered less news and more scandal every day. They coined the term **yellow journalism** for the sensational reporting style of the *World* and the *Journal*.

Women as Readers and Reporters Newspapers competed for women readers. They added special sections on fashion, social events, health, homemaking, and family matters. Newspapers rarely pushed for women's rights, however. Most were afraid to take bold positions that might anger some readers.

A few women worked as reporters. Nellie Bly of the *World* pretended to be insane in order to find out about treatment of the mentally ill. Her articles about cruelty in mental hospitals led to reforms.

New Reading Habits

Americans also read more books and magazines. New printing methods lowered the cost of magazines. Magazines also added eye-catching pictures to attract readers.

Each magazine had its special audience. *The Ladies' Home Journal* appealed mostly to middle-class women. By 1900, it had one million readers. Other magazines, such as *Harper's Monthly* and *The Nation*, specialized in politics or current events.

Low-priced paperbacks, known as **dime novels,** offered thrilling adventure stories. Many told about the "Wild West." Young people loved dime novels, but parents often disapproved. "Stories for children used to begin, 'Once upon a time . . . ,' a critic complained. "Now they begin, 'Vengeance, blood, death,' shouted Rattlesnake Jim.' "

Horatio Alger wrote more than 100 dime novels for children. Most told of poor boys who became rich and respected through hard work, luck, and honesty. "Rags-to-riches" stories offered the hope that even the poorest person could succeed in the United States.

New American Writers

In the 1880s, a new crop of American writers appeared. For the first time, Americans were reading more books by American authors than by British authors.

Primary Source

Rags to Riches

Paul the Peddler *is a typical Horatio Alger story. Below, Alger describes the book's hero:*

". . . He knew there were plenty of ways in which he could earn something. He had never tried [shining shoes], but still he could do it in case of emergency. He had sold papers, and succeeded fairly [well] in that line, and knew he could again. He had pitted himself against other boys, and the result had been to give him a certain confidence in his own powers and business abilities. . . .

Paul had learned to rely upon himself; [and] the influence of a good, though humble, home, and a [wise] mother had kept him aloof from the bad habits into which many street boys are led."

—Horatio Alger, *Paul the Peddler*

Analyzing Primary Sources

Based on this passage, what qualities and values would help Paul succeed?

Viewing History

A Realist Painting Philadelphia painter Thomas Eakins often depicted sports scenes. This 1873 painting, *The Biglin Brothers Racing,* shows two famous rowers of the time. **Drawing Conclusions** ***How would his study of anatomy have helped Eakins create this painting?***

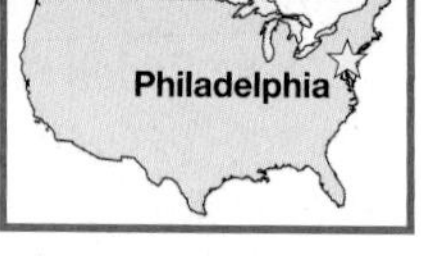

Realists One group of writers, called **realists,** tried to show the harsh side of life as it was. Many realists had worked as newspaper reporters. They had seen poverty and wanted to make people aware of the costs of urbanization and industrial growth.

Stephen Crane was best known for his Civil War novel, *The Red Badge of Courage.* Crane also wrote about the shattered lives of young city slum dwellers in novels like *Maggie: A Girl of the Streets.* Jack London, born in California, wrote about miners and sailors on the West Coast who put their lives at risk in backbreaking jobs.

Kate Chopin found an audience in women's magazines for her short stories about New Orleans life. Chopin's stories showed women breaking out of traditional roles.

Paul Laurence Dunbar was the first African American to make a living as a writer. He wrote poems, such as "We Wear the Mask," in a serious, elegant style. In other poems, he used everyday language to express the feelings of African Americans of the time.

Mark Twain The most famous and popular author of this period was Mark Twain, the pen name of Samuel Clemens. Twain had his first success in 1865 with his comical short story "The Celebrated Jumping Frog of Calaveras County."

Like many other writers, Twain used local color to make his stories more realistic. **Local color** refers to the speech and habits of a particular region. Twain captured the speech patterns of southerners who lived and worked along the Mississippi River.

In novels like *Huckleberry Finn,* Twain used homespun characters to poke fun at serious issues. Huck, a country boy, and Jim, an escaped slave, raft down the Mississippi River together in the days before the Civil War. Huck comes to respect Jim and to view slavery as wrong. Here, Huck talks about Jim's love for his family:

> "He was saying how the first thing he would do when he got to a free state he would go to saving up money, . . . and when he got enough he would buy his

wife, which was owned on a farm close to where Miss Watson lived; and then they would both work to buy the two children, and if their master wouldn't sell them, they'd get an Ab'litionist to go and steal them.❞

—Mark Twain, *The Adventures of Huckleberry Finn*

Although *Huckleberry Finn* became a classic, some schools and libraries refused to buy the book. They claimed that Huck was a crude character who would have a bad influence on "our pure-minded lads and lasses."

Painting Everyday Life

Like writers of the period, many artists sought to capture local color and the gritty side of modern life. In the late 1800s, leading artists painted realistic everyday scenes.

Paraphrasing Paraphrase the information about art during the late 1800s. Use your paraphrasing to fill in your outline.

During the Civil War, Winslow Homer drew scenes of brutal battles for magazines. Later, he gained fame for realistic paintings of the New England coast. Thomas Eakins learned anatomy and dissected dead bodies to be able to portray the human form accurately. Many of his paintings depicted sports scenes or medical operations. Henry Tanner, an African American student of Eakins, won fame for pictures of black sharecroppers. Later, Tanner moved to Paris to enjoy greater freedom.

Other American artists preferred to work in Europe, too. James Whistler left Massachusetts for Paris and London. His use of color and light influenced young European artists. Mary Cassatt (kuh SAT) also carved out a place for herself in the French art world. Cassatt painted bright, colorful scenes of people in everyday situations, especially mothers with their children.

★ ★ ★ Section 4 Assessment ★ ★ ★

Recall

1. **Identify** Explain the significance of **(a)** Chautauqua Society, **(b)** Joseph Pulitzer, **(c)** William Randolph Hearst, **(d)** Horatio Alger, **(e)** Stephen Crane, **(f)** Kate Chopin, **(g)** Paul Laurence Dunbar, **(h)** Mark Twain, **(i)** Thomas Eakins, **(j)** Mary Cassatt.
2. **Define** **(a)** compulsory education, **(b)** parochial, **(c)** yellow journalism, **(d)** dime novel, **(e)** realist, **(f)** local color.

Comprehension

3. How did American education change in the late 1800s?
4. Why did the number of American newspapers grow rapidly?
5. Identify three themes explored by realists in literature or art.

Critical Thinking and Writing

6. **Exploring the Main Idea** Review the Main Idea statement and the Setting the Scene story at the beginning of this section. Then, write a paragraph explaining the connection between education and new reading habits.
7. **Supporting a Point of View** Write a letter to Pulitzer or Hearst. Explain your views on his methods to increase newspaper circulation.

ACTIVITY

Writing a Museum Guide
Use the Internet to find other examples of American painting from 1865–1915. Choose one work, and prepare a write-up that might appear in a museum guide. Include the title, artist, and date, plus a description of the subject matter. For help in completing the activity, visit PHSchool.com, **Web Code mfd-2103.**

CHAPTER 21

Review and Assessment

Chapter Summary

Section 1
In the late 1800s, millions of "new immigrants" came to the United States in search of economic opportunity and freedom. As newcomers struggled to adjust, they were often torn between old traditions and American ways.

Section 2
Vast numbers of people migrated to cities, changing urban landscapes and creating new problems. Reformers began pressuring city governments for improvements in conditions.

Section 3
A building boom, new technology, and new leisure activities changed the way city dwellers lived. Organized baseball and entertainments such as vaudeville became very popular.

Section 4
The growth of public education was closely linked to other changes in American culture. In the North, most states passed compulsory education laws that required children to attend school.

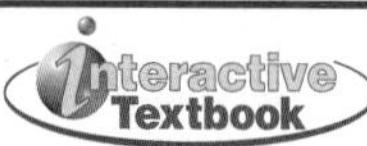

For additional review and enrichment activities, see the interactive version of *The American Nation,* available on the Web and on CD-ROM.

Chapter Self-Test For practice test questions for Chapter 21, visit PHSchool.com, **Web Code mfa-2104.**

Building Vocabulary

Use the chapter vocabulary words listed below to create a crossword puzzle. Exchange puzzles with a classmate. Complete the puzzles, and then check each other's answers.

1. **push factor**
2. **pull factor**
3. **acculturation**
4. **urbanization**
5. **tenement**
6. **skyscraper**
7. **suburb**
8. **vaudeville**
9. **ragtime**
10. **yellow journalism**

Reviewing Key Facts

11. Describe immigrant neighborhoods in American cities. (Section 1)
12. Why did cities set up building codes? (Section 2)
13. What services did religious organizations provide for the urban poor? (Section 2)
14. How did city planners deal with traffic problems? (Section 3)
15. How did schools prepare people for jobs in business and industry? (Section 4)

Critical Thinking and Writing

16. **Connecting to Geography: Regions** For each of the following factors, write a sentence explaining how it influenced the development of different neighborhoods within American cities: **(a)** ethnic makeup, **(b)** economic level, **(c)** transportation.
17. **Sequencing** Place the following developments in logical sequence: American cities boom, city governments do not provide adequate services, immigrants book passage on steamships, reforms help cities work better, peasants in Europe and Asia face economic hardships. Write a paragraph explaining how each development contributed to the next.
18. **Making Decisions** If you had been a city planner, would you have favored using city land and money to build public parks? List pros and cons. Then, explain your decision.
19. **Synthesizing Information** Make a diagram showing how the building of tenements, improvements in public education, and the move toward realism in literature were all linked to industrial growth.

Skills Assessment
Analyzing Primary Sources

Mary Antin, a Russian Jewish immigrant, came to the United States in 1890. Here, she speaks of the opportunities in her new home:

> "Education was free. That subject my father had written about repeatedly, as comprising his chief hope for us children, the essence of American opportunity, the treasure that no thief could touch, not even misfortune or poverty. It was the one thing that he was able to promise us when he sent for us; surer, safer than bread or shelter. . . . No application made, no questions asked, no examinations, rulings, exclusions. . . . The doors stood open for every one of us."
>
> —Mary Antin, *The Promised Land*

20. Why do you think Antin's father wanted to take his family out of Russia?
A. Jews were being persecuted in Russia.
B. Russia had expelled its Jewish population.
C. Passage to America was inexpensive.
D. Antin was opposed to communism.

21. What did Mary Antin describe as "the essence of American opportunity"?
A. abundant jobs
B. free land
C. the right to vote
D. free education

Applying Your Skills
Comparing Maps Over Time

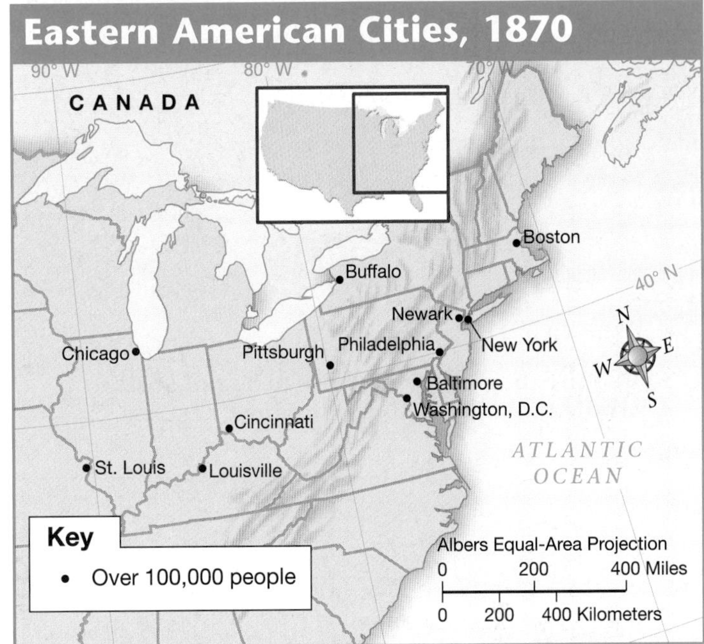

Compare this map with the one on page 599. Then, answer the questions that follow.

22. Which city's population passed the 100,000 mark between 1870 and 1900?
A. Philadelphia
B. Detroit
C. Albany
D. Baltimore

23. What changes would you expect to see on a later map of the same area?

Activities

Connecting With . . . Culture

Planning a Story With a partner, outline the plot for a "rags-to-riches" story like those written by Horatio Alger. Your main character is a young immigrant or a farmer who comes to live in the city in the late 1800s. Consider your character's hardships and how he or she becomes successful.

Connecting to Today

Comparing News Media Today, most newspapers operate their own Web sites. Use the Internet to find the Web site for a local newspaper. Compare the Web site with an edition of the newspaper. Then, write a letter to the editor explaining which is the best method for citizens to stay informed and why. For help in starting this activity, visit PHSchool.com, **Web Code mfd-2105.**

Researching

Preparing a News Report Use the Internet to find out more about the Chicago Fire of 1871. Then, with a small group, prepare a news report on the fire. Focus on the causes of the fire and its impact on the city. Include interviews with witnesses and an editorial on what the city should do in the future. For help in starting this activity, visit PHSchool.com, **Web Code mfd-2106.**

TEST PREPARATION

1 Which urban innovation was most closely linked to the growth of suburbs?

A Apartment buildings
B Streetcars
C Skyscrapers
D Department stores

Use the map <u>and</u> your knowledge of social studies to answer the following question.

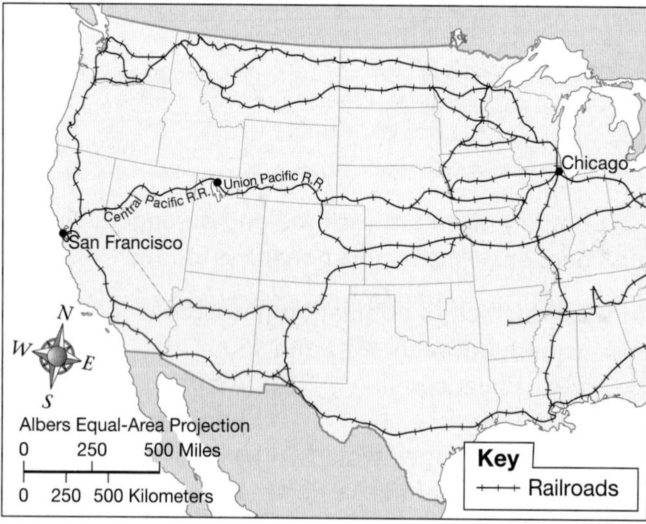

2 Which of the following questions would this map not help you answer?

A Where was the first transcontinental railroad completed?
B What railroad routes could a company use to ship goods from the Pacific Ocean to the Great Lakes?
C What geographic obstacles did western railroad builders have to overcome?
D What was the length of the shortest railway route from Chicago to San Francisco?

3 Which statement is true of both the Knights of Labor and the American Federation of Labor?

A It officially supported the use of strikes.
B It was open to both skilled and unskilled workers.
C Its goals included a shorter workday.
D Its goals included equal pay for men and women.

4 Which of the following was not a goal of the Populist party?

A Free silver
B Regulation of railroad rates
C Open immigration
D An income tax

Use the quotations <u>and</u> your knowledge of social studies to answer the following question.

John H. Vincent, 1886 [adapted]

"No man has a right to neglect his personal education, whether he be prince or plowboy."

"All knowledge, religious or worldly, is sacred."

"Between the ages of 20 and 80 lie a person's best educational opportunities."

5 The quotations most closely reflect the goals of what movement?

A The Chautauqua movement
B The settlement house movement
C The kindergarten movement
D The Social Gospel movement

Use the table <u>and</u> your knowledge of social studies to answer the following question.

United States Patents, 1861–1900

Five-Year Periods	Number of Patents
1861–1865	20,725
1866–1870	58,734
1871–1875	60,976
1876–1880	64,462
1881–1885	97,156
1886–1890	110,358
1891–1895	108,420
1896–1900	112,188

Source: *Historical Statistics of the United States*

6 Which statement is best supported by the table?

A The number of patents issued increased steadily from the Civil War to 1900.

B More patents were issued in 1880 than in 1870.

C More patents were issued between 1886 and 1895 than between 1876 and 1885.

D The average number of patents issued every year between 1891 and 1895 was 10,842.

7 Which of the following would be an example of vertical integration?

A The owner of an oil refinery buys up oil-drilling operations.

B The owner of a railroad buys up other railroads.

C A banker loans capital to two different copper-mining companies.

D Three different steel companies are run by the same board of directors.

8 In which of the following pairs was the first event a direct cause of the second?

A Spread of the Ghost Dance; Chivington Massacre

B Destruction of the buffalo; Battle of Little Bighorn

C Fort Laramie treaty; end of warfare between whites and Indians

D Discovery of gold in Black Hills; Sioux War

9 "The large mass of illiterate immigrants . . . is a menace, socially, industrially, and politically." Who would have been most likely to agree with this statement?

A Jane Addams

B A member of the American Protective Association

C An immigration official at Ellis Island

D Joseph Pulitzer

Writing Practice

10 "On balance, the rapid growth of industry in the late 1800s was beneficial to the nation." List two facts that support this statement. Then, explain whether you agree or disagree and why.

11 How were the reasons that settlers moved to the western frontier in the late 1800s similar to or different from the reasons that immigrants came to the United States?

Unit 7

A New Role for the Nation

UNIT OUTLINE

Chapter 22
The Progressive Era (1876–1920)

Chapter 23
Becoming a World Power (1865–1916)

Chapter 24
World War I (1914–1919)

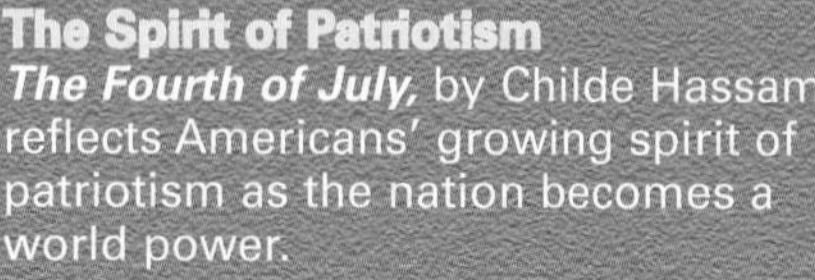

The Spirit of Patriotism
The Fourth of July, by Childe Hassam, reflects Americans' growing spirit of patriotism as the nation becomes a world power.

“Whether they will or no, Americans must begin to look outward. The growing production of the country demands it.”

—Alfred Thayer Mahan, naval officer (1897)

CHAPTER 22

The Progressive Era

1876–1920

1. Reform in the Gilded Age
2. The Progressives
3. Progressives in the White House
4. Women Win Reforms
5. Other Americans Seek Justice

Cartoon attacks on the spoils system

Jacob Riis's photo of a New York City slum apartment

AMERICAN EVENTS

1883 The Pendleton Act creates a commission to conduct exams for federal job seekers.

1890 With stark views of urban poverty, Jacob Riis's book *How the Other Half Lives* shocks middle-class readers.

1895 W.E.B. Du Bois becomes the first African American to receive a Ph.D. from Harvard University.

Presidential Terms: Ulysses S. Grant 1869–1877 | Rutherford B. Hayes 1877–1881 | James Garfield 1881 | Chester A. Arthur 1881–1885 | Grover Cleveland 1885–1889 | Benjamin Harrison 1889–1893 | Grover Cleveland 1893–1897 | William McKinley 1897–1901

1870 · 1885 · 1900

WORLD EVENTS

1893 ▲ New Zealand becomes the first nation to give women the right to vote.

The Vote for Women by 1919

By 1919, women in most states had won the right to vote in state and local elections.

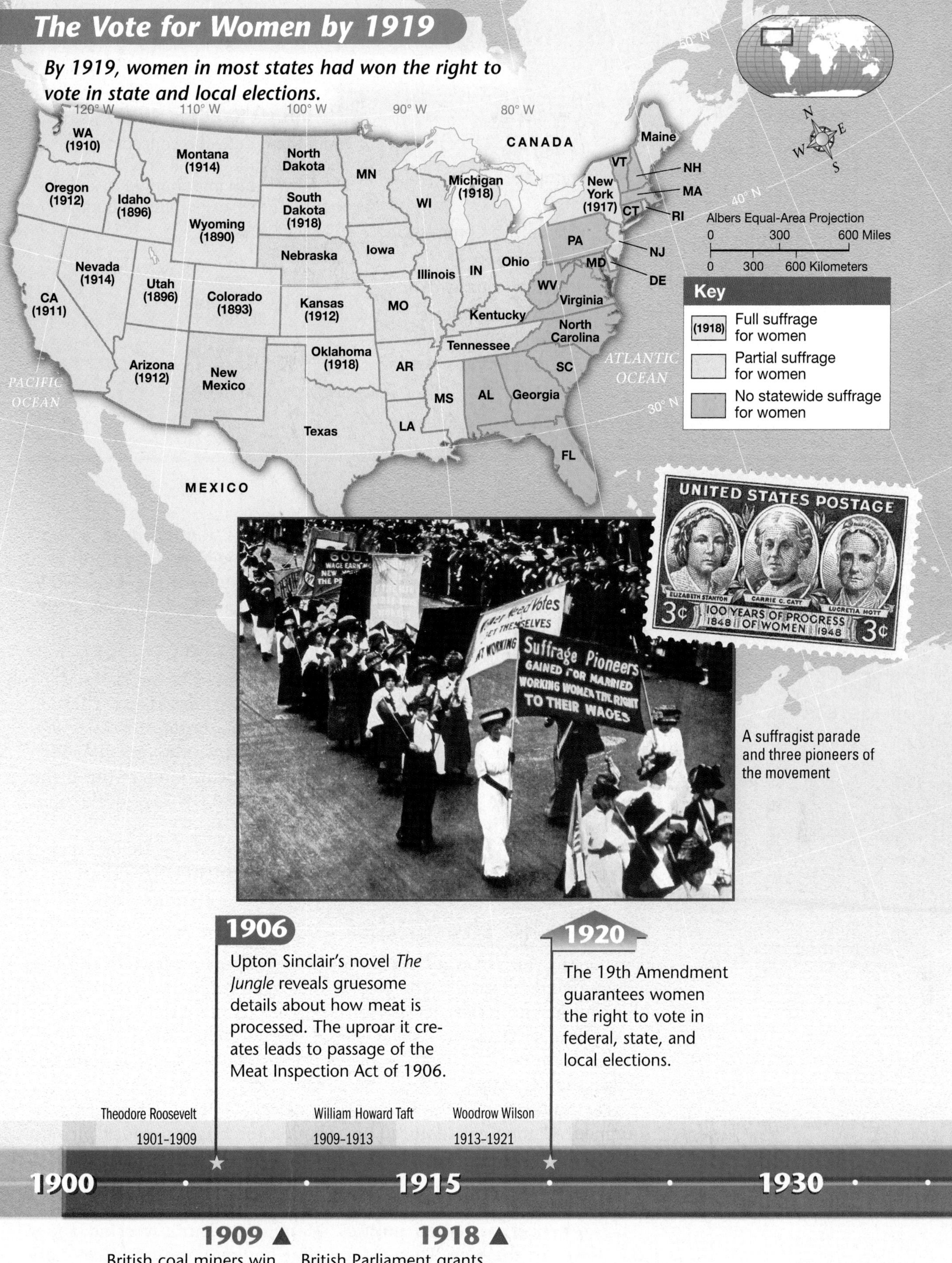

A suffragist parade and three pioneers of the movement

1906
Upton Sinclair's novel *The Jungle* reveals gruesome details about how meat is processed. The uproar it creates leads to passage of the Meat Inspection Act of 1906.

1920
The 19th Amendment guarantees women the right to vote in federal, state, and local elections.

Theodore Roosevelt 1901–1909
William Howard Taft 1909–1913
Woodrow Wilson 1913–1921

1900 · 1915 · 1930

1909 ▲
British coal miners win an eight-hour day.

1918 ▲
British Parliament grants the right to vote to women over the age of 30.

1 Reform in the Gilded Age

Prepare to Read

Objectives

In this section, you will
- Identify concerns that shaped politics during the Gilded Age.
- Explain how reformers tried to change the spoils system.
- List the laws that were passed to regulate big business.

Key Terms

Gilded Age
patronage
merit
Civil Service Commission
civil service
interstate commerce
Interstate Commerce Commission
Sherman Antitrust Act

Target Reading Skill

Main Idea Copy the concept web below. As you read, fill in each blank oval with important facts about reforms accomplished during the Gilded Age.

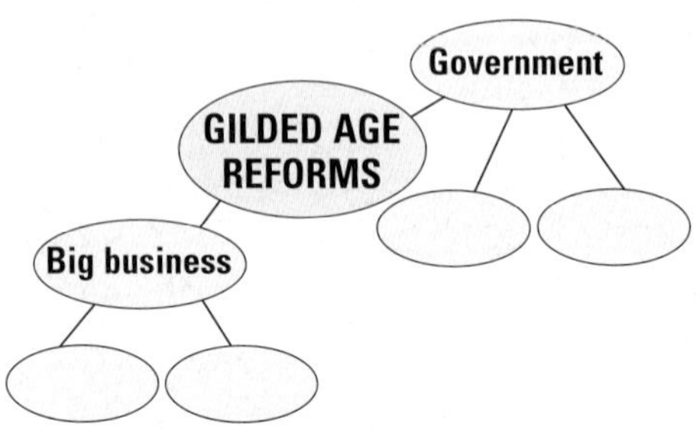

Main Idea During the Gilded Age, reformers worked to end political corruption and limit the power of big business.

An American palace

Setting the Scene The newly rich Martin family threw a huge and expensive party. They rented a fancy New York City hotel and transformed it to look like the palace of France's King Louis XIV. Critics condemned such extravagance. They pointed out that at the time, two in five Americans were out of work.

Wild spending by the wealthy was typical of the **Gilded Age** of the late 1800s. This era got its name from an 1873 novel by Mark Twain and Charles Dudley Warner titled *The Gilded Age.* ("Gilded" means coated with a thin layer of gold paint. It implies falseness beneath surface glitter.) For many Americans, the novel, which poked fun at the era's greed and political corruption, captured the spirit of the time. In the words of one observer, it was government "of, by, and for the rich."

The Gilded Age lasted from the 1870s through the 1890s. During this time, reformers struggled to clean up political corruption.

Politics in the Gilded Age

During the Gilded Age, political power was split between the two major parties. Usually, the North and West voted Republican, and the South voted Democrat. Neither party controlled Congress for more than a term or two, although Republicans held the White House for nearly 25 years. However, Presidents generally had less power than Congress during the period.

For Americans of the Gilded Age, elections provided great entertainment. Campaigns featured brass bands, torchlight parades, picnics, and long speeches. Americans marched, ate, drank, and listened. The turnout of voters was never again as high—almost 80 percent of eligible voters.

Two concerns shaped politics. Many Americans worried about the power of the rich. They feared that bankers, industrialists, and other wealthy men were controlling politics at the expense of the public good. The other worry was corruption, especially bribery and voter fraud. Reformers blamed much of the problem on the spoils system, the practice of rewarding political supporters with government jobs.

Reforming the Spoils System

The spoils system had grown since the days of Andrew Jackson. When a new President took office, job seekers swarmed into Washington. They demanded government jobs as rewards for their political support. Giving jobs to followers is called **patronage.**

Patronage often led to corruption. Some jobholders simply stole public money. Others had no skills for the jobs they were given. In New York, for example, one man was made court reporter even though he could neither read nor write.

Early Reform Efforts Calls for reform slowly brought change. In 1877, President Rutherford B. Hayes took steps toward ending the spoils system. He ordered an investigation of the New York customhouse. There, investigators found hundreds of appointed officials receiving high salaries but doing no work. Despite the protests of local Republican leaders, Hayes dismissed two customhouse officials. (See American Profile at right.)

In 1881, James Garfield entered the White House and was soon swamped with office seekers. He thought that government jobs should be awarded on the basis of **merit,** or ability, not politics.

That July, however, a disappointed office seeker, Charles Guiteau (gee TOH), shot the President. Garfield died two months later. The assassination sparked new efforts to end the spoils system.

Civil Service Exams Vice President Chester A. Arthur succeeded Garfield. Arthur was a product of the spoils system. In fact, he was one of the New York customhouse officials dismissed by Hayes a few years earlier! Yet, as President, Arthur worked with Congress to reform the spoils system.

In 1883, Congress passed the Pendleton Act. It created the **Civil Service Commission** to conduct exams for federal jobs. The **civil service** includes all federal jobs except elected offices and the military. The aim of the Civil Service Commission was to fill jobs on the basis of merit. People who scored highest on the civil service exams earned the posts.

At first, the Civil Service Commission controlled only a few federal jobs. However, under pressure from reformers, later Presidents placed more jobs under the Civil Service Commission. By 1900, the commission controlled about 40 percent of all federal jobs.

An American Profile

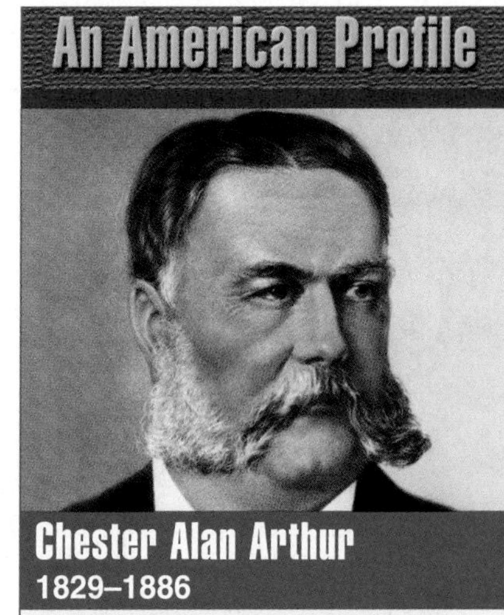

Chester Alan Arthur
1829–1886

Although Chester A. Arthur was an honorable man, he believed firmly in the spoils system. While running the New York customhouse, he employed far more people than the customhouse needed. These employees were loyal party workers.

In 1878, President Hayes fired Arthur. New York City bosses then turned on Hayes. To win them back, Republican leaders offered Arthur the vice presidential nomination.

To the horror of reformers, Arthur became President when President Garfield was assassinated in 1881. They were amazed when President Arthur went on to become a champion of civil service reform.

Why do you think President Arthur worked so hard to end the spoils system?

Regulating Big Business

Target Skill — Identify Main Ideas As you read this subsection, look for ways in which the government tried to regulate big business. Add this information to your concept web.

In 1877, Collis Huntington, builder of the Central Pacific Railroad, tried to bribe members of Congress to kill a railroad bill that would be unfavorable to his interests. He gave large amounts of money to members of Congress. "It costs money to fix things," Huntington explained.

Interstate Commerce Act The behavior of men like Huntington convinced many Americans that big businesses controlled the government. They demanded that something be done to limit the power of big business.

In response, the government began to regulate railroads and other large businesses. Under the Constitution, the federal government had the power to regulate **interstate commerce,** or business that crossed state lines. In 1887, President Grover Cleveland signed the Interstate Commerce Act. It forbade practices such as pools and rebates. (See Chapter 20.) It also set up the **Interstate Commerce Commission,** or ICC, to oversee the railroads.

At first, the ICC was weak. In court challenges, most judges ruled in favor of the railroads. Still, Congress had shown that it was ready to regulate big business. Later, Congress passed laws that made the ICC more effective.

Sherman Antitrust Act In 1888, President Cleveland lost his bid for reelection. Benjamin Harrison became President. In 1890, Harrison signed the **Sherman Antitrust Act.** The act prohibited businesses from trying to limit or destroy competition.

The Sherman Antitrust Act sounded strong, but enforcing it proved difficult. At first, judges ruled in favor of trusts. They held that the law was an illegal attempt by the government to control private property.

Instead of regulating trusts, the Sherman Antitrust Act was often used against labor unions. The courts said union strikes blocked free trade and thus threatened competition. Later on, as the reform spirit spread, the courts began to use the Sherman Act against monopolies.

★ ★ ★ Section 1 Assessment ★ ★ ★

Recall

1. **Identify** Explain the significance of **(a)** Gilded Age, **(b)** Chester A. Arthur, **(c)** Civil Service Commission, **(d)** Interstate Commerce Commission, **(e)** Sherman Antitrust Act.
2. **Define** **(a)** patronage, **(b)** merit, **(c)** civil service, **(d)** interstate commerce.

Comprehension

3. What two political concerns shaped politics during the Gilded Age?
4. What reforms were made to end the spoils system?
5. Describe two new laws that tried to limit the power of big business.

Critical Thinking and Writing

6. **Exploring the Main Idea** Review the Main Idea statement at the beginning of this chapter. Then, suppose that you have a government job as a result of patronage. Write two entries in your diary: one about how you got your job, and a second one telling what you think of replacing patronage with a civil service system.
7. **Drawing Conclusions** Why do you think early efforts to regulate big business had little success?

ACTIVITY

Go Online
PHSchool.com

Connecting to Today
Use the Internet to find out about current antitrust activities by the United States government. Select one recent antitrust case, and describe the major issues involved in it. Which side in the case do you think is right? For help in completing the activity, visit PHSchool.com, **Web Code mfd-2201.**

2 The Progressives

Prepare to Read

Objectives

In this section, you will
- Describe how corruption affected city governments.
- Explain why the muckrakers were an important force for reform.
- Identify the goals that the Progressives pursued.
- Summarize the political reforms that the Progressives achieved.

Key Terms

political boss
muckraker
Progressive
public interest
primary
initiative
referendum
recall
graduated income tax

Target Reading Skill

Cause and Effect As you read, complete the following chart to show how Progressive reforms shaped the era in three areas.

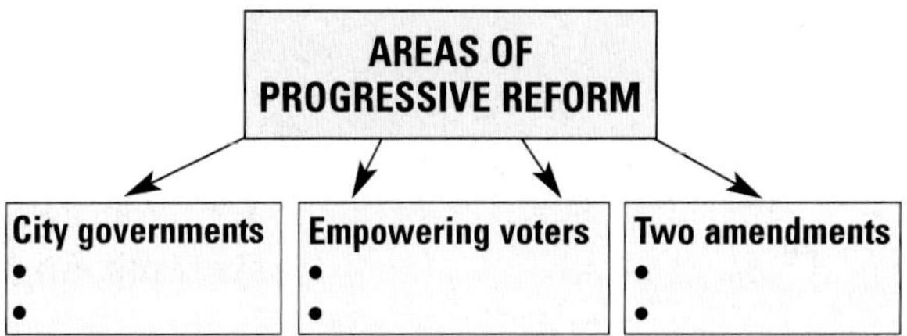

Main Idea Progressive reformers worked to end political corruption and give voters greater power.

Setting the Scene The Reverend Charles Parkhurst was furious about corruption in New York City. In one sermon, he called the city's politicians a "pack of administrative bloodhounds" who feed on the "flesh and blood of our citizenship."

A grand jury looked into these charges. They were outraged. However, their outrage was directed not against the wrongdoers but against Parkhurst. The grand jury condemned Parkhurst for encouraging the public to distrust government. Yet, Charles Parkhurst was only saying what most New Yorkers already knew. The city was riddled with corruption.

By the 1890s, more and more Americans were speaking out against corrupt politics. Soon, a new generation of reformers would fight to oust dishonest politicians and to give voters greater power.

Cartoonist Thomas Nast attacks political corruption

Reforming City Governments

How did city governments become so corrupt? As cities grew, they needed to expand services such as sewers, garbage collection, and roads. Often, politicians accepted money to give away these jobs. As a result, bribes and corruption became a way of life.

Political Bosses Powerful politicians, called **political bosses,** gained power in many cities. Political bosses also ruled county and state governments. Bosses controlled work done locally and demanded payoffs from businesses. City bosses were popular with the poor, especially with immigrants. They provided jobs and made loans to the needy. They handed out extra coal in winter and turkeys at Thanksgiving. In exchange, the poor voted for the boss or his chosen candidate.

Boss Tweed In New York City, Boss William Tweed carried corruption to new extremes. During the 1860s and 1870s, he cheated the city out of more than $100 million.

Journalists exposed Boss Tweed's wrongdoing. For example, cartoonist Thomas Nast pictured Tweed as a vulture feeding on the city. Nast's cartoons especially angered Tweed. His supporters might not be able to read, he said, but they could understand Nast's cartoons.

Faced with prison, Tweed fled to Spain. There, local police arrested him when they recognized him from Nast's cartoons. When Tweed died in jail in 1878, thousands of poor New Yorkers mourned for him.

Good-Government Leagues In many cities, reformers set up good-government leagues. Their goal was to replace corrupt officials with honest leaders.

The leagues had some successes. In Minneapolis, a corrupt mayor was indicted. Cleveland reformers helped elect Tom Johnson mayor. Johnson gave out contracts honestly, improved garbage and sewage systems, and set up services for the poor.

The Muckrakers

Reformers used the press to turn public opinion against corruption. Newspaper reporters described how corruption led to inadequate fire and police protection and poor sanitation services. Jacob Riis (REES), a photographer and writer, provided shocking images of slum life.

Crusading journalists like Riis became known as **muckrakers.** People said they raked the dirt, or muck, and exposed it to public view. One muckraker, Ida Tarbell, targeted the unfair practices of big business. Her articles about the Standard Oil Company led to demands for more controls on trusts.

In 1906, Upton Sinclair's novel *The Jungle* shocked the nation. Although the book was fiction it was based on facts. It revealed grisly details about the meatpacking industry. Sinclair told how the packers used meat from sick animals. He described how rats often got ground up in the meat, which was then dyed to make it seem healthy.

Muckrakers helped change public opinion. For years, middle-class Americans had ignored the need for reform. When they saw how dishonest politicians and businesses corrupted the nation—and even the food they ate—they, too, demanded change.

An American Profile

Ida Tarbell 1857–1944

Ida Tarbell was not afraid of challenges. At Allegheny College, she was the only woman in her graduating class. After college, she became editor of a literary journal.

Seeking new experiences, Tarbell took her entire savings and moved to Paris to study and write. She supported herself by writing for *McClure's Magazine.* In 1902, *McClure's* began publishing her most famous work, *The History of the Standard Oil Company.*

Tarbell became one of the best-known crusading journalists of her time. She also wrote biographies, including her own life story, when she was eighty.

Do you think Tarbell would have supported an organization working for greater rights for women? Why or why not?

The Progressives

By 1900, reformers were calling themselves **Progressives.** By that, they meant that they were forward-thinking people who wanted to improve American life. Progressives won many changes during the period from 1898 to 1917. As a result, this period is called the Progressive Era.

Progressives were never a single group with a single goal. Instead, they came from many backgrounds and backed different causes. They were united by a belief that the ills of society could be solved. Progressives wanted the government to act in the **public interest,** for the good of the people.

Both religion and science inspired Progressives. The Social Gospel movement of the late 1800s stressed the duty of Christians to

Progressive Political Reforms

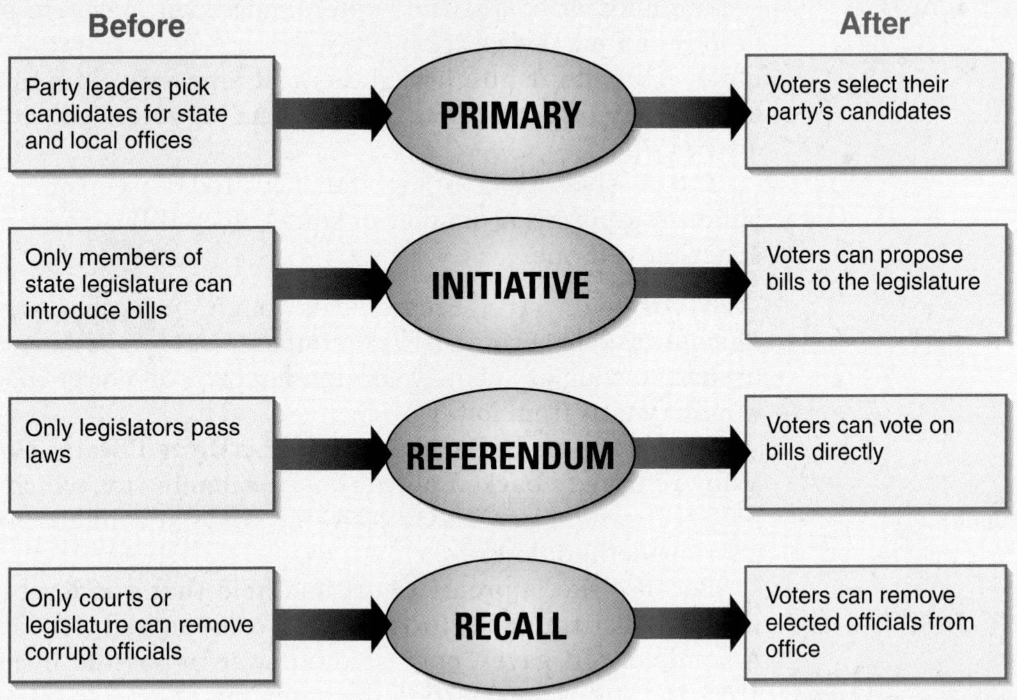

Before		After
Party leaders pick candidates for state and local offices	PRIMARY	Voters select their party's candidates
Only members of state legislature can introduce bills	INITIATIVE	Voters can propose bills to the legislature
Only legislators pass laws	REFERENDUM	Voters can vote on bills directly
Only courts or legislature can remove corrupt officials	RECALL	Voters can remove elected officials from office

GRAPHIC ORGANIZER *Skills*

In many states, Progressive reforms put more political power in voters' hands.

1. **Comprehension** **(a)** Who chooses political candidates in states with no primary? **(b)** How does the recall give more power to voters?
2. **Critical Thinking Drawing Conclusions** What responsibilities does a citizen have when voting on a referendum?

Civics

improve society. At the same time, Progressives used scientific studies and statistics to find ways to solve society's problems.

Progressives valued education. John Dewey, a Progressive educator, wanted schools to promote reform. Schools must teach democratic values by example, he argued. He therefore urged students to ask questions and to work together to solve problems.

Political Reforms

Among the leading Progressives was Robert La Follette of Wisconsin. "The will of the people shall be the law of the land," was his motto. His fighting spirit won him the nickname "Battling Bob."

The Wisconsin Idea As governor of Wisconsin, La Follette introduced various Progressive reforms that became known as the Wisconsin Idea. For example, he lowered railroad rates. The result was increased rail traffic, which helped both railroad owners and customers.

Empowering Voters Progressives like La Follette wanted voters to participate more directly in government. Since Andrew Jackson's time, party leaders had picked candidates for local and state offices. Progressives called, instead, for primaries. In a **primary,** voters choose their party's candidate for the general election. In 1903, Wisconsin was the first state to adopt a primary run by state government officials. By 1917, all but four states had done so.

Understand Effects How did Robert La Follette's Wisconsin Idea affect voters? Add this information to your chart.

Other reforms gave voters more power. They included the **initiative,** which gave voters the right to put a bill before a state legislature. A certain number of qualified voters must sign initiative petitions to propose a law. The **referendum** allowed voters to put a bill on the ballot and vote it into law. The **recall** allowed voters to remove an elected official from office. That reform let voters get rid of corrupt officials.

Progressives from other states visited Wisconsin to study La Follette's reforms. A number of states elected Progressive governors eager for reforms.

Two Amendments Progressives fought for other changes, too. They favored lowering tariffs on imported goods. If American industry had to compete against foreign imports, they argued, consumers would benefit from lower prices.

Some reforms led to changes in the United States Constitution. Many reformers backed a **graduated income tax,** which taxes people at different rates. The wealthy pay taxes at a higher rate than the poor or the middle class.

Because the Supreme Court had held that a federal income tax was unconstitutional, Progressives campaigned for a Sixteenth Amendment. It gave Congress the power to pass an income tax. By 1913, the states had ratified the amendment.

The states approved another amendment in 1913. Since 1789, state legislatures had elected senators. Powerful interest groups had sometimes bribed lawmakers to vote for certain candidates. Progressives wanted to end such abuses by having voters elect senators directly. In 1912, Congress approved the Seventeenth Amendment, which allowed for the direct election of senators. It was ratified a year later.

★ ★ ★ Section 2 Assessment ★ ★ ★

Recall

1. **Identify** Explain the significance of **(a)** William Tweed, **(b)** Ida Tarbell, **(c)** Progressive, **(d)** Robert La Follette.
2. **Define** **(a)** political boss, **(b)** muckraker, **(c)** public interest, **(d)** primary, **(e)** initiative, **(f)** referendum, **(g)** recall, **(h)** graduated income tax.

Comprehension

3. How did political bosses corrupt city governments?
4. How did the muckrakers help change public opinion?
5. Explain three major goals of Progressive reformers.
6. Describe two Progressive reforms that increased the political power of voters.

Critical Thinking and Writing

7. **Exploring the Main Idea** Review the Main Idea statement at the beginning of this section. Then, write at least four questions to ask muckrakers about their goals and achievements.
8. **Supporting a Point of View** La Follette and other Progressives believed that people would make the right decisions about their government if given the chance. Do you agree with that view? Explain.

ACTIVITY

Drawing a Political Cartoon You are Thomas Nast. Boss Tweed and his pals are stealing millions from the city you love. Draw a political cartoon to rouse public opinion against Tweed's corruption.

The Muckrakers

A number of best-selling books allowed reformers to get their message to the general public. The messages in these books shocked Americans and led to many important reforms.

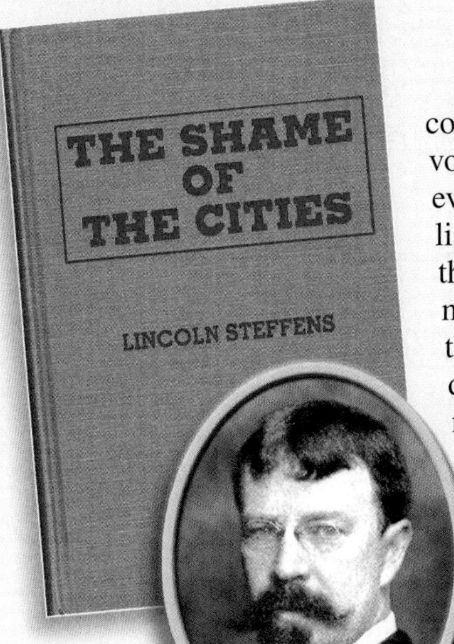

“The [political bosses] control the whole process of voting, and practice fraud at every stage. The assessor's list is the voting list, and the assessor is the [boss's] man. . . . The assessor pads the list with the names of dead dogs, children, and non-existent persons.”

—Lincoln Steffens, *The Shame of the Cities*, 1904

Lincoln Steffens (1866–1936)

Upton Sinclair (1878–1968)

“There was never the least attention paid to what was cut up for sausage; there would come all the way back from Europe old sausage that had been rejected, and that was moldy and white—it would be dosed with borax and glycerin, and . . . made over again for home consumption.”

—Upton Sinclair, *The Jungle*, 1906

“The farmer's profits were the object of attack from a score of different quarters. It was a flock of vultures descending upon a common prey—the commission merchant, the elevator combine, the mixing-house ring, the banks, the warehouse men, the laboring man, and, above all, the railroad.”

—Frank Norris, *The Octopus*, 1901

Frank Norris (1870–1902)

ACTIVITY

Think of yourself as a present-day muckraker. Make a list of up to five reforms you would like to see accomplished in the United States. Then, select one reform, and create a poster to encourage support for it.

3 Progressives in the White House

Prepare to Read

Objectives

In this section, you will

- Identify the key features of the Square Deal.
- Explain why Progressives first supported and then opposed William Howard Taft.
- List the major issues that affected the election of 1912.
- Summarize President Woodrow Wilson's policies.

Key Terms

trustbuster
Square Deal
Pure Food and Drug Act
conservation
national park
Bull Moose party
New Freedom
Federal Reserve Act
Federal Trade Commission

Target Reading Skill

Comparison and Contrast Copy the table below. As you read, complete the table by listing the achievements of the three "Progressive" Presidents.

ROOSEVELT	TAFT	WILSON
• Attacks bad trusts • •	• Sets up child labor office • •	• Backs Federal Trade Commission • •

Main Idea During the early 1900s, three Presidents worked for Progressive goals: Theodore Roosevelt, William H. Taft, and Woodrow Wilson.

San Francisco Chronicle.

PRESIDENT M'KINLEY SHOT BY AN ANARCHIST AT BUFFALO FAIR.

Two Bullets Fired by the Assassin, but Only One Penetrates the Body—Surgeons Hopeful of Recovery—An Attempt Made to Lynch the Cowardly Murderer.

WOUNDED AT A PUBLIC RECEPTION.

Stricken by a Man Who Grasped His Hand—Crowd Sought to Mete Out Swift Punishment.

A RECENT PORTRAIT OF PRESIDENT M'KINLEY.

DOCTORS DECLARE INJURIES SEVERE.

The Chances of Recovery Said to Be Against President—Cheering Reports Untrue.

President shot!

Setting the Scene An unemployed man stood nervously in line at the world's fair in Buffalo, New York. An anarchist, the man had a score to settle—with the President of the United States, William McKinley. When McKinley extended his hand, Leon Czolgosz (CHOHL goz) brushed it aside and fired two shots into the President. "Be easy with him, boys," gasped the wounded McKinley.

Doctors could not find the bullets lodged in the President's chest. They did not think to use the new X-ray machine on display at the fair.

On September 14, 1901, McKinley died. Vice President Theodore Roosevelt became President. At age 42, he was the youngest President to take office. He was also a strong supporter of Progressive goals.

Theodore Roosevelt

Teddy Roosevelt—or "TR," as he was called—came from a wealthy New York family. As a child, he suffered from asthma and was often sick. To build his strength, he lifted weights, ran, and boxed.

Political Ambitions TR could have enjoyed a life of ease. Instead, he decided to enter politics. He was determined to end corruption and work for the public interest.

TR's friends mocked his decision to devote his life to public service. They told him "that the men I met would be rough and brutal and unpleasant to deal with," he later recalled. He replied that he would not quit until he "found out whether I was really too weak to hold my own in the rough and tumble."

By age 26, Roosevelt was serving in the New York state legislature. Then, tragedy struck. In 1884, his mother and his young wife died on the same day. Overcome by grief, Roosevelt quit the legislature. He went west to work on a cattle ranch.

After two years, Roosevelt returned to the East and to politics. He served on the Civil Service Commission. He then headed New York City's police department and later became assistant secretary of the navy.

In 1898, the United States went to war against Spain. Roosevelt led a unit of troops in some daring exploits. He returned home to a hero's welcome and was elected governor of New York.

A Progressive Governor Since his days in the legislature, Roosevelt had pushed for reform. As governor, he continued to work for Progressive reforms. Other lawmakers called him a "goo goo," a mocking name for someone who wanted good government.

New York Republican bosses were relieved when Roosevelt resigned from the office of governor to become Vice President. Then, after President McKinley was shot in September 1901, Roosevelt became President. He was committed, he later wrote, to "making an old party Progressive."

TR and Big Business

Roosevelt promised to continue McKinley's probusiness policies. He was not against big business. In fact, he believed business was a positive force and that giant corporations were here to stay.

Roosevelt saw a difference, however, between good trusts and bad trusts. Good trusts, he said, were efficient and fair and should be let alone. Bad ones took advantage of workers and cheated the public. The government must either control them or break them up.

TR, the "Trustbuster" Roosevelt wanted to test the power of the government to break up bad trusts. In 1902, he asked the Attorney General, the government's chief lawyer, to bring a lawsuit against the Northern Securities Company. Northern Securities was a trust that had been formed to control competition among railroads. TR argued that the company used unfair business practices in violation of the Sherman Act.

At news of the lawsuit, stock prices fell on Wall Street, New York's center of business and finance. "Wall Street is paralyzed at the thought that a President of the United States would sink so low as to try to enforce the law," one newspaper joked. While business leaders worried, many ordinary Americans cheered the President.

In 1904, the Supreme Court ruled that Northern Securities had violated the Sherman Antitrust Act. It ordered the trust to be broken up. The decision was a victory for Progressives. For the first time, the Sherman Act had been used to break up trusts, not unions.

Next, Roosevelt had the Attorney General file suit against other trusts, including Standard Oil and the American Tobacco Company.

Viewing History

TR on the Campaign Trail

Theodore Roosevelt put tremendous energy into his speeches, shaking his fists in the air as he spoke. Here, Roosevelt is shown campaigning in Wyoming in 1903. Roosevelt's activities as an outdoorsman also helped his public image. After he refused to shoot a small captured bear, a toy company named a new product after the President: the Teddy bear. **Applying Information** ***How did Roosevelt's actions as President support his image as an energetic fighter?***

LINKING PAST AND PRESENT

▲ Past

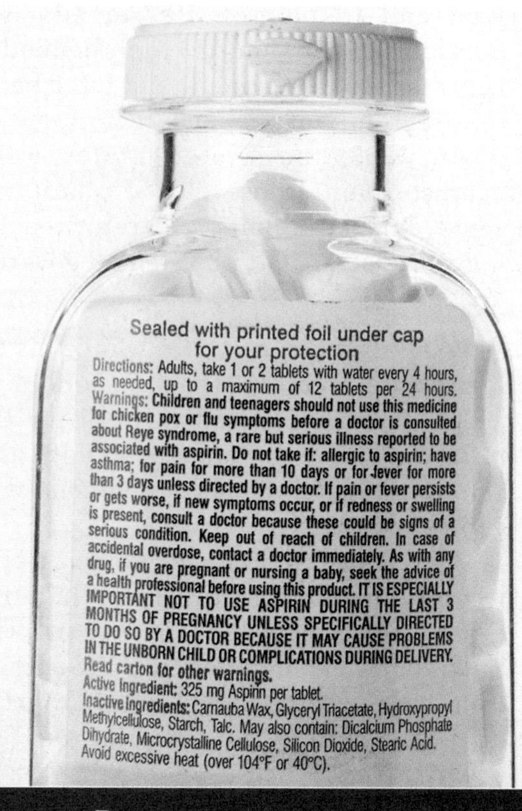

▲ Present

Viewing History

Protecting the Consumer

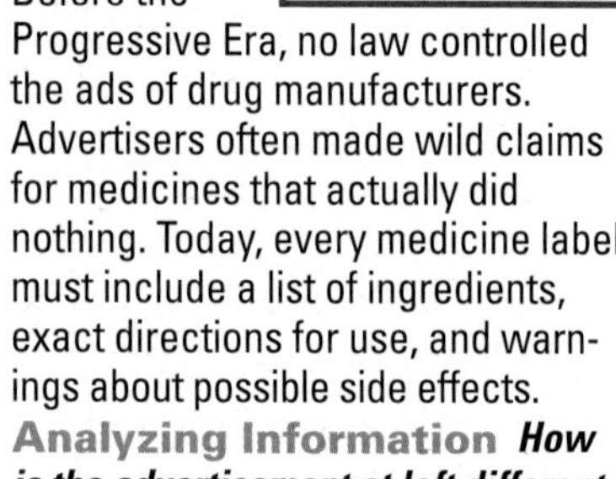

Before the Progressive Era, no law controlled the ads of drug manufacturers. Advertisers often made wild claims for medicines that actually did nothing. Today, every medicine label must include a list of ingredients, exact directions for use, and warnings about possible side effects. **Analyzing Information** ***How is the advertisement at left different from an ad for medicine that you might see in a magazine today?***

In time, the courts ordered the breakup of both trusts because they blocked free trade.

Some business leaders called Roosevelt a **trustbuster,** a person who wanted to destroy all trusts. "Certainly not," replied Roosevelt, only those that "have done something we regard as wrong." He preferred to control or regulate trusts, not "bust" them.

Support for Labor Roosevelt also clashed with mine owners. In 1902, Pennsylvania coal miners went on strike for better pay and a shorter workday. Mine owners refused to negotiate with the miners' union.

As winter approached, schools and hospitals ran out of coal. Furious at the mine owners, Roosevelt threatened to send in troops to run the mines. Finally, owners sat down with the union and reached an agreement. Roosevelt was the first President to side with labor.

The Square Deal

Roosevelt ran for President in his own right in 1904. During the campaign, he promised Americans a **Square Deal.** By this, he meant that everyone from farmers and consumers to workers and owners should have the same opportunity to succeed. That promise helped Roosevelt win a huge victory.

Railroads were a main target of the Square Deal. The Interstate Commerce Act of 1887 had done little to end rebates and other abuses. Roosevelt therefore urged Congress to outlaw rebates. In 1906, Congress gave the ICC the power to set railroad rates.

Consumers Roosevelt wanted reforms to protect consumers. He had been shocked by Upton Sinclair's novel *The Jungle.* In response, he sent more government inspectors to meatpacking houses. The owners refused to let them in.

Roosevelt then gave the newspapers copies of a government report that exposed conditions in meatpacking plants. The public was outraged. This forced Congress to pass a law in 1906 allowing more inspectors to enter meatpacking houses.

Muckrakers had exposed drug companies for making false claims about medicines. They also showed how food companies added harmful chemicals to canned foods. In 1906, Congress passed the **Pure Food and Drug Act,** which required food and drug makers to list ingredients on packages. It also tried to end false advertising and the use of impure ingredients.

Conserving Resources Roosevelt also took action to protect the nation's wilderness areas. To fuel industrial growth, lumber companies were cutting up whole forests. Miners were taking iron and coal from the earth at a frantic pace and leaving gaping holes.

Roosevelt loved the outdoors and worried about the destruction of the wilderness. He pressed for **conservation,** the protection of natural resources. "The rights of the public to natural resources outweigh private rights," he said.

Roosevelt wanted some forest areas left as wilderness. Others could supply needed resources. He wanted lumber companies to plant new trees in the forests they were clearing. Mining, too, should be controlled.

Under Roosevelt, the government set aside about 194,000 acres for national parks. A **national park** is an area set aside for people to visit. It is run by the federal government.

Taft and the Progressives

Roosevelt did not want to run for reelection in 1908. Instead, he backed William Howard Taft, his Secretary of War. Taft won easily. A confident Roosevelt said:

> "[Taft's] policies, principles, purposes, and ideals are the same as mine. The Roosevelt policies will not go out with Roosevelt."
>
> —Theodore Roosevelt in a letter to George Trevelyan, November 6, 1908

Roosevelt then left to hunt big game in Africa. He left behind an impressive record as a reformer. He also left the presidency more powerful than it had been at any time since the Civil War.

Taft's approach to the presidency was far different from Roosevelt's. Unlike the hard-driving, energetic Roosevelt, Taft was quiet and careful. Roosevelt loved power. Taft feared it.

Nevertheless, Taft supported many Progressive causes. He broke up even more trusts than TR had. He favored the graduated income tax, approved new safety rules for mines, and signed laws giving

Geography and History

The National Park System

The National Park System was established to protect land, wildlife, historic sites, and recreation areas. The government manages the parks so that visitors can enjoy the scenery without disturbing the land and wildlife.

Today, the National Park System protects about 350 separate areas. These include seashores, historic battlefields, and scenic trails. Dry Tortugas Park in Florida, for example, preserves marine wildlife and has an underwater nature trail. Death Valley National Park contains spectacular desert scenery and the lowest point in the Western Hemisphere. More than 200 million people visit national parks annually.

What benefit does the National Park System provide us?

government workers an eight-hour day. Under Taft, the Commerce Department set up an office to deal with the problems of child labor.

Despite such successes, Taft lost Progressive support. In 1909, he signed a bill that raised most tariffs. Progressives opposed the new law, arguing that tariffs raised prices for consumers. Also, Taft fired a high-level Forest Service official during a dispute over the sale of wilderness lands in Alaska. Progressives then accused the President of blocking conservation efforts.

1912: A Three-Way Election

When Roosevelt returned from Africa, he found Taft under attack by reformers. In 1912, TR decided to run against Taft for the Republican nomination. Although Roosevelt had much public support, Taft controlled the Republican party leadership. At its convention, the party nominated Taft.

The Bull Moose Party Progressive Republicans stormed out of the convention. They set up a new party and chose Roosevelt as their candidate. He accepted, saying "I feel as strong as a bull moose." Roosevelt's supporters became known as the **Bull Moose party.**

Woodrow Wilson Democrats chose Woodrow Wilson, a Progressive, as their candidate. Born in Virginia, Wilson was the son of a Presbyterian minister. As a boy, he made up his mind always to fight for what he thought was right. Wilson served as president of Princeton University and as governor of New Jersey. He was known as a brilliant scholar and a cautious reformer.

Together, Taft and Roosevelt won more votes than Wilson. However, they split the Republican vote. Their quarrel helped Wilson win the election of 1912.

Viewing History

A Cautious Reformer

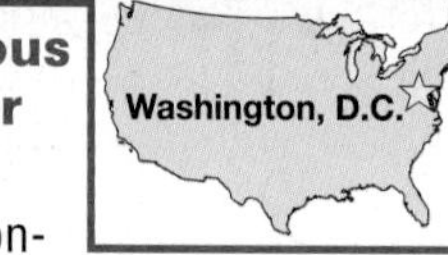

Woodrow Wilson's honesty and firm leadership inspired Progressives. Some Wilson supporters compared him with the nation's first President, George Washington, as can be seen by the attached song sheet. **Applying Information** ***What other Presidents might admirers of Washington and Wilson also like?***

Wilson in the White House

Woodrow Wilson's inaugural address reflected his strong sense of good and evil:

> "The nation has been deeply stirred, stirred by a solemn passion, stirred by the knowledge of wrong, of ideals lost, of government too often . . . made an instrument of evil. The feelings with which we face this new age of right and opportunity sweep across our heart-strings like some air out of God's own presence."
>
> —Woodrow Wilson, Inaugural Address, March 1913

Wilson asked honest, forward-looking Americans to stand at his side. "I will not fail them," he said.

The New Freedom At first, Wilson tried to break up trusts into smaller companies. By doing so, he hoped to restore the competition that had once existed in the American economy. "If America is not to have free enterprise, then she can have freedom of no sort whatever," he said. Wilson called his program the **New Freedom.**

To spur competition, Wilson asked Congress to lower the tariff. A lower tariff would favor imports and bring in foreign competition After a struggle, Congress did lower the tariff. To make up for lost revenues, it then passed a graduated income tax.

To regulate banking, Congress passed the **Federal Reserve Act** in 1913. It set up a system of federal banks. The system also gave the government the power to raise or lower interest rates and control the money supply.

Compare and Contrast

How did Woodrow Wilson's approach to trusts compare to Theodore Roosevelt's? Add this information to your chart.

Regulating Competition To ensure fair competition, President Wilson also persuaded Congress to create the **Federal Trade Commission** (FTC) in 1914. The FTC had the power to investigate companies and order them to stop using unfair practices to destroy competitors.

Wilson signed the Clayton Antitrust Act in 1914. He had wanted a much stronger law, but the new law did ban some business practices that limited free enterprise. In addition, it stopped antitrust laws from being used against unions, a major victory for labor.

Despite Wilson's successes, the Progressive movement slowed after 1914. By then, Progressives had achieved many of their goals. Also, the outbreak of war in Europe in 1914 occupied Americans. They worried that the war might soon affect them.

★ ★ ★ Section 3 Assessment ★ ★ ★

Recall

1. **Identify** Explain the significance of **(a)** Theodore Roosevelt, **(b)** Square Deal, **(c)** Pure Food and Drug Act, **(d)** William Howard Taft, **(e)** Bull Moose party, **(f)** Woodrow Wilson, **(g)** New Freedom, **(h)** Federal Reserve Act, **(i)** Federal Trade Commission.
2. **Define** **(a)** trustbuster, **(b)** conservation, **(c)** national park.

Comprehension

3. Describe three accomplishments of Theodore Roosevelt's Square Deal.
4. Why did opposition to Taft grow among reformers?
5. Why did the Republican party split in the 1912 election?
6. Name two accomplishments of Woodrow Wilson as President.

Critical Thinking and Writing

7. **Exploring the Main Idea** Review the Main Idea statement at the beginning of this section. Then, write a one-paragraph evaluation of the Progressive Presidents: Roosevelt, Taft, and Wilson.
8. **Drawing Inferences** "I'm glad to be going," said Taft as he left the White House in 1913. Why do you think he felt this way?

ACTIVITY

Expressing an Opinion

Use the Internet to find out what William Howard Taft did after he left the White House. Write a brief summary of Taft's later life. Then, write a paragraph describing what Presidents should do after their terms of office have expired. For help in completing the activity, visit PHSchool.com, **Web Code mfd-2202**.

Analyzing Political Cartoons

One way people respond to the issues of their time is to use humor. Political cartoons use humor and exaggeration to comment on issues and to persuade others to see a particular point of view.

The cartoon shown here makes a statement about President Theodore Roosevelt's handling of the meatpacking industry after he read Upton Sinclair's muckraking novel, *The Jungle*.

"A nauseating job, but it must be done."

Learn the Skill *To analyze a political cartoon, use the following steps:*

1. **Identify the symbols.** A political cartoon often uses symbols to help convey its message. Some symbols are well known, such as Uncle Sam. Others are used specifically for a particular cartoon.
2. **Study the words and images.** Political cartoons use few words, but those that do appear—as either labels or as a comment at the bottom—are significant.
3. **Analyze the meaning.** What is the point of view of the cartoonist?
4. **Interpret the cartoon.** Draw conclusions about the point of view the cartoon presents. How does the cartoonist feel about this issue?

Practice the Skill *Answer the following questions about the cartoon above:*

1. **(a)** What is the building behind Roosevelt? What does it stand for? **(b)** What is Roosevelt holding? What is it usually used for?
2. **(a)** What label is on the object Roosevelt is holding? **(b)** What is Roosevelt investigating? **(c)** Why is Roosevelt holding his nose?
3. What is the cartoonist saying in this cartoon?
4. **(a)** How do you think the cartoonist sees Roosevelt? **(b)** How do you think the cartoonist feels about the President and the meatpacking industry?

Apply the Skill *See the Chapter Review and Assessment.*

4 Women Win Reforms

Prepare to Read

Objectives

In this section, you will

- Describe how the women's suffrage movement helped bring about the Nineteenth Amendment.
- Identify the new opportunities women gained in education and employment.
- Explain why many women supported the campaign against alcohol.

Key Terms

National Woman Suffrage Association

suffragist

Nineteenth Amendment

WCTU

Eighteenth Amendment

Target Reading Skill

Sequence Copy this flowchart. As you read, fill in the boxes with some of the major events in women's struggle to win the right to vote. Add as many boxes as you need.

- **Seneca Falls Convention of 1848**

↓

- **National Woman Suffrage Association set up in 1869**

↓

(blank box)

Main Idea During the Progressive Era, many women fought for reforms and campaigned to win the right to vote.

Setting the Scene "Never was there such a sentence for such an offense as ours," wrote Rose Winslow from her jail cell. Winslow and other women were in jail for picketing the White House in 1917. Their cause was women's suffrage.

The women were held in solitary confinement. They then tried a new tactic: the hunger strike. In response, jailers fed them through tubes forced down their throats.

From the prison hospital, Winslow had notes smuggled out to tell people what was happening. Their hunger strike, she wrote, was meant to show "that women fighting for liberty may be considered political prisoners." She hoped it would save other women from suffering arrest and forced feedings.

During the Progressive Era, women continued their long battle for the right to vote. They also worked for other reforms, including pure food laws, an end to child labor, and a ban on the sale of alcohol.

Suffragists arrested outside the White House

Working for Women's Suffrage

The struggle of women for suffrage, or the right to vote, went back many years. As you have read, the Seneca Falls Convention in 1848 was the start of the organized women's rights movement. It called for many reforms, including women's suffrage.

After the Civil War, Elizabeth Cady Stanton and Susan B. Anthony renewed calls for suffrage. They had opposed the Fifteenth Amendment because it gave the vote to African American men but not to women. In 1869, Stanton and Anthony set up the **National Woman Suffrage Association,** a group that worked for a constitutional amendment to give women the right to vote.

Women Vote in the West In most states, leading politicians opposed women's suffrage. Still, in the late 1800s, women won the right to vote in four western states: Wyoming, Utah, Colorado, and

Idaho. Pioneer women had worked alongside men to build farms and cities. By giving women the vote, these states recognized the women's contributions.

When Wyoming applied for statehood in 1890, many members of Congress wanted it to change its law giving women the vote. Wyoming lawmakers replied: "We may stay out of the Union for 100 years, but we will come in with our women." Wyoming barely won admission.

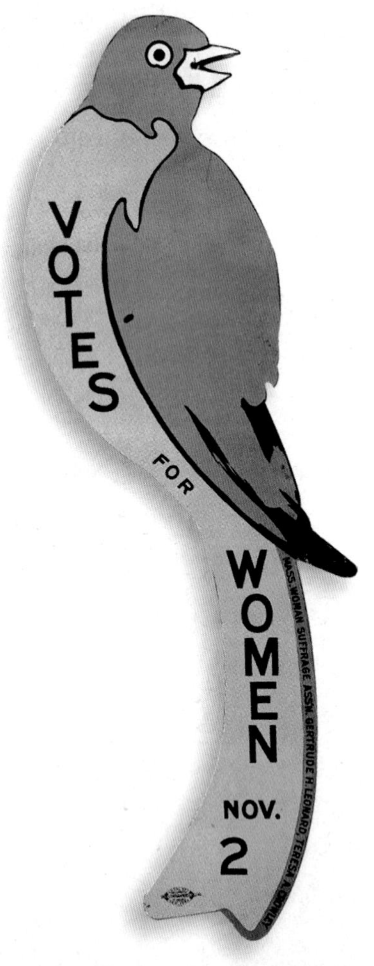

Viewing History

Suffrage Symbol

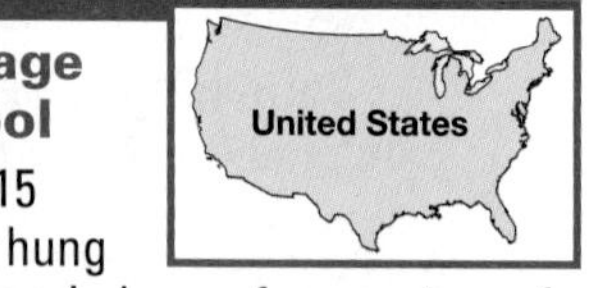

This 1915 banner hung from the windows of supporters of a constitutional amendment for women's suffrage. **Identifying Alternatives** ***Why do you think the designer used this bird as a symbol? What other symbols might the designer have used?***

Target Skill **Identify Sequence** What events on this page led to the passage of the Nineteenth Amendment? Add these events to your flowchart.

Growing Support for Suffrage In the early 1900s, the women's suffrage movement gained strength. More than 5 million women were earning wages outside the home. Although women were paid less than men, wages gave them some power. Many demanded a say in making the laws that affected them.

After Stanton and Anthony died, a new generation of leaders took up the cause. Among the most outspoken was Carrie Chapman Catt. She had worked as a school principal and a reporter before she became a leader of the National Woman Suffrage Association.

Catt was a brilliant organizer. She created a detailed plan to fight for suffrage, state by state. Across the nation, **suffragists,** or people who worked for women's right to vote, followed her strategy.

Slowly, their efforts succeeded. One by one, states in the West and Midwest gave women the vote. Generally, women in these states could vote only in state elections. At the same time, more and more women were demanding a constitutional amendment to give them the right to vote in all elections.

The Nineteenth Amendment

As the struggle dragged on, some suffragists, like Alice Paul, took more radical steps to win the vote. Paul had marched with British suffragists in London. She had been jailed and gone on hunger strikes to help British women win the vote. When Paul returned home, she fought for suffrage for American women.

Picketing the White House Soon after Wilson became President, he met with Paul and other suffragists. Wilson did not oppose women's suffrage, but he also did not back a constitutional amendment.

Paul told the President that suffragists wanted such an amendment. "And then," she recalled, "we sent him another delegation and another and another and another and another and another and another."

Early in 1917, Paul, Rose Winslow, and other women began to picket the White House. Within a few months, police started to arrest the silent protesters. Winslow and Paul were jailed for obstructing the sidewalk. A public outcry soon won their release. The women then resumed their picketing.

Victory at Last By early 1918, the tide had finally turned in favor of suffrage. President Wilson agreed to support the suffrage amendment. In 1919, Congress passed the **Nineteenth Amendment.** It guaranteed women the right to vote. By August 1920, three fourths of the states had ratified the amendment, which doubled the number of eligible voters.

Women Win New Opportunities

Besides working for the vote, women struggled to gain access to jobs and education. Most states refused to grant women licenses to practice law or medicine. Myra Bradwell taught herself law, just as Abraham Lincoln had done. Still, Illinois denied her a license in 1869 because she was a woman. In 1890, Illinois finally allowed her to practice law.

Higher Education Despite obstacles, a few women managed to get the higher education needed to enter the professions. In 1877, Boston University granted the first Ph.D. to a woman. Slowly, more women entered graduate schools and earned advanced degrees. By 1900, the nation had about 1,000 women lawyers and 7,000 women doctors.

Viewing History

Women Vote for President

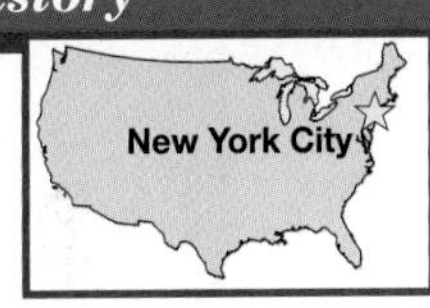

In the presidential election of 1920, lines outside polling places for the first time contained both men and women. This scene took place in New York City. **Applying Information** ***Which constitutional amendment made this scene possible?***

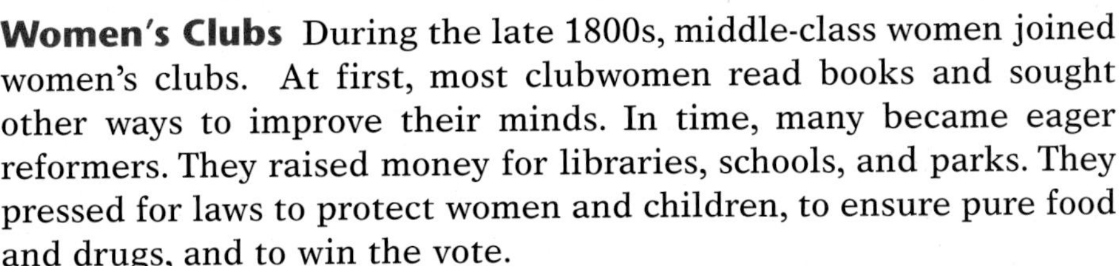

Women's Clubs During the late 1800s, middle-class women joined women's clubs. At first, most clubwomen read books and sought other ways to improve their minds. In time, many became eager reformers. They raised money for libraries, schools, and parks. They pressed for laws to protect women and children, to ensure pure food and drugs, and to win the vote.

Faced with racial barriers, African American women formed their own clubs, such as the National Association of Colored Women. They battled to end lynching and racial separation and worked for suffrage and other reforms.

Women Reformers During the Progressive Era, many women became committed to reforming society. Some women entered the new profession of social work. Others campaigned to end social evils, such as child labor. Florence Kelley investigated conditions in sweatshops. In time, she was made the chief factory inspector for the state of Illinois. Kelley's main concern, though, was child labor. She organized a boycott of goods produced by child labor. She helped publish a list of manufacturers whose factories met basic standards.

The Crusade Against Alcohol

The temperance movement to end the sale of alcoholic beverages began in the early 1800s. By 1900, the movement was gaining strength.

Women often led the temperance drive. Many wives and mothers recognized alcohol as a threat to their families. Drinking often caused violence and economic hardship at home.

For political reasons, women also opposed saloons, where alcohol was served. In saloons, male political bosses made political decisions out of the reach of women. Most saloons refused entry to women.

The WCTU In 1874, a group of women organized the Women's Christian Temperance Union, or **WCTU.** Frances Willard became its president in 1880. Willard recalled an incident at a Pittsburgh saloon:

> "The tall, stately lady who led us placed her Bible on the bar and read a psalm. . . . Then we sang "Rock of Ages" as I thought I had never sung it before. . . . This was my Crusade baptism."
>
> —Frances E. Willard, *Glimpses of Fifty Years, the Autobiography of an American Woman,* 1889

Willard spoke tirelessly about the evils of alcohol. She called for state laws to ban the sale of liquor. She also worked to close saloons. In time, Willard joined the suffrage movement, bringing many WCTU members along with her.

Carrie Nation was a more radical temperance crusader. She dedicated her life to fighting "demon rum." After her husband died from heavy drinking, Nation often stormed into saloons. Swinging a hatchet, she smashed beer kegs and liquor bottles. Nation won publicity, but her actions embarrassed the WCTU.

The Eighteenth Amendment Temperance crusaders wanted a constitutional amendment banning the sale of liquor. Support for such an amendment grew after 1917, when the United States entered World War I. Temperance supporters argued that grain used to make liquor should be used instead to feed American soldiers.

Temperance leaders finally persuaded Congress to pass the **Eighteenth Amendment** in 1917. By 1919, three fourths of the states had ratified it. The amendment made it illegal to sell alcoholic drinks anywhere in the United States.

★ ★ ★ Section 4 Assessment ★ ★ ★

Recall

1. **Identify** Explain the significance of **(a)** National Woman Suffrage Association, **(b)** Carrie Chapman Catt, **(c)** Alice Paul, **(d)** Nineteenth Amendment, **(e)** WCTU, **(f)** Frances Willard, **(g)** Carrie Nation, **(h)** Eighteenth Amendment.
2. **Define** suffragist.

Comprehension

3. Describe three highlights in the campaign to win women's suffrage through a constitutional amendment.
4. What new opportunities in jobs and education did women win during this period?
5. Why were women active in the crusade against alcohol?

Critical Thinking and Writing

6. **Exploring the Main Idea** Review the Main Idea statement at the beginning of this section. Then, create at least three slogans for banners and leaflets supporting the right of women to vote.
7. **Linking Past and Present** Frances Willard considered alcohol a threat to society. What threats does alcohol abuse pose today?

ACTIVITY

Writing a Song **You have worked for passage of the Nineteenth Amendment, and it has finally become law. Using a tune you know, write the lyrics of a song celebrating this success.**

5 Other Americans Seek Justice

Prepare to Read

Objectives

In this section, you will
- Identify the struggles African Americans faced during the Progressive Era.
- Describe the Mexican American experience.
- Explain how prejudice affected Asian Americans.
- List Native American losses suffered during this era.

Key Terms

lynch

NAACP

barrio

mutualista

"Gentlemen's Agreement"

Society of American Indians

Target Reading Skill

Clarifying Meaning As you read, prepare an outline of this section. Use roman numerals to indicate the major headings, capital letters for the subheadings, and numbers for the supporting details.

I. African Americans
  A. Booker T. Washington
    1.
    2.
  B. W.E.B. Du Bois
    1.
    2.
  C. Setbacks and successes
II. Mexican Americans

Main Idea African Americans and other Americans created their own communities and struggled for equality during the Progressive Era.

Setting the Scene San Angelo, Texas, built new schools for its white children in 1910. Parents of the town's 200 Mexican children protested. Their children were forced to go to separate "Mexican" schools. The buildings were old, and the children got little education.

When seven Mexican children tried to attend one of the new schools, officials barred their way. "To admit the Mexicans to white schools," said officials, "would be to demoralize the entire system."

During the Progressive era, reformers did little to prevent such injustice. Instead, a number of minority groups struggled alone to gain basic rights.

A segregated school in Arizona, 1913

African Americans

After Reconstruction, African Americans in the South lost many hard-won rights. Jim Crow laws led to segregation in schools, trains, and other public places. (See Chapter 18.) In the North, too, African Americans faced prejudice and discrimination. Landlords refused to rent homes in white areas to African Americans. Across the nation, African Americans were hired only for low-paying jobs.

The depression of 1893 made life even harder. In the South and elsewhere, jobless whites took out their anger on blacks. In the 1890s, more than 1,000 African Americans were **lynched**—murdered by mobs.

The murders outraged Ida B. Wells, an African American journalist. In her newspaper, *Free Speech*, Wells urged African Americans to protest the lynchings. She called for a boycott of streetcars and white-owned stores. Wells spoke out despite threats to her life.

Booker T. Washington During this period, Booker T. Washington spoke for many African Americans. He called on blacks and whites to live in harmony.

Tuskegee Institute

Two men are closely associated with the Tuskegee Institute in Tuskegee, Alabama. Booker T. Washington built Tuskegee into the nation's leading black industrial educational school. George Washington Carver revolutionized agricultural development in the South. The legacy of these two men, including Carver's work desk, has been preserved in Tuskegee today.

Virtual Field Trip For an interactive look at Tuskegee Institute, visit PHSchool.com, **Web Code mfd-2203.**

In *Up From Slavery*, his autobiography, Washington told his own success story. Although born into slavery, he had taught himself to read. As a youth, he worked in coal mines, attending schools whenever he could. In 1872, he graduated from the newly founded Hampton Institute. Nine years later, he helped found the Tuskegee Institute in Alabama to offer higher education to blacks.

African Americans, said Washington, must work patiently to move up in society. First, he urged them to learn trades and earn money. Then, they would have the power to demand equality.

Business tycoons like Andrew Carnegie and John D. Rockefeller backed Washington. They helped him build trade schools for African Americans. Presidents also sought his advice on racial issues.

W.E.B. Du Bois Other African Americans, like W.E.B. Du Bois (doo BOYS), took a different approach. Du Bois agreed with Booker T. Washington's view on the need for "thrift, patience, and industrial training." However, he added, "So far as Mr. Washington apologizes for injustice, . . . we must firmly oppose him." Instead of patiently accepting discrimination, Du Bois urged blacks to fight it actively.

In 1909, Du Bois, along with Jane Addams, Lincoln Steffens, and other reformers organized the National Association for the Advancement of Colored People, or NAACP. Blacks and whites in the NAACP worked for equal rights for African Americans.

Setbacks and Successes Most Progressives, though, gave little thought to the problems faced by African Americans. When black soldiers were accused of rioting in Brownsville, Texas, Teddy

Roosevelt had their whole regiment dishonorably discharged. Later, President Wilson ordered the segregation of black and white government workers. When blacks protested, Wilson replied that "segregation is not humiliating, but a benefit."

Despite many obstacles, some African Americans succeeded. George Washington Carver discovered hundreds of new uses for peanuts and other crops grown in the South. His writings about crop rotation changed southern farming practices. Sarah Walker, better known as Madame C. J. Walker, created a line of hair care products for African American women. She became the first American woman to earn more than $1 million.

Black-owned insurance companies, banks, and other businesses served the needs of African Americans. Other businesses provided personal services that whites refused to offer African Americans. Among these were restaurants, beauty parlors and barber shops, and funeral parlors. Black colleges trained young people for the professions. Churches like the African Methodist Episcopal Church were training grounds for African American leaders.

Mexican Americans

Thousands of Mexican Americans lived in the United States, especially in the Southwest and West. They lived in areas acquired by the United States under the Treaty of Guadalupe-Hidalgo and the Gadsden Purchase. In the early 1900s, however, large numbers of immigrants began arriving from Mexico.

In 1910, revolution and famine swept Mexico. Thousands of *Mexicanos*, or native-born Mexicans, fled their homeland into the United States. To them, it was *el norte*, "the north." The immigrants came from all levels of Mexican society. Many were poor farmers, but some came from middle-class and upper-class families. Although many Mexicanos later returned home, some remained.

Daily Life Mexican immigrants worked as field hands, built roads, and dug irrigation ditches. Some lived near the railroads they helped build. Still others worked in city factories, where they faced harsh conditions. They were paid less than white workers and were denied skilled jobs.

Like other immigrants, Mexicans created their own neighborhoods, or **barrios.** There, they preserved their language and culture, celebrated traditional festivals, and shared memories of Mexico. Los Angeles was home to the nation's largest barrio. Its population almost tripled between 1910 and 1920. Meanwhile, the migration was spreading to new parts of the United States. People who could not find work in the Southwest began moving to the Midwest and the Rocky Mountain region.

Mutual Aid Within the barrio, Mexican immigrants and Mexican Americans took many steps to help each other. Some formed ***mutualistas***, or mutual aid groups. These groups worked like other immigrant aid societies. Members of mutualistas pooled money to buy insurance and pay for legal advice. They also collected money for the sick and needy.

Primary Source

Teaching His Culture to Others

Mexican American author Victor Villasenor (VEE-yah-sen-yor) remembers an incident from his California youth. Victor heard a Latino elder telling Victor's mother about celebrating the Mexican holiday, Cinco de Mayo:

"This year, for the first time, we want to have a big celebration with a parade and extend it past the barrio into the Americano part of town so we can include the gringos in our celebration. You see, many of our people who came here during the Revolution, . . . are beginning to think that maybe this country is going to be our permanent home. So that's why we want to include the gringos and teach them of our Mexican traditions so we don't lose our culture."

—Victor Villasenor, *Rain of Gold*, 1991

Analyzing Primary Sources

Why did the elder want to teach his culture to Americans?

Asian Americans

In the 1870s, whites on the West Coast pressed Congress to pass the Chinese Exclusion Act. The Act, passed in 1882, kept Chinese from settling in the United States. With no new immigration, the Chinese population declined.

Newcomers From Japan Still, the demand for cheap labor remained high. White employers on the West Coast and in Hawaii therefore got around the Chinese Exclusion Act by hiring workers from other Asian countries, mainly the Philippines and Japan. More than 100,000 Japanese entered the United States in the early 1900s. Most had migrated to Hawaii to work on sugar plantations. When the United States annexed Hawaii in 1898, a number of Japanese saw the opportunity for a better life on the United States mainland.

Many newcomers from Japan were farmers. They settled on dry, barren land that Americans thought was useless. Through hard work and careful management of resources, the Japanese made their farms profitable. Soon, they were producing a large percentage of southern California's fruits and vegetables. Other newcomers worked in canneries, lumber mills, and mines.

Viewing History

Turning Swampland Into Farmland

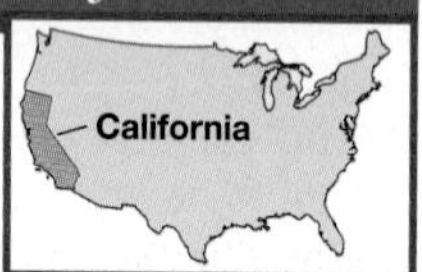

Chinese and Japanese farmers took land that no one else wanted and made it productive. These Chinese farmers are harvesting a vineyard in northern California. **Formulating Questions** ***Create an analytical question based on this picture.***

Hawaiian planters brought workers from Japan, Korea, and the Philippines. They deliberately hired workers from diverse groups. They hoped this would keep workers from uniting to demand better wages or improved working conditions. Like Mexican immigrants, Asian workers were paid less than whites and were denied promotion to skilled jobs.

A "Gentlemen's Agreement" Prejudice against immigrants from Asia remained high. Many white farmers and factory workers resented the success of the Japanese. In California, the Japanese were barred from owning land and from many economic pursuits. In 1906, San Francisco forced all Asian students, including Japanese children, to attend separate schools. Japan protested the insult, and the issue threatened to cause an international crisis.

Unions and other groups also put pressure on President Roosevelt to limit immigration from Japan. Because Japan was a growing naval power in the Pacific, Roosevelt tried to soothe Japanese feelings. He condemned the segregated schools and offered his own solution. If San Francisco ended its segregation order, he would restrict further Japanese immigration.

In 1907, Roosevelt reached a **"Gentlemen's Agreement"** with Japan. Japan would stop any more workers from going to the United

Target Skill — Summarize As you read this section, think about how you would summarize in two sentences the experience of Asian Americans during the Progressive era. Add this information to your outline.

States. The United States, in exchange, would allow Japanese women to join their husbands who were already in this country. Anti-Japanese feeling did not decrease with the Gentlemen's Agreement. In 1913, California passed a law which banned Asians who were not American citizens from owning land. Before long, the United States would take more drastic steps to stop immigration from Asia.

Native Americans

During the Progressive Era, Native Americans felt the effects of the Dawes Act of 1887. The act had divided reservation lands into family plots. With these lands, Indians were supposed to become farmers and enter mainstream American life.

What actually happened was quite different. Much of the land the families received was unsuited to farming. Also, many Indians had no farming tradition. They believed that the plains were an open place to ride and hunt—not something to divide into small parcels. Thus, many Native Americans simply sold their lands to speculators at very low prices. Within a short time after the Dawes Act became effective, speculators had swindled Native Americans out of millions of acres of reservation land.

In the early 1900s, a new generation of Native American leaders emerged. One group set up the **Society of American Indians.** It included artists, writers, Christian ministers, lawyers, and doctors from many Native American groups. The Society worked for social justice and tried to educate white Americans about Indian life. However, it supported policies to force Indians into the American mainstream by abolishing reservations. This created so much opposition among Native Americans that the Society went out of existence in 1925.

★ ★ ★ Section 5 Assessment ★ ★ ★

Recall

1. **Identify** Explain the significance of **(a)** Ida B. Wells, **(b)** Booker T. Washington, **(c)** W.E.B. Du Bois, **(d)** NAACP, **(e)** "Gentlemen's Agreement," **(f)** Society of American Indians.
2. **Define** **(a)** lynch, **(b)** barrio, **(c)** *mutualista.*

Comprehension

3. What problems did African Americans face during this era?
4. How did Mexican Americans protect their welfare in the United States?
5. What problems did Asian Americans face during the Progressive Era?
6. Why did Native Americans lose millions of acres of land during this period?

Critical Thinking and Writing

7. **Exploring the Main Idea** Review the Main Idea statement at the beginning of this section. Then, compare the experience of different minority groups during the Progressive Era.
8. **Identifying Points of View** "The way for people to gain their reasonable rights is not by voluntarily throwing them away." Do you think this statement was made by Washington or Du Bois? Explain.

Activity

Writing a Letter The year is 1912. You have fled famine and war in Mexico and have made a life in the United States. Write a letter to relatives back home about what they should expect if they decide to move to "el norte."

CHAPTER 22

Review and Assessment

Chapter Summary

Section 1
During the Gilded Age, reformers began working to end political corruption. Reforms included a civil service system and limits placed on big business.

Section 2
Progressive reformers achieved successes in their battle to end corruption in government and give voters more power. Progressives also fought for passage of the Sixteenth and Seventeenth amendments.

Section 3
As President, Theodore Roosevelt championed the Progressive agenda. The Progressives' unhappiness with President Taft in 1912 led to the election of Woodrow Wilson.

Section 4
Women's long fight to win the right to vote ended with the passage of the Nineteenth Amendment in 1920. Women also fought to reform education, end child labor, and ban the sale of alcohol.

Section 5
African Americans, Mexican Americans, Native Americans, and Asian Americans did not generally benefit from the reforms that improved the lives of other Americans.

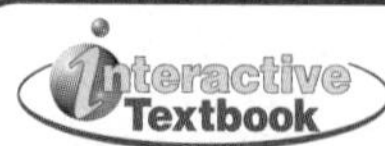

For additional review and enrichment activities, see the interactive version of *The American Nation,* available on the Web and on CD-ROM.

Chapter Self-Test For practice test questions for Chapter 22, visit PHSchool.com, **Web Code mfa-2204.**

Building Vocabulary

Use the chapter vocabulary words listed below to create a crossword puzzle. Exchange puzzles with a classmate and complete the puzzles.

1. **patronage**
2. **civil service**
3. **muckraker**
4. **primary**
5. **referendum**
6. **graduated income tax**
7. **trustbuster**
8. **conservation**
9. **suffragist**
10. **barrio**

Reviewing Key Facts

11. Why did reformers want to end the spoils system? (Section 1)
12. Explain three reforms of the Progressives that gave voters greater power. (Section 2)
13. Give two examples each of ways in which Roosevelt, Taft, and Wilson worked to achieve Progressive goals. (Section 3)
14. Explain the role played by women in the reforms of the Progressive Era. (Section 4)
15. How did Booker T. Washington and W.E.B. Du Bois disagree? (Section 5)

Critical Thinking and Writing

16. **Identifying Causes and Effects** List one event that resulted from each of the following: Nast publishes cartoons attacking Boss Tweed, Sinclair publishes *The Jungle,* Tarbell reveals business practices of Standard Oil.
17. **Comparing (a)** How did the role of President change during the administration of Theodore Roosevelt? **(b)** Suggest one reason for the change.
18. **Connecting to Geography: Movement** The migration of people is linked to both "push factors," which drive people to leave home, and "pull factors," which attract them to a new place. Explain the push and pull factors affecting the migration of Mexicans to "el norte" in the early 1900s.

Skills Assessment

Analyzing Primary Sources

A 1905 book explained the work of a "district leader" in New York City:

> "Nearly everybody goes to him for assistance of one sort or another, especially the poor of the tenements. . . . He will go to the police courts to put in a good word for the 'drunks and disorderlies' or pay their fines, if a good word is not effective. He will attend christenings, weddings, and funerals. He will feed the hungry and help bury the dead. A philanthropist? Not at all. He is playing politics all the time."
>
> —William L. Riordon, *Plunkitt of Tammany Hall*, 1905

19. What task might a district leader perform?
    - A. He builds tenements.
    - B. He hauls people into police court to answer the charges against them.
    - C. He pays a person's fine.
    - D. He makes donations to charities.
20. A district leader helps people because he wants to be
    - A. a philanthropist.
    - B. elected again.
    - C. kind.
    - D. a guest at happy occasions.

Applying Your Skills

Analyzing Political Cartoons

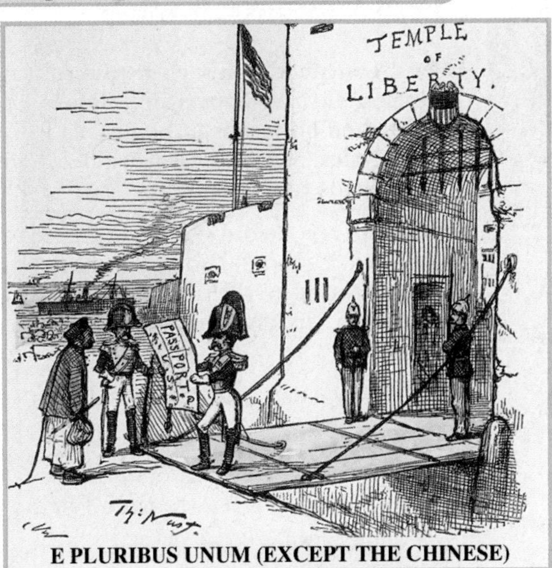

E PLURIBUS UNUM (EXCEPT THE CHINESE)

This Thomas Nast cartoon comments on immigration policy. Study the cartoon and answer the following questions:

21. The castle and the man in uniform on the moat stand for
    - A. China and the Chinese emperor
    - B. the United States and American laws
    - C. churches and a religious leader
    - D. Britain's monarch and King George V
22. What point is Thomas Nast trying to make in this cartoon?

Activities

Connecting With . . . Government and Citizenship

Creating a Timeline With a classmate or in a small group, create an illustrated timeline of key events in women's efforts to win the vote from 1789 to passage of the Nineteenth Amendment. Next to each event, note why it was important to the women's suffrage movement. Choose one event from your timeline that you think was a key turning point in the movement. Explain why you chose that event.

Connecting to Today

Creating a Database Since Theodore Roosevelt's days, the United States has greatly expanded its national parks. Use the Internet to create a database about the National Park Service. Include a brief history of the national park system, a list of at least 10 national parks, and some of the issues involved in protecting wildlife and wilderness areas. For help in starting this activity, visit PHSchool.com, **Web Code mfd-2205**.

Preparing a Report

Finding Resources on State Reforms Choose one of the Progressive political reforms discussed on pages 635–636: the initiative, the referendum, or the recall. Use the Internet to find at least three sites that contain information about the reform you have chosen. Then, write a report on that reform. For help in starting this activity, visit PHSchool.com, **Web Code mfd-2206**.

History Through Literature

Paul Laurence Dunbar

Paul Laurence Dunbar was the first African American to support himself entirely by writing. Before he died at the age of 33, Dunbar published hundreds of poems, as well as novels, short stories, and song lyrics. Much of his work dealt with the efforts of African Americans to win equality.

Vocabulary Before you read the selections, find the meanings of these words in a dictionary: **unwavering, didst, Ethiope, swarthy, consecrating, writ, blazoned, chrism, wert, bards, salient, devious, dispraise, dissension.**

Paul Laurence Dunbar
(1872–1906)

Ode to Ethiopia

O Mother Race! to thee I bring
This pledge of faith unwavering,
This tribute to thy glory.
I know the pangs which thou didst feel,
When Slavery crushed thee with its heel,
With thy dear blood all gory.

Sad days were those—ah, sad indeed!
But through the land the fruitful seed
Of better times was growing.
The plant of freedom upward sprung,
And spread its leaves so fresh and young—
Its blossoms now are blowing.

On every hand in this fair land,
Proud Ethiope's swarthy children stand
Beside their fairer neighbour;
The forests flee before their stroke,
Their hammers ring, their forges smoke,
They stir in honest labour.

They tread the fields where honour calls;
Their voices sound through senate halls
In majesty and power.
To right they cling; the hymns they sing
Up to the skies in beauty ring,
And bolder grow each hour.

Be proud, my race, in mind and soul;
Thy name is writ on Glory's scroll
In characters of fire.
High 'mid the clouds of Fame's bright sky
Thy banner's blazoned folds now fly,
And truth shall lift them higher.

Thou hast the right to noble pride,
Whose spotless robes were purified
By blood's severe baptism.
Upon thy brow the cross was laid,
And labour's painful sweat-beads made
A consecrating chrism.

No other race, or white or black,
When bound as thou wert, to the rack,
So seldom stooped to grieving;
No other race, when free again,
Forgot the past and proved them men
So noble in forgiving.

Go on and up! Our souls and eyes
Shall follow thy continuous rise;
Our ears shall list thy story
From bards who from thy root shall spring,
And proudly tune their lyres to sing
Of Ethiopia's glory.

With Sweat and Toil and Ignorance He Consumes His Life by Jacob Lawrence

Douglass

Ah, Douglass we have fall'n on evil days,
Such days as thou, not even thou didst know,
When thee, the eyes of that harsh long ago
Saw, salient, at the cross of devious ways,
And all the country heard thee with amaze.
Not ended then, the passionate ebb and flow,
The awful tide that battled to and fro;
We ride amid a tempest of dispraise.

Now, when the waves of swift dissension swarm,
And Honor, the strong pilot, lieth stark,
Oh, for thy voice high-sounding o'er the storm,
For thy strong arm to guide the shivering bark,
The blast-defying power of thy form,
To give us comfort through the lonely dark.

Analyzing Literature

1. How does Dunbar describe the period after Emancipation?

- **A** "Sad days were those—ah, sad indeed!"
- **B** "When Slavery crushed thee with its heel, . . . "
- **C** "The plant of freedom upward sprung, . . . "
- **D** "We have fall'n on evil days, . . ."

2. According to Dunbar, when was Frederick Douglass's voice heard by the whole nation?

- **A** When "we have fall'n on evil days, . . ."
- **B** In "Such days as thou, not even thou didst know, . . ."
- **C** "Long ago" in a harsher time
- **D** "Now, when the waves of swift dissension swarm, . . ."

3. **Critical Thinking and Writing** **Comparing and Contrasting** In both poems, Dunbar is addressing the struggles of African Americans. Yet, the moods of the two poems are different. How would you describe the difference?

CHAPTER 23

Becoming a World Power

1865–1916

1 A Pacific Empire
2 War With Spain
3 The United States in Latin America

Check (above) used to buy Alaska (upper left)

Captain Alfred Mahan

1867 Secretary of State William Seward purchases Alaska from Russia. Many Americans laugh at "Seward's Folly."

1870s The value of American foreign trade passes $1 billion a year.

1890 Captain Alfred Mahan publishes *The Influence of Sea Power Upon History.* He urges the United States to build up its navy.

AMERICAN EVENTS

Presidential Terms:

Andrew Johnson		Rutherford B. Hayes	James A. Garfield 1881 / Chester A. Arthur	Grover Cleveland
1865-1869	Ulysses S. Grant 1869-1877	1877-1881	1881-1885	1885-1889

1860 · 1875 · 1890

WORLD EVENTS 

▲ 1868 Japan begins rapid program to modernize.

1884 ▲ European powers agree to divide up most of Africa.

World Imperialism

During the Age of Imperialism, industrialized nations gained political and economic control over much of the world.

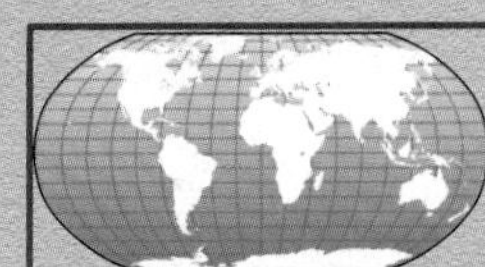

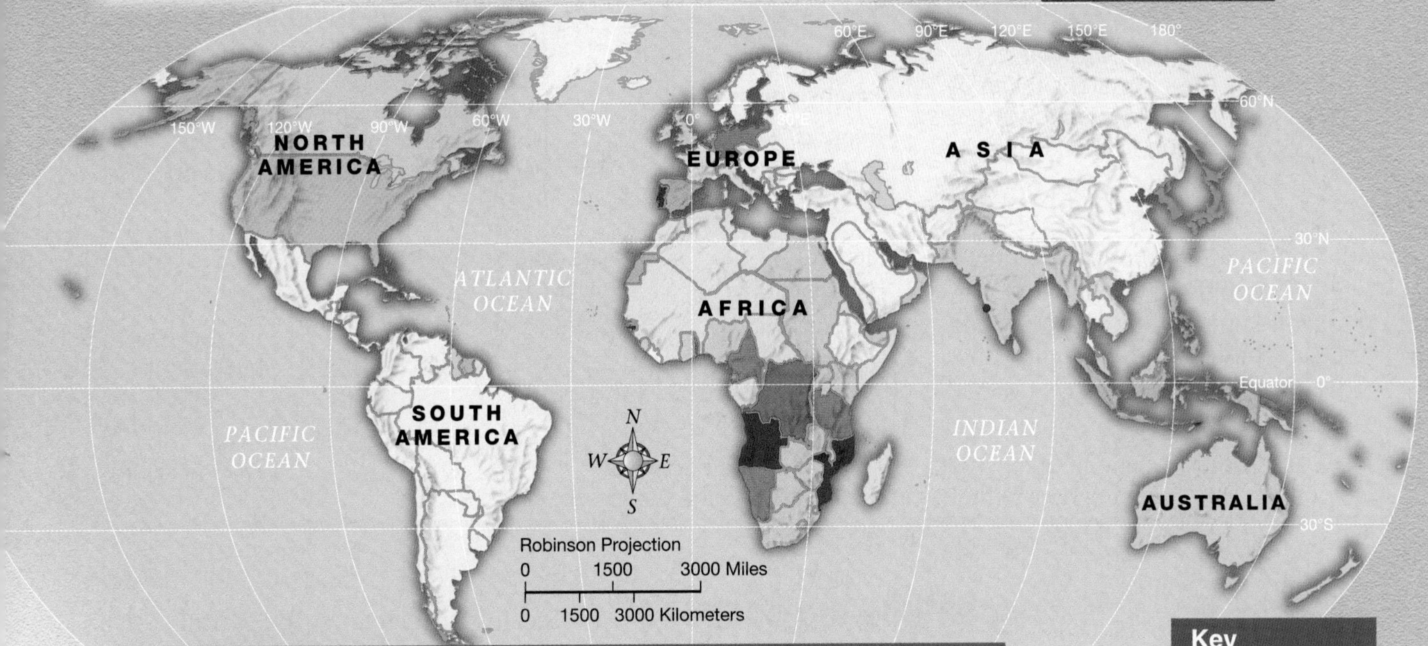
NORTH AMERICA
SOUTH AMERICA
EUROPE
ASIA
AFRICA
AUSTRALIA
ATLANTIC OCEAN
PACIFIC OCEAN
PACIFIC OCEAN
INDIAN OCEAN
150°W
120°W
90°W
60°W
30°W
0°
60°E
90°E
120°E
150°E
180°
60°N
30°N
Equator 0°
30°S
N
S
E
W
Robinson Projection
0 1500 3000 Miles
0 1500 3000 Kilometers
Key
Home countries and their colonies:
American
Belgian
British
Dutch
French
German
Italian
Japanese
Portuguese
Russian
Spanish

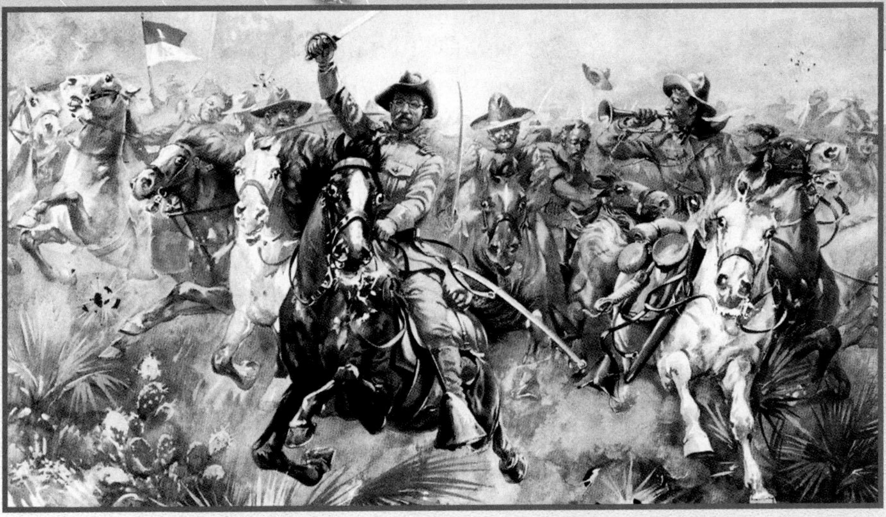

Theodore Roosevelt leading a charge in Cuba

1898
The Spanish-American War breaks out. American troops win quick victories in the Philippines and Cuba.

1904
President Theodore Roosevelt declares that the United States has the right to intervene in Latin America to preserve order.

1914
The Panama Canal opens.

Benjamin Harrison	Grover Cleveland	William McKinley	Theodore Roosevelt	William H. Taft	Woodrow Wilson
1889-1893	1893-1897	1897-1901	1901-1909	1909-1913	1913-1921

1890 · · **1905** · · **1920** ·

1895 ▲
Cubans rebel against Spanish rule.

▲ 1900
The Boxer Rebellion breaks out in China.

▲ 1910
The Mexican Revolution begins.

1 A Pacific Empire

Prepare to Read

Objectives

In this section, you will
- List the early steps taken by the United States toward expansion in the Pacific.
- Identify the causes of imperialism.
- Describe the U.S. conquest of Samoa and Hawaii.
- Summarize how Americans protected their trade with China.

Key Terms

isolationism
expansionism
Treaty of Kanagawa
annex
imperialism
racism
Great White Fleet
sphere of influence
Open Door Policy
Boxer Rebellion

Target Reading Skill

Reading Process Copy the concept web below. As you read, fill in the blank ovals with information about United States involvement in the Pacific. Add as many ovals as you need.

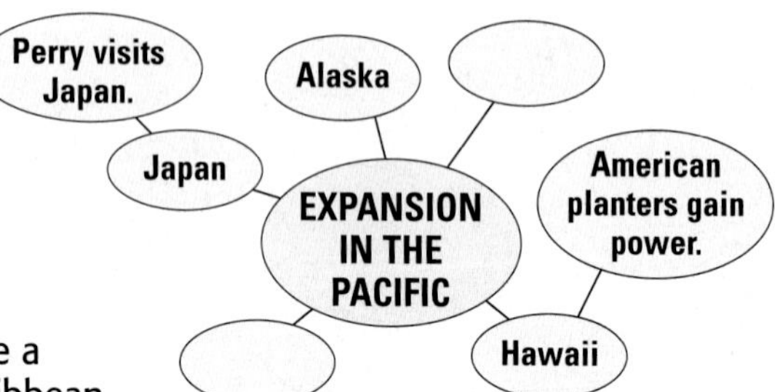

Main Idea At the end of the 1800s, the United States became a world power, acquiring new territories in the Pacific and the Caribbean.

The USS *Iowa*

Setting the Scene A tiny fleet of American ships sailed slowly out of Key West, Florida. Most of the ships had been built years before. Some were made of wood. "Two modern vessels of war," said a future admiral, "would have [destroyed us] in thirty minutes."

In the mid-1870s, the United States Navy ranked twelfth in the world, behind Denmark and Chile. Then, the nation began to build up its navy. By 1896, there were more than 10,000 American sailors in uniform and the navy ranked fifth in the world, with steel-plated battleships powered by steam. The expansion of the navy was but one sign that the United States was becoming a world power.

Isolation and Expansion

In his Farewell Address, George Washington had advised the nation to have little to do with the political affairs of other nations. Later Presidents continued this policy of **isolationism.** Americans had no wish to be dragged into Europe's frequent wars.

Early Expansion Yet, from its earliest existence, the American republic had also followed a policy of **expansionism,** or extending its national boundaries. Americans were constantly pressing westward across the continent.

At the same time, Americans conducted a lively foreign trade. Merchant ships carried American goods to Europe, as well as to Asian nations such as China. The island nation of Japan, however, refused to open its doors to American trade.

The Opening of Japan Fearing outsiders, Japanese rulers had cut themselves off from the world in the 1600s. They expelled all westerners. Only a few Dutch merchants were permitted to trade once a year at the port of Nagasaki. Any foreign sailors who were wrecked on the shores of Japan were not allowed to leave.

Americans wanted Japan to open its ports to trade, as well as to help shipwrecked sailors. To achieve these goals, President Millard Fillmore sent Commodore Matthew Perry to Japan. Perry entered Tokyo Bay with four warships in July 1853. The Japanese had never seen steam-powered ships.

Japanese rulers ordered the Americans to leave. Before departing, though, Perry presented Japanese officials with a letter from President Fillmore. It asked the Japanese to open trading relations with the United States. Perry said he would return the following year for an answer.

Perry returned in February 1854, this time with seven warships. Impressed by this show of strength, the Japanese emperor signed the **Treaty of Kanagawa.** In the treaty, Japan accepted demands to help shipwrecked sailors. It also opened two ports to American trade.

Perry's visit launched trade between Japan and the West. It also made the Japanese aware of the power of the western industrial nations. Japan soon set out to become a modern industrial nation itself, with the United States as one of its models.

Viewing History

American Ship in Japan

Japan

This woodcut shows an American steamship in Japan in 1861. By this time, the Japanese were no longer shocked by the sight of the ships they had called "floating volcanoes."

Applying Information ***Could this picture have been created 10 years earlier? Explain.***

Seward Looks to the Pacific

American interest in Asia and the Pacific continued. In the 1860s, Secretary of State William Seward wanted the United States to dominate trade in the Pacific. In 1867, he persuaded Congress to **annex,** or take over, Midway Island, in the middle of the Pacific Ocean. The island became part of the United States. Seward also made a bold deal to buy the vast territory of Alaska from Russia.

The Land Deal of the Century Seward saw Alaska as an important stepping stone for increasing United States trade in Asia and the Pacific. For their part, the Russians were eager to get rid of the territory, which was too far away to govern effectively.

One night in 1867, Seward was playing cards. Suddenly, he was interrupted by a message from the Russian ambassador. The czar, or emperor, of Russia was willing to sell Alaska to the United States for $7.2 million. Seward agreed to buy the land then and there.

"But your Department is closed," said the ambassador.

"Never mind that," Seward replied. "Before midnight you will find me at the Department, which will be open and ready for business."

Next morning, Seward completed the deal. The cost came to 2 cents an acre. The purchase of Alaska increased the area of the United States by almost one fifth.

"Seward's Folly" At the time, the purchase seemed foolish. Most Americans thought of Alaska as a barren land of icy mountains and

AmericanHeritage M A G A Z I N E

HISTORY **HAPPENED HERE**

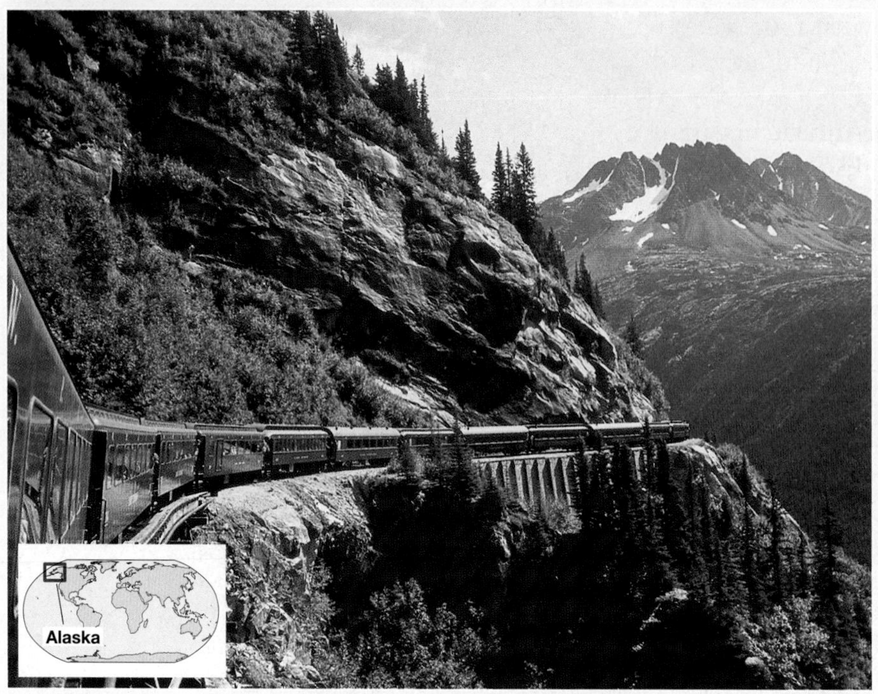

White Pass and Yukon Railroad

When the Alaska gold rush began, fortune seekers had to travel on foot. The journey became easier when the White Pass and Yukon Railroad opened. Construction began at Skagway, Alaska, in 1898. Today, you can ride a train along the same narrow trail that once carried gold seekers and supplies.

Virtual Field Trip For an interactive look at the White Pass and Yukon Railroad, visit PHSchool.com, **Web Code mfd-2301.**

frozen fish. They mockingly called the new territory "Seward's Ice Box" and referred to the purchase as "Seward's Folly."

Minds changed in the 1890s, after prospectors found gold in Alaska. Miners rushed to the new territory as they had once rushed to California. Since then, Seward's vision of Alaska as a valuable territory has proved correct. The lowlands of southern Alaska are well suited to farming. The land is also rich in timber, copper, petroleum, and natural gas. In 1959, Alaska became the forty-ninth state.

Imperialism

The period between 1870 and 1914 has often been called the Age of Imperialism. **Imperialism** is the policy of powerful countries seeking to control the economic and political affairs of weaker countries or regions. Between 1870 and 1914, European nations, such as Britain, Germany, and France, seized control of almost the entire continent of Africa and much of southern Asia. During this period, the United States and Japan also became imperial powers.

Why Imperialism? There were several reasons for the growth of imperialism. First, the industrial nations of Europe needed raw materials and new markets. European factories used raw materials from Africa and Asia to manufacture goods. Some of these goods would then be sold in Africa and Asia.

A second factor that shaped imperialism was **racism,** or the belief that one race is superior to another. Many Europeans felt that they had a duty to spread their religion and culture to people whom they considered to be less civilized. British writer Rudyard Kipling called this responsibility "the white man's burden." Such thinking ignored the fact that Africans and Asians already had rich cultures of their own.

A third cause was competition. When a European country colonized an area, it often closed the markets of that area to other countries. A European nation might take over an area just to keep rival nations out.

Americans Seek Empire Americans could not ignore Europe's race for colonies. By the 1890s, the United States was a world leader in both industry and agriculture. American factories turned out huge amounts of steel and other goods. American farms grew bumper crops of corn, wheat, and cotton. The nation was growing rapidly, and arguments in favor of expansion held great appeal.

Many people believed that the American economy would collapse unless the United States gained new foreign markets. Albert Beveridge of Indiana summed up the arguments for such commercial expansion:

> "Today we are raising more than we can consume. Today we are making more than we can use. Today our industrial society is congested; there are more workers than there is work. . . . Therefore we must find new markets for our produce, new occupations for our capital, new work for our labor."
>
> —Albert Beveridge, quoted in *Beveridge and the Progressive Era* (Bowers)

Expansionists also argued that Americans had a right and a duty to spread western culture. Josiah Strong, a Congregational minister, declared that Americans were "divinely commissioned" to bring democracy and Christianity "down upon Mexico, down upon Central and South America, out upon the islands of the sea."

Other expansionists stressed the need to make up for the vanishing frontier. For 100 years, the economy had boomed, as Americans settled the West. The 1890 census said, however, that the frontier was gone. People in crowded eastern cities had no new land to settle. The solution, said some, was to take new land overseas.

A New Navy One leading supporter of American imperialism was naval captain Alfred Mahan. In an influential 1890 book, *The Influence of Sea Power Upon History*, Mahan argued that the prosperity of the United States depended on foreign trade. Furthermore, he said, a bigger navy was needed to protect American merchant ships. "When a question arises of control over distant regions," Mahan wrote, "it must ultimately be decided by naval power."

In Mahan's view, the United States could not expand its navy unless it controlled naval bases throughout the world. Mahan was especially interested in acquiring harbors in the Caribbean and the Pacific as links to Latin America and Asia.

American Foreign Trade, 1865–1915

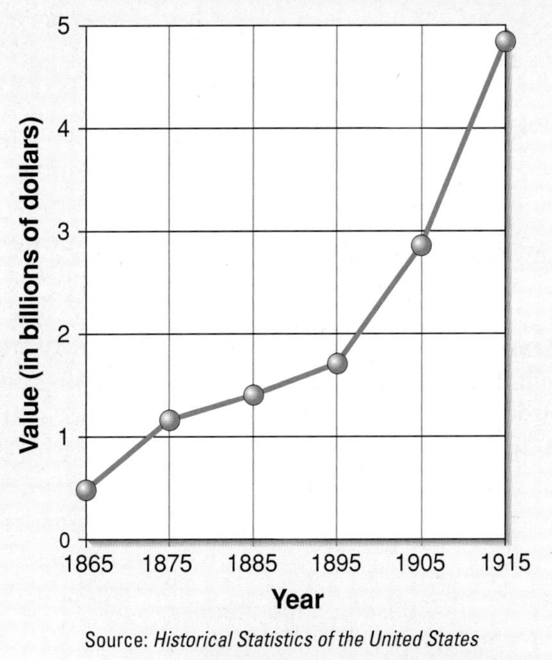

Source: *Historical Statistics of the United States*

GRAPH *Skills*

As American industry grew, so did trade between the United States and foreign countries.

1. **Comprehension** How much did the value of American imports and exports increase from 1885 to 1915?
2. **Critical Thinking Drawing Inferences** How is the information on this graph related to the growth of the United States Navy?

Even before Mahan's appeal, Congress had begun to enlarge and modernize the navy. By 1900, a powerful American navy was ready for action. Its steam-powered ships were called the **Great White Fleet** because their steel hulls were all painted white.

Rivalry Over Samoa

As naval power grew, the United States showed increasing interest in Samoa, a chain of islands in the South Pacific. Samoa had a fine harbor that could serve as a naval base and commercial port.

Germany and Great Britain also realized the value of the harbor. As the three nations competed for control, a military clash seemed likely. In 1889, German ships fired upon Samoan villages that were friendly to the Americans. For months, German and American sailors eyed each other nervously from their warships. Then, with tensions at their highest, a powerful storm sank ships of both countries. The disaster helped ease the crisis.

Later, the three nations arranged a peaceful settlement. The United States and Germany divided Samoa, while Britain received territories elsewhere in the Pacific. The United States had demonstrated that it would assert its power in the Pacific Ocean.

Taking Over Hawaii

Another Pacific territory that had long interested the United States was Hawaii. Hawaii is a chain of eight large islands and more than 100 smaller islands. Hawaii's rich soil, warm climate, and plentiful rainfall allow farmers to grow crops all year round.

GEOGRAPHY *Skills*

In the 1800s, the United States gained control of a number of territories in and around the Pacific Ocean.

1. **Location** On the map, locate **(a)** Alaska, **(b)** Hawaii, **(c)** Midway Island, **(d)** American Samoa, **(e)** Japan.
2. **Region** Based on longitude and latitude, which Pacific islands acquired by the United States were in the Western Hemisphere? The Southern Hemisphere?
3. **Critical Thinking Drawing Conclusions** Why would possession of the islands shown here be important to American trade with China and Japan?

The United States Expands in the Pacific

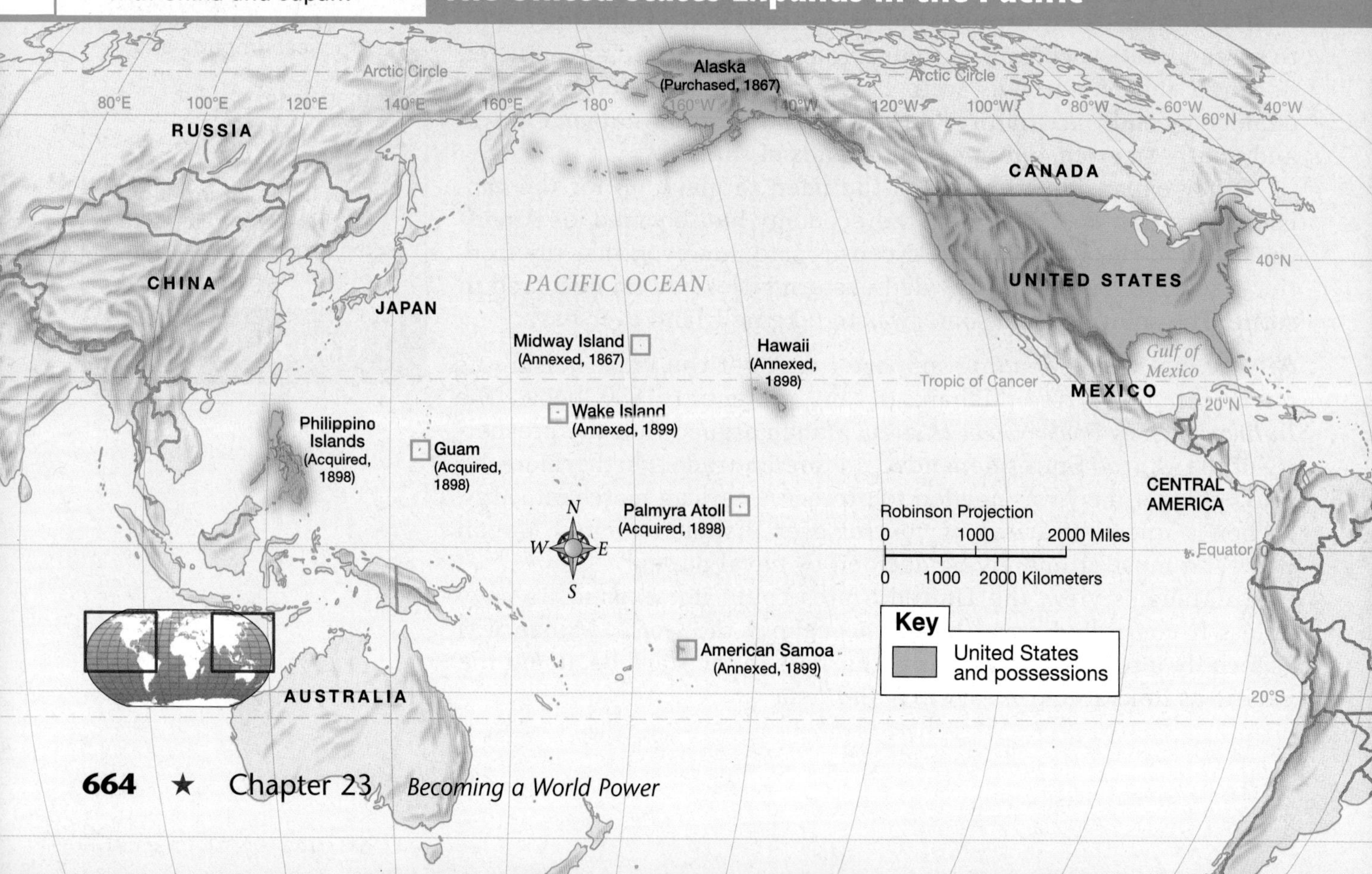

Westerners first learned about Hawaii in 1778. A British sea captain, James Cook, dropped anchor in the islands on his way to China. In the early 1800s, American ships bound for China began stopping in Hawaii, and a few American sailors and traders settled there.

Missionaries and Planters In 1820, American missionaries began arriving in Hawaii. They were eager to convert the Hawaiians to Christianity. The missionaries and other Americans became valued advisers to the rulers of Hawaii. Americans helped write Hawaii's first constitution in 1840.

By the mid-1800s, Americans had set up large sugar plantations in Hawaii. Needing cheap labor, the planters imported thousands of workers from China, Korea, the Philippines, and Japan. By 1900, one fourth of Hawaii's population had been born in Japan.

As the sugar industry grew, so did the wealth and political power of American planters. In 1887, they forced the Hawaiian king, Kalakaua, to accept a new constitution. It reduced royal power and increased the planters' influence.

Planters Rebel Kalakaua died in 1891. The new queen, Liliuokalani (lih lee oo oh kah LAH nee), cherished Hawaiian independence. Rejecting the new constitution, she sought to reduce the influence and privileges of planters and foreign merchants.

In 1893, the American planters rebelled against the queen's attempt to limit their power. The American ambassador called for United States marines to land on Hawaii and protect American lives. In fact, the marines helped topple the queen. Faced with American guns, Liliuokalani gave up her throne:

> "I yield to the superior force of the United States of America. . . . To avoid any collision of armed forces and perhaps the loss of life, I do this under protest, and impelled by said force, yield my authority."
>
> —Liliuokalani, letter to the United States government, 1893

Annexing Hawaii With Liliuokalani gone, the planters quickly set up a republic and asked the United States to annex Hawaii. A debate raged in Congress for months. President Grover Cleveland blocked moves to take over the islands. "Our interference in the Hawaiian Revolution of 1893 was disgraceful," he later said.

Congress finally annexed Hawaii in 1898, after Cleveland left office. Two years later, Hawaii became a United States territory. In 1959, Hawaii became the fiftieth state.

An American Profile

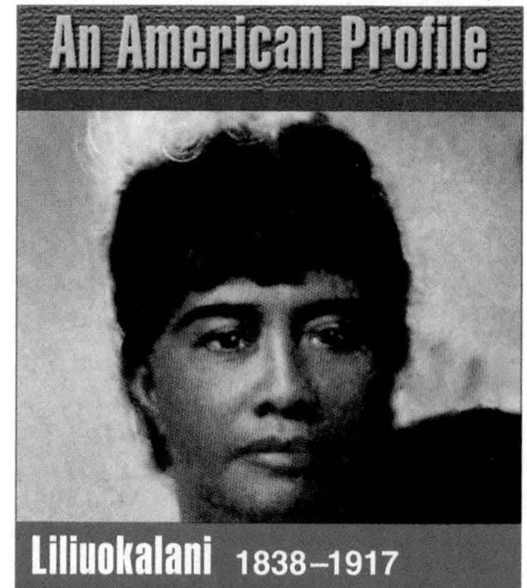

Liliuokalani 1838–1917

Liliuokalani did not reject all things foreign. As a child, she was educated by American missionaries. She later met Queen Victoria of England. She even married a non-Hawaiian, who died soon after she became queen. But as queen, she fought to reduce foreign influence.

Hawaii's last queen was also a talented songwriter. After Hawaii became a United States territory, she composed the famous "Aloha Oe," or "Farewell to Thee." Even after giving up her throne, she continued to fight, unsuccessfully suing the government for loss of property.

Why do you think Liliuokalani chose to take the actions she did?

Protecting Trade With China

Despite its new footholds in the Pacific, the United States was a latecomer to the race for Pacific and Asian territory. Britain, Germany, Japan, and other industrial nations were already competing for colonies in Asia. The rivalry was especially fierce in China.

Once the most advanced empire in the world, China had been weakened by years of civil war. In addition, China had refused to industrialize in the 1800s. It was unable to fight off industrial nations seeking profits from its vast resources and markets.

The Open Door In the late 1800s, Britain, France, Germany, Russia, and Japan carved spheres of influence in China. A **sphere of influence** was an area, usually around a seaport, where a nation had special trading privileges. Each nation made laws for its own citizens in its own sphere.

Use Prior Knowledge *Target Skill* Why was the United States at a disadvantage competing with the other powers?

The United States was eager to gain a share of the China trade. However, Secretary of State John Hay feared that the imperial powers would cut China off to American merchants. To prevent this, Hay sent a letter in 1899 to all the nations that had spheres of influence in China. He urged them to keep an "open door" in China permitting any nation to trade in the spheres of others. Reluctantly, the imperialist powers accepted the **Open Door Policy.**

The Boxers Rebel Many Chinese resented foreign influence. Some formed a secret society called the Righteous Fists of Harmony, or Boxers. In 1900, the Boxers attacked westerners, whom they called "foreign devils," all over China. More than 200 foreigners were killed. Hundreds of others were trapped in Beijing, the Chinese capital.

Foreign governments quickly organized an international army that included 2,500 Americans. Armed with modern weapons, they fought their way into Beijing. They freed the trapped foreigners and crushed the uprising.

Several nations saw the **Boxer Rebellion** as an excuse to seize more land in China. Secretary of State Hay sent another Open Door letter, urging all nations to respect China's independence. Britain, France, and Germany officially accepted Hay's letter. Fearing war, Japan and Russia quietly observed Hay's policy. Hay's Open Door letters showed that, to defend its interests, the United States was ready to take a larger role in world affairs.

★ ★ ★ Section 1 Assessment ★ ★ ★

Recall

1. **Identify** Explain the significance of **(a)** Matthew Perry, **(b)** Treaty of Kanagawa, **(c)** William Seward, **(d)** Alfred Mahan, **(e)** Great White Fleet, **(f)** Liliuokalani, **(g)** John Hay, **(h)** Open Door Policy, **(i)** Boxer Rebellion.
2. **Define** **(a)** isolationism, **(b)** expansionism, **(c)** annex, **(d)** imperialism, **(e)** racism, **(f)** sphere of influence.

Comprehension

3. How did the United States expand in the Pacific before 1870?
4. Why did the Age of Imperialism begin?
5. Why did American planters lead a rebellion in Hawaii?
6. **(a)** What was the goal of the Open Door Policy in China? **(b)** Did it succeed?

Critical Thinking and Writing

7. **Exploring the Main Idea** Review the Main Idea statement at the beginning of this section. Then, write two brief statements about American expansion from the viewpoints of William Seward and of Liliuokalani.
8. **Linking Past and Present** Do you think the United States could return to a policy of isolationism today? Write a paragraph giving reasons.

ACTIVITY

Go Online PHSchool.com

Connecting to Today
Use the Internet to find out about the role that is played by Alaska or Hawaii in the United States today. Prepare a page for an illustrated brochure focusing on the state's geography, people, resources, or culture. For help in completing the activity, visit PHSchool.com, **Web Code mfd-2302.**

Identifying Historical Trends

As you know, historical events are not isolated occurrences but are linked to events that preceded and that followed them. By examining different forms of evidence, you can determine how past events fit into the larger picture. This can help you identify historical trends.

In this excerpt, Albert Beveridge speaks in favor of building an American empire:

> "Distance and oceans are no arguments. The fact that all the territory our fathers bought and seized is [connected by land], is no argument. In 1819 Florida was farther from New York than Puerto Rico is from Chicago today; Texas, farther from Washington in 1845 than Hawaii is from Boston in 1898; California, more inaccessible in 1847 than the Philippines are now. The ocean does not separate us from lands of our duty and desire."
>
> —Albert Beveridge, "The March of the Flag"

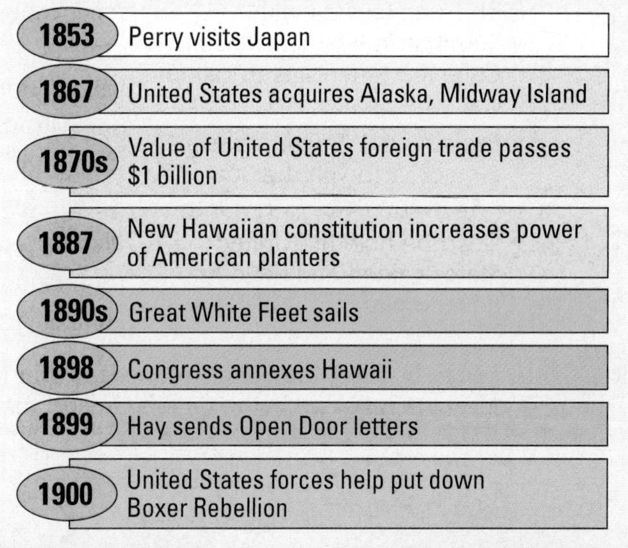

1853	Perry visits Japan
1867	United States acquires Alaska, Midway Island
1870s	Value of United States foreign trade passes $1 billion
1887	New Hawaiian constitution increases power of American planters
1890s	Great White Fleet sails
1898	Congress annexes Hawaii
1899	Hay sends Open Door letters
1900	United States forces help put down Boxer Rebellion

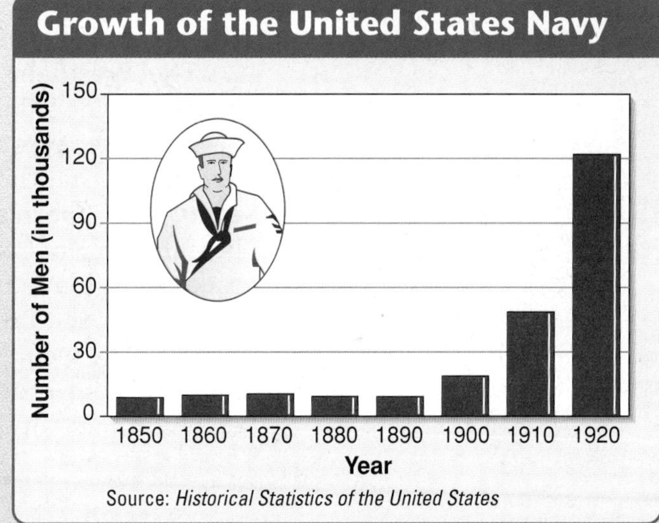

Source: *Historical Statistics of the United States*

Learn the Skill *To learn to identify historical trends, use the following steps:*

1. **Examine the evidence.** Study the materials and identify the key facts and issues.
2. **Look for connections among the different pieces of evidence.** What similarities can you find? How are they related?
3. **Identify historical trends.** What is the direction that these events are taking? What shifts in policy do they show?

Practice the Skill *Use the excerpt, the table, and the graph above to answer the following questions:*

1. **(a)** What kinds of events does the table show? **(b)** What is the main point Beveridge makes about overseas lands? **(c)** What change in the United States Navy does the graph show?
2. **(a)** Which events on the table are related to the subject of the graph? Explain. **(b)** How would Beveridge have reacted to the events on the table and the changes shown on the graph?
3. **(a)** What trend can you identify from these three pieces of evidence? **(b)** What other kinds of information might also reflect this trend?

Apply the Skill *See the Chapter Review and Assessment.*

2 War With Spain

Prepare to Read

Objectives

In this section, you will

- Summarize why tensions in Cuba led Americans to call for war with Spain.
- Explain how Americans won a quick victory in the Spanish-American War.
- Describe how the United States gained and ruled its new empire.

Key Terms

reconcentration
atrocity
yellow journalism
Spanish-American War
Rough Riders
Buffalo Soldiers
Platt Amendment
protectorate
Foraker Act

Target Reading Skill

Sequence Copy this flowchart. As you read, fill in the boxes with events relating to the growth of an American empire. The first and last boxes should help you get started.

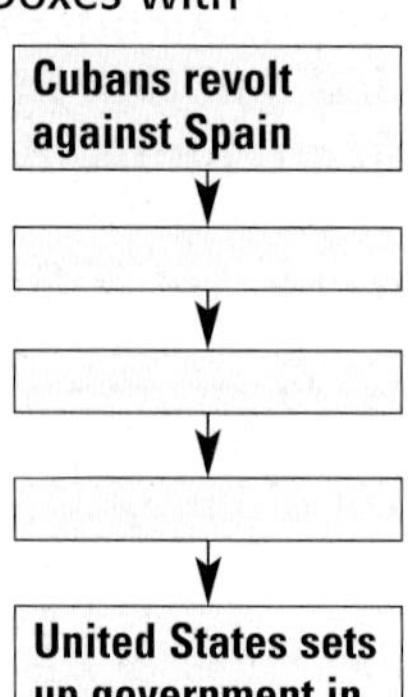

Main Idea In 1898, the Spanish-American War launched an age of American imperialism in the Caribbean and the Pacific.

William McKinley

Setting the Scene President William McKinley could not sleep. Night after night, he lay awake in his bedroom in the White House. He even had to seek the help of a doctor.

The President was worried about a looming war over Cuba, a Spanish-ruled island just 90 miles off the coast of Florida. Cuban patriots were in revolt against Spanish rule. Many Americans demanded that the President take action to help the Cubans. Almost every day, American newspapers reported stories of the cruelty and brutality of Spanish rule. The reports were often exaggerated, sometimes even made up. Nonetheless, they stirred American anger.

At first, the President resisted calls for war. But at 4 A.M. on April 25, 1898, a weary McKinley signed a declaration of war against Spain. The brief war that followed would launch the United States on its own age of imperialism in the Caribbean and the Pacific.

Tension in Cuba

For many years, Americans had looked longingly at Cuba. As early as 1823, Secretary of State John Quincy Adams had compared Cuba to a ripe apple. A storm, he said, might tear that apple "from its native tree"—the Spanish empire—and drop it into the hands of the United States.

By the 1890s, Spain's once-vast empire in the Western Hemisphere had shrunk to two islands in the Caribbean, Cuba and Puerto Rico. Then, Cuban rebels created the storm that Adams had hoped for.

"Cuba Libre!" In 1868, the Cuban people had rebelled against Spanish rule. The revolution was finally crushed after 10 years of fighting. Some of the revolutionaries fled to New York where they kept up the battle for freedom. Puerto Rican–born Lola Rodríguez de Tió wrote patriotic poems in support of Cuban independence. José Martí worked day and night raising funds and giving speeches in support of Cuban independence. He told sympathetic Americans of the Cuban struggle for freedom in his newspaper, *Patria.*

In 1895, Martí returned to Cuba. With cries of *Cuba Libre!*—"Free Cuba!"—rebels launched a new fight against Spain. Martí was killed early in the fighting, but the rebels battled on. Before long, they won control of much of the island.

The rebels burned sugar cane fields and sugar mills all over Cuba. They hoped that this would make the island unprofitable for Spain and persuade the Spanish to leave. The rebels killed workers who opposed them. They even blew up some passenger trains.

In response, Spain sent a new governor to Cuba, General Valeriano Weyler (WAY ee lair). Weyler used brutal tactics to crush the revolt. In a policy known as **reconcentration,** his men moved about half a million Cubans into detention camps so that they could not aid the rebels. At least 100,000 Cubans in reconcentration camps died from starvation and disease.

Viewing History

Rebels in Cuba

This print appeared in a United States newspaper in 1896. It shows Cuban rebels leading a charge against Spanish troops.

Identifying Points of View ***Do you think this artist wanted Americans to support Cuban independence from Spain? Explain.***

American Opinion Splits In the United States, people watched the revolt in nearby Cuba with growing concern. The United States had vital economic links to the island. Americans had invested about $50 million in Cuban sugar and rice plantations, railroads, tobacco, and iron mines. American trade with Cuba was worth about $100 million a year.

Opinion split over whether the United States should intervene in Cuba. Many business leaders opposed American involvement. They thought that it might hurt foreign trade. Other Americans, however, sympathized with Cuban desires for freedom. They called on the government to take action. Senator Henry Cabot Lodge of Massachusetts compared the Cuban rebels to the Patriots in the American Revolution:

> "They have risen against oppression, compared to which the oppression which led us to rebel against England is as dust in the balance; and they feel that for this reason, if no other, they should have the sympathy of the people of the United States."
>
> —Henry Cabot Lodge, Record of the 54th Congress, 1896

Americans Call for War

The press whipped up American sympathies for the people of Cuba. Two New York newspapers—Joseph Pulitzer's *World* and William Randolph Hearst's *Journal*—competed to print the most grisly stories

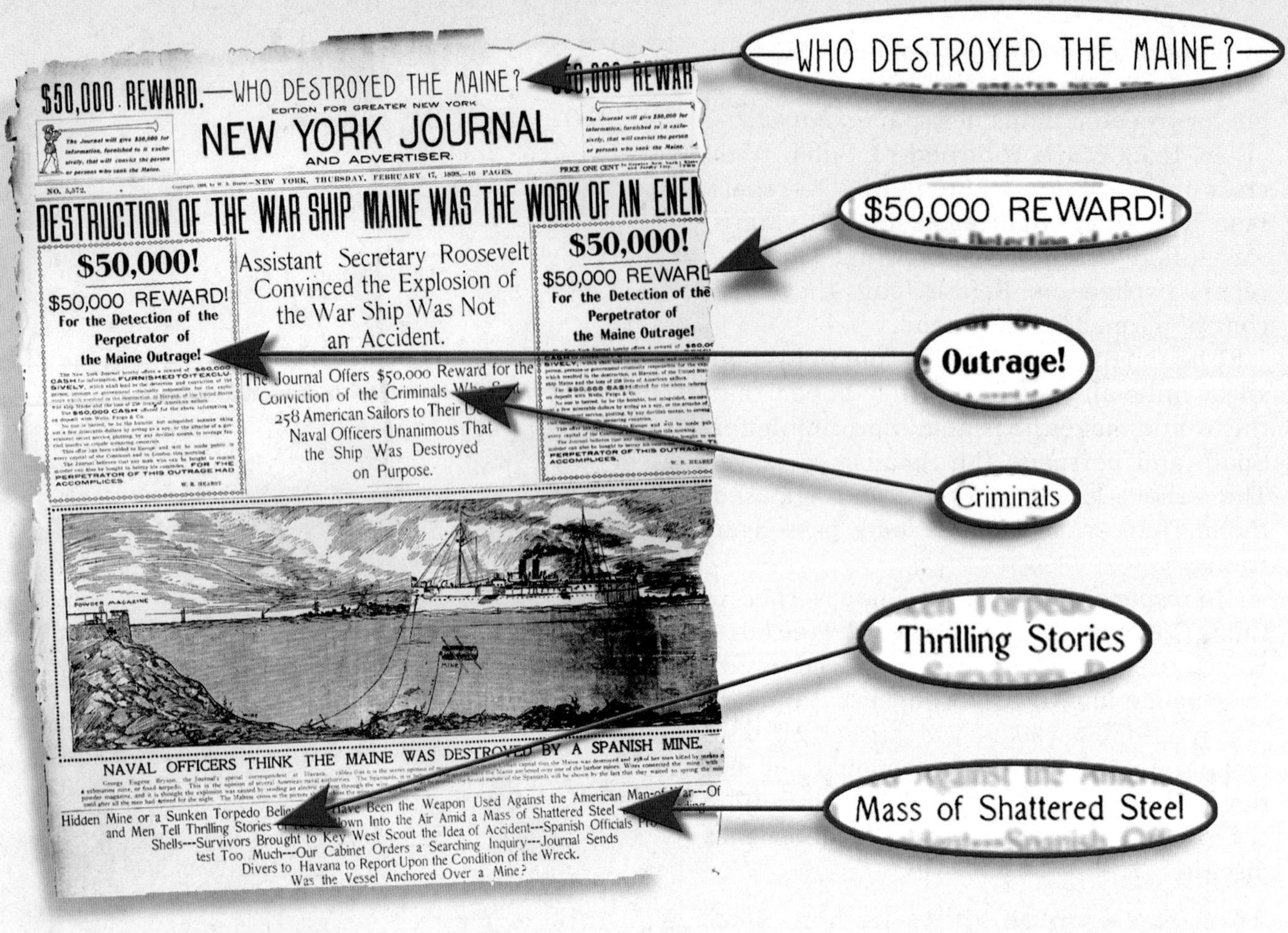

$50,000 REWARD.—WHO DESTROYED THE MAINE?—$50,000 REWAR

EDITION FOR GREATER NEW YORK

NEW YORK JOURNAL

AND ADVERTISER.

DESTRUCTION OF THE WAR SHIP MAINE WAS THE WORK OF AN ENEM

$50,000!

$50,000 REWARD!
For the Detection of the Perpetrator of the Maine Outrage!

Assistant Secretary Roosevelt Convinced the Explosion of the War Ship Was Not an Accident.

The Journal Offers $50,000 Reward for the Conviction of the Criminals Who Sent 258 American Sailors to Their Death. Naval Officers Unanimous That the Ship Was Destroyed on Purpose.

$50,000!

$50,000 REWARD
For the Detection of the Perpetrator of the Maine Outrage!

POWDER MAGAZINE

NAVAL OFFICERS THINK THE MAINE WAS DESTROYED BY A SPANISH MINE.

Hidden Mine or a Sunken Torpedo Believed to Have Been the Weapon Used Against the American Man-of-War---Officers and Men Tell Thrilling Stories of Being Blown Into the Air Amid a Mass of Shattered Steel and Exploding Shells---Survivors Brought to Key West Scout the Idea of Accident---Spanish Officials Protest Too Much---Our Cabinet Orders a Searching Inquiry---Journal Sends Divers to Havana to Report Upon the Condition of the Wreck. Was the Vessel Anchored Over a Mine?

WHO DESTROYED THE MAINE?

$50,000 REWARD!

Outrage!

Criminals

Thrilling Stories

Mass of Shattered Steel

Viewing History

Yellow Journalism

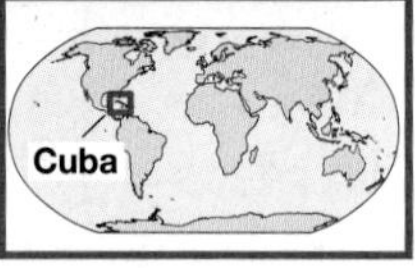

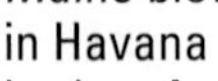

When the *Maine* blew up in Havana harbor, American newspapers were quick to point the finger of blame at Spain. Sensational pictures and language inflamed readers—and sold papers. **Analyzing Primary Sources** ***Why do you think the* New York Journal *included the words and phrases highlighted here?***

about Spanish **atrocities,** or wartime acts of cruelty and brutality. The publishers knew that war with Spain would boost sales of their newspapers.

Sensational Newspaper Stories To attract readers, Hearst and Pulitzer used **yellow journalism,** or reporting that relied on sensational stories and headlines. Often, these reports were biased or untrue. According to one story, a photographer bound for Cuba told Hearst that there was no war. "You supply the pictures," Hearst supposedly replied. "I'll supply the war." News stories described events in Cuba in graphic and horrifying detail.

Despite growing pressure, President Cleveland wanted to avoid war with Spain. He called the war fever in the United States an "epidemic of insanity." Stories in the press, he grumbled, were nonsense. When William McKinley became President in 1897, he also tried to keep the country neutral.

"Remember the *Maine!*" In 1898, fighting broke out in Havana, the Cuban capital. Acting promptly, President McKinley sent the battleship *Maine* to Havana to protect American citizens and property there.

On the night of February 15, the *Maine* lay at anchor in Havana harbor. Just after the bugler played taps, a huge explosion ripped through the ship. The explosion killed at least 260 of the 350 American sailors and officers on board.

The yellow press pounced on the tragedy. "DESTRUCTION OF THE WARSHIP *MAINE* WAS THE WORK OF AN ENEMY," screamed one New York newspaper. "THE WARSHIP *MAINE* SPLIT IN TWO BY AN ENEMY'S SECRET INFERNAL MACHINE?" blared the front page of another.

The real cause of the explosion remains a mystery. Most historians believe that a boiler blew up or there was an accident in the ship's own ammunition hold. But Americans, urged on by Pulitzer and Hearst, clamored for war. "Remember the *Maine!*" they cried.

Still hoping to avoid war, McKinley tried to get Spain to talk with the Cuban rebels. In the end, however, he gave in to war fever. On April 25, 1898, Congress declared war on Spain.

The Spanish-American War

The **Spanish-American War** lasted only four months. The battlefront stretched from the nearby Caribbean to the distant Philippine Islands off the coast of Southeast Asia.

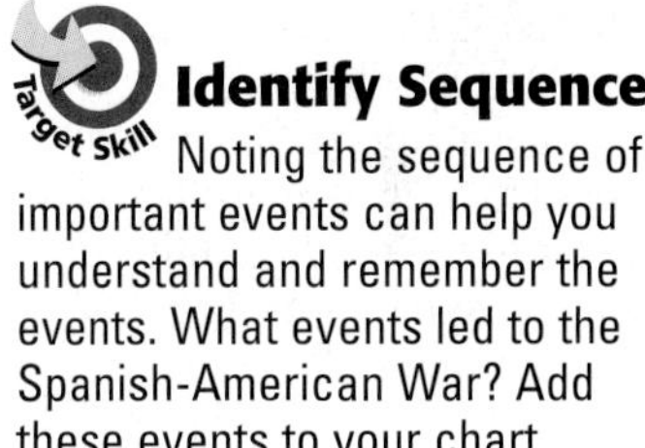

Identify Sequence Noting the sequence of important events can help you understand and remember the events. What events led to the Spanish-American War? Add these events to your chart.

Victory in the Philippines Two months earlier, Assistant Secretary of the Navy Theodore Roosevelt had begun making preparations for a possible war with Spain. Roosevelt quickly realized that a conflict with Spain would be fought not only in the Caribbean but wherever Spanish sea power lay. The Philippine Islands, a Spanish colony and Spain's main naval base in the Pacific, would be a major military objective.

Roosevelt believed it was important to attack the Spanish in the Philippines as soon as war began. He wired secret orders to Commodore George Dewey, commander of the Pacific fleet:

> "Secret and confidential. Order the squadron . . . to Hong Kong. Keep full of coal. In the event of declaration of war Spain, your duty will be to see that the Spanish squadron does not leave the Asiatic coast, and then offensive operations in Philippine Islands."
>
> —Theodore Roosevelt, Telegram, February 25, 1898

Dewey followed Roosevelt's instructions. Immediately after war was declared, the Commodore sailed his fleet swiftly to Manila, the main city of the Philippines. On April 30, 1898, Dewey's ships slipped into Manila harbor under cover of darkness. There, the Spanish fleet lay at anchor.

At dawn, Dewey told his flagship commander, Charles Gridley, "You may fire when you are ready, Gridley." Taking their cue, the Americans bombarded the surprised Spanish ships. By noon, the Spanish fleet had been destroyed.

By July, American ground troops had landed in the Philippines. As in Cuba, local people there had been fighting for independence from Spain for years. With the help of these Filipino rebels, led by Emilio Aguinaldo (ah gwee NAHL doh), the American forces quickly captured Manila.

War in Cuba Meanwhile, American troops had also landed in Cuba. The expedition was badly organized. Soldiers wore heavy woolen uniforms in the tropical heat, and they often had to eat spoiled food. Yet, most were eager for battle.

None was more eager than Theodore Roosevelt. When the war broke out, Roosevelt resigned his position as Assistant Secretary of the Navy. He then organized the First Volunteer Cavalry Regiment, later called the **Rough Riders.** The Rough Riders were a mixed crew, ranging from cowboys to college students and adventurers.

The Rough Riders joined regular troops in the most notable land battle of the war. During the fight for the key Cuban city of Santiago, Americans had to gain control of the San Juan Heights overlooking the city. Under withering fire, charging American forces took two strategic hills. African American members of the 9th and 10th Cavalries, nicknamed **Buffalo Soldiers,** played a major role in the bloody victory. John J. Pershing, commander of the 10th Cavalry, later described how the troops united in what came to be called the Battle of San Juan Hill:

> “White regiments, black regiments, regulars and Rough Riders, representing the young manhood of the North and South, fought shoulder to shoulder, unmindful of race or color, . . . mindful of their common duty as Americans.”
>
> —John J. Pershing, quoted in *The Life of General Pershing* (MacAdam)

Two days later, the Americans destroyed the Spanish fleet in Santiago Bay. The Spanish army in Cuba surrendered. American troops then landed on Puerto Rico and claimed the island.

A Quick End Spain was defeated. On August 12, Spain and the United States agreed to end the fighting. American losses in battle were fairly light—379 killed. However, more than 5,000 Americans died of other causes, such as yellow fever, typhoid, and malaria.

John Hay, who was soon to become Secretary of State, summed up American enthusiasm for the war. “It's been a splendid little war,” he wrote. A malaria-ridden veteran of the war had a different view: “I was lucky—I survived.”

An American Profile

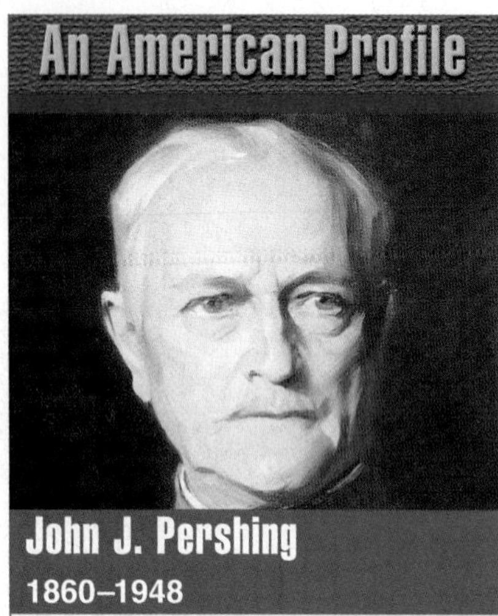

John J. Pershing
1860–1948

As war with Spain loomed, John Pershing was teaching military strategy at West Point. He immediately put in for active duty. "If I did not make every effort to obtain . . . field service," he wrote, "I should never forgive myself."

Throughout his 38-year career, Pershing was everywhere the army needed him, from the West to Cuba to France. But he also knew war's costs. Seeing a line of Cuban refugees, he said, "The suffering of the innocent is not the least of the horrors of war."

Why do you think Pershing was eager to serve in Cuba?

The Debate Over Empire

In a peace treaty signed in Paris in December 1898, Spain agreed to grant Cuba its freedom. Spain also gave the United States two islands: Puerto Rico in the Caribbean and Guam in the Pacific. Finally, in return for $20 million, Spain handed over the Philippines to the United States.

Before the Senate approved the treaty, a great debate occurred. Many Americans objected to the treaty. They said it violated American principles of democracy by turning the United States into a colonial power.

Expansionists favored the treaty. They said that the navy needed bases in the Caribbean and the Pacific. They pointed out that the Philippines and Puerto Rico offered new territory for American businesses. Also, many Americans agreed with President McKinley, who said that the United States would “uplift and civilize and

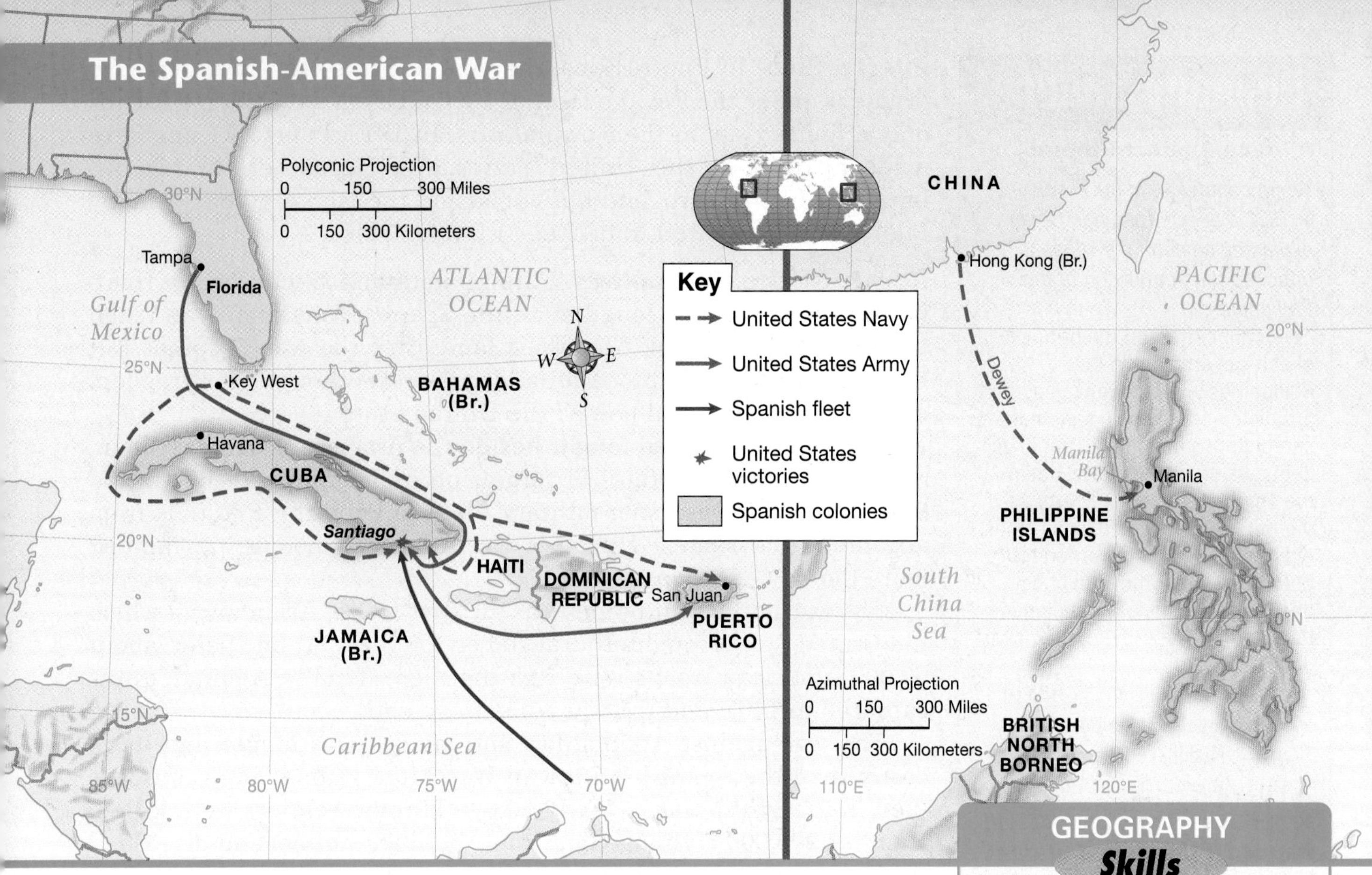

GEOGRAPHY *Skills*

The Spanish-American War was fought on two fronts that were half a world apart.

1. **Location** On the map, locate **(a)** Philippine Islands, **(b)** Manila Bay, **(c)** Cuba, **(d)** Santiago, **(e)** Havana.
2. **Movement** Describe the route that the United States Navy took to reach the Philippines.
3. **Critical Thinking Drawing Conclusions** Why do you think Dewey was able to trap the Spanish fleet in Manila Bay?

Christianize [the Filipinos]." In fact, most Filipinos already were Christians.

Urged on by McKinley, the Senate narrowly approved the peace treaty in February 1899. At last, the United States had acquired a true overseas empire.

Ruling an Empire

Americans had to decide how to rule their new territories. When the war with Spain began, the United States pledged to "leave the government and control of [Cuba] to its people." That promise, however, was not kept.

Cuba After the war, American soldiers remained in Cuba while the United States debated. Many in Congress believed that Cuba was not ready for independence. American business leaders feared that an independent Cuba might threaten their investments there.

In the end, the United States let the Cuban people write their own constitution. However, Cuba had to accept the **Platt Amendment.** The amendment allowed the United States to intervene in Cuba and gave the United States control of the naval base at Guantanamo Bay.

In effect, the amendment made Cuba an American **protectorate,** a nation whose independence is limited by the control of a more powerful country. The United States pulled its army out of Cuba in 1902. However, American soldiers would return to Cuba in 1906 and again in 1917.

Primary Source

A Voice Against Empire

While campaigning for President in 1900, William Jennings Bryan explained some of the reasons he opposed the acquisition of the Philippines:

"We cannot [reject] the principle of self-government in the Philippines without weakening that principle here. Lincoln said that the safety of this nation was not in its fleets, its armies, its forts, but in the spirit which prizes liberty as the heritage of all men, in all lands, everywhere, and he warned his countrymen that they could not destroy this spirit without planting the seeds of [tyranny] at their own doors."

— William Jennings Bryan, Official Proceedings of the Democratic National Convention, 1900

Analyzing Primary Sources

What does Bryan predict will happen if the United States rules over the Philippines?

Puerto Rico In Puerto Rico, the United States set up a new government under the Foraker Act of 1900. The act gave Puerto Ricans only a limited say in their own affairs. In 1917, Puerto Ricans were made citizens of the United States. Americans set up schools, improved health care, and built roads on the island. Even so, many Puerto Ricans wanted to be free of foreign rule.

Revolt in the Philippines Filipino nationalists had begun fighting for independence long before the Spanish-American War. When the United States took over their land after the war, Filipinos felt betrayed. Led by Emilio Aguinaldo, they now fought for freedom against a new imperial power: the United States.

Aguinaldo, who had fought beside the Americans against Spain, accused the United States of forgetting its beginnings. The United States, he said, was using military force to keep the Filipinos from attaining "the same rights that the American people proclaimed more than a century ago."

The war in the Philippines was the first all-out Asian war in which the United States fought. It dragged on for years. At one point, about 60,000 American troops were fighting there. Finally, Aguinaldo was captured in 1901, and the war came to an end.

The war against Aguinaldo's nationalists was longer and more costly than the Spanish-American War. More than 4,000 Americans died in the Philippines. Nearly 20,000 Filipino soldiers were killed. Another 200,000 civilians died from shelling, famine, and disease.

In 1902, the United States set up a government in the Philippines similar to the one in Puerto Rico. Filipinos, however, were not made American citizens because the United States planned to give them independence in the future. It was not until 1946, however, that the United States allowed Filipinos to govern themselves.

★ ★ ★ Section 2 Assessment ★ ★ ★

Recall

1. **Identify** Explain the significance of **(a)** Lola Rodríguez de Tió, **(b)** José Martí, **(c)** Valeriano Weyler, **(d)** Spanish-American War, **(e)** George Dewey, **(f)** Emilio Aguinaldo, **(g)** Rough Riders, **(h)** Buffalo Soldiers, **(i)** Platt Amendment, **(j)** Foraker Act.
2. **Define** **(a)** reconcentration, **(b)** atrocity, **(c)** yellow journalism, **(d)** protectorate.

Comprehension

3. Why did many Americans want to intervene in Cuba?
4. Describe the American victories in the Philippines and Cuba.
5. **(a)** Why did Americans disagree about the issue of empire? **(b)** How did the United States get involved in a war in the Philippines?

Critical Thinking and Writing

6. **Exploring the Main Idea** Review the Main Idea statement at the beginning of this section. Then, create a cause-and-effect chart for the Spanish-American War.
7. **Identifying Points of View** As John Hay, write a note to President McKinley giving reasons why you called the conflict with Spain "a splendid little war."

ACTIVITY

Drawing a Political Cartoon Draw a political cartoon about the debate over acquiring an empire. Take the viewpoint of either an expansionist or an opponent of imperialism.

3 The United States in Latin America

Prepare to Read

Objectives

In this section, you will
- Identify why the United States built the Panama Canal.
- Describe how Theodore Roosevelt used his "big stick" in Latin America.
- Explain why a crisis erupted between the United States and Mexico.

Key Terms

isthmus
corollary
Roosevelt Corollary
dollar diplomacy
moral diplomacy

Target Reading Skill

Main Idea As you read, prepare an outline of this section. Use roman numerals to indicate the major headings, capital letters for the subheadings, and numbers for the supporting details.

I. A Canal Across Panama
  A. Roosevelt's plan
    1. Reduce shipping costs
    2.
  B. Taking the Canal Zone
    1. Colombia refuses offer
    2.
II. Building the Canal
  A.
  B.

Main Idea Increasing economic ties led the United States to intervene in Latin American affairs.

Setting the Scene William Seward had dreamed of an American empire stretching southward. Under his plan, the United States would hold islands of the Caribbean as bases to protect a new water route across Central America. Mexico would be a state and Mexico City the capital of the new empire.

Seward's vision never came to pass. But as a new century dawned, the United States did stretch its power and influence across Latin America.

1901 cartoon

A Canal Across Panama

When Theodore Roosevelt became President in 1901, he was determined to build a canal through the Isthmus of Panama. An **isthmus** is a narrow strip of land connecting two larger bodies of land. Panama was an ideal location for a canal. Only 50 miles of land separated the Caribbean Sea and the Pacific Ocean.

Roosevelt's Plan Roosevelt knew that a canal through the isthmus would greatly benefit American commerce and military capability. By avoiding the long trip around South America, ships could shorten the journey from New York City to San Francisco by nearly 8,000 miles. Thus, a canal would reduce the cost of shipping goods. In addition, in the event of a war, the navy could quickly move ships back and forth between the Pacific Ocean and the Atlantic Ocean.

To build the canal, Roosevelt had to deal with Colombia, which owned the isthmus. Roosevelt asked Secretary of State John Hay to approach Colombia. Hay offered $10 million cash plus $250,000 a year to rent a strip of land across Panama.

Taking the Canal Zone When Columbia refused Roosevelt's offer, he was furious. "I do not think the [Colombian] lot of jack rabbits should be allowed permanently to bar one of the future highways of civilization," he exclaimed.

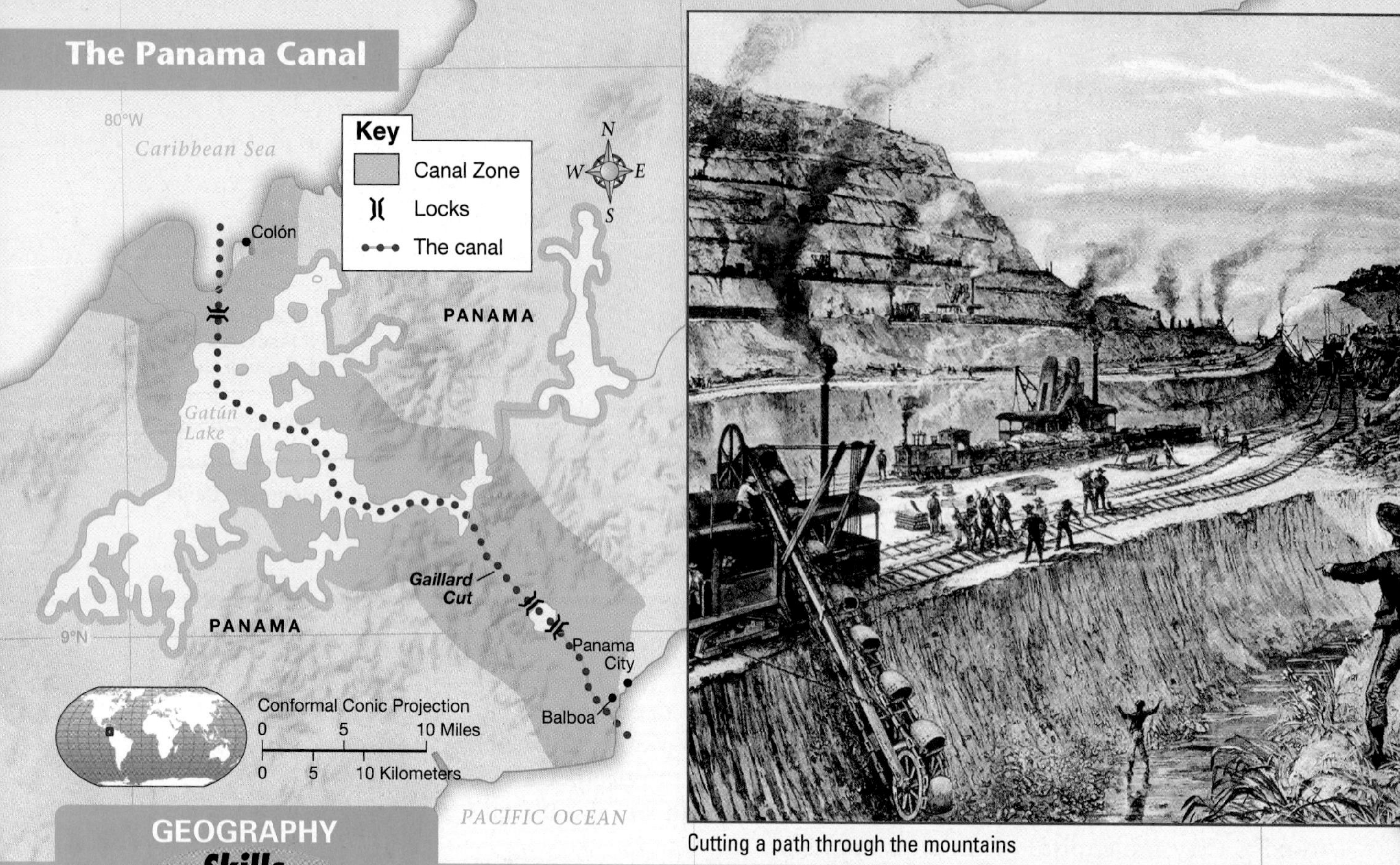

Cutting a path through the mountains

GEOGRAPHY *Skills*

The Panama Canal took almost 10 years to finish. The picture at right shows the digging of the Gaillard Cut.

1. **Location** On the map, locate **(a)** Caribbean Sea, **(b)** Pacific Ocean, **(c)** Canal Zone, **(d)** Gaillard Cut.
2. **Movement** In what direction did ships travel to get from the Caribbean Sea to the Pacific Ocean?
3. **Critical Thinking Synthesizing Information** Based on the map and picture, what were some of the difficulties that geography presented to canal builders?

At times like this, Roosevelt was fond of quoting an African proverb: "Speak softly and carry a big stick, and you will go far." He meant that words should be supported by strong action.

Roosevelt knew that some Panamanians wanted to break away from Colombia. He made it known that he would not help Colombia suppress the rebels. In fact, he might even support the rebellion.

On November 2, 1903, the American warship *Nashville* dropped anchor in the port of Colón, Panama. The next day, Panamanians rebelled against Colombia. American forces stopped Colombian troops from crushing the revolt. Panama then declared itself an independent republic. The United States recognized the new nation at once. Panama in turn agreed to let the United States build a canal on terms similar to those it had offered to Colombia.

Roosevelt's action in Panama angered many Latin Americans. It also upset some members of Congress. The President, however, proudly stated, "I took the Canal Zone and let Congress debate."

Building the Canal

Roosevelt now had the right to build his canal. However, before work could begin, Americans had to conquer a deadly enemy: disease.

Conquering Tropical Diseases With its tropical heat, heavy rainfall, and plentiful swamps, Panama was a "mosquito paradise." This presented serious difficulties for the canal builders. Mosquitoes carry two of the deadliest tropical diseases: malaria and yellow fever.

Dr. William Gorgas, an army physician, arrived in Panama in 1905 to help control the mosquitoes and the spread of disease. He ordered workers to locate all pools of water, where mosquitoes laid their eggs. Day after day, the workers drained swamps, sprayed tons of insecticide, and spread oil on stagnant water to kill mosquito eggs.

By 1906, Gorgas had won his battle. Yellow fever disappeared from Panama. Malaria cases dropped dramatically. Work on the Panama Canal could proceed.

The Big Dig Under the supervision of army engineer Colonel George Goethals, more than 40,000 workers struggled to dig the canal. Most were blacks from the West Indies. They blasted a path through mountains and carved out the largest artificial lake in the world up to that time. In all, they removed more than 200 million cubic yards of earth. Then, they built gigantic locks to raise and lower ships as they passed through the canal. Finally, in 1914, the first ocean-going steamship traveled through the Panama Canal.

The new waterway helped the trade of many nations. American merchants and manufacturers benefited most. They could now ship goods cheaply to South America and Asia. However, many Latin American nations remained bitter about the way in which the United States had gained control of the canal.

Cause *and* Effect

Causes

- Western frontier closes
- Businesses seek raw materials and new markets
- European nations compete for resources and markets

OVERSEAS EXPANSION

Effects

- United States develops strong navy
- Open Door Policy protects trade with China
- United States governs lands in Caribbean and Pacific
- United States builds Panama Canal
- United States sends troops to Latin American nations to protect its interests

Effects Today

- United States is global superpower
- Alaska and Hawaii are 49th and 50th states
- Puerto Rico, American Samoa, Guam, and U.S. Virgin Islands remain United States territories
- United States has close economic ties with Latin America and nations along the Pacific Ocean.

GRAPHIC ORGANIZER *Skills*

In the late 1800s, the United States gradually became more involved in foreign affairs.

1. **Comprehension** List three effects of United States involvement in Latin America.
2. **Critical Thinking Linking Past and Present** Which of the Effects Today listed here do you think is the most important? Explain.

The "Big Stick" in Latin America

The Panama Canal involved the United States more than ever in Latin America. Gradually, President Roosevelt and succeeding Presidents established a policy of intervening in Latin America. The United States was especially concerned when disturbances threatened American lives, property, and interests.

Roosevelt Extends the Monroe Doctrine In 1902, several European countries sent warships to force Venezuela to repay its debts. The United States did not want Europeans to interfere in Latin America. President Roosevelt decided that the United States must step in to keep Europeans out. He declared:

> "If we intend to say 'Hands off' to the powers of Europe, then sooner or later we must keep order ourselves."
>
> —Theodore Roosevelt, quoted in *T. R.: The Last Romantic* (Brands)

POLITICAL CARTOON *Skills*

Teddy Roosevelt and the Caribbean

This 1904 cartoon shows President Roosevelt using the navy to keep order in the Caribbean.

1. **Comprehension** What is the meaning of the object in Roosevelt's right hand?
2. **Understanding Main Ideas** What point is the cartoonist making about the relationship between the United States and Caribbean countries?
3. **Critical Thinking Identifying Points of View** Do you think the cartoonist approved of the Roosevelt Corollary? Explain.

THE BIG STICK IN THE CARIBBEAN SEA

In 1904, Roosevelt announced an important **corollary,** or addition, to the Monroe Doctrine. He claimed that the United States had a right to intervene in Latin America to preserve law and order. By using what he called "international police power," the United States could force Latin Americans to pay their debts to foreign nations. It would also keep those nations from meddling in Latin American affairs. For the next 20 years, Presidents used the **Roosevelt Corollary** to intervene in Latin America.

Dollar Diplomacy Roosevelt's successor, William Howard Taft, also favored a strong role in Latin America. However, he wanted to "substitute dollars for bullets." He urged American bankers to invest in Latin America. Taft's policy of building strong economic ties to Latin America became known as **dollar diplomacy.**

American investors responded eagerly. They helped build roads, railroads, and harbors in Latin America. These improvements increased trade, benefiting both the United States and local governments. The new railroads, for example, brought minerals and other resources to Latin American ports. From there, they were shipped all over the world.

Dollar diplomacy created problems, too. American businesses, such as the United Fruit Company, often meddled in the political affairs of host countries. Sometimes, the United States used military force to keep order. In 1912, when a revolution erupted in Nicaragua, the United States sent in marines to protect American investments.

Moral Diplomacy The next President, Woodrow Wilson, condemned the heavy-handed foreign policy of his predecessors. "The force of America," he said, "is the force of moral principle." The goals of Wilson's **moral diplomacy** were to condemn imperialism, spread democracy, and promote peace.

Nevertheless, Wilson ordered military intervention in Latin America more than any prior President. He sent marines to quell disturbances in Haiti in 1915 and in the Dominican Republic in 1916. American troops remained in Haiti until 1934.

The United States declared that its troops were restoring order and guarding American lives and property. Still, many Latin Americans denounced the United States for invading their countries and interfering in their internal affairs.

The United States and Mexico

Moral diplomacy faced its greatest test in Mexico. Porfirio Díaz, Mexico's president from 1884 to 1911, welcomed American investment. By 1912, Americans had invested about $1 billion to develop mines, oil wells, railroads, and ranches. Yet, most Mexicans remained poor. They worked the land of a few wealthy families, receiving very little for their labor.

Revolution in Mexico Mexicans rebelled against Díaz in 1910. The new leader, Francisco Madero, promised democratic reform. Then, in 1913, Madero was himself overthrown and killed by General Victoriano Huerta (WEHR tuh). As civil war raged, Wilson refused to recognize what he called Huerta's "government of butchers."

Wilson tried to stay neutral. He hoped that Mexico would develop a democratic government without American interference. As Huerta's

GEOGRAPHY *Skills*

In the early 1900s, the United States gained influence all around the Caribbean Sea.

1. **Location** On the map, locate **(a)** Colombia, **(b)** Panama, **(c)** Dominican Republic, **(d)** Haiti, **(e)** Honduras, **(f)** Puerto Rico.
2. **Region** Which of the areas shown on the map was governed directly by the United States?
3. **Critical Thinking Applying Information** Identify three places where Roosevelt's successors applied the Roosevelt Corollary.

The United States in the Caribbean

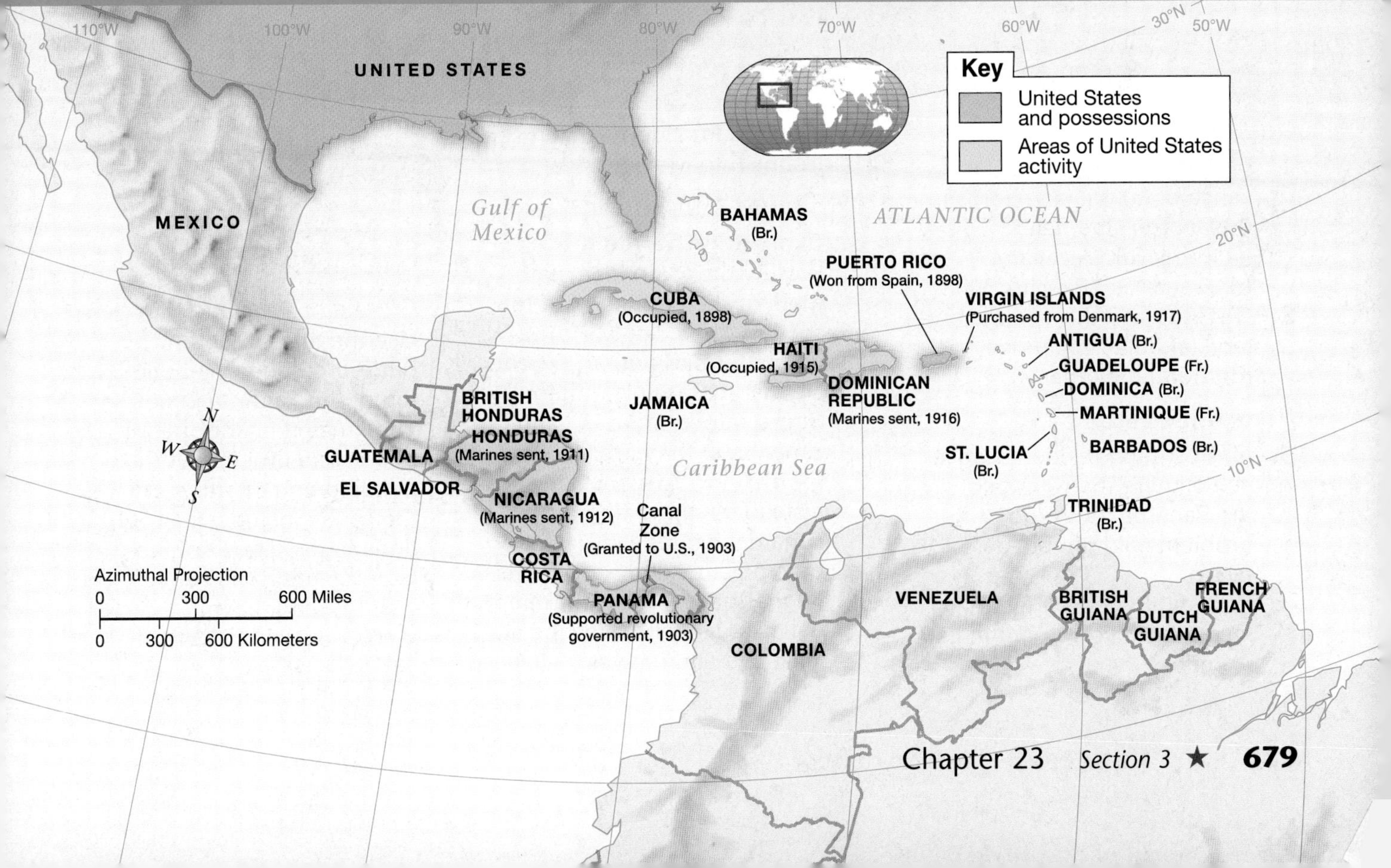

dictatorship grew more brutal, Wilson authorized the sale of arms to Huerta's rival, Venustiano Carranza.

Finally, a minor incident led to American intervention. In 1914, Huerta's troops arrested several American sailors. The sailors were quickly released and an apology issued. Still, Wilson ordered the United States Navy to occupy the Mexican port of Veracruz. Rallied by the American show of strength, Carranza's forces drove Huerta from power. The United States troops withdrew.

Identify Supporting Details

Which details describe the strained relations between the United States and Mexico?

Invading Mexico Still, civil war continued in Mexico. Now, General Francisco "Pancho" Villa hoped to overthrow Carranza. The United States supported Carranza.

In January 1916, Villa's soldiers removed 17 American citizens from a train in Mexico and shot them. In March, Villa raided the town of Columbus, New Mexico, killing 18 Americans. He hoped that his actions would weaken relations between the United States and the Carranza government. But the plan backfired.

Wilson sent General John J. Pershing with an army of several thousand soldiers into Mexico to capture Villa. When Mexico demanded that the troops be withdrawn, Wilson refused. Still, both Wilson and Carranza resisted calls for war. After 11 months, Wilson ordered Pershing to withdraw without capturing Villa. The United States had again shown its willingness to use force to protect its interests. The incident strained relations with Mexico.

As United States troops headed home from Mexico, many Americans realized that their nation's role in world affairs had dramatically changed over the years. Now, the United States stationed troops and ships in both Asia and Latin America. American business interests spanned the globe. It would be difficult for the United States to ignore the war that had been raging in Europe since 1914.

★ ★ ★ Section 3 Assessment ★ ★ ★

Recall

1. **Identify** Explain the significance of **(a)** William Gorgas, **(b)** George Goethals, **(c)** Roosevelt Corollary, **(d)** Francisco "Pancho" Villa.
2. **Define** **(a)** isthmus, **(b)** corollary, **(c)** dollar diplomacy, **(d)** moral diplomacy.

Comprehension

3. **(a)** How did President Roosevelt acquire the right to build the Panama Canal? **(b)** What problems did the builders face?
4. How did Roosevelt justify increased involvement in Latin America?
5. Why did President Wilson send troops into Mexico?

Critical Thinking and Writing

6. **Exploring the Main Idea** Review the Main Idea statement at the beginning of this section. Then, list two arguments for and two arguments against increasing United States intervention in Latin America in the early 1900s.
7. **Identifying Alternatives** Instead of supporting the Panamanian rebels against Colombia, what other actions might Roosevelt have taken to get a canal built? Describe at least two alternatives.

ACTIVITY

Creating a Timeline

Use the Internet to find out more about the building of the Panama Canal. Then, use this information to create a timeline of the building and opening of the canal. Include illustrations if you like. For help in completing the activity, visit PHSchool.com, **Web Code mfd-2303.**

Fighting the *Deadly* Mosquito

The French were the first to try building a canal across Panama. They began construction in 1881 but were defeated by disease. Mysterious illnesses were blamed on "swamp gas." In all, 22,000 workers died before the French abandoned their work in 1889.

When American crews arrived in 1905, disease began its deadly work again. But this time, scientists knew who the enemy was: a tiny, deadly mosquito that carried yellow fever.

When President Roosevelt announced plans to build a canal, many people predicted disaster. This 1904 cartoon shows the common view of Panama.

Dr. William Gorgas declared all-out war on mosquitoes. He installed screens on windows and doors and enforced a ban on uncovered water. An army of workers, like this one, sprayed insecticide on mosquito breeding grounds.

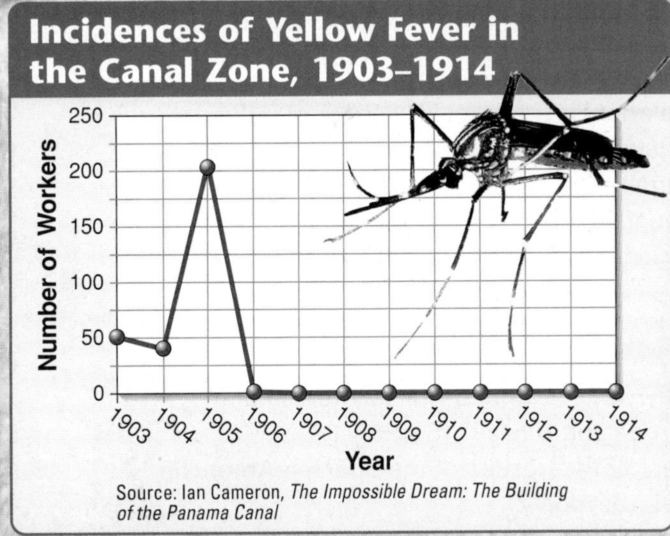

How successful was Gorgas? This graph shows the number of cases of yellow fever during the years the canal was being built.

Activity

To win his war on the mosquito, Gorgas needed an army of workers. Create a newspaper advertisement asking workers to come to Panama. Explain what they will be doing and why it is worth the risk.

CHAPTER 23 Review and Assessment

CHAPTER SUMMARY

Section 1
At the end of the nineteenth century, the United States began to build an overseas empire. The nation acquired Alaska, Hawaii, and other Pacific islands. The United States flexed its power and opened trade with Japan and China.

Section 2
After Cubans revolted against their Spanish rulers, the United States was drawn into a war with Spain. After a quick victory in the Spanish-American War, the United States acquired an empire that included Cuba and the Philippines.

Section 3
At the beginning of the twentieth century, the United States became more involved in Latin American affairs. U.S. support for Panama's independence from Colombia allowed the United States to build the Panama Canal. The United States intervened in Mexico's affairs after a civil war broke out there.

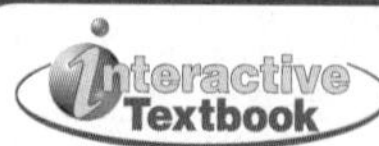

For additional review and enrichment activities, see the interactive version of *The American Nation,* available on the Web and on CD-ROM.

Chapter Self-Test For practice test questions for Chapter 23, visit PHSchool.com, **Web Code mfa-2304.**

Building Vocabulary

Review the meaning of the chapter vocabulary words listed below. Then, write a sentence for each word in which you define the word and describe its relation to the growing involvement of the United States in world affairs.

1. **isolationism**
2. **expansionism**
3. **annex**
4. **imperialism**
5. **racism**
6. **sphere of influence**
7. **yellow journalism**
8. **protectorate**
9. **dollar diplomacy**
10. **moral diplomacy**

Reviewing Key Facts

11. Why was the United States interested in Samoa and Hawaii? (Section 1)
12. Identify two results of the Spanish-American War. (Section 2)
13. What was the main idea of the Roosevelt Corollary? (Section 3)
14. How did Latin American nations react to United States intervention? (Section 3)

Critical Thinking and Writing

15. **Linking Past and Present** Captain Mahan insisted that the navy was the key to controlling events in distant regions. **(a)** List two supporting facts to show that his view was correct in 1890. **(b)** Do you think naval power is just as important today? Write a paragraph explaining your reasons.
16. **Making Decisions** If you had been President McKinley, would you have signed the declaration of war against Spain? List at least two reasons for and two reasons against. Then, write two or three sentences explaining your final decision.

17. **Connecting to Geography: Movement** Look at a map of the world. Write a description of the route that a merchant ship might take from New York to China in 1900. Then, write a description of the route the same ship could take in 1920.
18. **Comparing** Write a paragraph comparing the Latin American policies of Roosevelt, Taft, and Wilson. Describe how their goals and actions were similar or different.

Skills Assessment

Analyzing Primary Sources

Examine this cartoon and answer the questions that follow:

19. The large figure in the center represents
- **A.** the United States.
- **B.** China.
- **C.** Germany.
- **D.** Great Britain.

20. What policy does this cartoon illustrate?
- **A.** isolationism
- **B.** dollar diplomacy
- **C.** imperialism
- **D.** the Open Door Policy

Applying Your Skills

Identifying Historical Trends

Exports to Latin America, 1895–1915

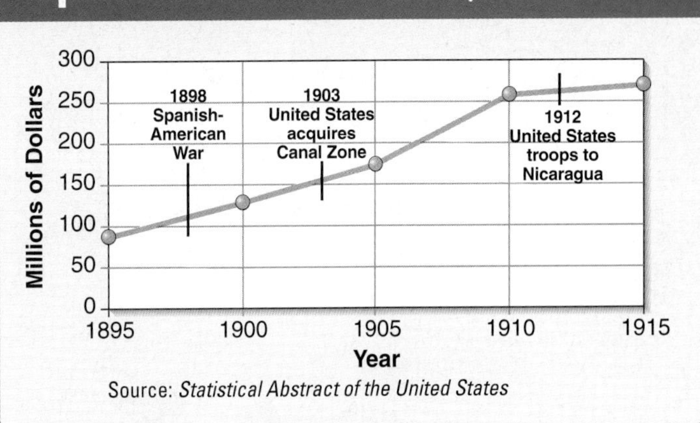

Source: *Statistical Abstract of the United States*

Use this graph and the cartoon on p. 678 to answer the following questions:

21. From this graph, you can conclude that
- **A.** exports to Latin America increased as a result of the Spanish-American War
- **B.** the Panama Canal made it easier to ship goods to Latin America
- **C.** imports from Latin America increased
- **D.** United States involvement in Latin America increased

22. How are the graph and the cartoon related to the same historical trend?

Activities

Connecting With . . . Geography

Creating a Master Map With the class, create a master map titled "Becoming a World Power." Use the information found on the various maps in this chapter. Draw a large base map showing the world from Asia to North America. Use one color to show the United States as it existed in 1865. Use a second color to show territories acquired after the Civil War and a third color to show areas in which the United States became involved. Draw a line around the entire area that might be called an "American empire."

Connecting to Today

Writing Headlines To understand the techniques of yellow journalism, select a recent news story. Use the Internet to find at least two different accounts relating to that story. Note facts and opinions. Then, write two headlines about that story, one factual and the other using the style of yellow journalism. For help in starting this activity, visit PHSchool.com, **Web Code mfd-2305.**

Finding Visual Evidence

Writing Captions Use the Internet to find photographs of the Spanish-American War. Write captions for two of them. Use the captions in this book as a model. For help in starting this activity, visit PHSchool.com, **Web Code mfd-2306.**

CHAPTER 24

World War I

1914–1919

The assassination of Archduke Ferdinand and his wife

Sinking of the *Lusitania*

AMERICAN EVENTS

1914 The assassination of Archduke Francis Ferdinand of Austria-Hungary and his wife leads to World War I. The United States remains neutral.

1915 Nearly 1,200 people, including 128 American citizens, die when a German submarine sinks the *Lusitania*.

1916 Avoiding war helps President Wilson win reelection.

Presidential Terms: Woodrow Wilson 1913–1921

1913 · 1915 · 1917

WORLD EVENTS

1914 ▲ World War I begins in Europe

1916 ▲ An estimated one million soldiers are killed and wounded in the Battle of Verdun.

World War I recruitment poster

Campaign urging men to enlist

1917
The United States enters the war.

1918
An armistice ends the war on November 11.

1919
The Senate rejects the Treaty of Versailles.

1921
The United States signs a peace treaty with Germany.

1917 — 1919 — 1921

▲ 1917
The Russian Revolution begins.

▲ 1918
An influenza epidemic kills millions worldwide.

1 War in Europe

Prepare to Read

Objectives

In this section, you will
- Identify the causes of World War I.
- Describe how war was fought in the trenches.
- Explain how Germany's use of submarine warfare affected American neutrality.

Key Terms

nationalism
militarism
terrorist
kaiser
Central Powers
Allied Powers
stalemate
propaganda
Lusitania

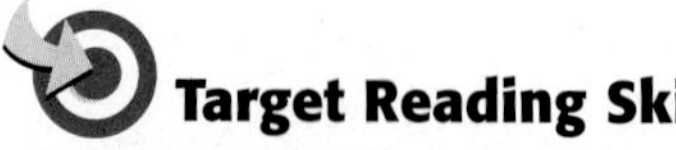

Target Reading Skill

Cause and Effect Copy the chart below. As you read, fill in the chart to show some of the causes of World War I. One cause has been filled in to help you get started. Add as many boxes as you need.

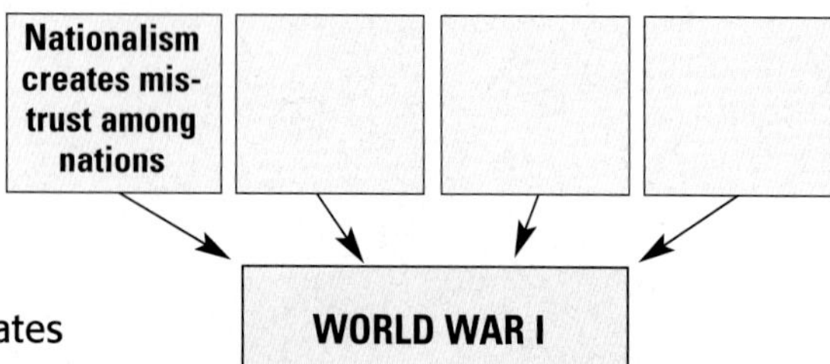

Main Idea When World War I erupted in 1914, the United States remained neutral.

Headline of assassination of Archduke Ferdinand and his wife

Setting the Scene In August 1914, Americans opened their papers to shocking news. War had erupted in Europe! A man in North Carolina wrote:

> “This dreadful conflict of the nations came to most of us as lightning out of a clear sky. The horror of it kept me awake for weeks, nor has the awfulness of it all deserted me.”
>
> —Robert N. Page, Letter, November 12, 1914

Most Americans believed that the war would not touch them. For a while, they were right. But soon, the war that had started in Europe spread across the globe.

Causes of the War

What caused the war in Europe? Tensions had been building there for years. When they erupted and war began in 1914, few Europeans were surprised.

Nationalism Extreme feelings of **nationalism,** or pride in one's nation, fueled the tension. In the 1870s, European nationalists demanded freedom and self-government. They believed that people with a common language and culture should throw off foreign rule and form their own countries.

While nationalism encouraged unity, it also created mistrust and bitter rivalry between nations. For example, France and Germany had gone to war in 1870. When France lost the war, it had to give Germany the iron-rich territory of Alsace-Lorraine. The French never forgot this blow to their national pride. They hoped for an opportunity to regain their lost territory.

In Eastern Europe, nationalism deepened hostility between Austria-Hungary and Russia. Russia encouraged Serbs and other minorities in Austria-Hungary to rise up against their rulers.

Recognize Multiple Causes

Which causes of World War I are discussed on this page? Add this information to your chart.

Imperialism and Militarism Imperialism also fueled rivalries among powerful nations. Between 1870 and 1914, Britain, France, Germany, Italy, and Russia scrambled for colonies in Africa, Asia, and the Pacific. Often, several nations competed for power in the same region. This competition sometimes led to wars in places far from Europe.

Militarism was a third source of tension. **Militarism** is the policy of building up strong armed forces to prepare for war. European nations expanded their armies and navies, creating new stresses. For example, Germany built up its navy. Britain responded by adding more ships to its fleet. This race for naval dominance strained relations between the two nations.

A Network of Alliances To protect themselves, European powers formed rival alliances. Germany organized the Triple Alliance with Austria-Hungary and Italy. France responded by linking itself to Russia and Britain in the Triple Entente (ahn TAHNT).

The alliance system posed a new danger. Allies agreed to support one another in case of an attack. Thus, a crisis involving one member of an alliance also affected that nation's allies. This meant that a minor incident could spark a major war. On June 28, 1914, that incident took place.

Viewing History

European Alliances

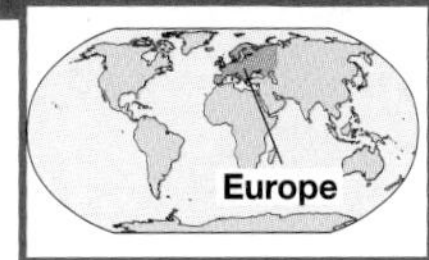

By 1914, the major European powers were involved in alliances. All were formed to produce powerful groups to protect one another in the event of an attack. Both the Allies and the Central Powers had millions of standing troops ready for war.

Applying Information ***What effect did alliances have on European armies?***

War Breaks Out

For years, nationalism had caused turmoil in the Balkan peninsula in southeastern Europe. There, the rival nations of Albania, Bulgaria,

Standing Armies of Europe

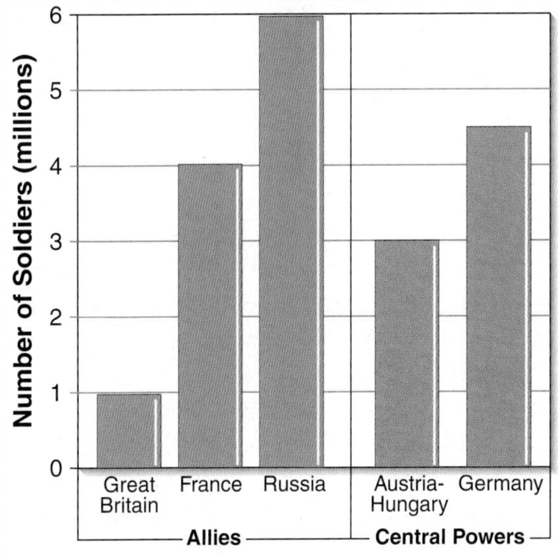

Source: *The International Internet Encyclopedia*

Greece, Montenegro, Romania, and Serbia battled for territory. At the same time, Balkan nationalists called on related ethnic groups in Austria-Hungary to throw off Austrian rule.

Assassination Sparks a Crisis In June 1914, a new crisis struck the region. Archduke Francis Ferdinand, heir to the throne of Austria-Hungary, was visiting Sarajevo, the capital of Bosnia. At the time, Bosnia was part of the Eastern European empire ruled by Austria-Hungary. Francis Ferdinand's visit angered members of the Black Hand, a Serbian terrorist group. A **terrorist** uses threats and violence to promote a cause. The Black Hand wanted Bosnia to break away from Austria-Hungary and join Serbia.

On June 28, the archduke and his wife, Sophie, rode through Sarajevo in an open car. Suddenly, a young terrorist named Gavrilo Princip stepped from the curb, waving a pistol. Taking aim, he fatally shot Francis Ferdinand and Sophie.

Alliance Against Alliance In the days that followed, Austria-Hungary accused the Serbian government of organizing the archduke's assassination. When Austria-Hungary threatened war, Russia moved to protect Serbia. Diplomats rushed to ease tensions, but they could not stop the system of alliances from running its fateful course.

On July 28, Austria-Hungary declared war on Serbia. The very next day, Russia ordered its forces to mobilize, or prepare for war. Austria-Hungary's ally, Germany, called on Russia to cancel the mobilization order. When it received no reply, Germany declared war on Russia on August 1.

On August 3, Germany declared war on Russia's ally France. The next day when German armies sliced through neutral Belgium on their march to France, Britain declared war on Germany. Long before, Britain had promised to defend Belgium if it were attacked.

In this way, what began as a local crisis in Bosnia exploded into a major war.

Viewing History

Trench Warfare

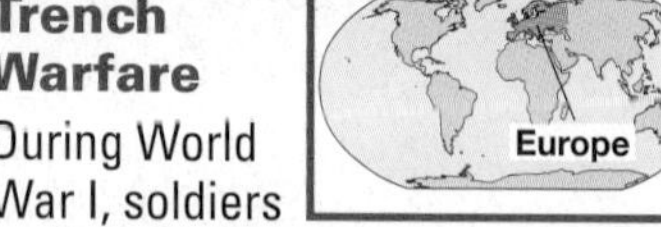

During World War I, soldiers on both sides fought from trenches that were usually 6 to 8 feet deep and 5 feet wide. Soldiers spent weeks in the muddy, rat-infested holes in the ground. **Analyzing Information** ***How did the trenches protect soldiers?***

Trench Warfare

"You will be home before the leaves have fallen from the trees," the **kaiser,** or German emperor, promised his troops as they marched off to war. Europeans on both sides of the conflict thought the war would end soon. They were mistaken. The war dragged on for four blood-soaked years, from 1914 to 1918. At the time, the conflict was called the Great War. Later, it became known as the First World War or World War I.

The war pitted the **Central Powers**—Germany, Austria-Hungary, Bulgaria and the Ottoman, or Turkish, Empire—against the **Allied Powers,** which were France, Britain, and Russia. In time, 21 other nations, including Italy, joined the Allies.

By November 1914, a German advance and an Allied counterattack had produced nothing but a deadly stalemate. A **stalemate** is a deadlock in which neither side is strong enough to defeat the other. For three years, the two armies fought huge battles, but with little to show for them.

Both sides dug in, creating a maze of trenches protected by barbed wire. Some trenches were shallow ditches. Others were elaborate tunnels that served as headquarters and first-aid stations. Between the front-line trenches of each side lay a "no man's land" of barbed wire.

In trench warfare, soldiers spent day after day shelling the enemy trenches. An attack would begin with hours of heavy artillery fire. Then, on orders from an officer, the troops charged "over the top" of the trenches. Armed with their rifles, soldiers raced across "no man's land" to attack the enemy. With luck, they might overrun a few trenches. Before long, the enemy would launch a counterattack, with similar results. In this way, the struggle went on, back and forth, over a few hundred yards of territory.

A new weapon used on both sides was gas—chlorine and mustard were two types. The clouds of gas floated into the trenches, choking and blinding the soldiers.

Because of the nature of trench warfare, most offensives were long and deadly. The Battle of Verdun lasted for 10 months in 1916. The Germans lost some 400,000 men trying to overrun French lines. The French lost even more lives defending their positions.

Meanwhile, in the East, the vast armies of Germany and Austria-Hungary faced off against those of Russia and Serbia. Stalemate and trench warfare brought mounting tolls there as well. By mid-1916, the Russians had lost more than one million soldiers. Yet, neither side could win a decisive victory.

Viewing History

Gas Masks Gas was one of the most feared weapons of World War I. Different kinds of gas caused choking, blindness, or severe skin blisters. Soldiers wore gas masks for protection against the fumes. **Applying Information** ***Why do you think nations later agreed to ban the use of poison gas?***

American Neutrality

When war broke out in Europe, the United States was determined to avoid being dragged into the conflict. The government adopted an official position of neutrality.

Public opinion, however, was divided, often along ethnic lines. Most Americans favored the Allies because of long-standing ties of language, history, and culture through Britain. Also, the United States and France had been allies in the American Revolution.

On the other hand, many of the 8 million Americans of German or Austrian descent favored the Central Powers. Millions of Irish Americans also sympathized with the Central Powers. They hated Britain, which had ruled Ireland for centuries. Many American Jews favored Germany against Russia. Some of them had fled persecution in Russia only a few years earlier.

Effects of the War The war had several immediate effects on the United States. First, the economy boomed as American farmers and manufacturers rushed to fill orders for war goods. By 1917, trade with the Allies had greatly increased. Trade with the Central Powers also increased but by a much smaller amount. This trade imbalance meant that the United States was not strictly neutral.

Both sides waged a propaganda war in the United States. **Propaganda** is the spreading of ideas that help a cause or hurt an opposing cause. Each side pictured the other as savage beasts who killed innocent civilians.

Primary Source

The *Lusitania*

Here are two editorials from two newspapers about the sinking of the Lusitania.

"Germany ought not to be left in . . . doubt how the civilized world regards her latest display of 'frightfulness.' . . . No plea of military necessity will [help Germany] before the . . . conscience of the world. . . . Some atrocities . . . fall under . . . universal condemnation . . ."

—New York *Nation,* May 13, 1915

"If ever the American people stood in need of calmness . . . it is at this hour. While every other nation is 'seeing red,' let us do what the German military authorities apparently have not done—count the cost [of any further action]. . . . We must protect our citizens, but we must find some other way [to do so] than war."

—Chicago *Standard,* May 13, 1915

Analyzing Primary Sources

What is the difference between the two editorials?

Submarine Warfare As a neutral nation, the United States claimed the right to trade with either side in the conflict. Early in the war, however, Britain blockaded German ports, hoping to starve Germany into surrender. In response, Germany set up a blockade around Britain. To enforce the blockade, Germany used a powerful new weapon—a fleet of submarines known as U-boats. German U-boats attacked any ship that entered or left British ports. This meant that neutral ships would also be attacked.

U-boat attacks on neutral shipping raised a storm of protest. Under international law, a country at war could stop and search a neutral ship suspected of carrying war goods. However, German submarines were not equipped to conduct a search. After surfacing, they simply torpedoed enemy and neutral ships, often killing scores of civilians.

Germany warned the United States and other neutral nations to keep their ships out of the blockade zone. President Wilson vowed to hold Germany responsible if its U-boats caused any loss of American life or property.

"Murder on the High Seas" Germany ignored Wilson's warning. On May 7, 1915, a German submarine torpedoed the ***Lusitania,*** a British passenger ship, off the coast of Ireland. Nearly 1,200 people died, including 128 Americans. An outraged Wilson threatened to break off diplomatic relations, or official ties, if Germany did not stop sinking passenger ships. Germany was not ready to strengthen the Allies by drawing the United States into the war. It agreed to restrict its submarine campaign. Before attacking any ship, U-boats would surface and give warning. This agreement, called the Sussex Pledge, kept the United States out of the war a little longer.

★ ★ ★ Section 1 Assessment ★ ★ ★

Recall

1. **Identify** Explain the significance of **(a)** Francis Ferdinand, **(b)** Central Powers, **(c)** Allied Powers, **(d)** *Lusitania*.
2. **Define** **(a)** nationalism, **(b)** militarism, **(c)** terrorist, **(d)** kaiser, **(e)** stalemate, **(f)** propaganda.

Comprehension

3. List three causes of tension in Europe in 1914.
4. How did trench warfare make offensives long and deadly?
5. How did President Wilson react to Germany's use of submarine warfare?

Critical Thinking and Writing

6. **Exploring the Main Idea** Review the Main Idea statement at the beginning of this section. Then, write a paragraph explaining why it would be difficult for the United States to remain neutral in World War I.
7. **Analyzing Information** How did the alliance system help bring about war?

Activity

Making a Diagram

Use the Internet to research trench warfare in World War I. Then, make an illustrated diagram of a typical network of trenches. Join with several other students to make a model based on your diagram. For help in completing the activity, visit PHSchool.com, **Web Code mfd-2401.**

2 From Neutrality to War

Prepare to Read

Objectives

In this section, you will
- Summarize how President Wilson tried to bring about peace.
- Explain why the United States moved toward war.
- Describe how the government prepared for and managed the war effort.
- Identify how the home front responded to the war.

Key Terms

warmonger
Zimmermann telegram
czar
Selective Service Act
draft
illiterate
bureaucracy
Liberty Bonds
pacifist
Socialist

Target Reading Skill

Sequence Copy the flowchart. As you read, fill in the boxes with the major events that led to the United States entry into World War I. The first and last boxes have been filled in for you. Add as many boxes as you need.

- Wilson issues a final plea for peace
-
-
- United States enters the war

Main Idea The United States tried to remain neutral, but the German submarine warfare finally brought the country into the war.

Setting the Scene In February 1916, Representative Jeff McLemore introduced a resolution in Congress. It warned Americans against traveling on armed ships of countries at war. If he could end American deaths by German torpedoes, McLemore hoped, the United States could remain at peace.

President Wilson did not like McLemore's idea. He was unwilling to accept any restrictions on the right of Americans to travel or work on armed vessels. Wilson pressured Congress to reject the McLemore resolution. Some members of his party were furious. "You have no right to ask me to follow this course," said one senator. "It may mean war for my country."

The senator's fears proved correct. A little more than a year later, German torpedoes brought more American deaths on the high seas, and President Wilson asked Congress for a declaration of war.

A German submarine

Wilson's Peace Efforts

President Wilson tried to bring both sides to peace talks. He believed that the United States, as a neutral nation, could lead warring nations to a fair peace, a "peace without victory." But Wilson's peace efforts failed.

Even as he was trying to make peace, Wilson knew that the United States might be drawn into the war. Thus, the President began to lobby for a stronger army and navy.

In 1916, Wilson ran for reelection against Republican Charles Evans Hughes. Although Hughes also favored neutrality, Democrats were able to portray him as a **warmonger,** or person who tries to stir up war. At the same time, they boosted Wilson's image with the slogan "He kept us out of war!"

The race was close. On election night, Hughes went to bed believing he had won. Just after midnight, his telephone rang. "The

Should the United States Declare War on Germany?

YES BECAUSE:

- Many Americans are outraged by German submarine warfare.
- Many Americans favor Britain and France.
- The Zimmermann telegram angered many Americans.
- American trade with the Allies is growing.

NO BECAUSE:

- The United States has a tradition of neutrality.
- Some Americans sympathize with the Central Powers.
- Wilson opposes the alliance with the Russian czar.
- Pacifists are opposed to joining the war.

GRAPHIC ORGANIZER *Skills*

As World War I progressed, the United States found it harder and harder to maintain neutrality.

1. **Comprehension** **(a)** List two factors that led the United States to try to remain neutral. **(b)** List two factors that pushed the nation toward war.
2. **Critical Thinking Supporting a Point of View** Should the United States have entered the war? Explain your reasons.

President cannot be disturbed," a friend told the caller. "Well, when he wakes up," the caller replied, "just tell him he isn't President." Late returns from California had given Wilson the election.

Moving Toward War

In January 1917, Wilson issued what proved to be his final plea for peace. It was too late. In a desperate effort to break the Allied blockade, Germany had already decided to renew submarine warfare. Germany warned neutral nations that after February 1, 1917, its U-boats would have orders to sink any ship nearing Britain. German leaders knew that renewed U-boat attacks would probably bring the United States into the war. They gambled that they would defeat the Allies before American troops could reach Europe.

To protest Germany's action, Wilson broke off diplomatic relations with Germany.

The Zimmermann Plot A few weeks later, a startling discovery moved the United States closer to war. In February, Wilson learned that Arthur Zimmermann, Germany's foreign secretary, had sent a secret note to the German minister in Mexico. The **Zimmermann telegram** instructed the minister to urge Mexico to attack the United States if the United States declared war on Germany. In return, Germany would help Mexico win back its "lost provinces" in the American Southwest, which would include all of Texas, Arizona, and New Mexico. When Americans heard about the Zimmermann telegram, anti-German feeling soared.

Revolution in Russia Two other events in early 1917 pushed the United States still closer to war. First, German submarines sank several American merchant ships. Second, a revolution in Russia drove Czar Nicholas II from power.

For hundreds of years, **czars,** or **Russian emperors,** had ruled with absolute power. Several times in the 1800s and early 1900s, Russians revolted against czarist rule. Their efforts ended in failure.

When the war in Europe began in 1914, Russians united behind the czar. However, as the war brought heavy losses at the front and economic hardship at home, discontent resurfaced. In March 1917, riots protesting the shortage of food turned into a revolution. The czar was forced to step down. Revolutionaries then set up the Provisional Government and called for democratic reforms.

President Wilson welcomed the Russian Revolution. He was a firm believer in democracy, and it was against his principles to be an ally of an absolute ruler. Without the czar, it would be easier for Wilson to support the Allied cause.

Target Skill: Identify Sequence Which events in the subsection "Moving Toward War" led to the U.S. declaration of war? Add these to your flowchart.

War Comes Finally, President Wilson went before Congress on April 2, 1917, to ask for a declaration of war. "The world must be made safe for democracy," he declared. His war message assured the American people that entering the war was not only just; it was noble.

Congress voted for war 455 to 56. Among those who voted against the declaration was Jeannette Rankin of Montana, the first woman elected to Congress. She hated war as much as she loved her country. "I want to stand by my country, but I cannot vote for war. I vote no!" she said.

On April 6, the President signed the declaration of war. It thrust Americans into the deadliest war the world had yet seen.

Preparing to Fight

The day after Congress declared war, George M. Cohan wrote a new song. The patriotic tune swept the nation. Its opening lines expressed the confidence that Americans felt:

> "Over there, over there,
> Send the word, send the word, over there,
> That the Yanks are coming . . . "
>
> —George M. Cohan, "Over There," 1917

Its closing message promised, "We'll be over, we're coming over, And we won't come back till it's over over there."

Americans had to do more than sing patriotic tunes, however. They had to prepare to fight—and quickly. The Allies needed everything from food to arms. Britain and France were on the verge of collapse. In Russia, soldiers were deserting to join the revolution.

Raising an Army Before it could fight, the United States needed to enlarge its armed forces. On May 18, 1917, Congress passed the **Selective Service Act.** It required all men from ages 21 to 30 to register for the military draft. A **draft** is a law requiring people of a certain age to serve in the military.

In the next 18 months, 4 million men and women joined the armed forces. People from every ethnic group enlisted. About 20,000 Puerto Ricans served in the armed forces, as did many Filipinos. Scores of soldiers were immigrants who had recently arrived in the United States.

Many Native Americans were not citizens, so they could not be drafted. Large numbers of Native Americans enlisted anyway. One family of Winnebago Indians provided 35 volunteers! They served together in the same unit.

At first, the armed forces did not allow African Americans in combat. When the government abandoned this policy, more than 2 million African Americans registered for the draft. Nearly 400,000 were accepted for duty. They were formed into segregated "black only" units that were commanded mostly by white officers. Still, African Americans rallied to the war effort.

Educating the Troops For many recruits, the Army offered several firsts. It was their first exposure to military authority and discipline.

An American Profile

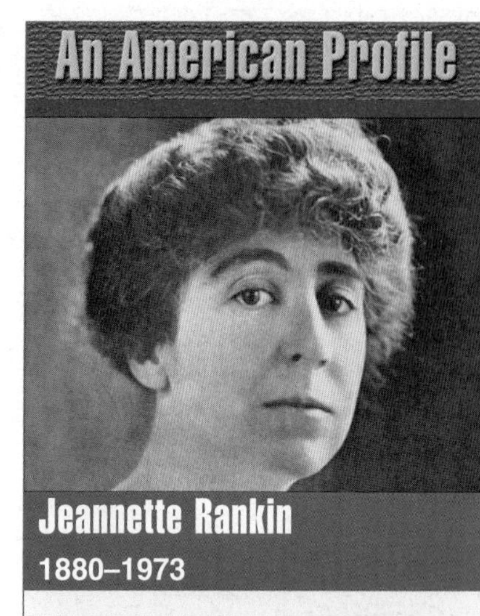

Jeannette Rankin
1880–1973

Jeannette Rankin championed the causes of women's rights and world peace.

Rankin worked to help women win the right to vote. In 1914, her home state of Montana granted that right. Two years later, she won election to the House of Representatives. Four days after she was sworn in, the House faced a vote on whether to enter World War I. Rankin voted no. Only 49 other members agreed.

For the next 20 years, she continued to work for peace. Serving again in Congress, she faced another war vote in December 1941. This time, she was the only member of the House to vote against entering World War II.

How did Rankin work for the causes she believed in?

It was the first time most had ventured outside their farms and villages, let alone outside their country. Some had never taken regular baths or eaten regular meals before. Others had never used indoor plumbing. About 25 percent were **illiterate,** that is, unable to read or write.

The army became a great educator. It taught millions of young Americans not only how to fight but also how to read, how to eat nutritious meals, and how to care for their daily health needs.

Shocking rates of illiteracy and other low test scores among recruits fueled a drive to reform public education. State and local school boards lengthened the school day and required students to spend more years in school. They raised teacher-training standards. More truancy officers patrolled the streets. By 1920, nearly 75 percent of all school-age children were enrolled in school.

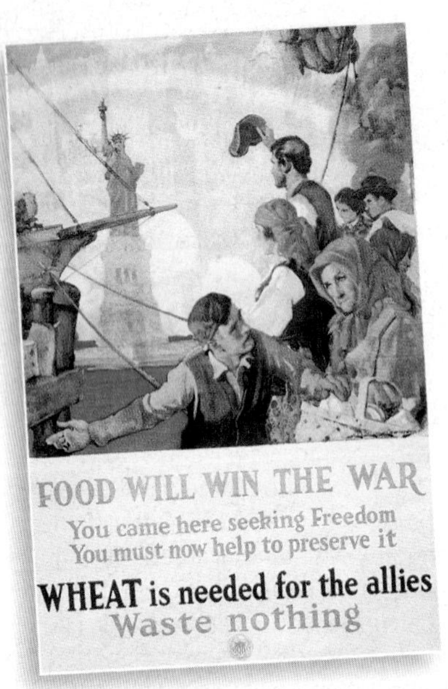

Viewing History

The Food Drive

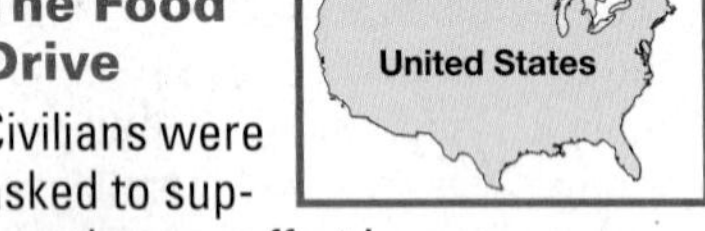

Civilians were asked to support the war effort in many ways. This poster urged families to eat less in order to save food for the soldiers. **Drawing Inferences** ***What group does this poster appeal to?***

Managing the War Effort

The United States reorganized its economy to produce food, arms, and other goods needed to fight the war. President Wilson set up government agencies to oversee the effort. A huge bureaucracy (byoo ROK ruh see) emerged to manage the war effort. A **bureaucracy** is a system of managing government through departments run by appointed officials.

Food Administration Wilson chose Herbert Hoover to be head of the Food Administration. Hoover's job was to boost food production. The nation had to feed its troops and send food to the Allies.

In keeping with the nation's democratic traditions, Hoover relied on cooperation rather than force. He tried to win support for his programs with publicity campaigns that encouraged Americans to act voluntarily. "Food Will Win the War," proclaimed one Food Administration poster.

Encouraged by rising food prices, farmers grew more crops. Citizens planted "victory gardens" to raise their own vegetables. People went without wheat on "wheatless Mondays," and without meat on "meatless Tuesdays." The food they saved helped the men in the trenches.

Managing Industry War caught the nation short of supplies. The military had on hand only around 600,000 rifles, 2,000 machine guns, and fewer than 1,000 pieces of artillery. Disorder threatened as the military competed with private industry to buy scarce materials.

To meet this crisis, President Wilson set up a new government agency, the War Industries Board. It told factories what they had to produce. It also provided for the sharing of limited resources and decided what prices should be set.

Without the support of workers, industry could not mobilize. In 1918, Wilson created the War Labor Board. It settled disputes over working hours and wages and tried to prevent strikes. With workers in short supply, unions were able to win better pay and working conditions. Railroad workers, for example, gained a large wage increase and an 8-hour workday. With the President supporting workers, union membership rose sharply and labor unrest declined.

The Home Front

Americans on the home front united behind the war effort. Movie stars, such as Charlie Chaplin and Mary Pickford, helped sell **Liberty Bonds.** By buying bonds, American citizens were lending money to the government to pay for the war. The sale of Liberty Bonds raised $21 billion, just over half of what the United States spent on the war.

To rally public support for the war, the government sent out 75,000 speakers known as "Four-Minute Men." Their name reminded people of the heroic minutemen of 1776. It also referred to the four-minute speeches the men gave at public events, movies, and theatrical productions. The speakers urged Americans to make sacrifices for the goals of freedom and democracy.

Women Workers As men joined the armed forces, women stepped into their jobs. Women received better pay in war industries than they had in peacetime. Still, they earned less than the men they replaced.

In factories, women assembled weapons and airplane parts. Some women drove trolley cars and delivered the mail. Others served as police officers, railroad engineers, or electric-lift truck drivers. By performing well in jobs once reserved for men, women helped change the view that they were fit only for "women's work." Unfortunately, most of the gains made by women later disappeared when the men returned to the work force at the end of the war. Thousands of women lost jobs as army defense workers.

Viewing History

New Opportunities for Women

Women workers became an essential part of the nation's war effort, taking jobs in war industries and defense plants. This woman worked in an ammunition factory. **Making Predictions** ***How do you think wartime work helped women win the right to vote?***

Anti-German Prejudice German Americans endured suspicion and intolerance during the war. Newspapers questioned their loyalty. Mobs attacked them on the streets. In 1918, a mob lynched Robert Prager, whose only crime was that he had been born in Germany. A jury later refused to convict the mob leaders.

Anti-German prejudice led some families to change their names. Schools stopped teaching the German language. Americans began referring to German measles as "liberty measles" and sauerkraut as "liberty cabbage."

Great Migrations The war spurred migration within the nation. Immigration from abroad had stopped. The draft drained cities and factories of needed workers. Cities soon swelled with newcomers.

During the war, almost a half million African Americans and thousands of Mexican Americans embarked on a great migration from the South and Southwest to cities in the North.

In northern cities, many blacks found better-paying jobs in war industries. As a result, black migration continued after the war ended. At the same time, however, they ran into prejudice and even violence. Competition for housing and jobs sometimes led to race riots. Thirty-nine African Americans were killed during a 1917 riot in East St. Louis, Illinois. A New York parade protested the deaths. Marchers carried signs demanding, "Mr. President, Why Not Make AMERICA Safe for Democracy?"

In the Southwest, ranchers pressed the government to let more Mexicans cross the border. Almost 100,000 Mexicans entered the

United States to work on farms, mostly in California and Texas. By 1920, Mexicans were the leading foreign-born group in California. Some Mexicans moved on to northern cities to work in factories.

Throughout the war, Mexicans worked in cotton and beet fields, in copper mines, and in steel mills. All these jobs were important to the war effort. Yet after the war, when veterans returned and unemployment grew, the United States tried to force Mexican workers to return to Mexico.

Opposition to the War Some Americans opposed the war. Among them were Progressives such as Jane Addams. Many of these critics were **pacifists,** people who refuse to fight in any war because they believe that war is evil.

Antiwar feeling also ran high among Socialists and radical labor groups. A **Socialist** believes that the people as a whole rather than private individuals should own all property and share the profits from all businesses. Socialists argued that the war benefited factory owners but not workers.

To encourage unity, Congress passed laws making it a crime to criticize the government or to interfere with the war effort. Nearly 1,600 men and women were arrested for breaking these laws. Eugene V. Debs, socialist candidate for President five times, was jailed for protesting the draft. The government also jailed "Big Bill" Haywood, head of the Industrial Workers of the World (IWW), a radical union. Using special powers granted under the wartime laws, government authorities ransacked the IWW's offices.

A few people questioned these laws. They argued that silencing critics violated the Constitution's guarantee of freedom of speech. Most Americans, however, felt that the laws were necessary in wartime.

Section 2 Assessment

Recall

1. **Identify** Explain the significance of **(a)** Zimmermann telegram, **(b)** Jeannette Rankin, **(c)** Selective Service Act, **(d)** Herbert Hoover, **(e)** Liberty Bonds.
2. **Define** **(a)** warmonger, **(b)** czar, **(c)** draft, **(d)** illiterate, **(e)** bureaucracy, **(f)** pacifist, **(g)** Socialist.

Comprehension

3. Describe Wilson's efforts to achieve peace.
4. Identify three events that moved the United States toward war.
5. How did the United States prepare for war?
6. How did the war ignite prejudice against some groups at home?

Critical Thinking and Writing

7. **Exploring the Main Idea** Review the Main Idea statement at the beginning of this section. Then, write a newspaper editorial about the United States entry into the war.
8. **Supporting a Point of View** Do you think that the government should have the right to silence critics during wartime? Give reasons to support your point of view.

ACTIVITY

Preparing a Speech
You are one of Wilson's Four-Minute Men. Prepare a short speech urging Americans to make sacrifices for the war effort. Arrange to present your speech to the class.

Recognizing Propaganda

On April 2, 1917, President Wilson stated that "the world must be made safe for democracy." A few days later, Congress declared war on Germany. At that time, many Americans still held strong antiwar feelings. To persuade Americans to support the decision and to mobilize for action, the government used propaganda. Propaganda is an effort to spread certain ideas and shape public opinion.

The poster shown here was used by the United States government to promote support for World War I. The term "Hun" was a negative name used for the Germans.

A propaganda poster

Learn the Skill *To recognize propaganda, use the following steps:*

1. **Identify the source.** If you know who is behind the propaganda, you can better evaluate the message.
2. **Note the frame of reference.** The place, time, and circumstances under which something is published can make a difference.
3. **Recognize the propaganda techniques.** Analyze the material to decide what approach it uses to persuade. One way is the use of negative images.
4. **Interpret the message.** What is the propaganda about? What point of view does it reflect?

Practice the Skill *Answer the following questions about the poster:*

1. Who is the publisher of the poster?
2. When was the poster published?
3. What propaganda technique is used in this poster?
4. What message do the words on the poster give?

Apply the Skill *See the Chapter Review and Assessment.*

3 Americans in Battle

Prepare to Read

Objectives

In this section, you will
- Identify the setbacks the Allies suffered in 1917 and early 1918.
- Explain how the American Expeditionary Force helped the Allies win the war.
- List the costs of the war.

Key Terms

Treaty of Brest-Litovsk
Harlem Hell Fighters
Battle of Belleau Wood
Battle of the Argonne Forest
armistice
abdicate
epidemic

Target Reading Skill

Main Idea As you read, prepare an outline. Use roman numerals to indicate the major headings of this section, capital letters for the subheadings, and numbers for the supporting details.

I. Setbacks for the Allies
  A. Russia makes a separate peace
    1. The Bolsheviks seize power
    2.
    3.
  B. The German "Peace Offensive"
    1.
    2.
II. The American Expeditionary Force in France

Main Idea The United States did not enter the First World War until 1917, but its fresh troops and supplies helped the Allies to victory.

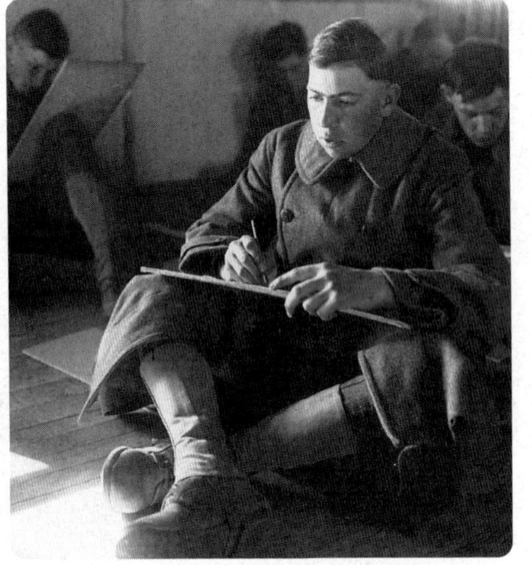

Allied soldier

Setting the Scene On the eve of battle in May 1918, Adrian Edwards, a young American soldier, wrote his mother from "somewhere in France." The letter was to be delivered in the event of his death. "Do not grieve," he wrote her,

> "... rather rejoice that you have given a son ... to save civilization, to prevent future wars, to punish the Germans, ... and to make the world safe for democracy."
>
> —Adrian Edwards, Letter, May 1918

Two days later, Adrian Edwards was killed, and his letter was sent home.

Two million American soldiers eventually served in France. Only a small number of them actually fought in battle. Still, they gave the war-weary Allies a much-needed boost to win the war.

Setbacks for the Allies

The first American troops reached France in June 1917. They quickly saw the desperate situation of the Allies. The Allies had lost millions of soldiers. Troops in the trenches were exhausted and ill. Civilians in Britain and France were near starvation.

Russia Makes a Separate Peace The outlook for the Allies grew even more bleak when Russia decided to withdraw from the war. In November 1917, a group known as the Bolsheviks seized power from Russia's Provisional Government. Led by Vladimir I. Lenin, the Bolsheviks wanted to stage a communist revolution in Russia.

Lenin embraced the ideas of Karl Marx, a German thinker of the 1800s. Marx had predicted that workers around the world would unite to overthrow the ruling class. After the workers revolted, they would do away with private property and set up a classless society. Lenin was determined to lead such a revolution in Russia.

Lenin opposed the war, arguing that it benefited only the ruling class. Once in power, he opened peace talks with Germany. In March 1918, Russia and Germany signed the **Treaty of Brest-Litovsk,** ending Russia's participation in the war. The treaty was harsh, requiring Russia to give up large amounts of land to Germany. Still, Lenin welcomed peace. With war ended, he could focus on the communist revolution.

The Allies saw the treaty as a betrayal. It gave Germany coal mines and other valuable resources in Russia. More important, with Russia out of the struggle, Germany now moved its armies away from the Russian, or eastern, front to support its armies on the western front in France.

The German "Peace Offensive" In early 1918, Germany mobilized its troops for an all-out attack on the Allies. By March 21, German forces had massed near the French town of Amiens. (See the map on this page.) The Germans were preparing what they called a "peace offensive." They hoped that a final push would end the war.

The offensive opened with dozens of German divisions lined up against a small British force. Late at night, 6,000 German cannons began pounding the British troops camped at Amiens. Despite the heavy fire, the British held on. The battle lasted for two weeks. At last, on April 4, the Germans gave up their attack.

The Germans continued their offensive elsewhere. By late May, they had smashed through Allied lines along the Aisne (EHN) River. On May 30, they reached the Marne River, just east of Château-Thierry (SHA toh tee ER ee). Paris lay only 50 miles away. At this point, American troops entered the war in force.

The American Expeditionary Force in France

By June 1918, American troops were reaching France in record numbers. More than one million American troops would arrive. Commanding the American Expeditionary Force (AEF) was General John J. Pershing. Pershing was already well known at home. He had led American troops into Mexico in 1916 to hunt for Mexican rebel leader Francisco "Pancho" Villa.

The Western Front

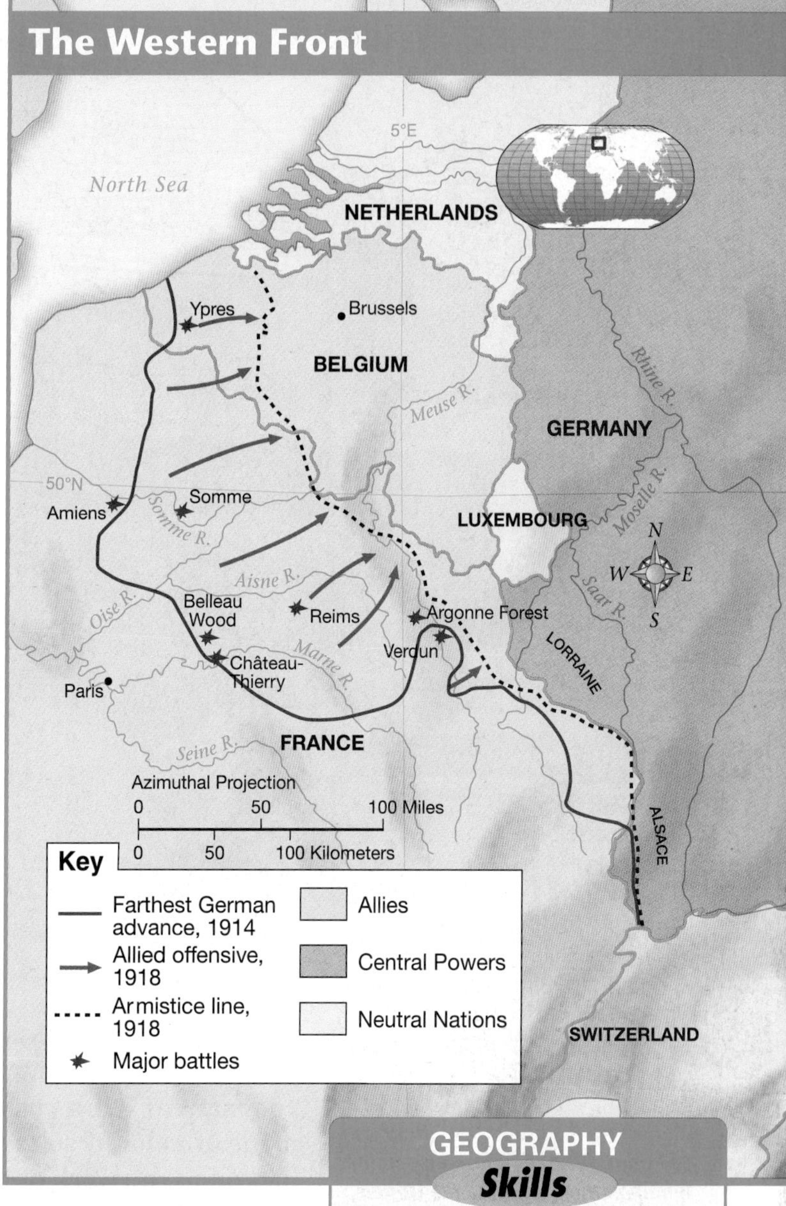

GEOGRAPHY *Skills*

Opposing armies battled back and forth across the Western Front. In 1918, the arrival of American troops gave fresh strength to the Allies.

1. **Location** On the map, locate **(a)** Paris, **(b)** Belleau Wood, **(c)** Aisne River, **(d)** Argonne Forest.
2. **Movement** **(a)** In what country did most of the fighting take place? **(b)** How close did German troops get to the French capital?
3. **Critical Thinking** According to this map, what effect did the arrival of American troops have in 1918?

Viewing History

The 369th Regiment

Nearly 2000 African American soldiers served in the 369th Regiment. Calling themselves the Harlem Hell Fighters, they served with distinction in the French Army. They were the first Americans to be awarded the *Croix de Guerre* (right), the French medal of honor. **Drawing Inferences** ***How do you think African American soldiers felt upon their return to the United States?***

Allied generals wanted the fresh troops to reinforce their own war-weary soldiers. Pershing refused. He insisted that American troops operate as separate units. The United States wanted to have an independent role in shaping the peace. Only by playing "a definite and distinct part" in the war would it win power at the peace table.

In the end, Pershing agreed to let some Americans fight with the British and French. At the same time, he set up an American operation to fight on its own.

Harlem Hell Fighters Among the first American units attached to the French Army was the 369th United States Infantry. This African American unit became known as the **Harlem Hell Fighters.** Although the United States allowed few African Americans to train for combat, the French respected the bravery of African American soldiers and were glad to fight side by side with them.

The Harlem Hell Fighters spent more time under fire than any other American unit. For their bravery, the French awarded them the *Croix de Guerre*, their highest military honor, and numerous other decorations.

After the war, New Yorkers greeted the returning Hell Fighters with a huge parade. "God bless you, boys!" they cheered. The unit commander felt a rush of joy. "They did not welcome us [as] a regiment of colored soldiers," he said, but as "a regiment of men who had done the work of men."

Marines Hold at Belleau Wood Meanwhile, the Germans were continuing their "peace offensive." As Germans rolled across the Aisne River, the French prepared to evacuate Paris.

In June 1918, American troops plunged into their first major battle in Belleau (BEH loh) Wood, outside Paris. A French general sent General James Harbord of the United States a message: "Have your men prepare entrenchments some hundreds of yards to the rear in case of need." Harbord sent back a firm reply: "We dig no trenches to fall back on. The marines will hold where they stand."

The **Battle of Belleau Wood** raged for three weeks. During a series of attacks and counterattacks, the inexperienced but combat-ready Americans performed bravely. Expert marksmen hit their targets from hundreds of yards away. Individual soldiers charged German machine gun nests. When one man fell, another stepped in promptly to take his place. The Americans suffered great casualties. But at last, on June 25, they emerged victorious from the woods. General Harbord passed along the good news: "Wood now exclusively U.S. Marine Corps."

Allies Win the War

In mid-July, the Germans launched another drive to take Paris. They pushed the Allies back until they came up against American troops. Within three days, the Allies, with American help, had forced the Germans to retreat.

The Allies now took the offensive. French Marshal Ferdinand Foch (FOHSH), commander of the Allied forces, ordered attacks along a line from Verdun to the North Sea. American forces stormed the area between the Meuse (MYOOZ) River and the Argonne Forest.

Battle of the Argonne Forest On September 26, 1918, in response to Foch's cry, "Everyone to battle!" more than one million American soldiers pushed into the Argonne Forest. This would be the final Allied offensive. Years of fierce fighting had left the land scarred with trenches and shell holes. The air still smelled of poison gas that had been used with deadly results against the men in the trenches in earlier battles.

At first, the Americans advanced despite heavy German fire. Then, rains and the thick woods slowed their movement. Small units drove forward to capture deadly German positions. Armed with a single rifle, Sergeant Alvin York of Tennessee wiped out a nest of German machine gunners. His brave act helped clear the way for advancing American troops. York became the most decorated American soldier of the war.

Finally, after 47 days, the Americans broke through the German defense. They had won the **Battle of the Argonne Forest.** However, the cost was high. Americans had suffered more than 100,000 casualties in the battle.

British, French, and Belgian forces also smashed through the German lines in their areas. By November, German forces were in retreat. After more than four years of fighting, the Great War was finally nearing its end.

Armistice Ends the War In September, German generals told the kaiser that the war could not be won. On October 4, Prince Max of Baden, head of the German cabinet, secretly cabled President Wilson:

> "To avoid further bloodshed, the German government requests the President to arrange the immediate conclusion of an armistice on land, by sea, and in the air."
>
> —Max, Prince of Baden, Cable, October 4, 1918

An **armistice** is an agreement to stop fighting. President Wilson set two conditions for an armistice. First, Germany must accept his plan for peace. Second, the German emperor must **abdicate,** or give up power.

While German leaders debated a response, rebellion simmered in the ranks. Daily, the German army lost ground. Morale plunged among the troops. German sailors mutinied. Several German cities threatened to revolt.

An American Profile

Alvin York 1887–1964

Alvin York was a deeply religious man. When the United States entered World War I, he asked to be made exempt from the draft because his religious beliefs would not allow him to kill. When his request was denied, York faced a terrible dilemma: to fight for his country or to follow his religious beliefs. He chose to do his duty as a soldier.

One day in France, he and his unit fought German soldiers armed with machine guns. Many Americans were killed. York killed 24 Germans. The remaining 132 surrendered to him! He was hailed as a hero and given the congressional Medal of Honor and a huge parade.

Why was York a reluctant hero?

On November 9, the German emperor was forced to resign. He and his son fled to Holland, and Germany became a republic. The new German leaders agreed to the armistice terms. At 11 A.M. on November 11, 1918—the eleventh hour of the eleventh day of the eleventh month—World War I ended at last.

Target Skill: Identify Supporting Details

Which details in the paragraphs in the subsection "The Costs of War" explain some of the results of World War I? Add these details to your outline.

The Costs of the War

The costs of the war were staggering. A generation of young Europeans lost their lives. Between 8 million and 9 million people died in battle—more than had died in all the wars fought during the previous 100 years. Almost 4 million Russian, French, and British soldiers were killed. Germany alone lost close to 2 million men. The United States lost over 100,000 men. Many more died of diseases. More than 20 million soldiers on both sides were wounded.

No one knows how many civilians died of disease, starvation, and other war-related causes. Some historians believe as many civilians died as soldiers.

Much of northern France lay in ruins. Millions of Germans were near starvation. In France and other nations, many children were left orphaned and homeless.

In 1918, as the world was reeling from the war, a new disaster struck. A terrible influenza epidemic spread around the globe. An **epidemic** is the rapid spread of a contagious disease among large numbers of people. Between 1918 and 1919, more than half a million Americans died in the flu epidemic. The death toll in other countries was even higher. All told, the epidemic killed more than 30 million people worldwide.

★ ★ ★ Section 3 Assessment ★ ★ ★

Recall

1. **Identify** Explain the significance of **(a)** Treaty of Brest-Litovsk, **(b)** Harlem Hell Fighters, **(c)** Battle of Belleau Wood, **(d)** Battle of the Argonne Forest.
2. **Define** **(a)** armistice, **(b)** abdicate, **(c)** epidemic.

Comprehension

3. Describe the situation of the Allies when the Americans arrived in 1917.
4. What role did American troops play in the Allied victory?
5. What conditions did Europeans face after the war?

Critical Thinking and Writing

6. **Exploring the Main Idea** Review the Main Idea statement at the beginning of this section. Then, write four or five newspaper headlines highlighting the role of American forces in bringing about the end of the war.
7. **Drawing Inferences** How do you think the Treaty of Brest-Litovsk affected future relations between the Allies and Russia?

ACTIVITY

Mental Mapping

Study the map of the Western Front on page 699. On a piece of paper, draw your own sketch map of the region. Label the major rivers and other bodies of water. Label the advances of the Allied army, the farthest advance of the German army, and the armistice army. Use color to shade Allied, Central, and neutral nations.

Honoring Our Veterans

World War I ended on November 11, 1918. Today, we celebrate that date as Veterans Day, a holiday to honor all of those who have served in the armed forces in war or peace.

"Veterans deserve to know that we as a people honor their service. Please honor their sacrifice. Pay tribute each day to their irreplaceable gift to our nation. And take a moment to thank tomorrow's veterans. It's never too early to let them know how deeply we recognize their passionate commitment to keep America safe."

—2000 Veterans Day Speech, Army Public Affairs Division

The first "unknown soldier" was one of four American dead taken from the French battlefields of World War I. He was honored at Arlington National Cemetery in 1921. Since then, unknowns from World War II and the Korean War have been buried in the "Tomb of the Unknowns." Here, a soldier solemnly stands guard at the tomb.

The Veterans of Foreign Wars (VFW) was started in 1899 by veterans of the Spanish-American War. Its membership now numbers more than 2 million. This nonprofit organization offers support to veterans. It also sponsors community projects, such as an annual essay contest for seventh, eighth, and ninth graders. Here, VFW members salute a passing parade.

Activity

With a group of classmates, plan a Veterans Day ceremony. Prepare the opening paragraph of a speech. (If you like, you may choose to focus on a specific veteran you know.) Design a banner or poster, and suggest a list of special activities for your community.

4 The Failed Peace

Prepare to Read

Objectives

In this section, you will
- Describe Wilson's fourteen-point peace plan.
- Explain what Wilson achieved at the Paris Peace Conference.
- Summarize why the Versailles Treaty failed to win support in the United States.

Key Terms

Fourteen Points
self-determination
League of Nations
Big Four
reparations
Treaty of Versailles
isolationist

Reading Process Copy the concept web below. As you read, fill in the blank ovals with important facts about the Paris Peace Conference. Add as many ovals as you need.

Main Idea President Woodrow Wilson went to the Paris Peace Conference with high hopes but failed to achieve his goal of a just and lasting peace.

Woodrow Wilson

Setting the Scene The USS *George Washington* slipped out of New York harbor and headed across the Atlantic. Thousands of people cheered at dockside. Planes in formation roared overhead.

On board the *George Washington* were President Woodrow Wilson and his advisers. They were sailing to France in late 1918 to help the Allies set the terms of peace. As the ship passed the Statue of Liberty, a hopeful Wilson waved his hat to the crowd. At last, he would have a chance to keep his promise of making the world "safe for democracy."

Woodrow Wilson was the first American President to meet foreign leaders on foreign soil. He was determined to do whatever was needed to achieve his vision of a just and lasting peace. In the end, however, Wilson failed. The other Allied leaders, it turned out, did not share his vision or his hopes.

Wilson's Fourteen-Point Peace Plan

In Europe, Wilson visited Paris, London, Milan, and Rome. Everywhere, cheering crowds welcomed him. He thought that the crowds shared his goal of peace without victory. In fact, he was wrong. The Europeans who greeted Wilson so warmly scoffed at his high-minded proposals for peace. They and their leaders were determined to punish the Germans for the war.

In January 1918, even before the war ended, Wilson outlined his peace plan. Known as the **Fourteen Points,** it was meant to prevent international problems from causing another war.

The first point in Wilson's plan called for an end to secret agreements. Secrecy, Wilson felt, had encouraged the web of rival alliances that had helped lead to war. Next, he called for freedom of the seas, free trade, and a limit on arms. He urged peaceful settlement of

The Hall of Mirrors

On June 28, 1919, Germany signed the Treaty of Versailles. This critical event took place in the Hall of Mirrors, which is part of the palace of Versailles.

Built to honor Louis XIV in the 1600s, the hall is decorated with seventeen large, richly decorated mirrors. At the time it was built, nearly all the materials available in the world to make mirrors were used in this lavish display.

Virtual Field Trip For an interactive look at the Hall of Mirrors, visit PHSchool.com, **Web Code mfd-2402.**

disputes over colonies. He also supported the principle of national **self-determination,** that is, the right of national groups to have their own territory and forms of government.

For Wilson, however, the fourteenth point was the most important. It called for a "general association of nations," or **League of Nations.** Its job would be to protect the independence of all countries—large or small. His goals were clear. He stated:

> "An evident principle runs through the whole program that I have outlined. It is the principle of justice to all peoples and nationalities, and their right to live on equal terms of liberty and safety with one another, whether weak or strong."
>
> —Woodrow Wilson, Speech, January 8, 1918

Wilson persuaded the Allies to accept the Fourteen Points as the basis for making peace. However, the plan soon ran into trouble. Some goals were too vague. Others conflicted with reality. In Paris, Wilson faced a constant battle to save his Fourteen Points. He discovered that the Allies were more concerned with protecting their own interests than with forging a lasting peace.

The Paris Peace Conference

Diplomats from more than 30 nations met in Paris and Versailles (vuhr SI) to negotiate five separate peace treaties known as the Peace of Paris. Key issues were decided by the leaders of the Allied nations known as the **Big Four:** Woodrow Wilson of the United States, David Lloyd George of Britain, Georges Clemenceau (kleh mahn SOH) of France, and Vittorio Orlando of Italy.

Disagreement Among the Allies Each leader had his own aims. Wilson had called for "peace without victory." He opposed punishing the defeated powers.

The other Allies, however, ached for revenge. Germany must pay, they said. They insisted on large **reparations,** or cash payments, for the losses they had suffered during the war. Further, they wanted to include a "war guilt clause" that would force Germany to accept responsibility for the war.

The Allies were also determined to prevent Germany from rebuilding its military strength. In particular, Clemenceau wanted to weaken Germany so that it could never again threaten France. "Mr. Wilson bores me with his Fourteen Points," he complained. "Why, God Almighty has only ten!"

The haggling continued for months. In the end, Wilson had to compromise on his Fourteen Points in order to save his key goals, especially the League of Nations. He would not budge on the League. With the League in place, he believed, any mistakes made in Paris could later be corrected.

Viewing History

Allied Leaders

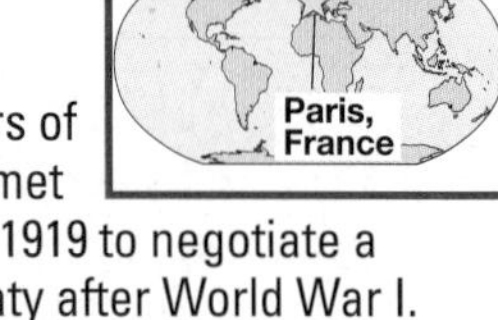

The leaders of the Allies met in Paris in 1919 to negotiate a peace treaty after World War I. Seated left to right are Vittorio Orlando, Premier of Italy; David Lloyd George, Prime Minister of Great Britain; Georges Clemenceau, Premier of France; and Woodrow Wilson, President of the United States. **Making Predictions** ***How do you think the Germans would respond to the Treaty of Versailles?***

Harsh Terms for Germany By June 1919, the **Treaty of Versailles,** the most important treaty of the Peace of Paris, was ready. None of the Allies was satisfied with it. Germany, which had not even been allowed to send delegates to the peace talks, was shocked by the terms of the treaty. Still, its representative had no choice but to sign.

Under the treaty, Germany had to take full blame for the war.

> "The Allied and Associated Governments affirm, and Germany accepts, the responsibility of Germany and her allies for causing all the loss and damage to which the Allied and Associated Governments and their nationals have been subjected as a consequence of the war imposed on them by the aggression of Germany and her allies."
>
> —The Versailles Treaty, June 28, 1919, Article 231

Germany also had to pay the Allies huge reparations, including the cost of pensions for Allied soldiers or their widows and children. The total cost of German reparations would come to over $300 billion.

Other provisions of the Treaty of Versailles were aimed at weakening Germany. The treaty severely limited the size of the German military. It returned Alsace-Lorraine to France. In addition, the treaty

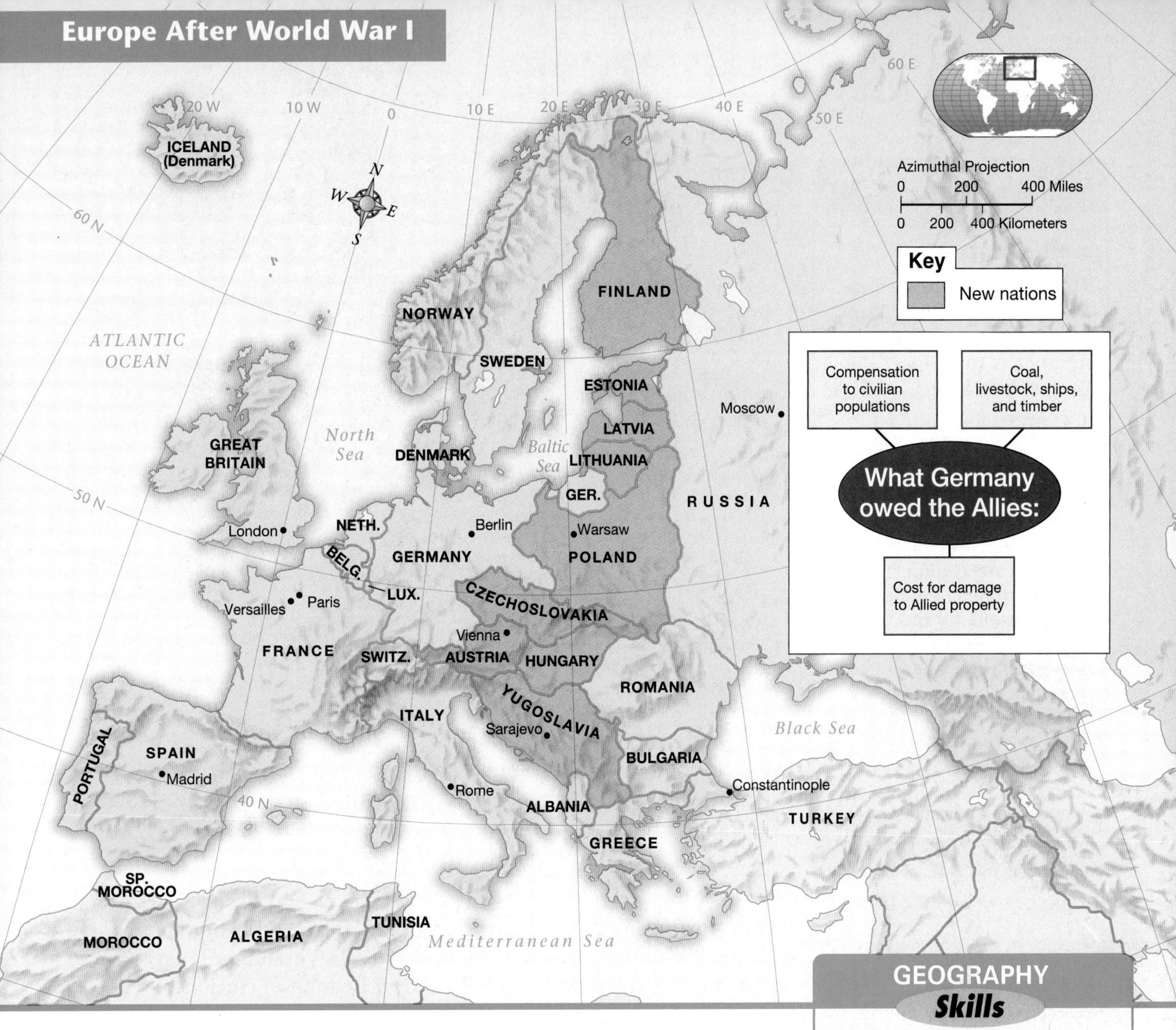

stripped Germany of its overseas colonies, which were put under the control of Britain or France. The Germans, wrote one reporter, "suffered a horrible humiliation."

A Few Victories for Wilson Wilson gained a few of his Fourteen Points, however. In Eastern Europe, the Allies provided for several new nations to be formed on the principle of self-determination, including Czechoslovakia and Yugoslavia. They were created out of lands once ruled by Germany, Russia, and Austria-Hungary. In addition, Poland regained its independence as a nation.

Some people were dissatisfied with the new boundaries. Many Germans, for example, had settled in Poland and Czechoslovakia. Before long, Germany would seek to regain control of German-speaking peoples in Eastern Europe.

To Wilson, however, his greatest achievement was persuading the Allies to include the League of Nations in the treaty. Wilson was certain that the League would prevent future wars by allowing nations

GEOGRAPHY *Skills*

A series of treaties ended World War I. The treaties created several new nations in Eastern Europe and restored independence in Poland.

1. **Location** On the map, locate **(a)** Poland, **(b)** Czechoslovakia, **(c)** Yugoslavia.
2. **Region** Which new nations bordered Russia?
3. **Critical Thinking Applying Information** Compare this map with the map of Europe at the beginning of the war on page 685. **(a)** How did Russia change? **(b)** What happened to Austria-Hungary?

POLITICAL CARTOON *Skills*

A Witches' Brew

This cartoon appeared at the time President Wilson hoped to encourage Americans to support the League of Nations.

1. **Comprehension** **(a)** What does the large pot, or cauldron, represent? **(b)** What are the witches doing?
2. **Understanding Main Ideas** According to the cartoon, why would it be dangerous for the United States to join the League?
3. **Critical Thinking Identifying Points of View** Do you think that this cartoonist was in favor of joining the League? Explain.

Civics 

to talk over their problems. If talk failed, members would join together to fight aggressors. "A living thing is born," he declared. The League "is definitely a guarantee of peace."

The Fight for the Versailles Treaty

When President Wilson returned home, he faced a new battle. He had to persuade the Senate to approve the Versailles Treaty and to approve American participation in the League of Nations.

Critics of the Treaty Most Americans favored the treaty. A vocal minority opposed it, however. Some said that it was too soft on the defeated powers. Many German Americans felt that it was too harsh. Some Republicans hoped to embarrass President Wilson, a Democrat, by rewriting or defeating the treaty. **Isolationists,** people who wanted the United States to stay out of world affairs, opposed the League of Nations. They were convinced that the League would lead to an "entangling alliance." Other people who were against the League felt that it did not have enough authority to solve any pressing economic problems. They thought that could lead to another war.

Critics of the treaty found a leader in Henry Cabot Lodge of Massachusetts. Lodge, a Republican, was chairman of the powerful Senate Foreign Relations Committee. Lodge accepted the idea of the League of Nations. However, he wanted changes in some provisions relating to the League. He believed that Americans were being asked to "subject our own will to the will of others."

Specifically, Lodge objected to Article 10 of the treaty. It called for the League to protect any member whose independence or territory was threatened. Lodge argued that Article 10 could involve the United States in future European wars. He wanted changes in the treaty that would ensure that the United States remained independent of the League. He also wanted Congress to have the power to decide on a case-by-case basis whether the United States would follow League policy.

Wilson believed that Lodge's changes would weaken the League. Advisers urged the President to compromise, to give up some of his demands in order to save the League. Wilson replied, "Let Lodge compromise." He refused to make any changes.

The Defeated Treaty As the battle grew hotter, the President took his case to the people. In early September 1919, Wilson set out across the country. He traveled nearly 8,000 miles and made 37 speeches in 29 cities. He urged Americans to let their senators know that they supported the treaty.

Wilson kept up a relentless pace. On September 25, the exhausted President complained of a headache. His doctors canceled the rest of the trip. Wilson returned to Washington. A week later, his wife found him unconscious. He had suffered a stroke that left him bedridden for weeks.

In November 1919, the Senate rejected the Versailles Treaty. "It is dead," Wilson mourned, "[and] every morning I put flowers on its grave." Gone, too, was Wilson's cherished goal—American membership in the League of Nations.

The United States did not sign a peace treaty with Germany until 1921. Many nations had already joined the League of Nations. Without the United States, though, the League failed to live up to its goal of protecting members against aggression. Wilson's dream of a world "safe for democracy" would have to wait.

Ask Questions
If you could have interviewed two senators, one who voted for and another who voted against the Versailles Treaty, what would you have asked them? How might they have responded?

★ ★ ★ Section 4 Assessment ★ ★ ★

Recall

1. **Identify** Explain the significance of **(a)** Fourteen Points, **(b)** League of Nations, **(c)** Big Four, **(d)** Treaty of Versailles, **(e)** Henry Cabot Lodge.
2. **Define** **(a)** self-determination, **(b)** reparations, **(c)** isolationist.

Comprehension

3. Describe the major points of Wilson's peace plan.
4. Why did Wilson's plan run into trouble at Versailles?
5. Why did the Senate reject the Versailles Treaty?

Critical Thinking and Writing

6. **Exploring the Main Idea** Review the Main Idea statement at the beginning of this section. Then, write a paragraph explaining why you think Wilson failed in his efforts to win "peace without victory."
7. **Making Predictions** **(a)** List three ways that the Treaty of Versailles punished Germany. **(b)** What do you think the effects of this harsh treatment might be?

ACTIVITY

Connecting to Today
The United States did not join the League of Nations. However, after World War II it helped to form the United Nations (UN). Use the Internet to find out more about American participation in the UN today. Write a brief report. For help in completing the activity, visit PHSchool.com, **Web Code mfd-2403.**

CHAPTER 24

Review and Assessment

Chapter Summary

Section 1
Nationalism, militarism, and alliances led to the outbreak of war in 1914. The Central Powers fought the Allied Powers in a bloody four-year conflict that became known as World War I. The United States remained neutral in the early years of the war.

Section 2
Wilson tried but failed to bring an end to the war in Europe. German U-boat attacks and the discovery of the Zimmerman telegram provoked the United States into declaring war in 1917. The war required the services of U.S. soldiers and the efforts of civilians at home.

Section 3
The arrival of U.S. troops in Europe turned the war around, leading to an Allied victory. Millions died as a result of the four-year conflict.

Section 4
President Wilson's fourteen-point peace plan contained ideas that he believed would prevent future wars. It also called for the establishment of a League of Nations. Nevertheless, the Treaty of Versailles imposed harsh terms on Germany. Isolationists in Congress kept the United States out of the League of Nations.

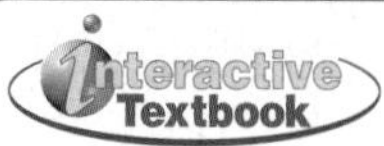

For additional review and enrichment activities, see the interactive version of *The American Nation,* available on the Web and on CD-ROM.

Chapter Self-Test For practice test questions for Chapter 24, visit PHSchool.com, **Web Code mfa-2404.**

Building Vocabulary

Review the meaning of the chapter vocabulary words listed below. Then, write a sentence for each word in which you define the word and describe its relation to World War I.

1. **nationalism**
2. **stalemate**
3. **draft**
4. **illiterate**
5. **pacifist**
6. **armistice**
7. **epidemic**
8. **self-determination**
9. **reparations**
10. **isolationist**

Reviewing Key Facts

11. What was the immediate cause of World War I? (Section 1)
12. What policy did the United States adopt at the outbreak of World War I? (Section 1)
13. Why did the United States declare war on Germany? (Section 2)
14. How did Russia's withdrawal from the war affect the Allied war effort? (Section 3)
15. **(a)** What were Wilson's goals for the peace? **(b)** Did he achieve them? Explain. (Section 4)

Critical Thinking and Writing

16. **Connecting to Geography: Interaction** How do you think trench warfare affected the land and resources of the battlefront area?
17. **Analyzing Information** **(a)** How did the United States regulate the economy during the war? **(b)** Why do you think Americans accepted government controls on the economy during World War I?
18. **Organizing Information** Review the subsection titled "The Home Front" on page 695. Make a concept web for the information presented in the subsection.
19. **Drawing Inferences** Many historians blame Wilson for the defeat of the Versailles Treaty in Congress. What reasons do you think they might give to support that position?

SKILLS ASSESSMENT

Analyzing Primary Sources

President Wilson made the following statement to journalist Frank I. Cobb in 1917. Read the statement, and answer the questions that follow:

> "[If you] lead this people into war, . . . they'll forget there ever was such a thing as tolerance. To fight you must be brutal and ruthless, and the spirit of ruthless brutality will enter into the very fiber of our national life, infecting Congress, the courts, the policeman on the beat, the man in the street. . . . Conformity would be the only virtue . . . and every man who refused to conform would have to pay the penalty."
>
> —President Wilson in conversation with Frank I. Cobb, 1917

20. According to Wilson, how would war affect U.S. citizens?
- **A.** It would cause them to become virtuous.
- **B.** It would turn them into nonconformists.
- **C.** It would have no effect on them.
- **D.** It would make them less tolerant and more brutal.

21. Wilson's view on war made him likely to
- **A.** support war as a show of U.S. strength.
- **B.** see a peaceful solution to avoid war.
- **C.** avoid war at any cost.
- **D.** support a draft of soldiers during peacetime.

APPLYING YOUR SKILLS

Recognizing Propaganda

This 1916 poster is the work of a Dutch artist. Study the poster. Answer the questions.

22. What organization distributed this poster?
- **A.** U.S. citizens in Belgium
- **B.** A relief group in Germany
- **C.** An English citizens' group in Belgium
- **D.** A Belgium relief committee in London

23. What propaganda techniques are used?

ACTIVITIES

Connecting With . . . Culture

Writing a Poem Read the poem written by British poet Siegfried Sassoon during the third year of the war.

> "You smug-faced crowds with kindling eye
> Who cheer when soldier lads march by,
> Sneak home and pray you'll never know
> The [place] where youth and laughter go."
>
> —Siegfried Sassoon, "Suicide in the Trenches," 1917

Then, review the lyrics of "Over There," the patriotic song by George M. Cohan, on page 693.

Why do you think the mood of these two works is so different? Express your answer in a short poem of your own.

Connecting to Today

A Television Documentary The Treaty of Versailles set up the nation of Yugoslavia. Use the Internet to find out about Yugoslavia today. Then, prepare a TV documentary showing Yugoslavia's development up to the present. *Hint:* In the late 1900s, civil war broke Yugoslavia into several independent states. For help in starting this activity, visit PHSchool.com, **Web Code mfd-2405.**

TEST PREPARATION

Use the table <u>and</u> your knowledge of social studies to answer the following question.

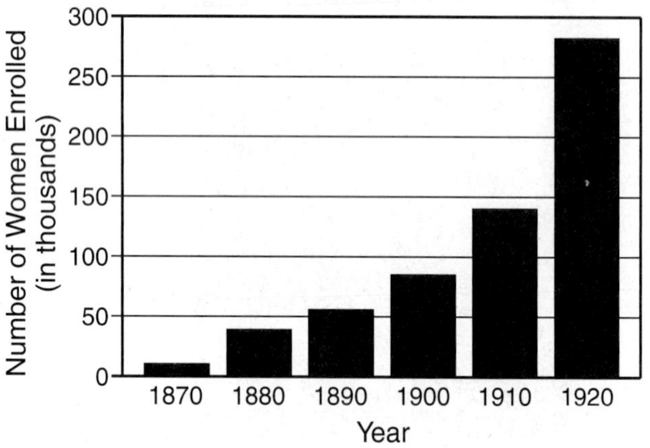

Source: Mabel Newcomer, *A Century of Higher Education for American Women*

1 Which decade saw the largest percentage increase in the number of women who attended colleges and universities?

A 1870s

B 1880s

C 1890s

D 1910s

2 Which of the following actions would be classified as an application of the Roosevelt Corollary?

A Roosevelt orders the navy to capture Manila Bay.

B Americans invest in railroads in South America.

C Taft sends United States marines to Nicaragua.

D Wilson refuses to recognize Huerta's government in Mexico.

3 W.E.B. Du Bois disagreed most strongly with Booker T. Washington on which issue?

A The importance of education for African Americans

B The need for African Americans to better their economic status

C How to fight discrimination against African Americans

D Whether black and white Americans should work together

Use the quotation <u>and</u> your knowledge of social studies to answer the following question.

Senator Robert M. La Follette, speech in the United States Senate, April 1917 (adapted)

"Countless millions are suffering from want and privation; countless other millions are dead and rotting on foreign battlefields. We are pledged by the President to make this fair, free, and happy land of ours the same shambles and bottomless pit of horror that we see in Europe today."

4 How would you summarize La Follette's position in the speech?

A The United States should not enter World War I.

B The United States should declare war on Spain.

C The United States should protest German submarine attacks.

D The United States should not join the League of Nations.

5 During World War I, which of the following did some Americans view as a violation of the First Amendment?

A Military draft law

B Laws to silence antiwar critics

C Segregation in the military

D Attacks on German Americans

6 Which of the following does not belong with the other three?

A Foraker Act

B Platt Amendment

C Battle of San Juan Hill

D Revolt in the Philippines

7 "A free, open-minded and absolutely impartial adjustment of all colonial claims based upon [the principle of self-determination]." Which of the following causes of World War I is addressed in this part of Woodrow Wilson's Fourteen Points?

A Militarism

B Imperialism

C The alliance system

D Extreme nationalism

8 The relationship of Thomas Nast to the downfall of Boss Tweed is most like which of the following?

A The relationship of Ida Tarbell to civil service reform

B The relationship of Theodore Roosevelt to conservation of natural resources

C The relationship of Carrie Chapman Catt to the Nineteenth Amendment

D The relationship of Upton Sinclair to the Pure Food and Drug Act

Use the map <u>and</u> your knowledge of social studies to answer the following question.

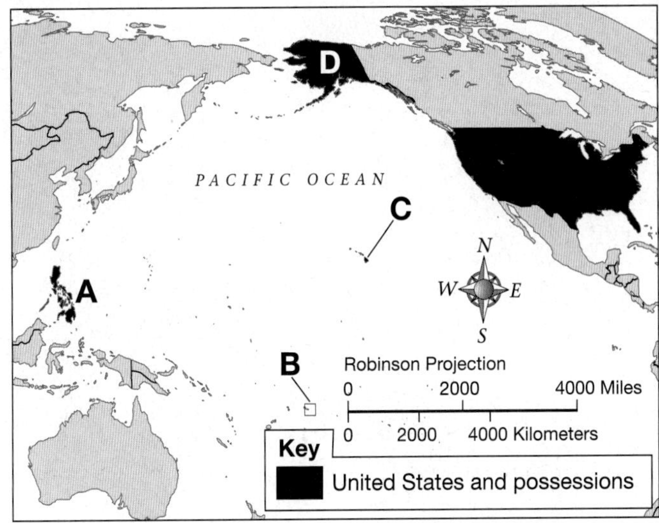

9 Which of the territories shown on the map is correctly matched with the method by which the United States acquired it?

A A—war

B B—purchase

C C—purchase

D D—annexation

Writing Practice

10 Compare and contrast the reasons that the government took steps to regulate the economy during the Progressive Era and during World War I. Include examples.

11 Historians consider Theodore Roosevelt one of the most important Presidents. Give reasons to support this viewpoint, using at least one example of domestic policy and one example of foreign policy. Then, make two generalizations about Roosevelt.

Unit 8 Prosperity, Depression, and War

UNIT OUTLINE

Hard Times
Drought Stricken Area, by Alexandre Hogue, mirrors the economic hardships that struck both rural and urban Americans in the 1930s.

“I see one-third of a nation ill-housed, ill-clad, ill-nourished.”

—President Franklin Delano Roosevelt (1937)

CHAPTER 25

The Roaring Twenties

1919–1929

1 Politics and Prosperity
2 New Ways of Life
3 The Roaring Twenties
4 A Nation Divided

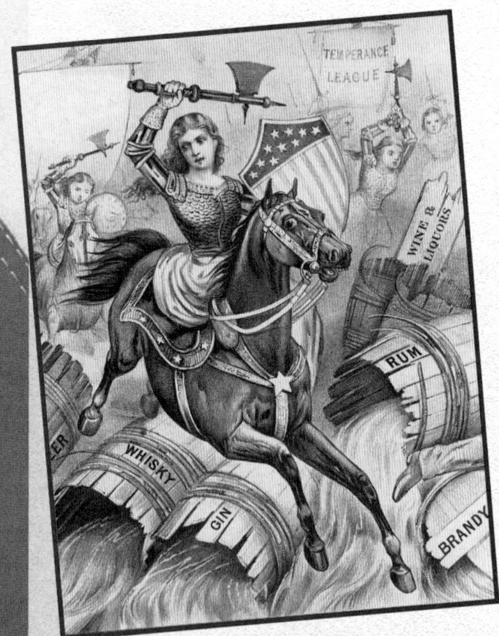

A poster supporting Prohibition

Telegraphic ticker from the 1920s

A stock certificate

AMERICAN EVENTS

1919 The Eighteenth Amendment bans the making or selling of alcoholic beverages.

1920s The economic boom of the 1920s boosts the stock market.

1921 The Emergency Quota Act limits immigration to the United States.

1923 The Senate Public Lands Committee begins investigating the Teapot Dome Scandal.

Presidential Terms: Woodrow Wilson 1913–1921 | Warren G. Harding 1921–1923

1918 · 1921 · 1924

WORLD EVENTS

▲ **1919** The Treaty of Versailles is signed.

▲ **1922** The Union of Soviet Socialist Republics is formed.

The Roaring Twenties

In the decade after World War I, a new energy swept the country. New dances, music, and fashions appeared, and the economy boomed.

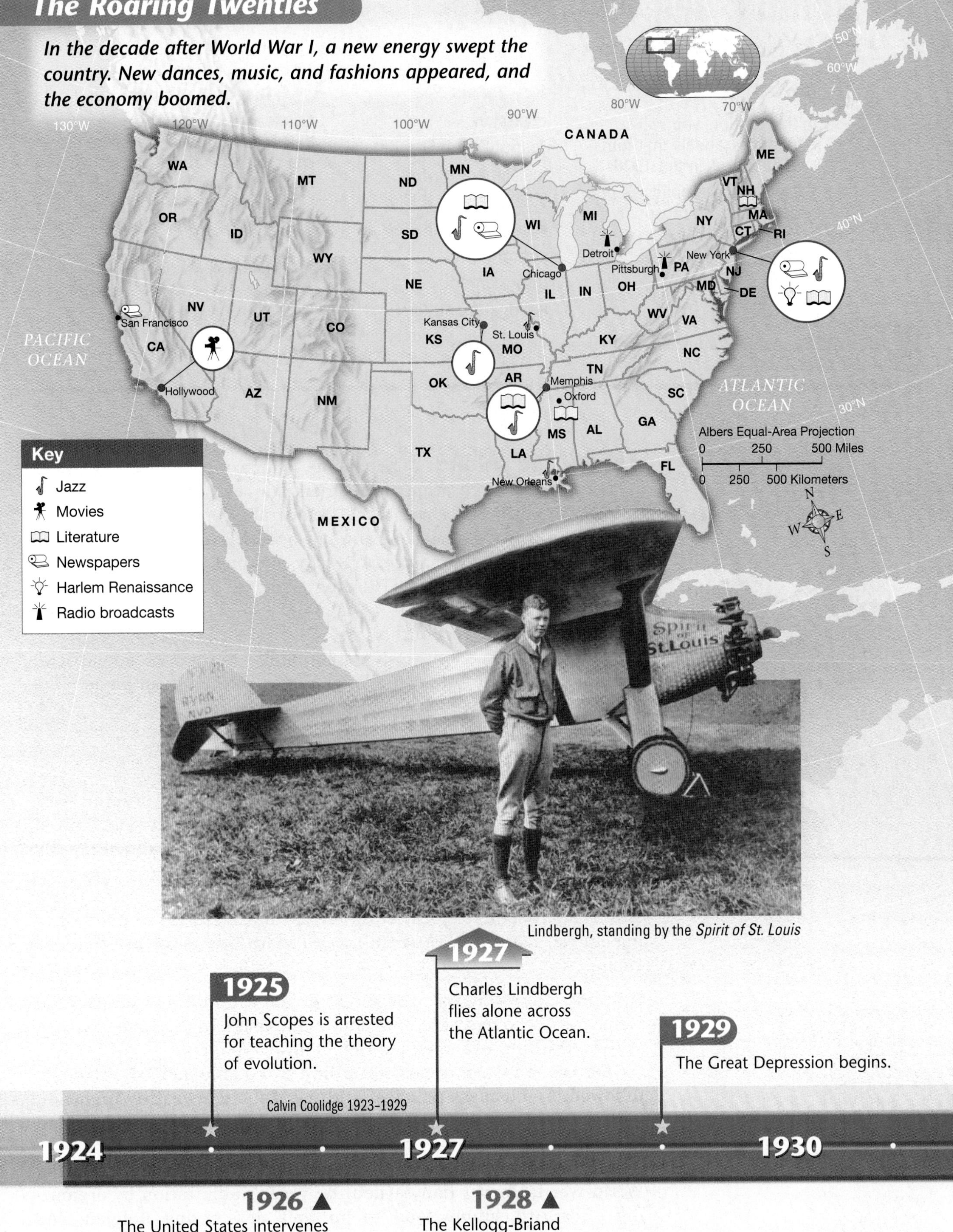

Lindbergh, standing by the *Spirit of St. Louis*

1 Politics and Prosperity

Prepare to Read

Objectives

In this section, you will
- Identify scandals that hurt Republicans in the 1920s.
- Explain how Coolidge's policies increased prosperity.
- Discuss the role the United States played in world affairs.

Key Terms

recession
Teapot Dome Scandal
installment buying
stock
bull market
communism
disarmament
Kellogg-Briand Pact

Target Reading Skill

Cause and Effect Copy the chart below. As you read, complete the chart to show the effects of Republican leadership on the United States during the 1920s. Add as many boxes as you need.

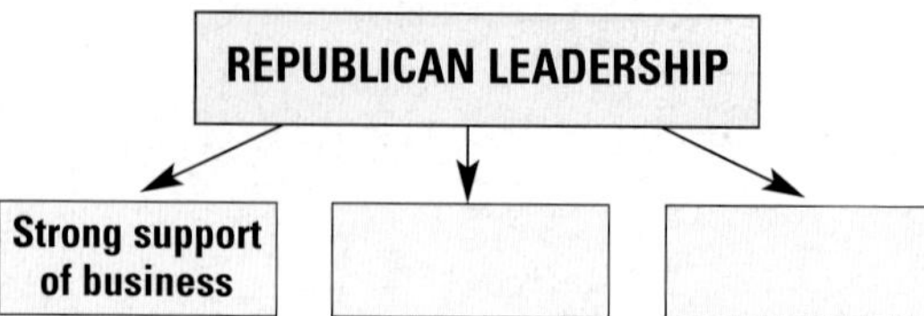

Main Idea As the Republican party returned to power in the 1920s, the economy boomed.

Warren G. Harding

Setting the Scene "The change is amazing," wrote a reporter just after the inauguration of President Warren G. Harding on March 4, 1921. Woodrow Wilson and the Democrats were out; Harding and the Republicans were in. Wilson had been ill, remote, and increasingly sour. Harding was warm, friendly, and open.

During the campaign, Harding's slogan had been "Back to Normalcy." By "normalcy," he meant "a regular steady order of things . . . normal procedure. . . ."

The 1920s turned out to be anything but normal. As one official said, the decade ushered in a "new era," of Republican leadership, booming prosperity, and changes in everyday life.

Republicans in Office

World War I had helped the economy. Europeans ordered vast amounts of supplies from American factories. After the United States entered the war in 1917, American factories expanded rapidly to meet the demand for military supplies.

When the war ended, more than 2 million soldiers came home and began to look for jobs. At the same time, factories stopped turning out war materials. The result was a sharp **recession,** or economic slump.

Harding Takes Office The recession fed voter discontent with the Democrats, who had held power for eight years. In the 1920 election, Warren Harding swamped his Democratic opponent.

For the top Cabinet posts, Harding chose able men who strongly followed pro-business policies. Andrew Mellon, a wealthy financier, became secretary of the treasury. Mellon balanced the budget and lowered taxes.

Herbert Hoover became the new secretary of commerce. During World War I, Hoover had earned the world's admiration by organizing efforts to supply food to millions of starving Belgians. As

POLITICAL CARTOON Skills

The Teapot Dome Scandal **This cartoon, published in 1924, comments on the Teapot Dome Scandal.**

1. **Comprehension** **(a)** Why are the officials running? **(b)** How do you think the White House will be affected?
2. **Understanding Main Ideas** What is the significance of the rolling oil tank?
3. **Identifying Points of View** According to the cartoon, how will this scandal affect the government?

Civics 

secretary of commerce, he worked to help American businesses expand overseas.

Corruption and Scandals To fill most other Cabinet posts, however, Harding brought in his old friends. They became known as the "Ohio Gang." Harding himself was honest and hard-working, but the Ohio Gang saw government service as a way to enrich themselves. A series of scandals resulted. For example, Harding made Charles Forbes head of the Veterans Bureau. Forbes was later convicted of stealing millions of dollars from the bureau.

Harding looked upon Forbes's crime as a betrayal. When rumors of new scandals surfaced, he grew even more distressed. In August 1923, Harding died of a heart attack. Many believed that the scandals contributed to his sudden death.

After Harding died, new scandals came to light. The most serious involved Secretary of the Interior Albert Fall. Two oil executives had bribed Fall. In return, he secretly leased them government land in California and at Teapot Dome, Wyoming. As a result of the **Teapot Dome Scandal,** Fall became the first Cabinet official ever sent to prison.

Coolidge Takes Office On the day Harding died, Vice President Calvin Coolidge was visiting his father's farm in Vermont. Coolidge recalled, "I was awakened by my father. . . . I noticed that his voice trembled." Coolidge's father, a justice of the peace, used the family Bible to swear his son in as President.

"Silent Cal" Coolidge was very different from Harding. Harding loved throwing parties and making long speeches. Coolidge was tight with both money and words. A woman reportedly told Coolidge she had bet that she could get him to say more than two words. "You lose," Coolidge replied.

Coolidge set out to repair the damage caused by the scandals. He forced the officials involved in scandals to resign. In 1924, Coolidge ran against Democrat John Davis and Progressive Robert La Follette. Voters chose to "Keep Cool With Coolidge" and returned the cautious New Englander to office.

Coolidge Prosperity

Like Harding, Coolidge believed that prosperity for all Americans depended on business prosperity. Coolidge cut regulations on business. He also named business leaders to head government agencies.

Industry Booms Coolidge's pro-business policies contributed to a period of rapid economic growth. People referred to this boom as "Coolidge prosperity." As factories switched to consumer goods, the postwar recession ended. From 1923 to 1929, the quantity of goods made by industry almost doubled.

For most Americans, incomes rose. As a result, they were able to buy a flood of new consumer products. Electric refrigerators, radios, phonographs, vacuum cleaners, and many other appliances took their places in American homes.

Businesses used advertising to boost sales of consumer goods. Advertisements encouraged people to think that their happiness depended on owning a wealth of shiny, new products.

Faced with so many goods, people often wanted to buy things they could not afford. In response, businesses allowed **installment buying,** or buying on credit. For example, buyers could take home a new refrigerator by putting down just a few dollars. Each month, they paid an installment until they had paid the full price, plus interest.

The new policy of "buy now, pay later" increased the demand for goods. At the same time, however, consumer debt jumped. By the end of the decade, consumers owed more than the amount of the federal budget.

A Soaring Stock Market The economic boom of the 1920s gave the stock market a giant boost. As you read in Chapter 20, corporations sold **stocks,** or shares of ownership, to investors. Investors made or lost money depending upon whether the price of the shares went up or down.

By the later 1920s, more people were investing in the stock market than ever before. Stock prices rose so fast that some people made fortunes almost overnight. Stories of ordinary people becoming rich drew others into the stock market. Such a period of increased stock trading and rising stock prices is known as a **bull market.**

Many people bought stocks on margin. Under this system, an investor bought a stock for as little as a 10 percent down payment. The buyer held the stock until the price rose, and then sold it at a profit. Margin buying worked as long as stock prices kept going up.

In 1928 and 1929, however, the prices of many stocks rose faster than the value of the companies themselves. A few experts warned

Connecting to Today

The Stock Market

Maybe you have heard a business reporter announce, "The Dow Jones is up." The reporter is referring to the Dow Jones Industrial Average, sometimes called "the Dow." The Dow is calculated by averaging the stock value of 30 large corporations.

Average prices of stocks are quoted in points rather than dollars. On a day when more people buy than sell shares in the Dow stocks, the Dow average might rise by, say, 30 points. On a very good day, the Dow may rise 100 or more points. Of course, on a bad day, it might go down by an equal amount.

Investors use many different sources of information to decide whether to buy or sell. They consider national and world events, corporate reports, and the opinions of financial experts. In the end, however, no one can really predict how the Dow will do in any given day, month, or even year.

Why is it hard to predict whether the Dow will go up or down?

that the bull market could not last forever. Still, most investors ignored the warnings.

A Limited Role in World Affairs

After World War I, the United States was the world's leading economic power. Europeans expected the United States to take a major role in world affairs. Presidents Harding and Coolidge wanted to keep the hard-won peace in Europe. However, they did not want to commit the United States to the job of keeping world peace. The United States sent observers to the League of Nations but refused to join. Most Americans supported this return to prewar isolationism.

Latin America During the war, Latin American nations had been cut off from Europe. As a result, United States trade and investment in Latin America increased. This trend continued after the war. However, the United States limited its role abroad for fear that more involvement might push the country into another war.

At times, the United States intervened to protect its economic interests in Latin America. In 1926, for example, a revolution broke out in Nicaragua, where Americans owned plantations and railroads. Coolidge sent marines to oversee new elections.

In 1927, Mexico announced plans to take over foreign-owned oil and mining companies. American investors called on President Coolidge to send in troops. Instead, Coolidge sent a diplomat, Dwight Morrow, to Mexico. After much hard bargaining, Morrow was able to work out a compromise with the Mexican government.

Viewing History

Consumer Credit

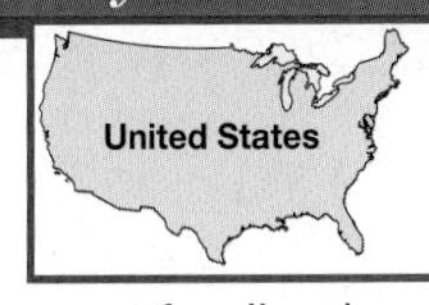

With installment plans and the appearance of mail-order catalogs, people bought radios, vacuum cleaners, and other new products on credit. Some stores showed attractive window displays of furniture available for purchase on credit. **Analyzing Information** ***How did Americans' ideas about owing money change in the 1920s?***

Understand Effects How did Republican leadership affect the U.S. role in world affairs? Note this information in your chart.

The Soviet Union Meanwhile, in the Soviet Union, V. I. Lenin created the world's first communist state.* **Communism** is an economic system in which all wealth and property are owned by the community as a whole.

The United States refused to recognize Lenin's government. Most Americans disliked communism. It shocked them when the Soviet government did away with private property and attacked religion. Yet, despite disapproval of the Soviet government, Congress voted $20 million in aid when famine threatened Russia in 1921. American aid may have saved as many as 10 million Russians from starvation.

Pursuing Peace An arms race in Europe had helped cause World War I. For this reason, many people in the 1920s favored the reduction of armed forces and weapons of war, or **disarmament.** Pacifist groups such as the Women's International League for Peace and Freedom, founded by Jane Addams, led the call for disarmament in the United States and Europe.

Presidents Harding and Coolidge also backed peace efforts. At the Washington Conference of 1921, the United States, Britain, and Japan agreed to limit the size of their navies. Seven years later, the United States and 61 other nations signed the **Kellogg-Briand Pact.** This treaty outlawed war.

The treaty, however, had a fatal flaw. It did not set up any means for keeping the peace. One nation could still use force against another without fear of punishment. Still, many hailed the Kellogg-Briand Pact as the beginning of a new age of peace.

---

* In 1922, Russia became the most powerful state in the newly created Union of Soviet Socialist Republics, or Soviet Union.

★ ★ ★ Section 1 Assessment ★ ★ ★

Recall

1. **Identify** Explain the significance of **(a)** Warren G. Harding, **(b)** Teapot Dome Scandal, **(c)** Calvin Coolidge, **(d)** Kellogg- Briand Pact.
2. **Define** **(a)** recession, **(b)** installment buying, **(c)** stock, **(d)** bull market, **(e)** communism, **(f)** disarmament.

Comprehension

3. How did corruption hurt the Republicans during the 1920s?
4. How did Americans benefit from "Coolidge prosperity"?
5. What role did most Americans in the 1920s think that the United States should take in world affairs? Explain.

Critical Thinking and Writing

6. **Exploring the Main Idea** Review the Main Idea statement at the beginning of this section. Then, explain why Calvin Coolidge made this statement: "The business of America is business."
7. **Making Predictions** During the 1920s, many Americans bought consumer goods on credit and stocks on margin. How would this make economic conditions worse after the economy began to slow down?

ACTIVITY

Connecting to Today
Mexico and the United States still share economic concerns. Use the Internet to find out about the North American Free Trade Agreement (NAFTA). Summarize the purpose of NAFTA. Then, discuss its effects today. For help in completing the activity, visit PHSchool.com, **Web Code mfd-2501.**

Determining Relevance

As you have read, many Americans enjoyed a new prosperity in the years following World War I. Numerous causes contributed to this economic growth in the 1920s. In examining these causes, it is important to determine how pertinent, or relevant, your information is to the topic. What logical connection exists between your topic and a piece of information?

Not only were radios a source of family entertainment and news, they also provided an effective means of selling consumer goods.

An advertisement for a radio

In 1922, Emily Post published a book on manners called *Etiquette*. This excerpt tells how a considerate guest should behave:

> "Courtesy demands that you, when you are a guest, shall show neither annoyance nor disappointment—no matter what happens. . . . If you neither understand nor care for dogs or children, and both insist on climbing all over you, you must seemingly like it."
>
> "You must pretend that six is a perfect dinner hour though you never dine before eight or . . . you must wait until eight-thirty or nine . . . though your dinner hour is six. . . ."
>
> —Emily Post, *Etiquette*, 1922

Learn the Skill *To determine if information is relevant, use the following steps:*

1. **Clarify the topic.** Be clear about the topic you are studying. Often, it is helpful to restate it in your own words.
2. **Examine the evidence.** Look carefully at the information you have. What does it represent?
3. **Determine the relevance.** How does the information relate to the topic? Ask yourself questions, for example, How would consumer spending contribute to economic growth?

Practice the Skill *Answer the following questions based on the chapter and the information on this page:*

1. Restate the topic in your own words.
2. **(a)** Which piece of information represents economic issues? **(b)** Which information is about another topic?
3. **(a)** How did the radio affect economic growth during the 1920s? **(b)** How is etiquette related to economic growth?

Apply the Skill *See the Chapter Review and Assessment.*

2 New Ways of Life

Prepare to Read

Objectives

In this section, you will
- Describe Prohibition.
- Identify the new rights gained by women.
- Explain how the automobile and a new popular culture changed American life.

Key Terms

Prohibition
bootleggers
repeal
League of Women Voters
Equal Rights Amendment
suburb

Target Reading Skill

Reading Process Copy the concept web below. As you read, fill in the blank ovals with the new ways of life that occurred during the 1920s. Add as many ovals as you need.

Main Idea New ideas and products and a new popular culture changed the values and customs of Americans during the 1920s.

Federal agents destroy barrels of illegal liquor

Setting the Scene At the stroke of midnight on the morning of January 16, 1920, church bells rang all across the United States. What some people called the "noble experiment" had begun. The experiment was **Prohibition,** a ban on the manufacture, sale, and transportation of liquor anywhere in the United States.

Supporters of Prohibition were overjoyed. Popular preacher Billy Sunday predicted that the ban on alcohol would cure a wide variety of social ills: "The slums will soon be only a memory. We will turn our prisons into factories and our jails into storehouses and corncribs. Men will walk upright now. Women will smile and children will laugh."

Only time would tell if the "noble experiment" would succeed or fail.

Prohibition was one of many developments that had a dramatic impact on society in the 1920s. New ideas, new products, and new forms of entertainment were rapidly changing the American way of life.

Prohibition

For nearly a century, reformers like the Woman's Christian Temperance Union had worked to ban alcoholic beverages. They finally achieved this when the states ratified the Eighteenth Amendment in January 1919. One year later, Prohibition went into effect.

In 1920, as today, alcohol abuse was a serious problem. Many Americans hoped the ban on liquor would improve American life. In fact, the ban did have some positive effects. Alcoholism declined during Prohibition. However, in the end, the ban did not work.

Evading the Law One reason that Prohibition failed was that many Americans found ways to get around the law. Some people manufactured their own alcohol in homemade stills. Others smuggled in liquor from Canada and the Caribbean. Because these smugglers sometimes hid bottles of liquor in their boots, they became known as **bootleggers.**

Illegal bars, called speak-easies, opened in nearly every city and town. In some ways, speak-easies made drinking liquor more popular than ever. To enforce the ban, the government sent out federal Prohibition agents. These "g-men" traveled across the United States, shutting down speak-easies, breaking up illegal stills, and stopping smugglers.

Rise of Organized Crime Prohibition gave a huge boost to organized crime. Every speak-easy needed a steady supply of liquor. Professional criminals, or gangsters, took over the job of meeting this need. As bootleggers earned big profits, crime became a big business. Gangsters divided up cities and forced speak-easy owners in their "territories" to buy liquor from them. Sometimes, gangsters used some of their profits to bribe police officers, public officials, and judges.

Repeal of Prohibition Gradually, more Americans began to think that Prohibition was a mistake. The ban reduced drinking but never stopped it. Even worse, argued critics, Prohibition was undermining respect for the law. Every day, millions of Americans were buying liquor in speak-easies. By the mid-1920s, almost half of all federal arrests were for Prohibition crimes.

By the end of the decade, many Americans were calling for the **repeal,** or cancellation, of Prohibition. In 1933, the states ratified the Twenty-first Amendment, which repealed the Eighteenth Amendment.* The noble experiment was over.

New Rights for Women

Another constitutional amendment, the Nineteenth Amendment, also changed American life, but in a very different way. Ratified in 1920, it gave women the right to vote.

Women Voters Women went to the polls nationwide for the first time in November 1920. Their votes helped elect Warren Harding President. Women did not vote as a group, however, as some people had predicted. Like men, some women voted for Republicans, and some for Democrats, and many did not vote at all.

In 1920, Carrie Chapman Catt, head of the National Woman Suffrage Association, set up the **League of Women Voters.** The organization worked to educate voters, as it does today. It also worked to guarantee other rights, such as the right of women to serve on juries.

Women served as delegates in the 1924 Republican and Democratic conventions. That year, the first two women governors were elected—Nellie Tayloe Ross of Wyoming and Miriam A. Ferguson of Texas.

As women in the United States voted for the first time, women in Puerto Rico asked if the new law applied to them. They were told

*To date, the Eighteenth Amendment is the only constitutional amendment that has ever been repealed.

An American Profile

Nellie Tayloe Ross

1876–1977

Nellie Tayloe Ross, the nation's first female governor, took office in Wyoming on January 5, 1925. Governor Ross had not sought a political career. She taught kindergarten for two years before her health failed. After she married, she was a homemaker and mother. Then, in 1922, her husband was elected governor of Wyoming. When he died in office, his supporters urged his widow to run for his vacant seat. Nellie Ross was elected governor. Later she became a popular speaker for the Democratic National Committee, and in 1933 she became the first female Director of the U.S. Mint.

Why do you think people urged Nellie Tayloe Ross to run for governor? Explain.

that it did not. Led by Ana Roqué de Duprey, an educator and writer, Puerto Rican women crusaded for the vote. In 1929, their crusade finally succeeded.

An Equal Rights Amendment Leaders in the suffrage movement also worked for other goals. Alice Paul, who had been a leading suffragist, pointed out that women still lacked many legal rights. For example, many professional schools still barred women, and many states gave husbands legal control over their wives' earnings. Paul called for a new constitutional amendment in 1923. Paul's proposed Equal Rights Amendment (ERA) stated that "equality of rights under the law shall not be denied or abridged by the United States or by any State on account of sex."

Many people feared that the ERA went too far. Some even argued that women would lose some legal safeguards, such as laws that protected them in factories. Paul worked vigorously for the ERA until her death in 1977. The amendment passed but was never ratified.

Changes for Working Women Women's lives changed in other ways in the 1920s. During World War I, thousands of women had worked outside the home for the first time. They filled the jobs of men who had gone off to war. When the troops came home, many women were forced to give up their jobs. Still, some remained in the work force.

For some women, working outside the home was nothing new. Poor women and working-class women had been cooks, servants, and seamstresses for many years. In the 1920s, they were joined by middle-class women who worked as teachers, typists, secretaries, and store clerks. A few women even managed to become doctors and lawyers despite discrimination.

Life at home also changed for women. More of them bought ready-made clothes than sewed for the whole family as they had done in the past. Electric appliances such as refrigerators, washers, irons, and vacuum cleaners made housework easier. On the other hand, such conveniences also encouraged some women to spend even more time on housework. Women who worked outside the home found that they had to work a second shift when they came home. Most husbands expected their wives to cook, clean, and care for children even if they held full-time jobs.

Predict

Read the subheadings of this section. Then, predict how the automobile affected American life in the 1920s. Read to check your predictions.

Impact of the Automobile

"Why on earth do you need to study what's changing this country?" one man asked the experts. "I can tell you what's happening in just four letters: A-U-T-O." In the 1920s, Americans traveled to more places and moved more quickly than ever before—all because of the automobile.

The auto industry played a central role in the business boom of the 1920s. Car sales grew rapidly during the decade. The auto boom spurred growth in related industries such as steel and rubber.

Affordable Cars Lower prices sparked the auto boom. By 1924, the cost of a Model T had dropped from $850 to $290. As a result, an American did not have to be rich to buy a car.

Car prices fell because factories became more efficient. As you have read, Henry Ford introduced the assembly line in his automobile factory in 1913. Before the assembly line, it took 14 hours to put together a Model T. In Ford's new factory, workers could assemble a Model T in 93 minutes.

Other companies copied Ford's methods. In 1927, General Motors passed Ford as the top automaker. Unlike Ford, General Motors sold cars in a variety of models and colors. Henry Ford had once boasted that people could have his cars in "any color so long as it's black." When General Motors introduced a low-priced car available in different colors, Ford lost many customers. Faced with the success of General Motors, he changed his mind. His next car, the Model A, came in different colors. Before long, car companies were offering new makes and models every year.

Viewing History

The Rise in Car Sales

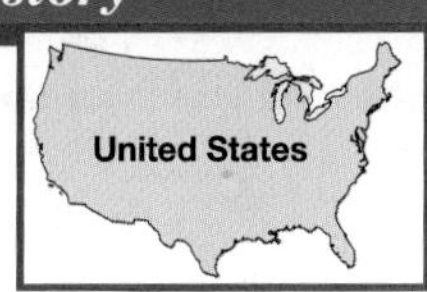

The explosion in automobile production resulted in lower prices. Now, more Americans were able to afford a car. By the late 1920s, nearly 80 percent of all registered cars in the world were in the United States.

Synthesizing Information ***Why do you think the automobile became a status symbol for some families?***

Economic Effects Car sales spurred growth in other parts of the economy. By 1929, some four million Americans owed their jobs to the automobile, directly or indirectly. Tens of thousands of people worked in steel mills, producing metal parts for cars. Others made tires, paint, and glass for cars. Some drilled for oil in the Southwest or worked in the oil refineries where crude petroleum was converted into usable gasoline.

The car boom had other effects. States and towns paved more roads and built new highways. In 1925, the Bronx River Parkway in New York was the first of many highways in parklike settings.

Gas stations, garages, car dealers, motels, and roadside restaurants sprang up across the country to serve the millions who traveled by car. In 1920, there were only about 1,500 filling stations in the entire United States. By 1929, there were more than 120,000. Mechanic shops, or places to repair automobiles, also became a necessity.

AmericanHeritage MAGAZINE

HISTORY **HAPPENED HERE**

Hollywood Boulevard

As the movie industry grew during the 1920s, so did the fame of Hollywood in California. It was the home of movie stars and the glittering world of the entertainment industry. In addition to the many places you can visit along historic Hollywood Boulevard, you can also see 2,000 bronze stars, each with a celebrity's name, embedded in the sidewalk.

Virtual Field Trip For an interactive look at Hollywood Boulevard, visit PHSchool.com, **Web Code mfd-2502.**

Social Effects Cars shaped life in the city and in the country. Many city dwellers wanted to escape crowded conditions. They moved to nearby towns in the country, which soon grew into suburbs. A **suburb** is a community located outside a city. With cars, suburban families could drive to the city even though it was many miles away. They could also drive to stores, schools, or work. No longer did people have to live where they could walk or take a trolley to work.

Another major shift came when suburban housewives refused to be confined to the passenger seat. Instead, they took their place behind the wheels of their own automobiles. As they did, they broke down still another barrier that separated the worlds of men and women.

In the country, cars brought people closer to towns, shops, and the movies. Such trips had taken several hours by horse and buggy. One farm woman bought a car before she got indoor plumbing. "You can't go to town in a bathtub," she explained.

Creating a Mass Culture

By making travel easier, cars helped Americans from different parts of the country learn more about one another. They played a role in creating a new national culture that crossed state lines.

New forms of entertainment also contributed to the rise of a mass culture. In the 1920s, rising wages and labor-saving appliances gave families more money to spend and more leisure time in which to spend it.

Radio Radio became very popular in the 1920s. The country's first radio station, KDKA, started broadcasting in Pittsburgh in 1920. By 1929, more than 10 million American families owned radios.

A new lifestyle emerged. Each night after dinner, families gathered around the radio to tune in to shows such as "Roxy and His Gang" or "Jack Frost's Melody Moments." Radio listeners enjoyed comedies and westerns, classical music and jazz, news reports and play-by-play sports broadcasts.

The Movies In the 1920s, the movie industry came of age. Southern California's warm, sunny climate allowed filming all year round. Soon, Hollywood became the movie capital of the world.

Movies contributed to the new mass culture. Millions of Americans went to the movies at least once a week. They thrilled to westerns, romances, adventures, and comedies. In small towns, theaters were bare rooms with hard chairs. In cities, they were huge palaces with red velvet seats.

The first movies had no sound. Audiences followed the plot by reading "title cards" that appeared on the screen. A pianist played music that went with the action.

Fans adored Hollywood movie stars. Cowboy stars like Tom Mix thrilled audiences with their heroic adventures. Clara Bow won fame playing restless, fun-seeking young women. The most popular star of all was comedian Charlie Chaplin, nicknamed "The Little Tramp." In his tiny derby hat and baggy pants, Chaplin presented a comical figure. His attempts to triumph over the problems of everyday life moved audiences to both laughter and tears.

In 1927, Hollywood caused a sensation when it produced *The Jazz Singer*. The film was a "talkie"—a movie with a soundtrack. Soon, all new movies were talkies.

Section 2 Assessment

Recall

1. **Identify** Explain the significance of **(a)** Prohibition, **(b)** Carrie Chapman Catt, **(c)** League of Women Voters, **(d)** Ana Roqué de Duprey, **(e)** Alice Paul, **(f)** Equal Rights Amendment, **(g)** Henry Ford, **(h)** Charlie Chaplin.
2. **Define (a)** bootleggers, **(b)** repeal, **(c)** suburb.

Comprehension

3. Why did Prohibition fail?
4. How did the Nineteenth Amendment change women's lives?
5. **(a)** How did the automobile affect the economy? **(b)** Discuss the effect of radio and the movies on the culture during the 1920s.

Critical Thinking and Writing

6. **Exploring the Main Idea** Review the Main Idea statement at the beginning of this section. Then, discuss two ideas that changed the way Americans lived during the 1920s.
7. **Analyzing Information** How did changes in technology contribute to new ways of life during the 1920s?

Activity

Writing Title Cards
You are a moviemaker producing a silent film about the Roaring Twenties. Write ten title cards for scenes that show what the decade was like.

3 The Roaring Twenties

Prepare to Read

Objectives

In this section, you will
- Identify the fads and fashions of the 1920s.
- Explain how a new group of writers and new jazz music affected American culture.
- Describe the Harlem Renaissance.
- Identify the heroes who were celebrated during the 1920s.

Key Terms

fad

flapper

jazz

expatriate

Target Reading Skill

Main Idea As you read, prepare an outline of this section. Use roman numerals to indicate the major headings of this section, capital letters for subheadings, and numbers for the supporting details. The sample below will help you get started.

I. New Fads and Fashions
  A. Following the latest fads
    1.
    2.
  B. Flappers set the style
    1.
    2.
II. The Jazz Age

Main Idea While new lifestyles and new ideas affected fashion and music, a new generation of writers rebelled by criticizing American life.

A dancing couple from the 1920s

Setting the Scene When asked about her favorite pastime, one young woman of the 1920s promptly replied, "I adore dancing. Who doesn't?" New dance crazes such as the Charleston, the Lindy Hop, and the Shimmy forever marked the decade as the "Jazz Age" and the "Roaring Twenties."

During the 1920s, new dances, new music, new games, and other new ways to have fun swept the country. For all the serious business of the 1920s, the decade also roared with laughter. At the same time, a new generation of writers were taking a critical look at American society.

New Fads and Fashions

"Ev'ry morning, ev'ry evening, ain't we got fun?" went a hit song of 1921. During the "Era of Wonderful Nonsense"—yet another nickname for the 1920s—fun came in many forms.

Following the Latest Fads Fads caught on, then quickly disappeared. A **fad** is an activity or a fashion that is taken up with great passion for a short time. Flagpole sitting was one fad of the 1920s. Young people would perch on top of flagpoles for hours, or even days. Another fad was the dance marathon, where couples danced for hundreds of hours at a time to see who could last the longest. Crossword puzzles and mah-jongg, a Chinese game, were other popular fads of the 1920s.

Identify Main Ideas What is the main idea of the subsection "New Fads and Fashions"? Include the main idea on your outline.

Dance crazes came and went rapidly. The most popular new dance was probably the Charleston. First performed by African Americans in southern cities like Charleston, South Carolina, the dance became a national craze after 1923. Moving to a quick beat, dancers pivoted their feet while kicking out first one leg, then the other, backward and forward.

Flappers Set the Style Perhaps no one pursued the latest fads more intensely than the **flappers.** These young women rebelled against traditional ways of thinking and acting. Flappers wore their hair bobbed, or cut short. They wore their dresses short, too—shorter than Americans had ever seen. Flappers shocked their parents by wearing bright red lipstick.

To many older Americans, the way flappers behaved was even more shocking than the way they looked. Flappers smoked cigarettes in public, drank bootleg alcohol in speak-easies, and drove fast cars. "Is 'the old-fashioned girl,' with all that she stands for in sweetness, modesty, and innocence, in danger of becoming extinct?" wondered one magazine in 1921.

Only a few young women were flappers. Still, they set a style for others. Slowly, older women began to cut their hair and wear make-up and shorter skirts. For many Americans, the bold fashions pioneered by the flappers symbolized a new sense of freedom.

The Jazz Age

Another innovation of the 1920s was **jazz.** Born in New Orleans, jazz combined West African rhythms, African American work songs and spirituals, and European harmonies. Jazz also had roots in the ragtime rhythms of composers like Scott Joplin.

Louis Armstrong was one of the brilliant young African American musicians who helped create jazz. Armstrong learned to play the trumpet in the New Orleans orphanage where he grew up. Armstrong had the ability to take a simple melody and experiment with the notes and the rhythm. This allowed his listeners to hear many different versions of the basic tune. Other great early jazz musicians included "Jelly Roll" Morton and singer Bessie Smith.

Jazz quickly spread from New Orleans to Chicago, Kansas City, and the African American section of New York known as Harlem. White musicians, such as trumpeter Bix Beiderbecke, also began to adopt the new style. Before long, the popularity of jazz spread to Europe as well.

Many older Americans worried that jazz and the new dances were a bad influence on the nation's young people. Despite their complaints, jazz continued to grow more popular. Today, jazz is recognized as an original art form developed by African Americans. It is considered one of the most important cultural contributions of the United States.

An American Profile

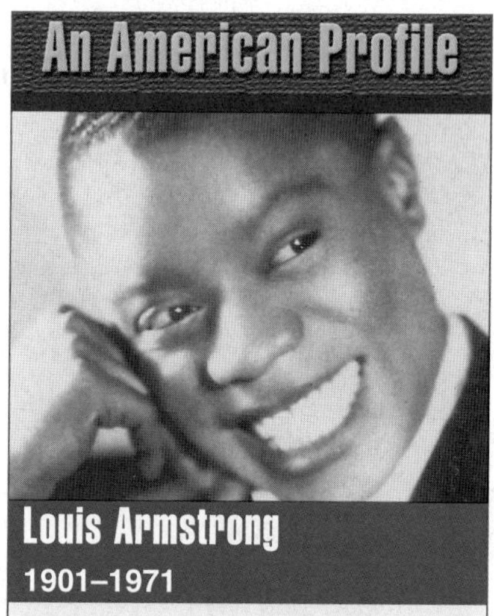

Louis Armstrong
1901–1971

Eleven-year-old Louis Armstrong often played a little tin horn on a rag wagon. He hoped people would throw rags and bottles into the wagon. Then, he could sell them for a penny. When he spotted a five-dollar cornet in a pawnshop window, he wondered what kind of music he could make with a real horn. He saved fifty cents a week and bought the horn. At 17, he was playing the cornet in New Orleans street parades. At 18, he joined a band on a riverboat. A listener later wrote, "That cornet [filled] the night with the hottest, the sweetest and purest jazz I'd ever heard."

Discuss Louis Armstrong's statement that at age 11, he was convinced he had music in his soul.

New Writers

A new generation of American writers earned worldwide fame in the 1920s. Many of them were horrified by their experiences in World War I. They criticized Americans for caring too much about money and fun. Some became so unhappy with life in the United States that they moved to Paris, France. There, they lived as **expatriates,** people who leave their own country to live in a foreign land.

Hemingway and Fitzgerald Ernest Hemingway was one of the writers who lived for a time in Paris. Still a teenager at the outbreak of World War I, he traveled to Europe to drive an ambulance on the Italian front. Hemingway drew on his war experiences in *A Farewell to Arms,* a novel about a young man's growing disgust with war. In *The Sun Also Rises,* he examined the lives of American expatriates in Europe.

Hemingway became one of the most popular writers of the 1920s. His simple but powerful style influenced many other writers.

The young writer who best captured the mood of the Roaring Twenties was Hemingway's friend F. Scott Fitzgerald. In *The Great Gatsby* and other novels, Fitzgerald examined the lives of wealthy young people who attended endless parties but could not find happiness. His characters included flappers, bootleggers, and moviemakers. Fitzgerald became a hero to college students and flappers, among others.

Viewing History

Sinclair Lewis

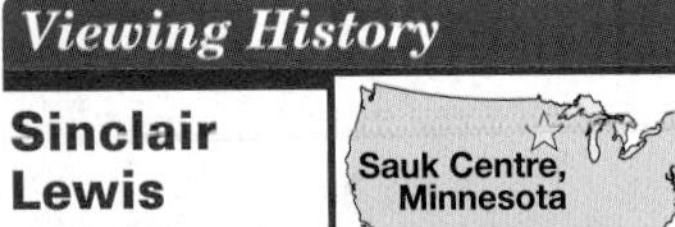

After living through the horror of World War I, many American writers criticized the values and lifestyles of the 1920s. The most outspoken critic was Sinclair Lewis. His novel *Main Street,* which mocked the values of small-town life in the United States, was an instant success. **Drawing Conclusions** ***Why do you think Lewis called his novel* Main Street?**

Other Writers Sinclair Lewis grew up in a small town in Minnesota and later moved to New York City. In novels such as *Babbitt* and *Main Street,* he presented small-town Americans as dull and narrow-minded. Lewis's attitude reflected that of many city dwellers toward rural Americans. In fact, the word *babbitt* became a popular nickname for a smug businessman uninterested in literature or the arts. In 1930, Lewis was the first American to win the Nobel Prize for literature.

Poet Edna St. Vincent Millay was enormously popular. She expressed the frantic pace of the 1920s in her verse, such as her short poem "First Fig":

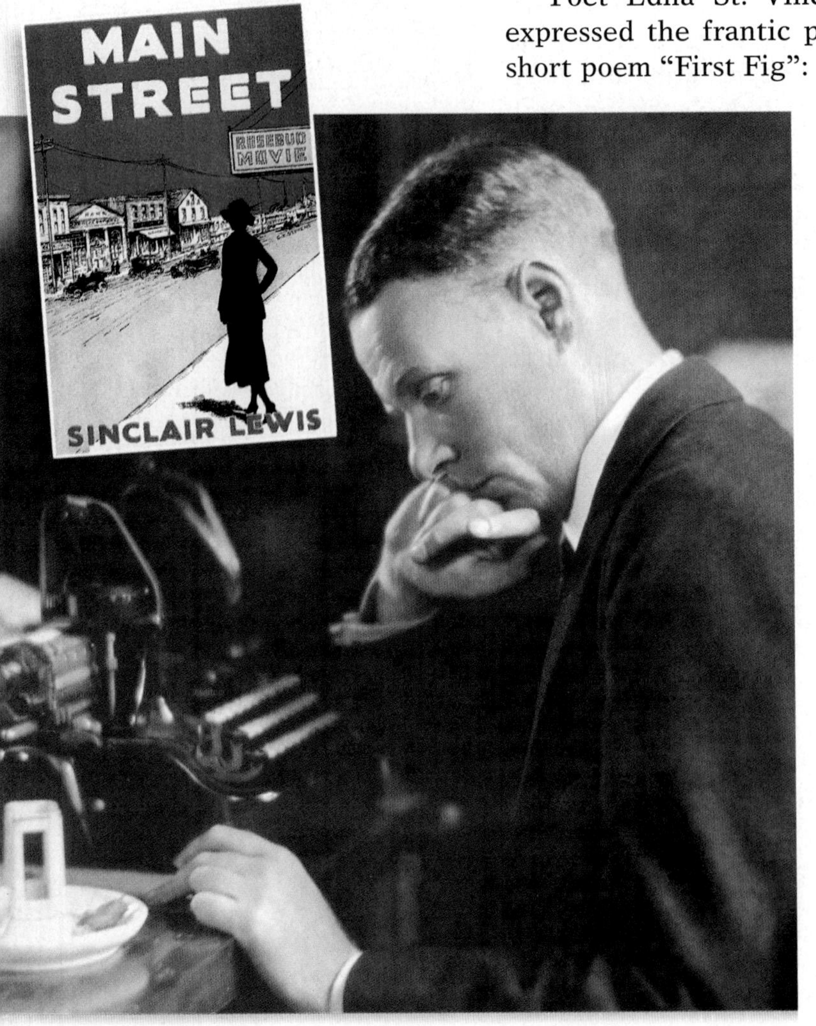

> "My candle burns at both ends; / It will not last the night; / But ah, my foes, and oh, my friends— / It gives a lovely light."
>
> —Edna St. Vincent Millay, "First Fig," 1920

Another writer, Eugene O'Neill, revolutionized the American theater. Most earlier playwrights had presented romantic, unrealistic stories. O'Neill shocked audiences with powerful, realistic dramas based on his years at sea. In other plays, he used experimental methods to expose the inner thoughts of tortured young people.

Harlem Renaissance

In the 1920s, large numbers of African American musicians, artists, and writers settled in Harlem, in New York City. "Harlem was like a great magnet for the Negro intellectual," said one black writer. This gathering of black artists and musicians led to the Harlem Renaissance, a rebirth of African American culture.

During the Harlem Renaissance, young black writers celebrated their African and

A Changing American Culture

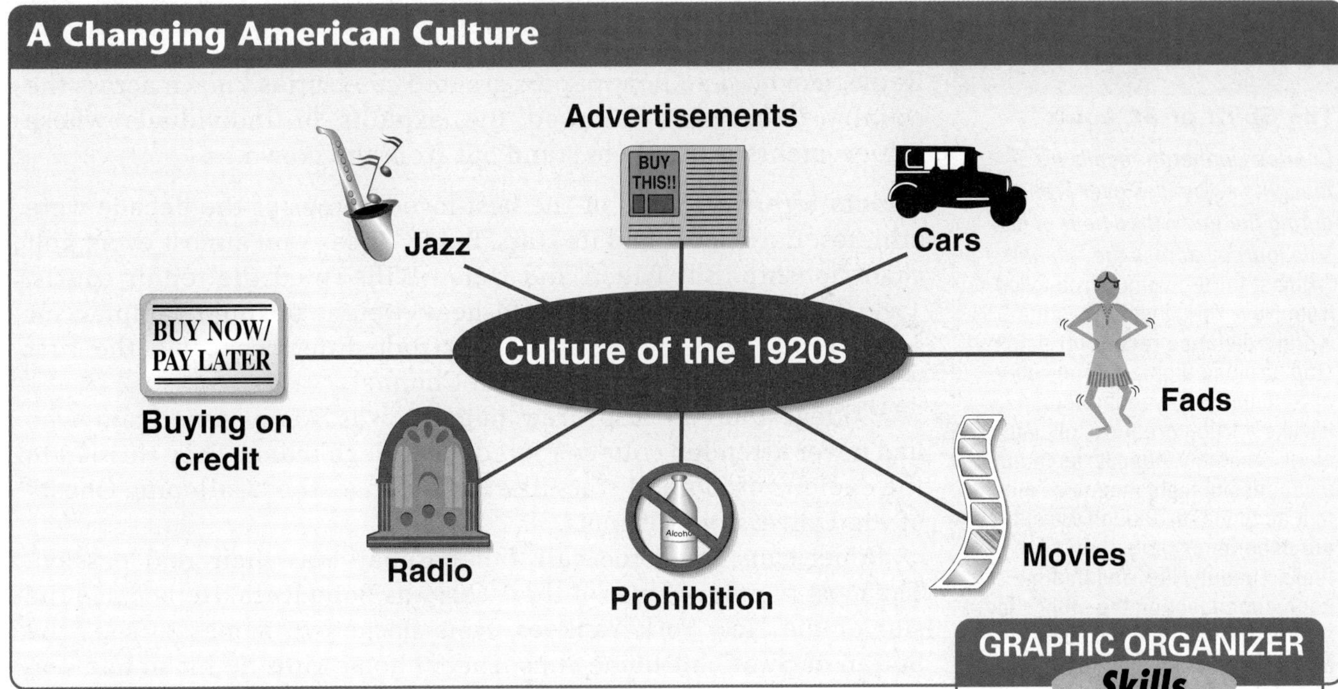

American heritages. They also protested prejudice and racism. For the first time, too, a large number of white Americans took notice of the achievements of black artists and writers.

Langston Hughes Probably the best-known poet of the Harlem Renaissance was Langston Hughes. He published his first poem, "The Negro Speaks of Rivers," soon after graduating from high school. The poem connected the experiences of black Americans living along the Mississippi River with those of ancient Africans living along the Nile and Niger rivers. Like other writers of the Harlem Renaissance, Hughes encouraged African Americans to be proud of their heritage.

In other poems, Hughes protested racism and acts of violence against African Americans. In addition to his poems, Hughes wrote plays, short stories, and essays about the black experience.

Other Writers Other poets such as Countee Cullen and Claude McKay also wrote of the experiences of African Americans. A graduate of New York University and Harvard, Cullen taught in a Harlem high school. In the 1920s, he won prizes for his books of poetry.

McKay came to the United States from Jamaica. In his poem "If We Must Die," he condemned the lynchings and other mob violence that black Americans suffered after World War I. The poem concludes with the lines "Like men we'll face the murderous, cowardly pack, / Pressed to the wall, dying but fighting back!"

Zora Neale Hurston, who grew up in Florida, wrote novels, essays, and short stories. Hurston grew concerned that African American folklore "was disappearing without the world realizing it had ever been." In 1928, she set out alone to travel through the South in a battered car. For two years, she collected the folk tales, songs, and prayers of black southerners. She later published these in her book *Mules and Men*.

GRAPHIC ORGANIZER *Skills*

The 1920s were a time of change in the United States. A number of new inventions, ideas, and practices contributed to this change.

1. **Comprehension** Identify two items on this graphic organizer that were linked to the economic boom of the 1920s.
2. **Critical Thinking Applying Information** **(a)** Which items shown here affected American leisure activities? **(b)** Of these, which are still popular?

An Age of Heroes

Radio, movies, and newspapers created celebrities known across the country. Americans followed the exploits of individuals whose achievements made them stand out from the crowd.

Sports Figures Some of the best-loved heroes of the decade were athletes. Each sport had its stars. Bobby Jones won almost every golf championship. Bill Tilden and Helen Wills ruled the tennis courts. Jack Dempsey reigned as world heavyweight boxing champion for seven years. At the age of 19, Gertrude Ederle became the first woman to swim across the English Channel.

College football also drew huge crowds. Many Americans who had never attended college rooted for college teams. They thrilled to the exploits of football stars like Red Grange, the "Galloping Ghost" of the University of Illinois.

Americans loved football, but baseball was their real passion. The most popular player of the 1920s was Babe Ruth. He became the star of the New York Yankees. Fans flocked to games to see "the Sultan of Swat" hit home runs. The 60 home runs he hit in one season set a record that lasted more than 30 years. His lifetime record of 714 home runs was not broken until 1974.

"Lucky Lindy" The greatest hero was Charles A. Lindbergh. On a gray morning in May 1927, he took off from an airport in New York to fly nonstop across the Atlantic Ocean—alone.

For more than 33 hours, Lindbergh piloted his tiny single-engine plane, the *Spirit of St. Louis,* over the stormy Atlantic. He carried no map, no parachute, and no radio. At last, he landed in Paris, France. The cheering crowd carried him across the airfield. "Lucky Lindy" returned to the United States as the hero of the decade.

Primary Source

The *Spirit of St. Louis*

Charles Lindbergh recalls his thoughts as he flies over France during the thirty-third hour of his solo journey across the Atlantic:

"Almost thirty-five hundred miles from New York. I've broken the world's distance record for a non-stop airplane flight. . . . The *Spirit of St. Louis* is a wonderful plane. It's like a living creature, gliding along smoothly, happily, as though a successful flight means as much to it as to me, as though we shared our experiences together, each feeling beauty, life, and death . . . each dependent on the other's loyalty. *We* have made this flight across the ocean, not *I* or *it.*"

—Charles Lindbergh, The *Spirit of St. Louis*, 1927

Analyzing Primary Sources

Why do you think Charles Lindbergh's sense of accomplishment shifted from himself to his partnership with his airplane?

Section 3 Assessment

Recall

1. **Identify** Explain the significance of **(a)** Louis Armstrong, **(b)** Ernest Hemingway, **(c)** F. Scott Fitzgerald, **(d)** Sinclair Lewis, **(e)** Eugene O'Neill, **(f)** Langston Hughes, **(g)** Countee Cullen, **(h)** Claude McKay, **(i)** Zora Neale Hurston, **(j)** Babe Ruth, **(k)** Charles Lindbergh.
2. **Define** **(a)** fad, **(b)** flapper, **(c)** jazz, **(d)** expatriate.

Comprehension

3. How did flappers reflect changes in American fashion?
4. What aspects of American life did writers criticize?
5. What themes did the writers of the Harlem Renaissance address in their works?
6. Why was Charles A. Lindbergh a hero?

Critical Thinking and Writing

7. **Exploring the Main Idea** Review the Main Idea statement at the beginning of this section. Then, describe three cultural achievements of the 1920s.
8. **Analyzing Ideas** Review Edna St. Vincent Millay's poem on page 732. How does it reflect the spirit of the 1920s?

ACTIVITY

The Winter Olympics

Before 1924, the Olympics featured only summer sports. In the 1920s, people began to want competition in winter sports. Use the Internet to research the 1924 Winter Olympics. Write a brief article for a sports magazine. For help in completing the activity, visit PHSchool.com, **Web Code mfd-2503.**

Connecting With... **Culture**

THE HARLEM RENAISSANCE

During the 1920s, the New York district of Harlem was the center of a surge of creative activity with lasting effects on American culture. Originally known as the Negro Movement, the Harlem Renaissance produced writers, artists, and jazz and blues musicians.

The best-known poet of the movement was Langston Hughes. Much of his poetry captures the rhythms of blues and jazz. Hughes also wove themes of the African American experience, history, and folklore into his work. Recognized as the Poet Laureate of Harlem, Hughes wrote more than 50 books.

The type of music known as the blues originated in the South in the late 1800s but reached a high point of development with the blues artists of the Harlem Renaissance. Their music contributed to the development of jazz and has influenced rock, folk, and country music. One of the most influential blues singers of the period was Bessie Smith, who became known as "Empress of the Blues." Her recordings were popular with black and white audiences alike.

Harlem was home to many popular nightclubs, where people came to dance, listen to jazz and blues musicians, and watch floorshows. The Cotton Club was one of the most well-known. Duke Ellington's band was the regular club band, later alternating with the band of Cab Calloway. Both of these musicians became legendary figures in jazz.

Duke Ellington

ACTIVITY

How would you celebrate the culture of your neighborhood? Write a poem or lyrics for a song that describes your pride in your neighborhood.

4 A Nation Divided

Prepare to Read

Objectives

In this section, you will

- Identify the Americans who did not share in the prosperity of the 1920s.
- Explain why Americans called for a limit on immigration.
- Discuss what the Scopes trial and the revival of the Klan revealed about society in the 1920s.
- Describe the election of 1928.

Key Terms

company union
sabotage
anarchist
deport
nativism
quota system

Target Reading Skill

Sequence Copy this flowchart. As you read, fill in the boxes with some of the major events described in this section that led to limits on immigration. The first and last boxes have been completed to help you get started. Add as many boxes as you need.

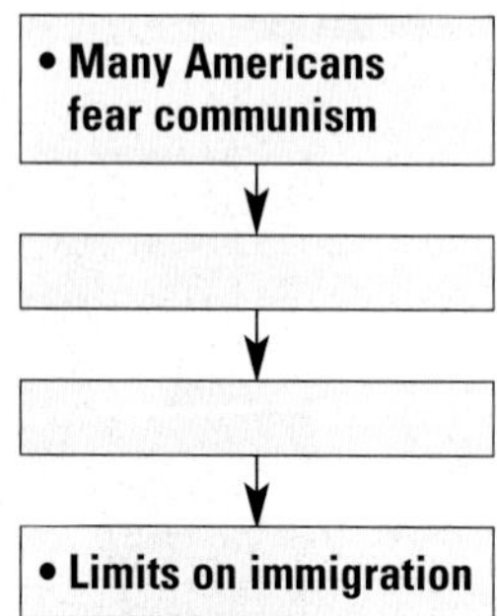

Main Idea In spite of the prosperity of the 1920s, the nation was divided between rich and poor, native-born and immigrant, and black and white.

Three farmers

Setting the Scene In the 1920s, John J. Raskob was convinced that everyone should be rich. Raskob had been an executive with General Motors. Now he listed his job simply as "capitalist." By investing wisely, he wrote, "anyone not only can be rich but ought to be rich."

Yet, most Americans in the 1920s were not rich. In 1929, at the height of "Coolidge prosperity," more than half of American families earned less than $2,000 a year. Farmers and factory workers were experiencing hardships. Most Americans could not afford the bare necessities, let alone the investments to make them rich.

Beneath the glittering prosperity of the 1920s, the economy was already in trouble.

The Perils of Prosperity

Many Americans did not share in the boom of the 1920s. Workers in the clothing industry, for example, were hurt by changes in women's fashions. Shorter skirts meant that less cloth was needed to make dresses. Coal miners also faced hard times as oil replaced coal as the major source of energy. Railroads slashed jobs because trains were losing business to cars and trucks.

Trouble on the Farm Farmers were hit the hardest. During World War I, Europeans had bought American farm products, sending prices up. Farmers borrowed money to buy more land and tractors. They planned to pay off these loans with profits from increased production.

When the war ended, however, European farmers were again able to produce enough for their own needs. As a result, prices for American farm products dropped sharply throughout the 1920s. Farmers were unable to pay their debts. By the end of the decade, the farmers' share of national income had shrunk by almost half.

Setbacks for Labor For labor unions, too, the 1920s were a disaster. During the war, unions had worked with the government to keep production high. Labor's cooperation contributed to victory. In return, union leaders expected the government to support labor.

During the war, wages had not kept up with prices. Now, with the war over, workers demanded higher pay. When employers refused, unions launched a wave of strikes. Management moved quickly to crush the strikes. Because the government did not step in to help them, workers felt betrayed and management gained power.

The strikes turned the public against labor. One strike in particular angered Americans. In 1919, the city of Boston fired 19 police officers who had tried to join the American Federation of Labor (AFL). Boston police struck in protest. The sight of police leaving their posts shocked the country.

The later 1920s saw even more setbacks for labor. In one court case after another, judges limited the rights of unions. At the same time, employers created **company unions,** labor organizations that were actually controlled by management. As a result, union membership dropped from 5 million in 1920 to 3.4 million by 1929. Without strong unions, labor had little power to win higher wages.

Viewing History

Seeking Justice for Sacco and Vanzetti

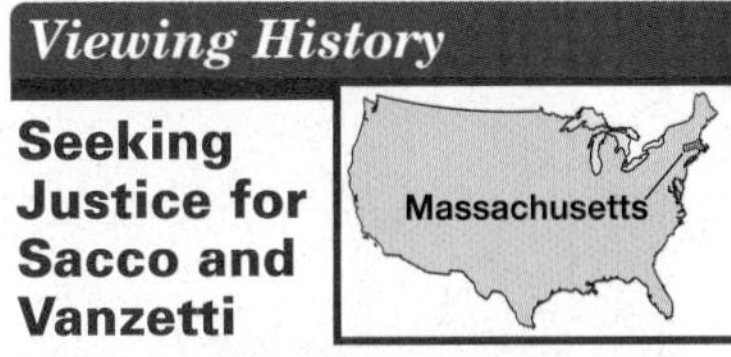

Did Sacco and Vanzetti get a fair trial? Many Americans did not think so. One artist created this poster calling for a new trial. Writers such as Edna St. Vincent Millay and Countee Cullen also supported the two Italian-born anarchists. In spite of protests, Sacco and Vanzetti were executed in 1927.

Analyzing Information ***Why did some people question the verdict in the Sacco and Vanzetti trial?***

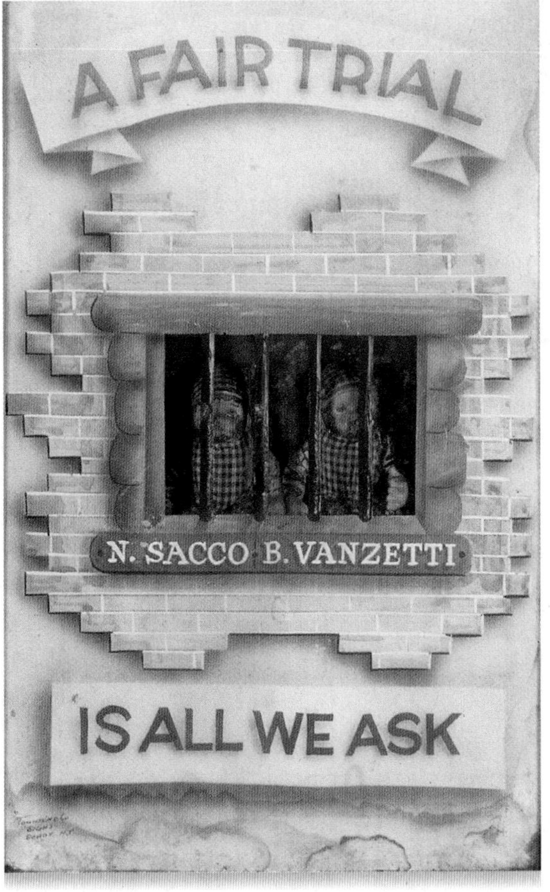

The Red Scare

During the war, Americans had been on the alert for enemy spies and **sabotage,** or the secret destruction of property or interference with work in factories. These wartime worries led to a growing fear of foreigners.

The rise of communism in the Soviet Union fanned that fear. Lenin, the communist leader, called on workers everywhere to overthrow their governments. Many Americans saw the strikes that swept the nation as the start of a communist revolution.

Hunting Up Radicals The actions of **anarchists,** or people who oppose organized government, added to the sense of danger. One group of anarchists plotted to kill well-known Americans, including John D. Rockefeller, the head of Standard Oil. Because many anarchists were foreign-born, their attacks led to an outcry against all foreigners.

The government took harsh actions against both anarchists and Communists, or "Reds." During the Red Scare, thousands of radicals were arrested and jailed. Many foreigners were **deported,** or expelled from the country.

Sacco and Vanzetti The trial of two Italian immigrants in Massachusetts came to symbolize the anti-foreign feeling of the 1920s. Nicola Sacco and Bartolomeo Vanzetti were arrested for robbery and murder in 1920. The two men admitted being anarchists but insisted they had committed no crime. A jury convicted them, however. Sacco and Vanzetti were then sentenced to death.

Viewing History

The Scopes Trial

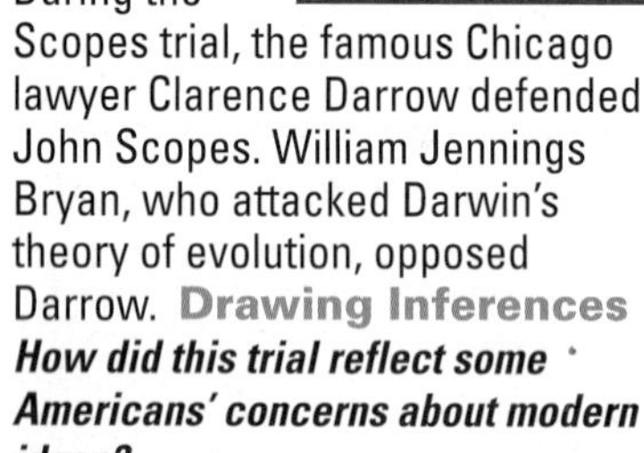

During the Scopes trial, the famous Chicago lawyer Clarence Darrow defended John Scopes. William Jennings Bryan, who attacked Darwin's theory of evolution, opposed Darrow. **Drawing Inferences** ***How did this trial reflect some Americans' concerns about modern ideas?***

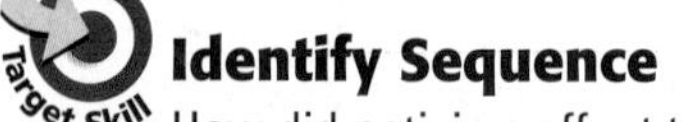

Identify Sequence How did nativism affect the United States in the 1920s? Add this information to your flowchart.

The Sacco and Vanzetti trial created a furor across the nation. The evidence against the two men was limited. The judge was openly prejudiced against the two immigrants. Many Americans thought that Sacco and Vanzetti were convicted, not because they were guilty, but because they were immigrants and radicals. The two men waited in jail during a six-year fight to overturn their convictions. Their appeals were turned down. In 1927, they were executed.

The issue of whether Sacco and Vanzetti received a fair trial has been debated ever since. In the meantime, many Americans felt the case proved that the United States had to keep out dangerous radicals.

Limiting Immigration

In the end, the Red Scare died down. Yet, anger against foreigners led to a new move to limit immigration. As you recall, this kind of anti-foreign feeling is known as **nativism.**

The Quota System After years of war, millions of Europeans hoped to find a better life in the United States. American workers feared that a flood of newcomers would force wages down. Others worried that communists and anarchists would invade the United States.

Congress responded by passing the Emergency Quota Act in 1921. The act set up a **quota system** that allowed only a certain number of people from each country to enter the United States. Only 3 percent of the people in any national group already living in the United States in 1910 could be admitted.

The quota system favored immigrants from Northern Europe, especially Britain. In 1924, Congress passed new laws that further cut immigration, especially from Eastern Europe, which was seen as a center of anarchism and communism. In addition, Japanese were added to the list of Asians denied entry to the country.

Newcomers From Latin America Latin Americans and Canadians were not included in the quota system. As a result, Mexican immigrants continued to move to the United States. Farms and factories in the Southwest depended on Mexican workers. The pay was low, and the housing was poor. Still, the chance to earn more money was a very powerful lure. By 1930, a million or more Mexicans had crossed the border.

The Jones Act of 1917 granted American citizenship to Puerto Ricans. Poverty on the island led to a great migration to the north. In 1910, about 1,500 Puerto Ricans lived on the mainland. By 1930, there were about 53,000.

The Scopes Trial

In the 1920s, cities drew thousands of people from farms and small towns. Those who stayed in rural areas often feared that new ways of life in the city were a threat to traditional values.

The clash between old and new values erupted in the small town of Dayton, Tennessee. At the center of the controversy was Charles Darwin's theory of evolution. Darwin, a British scientist, had claimed that all life had evolved, or developed, from simpler forms over a long period of time.

Some churches condemned Darwin's theory, saying it denied the teachings of the Bible. Tennessee, Mississippi, and Arkansas passed laws that banned the teaching of Darwin's theory. In 1925, John Scopes, a biology teacher in Dayton, taught evolution to his class. Scopes was arrested and tried.

Two of the nation's best-known figures opposed each other in the Scopes trial. William Jennings Bryan, who had run for President three times, argued the state's case against Scopes. Clarence Darrow, a Chicago lawyer who had helped unions and radicals, defended Scopes.

As the trial began, the nation's attention was riveted on Dayton. Reporters recorded every word of the battle between Darrow and Bryan. "Scopes isn't on trial," Darrow thundered at one point, "civilization is on trial." In the end, Scopes was convicted and fined. The laws against teaching evolution remain on the books, although they are rarely enforced.

The New Klan

Fear of change gave new life to an old organization. In 1915, a group of white men in Georgia declared the rebirth of the Ku Klux Klan. The original Klan had used terror to keep African Americans from voting after the Civil War. The new Klan had a broader aim: to preserve the United States for white, native-born Protestants.

The new Klan waged a campaign not only against African Americans, but also against immigrants, especially Catholics and Jews. Klan members burned crosses outside people's homes. They used whippings and lynchings to terrorize immigrants and African Americans. The Klan strongly supported efforts to limit immigration.

Primary Source

The Ku Klux Klan

Journalist and author William Allen White strongly opposed the Ku Klux Klan. He states his view in a letter to Herbert Swope, editor of the New York World:

"To make a case against a birthplace, a religion, or a race is wickedly un-American and cowardly. The whole trouble with the Ku Klux Klan is that it is based upon such deep foolishness that it is bound to be a menace to good government in any community."

—William Allen White, *Selected Letters of William Allen White,* 1899–1943

Analyzing Primary Sources

Why does White feel that prejudice is cowardly?

Viewing History

Marcus Garvey

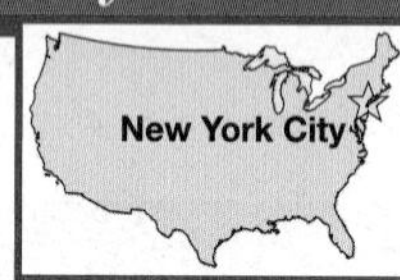

Known as "The Black Moses," Jamaican-born Marcus Garvey (at right in car) offered urban African Americans hope of relief from their difficult lives. The certificate at left is for a share of the *Black Star Line.* The ship was provided by Garvey's organization to take African Americans to Africa. **Drawing Conclusions** ***Why do you think African Americans were drawn to Garvey's message?***

Because of its large membership, the Klan gained political influence. In the mid-1920s, however, many Americans became alarmed at the Klan's growing power. At the same time, scandals surfaced that showed Klan leaders had stolen money from members. Klan membership dropped sharply.

Racial Tensions in the North African Americans had hoped that their service during World War I would weaken racism at home. However, returning black soldiers found that the South was still a segregated society. In the North, too, racial prejudice was widespread.

Many African Americans moved north during and after the war. They took factory jobs in Chicago, Detroit, New York, Philadelphia, and other large cities. The newcomers often found that the only jobs open to them were low-paying ones. Also, in many neighborhoods, whites refused to rent apartments to blacks.

At the same time, many blacks newly arrived from the South wanted to live near one another. As a result, areas with large black populations grew up in many northern cities.

Many northern white workers felt threatened by the arrival of so many African Americans. Racial tension grew. In 1919, less than eight months after the end of World War I, race riots broke out in several cities. The worst took place in Chicago, leaving 38 dead.

Marcus Garvey Shocked by the racism they found, African Americans looked for new ways to cope. Marcus Garvey became one of the most popular black leaders. He started the first widespread black nationalist movement in the United States. Garvey organized the Universal Negro Improvement Association. He hoped to promote unity and pride among African Americans. He believed that African Americans needed to rely on themselves rather than white people to get ahead. "I am the equal of any white man," Garvey said.

Garvey urged African Americans to seek their roots in Africa. Although few black Americans actually went to Africa, Garvey's "Back to Africa" movement built racial pride.

Election of 1928

By 1928, Republicans had led the nation for eight years. They pointed to prosperity as their outstanding achievement. Still, when asked about the upcoming election, President Coolidge said tersely, "I do not choose to run." Instead, Secretary of Commerce Herbert Hoover easily won the Republican nomination. The Democrats chose as their candidate Alfred E. Smith, a former governor of New York.

The contrast between the candidates revealed the tensions lurking below the surface of American life. Smith, the son of Irish immigrants, was the first Catholic to run for President. City dwellers, including many immigrants and Catholics, rallied around Smith. Hoover was a self-made millionaire from the Midwest. He won votes from rural Americans and big business. Supporters of Prohibition also supported Hoover because Smith favored repeal.

In the election, Smith won the country's 12 largest cities. Rural and small-town voters supported Hoover. He won by a landslide.

Americans hoped Hoover would keep the country prosperous. Less than a year after he took office, however, the economy would come crashing down.

★ ★ ★ Section 4 Assessment ★ ★ ★

Recall

1. **Identify** Explain the significance of **(a)** Red Scare, **(b)** Sacco and Vanzetti, **(c)** Emergency Quota Act, **(d)** Jones Act, **(e)** Scopes trial, **(f)** Ku Klux Klan, **(g)** Marcus Garvey, **(h)** Herbert Hoover, **(i)** Alfred E. Smith.
2. **Define** **(a)** company union, **(b)** sabotage, **(c)** anarchist, **(d)** deport, **(e)** nativism, **(f)** quota system.

Comprehension

3. Describe the problems farmers and labor unions faced.
4. What limits were placed on immigration?
5. **(a)** What was the Scopes trial? **(b)** Why was the Ku Klux Klan revived?
6. How did African Americans fight racism during the 1920s?
7. What did Americans hope Hoover could achieve?

Critical Thinking

8. **Exploring the Main Idea** Review the Main Idea statement at the beginning of this section. Then, describe the conditions that divided the nation during the 1920s.
9. **Supporting a Point of View** Do you think most veterans returning from World War I were pleased with conditions at home? Explain.

Activity

Writing a Speech It is 1928, and Herbert Hoover and Alfred E. Smith are running for President. You are a speechwriter. Write a brief speech that Hoover might use to win votes. Then, write a speech that Smith might use.

CHAPTER
25 Review and Assessment

Chapter Summary

Section 1
As the Republican party returned to power in the 1920s, the economy boomed. By the later 1920s, more people were investing in a soaring stock market. At the same time, in foreign affairs, the United States was returning to its prewar isolation.

Section 2
A surge of new ideas and products and a new popular culture were changing the American way of life during the 1920s. The Nineteenth Amendment, ratified in 1920, gave women the right to vote.

Section 3
While new lifestyles and new ideas affected fashion and music, a new generation of writers rebelled by criticizing American life. A gathering of black artists and musicians led to the Harlem Renaissance, a rebirth of African American culture.

Section 4
In spite of the prosperity of the 1920s, the nation was divided between rich and poor, native-born and immigrant, and black and white. The trial of two Italian immigrants, Sacco and Vanzetti, came to symbolize the anti-foreign feeling of the 1920s.

Interactive Textbook

For additional review and enrichment activities, see the interactive version of *The American Nation,* available on the Web and on CD-ROM.

Chapter Self-Test For practice test questions for Chapter 25, visit PHSchool.com, **Web Code mfa-2504.**

Building Vocabulary

Use the chapter vocabulary words listed below to create a crossword puzzle. Exchange puzzles with a classmate. Complete the puzzles, and then check each other's answers.

1. **recession**
2. **bull market**
3. **Prohibition**
4. **repeal**
5. **suburb**
6. **flapper**
7. **expatriate**
8. **company union**
9. **anarchist**
10. **deport**

Reviewing Key Facts

11. How did Harding and Coolidge support big business? (Section 1)
12. Describe the impact of Henry Ford on American business and society. (Section 2)
13. What trends in society did the new generation of writers in the 1920s find troubling? (Section 3)
14. What contributed to the spread of anti-immigrant feelings during the 1920s? (Section 4)

Critical Thinking and Writing

15. **Connecting to Geography: Interaction** Why did so many African Americans leave the rural South during and after World War I?
16. **Sequencing (a)** Which came first, the rise of communism in Russia or the Red Scare in the United States? **(b)** How did one event follow from the other? **(c)** Were those feelings justified? Explain.
17. **Analyzing Information** How might the general atmosphere of the 1920s have contributed to the failure of Prohibition?
18. **Linking Past and Present** Movie stars and sports figures were among the people considered heroes in the 1920s. Write a brief essay about people who are viewed as heroes today.

SKILLS ASSESSMENT

Analyzing Primary Sources

College football was a favorite sport in the 1920s. In the following excerpt, John R. Tunis writes about the national pastime.

> "Attempt to question the sacredness of football and any athletic director will immediately overwhelm you with a flood of unanswerable statistics. He will show that football is the godfather of games within and without the walls of the university, that with its gate receipts are built swimming pools and squash courts, that from its profits spring crews fully armed and golf and tennis teams fully clothed."
>
> —John R. Tunis, "The Great God Football," *Harper's Monthly*, November 1928

19. What does this passage tell you about how people regard the sport of football?
- **A.** It prepares athletes for other sports.
- **B.** They dislike it.
- **C.** They worship and respect it.
- **D.** It says nothing about people's feelings.

20. How did the prosperity of the 1920s help college football become a big business?
- **A.** People of the 1920s had money and time to attend nonwork activities.
- **B.** Television networks paid colleges for the rights to games.
- **C.** Fans could afford to buy sports merchandise.
- **D.** The deregulation of college football, not prosperity, led to its great profitability.

APPLYING YOUR SKILLS

Determining Relevance

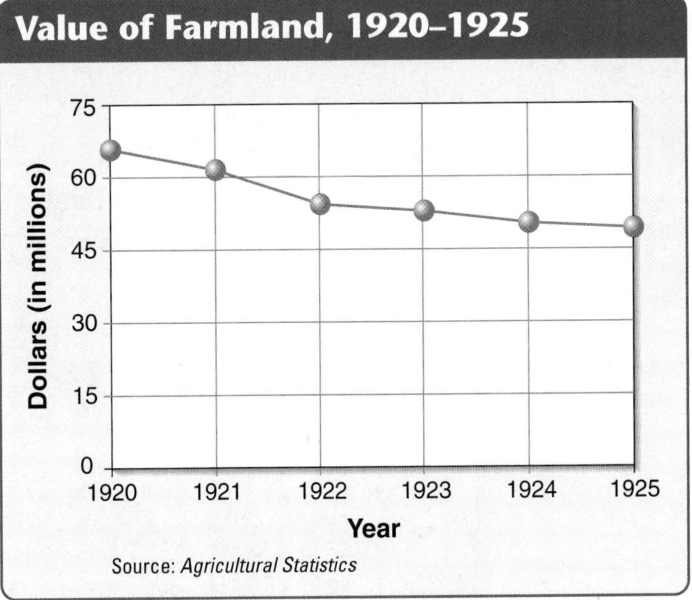

Source: *Agricultural Statistics*

21. What happened to the value of farmland between 1920 and 1925?
- **A.** The value doubled.
- **B.** The value declined for two years and then increased.
- **C.** The value fell steadily.
- **D.** There was no significant change.

22. Is this information relevant to the economy of the 1920s? Explain.

ACTIVITIES

Connecting With . . . Government and Citizenship

Understanding Freedom of Speech The First Amendment of the Constitution allows freedom of expression, even if the ideas expressed are not popular. Choose an incident from this chapter such as the Red Scare or the Scopes trial. Write an essay analyzing whether free speech was limited or violated. Be sure to discuss relevant issues of the time that may have contributed to the incident you chose.

Researching

Researching Modern Art Use the Internet to find information about an American artist of the 1920s such as Georgia O'Keeffe, Grant Wood, or Edward Hopper. Choose one artist and prepare a classroom presentation on his or her work. For help in starting this activity, visit PHSchool.com, **Web Code mfd-2506.**

CHAPTER 26

The Great Depression

1929–1941

1 The Great Crash
2 FDR and the New Deal
3 Response to the New Deal
4 The Nation in Hard Times

The depression spares no one: a 1932 cartoon

One-time millionaire selling apples on a street

AMERICAN EVENTS

1929 The stock market crash in October marks the beginning of the Great Depression.

1932 Jobless Bonus Army marchers protest for two months outside the Capitol building in Washington, D.C.

1933 Promising "a new deal" for the American people, Franklin D. Roosevelt becomes President.

Presidential Terms: Herbert Hoover 1929–1933 | Franklin D. Roosevelt 1933–1945

1929 · 1932 · 1935

WORLD EVENTS

▲ **1929** The depression spreads to Europe and then throughout the world.

1933 ▲ Adolf Hitler comes to power in Germany.

Drought and Dust Bowl During the Great Depression

Devastating drought and wind erosion ruined farmlands across much of the Great Plains in the 1930s.

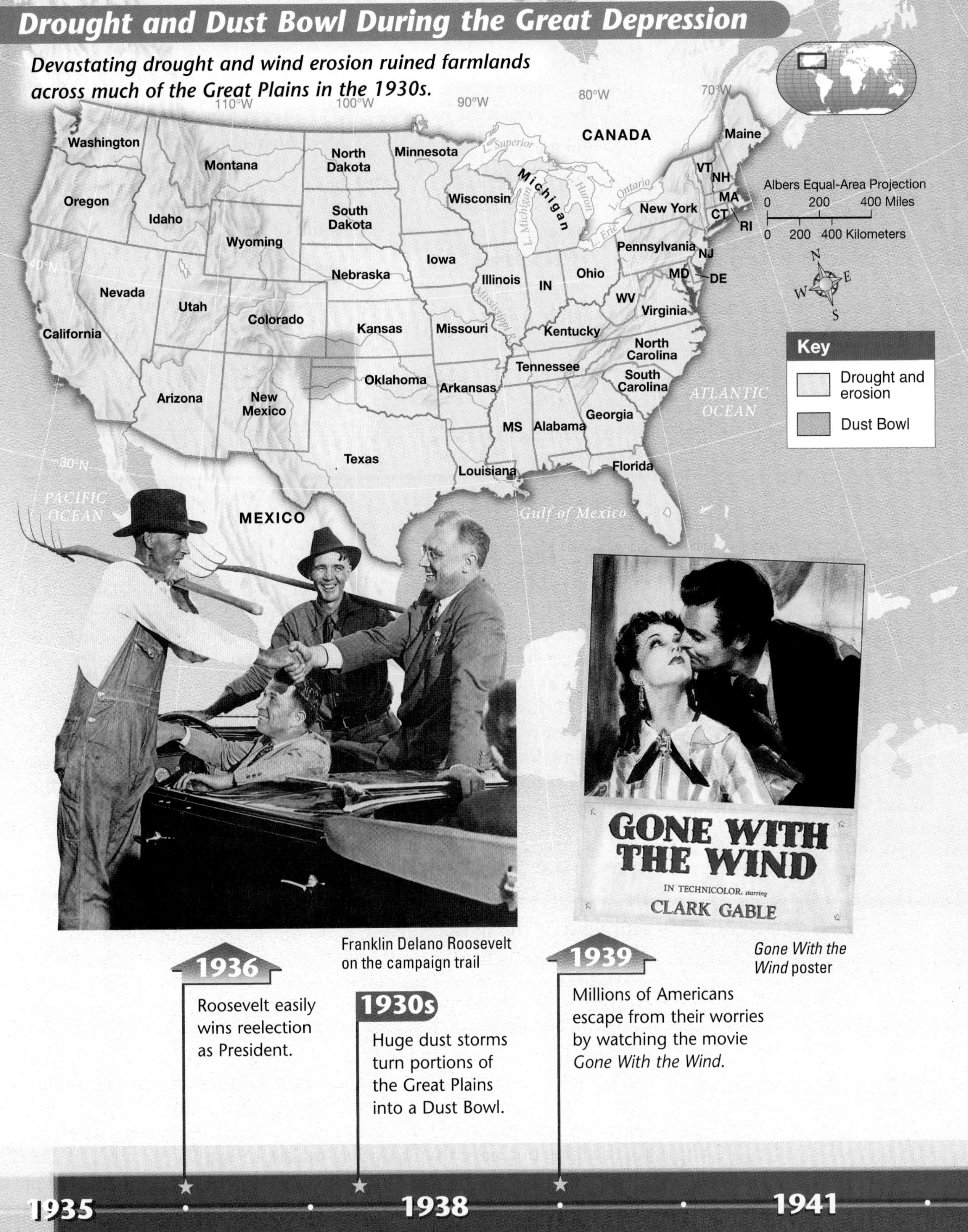

Franklin Delano Roosevelt on the campaign trail

Gone With the Wind poster

1936
Roosevelt easily wins reelection as President.

1930s
Huge dust storms turn portions of the Great Plains into a Dust Bowl.

1939
Millions of Americans escape from their worries by watching the movie *Gone With the Wind*.

1935 · **1938** · **1941**

1938 ▲
Mexico seizes foreign oil holdings.

1 The Great Crash

Prepare to Read

Objectives

In this section, you will
- Identify the signs of economic trouble that led to the crash of 1929 and the Great Depression.
- Describe how hard times affected American families.
- Explain how President Hoover's response to the depression led to the actions of the Bonus Army.

Key Terms

on margin
Black Tuesday
Great Depression
bankrupt
relief program
soup kitchen
public works
Hooverville
bonus

Target Reading Skill

Main Idea Copy the concept web below. Include three or four blank ovals. As you read, fill in each blank oval with information on the causes of the Great Depression.

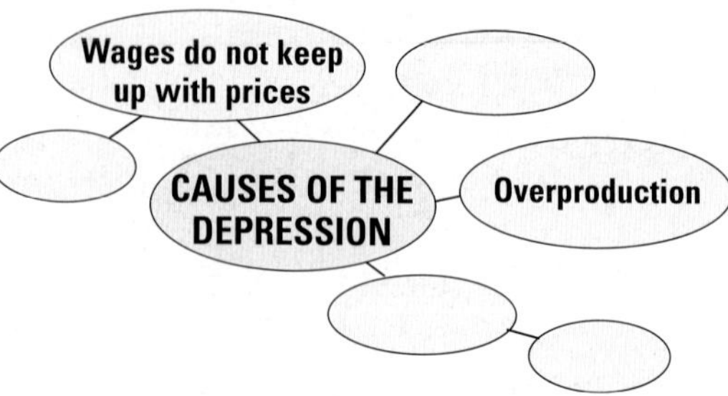

Main Idea The prosperity of the 1920s hid weaknesses in the economy that led to the Great Depression of the 1930s.

Before the crash

Setting the Scene Most Americans had great confidence in their new President, Herbert Hoover, when he was inaugurated in March 1929. For most of the 1920s, Hoover had served in the Cabinet as secretary of commerce. In that role, he had helped to create the greatest prosperity the country had ever seen. During the 1928 campaign, he assured voters, "we in America are nearer the final triumph over poverty than ever before in the history of any land."

Then, only seven months after Hoover's inauguration, the stock market crashed. The United States began a plunge into the worst economic depression in its history. Everywhere, stunned people asked, How could this have happened?

Signs of Economic Trouble

When Hoover took office in 1929, he saw a growing economy. Along with most of the nation's leaders, he did not recognize the signs of trouble.

Hoover did realize that some Americans had not shared in the prosperity of the 1920s. Some industries, such as textiles and soft-coal mining, had been depressed throughout the 1920s. For workers in those industries, a booming economy was something they only read about in the newspapers. The words on a Pennsylvania mining town tombstone reflected their feelings of frustration. "For forty years beneath the sod / With pick and spade I did my task / The coal king's slave, but now, thank God / I'm free at last."

Farmers also faced hard times. Throughout the 1920s, farm expenses had risen much faster than the prices that farmers received for their products. Farmers did not reduce production. As a result, prices for farm products stayed low and farmers' income fell. With it went much of their power to buy goods and pay off loans.

In the mid-1920s, the economy began to slow down. No one noticed the slowdown because at that time the government did not keep detailed statistics.

The Crash

By August 1929, some investors worried that the boom might soon end. They began selling their stocks. In September, more people decided to sell. The rash of selling caused stock prices to fall. Hoover reassured investors that the "business of the country . . . is on a sound and prosperous basis." Despite the President's calming words, the selling continued and stock prices tumbled.

Many investors had bought stocks on margin. Buyers of stocks **on margin** pay only part of the cost of the stock when they make the purchase. They borrow the rest from their stockbrokers. With prices falling, brokers asked investors to pay back what they owed. Investors who could not repay their loans had to sell their stock.

A panic quickly set in. Between October 24 and October 29, desperate people tried to unload millions of shares. As a result, stock prices dropped even further.

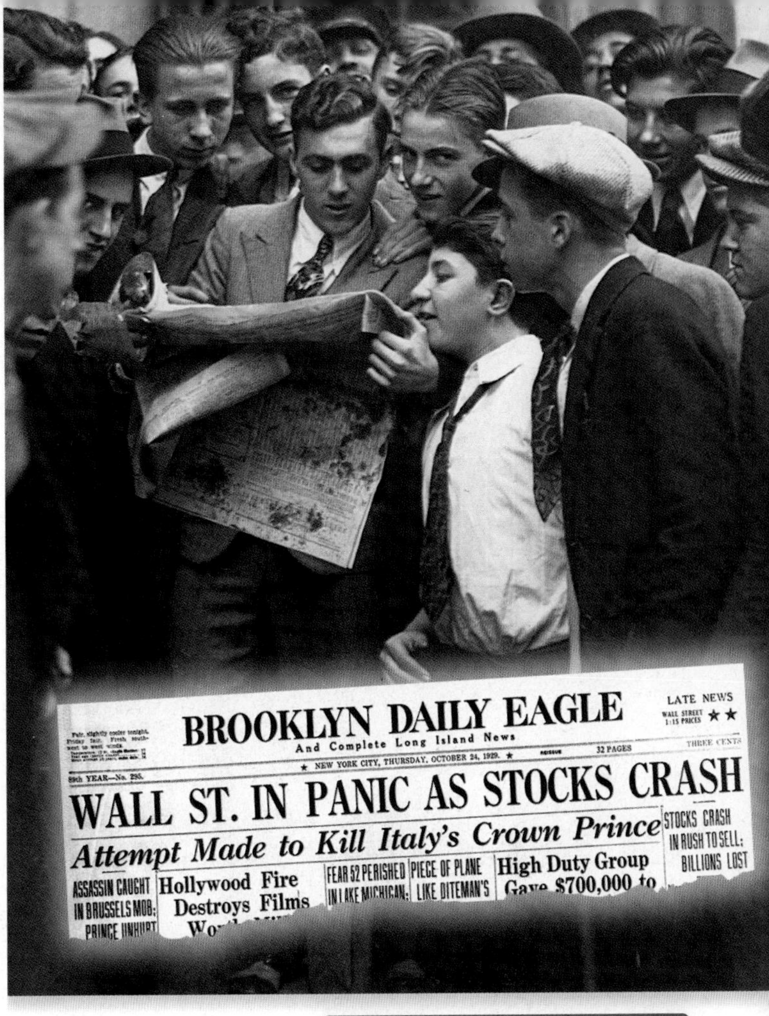

Viewing History

Panic on Wall Street! Screaming headlines announced the stock market crash of October 1929. Here, people gather on the street to read the alarming news. **Applying Information** ***What impact might headlines such as the one above have had on public confidence in the economy?***

When the stock market opened on Tuesday, October 29, a wild stampede of selling hit the New York Stock Exchange. Prices plunged because there were no buyers. People who thought they owned valuable stocks were left with worthless paper.

After **Black Tuesday,** as it came to be called, business leaders tried to restore confidence in the economy. John D. Rockefeller told reporters, "My son and I have for some days been purchasing some common stocks." Replied comedian Eddie Cantor, "Sure, who else has any money left?"

The Great Depression Begins

The period of economic hard times that followed the crash is known as the **Great Depression.** It lasted from 1929 to 1941.

The stock market crash did not cause the Great Depression, but it did shake people's confidence in the economy. As the depression worsened, people tried to understand how the prosperity of the 1920s had vanished.

Causes of the Great Depression Among the chief causes of the Great Depression was overproduction. American factories and farms produced vast amounts of goods in the 1920s. Yet, because wages did not keep up with prices, workers could not afford to buy many goods. Farmers also had little money for cars and other items. Soon, factories

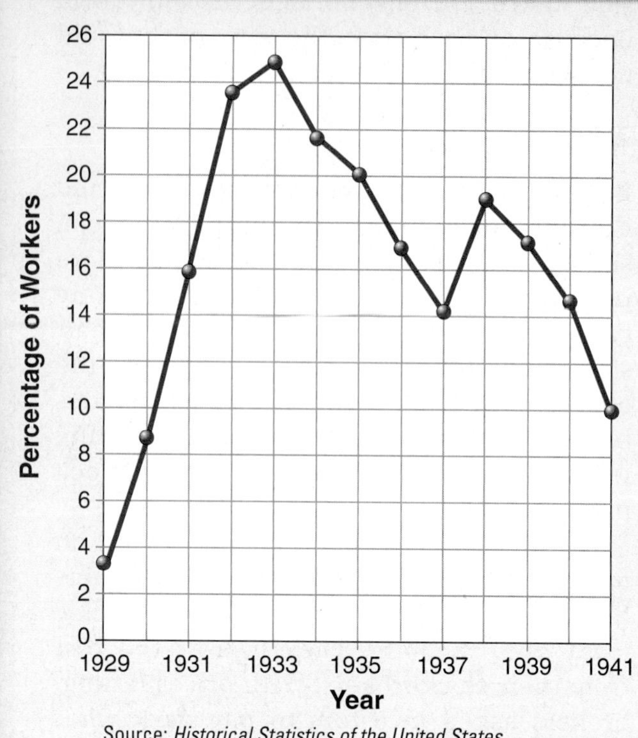

Source: *Historical Statistics of the United States*

Viewing History

Out of Work and Out of Luck

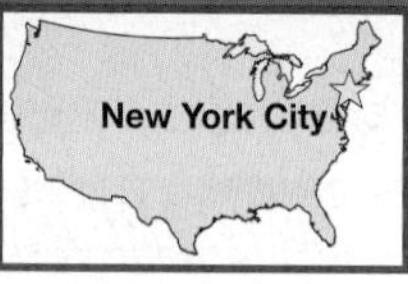

People were desperate for jobs during the depression. Painter Isaac Soyer captured the despair of unemployment in this painting. **Linking Past and Present** ***If an artist today painted a scene of job seekers, do you think the mood would be any different than it is in this Isaac Soyer painting?***

Identify Supporting Details

What information in the subsection "The Downward Spiral" identifies causes of the Great Depression? Add these details to your concept web.

and farms were producing more goods than people were buying. As orders slowed, factories closed or laid off workers.

Another cause of the depression was weakness in the banking system. During the 1920s, banks made unwise loans. For example, banks lent money to people who invested in the stock market. When the stock market crashed, borrowers could not repay their loans. Without the money from the loans, the banks could not give depositors their money when they asked for it. As a result, many banks were forced to close.

More than 5,000 banks closed between 1929 and 1932. When a bank closed, depositors lost the money that they had deposited in the bank. Often, a family's lifetime savings disappeared overnight.

The Downward Spiral After the stock market crash, the economy slid downhill at a fast pace. One disaster triggered another. The stock market crash, for example, ruined many investors. Without capital, or money, from investors, businesses could no longer grow and expand. Businesses could not turn to banks for capital because the banks were also in trouble.

As factories cut back on production, they cut wages and laid off workers. Unemployed workers, in turn, had little money to spend, so demand for goods fell further. In the end, many businesses went **bankrupt**—they were unable to pay their debts. As bankrupt businesses closed, even more people were thrown out of work.

The Great Depression led to a worldwide economic crisis. In the 1920s, the United States had loaned large sums to European nations so that they could repay their debts from World War I. When

American banks stopped making loans or demanded repayment of existing loans, European banks began to fail. The depression spread from nation to nation. By 1930, it had led to a worldwide economic collapse.

Hard Times

The United States had suffered earlier economic depressions. None, however, was as severe or lasted as long as the Great Depression. In earlier times, most Americans lived on farms and grew their own food. In the 1930s, millions of Americans lived in cities and worked in factories. When factories closed, the jobless had no money for food and no land on which to grow it.

Rising Unemployment As the depression spread, the unemployment rate soared. By the early 1930s, one in every four workers was jobless. Millions more worked shortened hours or took pay cuts. Many of the jobless lost their homes. On city streets, people sold apples and pencils, begged for money, and picked through garbage dumps for scraps of food.

The chance of finding work was small. On an average day, one New York job agency had 5,000 people looking for work. Only about 300 found jobs. In another city, police had to keep order as 15,000 women pushed and shoved to apply for six jobs cleaning offices. Some of the jobless shined shoes on street corners. Others set up sidewalk stands and sold apples.

The Human Cost During the depression, families suffered. Marriage and birth rates dropped. Hungry parents and children searched through city dumps and restaurant garbage cans. In one school, a teacher ordered a thin girl to go home to eat. "I can't," replied the girl. "This is my sister's day to eat."

The pressure of hard times led some families to split up. Fathers and even children as young as 13 or 14 years old left home to hunt for work. Their leaving meant the family had fewer people to feed.

Jobless men and women drifted from town to town looking for work. Some "rode the rails," living in railroad cars and hitching rides on freight trains. Louis Banks, a young African American, later described what it was like to ride the rails:

> "Twenty-five or thirty would be out on the side of the rail, white and colored. They didn't have no mothers or sisters, they didn't have no home, they were dirty, they had overalls on, they didn't have no food, they didn't have anything."
>
> — Louis Banks, Interview, 1970

Americans did their best to cope. Neighbors shared what little they had. Some families doubled up, taking in aunts, uncles, and cousins. Some families began to grow vegetables and can foods instead of shopping in stores.

The Great Depression shook Americans' belief in themselves. "No matter that others suffered the same fate, the inner voice whispered, 'I'm a failure,'" one unemployed man wrote.

Hoover Responds

President Hoover was deeply concerned about the suffering. However, Hoover did not believe that government should become directly involved in helping to end the business crisis. He feared that government might become too powerful. It was up to businesses, he felt, to work together to end the downslide.

Government Aid At first, Hoover also opposed government **relief programs**—programs to help the needy. Instead, the President urged business leaders to keep workers employed and to maintain wages.

Hoover also called on private charities to help the needy. Churches set up **soup kitchens,** places where the hungry could get a free meal. Ethnic communities organized their own relief efforts. In San Francisco's Chinatown, fraternal societies gave out food and clothing. Father Divine, an African American religious leader in New York's Harlem, fed 3,000 hungry people a day. Mexican Americans and Puerto Ricans turned to aid societies. Still, the numbers of the needy soon overwhelmed private charities.

Viewing History

On the Soup Kitchen Line

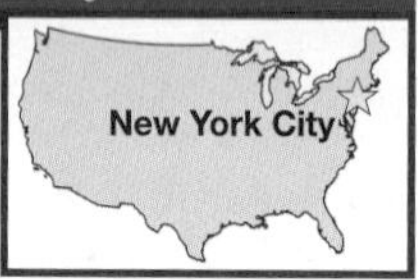

Long lines of hungry people were a common sight in towns and cities during the depression. These New Yorkers wait for a soup kitchen to open. **Drawing Inferences** ***What impact do you think eating at soup kitchens had on the self-esteem of these men?***

As conditions grew worse, Hoover realized that he had to take other steps. He set up public works programs. **Public works** are projects built by the government for public use. The government hired workers to build schools, construct dams, and pave highways. By providing jobs, these programs enabled people to earn money.

Hoover also asked Congress to approve the Reconstruction Finance Corporation, or RFC, in 1932. The RFC loaned money to banks, railroads, and insurance companies to help them stay in business. Saving these businesses, Hoover hoped, would save thousands of jobs.

The Depression Deepens Hoover did more to reverse hard times than any previous President. However, his efforts were too little and came too late. In 1931, as the third winter of the depression approached, more and more people joined the ranks of the hungry and homeless. "Men are sitting in the parks all day long and all night long," wrote one man in Detroit.

Many people blamed the President for doing too little. They gave the name **Hoovervilles** to the shacks where the homeless lived. People spoke of "Hoover blankets," the newspapers used by the homeless to keep warm when they slept outside. A cardboard patch that covered a hole in a shoe was called "Hoover leather." Men, women, and children lined up for "Hoover stew," the name they gave to the thin soup they received in soup kitchens.

The Bonus Army

While people waited for the government to help, one group of Americans took action. After World War I, Congress had voted to give veterans a **bonus,** or additional sum of money, to be paid in 1945. In 1932, more than 20,000 jobless veterans marched to Washington to demand the bonus right away. For two months, the Bonus Army, as the veterans were called, camped in a tent city along the Potomac River.

The House of Representatives voted to give the veterans the bonus at once, but the Senate rejected the bill. Senators thought that the cost would prevent government action to aid the country's recovery. Many discouraged veterans then went home. However, thousands of others remained, vowing to stay until 1945 if necessary.

Local police tried to force the veterans to leave. Battles with police left four people dead. Hoover then ordered General Douglas MacArthur to clear out the veterans. Using cavalry, tanks, machine guns, and tear gas, MacArthur moved into the camp and burned it to the ground. An editorial in the *Washington News* years later expressed the shock many Americans felt at the time:

> "What a pitiful spectacle is that of the great American Government, mightiest in the world, chasing unarmed men, women, and children with Army tanks. . . . If the Army must be called out to make war on unarmed citizens, this is no longer America."
>
> —*Washington News*, "The Summer of the BEF," November 23, 1946

After the attack on the Bonus Army, the President lost what little support he still had. Convinced that the country needed a change, Americans turned to a new leader.

Section 1 Assessment

Recall

1. **Identify** Explain the significance of **(a)** Herbert Hoover, **(b)** Black Tuesday, **(c)** Great Depression, **(d)** Hooverville.
2. **Define** **(a)** on margin, **(b)** bankrupt, **(c)** relief program, **(d)** soup kitchen, **(e)** public works, **(f)** bonus.

Comprehension

3. List two signs of economic trouble in the 1920s.
4. What impact did the Depression have on American families?
5. What was Hoover's response to the depression and to the Bonus Army?

Critical Thinking and Writing

6. **Exploring the Main Idea** Review the Main Idea statement at the beginning of this section. Then, write at least three questions that you would ask an economist in order to determine the causes of the Great Depression.
7. **Finding the Main Idea** Review the subsection "Hoover Responds" on page 750. **(a)** What is the main idea of the subsection? **(b)** State two facts that support the main idea.

ACTIVITY

Writing a News Report
Use the Internet to find information on the Bonus Army. Then, prepare the outline of a script for a TV news program reporting on the grievances of the Bonus Army veterans. For help in starting the activity, visit PHSchool.com, **Web Code mfd-2601.**

2 FDR and the New Deal

Prepare to Read

Objectives

In this section, you will
- Explain why voters elected Franklin D. Roosevelt as President in 1932.
- Describe the Hundred Days, and list its accomplishments.
- Summarize the New Deal's impact.
- Identify the economic reforms that were aimed at preventing another depression.

Key Terms

polio
bank holiday
fireside chat
Hundred Days
New Deal
Civilian Conservation Corps
National Recovery Administration
Tennessee Valley Authority

Target Reading Skill

Clarifying Meaning As you read, fill in the table with New Deal programs aimed at relief, recovery, or preventing another depression.

RELIEF FOR THE JOBLESS	PLANS FOR ECONOMIC RECOVERY	PREVENTING ANOTHER DEPRESSION
•	•	•
•	•	•

Main Idea The New Deal restored hope by providing programs that aimed at relief, recovery, and economic reform.

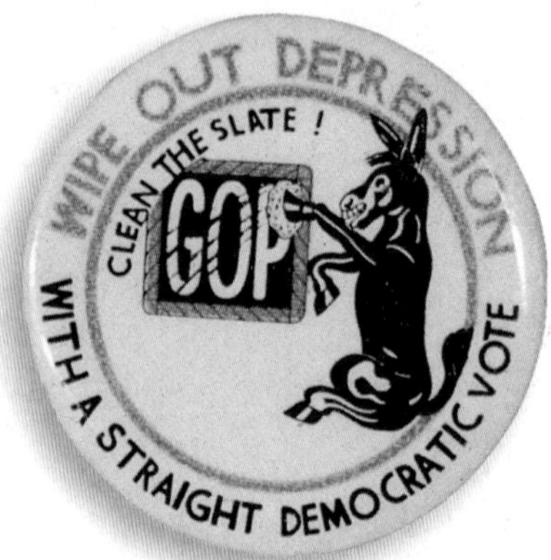

Looking for new leadership

Setting the Scene In Albany, New York, Governor Franklin Roosevelt read about the Bonus Army tragedy in the morning papers. Roosevelt was angry at the way Hoover had handled the marchers.

Roosevelt said he would have handled things differently. He understood the despair of the American people. He had told a friend, "I have looked into the faces of thousands of Americans. They have the frightened look of lost children. . . . They are saying: 'We're caught in something we don't understand.'"

Roosevelt knew that the government seemed helpless to most people. He saw that Americans looked for new leadership. In 1932, the Democrats chose him to run for President.

The election results gave Roosevelt his chance. His New Deal program began a new relationship between government and the economy. From then on, the federal government took an active role in managing the American economy.

Franklin D. Roosevelt

Franklin Delano Roosevelt, known as FDR, came from a wealthy, influential family. He attended Harvard University and Columbia Law School. In 1905, he married a distant cousin, Anna Eleanor Roosevelt.

During World War I, FDR served as assistant secretary of the navy. In 1920, he was the Democratic candidate for Vice President but lost in the Harding landslide.

A Devastating Disease Then, in the summer of 1921, Roosevelt was stricken with a severe case of polio. A disease caused by a virus, polio has been almost totally wiped out in the United States today. However, before the development of a vaccine in the 1950s, polio was a devastating disease. FDR's legs were totally paralyzed. He struggled for years to rebuild his strength.

In time, Roosevelt returned to public life. In 1928, he was elected governor of New York. Then, in 1932, the Democrats made him their presidential candidate. The Republicans again nominated Herbert Hoover, even though they knew he had little chance of winning.

A Call to Action Roosevelt set a new tone right from the start. He broke with tradition by flying to the Democratic convention to accept the nomination in person. Standing before the delegates, he declared: "I pledge myself to a new deal for the American people."

Roosevelt did not spell out what he meant by "a new deal." Still, he sounded a hopeful note. In campaign speeches, he promised to help the jobless, poor farmers, and the elderly.

Voters responded to FDR's confident manner and personal charm. On election day, he won a landslide victory. Democrats also gained many seats in Congress. On inauguration day, the new President addressed the American people with optimism:

> "This great nation will endure as it has endured, will revive and will prosper. So, first of all, let me assert my firm belief that the only thing we have to fear is fear itself—nameless, unreasoning, unjustified terror which paralyzes needed efforts to convert retreat into advance."
>
> —Franklin D. Roosevelt, Inaugural Address, March 4, 1933

President Roosevelt then issued a call to action. "This nation asks for action and action now," he said. Many Americans welcomed this energetic new President, especially since Hoover's more cautious approach had failed to end the nation's economic crisis.

The Hundred Days

During his campaign for the presidency, FDR had sought advice on how to fight the depression. He turned to a number of college professors who were experts on economic issues. These experts, nicknamed the Brain Trust, helped Roosevelt to plan bold new programs.

Once in office, President Roosevelt chose able advisers. Harold Ickes (IH keez), a Republican reformer from Chicago, became secretary of the interior. The President named social worker Frances Perkins the secretary of labor. Perkins was the first woman to hold a Cabinet post.

The new President moved forward on many fronts. He urged his staff to "take a method and try it. If it fails, admit it and try another. But above all try something."

Saving the Banks Roosevelt's first challenge was the nation's crumbling banking system. Many banks had closed. Fearful depositors had withdrawn their savings from other banks. People hid their money under mattresses or buried it in their yards.

The President knew that without sound banks, the economy could not recover. On his second day in office, he declared a **bank holiday**. He closed every bank in the country for four days. He then asked Congress to pass the Emergency Banking Relief Act. Under

American Profiles

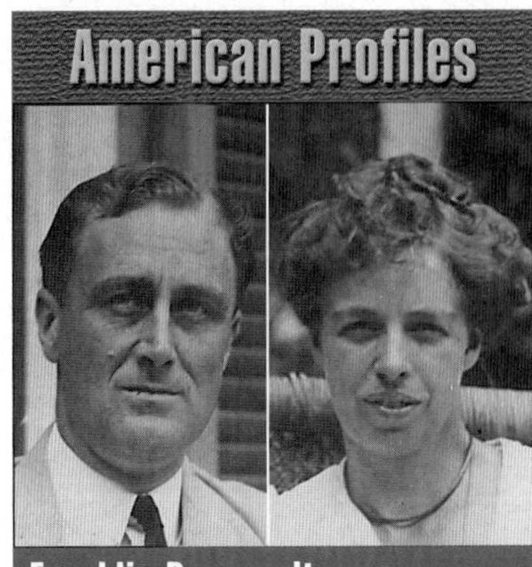

Franklin Roosevelt 1882–1945
Eleanor Roosevelt 1884–1962

Both Franklin and Eleanor Roosevelt came from wealthy and well-known families. Both believed that the wealthy had a responsibility to help those less fortunate. As President, FDR put this belief into action with his New Deal. As First Lady, Eleanor spoke out on issues ranging from conditions in coal mines to justice for African Americans. She also acted as the President's "eyes and ears," traveling about the country and reporting back to him.

After FDR's death in 1945, Eleanor won fame in her own right. From 1945 to 1953, she represented the United States at the United Nations.

Do wealthy people have a duty to aid those who are less fortunate? Explain.

this act, only those banks with enough funds to meet depositors' demands could reopen. Others had to stay closed.

A week after taking office, President Roosevelt spoke to Americans by radio. Under the new law, the President told the people, "it is safer to keep your money in a reopened bank than under your mattress."

The radio broadcast worked. FDR explained things so clearly, said humorist Will Rogers, that even the bankers understood the situation. Reassured by the President, depositors returned their money to banks, and the banking system grew stronger.

FDR gave 30 radio speeches while in office. He called them **fireside chats** because he spoke from a chair near a fireplace in the White House. All across the nation, families gathered around their radios to listen to Roosevelt. Many felt the President understood their problems.

A Flood of New Laws The bank bill was the first of many bills that FDR sent to Congress during his first three months in office. Between March 9 and June 16, 1933, Congress passed a record 15 major new laws. Even the President admitted he was "a bit shell-shocked" by the **Hundred Days,** as this period was called.

The bills covered programs from job relief to planning for economic recovery. Together, they made up Roosevelt's New Deal. The **New Deal** laid out three main goals: relief for the jobless, plans for economic recovery, and reforms to prevent another depression.

Paraphrase As you read the information under the next three blue headings, paraphrase the main accomplishments of the New Deal. Add this information to your table, placing each accomplishment in the correct column.

Relief for the Jobless

In 1933, when Roosevelt took office, 13 million Americans were out of work. The President asked Congress for a variety of programs to help the jobless.

CCC and FERA Among the earliest New Deal programs was the **Civilian Conservation Corps** (CCC). The CCC hired unemployed single men between the ages of 18 and 25. For $1 a day, they planted trees, built bridges, worked on flood-control projects, and developed new parks. The CCC served a double purpose. It conserved natural resources, and it gave jobs to young people. The Federal Emergency Relief Administration (FERA) gave federal money to state and local agencies. These agencies then distributed the money to the unemployed.

WPA The Works Progress Administration (WPA) came into existence in 1935. The WPA put the jobless to work making clothes and building hospitals, schools, parks, playgrounds, and airports.

The WPA also hired artists, photographers, actors, writers, and composers. Artists painted murals on public buildings. The Federal Theatre put on new plays for adults and children, as well as classics by such writers as Shakespeare.

WPA writers collected information about American life, folklore, and traditions. Some WPA writers interviewed African Americans who had lived under slavery. Today, scholars still use these interviews to learn firsthand about slave life.

San Antonio River Walk

The Works Progress Administration built hundreds of buildings, bridges, and highways during the depression. On the San Antonio River in Texas, WPA workers constructed a network of concrete walkways, bridges, and stairs. Today, tourists from around the world enjoy the hotels, shops, and restaurants along the San Antonio River Walk, or Paseo del Rio.

Virtual Field Trip For an interactive look at the River Walk, visit PHSchool.com, **Web Code mfd-2602.**

Critics accused the WPA of creating make-work projects that did little to benefit the nation in the long run. "People don't eat in the long run," replied a New Dealer. "They eat every day."

Promoting Recovery

To bring about recovery, the President had to boost both industry and farming. He developed programs that greatly expanded the government's role in the economy.

Helping Industry Overproduction and declining prices had been a major cause of the depression. Low prices during the depression had caused business to fail and created widespread unemployment. To help industry, New Dealers drew up plans to control production, stabilize prices, and keep workers on the job.

A key new law was the National Industrial Recovery Act (NIRA). Under this law, each industry wrote a code, or set of rules and standards, for production, wages, prices, and working conditions. The NIRA tried to end price cutting and worker layoffs.

To enforce the new codes, Congress set up the **National Recovery Administration** (NRA). Companies that followed the NRA codes stamped a blue eagle on their products. The government encouraged people to do business only with companies displaying the NRA eagle. The NRA soon ran into trouble, however. Many companies ignored the codes. Also, small businesses felt that the codes favored the biggest firms.

The NIRA also set up the Public Works Administration (PWA). It promoted recovery by hiring workers for thousands of public works projects. PWA workers built the Grand Coulee Dam in Washington, public schools in Los Angeles, two aircraft carriers for the navy, and a deep-water port in Brownsville, Texas. Despite these efforts, the PWA did little to bring about recovery.

Helping Farmers On farms, overproduction remained the main problem. Surpluses kept prices and farmers' incomes low. A surplus occurs when farmers produce more than they can sell.

To help farmers, the President asked Congress to pass the Agricultural Adjustment Act (AAA). Under the AAA, the government paid farmers not to grow certain crops. Roosevelt hoped that with smaller harvests, the laws of supply and demand would force prices to rise.

The government also paid farmers to plow surplus crops under the soil and to destroy surplus cows and pigs. Many Americans were outraged that crops and livestock were being destroyed when people in the cities were going hungry. Yet, the plan seemed necessary to help farmers recover and keep them growing food.

Viewing History

The Face of Courage

Depression-era photographers captured the sufferings of the rural poor in powerful images. This photograph by Dorothea Lange became a symbol of courage in the hard times. **Summarizing** ***Write a heading of no more than four words that summarizes what the photograph conveys to you.***

The Rural Electrification Administration (REA) was created to help people in rural areas get the same electrical service as people in urban areas. The REA provided money to extend electric lines to rural areas. The number of farms with electricity rose from 10 percent to 25 percent. Electricity helped save many farms from ruin. For example, with refrigeration, dairy farmers did not have to worry about milk going sour before it could be sent to market.

Tennessee Valley Authority Perhaps the boldest program of the Hundred Days was the **Tennessee Valley Authority** (TVA). It set out to remake the Tennessee River Valley. This vast region often suffered from terrible floods. Because the farmland was so poor, more than half the region's families were on relief.

The TVA was a daring experiment in regional planning. To control flooding, TVA engineers built 49 dams in seven states. (See the map on page 758.) The dams also produced cheap electric power. In addition to building dams, the TVA deepened river channels for shipping. It planted new forests to conserve soil and developed new fertilizers to improve farmland. The agency also set up schools and health centers.

The TVA sparked a furious debate. Critics argued that the government had no right to take business away from private companies in the region. Power companies in the Tennessee River Valley were especially outraged. They pointed out that the government, which did not have to make a profit for shareholders, could supply electrical power more cheaply than a private company could. Having to compete with the government, they said, might force them out of business.

Supporters replied that the TVA showed how the government could use its resources to help private enterprise. In the end, the program transformed a region of desperate poverty into a prosperous and productive area.

Preventing Another Depression

The third New Deal goal was to prevent another depression by reforming the economic system. During the Hundred Days, Congress passed laws regulating the stock market and the banking system. The Truth-in-Securities Act was designed to end the risky buying and selling of stocks in the hope of making a quick profit. Experts agreed that uncontrolled buying and selling was a leading cause of the 1929 crash.

Another law set up the Federal Deposit Insurance Corporation (FDIC). It insured savings accounts in banks approved by the government. If a bank insured by the FDIC failed, the government would make sure depositors received their money.

Later New Deal laws brought about other kinds of reforms. Laws regulated gas and electric companies. In 1938, a new law extended the Pure Food and Drug Act of 1906. It protected consumers by requiring manufacturers to list the ingredients in certain products. It also made sure that new medicines passed strict tests before they were put on the market.

★ ★ ★ Section 2 Assessment ★ ★ ★

Recall

1. **Identify** Explain the significance of **(a)** Franklin Roosevelt, **(b)** Hundred Days, **(c)** New Deal, **(d)** Civilian Conservation Corps, **(e)** National Recovery Administration, **(f)** Tennessee Valley Authority.
2. **Define (a)** polio, **(b)** bank holiday, **(c)** fireside chat.

Comprehension

3. What issues were responsible for FDR's victory in 1932?
4. What measures did the government take during the Hundred Days to end the depression?
5. What New Deal measures provided relief for the jobless and promoted recovery from the depression?
6. What laws were passed to prevent another depression?

Critical Thinking and Writing

7. **Exploring the Main Idea** Review the Main Idea statement at the beginning of this section. Then, write an outline for a speech that FDR might give to explain the goals of his New Deal programs.
8. **Drawing Inferences** What evidence in this section suggests the reasons why poor Americans were so drawn to the wealthy FDR?

ACTIVITY

Asking Questions

Write five questions that you might ask if you were conducting an interview with FDR. Include questions about his illness, his family, and the goals of the New Deal.

The TVA Today

The Tennessee Valley Authority has more than met the goals it set when it began in 1933. The TVA has helped people who live in the Tennessee Valley by generating electric power, promoting business growth, and supporting a healthy river system.

Americans can enjoy the clean waters of the TVA's lakes and rivers.

The TVA works with local communities to protect wildlife and clean up rivers and streams.

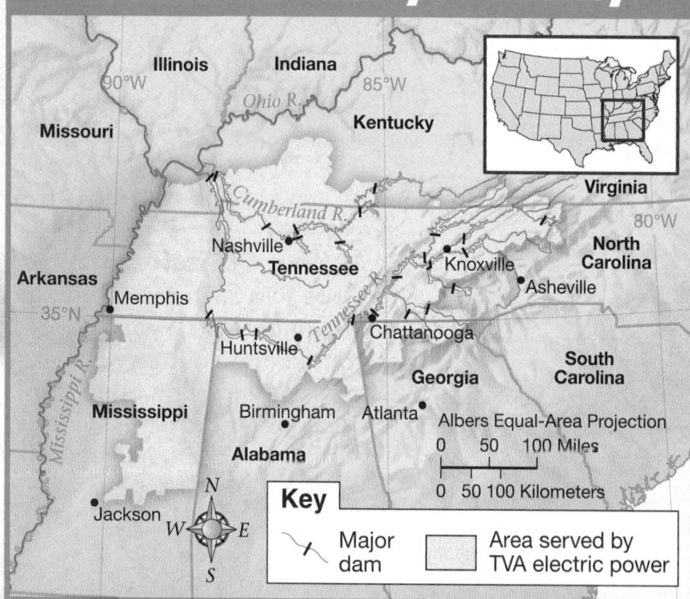

Since 1933, the TVA has built 49 giant dams and many smaller ones. The largest dams are shown on this map. The TVA is now the largest publicly owned power company in the United States. It provides electricity to eight million people who live in seven different states.

Dams built by the TVA provide electricity, control flooding, increase the region's water supply, and provide lakes for recreation.

ACTIVITY

Your family has lived in the Tennessee Valley since the 1920s. Your grandfather has told you what life was like before the TVA. Pick any song you know, and write lyrics to celebrate the accomplishments of the TVA.

3 Response to the New Deal

Prepare to Read

Objectives

In this section, you will
- Explain how New Deal critics proposed to end the depression.
- Identify why FDR tried to expand the Supreme Court.
- List the New Deal measures that reformed labor and social security.
- Evaluate the effects of the New Deal.

Key Terms

pension
National Labor Relations Act
collective bargaining
Congress of Industrial Organizations
sit-down strike
Social Security Act
deficit spending
national debt

Target Reading Skill

Cause and Effect As you read, complete the following chart to show some of the effects of the New Deal. One box has been filled in to help get you started. Add as many boxes as you need.

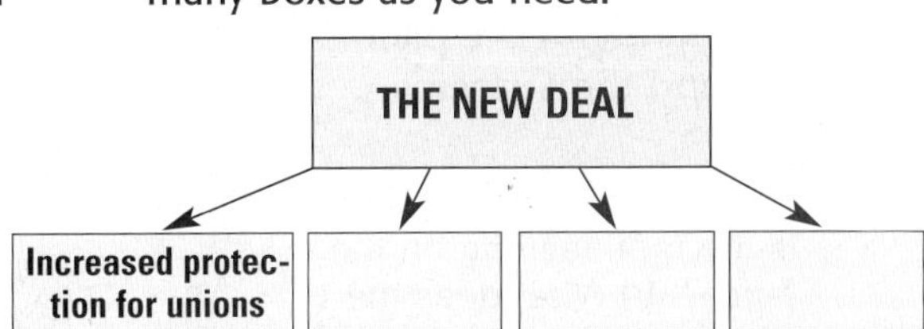

Main Idea As the New Deal came under criticism, Roosevelt launched a series of far-reaching reforms.

Setting the Scene By 1934, New Deal programs had restored hope, but they had not brought back prosperity. Although FDR was very popular, not all Americans supported him. Some people believed that government was doing too much—that it was interfering too much in people's lives. Others believed that it was doing too little—that it should take more drastic steps to aid the American people. One of the latter was Upton Sinclair, the novelist and muckraker who had written *The Jungle.*

In 1934, Sinclair ran for governor of California. Under the slogan "End Poverty in California," Sinclair proposed that the state rent or purchase unused factories and give them to workers. The workers could then keep what they manufactured.

Sinclair lost the election, but his good showing was a warning to Roosevelt. Voices of protest could be heard across the land. They reminded FDR that more needed to be done to end the depression.

A Roosevelt critic campaigns

Critics of the New Deal

Some of Roosevelt's most severe critics were people who had supported him in 1932. Among the most outspoken of these was Senator Huey Long of Louisiana. Long believed that the New Deal had not gone far enough to help the poor. Adopting the motto "Share Our Wealth," Long called for heavy taxes on the rich. He promised to use the tax money to provide every American family with a house, a car, and a decent annual income. Millions of people, especially the poor, cheered Long's idea. They overlooked the fact that he had used bribery and threats of violence to win political power.

A California doctor, Francis Townsend, also had a plan. The government, he said, had turned its back on older citizens. Townsend

POLITICAL CARTOON *Skills*

"Packing" the Supreme Court
This 1937 cartoon comments on the reaction of the Congress to the plan to expand the Supreme Court.

1. **Comprehension** **(a)** Who is the man leaning on the fence? **(b)** What does the donkey represent?
2. **Finding the Main Idea** How does the cartoonist show that the court-packing plan caused a huge uproar?
3. **Critical Thinking Interpreting a Political Cartoon** According to the cartoonist, what was the impact of Roosevelt's Supreme Court plan on party loyalty?

Civics

wanted everyone over age 60 to get a pension of $200 a month. A **pension** is a sum of money paid to people on a regular basis after they retire. People receiving the pension would have to retire, thus freeing up a job for someone else. They would also agree to spend the pension money at once to boost the economy.

On the other hand, many conservatives feared the new government programs. They formed the Liberty League to combat FDR's actions. The League complained that the New Deal interfered too much with business and with people's lives. The government, they warned, was taking away basic American freedoms.

FDR and the Supreme Court

In 1935, members of the Supreme Court began to attack the New Deal. In that year, the Supreme Court ruled that the National Industrial Recovery Act was unconstitutional. The NIRA, said the Court, gave too much power to the President and to the federal government. A year later, the Court struck down the Agricultural Adjustment Act. Then, it overturned eight other New Deal laws. To Roosevelt, the Supreme Court rulings threatened not only the New Deal but also his ability to lead the nation.

A Plan to Expand the Court Roosevelt waited until after the 1936 election to take action. In that election, he easily beat his Republican opponent, Alf Landon of Kansas.

Soon after his inauguration in January 1937, Roosevelt put forward a plan to enlarge the federal courts. He called for raising the number of Justices on the Supreme Court from 9 to 15. The change

New Deal Programs

PROGRAM	INITIALS	BEGUN	PURPOSE
Civilian Conservation Corps	CCC	1933	Provided jobs for young men to plant trees, build bridges and parks, and set up flood-control projects
Tennessee Valley Authority	TVA	1933	Built dams to provide cheap electric power to seven southern states; set up schools and health centers
Federal Emergency Relief Act	FERA	1933	Gave relief to unemployed and needy
Agricultural Adjustment Act	AAA	1933	Paid farmers not to grow certain crops
National Recovery Administration	NRA	1933	Enforced codes that regulated wages, prices, and working conditions
Public Works Administration	PWA	1933	Built ports, schools, and aircraft carriers
Federal Deposit Insurance Corporation	FDIC	1933	Insured savings accounts in banks approved by the government
Rural Electrification Administration	REA	1935	Loaned money to extend electricity to rural areas
Works Progress Administration	WPA	1935	Employed men and women to build hospitals, schools, parks, and airports; employed artists, writers, and musicians
Social Security Act	SSA	1935	Set up a system of pensions for the elderly, the unemployed, dependent children, and people with disabilities

CHART *Skills*

Congress passed dozens of laws as part of the New Deal. This chart describes 10 major New Deal programs created to fight the depression.

1. **Comprehension (a)** Which programs provided work for the unemployed? **(b)** Which provided financial aid?
2. **Critical Thinking Making Generalizations** Based on the "Begun" column in the chart, what generalization can you make about when most New Deal laws were passed?

would make it possible for him to appoint six new Justices who supported his programs.

Mixed Results The President's move raised a loud outcry. Both supporters and critics of the New Deal accused him of trying to "pack" the Court with Justices who supported his views. They saw his move as a threat to the principle of separation of powers.

For six months, the President fought for his plan. Even his allies in Congress deserted him. Finally, he withdrew his proposal.

Still, in the end, Roosevelt got the Supreme Court majority he wanted without a battle. One Justice who had voted against many New Deal laws changed his views. Another retired. Roosevelt filled his place with a new Justice who was favorable to his programs.

Labor Reforms

During the years of the New Deal, FDR supported programs to help workers. In 1935, Congress passed the **National Labor Relations Act,** or Wagner Act. Senator Robert Wagner of New York, the act's sponsor, was a strong supporter of labor.

Unions Grow Stronger The Wagner Act protected American workers from unfair management practices, such as firing a worker for joining a union. It also guaranteed workers the right to collective bargaining. **Collective bargaining** is the process by which a union representing a group of workers negotiates with management for a contract. Workers had fought for this right since the late 1800s.

Connecting to Today

Social Security

Americans rely on the Social Security system today as much as they did in the 1930s. Yet, population trends suggest that problems may lie ahead for the system. For one, a large number of people will be retiring between now and 2020. Also, people tend to live longer today than they did in the past. These two trends mean that the system will have to pay out more money. In fact, the system may soon be paying more out in benefits than it is bringing in from worker taxes.

The government is looking at ways to solve the problem. Many solutions have been proposed. They include making benefits smaller, raising taxes, and having people work more years before they retire.

What problem may affect the Social Security system?

Target Skill — Understand Effects In what ways do you think the New Deal "changed American government forever"?

The Wagner Act helped union membership grow from 3 million to 9 million during the 1930s. Union membership got a further boost when John L. Lewis set up the **Congress of Industrial Organizations** (CIO). The CIO represented workers in whole industries, such as steel, automobiles, and textiles.

With more members, unions increased their bargaining power. They also became a powerful force in politics.

Struggles and Victories Despite the Wagner Act, employers tried to stop workers from joining unions. Violent confrontations often resulted.

Workers then tried a new strategy. At the Goodyear Tire Factory in Akron, Ohio, workers staged a **sit-down strike.** They stopped all machines and refused to leave the factory until Goodyear recognized their union. The tactic worked. Workers at other factories made use of sit-down strikes until the Supreme Court outlawed them in 1939.

Social Security

On another front, the President sought to help the elderly. In the 1930s, the United States was the only major industrial nation that did not have a formal pension program. Roosevelt and Secretary of Labor Perkins pushed to enact an old-age pension program.

In September 1935, Congress passed the **Social Security Act.** The new law had three parts. First, it set up a system of pensions for older people. Payments from employers and employees supported this system.

Second, the new act set up the nation's first system of unemployment insurance. People who lost their jobs received small payments until they found work again. Third, the act gave states money to support dependent children and people with disabilities.

Critics condemned the Social Security law. Some liberals pointed out that it did not include farm workers, domestic servants, or the self-employed—many of whom were women or members of minority groups. Conservatives, on the other hand, saw Social Security as another way for the government to take money away from people who had jobs.

Despite these attacks, the Social Security system survived and expanded over the years. Today, it provides medical benefits and pensions to older Americans as well as unemployment insurance to workers.

The New Deal Balance Sheet

The New Deal changed American government forever. Ever since, Americans have debated whether the change was good or bad for the country.

Arguments Against the New Deal Before the 1930s, most Americans had little contact with the federal government. New Deal programs, however, touched almost every citizen. The federal government grew in size and power.

Many people worried about the increased power of government. They complained that the government was intruding in people's lives, threatening both individual freedoms and private property. These critics called for a return to the traditional policy of laissez faire—the idea that government should play as small a role as possible in the economy.

Critics also expressed alarm because the government was spending more than it took in. This practice of **deficit spending** was creating a huge increase in the **national debt,** or the total sum of money the government owes.

Finally, despite its vast spending, the New Deal had not achieved its major goal—ending the depression. In fact, full economic recovery did not come until 1941. By then, the United States was producing goods for nations fighting in World War II.

Arguments for the New Deal Supporters of the New Deal noted that FDR had steered the nation through the worst days of the depression. New Deal legislation had ended the banking crisis, protected farmers, and found work for millions of unemployed.

Supporters also argued that the government had a responsibility to use its power to help all its citizens, not just business and the wealthy. Programs like Social Security, New Dealers said, were necessary for national survival.

Most important of all, supporters argued, the New Deal had saved the nation's democratic system. Elsewhere in the world, people were turning to dictators to lead them out of hard times. President Roosevelt, on the other hand, restored the nation to economic health while preserving its liberties.

Over the years, Americans have continued to discuss the expanded role of government that began during the New Deal. The issue of whether government management of the economy helps or harms the free enterprise system remains a lively one today.

★ ★ ★ Section 3 Assessment ★ ★ ★

Recall

1. **Identify** Explain the significance of **(a)** National Labor Relations Act, **(b)** Congress of Industrial Organizations, **(c)** Social Security Act.
2. **Define** **(a)** pension, **(b)** collective bargaining, **(c)** sitdown strike, **(d)** deficit spending, **(e)** national debt.

Comprehension

3. How did New Deal critics propose to end the depression?
4. Why did many people oppose FDR's court-packing plan?
5. What New Deal laws dealt with labor reform and social security?
6. Was the New Deal good or bad for the country?

Critical Thinking and Writing

7. **Exploring the Main Idea** Review the Main Idea statement at the beginning of this section. Then, write a series of headlines that might have appeared in a newspaper of the times dealing with critics of the New Deal, FDR's plan to pack the Supreme Court, and New Deal measures after 1935.
8. **Analyzing Information** Using the chart on page 761, explain why labor unions strongly supported FDR.

Activity

Connecting to Today
Use the Internet to find out more about the impact of the New Deal on the way we live today. Then, organize a debate on the following topic: "The New Deal saved the free enterprise system." For help in completing the activity, visit PHSchool.com, **Web Code mdf-2603.**

Evaluating Long-Term Effects

Historical events may have both short-term and long-term effects. Short-term effects take place soon after an event, but long-term effects build up over time. Evaluating long-term effects is often helpful in understanding the present and anticipating the future.

Look at the chart of short-term and long-term effects of New Deal laws. Note that some of the long-term effects are totally different from the immediate effects of the New Deal.

Short-Term *and* Long-Term Effects

THE NEW DEAL

Short-Term Effects

- Social Security payments enable people to retire with pensions
- Union membership and power grow
- Farmers benefit from agricultural price supports
- The FDIC insures bank deposits
- The Securities and Exchange Commission oversees the stock market

Long-Term Effects

- Social Security protects millions of Americans but may not be able to pay full benefits in the future
- High-wage and low-wage earners continue to have different kinds of protection and benefits
- Americans have economic safeguards provided by the government
- A split between liberals and conservatives still affects public life

Learn the Skill *To evaluate long-term effects, use the following steps:*

1. **Identify the short-term effects.** Determine the immediate effects of an event.
2. **Identify the long-term effects.** Determine the consequences over time.
3. **Evaluate the long-term effects.** How do the lasting effects continue to influence people?

Practice the Skill *Study the chart and then answer the following questions:*

1. What was one short-term effect of the New Deal?
2. What is one long-term effect of the New Deal?
3. **(a)** How does the New Deal continue to affect Americans? **(b)** Why are some Americans worried about the future of Social Security? **(c)** Select one current political or social issue and describe how liberals and conservatives differ on that issue.

Apply the Skill *See the Chapter Review and Assessment.*

4 The Nation in Hard Times

Prepare to Read

Objectives

In this section, you will

- Identify the causes of the Dust Bowl.
- Explain how the depression affected women.
- Describe the New Deal's impact on African Americans and other Americans.
- Summarize how the arts reflected depression America.

Key Terms

Dust Bowl

migrant worker

Black Cabinet

civil rights

Indian New Deal

Target Reading Skill

Reading Process As you read, prepare an outline of this section. Use roman numerals to indicate the major headings, capital letters for the subheadings, and numbers for the supporting details. The sample below will help you get started.

I. The Dust Bowl
  A.
  B.
II. Women Face the Depression
  A.
  B. An active first lady
III. African Americans

Main Idea Many Americans found relief from the hard times of the Great Depression in the work of creative artists.

Setting the Scene In 1933, a reporter named Lorena Hickok set out from Washington on a government assignment. She was to report firsthand on conditions in rural areas. What she saw shocked even this veteran newswoman:

> "I visited one group of . . . miners and their families, who had been living in tents for two years. . . . It [was] fairly common to see children entirely naked. . . . And some had nothing at all, actually hadn't eaten for a couple of days."
>
> —Lorena Hickok, "Report From West Virginia," August 13–26, 1933

Few Americans suffered as much as the miners of West Virginia during the depression. Most people were able to eat adequately. Most still had some work. Some were helped by the New Deal; others were left out. Yet, almost all learned to live much more cheaply as they struggled to make ends meet.

Struggling to survive

The Dust Bowl

During much of the 1930s, states from Texas to the Dakotas suffered a severe drought. One region in the central Great Plains was especially hard hit. The topsoil dried out. High winds carried the soil away in blinding dust storms. As a result, this area became known as the **Dust Bowl.**

Buried Under Dust Dust storms buried farmhouses, fences, and even trees over large areas of the plains. People put shutters over doors and windows, but the dust blew in anyway. Even food crunched when it was chewed. One storm blew dust from Oklahoma to Albany, New York. A Kansas farmer sadly reported that he sat by his window counting the farms going by.

What caused the disaster? Years of overgrazing by cattle and plowing by farmers destroyed the grasses that once held the soil in place. The drought of the 1930s and high winds did the rest.

Migrant Workers Hardest hit by the drought and dust storms were poor farmers in Oklahoma and other Great Plains states. Hundreds of these "Okies" packed their belongings into cars and trucks and headed west. They became **migrant workers**—people who move from one region to another in search of work. They hoped to find jobs in the orchards and farms of California, Oregon, or Washington.

Once they reached the West Coast, the migrants faced a new hardship—they were not wanted. Local citizens feared that the newcomers would take away their jobs. Sometimes, angry crowds blocked the highways and sent the migrants away. Those migrants who did find work were paid little.

Viewing History

Scarce Jobs

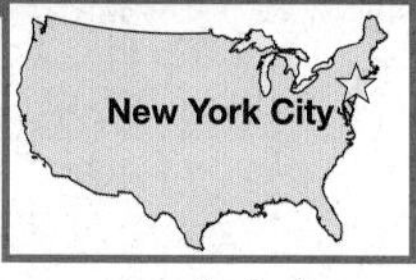

When the depression hit, opportunities for women faded. Programs like WPA provided some work, but not enough for all who needed employment. Here, women sew clothes in a WPA factory. **Identifying Causes and Effects** ***How did the depression affect the role of women in the family?***

Women Face the Depression

Traditional roles took on added importance during the depression. Homemakers had to stretch family budgets to make ends meet. Some women took in laundry to earn extra money. Others took in boarders to help pay the rent. Wives also found that unemployed husbands needed more nurturing to feel worthwhile.

Working women faced special problems during the depression. If jobs were available, employers hired men before they would hire women. In order to spread jobs around, the federal government refused to hire a woman if her husband had a job.

Women in the Workplace Despite such obstacles, millions of women earned wages in order to support themselves and their families. During the 1930s, the number of married women in the work force increased by 52 percent. Educated women took jobs as secretaries, schoolteachers, and social workers. Other women earned livings as maids, factory workers, and seamstresses.

Some women workers struck for better pay. In San Antonio, Texas, at least 80 percent of the pecan shellers were Mexican American women. When employers lowered their pay, a young worker, Emma Tenayuca, organized the shellers and led them off the job. Tenayuca said later, "I had a basic faith in the American idea of freedom and fairness. I felt something had to be done."

An Active First Lady Eleanor Roosevelt created a new role for the First Lady. Acting as the President's "eyes and ears," she toured the nation. She visited farms and Indian reservations and traveled deep into a coal mine. She talked to homemakers, studying the condition of their clothing on the washline to measure how well they were doing.

Target Skill **Ask Questions** What questions would you like to have asked Eleanor Roosevelt?

The First Lady did more than just aid the President. She used her position to speak out for women's rights, as well as other issues. In her newspaper column, "My Day," she called on Americans to live up to the goal of equal justice for all. By speaking out on social issues, Eleanor Roosevelt angered some people. However, many other Americans admired her strong stands.

African Americans

When the Great Depression hit, African American workers were often the first to lose their jobs. By 1934, black workers were suffering a 50 percent unemployment rate, more than twice the national average. Often, they were denied public works jobs. Some charities even refused to serve blacks at centers giving out food to the needy.

Eleanor Roosevelt and others close to the President urged him to improve the situation of African Americans. The President responded to their needs. For example, thousands of young black men learned a trade through the CCC.

In aiding African Americans, FDR won their support for the Democratic party. The President invited black leaders to the White House to advise him. These unofficial advisers became known as the **Black Cabinet.** They included Robert C. Weaver, a Harvard-educated economist, and Mary McLeod Bethune, a well-known Florida educator. Roosevelt appointed Bethune to head the National Youth Administration's Division of Negro Affairs. She was the first African American to head a government agency.

Often, Roosevelt followed the advice of the Black Cabinet. However, when African American leaders pressed the President to support an antilynching law, he refused. He feared that by doing so he would lose the support of southerners in Congress for his New Deal programs.

Many black leaders called on African Americans to unite to obtain their **civil rights**—the rights due to all citizens. African Americans used their votes, won higher-level government jobs, and kept up pressure for equal treatment. Slowly, they made a few gains. However, the struggle for civil rights would take many more years.

An American Profile

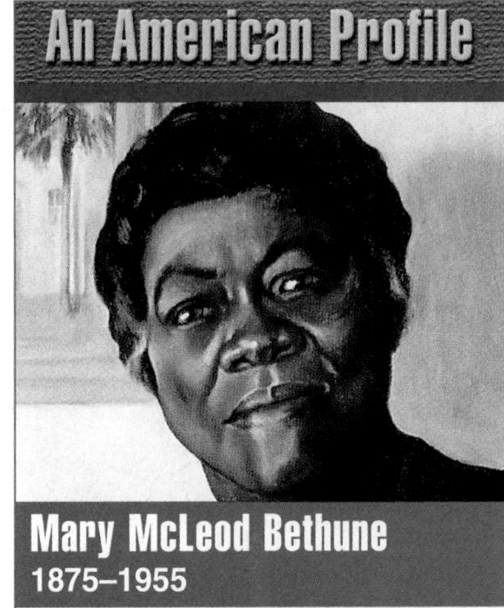

Mary McLeod Bethune
1875–1955

Mary McLeod Bethune was the 15th of 17 children born to a poor farm couple in South Carolina. As a child, Mary decided that she needed an education to fight her way out of poverty.

She was such a good student that she won numerous scholarships. After graduation, she taught and then founded a school in Florida. At first, she had only six students but after years of struggle, was able to raise the number to more than 300. For 40 years, Bethune served as president of what is today called Bethune-Cookman College. During this time, she founded and became the first president of the National Council of Negro Women.

Why do you think Bethune emphasized education so much?

Other Americans Face the Depression

The hard times of the Great Depression created fear and insecurity among many Americans. These feelings sometimes erupted in violence and discrimination against groups of Americans who were outside of the mainstream.

Mexican Americans By the 1930s, Mexican Americans worked in many cities around the country. A large number, however, were farmworkers in the West and Southwest. There, they faced discrimination in education and jobs and at the polls.

In good times, employers had encouraged Mexicans to move north and take jobs in factories or on farms. When hard times struck, however, many Americans wanted Mexicans to be sent back to their original country. More than 400,000 people were rounded up and sent to Mexico. Some of them were American citizens.

Asian Americans Some Americans resented Chinese, Japanese, and Filipino workers who competed with them for scarce jobs. Sometimes, violence against Asians erupted. Responding to pressure, the government sought to reduce the number of Asians in the United States. In 1935, FDR signed a law that provided free transportation for Filipinos who agreed to return to the Philippines and not come back.

Native Americans In 1924, Congress had granted all Native Americans citizenship. Still, most Indians continued to live in deep poverty. President Roosevelt encouraged new policies toward Native Americans.

In the 1930s, Congress passed a series of laws that have been called the **Indian New Deal.** The laws gave Native American nations greater control over their own affairs.

The President chose John Collier, a longtime defender of Indian rights, to head the Bureau of Indian Affairs. Collier ended the government policy of breaking up Indian landholdings. In 1934, Congress passed the Indian Reorganization Act (IRA). It protected and even expanded landholdings of Native American reservations. The Roosevelt administration also strengthened Native American governments by letting reservations organize corporations and develop their own business projects.

To provide jobs during the depression, the government set up the Indian Emergency Conservation Work Group. It employed Native Americans in programs of soil-erosion control, irrigation, and land development.

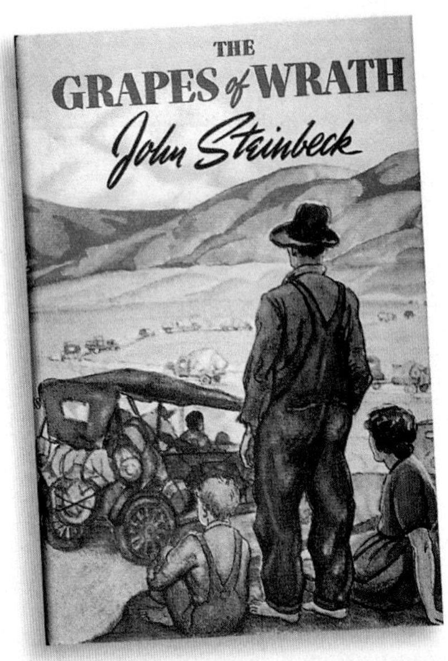

Primary Source

The Grapes of Wrath

In the novel The Grapes of Wrath, John Steinbeck told how suffering farmers headed west, hoping to find a better life in California:

"Carloads, caravans, homeless and hungry: . . . They streamed over the mountains, hungry and restless, . . . restless as ants, scurrying to find work to do—to lift, to push, to pull, to pick, to cut—anything, any burden to bear, for food. The kids are hungry. We got no place to live. Like ants scurrying for work, for food, and most of all for land.

We ain't foreign. Seven generations back Americans, and beyond that Irish, Scotch, English, German. One of our folks in the Revolution, an' they was lots of our folks in the Civil War—both sides. Americans."

—John Steinbeck, *The Grapes of Wrath* (1939)

Analyzing Primary Sources

Why were the migrants attracted to California?

The Arts of the Depression

Creative artists powerfully portrayed the hardships of depression life. Many writers depicted the hard times Americans faced across the country. In his 1939 novel *The Grapes of Wrath*, John Steinbeck told the heartbreaking story of the Okies streaming over the mountains trying to find new homes in California. (See Primary Source feature at left.)

Painting and Photography During the Depression Many painters turned to familiar themes. The huge murals of Thomas Hart Benton brought the history of the frontier to life. In *American Gothic*, Grant Wood painted an Iowa farmer and his daughter who look determined enough to survive any hardship.

The government sent out photographers to create a lasting record of American life during the Great Depression. The vivid photographs of Dorothea Lange (see page 756) showed the suffering of Dust Bowl farm families. Margaret Bourke-White photographed poor tenant farmers in the South.

Radio During the Depression Americans found ways to escape the hard times of the 1930s. Listening to the radio and going to the movies were among their favorite pastimes.

Every night, millions of Americans tuned in to their favorite radio programs. Comedians such as the husband-and-wife team,

George Burns and Gracie Allen, made people forget their troubles for a time. With so many people out of work, daytime radio shows became popular. People listened to dramas like "Ma Perkins" that told the story of families weathering the depression. Because soap companies sponsored many of these serials, the programs became known as soap operas.

Perhaps the most famous broadcast took place in 1938. On Halloween night, actor Orson Welles presented a "newscast" based on a science fiction novel, *The War of the Worlds*. Welles grimly reported the landing of invaders from the planet Mars. People who tuned in late mistook the program for a real newscast. Thousands of terrified people ran into the streets, seeking ways to escape the Martian invasion.

Movies During the Depression In the 1930s, moviemakers tried to restore Americans' faith in the future. Movies told optimistic stories about happy families or people finding love and success. Shirley Temple became a hugely popular star at the age of five. When Temple sang "On the Good Ship Lollipop," her upbeat spirit cheered up audiences.

One of the most popular movies was Walt Disney's *Snow White and the Seven Dwarfs*. It was the first full-length animated film. In 1939, Judy Garland won American hearts in *The Wizard of Oz*. The movie told of a young girl's escape from a bleak life in depression-era Kansas to the magical land of Oz.

The most expensively made and most popular movie of the 1930s was *Gone With the Wind*. It showed the Civil War in a romantic light. For more than three hours, many Americans forgot their worries as they watched the story of love and loss in the Old South. The movie also encouraged many Americans. They had survived hard times before. They would do so again.

Recall

1. **Identify** Explain the significance of **(a)** Dust Bowl, **(b)** Black Cabinet, **(c)** Mary McLeod Bethune, **(d)** Indian New Deal, **(e)** John Collier.
2. **Define** **(a)** migrant worker, **(b)** civil rights.

Comprehension

3. What was the Dust Bowl, and what problems did it create for American farmers?
4. What special hardships did women face during the Great Depression?
5. How did the depression affect African Americans, Mexican Americans, Asian Americans, and Native Americans?
6. How did the depression affect the creative arts?

Critical Thinking and Writing

7. **Exploring the Main Idea** Review the Main Idea statement at the beginning of this section. Then, make a list of the ways in which the arts filled needs during the depression.
8. **Analyzing Primary Sources** In *The Grapes of Wrath*, why does John Steinbeck compare the migrating farmers to ants?

ACTIVITY

Creating a Cartoon
Draw a political cartoon that might have appeared in an American newspaper in the 1930s. The cartoon should show the effects of the Great Depression on Dust Bowl farmers, working women, African Americans, Mexican Americans, or creative artists.

CHAPTER
26 Review and Assessment

Chapter Summary

Section 1
Leaders ignored signs of economic trouble during the prosperous twenties. The 1929 stock market crash marked the start of the Great Depression. Despite Hoover's efforts, both the economy and unemployment remained a problem.

Section 2
Elected President in 1932, Roosevelt established three goals to end the depression: relief for the jobless, plans for economic recovery, and reforms to prevent future depressions.

Section 3
While some people criticized Roosevelt's New Deal programs, FDR pushed for a series of far-reaching reforms. The Wagner Act strengthened unions, and the Social Security Act created a pension program as well as unemployment and disability insurance.

Section 4
A severe drought in the West produced a Dust Bowl, which ruined many farms. Women, African Americans, and other groups faced hard times. The arts provided a relief from the depression.

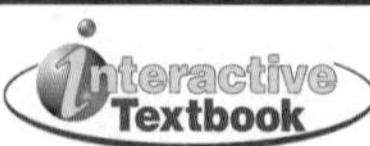

For additional review and enrichment activities, see the interactive version of *The American Nation,* available on the Web and on CD-ROM.

Chapter Self-Test For practice test questions for Chapter 26, visit PHSchool.com, **Web Code mfa-2604.**

Building Vocabulary

Write sentences using the chapter vocabulary words listed below, leaving blanks where the vocabulary words would go. Exchange your sentences with another student, and fill in the blanks in each other's sentences.

1. **on margin**
2. **bankrupt**
3. **soup kitchen**
4. **public works**
5. **bonus**
6. **pension**
7. **sit-down strike**
8. **national debt**
9. **migrant worker**
10. **civil rights**

Reviewing Key Facts

11. Why did Herbert Hoover not act more forcefully to end the depression? (Section 1)
12. What was the TVA, and why was it controversial? (Section 2)
13. How did the New Deal help farmers? (Section 2)
14. Why did Roosevelt try to enlarge the Supreme Court? (Section 3)
15. How did the depression affect women? (Section 4)

Critical Thinking and Writing

16. **Sequencing** **(a)** What problem did FDR tackle first upon taking office? **(b)** Why did he make this his first priority?
17. **Connecting to Geography: Interaction** **(a)** Name one major environmental problem in the world today. **(b)** How is it similar to, and how is it different from, the Dust Bowl problems of the 1930s?
18. **Analyzing Information** Why do you think African Americans suffered greater discrimination during the depression than during good times?
19. **Identifying Points of View** President Roosevelt urged his staff to "take a method and try it. If it fails, admit it and try another. But above all try something." How did this point of view reflect the nation's experience with Herbert Hoover?

Skills Assessment

Analyzing Primary Sources

During the depression, photographers captured the sufferings of the rural poor in powerful pictures. Study this photo, and then answer the questions that follow:

20. What evidence is there in the picture that the men are making a long trip?
- **A.** They are heading toward the train station.
- **B.** It is a long road with no traffic.
- **C.** They are carrying suitcases.
- **D.** Nothing in the photo suggests that they are making a long trip.

21. The men in the photograph were probably
- **A.** migrant workers.
- **B.** artists.
- **C.** models.
- **D.** government employees.

Applying Your Skills

Evaluating Long-Term Effects

Read this summary of the long-term impact of the New Deal and answer the questions that follow:

> " The great public works of the depression era—the bridges, dams, tunnels, public buildings, sewage systems, port facilities, and hospitals—remind us of this extraordinary period of government support for the national welfare. . . . In national and state parks and on mountain trails and oceanfront walks, Americans still reap advantages from the restoration and conservation work of the Civilian Conservation Corps. "
>
> —Cayton et al., *America: Pathways to the Present*

22. Which title best reflects the viewpoint of the author of the quotation?
- **A.** Our Crumbling Public Works
- **B.** Conserving Our Natural Heritage
- **C.** Failure of the New Deal
- **D.** The Heritage of the New Deal

23. **(a)** List three other long-term effects of FDR's presidency besides those mentioned in the quotation. **(b)** Select one long-term effect, and tell how it affects you today.

Activities

Connecting With . . . Civics

Understanding the Role of Charities
Working with a classmate, locate an organization in your community that helps people in need. Interview the leaders of the organization about what they do and where they get funds. Report to the class what you have learned.

Writing a Brief Biography

Depression-Era Leaders Use the Internet to research a person who was important during the Depression. Then, write a brief biography of that person. Focus on how he or she affected the course of history. Be sure to list the sources you used in writing your biography. For help in starting this activity, visit PHSchool.com, **Web Code mfd-2606.**

CHAPTER 27

The World War II Era

1935–1945

1 The Gathering Storm
2 World War II Begins
3 Americans in Wartime
4 The Allies Turn the Tide
5 The End of the War

Neutrality poster

Bombing of Pearl Harbor

AMERICAN EVENTS

1935 Congress passes the first Neutrality Act. The law is intended to keep the United States out of foreign conflicts.

1939 World War II begins as Germany invades Poland. Although the United States remains neutral, President Roosevelt seeks to aid the Allies, such as Britain and France.

1941 Japanese planes bomb the United States fleet at Pearl Harbor, Hawaii. The next day, the United States enters World War II on the Allied side.

Presidential Terms: Franklin D. Roosevelt 1933–1945

1935 · 1938 · 1941

WORLD EVENTS 

▲ **1935** Italy invades Ethiopia.

▲ **1937** Japan launches an all-out war against China.

1940 ▲ France surrenders to Germany.

Aggression in Europe

Under Adolf Hitler, Germany expanded across Europe, sparking the largest war in world history.

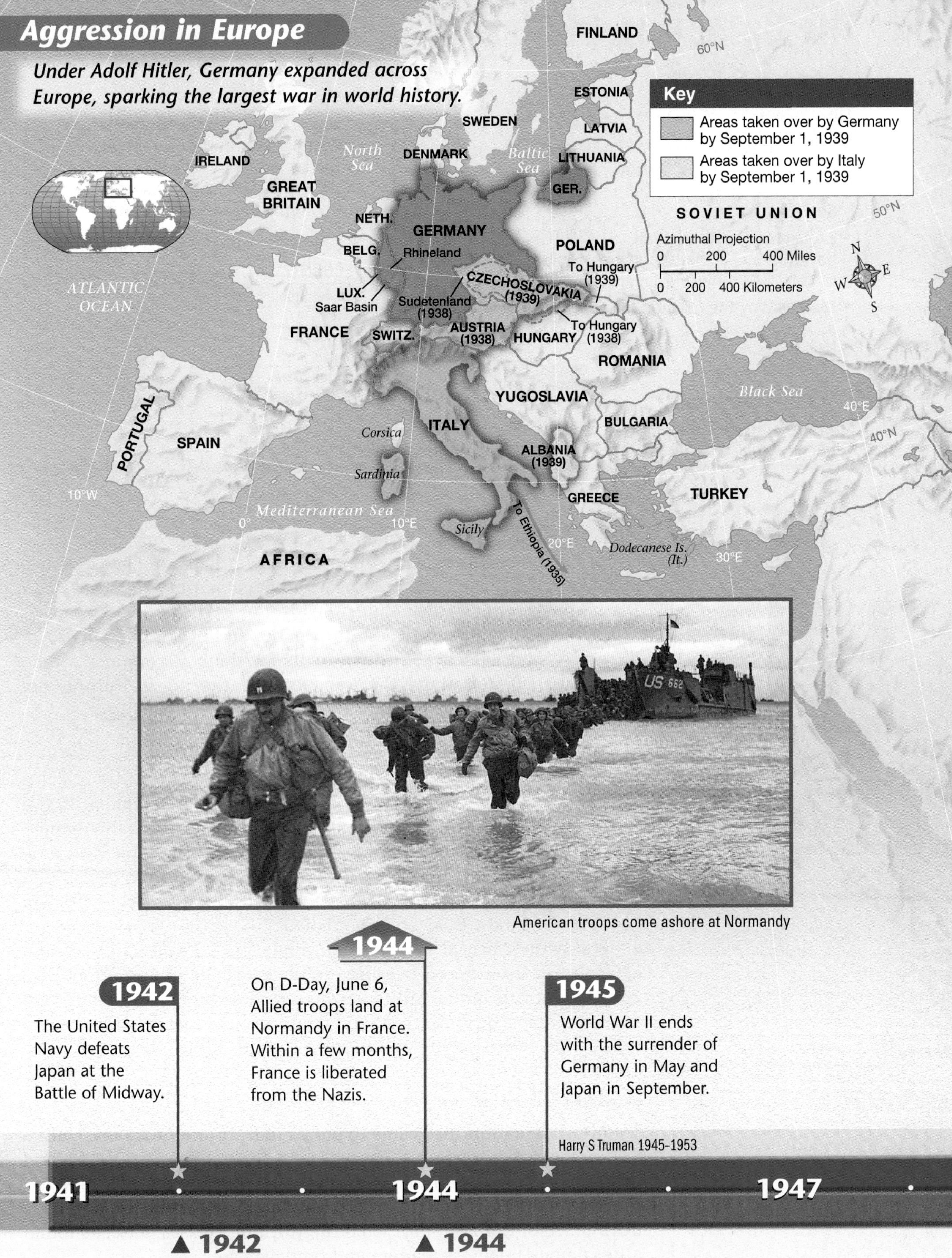

American troops come ashore at Normandy

1942
The United States Navy defeats Japan at the Battle of Midway.

1944
On D-Day, June 6, Allied troops land at Normandy in France. Within a few months, France is liberated from the Nazis.

1945
World War II ends with the surrender of Germany in May and Japan in September.

Harry S Truman 1945–1953

1941 · **1944** · **1947**

▲ 1942
Britain defeats German forces in Egypt.

▲ 1944
German troops are driven out of the Soviet Union.

1 The Gathering Storm

Prepare to Read

Objectives

In this section, you will
- Describe the kind of dictatorship Stalin set up in the Soviet Union.
- Explain how authoritarian governments came to power in Italy, Germany, and Japan.
- Discuss why the United States adopted a policy of isolationism.

Key Terms

totalitarian state
Fascism
aggression
Nazis
scapegoat
concentration camp
Neutrality Acts
Good Neighbor Policy

Target Reading Skill

Comparison and Contrast Copy the table below. As you read, complete the table with information about the world in the 1930s.

COUNTRY	LEADER	GOVERNMENT/ POLICIES
Soviet Union		
Italy		
Germany		
Japan		
United States		

Main Idea In the 1930s, as dictators elsewhere embarked on a path of aggression, the United States tried to stay out of the conflict.

Benito Mussolini

Setting the Scene A man strutted onto a balcony in Rome. A sea of people cheered in the plaza below. He thrust his jaw forward, puffed out his chest, raised his arm, and began a fiery speech. *"Duce! Duce!"* the crowd cried. "Leader! Leader!"

In the 1920s, Benito Mussolini set the style for a new breed of dictators, men with absolute power and visions of conquest. Some Americans worried about the war clouds gathering in Europe and Asia. But most hoped to isolate themselves from the conflict.

Stalin's Totalitarian State

As you have read, Lenin had set up a communist government in the Soviet Union. After Lenin's death in 1924, Joseph Stalin gained power. Stalin ruled as a totalitarian dictator. In a **totalitarian state, a single party controls the government and every aspect of people's lives.** Citizens must obey the government without question. Criticism of the government is severely punished.

Stalin took brutal measures to modernize Soviet industry and agriculture. He ordered peasants to hand over land and animals to government-run farms. Millions who resisted were executed or sent to labor camps. Stalin also staged trials and executions of his political enemies. Many confessed to false charges under torture.

Fascist Italy

Totalitarian leaders also came to power in Italy and Germany. Unlike Stalin, these dictators were Fascists (FAH shists). **Fascism** was rooted in militarism, extreme nationalism, and blind loyalty to the state. Fascist dictators vowed to create new empires. While Communists drew much of their support from the working classes, Fascists found allies among business leaders and landowners.

Mussolini In 1922, Benito Mussolini and his Fascist party seized power in Italy. He played on anger about the Versailles Treaty ending World War I. Many Italians felt cheated because the treaty did not grant Italy the territory it wanted. Mussolini also used economic unrest and fears of a communist revolution to win support.

Once in power, Mussolini outlawed all political parties except his own. He controlled the press and banned criticism of the government. Critics were jailed or simply murdered. In schools, children recited the motto "Mussolini Is Always Right!"

Conquering Ethiopia In the 1930s, Mussolini used foreign conquest to distract Italians from economic problems. Promising to restore the greatness of ancient Rome, he embarked on a program of military aggression. **Aggression** is a warlike act by one country against another without just cause.

Mussolini invaded the African nation of Ethiopia in 1935. The Ethiopians fought bravely. However, their cavalry and outdated rifles were no match for Italy's modern tanks and airplanes.

Ethiopian emperor Haile Selassie (HI lee suh LAS ee) asked the League of Nations for aid. The League responded weakly. Britain and France were caught up in their own economic problems and unwilling to risk another war. Without help, Ethiopia fell to the invaders.

Nazi Germany

In Germany, Adolf Hitler brought the National Socialist German Workers' Party, or **Nazis,** to power. Like Mussolini, Hitler played on anger about the Versailles Treaty. Germans bitterly resented the treaty because it blamed their country for World War I and made them pay heavy war costs.

Hitler Becomes Dictator Hitler assured Germans that they had not lost the war. Rather, he said, Jews and other traitors had "stabbed Germany in the back." The argument was false, but in troubled times people were eager to find a **scapegoat**—a person or group on whom to blame their problems.

Hitler was a powerful speaker and skillful politician. By the time depression struck, many Germans looked to him as a strong leader with answers to their problems.

In 1933, Hitler became chancellor, or head of the German government. Within two years, he ended democratic rule and created a militaristic totalitarian state. In Nazi Germany, the government controlled the press, the schools, and religion.

The following year, Hitler organized a week-long rally in Nuremberg. Crowds chanted slogans praising Hitler. Uniformed soldiers

Viewing History

Soviet Propaganda Poster

Soviet Union

The Soviet totalitarian state was built on the glorification of Stalin (left). This poster celebrated the adoption of a new Soviet constitution in 1937.

Evaluating Information ***What emotions did this propaganda poster try to stir in the Soviet people?***

Viewing History

Nazi Germany

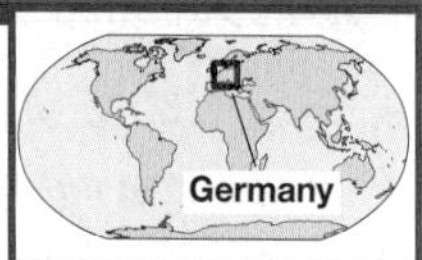

Adolf Hitler (left) was determined to build a mighty military machine. Here, lines of German troops march at the 1934 Nuremberg rally. Their banners display the swastika, symbol of the Nazi party. **Drawing Conclusions** ***What impact do you think pictures like these had on Germans? On people in neighboring countries?***

marched in endless parades and engaged in mock battles. American reporter William Shirer described the Nuremberg rally:

> ❝ It is difficult to exaggerate the frenzy of the three hundred thousand German spectators when they saw their soldiers go into action, heard the thunder of the guns, and smelt the powder. ❞
>
> —William L. Shirer, *Berlin Diary*

Attacks on Jews Hitler preached that Germans belonged to a race that was biologically superior to Jews, Gypsies, and other peoples. The Nazi government singled out the Jews for special persecution. Jews were deprived of their citizenship, forbidden to use public facilities, and driven out of almost every type of work. Later, Jews were rounded up and sent to **concentration camps,** prison camps for civilians who are considered enemies of the state. In time, as you will read, Hitler would unleash a plan to kill all the Jews in Europe.

The Nazi War Machine Hitler claimed that Germany had a right to expand to the east. In defiance of the Versailles treaty, he began to build up Germany's armed forces. Although the League of Nations condemned his actions, Hitler predicted that the rest of Europe would "never act. They'll just protest. And they will always be too late."

In 1936, German troops moved into the Rhineland, near the border with France and Belgium. France and Britain protested, but they took no action.

Target Skill **Compare and Contrast**

How did Germany's policies compare and contrast with Italy's? How were they similar? How were they different? Add this information to your table.

Military Rule in Japan

Japan's economy suffered severely in the Great Depression. As many Japanese grew impatient with their democratic government, military leaders took power. Like Hitler, these leaders preached racial superiority. They believed that the Japanese were purer than, and superior to, other Asians as well as non-Asians.

The military rulers set out to expand into Asia. In 1931, Japanese forces seized Manchuria in northeastern China. Manchuria was rich in coal and iron, two resources scarce in Japan. The Japanese set up a state in Manchuria called Manchukuo.

China called on the League of Nations for help. The League condemned Japanese aggression but did little else. The United States refused to recognize Manchukuo but took no action.

American Isolationism

In the United States, the strong isolationist mood of the 1920s continued. (See page 721.) As war clouds gathered overseas, Americans were determined to keep from becoming involved.

Neutrality Acts In 1935, Congress passed the first of a series of Neutrality Acts, which banned arms sales or loans to countries at war. Congress also warned Americans not to travel on ships of countries at war. By limiting economic ties with warring nations, isolationists hoped to stay out of any foreign conflict.

Good Neighbor Policy Closer to home, the United States tried to improve relations with Latin American nations. In 1930, President Hoover rejected the Roosevelt Corollary. (See Chapter 23.) The United States, he declared, no longer claimed the right to intervene in Latin American affairs.

Franklin Roosevelt also worked to build friendlier relations with Latin America. Under his Good Neighbor Policy, FDR withdrew American troops from Nicaragua and Haiti. He also canceled the Platt Amendment, which had limited the independence of Cuba.

As world tensions increased, the need to strengthen ties in the Americas became more pressing. On a visit to Argentina, Roosevelt warned that any foreign aggressor "will find a hemisphere wholly prepared to consult together for our mutual safety."

Primary Source

The Good Neighbor Policy

In this speech, President Roosevelt describes the results of his policy toward Latin America:

"The whole world now knows that the United States cherishes no predatory ambitions. We are strong; but less powerful nations know that they need not fear our strength. We seek no conquest: we stand for peace. . . . The twenty-one American republics are not only living together in friendship and in peace—they are united in the determination to so remain."

—Franklin D. Roosevelt, Speech at Chautauqua, New York, August 14, 1936

Analyzing Primary Sources

According to FDR, was the Good Neighbor Policy a success? Explain.

★ ★ ★ Section 1 Assessment ★ ★ ★

Recall

1. **Identify** Explain the significance of **(a)** Joseph Stalin, **(b)** Fascism, **(c)** Benito Mussolini, **(d)** Adolf Hitler, **(e)** Nazi, **(f)** Neutrality Acts, **(g)** Good Neighbor Policy.
2. **Define** **(a)** totalitarian state, **(b)** aggression, **(c)** scapegoat, **(d)** concentration camp.

Comprehension

3. Describe Stalin's totalitarian rule in the Soviet Union.
4. What factors helped dictators come to power in **(a)** Italy, **(b)** Germany, **(c)** Japan?
5. What were the goals of American isolationists?

Critical Thinking and Writing

6. **Exploring the Main Idea** Review the Main Idea statement at the beginning of this section. Then, make a list of at least two arguments for and two arguments against American isolationism in the 1930s.
7. **Drawing Inferences** Write a paragraph explaining why you think so many people were willing to reject democracy and turn to dictators in the 1930s.

ACTIVITY

Drawing a Political Cartoon Draw a political cartoon about the nature of totalitarian dictatorships. You might focus on how the government of a totalitarian state differs from the American system of government.

2 World War II Begins

Prepare to Read

Objectives

In this section, you will

- Describe how aggression led to war in Asia and Europe.
- Explain how the United States responded to the outbreak of World War II.
- Discuss why the United States finally entered the war.

Key Terms

Munich Conference
appeasement
Nazi-Soviet Pact
blitzkrieg
Axis
Allies
Battle of Britain
Lend-Lease Act
Atlantic Charter

Target Reading Skill

Cause and Effect Copy the causes chart below. As you read, fill in some of the events and developments that led to United States entry into World War II.

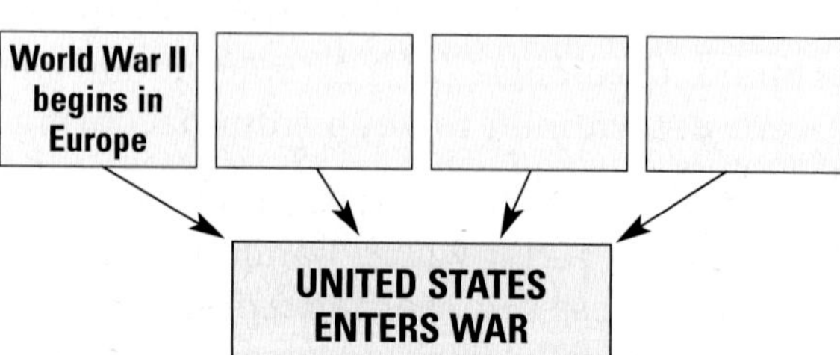

Main Idea Japanese and German aggression plunged the world into a war that eventually involved the United States.

Franklin Roosevelt

Setting the Scene On October 5, 1937, President Roosevelt addressed a large crowd in Chicago. He was there to see whether Americans were ready to abandon isolationism. Claiming that the "epidemic of world lawlessness" was spreading, he said:

> "There is no escape through mere isolation or neutrality. Those who cherish their freedom . . . must work together for the triumph of law and moral principles in order that peace, justice, and confidence may prevail in the world."
>
> —Franklin D. Roosevelt, "Quarantine Speech" October 5, 1937

Roosevelt's speech produced no change in the isolationist mood of Americans. "It is a terrible thing," he commented, "to look over your shoulder when you are trying to lead—and find no one there."

During the 1930s, neither the United States nor European nations were prepared to halt aggression in Europe or Asia. As the armies of Germany, Italy, and Japan conquered more territory, the democracies still hoped to avoid another world war.

Japan Sparks War in Asia

In 1937, Japan began an all-out war against China. Japanese planes bombed China's major cities. Thousands of people were killed. In the city of Nanjing alone, some 300,000 civilians and prisoners of war were murdered in a six-week massacre. Japanese troops defeated Chinese armies and occupied northern and central China.

The Japanese advance into China alarmed American leaders. They felt it undermined the Open Door Policy, which promised equal access to trade in China. It also threatened the Philippines, which the United States controlled. Nevertheless, isolationist feelings remained strong among the American people and kept the United States from taking a firm stand against the Japanese.

Germany Brings War to Europe

In Europe, Hitler continued his plans for German expansion. In 1938, just two years after occupying the Rhineland, Hitler annexed Austria. This action again violated the Treaty of Versailles. Once again, Britain and France took no action against Germany.

Later that year, Hitler claimed the Sudetenland, the western part of Czechoslovakia. He justified his demand by claiming that the Sudetenland contained many people of German heritage.

Appeasement Britain and France had signed treaties to protect Czechoslovakia but were reluctant to go to war. The two nations sought a peaceful solution. In September 1938, the leaders of Britain, France, Italy, and Germany met in Munich, Germany.

At the **Munich Conference,** Hitler promised that Germany would seek no further territory once it had acquired the Sudetenland. To preserve the peace, Britain and France agreed that Germany should have the Sudetenland. This practice of giving in to aggression in order to avoid war is known as **appeasement.**

The policy of appeasement failed. Nazi Germany seized the rest of Czechoslovakia the very next year. At last, Britain and France realized that they had to take a firm stand against Nazi aggression.

Viewing History

Japan Attacks China

The baby shown here miraculously survived the Japanese bombing of a train station in Shanghai, China. This famous photograph was widely circulated in the United States. **Drawing Conclusions** ***Why do you think this photograph became so well known? What effect do you think it had?***

Invasion of Poland Hitler next eyed Poland. In August 1939, he signed the **Nazi-Soviet Pact** with Stalin. The two rival dictators agreed not to attack each other. Secretly, they also agreed to divide Poland and other parts of Eastern Europe.

In September 1939, Hitler launched a **blitzkrieg,** or lightning war, against Poland. Unable to withstand up-to-date German planes and tanks, the Poles soon surrendered.

Meanwhile, the Soviet Union seized eastern Poland. Stalin's forces also invaded Finland and later annexed Estonia, Lithuania, and Latvia. Stalin claimed that these steps were needed to build Soviet defenses.

A Second World War

Two days after Hitler's invasion of Poland, Britain and France declared war on Germany. A new world war had begun.

World War II was truly a global conflict. Military forces fought all over the world. Italy, Japan, and six other nations joined Germany to form the **Axis** powers. Opposing the Axis powers were the **Allies.** Before the war was over, the Allies would include Britain, France, the Soviet Union, the United States, China, and 45 other countries.

Fall of France In the spring of 1940, Hitler's armies marched north and west. In April, they smashed through Denmark and Norway. In May, they overran Holland and Belgium and pushed into France. Hitler's ally, Italy, also attacked France.

Britain sent troops to help France resist the assault. The British and French, however, were quickly overpowered. By May, the Germans had forced them to retreat to Dunkirk, a French port on the English Channel. In a bold action, the British sent every available ship across the channel to rescue the trapped soldiers.

Unhindered, German armies entered France and marched on to Paris, the French capital. On June 22, 1940, barely six weeks later, France surrendered. The fall of France shocked the world.

Geography and History

Miracle at Dunkirk

The situation at Dunkirk looked hopeless. French and British troops had their backs to the North Sea. Advancing German troops pinned down the army, cutting off a possible retreat through ports on the English Channel. British Navy ships were too few to carry so many troops to safety in time.

In a massive effort, the British put to use nearly everything that could float. Civilians piloted fishing boats, private yachts, tugboats, motorboats, and ferries across the rough waters. Luckily, an approaching storm in the Atlantic had turned north before hitting the English Channel. By June 4, 1940, some 338,000 troops had been miraculously rescued from the beaches of Dunkirk.

Why do you think that so many civilians helped with the evacuation effort?

Battle of Britain Britain now stood alone. Even so, the new prime minister, Winston Churchill, was confident. He vowed:

> "We shall fight on the beaches, we shall fight on the landing grounds, we shall fight in the fields and in the streets . . . we shall never surrender."
>
> —Winston Churchill, Speech to House of Commons, June 4, 1940

German planes dropped bombs on London and other British cities during the **Battle of Britain.** British fighter pilots fought back, gunning down nearly 2,000 German planes. By late 1940, after months of bombing, Hitler gave up his planned invasion of Britain.

In the United States, people listened to radio reports from London. Hearing of Britain's brave stand against Hitler, Americans wondered how much longer they could stay out of the war.

The United States Moves Toward War

After the invasion of Poland, President Roosevelt announced that the United States would remain neutral. He knew that most Americans favored the Allies but did not want to go to war.

Recognize Multiple Causes

As you read this subsection and the next one, list the steps by which the United States became involved in World War II. Add this information to your chart.

Aid to the Allies Roosevelt sought ways to help the Allies. He asked Congress to repeal the neutrality law that banned the sale of arms to warring nations. Isolationists blocked the move, but FDR won a compromise. The United States could sell arms to the Allies under a "cash-and-carry" plan. The Allies had to pay cash for the goods and carry them away in their own ships.

By 1940, German submarines had sunk many British ships. Roosevelt agreed to give Britain 50 old American destroyers. In exchange, Britain gave the United States 99-year leases on military bases in Newfoundland and the Caribbean.

Prepared for War The United States also took several steps to prepare for war. Congress approved greater spending for the army and navy and set up a military draft. It was the first time young men were required to serve in the army during peace.

Isolationists opposed these moves, especially aid for Britain. "I have been forced to the conclusion that we cannot win this war for England, regardless of how much assistance we extend," warned Charles Lindbergh, the hero pilot of the 1920s. Many other

POLITICAL CARTOON *Skills*

The Nazi Threat
Dr. Seuss is best known for his children's books, but he also drew many political cartoons. This one appeared in an American newspaper in 1941.

1. **Comprehension** **(a)** What do the two birds represent? **(b)** What do the trees represent?
2. **Understanding Main Ideas** What is the attitude of the large bird toward the events going on around him?
3. **Critical Thinking Identifying Points of View** Do you think Dr. Seuss favored American neutrality in World War II? Explain.

Americans, however, felt that the United States had no choice. If Britain fell, Hitler might control the Atlantic Ocean.

A Third Term for FDR The threat of war persuaded FDR to run for a third term in 1940. His decision broke the precedent set by George Washington of serving only two terms as President.

Republicans nominated Wendell Willkie, an Ohio businessman. Willkie was a strong critic of FDR's New Deal. Still, he agreed with Roosevelt on many issues, such as sending aid to Britain. Both candidates also pledged not to send Americans into any foreign wars.

Republicans—and some Democrats—criticized Roosevelt for breaking the two-term tradition. Still, the voters gave FDR a clear victory. After his defeat, Willkie worked to win Republican support for Roosevelt's war aims.

Lend-Lease By late 1940, Britain was running out of cash. Roosevelt boldly suggested lending supplies to Britain. He proclaimed that Britain was defending democracy against totalitarian forces.

Despite opposition from isolationists, Congress passed the **Lend-Lease Act** in March 1941. It allowed sales or loans of war materials to "any country whose defense the President deems vital to the defense of the United States." Under Lend-Lease, the United States sent airplanes, tanks, guns, and ammunition to Britain. British merchant ships transported the goods, with escorts of American warships providing protection as far as Iceland.

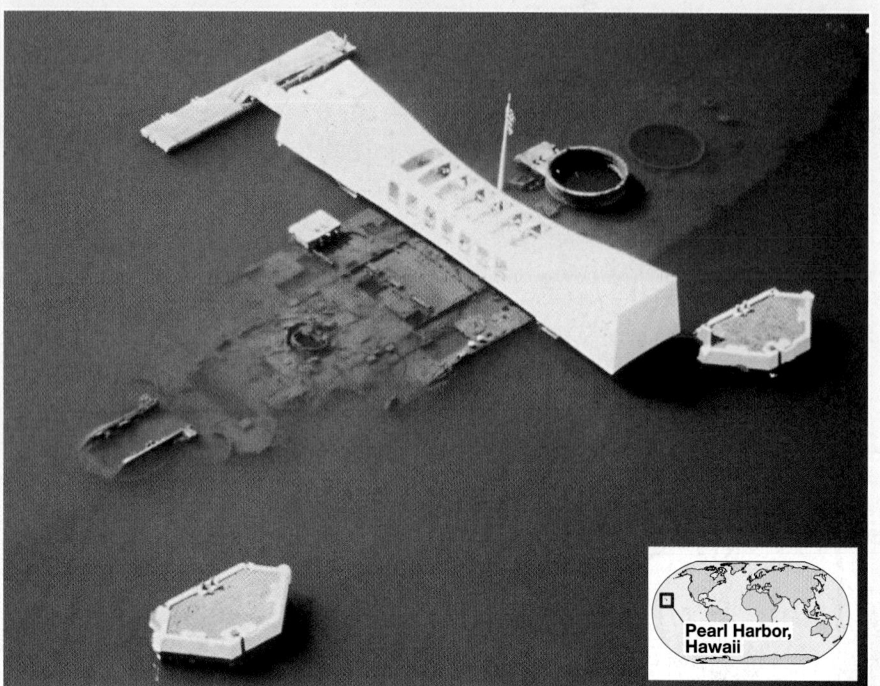

USS *Arizona* Memorial

On the morning of December 7, 1941, Japanese fighter planes bombed the United States fleet anchored at Pearl Harbor, Hawaii. The battleship Arizona *sank with 1,102 sailors inside. Today, you can take a navy shuttle to view the sunken hull of the* Arizona. *At the "remembrance exhibit," you can pay tribute to the first Americans to give their lives in World War II.*

Virtual Field Trip For an interactive look at the USS *Arizona* Memorial, visit PHSchool.com, **Web Code mfd-2701.**

In June 1941, Hitler launched a surprise invasion of the Soviet Union. The Soviets were now fighting on the Allied side. Although Roosevelt condemned Stalin's totalitarian rule, he extended Lend-Lease aid to the Soviet Union.

War Goals In August 1941, Roosevelt and Churchill issued the Atlantic Charter, which set goals for the postwar world. The two leaders agreed to seek no territory from the war. They pledged to support "the right of all peoples to choose the form of government under which they will live." The charter also called for a "permanent system of general security" similar to the League of Nations.

War Comes to the United States

To Roosevelt, Japanese aggressions in Asia were as alarming as Germany's advance through Europe. The Japanese had seized much of China. After Germany defeated France in 1940, Japan took control of French colonies in Southeast Asia. In September 1940, the Japanese signed an alliance with Germany and Italy.

An Embargo The United States tried to stop Japanese aggression by refusing to sell oil and scrap metal to Japan. This embargo angered the Japanese because they badly needed these resources. "Sparks will fly before long," predicted an American diplomat.

Japanese and American officials met in November 1941. Japan asked the United States to lift its trade embargo. The United States called on Japan to withdraw its armies from China and Southeast

Asia. Neither side would compromise. As the talks limped along, Japan completed plans for a secret attack on the United States.

Japan Attacks Pearl Harbor On Sunday morning, December 7, 1941, the American Pacific fleet was peacefully anchored at Pearl Harbor, Hawaii. Suddenly, Japanese planes swept through the sky. In less than two hours, they sank or seriously damaged 19 American ships, destroyed almost 200 planes, and killed about 2,400 people.

The attack was a desperate gamble by Japanese leaders. They knew they lacked the resources to win a long war with the United States. They believed, however, that Americans were weak and had no stomach for fighting. The Japanese thought the sneak attack would force the United States to beg for peace immediately. Instead, Pearl Harbor united Americans in their determination to fight.

The Japanese made two other mistakes. First, they failed to sink the aircraft carriers stationed at Pearl Harbor. The carriers were at sea at the time of the attack. Second, the Japanese did not bomb the fuel oil tanks in Hawaii. Oil and aircraft carriers would become two keys to American victory in the war that followed.

The next day, a grave President Roosevelt addressed Congress. "Yesterday, December 7, 1941—a date which will live in infamy—" he began. He told Congress and the nation:

> “No matter how long it may take us to overcome this premeditated invasion, the American people, in their righteous might, will win through to absolute victory.”
>
> —Franklin D. Roosevelt, War Message to Congress, December 8, 1941

Congress declared war on Japan. In response, Germany and Italy declared war on the United States. Americans were now united in the cause of freedom. Even isolationists backed the war effort.

★ ★ ★ Section 2 Assessment ★ ★ ★

Recall

1. **Identify** Explain the significance of **(a)** Munich Conference, **(b)** Nazi-Soviet Pact, **(c)** Axis, **(d)** Allies, **(e)** Winston Churchill, **(f)** Battle of Britain, **(g)** Wendell Willkie, **(h)** Lend-Lease Act, **(i)** Atlantic Charter.
2. **Define** **(a)** appeasement, **(b)** blitzkrieg.

Comprehension

3. **(a)** How did Britain and France respond to German aggression at first? **(b)** Why did they finally declare war on Germany?
4. Describe two actions the United States took to support the Allies.
5. What were the results of the attack on Pearl Harbor?

Critical Thinking and Writing

6. **Exploring the Main Idea** Review the Main Idea statement at the beginning of this section. Then, write a letter telling British and French leaders at the Munich Conference how you think they should respond to Nazi aggression.
7. **Drawing Conclusions** "Until December 7, 1941, the United States followed a neutral course." Do you agree or disagree? Write a paragraph explaining your reasoning.

ACTIVITY

Presenting a Scene
With two or three classmates, present a scene in which an American family listens to FDR's war message on the radio on December 8, 1941. Have the family discuss what they think the war will mean to them.

3 Americans in Wartime

Prepare to Read

Objectives

In this section, you will
- Describe how Americans mobilized the economy in World War II.
- Discuss the impact the war had on African Americans.
- Explain why Japanese Americans and other groups faced special problems during the war.

Key Terms

War Production Board
rationing
victory garden
Rosie the Riveter
"Double V" campaign
Tuskegee Airmen
compensation
bracero program

Target Reading Skill

Reading Process Copy the concept web below. As you read, fill in the blank ovals with information about Americans during World War II. Add as many ovals as you need.

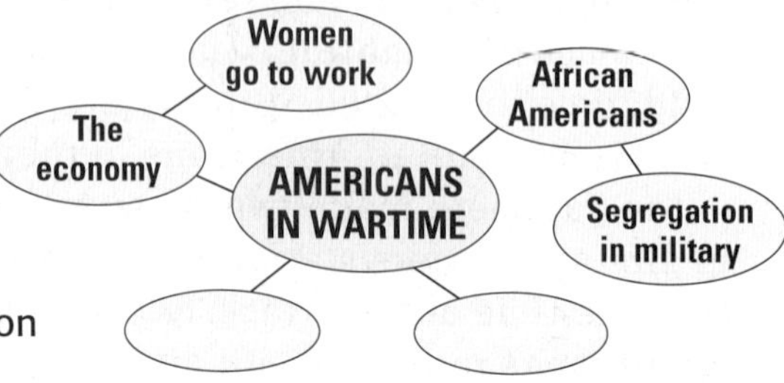

Main Idea Despite economic sacrifices, as well as discrimination faced by certain groups, Americans pulled together as never before to help defeat the enemy.

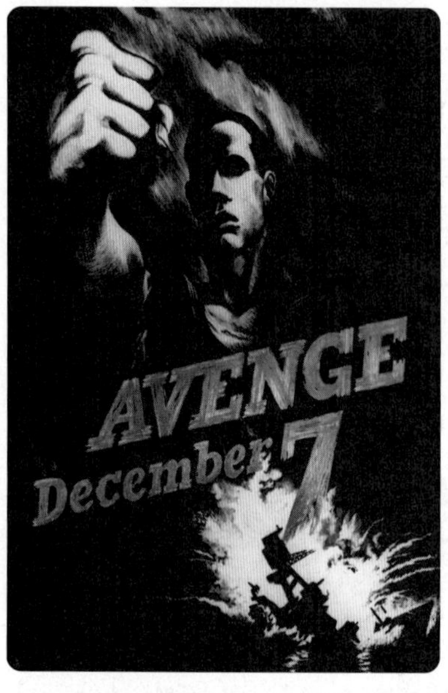

1942 American poster

Setting the Scene An English visitor was flying over the United States in 1943. Fresh from war-torn Europe, he was impressed by the calm below. There were no bombs falling or armies fighting. It was even hard to tell that the country was at war. Then, a flight attendant put his lunch tray in front of him. He recalled:

> "As I reached . . . to attack my butter pat, there, neatly inscribed on it, was the [command to] REMEMBER PEARL HARBOR. It needed the butter to remind one of the guns."
>
> —H. G. Nicholas, quoted in *V Was for Victory* (Blum)

The Japanese attack on Pearl Harbor plunged the United States into World War II. Americans united as never before. The cry "Remember Pearl Harbor" became a reminder that the efforts of Americans on the home front were vital to victory.

Mobilizing the Home Front

During World War II, more than 15 million Americans served in the military. Many millions more spent the war years at home, far from the battlefields. Winning the war depended on mobilizing the home front to support and supply the armed forces.

Combat Training In 1941, the military's first task was to train forces for combat. Army, navy, and air bases were built all over the country. Recruits were trained to fight in the jungles of the Pacific, the deserts of North Africa, and the towns and farmlands of Europe.

Women joined all the armed services. Women pilots logged 60 million air miles ferrying bombers from base to base, towing targets, and teaching men to fly. Although women were not allowed in combat, many served close to the front lines.

A Miracle of Production Even more than in World War I, the government controlled the economy during World War II. Government agencies set the prices of goods, negotiated with labor unions, and decided what should be produced.

The **War Production Board** helped factories shift from making consumer goods to making guns, ships, aircraft, and other war materials. Automobile makers, for example, switched to producing tanks and trucks.

A Nazi leader once scoffed that "Americans can't build planes, only electric iceboxes and razor blades." He was wrong. Americans performed a miracle of production. In 1942 alone, American workers produced more than 48,000 planes and shipped more than 8 million tons of goods.

As production of war materials grew, consumer goods became scarcer. The government imposed **rationing,** or limitations on the amounts of certain goods that people could buy. Americans used ration coupons to purchase coffee, sugar, meat, gasoline, and many other goods. When people ran out of coupons, they could not buy the items until new coupons were issued.

Viewing History

Rosie the Riveter

Rosie the Riveter became one of the most familiar images of World War II. In this magazine cover by popular artist Norman Rockwell, Rosie treads on a book written by Adolf Hitler. **Applying Information** ***How does this image reflect what you have read about women's contributions to the war effort?***

To combat food shortages, many Americans planted **victory gardens.** At the height of the war, more than 20 million victory gardens produced 40 percent of all vegetables grown in the country.

To pay for the war, the government raised taxes. It also borrowed money from millions of American citizens by selling war bonds. Movie stars took part in drives to sell bonds and boost patriotic spirit.

The war quickly ended the Great Depression. Unemployment fell as millions of jobs opened up in factories. Minority workers found jobs where they had been rejected in the past.

Women in the Wartime Economy

"If you can drive a car, you can run a machine." Newspapers and magazines echoed this call to American women to work for victory. "Why do we need women workers?" asked a radio announcer. "You can't build ships, planes, and guns without them."

Women responded to the urgent demand for their labor. Almost five million women entered the work force. They replaced the men who joined the armed services. Many women worked in offices. Millions more kept the nation's factories operating around the clock. Some welded, ran huge cranes, and tended blast furnaces. Others became bus drivers, police officers, and gas station attendants. The image of **Rosie the Riveter,** a fictional factory worker, became a symbol of American women's contribution to the war effort.

Because women were badly needed in industry, they were able to win better pay and working conditions. The government agreed that women and men should get the same pay for the same job. Many employers, however, found ways to avoid equal pay.

The war changed fashions for women. Instead of wearing skirts on the job, many women dressed in trousers. They wore overalls and tied scarves around their hair. More important, war work gave many women a new sense of confidence. One former welder recalled:

> "I will never regret my two years or more in the shipyards. It gave me a good start in life. . . . I decided that if I could learn to weld like a man, I could do anything it took to make a living."
>
> —Nova Lee McGhee Holbrook, quoted in *A Mouthful of Rivets* (Wise)

African Americans at War

When the war began, African Americans rallied to their nation's cause, as they had during World War I. This time, however, African Americans decided to pursue a **"Double V" campaign**—victory over the enemy abroad and victory over discrimination at home.

Fighting Discrimination at Home As industry geared up for war, factories replaced "No Help Wanted" signs with "Help Wanted, White" signs. Such discrimination angered African Americans.

In 1941, A. Philip Randolph, head of the Brotherhood of Sleeping Car Porters, called for a protest march on Washington. The government, he said, "will never give the Negro justice until they see masses—ten, twenty, fifty thousand Negroes on the White House lawn."

Government officials worried that such a march would feed Hitler's propaganda machine. After meeting with Randolph, FDR ordered employers that did business with the government to end

Viewing History

Relocation of Japanese Americans

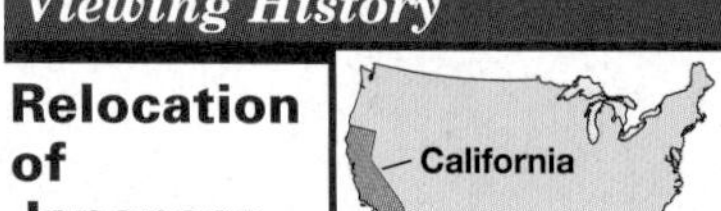

Here, American troops oversee the movement of Japanese American families on the West Coast to relocation camps. "Herd 'em up, pack 'em off" was the reaction of one newspaper columnist.

Identifying Points of View ***How do you think the families shown in this picture felt about what was happening?***

discrimination in hiring. As a result, the employment of skilled black workers doubled during the war.

However, as black employment increased, so did racial tension. Thousands of Americans—black and white—moved to cities to work in industry. Competition for scarce housing led to angry incidents. In 1943, race riots broke out in Detroit, New York, and other cities.

Courage Under Fire While FDR acted against discrimination in hiring, he refused to end segregation of the races in the military. Nearly a million African Americans enlisted or were drafted. They had to serve in all-black units commanded by white officers.

African Americans served heroically in all branches of the armed forces. One of the earliest heroes of the war was Dorie Miller, an African American sailor serving on the battleship *West Virginia.* During the attack on Pearl Harbor, Miller dragged his wounded captain to safety. Then, though he had no training as a gunner, Miller manned a machine gun to defend his ship against enemy planes. For heroism in action, Miller was awarded the Navy Cross.

In the army, African American soldiers formed artillery and tank units. African Americans in the navy served as gunners' mates and helped build bases in the Pacific. African American marines helped defend American posts against Japanese attacks. The **Tuskegee Airmen** were African American fighter pilots who trained at Tuskegee, Alabama. By the end of the war, the Tuskegee airmen had destroyed or damaged about 400 enemy aircraft.

The contributions of African Americans to the war effort increased their determination to win justice at home. After the war, black veterans would be at the forefront of a renewed campaign for civil rights.

An American Profile

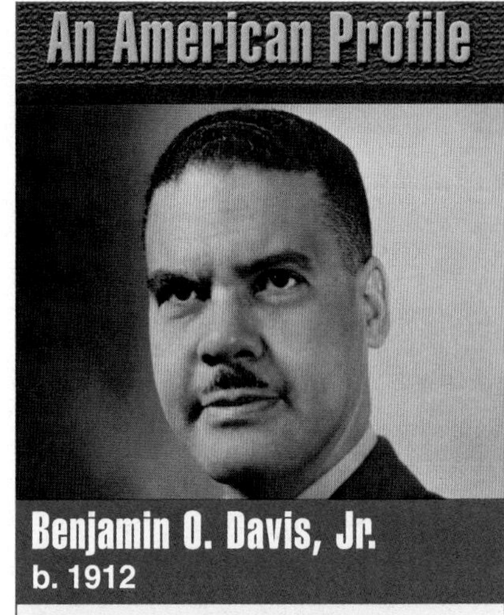

Benjamin O. Davis, Jr.
b. 1912

Benjamin O. Davis, Jr., had a history-making career. During World War II, he organized and took command of the Tuskegee Airmen. Davis flew 60 combat missions but rarely took credit for any victory. "The mission was always the dominating factor," he said. "It was a life and death operation, and it was important to our nation."

After the war, Davis helped end segregation in the Air Force. He flew combat again in the Korean War, and in 1959 he became the first African American to be awarded the rank of Major General.

What attitude did Davis have toward duty?

A Calamity for Japanese Americans

The war brought suffering to many Japanese Americans. Most lived on the West Coast or in Hawaii. Many of those on the West Coast were successful farmers and business people. For years, they had faced prejudice, in part because of their success.

Forced Relocation After the attack on Pearl Harbor, many people on the West Coast questioned the loyalty of Japanese Americans. Japanese Americans, they said, might act as spies and help Japan invade the United States. No evidence of disloyalty existed. Yet, President Roosevelt signed an order allowing the army to move Japanese Americans from their homes to "relocation camps." Many were American citizens by birth.

About 110,000 Japanese Americans were forced to sell their homes, farms, or businesses at great loss. "We didn't know where we were going," recalled Peter Ota, who was 15 at the time. "We didn't know what to take. A toothbrush, toilet supplies, some clothes. Only what you could carry." In the camps, Japanese Americans lived in crowded barracks behind barbed wire.

In the Service Despite unfair treatment, thousands of Japanese American men served in the armed forces. Most were put in segregated units and sent to fight in Europe. There, they won many honors

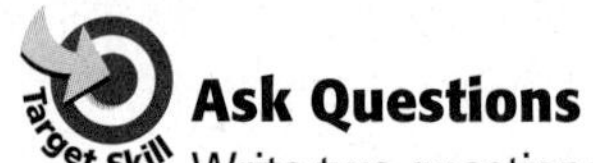

Ask Questions Write two questions you would like to have asked Japanese Americans about relocation camps or about service in World War II.

for bravery. The 442nd Nisei Regimental Combat Team became the most highly decorated military unit in United States history.

Years later, in 1988, Congress apologized to Japanese Americans who had been driven from their homes in World War II. Congress also approved **compensation,** or repayment for losses, in the amount of $20,000 to every survivor of the camps.

Other Groups Face Problems

Japanese Americans were not the only group to face wartime restrictions. About 11,000 German Americans and several hundred Italian Americans were also held in government camps as "enemy aliens." Other German Americans and Italian Americans faced curfews or travel restrictions.

A growing Mexican American population also faced problems. Because of the need for workers, the United States signed a treaty with Mexico in 1942. It allowed the recruitment of Mexican laborers to work in the United States. Under this **bracero program,** many Mexicans moved north to work on farms and railroads.

In June 1943, a group of sailors on leave attacked some young Mexican Americans, beating them on the streets. The incident led to several days of rioting in Los Angeles. Newspapers blamed the violence on the Mexican Americans. But in her newspaper column, Eleanor Roosevelt argued that the riots were the result of "longstanding discrimination against the Mexicans in the Southwest."

Still, like other groups, Mexican Americans served bravely in the military during World War II. Despite lingering problems at home, Americans were united in their resolve to push on to victory in Europe and the Pacific.

Section 3 Assessment

Recall

1. **Identify** Explain the significance of **(a)** War Production Board, **(b)** Rosie the Riveter, **(c)** "Double V" campaign, **(d)** A. Philip Randolph, **(e)** Tuskegee Airmen.
2. **Define** **(a)** rationing, **(b)** victory garden, **(c)** compensation, **(d)** bracero program.

Comprehension

3. Describe two economic policies that helped the American war effort.
4. What gains did African Americans make at home as a result of the war?
5. How did the war affect Japanese Americans on the West Coast?

Critical Thinking and Writing

6. **Exploring the Main Idea** Review the Main Idea statement at the beginning of this section. Then, write a letter from an American to a relative fighting overseas explaining why you are willing to make sacrifices for the war effort.
7. **Supporting a Point of View** Do you think the government is ever justified in suspending citizens' rights during wartime? Write a paragraph explaining your reasons.

ACTIVITY

Designing a Poster
With a partner, design a poster to encourage young Americans to serve in World War II. Your poster may focus on either military or nonmilitary service.

A WARTIME Economy

With the outbreak of World War II, the nation geared its economy to one goal: victory. The home front was alive with patriotic enthusiasm. Everyone, young and old, was expected to do his or her part.

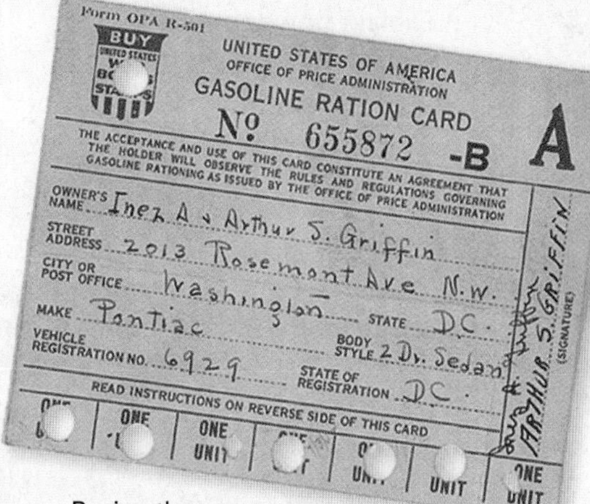

Form OPA R-501

BUY UNITED STATES WAR BONDS STAMPS

UNITED STATES OF AMERICA
OFFICE OF PRICE ADMINISTRATION
GASOLINE RATION CARD

Nº 655872 -B **A**

THE ACCEPTANCE AND USE OF THIS CARD CONSTITUTE AN AGREEMENT THAT THE HOLDER WILL OBSERVE THE RULES AND REGULATIONS GOVERNING GASOLINE RATIONING AS ISSUED BY THE OFFICE OF PRICE ADMINISTRATION

OWNER'S NAME Inez A. & Arthur S. Griffin
STREET ADDRESS 2013 Rosemont Ave N.W.
CITY OR POST OFFICE Washington STATE D.C.
MAKE Pontiac BODY STYLE 2 Dr. Sedan
VEHICLE REGISTRATION NO. 6929 STATE OF REGISTRATION D.C.

READ INSTRUCTIONS ON REVERSE SIDE OF THIS CARD

ONE UNIT | ONE UNIT | ONE UNIT | ONE UNIT | ONE UNIT | ONE UNIT | ONE UNIT

Arthur S. Griffin (SIGNATURE)

During the war, the government rationed essential items such as sugar, gasoline, coffee, meat, and even ketchup. Citizens were given ration books to keep track of the "points" allotted to each family.

SALVAGE IN WORLD WAR II

SAVE . . .	CAN BE MADE INTO . . .
30,000 razor blades	50 machine guns (.30 caliber)
30 lipstick tubes	20 ammunition cartridges
2,300 pairs of nylons	1 parachute
1 pound of fat	$\frac{1}{3}$ pound of gunpowder
2,500 tons of tin and 190,000 tons of steel	5,000 tanks

Source: The National D-Day Museum

Children went to the streets to collect scrap metal, paper, rubber—anything that could be recycled to help win the war. At left, members of New York's Tin Can Club Number One wash their day's haul. The chart (above) shows how some everyday products were turned into needed war materials.

ACTIVITY

You are a young person during World War II. Working in a small group, make a list of things that you and your friends could do at home and in the community to help win the war.

4 The Allies Turn the Tide

Prepare to Read

Objectives

In this section, you will
- List the defeats the Allies suffered in 1942.
- Explain how the Allied tactics helped turn the tide of battle in Europe.
- Summarize how the war in Europe ended.

Key Terms

Battle of Midway

Operation Overlord

D-Day

Battle of the Bulge

Target Reading Skill

Sequence Copy this flowchart. As you read, fill in the boxes with events that led to the Allied victory in Europe. Add as many boxes as you need.

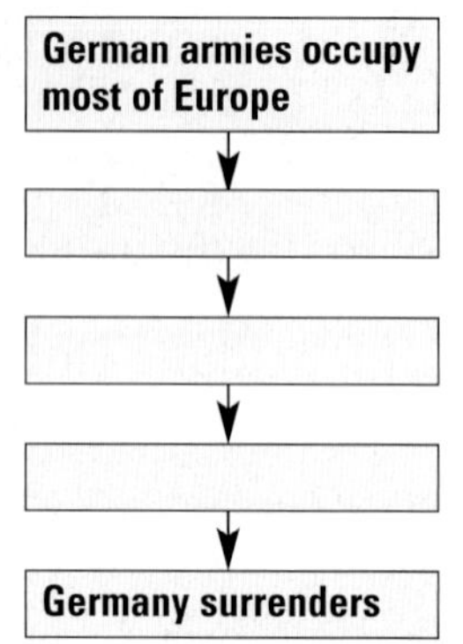

Main Idea Despite some early defeats, a series of Allied military successes helped to turn the tide of battle in Europe.

American World War II medal

Setting the Scene When Adolf Hitler learned of the Japanese attack on Pearl Harbor, he was delighted. "Now it is impossible for us to lose the war," he predicted. "We now have an ally who has never been vanquished in 3,000 years." Although Germany's alliance with Japan did not require it, Hitler promptly declared war on the United States.

At first, Hitler's prediction looked as if it might come true. In 1942, German armies occupied most of Europe and much of North Africa. Japan was sweeping across Asia and the Pacific. By 1944, however, the tide of battle had turned.

Bleak Days for the Allies

In early 1942, the situation looked bleak for the Allies. The German war machine seemed unbeatable. German submarines were sinking ships faster than the Allies could replace them. Most of Europe was in Axis hands.

Soviets Under Siege In the Soviet Union, German armies were closing in on Moscow, Leningrad, and Stalingrad. The Soviets resisted heroically. They burned crops and destroyed farm equipment so that the Germans could not use them.

Still, the German attack caused terrible hardships. During the 900-day siege of Leningrad, more than one million Russian men, women, and children died, mostly of starvation.

Japanese Advances Meanwhile, Japanese forces were on the move in the Pacific. After the bombing of Pearl Harbor, they seized Guam, Wake Island, Hong Kong, and Singapore. (See the map on page 797.)

General Douglas MacArthur commanded United States forces in the Pacific. With few troops, MacArthur had to defend a huge area. He directed American and Filipino troops in the defense of the

Philippines and the island of Bataan. They fought bravely against enormous odds. A reporter described the final defeat at Bataan:

> “Besieged on land and blockaded by sea, cut off from all sources of help in the Philippines and in America, these intrepid fighters have done all that human endurance could bear. . . . Bataan has fallen, but the spirit that made it stand—a beacon to all liberty-loving peoples of the world—cannot fall!”
>
> —Norman Reyes, "Voice of Freedom" broadcast, 1942

In the end, MacArthur was forced to withdraw. "I shall return," he vowed.

The Japanese pressed on. They captured Malaya, Burma, and the Dutch East Indies. They threatened India to the west and Australia and New Zealand to the south.

The Tide Turns

To succeed against the Axis powers, the Allies had to agree on a strategy. Even before Pearl Harbor, American and British leaders had decided that the Allies must defeat Germany and Italy first. Then, they would send their combined forces to fight Japan.

Japanese Defeats Adopting a "beat Hitler first" strategy did not mean abandoning the war in the Pacific. With the aircraft carriers that had survived the attack on Pearl Harbor, a naval task force met a Japanese fleet in the Coral Sea near Java in May 1942. After a three-day battle, the Japanese fleet turned back. It was the first

GEOGRAPHY Skills

Early in the war, the Axis powers gained control of much of Western Europe and North Africa. The tide later began to turn in favor of the Allies.

1. **Location** On the map, locate **(a)** El Alamein, **(b)** Stalingrad, **(c)** Sicily, **(d)** Normandy, **(e)** Berlin.
2. **Movement** In what year did Allied troops first enter Italy? Germany?
3. **Critical Thinking Drawing Conclusions** Why do you think the Allies did not attack France by way of the Spanish-French border?

World War II in Europe and Africa

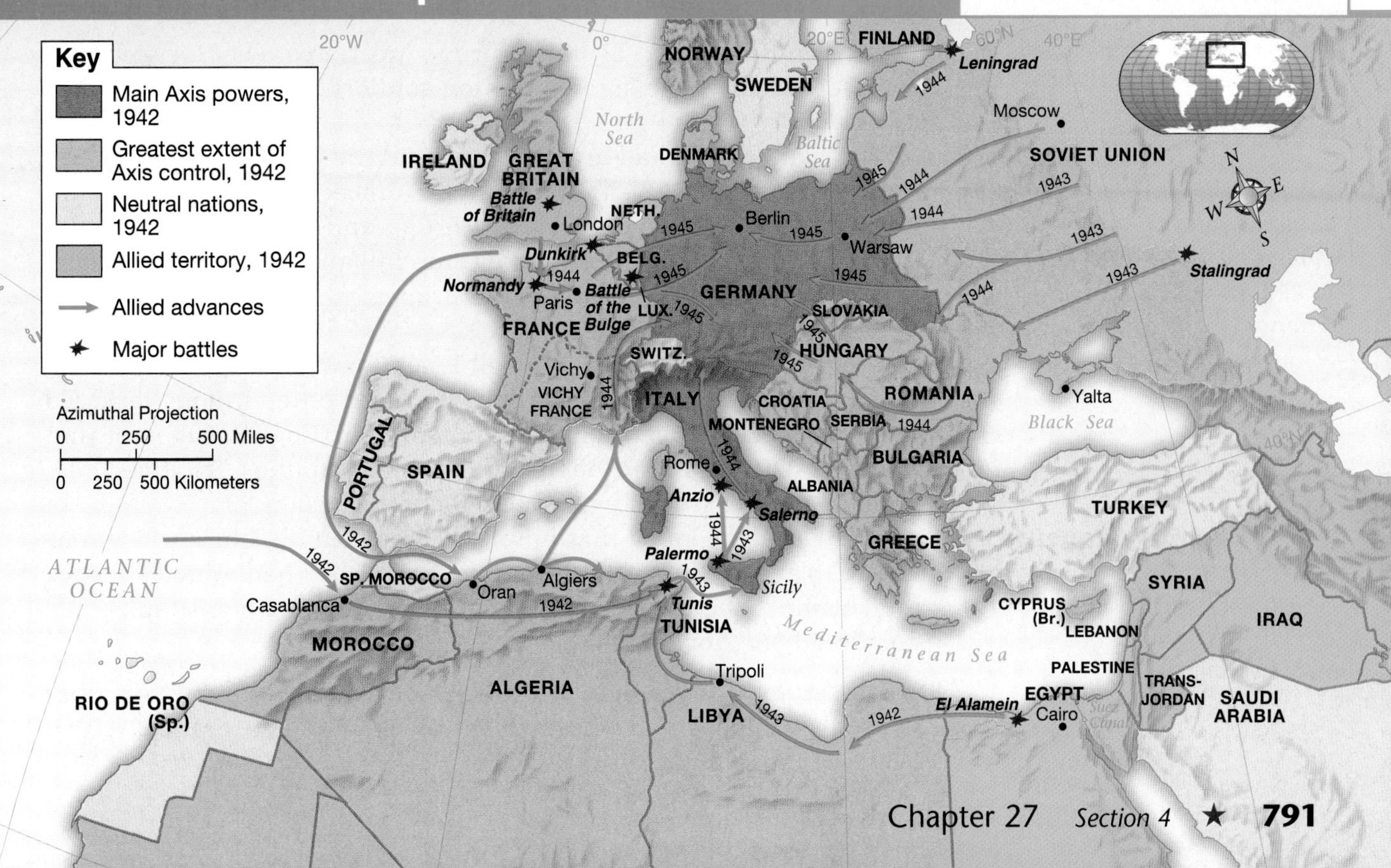

naval battle in history in which the ships never engaged one other directly. All the damage was done by airplanes from the carriers.

One month later, the United States Navy won a stunning victory at the Battle of Midway. American planes sank four Japanese aircraft carriers. The battle severely hampered the Japanese offensive. It also kept Japan from attacking Hawaii again.

Victories in North Africa Allied forces began to push back the Germans in North Africa. In October 1942, the British won an important victory at El Alamein in Egypt. German forces under General Erwin Rommel were driven west into Tunisia.

Meanwhile, American troops under the command of Generals Dwight D. Eisenhower, Omar Bradley, and George S. Patton landed in Morocco and Algeria. They then pushed east. Allied armies trapped Rommel's forces in Tunisia. In May 1943, his army had to surrender.

An American Profile

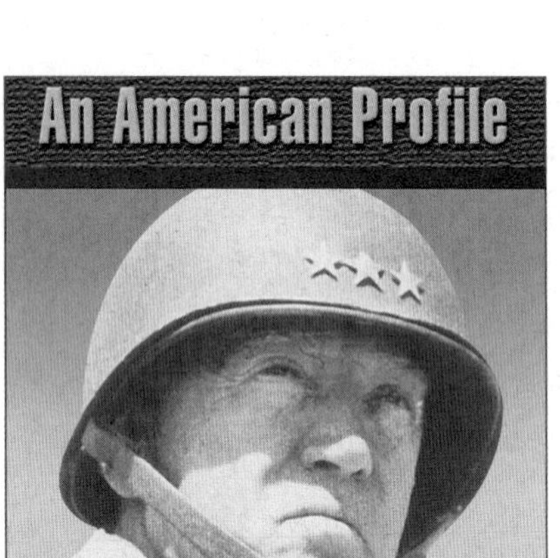

George S. Patton 1885–1945

A brilliant general, George Patton was known as "Old Blood and Guts" for his toughness and drive. "We'll win this war," he predicted, "by showing the Germans we've got more guts than they have." He led American tanks to victory after victory in North Africa.

Patton pushed his troops hard, but he was always ready to get down in the mud and blood with them. Once, marching alongside his men, he saw a soldier with a horribly wounded leg. Patton gave the soldier a dose of painkiller and stayed with the dying man until an ambulance arrived.

Why do you think Patton was willing to walk alongside his troops?

Success in Europe From bases in North Africa, the Allies organized the invasion of Italy. They used paratroopers and soldiers brought by sea to capture Sicily. In early September 1943, the Allies crossed from Sicily to the mainland of Italy.

By then, Mussolini had been overthrown. The Germans, however, still occupied much of Italy. In a series of bloody battles, the Allies slowly fought their way up the peninsula. On June 4, 1944, Allied troops marched into Rome. It was the first European capital to be freed from Nazi control.

The Soviet army repelled the Germans from Leningrad in 1943. At Stalingrad, after months of fierce house-to-house fighting, Soviet soldiers forced the German army to surrender. Slowly, the Soviet army pushed the Germans westward through Eastern Europe.

Opening a Second Front

Fighting in Russia and Eastern Europe was fierce. The Soviet Union would eventually lose some 9 million soldiers, more than any other country.

For years, Stalin had urged Britain and the United States to send armies across the English Channel into France. Such an attack would create a second front in Western Europe and ease pressure in the East. However, not until 1944 were Churchill and Roosevelt prepared to attempt an invasion of Western Europe.

Years of planning went into Operation Overlord, the code name for the invasion of Europe. General Eisenhower was appointed commander of Allied forces in Europe. He faced an enormous task. He had to organize a huge army, ferry it across the English Channel, and provide it with ammunition, food, and other supplies. By June 1944, almost 3 million troops were ready for the invasion.

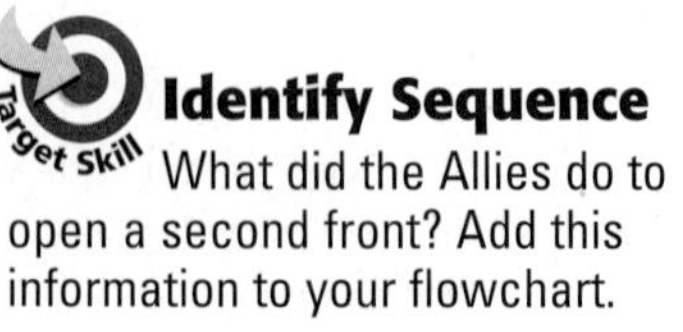

Identify Sequence What did the Allies do to open a second front? Add this information to your flowchart.

The Germans knew that an attack was coming, but not when or where. To guard against the Allied invasion, they had mined beaches and strung barbed wire. Machine guns and concrete antitank walls stood ready to stop an advance.

D-Day Invasion On June 6, 1944—D-Day, as it was known—a fleet of 4,000 Allied ships carried the invasion force to France. Allied

The Allies Advance

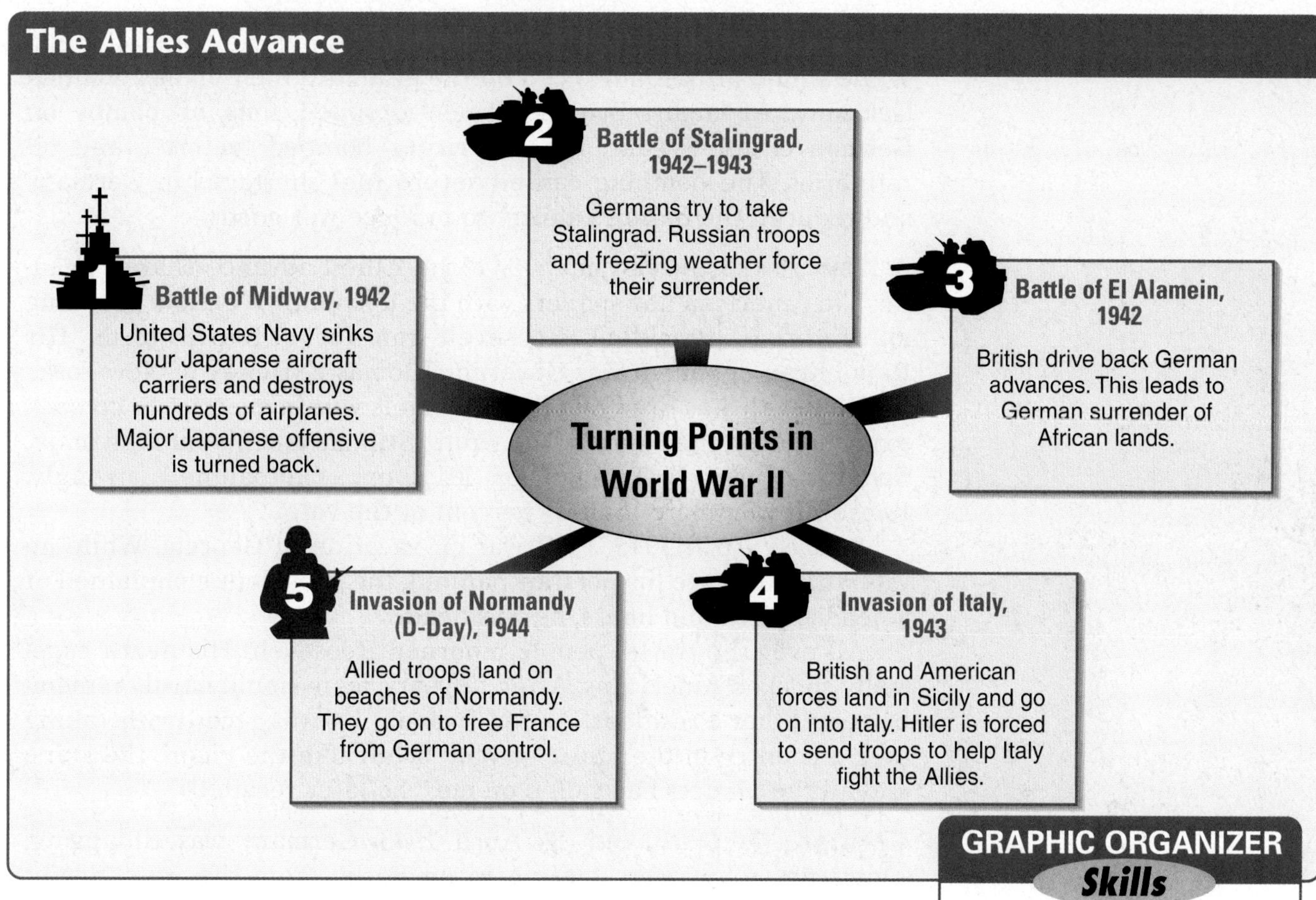

GRAPHIC ORGANIZER *Skills*

Several key victories helped the Allies turn the tide against the Axis powers.

1. **Comprehension** Which of the military actions described above was a turning point in the Pacific war?
2. **Critical Thinking Sequencing** Describe how one of the victories was a necessary first step to another.

troops scrambled ashore at Normandy. One American soldier who landed in the first wave recalled:

> “It all seemed unreal, a sort of dreaming while awake, men were screaming and dying all around me. . . . I honestly could have walked the full length of the beach without touching the ground, they were that thickly strewn about.”
>
> —Melvin B. Farrell, *War Memories*

Despite intense German gunfire and heavy losses, Allied forces pushed on. Every day, more soldiers landed to reinforce the advance.

On August 25, 1944, the Allies entered Paris. After four years under Nazi rule, the Parisians greeted their liberators with joy. Within a month, all of France was free.

Victory in Europe

By September, the Allies were moving east toward Germany. However, a shortage of truck fuel slowed the advance.

Advancing Toward Germany On December 16, 1944, German forces began a fierce counterattack. They pushed the Allies back, creating a bulge in the front lines. During the **Battle of the Bulge,** as it was later called, Audie Murphy emerged as the most honored American hero of the war. At one point, Murphy climbed aboard a burning tank. Alone and wounded, he used the tank's machine gun to hold off enemy troops on three sides.

The Battle of the Bulge slowed the Allies but did not stop them. While Allied armies advanced on the ground, Allied planes bombed Germany. At night, British airmen dropped tons of bombs on German cities. By day, the Americans bombed factories and oil refineries. The bombing caused severe fuel shortages in Germany and reduced the nation's ability to produce war goods.

A New President By mid-1944, the Allied advance shared headlines in American newspapers with the upcoming election. Breaking all tradition, President Roosevelt ran for a fourth term. His Republican opponent was Governor Thomas E. Dewey of New York.

Roosevelt was tired and ill. "All that is within me cries to go back to my home on the Hudson," he wrote. Still, he and his running mate, Senator Harry S Truman of Missouri, campaigned strongly. Roosevelt won more than 54 percent of the vote.

In early April 1945, FDR was on vacation in Georgia. While he was sitting to have his portrait painted, the President complained of a headache. Within hours, he was dead.

All over the world, people mourned Roosevelt. His death especially shocked Americans. After 12 years, many could hardly remember any other President. As for Truman, he was faced with taking over a country in the midst of war. "I felt like the moon, the stars, and all the planets had fallen on me," he later recalled.

Germany Is Defeated By April 1945, Germany was collapsing. American troops were closing in on Berlin from the west. Soviet troops were advancing from the east. On April 25, American and Soviet troops met at Torgau, 60 miles south of Berlin.

As Allied air raids pounded Berlin, Hitler hid in his underground bunker. Unwilling to accept defeat, he committed suicide. One week later, on May 7, 1945, Germany surrendered to the Allies. On May 8, the Allies celebrated the long-awaited V-E Day—Victory in Europe.

★ ★ ★ Section 4 Assessment ★ ★ ★

Recall

1. **Identify** Explain the significance of **(a)** Douglas MacArthur, **(b)** Battle of Midway, **(c)** Dwight D. Eisenhower, **(d)** Operation Overlord, **(e)** D-Day, **(f)** Battle of the Bulge, **(g)** Audie Murphy, **(h)** Harry S Truman.

Comprehension

2. Why did the war look bleak for the Allies in 1942?
3. How did the Allies open a second front in Europe?
4. Describe the final stage of the war in Europe.

Critical Thinking and Writing

5. **Exploring the Main Idea** Review the Main Idea statement at the beginning of this section. Then, choose two events described in this section. For each, write a headline and opening paragraph that might have appeared in an American newspaper.
6. **Making Decisions** If you had been an adviser to Franklin Roosevelt in 1944, would you have encouraged him to run for a fourth term in spite of ill health? Write a note to FDR explaining your reasons.

Activity

Go Online
PHSchool.com

Connecting to Today

Use the Internet to read other first-person accounts of the invasion of France. Then, write an essay about why you think Americans are still fascinated by D-Day. For help in completing the activity, visit PHSchool.com, **Web Code mfd-2702.**

Evaluating the Validity of Internet Sources

Today, there are dozens of Internet sites devoted to World War II, as well as to other historical topics. As a student of history, it is important to evaluate the different Web sites to determine how valid the information is. The page below is from a Web site devoted to the D-Day invasion of France.

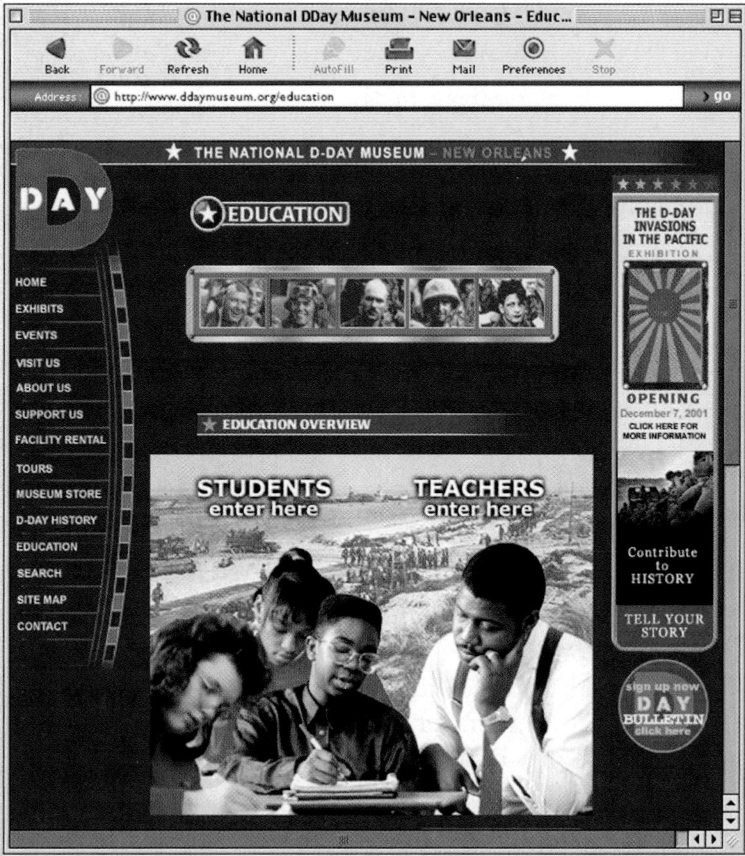

Source: The National D-Day Museum, 945 Magazine Street, New Orleans, LA

Learn the Skill *To learn how to evaluate Internet sources, use the following steps:*

1. **Determine the Web site's purpose.** Does the Web site provide information? Is it trying to sell something or to promote a particular point of view?
2. **Examine the information.** Does the site include visuals? Does it include firsthand accounts and other primary source materials?
3. **Compare the information to what you already know.** Does the information agree with what you have read in a textbook or other reliable print source? What other information is provided?
4. **Evaluate the source.** Is the source an established organization? Can you tell who provided the information?

Practice the Skill *Use the information given above to answer the following questions:*

1. What seems to be the purpose of this Web site?
2. **(a)** What kinds of information can you access from this page? **(b)** What other features and links does it include?
3. What additional information does this Web site provide to the facts given in your textbook?
4. **(a)** Who is the provider for this site? **(b)** If you were writing a paper about D-Day, do you think you could use the information provided on this Web site? Why or why not?

Apply the Skill *See the Chapter Review and Assessment.*

5 The End of the War

Prepare to Read

Objectives

In this section, you will
- Describe how American forces advanced in the Pacific.
- Explain why Japan finally surrendered.
- Discuss what made World War II the deadliest war in history.

Key Terms

island hopping
Navajo code-talkers
kamikaze
Potsdam Declaration
Bataan Death March
Holocaust
Nuremberg Trials

Target Reading Skill

Main Idea As you read, prepare an outline of this section. Use roman numerals to indicate the major headings, capital letters for the subheadings, and numbers for the supporting details.

I. War in the Pacific
   A. U.S. goals
      1.
      2.
   B. Island hopping
      1.
      2.
   C.
II. The Surrender of Japan
   A.
   B.

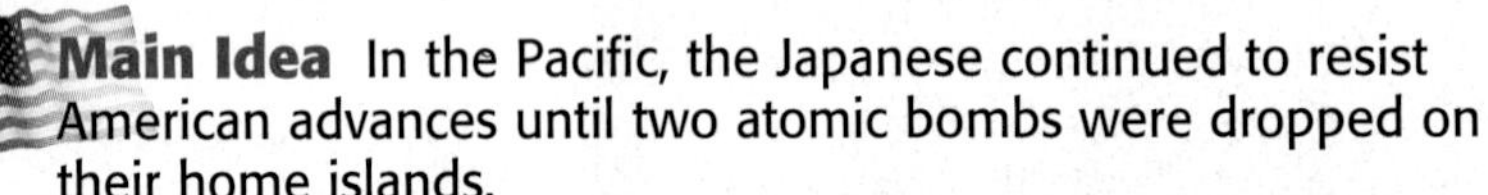

Main Idea In the Pacific, the Japanese continued to resist American advances until two atomic bombs were dropped on their home islands.

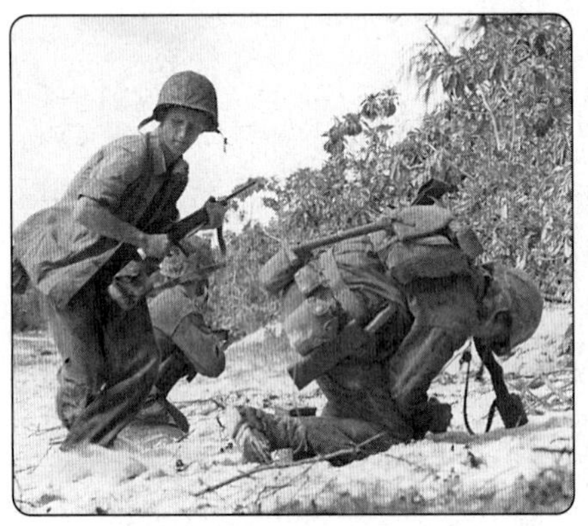

American troops at Saipan

Setting the Scene As Allied armies swept into Europe, a battle raged on the Pacific island of Saipan (si PAN). An American force of nearly 100,000 pounded a Japanese garrison of 32,000 troops. By the end, the Americans would suffer some 14,000 casualties. The Japanese would lose almost every soldier on Saipan.

Although greatly outnumbered, the Japanese fought to the bitter end. Many charged to their deaths shouting "*banzai*" ("ten thousand years") and carrying nothing but spears. Others jumped from cliffs to avoid capture. One reporter wondered, "Do the suicides . . . mean that the whole Japanese race will choose death before surrender?"

The surrender of Germany left only Japan to defeat. Still, as the battle of Saipan showed, the price of final victory could be immense.

War in the Pacific

While the war raged in Europe, the Allies kept up pressure on Japan. The United States had two main goals in the Pacific war: to regain the Philippines and to invade Japan.

Island Hopping To gain control of the Pacific Ocean, American forces used a strategy of capturing some Japanese-held islands and going around others. In this **island-hopping** campaign, each island that was won became another steppingstone to Japan.

A deadly routine developed. First, American ships shelled an island. Next, troops waded ashore under heavy gunfire. Then, in hand-to-hand fighting, Americans overcame fierce Japanese resistance.

Navajo soldiers made a key contribution to American strategy in the Pacific. Using their own language, they radioed vital messages from island to island. The Japanese intercepted the messages but were unable to understand these **Navajo code-talkers.**

In October 1944, American forces under General MacArthur finally returned to the Philippines. In hard-fought battles, the Americans then captured the islands of Iwo Jima (EE woh JEE muh) and Okinawa (oh kuh NAH wuh) from the Japanese.

Japanese leaders stressed an ancient code known as *Bushido,* or the Way of the Warrior. It emphasized loyalty, honor, and sacrifice. To surrender was to "lose face" or be dishonored. In suicide missions, **kamikaze** (kah muh KAH zee) pilots loaded old planes with bombs and then deliberately crashed them into Allied ships.

Attacking the Home Islands By April 1945, American forces were close enough to launch attacks against the Japanese home islands. American bombers pounded factories and cities. American warships bombarded the coast and sank ships. The Japanese people suffered terribly. Yet, their leaders promised a glorious victory.

United States military leaders made plans to invade Japan in the autumn. They warned that the invasion might cost between 150,000 and 250,000 American casualties.

The Surrender of Japan

Truman, Churchill, and Stalin met at Potsdam, Germany, in July 1945. While there, Truman received word that American scientists had successfully tested a secret new weapon, the atomic bomb. A single bomb was powerful enough to destroy an entire city. Some scientists believed that it was too dangerous to use.

From Potsdam, the Allied leaders sent a message warning Japan to surrender or face "prompt and utter destruction." Japanese

GEOGRAPHY *Skills*

After the Battle of Midway, the United States took the offensive against the Japanese Empire.

1. **Location** On the map, locate **(a)** Pearl Harbor, **(b)** Midway Island, **(c)** Philippine Islands, **(d)** Iwo Jima, **(e)** Okinawa, **(f)** Hiroshima.
2. **Movement** Which battle did the United States have to win before moving against Iwo Jima and Okinawa?
3. **Critical Thinking Drawing Conclusions** Based on this map, why do you think aircraft carriers were vital to American strategy in the Pacific?

World War II in the Pacific

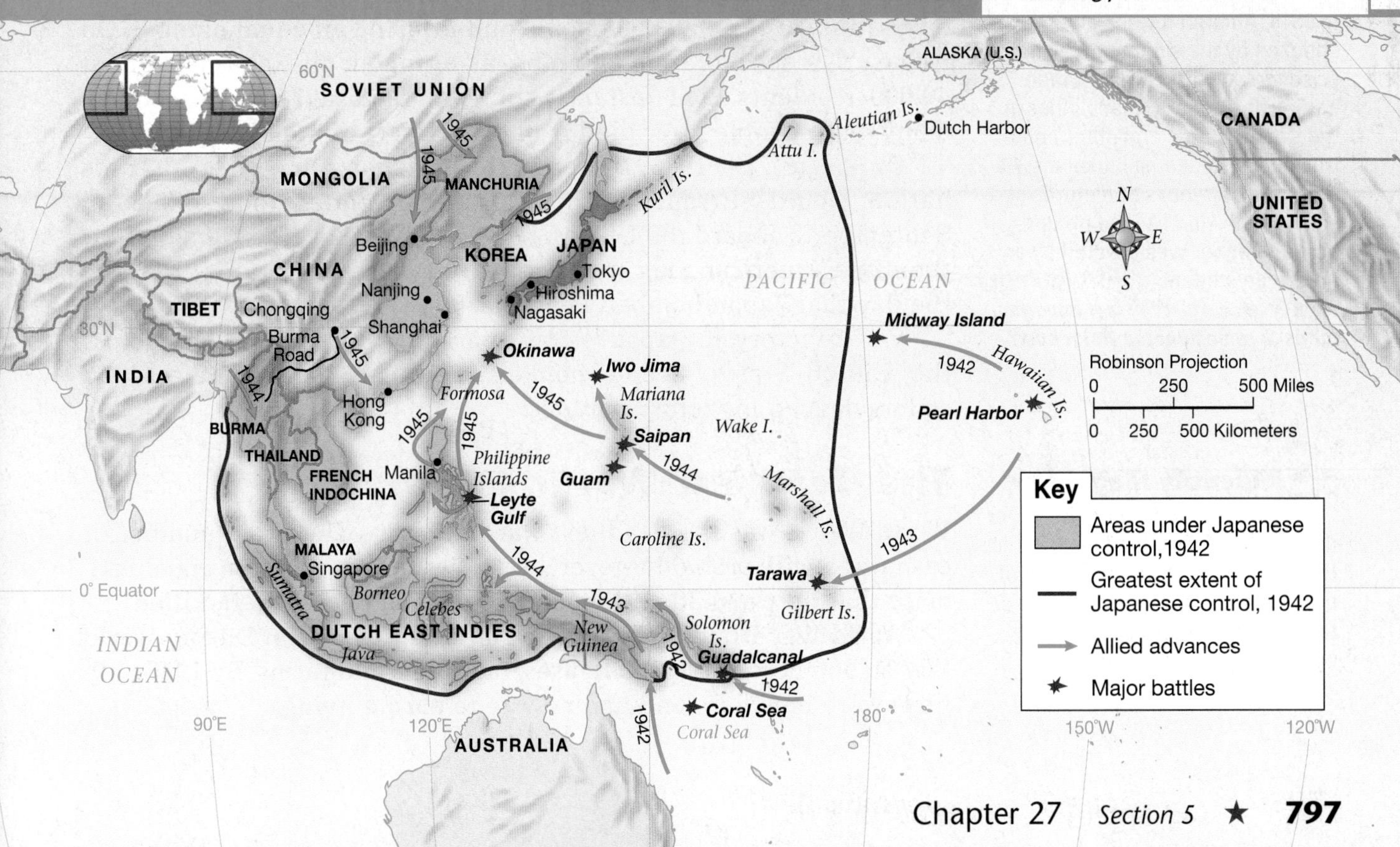

LINKING PAST AND PRESENT

▲ **Past**

▲ **Present**

Viewing History

Americans Remember the Holocaust

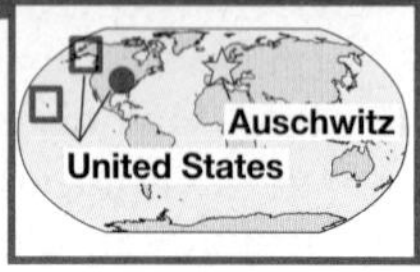

In 1945, American troops were shocked by the sight of Jewish prisoners in Nazi concentration camps (left). Today, many cities in the United States and other countries have Holocaust museums. At right, a visitor looks at pictures of some of the victims. The remembrance banner was created by an American student. **Linking Past and Present** ***Why is it important for us to remember the Holocaust?***

leaders did not know about the destructive power of the atomic bomb. They ignored the **Potsdam Declaration.**

On August 6, 1945, the American bomber *Enola Gay* dropped an atomic bomb on Hiroshima, Japan. The blast destroyed most of the city, killing at least 70,000 people and injuring an equal number. On August 9, a second atomic bomb was dropped, on Nagasaki. About 40,000 residents died instantly. In both Nagasaki and Hiroshima, many more people later died from the effects of atomic radiation.

On August 14, 1945, the emperor of Japan announced that his nation would surrender. The formal surrender took place on September 2 aboard the USS *Missouri* in Tokyo Bay. The warship flew the same American flag that had waved over Washington, D.C., on the day that Japan bombed Pearl Harbor.

V-J ("Victory in Japan") Day sparked wild celebrations across the United States. People honked their car horns. Soldiers and sailors danced in victory parades.

Target Skill **Identify Main Ideas** Read the paragraphs under the heading "The Deadliest War in History." Express the main idea of these paragraphs in a sentence or two. Add this information to your outline.

The Deadliest War in History

World War II was the deadliest war in history. The exact number of casualties will probably never be known. However, historians estimate that between 30 million and 60 million people were killed.

World War I had been fought mainly in trenches. During World War II, bombers destroyed houses, factories, and farms. By 1945, millions were homeless and had no way to earn a living.

After the war, Americans heard horrifying stories of the brutal mistreatment of prisoners of war. When the Japanese captured the Philippines in 1942, they forced about 75,000 American and Filipino prisoners to march 65 miles with little food or water. About 10,000 prisoners died or were killed during the **Bataan Death March.**

The Holocaust In the last months of the European war, Allied forces uncovered other horrors. The Allies had heard about Nazi death camps. As they advanced into Germany and Eastern Europe, they discovered the full extent of the **Holocaust,** the slaughter of Europe's Jews by the Nazis. During the war, the Nazis imprisoned Jews from Germany and the nations they conquered. More than 6 million Jews were tortured and murdered.

When Allied troops reached the death camps, they saw the gas chambers the Nazis had used to murder hundreds of thousands. The battle-hardened veterans wept at the sight of the dead and dying. After touring one death camp, General Omar Bradley wrote:

> "The smell of death overwhelmed us even before we passed through. . . . More than 3,200 naked, emaciated bodies had been flung into shallow graves."
>
> —Omar N. Bradley, *A General's Life*

Nearly 6 million Poles, Slavs, and Gypsies were also victims of the death camps. Nazis killed many prisoners of war, as well as people they considered unfit because of physical or mental disabilities.

War Crimes Trials As the full truth of the Holocaust was revealed, the Allies decided to put Nazi leaders on trial. In 1945 and 1946, they conducted war crimes trials in Nuremberg, Germany. As a result of the **Nuremberg Trials,** 12 Nazi leaders were sentenced to death. Thousands of other Nazis were imprisoned. The Allies also tried and executed Japanese leaders accused of war crimes.

Section 5 Assessment

Recall

1. **Identify** Explain the significance of **(a)** Navajo code-talkers, **(b)** Potsdam Declaration, **(c)** Bataan Death March, **(d)** Holocaust, **(e)** Nuremberg Trials.
2. **Define** **(a)** island hopping, **(b)** kamikaze.

Comprehension

3. What strategy did the United States follow in the Pacific?
4. How did the United States force Japan to surrender?
5. Why was World War II more deadly than World War I?

Critical Thinking and Writing

6. **Exploring the Main Idea** Review the Main Idea statement at the beginning of this section. Then, write the opening words of a speech President Truman might have given to explain why he decided to use the atomic bomb.
7. **Drawing Inferences** The Allies did not try enemy leaders as war criminals after World War I. Write a paragraph explaining why you think they conducted such trials after World War II and whether you agree with this decision.

Activity

Preparing a Report
Use the Internet to find out about the Manhattan Project, the secret government project to develop the atomic bomb. Write a summary of its goals and progress. For help in completing the activity, visit PHSchool.com, **Web Code mfd-2703.**

CHAPTER
27 Review and Assessment

Chapter Summary

Section 1
During the 1920s and 1930s, dictatorships and authoritarian governments arose in the Soviet Union, Italy, Germany, and Japan. The United States adopted a policy of isolationism during this period.

Section 2
Japanese and German aggression led to the outbreak of World War II. The United States began to prepare for war during the late 1930s. Japan's attack on Pearl Harbor sparked the U.S. entry into the war in 1941.

Section 3
The United States quickly mobilized after the outbreak of war. Women and African Americans played a key role in the war effort, but other groups faced wartime restrictions or discrimination.

Section 4
The Allies suffered serious setbacks in the early days of the war, but the tide began to turn in 1942. The Allied invasion of France in June 1944 led to Germany's eventual surrender in May 1945.

Section 5
The Pacific war continued after the end of hostilities in Europe, but Japan finally surrendered after the United States dropped atomic bombs on two of its cities. World War II was the deadliest war in history.

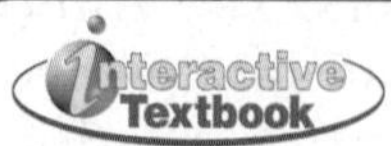

For additional review and enrichment activities, see the interactive version of *The American Nation,* available on the Web and on CD-ROM.

Chapter Self-Test For practice test questions for Chapter 27, visit PHSchool.com, **Web Code mfa-2704.**

Building Vocabulary

Review the chapter vocabulary words listed below. Then, use the words and their definitions to create a matching quiz. Exchange quizzes with another student. Check each other's answers when you are finished.

1. **totalitarian state**
2. **aggression**
3. **concentration camp**
4. **appeasement**
5. **blitzkrieg**
6. **rationing**
7. **victory garden**
8. **compensation**
9. **island hopping**
10. **kamikaze**

Reviewing Key Facts

11. What are the main features of Fascism? (Section 1)
12. What were the goals of the Atlantic Charter? (Section 2)
13. What role did women play in the American war effort? (Section 3)
14. Why was D-Day important? (Section 4)
15. Describe the terrible costs of World War II. (Section 5)

Critical Thinking and Writing

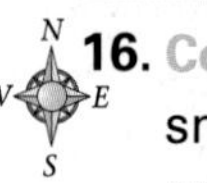

16. **Connecting to Geography: Place** Japan was a small island nation with limited natural resources. Identify two ways these characteristics of place affected World War II.
17. **Evaluating Information** What qualities do you think Dwight D. Eisenhower needed to succeed as commander of the Allied forces in Europe?
18. **Linking Past and Present** List three ways in which the world today might be different if the Axis powers had won World War II.

Skills Assessment

Analyzing Primary Sources

A reporter filed this account after flying with the team that dropped the atomic bomb on Nagasaki:

> "Observers in the tail of our ship saw a giant ball of fire rise as though from the bowels of the earth, belching forth enormous white smoke rings. Next they saw a giant pillar of purple fire, ten thousand feet high, shooting skyward with enormous speed. . . . It was a living thing, a new species of being, born right before our incredulous eyes."
>
> —William L. Laurence, *New York Times,* September 9, 1945

19. To what does Laurence compare the bombing?
- **A.** The tail of the airplane.
- **B.** The observers who were watching the explosion.
- **C.** A new species of being.
- **D.** The bowels of the earth.

20. Which one of the following words best describes Laurence's reaction to the bombing?
- **A.** saddened
- **B.** amazed
- **C.** angered
- **D.** completely neutral

Applying Your Skills

Evaluating the Validity of Internet Sources

The source information below might be found on an Internet site. Read the words and answer the questions that follow.

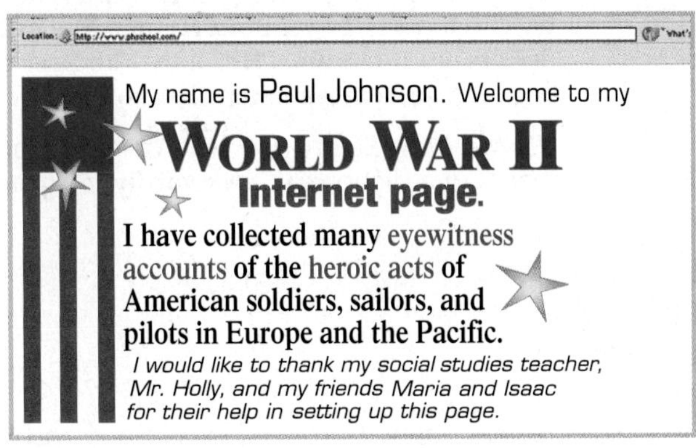
My name is Paul Johnson. Welcome to my

WORLD WAR II Internet page.

I have collected many eyewitness accounts of the heroic acts of American soldiers, sailors, and pilots in Europe and the Pacific.

I would like to thank my social studies teacher, Mr. Holly, and my friends Maria and Isaac for their help in setting up this page.

21. Based on the above statements alone, would you consider this Web site a valid source of information?
- **A.** Yes, because it is on the Internet.
- **B.** No, because it is not a government Web site.
- **C.** No, because it was created by a student.
- **D.** No, because Johnson does not identify where he found the stories.

22. What information would you need before using in a report any of the eyewitness stories found on this Web site?

Activities

Connecting With . . .

Culture

Interviewing Find somebody in your family or community who grew up during World War II. Prepare a series of 5–10 questions, and interview that person about memories of life on the home front, people whom they knew in the service, or the victory celebrations. Record the interview in writing or on tape, and present it to the class. (If you cannot find an appropriate person, use your questions to prepare a mock interview with a partner.)

Connecting to Today

Writing a Report Use the Internet to find out about the planning and building of the National World War II Memorial in the early 2000s. Write a report describing how the campaign started and how it proceeded. For help in starting this activity, visit PHSchool.com, **Web Code mfd-2705**.

Researching

Making a Map Use the Internet to find out more about one land or sea battle during World War II. Then, use this information to prepare a battle map that shows the locations and movements of opposing forces. For help in starting this activity, visit PHSchool.com, **Web Code mfd-2706**.

The Human Comedy

William Saroyan

Introduction **Published in 1943, *The Human Comedy* was one of the first novels to look at the American home front during World War II. The hero is 14-year-old Homer Macauley, who works after school delivering telegrams. Here, for the first time, he must bring a message telling a mother that her son has been killed in battle.**

Vocabulary Before you read the selection, find the meaning of these words in a dictionary: **awkwardly, disgrace.**

William Saroyan

Homer knew that Mrs. Rosa Sandoval was shocked to see him. Her first word was the first word of surprise. She said "Oh," as if instead of a messenger she had thought of opening the door to someone she had known a long time and would be pleased to sit down with. Before she spoke again she studied Homer's eyes and Homer knew that she knew the message was not a welcome one.

"You have a telegram?" she said.

It wasn't Homer's fault. His work was to deliver telegrams. Even so, it seemed to him that he was part of the whole mistake. He felt awkward and almost as if he *alone* were responsible for what had happened. At the same time he wanted to come right out and say, "I'm only a messenger, Mrs. Sandoval. I'm very sorry I must bring you a telegram like this, but it is only because it is my work to do so."

"Who is it for?" the Mexican woman said.

"Mrs. Rosa Sandoval, 1129 G Street," Homer said. He extended the telegram to the Mexican woman, but she would not touch it.

"Are you Mrs. Sandoval?" Homer said.

"Please," the woman said. "Please come in. I cannot read English. I am Mexican. I read only *La Prensa* which comes from Mexico City." She paused a moment and looked at the boy standing awkwardly as near the door as he could be and still be inside the house.

"Please," she said, "what does the telegram say?"

"Mrs. Sandoval," the messenger said, "the telegram says—"

But now the woman interrupted him. "But you must open the telegram and *read* it to me," she said. "You have not opened it."

"Yes ma'am," Homer said as if he were speaking to a school teacher who had just corrected him.

He opened the telegram with nervous fingers. The Mexican woman stooped to pick up the torn envelope, and tried to smooth it out. As she did so she said, "Who sent the telegram—my son Juan Domingo?

"No ma'am," Homer said. "The telegram is from the War Department."

"War Department?" the Mexican woman said.

"Mrs. Sandoval," Homer said swiftly, "your son is dead. Maybe it's a mistake. Everybody makes a mistake, Mrs. Sandoval. Maybe it wasn't your son. Maybe it was somebody else. The telegram *says* it was Juan Domingo. But maybe the telegram is wrong."

The Mexican woman pretended not to hear.

"Oh, do not be afraid, " she said. "Come inside. Come inside. I will bring you candy." She took the boy's arm and brought him to the table at the center of the room and there she made him sit.

"All boys like candy," she said. "I will bring you candy." She went into another room and soon returned with an old chocolate candy box. She opened the box at the table and in it Homer saw a strange kind of candy.

"Here," she said. "Eat this candy. All boys like candy."

Homer took a piece of the candy from the box, put it into his mouth, and tried to chew.

"You would not bring me a bad telegram," she said. "You are a good boy—like my little Juanito when he was a little boy. Eat another piece." And she made the messenger take another piece of the candy.

Homer sat chewing the dry candy while the Mexican woman talked. "It is our own candy," she said "from cactus. I make it for my Juanito when he come home, but *you* eat it. You are my boy too."

Now suddenly she began to sob, holding herself in as if weeping were a disgrace. Homer wanted to get up and run but he knew he would stay. He even thought he might stay the rest of his life. He just didn't know what else to do to try to make the woman less unhappy, and if she had *asked* him to take the place of her son, he would not have been able to refuse, because he would not have known how.

Mother and child of an American soldier

Analyzing Literature

1. What is Mrs. Sandoval's first reaction to finding out that she has received a telegram?
   - **A** Anger
   - **B** Relief
   - **C** Fear
   - **D** Sorrow

2. Why does Homer tell Mrs. Sandoval the telegram may be a mistake?
   - **A** He knows Juan Domingo is still alive.
   - **B** He wants to make Mrs. Sandoval feel better.
   - **C** He hopes to get a piece of candy.
   - **D** He does not care about Mrs. Sandoval's feelings.

3. **Critical Thinking and Writing** **Drawing Inferences** Write a paragraph explaining how you would have felt about working as a telegraph messenger during World War II.

TEST PREPARATION

1 Which of the following New Deal programs is correctly matched with one of its main goals?

A TVA: prevent another depression

B WPA: reduce unemployment

C CCC: provide relief for farmers

D FDIC: promote industrial recovery

Use the quotation and your knowledge of social studies to answer the following question.

> **Ernie Pyle, *Brave Men* (adapted)**
>
> "On the beach lay, expended, sufficient men and mechanism for a small war. They were gone forever now. And yet we could afford it . . . because we were on, we had our toehold, and behind us there were enormous replacements for this wreckage on the beach."

2 In the above passage, Pyle is describing the aftermath of what event?

A Bombing of Pearl Harbor

B Battle of Midway

C D-Day

D Bombing of Hiroshima

3 What was a chief goal of the quota system introduced in the 1920s?

A To end immigration

B To control sources of immigration

C To prevent labor unions from going on strike

D To limit union membership

4 Which of the following was not an economic effect of World War II?

A Increased production of consumer goods

B Rationing of gasoline and rubber

C Increase in taxes

D End of the Great Depression

Use the map and your knowledge of social studies to answer the following question.

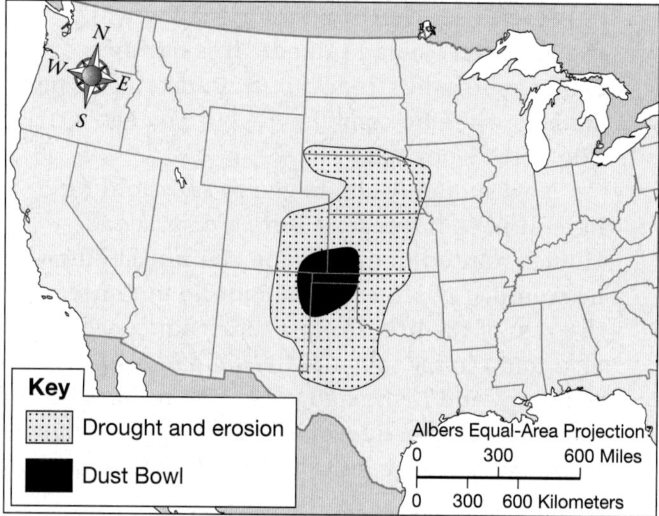

5 Which statement is best supported by this map?

A The most severe dust storms hit the state of Oklahoma.

B Drought and dust storms had no impact on California.

C Soil erosion was a severe problem in Kansas and Nebraska.

D Ten states were hit by drought and erosion during the depression.

6 Which of the following was not an effect of mass production of automobiles?

A It made automobiles less expensive to buy.

B It helped create a new mass culture.

C It stimulated the growth of other industries.

D It contributed to a decline in the rural population.

Use the graph <u>and</u> your knowledge of social studies to answer the following question.

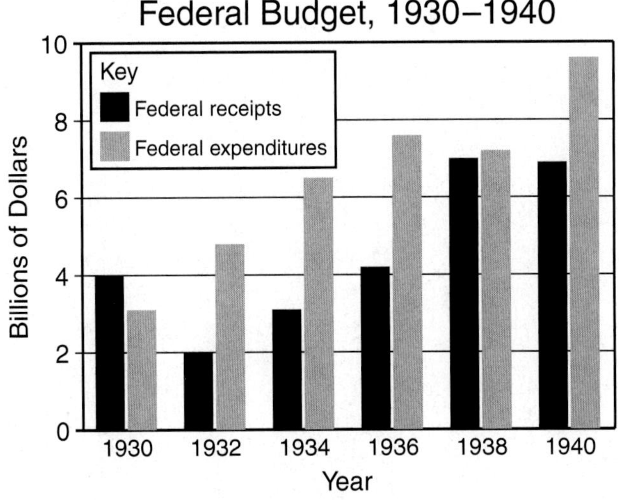

7 What development is best illustrated by this graph?

A Deficit spending as a result of the New Deal

B Economic impact of the stock market crash

C Government regulation of the economy under the New Deal

D Effects of World War II on the federal budget

8 "Writers of the 1920s were often critical of traditional American values." Which of the following facts best supports this generalization?

A Sinclair Lewis poked fun at small-town life.

B Langston Hughes expressed pride in his African heritage.

C F. Scott Fitzgerald included flappers as characters in many of his novels.

D Ernest Hemingway's simple, powerful writing style influenced a new generation of writers.

9 In which of the following pairs was the first event a direct cause of the second?

A Japan bombs Pearl Harbor; World War II begins

B France and Britain declare war on Germany; Hitler invades Poland

C Atlantic Charter is signed; United States sends aid to Britain

D Holocaust is revealed; Nuremberg Trials are held

Writing Practice

10 Compare and contrast the economic views and policies of Calvin Coolidge, Herbert Hoover, and Franklin Roosevelt.

11 "During World War II, Americans put aside their differences to work together for a common goal." Do you agree with this statement, disagree with this statement, or partly agree with this statement? Give reasons to support your answer.

Unit 9 The Bold Experiment Continues

A World Drawn Closer
In ***The World,*** Diana Ong shows the many people of the United States as part of a world that has grown increasingly closer together.

“We have a place, all of us, in a long story. . . . It is the American story; a story of flawed and fallible people, united across the generations by grand and enduring ideals.”
—President George W. Bush (2001)

CHAPTER 28

The Cold War Era

1945–1991

Cheering the Berlin Airlift

Rocketing into orbit

AMERICAN EVENTS

1948
United States planes break a Soviet blockade by bringing desperately needed food, fuel, and supplies to the people of Berlin.

1950
The Korean War begins.

1962
Friendship 7, with astronaut John Glenn aboard, blasts off for orbit around Earth.

Presidential Terms

Harry S Truman 1945–1953

Dwight D. Eisenhower 1953–1961

John F. Kennedy 1961–1963

Lyndon B. Johnson 1963–1969

1944 — 1956 — 1968

WORLD EVENTS

▲ **1946**
The Philippines gains its independence from the United States.

▲ **1959**
Fidel Castro comes to power in Cuba.

The Global Cold War

For more than 40 years, a bitterly contested Cold War divided the world into opposing camps.

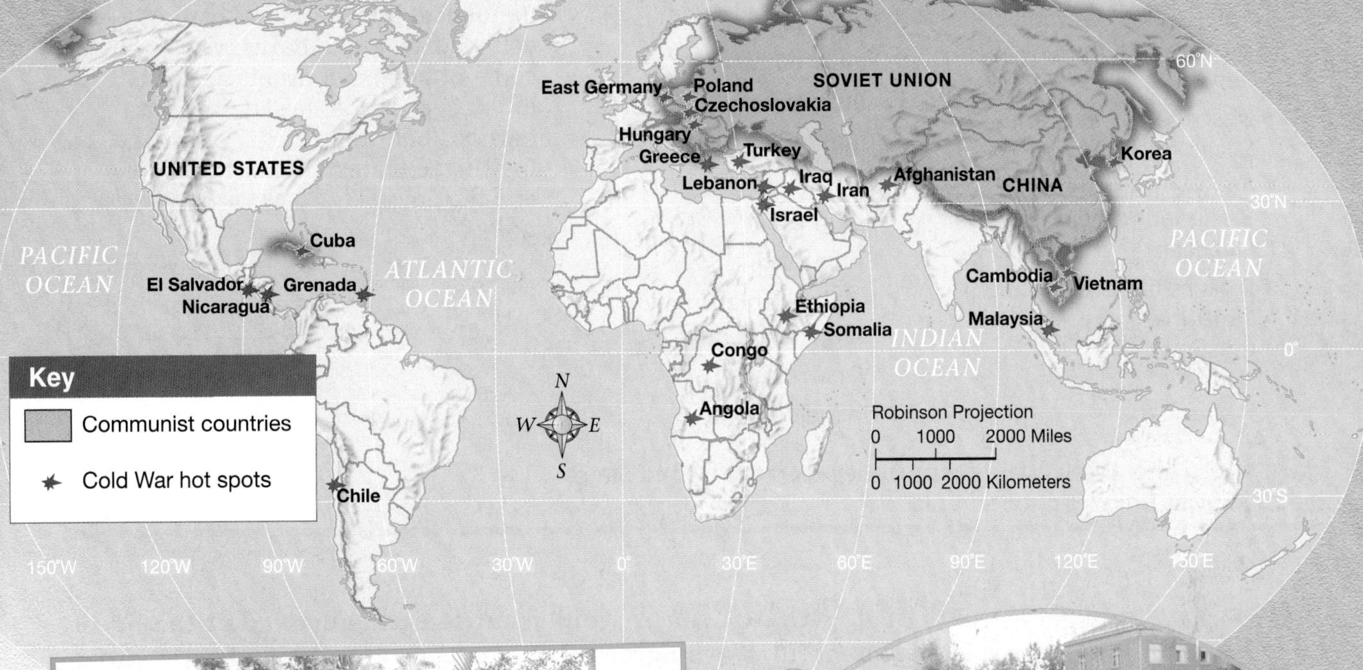

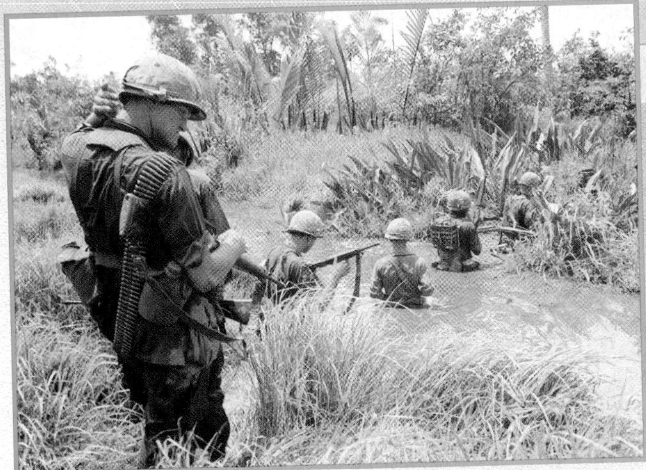
On patrol in Vietnam's Mekong Delta

Russian children and a toppled statue of one-time communist leader Vladimir Lenin

1968
More than a half million American troops are fighting in Vietnam.

1974
The United States removes the last of its combat troops from South Vietnam.

1991
Statues of former communist leaders are toppled as communism falls and the Soviet Union breaks up.

Richard M. Nixon 1969–1974	Gerald R. Ford 1974–1977	Jimmy Carter 1977–1981	Ronald Reagan 1981–1989	George H. W. Bush 1989–1993

1968 • • • **1980** • • • **1992** •

1975 ▲
Communists win control over all of South Vietnam, ending the Vietnam War.

1989 ▲
The Berlin Wall is torn down by the people of Berlin.

1 The Cold War Begins

Prepare to Read

Objectives

In this section, you will
- Explain how the Cold War began.
- Describe U.S. response to Soviet expansion.
- Analyze how the crisis over Berlin led to new Cold War alliances.
- Discuss the events during 1949 that increased Cold War tensions.

Key Terms

Cold War
satellite nation
containment
Truman Doctrine
Marshall Plan
Berlin Airlift
Berlin Wall
North Atlantic Treaty Organization
Warsaw Pact
United Nations

Target Reading Skill

Sequence Copy this flowchart. As you read, fill in the boxes with some of the major events described in this section that raised Cold War tensions between the United States and the Soviet Union.

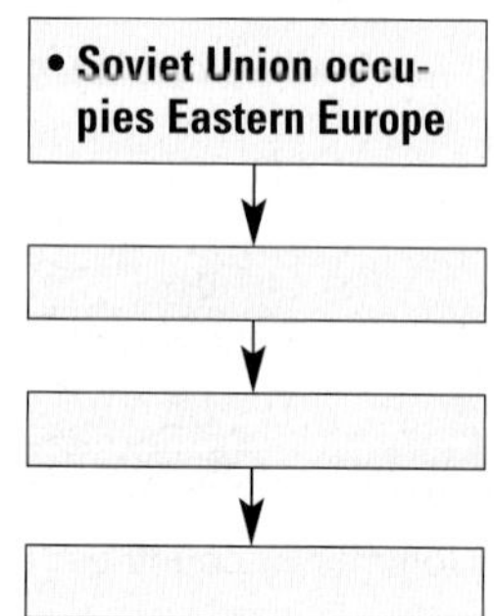

Main Idea After World War II, distrust between the United States and the Soviet Union led to the Cold War.

The Red Army marches

Setting the Scene An important telegram arrived at the State Department in Washington, D.C., in February 1946. It was from George Kennan, a top American diplomat in Moscow. Kennan was worried by the activities of the Soviet Union. At the time, communist forces were attempting to take over nations in Asia, Eastern Europe, and Southern Europe. As he later wrote, the Soviet Union was like a toy car "wound up and headed in a given direction, stopping only when it meets some unanswerable force."

Kennan especially worried about Soviet actions in Eastern Europe. There, Soviet dictator Joseph Stalin was using brutal methods to put communist governments in power. Kennan urged the United States to oppose these Soviet policies.

After World War II, the United States and the Soviet Union plunged into a new kind of war. They did not clash directly in battle. Instead, they competed for power around the world.

This intense rivalry became known as the **Cold War.** It lasted for nearly 50 years. The Cold War pitted the West (the United States and its allies) against the East (the Soviet Union and its allies).

Origins of the Cold War

During World War II, the United States, Britain, and the Soviet Union had worked together. Yet, even before the war ended, tensions surfaced among the Allies.

Growing Distrust The United States and Britain distrusted the Soviet Union. They disliked the communist rejection of religion and private property. They were angered by Soviet efforts to overthrow noncommunist governments. In fact, Soviet leaders boasted that communism would soon destroy free enterprise systems around the world.

The Soviets, in turn, distrusted the Western powers. They feared that the United States, now the world's most powerful nation, would use its military power to attack the Soviet Union. They feared that the United States would try to rebuild Germany in order to challenge the Soviet Union.

Broken Promises Before World War II ended, Soviet armies drove German forces out of the Soviet Union and Eastern Europe and back into Germany. As a result, Soviet troops occupied much of Eastern Europe.

Stalin promised to hold free elections "as soon as possible" in these Eastern European nations. He soon broke that promise. "A freely elected government in any of the Eastern European countries would be anti-Soviet," he said, "and that we cannot allow."

By 1948, Communists controlled the government of every Eastern European country. Except for Yugoslavia, these countries became satellite nations of the Soviet Union. A **satellite nation** is one that is dominated politically and economically by a more powerful nation. In each satellite nation, the Soviets backed harsh dictators. Citizens who protested were imprisoned or killed.

The "Iron Curtain" As early as 1946 the British statesman Winston Churchill had warned against Soviet expansion into Eastern Europe. Naming two cities that were located in the north and south of Europe, he said: "From Stettin in the Baltic to Trieste in the Adriatic, an iron curtain has descended across the Continent." The "iron curtain" cut off Soviet-run Eastern Europe from the democratic governments of the West.

Western fears of communism deepened as communist parties, backed by Stalin, achieved success in other parts of Europe. Italian Communists won many seats in the Italian parliament. In Greece, communist rebels waged a civil war to topple the Greek government. Communist-led unions conducted strikes that paralyzed the weak economies.

The United States Responds

President Harry S Truman was determined to keep Soviet influence contained within existing boundaries. Thus, his Cold War policy was known as **containment.**

The Truman Doctrine In March 1947, President Truman asked Congress for $400 million in military and economic aid for Greece and Turkey. Eventually, with American aid, both countries held off communist threats.

This program to encourage nations to resist communist expansion became known as the **Truman Doctrine.** Truman explained the need for this policy:

> "The free peoples of the world look to us for support in maintaining their freedoms. If we falter in our leadership, we may endanger the peace of the world—and we shall surely endanger the welfare of our own nation."
>
> —Harry Truman, Speech, March 12, 1947

An American Profile

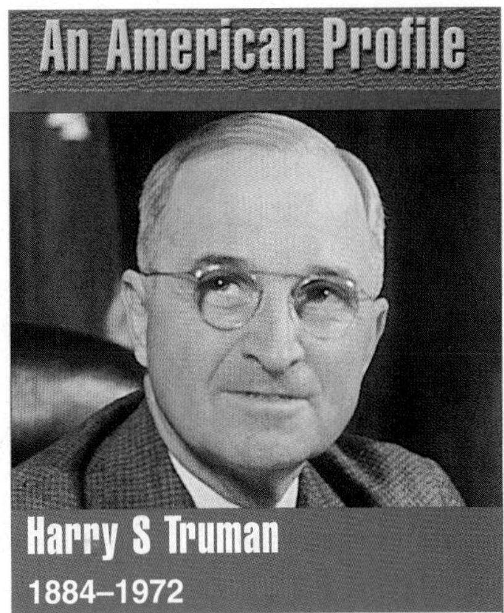

Harry S Truman
1884–1972

When the United States entered World War I, Harry Truman was 32 and barely able to see without glasses. He could easily have escaped the draft. But, Harry wanted to serve his country. So, he memorized the eye chart and was accepted.

Truman was sent to France as an artillery captain. During a night skirmish, he was on horseback when his unit came under fire from German positions. Abandoning their weapons, the soldiers began to run. In the panic, Truman was thrown from his horse. He remounted and, with shells exploding all around, shamed his men into returning to their guns. For the rest of the war, the unit fought bravely and well.

What leadership qualities did Truman show in combat?

The Marshall Plan Other European nations needed aid, too. The war had left Europe's homes, roads, and factories in ruins. When Secretary of State George Marshall toured Europe, he saw millions of homeless, hungry refugees.

Marshall feared that these conditions might encourage communist revolutions. So in June 1947, he proposed an ambitious plan to help Europe rebuild. The President and Congress accepted the **Marshall Plan.**

Between 1948 and 1952, the Marshall Plan provided more than $12 billion in aid to Western European countries. By helping these nations rebuild their economies, the Marshall Plan reduced the threat of communist revolutions in Western Europe.

Viewing History

Devastated Europe

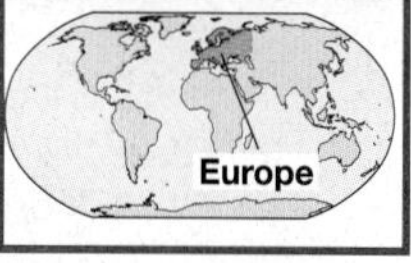

Like this German city, much of Europe lay in ruins after World War II. Homes, factories, roads, and farms had been destroyed. **Identifying Alternatives** ***What sort of aid do you think was most helpful to the people of Europe?***

Crisis Over Berlin

In 1948, a crisis developed in Berlin, Germany's largest city. After the war, the Allies had divided Germany into four zones. American, British, French, and Soviet troops each occupied a zone. Berlin, too, was divided among the four Allies, even though it lay inside the Soviet zone.

By 1948, the United States, Britain, and France wanted to reunite their zones. Stalin opposed that plan. A reunited Germany, he felt, would again be a threat to the Soviet Union. To show his determination to prevent a united Western Germany, Stalin closed all roads, railway lines, and river routes connecting Berlin with West Germany. The blockade cut off West Berlin from the rest of the world.

Berlin Airlift President Truman would not let West Berlin fall into Soviet hands. At the same time, he did not want to order American troops to open a path to West Berlin through the Soviet-occupied zone. That move could trigger war.

Instead, Truman approved a huge airlift. During the **Berlin Airlift,** hundreds of American and British planes carried tons of food, fuel, and other supplies to the two million West Berliners every day.

The airlift lasted for almost a year. Stalin finally saw that the West would not abandon West Berlin. In May 1949, he lifted the blockade. After the blockade, the United States, Great Britain, and France merged their zones into the Federal Republic of Germany, or West Germany.

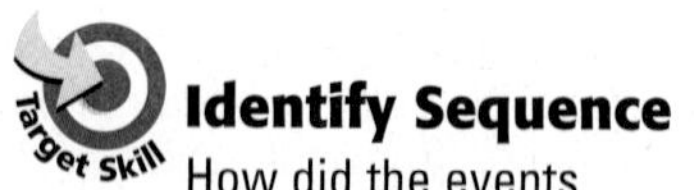

Identify Sequence How did the events described on this page add to the tension between the United States and the Soviet Union? Add these events to your flowchart.

Berlin Wall Both Germany and Berlin remained divided throughout the 1950s. With American aid, West Germany rebuilt its economy and became a prosperous nation. In time, the Soviet zone became the German Democratic Republic, or East Germany.

East Germany was much poorer than West Germany, and it had a government that was undemocratic. For years, East Germans fled communism by crossing into West Berlin. The flight of so many people embarrassed the communists.

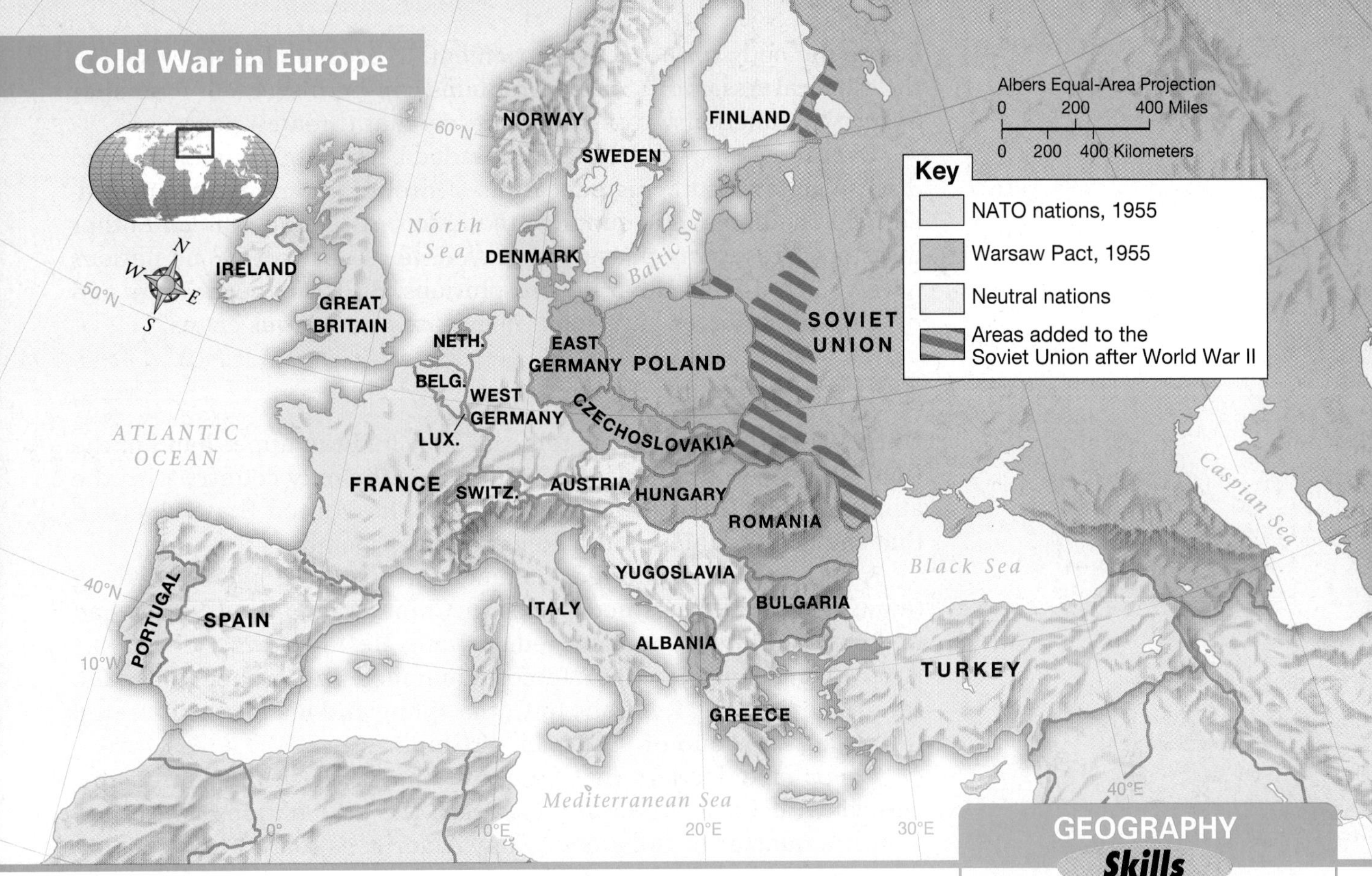

GEOGRAPHY *Skills*

By 1955, the United States and 14 other nations belonged to NATO. That same year, the Soviet Union and seven Eastern European nations formed the Warsaw Pact.

1. **Location** On the map, locate **(a)** the Soviet Union, **(b)** Poland, **(c)** East Germany, **(d)** West Germany, **(e)** Yugoslavia.
2. **Region** Which NATO nations bordered Warsaw Pact nations?
3. **Critical Thinking** **Drawing Conclusions** Why do you think most of the nations of Western Europe joined NATO?

In 1961, the East German government built a huge concrete wall topped with barbed wire. It sealed off East Berlin from West Berlin. East Berliners who tried to scale the wall were shot by East German border guards. The Berlin Wall cut off contact between families and friends. It became a bitter symbol of the Cold War that divided Europe and the world.

New Alliances

New military alliances emerged during the Cold War. A world peace-keeping organization was also set up.

Cold War Alliances To contain Soviet influences, the United States set up alliances with friendly nations. In 1949, it joined with many Western European countries to form the North Atlantic Treaty Organization, or NATO. A key NATO goal was to defend Western Europe against any Soviet threat.

In 1955, the Soviet Union formed its own military alliance, the Warsaw Pact. The Soviet Union dominated its Warsaw Pact neighbors, forcing them to follow its policies.

United Nations Many disputes were brought before a new world organization, the United Nations (UN). Fifty-one nations ratified the UN charter in October 1945. Over time, membership in the United Nations expanded as new nations were admitted.

Under the UN charter, member nations agree to bring disputes before the body for peaceful settlement. Every member has a seat in the General Assembly, where problems can be discussed. A smaller Security Council also discusses conflicts that threaten peace.

Over the years, the UN has succeeded best in fighting hunger and disease and in improving education. UN relief programs have provided food, medicine, and supplies to victims of famine, war, and other disasters. Preserving peace has proved more difficult. Some nations have rejected United Nations resolutions. Still, UN negotiators and peacekeeping forces have sometimes eased dangerous crises.

1949: Year of Shocks

Until 1949, most Americans felt that they had the upper hand in the Cold War. After all, the United States was the only country with the atomic bomb. Then in September 1949, the United States learned that the Soviet Union had tested an atomic bomb.

A second shock followed. Communist forces, led by Mao Zedong (mow dzuh DOONG), gained power in China. The United States had long backed the Nationalists, led by Jiang Jieshi (jyawng jeh SHEE).* After a long civil war, Mao's forces triumphed. In October 1949, Mao set up the People's Republic of China. Jiang and his forces retreated to Taiwan, an island off the coast of China.

Communist leaders in China and the Soviet Union often disagreed with each other. Yet together, the two nations controlled almost a quarter of the globe. Many Americans feared that communism would spread still farther.

* In earlier textbooks, this name is spelled Chiang Kai-shek.

★ ★ ★ Section 1 Assessment ★ ★ ★

Recall

1. **Identify** Explain the significance of **(a)** Cold War, **(b)** Truman Doctrine, **(c)** Marshall Plan, **(d)** Berlin Airlift, **(e)** Berlin Wall, **(f)** North Atlantic Treaty Organization, **(g)** Warsaw Pact, **(h)** United Nations.
2. **Define** **(a)** satellite nation, **(b)** containment.

Comprehension

3. Describe two reasons for the tensions that led to the Cold War.
4. How did the United States try to stop the spread of communism in Europe?
5. What military alliances emerged during the Cold War?
6. What two 1949 crises raised Cold War tensions?

Critical Thinking and Writing

7. **Exploring the Main Idea** Review the Main Idea statement at the beginning of this section. Then, write a dialog between a Soviet and an American diplomat on the causes of the Cold War.
8. **Drawing Inferences** After World War I, the United States refused to join the League of Nations. Why do you think it joined the United Nations after World War II?

Activity

Connecting to Today

Since World War II, the United States has played a leading role in international organizations such as NATO. Using the Internet, find out more about NATO's history. Then, describe some of NATO's activities today. For help in completing the activity, visit PHSchool.com, **Web Code mfd-2801.**

Predicting Consequences

Historical events often have effects that reach far into the future. To predict these consequences, it is necessary to weigh current evidence carefully. By drawing conclusions from a variety of sources, it is possible to make informed predictions about future developments.

This excerpt from a conversation with Joseph Stalin in 1945 addresses the growing split between the Soviet Union and the Western powers:

"In Poland, in the Balkans, and in China, everywhere agents [of the United States and Great Britain] spread the information that the war with us will break out any day now. . . . [They want] to push us away from our allies—Poland, Romania, Yugoslavia and Bulgaria. I asked them directly when they were starting the war against us. And they said 'What are you saying?' Whether in thirty years or so they want to have another war. . . . This would bring them great profit, particularly in the case of America, which is beyond the oceans and couldn't care less about the effects of the war. Their policy of sparing Germany testifies to that. He who spares the aggressor wants another war."

—Joseph Stalin, November 14, 1945

Learn the Skill *To predict consequences, use the following steps:*

1. **Identify the developments.** What events or developments have taken place? Are conflicts evident?
2. **Analyze information.** What facts are available? What opinions are given? What conclusions can be drawn?
3. **Predict possible future consequences.** How might present events affect the future? What trends are developing?

Practice the Skill *Answer the following questions based on Stalin's conversation and the cartoon above.*

1. **(a)** What prompted Stalin's angry comments? **(b)** What development prompted the cartoon from an American newspaper?
2. **(a)** What does Stalin expect future relations between the Western powers and the Soviet Union to be like? **(b)** What symbols does the cartoonist use to show the Soviet Union, France, Britain, and the United States?
3. Based on the speech and the cartoon, what consequences might you predict for future relations between the United States and the Soviet Union?

Apply the Skill *See the Chapter Review and Assessment.*

2 The Korean War Period

Prepare to Read

Objectives

In this section, you will

- Explain why the United States became involved in the conflict in Korea.
- Summarize how the fighting in Korea ended.
- Discuss the results of the hunt for communists at home.

Key Terms

38th parallel

demilitarized zone

perjury

censure

Target Reading Skill

Reading Process On a sheet of paper, draw a concept web like the one shown here. As you read this section, fill in each blank oval with important facts about how the Cold War affected the United States in the 1950s.

EFFECTS OF THE COLD WAR

North Korea attacks South Korea

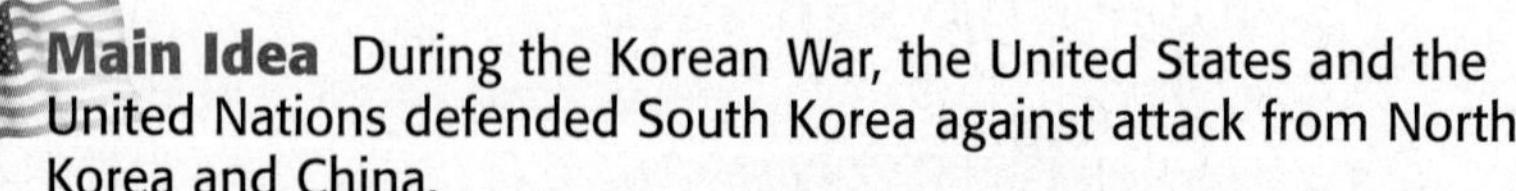

Main Idea During the Korean War, the United States and the United Nations defended South Korea against attack from North Korea and China.

Wounded in Korea

Setting the Scene The sound of exploding shells woke Joseph Darrigo early on June 25, 1950. Darrigo was an American military adviser to the South Korean army. He was stationed at the **38th parallel,** the dividing line between South Korea and communist North Korea.

Darrigo knew at once what was happening. The North Koreans were attacking across the 38th parallel. He hurried to alert a nearby military base but arrived too late. North Korean soldiers were already there. He later recalled:

> “Once they fired four or five bullets and I still hadn't been shot, I figured God was steering them away from me.”
>
> —Joseph Darrigo, Interview, 1995

Darrigo survived the attack, but many others did not.

The fighting that erupted that day in Korea was directly linked to the Cold War. It soon involved not only Koreans, but also the United Nations, the United States, China, and other powers.

The Korean Conflict

Korea is a peninsula in East Asia. Russia and China border it to the north and the west. Japan lies across the Sea of Japan to the east. In the past, these powerful neighbors often competed to control Korea. From 1910 to 1945, Japan ruled Korea as a colony.

Korea Divided As World War II ended, the United States and the Soviet Union agreed to a temporary division of Korea at the 38th parallel of latitude. Both nations agreed that Korea would soon be reunited.

As the Cold War deepened, however, Korea remained divided. The United States backed a noncommunist government in South Korea. The Soviet Union supported the communist government of

Taking a brief break from battle

North Korea. There was no agreement on when, or how, to reunite Korea.

Invasion In June 1950, North Korean troops swept across the 38th parallel into South Korea. The South Korean army was quickly overwhelmed. Within days, North Korean forces occupied Seoul (SOLE), capital of South Korea.

President Truman responded forcefully to the attack. He asked the United Nations to send a military force to Korea. The UN Security Council voted to set up a force, to be commanded by a general chosen by Truman. The President chose General Douglas MacArthur, who had commanded Allied forces in the Pacific during World War II. Although 16 nations joined the UN action in Korea, about 80 percent of the troops were American.

Landing at Inchon At first, UN forces were outnumbered and poorly supplied. Armed with new Soviet tanks, the North Koreans pushed steadily southward. They soon occupied almost all of South Korea.

MacArthur then launched a daring counterattack by sea. He landed United Nations forces at Inchon behind North Korean lines. Caught by surprise, the North Koreans were forced back across the 38th parallel.

MacArthur's original orders called for him only to drive the invaders out of South Korea. Truman and his advisers, however, wanted to punish North Korea for its aggression. They also wanted to unite

GEOGRAPHY *Skills*

When North Korean forces drove deep into South Korea, a United Nations force came to the aid of the South.

1. **Location** On the map, locate **(a)** North Korea, **(b)** South Korea, **(c)** 38th parallel, **(d)** Inchon, **(e)** Seoul, **(f)** Yalu River.
2. **Movement** Which side controlled Seoul **(a)** in September 1950, **(b)** in November 1950, **(c)** at the end of the war?
3. **Critical Thinking Making Predictions** Based on this map, do you think communist forces would have won control over all of Korea if the UN had not sent in troops?

Korea. With these goals in mind, they won UN approval for MacArthur to cross into North Korea.

China Enters the War While MacArthur advanced northward, the Chinese government warned that it would not "sit back with folded hands" if the United States invaded North Korea. As UN forces neared the Chinese border, masses of Chinese troops crossed the Yalu River into North Korea.

Once again, the fighting seesawed. The Chinese overwhelmed the UN forces, pushing them back deep into South Korea. Then, the UN forces regrouped and pushed the Chinese back into North Korea. By March 1951, UN troops had regained control of the south. The war then turned into a bloody deadlock.

An American Profile

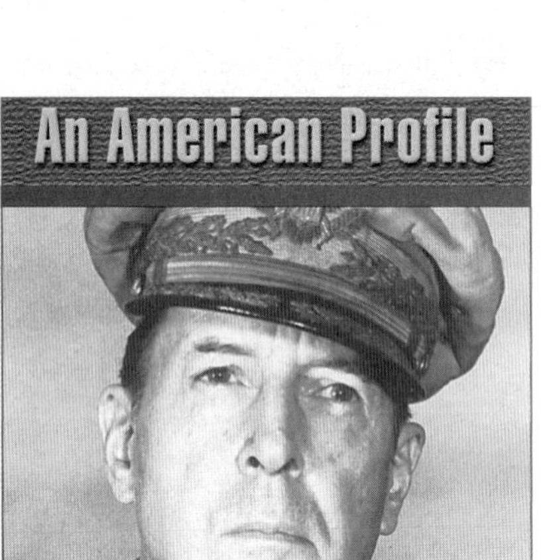

Douglas MacArthur
1880–1964

Douglas MacArthur was raised on army posts and attended the U.S. Military Academy at West Point. There, he achieved one of the highest records in Academy history. During World War I, he fought in France, winning numerous decorations for bravery and leadership.

In World War II, MacArthur commanded Allied forces fighting Japan in the Southwest Pacific. After the war, he led the Allied occupation of Japan. Under MacArthur, the power of the Japanese military was broken, land was distributed to poor farmers, and new rights were given to Japanese women.

What do you think was MacArthur's greatest accomplishment?

An End to the Fighting

During the deadlock, a serious disagreement arose between General MacArthur and President Truman. MacArthur felt that to win the war, UN forces must attack China. Truman feared that an attack on China might lead to a world war. He hoped to limit the war and restore the border between North Korea and South Korea at the 38th parallel.

Truman Fires MacArthur A frustrated MacArthur complained publicly that politicians in Washington were holding him back. "We must win," he insisted. "There is no substitute for victory." Angry that MacArthur was defying orders, Truman fired the popular general.

Truman's action outraged many Americans. They gave MacArthur a hero's welcome when he returned home. Truman, however, defended his decision. Under the Constitution, he pointed out, the President is commander in chief, responsible for key decisions about war and peace. MacArthur's statements, said Truman, undermined attempts to reach a peace settlement.

Armistice Peace talks began in mid-1951. At first there was little progress. Meanwhile, the deadly fighting continued.

Republicans nominated Dwight Eisenhower, the popular World War II general, as their presidential candidate in 1952. During the campaign, Eisenhower pledged that if he were elected, he would personally go to Korea. At the same time, he would work to get the stalled peace talks going again.

Eisenhower won the election and visited Korea within a few weeks of his victory. By then, both sides were eager for a cease-fire. The only remaining problem was the return of prisoners of war. After long negotiations, the two sides finally agreed to turn this issue over to an international commission.

Finally, in July 1953, the two sides signed an armistice to end the fighting. It redrew the border between North Korea and South Korea near the 38th parallel, where it had been before the war. Along the border, it also set up a **demilitarized zone** (DMZ), an area with no military forces. On either side of the DMZ, however, heavily armed troops dug in. They remain there today.

In a sense, the Korean War changed nothing. Korea remained divided. On the other hand, UN forces did push back North Korean forces. Through this action, the United States and its allies showed that they were ready to fight to prevent communist expansion.

Costs The human costs of the Korean War were staggering. About 54,000 Americans lost their lives in the war. Nearly 2 million Koreans and Chinese were also killed. Yet, the Korean war changed little in terms of borders. The cease-fire set the border between North and South Korea near the 38th parallel. This was close to where it had been before the war.

Viewing History

Peace Talks

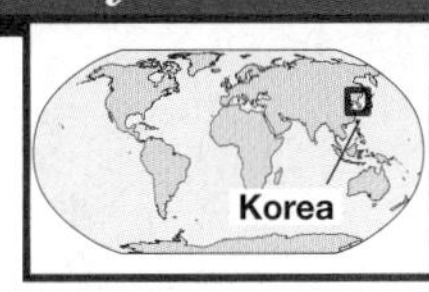

The Korean peace talks dragged on for two long years. Only in mid-1953, was an armistice finally signed. **Drawing Conclusions** ***Why do you think the United States accepted an armistice in Korea without a total victory?***

Hunting Communists at Home

For many Americans, the Korean War increased worries about Communists at home. Communist sympathizers and spies, they feared, might be secretly working to overthrow the government. These concerns helped spark a hunt for Communists within American society.

During the Great Depression, some Americans had turned against democracy and free enterprise. They had rejected the efforts of the New Deal as ineffective. To them, communism offered the only solution to the nation's deep economic troubles. In time, however, many American Communists recognized that Soviet leader Joseph Stalin was a brutal dictator, and they left the party.

Search for Spies Still, some remained avid Communists. Between 1946 and 1950, several people in the United States, Canada, and Britain were arrested as Soviet spies. In the United States, Ethel and Julius Rosenberg were sentenced to death for passing atomic secrets to the Soviets. Despite protests, both were executed in 1953. The Rosenberg case made many Americans wonder if other Soviet spies were living among them as ordinary citizens.

Americans also worried that there were Communists in high government positions. In 1950, Alger Hiss, a State Department official, was imprisoned for perjury, or lying under oath. Hiss had denied that he was part of a Soviet spy ring. Later evidence would suggest that Hiss and several other high government officials were passing secrets to the Soviet Union. It would also make it clear that Julius Rosenberg had indeed passed atomic secrets to the Soviets.

In 1947, President Truman ordered investigations of government workers to determine if they were loyal to the United States. Thousands of government employees were questioned. Some people were forced to resign. Many of those had done nothing disloyal to the United States.

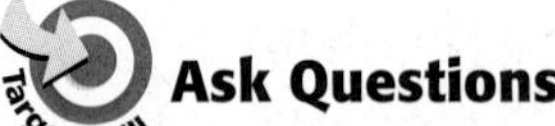

Ask Questions If you were able to interview Senator McCarthy after the "McCarthy era," what questions would you have asked him? How do you think he might have responded?

The McCarthy Era In 1950, Senator Joseph McCarthy of Wisconsin made a shocking announcement. He claimed to have a list of 205 State Department employees who were Communist party members. McCarthy was never able to prove his claims. Yet, McCarthy's dramatic charges won him national attention.

During the next four years, McCarthy's campaign spread suspicion across the nation. Businesses and colleges questioned employees. Many people were fired.

In 1954, the Senate held televised hearings to investigate a new McCarthy charge. He insisted that there were Communists in the United States Army. This time, McCarthy had gone too far. On national television, he came across as a bully, not a hero. His popularity plunged.

In December 1954, the Senate passed a resolution to censure, or officially condemn, McCarthy for "conduct unbecoming a member." As a result, McCarthy lost much of his support. By the time he died three years later, the Communist scare was mostly over.

Section 2 Assessment

Recall

1. **Identify** Explain the significance of **(a)** 38th parallel, **(b)** Douglas MacArthur, **(c)** Ethel and Julius Rosenberg, **(d)** Joseph McCarthy.
2. **Define** **(a)** demilitarized zone, **(b)** perjury, **(c)** censure.

Comprehension

3. Describe how the United States became involved in the conflict in Korea.
4. What was the outcome of the Korean War?
5. How did the McCarthy era grow out of the hunt for Communists at home?

Critical Thinking and Writing

6. **Exploring the Main Idea** Review the Main Idea statement at the beginning of this section. Then, write five headlines that trace the course of the Korean War from beginning to end.
7. **Linking Past and Present** Television played a key role in the downfall of Senator Joseph McCarthy. Give at least three examples of how television influences public opinion today.

ACTIVITY

Charting Military Spending
Use the Internet to research the military budgets of the United States from 1945 to 2000. Then, draw a line graph showing how spending increased during this period. For help in completing the activity, visit PHSchool.com, **Web Code mfd-2802.**

3 Regional Conflicts

Prepare to Read

Objectives

In this section, you will
- Discuss why the Cold War spread to Africa and Asia.
- Explain why Cuba became a crisis spot during the Cold War.
- Analyze why the United States intervened in Latin America during the Cold War.
- Describe how the Cold War led to an arms race.

Key Terms

superpower
exile
Bay of Pigs invasion
Cuban missile crisis
Alliance for Progress
Peace Corps
Organization of American States
National Aeronautics and Space Administration

Target Reading Skill

Comparison and Contrast As you read, complete this table listing Cold War conflicts and the actions taken by the superpowers.

REGION OR COUNTRY	ISSUE OR CONFLICT	SUPERPOWER ACTIONS
Africa and Asia		
Cuba	Castro set up communist government	
Other Parts of Latin America		

Main Idea Superpower rivalries heightened conflicts in many parts of the world during the Cold War.

Setting the Scene In September 1959, the Soviet leader, Nikita Khrushchev (KROOSH chawf), arrived in New York to address the United Nations. Khrushchev, who had gained power a few years after Stalin died in 1953, spoke calmly at first. He expressed hopes that the Cold War between the United States and the Soviet Union would end. Then, gradually his manner changed. Twice, he became so angry that he took off his shoe and pounded it on the table.

Khrushchev's trip to the UN symbolized the fact that the Cold War had become global. Although the Cold War had started in Europe, the United States and the Soviet Union now competed for allies and influence among the members of the United Nations.

Khrushchev at the United Nations

The Cold War in Africa and Asia

For years, many of the nations of Africa and Asia had been governed as colonies of European and other foreign powers. After World War II, many colonial people demanded and won independence. Some achieved independence peacefully. Others had to fight for it.

In the colonies, Communists often joined other groups to fight foreign control. Khrushchev called these struggles "wars of national liberation." Both openly and secretly, the Soviets gave economic and military aid to rebel forces.

The West tried to prevent the Soviets from expanding their influence. In their efforts, American leaders faced difficult choices. Should the United States provide aid to a colonial power? Should Americans use secret aid to counter the Soviets? Should they send troops into another nation to influence its internal affairs? In the end, the United States used all these tactics at one time or another to contain communism.

POLITICAL CARTOON *Skills*

American Comic Strips and Communism

This comic-strip panel appeared in an American comic book during the 1950s.

1. **Comprehension** **(a)** Who is the man standing by the globe? **(b)** Who are the other men seated at the table?
2. **Finding the Main Idea** What are the men discussing?
3. **Critical Thinking Identifying Points of View** What is the cartoonist's opinion of the communist world?

The Philippines The United States also had to deal with its own colony. In 1946, it withdrew from the Philippines, which it had acquired during the Spanish-American War. Crowds in Manila cheered as the American flag was lowered and the Filipino flag was hoisted high.

Since then, the Philippines has struggled to preserve a democratic government. It has suffered from poverty, local uprisings, and dictatorships. Under the rule of Ferdinand Marcos, who was in power from 1965 to 1986, opposition parties were repressed. In the years that followed, the Philippines struggled to find stable and honest government.

Cold War Rivalries in Africa During the 1950s and 1960s, more than 30 African nations won freedom from European rule. Both the United States and the Soviet Union sought allies among these new nations.

After independence, some new nations faced civil wars among rival ethnic or tribal groups. Some fought border wars with their neighbors. The superpowers backed opposing sides in these struggles. As a result, the Cold War turned local conflicts into international crises.

In East Africa, the United States and the Soviet Union took sides in a long war between Somalia and Ethiopia. The United States backed Somalia, while the Soviet Union supported Ethiopia. In southern Africa, the Cold War intensified a civil war in Angola.

India, Pakistan, and Indochina In 1947, India won independence from Britain. The Indian subcontinent was divided into two nations: India and Pakistan. Both the United States and the Soviet Union tried to win the support of these new nations.

Feeling threatened by the Soviet Union to its north, Pakistan became an ally of the United States. India accepted both American and Soviet aid but remained neutral in the Cold War.

French-ruled Indochina included present-day Laos, Cambodia, and Vietnam. In each country, separate nationalist groups fought for independence. The wars lasted for almost 30 years and eventually drew in the United States, as you will read in Section Four.

Crisis Over Cuba

By the 1960s, the United States and the Soviet Union had emerged as **superpowers**—nations with enough military, political, and economic strength to influence events worldwide. The rivalry between the superpowers led to clashes in many places, including Cuba, an island in the Caribbean.

In 1959, Fidel Castro led a revolution that set up a communist state in Cuba. Castro's government took over private companies, including many owned by American businesses. Thousands of Cubans, especially those from the upper and middle classes, fled to the United States.

Compare and Contrast

How did the United States react to Soviet intervention in Cuba? Add this information to your table.

Bay of Pigs Invasion The Soviet Union began supplying Cuba with large amounts of aid. The growing ties between the Soviet Union and Castro's Cuba worried American officials. Cuba lies just 90 miles off the coast of Florida.

In 1961, President John F. Kennedy approved a plan for Cuban exiles to overthrow Castro. **Exiles** are people who have been forced to leave their own country.

A force of about 1,200 Cuban exiles landed at the Bay of Pigs on Cuba's south coast. The invasion was badly planned. Castro's forces quickly rounded up and jailed the invaders. The **Bay of Pigs invasion** strengthened Castro in Cuba and embarrassed the United States.

Cuban Missile Crisis After the Bay of Pigs invasion, the Soviet Union gave Cuba more weapons. In October 1962, President Kennedy learned that the Soviets were secretly building missile bases on the island. If the bases were completed, atomic missiles could reach American cities within minutes.

Kennedy announced that American warships would stop any Soviet ship carrying missiles. The world waited tensely as Soviet ships steamed toward Cuba. At the last minute, the Soviet ships turned back. "We're eyeball to eyeball," said Secretary of State Dean Rusk, "and I think the other fellow just blinked."

Kennedy's strong stand led the Soviets to compromise. Khrushchev agreed to remove Soviet missiles from Cuba. In turn, the United States promised not to invade the island. Still the **Cuban missile crisis** had shaken both American and Soviet officials. In all the years of the Cold War, the world never came closer to a full-scale nuclear war.

Viewing History

Caribbean Conflict

Cuba

A United States plane flies low over a Soviet freighter during the Cuban missile crisis. Americans were checking the boat for any evidence of Soviet missiles aboard. **Identifying Alternatives** ***Were there other policies that President Kennedy could have followed to end the missile crisis? Explain.***

Intervening in Latin America

In the early 1900s, the United States had frequently intervened in the internal affairs of Latin American nations. Now,

Cold War tensions led the United States to resume its active role. A number of Presidents tried to contain communism in other Latin American nations.

Social and Economic Problems Latin America had long faced severe social and economic problems. A huge gap existed between the wealthy few and the majority of people. In most countries, rural people lived in desperate poverty. When the poor migrated to cities seeking work, they were often forced to live in shacks, without heat, light, or water.

Many poor Latin Americans saw communism as a solution to their problems. Communists called for land to be distributed to the poor and for governments to take over foreign corporations. Some non-Communists also supported this view.

Aid Programs Many American leaders agreed with the need for reform. They hoped that American aid would help make Latin American nations more democratic, ease the lives of the people, and lessen communist influence.

In 1961, President Kennedy created an ambitious aid program called the **Alliance for Progress.** He urged Latin American countries to make reforms to improve the lives of their people. In return, the United States contributed aid to build schools and hospitals and improve farming and sanitation services. The Alliance brought a few improvements, but it did not end the causes of poverty.

Kennedy also set up the **Peace Corps.** Under this program, American volunteers worked in developing countries as teachers, engineers, and technical advisers. Volunteers lived with local people for two years, teaching or giving technical advice.

The United States was also a leading member of the **Organization of American States,** or OAS. Through the OAS, the United States promoted economic progress in the Americas by investing in transportation and industry.

To battle communism, the United States also gave military aid to train and arm Latin American military forces. The United States spoke up for democracy and pressed governments to make reforms. Often, though, the United States ended up supporting military dictators because they opposed communism.

Intervention During the Cold War, the United States returned to a policy of intervention in Latin American affairs. Between 1950 and 1990, it intervened in Guatemala, the Dominican Republic, Panama, and Grenada.

During the 1970s and 1980s, civil wars raged in several Central American countries. Rebels in El Salvador and Guatemala fought to overthrow harsh governments. The United States backed the governments because they were strongly anticommunist.

The wars cost tens of thousands of lives. To escape the fighting, thousands of refugees fled to the United States.

In Nicaragua, a rebel group known as the Sandinistas overthrew a longtime dictator in 1979 and set up a socialist government. President Reagan, afraid that Nicaragua would become another

Geography and History

The Peace Corps

Peace Corps volunteers work hard during their two-year tour of duty. A volunteer might set up a health clinic, build an irrigation system, or start a new school. Many volunteers live in remote villages. All are expected to use the local language and live as the local people do.

Peace Corps members feel that they do much more than building, doctoring, and teaching. Said one:

"By communications on a person-to-person level the people of the world may some day eliminate the word [stranger]. Communication, after all, can breed understanding. And understanding can breed peace. I like to think that is what the Peace Corps is all about."

What are some jobs that Peace Corps volunteers do?

Cuba, aided a group opposed to the Sandinistas. They were known as "Contras," from the Spanish word for "against."

Many members of Congress disagreed with President Reagan's policy in Nicaragua. They passed laws banning military aid to the Contras. Even so, some people on the President's staff arranged for military aid secretly. When details of the arrangement became public, many Americans were outraged. Two Reagan officials were tried and convicted of lying to Congress, though the convictions were later successfully appealed

Finally, in 1990, Nicaragua held new elections. Nicaraguans rejected the Sandinistas and voted in new leaders.

The Arms Race

By the 1950s, both the Soviet Union and the United States had developed large stocks of nuclear bombs and missiles. Then, in 1957, the Soviet Union launched *Sputnik*, the world's first artificial satellite. Americans were stunned. If the Soviets had a rocket powerful enough to launch a satellite, could their rockets armed with atomic weapons reach the United States?

Sputnik sparked a new round of spending on weapons systems by both the Soviet Union and the United States. The United States soon launched its own satellites. Both superpowers now raced to send larger satellites farther into space. The United States also set up the **National Aeronautics and Space Administration,** or NASA. Its mission was to direct an American space program to compete with that of the Soviets.

By 1970, the two superpowers had stockpiles of weapons large enough to destroy each other many times over. With Soviet-American relations tense, it seemed possible that these weapons would someday be used.

★ ★ ★ Section 3 Assessment ★ ★ ★

Recall

1. **Identify** Explain the significance of **(a)** Bay of Pigs invasion, **(b)** Cuban missile crisis, **(c)** Alliance for Progress, **(d)** Peace Corps, **(e)** Organization of American States, **(f)** National Aeronautics and Space Administration.
2. **Define** **(a)** superpower, **(b)** exile.

Comprehension

3. How did superpower rivalries spread to Africa and Asia?
4. How did the superpowers come to the brink of war over Cuba?
5. What form did United States intervention in Latin America take during the Cold War?
6. Why did the Cold War superpowers become involved in an arms race?

Critical Thinking and Writing

7. **Exploring the Main Idea** Review the Main Idea statement at the beginning of the section. Then, list at least four examples of the global impact of the Cold War.
8. **Identifying Points of View** Why do you think that relations between the United States and Latin America were often strained during the Cold War?

ACTIVITY

Writing a Position Statement **You are an adviser to the President of the United States during the Cold War. The President is trying to decide whether the United States should support an anticommunist dictator in an Asian nation. Write a brief statement explaining your position.**

NASA and the Space Age

NASA grew out of the race between the United States and the Soviet Union to create a rocket that could reach outer space. Its greatest achievement was to land astronauts on the moon. This occurred on July 20, 1969, when *Apollo 11* astronaut Neil Armstrong set foot on the moon. His words were heard by millions of viewers worldwide: "One small step for a man, one giant leap for mankind."

NASA's space station Skylab was launched in 1973. It enabled astronauts to work and live in space for months.

In July 1969, American astronauts became the first humans to walk on the moon.

NASA's first astronaut team, 1959—(left to right) Walter Schirra, Alan Shepard, Virgil Grissom, Donald Slayton, John Glenn, Scott Carpenter, and Gordon Cooper—became instant American heroes.

This rock, collected by *Apollo* astronauts on the lunar surface, is billions of years old.

ACTIVITY

If you could make a time capsule to be placed by American astronauts on the moon, what objects would you put in it? List ten objects that would fit in a capsule about the size of a refrigerator that would give a good picture of life in the United States today.

4 The War in Vietnam

Prepare to Read

Objectives

In this section, you will
- Examine U.S. involvement in the Vietnam War.
- Discuss how the Vietnam War affected Americans at home.
- Explain how the Tet Offensive helped lead to the war's end.
- Analyze the Vietnam War's impact on the United States and Southeast Asia.

Key Terms

Vietcong
guerrilla
domino theory
Gulf of Tonkin Resolution
escalate
draft
Tet Offensive
Khmer Rouge
boat people

Target Reading Skill

Sequence Copy this flowchart. As you read, fill in the boxes with events that led to the communist takeover of Vietnam. Two boxes have been completed to help you get started. Add as many boxes as you need.

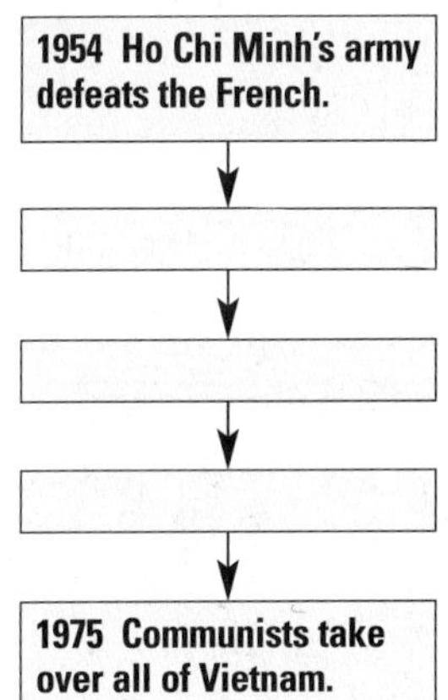

Main Idea In an effort to stop the spread of communism in Southeast Asia, the United States became involved in the long and unpopular Vietnam War.

Setting the Scene President Lyndon B. Johnson faced a difficult decision in May 1964. The United States was helping the government of South Vietnam battle communist rebels. Johnson had to decide whether to commit more forces to the struggle.

The President had doubts. "I don't think it's worth fighting for," he told a close adviser, "and I don't think we can get out. I don't see that we can ever hope to get out of there once we are committed."

The President never expressed those doubts publicly. In fact, he sent a growing number of Americans to fight in South Vietnam. Like many other Americans, he believed that the Vietnam War was justified because its goal was to stop the spread of communism.

While Lyndon Johnson was President, the fighting in Vietnam increased. It grew into the longest, most unpopular war in American history.

President Johnson and his generals

Early Involvement in Vietnam

Vietnam is a narrow country that stretches about 1,000 miles along the South China Sea. Since the late 1800s, it had been ruled by France as a colony.

The United States became involved in Vietnam slowly, step by step. During the 1940s, Ho Chi Minh (HO CHEE MIHN), a Vietnamese nationalist and a Communist, had led the fight for independence. Ho's army finally defeated the French in 1954.

An international peace conference divided Vietnam into two countries. Ho Chi Minh led communist North Vietnam. Ngo Dinh Diem (NOH DIN dee EHM) was the noncommunist leader of South Vietnam. In the Cold War world, the Soviet Union supported North Vietnam. The United States backed Diem in the south.

War in Southeast Asia

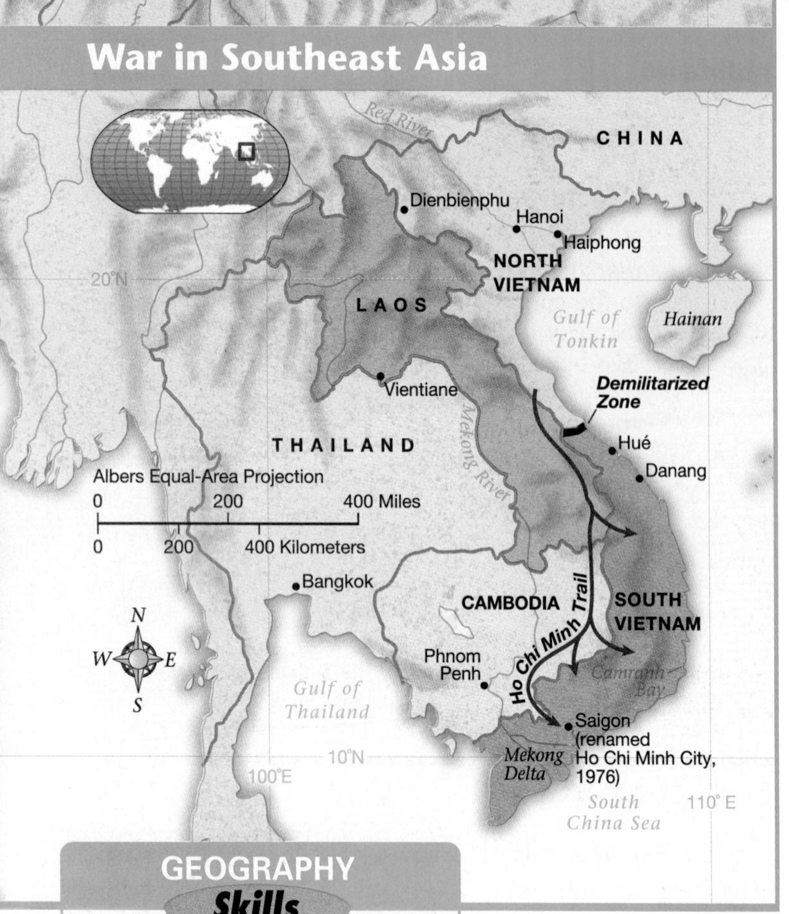

GEOGRAPHY *Skills*

During the Vietnam War, North Vietnam supplied arms to communist guerrillas in South Vietnam. The system of supply routes from the North was known as the Ho Chi Minh Trail.

1. **Location** On the map, locate **(a)** North Vietnam, **(b)** South Vietnam, **(c)** Gulf of Tonkin, **(d)** Hanoi, **(e)** Cambodia.
2. **Movement** Through which countries did the Ho Chi Minh Trail run?
3. **Critical Thinking Applying Information** According to the domino theory, what nations would be threatened if the Communists won control of South Vietnam?

Discontent Diem lost popular support during the 1950s. Many South Vietnamese thought that he favored wealthy landlords and was corrupt. He failed to help the nation's peasant majority and ruled with a heavy hand.

As discontent grew, many peasants joined the **Vietcong**—guerrillas who opposed Diem. **Guerrillas** (guh RIHL uhz) are fighters who make hit-and-run attacks on the enemy. They do not wear uniforms or fight in large battles. In time, the Vietcong became communist and were supported by North Vietnam. Vietcong influence quickly spread, especially in the villages.

American Aid Vietcong successes worried American leaders. If South Vietnam fell to communism, they believed, other countries in the region would follow—like a row of falling dominoes. This idea became known as the **domino theory.** The United States decided that it must keep South Vietnam from becoming the first domino.

During the 1950s and 1960s, Presidents Eisenhower and Kennedy sent financial aid and military advisers to South Vietnam. The advisers went to help train the South Vietnamese army, not to fight the Vietcong. Diem, however, continued to lose support. In November 1963, Diem was assassinated. A few weeks later, President John F. Kennedy was assassinated. Vice President Lyndon Baines Johnson became President.

The Fighting in Vietnam Expands

Lyndon Johnson was also determined to keep South Vietnam from falling to the communists. He increased aid to South Vietnam, sending more arms and advisers. Still, the Vietcong continued to make gains.

Gulf of Tonkin Resolution In August 1964, President Johnson announced that North Vietnamese torpedo boats had attacked an American ship patrolling the Gulf of Tonkin off the coast of North Vietnam. At Johnson's urging, Congress passed the **Gulf of Tonkin Resolution.** It allowed the President "to take all necessary measures to repel any armed attack or to prevent further aggression." Johnson used the resolution to order the bombing of North Vietnam and Vietcong-held areas in the south.

With the Gulf of Tonkin Resolution, the role of Americans in Vietnam changed from military advisers to active fighters. The war in Vietnam **escalated,** or expanded. By 1968, President Johnson had sent more than 500,000 troops to fight in Vietnam.

Jungle Warfare The Vietnam War differed from other wars that Americans had fought. Rather than trying to gain ground,

Americans attempted to destroy enemy positions. However, the Vietcong were hard to pin down. When Americans found an enemy stronghold, the guerrillas disappeared into the jungle. When the Americans left, the Vietcong returned. As a result, Americans found themselves going back again and again to fight in the same areas.

Worse still, American soldiers often could not tell which villagers were Vietcong. The enemy might be the old woman cooking rice outside her hut or the man walking down a village path. "The farmer you waved to from your jeep in the day," explained an American soldier, "would be the guy with the gun out looking for you at night."

The War at Home

As American casualties mounted, public support for the war faded. For the first time, Americans watched a war on television. They saw villages burned, children and old people caught in battle, and soldiers wounded and killed.

To raise troops, the United States expanded the **draft,** or system of mandatory enlistment. The draft affected American youth unequally. Many young middle-class men found ways to avoid the draft, such as attending college. As a result, many of the draftees sent to Vietnam were poor. A large number were African American and Latino.

By the mid-1960s, a growing number of Americans were protesting the war. The country split between "hawks" and "doves." Hawks supported the Vietnam War as a battle against communism. Doves opposed it. They saw it as a civil war involving the Vietnamese only.

The protests spread. On some college campuses, students staged marches and sit-ins, burned draft cards, and discussed how to avoid the draft.

Protesters charged that American lives and money were being wasted on an unjust war. The South Vietnamese government, they said, was corrupt and brutal, and the United States should not support it. They wanted the huge sums being spent on the war to be spent on social programs at home.

The antiwar protests fed a spirit of rebellion among young people. During the 1960s and early 1970s, many young people rejected traditional American values. They adopted new fashions in clothing and music. Their rebellious way of life often shocked their elders. Sadly, many experimented with illegal drugs. The use of these drugs took a tragic toll on the young and has remained a problem ever since.

The Tet Offensive: A Turning Point

In January 1968, the Vietcong launched surprise attacks on cities throughout South Vietnam. Guerrillas even stormed the American embassy in Saigon, the capital of South Vietnam. The attack became known as the **Tet Offensive** because it took place during Tet, the Vietnamese New Year's holiday.

In the end, American and South Vietnamese forces pushed back the enemy. Still, the Vietcong had won a major political victory. The

Primary Source

Memories of Vietnam

One steamy day in 1969, a young Marine named Paul O'Connell was in a foxhole when American jets providing air cover swooped low over his position:

"I took cover in a cave. . . . The jets came screaming in; and, just after you heard their jet roar, the earth shook; and the concussions left our ears ringing. One screaming jet after another. . . . I wondered if it was ever going to stop. I even wondered if the jets were on target; and if they were, it meant the enemy was very close to our positions. Finally, the bombing stopped; and the word was passed that it was okay to come out from our cover. . . . I decided I wasn't coming out from the cave. Never."

—Paul O'Connell, *Letters Home,* Vietnam Veterans Home Page

Analyzing Primary Sources

The bombing frightened O'Connell. Did this make him a poor soldier? Explain.

Vietnam Veterans Memorial

Since 1982, millions of Americans have visited the Vietnam Veterans Memorial in Washington, DC. The memorial is composed of two black granite walls inscribed with the names of more than 58,000 Americans killed in Vietnam. Says designer Maya Lin: "This memorial is for those who have died, and for us to remember."

Virtual Field Trip For an interactive look at the Vietnam Veterans Memorial, visit PHSchool.com, **Web Code mfd-2803.**

Target Skill **Identify Sequence** Why was the Tet Offensive a major victory for the Vietcong? Add the Tet Offensive to your flowchart in the correct sequence of events.

Tet Offensive showed that even with half a million American troops, no part of South Vietnam was safe from Vietcong attack. Many more Americans began to protest the war.

Hoping to restore calm to a nation rocked by protests, a weary President Johnson decided not to seek reelection in 1968. That year, Richard Nixon, a Republican, was elected President on a pledge to end the war.

The War Ends

President Nixon at first widened the war, hoping to weaken the enemy. For years, North Vietnamese soldiers had used trails in nearby Cambodia to supply their soldiers in South Vietnam. They also escaped to Cambodia when American and South Vietnamese units attacked.

In 1969, Nixon ordered the bombing of communist bases in Cambodia. Then, American and South Vietnamese forces invaded by land. These moves helped plunge Cambodia into its own civil war between communist and noncommunist forces.

United States Withdrawal Under pressure at home, President Nixon began to turn the war over to South Vietnam and withdraw American troops. Meanwhile, peace talks were held in Paris. In January 1973, the two sides reached a cease-fire agreement. The next year, the last American combat troops left Vietnam.

The United States continued to send large amounts of aid to South Vietnam. Even so, the South Vietnamese were unable to stop the North Vietnamese advance. In April 1975, communist forces captured Saigon. They renamed it Ho Chi Minh City. Soon after, Vietnam was united under a communist government.

Tragedy in Cambodia That year, the communist Khmer Rouge (kuh MER ROOJ) won the civil war in Cambodia. The Khmer Rouge imposed a brutal reign of terror on their own people. More than a million Cambodians starved to death or were killed.

In 1979, Vietnam invaded Cambodia and set up a new communist government. It was less harsh than the Khmer Rouge, but it could not end the fighting. Not until the 1990s would a shaky peace be restored in Cambodia.

Impact of the Vietnam War

The Vietnam War was a costly conflict. More than 58,000 American soldiers lost their lives. More than a million Vietnamese soldiers and perhaps half a million civilians died. The war shattered the Vietnamese economy.

After 1975, hundreds of thousands of people fled Vietnam and Cambodia. Refugees from Vietnam escaped in small boats. Many of these boat people drowned or died of hunger and thirst. Others made it to safety. Eventually, many were allowed to settle in the United States.

The Vietnam War was a painful episode in American history. Besides its huge cost, the war produced no victory and divided the nation. It left Americans wondering about how far the nation should go to fight communism.

★ ★ ★ Section 4 Assessment ★ ★ ★

Recall

1. **Identify** Explain the significance of **(a)** Ho Chi Minh, **(b)** Ngo Dinh Diem, **(c)** Vietcong, **(d)** Gulf of Tonkin Resolution, **(e)** Tet Offensive, **(f)** Khmer Rouge.
2. **Define** **(a)** guerrilla, **(b)** domino theory, **(c)** escalate, **(d)** draft, **(e)** boat people.

Comprehension

3. Describe the events that led the United States to play a major role in the Vietnam War.
4. List three ways that the Vietnam War affected Americans at home.
5. What was the relationship between the Tet Offensive and the war's end?
6. Describe the impact of the Vietnam War on the United States and Southeast Asia.

Critical Thinking and Writing

7. **Exploring the Main Idea** Review the Main Idea statement at the beginning of this section. Then, suppose you are an American soldier in Vietnam in 1968. Write a letter to your child explaining why you are there.
8. **Analyzing Information** How did the Cold War affect American policy in Vietnam?

ACTIVITY

Mental Mapping **Study the map showing War in Southeast Asia on page 828. On a piece of paper, draw your own sketch map of Vietnam. Label the names of countries, major bodies of water, the Ho Chi Minh Trail, and major cities. Use colors to outline and shade each country.**

5 The Cold War Ends

Prepare to Read

Objectives

In this section, you will
- Explain how President Richard Nixon changed the course of American foreign policy.
- Analyze why new Cold War tensions emerged after 1979.
- Describe conditions that caused communism to fall in the Soviet Union and Eastern Europe.
- Discuss how the Cold War affected American society.

Key Terms

détente

SALT Agreement

Star Wars

Solidarity

martial law

glasnost

summit meeting

Target Reading Skill

Main Idea As you read, prepare an outline of this section. Use roman numerals to indicate the major headings of this section, capital letters for the subheadings, and numbers for supporting details. The sample below will help you get started.

I. Changes in American Foreign Policy
A. The United States and China
B.
II. New Tensions
A. Soviet defeat
B.

Main Idea The Cold War dominated relations between the superpowers until the breakup of the Soviet Union in 1991 ended the Cold War.

The Berlin Wall comes down

Setting the Scene On a November night in 1989, television news programs carried a startling sight. There were Germans, young and old, swinging pickaxes and sledgehammers. Bit by bit, they were knocking down the huge concrete wall that had divided East Berlin from West Berlin for nearly 30 years.

Berliners from both sides of the wall danced, hugged, and kissed. East Berliners eagerly snatched up maps of West Berlin. For the first time, many East Berliners would be able to reunite with family and friends who were on the other side of the wall.

As you have read, communist East Germany had built the Berlin Wall to prevent its citizens from fleeing to the West. The wall had become a symbol of Cold War divisions. By the late 1980s, however, the Cold War was ending. All over Eastern Europe, nations were throwing off their communist rulers. The end of the Berlin Wall became the symbol of revolutionary changes throughout the communist world.

Changes in American Foreign Policy

In 1971, while Americans were still fighting in Vietnam, the Cold War showed signs of a thaw. President Nixon moved to ease world tensions. His first move was to seek improved relations with the People's Republic of China.

The United States and China Since 1949, the United States had refused to recognize Mao Zedong's communist government in China. Instead, it recognized the Chinese Nationalists, now confined to the island of Taiwan. The United States gave arms and aid to the Nationalists and supported their claim to being the legitimate government of all China.

Richard Nixon had long been one of the most outspoken opponents of recognizing the communist government in China. As President, though, Nixon allowed secret talks with Chinese officials that led to new openings for the two countries. To show its goodwill, China invited the American Ping-Pong team to a competition in Beijing.

To the surprise of many Americans, Nixon then visited the People's Republic of China in 1972. Television cameras captured the President walking along the Great Wall of China and attending state dinners with Chinese leaders. The visit was a triumph for Nixon and the start of a new era in relations with China. As tensions eased, the United States and China established formal diplomatic relations in 1979.

A Policy of Détente President Nixon followed his visit to China with another historic trip. In May 1972, he became the first American President to visit the Soviet Union since the beginning of the Cold War. The trip was part of Nixon's effort to reduce tensions between the superpowers. This policy was known as **détente** (day TAHNT).

Détente eased the Cold War by establishing more trade and other contacts between the superpowers. It also led them to sign a treaty to limit the number of nuclear warheads and missiles. The treaty was known as the **SALT Agreement.** (SALT stands for Strategic Arms Limitation Talks.)

The next two Presidents, Gerald Ford and Jimmy Carter, continued the policy of détente. Trade between the United States and the Soviet Union increased. Under President Ford, Soviet and American astronauts conducted a joint space mission. In 1979, President Carter met with Soviet leader Leonid Brezhnev (BREHZH nehf). They worked out the details of a SALT II Treaty.

New Tensions

Détente ended suddenly in 1979. In December, Soviet troops swept into Afghanistan, a mountainous nation on the Soviet Union's southern border. Soviet troops were sent there to help a pro-Soviet government that had just seized power.

A Soviet Defeat The United States condemned the Soviet invasion of Afghanistan. President Carter withdrew the SALT II Treaty from Senate approval hearings. The United States also refused to let

Cause *and* Effect

Causes

- Soviet Union takes control of Eastern European nations
- Communism gains influence in Western Europe, the Middle East, and Asia
- Western powers fear Soviet expansion

THE COLD WAR

Effects

- Arms race between United States and Soviet Union results in heavy military spending
- Western powers and Soviet Union create separate military alliances
- Armed conflicts erupt in Korea and Vietnam
- United States and Soviet Union compete for influence in developing nations

Effects Today

- United States is world's greatest military power
- Eastern Europe and Russia are struggling to create democratic governments
- Southeast Asian countries are still recovering from wars

GRAPHIC ORGANIZER *Skills*

For 45 years, the Cold War pitted the United States against the Soviet Union.

1. **Comprehension** **(a)** What events in Europe helped spark the Cold War? **(b)** Which effects of the Cold War involved Americans in actual fighting?
2. **Critical Thinking** **Analyzing Information** How did the Cold War help the United States become the world's greatest military power?

its athletes compete in the 1980 summer Olympic Games in Moscow.

Despite worldwide criticism, Soviet troops remained in Afghanistan for ten years. They suffered heavy losses as Afghan rebels, supplied by the United States, battled the communist government. The war in Afghanistan became so costly for the Soviets that it eventually contributed to the downfall of the Soviet Union. In 1989, the Soviets were forced to pull all troops out of Afghanistan.

Reagan's Strong Stand Ronald Reagan took office in 1981 firmly believing that the Soviet Union was "the focus of evil in the modern world." He called on Americans to "oppose it with all our might." Reagan also took a tough anticommunist stand in Latin America, as you have read.

Reagan wanted to deal with the Soviets from a position of strength. To achieve this, he persuaded Congress to increase military spending by more than $100 billion during his first five years in office. He also called for the development of a new weapons system that he hoped could destroy Soviet missiles from space. The system was nicknamed **Star Wars** after a popular movie of the time. Only the early stages of research were completed.

Viewing History

Improved Relations

Soviet premier Mikhail Gorbachev and President Ronald Reagan held three summit meetings. At this one, in 1987, they signed an arms control pact known as the INF Treaty. **Linking Past and Present** ***How have relations between Americans and Russians changed since 1987?***

During Reagan's first term in office, the two superpowers continued to view each other with deep mistrust. In December 1981, Poland's communist government cracked down on **Solidarity,** an independent labor union. Solidarity members had gone on strike at Polish shipyards to demand labor reforms. Under Soviet pressure, the Polish government imposed **martial law,** or emergency military rule, on the country.

President Reagan condemned the move. He urged the Soviets to allow Poland to restore basic human rights. The United States also put economic pressure on Poland to end martial law.

Decline of the Soviet Union

Cracks began to appear in the Soviet empire in the mid-1980s. Economic problems grew in part because of the huge sums the Soviets were spending on their military. There was little money left for producing consumer goods. Soviet citizens stood in line for hours waiting for poorly made products. They complained that the communist system was breaking down. The time was ripe for reform.

Target Skill **Identify Main Ideas** As you read, look for sentences that describe the main reasons for the decline of the Soviet Union.

Gorbachev's Reforms In 1985, a new Soviet leader, Mikhail Gorbachev (mee kah EEL GOR buh chawf), rose to power. He believed that only major reforms would allow the Soviet system to survive.

Gorbachev backed **glasnost,** the Russian term for speaking out openly. Glasnost, Gorbachev hoped, would lead citizens to find solutions to pressing economic and social problems. This new openness was a break with the past, when any criticism of government policies had been quickly silenced.

Summit Meetings Gorbachev realized that he could not solve the Soviet Union's economic problems without cutting military spending sharply. To do so, he had to have better relations with the United States.

President Reagan and Gorbachev met at several summit meetings. A **summit meeting** is a conference between the highest-ranking officials of different nations. Reagan agreed to these meetings because he approved of Gorbachev's new policy of openness.

In 1987, the two leaders signed an arms control pact called the Intermediate Nuclear Force (INF) Treaty. In it, both nations agreed to get rid of their stockpiles of short- and medium-range missiles. To prevent cheating, each side would have the right to inspect the other's missile sites. Two years later, Gorbachev withdrew Soviet troops from Afghanistan. This action removed another barrier to cooperation between the superpowers.

Communism Falls in Eastern Europe

For more than 50 years, the communist governments of Eastern Europe had banned any open discussion of political issues. As in the Soviet Union, only one political party, the Communist party, was allowed to win elections. People were denied many basic rights, such as freedom of speech.

At times, the Soviet Union had used force to maintain its control over the satellite nations. In 1956, Hungary had tried to follow its own independent course. The Soviet Union had sent in the Red Army, which brutally crushed the revolution. In 1968, Soviet troops marched into Czechoslovakia when a Czech leader tried to introduce some reforms.

Now, in the late 1980s, Eastern European governments could no longer control the rising demands of the people for democratic and economic reforms. With opposition so widespread, most of those governments did not dare to use military force to oppose change. Furthermore, the Soviet Union did not have the power to suppress these protests. It was too busy trying to solve its own problems.

In 1989, Poland held its first free elections in 50 years. Polish voters rejected communist candidates in favor of those put up by the trade union, Solidarity. Solidarity

Viewing History

Soviet Crackdown

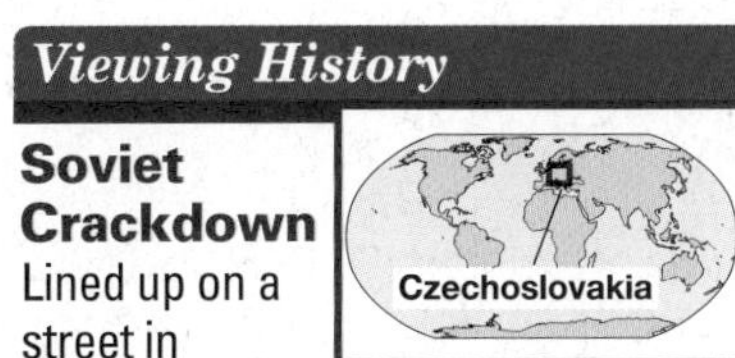

Lined up on a street in Prague, Czechoslovakia in August 1968, Soviet tanks are ready to put down any resistance by the Czech people. **Summarizing** ***In two sentences, summarize the ways by which the Soviet Union maintained control over Eastern Europe during the Cold War.***

leader, Lech Walesa (vah LEHN sah), had once been jailed by the Communists for almost a year. After the elections, he became head of a new Polish government.

One by one, Communist governments fell in Czechoslovakia, Hungary, Bulgaria, and Albania. In Romania, a violent revolt toppled the country's longtime communist dictator.

In East Germany, protests forced the Communists from power. As you have read, Berliners smashed through the wall that had divided their city for so long. By 1990, Germany was reunited under a democratic government.

Viewing History

Celebrating Communism's Fall

Russians carry the banner of their country through Moscow. The breakup of the Soviet Union marked the end of 45 years of bitter Cold War tensions. **Identifying Points of View** ***How do you think most Americans reacted to scenes such as this coming from Russia?***

The Soviet Union Collapses

The Soviet Union was made up of 15 different republics held together by a strong central government in Moscow. Under Soviet rule, the republics had few freedoms. All important policy decisions were made in Moscow.

By 1990, resentment of Moscow was high. Some Soviet people, including Lithuanians, Latvians, and Estonians, demanded self-rule. Attempting to quiet the unrest, Gorbachev allowed political parties to form. For nearly 70 years, the Soviet Union had been a one-party state.

Some of the new parties openly opposed the Communists. Hard-line communist officials were outraged. A group of them tried to oust Gorbachev. Their revolt did not last long. A Moscow politician, Boris Yeltsin, led thousands of Russians in protest. They surrounded the Parliament building and forced Soviet troops to pull back.

The attempted revolt weakened Gorbachev. In the months that followed, republic after republic declared its independence from the Soviet Union. In late 1991, Gorbachev resigned. By then, the Soviet Union had collapsed.

Fifteen new nations emerged from the old Soviet Union. Of these, Russia was the largest and most powerful. Under President Yeltsin, it began the difficult task of building a new economy based on a free-market system. In a free market, individuals decide what and how much to produce and sell. Under communism, the government had made such economic decisions.

The United States and Western European nations provided economic aid to Russia and the other republics. American experts offered advice to Russia's political and business leaders on the free-market system.

The United States was eager to see stable, democratic governments emerge in the old communist world. It also hoped that the new nations would become profitable trading partners.

Shifting to a free-market economy, however, brought terrible disruptions. Many people lost their jobs, their savings, and their sense of security. Crime and corruption grew. Many Russians began to wonder whether democracy could solve their country's many problems.

The Cold War: A Look Back

For almost 50 years, the Cold War deeply affected American life. Students in the 1950s practiced crouching under their desks in case of atomic attack. Hundreds of thousands of Americans went off to fight in the Korean and Vietnam wars. About 112,000 of them did not return.

Americans cheered the end of the Cold War and the emergence of democratic governments in Eastern Europe. Victory was costly, though. From 1946 to 1990, the United States spent over $6 trillion on national defense. The development of nuclear weapons and the arms race had created new dangers for the world. During and after the Cold War, other nations besides the superpowers tried to develop their own nuclear weapons.

The Cold War had divided Americans at times. The search for Communists in the 1950s had created an atmosphere of fear and suspicion. The Vietnam War had split the American public in an often-bitter debate.

Americans had strongly disagreed about foreign policy during the Cold War. Despite these disagreements, Americans valued their freedom, especially the right to free speech and open debate. Although some argued over how the Cold War was fought, Americans could agree that freedom was worth fighting for.

★ ★ ★ Section 5 Assessment ★ ★ ★

Recall

1. **Identify** Explain the significance of **(a)** SALT Agreement, **(b)** Ronald Reagan, **(c)** Star Wars, **(d)** Solidarity, **(e)** Mikhail Gorbachev, **(f)** glasnost, **(g)** Boris Yeltsin.
2. **Define** **(a)** détente, **(b)** martial law, **(c)** summit meeting.

Comprehension

3. What foreign policy changes did President Nixon make?
4. How did the Soviet invasion of Afghanistan cause tensions between the superpowers?
5. Give two reasons why communism collapsed in the Soviet Union and Eastern Europe.
6. Describe two results of the Cold War.

Critical Thinking and Writing

7. **Exploring the Main Idea** Review the Main Idea statement at the beginning of this section. Then, make a list of the ten most important events of the Cold War. Rank the events in order of importance. Explain your ranking.
8. **Solving Problems** **(a)** Describe two ways in which the United States could help former communist nations make the shift to democracy. **(b)** Do you think that the United States should provide such help? Why or why not?

Activity

Writing a News Dispatch **You are a foreign correspondent for a leading American newspaper. Write two reports to send to your newspaper, dated 1989 and 1991. In each report, describe the events leading to the collapse of the Soviet Union.**

CHAPTER
28 Review and Assessment

CHAPTER SUMMARY

Section 1
Distrust among the nations that had defeated the Axis powers triggered a Cold War. The post-WWII period was marked by the Berlin crisis, new alliances, the Soviet development of the atomic bomb, and the fall of China to communists.

Section 2
The Korean War in the early 1950s increased tensions between the two superpowers and led to the hunt for communists in the United States.

Section 3
The Cold War spread to Africa, Asia, and Latin America. The two superpowers clashed during the Cuban missile crisis. The arms race and the space race pitted the superpowers against one another.

Section 4
The United States became involved in the Vietnam War in an effort to stop the spread of communism. After the Tet Offensive, many Americans began to oppose the Vietnam War. The Communist North's capture of Saigon after the U.S. withdrawal from South Vietnam brought the long war to an end.

Section 5
President Nixon negotiated with China and the Soviet Union to try to ease tensions, but events produced new conflicts. Free elections in Eastern Europe and the collapse of the Soviet Union marked the end of the Cold War.

Building Vocabulary

Use the chapter vocabulary words listed below to create a crossword puzzle. Exchange puzzles with a classmate. Complete the puzzles, and then check each other's answers.

1. **containment**
2. **demilitarized zone**
3. **perjury**
4. **superpower**
5. **exile**
6. **guerrilla**
7. **escalate**
8. **détente**
9. **martial law**
10. **summit meeting**

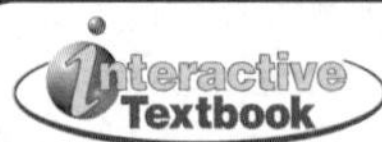

For additional review and enrichment activities, see the interactive version of *The American Nation,* available on the Web and on CD-ROM.

Chapter Self-Test For practice test questions for Chapter 28, visit PHSchool.com, **Web Code mfa-2804.**

Reviewing Key Facts

11. Describe two actions President Truman took to combat the spread of communism in Europe after World War II. (Section 1)
12. What impact did the Korean War have on events in the United States? (Section 2)
13. Give one example of how superpower rivalries affected nations around the world. (Section 3)
14. Describe three results of the Vietnam War. (Section 4)
15. Describe President Reagan's policies toward the Soviet Union. (Section 5)

Critical Thinking and Writing

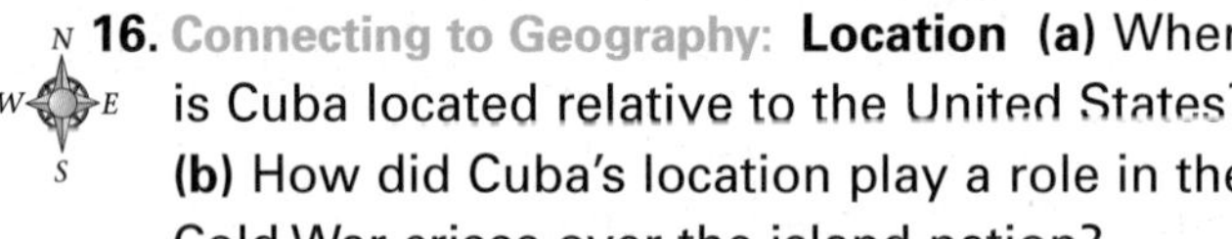

16. **Connecting to Geography: Location (a)** Where is Cuba located relative to the United States? **(b)** How did Cuba's location play a role in the Cold War crises over the island nation?
17. **Comparing** Compare and contrast the Korean War and the Vietnam War in terms of **(a)** results, **(b)** popular support.
18. **Sequencing (a)** Which began first: glasnost or the breakup of the Soviet Union? **(b)** Explain why these two events occurred in the order in which they did, not the other way around.

Skills Assessment

Analyzing Primary Sources

American cartoonists expressed the fears of Americans about the Cold War's rising tensions. This cartoon is from a 1947 newspaper.

19. What does the basketball symbolize?
- **A.** *Sputnik*
- **B.** a falling meteorite
- **C.** European recovery
- **D.** the Marshall Plan

20. The man blocking the basketball is Joseph Stalin. He is blocking the basketball because
- **A.** The United States opposes European recovery.
- **B.** The USSR opposes the U.S.-backed Marshall Plan.
- **C.** The United States opposes the USSR-backed Marshall Plan.
- **D.** The United States and the Soviet Union oppose European recovery.

Applying Your Skills

Predicting Consequences

This 1946 telegram would later prove valuable to those who tried to predict the consequences of Soviet propaganda on the Russian people:

> “[Communist propaganda] does not represent natural outlook of Russian people. Latter are, by and large, friendly to outside world, . . . eager above all to live in peace and enjoy fruits of their own labor. Party line only represents [ideas] which official propaganda machine puts forward with great skill. . . .”
>
> —George Kennan, telegram to the State Department, February 22, 1946

21. A government official could conclude that Kennan thought that the Soviet people
- **A.** were ready to rebel against their government.
- **B.** would never challenge their government.
- **C.** would eventually turn against their government's policies.
- **D.** were especially warlike and anti-American.

22. **(a)** In what ways did Soviet policies prevent the Soviet people from enjoying the "fruits of their own labor"? **(b)** What challenges lie ahead for Russia's rulers today based on Kennan's 1946 statements?

Activities

Connecting With . . . Culture

Writing Slogans Write three slogans that might have appeared on posters during the Cold War period. Topics might include the search for communists in the United States during the 1950s, Truman versus MacArthur, the Berlin Wall, the Vietnam War, the fall of communism in the Soviet Union, the Cuban missile crisis.

Connecting to Today

Creating a Brochure Use the Internet to find out about the Korean War Veterans Memorial. Make a tourist brochure describing the memorial, its design, its meaning for veterans and others, and its place in American history. For help in starting this activity, visit PHSchool.com, **Web Code mfd-2805.**

CHAPTER 29

Prosperity, Rebellion, and Reform

1945–1980

1 Postwar Policies and Prosperity
2 The Civil Rights Movement
3 Protest, Reform, and Doubt
4 The Crusade for Equal Rights

Jackie Robinson

President Johnson signs the 1964 Civil Rights Act

AMERICAN EVENTS

1947 Jackie Robinson breaks the color barrier in baseball.

1950s The baby boom increases the United States population.

1963 Civil rights supporters protesting discrimination march on Washington, D.C.

1964 The Civil Rights Act of 1964 is passed.

Presidential Terms: Harry S. Truman 1945–1953 | Dwight D. Eisenhower 1953–1961 | John F. Kennedy 1961–1963

1945 · 1955 · 1965

WORLD EVENTS

▲ **1950** The Korean War begins.

▲ **1957** Ghana becomes the first West African colony to win its independence.

Centers of the Human Rights Movement

During the protests of the 1960s and 1970s African Americans, women, and other minorities demanded that their civil rights be recognized and respected.

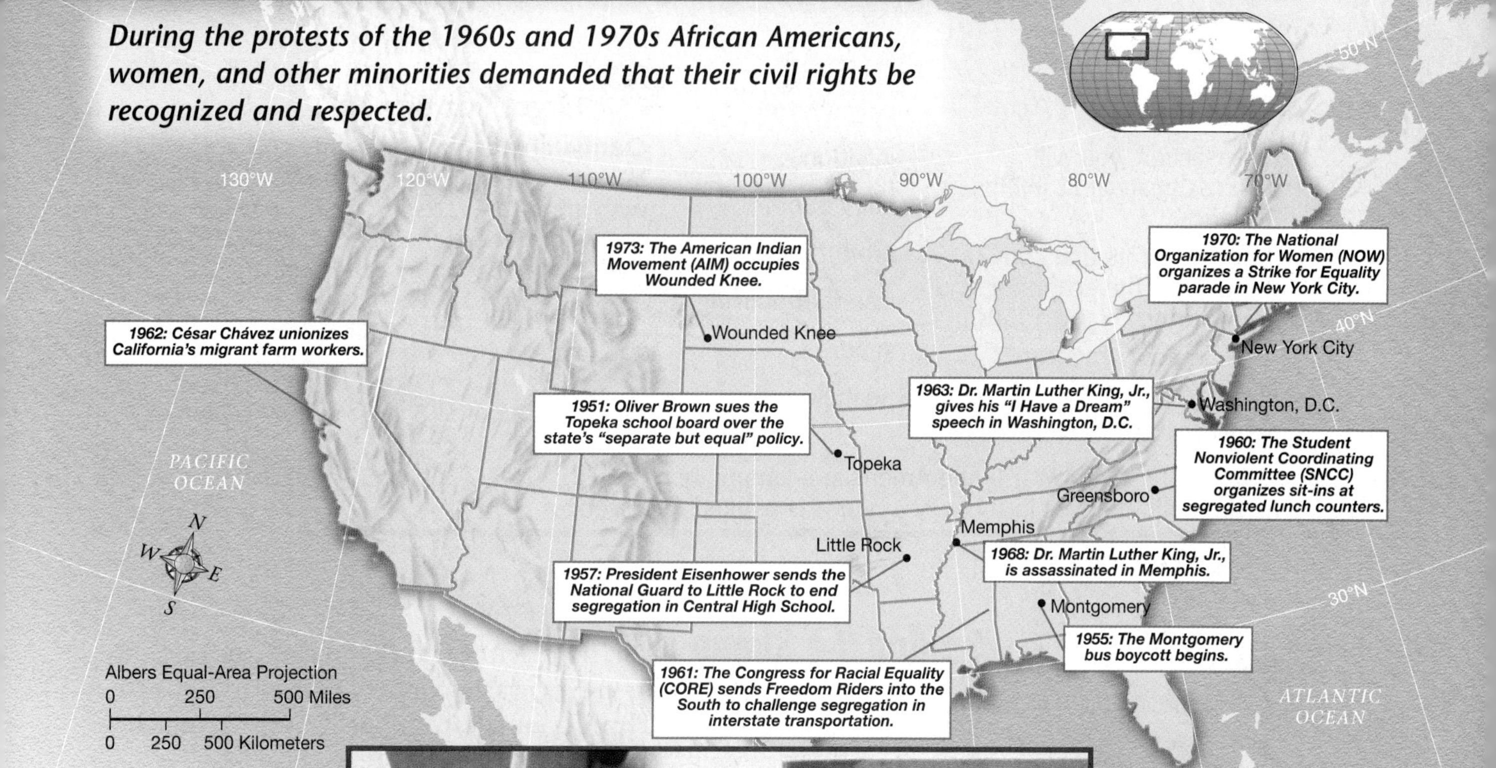

130°W 120°W 110°W 100°W 90°W 80°W 70°W

50°N 40°N 30°N 20°N

1973: The American Indian Movement (AIM) occupies Wounded Knee.

1970: The National Organization for Women (NOW) organizes a Strike for Equality parade in New York City.

1962: César Chávez unionizes California's migrant farm workers.

Wounded Knee

New York City

1963: Dr. Martin Luther King, Jr., gives his "I Have a Dream" speech in Washington, D.C.

Washington, D.C.

1951: Oliver Brown sues the Topeka school board over the state's "separate but equal" policy.

Topeka

1960: The Student Nonviolent Coordinating Committee (SNCC) organizes sit-ins at segregated lunch counters.

Greensboro

PACIFIC OCEAN

Memphis

Little Rock

1968: Dr. Martin Luther King, Jr., is assassinated in Memphis.

1957: President Eisenhower sends the National Guard to Little Rock to end segregation in Central High School.

Montgomery

1955: The Montgomery bus boycott begins.

Albers Equal-Area Projection

0 250 500 Miles

0 250 500 Kilometers

1961: The Congress for Racial Equality (CORE) sends Freedom Riders into the South to challenge segregation in interstate transportation.

ATLANTIC OCEAN

Richard M. Nixon

1974

Threatened with impeachment, Richard M. Nixon becomes the first President to resign.

Lyndon B. Johnson 1963-1969	Richard M. Nixon 1969-1974	Gerald R. Ford 1974-1977	Jimmy Carter 1977-1981

1965 · · · · **1975** · · · · **1985** · ·

▲ 1960s
The United States involvement in Vietnam grows.

▲ 1975
The Helsinki Agreement defines basic human rights.

1 Postwar Policies and Prosperity

Prepare to Read

Objectives

In this section, you will
- Discuss postwar problems in America.
- List the factors that contributed to the economic and baby booms of the 1950s.
- Explain how American lifestyles changed in the 1950s.

Key Terms

inflation

baby boom

productivity

standard of living

suburb

beatnik

Target Reading Skill

Clarifying Meaning Copy the concept web below. As you read, fill in the blank ovals with important facts about the way life changed in the United States in the 1950s. Add as many ovals as you need.

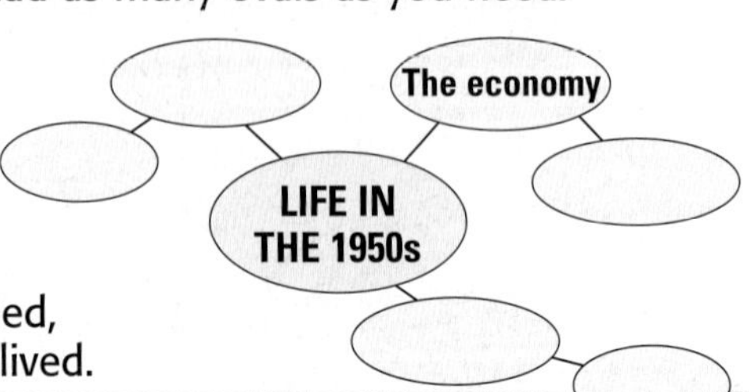

Main Idea After World War II, the American economy boomed, bringing dramatic changes in the way Americans worked and lived.

A 1950 car ad

Setting the Scene

A British visitor coming to the United States in 1948 was amazed. "There never was a country more fabulous than America," he observed. Three years after World War II, much of Europe still lay in ruins. But America, he wrote,

> “ sits bestride the world like a Colossus. . . . Half of the wealth of the world, more than half of the productivity, nearly two-thirds of the world's machines are concentrated in American hands; the rest of the world lies in the shadow of American industry. ”
>
> —Robert Payne, 1949

In the decades after World War II, the United States experienced a boom like no other in its history. The population mushroomed, the economy prospered, and Americans enjoyed the highest standard of living any people had ever known.

From War to Peace

When the war ended in 1945, two thirds of all American men between the ages of 18 and 34 were in uniform. Experts feared that without wartime production, many returning soldiers might find no jobs. Unemployment would rise, and the economy would tumble.

Economic Difficulties Even before the war ended, Congress passed the GI Bill of Rights* to help returning veterans. Under this law, the government spent billions of dollars to help veterans set up farms and businesses. Many GIs received loans to pay for college or a new home. It also provided a full year of unemployment benefits for veterans who could not find work.

*GI stands for "government issue." During World War II, GI came to mean any member of the United States armed forces.

Inflation, or rising prices, was a major postwar problem. During the war, the government had controlled prices and wages. After the war, the controls ended. The price of goods rose.

Workers demanded higher wages to pay for the price increases. When employers refused, labor unions called strikes.

President Harry Truman was sympathetic to workers but feared that higher wages would only add to inflation. He urged strikers to return to work.

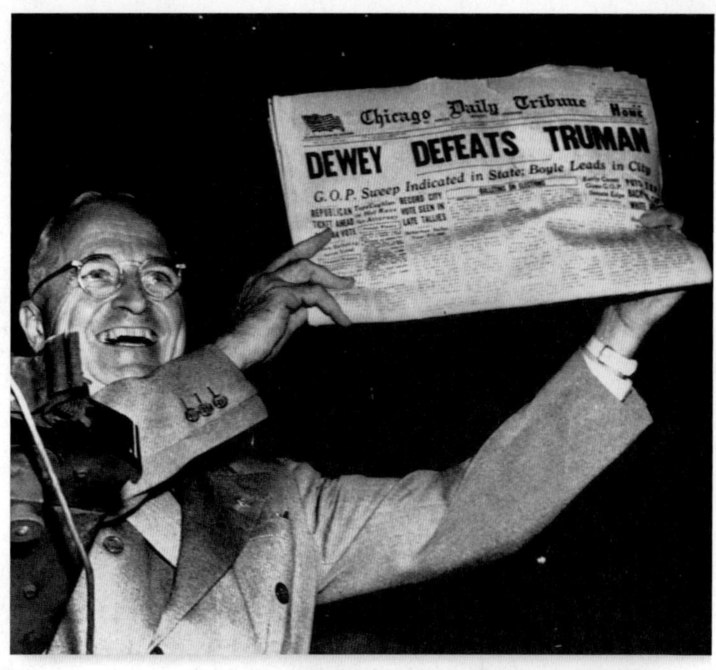

Viewing History

A Truman Victory

St. Louis

Based on early results, the *Chicago Daily Tribune* declared Truman the loser in the 1948 election. Here, Truman proudly displays the newspaper headline. **Draw Inferences** ***What does this headline suggest about the election?***

Truman's Surprise Victory As the election of 1948 approached, President Truman and his Democratic party seemed doomed to defeat. Labor strikes and soaring prices had already helped Republicans win a majority in both the House and the Senate for the first time since the 1920s. Among Democrats, unhappy liberals and conservatives deserted Truman to form parties of their own. The Republicans confidently nominated Governor Thomas Dewey of New York for President.

Truman fought back. During his campaign, Truman traveled thousands of miles across the country by train. At every stop, he attacked the Republicans as "do-nothings" and "gluttons of privilege." When all the votes were counted, Truman won a surprise victory over Dewey.

A New Round of Reform During his presidency, Truman proposed a new round of reform called the Fair Deal. He wanted to extend the liberal policies of his predecessor, Franklin D. Roosevelt.

In Congress the Fair Deal faced heavy opposition from conservative Democrats and Republicans. Only a few of the proposals passed: a higher minimum wage, expanded Social Security benefits, and loans for buying low-cost houses. Congress rejected most of Truman's reforms, including a bold plan to provide government-financed health insurance.

The Eisenhower Years In 1952, President Truman chose not to run for reelection. Democrats nominated Adlai Stevenson of Illinois. Republicans chose General Dwight D. Eisenhower, a hero of World War II. Eisenhower, known as "Ike," promised to end the conflict in Korea and lead Americans through the Cold War.

For the first time, television played a major role in a presidential campaign. Instead of long speeches, Republicans used 20-second TV "spots" of Ike responding to questions from hand-picked citizens. Complained one critic: "It was selling the President like toothpaste." Still, enough voters were impressed with Ike's military experience and foreign policy skills to give him a landslide victory.

Like most Republicans, President Eisenhower believed in limiting federal spending and reducing federal regulation of the economy. He called his political course the "straight road down the middle."

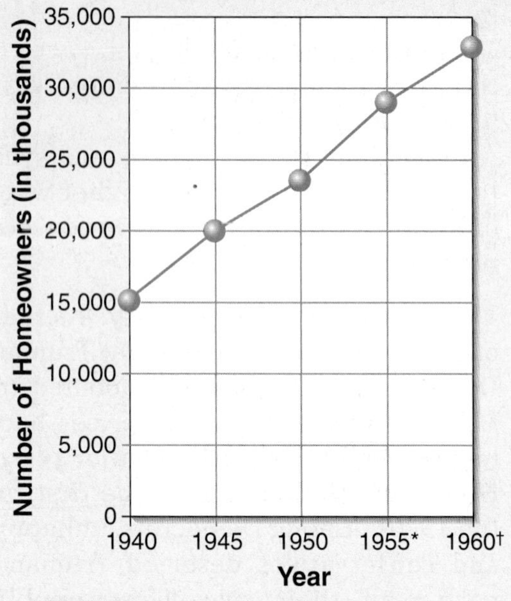

Viewing History

An Increase in Home Ownership

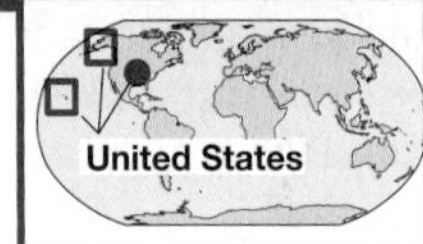

With growing families and larger incomes, more people sought new houses in the suburbs. Between 1947 and 1965, at least 1.25 million new houses were built each year. More than one half of those were in the suburbs. **Analyzing Information** ***Why do you think more people chose to live in the suburbs?***

He favored cutting the federal budget but expanding Social Security benefits and some other New Deal programs.

Most Americans supported Eisenhower's middle-of-the-road approach. In the 1956 presidential election, voters reelected Ike to a second term of office.

An Economic and Baby Boom

During the Great Depression and World War II, many Americans had put off having families. When the war ended and prosperity returned, the number of births soared.

Population experts called the phenomenon a **baby boom.** In the 1930s, the population of the United States had grown by only 9 million. In the 1940s it grew by 19 million and in the 1950s by an astounding 29 million! Most couples married young, had an average of three children, and completed their families by their late twenties.

Improvements in health care and nutrition contributed to the baby boom. Better care for pregnant women and newborn infants meant that more babies survived. Fewer children died from childhood diseases than had died in the past.

Economic Boom In addition to the baby boom, there was an economic boom. The economy rapidly expanded in the postwar years. When an economy expands, more goods are produced and sold and more jobs are created.

Federal projects also increased factory production. The government spent more money to build new roads, houses, and schools. In the middle of the Cold War, government spending on military goods spurred the economy, too.

New technology added to the boom by promoting steady rises in **productivity,** or the average output per worker. Corporations began using computers to perform calculations and keep records.

High productivity allowed the United States to manufacture and consume, or use, more goods than any other country. Increased productivity also led to a workweek that averaged 40 hours. Americans now had more leisure time.

Target Skill **Summarize** Write one or two sentences summarizing the two "booms" in the United States after World War II.

Lifestyles of the 1950s

The economic boom raised Americans' **standard of living,** an index based on the amount of goods, services, and leisure time people have. Americans bought washing machines, vacuum cleaners, televisions, automobiles, and many other consumer goods.

Because so many of their purchases revolved around home and family, few Americans worried that they were saving little. Instead, most Americans enjoyed a life in which they had more money to spend. This consumer spending reshaped the country.

Suburban Living With their newfound wealth, many people bought homes in the **suburbs,** or communities outside the cities. The GI Bill encouraged home building in the suburbs by offering low-interest loans to veterans. During the 1950s, suburbs grew 40 times faster than cities.

Builder William Levitt pioneered a new way of building suburban houses. He bought large tracts of land and then divided them into small lots. On each lot, he built a house identical to every other house in the tract. Because these houses were mass-produced, they cost much less to build than custom-made houses. They could also be constructed rapidly. Using preassembled materials, teams of carpenters, plumbers, and electricians could put up a Levitt house in 16 minutes.

Levitt began his first big project in 1947, on Long Island, where he put up 17,000 new homes. It was the largest housing development ever built by an American. Levitt called the project Levittown. African Americans were barred from owning or renting in Levittown. Levitt feared that if he sold to blacks, whites would not buy.

Shopping centers with modern department stores sprang up near the suburban housing developments. There were eight shopping centers in 1946. By the end of the 1950s, there were 4,000. No longer did consumers have to travel to the city to buy what they wanted. Shiny new shopping centers were only a short drive away.

As millions flocked to the suburbs, central cities began a slow decline. Suburbs and shopping centers drained cities of businesses and taxes. Since most of those who moved were white, some critics complained that the United States was turning into a nation of "chocolate cities and vanilla suburbs."

Sunbelt Living Americans also flocked to the Sunbelt, a region stretching across the southern rim of the country. States from Florida to Texas and California began to experience dramatic growth.

LINKING PAST AND PRESENT

▲ Past

▲ Present

Viewing History

The Cinema

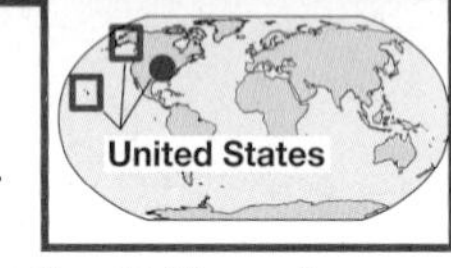

Drive-in theaters became popular during the 1940s and peaked in the 1950s. Customers could buy snacks and enjoy a movie while sitting in their cars. Today, movie fans can watch their favorite movies at home. Most movies are available on video cassettes or DVD (digital video disc) which can be bought or rented from a local video store.

Evaluating Information

What does the popularity of the drive-in movie tell you about the 1950s?

For Americans on the move, the Sunbelt, both then and now, had many lures: a warm climate; good jobs; a prosperous economy based on agriculture, oil, and electronics; and national defense industries. Businesses still move to the region for its low taxes and growing work force. The work force included recent immigrants from Latin America and Asia. Like many ambitious newcomers, they were willing to work hard for low pay.

Car Crazy During the 1950s, cars became more important to daily life. People living in the suburbs or the Sunbelt usually needed a car to drive to work. By 1960, 9 out of 10 families living in the suburbs owned a car. Since few people bought foreign cars, the American automobile companies, such as General Motors, profited greatly.

To accommodate the increase in automobiles, the federal government built thousands of miles of highways. In 1956, Congress passed the Federal Aid Highway Act. This act called for a network of high-speed roads linking the nation. It set aside $41 billion to build 40,000 miles of highway.

The new highway system boosted the economy, especially the automobile and trucking industries. Americans could travel more easily for business or pleasure. As a result, a new roadside culture of motels and fast-food restaurants emerged.

Television Television caught on slowly. However, as TV sets shrank in price and grew in size, almost everybody wanted one. Nine out of 10 households had at least one television by 1960.

Television brought news and entertainment into people's homes. Commercials encouraged spending and buying. Television also helped to make the 1950s a time when people wanted to look and act the same as everyone else. Many programs presented the same single view of the ideal middle-class family. Fathers knew best, mothers were loving and supportive, and children were always obedient.

Rock Music In the mid-1950s, a new type of music appeared. Rock-and-roll combined the sounds of rhythm, blues, country, and gospel with a hard-driving beat. Adults worried that the music was too wild. However, many teenagers liked rock-and-roll because it provided an opportunity for them to show their independence. *Teenager* was a word first used in the 1950s to describe someone between 13 and 19 years old.

African American singers Chuck Berry and Little Richard gained national fame. From Texas came Buddy Holly, and from California, Latino singer Richie Valens. No one attracted more attention than Memphis's Elvis Presley. His slick hair, sideburns, and steamy dancing alarmed parents but made Elvis a hit with teenagers. They dressed like him, bought his records, and nicknamed him "the King."

Signs of Discontent Not all Americans in the 1950s were happy about the emphasis on getting and spending. A small group of writers and artists criticized what they saw as the growing materialism of American society and its lack of individuality. Novelist Jack Kerouac coined the term *beat*, meaning "weariness with all forms of the modern industrial state." Middle-class observers called Kerouac and others like him **beatniks.** Still, Kerouac's best-selling novel, *On the Road,* influenced many young Americans.

Most Americans paid little attention to these signs of discontent. Soon, however, a growing outcry could not be ignored.

Section 1 Assessment

Recall

1. **Identify** Explain the significance of **(a)** GI Bill of Rights, **(b)** Fair Deal, **(c)** Dwight D. Eisenhower, **(d)** Levittown, **(e)** Sunbelt, **(f)** Federal-Aid Highway Act, **(g)** Elvis Presley, **(h)** Jack Kerouac.
2. **Define** **(a)** inflation, **(b)** baby boom, **(c)** productivity, **(d)** standard of living, **(e)** suburb, **(f)** beatnik.

Comprehension

3. What economic difficulties did Americans face immediately after World War II?
4. Discuss the significance of the baby boom of the late 1940s.
5. Describe the effect of television on American life in the 1950s.

Critical Thinking and Writing

6. **Exploring the Main Idea** Review the Main Idea statement at the beginning of this section. Then, write two generalizations about the way most Americans lived in the 1950s.
7. **Identifying Points of View** Why did some people dislike the cultural changes that were occurring in the 1950s?

Activity

Writing Interview Questions **As a news reporter, you are assigned to write an article on how the United States changed during the 1950s. Write five questions that you would ask someone who had lived during those years. Each question should be based on one of the headings in this section.**

The Early Days of Television

After coast-to-coast broadcasting began in 1951, the number of TV sets soared from 6 million to 60 million within a decade. Americans were fascinated with the broad range of visual entertainment available at home, and television quickly became a part of the American culture.

I Love Lucy became an overnight sensation in 1951 and went on to become the most popular situation comedy in the history of television. More than 70 percent of the nation's TV sets were tuned in to the show when characters Lucy and Ricky Ricardo became parents to "Little Ricky."

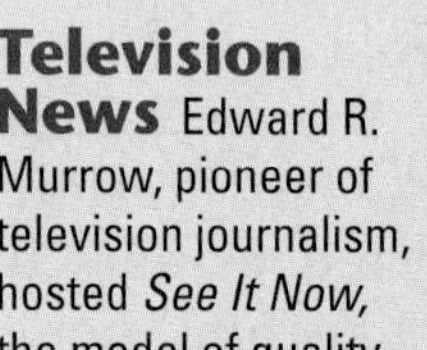

Television News Edward R. Murrow, pioneer of television journalism, hosted *See It Now,* the model of quality TV documentaries. On *Person to Person,* Murrow spoke from his TV studio to celebrities in their homes. Walter Cronkite, another well-known journalist, hosted *You Are There,* newsreels of historic events.

TV families of the 1950s were warmly portrayed in such shows as *Father Knows Best* (shown here), *Lassie, Leave It to Beaver,* and *The Adventures of Ozzie and Harriet.*

The Howdy Doody Show was the most popular children's show of the 1950s.

Activity

Use the Internet to find out about the quiz show scandal of 1959. Why do you think TV networks replaced high-stakes quiz shows with Westerns and detective shows in the aftermath of the scandal?

2 The Civil Rights Movement

Prepare to Read

Objectives

In this section, you will
- Explain how discrimination affected the lives of minorities in the United States.
- Discuss the role the courts played in helping African Americans and Mexican Americans gain civil rights.
- Describe the role of Martin Luther King, Jr., in the Montgomery bus boycott.

Key Terms

segregation

integration

civil rights movement

boycott

civil disobedience

Target Reading Skill

Sequence Copy this flowchart. As you read, describe the events that began to end segregation during the late 1940s and 1950s. The first and last boxes have been completed to help you get started. Add as many boxes as you need.

The NAACP becomes more active in working against segregation

↓

(blank)

↓

(blank)

↓

Groups against segregation

Main Idea After World War II, African Americans and other minorities began to demand their full civil rights and an end to discrimination.

Setting the Scene Driving north from the South every summer, young George knew that the trip must be carefully planned. The family had to take food and water. But, they also had to map out which roads to take and where to stop. In the racially divided South, blacks were not always welcome. Going to the restroom was a difficult problem during the trip. At stop after stop, George saw signs that read "Whites only" or "No coloreds allowed."

George later became a college president but only after decades of struggle had broken down barriers of discrimination. Across the United States, African Americans and other racial minorities faced discrimination not just on the road but also in jobs, housing, and education. After World War II, their struggles for equality and civil rights intensified.

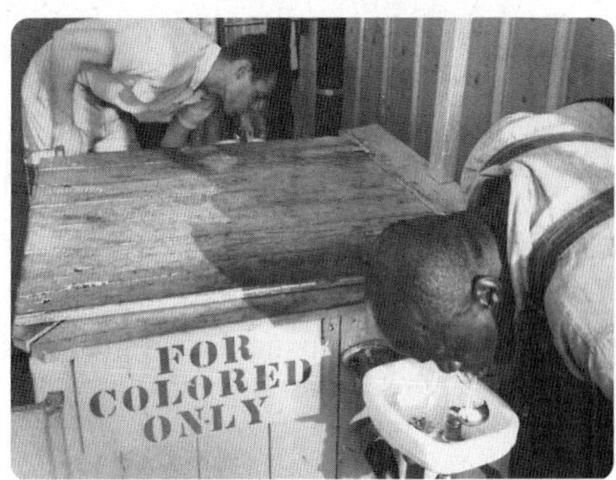

A segregated water fountain

Discrimination Creates Barriers

Throughout the nation, discrimination limited the lives of millions of Americans. Qualified African Americans found themselves barred from good jobs and decent housing in the North. In the South, laws enforced strict separation, or **segregation**, of the races in schools, theaters, restaurants, and other public places. Facilities for blacks were inferior to those for whites.

Discrimination also limited Mexican Americans and other Latinos. They were not subject to strict segregation laws. However, other laws—as well as traditions—worked against them. In the Southwest, all-white schools closed their doors to Mexican American children. Instead, poorly equipped "Mexican schools" served them. Custom kept Mexican Americans from living in certain neighborhoods or using certain hotels or restaurants. Often, better-paying jobs were not open to them.

Breaking Down the Barriers For African Americans, the NAACP (National Association for the Advancement of Colored People) led the drive against discrimination. During World War II, NAACP membership rocketed from 50,000 to 500,000. Under Thurgood Marshall, its Legal Defense Fund mounted several court battles against segregation. It also helped blacks register to vote and fought for equal opportunity in housing and employment.

Historic Firsts There were two significant events in the 1940s in the fight against segregation. Jackie Robinson broke the color barrier in Major League Baseball in 1947 when he joined the Brooklyn Dodgers. He was even named rookie of the year. Not since Moses Fleetwood Walker had a black player joined the major leagues. Walker was the first African American player to join a major league team in 1884.

Under pressure from civil rights groups, President Truman ordered **integration,** or the mixing of different racial groups, in the armed forces in 1948. During the Korean War, black and white soldiers fought side by side.

After risking their lives abroad, veterans were unwilling to accept discrimination at home. Often they became leaders in the struggle for equal rights. "Veterans," explained an observer, "have acquired a new courage, and have become more vocal in protesting inequalities."

An American Profile

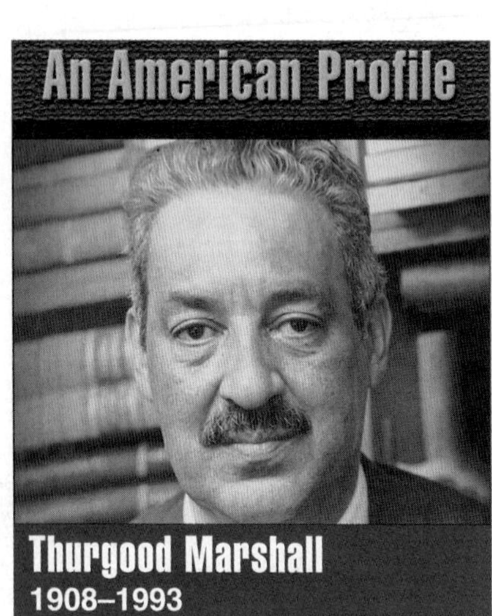

Thurgood Marshall
1908–1993

Thurgood Marshall made history at the United States Supreme Court. In 1954, he argued before the Court the case that ended the practice of separate schools for white and black students—*Brown* v. *Board of Education of Topeka.* Later, he became the first African American to become a justice of the Supreme Court.

After Marshall had graduated from law school, he joined a team of lawyers working for the NAACP. Marshall's plan was to chip away at the laws that treated African Americans unfairly. He argued 32 cases before the Supreme Court and won 29 times.

How did Marshall work to gain racial equality for African Americans?

The Court Fight for Civil Rights

During the 1950s, African Americans and Mexican Americans stepped up the struggle for equality. They took their cases to court but also protested in the streets. Their efforts became known as the **civil rights movement.**

In Schools The U.S. Supreme Court had decided in 1896 in *Plessy* v. *Ferguson* that "separate but equal" facilities for blacks and whites were constitutional. During the 1940s, the NAACP did not attack this idea head on. Instead, its lawyers argued that an individual facility like a state college or law school was not equal to the local white school.

Such a legal strategy might improve black schools and other segregated facilities case by case, but those cases did little to end segregation. By the early 1950s, laws in 21 states and the District of Columbia still enforced separate black and white public schools. Virtually all of the black schools were inferior to the white ones.

Oliver Brown of Topeka, Kansas, decided to challenge the Kansas law. He asked the local school board to let his daughter, Linda, attend a nearby white school rather than the distant black school to which she had been assigned. When board members refused, Brown filed a suit against the school board with the help of the NAACP. The case of *Brown* v. *Board of Education of Topeka* reached the Supreme Court.

To present the case in court, Brown hired lawyer Thurgood Marshall, who specialized in civil rights cases. Marshall had served as legal director of the NAACP for more than ten years. He decided to challenge the whole idea of "separate but equal." Segregated schools, he argued, could never provide equal education. By their very nature, said Marshall, segregated schools violated the Fourteenth Amendment, which gave "equal protection" to all citizens.

The Supreme Court ruled in Brown's favor in 1954. Chief Justice Earl Warren noted that segregation affected the "hearts and minds" of black students "in a way unlikely ever to be undone." The unanimous decision declared:

> ❝ We conclude that in the field of public education, the doctrine of 'separate but equal' has no place. Separate educational facilities are always unequal. ❞

Desegregating Public Schools A year later, the Court ordered the schools to be desegregated "with all deliberate speed." In a few places, schools were integrated without much trouble. In many others, officials resisted. White politicians in these places decided that the phrase "with all deliberate speed" could mean they could take years to integrate their schools. Or, perhaps they would never obey the decision.

Arkansas Governor Orval Faubus called out the National Guard in 1957 in order to keep African American students from attending all-white Central High School in Little Rock. President Eisenhower finally sent in federal troops because the Arkansas governor was defying a federal law. Under their protection, black students entered Central High.

Eisenhower was the first President since Reconstruction to use armed federal troops in support of African American rights. The action showed that the federal government could play a key role in protecting civil rights.

On Juries Mexican Americans organized their own fight for civil rights. Mexican American veterans founded the American GI Forum of the United States (AGIF) in 1948 in order to campaign for equal rights. Similar to the NAACP, the AGIF supported legal challenges to discrimination.

In 1954, the same year as *Brown* v. *Board of Education,* Mexican Americans won an important legal battle when the Supreme Court ruled on the case of *Hernández* v. *Texas.*

Pete Hernández, a Mexican American, had been convicted of murder by an all-white jury in Texas. Among the lawyers who appealed his conviction was Gus Garcia, one of the leaders of the AGIF. Attorney James DeAnda, another Mexican American, also helped. He had previously worked to desegregate areas of Corpus Christi, Texas, where Mexican Americans were not allowed to buy houses.

Hernández's lawyers argued that Mexican Americans in Texas were denied equality under the law because they were excluded from juries. The Supreme Court agreed. It overturned the conviction and ended the exclusion of Mexican Americans from Texas juries. In the future, other minority groups would use this decision to help win their civil rights.

Primary Source

The Little Rock Nine

Elizabeth Eckford was one of the original nine African American students to attend Central High School in Little Rock. Years later, she described her experience:

"I tried to find a friendly face somewhere in the mob. I looked at [a white girl] again and she spat on me. . . . Then I saw a bench at the bus stop. When I got there, I don't think I could have gone another step. I sat down and the mob crowded up and began shouting all over again. Just then a white man sat down beside me, put his arm around me and patted my shoulder. He raised my chin and said, 'Don't let them see you cry.'"

—Elizabeth Eckford, in an interview

Analyzing Primary Sources

Why did the man tell Eckford not to let the other students see her cry?

Rosa Parks

Walking to work

Viewing History

The Montgomery Bus Boycott

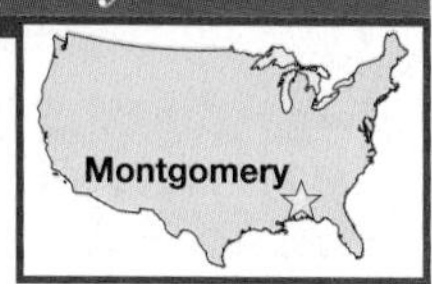

The yearlong boycott, which began with Rosa Parks's refusal to give up her seat to a white passenger on a bus, gripped the nation's attention. African Americans walked to work, and Martin Luther King, Jr., gained prominence as an important civil rights leader. King is shown here during his arrest and with his wife (facing page) and other demonstrators. **Applying Information** ***How did African Americans use economic pressure to gain equal rights?***

The Montgomery Bus Boycott

Court cases were not enough to end discrimination, as Rosa Parks discovered in December 1955. She was riding home from work on a crowded bus in Montgomery, Alabama. The driver ordered her to move to the back of the bus so that a white man could have her seat, as Alabama's segregation laws required. Parks, a well-known activist and a former secretary of the local chapter of the NAACP, refused to leave her seat. She was arrested and put in jail.

Rosa Parks's arrest angered African Americans in Montgomery. That night, several women from the NAACP composed a letter asking all African Americans to **boycott,** or refuse to use, the buses. The boycott, they hoped, would hurt the city financially and force an end to segregation on the buses. The women distributed thousands of copies of the letter to the African Americans of Montgomery.

To support the protest, Montgomery's black leaders formed a new organization, the Montgomery Improvement Association (MIA). They chose Dr. Martin Luther King, Jr., a Baptist minister, as its head.

Dr. King spoke at a meeting in the Holt Street Baptist Church. Hundreds packed the church. Thousands more stood outside. "We are here this evening . . . for serious business," King began. "Yes, yes!" the crowd shouted. As the crowd cheered him on, King continued:

> “You know, my friends, there comes a time when people get tired of being trampled over by the iron feet of oppression. . . . We are determined here in Montgomery . . . to work and fight until justice runs down like water, and righteousness like a mighty stream!”
>
> —Martin Luther King, Jr., Speech, December 2, 1955

On December 5, 1955, most African Americans in Montgomery refused to travel by bus.

Target Skill: Identify Sequence What important events led to the Montgomery bus boycott? Read to learn what events came as a result of the boycott. Add these events to your flowchart.

King is arrested

A successful end

The Boycott Continues The boycott lasted from December 5 to December 20 of the next year. MIA carpools took some 20,000 African Americans to and from work each day. Many people simply walked. One elderly woman coined a phrase that became a motto of the boycott: "My feets is tired, but my soul is rested."

Angry whites fought back. Employers threatened to arrest African Americans if they did not abandon the boycott. Police handed out traffic tickets to harass boycotters and they frequently stopped African American drivers and demanded to see their licenses.They arrested King for speeding and kept him in jail for several days. King's house was bombed. Still, the boycott continued.

King insisted that his followers limit their actions to **civil disobedience,** or nonviolent protests against unjust laws. He said, "We must use the weapon of love. We must have compassion and understanding for those who hate us."

Throughout the bus boycott, African American churches were vital to its success. Churches played a central role in the lives of African Americans across the country. In Montgomery, mass meetings were held in black churches. There, boycotters sang together, prayed together, and listened to stories of sacrifice. The churches kept morale high, provided leadership, and helped boycotters give each other courage and inspiration.

Finally, the MIA filed a federal lawsuit to end bus segregation in Montgomery. In 1956, almost a year after Rosa Parks had refused to move to the back of the bus, the Supreme Court ruled that segregation on Alabama buses was unconstitutional. The Montgomery bus company agreed to integrate the buses and to hire black bus drivers.

Wide-reaching Effects The effects of the bus boycott reached far beyond Montgomery. The boycott brought the civil rights movement to national attention. It launched nonviolent protest as a key tactic in the struggle for equality. Finally, the boycott introduced the nation to a new generation of African American leaders. Many were ministers from African American churches.

Martin Luther King, Jr.

One of the most important of these new national figures was boycott leader Martin Luther King, Jr. He was the son of a prominent Baptist minister. King had graduated from Morehouse College, a leading black college. Later, he had earned a Ph.D. in religion and served as pastor of an African American church in Montgomery.

King had studied a wide range of philosophers and political thinkers. He had come to admire especially Mohandas Gandhi, a lawyer who had pioneered the use of nonviolence to end British rule in India.

Following the Montgomery victory, King and other African American leaders founded the Southern Christian Leadership Conference (SCLC) to carry on the crusade for civil rights. The group, consisting of nearly 100 black ministers, elected King president and the Reverend Ralph Abernathy treasurer. The SCLC urged African Americans to fight injustice by using civil disobedience:

> “Understand that nonviolence is not a symbol of weakness or cowardice, but as . . . demonstrated, nonviolent resistance transforms weakness into strength and breeds courage in the face of danger.”
>
> — SCLC statement, January 10–11, 1957

Still, discrimination and segregation remained widespread. The civil rights movement of the 1950s would soon grow into a howling wind of protest that would sweep across the country.

★ ★ ★ Section 2 Assessment ★ ★ ★

Recall

1. **Identify** Explain the significance of **(a)** NAACP, **(b)** Jackie Robinson, **(c)** *Brown* v. *Board of Education of Topeka,* **(d)** Thurgood Marshall, **(e)** AGIF, **(f)** *Hernández* v. *Texas,* **(g)** Rosa Parks, **(h)** Martin Luther King, Jr.
2. **Define** **(a)** segregation, **(b)** integration, **(c)** civil rights movement, **(d)** boycott, **(e)** civil disobedience.

Comprehension

3. Describe how discrimination limited the lives of minorities.
4. Discuss the impact of the *Brown* v. *Board of Education of Topeka* decision.
5. Discuss the methods that Dr. Martin Luther King, Jr., used to help end segregation on Montgomery's buses.

Critical Thinking and Writing

6. **Exploring the Main Idea** Review the Main Idea statement at the beginning of this section. Then, make a concept web with facts about the early civil rights movement.
7. **Supporting a Point of View** Do you think that civil disobedience is an effective method of protest? Explain.

ACTIVITY

Researching Civil Rights Cases

Use the Internet to find out about court cases that challenged segregation in education before *Brown* v. *Board of Education of Topeka.* With a partner, prepare a chart with interesting facts about each case. For help in completing the activity, visit PHSchool.com, **Web Code mfd-2901.**

Interpreting Oral History

As time passes, events of the present quickly become events of the past—a part of history. Often, you can learn about recent historical events by interpreting the recollections of people who were present. These memories can help you understand what people thought and how they felt. Many recollections come to us as oral history that is later written down.

A black activist, John Lewis was one of the leaders in the 1965 march through Selma, Alabama. He describes events as he leads a group of demonstrators through the streets.

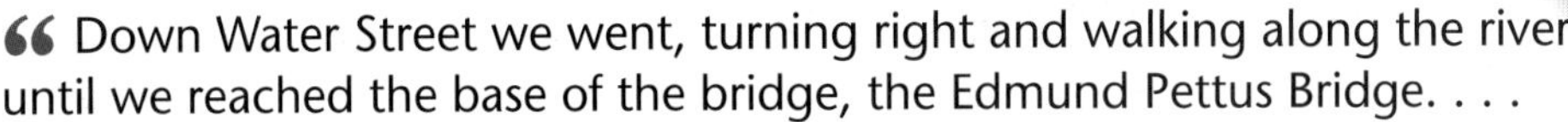

“ Down Water Street we went, turning right and walking along the river until we reached the base of the bridge, the Edmund Pettus Bridge. . . .

When we reached the crest of the bridge, I stopped dead still. . . .

There, facing us at the bottom of the other side, stood a sea of blue-helmeted, blue-uniformed Alabama state troopers, line after line of them, dozens of battle-ready lawmen stretched from one side of U.S. highway 80 to the other. . . . the officer in charge . . . stepped forward, holding a small bull-horn up to his mouth.

'This is an unlawful assembly. . . . Your march is not conducive to the public safety. You are ordered to disperse and go back to your church or to your homes.'

I wasn't about to turn around. We were there. We couldn't turn and go back even if we wanted to. . . . There was only one option left that I could see.

'We should kneel and pray.' . . . We turned and passed the word back to begin bowing down in a prayerful manner. But that word didn't get far. It didn't have time. One minute after he issued his warning . . . Major Cloud issued an order . . . 'Troopers. Advance!' ”

Learn the Skill *To interpret oral history, use the following steps:*

1. **Examine the evidence.** What information does it give? What period or event is being discussed?
2. **Identify the point of view.** How does the speaker "see" the event?
3. **Determine the reliability.** What was the person's role in the event? How might that role affect his or her recollections?
4. **Interpret the recollection.** What can you learn from this oral history? What conclusions can you draw?

Practice the Skill *Answer the following questions based on the passages above:*

1. What event is Lewis describing?
2. What was Lewis's viewpoint on the march?
3. **(a)** What was Lewis's role in the events he recalls? **(b)** How reliable would you judge the account to be?
4. What did you learn from the account of John Lewis?

Apply the Skill *See the Chapter Review and Assessment.*

3 Protest, Reform, and Doubt

Prepare to Read

Objectives

In this section, you will
- List the goals of Presidents Kennedy and Johnson.
- Explain why protests increased in the 1960s.
- Describe the issues President Nixon faced.
- Identify the principles guiding the Carter administration.

Key Terms

counterculture movement

silent majority

stagflation

Target Reading Skill

Reading Process As you read, prepare an outline of this section. Use roman numerals to indicate the major headings, capital letters for the subheadings, and numbers for the supporting details.

I. Kennedy in the White House
  A. Election of 1960
    1. The issue of Kennedy's religion
    2.
  B. Kennedy's policies
    1. Poverty program
    2.
  C. Tragedy in Dallas

Main Idea The 1960s was a decade filled with problems: political assassinations, scandals, political crises, and protest movements.

John F. Kennedy

Setting the Scene John F. Kennedy took the presidential oath of office on January 20, 1961. At 43, he was the youngest man ever elected President and the first to be born in the twentieth century. "Let the word go forth," he said, "that the torch has been passed to a new generation of Americans."

Kennedy's youth and idealism had inspired Americans during the campaign. Now he called them to service:

> "The trumpet summons us again . . . to bear the burden of a long twilight struggle . . . against the common enemies of man: tyranny, poverty, disease, and war itself. . . . And so, my fellow Americans: ask not what your country can do for you—ask what you can do for your country."
>
> —John F. Kennedy, Inaugural Address, January 20, 1961

For all his youth and high hopes, Kennedy and the Presidents who followed him faced tough challenges. The 1960s and 1970s were years of idealism. They also turned out to be a time of uncertainty, tragedy, and turmoil for Americans of all ages.

Kennedy in the White House

The election of 1960 pitted Republican Vice President Richard Nixon against Kennedy, a Democrat and Senator from Massachusetts.

Election of 1960 The election was a close contest. Many Americans voted against Kennedy because they felt he did not have enough experience to be President. Others worried about Kennedy's religion, Catholicism. No Roman Catholic had ever been President. Many Americans feared that Kennedy might be more loyal to the Roman Catholic Church than to the country. Kennedy reassured voters that he believed in the separation of church and state.

Kennedy Space Center

The history of United States space exploration is on display at the Kennedy Space Center in Florida. Visitors can view IMAX movies, walk among actual rockets, explore a simulated space station, and climb aboard a full-sized replica of a space shuttle. Exhibits honor the past achievements of American astronauts and highlight goals for the future.

Virtual Field Trip For an interactive look at the Kennedy Space Center, visit PHSchool.com, **Web Code mfd-2902.**

Television turned the tide for Kennedy. In the first televised debates ever held in a presidential campaign, Kennedy appeared youthful and confident. Nixon, recovering from a recent illness, looked tired and nervous. Kennedy won the election by a narrow margin.

Kennedy's Policies During the campaign, Kennedy had been shocked to find hungry families living in the United States. "Just imagine," he said, "kids who never drank milk!" As President, he urged Congress to pass laws to help the millions of Americans living in poverty.

Congress blocked the President's poverty programs. But it did fund the Peace Corps—volunteers sent to teach or provide technical help in developing nations. It also approved Kennedy's proposal to explore the "new frontier" of space. Before any other proposals could be enacted, a tragic event cut down the young President and shattered the nation.

Tragedy in Dallas On November 22, 1963, Kennedy traveled to Dallas, Texas, on a political tour. As his convertible passed cheering crowds, shots rang out. The President slumped in his seat. Later, John F. Kennedy died. That afternoon, Vice President Lyndon Johnson was sworn in as President.

A special government commission headed by Chief Justice Earl Warren later concluded that a lone gunman, Lee Harvey Oswald, had murdered the President. After his arrest, Oswald himself was killed

Viewing History

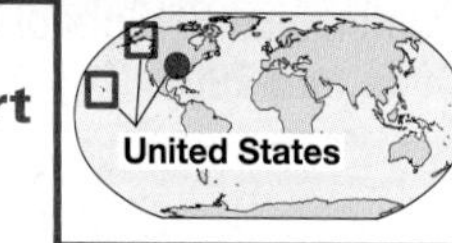

Getting a Head Start President Johnson favored programs to help young people. Head Start programs helped children from low-income families prepare for elementary school. Here, Lady Bird Johnson joins in a special ceremony. The two boys (top right) are having fun with clay. **Analyzing Information** ***How might this program benefit young children? Explain.***

by another gunman. Today, most historians agree with the Warren Commission.

Johnson's Great Society

"Let us continue," said Johnson. He steered many of Kennedy's proposals through Congress. In November 1964, voters returned him to the White House in a landslide victory. Johnson had his own program. He called it the Great Society. It boldly aimed at creating a decent living standard for every American. In a first step, Johnson declared a "war on poverty."

Congress had not supported Kennedy's poverty program. However, Johnson was much more persuasive. He cornered members of Congress. Johnson successfully used his years of political experience to help get what he wanted. In just two years in office, Johnson pushed 50 new laws through Congress.

The Great Society had many programs. Under Medicare, the government helped pay hospital costs for senior citizens. Medicaid gave states money to help poor citizens with medical bills. A new Office of Economic Opportunity created job-training programs for the unemployed. It gave loans to needy farmers and to businesses in poor sections of cities.

Programs to build housing for low-income and middle-income families were also part of the Great Society. To carry out these programs, Congress established the Department of Housing and Urban Development, or HUD. Robert Weaver headed the department. He was the first African American ever appointed to the Cabinet.

The Great Society had a mixed record. It aided the poor but at great cost to taxpayers. Government grew in size and intruded on people's lives as never before. Corruption sometimes plagued antipoverty programs. Still, Medicare, Medicaid, and other reforms helped millions and became permanent parts of American life.

Protest Movements

Despite these social reforms, protest movements grew in the 1960s. The civil rights movement expanded. Opposition to the war in Vietnam grew. Some young people began to reject the values and lifestyles of their parents.

The Counterculture Movement Many young Americans joined the counterculture movement. They criticized competition and the drive for personal success. Instead of going to college, they "dropped out." Instead of traditional families, they lived together in groups or communes. Many listened to new forms of rock music. Some "turned on," or experimented with illegal drugs.

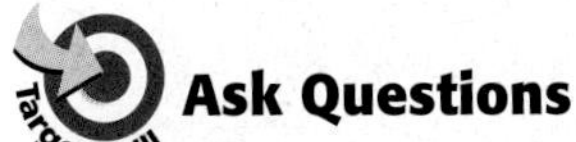

Ask Questions What questions would you ask members of the counterculture about their views of the 1960s and 1970s and their views of today?

Inspired by the civil rights movement, counterculture protesters called for peace, justice, and social equality. They wore torn, faded jeans and work shirts to blur the differences between rich and poor. Men grew long hair and beards. Women refused to put on makeup. All wanted to look more natural and less like their parents.

Like the beatniks of the 1950s, members of the counterculture said American life was empty and materialistic. Some turned to eastern religions such as Buddhism in search of spiritual meaning.

The Antiwar Movement As more and more young men were sent to fight in the Vietnam War, an antiwar movement gained strength. Protesters staged rallies, burned draft cards, and refused to serve in the military. Many of the largest demonstrations took place on college campuses.

By 1968, the antiwar movement was peaking. As a result, President Johnson's popularity plummeted. To avoid angry protesters, Johnson stayed in the White House more and more. He decided against running for the presidency again.

The Election of 1968 Johnson's decision opened the way for other Democrats to seek their party's nomination in 1968. New York senator Robert Kennedy, brother of the late President, made a strong run. While campaigning in Los Angeles, however, Kennedy was killed by a Palestinian who opposed the senator's support for Israel. The Democrats selected Vice President Hubert Humphrey as their candidate. The Republicans again nominated former Vice President Richard Nixon. Nixon promised "peace with honor" in Vietnam and "law and order" at home. Alabama governor George Wallace entered the race as a third-party candidate. Helped by this and by divisions among Democrats over the Vietnam War, Nixon won a narrow victory.

The Nixon Years

As President, Nixon tried to reduce government involvement in people's lives. He cut funds for many Great Society programs, including job training, education, and low-income housing. He also sought to return power to the states. He called this transfer of power the "New Federalism."

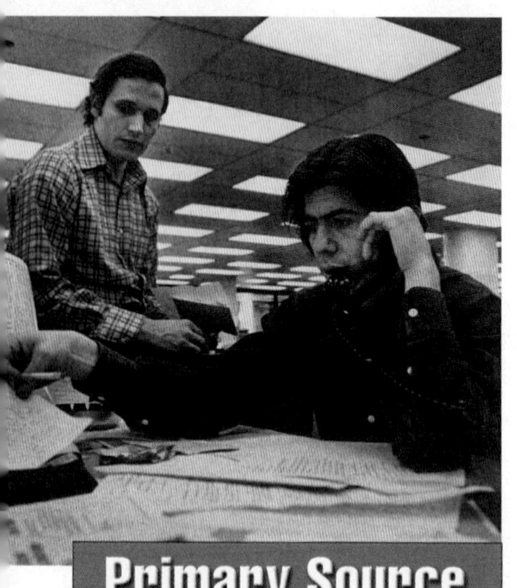

Primary Source

All the President's Men

Bob Woodward and Carl Bernstein were two Washington Post *reporters. Here is what they learned the first day on the Watergate story:*

"The first paragraph of the [*Post's* first Watergate story] read: 'Five men, . . . were arrested at 2:30 A.M. yesterday in what authorities described as an elaborate plot to bug the offices of the Democratic National Committee.'. . .

After midnight, Woodward received a call from Eugene Bachinski, a *Post* reporter. . . .

Bachinski had something from one of his police sources. Two address books, belonging to two of the Miami men arrested inside the Watergate, contained the name and phone number of an E. Howard Hunt, with the small notations 'W.House' and 'W.H.'"

—Bob Woodward and Carl Bernstein, *All the President's Men*, 1974

Analyzing Primary Sources

What information linked the burglary to the Nixon administration?

Law and Order During the campaign, Nixon said that he wanted to help what he called the **silent majority.** These Americans were disturbed by the unrest of the 1960s but did not protest publicly. They were, Nixon explained, the "great majority of Americans, the nonshouters, the nondemonstraters."

True to his campaign promise, Nixon began a "law-and-order" program. Federal funds were used to help local police departments. Nixon also named four conservative justices to the Supreme Court. They tended to favor dealing harshly with lawbreakers.

The Space Program Nixon inherited the space program from Kennedy and Johnson. Its greatest triumph came in 1969 just as Nixon took office. In 1969, two astronauts landed a small craft on the moon's surface. With millions of television viewers around the world watching, Neil A. Armstrong became the first person to step onto the moon. "That's one small step for a man—one giant leap for mankind," he radioed back to Earth. American astronauts visited the moon five more times.

The Economy During the Nixon years, the economy suffered from **stagflation,** a combination of rising prices, high unemployment, and slow economic growth. To halt inflation, Nixon froze wages and prices. To stimulate economic growth, he increased federal spending.

Still, economic problems would not go away. Increased federal spending caused federal budget deficits, that is, the government spent more than it received in revenues. Early in Nixon's second term, an oil embargo put added pressure on the economy. Higher energy prices caused the price of goods to rise even more.

Scandal Brings Down a President In Nixon's second term in office, a scandal brought the President down. It began while Nixon was campaigning for reelection. On June 17, 1972, police caught five men breaking into Democratic party headquarters in the Watergate apartment building in Washington, D.C. Evidence linked the burglars to Nixon's reelection committee. The President assured the public that no one in the White House was involved in the Watergate Affair.

Despite Nixon's denials, a Senate committee began public hearings in May 1973. The hearings revealed that Nixon had made secret tape recordings of conversations in his office. These tapes showed that the President and several close advisers had tried to cover up the truth about the Watergate break-in.

In the middle of the Watergate Affair, another scandal erupted. Vice President Spiro Agnew was accused of taking bribes and was forced to resign. The President chose Representative Gerald R. Ford of Michigan to replace him. The Watergate crisis came to a head in July 1974. A House of Representatives committee passed articles of impeachment against the President. One charge was obstructing, or blocking, justice. Even the President's strongest defenders found the evidence convincing. In August 1974, before an impeachment trial could begin, Richard Nixon became the first President to resign from office.

Ford Pardons Nixon Gerald Ford, the new President, had a difficult job. He faced a troubled economy and the challenge of helping the nation emerge from a major political scandal. In response to the nation's troubled mood, President Ford granted Nixon a "full, free, and absolute pardon." He did so a month after Nixon resigned. Some felt that Nixon should have been brought to trial. Ford, however, wanted to save the country from a bitter debate over Watergate. Ford lost a great deal of public support because of that decision.

Carter in the White House

In 1976, Republicans nominated Ford for President. Democrats chose Jimmy Carter, the former governor of Georgia.

Carter had no experience in Washington but used to his advantage the fact that he was a Washington outsider. He pointed out that "the vast majority of Americans . . . are also outsiders." After years of scandal in Washington, Carter's fresh face and promises of a new approach carried him to a narrow victory.

Carter's term began with a whirlwind of activity. In his first year, the new President sent Congress almost a dozen major bills. They included reforms in the Social Security system and in the tax code. But Carter's lack of experience in Washington hurt him. Congress refused to support his legislation.

The President did not fare much better with the problem of high inflation. When the government tried to slow inflation, prices only kept rising. Many families had trouble paying for food, clothing, and rent.

In foreign affairs, Carter was a strong defender of human rights. The United States had signed the Helsinki Agreement just before he took office. Thirty-five nations pledged to respect basic rights such as religious freedom and freedom of speech. The United States, Carter said, should keep this pledge and not aid countries that violated human rights.

Section 3 Assessment

Recall

1. **Identify** Explain the significance of **(a)** Peace Corps, **(b)** Warren Commission, **(c)** Great Society, **(d)** Medicare, **(e)** Medicaid, **(f)** Neil Armstrong, **(g)** Watergate Affair, **(h)** Gerald Ford, **(i)** Jimmy Carter, **(j)** Helsinki Agreement.
2. **Define** **(a)** counterculture movement, **(b)** silent majority, **(c)** stagflation.

Comprehension

3. Describe two Great Society programs that became law.
4. How did some Americans oppose United States involvement in the Vietnam War?
5. Explain how Nixon tried to deal with **(a)** stagflation, **(b)** the Watergate Affair.
6. Did Carter achieve the goals of his domestic program? Explain.

Critical Thinking and Writing

7. **Exploring the Main Idea** Review the Main Idea statement at the beginning of this section. Then, discuss the efforts of Presidents during the 1960s and 1970s to bring about reform.
8. **Comparing** Compare Presidents Kennedy, Johnson, Nixon, and Carter in terms of their relationships with Congress.

Activity

Making Information Pamphlets
Use the Internet to learn more about Medicare and Medicaid. Who is eligible? What are the benefits? How can a person apply? Use the information to make pamphlets about the programs. For help in completing the activity, visit PHSchool.com, **Web Code mfd-2903.**

4 The Crusade for Equal Rights

Prepare to Read

Objectives

In this section, you will
- Discuss the African American drive for equal rights.
- Explain why the women's movement grew stronger.
- Compare how different groups tried to achieve equal rights.

Key Terms

sit-in

affirmative action

migrant worker

bilingual

Target Reading Skill

Cause and Effect Copy the chart below. As you read, complete the chart to show some of the effects of the protests by groups demanding equal rights. Add as many entries as you need.

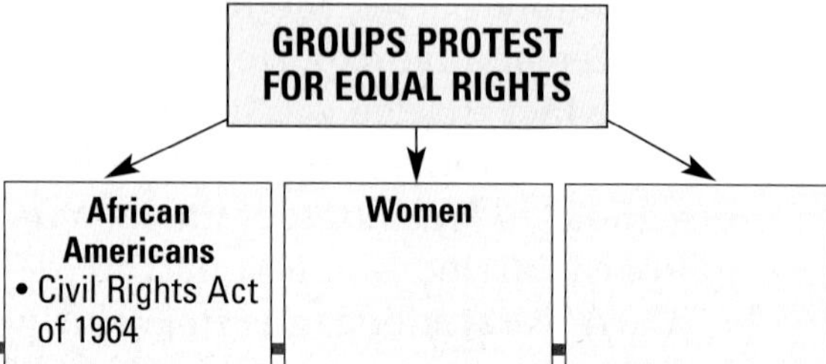

Main Idea In the 1960s and 1970s, a crusade for equal rights swept across the country, producing a new era of protest and reform.

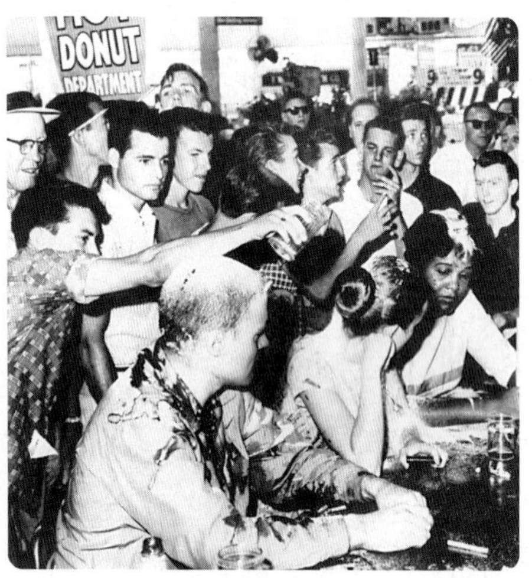

Sit-in at a lunch counter

Setting the Scene In 1963 Anne Moody was a senior in college when she and two friends sat down at a "whites only" lunch counter in Jackson, Mississippi. The waitress told them to move to the black section. Anne and her friends, all African Americans, stayed put. "We would like to be served," Anne said politely.

A crowd of whites pulled them from their seats. They beat one of Anne's friends, who was promptly arrested. When Anne and her other friend returned to their seats, they were joined by a white woman from her school. "Now there were three of us," Anne recalled, "and we were integrated." The crowd smeared them with ketchup and mustard and dragged them from the lunch counter.

Anne and her friends were using a form of protest called **sit-ins**, in which people sit and refuse to leave. The first sit-in took place at a lunch counter in Greensboro, North Carolina, in 1960. During the 1960s, thousands of blacks and whites were conducting sit-ins at public places across the South. The protests signaled a new determination to end segregation and discrimination.

African Americans Crusade for Equality

Across the South, segregation laws limited the rights of black Americans not only at lunch counters but also in bus stations, restrooms, and other public facilities. In the 1960s, sit-ins and other forms of protest fanned the crusade for equality.

Nonviolent Direct Action Civil rights groups planned the protests, but it was often young people like Anne Moody who carried them out. The Congress of Racial Equality (CORE), for example, organized "Freedom Rides." Busloads of young Freedom Riders—black and white—rode from town to town to integrate bus terminals in the South.

These early civil rights groups held firmly to the tactics of what Martin Luther King, Jr., called "nonviolent direct action." Sit-ins, boycotts, marches, and other peaceful methods were used to achieve their goals.

Police sometimes responded by using attack dogs or water hoses against protesters. Houses and churches of black leaders were bombed. Civil rights workers—black and white—were sometimes injured or killed. By remaining nonviolent, protesters gained a moral advantage and the sympathy of many Americans.

In 1963, more than 200,000 Americans marched on Washington, D.C. They wanted Congress to pass laws to end discrimination and to help the poor. Among the speakers that day was Martin Luther King, Jr. In a now-famous speech, he proclaimed:

> ❝ When we let freedom ring . . . we will be able to speed up that day when all of God's children, black men and white men, Jews and Gentiles, Protestants and Catholics, will be able to join hands and sing in the words of the old Negro spiritual, 'Free at last! Free at last! Thank God Almighty, we are free at last!' ❞
>
> —Martin Luther King, Jr., Speech, August 28, 1963

Federal Civil Rights Laws The demonstrations spurred Presidents Kennedy and Johnson to press for federal civil rights laws. Kennedy failed, but Johnson succeeded in pushing through the Civil Rights Act of 1964, which protected the right of all citizens to vote. It also outlawed discrimination in hiring and ended segregation in public places.

At the Democratic National Convention in 1964, Fannie Lou Hamer, an African American, told of her experiences while trying to register to vote in Mississippi. Her efforts, along with the help of others, were successful in gaining voting rights.

In 1965, the Voting Rights Act allowed federal officials to register voters in states practicing discrimination. It also ended literacy tests used to block African Americans from voting. As a result, tens of thousands of African Americans voted for the first time.

The new civil rights laws did not end all discrimination. In the North, no formal system of segregation existed. Informally, though, housing in certain neighborhoods and employment in many companies remained closed to African Americans.

Black Power Some African Americans believed that nonviolent protest had failed. The Black Panthers and other radical groups told African Americans to arm themselves. Blacks, they said, had to be ready to protect themselves and to fight for their rights.

Black Muslims, such as Malcolm X, argued that African Americans could succeed only if they separated from white society. Before being assassinated in 1965, Malcolm X began to change his views. He called for "a society in which there could exist honest white-black brotherhood."

Both moderates and radicals found common ground in talk of "black power." They urged African Americans to achieve economic independence by starting their own businesses and shopping in black-owned stores. Leaders also called for "black pride," encouraging African Americans to learn more about their heritage and culture.

An American Profile

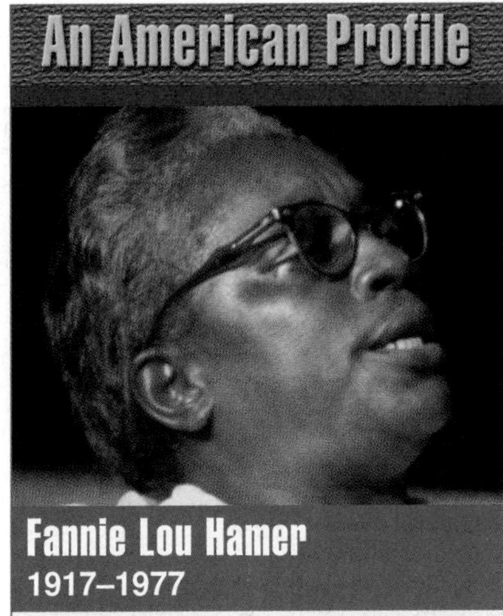

Fannie Lou Hamer
1917–1977

When Fanny Lou Hamer was born, African Americans had few rights. They faced discrimination that denied them chances to get ahead. For nearly 50 years, Hamer lived a quiet, hard-working life.

One day, members of civil rights groups came to Hamer's area. They wanted volunteers to help win voting rights for blacks. Hamer joined the effort—even though she suffered in several ways as a result. She lost her job. Her family had to move. She was arrested and severely beaten. Still, she continued to work for the cause. In 1964, Hamer became a leader of the Mississippi Freedom Democratic Party. In this role, she won fame.

How did Hamer show her dedication to civil rights?

Viewing History

Marching for Women's Rights

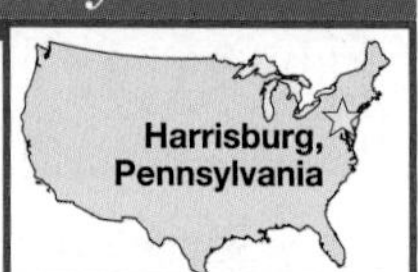

American women became politically active during the 1960s and 1970s. Many joined the efforts of the National Organization for Women. Here, women march together to express their solidarity. **Applying Information** ***What causes are important to these women?***

Protest Turns Violent In crowded city neighborhoods, many blacks were angry about discrimination, lack of jobs, and poverty. Beginning in 1965, their anger boiled over into violence. During six days in August, rioters in Watts, a black neighborhood in Los Angeles, set fire to buildings and looted stores. Some 4,000 people were arrested, 34 were killed, and 1,000 were injured. Over the next two years, Chicago, Detroit, and dozens of other cities exploded with violence, destruction, and death.

King Is Killed Martin Luther King, Jr., continued to preach nonviolence. In April 1968, he went to Memphis, Tennessee, to support a strike of black sanitation workers. When he stepped outside his motel room, a white gunman killed him.

King's life has continued to inspire Americans to work for peaceful change. To honor his memory, his birthday was declared a national holiday in 1986.

Some Results The civil rights movement began to show some results in the 1970s. African Americans won public offices in small towns and large cities. Atlanta, Cleveland, Detroit, New Orleans, and Los Angeles had all elected black mayors by 1979.

African Americans also made gains in the federal government. In 1967, Edward Brooke of Massachusetts became the first black senator since Reconstruction. A year later, President Johnson appointed Thurgood Marshall to the Supreme Court.

Many businesses and universities adopted **affirmative action** programs. These programs sought to hire and promote minorities, women, and others who had faced discrimination. By the 1970s, more African Americans were entering such professions as medicine and law. Yet, for all their efforts, blacks still had to contend with bias in hiring, promotions, and pay.

The Women's Rights Movement

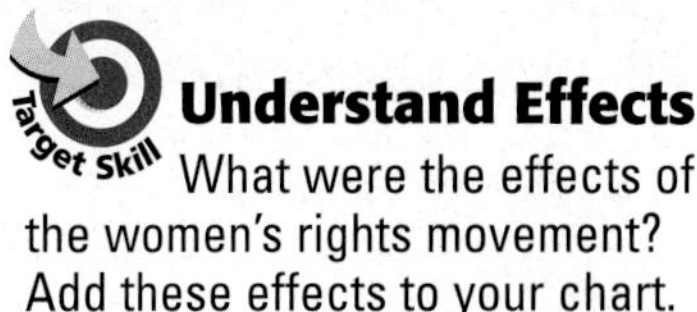

Understand Effects What were the effects of the women's rights movement? Add these effects to your chart.

Women had long fought inequality. Since the 1960s, their drive for equal rights has been known as the Women's Rights Movement.

In the workplace qualified women found that male employers were unwilling to hire them for certain jobs, and they were usually paid less than men, even for the same work. They were fired before men and promoted less quickly.

In 1966, writer Betty Friedan helped to set up the National Organization for Women (NOW), which worked for equal rights for women in jobs, pay, and education. It also helped women bring discrimination cases to court and campaigned for maternity leave and child-care centers. Urging women to be more politically active, NOW organized the Strike for Equality Parade down New York's Fifth Avenue in 1970. Some 50,000 women marched.

New laws helped women make some gains. The Equal Pay Act of 1963 required equal pay for equal work. The Civil Rights Act of 1964 outlawed discrimination in hiring based on gender and on race.

In the 1970s, the women's movement suffered a major defeat. In 1972, Congress passed a proposal for the Equal Rights Amendment (ERA) to the Constitution. The amendment would ban discrimination based on gender. However, Phyllis Schlafly and other conservative women led a successful campaign against ratification of the amendment. They said the ERA would lead to women being drafted into the military and would harm the traditional family. Despite this defeat, the women's movement brought women more power and equality.

The Latino Drive for Equality

By the end of the 1970s, more than 10 million Latinos lived in the United States. Like African Americans, women, and other minorities, Latinos worked for equal rights.

Mexican Americans Mexican Americans are the largest group of Latinos living in the United States. From 1960 to 1980, the greatest number of immigrants to the United States came from Mexico.

Many Mexican Americans lived and worked in cities. Many more labored as **migrant workers** who traveled from farm to farm looking for work. Low wages and harsh working conditions made life difficult for them. Discrimination made things worse. Mexican Americans were often barred from better-paying jobs and from better neighborhoods. Few schools offered programs for those whose first language was Spanish. Migrants moved so often that it was hard for their children to attend school regularly.

Puerto Rican Americans Latinos in the eastern United States often came from Puerto Rico. In the 1950s, thousands left Puerto Rico in search of work in the United States. Many took jobs in the factories of New York City, New Jersey, Connecticut, and Pennsylvania. Some went to Boston, Chicago, and San Francisco. Puerto Ricans also faced discrimination in housing and jobs wherever they settled.

Milestones of the Human Rights Movement

1975	Voting Rights Act
1973	AIM Occupation of Wounded Knee
1966	Founding of NOW
1965	Voting Rights Act
1964	Civil Rights Act
1963	March on Washington
1960	Greensboro lunch counter sit-in
1955	Montgomery bus boycott
1954	*Brown* v. *Board of Education*

VOTE

GRAPHIC ORGANIZER *Skills*

The period from the mid-1950s to the mid-1970s was an eventful time for the human rights movement.

1. **Comprehension** In which decade was the human rights movement most active?
2. **Critical Thinking Identifying Points of View** Which milestone on this chart was part of the women's rights movement?

Cuban Americans A third group of Latinos came in two waves from Cuba. Between 1959 and 1962, some 200,000 people fled to southern Florida when Fidel Castro set up a communist government in Cuba. These immigrants were often middle class and well educated. They adapted quickly to their new home. A second wave of immigrants came in 1980 after Castro allowed thousands of people to leave the island. Most of the new refugees were unskilled. They had a hard time making a living.

As their numbers grew, Cuban Americans became a force in southern Florida. Miami took on a new look. Shop windows displayed signs in Spanish. Cuban restaurants and shops opened. Cubans published Spanish-language newspapers and operated radio and television stations. Cuban American politicians were soon elected.

Latinos Organize In the 1960s, new Latino organizations sought change. César Chávez formed a union of migrant workers, the United Farm Workers. When farm owners refused to talk to the union, Chávez called for a nationwide boycott of farm products. In the end, the owners recognized the union, and workers won higher wages.

By the mid-1960s, Latinos began to publicly take pride in their history and culture. Mexican Americans called themselves Chicanos, a name that comes from the Spanish word *Mexicano.*

Latino groups also registered voters and made sure that voting laws were enforced. These new voters helped to elect more Latino officials to represent their interests.

One result of these efforts was the Voting Rights Act of 1975. It required areas with many non-English-speaking citizens to hold bilingual elections. **Bilingual** means in two languages. In a bilingual election, information is provided in more than one language. With a ballot that was written in Spanish, it was easier for Latinos to vote.

The Bilingual Education Acts of 1968 and 1973 promoted bilingual programs in public schools with Spanish-speaking and Asian students.

Asian Americans Asian Americans joined the civil rights movement. In 1968, students at the University of California at Berkeley founded the Asian American Political Alliance (AAPA). Students of Chinese, Japanese, Filipino, and other Asian descent joined to promote the rights and culture of Asian Americans. As a result, between 1968 and 1973, universities across the nation created programs in Asian American studies.

Native Americans Native Americans also worked for their full rights. They claimed rights not only as individuals but also as members of tribal groups. Over the years, the federal government had recognized tribal governments by signing treaties with them.

During the late 1940s and the 1950s, the federal government tried to break up tribal governments. They also encouraged Indians to leave the reservations. By the late 1960s, more than half of all American Indians lived off the reservations, mainly in cities. Gradually, city life weakened traditional tribes and customs.

Native Americans organized against these government policies. The National Congress of American Indians regularly sent delegations to Washington to defend Indian rights.

The American Indian Movement (AIM) protested the treatment of Indians. In 1973, AIM members occupied Wounded Knee, South Dakota, for several weeks. As you have read, the United States Army had killed nearly 300 Indians at Wounded Knee in 1890. AIM wanted to remind people of the government's failure to deal fairly with American Indians. Protests and court cases have won sympathy for Indian causes and more rights for Native Americans.

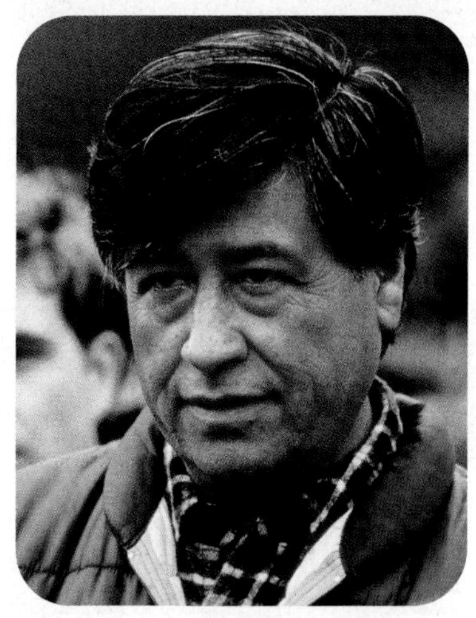

Viewing History

Migrant Workers Unite

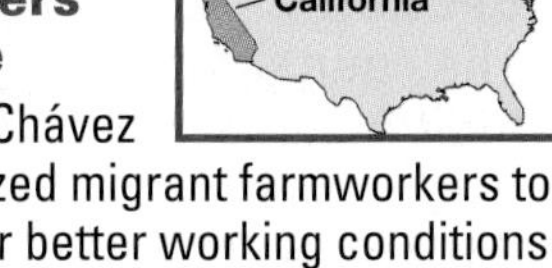

César Chávez organized migrant farmworkers to rally for better working conditions and higher wages. **Applying Information** ***Why might it have been difficult to organize migrant farmworkers?***

Section 4 Assessment

Recall

1. **Identify** Explain the significance of **(a)** Freedom Ride, **(b)** Civil Rights Act of 1964, **(c)** Voting Rights Act, **(d)** Black Panthers, **(e)** Malcolm X, **(f)** National Organization for Women, **(g)** César Chávez, **(h)** Bilingual Education Acts, **(i)** Asian American Political Alliance, **(j)** American Indian Movement.
2. **Define** **(a)** sit-in, **(b)** affirmative action, **(c)** migrant worker, **(d)** bilingual.

Comprehension

3. How did African Americans fight for equal rights?
4. What was the purpose of NOW?
5. Describe the success of groups seeking equal rights.

Critical Thinking and Writing

6. **Exploring the Main Idea** Review the Main Idea statement at the beginning of this section. Then, write a paragraph about how the civil rights movement paved the way for other groups to work for equal rights.
7. **Drawing Conclusions** Why do you think the political goals of Cuban Americans differed from those of Mexican Americans? Explain.

Activity

Debating an Issue

Dr. Martin Luther King, Jr., and Malcolm X are at a meeting before Malcolm X changed his views in 1965. Write a dialogue between the two leaders debating how to end discrimination against African Americans.

CHAPTER 29

Review and Assessment

Chapter Summary

Section 1
The postwar period presented challenges for the nation, including inflation. However, prosperity returned, leading to both an economic boom and a baby boom. Trends during the 1950s included the growth of suburbs, a population boom in the South, and the development of rock-and-roll as a popular medium of expression.

Section 2
The courts, the Montgomery bus boycott, and Martin Luther King, Jr., played major roles in the battle against discrimination after World War II. Barriers that had long held back African Americans and other groups began to fall.

Section 3
Presidents Kennedy and Johnson supported programs that would help America's underprivileged. Antiwar protests and other protests marked the 1960s. During the 1970s and 1980s, Presidents Nixon, Ford, and Carter confronted economic and foreign policy issues.

Section 4
African Americans, women, Latinos, and other groups fought for equal rights in the 1960s and 1970s. These groups made some gains but continue to work toward equality.

Building Vocabulary

Review the chapter vocabulary words listed below. Then, use the words and their definitions to create a matching quiz. Exchange quizzes with another student. Check each other's answers when you are finished.

1. **inflation**
2. **productivity**
3. **beatnik**
4. **boycott**
5. **civil disobedience**
6. **counterculture**
7. **silent majority**
8. **stagflation**
9. **affirmative action**
10. **bilingual**

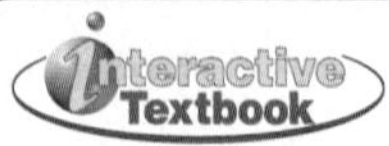

For additional review and enrichment activities, see the interactive version of *The American Nation*, available on the Web and on CD-ROM.

Chapter Self-Test For practice test questions for Chapter 29, visit PHSchool.com, **Web Code mfa-2904.**

Reviewing Key Facts

11. Describe two factors that helped the economy to expand after World War II. (Section 1)
12. What three victories occurred in the civil rights movement during the 1950s? (Section 2)
13. Explain Nixon's views on the role of the federal government in people's lives. (Section 3)
14. Describe one way in which each of the following groups fought against injustice: **(a)** African Americans, **(b)** Latino Americans, **(c)** Asian Americans, **(d)** Native Americans, **(e)** women. (Section 4)

Critical Thinking and Writing

15. **Applying Information** How did the government support the Supreme Court's decision in *Brown* v. *Board of Education of Topeka?*
16. **Connecting to Geography: Movement** What were the causes and effects of the growth of the suburbs in the 1950s?
17. **Linking Past and Present** One of the reforms of the civil rights era was the establishment of bilingual education. Today, some people question the benefits of that program. Do you agree or disagree? Explain.
18. **Synthesizing Information** Which laws passed during Johnson's or Kennedy's presidency do you think have had the most lasting effect on American society? Explain.

Skills Assessment

Analyzing Primary Sources

Vice President Gerald Ford became President on August 9, 1974, after Richard Nixon resigned. Read the following excerpt from the speech Ford made to the nation that day.

> "My fellow Americans, our long national nightmare is over. Our Constitution works; [ours] is a Government of laws and not of men. . . . As we restore the internal wounds of Watergate, more painful and more poisonous than those of foreign wars, . . . let us restore the golden rule to our political process, and let brotherly love purge our hearts of suspicion and hate."
>
> —Gerald Ford, speech on August 9, 1974

19. Of what national nightmare is Ford speaking?
    - **A.** Foreign wars
    - **B.** Watergate
    - **C.** The rule of law
    - **D.** The political process
20. Based on this speech, how do you know that Ford is likely to pardon Nixon?
    - **A.** The Constitution requires it.
    - **B.** Nixon refused to step down until Ford agreed to pardon him.
    - **C.** It is not clear that Ford will pardon Nixon.
    - **D.** He speaks of being loving instead of suspicious and hateful.

Applying Your Skills

Interpreting Oral History

The Apollo 11 crew landed on the moon July 20, 1969. Michael Collins was part of the team along with Neil Armstrong and Edwin Aldrin. This is Collins's account of the trip. Read the passage and answer the questions.

> "The moon I had known all my life, that small, flat yellow disk in the sky [was] replaced by the most awesome sphere I had ever seen.
>
> It was huge. . . . I could almost reach out and touch it. It was between us and the sun [which] created a halo around it [and made] the moon's surface dark and mysterious. . . . It didn't look like a very friendly place, but Neil summed it up: 'It's worth the price of the trip.'"
>
> —Michael Collins, *Flying to the Moon and Other Strange Places*

21. How does Collins describe the moon?
    - **A.** It is a large, orange disk.
    - **B.** It is large, round, and mysterious.
    - **C.** It is a flat, blue disk.
    - **D.** It is huge with a bluish rim.
22. **(a)** What do you think Armstrong's statement means? **(b)** What did you learn from this account?

Activities

Connecting With . . . Government and Citizenship

President Lyndon B. Johnson made the following statement at a staff meeting in 1965:

> "Look, I've just been elected and right now we'll have a honeymoon with Congress. . . . I'll have a good chance to get my program through.
>
> But after I make my recommendation, I'm going to start to lose the power and authority I have. . . ."

Think about what you have read about Presidents in this chapter and what you know about past Presidents. Then, write a paragraph discussing whether or not Presidents lose their popularity and power while in office.

Protest Songs

Analyzing Song Lyrics Protest songs were popular in the 1960s and 1970s. Use the Internet to research three songs. Explain how the lyrics related to social and political issues of the era. For help in starting the activity, visit PHSchool.com, **Web Code mfd-2906.**

CHAPTER 30

The Nation in a New World

1970–PRESENT

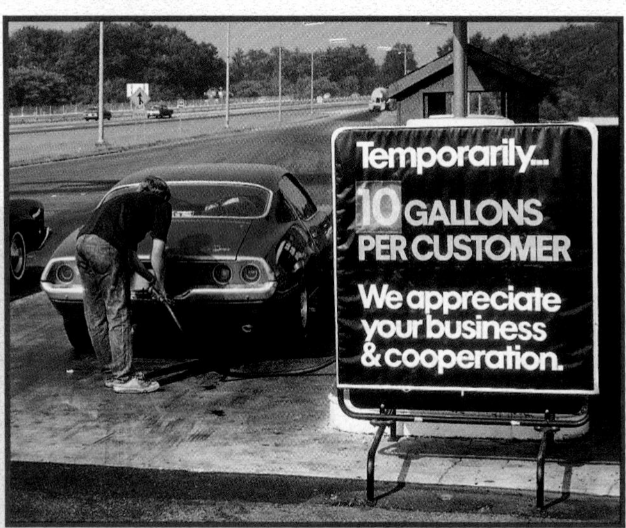

Rationing gas during the oil embargo

Ronald Reagan

AMERICAN EVENTS

1973 Oil-producing Arab nations cut off oil shipments to the United States. The oil embargo causes severe fuel shortages.

1980 Ronald Reagan is elected President. Reagan ushers in a new conservative era as he promises to reduce the size of government.

1990 The Americans With Disabilities Act outlaws discrimination against people with physical or mental impairments.

Presidential Terms: Richard M. Nixon 1969–1974 | Gerald R. Ford 1974–1977 | Jimmy Carter 1977–1981 | Ronald Reagan 1981–1989

1970 · 1980 · 1990

WORLD EVENTS

1979 ▲ Israel and Egypt sign a peace treaty.

1989 ▲ China crushes prodemocracy demonstrations.

North American Trade

In 1993, the North American Free Trade Agreement encouraged the growth of United States trade with Canada and Mexico.

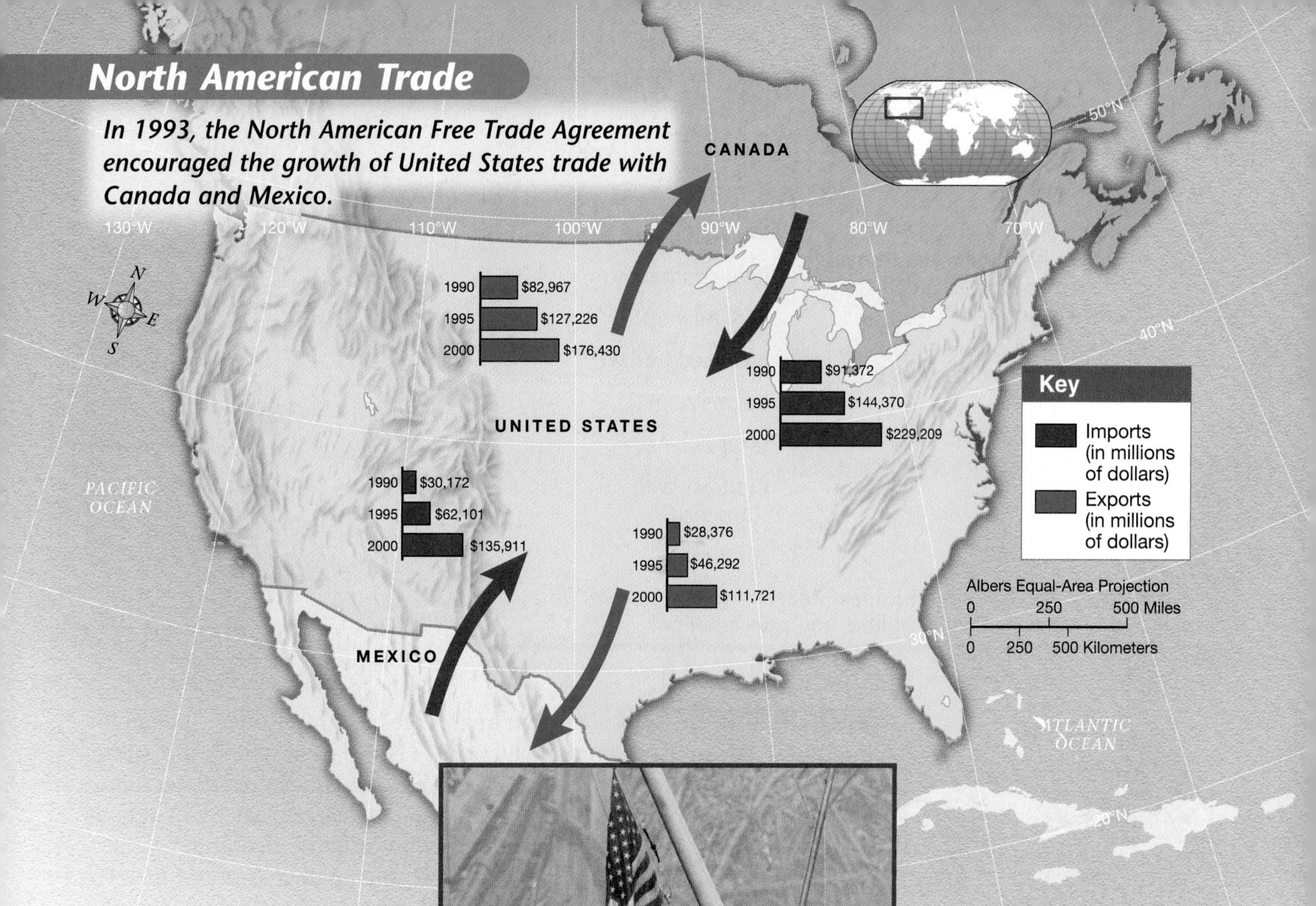

Firefighters in the rubble of the World Trade Center

1990s

The Internet booms as more people use computers to communicate, get information, and do business.

2001

After terrorist attacks on the Pentagon and New York's World Trade Center, President Bush launches a campaign to defeat world terrorism.

George H. W. Bush 1989–1993 | William J. Clinton 1993–2001 | George W. Bush 2001–

1990 · 2000 · 2010

▲ 1991

The Soviet Union breaks apart.

▲ 1998

India and Pakistan test nuclear weapons.

1 The Conservative Revolt

Prepare to Read

Objectives

In this section, you will
- Explain how President Ronald Reagan forwarded a conservative agenda.
- Identify the problems Presidents George H.W. Bush and Bill Clinton faced.
- Describe the major events of George W. Bush's presidency.

Key Terms

Moral Majority
Reaganomics
deregulation
balanced budget
downsizing
recession
Contract With America
surplus

Target Reading Skill

Sequence Copy this flowchart. As you read, fill in the boxes with key events during the terms of President Reagan and his successors. Add as many boxes as you need.

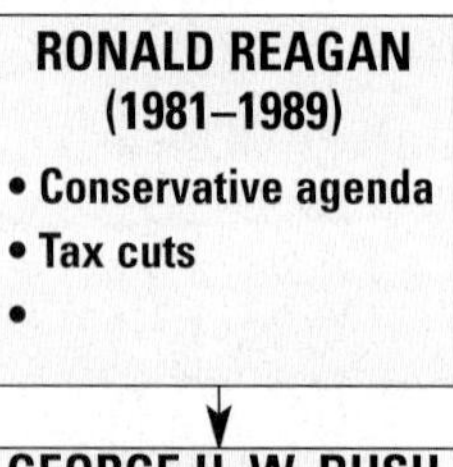

GEORGE H. W. BUSH
(1989–1993)

Main Idea The election of Ronald Reagan in 1980 ushered in a new era of conservatism in politics and public policy.

1980 Reagan campaign button

Setting the Scene The sun beamed as Ronald Reagan began his inaugural address on January 20, 1981. The day matched the sunny optimism of the new President. Just shy of his seventieth birthday, Reagan brought new ideas to Washington. "Government," he said, "is not the solution to our problems, government is the problem."

Ronald Reagan led a conservative revolt against years of government expansion. In two terms as President, he began to move the nation in a new direction.

The Conservative Agenda

Ronald Reagan swept into office on a conservative tide. More Americans had come to agree with him that high taxes and "big government" were causing many national problems. These ideas contrasted sharply with the dominant ideas of the 1960s and 1970s.

Limiting Government Since the 1930s, the federal government had grown steadily. President Franklin D. Roosevelt had begun this trend to help people through the Great Depression. Harry Truman, John Kennedy, and Lyndon Johnson continued the expansion. These liberal presidents believed that government should play a large role in managing the economy and providing social programs.

Beginning in the 1960s, a conservative movement warned against growing federal power. Arizona senator Barry Goldwater led the way. He argued for smaller government nearer the people:

> "Our towns and our cities, then our counties and our states, then our regional compacts—and only then the national government. That, let me remind you, is the ladder of liberty built by decentralized power."
>
> —Barry Goldwater, Speech at Republican National Convention, July 16, 1964

By the 1980s, conservatives dominated the Republican party. Led by Ronald Reagan, they believed that federal social programs had become too costly and that federal regulations kept businesses from growing. State and local governments, they argued, were closest to the people and should decide what regulations were needed.

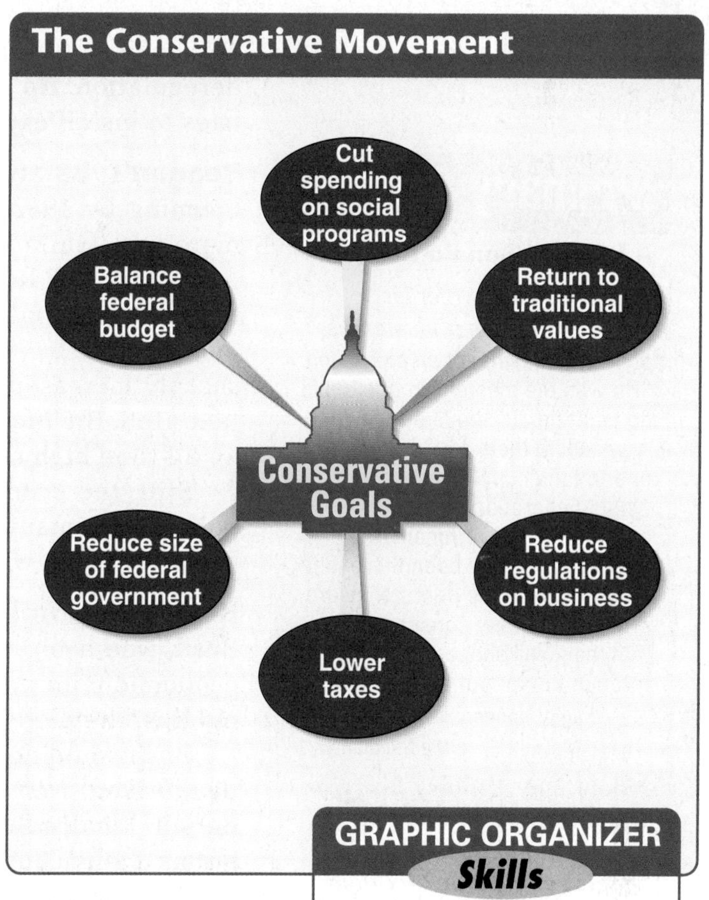

GRAPHIC ORGANIZER **Skills**

The conservative movement had social, political, and economic goals.

1. **Comprehension** Which of the goals shown here are primarily related to economics?
2. **Critical Thinking Applying Information** Ronald Reagan said he wanted to "get government off the back of the people." Which of the goals shown here support this statement?

Civics 

Traditional Values After decades of social change, many conservatives called for a return to traditional values. These included religion, family, and patriotism.

Reflecting the renewed emphasis on traditional values, evangelical Christian churches grew rapidly during the 1970s and 1980s. Evangelicals stressed personal conversion and sought to convert others. Evangelical ministers used television to widen their audience.

Many evangelicals took an active role in conservative political causes. In 1979, the Reverend Jerry Falwell founded the **Moral Majority.** The group aided political candidates who favored conservative religious goals, such as a constitutional amendment to allow organized prayer in public schools. In 1980, strong support from the Moral Majority and other conservative religious organizations helped to put Ronald Reagan in the White House.

The Reagan-Bush Era

Reagan was a handsome man with a relaxed, friendly air. He had been a movie star before winning election as governor of California. His skill at presenting ideas in terms that ordinary people could understand earned him the nickname the Great Communicator.

In 1980, Reagan defeated Jimmy Carter for President. After an era of protests, scandals, and high prices, voters embraced Reagan's promise to "Make America Great Again." He was reelected in 1984 by an even wider margin.

Reaganomics The new President's first priority was his economic program, often called **Reaganomics.** He persuaded Congress to cut taxes. Reagan hoped that taxpayers would use the extra money to buy more and save more. Buying more would spur business growth. Saving more would allow banks to invest in new business ventures.

Reaganomics also involved cutting federal spending to reduce the size of government. The President persuaded Congress to slow down spending increases on social programs such as welfare and aid to education. Critics charged that those cuts hurt the poor, the elderly, and children. Supporters responded that Reagan was just trimming programs that did not work.

A third goal of Reaganomics was **deregulation,** or reduction of restrictions on businesses. Earlier Presidents had slowly begun to deregulate a few industries. Reagan increased the pace and scope of deregulation. He opposed all laws, for example, that required industries to install expensive antipollution devices.

Primary Source

A View of Ronald Reagan

A former speechwriter for President Reagan evaluates his style and his impact on the nation:
"He was the master. No one could do what he did, move people that way, talk to them so that they understood. . . . He brought a whole generation of young activists into government; they never would have been there if he hadn't opened the doors; they are creating the new conservatism that may well shape our politics through the turn of the century."
— Peggy Noonan, *What I Saw at the Revolution*

Analyzing Primary Sources
Do you think Noonan's prediction about Reagan's impact came true? Explain.

Reagan's Balance Sheet After a slow start, the economy was booming by 1982. When Reagan left office, there were 16 million more jobs, while inflation had been held in check.

Another of Reagan's goals—a balanced budget—proved harder to achieve. A **balanced budget** requires the government to spend only as much as it takes in. But with Cold War tensions high, Reagan sharply increased military spending. As military spending rose and taxes fell, the budget deficit soared. For 1986, the deficit jumped to an all-time high of $240 billion.

Still, the economy continued to expand, and Reagan remained popular. For many Americans, he had succeeded in restoring faith in the presidency, which had been so badly tarnished in recent years.

Bush's Economic Troubles Reagan's Vice President, George H. W. Bush, won a big victory in 1988. Bush vowed to continue Reagan's economic policies, cutting the deficit without raising taxes. "Read my lips," he pledged during the campaign. "No new taxes."

Bush could not keep his promise. By 1990, he and Congress were deadlocked over which government programs to cut to reduce the deficit. Finally, Bush agreed to raise taxes to save some popular programs. Many conservatives felt betrayed.

As taxes rose, the economy grew weaker. To make matters worse, a banking crisis developed. Deregulation had led some banks to make risky loans. When those loans were not repaid, many banks failed. Without bank loans, the economy slowed. Many businesses cut costs by **downsizing,** or reducing their workforces. Downsizing increased business profits but also increased joblessness.

These conditions soon produced a recession. A **recession** is an economic slump that is milder than a depression. The recession continued for more than a year.

Conservatives on the Court Reagan and Bush appointed a total of five Justices to the Supreme Court. (One of Reagan's choices, Sandra Day O'Connor, was the first woman to serve on the Court.) The new Justices were more conservative than those they replaced.

The more conservative Court placed new limits on the rights of suspected criminals, as well as on the right of prisoners to appeal convictions. The Court made it harder for workers to win job discrimination cases. It also reduced busing, which some school districts had used since the 1960s to achieve racial integration in public schools.

Target Skill **Identify Sequence** Read the subsection "Clinton and the Conservatives." What key events marked Bill Clinton's presidency? Add these to your flowchart.

Clinton and the Conservatives

Bush faced a stiff reelection challenge in 1992. Recession and unemployment continued. Bickering between Congress and the President left voters unhappy with Washington politics. The Democratic nominee, Arkansas governor Bill Clinton, promised more government involvement in areas ignored by Reagan and Bush.

On Election Day, voters signaled their dissatisfaction. Only 38 percent voted for Bush. Clinton received less than half the popular

POLITICAL CARTOON *Skills*

Clinton and the Congress **The 1994 elections left the nation with a Democrat as President and a Republican-controlled Congress. In this cartoon from a Singapore newspaper, the elephant is used as the traditional symbol of the Republican party.**

1. **Comprehension** **(a)** Who is operating the boat? **(b)** Can Clinton move in the direction he wants without their help? Why or why not?
2. **Understanding Main Ideas** What is the cartoonist saying about the situation in Washington after the 1994 congressional elections?
3. **Critical Thinking Identifying Points of View** Can you tell whether this cartoonist favored the President or the Congress? Explain.

Civics 

vote—43 percent. The remaining 19 percent went to Ross Perot, a Texas billionaire who ran as an independent candidate.

A Middle Road President Clinton followed a middle-of-the-road course. On the one hand, he moved cautiously when he persuaded Congress to increase some taxes and reduce spending. For the first time in over 40 years, the federal deficit began a steady decline.

On the other hand, Clinton pushed for bold reform of the health care system. In 1994, some 37 million Americans had no health insurance. Clinton called for a national system of health insurance for almost all Americans. After heated debate, however, Congress defeated the plan. Many Americans worried that it would be too costly and involve the government too deeply in their lives.

To many Americans, the struggle over health care showed that Washington was paralyzed. Democrats controlled both Congress and the White House, yet the President could not get his own plan enacted.

Conservatives Win Control Voter frustration helped Republicans win a resounding victory in the 1994 congressional elections. For the first time since the 1950s, Republicans held a majority in both the Senate and the House of Representatives. "It was a revolution," cheered Toby Roth, a Wisconsin Republican.

Newt Gingrich of Georgia became Speaker of the House. Under his leadership, House Republicans drew up a **"Contract With America."** This set of proposed laws included trimming social welfare programs, reducing environmental regulations, and slashing taxes.

The President attacked many of the proposals as unfair to poor and middle-class Americans. After a bitter fight, he compromised with Congress on a plan to balance the federal budget by the year

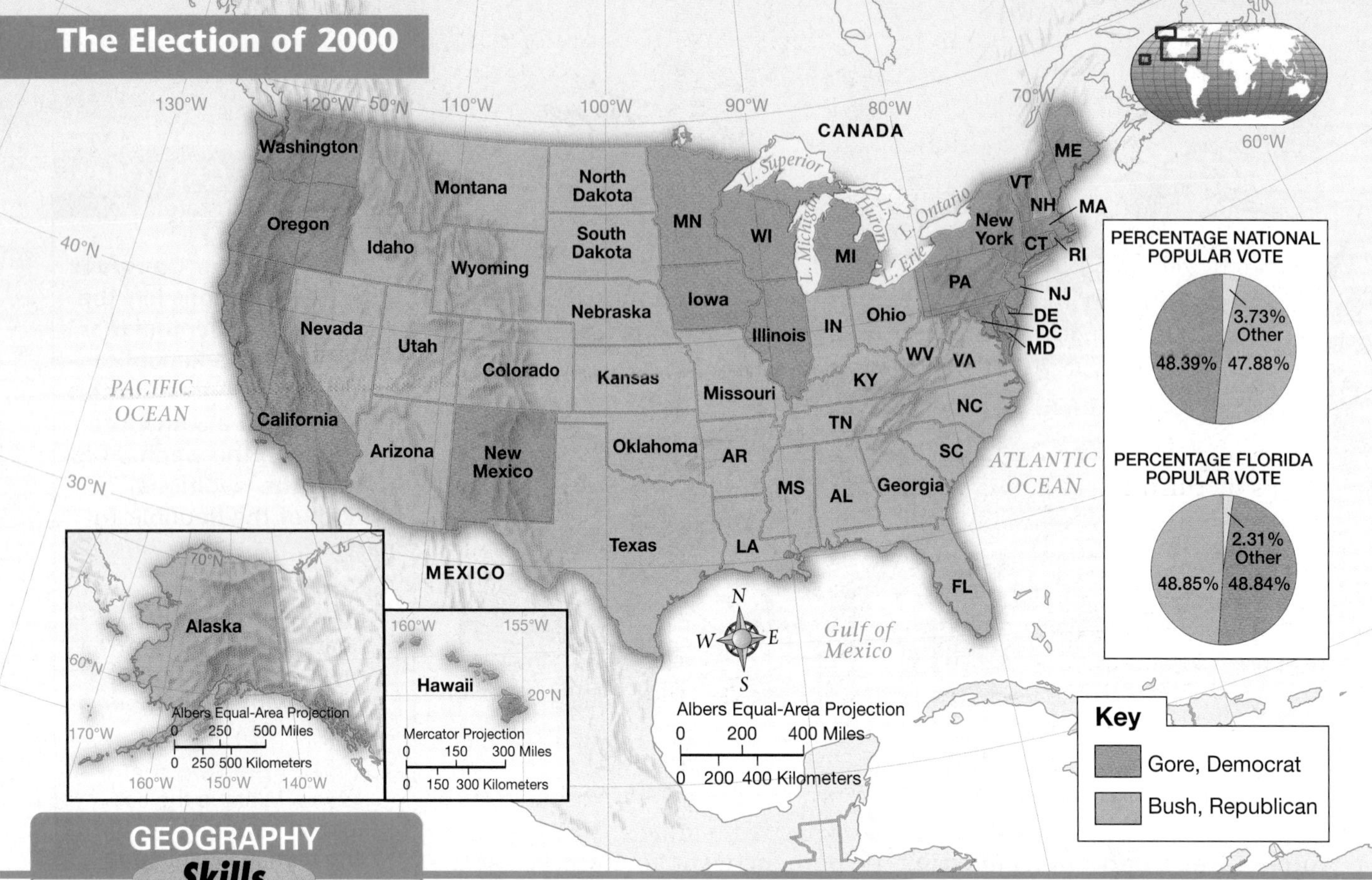

GEOGRAPHY Skills

The presidential election of 2000 was the most disputed race since 1876.

1. **Location** On the map, locate **(a)** Florida, **(b)** Tennessee, **(c)** Texas.
2. **Region** In what areas of the country did Al Gore receive his strongest support?
3. **Critical Thinking Drawing Conclusions** What role did candidates of other parties play in the election?

2002. In fact, the economy grew so strongly that in 1998 the government reported a budget **surplus,** in which income exceeded spending. Over the next two years, the surplus grew even larger.

Congress and Clinton also compromised on welfare reform. The government limited the length of time a person could receive welfare benefits. In this way, it hoped to encourage unemployed Americans to find jobs.

Impeachment and Trial In 1996, Clinton easily won reelection. Yet, controversy engulfed his second term. Federal prosecutors investigated Clinton for real estate dealings while he was governor of Arkansas. Prosecutors found no evidence of lawbreaking. However, they did accuse the President of lying under oath about an improper relationship with a White House intern.

Amid heated debate, the House voted to impeach the President. For only the second time in history, the Senate tried a President. In February 1999, Clinton was acquitted. All 45 Democratic senators supported the President. All but five Republicans voted to convict.

The Bush II Era

In the presidential election of 2000, the Republicans nominated Texas governor George W. Bush, son of former President George H. W. Bush. Along with vice presidential nominee Richard Cheney, Bush campaigned to return "honor and decency" to the White House and to end party bickering in Washington.

Vice President Al Gore ran for the Democrats. His running mate, Senator Joseph Lieberman of Connecticut, was the first Jewish candidate nominated for Vice President by a major party. The Democrats promised to continue the policies of the Clinton years.

Dispute Over Florida Gore won the popular vote by a narrow margin. But the electoral vote remained in doubt because of disputed ballots in Florida. There, Bush clung to a slim lead.

In a number of counties, the vote count was in dispute. Both sides took their cases to court. In December, the Supreme Court ruled that the Florida recount would have to stop. Gore conceded, and Bush was declared the winner.

Bush as President In his first years in office, Bush won major victories by fulfilling campaign pledges to lower taxes and to raise academic standards for public schools. He reduced taxes with the largest cuts since the Reagan era. Critics worried that tax cuts would slow recovery from an economic recession.

The President also pushed through Congress the "No-Child-Left-Behind" Act of 2002. It required public schools to demonstrate the success of their programs by testing students' reading and math skills at various grades.

On September 11, 2001, the Bush presidency was forever changed by terrorist attacks on the Pentagon and New York's World Trade Center. George Bush led the nation as it fought back against the attackers. Bush's popularity soared.

In 2002, the Republicans won control of both the House and Senate. Confident of popular support, Bush undertook the greatest shift in American foreign policy since the United States adopted a policy of containment shortly after World War II.

Section 1 Assessment

Recall

1. **Identify** Explain the significance of **(a)** Ronald Reagan, **(b)** Moral Majority, **(c)** Reaganomics, **(d)** George H. W. Bush, **(e)** Bill Clinton, **(f)** Newt Gingrich, **(g)** Contract With America, **(h)** George W. Bush, **(i)** Al Gore.
2. **Define** **(a)** deregulation, **(b)** balanced budget, **(c)** downsizing, **(d)** recession, **(e)** surplus.

Comprehension

3. Describe two conservative goals of Ronald Reagan.
4. How did Bill Clinton compromise with conservatives?
5. How did the September 11, 2001, attacks on the Pentagon and World Trade Center affect George W. Bush's presidency?

Critical Thinking and Writing

6. **Exploring the Main Idea** Review the Main Idea statement at the beginning of this section. Then, write a paragraph explaining why Ronald Reagan's presidency has been called a "revolution."
7. **Drawing Conclusions** List three reasons that appointing Justices to the Supreme Court is one of the President's most important powers under the Constitution.

ACTIVITY

Composing Slogans
You are a campaign worker for one of the Presidents discussed in this section. Write two slogans that President could have used in an election campaign. You may want to present your slogan as part of a poster or button.

2 American Leadership in a New World

Prepare to Read

Objectives

In this section, you will
- Describe the changes caused by the end of the Cold War.
- Explain how the United States helped promote democracy.
- Describe the U.S. role in world affairs.
- Summarize why nuclear arms remained a threat.

Key Terms

mediator

apartheid

sanctions

Dayton Accord

Strategic Arms Reduction Treaty

Target Reading Skill

Reading Process Copy the table below. As you read, complete the table with information about the role of the United States in the post–Cold War world.

PROMOTING DEMOCRACY	RESOLVING CONFLICT
• South Africa: sanctions against apartheid •	• Yugoslavia •

Main Idea After the Cold War, the United States led the search for peace and stability in the world.

American flags

Setting the Scene "We were suddenly in a unique position," said Brent Scowcroft, "without experience, without precedent, and standing alone at the height of power." Scowcroft was referring to the end of the Cold War, when he was National Security Advisor to President George H. W. Bush. The superpower rivalry between the United States and the Soviet Union was gone "in a blink of an eye," he wrote. Now Americans faced a new world:

> ❝ It was, it is, an unparalleled situation in history, one which presents us with the rarest opportunities to shape the world and the deepest responsibility to do so wisely. ❞
>
> — George H. W. Bush and Brent Scowcroft, *A World Transformed*

Despite the end of the Cold War, conflict still threatened many areas of the world. As the last superpower, the United States led the search for a new international order that would bring stability and lasting peace to the world.

The Lone Superpower

As you have read, the Soviet Union split apart in 1991. The breakup brought an end to the Cold War. The United States remained the world's lone superpower.

Americans debated their function in the post–Cold War world. Some people wanted to reduce the role of the United States in world affairs. "In the post–Cold War world, we will no longer require our people to carry an unfair burden for the rest of humanity," said Representative Dana Rohrabacher.

Others argued that the nation must not retreat from the world. Like Brent Scowcroft, they thought that the United States had a responsibility to use its power wisely. "The United States must lead, period," declared Speaker of the House Newt Gingrich.

Neither President George H.W. Bush nor President Bill Clinton turned his back on the world. Both realized that fostering freedom and democracy abroad would only strengthen the United States at home.

Promoting Global Democracy

The desire of Presidents Bush and Clinton to promote global democracy supported a process that was already underway. Political freedom was spreading across the globe. With it came economic freedom, the promotion of free markets with less interference from the state. In the last years of the 20th century, the United States encouraged both of these trends. American leadership met with both failures and successes.

American leadership took many forms. Sometimes the United States worked to influence foreign governments through quiet diplomacy or economic pressure. Sometimes it acted as a mediator. A **mediator** is an agent that helps conflicting parties iron out their differences. Occasionally the United States used military force, often in cooperation with other nations.

Asia In 1986, thousands of Filipinos protested the rule of dictator Ferdinand Marcos. They accused Marcos of fraud in a recent presidential election. Proclaiming "people power," they refused to recognize Marcos as president. After weeks of demonstrations, the Philippine army joined the demonstrations. Marcos fled. The United States backed Corazon Aquino, the woman who had run against him. During the 1990s, the United States continued to provide economic aid for the young Filipino democracy.

Other nations in Asia had mixed success with political reforms. In the 1980s and 1990s, fierce protests shook corrupt, undemocratic governments in South Korea and Indonesia. The protests led to freer elections and the possibility of greater democratic reforms.

China After President Nixon's historic visit to China, many hoped that the communist nation would begin to reform. During the 1980s, China did begin to build a free market economy. However, Chinese leaders refused to accept political reforms.

In 1989, students and workers launched a bold campaign to bring democracy to China. Hundreds of thousands gathered at Tiananmen Square in the nation's capital, Beijing. However, the army crushed the demonstrations. Many people were killed or arrested.

President George H. W. Bush disapproved of the crackdown but took no strong action against the Chinese government. He hoped to influence China by keeping communication open. President Clinton followed a similar policy. On a 1998 visit to China, he pledged to strengthen ties between the two nations. At the same time, he publicly debated human rights issues with China's president.

In 2001, China won its bid to host the 2008 Olympic games. Many hoped that the worldwide attention brought by the Olympics would encourage reform.

An American Profile

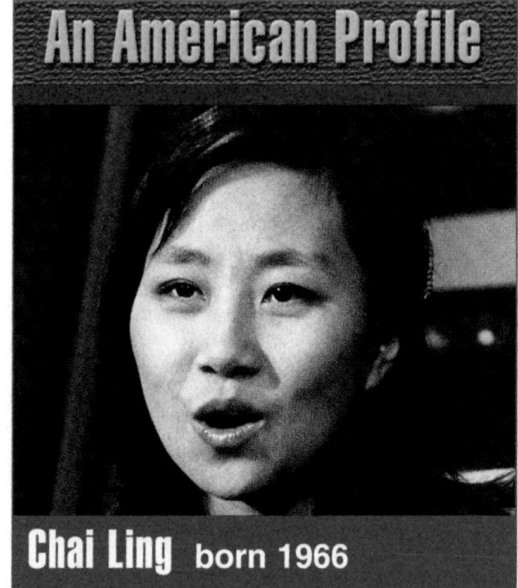

Chai Ling born 1966

A student at Beijing University, Chai Ling was known for her forceful leadership skills. At age 23, she became chief commander of the democracy movement in China.

After the army crushed the protests in Tiananmen Square, Chai Ling was one of the most wanted women in China. She escaped to Hong Kong, nailed inside a wooden crate in the hold of a leaky boat. In time, she came to the United States. She became a software entrepreneur while continuing to work for reform in China. Chai Ling has twice been nominated for the Nobel Peace Prize.

Why do you think Chai Ling chose to immigrate to the United States?

Cuba and North Korea Other communist nations refused to reform even when their people faced hard times. The fall of the Soviet Union deprived Cuba of its main source of trade and economic aid. As the Cuban economy spiraled downward, some 30,000 Cubans fled by boat to the United States. Still, after four decades, Fidel Castro remained in power.

In 1994, the United States signed an agreement with Cuba to allow Cubans to emigrate more freely. At the same time, the United States continued to enforce a 40-year-old embargo aimed at toppling Castro.

On the Korean peninsula, the Cold War remained alive. There, communist North Korea and democratic South Korea armed against each other. In the 1990s, famine struck North Korea. The famine was worsened by the economic policies of the North Korean dictator, Kim Jong Il. To make matters worse, the North Koreans announced in 2003 that they were resuming their nuclear arms program. This violated a treaty North Korea had signed with the United States, South Korea, Japan, and other nations. Experts worried that nuclear weapons in the hands of the North Koreans could be used to threaten the region and to supply terrorists.

South Africa The cause of global democracy had its most dramatic success in South Africa. Since 1948, the government of South Africa had enforced a policy of **apartheid** (uh PAHR tayt), or strict separation of races. The nation's nonwhite majority was segregated. By law, nonwhites and whites were required to use separate facilities. Nonwhites were allowed no voice in the government.

In 1986, Congress approved economic sanctions against South Africa to force an end to apartheid. **Sanctions** are measures aimed at making a country change its policy. American companies were forbidden to invest in South Africa or import South African products.

In the 1990s, South Africa moved to end minority rule. Under a new constitution, all races were permitted to vote for the first time in 1994. Nelson Mandela, a black who had spent 27 years in prison for opposing apartheid, was elected president. When Mandela retired, his deputy president, Thabo Mbeki, won election in 1999.

Russia and Eastern Europe

After the Cold War, the nations that rejected communism struggled to adapt to their new freedoms. As the governments sold off state-run businesses to private enterprises, their economies were not able to adjust. The result was high unemployment and high inflation.

Russian president Boris Yeltsin sought to build a stable democracy. His efforts faltered when he failed to put down an independence movement in the Russian province of Chechnya. After Yeltsin resigned in 2000, Vladimir Putin took over. Putin, a former communist official, was known for his ability to use power behind the scenes. As president, he wrestled with economic problems and the

Chechnya rebellion. He also sought to build closer ties with China and the nations of Europe.

Civil War in Bosnia In Eastern Europe, Yugoslavia faced a civil war. Yugoslavia was made up of several republics, including Croatia, Serbia, and Bosnia-Herzegovina. In 1991, Croatia and Bosnia declared their independence. However, Serbs in Croatia and Bosnia wanted to remain part of Yugoslavia. With help from Serbia, they fought to prevent the new governments from splitting away. During four years of civil war, more than 250,000 people died, including many children and teenagers.

To end the violence, the United States sponsored a meeting in Dayton, Ohio. There an agreement was hammered out. To help guarantee the peace agreement, President Clinton sent about 20,000 American troops to Bosnia. There, they joined NATO and Russian forces in a peacekeeping mission. The troops helped to restore order.

Crisis in Kosovo Kosovo, a province within Serbia, also sought greater independence. The Albanians living there were in the majority and resented Serbian rule.

In 1998, Serbs launched a series of attacks against Albanian rebels in Kosovo. Hundreds of thousands of Albanians fled the province. Many thousands of others were killed or wounded.

President Clinton condemned the attacks as "feeding the flames of ethnic and religious division." In March 1999, American air forces joined the air forces of other NATO nations in bombing Serbia. This forced Serbian troops to leave Kosovo. NATO peacekeeping forces then entered the province. The violence in Kosovo ended. Still, rebuilding has been a slow process.

GEOGRAPHY *Skills*

After the Cold War ended, Eastern Europe underwent a period of change and conflict.

1. **Location** On the map, locate **(a)** Russia, **(b)** Croatia, **(c)** Bosnia-Herzegovina, **(d)** Albania.
2. **Region** Compare this map to the map on page 813. Which nations shown here had been part of the Soviet Union?
3. **Critical Thinking Drawing Inferences** Which Western nations do you think would be most concerned about refugees from Serbia & Montenegro?

Easing Conflict Elsewhere

Sometimes the American effort to bring stability to war-torn regions ended in tragedy. In 1992, American forces led a UN mission attempting to end civil war and famine in the African nation of Somalia. However, neither the American troops nor the UN were able to end the civil war. Gradually, the Americans found themselves the target of hostility. In 1993, 18 U.S. Army Rangers died in fighting while trying to restore order in the capital of Mogadishu. Shortly after, the United States withdrew its troops from Somalia.

The United States used diplomacy to ease conflict in Northern Ireland. The many Catholics there wanted the region to be reunited with Ireland. Most Protestants wanted to remain under British rule. From 1969 to 1998, more than 3,000 people died in the fighting.

The United States sent former Senator George Mitchell of Maine to aid Northern Ireland peace talks. He helped to produce an agreement in April 1998. Although the peace process was slow and often troubled, a lasting peace settlement seemed within reach.

The Threat of Nuclear Arms

Use Prior Knowledge

Compare the new arms race described here to the Cold War arms race between the United States and the Soviet Union described in Chapter 28.

As the former Soviet Union collapsed, the world faced a menacing challenge, the spread of nuclear weapons. The United States and Russia still had thousands of nuclear missiles in their possession. Other nations were developing nuclear weapons, too.

Reducing Nuclear Arms The United States and the old Soviet Union had already agreed to several treaties reducing nuclear arms. In 1991, they signed the most important agreement yet, the Strategic Arms Reduction Treaty, or START. Even more reductions followed in 1993. In 2002, Presidents Bush and Putin agreed to cut their nuclear missiles by more than half over ten years.

A New Arms Race Despite such progress, a new arms race loomed. In 1998, India announced that it had conducted five nuclear tests. Two weeks later, Pakistan, its neighbor and deadly rival, exploded five nuclear devices of its own. World leaders saw the tests as the beginning of a dangerous new arms race. President Clinton called for economic sanctions against both India and Pakistan but with little effect.

 Section 2 Assessment   

Recall

1. **Identify** Explain the significance of **(a)** Corazon Aquino, **(b)** Nelson Mandela, **(c)** Dayton Accord, **(d)** Strategic Arms Reduction Treaty.
2. **Define (a)** mediator, **(b)** apartheid, **(c)** sanctions.

Comprehension

3. How did Americans differ about the role of the United States after the end of the Cold War?
4. Give two examples of how the United States encouraged democracy in other countries.
5. What role did the United States play in Bosnia?
6. Why did the dispute between India and Pakistan threaten the security of nations around the world?

Critical Thinking and Writing

7. **Exploring the Main Idea** Review the Main Idea statement at the beginning of this section. Then, write a letter to the President expressing your view of the role of the United States in the post–Cold War world.
8. **Identifying Alternatives** List at least two alternative courses President Bush might have followed when China crushed the pro-democracy movement in 1989.

Activity

Making a Map

Use the Internet to find out which nations of the world have nuclear weapons. On an outline map of the world, use a color code to show countries that are known or suspected to have nuclear weapons. For help in completing the activity, visit PHSchool.com, **Web Code mfd-3001.**

3 The Spread of Regional Conflict

Prepare to Read

Objectives

In this section, you will
- Identify the U.S. role in the Arab-Israeli conflict.
- Explain how America became involved in conflicts in Iran and Iraq.
- Discuss the U.S. response to terrorist attacks in September 2001.

Key Terms

OPEC

Camp David Accords

PLO

Persian Gulf War

terrorism

Target Reading Skill

Cause and Effect Copy the effects chart below. As you read, fill in some of the events and developments that followed American involvement in regional conflicts.

Main Idea A series of regional conflicts in the Middle East eventually spread to the United States.

Setting the Scene On the evening of September 11, 2001, Americans across the nation gathered in grief. Many people wept openly. Some held candles. On the steps of the Capitol Building, the leaders of Congress, Democrats and Republicans alike, stood shoulder to shoulder, united in a new resolve "to fight evil."

The candlelight vigils marked the end of a tragic day. That morning, hijackers from the Middle East had flown two airliners into the Twin Towers of the World Trade Center, symbols of American financial might. The towers burned and collapsed. A third hijacked plane struck American military headquarters at the Pentagon. A fourth crashed in Pennsylvania. More than 3,000 people died.

The events of September 11 produced dramatic changes in American foreign policy. To the task of promoting global democracy, President Bush added a new goal: to fight terrorism both at home and abroad. He also resolved to end regional conflicts before they spread again.

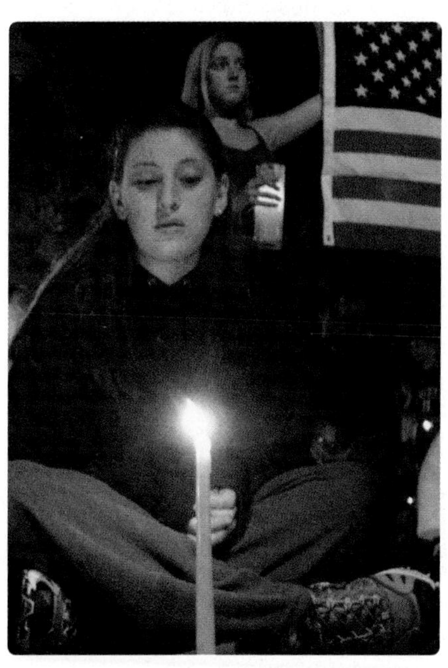

Americans honor attack victims

The Arab-Israeli Conflict

Conflict had long troubled the Middle East, a region extending from southwestern Asia across North Africa. Over the centuries, friction among religious groups has led to discord and violence. European attempts to colonize the Middle East and, more recently, competition for large oil reserves in the region have added to tensions.

The United States has conflicting interests in the Middle East. It has strongly supported the Jewish state of Israel. Yet, it also has ties to the Islamic Arab states that dominate the region. Arab nations such as Saudi Arabia supply much of the oil used by Americans.

Israelis and Arabs In the late 1800s, European Jews arrived in Palestine along the Mediterranean coast. They hoped to create a Jewish state in their ancient homeland. Jewish settlement grew in the 1930s as European Jews fled Nazi persecution. In 1948, Arabs rejected a plan to divide the land into one Jewish and one Palestinian state. Jews in Palestine announced the creation of the state of Israel. The United States and other nations quickly recognized the new nation.

Neighboring Arab nations refused to recognize the Jewish state. Instead, they attacked. But Israel won the 1948 war. More than 500,000 Palestinian Arabs fled to refugee camps in nearby states. Most were not permitted to return after the war and were not paid for their lands and homes. Arab nations attacked again in 1967 and 1973. In these wars, Israel won portions of Egypt, Jordan, and Syria. Arabs called these lands the "occupied territories."

The United States sent aid to Israel in the 1973 war. Arab members of **OPEC,** the Organization of Petroleum Exporting Countries, retaliated. They cut off oil shipments to the United States and slowed down oil production. OPEC finally lifted the oil embargo in 1974.

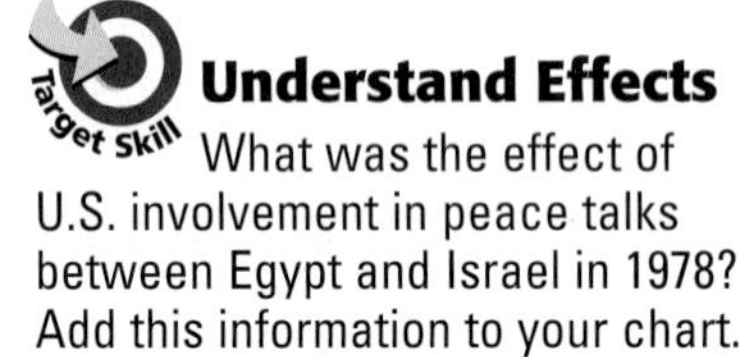

Understand Effects What was the effect of U.S. involvement in peace talks between Egypt and Israel in 1978? Add this information to your chart.

Egyptian president Anwar el-Sadat took a bold step toward peace in 1977. He became the first Arab head of state to visit Israel. When peace talks between the two nations broke down, President Jimmy Carter invited Sadat and Israeli Prime Minister Menachem Begin (muh NAHK uhm BAY gihn) to Camp David, the President's retreat in Maryland. In the **Camp David Accords** of 1978, Israel agreed to return the Sinai Peninsula to Egypt and Egypt agreed to recognize Israel. The two nations signed a peace treaty in 1979.

The Palestinian Issue Palestinian Arabs waged guerrilla war against Israel. Under Israeli rule, Palestinians in the occupied territories had limited rights. Those living outside Israel wanted to return to their homeland under a Palestinian government. Many supported the Palestine Liberation Organization, or **PLO.** Its leader, Yasir Arafat, stated that the goal of the PLO was to destroy Israel.

In 1987, Palestinians in the occupied territories took to the streets to protest Israeli rule. The unrest, called the *Intifada,* focused attention on the need to end the Israeli-Palestinian conflict.

After years of effort, the United States persuaded Israel and the PLO to come to the bargaining table. In 1993, the longtime enemies signed a pact in Washington, D.C. The PLO agreed to recognize Israel's right to exist and promised to give up violence. Israel agreed to limited self-rule for Palestinian parts of the Gaza Strip and West Bank. Palestinians and Israelis seemed to be moving toward peace. Yet by 2002, escalating violence threatened the fragile peace.

In 2003, President George W. Bush led a renewed effort to settle the conflict. His "roadmap to peace" called for the creation of a democratic Palestine and guarantees of survival and security for Israel. Israeli and Palestinian leaders accepted it. However, Palestinian militants launched a series of suicide bombings in Israel to disrupt the peace process. In response, Israel attacked Palestinian targets. The peace process seemed to be collapsing. Nevertheless, Palestinian and Israeli leaders continued to work towards a lasting peace agreement encouraged by the United States.

Conflict With Iran and Iraq

The United States was deeply involved in other Middle East conflicts. In 1953, the United States helped to overthrow the elected government of Iran and to return the dethroned Shah Muhammad Reza

Pahlavi to power. Then, in 1979, a revolution forced the unpopular shah to flee. A religious leader, the Ayatollah Khomeini (i yuh TOH luh koh MAYN ee), took control of Iran.

Iran Hostage Crisis The shah had been a firm ally of the United States. The Ayatollah was strongly anti-American. Where the shah had favored westernizing Iran, the new ruler wanted to return to the strict traditions of Islam. Neither, however, favored democracy.

In November 1979, President Carter let the shah enter the United States for medical treatment. In response, Iranian revolutionaries seized the American embassy and took 53 Americans hostage. The hostages were not freed until January 1981. The hostage crisis poisoned American relations with Iran for decades.

The Persian Gulf War In August 1990, Saddam Hussein, the dictator of Iraq, sent 100,000 troops to invade oil-rich Kuwait. President George H.W. Bush feared that the invasion was the start of a larger plan to gain control of Middle East oil.

Saddam Hussein ignored demands from the United States and the UN to withdraw from Kuwait. The UN then imposed a trade boycott on Iraq. When Saddam still refused to leave Kuwait, the United States and its UN allies launched an air attack on Iraq. This was followed by a massive attack on Iraqi troops in Kuwait and Iraq. Troops from 28 nations—including some Arab countries—joined the effort. It took only six weeks to defeat the Iraqis and free Kuwait.

Although the war was over, the UN boycott against Iraq continued. The goal was to force Saddam Hussein to stop his chemical and biological weapons programs. However, Hussein refused to cooperate with UN arms inspectors.

GEOGRAPHY *Skills*

Oil wealth and religious conflict have helped shape events in the Middle East.

1. **Location** On the map, locate **(a)** Israel, **(b)** Egypt, **(c)** Iran, **(d)** Iraq, **(e)** Kuwait, **(f)** Afghanistan.
2. **Region** In what area are the most oil fields located?
3. **Critical Thinking Applying Information** **(a)** If this were a map printed in 1978, what color would the Sinai Peninsula be? **(b)** Why did this situation change?

The Middle East

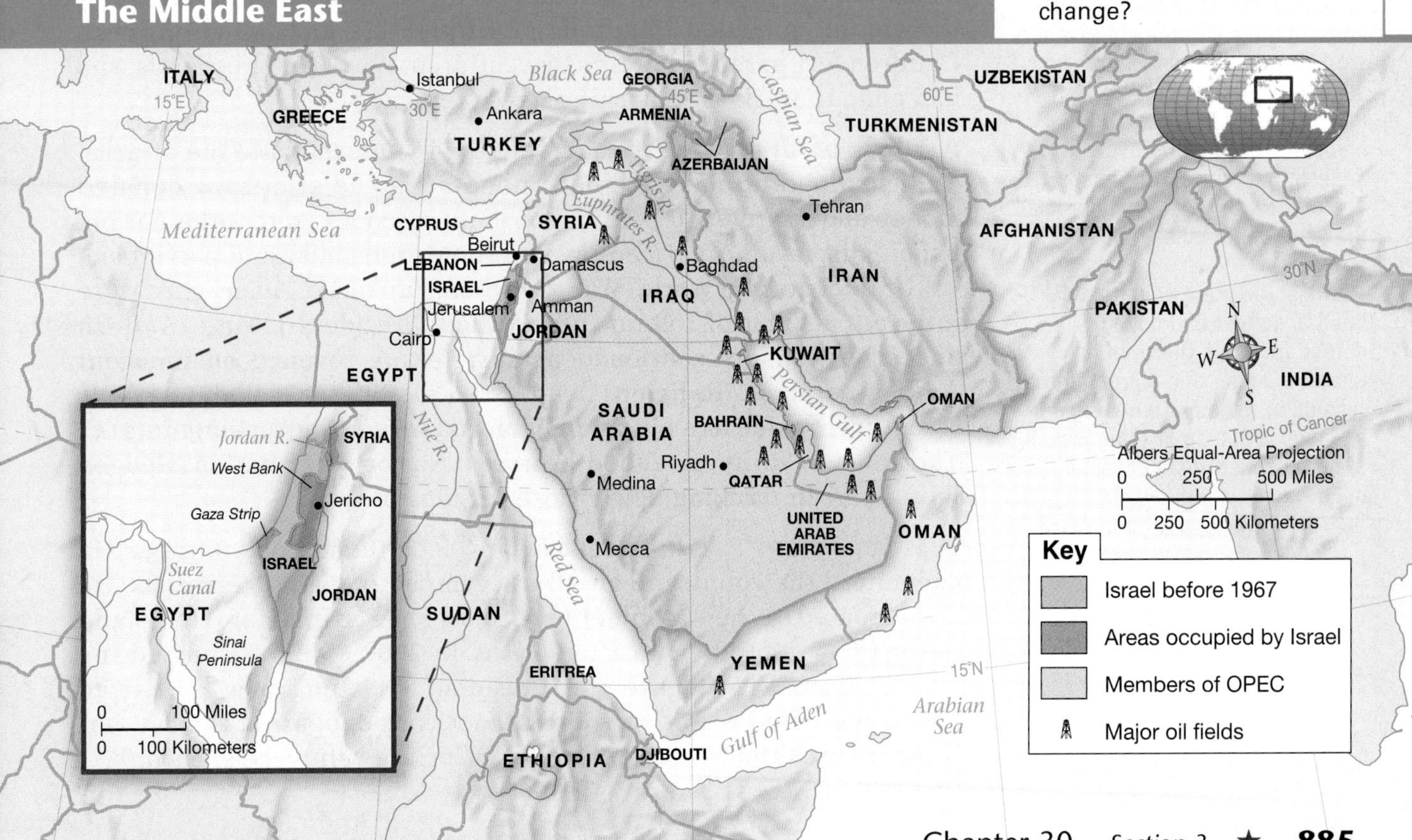

Primary Source

The Nation Is Attacked

Nine days after the September 11 attacks, President Bush addressed Congress and the nation:

"We have seen the state of our union in the endurance of rescuers working past exhaustion. We've seen the unfurling of flags, the lighting of candles, the giving of blood, the saying of prayers in English, Hebrew, and Arabic. . . . The entire world has seen for itself the state of our union, and it is strong.

Tonight we are a country awakened to danger and called to defend freedom. Our grief has turned to anger and our anger to resolution. Whether we bring our enemies to justice or bring justice to our enemies, justice will be done."

—George W. Bush, Address to Congress, September 20, 2001

Terrorism and the United States

After the 1960s, terrorist bombings, kidnappings, and hijackings became more common in Europe, the Middle East, and elsewhere. **Terrorism** is the deliberate use of violence to spread fear and to achieve political goals. Often the victims are civilians and the targets symbolic, such as embassies or centers of economic power. In troubled areas such as Northern Ireland and Israel, acts of terror played a key role in conflicts.

Americans and Terrorism In the Middle East, some radical Muslim groups sponsored terrorism. They were angered by the Persian Gulf War, by United States support for Israel, and by other American policies. Extremists also saw American culture as immoral, and offensive to their own very strict brand of Islam.

As a result, fanatical groups targeted American sites overseas for terrorist acts. In 1988, an explosion killed 270 people on an American passenger airliner over Scotland. Between 1998 and 2000, bombs hit two United States embassies in Africa and a navy ship off the coast of Yemen in the Middle East.

Attacks on the United States Terrorism from abroad spread to the United States itself. In 1993, a bomb damaged the World Trade Center in New York. Six Arab men were later convicted of the crime.

On September 11, 2001, as you have read, terrorists slammed three airliners into the World Trade Center and the Pentagon. On a fourth hijacked airliner, courageous passengers fought back. The plane crashed in a field in Pennsylvania. All on board were killed, but the plane was prevented from hitting any target on the ground.

The Human Cost The terrorist attacks of September 11 took more lives than the Japanese attack on Pearl Harbor in 1941. In New York, the victims included hundreds of firefighters and police officers. Children lost parents. Parents lost children. Wives and husbands who had gone to work that morning never returned.

A Spirit of Unity Americans were quick to respond to the attacks. Millions lined up to give blood, aided in rescue efforts, or donated money and supplies to help victims and rescuers. Across the nation, people displayed American flags to show their unity and patriotism.

Unlike during World War II, when Japanese Americans were interred, a spirit of tolerance prevailed. President George W. Bush and other leaders cautioned against taking revenge on innocent Arab Americans. Religious leaders of all faiths, including Islam, stood side by side at a national memorial service in Washington, D.C. The spirit of unity extended overseas. Nation after nation pledged its support in tracking down those responsible.

War on Terrorism President Bush voiced the nation's outrage. He committed the country to an all-out campaign against terrorists. He also created a new cabinet-level post, the Office of Homeland Security, to defend against terrorism. In 2002, Congress passed the USA Patriot Act. It gave the President sweeping new powers to arrest suspected terrorists. Most Americans supported the act, but some worried that it violated rights of privacy and free speech.

Early on, Bush blamed al-Qaida (KI duh), a terrorist network, led by a wealthy Saudi, Osama bin Laden. Bin Laden was hiding in Afghanistan, protected by a brutal dictatorship, the Taliban. Bush vowed to bring bin Laden to justice.

The campaign against terrorism moved along three fronts: diplomatic, economic, and military. First, the President asked other nations to stand with the United States against terrorism. Second, Bush sought to find and block the money supplies of terrorist organizations. Third, American forces attacked military sites and terrorist training camps in Afghanistan. With the aid of Afghan rebels, American forces soon toppled the Taliban. Still, the search for Osama bin Laden continued.

Ousting Saddam In his 2002 State of the Union address, President Bush charged that an "axis of evil"—consisting of Iraq, Iran, and North Korea—was endangering the world. These nations, he said, oppressed their people, sponsored terrorism, and were developing weapons of mass destruction (WMD). President Bush was particularly concerned with the activities of Iraq's Saddam Hussein. Bush worried that under Saddam's leadership, Iraq was developing weapons of mass destruction that could be used by governments in the Middle East or supplied to terrorists.

Despite opposition from France, Germany, Russia, and other countries, the United States invaded Iraq in March 2003. Technology played a key role in the conflict. Laser-guided missiles and other advanced weapons hit Iraqi targets with precision. Lightning air and ground strikes by a coalition of forces led by the United States toppled the Iraqi regime in just six weeks. Iraqi leaders, including Saddam, went into hiding. One by one, many of the top leaders were tracked down. In December 2003, Saddam was captured. However, guerrilla activities persisted in Iraq. It seemed that the tough task of rebuilding the country would take many years.

Section 3 Assessment

Recall

1. **Identify** Explain the significance of **(a)** OPEC, **(b)** Camp David Accords, **(c)** PLO, **(d)** Ayatollah Khomeini, **(e)** Saddam Hussein, **(f)** Persian Gulf War, **(g)** Osama bin Laden.
2. **Define** terrorism.

Comprehension

3. How did the United States try to promote peace between Israel and its Arab neighbors?
4. Identify the causes of the war of 2003 against Iraq.
5. Describe the aftermath of the terrorist attacks in 2001.

Critical Thinking and Writing

6. **Exploring the Main Idea** Review the Main Idea statement at the beginning of this section. Then, list reasons for and against getting involved in regional conflicts.
7. **Identifying Causes and Effects** Write a paragraph explaining how oil has shaped how Americans respond to events in the Middle East.

Activity

Writing a Dialogue
Write and stage a television panel discussion about the events of September 11, 2001, and their aftermath. Your dialogue should focus on what a hero is and how the heroes of that event should be honored.

4 A Global Economy

Prepare to Read

Objectives

In this section, you will
- Explain how changes in international trade affected the United States.
- List problems the environment posed for the global economy.
- Discuss how the new networked world of information changed the global economy.

Key Terms

trade deficit
North American Free Trade Agreement
environmentalist
Environmental Protection Agency
renewable resource
global warming
Internet
e-commerce

Target Reading Skill

Clarifying Meaning Copy the concept web below. As you read, fill in the blank ovals with information about the new global economy. Add as many ovals as you need.

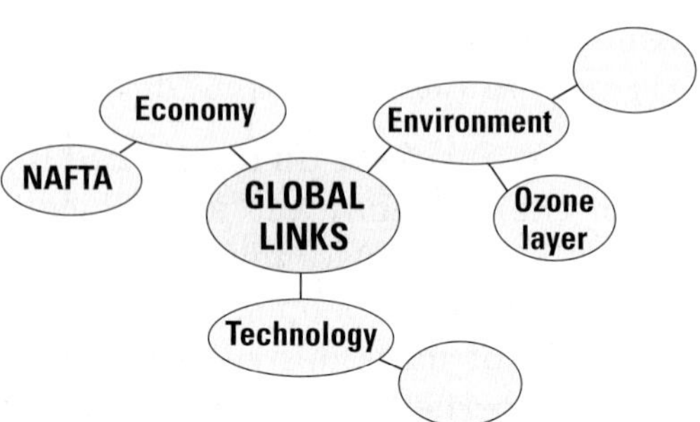

Main Idea Global economic links, the global environment, and a global information network tie the modern world together.

Japanese currency

Setting the Scene The trouble began in Asia. First, the booming economy of Japan turned sharply downward in the mid-1990s. Then, in 1997, banks in Thailand began to fail. From there, the financial crisis spread to other Asian powerhouses—South Korea, Indonesia, and Hong Kong.

The crisis threatened to engulf the world. Asian nations bought fewer raw materials and manufactured goods. Soon, nations in Latin America, the Middle East, and Europe were feeling the crunch. Led by the United States, international organizations pumped over $200 billion into these shaky economies. Such actions averted a global financial collapse.

The world was so tightly connected that financial trouble in far-off Asia could ripple quickly across the globe. The global environment and the new global network of information also affected the global economy. Each challenged the United States to strive for greater cooperation with other nations.

Competition and Cooperation

As the Asian financial crisis shows, American businesses operate in a global economy. In recent decades, trade with other nations has grown dramatically. In 1970, foreign trade made up about 10 percent of the American economy. By 2000, foreign trade amounted to about 25 percent.

Tough Competition In this growing world economy, the United States faces tough competition from industrialized countries in Europe and Asia. In general, American companies pay their workers higher wages than companies in most other nations. As a result, foreign products are often cheaper to manufacture and less expensive to buy than American ones.

Foreign competition has led to trade deficits for the United States. A **trade deficit** occurs when a nation buys more goods and services from foreign countries than it sells to them. To reduce this deficit, many American firms have built more efficient factories in order to lower costs. They have also tried to increase sales abroad by producing better products than foreign rivals.

Some people have called upon the government to protect American industries by raising tariffs on foreign goods. Others oppose high tariffs. They warn that other nations might raise their own tariffs in response, leading to costly "trade wars."

Removing Trade Barriers Opponents of tariffs won a victory in 1993. After bitter debate, Congress ratified the **North American Free Trade Agreement** (NAFTA). In this treaty, the United States and its neighbors, Canada and Mexico, agreed to cooperate in removing tariffs and other trade barriers among them.

Most economists agreed that NAFTA encouraged new trade and created jobs. However, critics pointed out that NAFTA hurt some industries and the environment. Auto parts makers moved factories to Mexico, where wages were lower. Also, foreign countries did not have the same strict antipollution laws as the United States.

In 1997, Congress refused to give President Clinton extra powers to negotiate more free-trade agreements. The debate over foreign trade continued into the new century.

Foreign Trade, 1950–2000

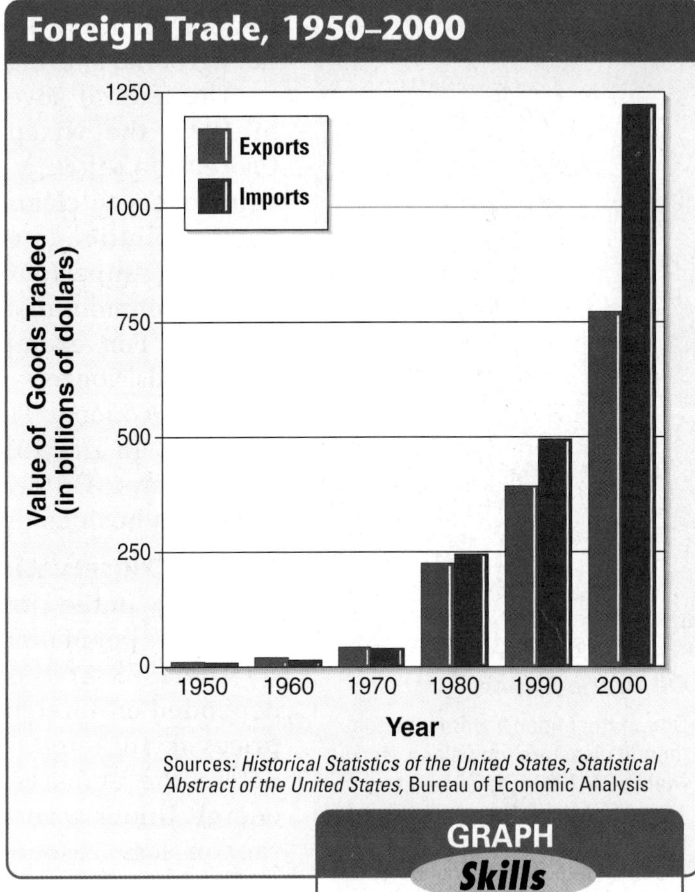

Sources: *Historical Statistics of the United States, Statistical Abstract of the United States,* Bureau of Economic Analysis

GRAPH *Skills*

Many Americans worry because the United States imports more goods than it exports. This situation is called a trade deficit.

1. **Comprehension** According to this graph, during what decade did the United States develop a trade deficit?
2. **Critical Thinking Analyzing Information** During the 1990s, which grew more—imports or exports? Explain.

Economics $

The Environment and the Global Economy

No issue has more global impact than the environment. Environmental problems do not stop at national borders. But not all nations agree on what needs to be done or on the price to be paid to protect the environment.

The Environmental Movement In the United States, marine biologist Rachel Carson sounded the alarm on environmental dangers. In 1962, she charged that chemical pesticides were poisoning the planet. Her book *Silent Spring* described a bleak future:

> "It was a spring without voices. On the mornings that had once throbbed with the dawn chorus of robins, catbirds, doves, jays, wrens . . . there was now no sound; only silence lay over the fields and woods and marsh."
>
> —Rachel Carson, *Silent Spring*

Reformers known as **environmentalists** called attention to environmental dangers. Chemical wastes turned rivers into sewers.

Factory smokestacks belched foul-smelling fumes. Massive tankers ran aground, spilling oil into the sea.

The federal government responded to environmental concerns. In 1970, the Nixon administration created the **Environmental Protection Agency** (EPA). The Clean Air Act of 1970 required automakers to clean up car exhausts. The Clean Water Act of 1972 fought pollution in rivers and lakes. The Waste Cleanup Act of 1980 created a "superfund" to clean up chemical dumps.

Environmentalists have faced opposition, often on economic grounds. For example, while environmentalists try to preserve forestlands, loggers point out that forest products are vital to the nation's economy. They also warn that restrictions on logging may cost jobs. In the 1980s, President Reagan sought to ease environmental laws. He argued that strict regulation was too costly for American businesses.

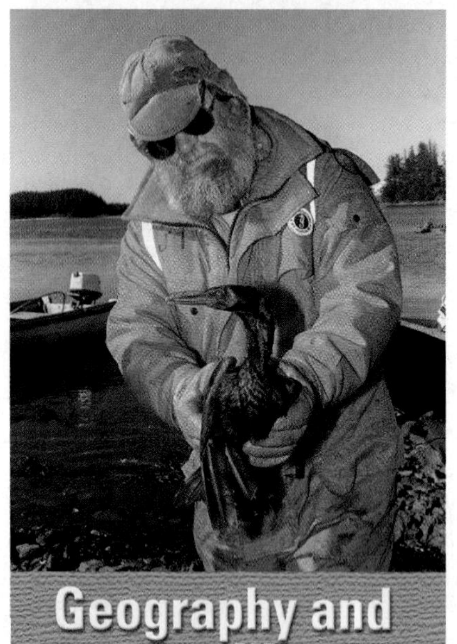

Geography and History

Oil in the Sound

One of the nation's worst environmental disasters took place on March 24, 1989. The oil tanker *Exxon Valdez* struck a submerged reef, spilling 11 million gallons of crude oil into Prince William Sound on Alaska's southern coast. For hours, oil poured into the waters of one of the most environmentally sensitive regions of the world. The fragile ecosystem contains whales, sea lions, seals, bears, deer, sea otters, salmon, and the tiny plankton upon which larger creatures feed.

Within a week, thousands of dead birds and animals littered the shoreline. Workers from around the world rushed to Alaska to capture and clean oil-soaked survivors.

Why do you think people far from Alaska were concerned about the effects of an oil spill on animals in a remote sound?

Energy Conservation Environmentalists also directed attention to energy use in the United States. Americans make up only 5 percent of the world's population but consume over a quarter of its energy supply.

The 1973 Arab oil embargo showed Americans how much they depended on foreign energy sources. When oil shipments resumed, prices skyrocketed. Within 10 years, fuel cost four times as much as before the embargo. In response, Americans worked to conserve energy. Under government pressure, carmakers produced autos that ran on less gasoline. Homeowners added insulation to cut the amount of fuel used in homes.

Americans have also sought to develop other sources of energy. Many factories have switched from oil to coal. The United States has about one quarter of the world's usable coal reserves. Coal, however, is a dirtier fuel than oil. Coal-burning plants must use expensive devices to reduce the smoke and acids they emit into the air. Such devices add to the cost of using coal.

Today, nuclear plants generate about one fifth of the nation's electric power. Still, nuclear power is costly, and it produces long-lasting radioactive wastes that are difficult to dispose of. Even worse, an accident at a nuclear power plant could release harmful radioactive gases into the air.

Other scientists are working to harness renewable resources such as sun or wind power. A **renewable resource** is one that can be quickly replaced by nature. However, solar energy, or sun power, is expensive for many uses.

In 2001, a series of blackouts hit homes and businesses in California. Utility companies failed to provide enough electricity to meet consumer demand. The California blackouts highlighted the continuing problem of energy use.

Global Cooperation Environmental problems across the globe led nations to cooperate. In 1992, President George H. W. Bush joined other world leaders at the Earth Summit in Brazil. The goal of the conference was to discuss key environmental issues.

One issue involved rising global temperatures. A prolonged period of warmer-than-usual weather led some scientists to believe that the Earth's atmosphere was warming up. Human activities, such as

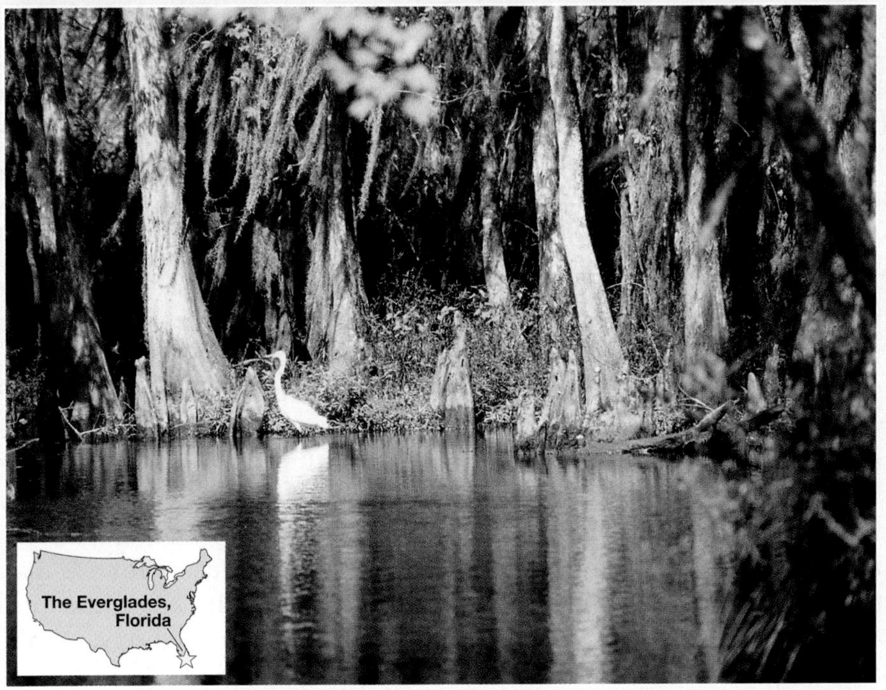

Everglades National Park

The Everglades is the largest subtropical wilderness in the United States. Starting in the 1960s, Florida resident Marjorie Stoneman Douglas began a historic battle to protect the area's vital water supplies and its rare plant and animal life. Today, you can camp, hike, or canoe in the area that Douglas called "one of the unique regions of the Earth."

Virtual Field Trip For an interactive look at the Everglades, visit PHSchool.com, **Web Code mfd-3002.**

driving cars and operating factories, were adding carbon dioxide to the atmosphere. Carbon dioxide holds in heat that would otherwise escape into space. The scientists predicted a slow but steady rise in the world's average temperature. This **global warming,** they warned, might one day turn green fields into deserts! Leaders at the Earth Summit pledged to reduce the amounts of carbon dioxide their countries released into the atmosphere.

Some scientists disagreed with the global warming theory. They pointed out that the Earth had gone through many cold and warm cycles in the past. In 2001, President George W. Bush announced that the United States would slow efforts to control carbon dioxide emissions. He believed there was not enough evidence of environmental damage to warrant the cost to American businesses.

A second problem raised at the Earth Summit involved the layer of ozone gas that surrounds the earth miles above its surface. This layer blocks out damaging ultraviolet rays from the sun. In the 1980s, scientists warned that gases used in homes and industries were creating holes in the ozone layer. Especially dangerous were gases used in aerosol cans, refrigerators, and air conditioners. Nations all over the world agreed to phase out their use.

A Networked World

Today, technology ties the world together as never before. Cellular phones and pagers have changed the way people live and do business. No device has had greater impact than the computer.

A Computer Revolution In the 1950s, most people had barely heard of computers. Computing was done on mainframes, large and expensive machines found only in big businesses, universities, or government offices. One mainframe could fill a room and weigh 30 tons or more.

Summarize As you read, summarize how technology has affected global links. Add this information to your concept web.

Slowly scientists began to make computers smaller and smaller. But even small computers required complex programs to run them. Then, in the 1970s, a Harvard dropout named Bill Gates developed a new program that allowed ordinary people to operate computers. By the 1980s, powerful personal computers could be found in homes, small businesses, and schools.

The Internet During the 1960s, a scientist at the Massachusetts Institute of Technology dreamed of connecting computers all over the world into a single "Galactic Network." Eventually this idea evolved into the Internet, a series of interconnected computers that gave users access to computerized information. Through the Internet, computer users could exchange information.

Personal computers and the Internet have produced an information revolution. A world of facts and figures is now available at an instant to anyone with access to a computer and a modem. E-mail has become more popular than the postal mail. In 2001, the post office handled about 670 million letters and packages a day. At the same time, about 3.5 billion e-mails were being sent daily.

Computers and the Internet revolutionized business. They increased efficiency and productivity and allowed more people to work at home and still be in touch with their offices. E-commerce, or business and trade over the Internet, boomed. In 2001, a survey reported that three out of every four American consumers said that they had made a purchase online within the previous year.

★ ★ ★ Section 4 Assessment ★ ★ ★

Recall

1. **Identify** Explain the significance of **(a)** North American Free Trade Agreement, **(b)** Rachel Carson, **(c)** Environmental Protection Agency, **(d)** Bill Gates, **(e)** Internet.
2. **Define** **(a)** trade deficit, **(b)** environmentalist, **(c)** renewable resource, **(d)** global warming, **(e)** e-commerce.

Comprehension

3. How did the United States develop a trade deficit?
4. Describe two environmental problems the United States and the world faced.
5. How did the development of the Internet affect business?

Critical Thinking and Writing

6. **Exploring the Main Idea** Review the Main Idea statement at the beginning of this section. Then, write a paragraph explaining whether you think the new world of global links is good or bad for the nation.
7. **Making Decisions** Would you be willing to give up or pay a higher price for many products in order to protect the environment? State your decision and list the reasons.

Activity

Writing an Advertisement It is 1980, and the Internet is a new idea. Write and design an advertisement encouraging schools, businesses, or private citizens to sign up for the Internet. Explain the benefits of the service.

Connecting With... **Economics**

Oil: A Valuable Resource

Throughout history, natural resources—from water to spices—have shaped politics, caused wars, and led to the rise and fall of nations. Today, oil plays such a role in the global economy. Oil shortages and rising oil prices touch everybody.

Giant derricks remove crude oil from the ground or the bottom of the sea. What happens if the companies or nations that sell the crude oil cut back on production or raise the price? People have to pay more for gasoline, heating oil, and a wide variety of other products.

What do sneakers, candles, and lipsticks have in common? They are all manufactured using petroleum—along with ink, bubble gum, transparent tape, telephones, crayons, dolls, and skate wheels. If oil prices go up, so will the prices of these products that we all use.

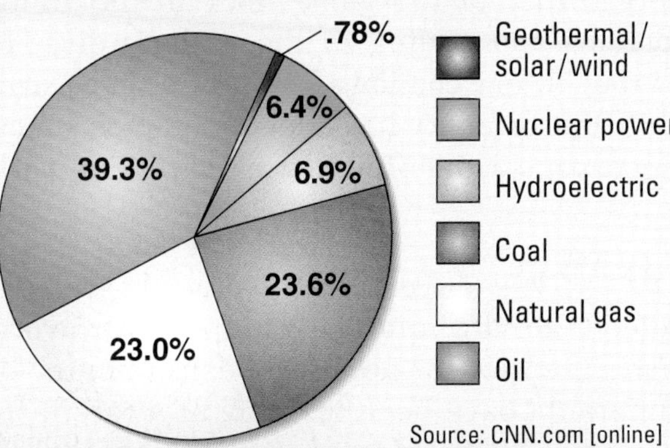

Oil is not the only source of energy in the world. But, as this pie chart shows, it is still the most vital to the world's economy.

Activity

Oil is a basic ingredient in plastics. Make a list of plastic products that you use every day. Then, see if you can identify alternatives for each that are not made of plastic. Make a poster that shows three plastic products and your ideas for substitutes.

5 New Challenges for the Nation

Prepare to Read

Objectives

In this section, you will
- Identify the new immigrants.
- List the groups that added their voices to the call for equal rights.
- Discuss the challenges the United States faces in the twenty-first century.

Key Terms

refugee
illegal alien
Immigration Reform and Control Act
American Indian Religious Freedom Act
mainstreaming
Americans With Disabilities Act
American Association of Retired Persons

Target Reading Skill

Main Idea As you read, prepare an outline of this section. Use roman numerals to indicate the major headings, capital letters for the subheadings, and numbers to indicate supporting details.

I. The New Immigrants
- **A. Changing patterns**
  - **1. Asian immigration**
  - **2.**
- **B. New policies**
  - **1.**
  - **2.**

II. The Struggle for Equal Rights Continues
- **A.**
- **B.**

Main Idea New immigrants and continuing struggles for equal rights brought a new look to the American dream of liberty and freedom.

Immigrants take citizenship oath

Setting the Scene In an auditorium in Austin, Texas, a woman from India stood clutching a small American flag. Nearby stood another woman from Jordan. Karolyn Mora, who had come from Costa Rica five years earlier, was also there. She confessed:

> "When I first came, I felt like a stranger, but now I feel like I am part of America. That's all I wanted—the American dream."
>
> —Karolyn Mora, Interview, April 6, 2001

These women were among 473 immigrants from 73 countries who had just become American citizens. Officials at the ceremony in the spring of 2001 had never seen so many nations represented before.

Immigrants from every corner of the globe flock to the United States, pursuing their dreams and adding to the nation's diversity. Increasing diversity has brought new challenges as groups have struggled to protect their rights. But diversity has added strengths, among them an uncommon ability to cope with difference in a shrinking world.

The New Immigrants

In 1965, Congress ended the old quota system that favored Europeans. New laws made it easier for non-Europeans to enter the country. Since then, immigrants have been arriving at a rate faster than at any time since the early 1900s. Most recent immigrants have come from Latin America, the Caribbean, and Asia.

Changing Patterns Asian Americans are the nation's fastest-growing ethnic group. Wars and famines pushed many Asians into other parts of the world. After the Vietnam War, "boat people" from Southeast Asia sought refuge in the United States. Many immigrants from the Philippines, India, and Korea sought economic opportunity.

Many Latin American immigrants were refugees from civil wars in Nicaragua, El Salvador, and Guatemala during the 1980s. **Refugees** are people who flee their homelands to seek safety elsewhere. Others fled harsh governments in Cuba and Chile or poverty in Mexico and other nations. By 2001, Latin Americans and their descendants were the largest ethnic group in the country.

Hundreds of thousands of immigrants have also come from islands of the Caribbean. These people bring a rich mixture of African, European, Native American, and other backgrounds.

New immigration patterns have fueled a debate over what it means to be American. Many new citizens are eager to adopt American ways. At the same time, they do not want to abandon their old traditions.

Identify Main Ideas What are the main ideas of the subsections following "The Struggle for Equal Rights Continues"? Add these main ideas to your outline.

New Policies New immigrants must apply for admission. Those with relatives in the United States or with valuable job skills are most likely to be accepted. Thousands of others are turned down. Those entering without permission are **illegal aliens.**

To reduce illegal immigration, Congress passed the **Immigration Reform and Control Act** in 1986. It allowed people who arrived illegally before 1982 to stay and apply for citizenship. But the act tried to discourage future illegal immigration by imposing fines on employers who hired undocumented, or illegal, workers.

Rising costs of medical care, education, and other services for illegal immigrants strained the resources of several states. In 1994, California adopted a controversial law that banned schooling and most health services for illegal aliens. Two years later, Congress passed a new law allowing local police to arrest illegal immigrants.

The Struggle for Equal Rights Continues

As you read, in the 1960s, the struggle for equal rights expanded from African Americans to other groups. While these Americans achieved significant successes, challenges remained.

African Americans African Americans made notable advances in government. In 1989, Douglas Wilder of Virginia became the first black elected governor of a state. That same year, General Colin Powell was named chairman of the Joint Chiefs of Staff. Later, as Secretary of State, Powell was a key figure in the campaign against terrorism.

The civil rights movement had opened new jobs and educational opportunities. By 1998, 92 percent of African Americans seeking jobs found employment, compared with 87 percent in 1980. The black middle class grew steadily. More African Americans were attending college than ever before, and fewer lived below the poverty level.

Despite such successes, many African Americans continued to battle economic hardship. The wages of African Americans lagged behind those of whites. Unemployment for blacks was over twice that for whites. Poverty and lack of education trapped many African Americans in urban slums. In 2000, African Americans still remained less well educated and owned less property than whites.

Native Americans After shrinking for centuries, the American Indian population is growing. By 2000, it had reached about 2.4 million. Over half live in urban areas. Another third live on reservations.

An American Profile

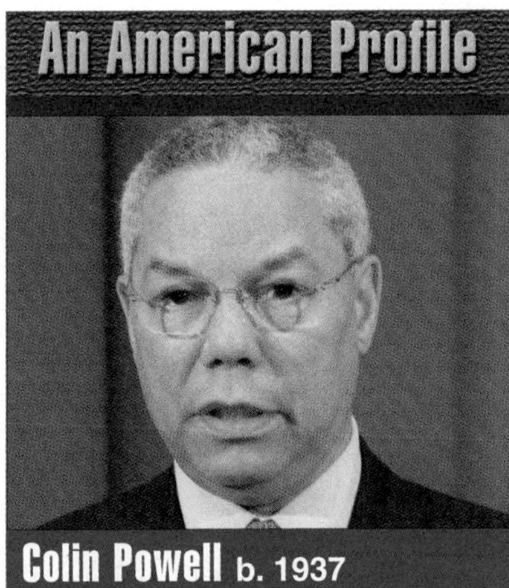

Colin Powell b. 1937

In Colin Powell's family, every child was expected to work for a college education. After earning degrees in geology and business administration, he joined the army. He won a Purple Heart in Vietnam.

Powell helped found America's Promise to encourage Americans to volunteer for public service. A reporter wrote, "Spend an hour talking with General Colin Powell about his crusade to save America's kids and, despite the many problems that confront today's youngsters, you come away enthused and optimistic about the next generation."

Why do you think Colin Powell has been named one of the most admired Americans?

Women Working Outside the Home, 1960–2000

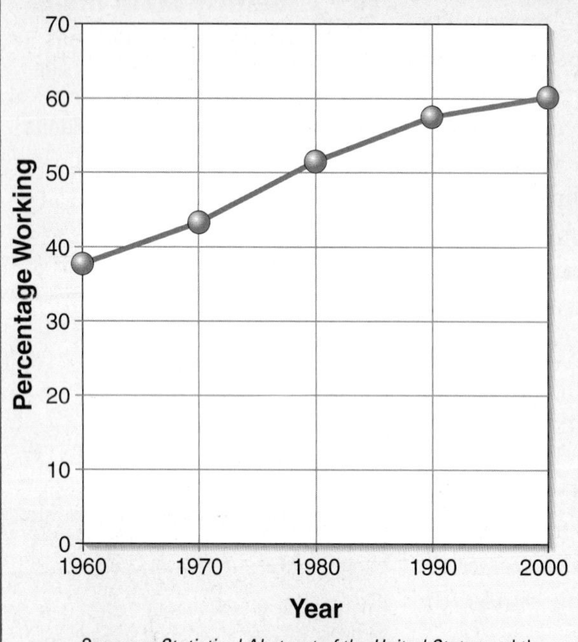

Sources: *Statistical Abstract of the United States* and the Women's Bureau of the U.S. Department of Labor

GRAPH *Skills*

For most of the nation's history, most women did not work outside the home. That situation changed after the 1960s.

1. **Comprehension** During what decade did the majority of women work outside the home for the first time?
2. **Critical Thinking Making Predictions** Do you think the trend shown on this graph will continue? Why or why not?

Economics 

By 1970, the federal government had ended its policy of encouraging Indians to leave their reservations. Native American tribes and organizations won greater power to govern themselves. The **American Indian Religious Freedom Act** of 1978 directed federal agencies not to interfere with Native American religious practices.

Native American groups have worked to develop economic independence. Many reservations set up banks, factories, and other businesses. Several tribes opened their own colleges and universities.

Women The women's rights movement continued to press for equal treatment of women. Progress came but not as quickly or completely as many women hoped.

In government, women have taken more prominent roles, especially on the local and state levels. On the national level, women won more seats in Congress. By the late 1990s, two of the nine Supreme Court Justices were women. In 1997, Madeleine Albright became the first female secretary of state, the highest-ranking cabinet position.

About 60 percent of American women worked outside the home by 2000. Women held jobs once closed to them, from firefighters to professional basketball players. As more women were promoted to higher positions in business, their incomes rose. The gap between women's and men's wages narrowed but did not disappear. On average, women earned less than 75 percent of what men earned.

An increasing number of single women were heads of households. More than half the children in these households lived in poverty. Working mothers also had the problem of finding affordable, adequate day care.

New Voices for Change

Other groups of Americans organized to promote change. These groups cut across racial, ethnic, and gender lines.

Americans With Disabilities Americans with disabilities joined the battle for equal rights. Veterans of Vietnam and other wars took a leading role. Many had lost limbs or become paralyzed serving their country. They insisted on their right to gain entrance to public buildings and transportation and to make a living.

People in wheelchairs often had limited access to public transportation and buildings. Disabled rights organizations pressed for laws requiring reserved parking spaces, ramped curbs, and wheelchair lifts on buses.

A 1975 law ensured access to public schools for children with disabilities. Some schools began **mainstreaming,** or placing children with special needs in regular classes. Others schools offered small classes with specialized help.

In 1990, Congress passed the Americans With Disabilities Act. The new law outlawed discrimination in hiring people with physical or mental impairments. It also required employers to provide "reasonable accommodations," such as ramps for workers in wheelchairs.

Older Americans The American population is aging rapidly. Birth rates have declined, and medical care is improving. As "baby boomers" born in the 1940s and 1950s age, the number of senior citizens will jump dramatically. By 2000, one American in eight was over the age of 65. That number may reach one in five by 2030.

The aging population presents challenges to both older and younger Americans. Who will care for these seniors? How will they pay their medical bills? What role will the government play?

Organizations such as the American Association of Retired Persons (AARP) pay special attention to issues of concern to older Americans. These include Social Security and Medicare, which provide pensions and medical assistance to the elderly. As their membership grows, such groups gain political power. Older citizens also gain influence by exercising their power to vote in great numbers.

Viewing History

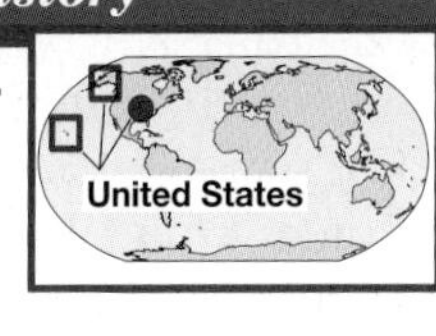

Accommodating Americans With Disabilities

Today, many laws require businesses and public buildings to provide access and services for people with disabilities. These accommodations include wheelchair lifts on buses (above). **Drawing Conclusions** ***How can accommodations like this help Americans with disabilities to achieve economic independence?***

Challenges for a New Century

At the dawn of the twenty-first century, Americans face both opportunities and challenges. The nation is changing and so is the rest of the world. As Americans adjust, they find themselves tested anew.

Terrorism The attacks on the World Trade Center and Pentagon in 2001 were part of a global campaign of terror. But terrorism could be homegrown as well. In 1995, a blast at a federal building in Oklahoma City killed 168 people. Two Americans who resented the government were convicted for the Oklahoma City bombing.

In the wake of the 2001 attacks, a new form of terrorism emerged. Pieces of mail were infected with the disease anthrax. Most of the people exposed were treated in time, but a number died.

In October 2001, Congress voted to give law enforcement agencies broad new powers to fight terrorism. Americans had to face the challenge of safeguarding the nation without sacrificing the basic rights and freedoms guaranteed by the Constitution.

Violence and Drug Abuse In 1999, two students at a Colorado high school opened fire on fellow students, killing 15 people. The shocking incident was one of several school shootings that led Americans to debate how such violence could be prevented.

Another serious problem is drug abuse. Schools are in the front lines here, too, as they try to protect students from dangerous and illegal substances such as cocaine and heroin.

Americans are torn between two approaches to fighting illegal drugs. Some see drug abuse as a social problem. They favor using treatment centers to help drug users. To others, drug abuse is a criminal problem. They want stiffer penalties for drug dealers and users. The United States has spent billions of dollars pursuing drug smugglers and dealers. Yet, drug abuse remains widespread.

Meeting Challenges Anew The United States faces complex issues and great dangers in the new century. Yet, Americans have met such challenges before. In 1776, the problems were so great that many believed the new nation would not survive. Instead, it grew into a superpower and a model for democracies everywhere.

From the beginning, the motto of the United States has been *E pluribus unum*—"Out of many, one." The motto reflects the unity of the nation's many regions and people. Together with democracy, diversity lies at the source of the nation's strength.

President John F. Kennedy struck those themes as he took the oath of office in 1961. He called on his "fellow Americans" to serve their democratic republic: "Ask not what your country can do for you—ask what you can do for your country." Less remembered is the challenge he issued to a divided world in his next breath:

> "My fellow citizens of the world, ask not what America will do for you, but what together we can do for the freedom of man."
>
> —John F. Kennedy, Inaugural Address, January 20, 1961

At the dawn of the twenty-first century, America again beckons the world to join the common cause of freedom. Only by overcoming our differences and relying on one another's strengths can Americans and their "fellow citizens of the world" succeed.

★ ★ ★ Section 5 Assessment ★ ★ ★

Recall

1. **Identify** Explain the significance of **(a)** Immigration Reform and Control Act, **(b)** Colin Powell, **(c)** American Indian Religious Freedom Act, **(d)** Americans With Disabilities Act, **(e)** American Association of Retired Persons.
2. **Define** **(a)** refugee, **(b)** illegal alien, **(c)** mainstreaming.

Comprehension

3. How did immigration patterns change in the late 1900s?
4. Describe one issue concerning each of the following: **(a)** African Americans, **(b)** women, **(c)** Americans with disabilities.
5. What two approaches have Americans taken to meet the challenge of drug abuse?

Critical Thinking and Writing

6. **Exploring the Main Idea** Review the Main Idea statement at the beginning of this section. Then, write a letter to new immigrants to the United States. Describe what will be expected of them and what they can expect in return.
7. **Drawing Conclusions** Write a paragraph explaining why younger Americans should be concerned about issues affecting older people.

Activity

Connecting to Today

Use the Internet to find out about recent programs designed to prevent violence in schools. Then, write up an action plan explaining how you might deal with the problem in your own school. For help in completing the activity, visit PHSchool.com, **Web Code mfd-3003.**

Transferring Information

Historical information comes in many forms. Sometimes, it is helpful to organize information so that you can compare it with other data.

The data below relate to sources of immigration in 1900. These data have been used to create the pie chart below.

Asia	4 percent
Americas	1.2 percent
Europe	94.7 percent
Africa	less than 1 percent
Other	less than 1 percent

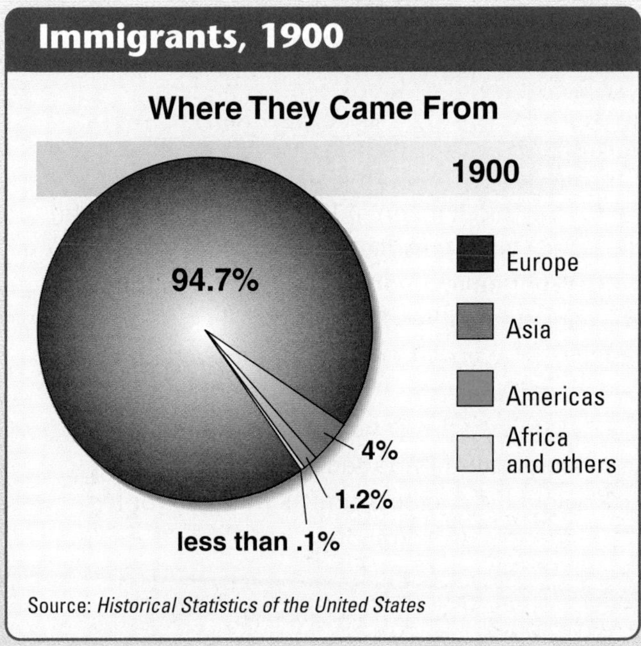

The paragraph below describes modern immigration trends.

Immigration patterns have changed. In 1998, the largest percentage—45.2—came from the Americas. Another sizable percentage—33.2—were people from Asia. Africans now made up 6.2 percent, while Europeans accounted for 13.7 percent. About 1.7 percent of immigrants came from other places.

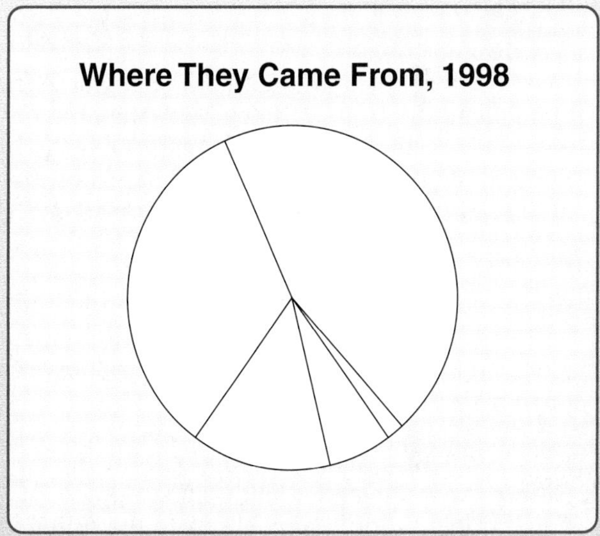

Learn the Skill *To learn how to transfer information, use the following steps:*

1. **Identify the raw data.** As you read a selection, note the facts given. If many statistics are included, think about how you might organize them so that they are easier to see and use.
2. **List the data.** Compile a list of the facts. Organize the percentages from greatest to least.
3. **Transfer the data.** To make a pie chart, divide a circle into parts that add up to 100. Color a portion of the circle to represent each percentage you want to include. Label the chart.
4. **Draw conclusions based on the data.** What can you learn by looking at the data in this form?

Practice the Skill *Use the information above to answer the following questions:*

1. What percentage of immigrants to the United States in 1998 were from Europe? From Asia?
2. **(a)** List the data in the paragraph in order of percentage. **(b)** Where did the largest group of immigrants come from in 1998?
3. Copy the blank pie chart, and fit the data from the paragraph into it. Use the same color code as in the completed pie chart.
4. Describe how immigration patterns changed between 1900 and 1998.

Apply the Skill *See the Chapter Review and Assessment.*

CHAPTER 30

Review and Assessment

Chapter Summary

Section 1
The election of Ronald Reagan in 1980 brought a new era of conservatism in politics and public policy. Reagan persuaded Congress to cut taxes and cut federal spending. President George H.W. Bush continued some of Reagan's policies but lost to Bill Clinton when the economy soured.

Section 2
After the Cold War, the United States worked to promote global democracy and ease regional conflicts. However, the continuing arms race posed new threats to world peace.

Section 3
A series of conflicts in the Middle East increasingly involved the United States. With the attack by al-Qaida on New York and Washington, D.C., on September 11, 2001, the United States launched an all-out campaign against world terrorism.

Section 4
Global economic links, the global environment, and a global information network tie the modern world together. Events in far off places now can have major impacts on our lives.

Section 5
New immigrants and continuing struggles for equal rights brought a new look to the American dream of liberty and freedom. At the same time, Americans faced new challenges trying to control violence and drug use and stem terrorism directed against the United States.

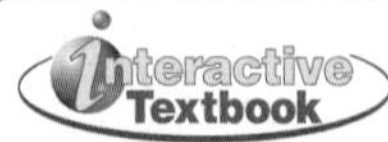

For additional review and enrichment activities, see the interactive version of *The American Nation,* available on the Web and on CD-ROM.

Chapter Self-Test For practice test questions for Chapter 30, visit PHSchool.com, **Web Code mfa-3004.**

Building Vocabulary

Write sentences using the words listed below, leaving blanks where the words would go. Exchange your sentences with another student, and fill in the blanks in each other's sentences.

1. **deregulation**
2. **downsizing**
3. **recession**
4. **sanctions**
5. **trade deficit**
6. **environmentalist**
7. **renewable resource**
8. **e-commerce**

Reviewing Key Facts

9. How did conservatives view the role of the federal government? (Section 1)
10. What policy did the United States follow toward Cuba? (Section 2)
11. What were the results of the Persian Gulf War? (Section 3)
12. Why was the development of smaller computers important? (Section 4)
13. How did the economic status of women change? (Section 5)

Critical Thinking and Writing

14. **Supporting a Point of View** President Bill Clinton said that Americans must "overcome a dangerous and growing temptation . . . to focus solely on the problems we face here in America." Write a paragraph explaining whether you agree and why.
15. **Comparing** Review what you read in Chapter 27 about American reaction to the bombing of Pearl Harbor. How was reaction to the terrorist attacks of 2001 similar?
16. **Connecting to Geography: Interaction** How do environmentalists and their opponents reflect differing views of human-environment interaction?

Skills Assessment

Analyzing Primary Sources

Journalist Tom Brokaw spoke to a college graduating class about the future:

> “No piece of software, no server or search engine will offer you the irreplaceable rewards of a loving personal relationship, the strength and comfort of a real community of shared values and common dreams, the moral underpinning of a life lived well, whatever the financial scorecard. Nor will this new technology make you more racially tolerant . . . more courageous to take a firm stand for what you know is right.”
>
> —Tom Brokaw, Speech at Santa Fe College, May 15, 1999

17. Which of the following best explains the main idea of this selection?

- **A.** The world is progressing through advances made by science.
- **B.** Technology needs to serve the public.
- **C.** Machines may cause great evil.
- **D.** Technology cannot replace the bonds between people and their communities.

18. What civic value does Brokaw mention?

- **A.** a community of shared values and common dreams
- **B.** a community that is well armed
- **C.** a community that rejects technology because of its concern to preserve jobs
- **D.** a community that supports technology because it makes us more affluent

Applying Your Skills

Transferring Information

The chart below gives raw data about United States exports in 1999. Examine the data, and answer the questions that follow.

U.S. Exports by Region

REGION	PERCENTAGE OF U.S. EXPORTS
Europe	24.7
NAFTA (Canada and Mexico)	36.4
Other Latin American Countries	8.0
Asia	27.4
Australia and Oceania	2.1
Africa	1.4

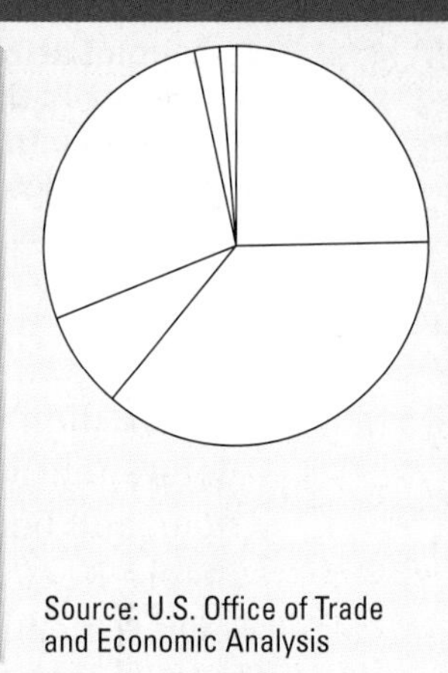

Source: U.S. Office of Trade and Economic Analysis

19. What percentage of United States exports went to Canada and Latin America in 1999?

- **A.** 36.4 percent
- **B.** 8 percent
- **C.** 44.4 percent
- **D.** cannot tell from the data given

20. Copy the blank pie chart shown here. Use the data given in the table to create a pie chart.

Activities

Connecting With . . . Culture

Creating a Banner Think about the motto of the United States, *E pluribus unum*—“Out of many, one.” Then, with a partner, design and create a banner around this theme. Use words and symbols to express what this motto means to you.

Connecting to Today

Use the Internet to find out about changes in the population of the United States over the last 50 years. You may focus on ethnic makeup, immigration, age, family income, or another topic. Use the information you discover to create a graph. For help in starting this activity, visit PHSchool.com, **Web Code mfd-3005.**

The House on Mango Street

Sandra Cisneros

Sandra Cisneros

Introduction **Born in Chicago, Sandra Cisneros was one of the first Mexican American novelists to achieve widespread success. Her best-known book is *The House on Mango Street,* published in 1984. In a series of short episodes, the book paints a vivid picture of life in a Latino neighborhood in a large American city. The fictional narrator is Esperanza Cordero, the young daughter of Mexican immigrants. In the opening episode of the book, below, Esperanza describes her feelings when her family moves from one part of Chicago to another.**

We didn't always live on Mango Street. Before that we lived on Loomis on the third floor, and before that we lived on Keeler. Before Keeler it was Paulina, and before that I can't remember. But what I remember most is moving a lot. Each time it seemed there'd be one more of us. By the time we got to Mango Street we were six—Mama, Papa, Carlos, Kiki, my sister Nenny and me.

The house on Mango Street is ours, and we don't have to pay rent to anybody, or share the yard with the people downstairs, or be careful not to make too much noise, and there isn't a landlord banging on the ceiling with a broom. But even so, it's not the house we'd thought we'd get.

We had to leave the flat on Loomis quick. The water pipes broke and the landlord wouldn't fix them because the house was too old. We had to leave fast. We were using the washroom next door and carrying water over in empty milk gallons. That's why Mama and Papa looked for a house, and that's why we moved into the house on Mango Street, far away, on the other side of town.

They always told us that one day we would move into a house, a real house that would be ours for always so we wouldn't have to move each year. And our house would have running water and pipes that worked. And inside it would have real stairs, not hallway stairs, but stairs inside like the houses on T.V. And we'd have a basement and at least three washrooms so when we took a bath we wouldn't have to tell everybody. Our house would be white with trees around it, a great big yard and grass growing without a fence. This was the house Papa talked about when he held a lottery ticket and this was the house Mama dreamed up in the stories she told us before we went to bed.

But the house on Mango Street is not the way they told it at all. It's small and red with tight steps in front and windows so small you'd think they were holding their breath. Bricks are crumbling in place, and the front door is so swollen you have to push hard to get in. There is no front yard, only four little elms the city planted by the curb. Out back is a small garage for the car we don't own yet and a small yard that looks smaller between the two buildings on either side. There are stairs in our house, but they're ordinary hallway stairs, and the house has only one washroom. Everybody has to share a bedroom—Mama and Papa, Carlos and Kiki, me and Nenny.

Once when we were living on Loomis, a nun from my school passed by and saw me playing out front. The laundromat downstairs had been boarded up because it had been robbed two days before and the owner had painted on the wood YES WE'RE OPEN so as not to lose business.

Where do you live? she asked.

There, I said pointing up to the third floor.

You live *there?*

Latino family in a mural in San Francisco, California

There. I had to look where she pointed—the third floor, the paint peeling, wooden bars Papa had nailed on the windows so we wouldn't fall out. You live *there?* The way she said it made me feel like nothing. *There.* I lived there. I nodded.

I knew then I had to have a house. A real house. One I could point to. But this isn't it. The house on Mango Street isn't it. For the time being, Mama says. Temporary, says Papa. But I know how those things go.

Analyzing Literature

1. What is one reason Esperanza is disappointed in the family's new home on Mango Street?

- **A** The new house has broken water pipes.
- **B** The new house is located above a laundromat.
- **C** The new house does not have its own front yard.
- **D** The new house is located on the poor side of town.

2. How does Esperanza feel when she is talking to the nun?

- **A** She is ashamed of the place where she lives.
- **B** She is proud that the nun spoke to her.
- **C** She is angry with her parents.
- **D** She is hopeful about the new house on Mango Street.

3. **Critical Thinking and Writing** **Comparing** How are the hopes, feelings, and experiences of Esperanza and her parents similar to those of earlier immigrants and their families?

TEST PREPARATION

Use the map <u>and</u> your knowledge of social studies to answer the following question.

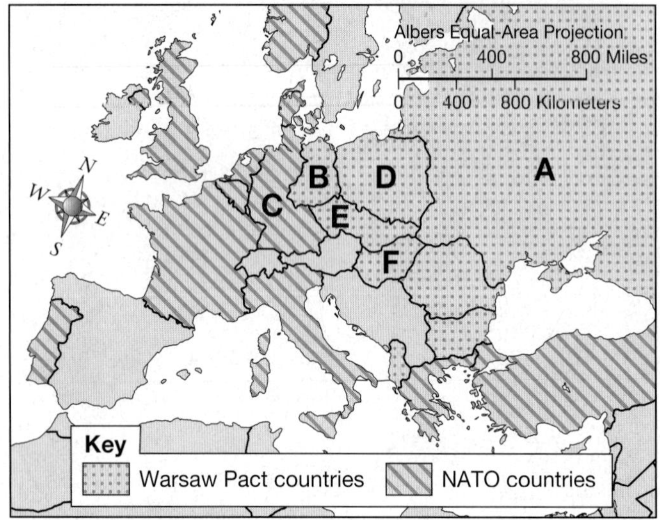

1 During the Cold War, the relation of nation A to nation D was the same as which of the following?

A Nation B to nation C

B Nation E to nation F

C Nation A to nation E

D Nation C to nation D

2 Which of the following does not belong with the other three?

A Fair Deal

B William Levitt

C GI Bill of Rights

D Decline of inner cities

3 Which of the following was not an effect of the oil embargo of the 1970s?

A Increased inflation

B Call for energy conservation

C Persian Gulf War

D Fuel shortages

4 Which of the following statements is true of both the Korean War and the war in Vietnam?

A The war bitterly divided Americans at home.

B American involvement in the fighting escalated gradually over several years.

C After fighting ended, tensions remained high between the North and the South.

D The Soviet Union backed the communist North, but did not face the United States directly.

Use the quotation <u>and</u> your knowledge of social studies to answer the following question.

> "We conclude that . . . the doctrine of 'separate but equal' has no place. Separate . . . facilities are inherently unequal."

5 The above passage is an excerpt from what document?

A Supreme Court decision in *Plessy* v. *Ferguson*

B Supreme Court decision in *Brown* v. *Board of Education*

C Martin Luther King's "I Have a Dream" speech

D Civil Rights Act of 1964

6 Which of the following events was an effect of the other three?

A Military spending strains Soviet economy.

B Soviet republics declare independence.

C Cold War ends.

D Gorbachev and Reagan meet.

Use the graph and your knowledge of social studies to answer the following question.

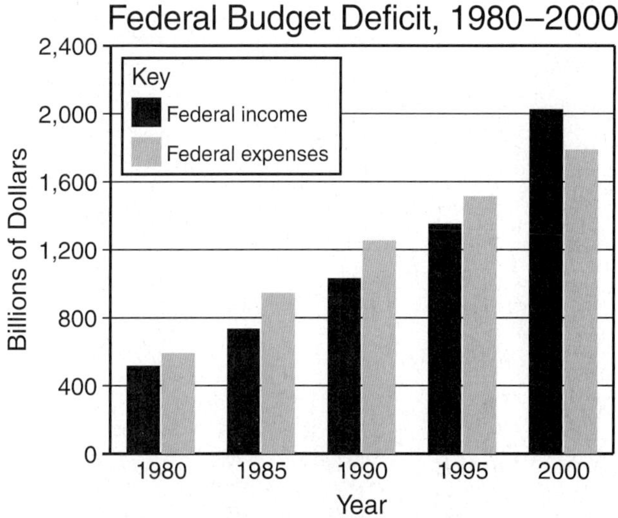

7 Which is a valid conclusion that can be drawn from this graph?

A The budget deficit increased during President Reagan's term.

B President Clinton reduced federal spending.

C In 1992, the budget deficit was about $500 billion.

D The budget deficit decreased steadily throughout the 1990s.

8 The relationship of Barry Goldwater to the conservative revolution is most like which of the following?

A The relationship of Ronald Reagan to the Cold War

B The relationship of Rachel Carson to the environmental movement

C The relationship of Malcolm X to the civil rights movement

D The relationship of George Bush to the Persian Gulf War

9 The Watergate affair best illustrates which principle of the Constitution?

A Judicial review

B Federalism

C Popular sovereignty

D Checks and balances

Writing Practice

10 "Both the Cold War and the civil rights movement were related to a belief in American democracy." Explain the meaning of this statement and whether or not you agree with it. Include supporting details from your reading.

11 Describe the immediate effects of the 2001 terrorist attacks on New York and Washington, D.C. Explain why you think such crises often unite Americans.

Reference Section

Washington Crossing the Delaware
by Emanuel Gottlieb Leutze

Presidents of the United States

1 George Washington (1732–1799)

Years in office: 1789–1797
Party: none
Elected from: Virginia
Vice President: John Adams

2 John Adams (1735–1826)

Years in office: 1797–1801
Party: Federalist
Elected from: Massachusetts
Vice President: Thomas Jefferson

3 Thomas Jefferson (1743–1826)

Years in office: 1801–1809
Party: Democratic Republican
Elected from: Virginia
Vice President: 1) Aaron Burr, 2) George Clinton

4 James Madison (1751–1836)

Years in office: 1809–1817
Party: Democratic Republican
Elected from: Virginia
Vice President: 1) George Clinton, 2) Elbridge Gerry

5 James Monroe (1758–1831)

Years in office: 1817–1825
Party: Democratic Republican
Elected from: Virginia
Vice President: Daniel Tompkins

6 John Quincy Adams (1767–1848)

Years in office: 1825–1829
Party: National Republican
Elected from: Massachusetts
Vice President: John Calhoun

7 Andrew Jackson (1767–1845)

Years in office: 1829–1837
Party: Democratic
Elected from: Tennessee
Vice President: 1) John Calhoun, 2) Martin Van Buren

8 Martin Van Buren (1782–1862)

Years in office: 1837–1841
Party: Democratic
Elected from: New York
Vice President: Richard Johnson

9 William Henry Harrison* (1773–1841)

Years in office: 1841
Party: Whig
Elected from: Ohio
Vice President: John Tyler

10 John Tyler (1790–1862)

Years in office: 1841–1845
Party: Whig
Elected from: Virginia
Vice President: none

11 James K. Polk (1795–1849)

Years in office: 1845–1849
Party: Democratic
Elected from: Tennessee
Vice President: George Dallas

12 Zachary Taylor* (1784–1850)

Years in office: 1849–1850
Party: Whig
Elected from: Louisiana
Vice President: Millard Fillmore

***Died in office**

Presidents of the United States

13 Millard Fillmore (1800–1874)

Years in office: 1850–1853
Party: Whig
Elected from: New York
Vice President: none

14 Franklin Pierce (1804–1869)

Years in office: 1853–1857
Party: Democratic
Elected from: New Hampshire
Vice President: William King

15 James Buchanan (1791–1868)

Years in office: 1857–1861
Party: Democratic
Elected from: Pennsylvania
Vice President: John Breckinridge

16 Abraham Lincoln** (1809–1865)

Years in office: 1861–1865
Party: Republican
Elected from: Illinois
Vice President: 1) Hannibal Hamlin, 2) Andrew Johnson

17 Andrew Johnson (1808–1875)

Years in office: 1865–1869
Party: Republican
Elected from: Tennessee
Vice President: none

18 Ulysses S. Grant (1822–1885)

Years in office: 1869–1877
Party: Republican
Elected from: Illinois
Vice President: 1) Schuyler Colfax, 2) Henry Wilson

19 Rutherford B. Hayes (1822–1893)

Years in office: 1877–1881
Party: Republican
Elected from: Ohio
Vice President: William Wheeler

20 James A. Garfield** (1831–1881)

Years in office: 1881
Party: Republican
Elected from: Ohio
Vice President: Chester A. Arthur

21 Chester A. Arthur (1829–1886)

Years in office: 1881–1885
Party: Republican
Elected from: New York
Vice President: none

22 Grover Cleveland (1837–1908)

Years in office: 1885–1889
Party: Democratic
Elected from: New York
Vice President: Thomas Hendricks

23 Benjamin Harrison (1833–1901)

Years in office: 1889–1893
Party: Republican
Elected from: Indiana
Vice President: Levi Morton

24 Grover Cleveland (1837–1908)

Years in office: 1893–1897
Party: Democratic
Elected from: New York
Vice President: Adlai Stevenson

****Assassinated**

25 William McKinley** (1843–1901)

Years in office: 1897–1901
Party: Republican
Elected from: Ohio
Vice President: 1) Garret Hobart, 2) Theodore Roosevelt

26 Theodore Roosevelt (1858–1919)

Years in office: 1901–1909
Party: Republican
Elected from: New York
Vice President: Charles Fairbanks

27 William Howard Taft (1857–1930)

Years in office: 1909–1913
Party: Republican
Elected from: Ohio
Vice President: James Sherman

28 Woodrow Wilson (1856–1924)

Years in office: 1913–1921
Party: Democratic
Elected from: New Jersey
Vice President: Thomas Marshall

29 Warren G. Harding* (1865–1923)

Years in office: 1921–1923
Party: Republican
Elected from: Ohio
Vice President: Calvin Coolidge

30 Calvin Coolidge (1872–1933)

Years in office: 1923–1929
Party: Republican
Elected from: Massachusetts
Vice President: Charles Dawes

31 Herbert C. Hoover (1874–1964)

Years in office: 1929–1933
Party: Republican
Elected from: California
Vice President: Charles Curtis

32 Franklin D. Roosevelt* (1882–1945)

Years in office: 1933–1945
Party: Democratic
Elected from: New York
Vice President: 1) John Garner, 2) Henry Wallace, 3) Harry S Truman

33 Harry S Truman (1884–1972)

Years in office: 1945–1953
Party: Democratic
Elected from: Missouri
Vice President: Alben Barkley

34 Dwight D. Eisenhower (1890–1969)

Years in office: 1953–1961
Party: Republican
Elected from: New York
Vice President: Richard M. Nixon

35 John F. Kennedy** (1917–1963)

Years in office: 1961–1963
Party: Democratic
Elected from: Massachusetts
Vice President: Lyndon B. Johnson

36 Lyndon B. Johnson (1908–1973)

Years in office: 1963–1969
Party: Democratic
Elected from: Texas
Vice President: Hubert Humphrey

***Died in office**
****Assassinated**

37 Richard M. Nixon*** (1913–1994)

Years in office:
1969–1974
Party:
Republican
Elected from:
New York
Vice President:
1) Spiro Agnew,
2) Gerald R. Ford

38 Gerald R. Ford (b. 1913)

Years in office:
1974–1977
Party:
Republican
Appointed from:
Michigan
Vice President:
Nelson Rockefeller

39 Jimmy Carter (b. 1924)

Years in office:
1977–1981
Party:
Democratic
Elected from:
Georgia
Vice President:
Walter Mondale

40 Ronald W. Reagan (b. 1911)

Years in office:
1981–1989
Party:
Republican
Elected from:
California
Vice President:
George H.W. Bush

41 George H.W. Bush (b. 1924)

Years in office:
1989–1993
Party:
Republican
Elected from:
Texas
Vice President:
J. Danforth Quayle

42 William J. Clinton (b. 1946)

Years in office:
1993–2001
Party:
Democratic
Elected from:
Arkansas
Vice President:
Albert Gore, Jr.

43 George W. Bush (b. 1946)

Years in office:
2001–
Party:
Republican
Elected from:
Texas
Vice President:
Richard Cheney

***Resigned

Gazetteer of American History

This gazetteer, or geographic dictionary, lists places that are important in American history. The approximate latitude and longitude are given for cities, towns, and other specific locations. See text page 4 for information about latitude and longitude. In the Gazetteer, each listing usually includes two numbers in parentheses. The first number refers to the text page where you can find out about the place. The second appears in slanted, or *italic,* type and refers to a map (*m*) where the place is shown.

A

Abilene (39°N/97°W) (p. 554, *m548*)
Afghanistan (p. 833, *m916–917*)
Africa (p. 52, *m51*)
Alabama (p. 914, *m918–919*)
Alamo (29°N/99°W) (p. 387, *m386*)
Alaska (p. 914, *m918–919*)
Albany (43°N/74°W) (p. 143, *m142*)
Andes (p. 39)
Antarctica (*m916–917*)
Appalachian Mountains (p. 13, *m12*)
Appomattox Court House (37°N/79°W) (p. 509, *m509*)
Arctic Ocean (p. 11, *m12*)
Argentina (p. 349, *m349*)
Argonne Forest (49°N/6°E) (p. 703, *m701*)
Arizona (p. 914, *m918–919*)
Arkansas (p. 914, *m918–919*)
Armenia (p. 601, *m916–917*)
Asia (p. 50, *m916–917*)
Atlanta (34°N/84°W) (p. 508, *m470*)
Atlantic Ocean (p. 11, *m916–917*)
Atlantic Plain (p. 13, *m12*)
Australia (*m916–917*)
Austria Hungary (p. 687, *m685*)

B

Baltimore (39°N/77°W) (p. 323, *m323*)
Beijing (40°N/116°E) (p. 666, *m797*)
Belleau Wood (49°N/3°E) (p. 702, *m701*)
Bering Sea (p. 69, *m37*)
Berlin (53°N/13°E) (p. 812)
Bosnia (p. 880, *m916–917*)
Boston (42°N/71°W) (p. 102, *m103*)
Brazil (p. 350, *m349*)
Breed's Hill (42°N/71°W) (p. 170)
Buena Vista (26°N/101°W) (p. 396, *m395*)
Buffalo (43°N/79°W) (p. 341, *m340*)
Bunker Hill (42°N/71°W) (p. 170)

C

Cahokia (39°N/90°W) (p. 189, *m187*)
California (p. 914, *m918–919*)
Cambodia (p. 830, *m828*)
Canada (p. 145, *m916–917*)
Canadian Shield (p. 13, *m12*)
Caribbean Sea (p. 69, *m76*)
Central America (p. 40, *m349*)
Central Plains (p. 13, *m12*)
Chancellorsville (38°N/78°W) (p. 493, *m491*)
Charleston (33°N/80°W) (p. 115, *m115*)
Chesapeake Bay (p. 114, *m115*)
Chicago (42°N/88°W) (p. 410, *m918–919*)
China (p. 53, *m916–917*)
Chisholm Trail (p. 553, *m548*)
Cincinnati (39°N/84°W) (p. 410, *m918–919*)
Cleveland (41°N/82°W) (*m918–919*)
Coastal Plains (p. 13, *m12*)
Colombia (p. 675, *m679*)
Colorado (p. 914, *m918–919*)
Colorado River (p. 914, *m918–919*)
Columbia River (p. 310, *m308*)
Concord (43°N/71°W) (p. 159, *m170*)
Connecticut (p. 914, *m918–919*)
Cowpens (35°N/82°W) (p. 192, *m192*)
Cuba (22°N/79°W) (p. 668, *m673*)
Cumberland Gap (37°N/84°W) (p. 148, *m329*)
Cuzco (14°S/72°W) (p. 39, *m35*)
Czechoslovakia (p. 709, *m709*)

D

Dallas (33°N/97°W) (p. 7, *m918–919*)
Delaware (p. 914, *m918–919*)
Delaware River (p. 85, *m90*)
Denver (40°N/105°W) (*m548*)
Detroit (42°N/83°W) (p. 321, *m323*)
District of Columbia (p. 281, *m918–919*)
Dominican Republic (p. 679, *m679*)
Dunkirk (51°N/2°E) (p. 780, *m791*)
Dust Bowl (p. 765, *m745*)

E

Egypt (p. 884, *m885*)
El Alamein (31°N/29°E) (p. 792, *m791*)
El Salvador (p. 824, *m916–917*)
England (p. 81, *m82*)
English Channel (p. 780)
Equator (p. 4, *m916–917*)
Erie Canal (p. 340, *m340*)
Europe (p. 68, *m916–917*)

F

Florida (p. 914, *m918–919*)
Fort Donelson (37°N/88°W) (p. 494, *m507*)
Fort Henry (37°N/88°W) (p. 494, *m507*)
Fort McHenry (39°N/77°W) (p. 323)
Fort Necessity (40°N/79°W) (p. 143, *m142*)
Fort Pitt (40°N/80°W) (p. 144, *m187*)
Fort Sumter (33°N/80°W) (p. 481)
Fort Ticonderoga (44°N/74°W) (p. 144, *m142*)
France (p. 83, *m916–917*)
Fredericksburg (38°N/78°W) (p. 493, *m491*)

G

Gadsden Purchase (p. 397, *m379*)
Gaza Strip (31°N/34°E) (p. 884, *m885*)
Georgia (p. 914, *m918–919*)
Germany (p. 415, *m916–917*)
Gettysburg (40°N/77°W) (p. 506, *m491*)
Goliad (29°N/97°W) (p. 388, *m386*)

Q

R

S

T

U

V

W

Y

The Fifty States

State	Date of Entry to Union (Order of Entry)	Land Area in Square Miles	Population (In Thousands)	Number of Representatives in House*	Capital	Largest City
Alabama	1819 (22)	50,750	4,447	7	Montgomery	Birmingham
Alaska	1959 (49)	570,374	627	1	Juneau	Anchorage
Arizona	1912 (48)	113,642	5,131	8	Phoenix	Phoenix
Arkansas	1836 (25)	52,075	2,673	4	Little Rock	Little Rock
California	1850 (31)	155,973	33,872	53	Sacramento	Los Angeles
Colorado	1876 (38)	103,730	4,301	7	Denver	Denver
Connecticut	1788 (5)	4,845	3,406	5	Hartford	Bridgeport
Delaware	1787 (1)	1,955	784	1	Dover	Wilmington
Florida	1845 (27)	53,997	15,982	25	Tallahassee	Jacksonville
Georgia	1788 (4)	57,919	8,186	13	Atlanta	Atlanta
Hawaii	1959 (50)	6,423	1,212	2	Honolulu	Honolulu
Idaho	1890 (43)	82,751	1,294	2	Boise	Boise
Illinois	1818 (21)	55,593	12,419	19	Springfield	Chicago
Indiana	1816 (19)	35,870	6,080	9	Indianapolis	Indianapolis
Iowa	1846 (29)	55,875	2,926	5	Des Moines	Des Moines
Kansas	1861 (34)	81,823	2,688	4	Topeka	Wichita
Kentucky	1792 (15)	39,732	4,042	6	Frankfort	Louisville
Louisiana	1812 (18)	43,566	4,469	7	Baton Rouge	New Orleans
Maine	1820 (23)	30,865	1,275	2	Augusta	Portland
Maryland	1788 (7)	9,775	5,296	8	Annapolis	Baltimore
Massachusetts	1788 (6)	7,838	6,349	10	Boston	Boston
Michigan	1837 (26)	56,809	9,938	15	Lansing	Detroit
Minnesota	1858 (32)	79,617	4,919	8	St. Paul	Minneapolis
Mississippi	1817 (20)	46,914	2,845	4	Jackson	Jackson
Missouri	1821 (24)	68,898	5,595	9	Jefferson City	Kansas City
Montana	1889 (41)	145,556	902	1	Helena	Billings
Nebraska	1867 (37)	76,878	1,711	3	Lincoln	Omaha
Nevada	1864 (36)	109,806	1,998	3	Carson City	Las Vegas
New Hampshire	1788 (9)	8,969	1,236	2	Concord	Manchester
New Jersey	1787 (3)	7,419	8,414	13	Trenton	Newark
New Mexico	1912 (47)	121,365	1,819	3	Santa Fe	Albuquerque
New York	1788 (11)	47,224	18,976	29	Albany	New York
North Carolina	1789 (12)	48,718	8,049	13	Raleigh	Charlotte
North Dakota	1889 (39)	68,994	642	1	Bismarck	Fargo
Ohio	1803 (17)	40,953	11,353	18	Columbus	Columbus
Oklahoma	1907 (46)	68,679	3,451	5	Oklahoma City	Oklahoma City
Oregon	1859 (33)	96,003	3,421	5	Salem	Portland
Pennsylvania	1787 (2)	44,820	12,281	19	Harrisburg	Philadelphia
Rhode Island	1790 (13)	1,045	1,048	2	Providence	Providence
South Carolina	1788 (8)	30,111	4,012	6	Columbia	Columbia
South Dakota	1889 (40)	75,898	755	1	Pierre	Sioux Falls
Tennessee	1796 (16)	41,220	5,689	9	Nashville	Memphis
Texas	1845 (28)	261,914	20,852	32	Austin	Houston
Utah	1896 (45)	82,168	2,233	3	Salt Lake City	Salt Lake City
Vermont	1791 (14)	9,249	609	1	Montpelier	Burlington
Virginia	1788 (10)	39,598	7,079	11	Richmond	Virginia Beach
Washington	1889 (42)	66,582	5,894	9	Olympia	Seattle
West Virginia	1863 (35)	24,087	1,808	3	Charleston	Charleston
Wisconsin	1848 (30)	54,314	5,364	8	Madison	Milwaukee
Wyoming	1890 (44)	97,105	494	1	Cheyenne	Cheyenne
District of Columbia		61	572	1 (nonvoting)		

Self-Governing Areas, Possessions, and Dependencies	Land Area in Square Miles	Population (In Thousands)	Capital
Puerto Rico	3,515	809	San Juan
Guam	209	155	Agana
U.S. Virgin Islands	132	121	Charlotte Amalie
American Samoa	77	65	Pago Pago

Sources: Department of Commerce, Bureau of the Census

*As of 108th Congress.

State Flags

Alabama

Alaska

Arizona

Arkansas

California

Colorado

Connecticut

Delaware

Florida

Georgia

Hawaii

Idaho

Illinois

Indiana

Iowa

Kansas

Kentucky

Louisiana

Maine

Maryland

Massachusetts

Michigan

Minnesota

Mississippi

Missouri

Montana

Nebraska

Nevada

New Hampshire

New Jersey

New Mexico

New York

North Carolina

North Dakota

Ohio

Oklahoma

Oregon

Pennsylvania

Rhode Island

South Carolina

South Dakota

Tennessee

Texas

Utah

Vermont

Virginia

Washington

West Virginia

Wisconsin

Wyoming

The World: Political

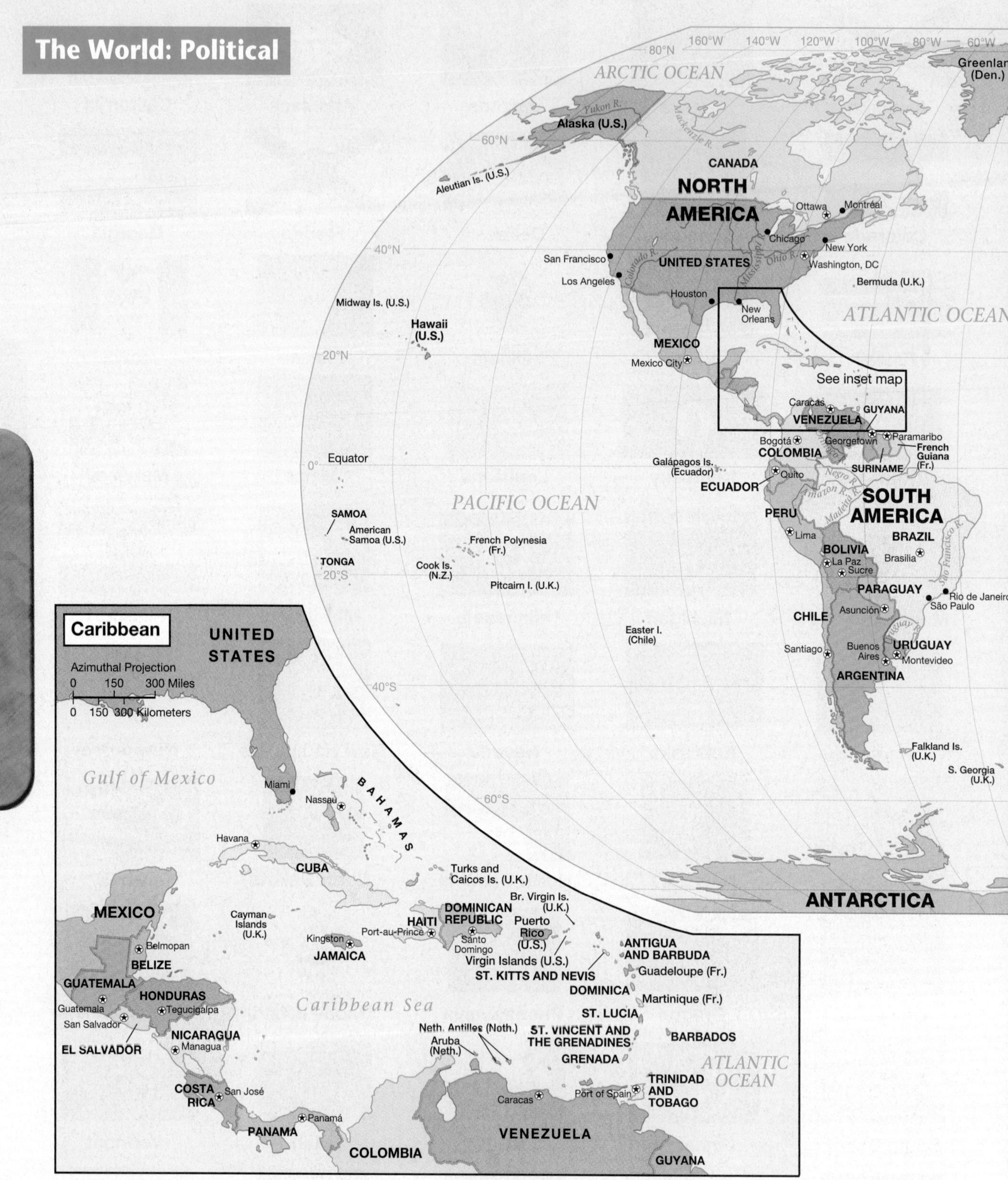

Geographic Atlas

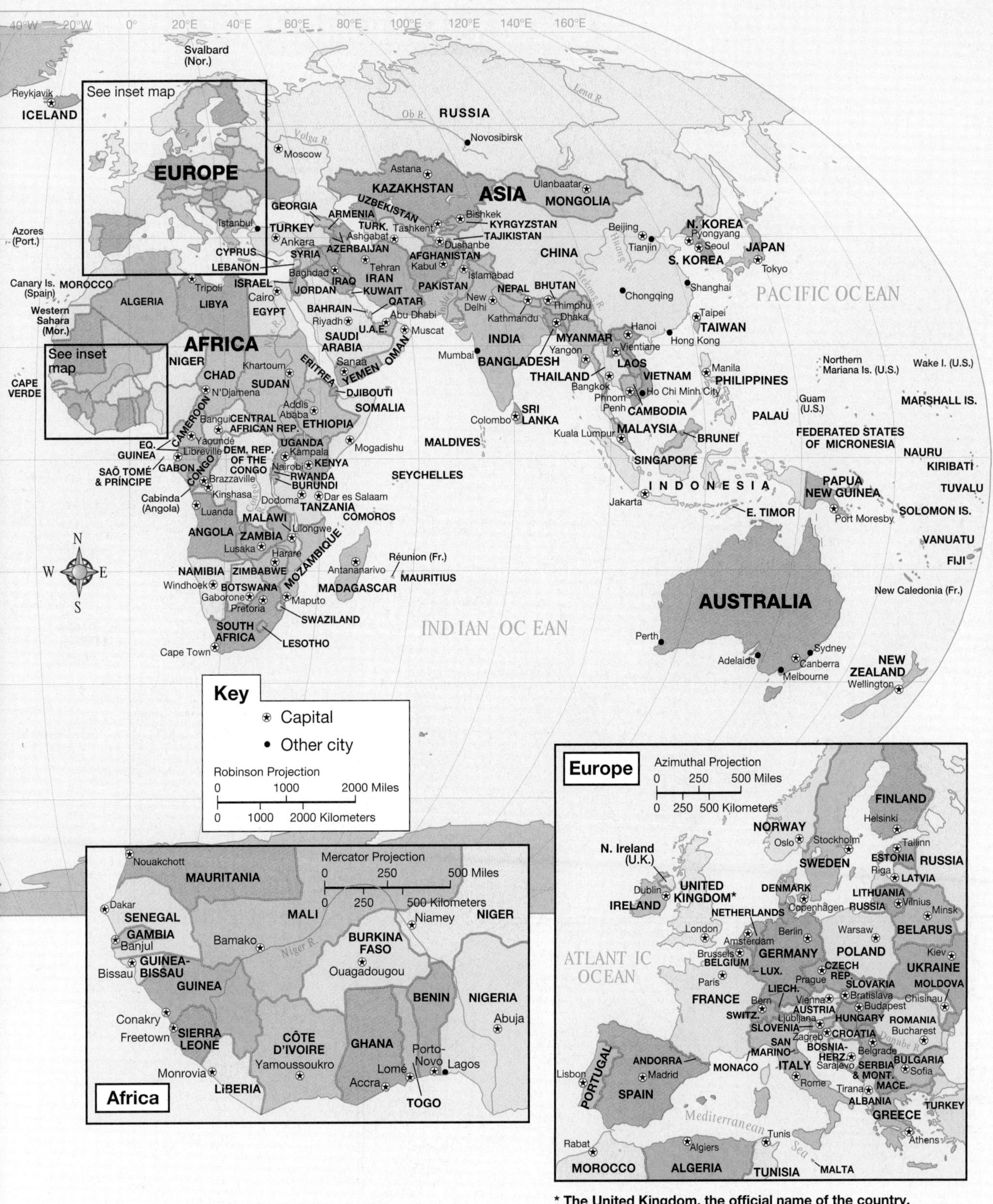

* The United Kingdom, the official name of the country, is more often referred to as Great Britain.

Geographic Atlas

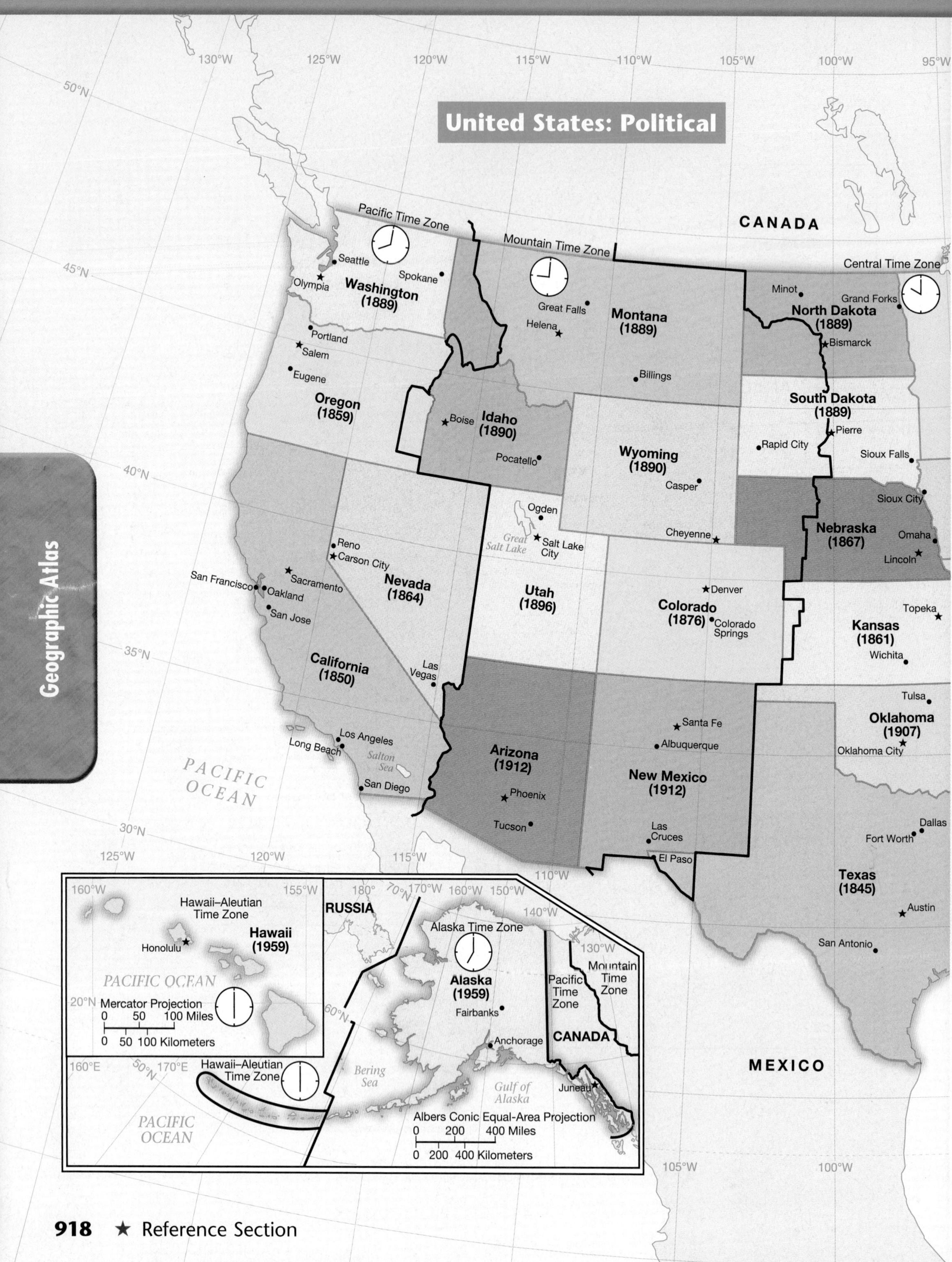
United States: Political
CANADA
Pacific Time Zone
Mountain Time Zone
Central Time Zone
Washington (1889)
Seattle
Olympia
Spokane
Oregon (1859)
Portland
Salem
Eugene
Idaho (1890)
Boise
Pocatello
Montana (1889)
Great Falls
Helena
Billings
Wyoming (1890)
Casper
Cheyenne
North Dakota (1889)
Minot
Grand Forks
Bismarck
South Dakota (1889)
Pierre
Rapid City
Sioux Falls
Nebraska (1867)
Sioux City
Omaha
Lincoln
Nevada (1864)
Reno
Carson City
Las Vegas
California (1850)
Sacramento
San Francisco
Oakland
San Jose
Los Angeles
Long Beach
San Diego
Salton Sea
Utah (1896)
Ogden
Great Salt Lake
Salt Lake City
Colorado (1876)
Denver
Colorado Springs
Kansas (1861)
Topeka
Wichita
Arizona (1912)
Phoenix
Tucson
New Mexico (1912)
Santa Fe
Albuquerque
Las Cruces
El Paso
Oklahoma (1907)
Tulsa
Oklahoma City
Texas (1845)
Dallas
Fort Worth
Austin
San Antonio
MEXICO
PACIFIC OCEAN
Hawaii–Aleutian Time Zone
Hawaii (1959)
Honolulu
PACIFIC OCEAN
Mercator Projection
0 50 100 Miles
0 50 100 Kilometers
RUSSIA
Alaska Time Zone
Alaska (1959)
Fairbanks
Anchorage
Juneau
Pacific Time Zone
Mountain Time Zone
CANADA
Bering Sea
Gulf of Alaska
Hawaii–Aleutian Time Zone
PACIFIC OCEAN
Albers Conic Equal-Area Projection
0 200 400 Miles
0 200 400 Kilometers

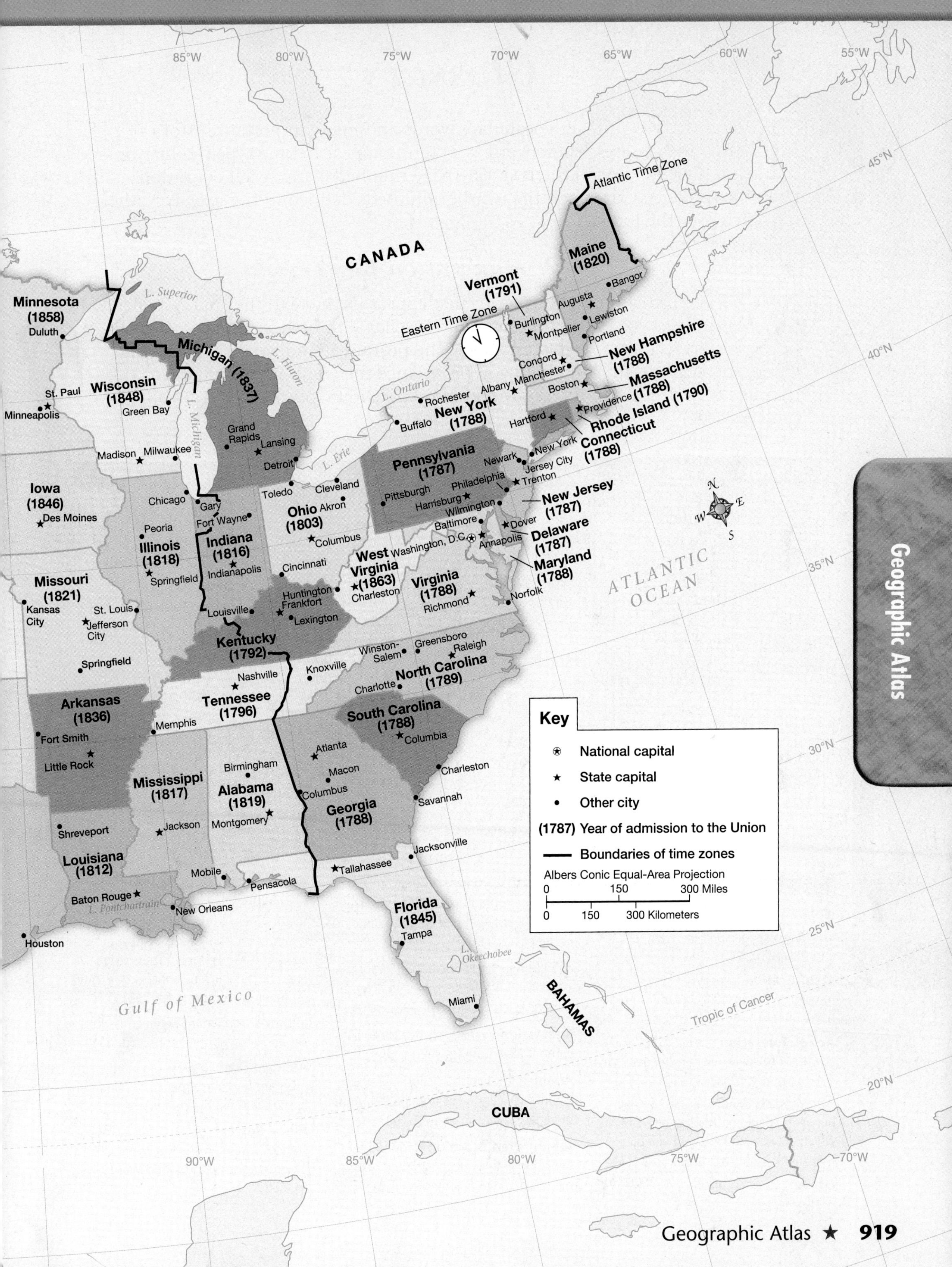

Geographic Atlas

Glossary

This glossary defines all vocabulary words and many important historical terms and phrases. These words and terms appear in blue type the first time that they are used in the text. The page number(s) after each definition refers to the page(s) on which the word or phrase is defined in the text. For other references, see the index.

Pronunciation Key

When difficult names or terms first appear in the text, they are respelled to help you with pronunciation. A syllable printed in small capital letters receives the greatest stress. The pronunciation key below lists the letters and symbols that will help you pronounce the word. It also includes examples of words using each of the sounds and shows how each word would be pronounced.

Symbol	Example	Respelling
a	hat	(hat)
ay	pay, late	(pay), (layt)
ah	star, hot	(stahr), (haht)
ai	air, dare	(air), (dair)
aw	law, all	(law), (awl)
eh	met	(meht)
ee	bee, eat	(bee), (eet)
er	learn, sir, fur	(lern), (ser), (fer)
ih	fit	(fiht)
i	mile	(mīl)
ir	ear	(ir)
oh	no	(noh)
oi	soil, boy	(soil), (boi)
oo	root, rule	(root), (rool)
or	born, door	(born), (dor)
ow	plow, out	(plow), (owt)

Symbol	Example	Respelling
u	put, book	(put), (buk)
uh	fun	(fuhn)
yoo	few, use	(fyoo), (yooz)
ch	chill, reach	(chihl), (reech)
g	go, dig	(goh), (dihg)
j	jet, gently bridge	(jeht), (JEHNT lee), (brihj)
k	kite, cup	(kīt), (kuhp)
ks	mix	(mihks)
kw	quick	(kwihk)
ng	bring	(brihng)
s	say, cent	(say), (sehnt)
sh	she, crash	(shee), (krash)
th	three	(three)
y	yet, onion	(yeht), (UHN yuhn)
z	zip, always	(zihp), (AWL wayz)
zh	treasure	(TREH zher)

Glossary

A

abdicate give up power (p. 701)

abolitionist person who wanted to end slavery (p. 440)

acculturation process of holding on to older traditions while adapting to a new culture (p. 604)

Act of Toleration a 1649 Maryland law that provided religious freedom for all Christians (p. 114)

Adams-Onís Treaty an 1821 treaty between Spain and the United States in which Spain agreed to give Florida to the United States (p. 350)

adobe sun-dried brick (p. 41)

affirmative action program to provide more job and education opportunities for people who faced discrimination in the past (p. 864)

AFL (American Federation of Labor) an organization of trade unions that represented skilled workers (p. 592)

aggression warlike act by one country without just cause (p. 775)

Alamo old Spanish mission in Texas where Mexican forces under Santa Anna besieged Texans in 1836 (p. 387)

Albany Plan of Union proposal by Benjamin Franklin to create one government for the 13 colonies (p. 143)

Alien and Sedition acts in 1798, Federalist-supported laws that permitted the President to expel foreigners, made it harder for immigrants to become citizens, and allowed for citizens to be fined or jailed if they criticized the government or its officials (p. 293)

alliance agreement between nations to aid and protect one another (p. 85)

Alliance for Progress economic aid program for Latin America developed by President Kennedy (p. 824)

Allied Powers military alliance of France, Britain, Russia, Italy, and 20 other nations during World War I (p. 688)

Allies World War II military alliance of Britain, France, the Soviet Union, the United States, China, and 45 other countries (p. 779)

ally nation that works with another nation for a common purpose (p. 183)

altitude height above sea level (p. 15)

amend change (p. 218)

American Association of Retired Persons (AARP) organization that monitors issues of concern to older Americans (p. 897)

American Colonization Society early 1800s organization that proposed to end slavery by helping African Americans move to Africa (p. 440)

American Indian Religious Freedom Act a 1978 law that directed federal agencies not to interfere with Native American religious practices (p. 896)

American System program for economic growth promoted by Henry Clay in the early 1800s; called for high tariffs on imports (p. 345)

Americans With Disabilities Act law passed in 1990 that prohibits discrimination in hiring people with physical or mental impairments (p. 897)

amnesty government pardon (p. 517)

anarchist person who opposes organized government (pp. 592, 737)

annex to add on or take over (pp. 389, 661)

anthropology the study of how people and cultures develop (p. 30)

Antifederalists people who opposed the Constitution and a strong national government (p. 215)

apartheid strict separation of races practiced in South Africa (p. 880)

appeal to ask that a decision be reviewed by a higher court (p. 256)

appeasement practice of giving in to aggression in order to avoid war (p. 779)

Appomattox Court House Virginia town that was the site of the Confederate surrender in 1865 (p. 509)

apprentice person who learns a trade or craft from a master (p. 128)

archaeology the study of evidence left by early peoples in order to find out about their way of life (p. 22)

armistice an agreement to stop fighting (p. 701)

arsenal place where guns are stored (p. 476)

Articles the main body of the Constitution, which establishes the framework for the United States government (p. 249)

Articles of Confederation first American constitution, passed in 1777, which created a loose alliance of 13 independent states (p. 201)

artifact object made by humans (p. 22)

artisan skilled worker (p. 413)

assembly line method of production in which workers stay in one place as products edge along past them on a moving belt (p. 588)

astrolabe navigational instrument used to determine latitude (p. 59)

Atlantic Charter a 1941 program developed by the United States and Britain that set goals for the postwar world (p. 782)

atrocity act of cruelty and brutality (p. 670)

authenticity the quality or condition of being genuine (p. 21)

Axis World War II military alliance of Germany, Italy, Japan, and six other nations (p. 779)

B

baby boom large increase in the birthrate from the late 1940s through the early 1960s (p. 844)

Bacon's Rebellion a 1676 raid led by Nathaniel Bacon against the governor and Native Americans in Virginia (p. 114)

balanced budget condition that exists when the government spends only as much as it takes in (p. 874)

bank holiday closing of banks for four days during the Great Depression (p. 753)

Bank of the United States bank set up in 1791 to hold government deposits and to issue paper money to pay government bills (p. 281)

bankrupt unable to pay debts (p. 748)

barrio Mexican neighborhood in the United States (p. 651)

Bataan Death March long trek across the Philippines that American and Filipino prisoners of war were forced to make by the Japanese in 1942 (p. 799)

Battle of Antietam an 1862 Civil War battle in Maryland (p. 493)

Battle of Belleau Wood hard-fought American victory over the Germans in France in 1918 (p. 700)

Battle of Britain Germany's failed attempt to subdue Britain in 1940 in preparation for invasion (p. 780)

Battle of Bull Run first major battle of the Civil War; fought in Virginia in 1861 (p. 491)

Battle of Bunker Hill in 1775, first major battle of the Revolution (p. 170)

Battle of Chancellorsville an 1863 Civil War battle in Virginia; important victory for the Confederacy (p. 493)

Battle of Cowpens a 1781 battle in South Carolina where Americans won an important victory over the British (p. 192)

Battle of Fredericksburg an 1862 Civil War battle in Virginia; one of the Union's worst defeats (p. 493)

Battle of Gettysburg an 1863 Civil War battle in Pennsylvania that ended a Confederate invasion of the North (p. 506)

Battle of Lake Erie In the War of 1812, an American victory led by Oliver Perry against the British (p. 322)

Battle of Long Island a 1776 battle in New York in which more than 1,400 Americans were killed, wounded, or captured (p. 181)

Battle of Midway a 1942 battle in the Pacific during which American planes sank four Japanese aircraft carriers (p. 792)

Battle of New Orleans At the end of the War of 1812, a battle between British and American forces that ended in an American victory (p. 324)

Battle of San Jacinto an 1836 battle between Texans and Mexicans during the Texas war for independence from Mexico (p. 388)

Battle of Saratoga in 1777, the first major American victory in the Revolution (p. 183)

Battle of Shiloh an 1862 Civil War battle in Tennessee that ended in a Union victory (p. 494)

Battle of the Argonne Forest defeat of the Germans by French and American troops in France in October 1918 (p. 701)

Battle of the Bulge German counterattack in December 1944 that temporarily slowed the Allied invasion of Germany (p. 793)

Battle of Tippecanoe In 1811, battle over white settlement in the Indiana Territory (p. 318)

Battle of Trenton a 1776 battle in New Jersey in which George Washington's troops captured a Hessian encampment (p. 182)

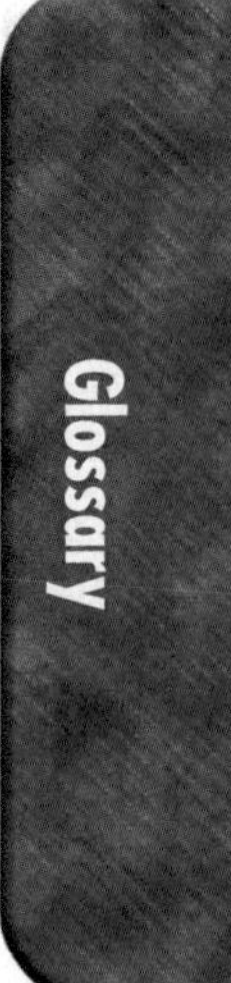

Battle of Verdun prolonged World War I battle in which more than 1 million died or were wounded (p. 689)

Battle of Yorktown 1781 American victory in Virginia that forced the British to surrender (p. 193)

battles of Lexington and Concord in 1775, conflicts between Massachusetts colonists and British soldiers that started the Revolutionary War (p. 160)

Bay of Pigs invasion failed invasion of Cuba in 1961 when a force of 1,200 Cuban exiles, backed by the United States, landed at the Bay of Pigs (p. 823)

Bear Flag Republic nickname for California after it declared independence from Mexico in 1846 (p. 396)

beatnik 1950s person who criticized American culture for conformity and devotion to business (p. 847)

Berlin Airlift American and British relief effort to airlift supplies to West Berliners from 1948 to 1949 (p. 812)

Berlin Wall wall built by the communist East German government in 1961 to seal off East Berlin from West Berlin (p. 813)

Bessemer process method developed in the 1850s to produce stronger steel at a lower cost (p. 578)

bias a leaning toward or against a certain person, group, or idea (p. 22)

Big Four leaders of Britain, France, the United States, and Italy after World War I (p. 706)

bilingual in two languages (p. 866)

bill proposed law (p. 253)

bill of rights written list of freedoms the government promises to protect (pp. 123, 200)

Bill of Rights first 10 amendments to the United States Constitution (p. 218)

Black Cabinet group of black leaders who unofficially advised President Franklin D. Roosevelt concerning the situation of African Americans (p. 767)

black codes Southern laws that severely limited the rights of African Americans after the Civil War (p. 521)

Black Tuesday (October 29, 1929) day the stock market crashed, signaling start of the Great Depression (p. 747)

blitzkrieg the swift attacks launched by Germany in World War II (p. 779)

blockade the shutting of a port to keep people or supplies from moving in or out (p. 171)

boat people after the Vietnam War, refugees who escaped from Vietnam in small boats (p. 831)

bond certificate that promises to repay money loaned, plus interest, on a certain date (p. 280)

bonus additional sum of money (p. 751)

Bonus Army veterans who marched to Washington in 1932 to demand immediate payment of a World War I bonus (p. 751)

boom period of swift economic growth (p. 419)

bootlegger person who smuggled liquor into the United States during Prohibition (p. 725)

Border Ruffians proslavery bands from Missouri who often battled antislavery forces in Kansas (p. 470)

border state slave state that remained in the Union during the Civil War (p. 487)

Boston Massacre a 1770 conflict in which five colonists were killed by British troops (p. 152)

Boston Tea Party a 1773 protest in which colonists dressed as Indians dumped British tea into Boston harbor (p. 157)

Boxer Rebellion uprising in China against westerners and Western influence in 1900 (p. 666)

boycott to refuse to buy or use certain goods or services (pp. 150, 852)

bracero program recruitment of Mexican laborers to work in the United States during World War II (p. 788)

Buffalo Soldiers nickname for the African American members of the 9th and 10th Cavalries during the Spanish-American War (p. 672)

building code standards for construction and safety of buildings (p. 609)

bull market period of increased stock trading and rising stock prices (p. 720)

Bull Moose party Progressive Republicans who supported Theodore Roosevelt during the election of 1912 (p. 642)

bureaucracy system of managing government through departments run by appointed officials (p. 695)

burgess representative to the colonial Virginia government (p. 90)

C

Cabinet group of officials who head government departments and advise the President (p. 279)

Camp David Accords 1979 peace treaty between Israel and Egypt in which Israel agreed to return the Sinai Peninsula to Egypt and Egypt agreed to recognize Israel (p. 884)

capital money raised for a business venture (p. 331)

capitalist person who invests in a business to make a profit (p. 331)

caravan group of people who travel together for safety (p. 52)

carpetbagger uncomplimentary nickname for a northerner who went to the South after the Civil War (p. 527)

cartographer mapmaker (p. 8)

cash crop crop sold for money at market (p. 111)

cash economy economy in which people exchange money for goods and services (p. 27)

cattle drive herding and moving cattle (p. 553)

caucus private meeting; often a political meeting (p. 364)

causeway raised road made of packed earth (p. 38)

cavalry troops on horseback (p. 184)

cede to give up (pp. 202, 396)

censure to officially condemn (p. 820)

Central Powers military alliance of Germany, Austria-Hungary, Bulgaria, and the Ottoman Empire during World War I (p. 688)

Chapultepec fort outside of Mexico City; site of an 1847 battle between the United States and Mexico (p. 396)

charter legal document giving certain rights to a person or company (p. 88)

Chautauqua Society traveling adult education program in the 1800s (p. 618)

checks and balances a principle of the United States Constitution that gives each branch of government the power to check the other branches (p. 251)

Chinese Exclusion Act 1882 law that barred Chinese laborers from entering the United States (p. 605)

chronology sequence of events over time (p. 25)

circumnavigate travel all the way around the Earth (p. 71)

citizen person who owes loyalty to a particular nation and is entitled to all its rights and protections (p. 265)

city-state large town that has its own government and controls the surrounding countryside (p. 52)

civic virtue the willingness to work for the good of the nation or community even at great sacrifice (p. 266)

civics the study of the rights and responsibilities of citizens (p. 29)

civil relating to lawsuits involving the private rights of individuals (p. 261)

civil disobedience idea that people have a right to disobey laws they consider to be unjust, if their consciences demand it (pp. 451, 853)

civil rights the rights due to all citizens (p. 767)

civil rights movement the efforts of African Americans to win equal rights (p. 850)

civil service all federal jobs except elected offices and those in the military (p. 631)

Civil Service Commission government agency created by the Pendleton Act of 1883 to fill federal jobs on the basis of merit (p. 631)

civil war war between people of the same country (p. 465)

Civil War amendments the Thirteenth, Fourteenth, and Fifteenth amendments to the United States Constitution (p. 261)

civilian nonmilitary (p. 249)

Civilian Conservation Corps New Deal program that hired unemployed men to work on natural conservation projects (p. 754)

clan group of two or more related families (p. 48)

Clermont steamboat built in 1807 by Robert Fulton; first steamboat to be commercially successful in American waters (p. 339)

climate average weather of a place over a period of 20 to 30 years (p. 15)

clipper ship fast-sailing ship of the mid-1800s (p. 410)

Cold War after World War II, long period of intense rivalry between the Soviet Union and the United States (p. 810)

collective bargaining process by which a union representing a group of workers negotiates with management for a contract (pp. 592, 761)

colony group of people who settle in a distant land but are still ruled by the government of their native land (p. 70)

Columbian Exchange the global exchange of goods and ideas resulting from the encounter between the peoples of the Eastern and Western hemispheres (p. 71)

committee of correspondence letter-writing campaign that became a major tool of protest in the colonies (p. 153)

Common Sense a 1776 essay by Thomas Paine that urged the colonies to declare independence (p. 173)

communism economic system in which all wealth and property are owned by the state (p. 722)

company union labor organization that is actually controlled by management (p. 737)

compensation repayment for losses (p. 788)

Comprehensive Test Ban Treaty agreement proposed in 1996 to end all testing of nuclear weapons (p. 882)

compromise settlement in which each side gives up some of its demands in order to reach an agreement (p. 208)

Compromise of 1850 agreement over slavery by which California joined the Union as a free state and a strict fugitive slave law was passed (p. 465)

compulsory education requirement that children attend school to a certain grade or age (p. 617)

concentration camp prison camp for civilians who are considered enemies of the state (p. 776)

confederation league of independent states or nations (p. 317)

Congress of Industrial Organizations (CIO) labor organization founded in the 1930s to represent workers in basic mass-production industries (p. 762)

conquistador name for the Spanish explorers who claimed lands in the Americas for Spain (p. 74)

conservation protection of natural resources (p. 641)

Conservatives during Reconstruction, white southerners who resisted change (p. 527)

consolidate combine (p. 575)

constitution document that sets out the laws, principles, organization, and processes of a government (p. 200)

Constitutional Convention gathering of state representatives on May 25, 1787, to revise the Articles of Confederation (p. 206)

consumer user of goods and services (p. 27)

containment the policy of trying to prevent the spread of Soviet influence beyond where it already existed (p. 811)

Continental Army army established by the Second Continental Congress to fight the British (p. 169)

continental divide mountain ridge that separates river systems flowing toward opposite sides of a continent (p. 309)

Contract With America 1994 legislative package that included trimming social welfare programs and slashing taxes (p. 875)

cooperative group of farmers who pool their money to buy seeds and tools wholesale (p. 565)

Copperhead northerner who opposed using force to keep the southern states in the Union (p. 501)

corduroy road road made of logs (p. 339)

corollary addition to an earlier stated principle (p. 678)

corporation business that is owned by investors (p. 580)

corral enclosure for animals (p. 545)

"cottonocracy" name for the wealthy planters who made their money from cotton in the mid-1800s (p. 422)

counterculture movement protest movement in the 1960s that rejected traditional values and culture (p. 859)

coureur de bois French colonist who lived in the woods as a fur trapper (p. 83)

cow town settlement that grew up at the end of a cattle trail (p. 554)

creole person born in Spain's American colonies to Spanish parents (pp. 78, 348)

Crusades between 1100 and 1300, series of wars fought by Christians to control the Holy Land (p. 58)

Cuban missile crisis major Cold War confrontation in 1962 (p. 823)

cultivate to prepare and use land for planting crops (p. 419)

culture entire way of life developed by a people (pp. 22, 40)

culture area region in which people share a similar way of life (p. 42)

currency money (p. 202)

czar Russian emperor (p. 692)

D

D-Day (June 6, 1944) day of the invasion of Western Europe by Allied forces (p. 792)

dame school school run by a woman, usually in her own home (p. 128)

Dayton Accord 1995 peace agreement negotiated among Bosnia, Croatia, and Serbia (p. 881)

debtor person who cannot pay money he or she owes (pp. 116, 436)

Declaration of Independence a 1776 document stating that the 13 English colonies were a free and independent nation (p. 175)

deficit spending government practice of spending more than is taken in from taxes (p. 763)

demilitarized zone (DMZ) area from which military forces are prohibited (p. 818)

democratic ensuring that all people have the same rights (p. 302)

Democratic Republican supporter of Thomas Jefferson (p. 289)

Democrats supporters of Andrew Jackson; included frontier farmers and factory workers (p. 364)

department store large retail store offering a variety of goods organized in separate departments (p. 613)

deport expel from a country (p. 737)

depression period when business activity slows, prices and wages fall, and unemployment rises (pp. 204, 373)

deregulation reduction of restrictions on businesses (p. 873)

détente policy to reduce tensions between two countries (p. 833)

dictatorship government in which one person or a small group holds complete authority (pp. 212, 386)

diffusion process of spreading ideas from one culture to another (p. 43)

dime novel in the late 1800s, low-priced paperbacks offering adventure stories (p. 619)

direct democracy form of government in which ordinary citizens have the power to govern (p. 57)

disarmament reduction of armed forces and weapons of war (p. 722)

discrimination policy that denies equal rights to certain groups of people (p. 417)

dividend share of a corporation's profit (p. 580)

dollar diplomacy President Taft's policy of building strong economic ties to Latin America (p. 678)

domestic tranquillity peace and order at home (p. 249)

domino theory belief that if South Vietnam fell to communism, other countries in the region would also fall to communism (p. 828)

"Double V" campaign African American civil rights campaign during World War II (p. 786)

downsizing reducing a workforce (p. 874)

draft law that requires people of a certain age to enlist in the military (pp. 502, 693, 829)

Dred Scott* v. *Sandford an 1857 Supreme Court case that brought into question the federal power over slavery in the territories (p. 471)

Dust Bowl region in the central Great Plains that was hit by a severe drought during the 1930s (p. 765)

E

e-commerce business and trade over the Internet (p. 892)

Earth Summit meeting of world leaders in 1992 to discuss key environmental issues (p. 890)

economics the study of how people manage limited resources to satisfy their wants and needs (p. 26)

Eighteenth Amendment 1917 constitutional amendment that made it illegal to sell alcoholic drinks (p. 648)

electoral college group of electors from every state who meet every four years to vote for the President and Vice President of the United States (p. 255)

elevation height above sea level (p. 13)

emancipate to set free (p. 497)

Emancipation Proclamation Lincoln's 1863 declaration freeing slaves in the Confederacy (p. 497)

embargo ban on trade (p. 314)

Embargo Act an 1807 law that imposed a total ban on foreign trade (p. 314)

encomienda land granted to Spanish settlers that included the right to demand labor or taxes from Native Americans (p. 78)

English Bill of Rights a 1689 document that guaranteed the rights of English citizens (pp. 123, 213)

Enlightenment movement in Europe in the 1600s and 1700s that emphasized the use of reason (p. 129)

Environmental Protection Agency federal government agency that works to reduce pollution (p. 890)

environmentalist person who works to reduce pollution and protect the natural environment (p. 889)

epidemic rapid spread of a contagious disease (p. 702)

Equal Rights Amendment a 1923 proposed constitutional amendment intended to prohibit all discrimination based on sex; the amendment was never ratified (p. 726)

Era of Good Feelings the eight years of James Monroe's presidency, from 1817 to 1825 (p. 343)

Erie Canal artificial waterway opened in 1825 linking Lake Erie to the Hudson River (p. 340)

erosion gradual wearing away (p. 13)

escalate to expand (p. 828)

established church chosen religion of a state (p. 94)

executive branch branch of government that carries out laws (p. 208)

exile person who has been forced to leave his or her own country (p. 823)

expansionism policy of extending a nation's boundaries (p. 660)

expatriate person who renounces his or her own country and takes up residence in a foreign land (p. 731)

expedition long voyage of exploration (p. 308)

export trade product sent to markets outside a country (p. 120)

extended family family group that includes grandparents, parents, children, aunts, uncles, and cousins (pp. 53, 425)

F

faction opposing group within a party (p. 287)

factory system method of producing goods that brought workers and machinery together in one place (p. 331)

fad activity or fashion that is very popular for a short time (p. 730)

famine severe food shortage (p. 415)

Farewell Address final official speech of Presidents as they exit office (p. 286)

Fascism political system that is rooted in militarism, extreme nationalism, and blind loyalty to the state (p. 774)

Federal Reserve Act a 1913 law that set up a system of federal banks and gave government the power to control the money supply (p. 643)

Federal Trade Commission (FTC) government agency created in 1914 to ensure fair competition (p. 643)

federalism a principle of the United States Constitution that establishes the division of power between the federal government and the states (p. 251)

Federalist supporter of a strong federal government (pp. 215, 289)

Federalist Papers series of essays by Federalists James Madison, Alexander Hamilton, and John Jay in support of ratifying the Constitution (p. 216)

Glossary

feudalism system of rule by lords who ruled their own lands but owed loyalty and military service to a monarch (p. 58)

Fifteenth Amendment an 1869 amendment to the United States Constitution that forbids any state to deny African Americans the right to vote because of race (p. 524)

54th Massachusetts Regiment African American unit in the Union Army (p. 499)

fireside chat radio speech given by President Franklin D. Roosevelt while in office (p. 754)

First Amendment amendment to the United States Constitution that safeguards basic individual liberties (p. 260)

First Continental Congress in 1774, meeting of delegates from 12 colonies in Philadelphia (p. 158)

first global age era at beginning of 1400s, when long-distance trade and travel increased dramatically (p. 50)

flapper young woman in the 1920s who rebelled against traditional ways of thinking and acting (p. 731)

flatboat boat with a flat bottom used for transporting heavy loads on inland waterways (p. 337)

Foraker Act law passed by Congress in 1900 under which the United States gave Puerto Ricans a limited say in government (p. 674)

foreign policy actions that a nation takes in relation to other nations (p. 285)

Fort Wagner fort in South Carolina that was the site of an attack by the African American 54th Massachusetts Regiment in 1863 (p. 499)

forty-niner one of the more than 80,000 people who joined the gold rush to California in 1849 (p. 400)

Founding Fathers leaders who laid the groundwork for the United States (p. 211)

Fourteen Points President Wilson's goals for peace after World War I (p. 706)

Fourteenth Amendment an 1868 amendment to the United States Constitution that guarantees equal protection of the laws (p. 522)

free enterprise system economic system in which businesses are owned by private citizens who decide what to produce, how much to produce, and what prices to charge (pp. 28, 581)

free market economic system in which goods and services are exchanged with little regulation (p. 303)

Free-Soil party bipartisan antislavery party founded in the United States in 1848 to keep slavery out of the western territories (p. 462)

freedmen men and women who had been slaves (p. 517)

Freedmen's Bureau government agency founded during Reconstruction to help former slaves (p. 517)

French and Indian War a war that took place from 1754 to 1763 that led to the end of French power in North America (p. 142)

French Revolution a 1789 rebellion in France that ended the French monarchy for a time (p. 284)

frigate fast-sailing ship with many guns (p. 292)

fugitive runaway (p. 464)

Fugitive Slave Act law passed in 1850 that required all citizens to aid in the capture of runaway slaves (p. 465)

Fundamental Orders of Connecticut a 1639 plan of government in the Puritan colony in Connecticut (p. 104)

G

Gadsden Purchase strip of land in present-day Arizona and New Mexico for which the United States paid Mexico $10 million in 1853 (p. 397)

gauge width of a train track (p. 574)

General Court elected representative assembly in the Massachusetts Bay Colony (p. 103)

general welfare well-being of all the citizens of a nation (p. 249)

"Gentlemen's Agreement" a 1907 agreement between the United States and Japan to limit Japanese immigration (p. 652)

gentry highest social class in the 13 English colonies (p. 126)

geography the study of people, their environments, and their resources (p. 4)

Gibbons* v. *Ogden an 1814 case in which the Supreme Court upheld the power of the federal government to regulate commerce (p. 346)

Gilded Age the period in American history lasting from the 1870s to the 1890s, marked by political corruption and extravagant spending (p. 630)

glacier thick sheet of ice (p. 36)

glasnost policy in the Soviet Union of speaking openly about problems (p. 835)

global warming the slow but steady rise in the world's average temperature (p. 891)

Glorious Revolution in 1688, movement that brought William and Mary to the throne of England and strengthened the rights of English citizens (p. 123)

Good Neighbor Policy President Franklin Roosevelt's policy intended to strengthen friendly relations with Latin America (p. 777)

graduated income tax tax on earnings that charges different rates for different income levels (p. 636)

grandfather clause law that excused a voter from a literacy test if his father or grandfather had been eligible to vote on January 1, 1867 (p. 532)

Great Awakening religious movement in the English colonies in the early 1700s (p. 127)

Great Compromise plan at the Constitutional Convention that settled the differences between large and small states (p. 208)

Great Depression worst period of economic decline in United States history, beginning in 1929 (p. 747)

Great White Fleet name for the steam-powered ships of the enlarged and modernized American navy of the early 1900s (p. 664)

Green Mountain Boys Vermont colonial militia led by Ethan Allen that made a surprise attack on Fort Ticonderoga (p. 169)

guerrilla fighter who uses hit-and-run attacks (pp. 192, 828)

Gulf of Tonkin Resolution Congressional resolution passed in 1964 that authorized military action in Vietnam (p. 828)

Gullah combination of English and West African languages spoken by African Americans in the South Carolina colony (p. 126)

H

habeas corpus the right not to be held in prison without first being charged with a specific crime (pp. 213, 502)

Harlem Hell Fighters the African American infantry unit that fought with the French Army in World War I (p. 700)

Hartford Convention gathering of New Englanders to protest the War of 1812 by threatening to secede from the Union (p. 325)

Haymarket Riot labor rally in Chicago in 1886 that ended in violence when a bomb exploded (p. 592)

Holocaust slaughter of Europe's Jews by the Nazis before and during World War II (p. 799)

Hooverville group of shacks in which the homeless lived during the Great Depression (p. 750)

House of Burgesses representative assembly in colonial Virginia (p. 90)

House of Representatives the larger of the two bodies that make up the legislative branch of the United States government (p. 252)

Hudson River School group of American artists who painted landscapes of New York's Hudson River Valley in the mid-1800s (p. 448)

Hull House settlement house founded by Progressive reformer Jane Addams in Chicago in 1889 (p. 610)

Hundred Days first hundred days of President Franklin D. Roosevelt's presidency (p. 754)

I

ILGWU (International Ladies' Garment Workers Union) union of garment workers formed in 1900 (p. 593)

illegal alien immigrant who enters a country without permission (p. 895)

illiterate unable to read or write (p. 694)

immigrant person who enters another country in order to settle there (p. 266)

Immigration Reform and Control Act law that allowed people who arrived illegally in the United States before 1982 to apply for citizenship (p. 895)

impeach to bring charges of serious wrongdoing against a public official (pp. 257, 523)

imperialism policy of powerful countries seeking to control the economic and political affairs of weaker countries or regions (p. 662)

import trade product brought into a country (p. 120)

impressment practice of forcing people into military service (p. 313)

inauguration ceremony in which the President officially takes the oath of office (p. 278)

income tax a tax on people's earnings (p. 502)

incriminate to give evidence against (p. 260)

indentured servant person who agreed to work without wages for a period of time in exchange for passage to the colonies (p. 126)

Indian New Deal series of laws passed in the 1930s that gave Native American nations greater control over their own affairs (p. 768)

Indian Removal Act law passed in 1830 that forced many Native Americans to move west of the Mississippi River (p. 372)

indigo plant used to make a valuable blue dye (p. 115)

individualism concept that stresses the importance of each individual (p. 451)

Industrial Revolution gradual process by which machines replaced hand tools (p. 330)

inflation a rise in prices and a decrease in the value of money (pp. 503, 565, 843)

infrastructure system of roads, bridges, and tunnels (p. 263)

initiative process by which voters can put a bill directly before the state legislature (pp. 263, 636)

installment buying buying on credit (p. 720)

integration mixing of different racial or ethnic groups (p. 850)

interchangeable parts identical, machine-made parts for a tool or an instrument (p. 332)

internal improvements improvements to roads, bridges, and canals (p. 346)

Internet series of interconnected computers that allow users to access and exchange computerized information (p. 892)

interstate commerce business that crosses state lines (pp. 346, 632)

Interstate Commerce Commission (ICC) government agency organized to oversee railroad commerce (p. 632)

intervention direct involvement (p. 351)

Intolerable Acts series of laws passed in 1774 to punish Boston for the Tea Party (p. 157)

irrigation bringing water to dry lands (p. 6)

Islam monotheistic religion founded by the prophet Muhammad in the early 600s (p. 50)

island hopping during World War II, Allied strategy of capturing Japanese-held islands to gain control of the Pacific Ocean (p. 796)

isolationist after World War I, American who wanted the United States to stay out of world affairs (pp. 660, 708)

isthmus narrow strip of land connecting two larger bodies of land (pp. 11, 675)

J

Jay's Treaty a 1795 agreement between Britain and the United States that called for Britain to pay damages for seized American ships and to give up forts it still held in the West (p. 286)

jazz music style that developed from blues, ragtime, and other earlier styles (p. 731)

jerky dried meat (p. 545)

Jim Crow laws laws that separated people of different races in public places in the South (p. 532)

judicial branch branch of government that decides if laws are carried out fairly (p. 208)

judicial review power of the Supreme Court to decide whether the acts of a President or laws passed by Congress are constitutional (p. 305)

Judiciary Act a 1789 law that created the structure of the Supreme Court and set up a system of district courts and circuit courts for the nation (p. 279)

jury duty the responsibility of every citizen to serve on a jury when called (p. 268)

K

kachina masked dancer at religious ceremonies of the Southwest Indians (p. 47)

kaiser title of the German emperor (p. 688)

kamikaze World War II Japanese pilot trained to make a suicidal crash attack, usually upon a ship (p. 797)

Kansas-Nebraska Act an 1854 law that established the territories of Nebraska and Kansas, giving the settlers the right of popular sovereignty to decide on the issue of slavery (p. 468)

Kellogg-Briand Pact a 1928 treaty outlawing war (p. 722)

Kentucky and Virginia resolutions declarations passed in 1798 and 1799 that claimed that each state has the right to decide whether a federal law is constitutional (p. 293)

Khmer Rouge communist party in Cambodia that imposed a reign of terror on Cambodian citizens (p. 831)

kinship sharing a common ancestor (p. 53)

"kitchen cabinet" group of unofficial advisers to Andrew Jackson who met with him in the White House kitchen (p. 367)

Knights of Labor an American labor organization founded in 1869 to protect the rights of workers (p. 591)

Know-Nothing party political party of the 1850s that was anti-Catholic and anti-immigrant (p. 416)

Ku Klux Klan secret society organized in the South after the Civil War to reassert white supremacy by means of violence (p. 527)

L

laissez faire idea that government should play as small a role as possible in economic affairs (p. 303)

Lancaster Turnpike road built in the 1790s by a private company, linking Philadelphia and Lancaster, Pennsylvania (p. 339)

Land Ordinance of 1785 law setting up a system for settling the Northwest Territory (p. 203)

latitude distance north or south from the equator (p. 4)

lawsuit legal case brought to settle a dispute between a person or group (p. 471)

League of Nations association of nations formed after World War I under Wilson's Fourteen Points plan (p. 705)

League of the Iroquois alliance of the five Iroquois nations (p. 48)

League of Women Voters organization established in 1920 to promote rights for women (p. 725)

legislative branch branch of government that passes laws (p. 208)

legislature group of people who have the power to make laws (p. 122)

Lend-Lease Act during World War II, the law that allowed the United States to sell arms and equipment to Britain (p. 781)

libel act of publishing a statement that may unjustly damage a person's reputation (p. 130)

The Liberator most influential antislavery newspaper; begun by William Lloyd Garrison in 1831 (p. 440)

liberty freedom (p. 249)

Liberty Bonds bonds sold by the United States government to raise money for World War I (p. 695)

limited government a principle of the United States Constitution that states that government has only the powers that the Constitution gives it (p. 250)

literacy test examination to see if a person can read and write; used in the past to restrict voting rights (p. 532)

local color speech and habits of a particular region (p. 620)

local government government on the county, parish, city, town, village, or district level (p. 263)

locomotive engine that pulls a railroad train (p. 409)

lode rich vein of gold, silver, or other valuable ore (p. 547)

Lone Star Republic nickname for Texas after it won independence from Mexico in 1836 (p. 389)

longitude distance east or west from the Prime Meridian (p. 4)

Louisiana Purchase vast territory between the Mississippi River and Rocky Mountains, purchased from France in 1803 (p. 308)

Lowell girl young woman who worked in the Lowell Mills in Massachusetts during the Industrial Revolution (p. 333)

Loyalist colonist who remained loyal to Britain (p. 170)

Lusitania British passenger ship that was torpedoed by a German U-boat in 1915; 1,200 people died, including 128 Americans (p. 690)

lynch for a mob to illegally seize and execute someone (pp. 401, 649)

M

Magna Carta signed in 1215, a British document that contained two basic ideas: monarchs themselves have to obey the laws, and citizens have basic rights (pp. 90, 213)

mainstreaming placing children with special needs in regular classes (p. 896)

majority more than half (p. 362)

Manifest Destiny 1800s belief that Americans had the right to spread across the continent (p. 393)

manor district ruled by a lord, including the lord's castle and the lands around it (p. 58)

map projection way of drawing Earth on a flat surface (p. 8)

Marbury* v. *Madison an 1803 court case in which the Supreme Court ruled that it had the power to decide whether laws passed by Congress were constitutional (p. 305)

Marshall Plan American plan to help European nations rebuild their economies after World War II (p. 812)

martial law rule by the army instead of the elected government (pp. 487, 834)

martyr person who dies for his or her beliefs (p. 476)

Mason-Dixon Line boundary between Pennsylvania and Maryland that divided the Middle Colonies from the Southern Colonies (p. 113)

mass production process of making large quantities of a product quickly and cheaply (p. 588)

Mayflower Compact a 1620 agreement for ruling the Plymouth Colony (p. 95)

McCulloch* v. *Maryland an 1819 case in which the Supreme Court ruled that states had no right to interfere with federal institutions within their borders (p. 346)

mediator agent who helps conflicting parties iron out their differences (p. 879)

mercantilism theory that a nation's economic strength came from keeping a strict control over its colonial trade (p. 120)

mercenary soldier who fights merely for pay, often for a foreign country (p. 171)

merit ability (p. 631)

mestizo in Spain's American colonies, person of mixed Spanish and Indian background (p. 78)

Mexican Cession Mexican territories of California and New Mexico given to the United States in 1848 (p. 396)

middle class in the 13 English colonies, a class that included skilled craftworkers, farmers, and some tradespeople (p. 126)

migrant worker person who moves from one region to another in search of work (pp. 766, 865)

militarism the policy of building up strong armed forces to prepare for war (p. 687)

militia army of citizens who serve as soldiers during an emergency (p. 158)

minuteman colonial militia volunteer who was prepared to fight at a minute's notice (p. 159)

mission religious settlement run by Catholic priests and friars (p. 78)

missionary person who tries to spread certain religious beliefs among a group of people (pp. 56, 84)

Missouri Compromise agreement, proposed in 1819 by Henry Clay, to keep the number of slave and free states equal (p. 460)

Monitor ironclad Union warship (p. 492)

monopoly a company or group having control of all or nearly all of the business of an industry (p. 581)

Monroe Doctrine President Monroe's foreign policy statement warning European nations not to interfere in Latin America (p. 351)

moral diplomacy President Wilson's policy of condemning imperialism, spreading democracy, and promoting peace (p. 679)

Moral Majority religious organization that backed conservative political causes in the 1980s (p. 873)

Mormons members of the Church of Jesus Christ of Latter-Day Saints founded by Joseph Smith in 1830 (p. 398)

Mound Builders the name for various North American cultures that built large earth mounds beginning about 3,000 years ago (p. 41)

mountain man trapper who explored and hunted in Oregon Territory in the early 1800s (p. 381)

moving assembly line method of production in which workers stay in one place as products edge along a moving belt (p. 588)

muckraker journalist who exposed corruption and other problems of the late 1800s and early 1900s (p. 634)

mudslinging the use of insults to attack an opponent's reputation (p. 374)

Munich Conference a 1938 meeting of the leaders of Britain, France, Italy, and Germany at which an agreement was signed giving part of Czechoslovakia to Hitler (p. 779)

mutualista Mexican American mutual aid group (p. 651)

N

NAACP (National Association for the Advancement of Colored People) organization founded in 1909 to work toward equal rights for African Americans (p. 650)

National Aeronautics and Space Administration (NASA) government agency that directs the American space program (p. 825)

national debt total sum of money that a government owes to others (pp. 280, 763)

National Labor Relations Act law passed in 1935 that protects American workers from unfair management practices (p. 761)

national park area set aside by the federal government for people to visit (p. 641)

National Recovery Administration government agency set up during the Great Depression to enforce new codes designed to stabilize industry (p. 755)

National Road first federally funded national road project, begun in 1811 (p. 339)

National Woman Suffrage Association group set up in 1869 to work for a constitutional amendment to give women the right to vote (p. 645)

nationalism excessive pride in one's nation (pp. 318, 686)

nativism antiforeign belief opposed to immigration (p. 738)

natural resources materials that humans can take from the environment to survive and satisfy their needs (p. 5)

natural rights rights that belong to all people from birth (p. 175)

naturalize to complete the official process for becoming a citizen (p. 265)

Nauvoo Mormon community built on the banks of the Mississippi River in Illinois in the 1840s (p. 398)

Navajo code-talkers during World War II, Navajo soldiers who used their own language to radio vital messages during the island-hopping campaign (p. 796)

Navigation Acts series of English laws in the 1650s that regulated trade between England and its colonies (p. 121)

Nazi member of the National Socialist German Workers' Party (p. 775)

Nazi-Soviet Pact agreement signed between Hitler and Stalin in 1939 in which the two dictators agreed not to attack each other (p. 779)

Negro Fort settlement of fugitive African American slaves in the Spanish colony of Florida (p. 350)

network system of connected railroad lines (p. 575)

neutral not taking sides in a conflict (p. 285)

Neutrality Acts series of laws passed by Congress in 1935 that banned arms sales or loans to countries at war (p. 777)

Neutrality Proclamation a 1793 statement by President Washington that the United States would not support or aid either France or Britain in their European conflict (p. 285)

New Deal program of President Franklin D. Roosevelt to end the Great Depression (p. 754)

New Freedom President Wilson's program to break up trusts and restore American economic competition (p. 643)

New Jersey Plan plan at the Constitutional Convention, favored by smaller states, that called for three branches of government with a single-chamber legislature (p. 208)

New Mexico Territory huge region in the Southwest owned by Mexico in the 1800s (p. 391)

"New South" term to describe the South in the late 1800s when efforts were made to expand the economy by building up industry (p. 533)

Nineteenth Amendment a 1919 amendment to the United States Constitution that gives women the right to vote (pp. 261, 646)

nominating convention meeting at which a political party chooses a candidate (p. 364)

Nonintercourse Act an 1809 law that allowed Americans to carry on trade with all nations except Britain and France (p. 314)

North American Free Trade Agreement (NAFTA) treaty among the United States, Canada, and Mexico to gradually remove tariffs and other trade barriers (p. 889)

North Atlantic Treaty Organization (NATO) alliance formed in 1949 by the United States and Western European nations to fight Soviet aggression (p. 813)

Northwest Ordinance a 1787 law that set up a government for the Northwest Territory (p. 203)

northwest passage a waterway through or around North America (p. 81)

nullification idea that a state has the right to nullify, or cancel, a federal law that the state leaders consider to be unconstitutional (p. 371)

Nullification Act act passed by South Carolina that declared the 1832 tariff illegal (p. 371)

Nuremberg Trials Nazi war crimes trials held in 1945 and 1946 (p. 799)

O

Olive Branch Petition peace petition sent to King George by colonial delegates after the battles of Lexington and Concord (p. 168)

on margin practice that allows people to buy stock with a down payment of a portion of the full value (p. 747)

OPEC (Organization of Petroleum Exporting Countries) multinational organization that sets a common policy for the sale of petroleum (p. 884)

Open Door Policy policy issued by Secretary of State John Hay in 1899 that allowed a nation to trade in any other nation's sphere of influence in China (p. 666)

Operation Overlord code name for the Allied invasion of Europe in 1944 (p. 792)

Oregon Country term used in the early 1800s for the region that includes present-day Oregon, Washington, Idaho, and parts of Wyoming, Montana, and Canada (p. 380)

Oregon Trail route to Oregon used by wagon trains in the 1800s (p. 383)

Organization of American States (OAS) international organization that promotes peace and economic progress in the Americas (p. 824)

override to overrule, as when Congress overrules a presidential veto (p. 257)

P

pacifist person who objects to any war; believes war is evil (p. 696)

Palestine Liberation Organization (PLO) Palestinian-Arab organization founded in 1964 to destroy Israel, mainly through the use of armed force (p. 884)

Parliament representative assembly in England (p. 90)

parochial church-sponsored; often used to refer to church-sponsored schools (p. 617)

patent license for a new invention (p. 584)

Patriot colonist who favored war against Britain (p. 169)

patriotism feeling of love and devotion toward one's country (p. 266)

patronage the practice of awarding government jobs to political supporters (p. 631)

patroon owner of a large estate in a Dutch colony (p. 109)

Peace Corps government organization that sends American volunteers to developing countries to teach or give technical advice (p. 824)

peninsulare person from Spain who held a position of power in a Spanish colony (p. 78)

Pennsylvania Dutch German-speaking Protestants who settled in Pennsylvania (p. 110)

pension sum of money paid to people on a regular basis after they retire (p. 760)

perjury to lie under oath (p. 820)

persecution mistreatment or punishment of a group of people because of their beliefs (p. 94)

Persian Gulf War a 1991 war in which the United States and its UN allies drove invading Iraqi forces out of neighboring Kuwait (p. 885)

petition formal written request to someone in authority that is signed by a group of people (p. 149)

Pickett's Charge failed Confederate charge at the Battle of Gettysburg (p. 506)

Pilgrims in the 1600s, English settlers who sought religious freedom in the Americas (p. 93)

Pinckney Treaty a 1795 agreement with Spain that let Americans ship their goods down the Mississippi River and store them in New Orleans (p. 306)

pit house house in the Arctic region dug into the ground and covered with wood and skins (p. 43)

Plains of Abraham a field near Quebec; site of a major British victory over the French in the French and Indian War (p. 144)

plantation large estate farmed by many workers (p. 80)

Platt Amendment amendment to the 1902 Cuban constitution that allowed the United States to intervene in Cuba (p. 673)

Plessy* v. *Ferguson an 1896 court case in which the Supreme Court ruled that segregation in public facilities was legal as long as the facilities were equal (p. 532)

pogrom in Eastern Europe, an organized attack on a Jewish community (p. 600)

polio highly infectious disease that causes inflammation of the nerve cells of the brain stem and spinal cord, leading to paralysis (p. 752)

political boss powerful politician who controls work done locally and demands payoffs from businesses (p. 633)

political science the study of government (p. 29)

poll tax tax required before a person can vote (p. 532)

Pontiac's War a 1763 conflict between Native Americans and the British over settlement of Indian lands in the Great Lakes area (p. 147)

pool system in which several railroad companies agreed to divide up the business in an area (p. 576)

popular sovereignty in the mid-1800s, a term referring to the idea that each territory could decide for itself whether or not to allow slavery (pp. 250, 462)

potlatch ceremonial dinner held by some Native Americans of the Northwest Coast to show off their wealth (p. 44)

Potsdam Declaration message sent by the Allies in July 1945 calling for Japanese surrender (p. 798)

preamble introduction to a declaration, constitution, or other official document (pp. 175, 248)

precedent act or decision that sets an example for others to follow (pp. 96, 278)

precipitation water that falls in the form of rain, sleet, hail, or snow (p. 15)

predestination Protestant idea that God decided in advance which people would attain salvation after death (p. 435)

presidio fort where soldiers lived in the Spanish colonies (p. 77)

primary election in which voters choose their party's candidate for the general election (p. 635)

primary source firsthand information about people or events (p. 20)

Proclamation of 1763 law forbidding English colonists to settle west of the Appalachian Mountains (p. 147)

productivity average output per worker (p. 845)

profiteer person who takes advantage of a crisis to make money (p. 503)

Progressive reformer in the late 1800s and early 1900s who wanted to improve American life (p. 634)

Prohibition ban on the manufacture, sale, and transportation of liquor anywhere in the United States from 1920 to 1933 (p. 724)

propaganda spreading of ideas to help a cause or hurt an opposing cause (p. 689)

proprietary colony English colony in which the king gave land to proprietors in exchange for a yearly payment (p. 109)

protectorate nation whose independence is limited by the control of a more powerful country (p. 673)

Protestant Reformation movement to reform the Roman Catholic Church in the 1500s; led to the creation of many different Christian churches (p. 83)

psychology the study of how people think and behave (p. 30)

public interest the good of the people (p. 634)

public school school supported by taxes (p. 128)

public works projects built by the government for public use (p. 750)

pueblo a town in the Spanish colonies; Anasazi village (pp. 41, 77)

pull factor condition that attracts people to move to a new area (p. 600)

Pure Food and Drug Act a 1906 law that requires food and drug makers to list ingredients on packages (p. 641)

Puritans group of English Protestants who settled the Massachusetts Bay Colony (p. 102)

push factor condition that drives people from their homeland (p. 600)

Q

Quakers Protestant reformers who believe in the equality of all people (p. 110)

Quebec Act law that set up a government for Canada and protected the rights of French Catholics (p. 158)

quipu device made of cord or string with knots that stood for quantities; used by the Incas to keep accounts and records (p. 40)

quota system system that limited immigration by allowing only a certain number of people from each country to immigrate to the United States (p. 738)

Quran sacred book of Islam (p. 51)

R

racism belief that one race is superior to another (pp. 119, 662)

radical person who wants to make drastic changes in society (p. 173)

Radical Reconstruction period beginning in 1867, when the Republicans, who had control in both houses of Congress, took charge of Reconstruction (p. 523)

Radical Republican member of Congress during Reconstruction who wanted to ensure that freedmen received the right to vote (p. 522)

ragtime popular music of the late 1800s that had a lively, rhythmic sound (p. 615)

ratify to approve (p. 194)

rationing limitations on the amount of certain goods that people can buy (p. 785)

Reaganomics President Reagan's economic program that cut taxes, cut federal spending on social programs, and increased military spending (p. 873)

realist writer or artist who shows life as it really is (p. 620)

rebate discount (p. 576)

recall process by which voters can remove an elected official from office (p. 636)

recession economic slump that is milder than a depression (pp. 718, 874)

reconcentration policy of moving large numbers of people into camps for political or military purposes (p. 669)

Reconstruction rebuilding of the South after the Civil War (p. 517)

Reconstruction Act an 1867 law that threw out the southern state governments that had refused to ratify the Fourteenth Amendment (p. 523)

referendum process by which people vote directly on a bill (p. 636)

refuge place where one is safe from persecution (p. 399)

refugee person who flees his or her homeland to seek safety elsewhere (p. 895)

relief program government program to help the needy (p. 750)

religious tolerance willingness to let others practice their own beliefs (p. 104)

Renaissance burst of learning in Europe from the late 1300s to about 1600 (p. 59)

rendezvous yearly meeting where mountain men traded furs (p. 382)

renewable resource resource that can be quickly replaced by nature (p. 890)

reparations cash payments made by a defeated nation to a victorious nation to pay for losses suffered during a war (p. 706)

repeal to cancel (pp. 150, 725)

representative government political system in which voters elect representatives to make laws for them (p. 90)

republic system of government in which citizens choose representatives to govern them (pp. 57, 211)

Republic of Great Colombia independent state composed of the present-day nations of Venezuela, Colombia, Ecuador, and Panama; established in 1819 (p. 349)

Republican party political party established in the United States in 1854 with the goal of keeping slavery out of the western territories (p. 473)

reservation limited area set aside for Native Americans (p. 558)

resident alien noncitizen living in the country (p. 266)

revival large outdoor religious meeting (p. 435)

Roosevelt Corollary statement by Theodore Roosevelt that the United States had a right to intervene in Latin America to preserve law and order (p. 678)

Rosie the Riveter fictional factory worker who became a symbol of working women during World War II (p. 785)

Rough Riders military unit organized by Theodore Roosevelt during the Spanish-American War (p. 672)

royal colony colony under the direct control of the English crown (p. 109)

rugged individualist person who follows his or her own independent course in life (p. 381)

S

Sabbath holy day of rest (p. 106)

sabotage secret destruction of property or interference with production in a factory or other workplace (p. 737)

sachem member of the tribal chief council in the League of the Iroquois (p. 48)

SALT Agreement (Strategic Arms Limitation Talks) treaty between the United States and the Soviet Union to limit the number of nuclear warheads and missiles (p. 833)

salvation everlasting life (p. 56)

Salvation Army an international charitable organization (p. 609)

sanctions measures designed to make a country change its policy (p. 880)

Santa Fe Trail route to Santa Fe, New Mexico, that was used by traders in the 1800s (p. 392)

satellite nation nation that is dominated politically and economically by a more powerful nation (p. 811)

savanna region of grasslands (p. 52)

scalawag white southerner who supported the Republicans during Reconstruction (p. 526)

scapegoat person or group who is made to bear the blame for others (p. 775)

secede to withdraw from membership in a group (p. 463)

Second Amendment amendment to the United States Constitution related to the right to bear arms (p. 260)

Second Great Awakening widespread religious movement in the United States in the early 1800s (p. 435)

secondary source account provided after the fact by people who did not directly witness or participate in the event (p. 21)

sectionalism loyalty to a state or section rather than to the whole country (p. 345)

sedition stirring up rebellion against a government (p. 293)

segregation legal separation of people based on racial, ethnic, or other differences (pp. 532, 849)

Selective Service Act law passed by Congress in 1917 that required all men from ages 21 to 30 to register for the military draft (p. 693)

self-determination right of national groups to have their own territory and forms of government (p. 705)

self-sufficient able to produce enough for one's own needs (p. 392)

Seminole War conflict that began in Florida in 1817 when the Seminoles resisted removal (p. 373)

Senate the smaller of the two bodies that make up the legislative branch of the United States government (p. 253)

Seneca Falls Convention an 1848 meeting at which leaders of the women's rights movement called for equal rights for women (p. 445)

separation of powers principle by which the powers of government are divided among separate branches (p. 214)

settlement house community center organized in the late 1800s to offer services to the poor (p. 609)

sharecropper person who rents a plot of land from another person and farms it in exchange for a share of the crop (p. 529)

Shays' Rebellion a 1786 revolt in Massachusetts led by farmers in reaction to high taxes (p. 204)

Sherman Antitrust Act an 1890 law that banned the formation of trusts and monopolies in the United States (pp. 582, 632)

siege military blockade or bombardment of an enemy town or position in order to force it to surrender (pp. 193, 387, 506)

silent majority term for Americans who were disturbed by unrest in the 1960s but did not protest publicly (p. 860)

Silk Road overland trade routes linking China to the Middle East (p. 52)

sit-down strike strike in which workers refuse to leave the workplace until a settlement is reached (p. 762)

sit-in form of protest in which people sit and refuse to leave (p. 862)

skyscraper tall building with many floors supported by a lightweight steel frame (p. 612)

slave code laws that controlled the lives of enslaved African Americans and denied them basic rights (pp. 119, 424)

smuggling importing or exporting goods in violation of trade laws (p. 314)

Social Gospel movement within American Protestantism in the late 1800s that attempted to apply biblical teachings to society's problems (p. 609)

social reform an organized attempt to improve what is unjust or imperfect in society (p. 434)

social sciences studies that relate to human society and social behavior (p. 29)

Social Security Act a 1935 law that set up a system of pensions for older people and set up the nation's first system of unemployment insurance (p. 762)

Socialist person who supports community ownership of property and the sharing of all profits (p. 696)

Society of American Indians group that worked for social justice and tried to push Native Americans into the American mainstream (p. 653)

sociology the study of how people behave in groups (p. 30)

sod house house built of soil held together by grass roots (p. 564)

sodbuster farmer on the Great Plains in the late 1800s (p. 564)

Solidarity independent labor union that challenged Poland's communist government (p. 834)

soup kitchen place where food is provided to the needy at little or no charge (p. 750)

Spanish-American War war between Spain and the United States in 1898 (p. 671)

speculator someone who invests in a risky venture in the hope of making a large profit (p. 280)

sphere of influence area where a nation had special trading privileges (p. 666)

spinning jenny machine developed in 1764 that could spin several threads at once (p. 331)

spoils system practice of rewarding supporters with government jobs (p. 366)

Square Deal Theodore Roosevelt's campaign promise that all groups would have an equal opportunity to succeed (p. 640)

stagflation combination of rising prices, high unemployment, and slow economic growth (p. 860)

stalemate deadlock in which neither side is strong enough to defeat the other (p. 688)

Stamp Act a 1765 law that placed new duties on legal documents, and taxed newspapers, almanacs, playing cards, and dice (p. 149)

standard of living index based on the amount of goods, services, and leisure time people have (p. 845)

Star Wars President Reagan's proposed weapons system to destroy Soviet missiles from space (p. 834)

states' rights the right of states to limit the power of the federal government (pp. 293, 370)

Statue of Liberty a large statue symbolizing hope and freedom on Liberty Island in New York Harbor (p. 602)

steerage on a ship, the cramped quarters for passengers paying the lowest fares (p. 601)

stock share of ownership in a corporation (pp. 580, 720)

Strategic Arms Reduction Treaty (START) a 1991 treaty signed by the United States and Soviet Union to reduce nuclear weapons (p. 882)

strike refusal by workers to do their jobs until their demands are met (p. 414)

strikebreaker replacement for a striking worker (p. 591)

subsidy financial aid or land grant from the government (p. 550)

suburb residential area on the outskirts of a city (pp. 613, 728, 845)

suffrage the right to vote (p. 361)

suffragist person who worked for women's right to vote (p. 646)

summit meeting conference between the highest-ranking officials of different nations (p. 835)

superpower nation with the military, political, and economic strength to influence events worldwide (p. 823)

Supreme Court highest court in the United States established by the Constitution (p. 256)

surplus extra; condition that exists when income exceeds spending (pp. 37, 876)

Sutter's Mill location where gold was discovered in California in 1848, setting off the gold rush (p. 400)

Swahili language that blends Arab words and local African languages spoken widely in East Africa (p. 52)

sweatshop workplace where people labor long hours in poor conditions for low pay (p. 591)

T

tariff tax on foreign goods brought into a country (p. 281)

Tariff of Abominations tariff passed by Congress in 1828 that favored manufacturing in the North (p. 370)

Tea Act a 1773 law that let the British East India Company bypass tea merchants and sell directly to colonists (p. 156)

Teapot Dome Scandal, political scandal during President Harding's administration (p. 719)

Tejano person of Mexican descent born in Texas (p. 386)

telegraph communications device that sends electrical signals along a wire (p. 409)

temperance movement campaign against alcohol consumption (p. 436)

Ten Percent Plan Lincoln's plan that allowed a southern state to form a new government after 10 percent of its voters swore an oath of loyalty to the United States (p. 517)

tenement small apartment in a city slum building (p. 607)

Tennessee Valley Authority New Deal program that built dams to control flooding and produce cheap electric power (p. 756)

tepee tent made by stretching buffalo skins on tall poles (p. 545)

terrace wide shelf of land cut into a hillside (p. 40)

terrorism deliberate use of violence to spread fear and achieve political goals (pp. 688, 886)

Tet Offensive North Vietnamese and Vietcong surprise attack on American forces in Vietnam on the Vietnamese New Year's holiday in 1968 (p. 829)

Thanksgiving day at the end of the harvest season set aside by the Pilgrims to give thanks to God (p. 97)

thematic map map that deals with a specific topic, such as population, natural resources, or elections (p. 9)

Thirteenth Amendment an 1865 amendment to the United States Constitution that bans slavery throughout the nation (p. 519)

38th parallel dividing line between South Korea and North Korea (p. 816)

Three-Fifths Compromise agreement at the Constitutional Convention that three fifths of the slaves in any state be counted in its population (p. 209)

total war all-out war that affects civilians at home as well as soldiers in combat (p. 508)

totalitarian state country where a single party controls the government and every aspect of people's lives (p. 774)

town meeting meeting in colonial New England where settlers discussed and voted on issues (p. 107)

Townshend Acts laws passed in 1767 that taxed goods such as glass, paper, paint, lead, and tea (p. 150)

trade deficit condition that exists when a nation buys more goods and services from foreign countries than it sells to them (p. 889)

trade union association of trade workers formed to gain higher wages and better working conditions (pp. 414, 592)

Trail of Tears forced journey of the Cherokee Indians from Georgia to a region west of the Mississippi during which thousands of Cherokees died (p. 372)

traitor person who betrays his or her country (p. 175)

transatlantic crossing or spanning the Atlantic Ocean (p. 585)

transcendentalists New England writers and thinkers who believed that the most important truths in life transcended, or went beyond, human reason (p. 450)

transcontinental railroad railroad that stretches across a continent from coast to coast (p. 549)

travois sled pulled by a dog or horse (p. 545)

treason actions against one's country (p. 476)

Treaty of Brest-Litovsk a 1918 treaty between Russia and Germany that ended Russia's involvement in World War I (p. 699)

Treaty of Ghent peace treaty signed by Britain and the United States at the end of the War of 1812 (p. 325)

Treaty of Greenville treaty signed by some Native Americans in 1795, giving up land that would later become part of Ohio (p. 317)

Treaty of Guadalupe-Hidalgo an 1848 treaty in which Mexico gave up California and New Mexico to the United States for $15 million (p. 396)

Treaty of Kanagawa an 1854 treaty between Japan and the United States that opened up ports to American trade in Japan (p. 661)

Treaty of Paris a 1763 agreement between Britain and France that ended the French and Indian War (p. 145); peace treaty between the United States and Britain, ratified in 1783, that recognized the United States as an independent nation (p. 194)

Treaty of Versailles treaty signed on June 28, 1919, by Germany and the Allies; formally placed the responsibility for the war on Germany and its allies (p. 706)

Triangle Fire fire in 1911 at the Triangle Shirtwaist Factory in New York City that killed nearly 150 workers (p. 593)

triangular trade colonial trade route between New England, the West Indies, and Africa (p. 121)

tribe community of people that share common customs, language, and rituals (p. 42)

tributary stream or smaller river that flows into a larger one (p. 15)

tribute bribe (p. 313)

Truman Doctrine President Truman's policy of giving U.S. aid to nations threatened by communist expansion (p. 811)

trust group of corporations run by a single board of directors (p. 581)

trustbuster person who wanted to destroy all trusts (p. 640)

turning point moment in history that marks a decisive change (p. 70)

turnpike road built by a private company that charges a toll to use it (p. 339)

Tuskegee Airmen African American fighter pilots who trained in Tuskegee, Alabama, during World War II (p. 787)

tutor private teacher (p. 128)

Twenty-sixth Amendment amendment to the United States Constitution that lowered the minimum voting age from 21 to 18 (p. 261)

U

U-boat German submarine used in World War I and World War II (p. 690)

unamendable unable to change (p. 479)

Uncle Tom's Cabin an 1852 novel by Harriet Beecher Stowe written to show the evils of slavery and the injustice of the Fugitive Slave Act (p. 466)

unconstitutional not permitted by the Constitution (pp. 257, 288)

Underground Railroad network of abolitionists who secretly helped slaves escape to freedom (p. 441)

United Nations world organization established in 1945 to provide peaceful resolutions to international conflicts (p. 813)

United Provinces of Central America federation established in 1823, containing the present-day nations of Guatemala, El Salvador, Honduras, Nicaragua, and Costa Rica (p. 349)

urbanization movement of population from farms to cities (pp. 335, 606)

V

Valley Forge Pennsylvania site of Washington's Continental Army encampment during the winter of 1777–1778 (p. 185)

vaquero Spanish or Mexican cowhand (pp. 392, 553)

vaudeville variety show made popular in the late 1800s that included comedians, song-and-dance routines, and acrobats (p. 615)

vertical integration practice in which a single manufacturer controls all of the steps used to change raw materials into finished products (p. 579)

veto to reject, as when the President rejects a law passed by Congress (p. 257)

victory garden during World War II, vegetable garden planted to combat food shortages in the United States (p. 785)

Vietcong Vietnamese guerrillas who opposed the noncommunist government of South Vietnam (p. 828)

vigilante self-appointed enforcer of the law (pp. 401, 549)

Virginia ironclad warship used by the Confederates to break the Union blockade (p. 492)

Virginia Plan plan at the Constitutional Convention that called for a strong national government with three branches and a two-chamber legislature (p. 208)

W

Wade-Davis Bill an 1864 plan for Reconstruction that denied the right to vote or hold office to anyone who had volunteered to fight for the Confederacy (p. 517)

War Hawks members of Congress from the South and the West who called for war with Britain prior to the War of 1812 (p. 318)

War Production Board government agency created during World War II to help factories shift from making consumer goods to making war materials (p. 785)

warmonger person who tries to stir up war (p. 691)

Warsaw Pact military alliance, established in 1955, of the Soviet Union and other communist states in Europe (p. 813)

WCTU (Women's Christian Temperance Union) group organized in 1874 that worked to ban the sale of liquor in the United States (p. 648)

weather condition of the earth's atmosphere at a given time and place (p. 15)

Whigs members of John Quincy Adams's former National Republican party (p. 363)

Whiskey Rebellion a 1794 protest over a tax on all liquor made and sold in the United States (p. 282)

wholesale buying or selling something in large quantities at lower prices (p. 565)

Wilmot Proviso law passed in 1846 that banned slavery in any territories won by the United States from Mexico (p. 461)

Wisconsin Idea series of Progressive reforms introduced in the early 1900s by Wisconsin governor Robert La Follette (p. 635)

women's rights movement organized campaign to win property, education, and other rights for women (p. 446)

writ of assistance legal document that allowed British customs officials to inspect a ship's cargo without giving a reason (p. 150)

X

XYZ Affair a 1797 French attempt to bribe the United States by demanding money before discussing French seizure of neutral American ships (p. 292)

Y

Yankee nickname for New England merchants who dominated colonial trade (p. 121)

yellow journalism news reporting, often biased or untrue, that relies on sensational stories and headlines (pp. 619, 670)

Young Men's Hebrew Association (YMHA) organization founded in Baltimore in 1854 to provide community services to Jewish neighborhoods (p. 609)

Z

Zimmermann telegram a 1917 telegram sent from Germany's foreign secretary to the German minister in Mexico instructing the minister to urge Mexico to attack the United States if the United States declared war on Germany (p. 692)

Spanish Glossary

A

abdicate/abdicar entregar el poder (pág. 701)

abolitionist/abolicionista persona que quería acabar la esclavitud (pág. 440)

acculturation/aculturación proceso por el cual se mantienen viejas tradiciones mientras se va adoptando otra cultura (pág. 604)

Act of Toleration/Acta de Tolerancia ley aprobada por la asamblea de Maryland en 1649 que aseguraba la libertad religiosa para todos los cristianos (pág. 114)

Adams-Onís Treaty/Tratado de Adams-Onís tratado de 1821 entre España y Estados Unidos según el cual España se comprometía a entregar Florida a Estados Unidos (pág. 350)

adobe/adobe ladrillo secado al sol (pág. 41)

affirmative action/acción afirmativa programa que proporciona más oportunidades de trabajo y educación a personas que sufrieron discriminación en el pasado (pág. 864)

AFL/*AFL* (Federación Americana de Trabajadores) organización de sindicatos que representaba a trabajadores cualificados (pág. 592)

aggression/agresión acto similar a un acto de guerra de un país contra otro sin que haya una causa justa (pág. 775)

Alamo/Álamo vieja misión española situada en Texas donde las fuerzas mexicanas bajo las órdenes de Santa Anna asediaron a los texanos en 1836 (pág. 387)

Albany Plan of Union/Plan de Unión de Albany propuesta de Benjamin Franklin que consistía en crear un solo gobierno para las 13 colonias (pág. 143)

Alien and Sedition acts/Actas de Extranjería y de Sedición leyes apoyadas por los federalistas que permitían que el presidente expulsara a extranjeros o dificultara que obtuvieran la ciudadanía, y multara o encarcelara a ciudadanos por criticar al gobierno (pág. 293)

alliance/alianza acuerdo entre naciones para ayudarse y protegerse mutuamente (pág. 85)

Alliance for Progress/Alianza para el Progreso programa que desarrolló el presidente Kennedy para promover reformas sociales en América Latina (pág. 824)

Allied Powers/potencias aliadas alianza militar entre Francia, Inglaterra, Rusia, Italia y 20 otras naciones durante la Primera Guerra Mundial (pág. 688)

Allies/aliados alianza militar entre Inglaterra, Francia, la Unión Soviética, Estados Unidos, China y otros 45 países (pág. 779)

ally/aliado nación que trabaja con otra nación hacia una meta común (pág. 183)

altitude/altura elevación sobre el nivel del mar (pág. 15)

amend/reformar cambiar (pág. 218)

American Association of Retired Persons/Asociación Americana de Personas Jubiladas (AARP) organización que lleva a cabo el seguimiento y control de los asuntos de interés para personas de edad más avanzada (pág. 897)

American Colonization Society/Sociedad de Colonización Americana organización de principios del siglo XIX que proponía ayudar a los afroamericanos a que se mudaran a África (pág. 440)

American Indian Religious Freedom Act/Ley de Libertad Religiosa de los Indígenas Estadounidenses ley de 1978 que obligó a las agencias federales a no obstaculizar las prácticas religiosas de los indígenas (pág. 896)

American System/sistema estadounidense programa para fomentar el crecimiento económico, promovido por Henry Clay a principios del siglo XIX; proponía imponer altas tasas a las importaciones (pág. 345)

Americans With Disabilities Act/Ley de los Estadounidenses Discapacitados ley de 1990 que prohibe la discriminación al contratar a personas con dificultades físicas o mentales (pág. 897)

amnesty/amnistía perdón del gobierno (pág. 517)

anarchist/anarquista persona que se opone a todas las formas de gobierno organizado (págs. 592, 737)

annex/anexar agregar; incorporar un territorio (págs. 389, 661)

anthropology/antropología estudio de cómo se desarrollan las personas y las culturas (pág. 30)

Antifederalists/antifederalistas personas que se oponían a la constitución y a un gobierno nacional fuerte (pág. 215)

apartheid/apartheid separación estricta de las razas practicada anteriormente en Sudáfrica (pág. 880)

appeal/apelar pedir a una corte de mayor autoridad que reconsidere una decisión (pág. 256)

appeasement/apaciguamiento aceptación de agresiones para evitar una guerra (pág. 779)

Appomattox Court House/Appomattox Court House ciudad de Virginia en donde la Confederación se rindió en 1865 (pág. 509)

apprentice/aprendiz persona que aprende un oficio o artesanía de un maestro (pág.128)

archaeology/arqueología estudio de las evidencias dejadas por culturas antiguas con el objeto de conocer su forma de vida (pág. 22)

armistice/armisticio acuerdo para detener el combate (pág. 701)

arsenal/arsenal depósito de armas (pág. 476)

Articles/artículos parte principal de la constitución que establece la estructura del gobierno de Estados Unidos (pág. 249)

Articles of Confederation/Artículos de la Confederación primera constitución de Estados Unidos; aprobada en 1777, creó una alianza tenue entre los 13 estados independientes (pág. 201)

artifact/artefacto objeto hecho por seres humanos (pág. 22)

artisan/artesano trabajador manual cualificado (pág. 413)

assembly line/cadena de montaje método de producción según el cual los trabajadores permanecen en un lugar fijo mientras los productos pasan frente a ellos sobre una cinta transportadora (pág. 588)

astrolabe/astrolabio instrumento de navegación que se usa para determinar la latitud (pág. 59)

Atlantic Charter/Cédula del Atlántico programa creado por Estados Unidos e Inglaterra en 1941, que estableció objetivos para el mundo en la posguerra (pág. 782)

atrocity/atrocidad acto de crueldad y brutalidad (pág. 670)

authenticity/autenticidad condición de ser genuino (pág. 21)

Axis/eje alianza militar durante la Segunda Guerra Mundial entre Alemania, Italia, Japón y otras seis naciones (pág. 779)

B

baby boom/*baby boom* gran incremento de la tasa de natalidad en Estados Unidos desde finales de la década de1940 hasta principios de la década de 1960 (pág. 844)

Bacon's Rebellion/rebelión de Bacon revuelta liderada en 1676 por Nathaniel Bacon en contra del gobernador y de los indígenas de Virginia (pág. 114)

balanced budget/presupuesto equilibrado condición que se da cuando el gobierno sólo gasta la cantidad que recibe (pág. 874)

bank holiday/feriado bancario cierre de los bancos por cuatro días durante la Gran Depresión (pág. 753)

Bank of the United States/Banco de Estados Unidos banco establecido en 1791 para retener los depósitos del gobierno y emitir papel moneda para el pago de las cuentas del gobierno y otorgar préstamos a granjeros y comerciantes (pág. 281)

bankrupt/en bancarrota sin capacidad para pagar las deudas (pág. 748)

barrio/barrio término que se refiere vecindarios de población mexicano-americana (pág. 651)

Bataan Death March/marcha de la muerte de Bataan viaje largo y difícil a través de Filipinas que los japoneses obligaron a realizar a prisioneros de guerra estadounidenses y filipinos en 1942 (pág. 799)

Battle of Antietam/batalla de Antietam sangrienta batalla librada en Maryland en 1862 durante la Guerra Civil (pág. 493)

Battle of Belleau Wood/batalla del bosque de Belleau difícil victoria de Estados Unidos sobre Alemania, en Francia en 1918 (pág. 700)

Battle of Britain/batalla de Inglaterra intento fracasado de Alemania de someter a Inglaterra en 1940, como preparación para una invasión (pág. 780)

Battle of Bull Run/batalla de Bull Run primera gran batalla de la Guerra Civil, librada en Virginia en 1861 (pág. 491)

Battle of Bunker Hill/batalla de Bunker Hill primera gran batalla de la Revolución; librada en 1775 (pág. 170)

Battle of Chancellorsville/batalla de Chancellorsville batalla librada en Virginia en 1863 durante la Guerra Civil; fue una victoria importante para la Confederación (pág. 493)

Battle of Cowpens/batalla de Cowpens batalla de 1781 librada en Carolina del Norte; fue una victoria importante de los colonos sobre los británicos (pág. 192)

Battle of Fredericksburg/batalla de Fredericksburg batalla librada en Virginia en 1862 durante la Guerra Civil; fue una de las peores derrotas de la Unión (pág. 493)

Battle of Gettysburg/batalla de Gettysburg batalla librada en Pennsylvania en 1863 durante la Guerra Civil; evitó que los Confederados invadieron el Norte (pág. 506)

Battle of Lake Erie/batalla del lago Erie batalla de la guerra de 1812; las fuerzas de Estados Unidos, lideradas por Oliver Perry, vencieron a los británicos (pág. 322)

Battle of Long Island/batalla de Long Island batalla de 1776 en Nueva York en la que más de 1,400 colonos murieron, resultaron heridos o fueron capturados (pág. 181)

Battle of Midway/batalla de Midway batalla de 1942 en el Pacífico en la que aviones de Estados Unidos hundieron cuatro portaviones japoneses (pág. 792)

Battle of New Orleans/batalla de Nueva Orleáns al final de la guerra de 1812, batalla en la que las fuerzas de Estados Unidos vencieron a los británicos (pág. 324)

Battle of San Jacinto/batalla de San Jacinto batalla de 1836 entre texanos y mexicanos durante la guerra en la que Texas tretaba de independizarse de México (pág. 388)

Battle of Saratoga/batalla de Saratoga en 1777, primera victoria importante de la Revolución (pág. 183)

Battle of Shiloh/batalla de Shiloh batalla librada en 1862 en Tennessee, que terminó en una victoria de la Unión (pág. 494)

Battle of the Argonne Forest/batalla del bosque de Argonne derrota de los alemanes en Francia en octubre de 1918 por las tropas francesas y estadounidenses (pág. 701)

Battle of the Bulge/batalla de Bulge contraataque alemán en diciembre de 1944, que atrasó por un tiempo la invasión de los aliados a Alemania (pág. 793)

Battle of Tippecanoe/batalla de Tippecanoe batalla de 1811 a propósito de las colonizaciones blancas en el territorio de Indiana (pág. 318)

Battle of Trenton/batalla de Trenton batalla de 1776 librada en Nueva Jersey en la que las tropas de George Washington capturaron un campamento de Hessian (pág. 182)

Battle of Verdun/batalla de Verdún batalla prolongada de la Primera Guerra Mundial en la que murieron o fueron heridas más de un millón de personas (pág. 689)

Battle of Yorktown/batalla de Yorktown victoria de los colonos en Virginia en 1781 que obligó a los británicos a rendirse (pág. 193)

battles of Lexington and Concord/batallas de Lexington y Concord conflictos de 1775 entre colonos de Massachusetts y soldados británicos que dieron origen a la Revolución Americana (pág. 160)

Bay of Pigs invasion/invasión de la bahía de los Cochinos intento fallido de invadir Cuba en 1961 por cubanos anticastristas (pág. 823)

Bear Flag Republic/República de la Bandera del Oso sobrenombre de California después de declararse independiente de México en 1846 (pág. 396)

beatnik/*beatnik* en la década de 1950, persona que criticaba a la cultura estadounidense por su conformidad y devoción por los negocios (pág. 847)

Berlin Airlift/puente aéreo de Berlín operación de ayuda llevada a cabo por aviones estadounidenses y británicos para transportar suministros a los habitantes de Berlín occidental durante el bloqueo soviético de 1948 a 1949 (pág. 812)

Berlin Wall/muro de Berlín muro construido por el gobierno comunista de Alemania oriental en 1961 para aislar Berlín oriental de Berlín occidental (pág. 813)

Bessemer process/sistema Bessemer método inventado en la década de 1850 para producir un acero más resistente a un menor costo (pág. 578)

bias/prejuicio inclinación a favor o en contra de cierta persona, grupo o idea (pág. 22)

Big Four/los cuatro grandes los líderes de las naciones aliadas (Gran Bretaña, Estados Unidos, Francia e Italia) después de la Primera Guerra Mundial (pág. 706)

bilingual/bilingüe en dos idiomas (pág. 866)

bill/proyecto de ley ley que se propone para su aprobación (pág. 253)

bill of rights/declaración de derechos lista escrita de las libertades que el gobierno promete proteger (págs. 123, 200)

Bill of Rights/Declaración de Derechos las primeras 10 enmiendas de la Constitución de Estados Unidos (pág. 218)

Black Cabinet/Gabinete Negro líderes afroamericanos que asesoraban extraoficialmente al presidente Franklin D. Roosevelt en asuntos importantes para los afroamericanos (pág. 767)

black codes/códigos de negros leyes aprobadas por los estados del Sur después de la Guerra Civil que limitaban con severidad los derechos de los afroamericanos (pág. 521)

Black Tuesday/Martes Negro (29 de octubre de 1929) día en que calló el mercado de valores, marcando el comienzo de la Gran Depresión (pág. 747)

blitzkrieg/*blitzkrieg* palabra alemana que significa guerra relámpago, los rápidos ataques lanzados por Alemania en la Segunda Guerra Mundial (pág. 779)

blockade/bloqueo cierre de un puerto para que ni las personas ni las provisiones entren o salgan (pág. 171)

boat people/balseros después de la guerra de Vietnam, refugiados que huyeron de Vietnam en pequeñas embarcaciones (pág. 831)

bond/bono certificado que promete el pago de dinero que se ha prestado, más el interés, en una determinada fecha (pág. 280)

bonus/bono cantidad adicional de dinero (pág. 751)

Bonus Army/ejército del bono veteranos que marcharon hacia Washington en 1932 para exigir que se aprobara un proyecto de ley que proveía el pago inmediato del bono que les correspondía por la Primera Guerra Mundial (pág. 751)

bootlegger/contrabandista persona que introducía de contrabando bebidas alcohólicas en Estados Unidos durante la época de la Ley Seca (pág. 725)

Border Ruffians/rufianes de frontera bandas proesclavistas que a menudo combatían las fuerzas antiesclavistas en Kansas (pág. 470)

border state/estado de frontera estado esclavista que permaneció en la Unión durante la Guerra Civil (pág. 487)

Boston Massacre/masacre de Boston conflicto de 1770 entre colonos y tropas británicas en el que se dio muerte a cinco colonos (pág. 152)

Boston Tea Party/Fiesta del Té de Boston protesta de 1773 en la que los colonos se vistieron de indígenas y lanzaron el té de los británicos a la bahía de Boston (pág. 157)

Boxer Rebellion/rebelión de los Boxers revuelta contra Occidente y la influencia occidental en China en 1900 (pág. 666)

boycott/boicot rechazar la compra o el uso de ciertos bienes o servicios (págs. 150, 852)

bracero program/programa de braceros contratación de jornaleros mexicanos para trabajar en Estados Unidos durante la Segunda Guerra Mundial (pág. 788)

Buffalo Soldiers/soldados búfalos sobrenombre de los afroamericanos integrantes de los batallones de caballería noveno y décimo durante la guerra Hispano-Americana (pág. 672)

building code/código de construcción normas para la construcción y seguridad de los edificios (pág. 609)

bull market/mercado alcista período en el cual la compraventa de acciones aumenta y suben los precios de las acciones (pág. 720)

Bull Moose party/partido del alce republicanos progresistas que apoyaron a Theodore Roosevelt durante la elección de 1912 (pág. 642)

bureaucracy/burocracia sistema de administración del gobierno mediante departamentos dirigidos por funcionarios nombrados (pág. 694)

burgess/burgués representante del gobierno colonial de Virginia (pág. 90)

C

Cabinet/gabinete grupo de funcionarios que dirigen departamentos gubernamentales y aconsejan al presidente (pág. 279)

Camp David Accords/acuerdos de Camp David tratado de paz firmado en 1997 entre Israel y Egipto en el que Israel accedió a devolver a Egipto la península de Sinaí y Egipto accedió a reconocer a Israel (pág. 884)

capital/capital dinero con el que se inicia un negocio (pág. 331)

capitalist/capitalista persona que invierte en un negocio con el fin de obtener beneficios (pág. 331)

caravan/caravana grupo de personas que viajaban juntas por razones de seguridad (pág. 52)

carpetbagger/*carpetbagger* sobrenombre despreciativo dado a los norteños que se mudaron al Sur después de la Guerra Civil (pág. 527)

cartographer/cartógrafo persona que hace mapas (pág. 8)

cash crop/cosecha de contado cosecha vendida por dinero en el mercado (pág. 111)

cash economy/cultivo comercial economía en la que se intercambian dinero por mercancías y servicios (pág. 27)

cattle drive/arreo de ganado conducir y llevar ganado, normalmente hacia las vías del ferrocarril (pág. 553)

caucus/reunión encuentro privado, a menudo de carácter político (pág. 364)

causeway/paso elevado camino elevado hecho con tierra comprimida (pág. 38)

cavalry/caballería tropas a caballo (pág. 184)

cede/ceder entregar (págs. 202, 396)

censure/censurar condenar oficialmente (pág. 820)

Central Powers/potencias centrales alianza militar entre Alemania, el Imperio Austro-Húngaro, Bulgaria y el Imperio Otomano durante la Primera Guerra Mundial (pág. 688)

Chapultepec/Chapultepec fuerte en las afueras de Ciudad de México donde ocurrió una batalla entre Estados Unidos y México en 1847 (pág. 396)

charter/carta legal documento que da ciertos derechos a una persona o compañía (pág. 88)

Chautauqua Society/sociedad chautauqua movimiento itinerante para la educación de adultos del siglo XIX (pág. 618)

checks and balances/controlar y equilibrar principio de la Constitución de Estados Unidos que da a cada rama del gobierno el poder de vigilar las otras ramas (pág. 251)

Chinese Exclusion Act/Ley de la Exclusión China ley aprobada por el Congreso en 1882 que prohibía a los trabajadores chinos entrar a Estados Unidos (pág. 605)

chronology/cronología secuencia de sucesos a través del tiempo (pág. 25)

circumnavigate/circunnavegar viajar alrededor de la Tierra (pág. 71)

citizen/ciudadano persona que debe lealtad a una nación particular y se beneficia de la protección y de todos los derechos de dicha nación (pág. 265)

city-state/ciudad estado ciudad grande que tiene su propio gobierno y controla el campo que la rodea (pág. 52)

civic virtue/virtud cívica deseo de trabajar por el bien de una nación o comunidad aun a costa de grandes sacrificios (pág. 266)

civics/educación cívica estudio de los derechos y responsabilidades de los ciudadanos (pág. 29)

civil/civil se refiere a los juicios sobre derechos privados de los individuos (pág. 261)

civil disobedience/desobediencia civil idea de que las personas tienen derecho a desobedecer las leyes que consideren injustas, si su conciencia lo exige (págs. 451, 853)

civil rights/derechos civiles los derechos que corresponden a todos los ciudadanos (pág. 767)

civil rights movement/movimiento de los derechos civiles lucha de los afroamericanos para conseguir igualdad de derechos (pág. 850)

civil service/servicio civil todos los puestos federales excepto los que se eligen por votación y los puestos militares (pág. 631)

Civil Service Commission/Comisión de Servicio Civil agencia del gobierno creada en 1883 para asignar puestos federales basándose en el mérito de los candidatos (pág. 631)

civil war/guerra civil guerra entre personas del mismo país (pág. 465)

Civil War amendments/enmiendas de la Guerra Civil enmiendas Trece, Catorce y Quince de la Constitución de Estados Unidos (pág. 261)

civilian/civil no militar (pág. 249)

Civilian Conservation Corps/ Cuerpo de Conservación Civil programa del Nuevo Acuerdo que daba trabajo a hombres solteros y desempleados en proyectos de conservación de la naturaleza en todo el país (pág. 754)

clan/clan grupo de dos o más familias emparentadas (pág. 48)

Clermont/Clermont barco de vapor construido en 1807 por Robert Fulton; primero en obtener éxito comercial en aguas de Estados Unidos (pág. 339)

climate/clima promedio del tiempo de un lugar en un período de 20 a 30 años (pág. 15)

clipper ship/clíper barco de mediados del siglo XIX que navegaba velozmente (pág. 410)

Cold War/Guerra Fría después de la Segunda Guerra Mundial, largo período de intensa rivalidad entre la Unión Soviética y Estados Unidos (pág. 810)

collective bargaining/negociación colectiva proceso por el cual un sindicato que representa un grupo de trabajadores negociaba un contrato con la dirección de la empresa (págs. 592, 761)

colony/colonia grupo de personas que se establece en una tierra distante pero sigue bajo la dirección del gobierno de su tierra natal (pág. 70)

Columbian Exchange/intercambio colombino intercambio global de bienes e ideas que resulta del encuentro entre los pueblos de los hemisferios occidental y oriental (pág. 71)

committee of correspondence/ comité de correspondencia campaña que consistió en escribir cartas y se convirtió en un importante instrumento de protesta en la colonia (pág. 153)

Common Sense/Sentido común ensayo de Thomas Paine publicado en 1776 que instaba a las colonias a declarar la independencia (pág. 173)

communism/comunismo sistema económico según el cual toda la propiedad y la riqueza pertenecen al Estado (pág. 722)

company union/sindicato de empresa organización de trabajadores cuyo control recae realmente en la dirección de la empresa (pág. 737)

compensation/compensación pago por pérdidas (pág. 788)

Comprehensive Test Ban Treaty/ Tratado de Prohibición de Ensayos Nucleares acuerdo propuesto en 1996 con el fin de terminar todas las pruebas de armas nucleares (pág. 882)

compromise/compromiso documento en el que cada lado cede en algunas de sus posiciones para poder llegar a un acuerdo (pág. 208)

Compromise of 1850/Compromiso de 1850 acuerdo con respecto a la esclavitud según el cual California se sumó a la Unión como estado libre, y se aprobó una estricta ley sobre esclavos fugitivos (pág. 465)

compulsory education/educación obligatoria requisito de que los niños fueran a la escuela hasta un cierto grado o una cierta edad (pág. 617)

concentration camp/campo de concentración campo de prisioneros civiles que se consideraban enemigos del Estado (pág. 776)

confederation/confederación liga de estados o naciones independientes (pág. 317)

Congress of Industrial Organizations/Congreso de Organizaciones Industriales (CIO) organización de trabajadores fundada en la década de 1930 para representar a los trabajadores de las industrias básicas de producción en masa (pág. 762)

conquistador/conquistador término que se refiere a los exploradores españoles que conquistaron en el nombre de España tierras en las Américas (pág. 74)

conservation/conservación protección de los recursos naturales (pág. 641)

Conservatives/conservadores durante la Reconstrucción, los blancos del Sur que se resistían al cambio (pág. 527)

consolidate/consolidar reunir, juntar (pág. 575)

constitution/constitución documento que establece las leyes, principios, organización y sistema de un gobierno (pág. 200)

Constitutional Convention/ Convención Constitucional reunión de los representantes de los estados realizada el 25 de mayo de 1787 para revisar los Artículos de la Confederación (pág. 206)

consumer/consumidor el que usa bienes y servicios (pág. 27)

containment/contención política que consistía en tratar de impedir la extensión de la influencia soviética más allá de donde ya existía (pág. 811)

Continental Army/Ejército Continental ejército establecido por el Segundo Congreso Continental para luchar contra los británicos (pág. 169)

continental divide/divisoria continental cadena de montañas que separa sistemas fluviales que corren en direcciones opuestas en un continente (pág. 309)

Contract With America/contrato con América paquete legislativo aprobado en1994 por los republicanos de la Cámara de Representantes que incluía el recorte de los programas de asistencia social, la reducción de la normativa medioambiental y la bajada de impuestos (pág. 875)

cooperative/cooperativa grupo de granjeros que contribuyen con dinero para comprar semillas o herramientas al por mayor (pág. 565)

Copperhead/Copperhead norteño que oponía el uso de la fuerza para mantener los estados del Sur dentro de la Unión (pág. 501)

corduroy road/camino de troncos camino hecho con troncos (pág. 339)

corollary/corolario añadidura a un principio enunciado anteriormente (pág. 678)

corporation/corporación negocio cuyos dueños son los inversionistas (pág. 580)

corral/corral recinto para animales (pág. 545)

"cottonocracy"/"algodocracia" sobrenombre dado a dueños de plantaciones ricos que hicieron su dinero con el algodón a mediados del siglo XIX (pág. 422)

counterculture/contracultura movimiento de protesta de la década de 1960 que rechazaba los valores y la cultura estadounidenses tradicionales (pág. 859)

coureur de bois/coureur de bois colonos franceses que cazaban animales por sus pieles (pág. 83)

cow town/pueblo vaquero asentamiento formado al final de una ruta de ganado (pág. 554)

creole/criollo persona de padres españoles nacida en las colonias españolas de América (págs. 78, 348)

Crusades/Cruzadas guerras en las que los cristianos lucharon por el control de la Tierra Santa entre 1100 y 1300 (pág. 58)

Cuban missile crisis/crisis de los misiles en Cuba enfrentamiento de gran importancia en 1962 en el que Estados Unidos bloqueó el intento soviético de poner misiles atómicos en Cuba (pág. 823)

culture/cultura forma de vida de un pueblo (págs. 22, 40)

culture area/área cultural región en la que las personas tienen una forma de vida similar (pág. 42)

currency/moneda dinero circulante (pág. 202)

czar/zar emperador de Rusia (pág. 692)

D

D-Day/Día D 6 de junio de 1944, día de la invasión de Europa occidental por las potencias aliadas (pág. 792)

dame school/escuela de damas escuela privada dirigida por una mujer, generalmente en su propia casa (pág. 128)

Dayton Accord/Acuerdo de Dayton acuerdo de paz negociado en 1995 entre Bosnia, Croacia y Serbia (pág. 881)

debtor/deudor persona que no puede pagar el dinero que debe (págs. 116, 436)

Declaration of Independence/ Declaración de Independencia documento de 1776 que declaraba que las 13 colonias formaban una nación independiente (pág. 175)

deficit spending/gasto deficitario práctica del gobierno de gastar más de lo que se recauda por impuestos (pág. 763)

demilitarized zone/zona desmilitarizada (DMZ) área en la que las fuerzas militares están prohibidas (pág. 818)

democratic/democrático que asegura que todas las personas tengan los mismos derechos (pág. 302)

Democratic Republican/republicano demócrata partidario de Thomas Jefferson (pág. 289)

Democrats/demócratas quienes apoyaban a Andrew Jackson, incluyendo granjeros de frontera y trabajadores de fábrica (pág. 364)

department store/gran almacén tienda que ofrece al por menor una variedad de artículos organizados en departamentos separados (pág. 613)

deport/deportar expulsar de un país (pág. 737)

depression/depresión período en que la actividad comercial disminuye, los precios y los salarios bajan, y aumenta el desempleo (págs. 204, 373)

deregulation/desregulación reducción al control de las empresas (pág. 873)

détente/detente política de reducir las tensiones entre las superpotencias (pág. 833)

dictator/dictador gobernante que tiene poder y autoridad absolutos (pág. 386)

dime novel/novelas de diez centavos a finales del siglo XIX, libros de aventuras con tapa blanda y baratos (pág. 619)

direct democracy/democracia directa forma de gobierno según la cual los ciudadanos comunes tienen el poder de gobernar (pág. 57)

disarmament/desarme reducción de las fuerzas militares y el armamento (pág. 722)

discrimination/discriminación política que niega derechos igualitarios a ciertos grupos de personas (pág. 417)

dividend/dividendo parte de las ganancias de una corporación (pág. 580)

dollar diplomacy/diplomacia del dólar política del presidente Taft que consistía en tratar de crear fuertes lazos económicos con Latinoamérica (pág. 678)

domestic tranquility/tranquilidad interna orden y paz interna de una nación (pág. 249)

domino theory/teoría del dominó convencimiento de que si Vietnam del Sur sucumbía al comunismo, otros países cercanos seguirían el mismo camino (pág. 828)

"Double V" campaign/campaña "Doble V" campaña por los derechos civiles de los afroamericanos durante la Segunda Guerra Mundial (pág. 786)

downsizing/reducción de plantilla reducir el número de trabajadores (pág. 874)

draft/leva ley que obliga a las personas de cierta edad a alistarse en el servicio militar (págs. 502, 693, 829)

Dred Scott v. Sandford/Dred Scott versus Sandford un caso que llegó a la Corte Suprema en 1857 y puso en duda el poder federal con respecto a la esclavitud en los territorios (pág. 471)

Dust Bowl/Cuenca de Polvo región del centro de las Grandes Llanuras que sufrió una gran sequía en la década de 1930 (pág. 765)

E

e-commerce/comercio electrónico negocios y comercio por Internet (pág. 892)

Earth Summit/Cumbre de la Tierra reunión de los líderes mundiales en 1992 para dialogar acerca de los principales asuntos medioambientales (pág. 890)

economics/economía el estudio de cómo las personas manejan recursos limitados para satisfacer sus deseos y necesidades (pág. 26)

Eighteenth Amendment/Enmienda Decimoctava enmienda a la Constitución de Estados Unidos aprobada en 1917 que declaraba ilegal la venta de bebidas en el país (pág. 648)

electoral college/colegio electoral grupo de electores de cada estado que cada cuatro años vota para elegir al presidente y vicepresidente de Estados Unidos (pág. 255)

elevation/elevación altura por encima del nivel del mar (pág. 13)

emancipate/emancipar liberar (pág. 497)

Emancipation Proclamation/ Proclama de Emancipación declaración de 1863 del presidente Lincoln que liberaba a los esclavos de la Confederación (pág. 497)

embargo/embargo prohibición de comerciar (pág. 314)

Embargo Act/Acta de Embargo ley de 1807 que impuso la prohibición total al comercio exterior (pág. 314)

encomienda/encomienda tierra otorgada por el gobierno español a los colonos españoles; incluía el derecho a exigir trabajo o impuestos a los indígenas (pág. 78)

English Bill of Rights/Declaración de Derechos Inglesa documento de 1689 que garantizaba los derechos de los ciudadanos ingleses (págs. 123, 213)

Enlightenment/Ilustración movimiento europeo de los siglos XVII y XVIII que enfatizaba el uso de la razón (pág. 129)

Environmental Protection Agency/Agencia de Protección Medioambiental agencia del gobierno federal que tiene como cometido hacer cumplir la normativa medioambiental (pág. 890)

environmentalist/ecologista persona que lucha por reducir la polución y proteger el medio ambiente (pág. 889)

epidemic/epidemia dispersión rápida de una enfermedad contagiosa (pág. 702)

Equal Rights Amendment/ Enmienda por la Igualdad de Derechos enmienda constitucional propuesta en 1923, que tenía como objetivo prohibir toda discriminación sexual; la enmienda nunca fue aprobada (pág. 726)

Era of Good Feelings/era de los buenos sentimientos los ocho años de la presidencia de James Monroe, de 1817 a 1825 (pág. 343)

Erie Canal/canal de Erie canal artificial construido en 1825 que unía el lago Erie con el río Hudson (pág. 340)

erosion/erosión desgaste gradual (pág. 13)

escalate/extender intensificar (pág. 828)

established church/iglesia oficial religión elegida por un Estado (pág. 94)

execute/ejecutar llevar a cabo (pág. 201)

executive branch/rama ejecutiva rama del gobierno que hace cumplir las leyes (pág. 208)

exile/exiliado persona forzada a abandonar su propio país (pág. 823)

expansionism/expansionismo política que consiste en extender los límites de una nación (pág. 660)

expatriate/expatriado persona que renuncia a su propio país y pasa a residir en el extranjero (pág. 731)

expedition/expedición largo viaje de exploración (pág. 308)

export/producto de exportación artículo comercial que se envía a mercados extranjeros (pág. 120)

extended family/familia extendida grupo familiar que incluye abuelos, padres, hijos, tías, tíos y primos (págs. 53, 425)

F

faction/facción grupo de oposición dentro de un partido (pág. 287)

factory system/systema de fábricas método de producción que reunió en un mismo lugar trabajadores y maquinaria (pág. 331)

fad/novedad actividad o moda pasajera que se adopta con gran pasión por poco tiempo (pág. 730)

famine/hambruna severa escasez de alimentos (pág. 415)

Farewell Address/discurso de despedida el último discurso de los presidentes al expirar sus mandatos (pág. 286)

Fascism/fascismo sistema político basado en el militarismo, el nacionalismo extremo y la lealtad ciega al Estado (pág. 774)

Federal Reserve Act/Ley de la Reserva Federal ley de 1913 que estableció un sistema de bancos federales y dio al gobierno el poder de controlar el suministro de dinero (pág. 643)

Federal Trade Commission (FTC)/ Comisión Federal de Comercio (FTC) agencia del gobierno creada en 1914 para asegurar la competencia justa (pág. 643)

federalism/federalismo principio de la Constitución de Estados Unidos que establece la división de poderes entre el gobierno federal y los estados (pág. 251)

Federalist/federalista partidario de la Constitución quien estaba a favor de un gobierno federal o nacional fuerte (págs. 215, 289)

The Federalist Papers/Los Ensayos Federalistas ensayos escritos por los Federalistas James Madison, Alexander Hamilton y John Jay que apoyaban la ratificación de la Constitución (pág. 216)

feudalism/feudalismo sistema de gobierno en el que los señores regían sus propias tierras pero debían lealtad y servicio militar a un monarca (pág. 58)

Fifteenth Amendment/Enmienda Decimoquinta enmienda a la Constitución de Estados Unidos aprobada en 1869 que prohibe a los estados negar a los afroamericanos el derecho al voto por causa de su raza (pág. 524)

54th Massachusetts Regiment/ regimiento 54° de Massachusetts unidad afroamericana del ejército de la Unión (pág. 499)

fireside chat/charla alrededor del fuego discurso por radio del presidente Franklin D. Roosevelt durante su presidencia (pág. 754)

First Amendment/Primera Enmienda enmienda a la Constitución de Estados Unidos que protege las libertades individuales básicas (pág. 260)

First Continental Congress/Primer Congreso Continental reunión de delegados de 12 colonias en Filadelfia en 1774 (pág. 158)

first global age/primera era global época a comienzos del siglo XV en la que el comercio y los viajes aumentaron notablemente (pág. 50)

flapper/*flapper* mujer joven que en la década de 1920 se revelaba contra los maneras tradicionales de pensar y actuar (pág. 731)

flatboat/carguero de poco fondo embarcación que se usa para transportar carga pesada en rutas acuáticas de tierra adentro (pág. 337)

Foraker Act/Ley de Foraker ley aprobada por el Congreso en 1900 bajo la cual Estados Unidos dio a los puertorriqueños una voz limitada en sus propios asuntos (pág. 674)

foreign policy/política exterior acciones de una nación en relación con otras naciones (pág. 285)

Fort Wagner/fuerte Wagner fuerte de Carolina del Sur objeto de un ataque en 1863 por parte del Regimiento 54° de Massachusetts (pág. 499)

forty-niner/persona del cuarenta y nueve una de los más de 80,000 personas que en 1849 se unieron a la fiebre del oro (pág. 400)

Founding Fathers/padres de la patria líderes que dieron los primeros pasos para la formación de Estados Unidos (pág. 211)

Fourteen Points/los catorce puntos los objetivos del presidente Wilson para los tiempos de paz después de la Primera Guerra Mundial (pág. 704)

Fourteenth Amendment/Enmienda Decimocuarta enmienda a la Constitución de Estados Unidos aprobada en 1868 que garantiza la protección igualitaria de las leyes (pág. 522)

free enterprise system/sistema de libre empresa sistema económico en el cual los negocios son de los ciudadanos privados, y ellos deciden qué producir, cuánto producir, dónde vender los productos y qué precios cobrar (págs. 28, 581)

free market/mercado libre sistema económico en el cual los bienes y servicios se intercambian con pocas restricciones (pág. 303)

Free-Soil party/partido del territorio libre partido antiesclavista fundado en 1848 en Estados Unidos, para mantener la esclavitud fuera de los territorios del oeste (pág. 462)

freedmen/libertos hombres y mujeres que habían sido esclavos (pág. 517)

Freedmen's Bureau/Oficina de Libertos agencia del gobierno de Estados Unidos fundada durante la Reconstrucción para ayudar a los libertos (pág. 517)

French and Indian War/guerra Franco-Indígena guerra ocurrida de 1754 a 1763 que acabó con el poder francés en América del Norte (pág.142)

French Revolution/Revolución Francesa rebelión que tuvo lugar en Francia en 1789 y que acabó con la monarquía por un tiempo (pág. 284)

frigate/fragata barco armado con muchos cañones que navega rápidamente (pág. 292)

fugitive/fugitivo persona que huye (pág. 464)

Fugitive Slave Act/Acta de los Esclavos Fugitivos ley de 1850 que exigía a todos los ciudadanos colaborar en la captura de esclavos fugitivos (pág. 465)

Fundamental Orders of Connecticut/Órdenes Fundamentales de Connecticut plan de gobierno de la colonia puritana de Connecticut en 1639 (pág. 104)

G

Gadsden Purchase/Compra de Gadsden banda de tierra entre lo que es hoy Arizona y Nuevo México, por la cual Estados Unidos pagó a México $10 millones en 1853 (pág. 397)

gauge/entrevía distancia entre las vías del tren (pág. 574)

General Court/Corte General asamblea representativa elegida de la colonia de la bahía de Massachusetts (pág. 103)

general welfare/bienestar general bienestar de todos los ciudadanos de una nación (pág. 249)

"Gentlemen's Agreement"/"acuerdo entre caballeros" acuerdo de 1907 entre Estados Unidos y Japón para limitar la inmigración japonesa (pág. 652)

gentry/alta burguesía la clase social más alta en las 13 colonias inglesas (pág. 126)

geography/geografía el estudio de las personas, su medio ambiente y sus recursos (pág. 4)

Gettysburg Address/discurso de Gettysburg discurso pronunciado en 1863 por el presidente Lincoln después de la batalla de Gettysburg (pág. 507)

Gibbons v. Ogden/Gibbons versus Ogden caso judicial de 1814 en el que la Corte Suprema confirmó el poder del gobierno federal para regular el comercio (pág. 346)

Gilded Age/Época Dorada período en la historia estadounidense durante las últimas dos décadas del siglo XIX, marcado por la corrupción política y e derroche (pág. 630)

glacier/glaciar capa gruesa de hielo (pág. 36)

glasnost/*glasnost* política de hablar abiertamente de los problemas de la Unión Soviética (pág. 835)

global warming/calentamiento global subida lenta pero ininterrumpida de la temperatura media de la Tierra (pág. 891)

Glorious Revolution/Revolución Gloriosa movimiento de 1688 que llevó a William y a Mary al trono de Inglaterra y reforzó los derechos de los ciudadanos ingleses (pág. 123)

Good Neighbor Policy/política de buena vecindad política del presidente Franklin Roosevelt que tenía como objetivo reforzar las relaciones de amistad con América Latina (pág. 777)

graduated income tax/impuesto sobre la renta escalonado impuesto sobre las ganancias que aplica porcentajes distintos según los diferentes niveles de renta (pág. 636)

grandfather clause/cláusula del abuelo ley que eximía a un votante de la prueba de alfabetización si su padre o su abuelo había sido elegible para votar el 1° de enero de 1867 (pág. 532)

Great Awakening/Gran Despertar movimiento religioso que tuvo lugar a principios del siglo XVIII en las colonias inglesas (pág. 127)

Great Compromise/Gran Compromiso plan de la Convención Constitucional que resolvió los conflictos entre los estados grandes y los pequeños (pág. 208)

Great Depression/Gran Depresión el peor período de decadencia económica de Estados Unidos; comenzó en 1929 (pág. 747)

Great White Fleet/Gran Flota Blanca nombre de los barcos de vapor de la marina de Estados Unidos, agrandados y modernizados, a principios del siglo XX (pág. 664)

Green Mountain Boys/los muchachos de *Green Mountain* milicia colonial de Vermont liderada por Ethan Allen que llevó a cabo un ataque sorpresa al fuerte Ticonderoga (pág. 169)

guerrilla warfare/guerrillero uso de tácticas militares de ataque y fuga inmediata (págs. 192, 828)

Gulf of Tonkin Resolution/Resolución del Golfo de Tonkín resolución aprobada por el Congreso en 1964 que autorizó la intervención militar en Vietnam (pág. 828)

Gullah/*Gullah* combinación del idioma inglés y de lenguas de África occidental que hablaban los afroamericanos en la colonia de Carolina de Sur (pág. 126)

H

habeas corpus/habeas corpus derecho por el cual no puede encarcelarse a ninguna persona a menos que se le acuse de haber cometido un crimen específico (págs. 213, 502)

Harlem Hell Fighters/luchadores infernales de Harlem unidad de infantería compuesta por afroamericanos que luchó junto con el ejército francés en la Primera Guerra Mundial (pág. 700)

Hartford Convention/Convención de Hartford reunión de delegados de Nueva Inglaterra durante la guerra de 1812 que amenazó con separarse de la Unión como protesta contra la guerra (pág. 325)

Haymarket Riot/revuelta Haymarket mitin laboral que tuvo lugar en Chicago en 1886, encabezado por un grupo pequeño de anarquistas, terminó violentamente al explotar una bomba (pág. 592)

Holocaust/Holocausto masacre de judíos europeos por parte de los nazis antes durante la Segunda Guerra Mundial (pág. 799)

Hooverville/Hooverville conjunto de casuchas miserables donde vivían las personas que no tenían un hogar durante la Gran Depresión (pág. 750)

House of Burgesses/Casa de los Burgueses asamblea de representantes de la Virginia colonial (pág. 90)

House of Representatives/Cámara de Representantes el mayor de los dos cuerpos que forman la rama legislativa del gobierno de Estados Unidos (pág. 252)

Hudson River School/escuela del río Hudson grupo de pintores estadounidenses que pintaban paisajes del valle del río Hudson en Nueva York, a mediados del siglo XIX (pág. 448)

Hull House/casa Hull centro comunitario fundado en Chicago por la reformadora progresista Jane Addams en 1889 (pág. 610)

Hundred Days/los cien días los primeros 100 días de la presidencia de Franklin D. Roosevelt (pág. 754)

I

ILGWU/*ILGWU* Sindicato Internacional de Trabajadoras de la Industria del Vestido, fundado en 1900 (pág. 593)

illegal alien/extranjero ilegal inmigrante que entra en un país sin autorización (pág. 895)

illiterate/analfabeto que no sabe leer ni escribir (pág. 694)

immigrant/inmigrante persona que se establece en otro país (pág. 266)

Immigration Reform and Control Act/Ley de Reforma y Control de la Inmigración ley que permitía que las personas que llegaron de forma ilegal a Estados Unidos antes de 1982 pudieran quedarse en el país y solicitar la residencia (pág. 895)

impeach/juicio político acusar formalmente de faltas serias a un representante político (págs. 257, 523)

imperialism/imperialismo política de los países poderosos que tratan de controlar los asuntos económicos y políticos de los países o regiones más débiles (pág. 662)

import/producto de importación artículo comercial que se ha introducido a un país (pág. 120)

impressment/leva práctica de forzar a las personas a que hagan el servicio militar (pág. 313)

inauguration/toma de mando ceremonia en la cual el presidente jura su cargo (pág. 278)

income tax/impuesto a los ingresos un impuesto al dinero que las personas ganan (pág. 502)

incriminate/incriminar presentar evidencias en contra de alguien (pág. 260)

indentured servant/sirviente por contrato persona que aceptaba trabajar sin pago por un tiempo a cambio de un pasaje a las colonias (pág. 126)

Indian New Deal/Nuevo Acuerdo Indígena leyes aprobadas en 1930 que dieron a las naciones de los indígenas un mayor control en sus propios asuntos (pág. 768)

Spanish Glossary

Indian Removal Act/Acta de Reubicación de los Indígenas ley aprobada en 1830 que forzaba a muchos indígenas a mudarse hacia el oeste del río Mississippi (pág. 372)

indigo/índigo planta usada para hacer una valiosa tintura azul (pág. 115)

individualism/individualismo concepto que destaca la importancia de cada individuo (pág. 451)

Industrial Revolution/Revolución Industrial proceso gradual en el que las máquinas reemplazaron a las herramientas manuales (pág. 330)

inflation/inflación aumento de los precios y desvalorización del dinero (págs. 503, 565, 843)

infrastructure/infraestructura sistema de caminos, puentes y túneles (pág. 263)

initiative/iniciativa proceso por el cual los votantes pueden presentar un proyecto de ley directamente ante la legislación del estado (págs. 263, 636)

installment buying/compra a plazo comprar a crédito (pág. 720)

integration/integración mezcla de diversos grupos raciales o étnicos (pág. 850)

interchangeable parts/partes intercambiables partes o repuestos idénticos para herramientas o instrumentos hechos a máquina (pág. 332)

internal improvements/mejoras internas mejoras hechas a caminos, puentes y canales (pág. 346)

Internet/Internet ordenadores unidos de manera que los usuarios puedan acceder e intercambiar información (pág. 892)

interstate commerce/comercio interestatal negocio que se lleva a cabo cruzando los límites de dos o más estados (págs. 346, 632)

Interstate Commerce Commission (ICC)/Comisión de Comercio Interestatal (ICC) agencia del gobierno que vigila el comercio ferroviario (pág. 632)

intervention/intervención participación directa (pág. 351)

Intolerable Acts/Actas Intolerables leyes aprobadas en 1774 para castigar a Boston por la Fiesta del Té (pág. 157)

irrigation/irrigación riego de tierras áridas (pág. 6)

Islam/islam religión monoteísta fundada por el profeta Mahoma a principios del siglo VII (pág. 50)

island hopping/de isla en isla estrategia de los aliados durante la Segunda Guerra Mundial, que consistía en capturar islas ocupadas por los japoneses para obtener el control del Pacífico (pág. 796)

isolationism/aislacionismo política que consiste en tener poca relación con los asuntos políticos de las naciones extranjeras (págs. 660, 708)

isthmus/istmo estrecha franja de tierra que une dos áreas de terreno más extensas (págs. 11, 675)

J

Jay's Treaty/Tratado de Jay acuerdo de 1795 entre Gran Bretaña y Estados Unidos que requería que Gran Bretaña pagara por los daños ocasionados por la captura de barcos estadounidenses, y devolviera los fuertes que aún ocupaba en el Oeste (pág. 286)

jazz/*jazz* estilo musical que se desarrolló a partir del *blues*, el *ragtime* y otros estilos anteriores (pág. 731)

jerky/tasajo carne secada (pág. 545)

Jim Crow laws/leyes de Jim Crow leyes que separaban en los lugares públicos del Sur a las personas de diferentes razas (pág. 532)

judicial branch/rama judicial rama del gobierno que decide si las leyes se practican de manera justa (pág. 208)

judicial review/revisión judicial poder de la Corte Suprema para decidir si los actos de un presidente o las leyes aprobadas por el Congreso son constitucionales (pág. 305)

Judiciary Act/Acta Judicial ley de 1789 que creó la estructura de la Corte Suprema y estableció un sistema de cortes de distrito y cortes de circuito a nivel nacional (pág. 279)

jury duty/el deber de servir en un jurado obligación de todo ciudadano de servir en un jurado cuando se le llama (pág. 268)

K

kachina/kachina bailarín enmascarado que participaba en ceremonias religiosas de los indígenas del Sudoeste (pág. 47)

kaiser/*kaiser* título del emperador alemán entre 1871 y 1918 (pág. 688)

kamikaze/kamikaze piloto japonés entrenado durante la Segunda Guerra Mundial para estrellarse en un ataque suicida, generalmente contra un barco (pág. 797)

Kansas-Nebraska Act/Acta de Kansas-Nebraska ley de 1854 que estableció los territorios de Kansas y Nebraska, dando a los colonos el derecho de soberanía popular para decidir con respecto a la esclavitud (pág. 468)

Kellogg-Briand Pact/Pacto de Kellog-Briand tratado de 1928 que declaraba ilegal la guerra (pág. 722)

Kentucky and Virginia resolutions/Acuerdos de Kentucky y Virginia declaraciones aprobadas en 1798 y 1799 que reivindicaban para los estados el derecho de decidir si una ley federal era constitucional (pág. 293)

Khmer Rouge/Khmer Rojo partido comunista en Camboya que impuso un verdadero imperio de terror en los camboyanos (pág. 831)

kinship/parentesco cuando se tienen antepasados en común (pág. 53)

"kitchen cabinet"/"gabinete de cocina" grupo de consejeros extra oficiales de Andrew Jackson que se reunía con él en la cocina de la Casa Blanca (pág. 367)

Knights of Labor/*Knights of Labor* organización laboral estadounidense fundada en 1869 para proteger los derechos de los trabajadores (pág. 591)

Know-Nothing Party/partido Know-Nothing partido político de la década de 1850 que estaba en contra del catolicismo y de la inmigración (pág. 416)

Ku Klux Klan/Ku Klux Klan sociedad secreta organizada en el Sur después de la Guerra Civil para afirmar la supremacía blanca por medio de la violencia (pág. 527)

L

laissez faire/*laissez faire* idea de que el gobierno debería tener una función mínimo en los asuntos económicos (pág. 303)

Lancaster Turnpike/carretera de peaje a Lancaster camino de peaje construido en la década de 1790 por una compañía privada; unía a Filadelfia con Lancaster, Pennsylvania (pág. 339)

Land Ordinance of 1785/ Ordenanza de Tierras de 1785 ley que establecía un sistema para colonizar el Territorio del Noroeste (pág. 203)

latitude/latitud distancia hacia el norte o el sur del ecuador (pág. 4)

lawsuit/demanda caso legal iniciado para dirimir una disputa entre personas o grupos (pág. 471)

League of Nations/Liga de las Naciones asociación de naciones formada después de la Primera Guerra Mundial bajo el plan de Los Catorce Puntos de Wilson (pág. 705)

League of the Iroquois/Liga de los Iroquois alianza de las cinco naciones de los iroquois (pág. 48)

League of Women Voters/Liga de Mujeres Votantes organización establecida en 1920 para garantizar los derechos de las mujeres (pág. 725)

legislative branch/rama legislativa rama del gobierno que aprueba las leyes (pág. 208)

legislature/legislatura grupo de personas que tiene el poder de hacer leyes (pág. 122)

Lend-Lease Act/Ley de Préstamo-Alquiler durante la Segunda Guerra Mundial, ley que permitió a Estados Unidos vender armas y equipamiento a Inglaterra (pág. 781)

libel/libelo acto de publicar afirmaciones que pueden dañar injustamente la reputación de una persona (pág. 130)

The Liberator/The Liberator el periódico antiesclavista más influyente, fundado por William Lloyd Garrison en 1831 (pág. 440)

liberty/libertad independencia (pág. 249)

Liberty Bonds/bonos de la libertad bonos vendidos por el gobierno de Estados Unidos para recaudar dinero para la Primera Guerra Mundial (pág. 695)

limited government/gobierno limitado principio de la Constitución de Estados Unidos que establece que el gobierno sólo tiene los poderes que la constitución le otorga (pág. 250)

literacy test/prueba de alfabetización examen para determinar si una persona sabe leer y escribir; se usaba para restringir el derecho al voto (pág. 532)

local color/color local habla y costumbres de una región determinada (pág. 620)

local government/gobierno local gobierno del condado, distrito de condado, ciudad, pueblo, villa o distrito (pág. 263)

locomotive/locomotora máquina que arrastra un tren (pág. 409)

lode/filón veta rica en oro, plata u otro mineral valioso (pág. 547)

Lone Star Republic/República de la Estrella Solitaria sobrenombre de Texas después que obtuvo su independencia de México en 1836 (pág. 389)

longitude/longitud distancia hacia el este o el oeste del primer meridiano (pág. 4)

Louisiana Purchase/Compra de Luisiana vasto territorio entre el río Mississippi y las Montañas Rocosas que se le compró a Francia en 1803 (pág. 308)

Lowell girl/chica Lowell mujer joven que trabajaban en las fábricas de Lowell, Massachusetts durante la revolución industrial (pág. 333)

Loyalist/*loyalist* colono que permaneció leal a Gran Bretaña (pág. 170)

Lusitania /Lusitania barco de pasajeros inglés que fue torpedeado por un submarino alemán en 1915; 1,200 personas murieron incluyendo 128 estadounidenses (pág. 690)

lynch/linchar captura y ejecución ilegal de una persona por parte de una multitud (págs. 401, 649)

M

Magna Carta/Carta Magna documento británico de 1215 cuyas dos ideas básicas sostienen que incluso los monarcas tienen que obedecer la ley y que los ciudadanos tienen derechos básicos (págs. 90, 213)

mainstreaming/mainstreaming integración de los niños con necesidades especiales en clases normales (pág. 896)

majority/mayoría más de la mitad (pág. 362)

Manifest Destiny/destino manifiesto creencia que se diseminó en el siglo XIX de que los estadounidenses tenían el derecho y la obligación de ocupar todo el continente, hasta el Pacífico (pág. 393)

manor/señorío distrito regido por un Señor que incluía su castillo y las tierras que lo rodeaban (pág. 58)

map projection/proyección cartográfica dibujo de la Tierra sobre una superficie plana (pág. 8)

Marbury* v. *Madison/Marbury versus Madison caso judicial de 1803 en el cual la Corte Suprema dictaminó que tenía el poder de decidir si las leyes aprobadas por el Congreso eran constitucionales (pág. 305)

Marshall Plan/plan Marshall plan estadounidense para ayudar a los países europeos a reconstruir sus economías después de la Segunda Guerra Mundial (pág. 812)

martial law/ley marcial gobierno de militares en vez de un gobierno electo (págs. 487, 834)

martyr/mártir persona que muere por sus creencias (pág. 476)

Mason-Dixon Line/línea de Mason-Dixon límite entre Pennsylvania y Maryland que dividía las colonias centrales de las colonias del sur (pág. 113)

mass production/producción en masa proceso que consiste en hacer grandes cantidades de un producto, con gran rapidez y a bajo costo (pág. 588)

Mayflower Compact/acuerdo Mayflower acuerdo de 1620 para gobernar la colonia de Plymouth (pág. 95)

McCulloch* v. *Maryland/Mc Cullock versus Maryland caso judicial de 1819 en el que la Corte Suprema dictaminó que los estados no tenían derecho a interferir en las instituciones federales aunque estuvieran en su territorio (pág. 346)

mediator/mediador agente que ayuda a las partes en conflicto a resolver sus diferencias (pág. 879)

mercantilism/mercantilismo teoría de que el poder económico de una nación provenía de mantener un estricto control sobre el comercio de las colonias (pág. 120)

mercenary/mercenario soldado que lucha exclusivamente por dinero, a menudo para un país extranjero (pág. 171)

merit/mérito habilidad (pág. 631)

mestizo/mestizo en las colonias españolas de las Américas, la persona que tiene mezcla indígena y española (pág. 78)

Mexican Cession/cesión mexicana territorio mexicano de California y Nuevo México que se entregó a Estados Unidos en 1848 (pág. 396)

middle class/clase media en las 13 colonias inglesas, la clase social que incluía artesanos cualificados, granjeros y algunos comerciantes (pág. 126)

migrant worker/trabajador itinerante persona que se traslada de una región a otra en busca de trabajo (págs. 766, 865)

militarism/militarismo política que consiste en reforzar las fuerzas armadas como preparación para la guerra (pág. 687)

militia/milicia ejército de ciudadanos que sirven como soldados en una emergencia (pág. 158)

minuteman/miliciano de la Guerra de Independencia voluntario de una milicia colonial que estaba siempre listo para luchar (pág. 159)

mission/misión colonia religiosa administrada por frailes y monjas católicas (pág. 78)

missionary/misionero persona que enseña sus creencias religiosas a otros (págs. 56, 84)

Missouri Compromise/compromiso de Missouri acuerdo, propuesto en 1819 por Henry Clay, para mantener igual el número de estados esclavistas y antiesclavistas (pág. 460)

Monitor/Monitor buque de guerra blindado de la Unión (pág. 492)

monopoly/monopolio compañía o agrupación que tiene control de toda o casi toda una industria (pág. 581)

Spanish Glossary

Monroe Doctrine/Doctrina Monroe política exterior del presidente Monroe que prevenía a las naciones europeas de no intervenir en América Latina (pág. 351)

moral diplomacy/diplomacia moral política del presidente Wilson que consistía en condenar el imperialismo, extender la democracia y promover la paz (pág. 679)

Moral Majority/Mayoría Moral organización religiosa que apoyaba causas políticas conservadoras en la década de 1980 (pág. 873)

Mormons/mormones miembros de la Iglesia de Jesucristo de los Santos de los Últimos Días fundada en 1830 por José Smith (pág. 398)

Mound Builders/constructores de montículos nombre de varias culturas de América del Norte que construyeron grandes montículos de tierra, comenzando hace unos 3,000 años (pág. 41)

mountain man/hombre de montaña cazador que exploraba Oregón a principios del siglo XIX (pág. 381)

moving assembly line/cadena de ensamblaje en movimiento método de producción según el cual los trabajadores permanecen en un lugar mientras que los productos pasan frente a ellos en una cinta transportadora (pág. 588)

muckraker/*muckraker* periodista que ponía en evidencia la corrupción y otros problemas a finales del siglo XIX y principios del siglo XX (pág. 634)

mudslinging/detractar uso de insultos para atacar la reputación de un oponente (pág. 374)

Munich Conference/Conferencia de Munich reunión en 1938 entre los líderes de Inglaterra, Francia, Italia y Alemania en la que se acordó entregar a Hitler parte de Checoslovaquia (pág. 779)

mutualista/mutualista grupo de ayuda mutua de los estadounidenses de origen mexicano (pág. 651)

N

NAACP/*NAACP* (Asociación Nacional para el Avance de la Gente de Color) organización establecida para luchar por la igualdad de derechos de los afroamericanos (pág. 650)

National Aeronautics and Space Administration/Administración Nacional de la Aeronáutica y el Espacio (NASA) agencia gubernamental que dirige el programa espacial estadounidense (pág. 825)

national debt/deuda nacional cantidad total de dinero que un gobierno debe (págs. 280, 763)

National Labor Relations Act/Ley Nacional de Relaciones Laborales ley aprobada en 1935 que protege a los trabajadores de Estados Unidos de prácticas injustas por parte de sus patrones (pág. 761)

national park/parque nacional área que el gobierno federal reserva para que las personas la visiten (pág. 641)

National Recovery Administration/ Administración para la Recuperación Nacional agencia gubernamental establecida durante la Gran Depresión para asegurar el cumplimiento de nuevos códigos diseñados para estabilizar la industria (pág. 755)

National Road/Caminos Nacionales primer proyecto nacional de caminos financiado federalmente, que se inició en 1811 (pág. 339)

National Woman Suffrage Association/Asociación Nacional para el Sufragio de la Mujer grupo fundado en 1869 para luchar por una enmienda constitucional que concediera a las mujeres el derecho al voto (pág. 645)

nationalism/nacionalismo orgullo excesivo en la propia nación (págs. 318, 686)

nativist/nativista persona a favor de que se limitara la immigración y Estados Unidos se reservara para los protestantes blancos nacidos en el país (págs. 416, 604, 738)

natural resources/recursos naturales materiales que los seres humanos toman del medio ambiente para sobrevivir y satisfacer sus necesidades (pág. 5)

natural rights/derechos naturales derechos que corresponden a todas las personas desde su nacimiento (pág. 175)

naturalize/naturalizarse proceso oficial para convertirse en ciudadano (pág. 265)

Nauvoo/Nauvoo comunidad mormona formada en la década de 1840 en los bancos del río Mississippi en Illinois (pág. 398)

Navajo code-talkers/navajos que hablaban en código en la Segunda Guerra Mundial, soldados navajos que usaban su propio lenguaje para enviar por radio mensajes vitales para la campaña "de isla en isla" (pág. 796)

Navigation Acts/Actas de Navegación leyes aprobadas por el parlamento inglés a finales del siglo XVII que regulaban el comercio entre Inglaterra y las colonias (pág. 121)

Nazi/nazi miembro del partido Nacional Socialista de Trabajadores Alemanes liderado por Adolf Hitler (pág. 775)

Nazi-Soviet Pact/pacto nazi-soviético acuerdo firmado entre Hitler y Stalin en 1939 por el cual los dos dictadores se comprometieron a no atacarse mutuamente (pág. 779)

Negro Fort/Fuerte de los Negros asentamiento de esclavos afroamericanos fugitivos en la colonia española de Florida (pág. 350)

network/red sistema de vías de ferrocarril que se comunican (pág. 575)

neutral/neutral que no toma partido en un conflicto (pág. 285)

Neutrality Acts/Leyes de Neutralidad leyes aprobadas por el Congreso en 1935 que prohibían la venta o préstamo de armas a los países que estuvieran en guerra (pág. 777)

Neutrality Proclamation/ Declaración de Neutralidad declaración de 1793 hecha por el presidente Washington que estipulaba que Estados Unidos no apoyaría ni ayudaría a Francia ni a Gran Bretaña en su conflicto europeo (pág. 285)

New Deal/Nuevo Acuerdo programa del presidente Franklin D. Roosevelt para poner fin a la Gran Depresión (pág. 754)

New Freedom/nueva libertad programa del presidente Wilson para acabar con los *trusts* y restituir la competencia económica en Estados Unidos (pág. 643)

New Jersey Plan/Plan de Nueva Jersey plan de la Convención Constitucional apoyado por los estados pequeños que requería tres ramas del gobierno con una legislatura de cámara única (pág. 208)

New Mexico Territory/Territorio de Nuevo México extensa región del suroeste que pertenecía a México en el siglo XIX (pág. 391)

"New South"/"Nuevo Sur" término de fines de siglo XIX que describía el Sur cuando se esforzaba por expandir la economía a través de la industria (pág. 533)

Nineteenth Amendment/Enmienda Decimonovena enmienda a la Constitución de Estados Unidos que da a las mujeres el derecho al voto (págs. 261, 646)

nominating convention/convencíon de postulaciones reuníon en la cual un partido político elige sus candidatos (pág. 364)

Nonintercourse Act/Acta de No Intercambio ley de 1809 que permitía a los estadounidenses comerciar con todas las naciones excepto Francia y Gran Bretaña (pág. 314)

Spanish Glossary

North American Free Trade Agreement/Tratado de Libre Comercio Norteamericano (TLC) tratado entre Estados Unidos, Canadá y México para eliminar gradualmente aranceles y otras barreras al comercio (pág. 889)

North Atlantic Treaty Organization/Organización del Tratado del Atlántico Norte (OTAN) alianza constituida en 1949 por Estados Unidos y países de Europa occidental para combatir la agresión soviética (pág. 813)

Northwest Ordinance/Ordenanza del Noroeste artículo de 1787 que establecía un gobierno para el Territorio del Noroeste (pág. 203)

northwest passage/pasaje noroeste pasaje de agua a través o alrededor de América del Norte (pág. 81)

nullification/anulación idea de que un estado tiene el derecho de anular o cancelar una ley federal que se considere inconstitucional (pág. 371)

Nullification Act/Acta de Anulación acta aprobada por Carolina del Sur que declaraba ilegal la tasa de 1832 (pág. 371)

Nuremberg Trials/juicios de Nuremberg en 1945 y 1946, juicios a los crímenes de guerra de los nazis (pág. 799)

O

Olive Branch Petition/Petición de la Rama de Olivo petición de paz enviada al rey George por los delegados coloniales después de las batallas de Lexington y Concord (pág. 168)

on margin/con margen práctica que permite a las personas comprar acciones abonando una entrada del diez por ciento del valor total (pág. 747)

OPEC/OPEP (Organización de Países Exportadores de Petróleo) organización internacional que establece una política común para la venta de petróleo (pág. 884)

Open Door Policy/política de puertas abiertas política promulgada por el Secretario de Estado John Hay en 1899 que permitía a una nación comerciar con China en la esfera de influencia de cualquier otra nación (pág. 666)

Operation Overlord/operación Overlord nombre en código de la invasión de los aliados en Europa, ocurrida en 1944 (pág. 792)

Oregon Country/Territorio de Oregón término usado a principios del siglo XIX para designar lo que es hoy Oregón, Washington, Idaho y partes de Wyoming, Montana y Canadá (pág. 380)

Oregon Trail/camino de Oregón ruta hasta Oregón usada por los trenes de carga en el siglo XIX (pág. 383)

Organization of American States/Organización de Estados Americanos (OEA) organización internacional que promueve la paz y el progreso económico en las Américas (pág. 824)

override/invalidar no admitir, como cuando el Congreso decide no admitir el veto presidencial (pág. 257)

P

pacifist/pacifista persona que se opone a todas las guerras porque cree que todas las guerras son malignas (pág. 696)

Parliament/Parlamento en Inglaterra, asamblea representativa (pág. 90)

parochial/parroquial de la iglesia; usado a menudo para referirse a las escuelas auspiciadas por la iglesia (pág. 617)

patent/patente licencia para un nuevo invento (pág. 584)

Patriot/patriota colono que estaba a favor de la guerra contra Gran Bretaña (pág. 169)

patriotism/patriotismo sentimiento de amor y devoción hacia el propio país (pág. 266)

patronage/patronato práctica de otorgar puestos gubernamentales a los partidarios políticos (pág. 631)

patroon/patrón dueño de una gran propiedad en una colonia holandesa (pág. 109)

Peace Corps/Cuerpo de Paz organización del gobierno que envía voluntarios estadounidenses a países en desarrollo para dar asistencia técnica (pág. 824)

peninsulare/peninsular término que se refiere a un español que tenía una posición de poder en una colonia española (pág. 78)

Pennsylvania Dutch/holandeses de Pennsylvania protestantes de lengua alemana que se establecieron en Pennsylvania (pág. 110)

pension/pensión suma de dinero que se paga a las personas regularmente después de jubilarse (pág. 760)

perjury/perjurio mentir bajo juramento (pág. 820)

persecution/persecución maltrato o castigo a un grupo de personas a causa de sus creencias (pág. 94)

Persian Gulf War/guerra del Golfo Pérsico guerra en 1991 en la que Estados Unidos y sus aliados en las Naciones Unidas expulsaron a las fuerzas invasoras de Iraq del contiguo territorio de Kuwait (pág. 885)

petition/petición solicitud formal firmada por un grupo de personas dirigida a alguien de mayor autoridad (pág. 149)

Pickett's Charge/ataque a Pickett ataque la Confederación como parte de la batalla de Gettysburg que fracasó (pág. 506)

Pilgrims/peregrinos colonos ingleses que, en el siglo XVII, procuraron libertad religiosa en las Américas (pág. 93)

Pinckney Treaty/Tratado de Pinckney acuerdo de 1795 con España que permitió a Estados Unidos transportar sus mercancías por el río Mississippi y almacenarlas en Nueva Orleáns (pág. 306)

pit house/casa subterránea casa de la región ártica cavada en la tierra y cubierta con madera y pieles (pág. 43)

Plains of Abraham/Planicies de Abraham campo cerca de Quebec donde en la guerra Franco-Indígena tuvo lugar una importante victoria de los británicos frente a los franceses (pág. 144)

plantation/plantación gran propiedad cultivada por muchos trabajadores (pág. 80)

Platt Amendment/Enmienda Platt enmienda de 1902 a la constitución cubana, que permitía a Estados Unidos intervenir en Cuba (pág. 673)

Plessy* v. *Ferguson*/*Plessy versus Ferguson un caso legal de 1896 en el cual la Suprema Corte dictaminó que la segregación en las instalaciones públicas era legal si las instalaciones eran iguales (pág. 532)

PLO/OPL (Organización para la Liberación de Palestina) organización palestino-árabe fundada en 1964 con el fin de destruir a Israel, principalmente a través del uso de fuerza armada (pág. 884)

pogrom/*pogrom* en la Europa del este, ataque organizado a una comunidad judía (pág. 600)

polio/polio enfermedad infecciosa que inflama las células nerviosas de la base del cerebro y la columna vertebral, produciendo parálisis (pág. 752)

political boss/capo político político poderoso que controla el trabajo que se realiza localmente y exige sobornos a los negocios (pág. 633)

political science/ciencias políticas el estudio del gobierno (pág. 29)

poll tax/impuesto al voto impuesto que se requería antes de que las personas pudieran votar (pág. 532)

Pontiac's War/guerra de Pontiac conflicto de 1763 entre indígenas y británicos sobre la colonización de tierras indígenas de los Grandes Lagos (pág. 147)

pool/mancomunidad sistema por el cual varias compañías de ferrocarril se ponen de acuerdo en repartirse el negocio de cierta área (pág. 576)

popular sovereignty/soberanía popular a mediados del siglo XIX, término que se refería a la idea de que cada territorio podía decidir por sí mismo si permitir la esclavitud (págs. 250, 462)

potlatch/*potlatch* cena ceremonial realizada por algunos indígenas de la costa noroeste para mostrar su riqueza (pág. 44)

Potsdam Declaration/Declaración de Potsdam mensaje enviado por los aliados a los japoneses en julio de 1945 pidiéndoles que se rindieran (pág. 798)

preamble/preámbulo introducción a una declaración, constitución u otro documento oficial (págs. 175, 248)

precedent/precedente acta o decisión que sirve de ejemplo a las que siguen (págs. 96, 278)

precipitation/precipitación agua que cae en forma de lluvia, cellisca, granizo o nieve (pág. 15)

predestination/predestinación idea protestante según la cual Dios decidía de antemano quiénes, después de muertos, se salvarían (pág. 435)

presidio/presidio fuerte de las colonias españolas donde vivían los soldados (pág. 77)

primary election/elección primaria elección en la que los votantes eligen los candidatos de su partido para la elección general (pág. 635)

primary source/fuente original información directa acerca de personas o sucesos (pág. 20)

Proclamation of 1763/Proclama de 1763 ley que prohibía a los colonos ingleses establecerse al oeste de los montes Apalaches (pág. 147)

productivity/productividad producción media por trabajador (pág. 845)

profiteer/aprovechador persona que aprovecha una crisis para hacer dinero (pág. 503)

Progressive/progresista reformista de finales del siglo XIX y principios del siglo XX que quería mejorar la calidad de vida en Estados Unidos (pág. 634)

Prohibition/Ley Seca prohibición a la fabricación, venta y transporte de bebidas alcohólicas en todo el territorio de Estados Unidos entre 1920 y 1933 (pág. 724)

propaganda/propaganda difusión de ideas para apoyar una causa o perjudicar la causa opuesta (pág. 689)

proprietary colony/colonia de propietarios colonia inglesa en la cual el rey daba tierras a propietarios a cambio de un pago anual (pág. 109)

protectorate/protectorado nación cuya independencia está limitada por el control de un país más poderoso (pág. 673)

Protestant Reformation/reforma protestante movimiento del siglo XVI para reformar la iglesia católica romana y que llevó a la creación de muchas iglesias cristianas (pág. 83)

psychology/sicología el estudio del modo de pensar y comportarse de los seres humanos (pág. 30)

public interest/interés público lo que es bueno para el pueblo (pág. 634)

public school/escuela pública escuela financiada por los impuestos (pág. 128)

public works/obras públicas proyectos construidos por el gobierno para uso público (pág. 750)

pueblo/pueblo ciudad de las colonias españolas; aldea de los anazasi (págs. 41, 77)

pull factor/factor de atracción condiciones que atraen a la gente a mudarse a otra área (pág. 600)

Pure Food and Drug Act/Ley de los Alimentos y Medicamentos Puros ley de 1906 que exige a los fabricantes de alimentos y medicamentos que indiquen los ingredientes en los envases (pág. 641)

Puritans/puritanos grupo de protestantes ingleses que se establecieron en la colonia de la bahía de Massachusetts (pág. 102)

push factor/factor de rechazo condiciones que hacen que la gente se vaya de sus lugares de origen (pág. 600)

Q

Quakers/cuáqueros reformistas protestantes que creen en la igualdad de todas las personas (pág. 110)

Quebec Act/Acta de Quebec ley que establecía un gobierno para Canadá y protegía los derechos de los católicos franceses (pág. 158)

quipu/quipu artefacto hecho de cuerda o tiras con nudos que representaban cantidades; usado por los incas para sus registros y contabilidad (pág. 40)

quota system/sistema de cupos sistema que limita la inmigración permitiendo que sólo un número determinado de personas de cada país entre a Estados Unidos (pág. 738)

Quran/Corán libro sagrado del islam (pág. 51)

R

racism/racismo creencia en la superioridad de una raza con respecto a otra (págs. 119, 662)

radical/radical persona que quiere realizar cambios drásticos en la sociedad (pág. 173)

Radical Reconstruction/reconstrucción radical período que comenzó en 1867 cuando los Republicanos, que tenían el control de ambas cámaras, se hicieron cargo de la Reconstrucción (pág. 523)

Radical Republican/republicano radical en la época de la Reconstrucción, miembro del Congreso que quería asegurarse de que los libertos recibieran el derecho a votar (pág. 522)

ragtime/*ragtime* música popular de finales del siglo XIX, rítmica y alegre (pág. 615)

ratify/ratificar aprobar (pág. 194)

rationing/racionamiento limitación en la cantidad disponible para la venta al público de ciertos artículos (pág. 785)

Reaganomics/*reaganomics* programa económico del presidente Reagan que bajó los impuestos, bajó los gastos federales en programas de asistencia social y aumentó los gastos militares (pág. 873)

realist/realista escritor o pintor que muestra la vida tal como es (pág. 620)

rebate/rebaja descuento (pág. 576)

recall/impugnación proceso por el cual los votantes pueden destituir del cargo a un funcionario electo (pág. 636)

recession/recesión disminución de la actividad económica que es más leve que una depresión (págs. 718, 874)

reconcentration/reconcentración política de trasladar grandes cantidades de personas a campos especiales con intención militar o política (pág. 669)

Reconstruction/Reconstrucción reconstrucción del Sur después de la Guerra Civil (pág. 517)

Reconstruction Act/Acta de la Reconstrucción ley de 1867 que anuló los gobiernos de los estados del Sur que se habían negado a ratificar la Enmienda Decimocuarta (pág. 523)

referendum/referéndum proceso por el cual las personas votan directamente con respecto a un proyecto de ley (pág. 636)

refuge/refugio lugar donde se está libre de persecuciones (pág. 399)

refugee /refugiado persona que abandona su tierra natal en busca de seguridad en otro lugar (pág. 895)

relief program/programa de ayudas programa del gobierno para ayudar a los necesitados (pág. 750)

religious tolerance/tolerancia religiosa deseo de permitir que otros practiquen sus propias creencias (pág. 104)

Renaissance/Renacimiento explosión europea de conocimientos que tuvo lugar desde finales del siglo XIV hasta el siglo XVI (pág. 59)

rendezvous/*rendezvous* encuentro anual en el cual los hombres de montaña intercambiaban pieles (pág. 382)

renewable resource/recurso renovable recurso que puede ser reemplazado rápidamente por la propia naturaleza (pág. 890)

reparations/reparaciones después de una guerra, entregas de dinero por parte de una nación vencida a la nación vencedora para pagar por las pérdidas sufridas durante la guerra (pág. 706)

repeal/revocar cancelar (págs. 150, 725)

representative government/gobierno representativo sistema político según el cual los votantes eligen a los representantes que dictarán las leyes (pág. 90)

republic/república sistema de gobierno en el cual los ciudadanos eligen representantes para que los gobiernen (págs. 57, 211)

Republic of Great Colombia/República de la Gran Colombia estado independiente fundado en 1819, compuesto por lo que hoy son Venezuela, Colombia, Ecuador (pág. 349)

Republican party/partido republicano partido político establecido en 1854 en Estados Unidos, con el fin de mantener la esclavitud fuera de los territorios del oeste (pág. 473)

resident alien/extranjero residente persona que vive en el país sin ser ciudadano (pág. 266)

revival/reunión evangelista gran encuentro religioso al aire libre (pág. 435)

Roosevelt Corollary/corolario de Roosevelt declaración del presidente Theodore Roosevelt según la cual Estados Unidos tenía el derecho a intervenir en Latinoamérica para preservar la ley y el orden (pág. 678)

Rosie the Riveter/Rosie la Remachadora trabajadora de una fábrica ficticia que se convirtió en el símbolo de la contribución de las mujeres estadounidenses al esfuerzo que supuso la Segunda Guerra Mundial (pág. 785)

Rough Riders/jinetes rudos sobrenombre de la unidad organizada por Theodore Roosevelt durante la guerra entre España y Estados Unidos (pág. 672)

royal colony/colonia real colonia bajo el control directo de la corona inglesa (pág. 109)

rugged individualist/individualista recalcitrante persona que sigue en la vida su propio camino independiente (pág. 381)

S

Sabbath/sabbat día de descanso religioso (pág. 106)

sabotage/sabotaje destrucción secreta de propiedades o interrupción de la producción en una fábrica u otro lugar de trabajo (pág. 737)

sachem/*sachem* miembro del consejo tribal de jefes de la Liga de los Iroquois (pág. 48)

SALT Agreement/Tratado *SALT* (discursos sobre limitación de armas estratégicas) tratado firmado por Estados Unidos y la Unión Soviética para limitar el número de cabezas nucleares y misiles (pág. 833)

salvation/salvación vida eterna (pág. 56)

Salvation Army/Ejército de Salvación organización internacional de caridad (pág. 609)

sanctions/sanciones medidas diseñadas para obligar a un país a cambiar su política (pág. 880)

Santa Fe Trail/camino de Santa Fe ruta a Santa Fe, Nuevo México, que usaban los comerciantes en el siglo XIX (pág. 392)

satellite nation/país satélite país dominado política y económicamente por otro más poderoso (pág. 811)

savanna/sabana región de pastos (pág. 52)

scalawag/*scalawag* blanco sureño que apoyaba a los Republicanos durante la Reconstrucción (pág. 526)

scapegoat/chivo expiatorio persona o grupo sobre el que se descargan las culpas de otros (pág. 775)

secede/separarse retirarse como miembro de un grupo (pág. 463)

Second Amendment/Segunda Enmienda enmienda a la Constitución de Estados Unidos que se refiere al derecho a tener armas (pág. 260)

Second Great Awakening/Segundo Gran Despertar extenso movimiento religioso en Estados Unidos a principios de siglo XIX (pág. 435)

secondary source/fuente secundaria relato de los hechos proporcionado por personas que no participaron directamente o presenciaron los hechos ocurridos (pág. 21)

sectionalism/seccionalismo lealtad a un estado o región antes que a todo el país (pág. 345)

sedition/sedición rebelión en contra de un gobierno (pág. 293)

segregation/segregación separación de las personas por razones de raza, etnia u otras características (págs. 532, 849)

Selective Service Act/Ley de Servicio Selectivo ley aprobada por el Congreso en 1917 que requería que todos los hombres de 21 a 30 años se inscribieran para el servicio militar (pág. 693)

self-determination/autodeterminación derecho de los grupos nacionales a tener su propio territorio y formas de gobierno (pág. 705)

self-sufficient/autosuficiente capaz de producir lo suficiente para satisfacer las necesidades propias (pág. 392)

Seminole War/guerra de los Seminoles conflicto que se inició en Florida en 1817 cuando los indios seminoles resistieron ser trasladados (pág. 373)

Senate/Senado el menor de los dos cuerpos que constituyen la rama legislativa del gobierno de Estados Unidos (pág. 253)

Seneca Falls Convention/convención de Seneca Falls un encuentro de 1848 en el cual líderes del movimiento por los derechos femeninos reclamaron derechos igualitarios para la mujer (pág. 445)

separation of powers/separación de poderes principio según el cual los poderes del gobierno se dividen en ramas separadas (pág. 214)

settlement house/centro comunitario establecimiento organizado a finales del siglo XIX para ofrecer servicios a los pobres (pág. 609)

sharecropper/aparcero persona que alquila un terreno de otra persona y lo trabaja a cambio de parte de la cosecha (pág. 529)

Shays' Rebellion/rebelión de Shays revuelta de Massachussetts liderada por granjeros en 1786 en reacción a los altos impuestos (pág. 204)

Sherman Antitrust Act/Ley Antimonopolio de Sherman ley de 1890 que prohibía la formación de *trusts* y monopolios en Estados Unidos (págs. 582, 632)

siege/sitio cerco por parte del ejército de una ciudad o posición enemiga, seguido de bloqueo o bombardeo para obligarla a que se rinda (págs. 193, 387, 506)

silent majority/mayoría silenciosa término empleado para referirse a los estadounidenses que estaban preocupados por los disturbios de la década de 1960 pero no protestaban por ello públicamente (pág. 860)

Silk Road/Ruta de la Seda rutas terrestres que unían China con el Oriente Medio (pág. 52)

sit-down strike/huelga en el lugar de trabajo huelga en la cual los obreros se niegan a salir del lugar donde trabajan hasta que se llegue a un acuerdo (pág. 762)

sit-in/sentada forma de protesta en la que la gente se sienta y se resiste a marcharse (pág. 862)

skyscraper/rascacielos edificio alto de muchos pisos sostenido por un armazón de acero de poco peso (pág. 612)

slave codes/códigos de la esclavitud leyes que controlaban la vida de los esclavos afroamericanos y les negaban los derechos básicos (págs. 119, 424)

smuggling/contrabando importar o exportar mercancías violando las leyes de comercio (pág. 314)

Social Gospel/evangelio social movimiento del protestantismo estadounidense de finales del siglo XIX que intentaba aplicar las enseñanzas de la Biblia a los problemas sociales (pág. 609)

social reform/reforma social intento organizado de mejorar lo que es injusto o imperfecto en la sociedad (pág. 434)

social sciences/ciencias sociales estudios que se refieren a la sociedad y a la conducta social (pág. 29)

Social Security Act/Ley de la Seguridad Social ley de 1935 que estableció un sistema de pensiones para personas mayores y el primer sistema nacional de seguro de desempleo (pág. 762)

Socialist/socialista persona que está a fovor de que las propiedades pertenezcan a la comunidad y se compartan todas las ganancias (pág. 696)

Society of American Indians/ Sociedad de Indígenas Estadounidenses agrupación que luchaba por la justicia social y la participación de indígenas en la corriente social principal de Estados Unidos (pág. 653)

sociology/sociología estudio del comportamiento de las personas en grupos (pág. 30)

sod house/casa de tepe casa construida con tierra sujetada con raíces de hierbas (pág. 564)

sodbuster/*sodbuster* granjero de las Grandes Llanuras de a finales del siglo XIX (pág. 564)

Solidarity/Solidaridad sindicato independiente que desafió al gobierno comunista de Polonia (pág. 834)

soup kitchen/olla popular lugar donde se proporciona comida gratis o por un precio mínimo a los necesitados (pág. 750)

Spanish-American War/guerra Hispano-Americana guerra entre España y Estados Unidos en 1898, que tuvo como resultado que España cediera Puerto Rico, Filipinas y Guam a Estados Unidos, y otorgara la independencia a Cuba (pág. 671)

speculator/especulador alguien que invierte dinero en un negocio arriesgado con la esperanza de obtener grandes ganancias (pág. 280)

sphere of influence/esfera de influencia zona donde una nación tenía privilegios comerciales especiales (pág. 666)

spinning jenny/hiladora de varios husos máquina inventada en 1764 que hilaba varios hilos al mismo tiempo (pág. 331)

spoils system/sistema de sinecuras práctica que recompensaba a los partidarios de un gobierno otorgándoles empleos en dicho gobierno (pág. 366)

Square Deal/acuerdo justo la promesa de Theodore Roosevelt durante su campaña de que todos los grupos tendrían las mismas oportunidades de éxito (pág. 640)

stagflation/estagflación combinación de alza de precios, alto desempleo y lento crecimiento económico (pág. 860)

stalemate/punto muerto empate en el cual ninguno de los lados es suficientemente fuerte como para derrotar al otro (pág. 688)

Stamp Act/Acta de los Sellos ley de 1765 que imponía nuevas obligaciones a los documentos legales y gravaba con impuestos los periódicos, almanaques, naipes y dados (pág. 149)

standard of living/nivel de vida índice basado en la cantidad de bienes, servicios y tiempo libre que tienen las personas (pág. 845)

Star Wars/guerra de las galaxias sistema armamentístico propuesto por el presidente Reagan con el objeto de destruir los misiles soviéticos desde el espacio (pág. 834)

states' rights/derechos de los estados el derecho de los estados a limitar el poder del gobierno federal (págs. 293, 370)

Statue of Liberty/estatua de la Libertad estatua monumental situada en la isla Liberty, en la bahía de Nueva York, que simboliza la esperanza y la libertad (pág. 602)

steerage/tercera clase en un barco, la zona hacinada en que viajan los pasajeros con los billetes más baratos (pág. 601)

stock/acción participación en la propiedad de una corporación (págs. 580, 720)

Strategic Arms Reduction Treaty/ Tratado de Reducción de Armas Estratégicas (START) tratado firmado en 1991 por Estados Unidos y la Unión Soviética para reducir las armas nucleares (pág. 882)

strike/huelga acción, por parte de los trabajadores, de negarse a hacer su trabajo hasta que se acepten sus condiciones (pág. 414)

strikebreaker/rompehuelgas el que reemplaza a un trabajador que está de huelga (pág. 591)

subsidy/subsidio ayuda financiera o concesión de tierras por parte del gobierno (pág. 550)

suburb/suburbio área residencial en las afueras de una ciudad (págs. 613, 728, 845)

suffrage/sufragio derecho a votar (pág. 361)

suffragist/sufragista persona que lucho por conseguir el derecho al voto de las mujeres (pág. 646)

summit meeting/cumbre reunión entre los gobernantes de mayor rango de distintas naciones (pág. 835)

superpower/superpotencia país con suficiente fuerza militar, política y económica como para ejercer su influencia por todo el mundo (pág. 823)

Supreme Court/Corte Suprema corte de máxima autoridad de Estados Unidos, establecida por la Constitución (pág. 256)

surplus/superávit excedente; condición que se da cuando los ingresos superan a los gastos (págs. 37, 876)

Sutter's Mill/Sutter's Mill lugar donde se descubrió oro en 1848, lo cual inició la fiebre del oro (pág. 400)

Swahili/swahili idioma que mezcla palabras árabes con las lenguas africanas locales, hablado en gran parte de África oriental (pág. 52)

sweatshop/taller del sudor fábrica donde la gente trabaja muchas horas en malas condiciones y por poco dinero (pág. 591)

T

tariff/tasa de importación impuesto que afecta a bienes extranjeros que se importan a un país (pág. 281)

Tariff of Abominations/Tasa de Abominaciones tasa aprobada por el Congreso en 1828 que favorecía a la industria del Norte (pág. 370)

Tea Act/Acta del Té ley de 1773 que permitía a la Compañia Británica de las Indias Orientales prescindir de los comerciantes de té y vender sus productos directamente a los colonos (pág. 156)

Teapot Dome Scandal/escándalo *Teapot Dome* escándalo politico durante la administración del presidente Harding (pág. 719)

Tejano/tejano person nacida en Texas de origen mexicano (pág. 386)

telegraph/telégrafo mecanismo para comunicarse que envía señales eléctricas por un cable (pág. 409)

temperance movement/movimiento por la temperancia campaña en contra del consumo de alcohol (pág. 436)

Ten Percent Plan/Plan del Diez Por Ciento plan del Lincoln que permitía que un estado del Sur formara un nuevo gobierno después de que el diez por ciento de sus votantes juraran lealtad a Estados Unidos (pág. 517)

tenement/apartamento de inquilinato pequeño apartamento en un barrio pobre de la ciudad (pág. 607)

Tennessee Valley Authority/Autoridad del Valle del Tennessee programa del Nuevo Acuerdo para la construcción de diques que controlaban las inundaciones y producían energía eléctrica a un precio económico (pág. 756)

tepee/tipi tienda construida con pieles de búfalo, estirada entre altos palos (pág. 545)

terrace/terraza amplio escalón de tierra que se cava en la ladera de una colina (pág. 40)

terrorism/terrorismo uso deliberado de actos arbitrarios de violencia con el fin de conseguir un determinado fin político (págs. 688, 886)

Tet Offensive/ofensiva *Tet* ataque orpresivo contra las fuerzas estadounidenses estacionadas en Vietnam en Año Nuevo vietnamita en 1968 (pág. 829)

Thanksgiving/Día de Acción de Gracias día al final de la temporada de cosecha que los peregrinos reservaban para dar gracias a Dios (pág. 97)

thematic map/mapa temático mapa sobre un tema específico, como población, recursos naturales o elecciones (pág. 9)

Thirteenth Amendment/Enmienda Decimotercera enmienda de 1865 a la Constitución de Estados Unidos que prohibe la esclavitud en toda la nación (pág. 519)

38th parallel/paralelo 38 línea divisoria entre Corea del Sur y Corea del Norte (pág. 816)

Three-Fifths Compromise/Compromiso de los Tres Quintos acuerdo logrado en la Convención Constitutional, según el cual las tres quintas partes de los esclavos de cada estado se contarían como parte de la población (pág. 209)

total war/guerra total guerra absoluta que afecta tanto a los civiles en sus casas como a los soldados en combate (pág. 508)

totalitarian state/estado totalitario país en el cual un único partido controla el gobierno y todos los aspectos de la vida de las personas (pág. 774)

town meeting/cabildo abierto reunión en Nueva Inglaterra durante la colonia donde los colonos discutían y votaban (pág. 107)

Townshend Acts/Actas de Townshend leyes aprobadas en 1767 que gravaban con impuestos bienes como vidrio, papel, pintura, plomo y té (pág. 150)

trade deficit/déficit comercial condición que se da cuando un país compra a otros países más bienes y servicios de los que vende (pág. 889)

trade union/gremio asociación de trabajadores de un mismo oficio formada para acceder a una paga mayor y a mejores condiciones de trabajo (págs. 414, 592)

Trail of Tears/Ruta de Lágrimas viaje forzado de los indígenas cheroquíes de Georgia hacia la región al oeste del Mississippi en el cual miles de indígenas murieron (pág. 372)

traitor/traidor persona que traiciona a su país (pág. 175)

transatlantic/transatlántico a través del Atlántico (pág. 585)

transcendentalist/trascendentalista escritores de Nueva Inglaterra que creían que las verdades más importantes de la vida trascendían, o estaban más allá, de la razón humana (pág. 450)

transcontinental railroad/ferrocaril transcontinental ferrocarril que cruza un continente de costa a costa (pág. 549)

travois/*travois* trineo arrastrado por un perro o caballo (pág. 545)

treason/traición acciones contra el propio país (pág. 476)

Treaty of Brest-Litovsk/Tratado de Brest-Litovsk tratado de 1918 entre Rusia y Alemania que puso fin a la participación rusa en la Primera Guerra Mundial (pág. 699)

Treaty of Ghent/Tratado de Gante tratado de paz firmado por Gran Bretaña y Estados Unidos a fines de la guerra de 1812 (pág. 325)

Treaty of Greenville/Tratado de Greenville tratado firmado por algunos indígenas en 1795, por el cual entregaron tierra que más tarde formaría parte de Ohio a cambio de dinero (pág. 317)

Treaty of Guadalupe-Hidalgo/Tratado de Guadalupe-Hidalgo tratado de 1848 por el cual México entregó California y Nuevo México a Estados Unidos a cambio de $15 millones (pág. 396)

Treaty of Kanagawa/Tratado de Kanagawa tratado de 1854 entre Japón y Estados Unidos que abrió los puertos para el comercio estadounidense con Japón (pág. 661)

Treaty of Paris/Tratado de París acuerdo de 1763 entre Francia y Gran Bretaña que puso fin a la guerra Franco-Indígena, (pág. 145); acuerdo de 1783 entre Estados Unidos y Gran Bretaña que reconoció a Estados Unidos como una nación independiente (pág. 194)

Treaty of Versailles/Tratado de Versailles tratado firmado el 28 de junio de 1919 por Alemania y por los aliados; atribuía formalmente a Alemania y a sus aliados la responsabilidad por la guerra (pág. 706)

Triangle Fire/incendio de Triangle incendio de 1911 en la fábrica *Triangle Shirtwaist* de Nueva York, donde murieron casi 150 trabajadores (pág. 593)

triangular trade/comercio triangular ruta de comercio colonial entre Nueva Inglaterra, las Antillas y África (pág. 121)

tribe/tribu comunidad de personas que tienen las mismas costumbres, lenguaje y rituales (pág. 42)

tributary/tributario arroyo o río pequeño que desemboca en un río mayor (pág. 15)

tribute/tributo contribución de dinero (pág. 313)

Truman Doctrine/doctrina Truman política del presidente Truman de suministrar ayuda estadounidense a los países amenazados por la expansión comunista (pág. 811)

trust/*trust* grupo de corporaciones gobernadas por un solo consejo administrativo (pág. 581)

trustbuster/que lucha contra los *trusts* persona que desea destruir todos los *trust* (pág. 640)

turning point/momento decisivo momento histórico que indica un cambio fundamental (pág. 70)

turnpike/camino de peaje camino construido por una compañía privada que cobra un peaje por su uso (pág. 339)

Tuskegee Airmen/aviadores de Tuskegee pilotos afroamericanos de aviones de guerra entrenados en

Spanish Glossary

Tuskegee, Alabama, en la Segunda Guerra Mundial (pág. 787)

tutor/tutor maestro privado (pág. 128)

Twenty-sixth Amendment/ Enmienda Vigesimosexta enmienda a la Constitución de Estados Unidos que redujo de 21 a 18 años la edad mínima requerida para votar (pág. 261)

U

U-boat/submarinos *U-boat* submarinos alemanes usados en la Primera y Segunda Guerra Mundial (pág. 690)

Uncle Tom's Cabin/La Cabaña del Tío Tom novela de Harriet Beecher Stowe en contra de la esclavitud y el Acta de Esclavos Fugitivos (pág. 466)

unconstitutional/inconstitucional que no está permitido por la Constitución (págs. 257, 288)

Underground Railroad/Ruta Clandestina red de abolicionistas negros y blancos que ayudaban en secreto a huir a los esclavos hacia la libertad en el norte de Estados Unidos o Canadá (pág. 441)

United Nations/Naciones Unidas organización mundial establecida en 1945 para proporcionar soluciones pacíficas a los conflictos internacionales (pág. 813)

United Provinces of Central America/Provincias Unidas de América Central federación fundada en 1823 las actuales Guatemala, El Salvador, Honduras, Nicaragua y Costa Rica (pág. 349)

urbanization/urbanización traslado de la población de las granjas a las ciudades (págs. 335, 606)

V

Valley Forge/Valley Forge lugar de Pennsylvania donde estaba el campamento del Ejército Continental comandado por Washington durante el invierno de 1777 y 1778 (pág. 185)

vaquero/vaquero término que se refiere a ganaderos mexicanos o hispanos (págs. 392, 553)

vaudeville/*vaudeville* espectáculo de variedades popularizado a finales del siglo XIX, que incluía comediantes, actuaciones de canto y baile, y acróbatas (pág. 615)

vertical integration/integración vertical práctica por la cual un solo fabricante controla todos los pasos necesarios para transformar la materia prima en productos terminados (pág. 579)

veto/veto rechazar, como cuando el presidente rechaza una ley que ha sido aprobada por el Congreso (pág. 257)

victory garden/huerta de la victoria durante la Segunda Guerra Mundial, huerta que se plantaba para combatir la escasez de alimentos en Estados Unidos (pág. 785)

Vietcong/*Vietcong* guerrilleros vietnamitas que se oponían al gobierno no comunista de Vietnam del Sur (pág. 828)

vigilante/vigilante alguien que se designa a sí mismo para hacer cumplir la ley (págs. 401, 549)

Virginia/Virginia buque de guerra blindado que usaron los Confederados para quebrar el bloqueo de la Unión (pág. 492)

Virginia Plan/Plan de Virginia plan de la Convención que recomendaba un gobierno nacional fuerte con tres ramas y una legislatura de dos cámaras (pág. 208)

W

Wade-Davis Bill/Proyecto de Wade-Davis plan de 1864 para la Reconstrucción que negaba el derecho al voto o el acceso a la función pública a quienes se habían ofrecido a luchar por la Confederación (pág. 517)

War Hawks/halcones de guerra miembros del Congreso que representaban al Oeste y al Sur y que instaban a la guerra contra Gran Bretaña antes de la guerra de 1812 (pág. 318)

War Production Board/Junta de Producción de Guerra agencia del gobierno creada durante la Segunda Guerra Mundial para ayudar a las fábricas a producir materiales de guerra en lugar de bienes de consumo (pág. 785)

warmonger/belicista persona que fomenta la guerra (pág. 691)

Warsaw Pact/Pacto de Varsovia alianza militar de la Unión Soviética con otros países comunistas de Europa establecida en 1955 (pág. 813)

WCTU/*WCTU* (Asociación de las Mujeres Cristianas por la Abstinencia) grupo organizado en 1874 que luchó por la prohibición de la venta de bebidas alcohólicas en Estados Unidos (pág. 648)

weather/tiempo condición de la atmósfera terrestre en un lugar y momento determinado (pág. 15)

Whigs/*Whigs* miembros del viejo Partido Republicano Nacional, liderado por John Quincy Adams (pág. 363)

Whiskey Rebellion/rebelión del whisky protesta de 1794 con respecto a un impuesto aplicado a todas las bebidas alcohólicas producidas y vendidas en Estados Unidos (pág. 282)

wholesale/venta al por mayor comprar o vender algo en grandes cantidades a precios reducidos (pág. 565)

Wilmot Proviso/Cláusula de Wilmot ley aprobada en 1846 que proscribía la esclavitud en todos los territorios ganados a México por Estados Unidos (pág. 461)

Wisconsin Idea/idea de Wisconsin serie de reformas progresistas introducidas a principios del siglo XX por el gobernador de Wisconsin Robert La Follette (pág. 635)

women's rights movement/ movimiento por los derechos femeninos campaña organizada para obtener el derecho a la propiedad, la educación y otros derechos para la mujer (pág. 446)

writ of assistance/mandato de asistencia documento legal que permitía a los funcionarios de la aduana inglesa realizar la inspección de la carga de un barco sin tener que alegar razón alguna (pág. 150)

X

XYZ Affair/*Affair XYZ* intento francés de 1797 de sobornar a Estados Unidos exigiendo pagos antes de que comenzaran las conversaciones sobre la captura por parte de los franceses de barcos estadounidenses neutrales (pág. 292)

Y

Yankee/yankis sobrenombre de los comerciantes de Nueva Inglaterra que dominaban el comercio colonial (pág. 121)

yellow journalism/periodismo amarillo periodismo que publica noticias a menudo falsas o mal intencionadas y se apoya en artículos y titulares sensacionalistas (págs. 619, 670)

Young Men's Hebrew Association (YMHA)/Asociación Hebrea de Jóvenes (YMHA) organización fundada en Baltimore en 1845 para ofrecer servicios comunitarios en los barrios judíos (pág. 609)

Z

Zimmermann telegram/telegrama de Zimmermann telegrama enviado en 1917 por el secretario de asuntos exteriores de Alemania al ministro alemán en México, dándole órdenes de instigar a México a que atacara a Estados Unidos en caso de que éstos declarasen la guerra a Alemania (pág. 692)

Page numbers that are italicized refer to illustrations or quotations. An *m, p, c, g,* or *go* after a page number refers to a map *(m)*, picture *(p)*, chart *(c)*, graph *(g)*, or graphic organizer *(go)* on that page. A *q* refers to a quote within the text. A *ps* refers to a primary source feature.

A

B

Index

Index

Index

F

G

H

Index

Index

Index

Q

R

S

Index

Index

Index

X

Y

Z

Credits

Staff Credits

The people who made up *The American Nation* team—representing design services, editorial, editorial services, electronic publishing technology, manufacturing and inventory planning, market research, marketing services, online services and multimedia development, planning and budgeting, product planning, production services, project office, publishing processes, and rights and permissions—are listed below. Bold type denotes the core team members.

Ernest Albanese, Robert Aleman, Diane Alimena, **Margaret Antonini,** Rachel Avenia-Prol, Penelope Baker, Renée Beach, Rhett Conklin, **Lisa DelGatto,** Marlies Dwyer, Libby Forsyth, Doreen Galbraith, Catalina Gavilanes, **Nancy Gilbert,** Evan Holstrom, **John Kingston,** Vicki Lamb, Mary Sue Langan, Carol Lavis, **Marian Manners,** Vickie Menanteaux, Carrie O'Connor, James O'Neill, **Robert Prol, Maureen Raymond,** Bruce Rolff, Gerry Schrenk, Mildred Schulte, Melissa Shustyk, Annette Simmons, Robin Sullivan, Frank Tangredi.

Additional Credits

Greg Abrom, Susan Andariese, Rui Camarinha, John A. Carle, Orquidea Cepin, Lisa Ferrari, Jacki Hasko, Beth Hyslip, Raegan Keida, Elizabeth Kiszonas, Steve Lewin, Kathleen Mercandetti, Art Mkrtchyan, Kenneth Myett, Xavier W. Niz, Ray Parenteau, Andrew Roney, Robert Siek, Jeff Zoda.

Text Credits

Grateful acknowledgment is made to the following for copyrighted material

The Mother of Nations Excerpt from *The Mother of Nations* by Joseph Bruchac. Copyright © 1989 by Joseph Bruchac. Published by The Crossing Press, 1989. Reprinted by permission.

I Have A Dream *I Have A Dream* by Dr. Martin Luther King, Jr. Copyright © 1963 by Martin Luther King, Jr. Copyright renewed 1991 by Coretta Scott King. Reprinted by arrangement with The Heirs to the Estate of Martin Luther King, Jr., c/o Writer's House, Inc. as agent for the proprietor.

John D. Rockefeller, Sr., Poem Copyright © 1937 John D. Rockefeller, Sr.

The Little Rock Nine Excerpt from interview with Elizabeth Eckford, 1957. Copyright © 1957.

Note: Every effort has been made to locate the copyright owner of material used in this textbook. Omissions brought to our attention will be corrected in subsequent editions.

Map and Art Credits

Maps: Mapping Specialists Limited; **Art: 18–19** John Edwards & Associates; **Charts and Graphs:** Kathleen Mercandetti.

Photo Credits

Frequently cited sources are abbreviated as follows: GC, The Granger Collection, New York; AP, AP/Wide World Photos; CP, Culver Pictures, Inc.; LOC, Library of Congress; NWPA; North Wind Picture Archives; PR, Photo Researchers, Inc.; SS, SuperStock

Photo Research: Omni-Photo Communications, Inc.

Cover and Title Page: Richard Walker/Pearson Education/PH School. Drum: Collections of the Fort Ticonderoga Museum; **ii** *m.* Collections of the Fort Ticonderoga Museum; *t.* Richard Walker/ Pearson Education/PH School; **iv** Richard Walker/Pearson Education/PH School; **vi** *t.* North American kachina doll, Hopi tribe. Horniman Museum. ©Michael Holford; *b.* GC; **vii** *t.* Howard Chandler Christy, *Scene at the Signing of the Constitution,* April 1940. Architect of the Capitol; *b.* Courtesy of The Bostonian Society, Old State House; **viii** *t.* ©Copyright 2003 PhotoDisc, Inc.; **ix** *t.* National Museum of American History, Department of Social History, Political History Collection, Smithsonian Institution; *b.* ©1993 NWPA; **x** *t. Attack at Battery Wagner* © 1993 Tom Lovell © 1993 The Greenwich Workshop, Inc. Courtesy of The Greenwich Workshop, Inc., Shelton CT; **xi** *b.* SS; **xii** *t.* GC; *b.* National Museum of American History, Smithsonian Institution; **xiii** *t.* ©AP; *b.* Dallas Museum of Art, Texas, USA/The Bridgeman Art Library, London/ New York; **xiv** *t.* NOW, ©1992; *b.* SS; **xv** National Archives, photo no. 102-LH-1948; **xx** ©Copyright 2003 PhotoDisc, Inc.; **xxiii** LOC; **xxv** GC; **xxviii** Michael Newman/PhotoEdit; **xxxi** Walter Hodges/Getty Images, Inc.; **xl–1** Leigh, William Robinson. *Grand Canyon,* 1911. Oil on canvas, 66" x 99". Collection of The Newark Museum, Gift of Henry Washington Wack, 1930. Inv.: 30.203. The Newark Museum, Newark, New Jersey, USA. Art Resource, NY; **2** *l.* Jacques Le Moyne, *Chief Athore and Rene de Laudonniere.* Gouache and metallic pigments on vellum, with traces of black chalk outlines, 27 June 1564. Print Collection, Miriam and Ira D. Wallach Division of Art, Prints and Photographs, The New York Public Library, Astor, Lenox and Tilden Foundations; *r.* ©Hulton Getty/Archive Photos; **3** *l.* GC; *r.* Stone; **4** ©Bettmann/CORBIS; **6** ©H. De Lespinasse/The Image Bank; **11** ©1988 Addison Geary/ Stock Boston; **13** ©UPI-Bettmann/ CORBIS; **14** *t.* ©Adam Jones/PR; *m.* ©Ansel Adams Publishing Rights Trust/CORBIS; **20** Courtesy of Simon & Schuster; **21** ©Punch-Bill Tidy/Rothco; **23** *m.l.* Courtesy of the Massachusetts Historical Commission, Office of the Secretary of the Commonwealth, City Square Archaeological District, Boston; *m.r.* Courtesy of the Massachusetts Historical Commission, Office of the Secretary of the Commonwealth, American Glass Company site, South Boston; *b.* ©Cary Wolinsky/ Stock Boston; **26** Stone; **27** *t.r.* ©2000 The Stock Market/Roger Ball; *t.* ©1997 The Stock Market/ Bill Stormont; **28** Denise DeLuise/ First Image West, Inc.; **31** *t.l.* ©Roman Soumar/CORBIS; Junior Achievement; *t.l.* Hulton Getty/ Liaison Agency, Inc.; *t.r.* From the Walker Collection of A'Lelia Bundles; *t.r.* From the Walker Collection of A'Lelia Bundles; **34** GC; **35** *l.* © Dorling Kindersley. Courtesy of St. Bride Printing; *r.* Diego Rivera, *The Great City of Tenochtitlan,* 1945. Detail of mural, 4.92 x 9.71 m. Patio Corridor, National Palace, Mexico City, D.F., Mexico. Schalkwijk/Art Resource, NY; **36** ©Lowell Georgia/CORBIS; **40** ©NWPA; **41** ©Craig Aurness/ CORBIS; **42** ©Denver Art Museum. Accession #1968.330A; **43** *t.r.* ©British Museum; *t.r.* ©British Museum; **45** *t.l.* Inuit polar bears, 14th–15th century. University of British Columbia/The Bridgeman Art Library, London/ New York; *t.l.* Two Basket Hats .7464: Twined: hazel shoots, willow root, conifer root, bear grass, maidenhair, fern stems/ .7515: Twined: conifer root and bear grass wefts. The Brooklyn Museum 05.588.7464 + 05.588.7515 Museum Expedition 1905, Museum Collection Fund. ©Justin Kerr/The Brooklyn Museum; *t.l.* North American kachina doll, Hopi tribe. Horniman Museum. ©Michael Holford; *t.l.* The University Museum, University of Pennsylvania (Neg. T4-303); *t.r.* ©2003 British Museum; *t.r.* Werner Forman Archive, Smithsonian Institution, Washington, DC/Art Resource, NY; *t.r.* ©Canadian Museum of Civilization, Photo S93-9725; **46** Knife River Indian Villages National Historic Site, National Park Service Photo by Fred Armstrong; **47** Neg./Trans. no. K 10302. Courtesy Department of Library Services, American Museum of Natural History; **50** GC; **52** ©Aldona Sabalis/PR; **53** *b.r.* GC; *b.* ©ChinaStock Photo Library. All rights reserved; **55** GC; **57** Art Resource, NY; **58** Limbourg Brothers. The Month of October. Sowing. Detail. Chateau du Louvre. Tres Riches Heures du Duc de Berry. Musee Conde, Chantilly, France. Giraudon/Art Resource, NY; **60** Ivory salt cellar, Benin, 16th century. Nationalmuseet, Copenhagen, Denmark/Bridgeman Art Library, London/New York; **61** ©Copyright 2003 PhotoDisc, Inc.; **63** Florentine Codex, (16th century). Ms Palat. 218–220 Book IX Montezuma II (1466–1520) receiving tributes, from an account of the Aztecs written and illustrated by Bernardino de Sahagun, Spanish, mid 16th century. Biblioteca Medicea-Laurenziana, Florence, Italy/Bridgeman Art Library, London/New York; **64** Prentice Hall; **65** Courtesy Haudenosaunee Onondaga Nation and the New York State Museum; **66** *l.* Sebastiano del Piombo (ca. 1485–1547), *Christopher Columbus.* All rights reserved. Copyright © by the Metropolitan Museum of Art, NY; *r.* ©Wolfgang Kaehler/CORBIS; **67** Equity Management Inc.; **68** Werner Forman Archive/Statens Historiska Museum, Stockholm/ Art Resource, NY; **69** *b.r.* Rare Books Division, New York Public Library; *b.l.* Museum fur Kunst und Gewerbe, Hamburg; **74** Photograph courtesy Florida Division of Historical Resources, Bureau of Archaeological Research; **75** *Hernando Cortes (1485–1547, Spanish conquistador) meeting Indians of Tlaxcala region, Mexico, folio 207R of 1579 manuscript* Historia de las Indias by Diego Duran. ©The Art Archive/Biblioteca Nacional Madrid/Dagli Orti; **81** Image Select/Art Resource, NY; **83** *m.* ©Fotopic/Omni-Photo Communications, Inc.; *b.r.* ©NWPA; **85** GC; **86** ©Esbin/ Anderson/Omni-Photo Communications, Inc.; **87** Courtesy of The Association for the Preservation of Virginia Antiquities; **88** *t.* ©Richard T. Nowitz/CORBIS; *t.l. Captain John Smith, 1st Governor of Virginia,* c. 1616 (oil on canvas) by English School (17th

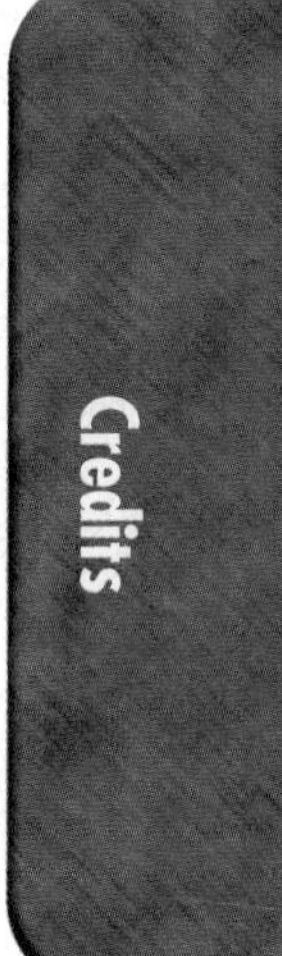

century). The Berger Collection at the Denver Art Museum, USA/The Bridgeman Art Library, London/ New York; **89** *Pocahontas 1616* (detail), National Portrait Gallery, Smithsonian Institution/Art Resource, NY; **92** *b.* Jack Clifton, *First Legislature in the New World.* Oil on canvas. State Capitol, Commonwealth of Virginia. Courtesy The Library of Virginia; Courtesy Cassell & Co.; From "The Chronicle of Western Fashion" by John Peacock, published by Harry N. Abrams, Inc., New York. Used by permission of Thames & Hudson; **93** Courtesy of the Pilgrim Society, Plymouth, Massachusetts; **95** ©Bettmann/CORBIS; **96** ©Ted Curtin/Stock Boston; **100** *l.* GC; *r.* The Historical Society of Pennsylvania (HSP), *Silver Gorget* by Joseph Richardson [S-8-120]; **101** *l.* Peale, Charles Wilson (1741–1827), *Jonathan Edwards.* Engraved by J. D. Gross. Peale Museum; *r.* Courtesy of the LOC; **102** John Lewis Stage; **104** ©Bettmann/CORBIS; **105** GC; **106** ©Stone; **108** Chippendale mahogany side chair, Philadelphia, 1765–1770. From the collection of May and Howard Joynt/Christie's Images; **109** GC; **113** GC; **117** Photographer: Ron Blunt. Courtesy of Drayton Hall, Charleston, South Carolina. A property of the National Trust for Historic Preservation. All Rights Reserved; **118** Courtesy, American Antiquarian Society; **120** CP; **121** *Moses Marcy,* unknown artist. Oil on wood overmantel panel from the Moses Marcy House, Southbridge, MA, mid-18th century (no longer standing). Old Sturbridge Village, Southbridge, MA. [20.19.1] Photo by Henry E. Peach; **124** GC; **125** Brady/ Prentice Hall, Inc.; **127** GC; **129** *t.l.* GC; *t.r.* ©Aaron Haupt/PR; **131** *t.* Chamberlin Mason (English, died 1787), *Portrait of Benjamin Franklin,* 1762 (detail). Oil on canvas, $50\frac{3}{8}$" x $40\frac{3}{4}$". [56-88-1] Philadelphia Museum of Art: Gift of Mr. and Mrs. Wharton Sinkler; *m.r., m.b.* Courtesy of the Historical and Interpretive Collections of The Franklin Institute, Philadelphia, PA. Photo by Charles F. Penniman, Jr.; *l.* Musee de l'Amitie Franco-Americaine, Bierancourt, France. ©Photograph by Erich Lessing/Art Resource, NY; **138** GC; **139** *l.* GC; *r.* GC; **140** GC; **141** GC; **146** Courtesy of the LOC; **147** *b.l.* GC; *b.r.* GC; **149** Colonial Williamsburg Foundation; **151** *t.l.* Dawe, Phillip (c. 1750–c.1785). *The Bostonians Paying the Excise-Man or Tarring & Feathering.* London, 1774. Colored Engraving. The Gilder Lehman Collection on deposit at the Pierpont Morgan Library. GL 4961.01. Photography: Joseph Zehavi. The Pierpont Morgan Library. Art Resource, NY; *t.r.* AP Photo/Tony Dejak; **152** GC; **154** GC; **155** Courtesy, American Antiquarian Society; **156** Samuel Adams (1722–1803) American Revolutionary politician, chief agitator of the Boston Tea Party by Anonymous. Museum of Fine Arts, Boston, MA, USA/The Bridgeman Art Library, London/New York; **157** *t.* GC; *m.r.* Courtesy of The Bostonian Society, Old State House; **159** Lisa Poole/AP; **164** AP; **165** GC; **166** *l.* GC; *r.* Courtesy of The Bostonian Society, Old State House; **167** *l. Marquis de Lafayette* by Francesco-Guiseppe Casanova, ca. 1781–85, oil on canvas, 18.5 x 16.5 in., accession 1939.9. Collection of The New-York Historical Society; *r.* Gallery of the Republic; **168** West Point Museum Collections, United States Military Academy, West Point, New York. Presented by F. Donald Campbell, No 18,947. Photograph by Paul Warchol, New York; **169** GC; **172** GC; **173** *m.r.* Independence National Historical Park Collection; *m.r.* GC; **177** Letraset Phototone; **176–177** GC; **181** GC; **186** Unknown artist, *Black Privateer,* panel 4, panel reverse F, oil, ca. 1780. Courtesy of Alexander A. McBurney, M.D.; **187** Valentine Museum, Richmond, Virginia; **189** © Bettmann/ CORBIS; **190** *t.l.* GC; *t.r.* ©1996 NWPA; *b.* GC; **191** Courtesy of Ted Speigel; **194** ©Christine Pemberton/Omni-Photo Communications, Inc.; **197** Courtesy of the LOC; **198** *l.* GC; *r.* GC; *m.* National Museum of American History, Department of Social History, Political History Collection, Smithsonian Institution; **199** Bas-relief sculpture depicting the signing of the United States Constitution at the South entrance of the Nebraska State Capitol, Lincoln, Nebraska. Image provided by Nebraska Capitol Collections; **200** *Thomas Jefferson.* Unknown artist. Oil on fragment of white marble. Photography by Jeff Goldman, 1986. Maryland Historical Society, Baltimore, Maryland; **202** ©Bettmann/CORBIS; **205** *m.r.* ©NWPA; *b.* ©NWPA; **206** ©Leif Skoogfors/Woodfin Camp & Associates; **207** ©Grace Davies/ Omni-Photo Communications, Inc.; **208** Peale, Charles Wilson, *James Madison,* 1783. Courtesy of the LOC; **209** Christy, Howard Chandler, *Scene at the Signing of the Constitution,* April 1940. Architect of the Capitol; **211** GC; **212** *t.* ©Nathan Beck/Omni-Photo Communications, Inc.; *t.l.* Jean-Antoine Houdon (1741–1828), *Benjamin Franklin* (ca. 1778). Plaster bust, 84.2 x 66.6 x 41.1 cm. Gift of the estate of George Francis Parkman, 1908. Boston Athenaeum; **215** National Museum of American History, Smithsonian Institution; **221** Courtesy of the American Antiquarian Society; **246** *l.* ©Joseph Sohm, Chromosohm Inc./ CORBIS; *r.* GC; **247** *l.* National Museum of American History, Smithsonian Institution; *r.* ©Paul Conklin/PhotoEdit; **248** Cover, *Time Magazine,* Nov. 20, 2000, Vol. 156, No. 21.TimePix, Inc.; **249** *l.* ©Copyright 2001 PhotoDisc, Inc.; *r.* ©1997 Corbis Stock Market/Ed Wheeler; **252** GC; **255** ©Spencer Grant/Stock Boston; **257** ©Arthur Grace/Stock Boston; **259** ©Stock Boston; **262** ©Stephen Varone/ Omni-Photo Communications, Inc.; **263** ©Michael Mancuso/Omni-Photo Communications, Inc.; **265** *People Weekly* ©1997 Andrew Kaufman; **266** Art Resource, NY; **267** ©The New Yorker Collection 2003, Barney Tobey, from cartoonbank.com. All Rights Reserved; **269** George Jones III/PR; **274–275** John Hill, *Junction of the Erie and Northern (Champlain) Canals.* Aquatint, Number 34684. Courtesy of The New-York Historical Society; **276** *l. George Washington Banner:* watercolor, graphite and pen ink on paper. .733 x .534 m. ($28\frac{3}{4}$ in. x $21\frac{1}{16}$ in.). Index of American Design, ©1993 National Gallery of Art. Photograph ©Board of Trustees, National Gallery of Art, Washington DC; *r.* Courtesy of the LOC; *c.* Courtesy of the LOC; **277** Copyright © By the Metropolitan Museum of Art, NY; **278** ©2000 NWPA; **279** ©Chromosohm/Sohm MCMXCII/PR; **280** GC; **283** *l.* Isaac Fowle (1818–1853), *Lady with a Scarf Figurehead.* Courtesy of The Bostonian Society/Old State House; *t.r. Swordsman Whirligig,* c. 1870. Carved, polychromed wood, 44.5 x 12.7 x 9.5 (excluding base) ($17\frac{1}{2}$ x 5 x $3\frac{3}{4}$). ©Shelburne Museum, Shelburne, Vermont (27.FW-43). Photograph by Ken Burris; *m.* GC; *b.r. Gabriel,* c. 1800. Sawn, polychromed wood with iron reinforcements. 33 x 85.1 x 1.3 (13 x $33\frac{1}{2}$ x $\frac{1}{2}$). Found in Ridgefield, Connecticut. ©Shelburne Museum, Shelburne, Vermont (27.FW-2). Photograph by Ken Burris; **284** ©Jorn Fabricius; **285** ©Gianni Dagli Orti/CORBIS; **287** *E pluribus unum Eagle.* Wood, hand-carved and painted. ©Shelburne Museum, Shelburne, Vermont (27.FE-37). Photograph by Ken Burris; **288** CP; **291** GC; **292** GC; **297** *Arrival of Gen. George Washington in New York City, April 23, 1789,* n.d., oil on canvas, 93 /4 x 142 in., by Arsene Hippolyte Rivey, negative no. 7161, accession number 1939.216. ©Collection of The New-York Historical Society; **298** Photofest; **299** Photofest; **300** *l.* ©Lawrence Migdale/Stock Boston; *r.* GC; **301** From the collection of Mac G. and Janelle C. Morris; **302** Courtesy of the LOC; **304** *t.l.* Photograph ©1995 Fred J. Maroon; *inset* Photograph ©1995 Fred J. Maroon; **306** William Clark's elkskin-bound journal, open view showing entry for Saturday, 26 October 1805 leather and paper by Clark, William (entries), 1805 Objects 109. Missouri Historical Society; **307** GC; **308** National Museum of American History, Department of Social History, Political History Collection, Smithsonian Institution, Photo No. 95-3550; **309** ©Stock Montage, Inc.; **311** *t.l.* Missouri Historical Society, St. Louis (Neg. # L/A 407); *t.c.* ©Anthony Mercieca/PR; *t.r.* ©1985 William H. Mullins/PR; *b.l.* ©Tim Davis/PR; *b.r.* ©Tim Davis/PR; **312** GC; **313** *m.r.* Chinese export porcelain saucer (after 1743). Reconstruction. Overglaze enameled in red, black and gold; "Altar of Love" pattern. D: 11.4 cm (4.5 in.) Provenance: Garden Wall [ER 294C (SC 550)]. Photo by Edward Owen. Monticello/Thomas Jefferson Memorial Foundation, Inc.; *b.r. View of the Foreign Factories in Canton* (detail), oil on glass, c. 1800–1815. OH: 28.250, OW: 40.000. Courtesy, Winterthur Museum; **316** The Field Museum of Natural History, #A93851c; **318** GC; **320** West Point Museum Collections, United States Military Academy, West Point, New York. Presented by F. Donald Campbell, No 14,874. Photograph by Paul Warchol, New York; **321** U. S. Navy Photo; **322** GC; **324** GC; **328** *l.* ©Bettmann/ CORBIS; *r.* GC; **329** *l.* GC; *r.* GC; **330** Courtesy of the Beverly Historical Society and Museum, Beverly, MA. Accession #29153; **331** Unidentified American, mid-19th century, *View of the Iron Works, Canton, Massachusetts,* about 1850. Detail. Oil on canvas, 68.9 x 86.68 cm ($27\frac{1}{8}$ x $34\frac{1}{8}$ in.) Museum of Fine Arts, Boston: Gift of Maxim Karolik for the M. and M. Karolik Collection of American Paintings, 1815–1865. [62.274]; **333** GC; **334** *t.l.* Circus World Museum; *t.r.* ©Danielle B. Hayes/ Omni-Photo Communications, Inc.; **336** GC; **337** *Travel by Stagecoach Near Trenton, New Jersey.* By the Metropolitan Museum of Art, NY; Rogers Fund, 1942 (42.95.11); **338** Conner Prairie Village; **340** George Caleb Bingham (1811–1879), *Raftsmen Playing Cards* (detail), 1847. Oil on canvas, $28\frac{1}{16}$ x $38\frac{1}{16}$ in. (71.3 x 96.7 cm.) The Saint Louis Art Museum, St. Louis, Missouri. Purchase: Ezra H. Linley Fund (B-180), 50:1934; **342** ©2001 NWPA; **343** ©Bettmann/CORBIS; **344** Lowell Historical Society; **348** Ted Donovan/Photos de BajaMex; **350** Florida State Archives; **356–357** Oscar E. Berninghaus, *Westward Ho! Early*

Overland Transportation, 1840s. SS; **358** *r.* GC; *l. Politics in an Oyster House* by Richard Caton Woodville, Walters Art Gallery, Baltimore; **359** *l.* GC; *r.* The Historical Society of Pennsylvania (HSP), *Nicholas Biddle* by Henry Inman. Oil on canvas, 1839. 88.9 x 68.6 cm (35 x 27 in). [1978.21]; **360** Courtesy of the Museum of the City of New York; **365** Courtesy of the LOC; **367** GC; **370** *m.l.* Index Stock Imagery, Inc.; *m.r.* GC; **371** GC; **372** National Park Service, Martin Van Buren National Historic Site; **375** *t.r.* National Portrait Gallery, Smithsonian Institution/Art Resource, NY; *b.* National Museum of American History, Department of Social History, Political History Collection, Smithsonian Institution; **377** Collection of The New York Historical Society; **378** *l.* CP; *r. The Last Stand at the Alamo, 6th March 1836* (illustration) by Wyeth, Newell Convers (1882–1945). Private Collection/Art Resource, NY; **379** *l.* ©David Hiser/Network Aspen; *r.* GC; **380** ©1992 NWPA; **382** CP; **383** *t.r.* ©1993 NWPA; *m.r.* Courtesy of the Lane County Historical Museum; **385** *"There is still time to escape! . . ." Col. William B. Travis at the Alamo, San Antonio, Texas, March 3, 1836.* Detail. Illustration by Norman Price. The Daughters of the Republic of Texas Library [CN96.266]; **387** ©Bob Daemmrich; **388** *t.* Archives Division–Texas State Library; *m.l.* Courtesy of the Texas Memorial Museum; **391** ©2000 NWPA; **393** George Peter Alexander Healy, *James K. Polk,* 1846 (detail). Oil on canvas, 30½ x 25½ in. In the Collection of The Corcoran Gallery of Art, Museum Purchase, Gallery Fund [79.14]; **394** ©1996 NWPA; **396** GC; **397** Corel Professional Photos CD-ROM™; **398** CP; **403** *t.* ©2001 PhotoDisc, Inc.; *m.* Collection of Norm Wilson. Courtesy of the Oakland Museum of California; *b.* Seaver Center for Western History Research, Natural History Museum of Los Angeles County. Museum Collection Number 277; **406** *l.* ©NWPA; *r.* ©2000 NWPA; **407** ©2001 NWPA; **408** ©Elizabeth Whiting & Associates/CORBIS; **409** *t.* CP; *b.* Photograph by Michael Freeman and Robert Golden. National Museum of American History, Smithsonian Institution; **412** *t.r* GC; *m.* GC; *r.* GC; **413** American Textile History Museum, Lowell, Massacusetts. [P1449.1091D]; **416** © Richard Haynes; **418** ©Robert Finken/PR; **419** Smithsonian Institution; **422** *Katie Darling,* ex-slave, Marshall. (Lot 13262-7, 53 [P&P]). From 5 x 3.25 in. silver gelatin print. Created August 3, 1937. Courtesy of the LOC; **423** GC; **424** *inset* CP; *b.* GC; **430** Cabinet photograph by Gilbert Studios, Washington DC. Gold-toned albumin print. Courtesy Oxford University Press Inc.; **431** ©John Lei/Omni-Photo Communications, Inc.; **432** *l.* GC; *m.* GC; *r.* Courtesy of the Massachusetts Historical Society; **433** *l.* Adelaide Johnson, *Portrait monument to Lucretia Mott, Elizabeth Cady Stanton and Susan B. Anthony.* Marble, c. 1920. Architect of the Capitol; *r.* GC; **434** Courtesy Old New-Gate Prison, East Granby, Connecticut. Photo Thomas P. Benincas, Jr. Connecticut Historical Commission; **436** *The Tree of Temperance,* 1855. Published by A. D. Fillmore, Cincinnati, Ohio. Lithograph on wove paper; 27.1 x 20.4 cm (sheet, trimmed to image). No 1855-2. Courtesy of the LOC; **438** ©1993 NWPA; *b.* GC; **439** The Trustees of the Wedgwood Museum, Barlaston, Staffordshire, England; **440** ©1998 NWPA; **441** Photo courtesy Ernest Pappas; **443** *Reward Poster, April 3, 1860* (letterpress broadside) by American School, (19th Century). Private Collection/The Bridgeman Art Library, London/New York; **444** *l.* GC; *r.* GC; **445** CP; **446** *t.r.* © David Weintraub/PR; *l.* Courtesy of the LOC; **448** CP; **449** Asher Brown Durand, *Kindred Spirits.* Oil on canvas, 1849. GC; **450** Courtesy of Richard Masloski; **456–457** Winslow Homer, *A Rainy Day in Camp,* 1871. The Metropolitan Museum of Art, Gift of Mrs. William F. Milton, 1923. (23.77.1) Copyright ©2003 The Metropolitan Museum of Art; **458** *l.* Courtesy of the Illinois State Historical Library; *r.* Eastman Johnson, *A Ride for Liberty—the Fugitive Slaves.* The Brooklyn Museum; **459** *l.* GC; *r.* Ft. Sumter National Monument.; **460** The American Philosophical Society; **461** *b.l.* GC; *b.r.* GC; **463** GC; **464** GC; **467** *t.r.* Courtesy of the LOC; *m.* Courtesy of the LOC; *b.l.* ©Stock Montage, Inc.; **468** GC; **471** ©CORBIS; **473** National Portrait Gallery, Smithsonian Institution; **474** Currier & Ives, *The Right Man for the Right Place,* 1856. Lithograph on wove paper, 27 x 34 cm. Courtesy of the LOC; **477** Copyright © by the Metropolitan Museum of Art, NY; **478** Courtesy of the Illinois State Historical Library; **480** National Geographic Society; **481** GC; **483** GC; **484** ©1997 NWPA; **485** *l.* Courtesy of the LOC; *r.* CP; **486** West Point Museum Collections, United States Military Academy, West Point, New York; **489** ©Omni-Photo Communications, Inc.; **490** Smithsonian Institute; **494** Photograph by Matthew Brady. ©CORBIS; **495** ©2001 NWPA; **496** *Unidentified African-American Civil War soldier.* Tintype, unknown photographer, no date. Chicago Historical Society, ICHi-08068; **498** *Attack at Battery Wagner* © 1993 Tom Lovell © 1993 The Greenwich Workshop, Inc. Courtesy of The Greenwich Workshop, Inc., Shelton CT; **500** *Home Coming, 1865,* watercolor by William L. Sheppard. The Museum of the Confederacy, Richmond, Virginia. Copy Photography by Katherine Wetzel; *l.* Massachusetts Commandery, Military Order of the Loyal Legion and the U.S. Army Military History Institute; *t.l.* U.S. Army Military History Institute; *m.l.* U.S. Army Military History Institute; **501** *r.* ©Eric Kroll/Omni-Photo Communications, Inc.; **505** ©CORBIS; **506** GC; **511** Courtesy of the LOC; **513** Photograph by Matthew Brady. CP; **514** *l.* CP; *r.* CP; *m. Upholstered walnut parlor rocking chair.* Used by President Abraham Lincoln at Ford's Theatre, Washington, DC, April 14, 1865. H: 10.00 x 106.68 cm., W: 36.625 in., L: 34.5 in. (29.1451.1). From the Collections of Henry Ford Museum and Greenfield Village, No. 11-A-35(A); **515** *l.* GC; *r.* GC; **516** ©Bern Keating; **517** GC; **518** Courtesy of Ford's Theatre, Washington, DC. Photo by Andrew Lautman; **521** AP Photo/Lou Krasky; **523** GC; **525** *t.* ©Copyright 2001 PhotoDisc, Inc.; *b.* ©Bettmann/CORBIS; **526** ©1994 NWPA; **527** GC; **528** GC; **530** SS; **532** ©1998 NWPA; **536** The National Portrait Gallery, Smithsonian Institution; **537** ©Copyright 2003 PhotoDisc, Inc.; **540–541** Peter Severin Kroyer (1851–1909), *The Biermeister & Main Steel Forge.* Statens Museum for Kunst, Copenhagen, Denmark/Bridgeman Art Library, London/SS; **542** *l.* GC; *r.* Image #:3273(3). Photo by: Lee Boltin. American Museum of Natural History Library; **543** GC; **544** Photo by I. G. Holmes, Panhandle-Plains Historical Society; **545** GC; **547** CP; **550** SS; **552** SS; **554** *l.* CP; *m.b.* SS; *m.t.* ©John Lei/Omni-Photo Communications, Inc.; *t.r.* Grace Davies/Omni-Photo Communications, Inc *m.r.* ©Copyright 2003 PhotoDisc, Inc.; **557** SS; **558** ©Lawrence Migdale/Stock Boston; **559** GC; **562** GC; **563** GC; **565** ©CORBIS; **567** *b.* SS; *t.* ©1999 NWPA; **570** Permission granted by Troll Communications, LLC; **571** CP; **572** *l.* Courtesy of the LOC; *r.* GC; **573** *l.* GC; *r.* Courtesy Ford Motor Company; **574** CP/SS; **576** Courtesy of the LOC; **578** ©2001 NWPA; **579** GC; **583** *t.* GC; *b.* GC; *m.l.* GC; **584** ©Schenectady Museum; Hall of Electrical History Foundation/CORBIS; **585** CP; **586** *l.* National Park Service, U.S. Department of Interior, Edison National Historic Site; *inset* ©Breton Littlehales/National Geographic Society; **588** From the collections of Henry Ford Museum & Greenfield Village; **590** CP; **591** Mary Kenney O'Sullivan, mid 1900s. Cabinet card by Purdy, Boston, Massachusetts. The Schlesinger Library, Radcliffe Institute, Harvard University; **593** ©CORBIS; **595** *t.r.* ©Bettmann/CORBIS; *l.* ©PR; *m.r.* Courtesy National Archives, photo no. 102-LH-1948; **597** *r.* Courtesy of the LOC; **598** *l.* GC; *r.* © Grace Davies/Omni-Photo Communications, Inc.; **599** ©2001 NWPA; **600** ©Bettmann/CORBIS; **601** GC; **602** ©Kevin Fleming/CORBIS; **604** AP; **606** GC; **608** *l.* Brown Brothers; *r.* GC; **609** GC; **613** © NWPA; **614** *inset* CP; *l.* GC; **615** New York Public Library at Lincoln Center; **616** *b.* ©1989 NWPA; *t.* AP; **617** ©2001 NWPA; **618** *l.* GC; *r.* GC; **619** Brown Brothers; **620** GC; **626–627** *The Fourth of July* (detail), 1916, Frederick Childe Hassam (1859–1935)/Christie's Images; **628** *l.* ©1995 NWPA; *r.* Courtesy of the LOC; **629** *m.* ©1989 NWPA; *r.* Equity Management Inc./United States Postal Service; **630** © Richard Cheek for the Preservation Society of Newport County; **631** GC; **633** GC; **634** Courtesy of the LOC; **637** *m.t.* GC; *t.r. The Jungle* by Upton Sinclair. Cover of the 1995 Barnes and Noble Classics edition. Cover design by Tom McKeveny. Cover painting: Bill Jacklin, *Two Chimneys II,* 1986, private collection, courtesy of the artist; *m.l.* CP; *b.* GC; *inset The Epic of the Wheat: The Octopus:* A Story of California by Frank Norris. Cover of the 1994 Penguin Twentieth-Century Classics reissue edition. Cover painting: *His Private Car* by LeComte Stewart. Courtesy of The Museum of Church History and Art, Salt Lake City, Utah. Photograph © The Church of Jesus Christ of Latter Day Saints, 1985. All rights reserved; **637** *t.l.* Amereon, Limited; **638** GC; **639** *inset* National Museum of American History, Smithsonian Institution; *t.r.* Photo by R. Y. Young. Courtesy of the LOC; **640** *l.* CP; *r.* Silver Burdett Ginn; **642** *t.l.* GC; *inset* Courtesy of The New-York Historical Society; **644** CP; **645** ©CORBIS; **646** Sally Anderson-Bruce; **647** © Bettmann/CORBIS; **649** Courtesy of the Arizona Historical Society/ Tucson, accession number 69472; **650** Courtesy National Park Service, Museum Management Program and Tuskegee Institute National Historic Site. Photo by Eric Long; **652** Chinese Immigrants Harvesting at J. deBarth Short Vineyards, San Marino, CA. California Historical Society, San Francisco, FN-23451; **655** ©2001 NWPA; **656** GC; **657** Jacob Lawrence, Harriet Tubman Series,

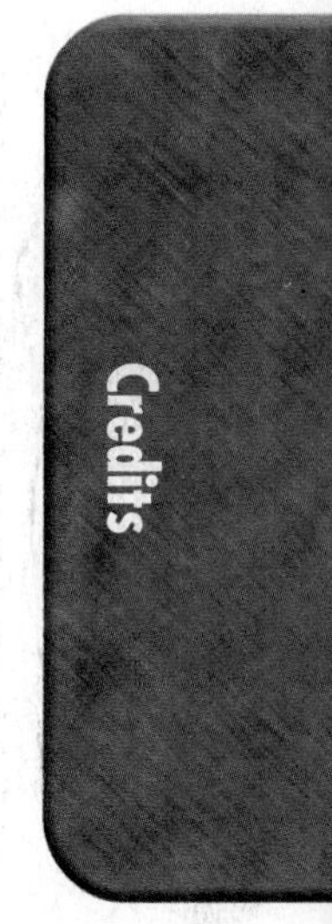

No. 1, (detail) 1939–40. "With sweat and toil and ignorance he consumes his life to pour the earnings into channels from which he does not drink."-Harriet Ward Beecher. Collection of Hampton University Museum, Hampton, Virginia. © Gwendolyn Knight Lawrence, courtesy of the Jacob and Gwendolyn Lawrence Foundation; **658** *m.* Courtesy National Archives, photo no. (RP0016); *r.* GC; *l.* ©Jeff Greenberg/ Omni-Photo Communications, Inc.; **659** GC; **660** © CORBIS; **661** American Naval vessel in a Japanese harbour, 1861 (color woodcut) by Japanese School, (19th century). LOC, Washington, DC, USA/The Bridgeman Art Library, London/New York; **662** ©Jeff Greenberg/PR; **665** GC; **668** GC; **669** GC; **670** GC; **672** SS; **675** ©1996 NWPA; **676** GC; **678** GC; **681** *b.* ©Agence France Presse/ CORBIS; *b.r.* © David M. Schleser/ PR; *t.* GC; **683** CP; **684** *l.* GC; *r.* ©Bettmann/CORBIS; **685** *r.* © National Archives/PR; *l.* Courtesy of the LOC; **686** GC; **687** GC; **688** *l.* ©1989, FPG International LLC; **689** ©1999, Kerry Wetzel/FPG International LLC; **691** © CORBIS; **693** GC; **694** GC; **695** © 1988, FPG International LLC; **697** GC; **698** National Archives; **700** GC; ©Gamma Press US, Inc.; **701** AP; **703** *b.* © CORBIS; *t.r.* ©Jack Kurtz/Impact Visuals; *inset* Courtesy of the Veterans of Foreign Wars of the United States; *background image* ©PhotoDisc, Inc.; **704** National Portrait Gallery, Smithsonian Institution/Art Resource, NY; **705** Palace of Versailles, France/SS; **706** AP; **708** CP; **711** *r.* The Imperial War Museum, London, Louis Raemakers and "*In Belgium, Help*" **714–715** Alexandre Hogue (1898–1994), *Drought Stricken Area,* 1934 (detail) , Oil on canvas. Dallas Museum of Art, Texas, USA/The Bridgeman Art Library, London/New York; **716** *l.* Courtesy of the LOC; *r.* New York Stock Exchange Archives; **717** AP; **718** Warren Gamaliel Harding (detail) by Margaret Lindsay Williams (1887–1960). Oil on canvas. (Accession No. NPG66.21), 135.9 x 99.7 cm (53½ x 39¼ in.) The National Portrait Gallery, Smithsonian Institution; **719** GC; **721** *l.* Courtesy of Spiegel; *r.* Brown Brothers; **723** GC; **724** CP; **725** Brown Brothers; **727** ©1999 FPG International LLC; **728** ©Robert Landau/CORBIS; **730** Photofest; **731** Photofest; **732** *inset* ©AP. Original art by C. K. Stevens; *b.* ©1999, Thompson/FPG International LLC; **735** *r.* CP; *m.l.* SS; *b.* SS; *l.* ©Janet Sommer/ Archive Photos; **736** Hulton Getty/Liaison Agency; **737** Collection of David J. and Janice L. Frent; **738** CP; **740** *t.* GC; *inset* From Black Moses: The Story of Marcus Garvey and the University Negro Improvement Association by E. David Cronon, ©1955, 1969, Madison: University of Wisconsin Press. Used by permission of the publisher; **744** *r.* AP; *l.* GC; **745** *l.* ©1992 Photoworld/FPG International LLC; *r.* GC; **746** AP; **747** *inset* ©UPI-Bettmann/CORBIS; ©Bettmann/CORBIS; **748** Isaac Soyer, *Employment Agency* (detail). Collection of Whitney Museum of American Art; **750** SS; **752** Franklin Delano Roosevelt Library, Hyde Park, NY; **753** ©1999 FPG International LLC; **755** ©Sandy Felsenthal/CORBIS; **756** Courtesy of the LOC; **758** *t.r.* Tennessee Valley Authority; *r.* AP; *t.l.* Tennessee Valley Authority; **759** ©CORBIS; **760** GC; **762** ©Wally McNamee/CORBIS; **765** Courtesy National Archives **766** ©Bettmann/CORBIS; **767** GC; **768** GC; **771** Courtesy of the LOC; **772** *l.* GC; *r.* GC; **773** SS; **774** GC; **775** Collection Kharbine-Tapabor, Paris, France/The Bridgeman Art Library, London/New York; **776** *inset* ©Heinrich Hoffman/CORBIS; *t.* CP; **778** SS; **779** Courtesy National Archives, War and Conflict, #993, #1131; **781** From the book, *Dr. Seuss Goes to War: The World War II Editorial Cartoons of Theodor Seuss Geisel* by Richard H. Minear. Published in cooperation with the Dr. Seuss Collection at the University of California at San Diego; **782** ©H. K. Owen/ Black Star; **784** ©Hulton Getty/ Getty Images/Three Lions/Archive Photos; **785** Printed by permission of the Norman Rockwell Family Trust. Copyright ©2001, The Norman Rockwell Family Trust; **786** CP; **787** ©Bettmann/CORBIS; **789** *l.* AP; *r.* National Museum of American History, Smithsonian Institution; **790** ©Tria Giovan/ CORBIS; **792** ©Anthony Potter Collection/Hulton Getty/Archive Photos; **795** National D-Day Museum; **796** CP; **798** *r.* ©Mike Segar/Archive Photos; *l.* AP; *b.r.* Pete Souza/Liaison Agency; **802** ©Hulton Getty/Archive Photos; **803** ©Hulton Getty/Getty Images/ Anthony Potter Collection/Archive Photos; **806–807** Diana Ong, *4 The World.* SS; **808** *l.* ©Bettmann/ CORBIS; *r.* NASA; **809** *r.* AP; *l.* AP **810** ©Bettmann/CORBIS; **811** ©Bettmann/CORBIS; **812** CP; **815** GC; **816** GC; **817** GC; **818** SS; **819** AP **821** AP; **822** Michael Barson/Past Pefect; **823** ©Hulton Getty/MPI/Archive Photos; **824** CP; **826** *m.r.* ©Bettmann/CORBIS; *l.* NASA; *t.r.* ©NASA/Roger Ressmeyer/CORBIS; *m.b.* ©Roger Ressmeyer/CORBIS; **827** ©Bettmann/CORBIS; **830** SS; **832** AP Photo/Lutz Schmidt; **834** ©White House/Hulton Getty/ Archive Photos; **835** ©Hulton Getty/Archive Photos; **836** © CORBIS; **839** ©LOC/CORBIS; **840** *l.* AP; *r.* AP; **841** ©Reuters NewMedia Inc./CORBIS; **842** "Two fine cars for the price of one!" Advertisement No. 7141-A, Prepared by J. Walter Thompson Company, 1953. Courtesy of Duke University, Hartman Center for Sales, Advertising & Marketing History, J. Walter Thompson Archives; **843** ©Frank Cancellare/ Bettmann/CORBIS; **844** ©Bettmann/CORBIS; **846** *l.* ©Bettmann/CORBIS; *r.* David Young-Wolff/PictureQuest; **848** *t.l.* Photofest; *m.* ©NBC TV/Hulton Getty/Archive Photos; *b.l.* Photofest; *t.r.* ©Copyright 2001 PhotoDisc, Inc.; *inset* Archive Photos/ PictureQuest; **849** ©Bettmann/ CORBIS; **850** AP; **851** ©Bettmann/ CORBIS; **852** *l.* ©Bettmann/CORBIS; *r.* ©Grey Villet/TimePix, Inc.; **853** *m.* ©Bettmann/CORBIS; *r.* ©Bettmann/CORBIS; **855** ©Bettmann/CORBIS; **856** AP; **857** ©CORBIS; **858** *inset* AP Photo/ Hattiesburg (MS) American, Joe Lovett; *t.* ©Hulton Getty/Archive Photos; **860** ©Bettmann/CORBIS; **862** AP Photo/Jackson (MS) Daily News, Fred Blackwell; **863** ©Flip Schulke/CORBIS; **864** *t.* Stock Boston; *inset* National Organization for Women, ©1992; **867** ©Philip Jon Bailey/Stock Boston; **870** *l.* ©Mike Mazzaschi/ Stock Boston; *r.* ©A. Ramey/ PhotoEdit; **871** ©2001 *The Record* (Bergen County, NJ) Thomas E. Franklin, staff photographer/ CORBIS/SABA; **872** National Museum of American History, Department of Social History, Political History Collection, Smithsonian Institution; **875** Lianhe Zaobao Heng/Cartoonists & Writers Syndicate/ cartoonweb.com; **878** ©Bob Daemmrich/Stock Boston; **879** ©Reuters/Christine Grunnet/ Archive Photos; **883** AP; **886** Mark Wilson/Getty Images/Liaison Agency; **888** ©David R. Austen/ Stock Boston; **890** ©AFP/Chris Wilkins/CORBIS; **891** ©Myrleen Ferguson Cate/PhotoEdit; **892** *l.* ©Owen Franken/Stock Boston; *t.r.* ©Michael Newman/PhotoEdit; *b.r.* ©1988 Peter L. Chapman/Stock Boston; *m.r.* ©Phyllis Ricardi/Stock Boston; **894** ©Michael Newman/ PhotoEdit; **895** © Reuters NewMedia Inc./CORBIS; **897** *r.* ©Bob Daemmrich/Stock Boston; **902** AP Photo/Dana Tynan; **903** ©1991 Robert Fried/Stock Boston; **906** *Washington Crossing the Delaware,* Emanuel Leutze, GC; **907–910:** portrait nos.1, 2 ,4, 5, 6, 9, 10, 12, 14, 15, 18, 20, 21, 25, 26, 27, 35, National Portrait Gallery, Smithsonian Institution/Art Resource, NY; nos. 3, 7, 8, 9,11,13, 16, 17, 19, 22, 23, 24, 28, 29, 30, 31, 32, 33, 34, 36, 37, 38, 39, 40, 41, 42, White House Collection, copyright White House Historical Association; #43: © Bob Daemmrich/Stock, Boston, Inc./PictureQuest; *b.r.* GC; *b.* ©Peter Poulides/Stone/Getty Images; **END1** National Museum of American History, Smithsonian Institution, photo id: 95-1155/4; **END2** *t.* Doug Armand/Stone

The American Flag

The Flag That Inspired Our National Anthem

During the War of 1812, Mary Young Pickersgill was hired to make a new flag for Fort McHenry in Baltimore harbor. She was told to make a huge flag.

Pickersgill's flag was so large that, when it was hung at Fort McHenry, it could be seen far and wide. In fact, Francis Scott Key could see the flag from eight miles away during the bombardment of the fort by British warships. Its "broad stripes and bright stars" inspired him to write the poem, "The Star-Spangled Banner." The poem was later set to music. In 1931, Congress made "The Star-Spangled Banner" the national anthem of the United States.

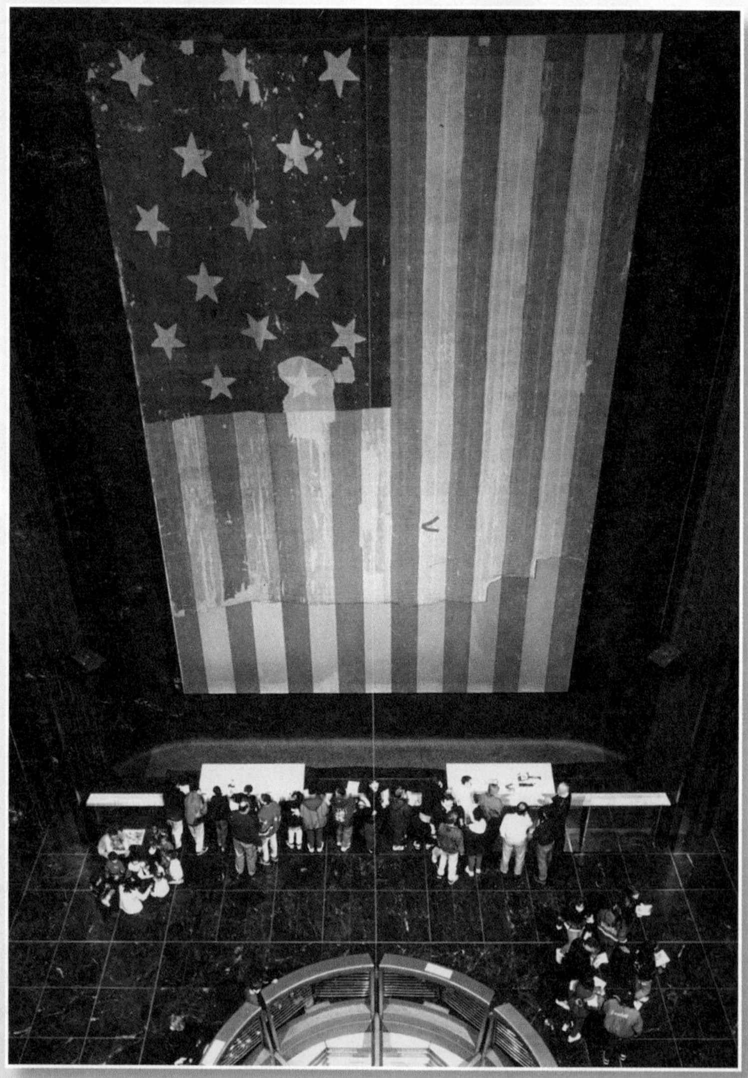

Today, the original Star-Spangled Banner hangs at the Smithsonian Institution in Washington, D.C.